MARKETING

M A

RKETING
Concepts and Strategies
Sixth Edition

William M. Pride
TEXAS A & M UNIVERSITY

O. C. Ferrell
TEXAS A & M UNIVERSITY

HOUGHTON MIFFLIN COMPANY   BOSTON

DALLAS   GENEVA, ILLINOIS   PRINCETON, NEW JERSEY   PALO ALTO

ABOUT THE COVER

Three blue squares, identical in color and size, are shown in different environments. Your perception of the square changes depending on the color that surrounds it. How a consumer perceives a product or organization depends on the environment in which it is presented—and this environment is created in part by marketing.

Part Opener photographs: I, Mason Morfit; II, Bill Varie/The Image Bank; III, Lou Jones/The Image Bank; IV, Larry Dale Gordon/The Image Bank; V, Lou Jones/The Image Bank; VI, Gary Gladstone/The Image Bank; VII, R. & M. Magruder/The Image Bank

Figure Illustrations: Boston Graphics, Inc.

Printed in the U.S.A.

Library of Congress Catalog Card Number: 88-81358

ISBN: 0-395-36938-X

BCDEFGHIJ-VH-9543210-89

To Nancy, Michael, and Allen Pride

To O. C. Ferrell, Sr., and Kathlene Ferrell

Brief Contents

Contents

WITHDRAWN

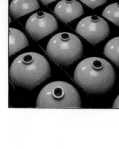

Part VI
Marketing Management   626

18. Strategic Market Planning   628

Preface

The Sixth Edition: Strategic and Accessible

A marketing textbook must change often to keep pace with new developments in the teaching and practice of marketing. In this edition, we focus on the concepts most relevant to the development and implementation of marketing strategies. To make the sixth edition as informative, accessible, complete, and interesting as possible,

▶ We have focused more on strategic marketing, a change signaled by the new subtitle: *Concepts and Strategies*. The book opens with an overview of strategic marketing. A complete chapter on strategic market planning is included as well. Strategy and decision making are emphasized in cases and examples. A new, detailed strategic case at the end of each of the book's parts helps students integrate the concepts discussed in each part.
▶ We have included more examples demonstrating the marketing of real, current products and organizations, from Levi's 501 jeans to Federal Express. Each chapter has two cases, half of which are new, and two new, longer applications that illustrate or extend the discussions in the main text.
▶ We have created a more open, attractive visual presentation of the material to stimulate readers' interest in the subject.

In addition, we have made the writing more lively, readable, and concise, and updated the entire book, making major changes and additions including

▶ Expanded coverage of ethics and social responsibility (Chapter 2) and of ethical decisions in marketing research (Chapter 6)
▶ Extended discussion of lifestyle segmentation and regional marketing (Chapter 3)
▶ Revised and expanded treatment of social class and subliminal influence (Chapter 4)
▶ More complete coverage of criteria for channel selection and of legal issues in channel management (Chapter 9)
▶ A reorganized and more substantive look at topics in retailing and physical distribution (Chapters 11 and 12)

- More detailed discussion of telemarketing, sales-force compensation and motivation, and couponing (Chapter 15)
- A new section on centralization and decentralization and a more comprehensive treatment of marketing implementation (Chapter 19)
- More thorough investigation of international marketing research (Chapter 22)

Despite these changes, we believe that users of earlier editions of *Marketing* will find in this sixth edition the same strengths that have made previous editions so popular. Like its predecessors, this edition explores the depth and breadth of the field, combining detailed real examples with comprehensive coverage of marketing concepts and strategies used widely outside of the business world as well as in it. By focusing on the universal concerns of marketing decision makers, we demonstrate that marketing is a challenging, relevant field of study and a part of our world that influences almost everything we do.

Features of the Sixth Edition

As always, our goal is to provide a comprehensive and practical introduction to marketing, easy both to teach and to read. The entire book is structured to excite students about marketing and to make learning comprehensive and efficient.

- *Learning objectives* open each chapter, providing students an overview of new concepts.
- A *vignette* introduces each chapter's marketing issues.
- *Examples* of familiar products and organizations make concrete and specific the generalizations of marketing theory.
- Two longer *applications* in each chapter, focusing on recognizable firms and products, extend the discussion of marketing topics and decisions.
- Numerous *figures, tables, and photographs* augment the text and increase comprehension.
- A complete chapter *summary* reviews the major topics discussed.
- A *list of important terms* (highlighted in the text) provides a study aid, helping students expand their marketing vocabulary.
- *Discussion and review questions* encourage further study and exploration of chapter material.
- Two concise, stimulating *cases* provoke discussion at the end of each chapter.
- A *diagram of the text's organization* at the beginning of each part shows students how material in the upcoming part relates to the rest of the book.
- A *strategic case* at the end of each part helps students integrate concepts from throughout that part.
- A *glossary* at the end of the text defines more than 625 important marketing terms.
- *Appendices* discuss career opportunities in marketing and provide additional insights into financial analysis in marketing.
- A *name index* and a *subject index* enable students to find topics of interest quickly.

Text Organization

We have organized the seven parts of *Marketing: Concepts and Strategies* to give students a theoretical and practical understanding of marketing decision making. Part I presents an overview of marketing, discusses general marketing concepts, and considers the marketing environment, types of markets, target market analysis, buyer behavior, and marketing research. Part II focuses on the conceptualization, development, and management of products. Part III examines marketing channels, institutions, and physical distribution. Part IV covers promotion decisions and methods, including advertising, personal selling, sales promotion, and publicity. Part V is devoted to pricing decisions and Part VI to marketing management and discussions of strategic market planning, organization, implementation, and control. Part VII explores strategic decisions in industrial, service, nonbusiness, and international marketing.

In addition to numerous instructor support materials (discussed in the front of the instructor's manual), the package for this text includes aids to both teaching and learning:

▶ A study guide helps students review and integrate material.
▶ *Marketing Cases* supplements the cases in the text with 42 others that demonstrate how marketing decisions are made.
▶ *Marketing: A Simulation* gives student teams working on microcomputers valuable experience in making marketing decisions.
▶ *Microstudy Plus,* a self-instructional program for microcomputers, reinforces learning of key concepts.

Through the years, professors and students have sent us many helpful suggestions for improving the text. We invite your comments, questions, or criticisms. We want to do our best to provide materials that enhance the teaching and learning of marketing concepts and strategies. Your suggestions will be sincerely appreciated.

WILLIAM M. PRIDE

O. C. FERRELL

Acknowledgments

Like most textbooks, this one reflects the ideas of a multitude of academicians and practitioners who have contributed to the development of the marketing discipline. We appreciate the opportunity to present their ideas in this book.

A number of individuals have made many helpful comments and recommendations in their reviews of this or earlier editions. We appreciate the generous help of these reviewers.

Timothy Hartman
Ohio University

Sheldon Somerstein
City University of New York

Linda K. Anglin
Mankato State University

Winston Ring
University of Wisconsin

William Lundstrom
Old Dominion University

Shanna Greenwalt
Southern Illinois University

Philip Kemp
DePaul University

Ernest F. Cooke
Memphis State University

Paul N. Bloom
University of North Carolina

George C. Hozier
University of New Mexico

Jay D. Lindquist
Western Michigan University

Robert F. Dwyer
University of Cincinnati

David R. Rink
Northern Illinois University

John Buckley
Orange County Community College

Thomas Ponzurick
West Virginia University

Barbara Unger
Western Washington University

Harrison L. Grathwol
University of Washington

Robert D. Hisrich
University of Tulsa

Charles L. Hilton
Eastern Kentucky University

Roy Klages
State University of New York at Albany

William G. Browne
Oregon State University

Poondi Varadarajan
Texas A & M University

Lee R. Duffus
University of Tennessee

Glen Riecken
East Tennessee State University

W. R. Berdine
California State Polytechnic Institute

Charles L. Lapp
University of Dallas

Thomas V. Greer
University of Maryland

Patricia Laidler
Massasoit Community College

Stan Madden
Baylor University

Elizabeth C. Hirschman
Rutgers—The State University

Peter Bloch
Louisiana State University

Linda Calderone
*State University of New York
Agricultural and Technical College
at Farmingdale*

Barbara Coe
North Texas State University

Alan R. Wiman
Rider College

Donald L. James
Fort Lewis College

Terrence V. O'Brien
Northern Illinois University

Joseph Guiltinan
Notre Dame

Kent B. Monroe
Virginia Polytechnic Institute

William Staples
University of Houston—Clear Lake

Richard J. Semenik
University of Utah

Pat J. Calabro
University of Texas at Arlington

James F. Wenthe
University of Georgia

Richard C. Becherer
Wayne State University

Thomas E. Barry
Southern Methodist University

Mark I. Alpert
University of Texas at Austin

Richard A. Lancioni
Temple University

Steven Shipley
Governor's State University

Paul J. Solomon
University of South Florida

Michael Peters
Boston College

Terence A. Shimp
University of South Carolina

Kenneth L. Rowe
Arizona State University

Allan Palmer
University of North Carolina at Charlotte

Stewart W. Bither
Pennsylvania State University

John R. Brooks, Jr.
West Texas State University

Carlos W. Moore
Baylor University

Charles Gross
Illinois Institute of Technology

Hugh E. Law
East Tennessee University

Dillard Tinsley
Stephen F. Austin State University

John R. Huser
Illinois Central College

David J. Fritzsche
University of Portland

David M. Landrum
Central State University

Robert Copley
University of Louisville

Robert A. Robicheaux
University of Alabama

Sue Ellen Neeley
University of Houston—Clear Lake

Otto W. Taylor
*State University of New York
Agricultural and Technical College
at Farmingdale*

Michael L. Rothschild
University of Wisconsin—Madison

Thomas Falcone
Indiana University of Pennsylvania

William L. Cron
Southern Methodist University

Sumner M. White
Massachusetts Bay Community College

Del I. Hawkins
University of Oregon

Ralph DiPietro
Montclair State College

Norman E. Daniel
Arizona State University

Bruce Stern
Portland State University

Beheruz N. Sethna
Clarkson College

Stephen J. Miller
Oklahoma State University

Dale Varble
Indiana State University

William M. Kincaid, Jr.
Oklahoma State University

John McFall
San Diego State University

James D. Reed
Louisiana State University—Shreveport

Ken Jensen
Bradley University

Arthur Prell
Lindenwood College

David H. Lindsay
University of Maryland

Claire F. Sullivan
Bentley College

Joseph Hair
Louisiana State University

Roger Blackwell
Ohio State University

James C. Carroll
University of Southwestern Louisiana

Guy Banville
Creighton University

Jack M. Starling
North Texas State University

Lloyd M. DeBoer
George Mason University

Dean C. Siewers
Rochester Institute of Technology

Benjamin J. Cutler
Bronx Community College

Gerald L. Manning
Des Moines Area Community College

Hale Tongren
George Mason University

Lee Meadow
Bentley College

Ronald Schill
Brigham Young University

Don Scotton
Cleveland State University

George Glisan
Illinois State University

Jim L. Grimm
Illinois State University

John I. Coppett
Iowa State University

Roy R. Grundy
College of DuPage

Steven J. Shaw
University of South Carolina

Melvin R. Crask
University of Georgia

J. Paul Peter
University of Wisconsin—Madison

Bert Rosenbloom
Drexel University

Terry M. Chambers
Appalachian State University

Rosann L. Spiro
Indiana University

Joseph Cangelosi
East Tennessee State University

Keith Murray
Northeastern University

Robert Solomon
Stephen F. Austin State University

Joseph Ballinger
Stephen F. Austin State University

Douglas Korneman
Milwaukee Area Technical College

John Lavin
Waukesha County Technical Institute

Lyndon Simkin
University of Warwick

Robert Grafton-Small
University of Strathclyde

Bodo Schlegelmilch
University of Edinburgh

Victor Quinones
University of Puerto Rico

Ken Wright
West Australia College of Advanced Education—Churchland Campus

Tinus Van Drunen
Universiteit Twente (Netherlands)

Larry Chonko
Baylor University

Jackie Brown
University of San Diego

Bernard LaLonde
Ohio State University

Yvonne Karsten
Mankato State University

George Avellano
Central State University

Salah S. Hassan
Skidmore College

Brian Meyer
Mankato State University

Blaine S. Greenfield
Bucks County Community College

George Wynn
James Madison University

Hal Teer
James Madison University

For contributing cases we are indebted to David Loudon, C. W. McConkey, and Maynard M. Dolecheck, Northeast Louisiana University; James Kennedy, Angelina College; and Donald Sapit, Sigma Marketing Concepts. We especially thank Jim L. Grimm, Illinois State University, for drafting the appendix on financial analysis in marketing.

Our special thanks go to Mary Gilly, University of California at Irvine, for developing the casebook, *Marketing Cases*. For creating *Marketer: A Stimulation*, we wish to thank Jerald R. Smith, University of Louisville. A great deal of thanks also go to Edwin C. Hackleman for developing the computerized test preparation program and for creating *Microstudy Plus*. We are deeply grateful to Lyn Gattis and Gwyneth M. Vaughn for their extreme diligence in providing editorial suggestions and support. For many types of technical assistance we thank Lisa Collins, Neil C. Herndon, Jr., Scott Saunders, Eric Voss, Dale Hoelscher, and Wendy Reed.

O. C. Ferrell expresses appreciation to the University of Michigan, School of Business and Marketing faculty, for resources and support while he was a visiting professor during 1988.

MARKETING

I. An Analysis of Marketing Opportunities

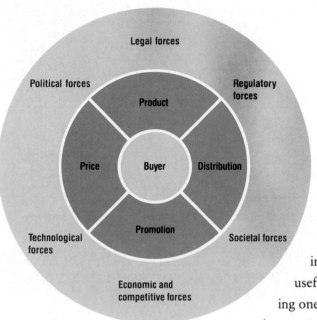

Legal forces

Political forces

Regulatory forces

Product

Price

Buyer

Distribution

Technological forces

Promotion

Societal forces

Economic and competitive forces

In Part I we introduce the field of marketing and provide a broad perspective from which to explore and analyze various components of the marketing discipline. In the first chapter we define marketing and discuss why an understanding of it is useful in many aspects of everyday life, including one's career. We provide an overview of general strategic marketing issues such as market opportunity analysis, target markets, and marketing mix development. Marketers should understand how environmental forces can affect customers and their responses to marketing strategies. In Chapter 2 we discuss political, legal, regulatory, societal, economic and competitive, and technological forces in the environment. In Chapter 3 we focus on one of the major steps in the development of a marketing strategy: selecting and analyzing target markets. Understanding elements that affect buying decisions enables marketers to better analyze customers' needs and evaluate how specific marketing strategies can satisfy those needs. In Chapter 4 we discuss consumer buying decision processes and factors that influence buying decisions. In Chapter 5 we stress organizational markets, organizational buyers, the buying center, and the organizational buying decision process. In Chapter 6 we analyze the role of a marketing information system and describe the basic steps in the marketing research process.

1. An Overview of Strategic Marketing

OBJECTIVES

- ▶ To learn representative definitions of marketing, and to understand the definition of marketing used in this text.

- ▶ To understand why a person should study marketing.

- ▶ To gain insight into the basic elements of the marketing concept and its implementation.

- ▶ To understand the major components of a marketing strategy.

- ▶ To acquire an overview of general strategic marketing issues such as market opportunity analysis, target market selection, and marketing mix development.

*S*touffer Food Corp., a producer of prepared frozen foods, several years ago conducted research that showed that purchases by larger families (those with two or more children) made up a significant portion of company sales. In response to these findings, Stouffer developed the Family Casserole line and marketed it in packages containing servings for four or more people. The line flopped because Stouffer's research failed to detect "split-menu dining"—a growing trend among larger, more active families. Such families are not always able to eat together, and even when they do, family members do not necessarily eat the same thing. Thus consumers buying Stouffer products tend to purchase smaller packages, suitable for one- or two-person servings. The failure of the Family Casserole line alerted Stouffer to the split-menu trend. "The fragmentation of eating has become much more normal than random," says Linda Smithson, director of Pillsbury Co.'s consumer center. All food manufacturers are concerned about the decline and projected ultimate death of the family meal. New products are being continually developed to appeal to diverse eating habits.

In contrast, Stouffer's Lean Cuisine line has been a success (see Figure 1.1). Stouffer's research indicated that women, smaller families, and single-person households would purchase the dinners. Stouffer found that working women wanted to watch their weight and to serve their families nourishing meals with minimal preparation. Stouffer's failure and success illustrate the necessity of both research into and accurate assessment of buyers' needs.

Although Stouffer's Family Casserole line failed, two Brenham, Texas, women have taken advantage of the same market niche to sell their family sized

FIGURE 1.1

Stouffer's successful
Lean Cuisine line
targets the single-
family household
(SOURCE: Stouffer
Food Corporation)

frozen casseroles. As Stouffer did, Virginia and Barbara Gaskamp recognized that more women are working outside the home and do not have the time to prepare nutritious meals. These working women, as well as couples who both work but have no children (known as dinks—double income, no kids), are willing to purchase large-sized, easy-to-prepare nutritious meals. The Gaskamps' Market Place Casseroles come in one- or two-pound sizes packaged in an aluminum tray, and they are priced competitively. The company recently changed its packaging so consumers are able to microwave the casseroles, making them more convenient.

In 1986, Market Place Casseroles sold $90,000 worth of the frozen casseroles. In 1987, sales were $185,000, and 1988 sales were expected to be double those of 1987. The casseroles have been so successful thus far because they are home-cooked with high-quality ingredients, and they are promoted on that basis. These dinners specifically meet the needs of the target market: working women in both large and small active families who simply do not have time to prepare nutritious meals. The company is small enough that it can take advantage of small niches in the market that are not profitable for a larger company such as Stouffer. The company also profits from the Gaskamps' local reputation for good, home-cooked food.

We can thus see that significant changes in the overall population can have a decisive impact on the success of a product. Marketers engage in research both to analyze and anticipate such changes, but important trends in consumer behavior may be overlooked, causing product failure, as is what happened with Stouffer's Family Casseroles. Also, a smaller company can sometimes more efficiently use its resources and knowledge of a market than a larger company to meet the needs of a specific group within a large target market.[1]

T HIS FIRST CHAPTER is an overview of the marketing concepts and decisions covered in the text. Initially, we develop a definition of marketing and explain each element of the definition. Then we look at several reasons why people should study marketing and point out that marketing activities pervade our everyday lives. We introduce the marketing concept and consider several issues associated with implementing it. Next we discuss the major tasks of strategic marketing management: market opportunity analysis, target market selection, marketing mix development, and management of marketing activities. We conclude our overview by discussing the organization of this text.

Marketing Defined

If you ask several people what **marketing** is, they will respond with a variety of descriptions. Marketing encompasses many more activities than most people think. Remember, though, that any definition is merely an abstract description of a broad concept. No definition perfectly describes the concept to which it refers. Marketing is practiced and studied for many different purposes and so has been, and continues to be, defined in many ways, whether for academic, research, or applied business purposes. Following are three such definitions:

1. Marketing is the process of planning and executing the conception, pricing, promotion, and distribution of ideas, goods, and services to create exchanges that satisfy individual and organizational objectives.[2]

1. Based on information from Betsy Morris, "Are Square Meals Headed for Extinction?" *Wall Street Journal,* March 15, 1988, Section 2, p. 1; Ann Lloyd, "The Lean Cuisine Story," *American Demographics,* December 1984, p. 16; a marketing study on Stouffer's Lean Cuisine prepared by Jimmy Ashley, Jewel Hervey, Jim Paquin, Mike Quinnelly, Karen Reyes, and Lance Scott, Texas A&M, 1987; a marketing study on Market Place Casseroles prepared by Gerhard Baumann, Jill Hubred, Alan Blankley, and Chris Smith, Texas A&M, 1987.
2. "AMA Board Approves New Marketing Definition," *Marketing News,* Mar. 1, 1985, p. 1.

2. Micro-marketing is the performance of activities that seek to accomplish an organization's objectives by anticipating customer or client needs and directing a flow of need satisfying goods and services from producer to customer or client.[3]
3. Marketing is the set of individual and social activities concerned with the initiation, resolution, and/or acceptance of exchange relationships.[4]

All these definitions contribute something to our development of a definition of marketing. One study found that the first definition, which was developed by the American Marketing Association, has been widely accepted by academics and marketing managers. This same study found that academics view exchange as the most important concept in a marketing definition, whereas managers view customer satisfaction as the most important concept in a definition.[5]

The second definition emphasizes that marketing focuses on activities to satisfy customers. The third definition focuses on marketing as activities that initiate or resolve exchange relationships. Although earlier definitions restricted marketing as a business activity, these definitions are broad enough to indicate that marketing also occurs in nonbusiness situations as practiced by nonbusiness organizations.

We agree with many aspects of these three definitions, but we believe that our slightly broader definition encompasses the best features of these definitions plus one additional dimension: marketing activities occur in a dynamic environment. That environment determines what types of activities will develop effective exchanges. We will describe in detail our definition of marketing:

Marketing consists of individual and organizational activities that facilitate and expedite satisfying exchange relationships in a dynamic environment through the creation, distribution, promotion, and pricing of goods, services, and ideas.

In this definition, marketing is viewed as a diverse group of activities directed at various products and performed within many types of organizations. In marketing exchanges, any product may be involved. We assume only that individuals and organizations expect to gain a reward in excess of the costs incurred. So that our definition will be fully understood, we now examine each component more closely.

Marketing Consists of Activities

Numerous activities are required to market products effectively. Some activities can be performed by producers. Some can be accomplished by intermediaries, who buy from producers or other intermediaries so that they can resell the products. And some activities may even be performed by purchasers. Marketing does not include all human and organizational activities; it encompasses only those activities aimed at facilitating and expediting exchanges. Table 1.1 lists several major categories and examples of marketing activities. Note that this list is not all-inclusive; each activity could be subdivided into numerous, more specific activities.

3. Jerome McCarthy and William Perreault, Jr., *Basic Marketing: A Managerial Approach* (Homewood, IL: Irwin, 1987), p. 8.
4. Richard P. Bagozzi, *Principles of Marketing Management* (Chicago: Science Research Associates, 1986), p. 5.
5. O. C. Ferrell and George Lucas, "An Evaluation of Progress in the Development of a Definition of Marketing," *Journal of the Academy of Marketing Science,* Fall 1987, p. 17.

TABLE 1.1

Possible decisions and
activities associated
with marketing mix
variables

MARKETING MIX VARIABLES	POSSIBLE DECISIONS AND ACTIVITIES
PRODUCT	Develop and test-market new products; modify existing products; eliminate products that do not satisfy customers' desires; formulate brand names and branding policies; create product warranties and establish procedures for fulfilling warranties; plan packages, including materials, sizes, shapes, colors, and designs
DISTRIBUTION	Analyze various types of distribution channels; design appropriate distribution channels; design an effective program for dealer relations; establish distribution centers; formulate and implement procedures for efficient product handling; set up inventory controls; analyze transportation methods; minimize total distribution costs; analyze possible locations for plants and wholesale or retail outlets
PROMOTION	Set promotional objectives; determine major types of promotion to be used; select and schedule advertising media; develop advertising messages; measure the effectiveness of advertisements; recruit and train salespersons; formulate compensation programs for sales personnel; establish sales territories; plan and implement sales promotion efforts such as free samples, coupons, displays, sweepstakes, sales contests, and cooperative advertising programs; prepare and disseminate publicity releases
PRICE	Analyze competitors' prices; formulate pricing policies; determine method or methods used to set prices; set prices; determine discounts for various types of buyers; establish conditions and terms of sales

Marketing Is Performed by Individuals and Organizations

Marketing pervades many relationships among individuals, groups, and organizations. All types of organizations perform marketing activities to facilitate exchanges. Businesses as well as nonbusiness organizations such as colleges and universities, charitable organizations, and community theaters and hospitals perform marketing activities. For example, colleges and universities and their students engage in exchanges. To receive knowledge, entertainment, room, board, and a degree, students give up time, money, effort, perhaps services in the form of labor, and opportunities to do other things. In return, the institutions provide instruction, food, medical services, entertainment, recreation, and the use of land and facilities. Even the sole owner and operator of a small neighborhood store decides which products will satisfy customers, arranges deliveries to the store, prices inventory, displays products, advertises, and assists customers.

Marketing Facilitates Satisfying Exchange Relationships

For an **exchange** to take place, **four** conditions must exist. First, two or more individuals, groups, or organizations must participate. Second, each party must possess something of value **that the** other party desires. Third, each party must be willing to give up its "something of value" to receive the "something of value" the other party holds. The objective of a marketing exchange is to receive something that is desired more than what is given up to get it, that is, a reward in excess of costs. Fourth, the parties to the exchange must be able to communicate with each other to make their somethings of value available.[6] Figure 1.2 illustrates the process of exchange. As the arrows indicate, the two parties communicate to make their somethings of value available to each other. Note, though, that an exchange will not necessarily take place just because these four conditions exist. However, even if there is no exchange, marketing activities still have occurred. The somethings of value held by the two parties are most often products and/or financial resources such as money or credit. When an exchange occurs, products are traded for either other products or financial resources.

The exchange should be *satisfying* to both the buyer and the seller. In a study of marketing managers, 32 percent indicated that creating customer satisfaction was the most important concept in a definition of marketing.[7] Expediting exchange to facilitate satisfaction is the core concept of marketing. All marketing activities should be oriented toward creating and sustaining satisfying exchanges. To maintain an exchange relationship, both the buyer and the seller must be satisfied. The buyer must be satisfied with the good, service, or idea obtained in the exchange. The seller must receive something of value that permits satisfaction; this is often financial reward(s).

The most significant strategic choice any firm makes is deciding what customers are to be served.[8] A seller's satisfaction may derive from doing business with a particular customer or customer group, from making a profit through a particular exchange relationship, or perhaps from achieving another organizational objective.

6. Philip Kotler, *Marketing Management: Analysis, Planning, Implementation, and Control,* 6th ed. (Englewood Cliffs, N.J.: Prentice-Hall, 1988), p. 6.
7. O. C. Ferrell and George Lucas, "An Evaluation of Progress in the Development of a Definition of Marketing," *Journal of the Academy of Marketing Science,* Fall 1987, p. 20.
8. Frederick E. Webster, Jr., "Marketing Strategy in a Slow Growth Economy," *California Management Review,* Spring 1986, p. 101.

FIGURE 1.2

Exchange between buyer and seller

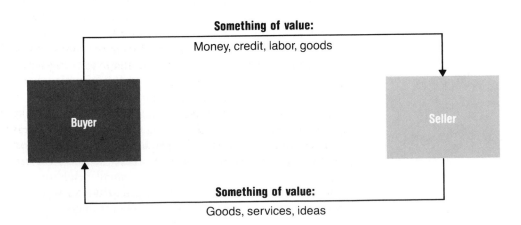

FIGURE 1.3

Ford promotes on-going development of quality cars and trucks (SOURCE: Courtesy of the Ford Motor Company)

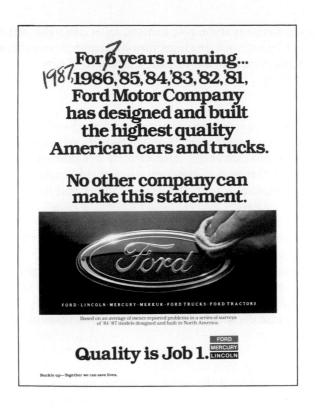

Maintaining a positive relationship with buyers is an important goal for a seller, regardless of whether the seller is marketing cereal, laundry equipment, financial services, or an electric generating plant. Through buyer-seller interaction, the buyer develops expectations about the seller's future behavior. To fulfill these expectations, the seller must deliver on promises made. Over time, a healthy buyer-seller relationship results in interdependencies between the two parties. The buyer depends on the seller to provide information, parts, and service; to be available; and to provide satisfying products in the future. For example, in Figure 1.3, Ford surveys report that they are designing and building the highest quality cars and trucks of the past seven years. The seller depends on the buyer to continue to make purchases from the seller and to seek information. The 60,000- and 70,000-mile limited warranties on many new American automobiles illustrate an attempt to create long-term buyer-seller relationships.

There is a growing trend among consumer goods companies to establish communication channels with buyers to maintain long-term relationships. For example, many such companies now have toll-free numbers consumers can call to make inquiries, make complaints, ask for information, or the like. In a number of industries—large appliances, computers, telecommunications hardware, office automation, farm equipment, and industrial machinery—service support is emerging as the major area in which firms will soon be striving for competitive advantage.[9] Large projects or products, such as a weapons system, require considerable

9. Midland M. Lele, "How Service Needs Influence Product Strategy," *Sloan Management Review,* Fall 1986, p. 63.

interaction between the buyer and the seller after the sale and before and after delivery. Sellers of such products must be prepared to maintain favorable relationships with the buyer for a long period. The sale, in this case, is just the beginning of the relationship.[10]

Marketing Occurs in a Dynamic Environment

The marketing environment consists of many changing forces: laws, regulations, actions of political officials, societal pressures, changes in economic conditions, and technological advances. Each of these dynamic forces has an impact on how effectively marketing activities can facilitate and expedite exchanges. We explore such environmental forces later in this chapter and in Chapter 2.

Marketing Involves Product Development, Distribution, Promotion, and Pricing

Marketing is more than just advertising or selling the product. Marketing people get involved with designing and developing a product. Marketing focuses on making the product available at the right place, at the right time, at a price that is acceptable to customers and on informing customers in a way that helps them determine if the product is consistent with their needs. Later in this chapter we discuss in more detail the areas of product development, distribution, promotion, and pricing.

Marketing Focuses on Goods, Services, and Ideas

We already have used the word *product* a number of times in this chapter. For purposes of analysis in this text, a **product** is viewed as being a good, a service, or an idea. A **good** is a physical entity one can touch. A **service** is the application of human and mechanical efforts to people or objects. Services such as bank services and long-distance telephone services are just as real as goods, but an individual cannot actually touch them. Examples of marketers that deal in services include airlines, dry cleaners, beauty shops, financial institutions, hospitals, day care centers, and carpet cleaners. **Ideas** include concepts, philosophies, images, and issues. For instance, Weight Watchers International Inc., for a fee, gives its members ideas to help them lose weight and control their eating habits. Other marketers of ideas include political parties, churches, and schools.

Why Study Marketing?

After considering the definition of marketing, one can understand some of the obvious reasons why the study of marketing is relevant. In this section we discuss several perhaps less obvious reasons why one should study marketing.

Marketing Activities Are Used in Many Organizations

From 25 to 33 percent of all civilian workers in the United States perform marketing activities. A variety of interesting and challenging career opportunities are available in the marketing field. Some of these opportunities are personal selling, advertising, packaging, transportation, storage, marketing research, product devel-

10. Theodore Levitt, "After the Sale Is Over," *Harvard Business Review*, Sept.–Oct. 1983, pp. 87–93.

FIGURE 1.4
The National Wildlife
Federation uses mar-
keting to gain support
(SOURCE: Courtesy of
the National Wildlife
Federation)

opment, wholesaling, and retailing. In addition, many individuals who work for nonbusiness organizations are involved in marketing activities. Marketing skills are used to promote political, cultural, church, civic, and charitable activities. The advertisement in Figure 1.4 encourages support of the National Wildlife Federation, a nonprofit organization. Whether a person earns a living through marketing activities or performs them without compensation in nonbusiness settings, marketing knowledge and skills are valuable assets.

Marketing Activities Are Important to Businesses and the Economy

A business organization must sell products to survive and to grow. Marketing activities directly or indirectly help sell the organization's products. By doing so, they generate financial resources that can be used to develop innovative products. New products allow a firm to better satisfy customers' changing needs, which in turn enables the firm to generate more profits. For example, each year *Fortune* publishes a list of what its staff considers the top products. Recently, among these products of the year were the Acura Legend Coupe, E.I. du Pont de Nemours & Co., Inc.'s Stainmaster carpet, the American Express Optima card, digital audiotape machines, disposable cameras, Mevacor (a drug that lowers cholesterol), Casio's SF-4000 digital diary, and Interplak (an electric toothbrush to eliminate plaque).[11] All these products produce considerable profit for the firms that introduced them. For example, Stainmaster carpet is the most successful product Du

11. John Steinbreder, "Products of the Year," *Fortune*, Dec. 7, 1987, pp. 121–125.

Pont has ever introduced, and more than 400,000 Interplak electric toothbrushes were sold in 1987, the first year they were introduced.

Our highly complex, industrialized economy depends heavily on marketing activities. They help produce the profits that are essential not only to the survival of individual businesses but to the health and ultimate survival of the economy as a whole. Profits are essential to economic growth because without them, businesses find it difficult, if not impossible, to buy added raw materials, hire more employees, attract more capital, and produce the additional products that in turn make more profits.

Marketing Knowledge Enhances Consumer Awareness

Besides contributing to the well-being of our nation, marketing activities pervade our everyday lives. In fact, they help us achieve many improvements in the quality of our lives. Still, critics contend that commonplace products are marketed so zealously that they get attention out of all proportion to their merit.[12]

Studying marketing activities allows us to weigh their costs, benefits, and flaws more effectively. We can see where they need to be improved and how to accomplish that goal. For example, if you have had an unsatisfactory experience with a warranty, you may have wished that laws were enforced more strictly to make sellers fulfill their promises. In the same vein, you may have wished that you had more information about a product—or more accurate information—before you made the purchase. Understanding marketing enables us to evaluate the corrective measures (such as laws, regulations, and industry guidelines) that may be required to stop unfair, misleading, or unethical marketing practices. The results of a national survey presented in Table 1.2 indicate that there is a considerable lack of knowledge about marketing activities, as reflected by the sizable proportion of respondents who agree with the myths in the table.

Marketing Costs Consume a Sizable Part of Buyers' Dollars

The study of marketing will make you aware that many marketing activities are necessary to provide people with satisfying goods and services. Obviously, these marketing activities cost money. In fact, about one-half of a buyer's dollar goes for marketing costs. A family with a monthly income of $2,000 and who allocates $400 to taxes and savings spends about $1,600 for goods and services. Of this amount, $800 goes for marketing activities. Clearly, if marketing expenses consume that much of your dollar, you should know how this money is used.

The Marketing Concept

Some organizations have tried to be successful by buying land, building a plant, equipping it with people and machines, and then making a product that they believe the world needs. However, these organizations frequently fail to attract people with what they have to offer because they defined their business as "making a product" rather than "helping potential customers satisfy their needs and

12. "In Today's Marketplace, It's Hype, Hype, Hype," *U.S. News and World Report,* Dec. 5, 1983, p. 51.

wants." An organization that adopts and properly implements the marketing concept should not have difficulty attracting customers.

The marketing concept is not a second definition of marketing. It is a way of thinking—a management philosophy about an organization's entire activities. This philosophy affects all efforts of the organization, not just the marketing activities.

Basic Elements of the Marketing Concept

According to the **marketing concept,** an organization should try to satisfy the needs of customers or clients through a coordinated set of activities that also allows the organization to achieve its goals. Customer satisfaction is the major aim of the marketing concept. In Figure 1.5, General Electric recognizes the importance of the marketing concept by helping ensure customer satisfaction with a 90-day refund or exchange policy. First, a business organization must find out what will satisfy customers. With this information, the business can create satisfying products. But that is not enough. The business then must get these products to the customers. Nor does the process end there. The business must continue to alter, adapt, and develop products to keep pace with customers' changing desires and preferences. For example, consumers' snack-food preferences have changed toward foods with fewer calories. General Foods Corp. now offers reduced-calorie snacks to serve this need. The marketing concept stresses the importance of customers and emphasizes that marketing activities begin and end with them.

TABLE 1.2

National survey results regarding marketing myths

MYTHS	STRONGLY AGREE	SOMEWHAT AGREE	NEITHER AGREE NOR DISAGREE	SOMEWHAT DISAGREE	STRONGLY DISAGREE	NO RESPONSE
Marketing and selling are about the same thing	11.9% (245)	31.4% (645)	23.2% (476)	21.0% (431)	11.4% (234)	1.2% (24)
A grocery store owner takes home at least $3 for every $10 bag of groceries sold	19.5% (400)	23.8% (486)	30.3% (619)	14.9% (305)	11.0% (226)	0.4% (9)
Products that are advertised a great deal cost more	30.5% (625)	36.1% (741)	13.7% (282)	13.1% (270)	5.7% (117)	1.0% (20)
Wholesalers make high profits that significantly increase prices consumers pay	35.4% (725)	37.7% (771)	15.9% (326)	8.0% (164)	2.4% (49)	0.5% (10)
Marketing is the same thing as advertising	12.9% (265)	35.7% (734)	22.7% (465)	19.8% (406)	7.7% (157)	1.3% (28)

SOURCE: William M. Pride and O. C. Ferrell; a national survey of U.S. households, 1985.

In attempting to satisfy customers, businesses must consider not only short-run, immediate needs but also broad, long-term desires. Trying to satisfy customers' current needs by sacrificing their long-term desires will only create strong dissatisfaction in the future. For example, people want efficient, low-cost energy to power their homes and automobiles, yet they clearly react adversely to energy producers who pollute the air and water, kill wildlife, or cause disease or birth defects in future generations. To meet these short- and long-run needs and desires, a firm must coordinate all its activities. Production, finance, accounting, personnel, and marketing departments must work together.

Please do not think that the marketing concept is a highly philanthropic philosophy aimed at helping customers at the expense of the business organization. A firm that adopts the marketing concept must not only satisfy its customers' objectives but also achieve its own goals or it will not stay in business long. The overall goals of a business might be directed toward increasing profits, market shares, sales or be a combination of the three goals. The marketing concept stresses that a business organization can best achieve its goals by providing customer satisfaction. Implementing the marketing concept should benefit the organization as well as its customers. A firm can be successful only through coordination of all the organization's activities with the aim of meeting its objectives.

Evolution of the Marketing Concept

The marketing concept may seem like an obvious and sensible approach to running a business. However, business people have not always believed that the best way to make sales, and profits, is to satisfy customers. A famous example is Henry Ford's philosophy: "The customers can have any color car they want as long as it is black." The philosophy of the marketing concept emerged in the third major era in the history of U.S. business, preceded by the production and the sales eras. Surprisingly, nearly forty years after the marketing era began, many businesses still have not adopted the marketing concept.

The Production Era   During the second half of the nineteenth century, the Industrial Revolution came into its own in the United States. Electricity, rail transportation, the division of labor, the assembly line, and mass production made it possible to manufacture products more efficiently. As a result of new technology and new ways of using labor, products streamed out of factories into the marketplace, where consumer demand for manufactured goods was strong. This **production orientation** continued into the early part of this century, encouraged by the scientific management movement that, to increase worker productivity, championed rigidly structured jobs and pay based on output.

The Sales Era   Beginning in the 1920s, the strong consumer demand for products subsided. Businesses realized that products, which by this time could be made relatively efficiently, would have to be "sold" to consumers. From the mid-1920s to the early 1950s, businesses looked on sales as the major means of increasing profits. As a result, this period came to have a **sales orientation.** Business people believed that the most important marketing activities were personal selling and advertising.

FIGURE 1.5

General Electric provides a 90-day refund or exchange policy to ensure customer satisfaction (SOURCE: Courtesy of General Electric Appliances)

The Marketing Era By the early 1950s, some business people began to recognize that efficient production and extensive promotion of products did not guarantee that customers would buy them. These businesses, and many others since then, found that they must first determine what customers want and then produce it, rather than simply make products and try to change customers' needs to fit what is produced. As more and more organizations realized that the measurement of customers' needs is where everything begins, U.S. business moved into the marketing era, the era of **customer orientation**. Today, U.S. businesses are beginning to recognize that their destiny and success will be determined by the world economic and business environment. Because of improved world transportation and communications, what happens in Japan and Europe is just as important as what happens in the United States. Many businesses are expanding their customer orientation, not just within the United States but worldwide. This expansion is requiring new marketing philosophies that attempt to either standardize products for customers around the world or customize products for customers in specific countries. For example, General Motors Corp. is now exporting its Chevrolet Corsica and Beretta and Pontiac Grand Am to Japan.[13] Pepsi-Cola and Pizza Hut pizza are sold in the Soviet Union. McDonald's Corp. has twenty-five stores, Burger King has six stores, and Pizza Hut, Inc. and KFC (Kentucky Fried Chicken) Corporation each have seven stores in Hong Kong.[14] Gillette European Personal Care Division has

13. Jacob M. Schlesinger, "GM to Expand to Japan as Fuji Weighs Expansion of Planned U.S. Unit," *Wall Street Journal,* Nov. 13, 1987, p. 2.
14. Maggie Fox, "Fast Food Heats Up in Hong Kong," *Advertising Age,* Oct. 26, 1987, p. 78.

developed a deodorant for multiple European nationalities. Natrel Plus is a more expensive deodorant made from a plant extract. The product is being sold in the United Kingdom, Ireland, Sweden, Norway, Holland, Finland, and France.[15]

Implementing the Marketing Concept

A philosophy may look good on paper. It may sound reasonable and even noble. But that does not mean it can be put into practice easily. The marketing concept is a case in point. To implement it, an organization must focus on some general conditions and must also be cognizant of several problems. Because of these conditions and problems, the marketing concept has yet to be fully accepted by American business.

Because the marketing concept affects all types of business activities, not only marketing activities, the top management of an organization must adopt it whole-heartedly. High-level executives must incorporate the marketing concept into their personal philosophies of business management so completely that it is the basis for all the goals and decisions they set for their firms. They must convince other members of the organization to accept the changes in policies and operations that flow from their acceptance of the marketing concept.

As the first step, management must establish an information system that enables it to discover customers' real needs and to use that information internally to create satisfying products. Because an information system of this sort is almost always expensive, management must be willing to commit a substantial amount of money and time for development and maintenance. Without an adequate information system, an organization cannot be customer oriented.

Management's second major task may well be restructuring the organization. We pointed out that if a firm is to satisfy customers' objectives as well as its own, it must coordinate all activities. To achieve this coordination, the internal operations and the overall objectives of one or more departments may need restructuring. If the head of the marketing unit is not a member of the organization's top-level management, the situation should be rectified. Some departments may have to be abolished and new ones created. Implementing the marketing concept demands the support not only of top management but of managers and staff at all levels within the organization.

Even when the basic conditions of establishing an information system and reorganizing the firm are satisfied, it is not certain that the firm's new marketing approach will function perfectly. First, there is a limit to a firm's ability to satisfy customers' needs for a particular product. In a mass production economy, most business organizations cannot tailor products to fit the exact needs of each customer. Second, although a firm may try to learn what customers want, it may be unable to do so. Even when a firm correctly identifies customers' needs, the firm's personnel often have a hard time actually developing a product to satisfy those needs. Many companies spend considerable time and money to research customers' needs and yet still create some products that do not sell well. Third, by satisfying one segment of society, a firm sometimes contributes to the dissatisfaction of other segments. Government and nonbusiness organizations also experience this problem. Fourth, a firm may have trouble maintaining employee morale during any

15. Ron Melk, "Gillette's Natrel Approach to Europe," *Adweek's Marketing Week,* Mar. 14, 1988, p. 14.

restructuring that may be required to coordinate the activities of various departments. Management must clearly enunciate the reasons for the changes and communicate its own enthusiasm for the marketing concept.

Strategic Marketing Management

Marketing management is a process of planning, organizing, implementing, and controlling marketing activities to facilitate and expedite exchanges effectively and efficiently. Effectiveness and efficiency are important dimensions of this definition. *Effectiveness* is the degree to which an exchange helps achieve an organization's objectives. The quality of exchanges relative to an organization's objectives may range from highly desirable to highly undesirable. A major purpose of the marketing management process is to facilitate desirable exchanges. *Efficiency* is the minimization of resources an organization must spend to achieve a specific level of desired exchanges. Thus the overall goal of marketing management is to facilitate highly desirable exchanges and to minimize as much as possible the costs of doing so.

Our definition of marketing states that activities are performed to facilitate and expedite exchanges. When marketing managers attempt to properly manage marketing activities, they must deal with two broad sets of variables: those relating to the marketing mix and those that make up the marketing environment. The marketing mix decision variables—product, distribution, promotion, and price—are factors over which an organization has control. As Figure 1.6 shows, these variables are constructed around the buyer. The marketing environment variables are political, legal, regulatory, societal, economic and competitive, and technological forces. These factors are subject to less control by an organization, but they affect buyers and marketing managers' decisions regarding marketing mix variables.

To achieve the broad goal of facilitating and expediting desirable exchanges, marketing management in an organization is responsible for developing and managing marketing strategies. Strategy—a word derived from the ancient Greek *strategia,* meaning "the art of the general"—is concerned with the key decisions required to reach an objective or set of objectives. A marketing strategy articulates a plan for the best use of the organization's resources and advantages to meet its objectives. Specifically, a **marketing strategy** encompasses selecting and analyzing a target market (the group of people whom the organization wants to reach) and creating and maintaining an appropriate **marketing mix** (product, distribution, promotion, and price) that will satisfy those people.

To develop and manage marketing strategies, an organization's marketing management must focus on several generic marketing management tasks: market opportunity analysis, target market selection, marketing mix development, and management of marketing activities. Figure 1.7 shows these tasks, along with the chapters of this book in which these tasks are discussed.

Market Opportunity Analysis

Customer desire for almost any product diminishes over time. Few organizations can assume that products popular today will be of interest to buyers ten years from now. An organization's long-term survival depends on finding new products and markets.

FIGURE I.6

Components of the marketing mix and marketing environment

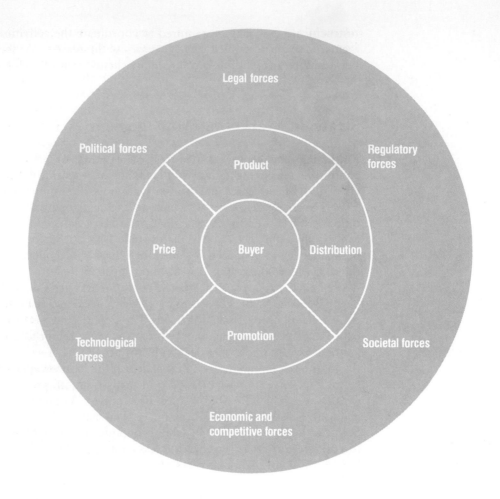

An organization can consider a variety of alternatives through which it can grow and sustain itself. An organization can modify existing products (for example, All Bran cereal could increase its fiber content to address increasing health consciousness among customers), introduce new products (such as Gillette Co.'s recent introduction of Good News disposable razors with a pivot head to replace the earlier Good News version that did not have a pivot head),[16] and delete some that customers no longer desire (such as the Beta videorecorders). A firm may attempt to market its products to a greater number of individuals in its existing markets. Various efforts may be initiated to convince current customers to use more of a product, or marketing managers may decide to expand the geographic boundaries of a market. Diversification into new product offerings through internal efforts or through acquisitions of other organizations may be viable options for a firm. An organization's ability to pursue any of these alternatives successfully depends on the organization's internal characteristics and the forces within the marketing environment.

16. P. Rajan Varadarajan, "Marketing Strategies in Action," *Business,* January–March 1986, p. 11.

Internal Organizational Factors   The primary factors inside an organization that should be considered when analyzing market opportunities are organizational objectives, financial resources, managerial skills, organizational strengths and weaknesses, and cost structures. Most organizations that plan to flourish over time have overall objectives. Some market opportunities may be consistent with these objectives, but others are not. To pursue opportunities that are inconsistent with the firm's overall objectives is hazardous. Frequently, the pursuit of such opportunities ends in failure or forces the firm to alter its long-term objectives. The Application on page 23 illustrates how Harley-Davidson Motor Co., Inc. has had to reassess its opportunities and deploy the right resources to recover from a decreasing share in the motorcycle industry.

Obviously, a firm's financial resources place a constraint on the type of market opportunities that can be pursued. An organization typically does not develop projects that can result in an economic catastrophe. However, there are situations in which the firm has little choice but to invest in a high-risk opportunity because the costs of not pursuing the project are so high.

Management's skills and experience limit the types of opportunities that an organization can pursue. Especially when a firm is exploring the possibility of entering unfamiliar markets with new products, a good deal of caution should be exercised. When managerial experience and skills are lacking, they sometimes can be acquired by hiring managerial personnel.

Most organizations have certain strengths and weaknesses. Because of the types of operations that a firm has engaged in, it normally has employees with specialized

FIGURE 1.7

Generic marketing
management tasks

Generic marketing management tasks

Market opportunity analysis and target market selection

- The Marketing Environment (Chapter 2)
- Target Market Evaluation (Chapter 3)
- Consumer Markets and Buying Behavior (Chapter 4)
- Organizational Markets and Buying Behavior (Chapter 5)
- Marketing Research and Information Systems (Chapter 6)

Marketing mix development

- Product Decisions (Chapters 7 and 8)
- Distribution Decisions (Chapters 9, 10, 11, and 12)
- Promotion Decisions (Chapters 13, 14, and 15)
- Price Decisions (Chapters 16 and 17)

Management of marketing activities

- Strategic Market Planning (Chapter 18)
- Organization, Implementation, and Control (Chapter 19)

skills and technological information. These characteristics can be a strength when launching marketing strategies that require them. However, they may be a weakness if the firm tries to compete in new, unrelated product areas.

An organization's cost structure may be advantageous if certain opportunities are pursued and disadvantageous if other market opportunities are pursued. The cost structure can be affected by such factors as geographic location, employee skill mix, access to raw materials, and type of equipment and facilities.

Marketing Environment Forces   The **marketing environment** of political, legal, regulatory, societal, economic and competitive, and technological forces surrounds the buyer and the marketing mix (see Figure 1.6). Business strategists know that they cannot predict the marketing environment with certainty. Even so, over the years, businesses have become more systematic in taking external conditions into consideration when planning their competitive actions.[17] The forces in the marketing environment affect in three general ways a marketer's ability to facilitate and expedite exchanges. First, the marketing environment influences customers. It affects lifestyles, standards of living, and preferences and needs for products. Because a marketing manager tries to develop and adjust the marketing mix to satisfy consumers, the effects of environmental forces on customers also have an indirect impact on the marketing mix components. Second, forces in the marketing environment directly influence whether and how a marketing manager can perform certain marketing activities. Third, the environmental forces may affect a marketing manager's decisions and actions by influencing buyers' reactions to the firm's marketing mix.

Although forces in the marketing environment sometimes are considered "uncontrollables," a marketing manager may be able to influence one or more of them. However, marketing environment forces fluctuate quickly and dramatically, which is one reason why marketing is so interesting and challenging. Because these forces are highly interrelated, a change in one may cause others to change.

Even though environmental changes produce uncertainty for marketers and, at times, have severe adverse effects on marketing efforts, they also can create opportunities. Thus a marketer must be aware of changes in environmental forces not only to adjust to and influence them but to capitalize on the opportunities they provide. The remainder of this section briefly describes environmental forces. In Chapter 2 we explore each major environmental force in greater depth.

Our political institutions enact laws and create regulatory units that affect business organizations. More broadly, **political forces** strongly influence our country's economic and political stability. They do so through decisions that affect domestic matters and through their authority to negotiate trade agreements and determine foreign policy. If government officials have negative opinions about a firm or an industry, they may pass and enforce laws that place severe constraints on the firm or industry's ability to market products. In addition, the government purchases many products in tremendous quantities and offers several kinds of loans that can aid businesses. Political officials thus may affect firms' financial positions by awarding or failing to award government contracts or loans.

17. Gene R. Laczniak and Robert F. Lusch, "Environment and Strategy in 1995: A Survey of High-Level Executives," *Journal of Consumer Marketing,* Spring 1986, p. 28.

Harley-Davidson Shifts into High Gear

Harley-Davidson Motor Co., Inc., the Milwaukee-based maker of big, heavy motorcycles (often called "hogs"), led the U.S. heavyweight motorcycle market until the late 1970s. The company's market share slipped largely because of competition from Japanese motorcycles (Harley owners refer to Japanese bikes as "rice burners"). Harley-Davidson's reputation also suffered because their products were of inferior quality. At one point, the company's biggest competitor, Honda Motor Co., Ltd., held more than half of the U.S. market, whereas Harley-Davidson held on to a tiny 4 percent. The Japanese bikes are often cheaper; Honda's comparably sized motorcycles cost about $500 less than Harley-Davidson's. Harley received help from the U.S. government in 1983 in the form of a five-year tax on heavy motorcycles imported from Japan, but Harley had to solve its other problems alone.

The company focused first on improving old products and developing new ones. Customers had been complaining about the deteriorating quality of Harley bikes, and many people called Harley's flagship V engine an antique. The company updated the V engine and eliminated many of its problems. Harley-Davidson also turned to Japanese manufacturing and management techniques to cut costs and improve product quality. It introduced several midsized bikes with lower price tags. Its Sportster model sells for $3,995, although top-of-the-line Harley-Davidson road cruisers still fetch up to $12,000.

In the past, Harley-Davidson aimed its bikes at two main groups: the "bikers" and the "towers." The bikers fit the popular conception of motorcycle riders, with their leather jackets, tattoos, and Harley insignia. The towers are conventional blue-collar workers who tend to take longer trips than do owners of smaller motorcycles. The company has survived the last few years largely because of these loyal customers and dedicated dealers. Some of Harley-Davidson's better known customers include Malcolm Forbes (publisher of *Forbes* magazine) and members of the Hell's Angels and the California Highway Patrol.

However, more white-collar professional people are now riding hogs. In fact, 10 percent of hog riders are women. The white-collar market particularly values the luxury, durability, and classic image that Harley represents. Harley-Davidson is expanding its marketing activities to include these consumers, although they will not forget the loyal bikers and towers. The company promotes its hogs to these groups with a new all-American image and by sponsoring motorcycle rallies.

The company's shift in marketing strategy resulted in an increase in market share, to almost 40 percent of the U.S. heavy and midsized motorcycle market. The company's situation improved so much that it asked the government to withdraw the tariff on heavy Japanese bikes one year early. The company will not compete with the Japanese for the small-bike market, but it plans to compete head-on in the heavy and midsized bike markets, where its hogs have a quality edge.

Harley-Davidson achieved its return to success through dedication to its customers and emphasis on durability and high quality. Although Harley-Davidson is the last of more than 150 U.S. motorcycle manufacturers, its chance for success in the future is enhanced because they are following one of the company's oldest axioms: Harley-Davidson sells more than just motorcycles, they sell a special loyalty and image to their customers.

SOURCES: Michael Oneal, "Full Cycle," *Continental*, November 1987, pp. 20–24; Rod Willis, "Harley-Davidson Comes Roaring Back," *Management Review*, March 1986, pp. 20–27; John A. Conway, "Follow Through: Harley Back in High Gear," *Forbes*, Apr. 20, 1987, p. 8.

Legislation and the interpretation of laws give rise to **legal forces.** Marketing decisions and activities are restrained and controlled by a multitude of laws, many enacted either to preserve a competitive atmosphere or to protect consumers. Laws tend to influence marketing activities directly, but their real effects on the marketing mix components depend largely on how marketers and the courts interpret the laws. For example, wide-open competition in the drug market is one result of a unanimous decision of the U.S. Supreme Court in favor of generic medications. This decision permits pharmacists to substitute a less expensive form of a drug for a brand-name medication when filling prescriptions.[18]

Regulatory forces arise from regulatory units at the local, state, and federal levels. These units create and enforce numerous regulations that affect marketing decisions. At times government regulatory agencies, especially at the federal level, sponsor meetings to encourage firms in a particular industry to develop guidelines to stop questionable practices. Industry leaders usually cooperate in such cases because they recognize that the next step may be government regulation. Government is not the only source of regulations affecting marketers, however; individual firms and trade organizations also exert regulatory pressures on themselves and their members.

Most American consumers seek a high standard of living and an enjoyable quality of life. **Societal forces** pressure marketers to provide such living standards and lifestyles through socially responsible decisions and activities. Today, thirty to forty thousand local consumer groups are well prepared and educated to monitor and, if need be, fight industries on an issue-by-issue basis.[19] This proliferation is just one example of how people in our society form interest groups to let marketers know what they want. In general, such groups desire not only a high standard of living but a high-quality environment. In addition, they insist on honest marketing and attention to product safety. For example, pressure from consumer groups claiming McDonald's Chicken McNuggets and Filet-O-Fish sandwiches were too

18. Pravet Choudhury, "High Court Clears the Way for Generic Drug Competition," *Marketing News,* Mar. 4, 1983, p. 6.
19. John Elkins, "Social Trends Dictate Changes in American Approach to Business," *Marketing News,* June 24, 1983, p. 16.

fatty resulted in the company's switching from beef and vegetable shortening to pure vegetable shortening, which has a considerably lower fat content.[20]

To a large extent **economic forces** determine the strength of a firm's competitive atmosphere. The intensity of competition is affected by three primary factors: the number of businesses that control the supply of a product, how easily a firm can enter the industry, and how much demand there is for the product relative to supply. Economic factors affect the impact of marketing activities because they determine the size and strength of demand for products. Two general determinants of demand are buyers' ability to purchase and their willingness to purchase. Changes in general economic conditions have a great bearing on these two factors.

There are two ways **technological forces** influence marketers' decisions and activities. First, the forces have great impact on people's everyday lives. Technology affects our lifestyles and standards of living that in turn influence our desires for products and our reactions to the marketing mixes offered by business organizations. Second, technological developments may have a direct impact on creating and maintaining a marketing mix because they may affect all its variables: product, distribution, promotion, and price. The technologies of communication, transportation, computers, metals, and packaging have influenced the types of products produced as well as promotion, pricing, and distribution. In Figure 1.8, Boeing promotes their commitment to developing technologies in the aerospace industry.

This brief description of marketing environment forces suggests some of their possible effects on marketing decisions and activities. If marketers hope to create and maintain effective marketing strategies, they must recognize that dynamic environmental forces can create both marketing problems and marketing opportunities. They must therefore be able to adjust marketing strategies to major changes in the marketing environment.

Marketing Strategy: Target Market Selection

A **target market** is a group of persons for whom a firm creates and maintains a marketing mix that specifically fits the needs and preferences of that group. When choosing a target market, marketing managers try to evaluate possible markets to see how entering them would affect the firm's sales, costs, and profits. Marketers also attempt to determine if the organization has the resources to produce a marketing mix that meets the needs of a particular target market and if satisfying those needs is consistent with the firm's overall objectives. They also analyze the size and number of competitors already selling in the possible target market.

Marketing managers may define a target market to include a relatively small number of people, or they may define it to encompass a vast group of people. For example, women are the newest target market of sports marketers. More than half of all women participate in sports, and there has been a dramatic increase in the number of women athletes. Moreover, women hold 65 percent of health club memberships. Miller Lite is attempting to use this information in aiming advertisements at women involved in sports.[21] Although it may focus its efforts on one

---

20. Jonathan Dahl, "McDonald's to Fry Its Kettle of Fish in a Different Fat," *Wall Street Journal,* May 9, 1986, p. 21.
21. Carol Kleiman, "Women Are Newest Target Group of Sports Marketing," *Eagle,* May 11, 1986, p. 5E.

target market through a single marketing mix, a business often focuses on several target markets by developing and employing multiple marketing mixes.

Target market selection is crucial to generating productive marketing efforts. On numerous occasions a business has failed because its management did not identify the specific customer group at which the organization was aiming its products and marketing efforts. Business organizations that try to be "all things to all people" typically end up not satisfying the needs of any customer group very well. It is important for an organization's management to designate which customer groups the firm is trying to serve and to have some information about these customers. The identification and analysis of a target market provides a foundation on which a marketing mix can be developed.

Marketing Strategy: Marketing Mix Development

The marketing mix consists of four major components: product, distribution, promotion, and price. As discussed earlier, these components are called marketing mix decision variables because a marketing manager can vary the type and amount of each element. One primary goal is to create and maintain a marketing mix that satisfies consumers' needs for a general product type. Notice in Figure 1.6 that the marketing mix is built around the buyer (as is stressed by the marketing concept). Also, bear in mind that the marketing mix variables are affected in many ways by the marketing environment variables.

Marketing mix variables often are viewed as "controllable" variables because they can be changed. However, there are limits to how much these variables can be altered. For example, because of economic conditions or government regulations, a manager may not be free to adjust prices from one day to the next. Changes in sizes, colors, shapes, and designs of most tangible goods are expensive; therefore such product features cannot be altered very often. In addition, promotional campaigns and the methods used to distribute products ordinarily cannot be changed overnight.

Marketing managers must develop a marketing mix that precisely matches the needs of the people in the target market. Before they can do this, they have to collect in-depth, up-to-date information about those needs. (Our chapter-opening story about Stouffer exemplifies a firm that incorrectly assessed buyers' needs in one case and yet was able to accurately assess needs in another situation.) The information might include data regarding the age, income, race, sex, and educational level of people in the target market; their preferences for product designs, features, colors, and textures; their attitudes toward competitors' products, services, advertisements, and prices; and the frequency and intensity with which they use the product. With these kinds of data, marketing managers are better able to develop a product, distribution, promotion, and price that satisfy the people in the target market.

Now let us look more closely at the decisions and activities related to each marketing mix variable (product, distribution, promotion, and price). Table 1.1 is a partial list of the numerous decisions and activities associated with each marketing mix variable.

The Product Variable As noted earlier, a product can be a good, a service, or an idea. The actual physical production of products is not a marketing activity. However, marketers do research consumers' product wants and design products to

FIGURE 1.8

Boeing recognizes the importance of developing new technology and products for the future (SOURCE: The Boeing Company)

achieve the desired characteristics. They may also create and alter packages and brand names. This aspect of the marketing mix is known as the **product variable.** Repair and warranty services also may be a part of the decisions included in the product variable.

Product variable decisions and related activities are important because they are involved directly with creating want-satisfying products. To maintain a satisfying set of products that will help an organization achieve its goals, a marketer must be able to develop new products, modify existing ones, and eliminate those that no longer satisfy buyers and yield acceptable profits. For example, after realizing that sales at lunch time accounted for only 15 to 18 percent of its total revenue, Pizza Hut conducted a study to see if people wanted pizza for lunch. The study indicated that customers liked pizza for lunch, provided they could get it quickly. This revealed a market opportunity. Pizza Hut redesigned kitchens and developed equipment for quick preparation of a five-minute personal-size pizza.[22]

The Distribution Variable   To satisfy consumers, products must be available at the right time in a convenient and accessible location. In dealing with the **distribution variable,** a marketing manager attempts to make products available in the quantities desired to as many customers as possible and to hold the total inventory,

22. P. Rajan Varadarajan, "Marketing Strategies in Action," *Business,* January–March 1986, p. 15.

transportation, and storage costs as low as possible. A marketing manager may become involved in selecting and motivating intermediaries (wholesalers and retailers), establishing and maintaining inventory control procedures, and developing and managing transportation and storage systems.

As an example of the importance of the distribution variable in the marketing mix, management at Adolph Coors Co. dramatically increased sales when it expanded its distribution into six southeastern states, which represented the fastest-growing beer market in the United States. Instead of relying on inexperienced wholesalers, Coors tapped into an existing network of Schlitz distributors that needed extra business. This distribution strategy allowed Coors to gain 10 percent of the Florida market in a very short time.[23]

The Promotion Variable   The **promotion variable** is used to facilitate exchanges by informing one or more groups of people about an organization and its products. Promotion is used for various reasons. For example, it might be used to increase public awareness of an organization, a new product, or a new brand. In addition, promotion is used to educate consumers about product features or to urge people to adopt a particular position on a political or social issue. It may also be used to renew interest in a product whose popularity is waning. The Application on page 29 is an example of The Coca-Cola Company's creative use of promotion to generate awareness of New Coke (see Figure 1.9). Coke used a popular persona, Max

23. John J. Curran, "Beer Stocks with Yeasty Promise," *Fortune,* Oct. 17, 1983, pp. 179–180.

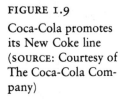

FIGURE 1.9

Coca-Cola promotes its New Coke line (SOURCE: Courtesy of The Coca-Cola Company)

M-M-Max Headroom

Organizations frequently use a person or symbol to communicate with consumers and to help consumers identify with the organization and its products. A spokesperson is particularly useful when he or she appeals to a specific group of people with whom the organization would like to communicate. Probably the best-known company spokesthing of the 1980s is Max Headroom, for Coca-Cola's "C-C-Catch the Wave" advertising campaign. Max appeared as the head "cokeologist" in Coke's futuristic commercials, exhorting young cokeologists not to say the dreaded "P-word" (Coke's main rival, Pepsi-Cola). Max also appeared on T-shirts and bumper stickers. The computer-generated persona delighted small children and adults alike with his stuttering wit, but he was especially popular with the younger generations that Coca-Cola wanted to reach.

Peter Wagg and Chrysalis Visual Programming created Max to host a rock and popular music video show in London. Home Box Office ran a one-hour movie that developed Max's persona, later expanded for the American television series *Max Headroom*. In the series, Max started out as investigative reporter Edison Carter. The reporter discovered that his own Network 23 was using "blipverts," compressed television commercials, to keep its viewers from changing channels. Network executives tried to stop Carter from exposing the story; their efforts culminated in a motorcycle chase through a parking garage, where Edison Carter crashed. The last thing Carter saw before he died was a sign that read "Maximum Headroom." Network 23 tried to cover up the accident by re-creating Carter on a computer, but they wound up with Max Headroom, and of course, a memorable new television series.

Max appealed to a generation of young consumers who are far more computer literate than any generation before them. This is also the generation who grew up watching movies such as *Star Wars* and *Mad Max* (no relation to Max Headroom), from which *Max Headroom* seemed to borrow certain futuristic elements.

Coca-Cola saw Max Headroom's potential immediately. Max is funny, colorful, bold, and perfect—because he is computer generated. These are the characteristics Coca-Cola wanted the soda-consuming youth market to perceive in its reformulated Coke. Max championed good causes on his television show and helped his friends fight evil and injustice. Max Headroom also gave young viewers a hero. Such a persona gives consumers a good feeling; maybe a little bit of that feeling rubbed off on Coke's image too.

Max Headroom reminded his viewers to drink Coke, every time they saw him on a billboard, T-shirt, and even on his television series. In fact, research conducted by Video Storyboard Tests, Inc. found that more consumers remembered Max Headroom commercials than any other commercial at the time. Coke retired Max in 1987 but he was brought back in 1988 for a new advertising campaign. Max Headroom, in 1988, took advantage of an election year to appear as a mock candidate with the themeline to the advertisements, "New Coke. Think About It."

Every organization needs someone, or something, to help communicate with its targeted consumers, but only Coca-Cola is lucky enough to have Max Headroom on its marketing staff.

SOURCES: " 'Ultimate Talking Head' C-C-Catches Fancy of Youth," *Marketing News,* Sept. 26, 1986, pp. 1, 19; "The 100 Leading National Advertisers," 1987 edition, *Advertising Age,* Sept. 24, 1987, p. 75; Scott Ticer, "Max Headroom Speaks the Dreaded 'P-Word,' " *Business Week,* Mar. 16, 1987, pp. 40–41; Jeffrey Scott, "Coca-Cola to Stick with 'New Coke' as Brand Flounders in No. 10 Spot," *Adweek's Marketing Week,* Feb. 22, 1988; and *Max Headroom,* the ABC television series, 1986 and 1987 seasons.

Headroom, in advertisements. The *Max Headroom* television series gave Coke even more publicity. Part 4 looks closely at such promotion activities as advertising, publicity, personal selling, and sales promotion.

The Price Variable   In the area of the **price variable,** marketing managers usually have a hand in establishing pricing policies and determining product prices. Price is important to consumers because they are concerned about the value obtained in an exchange. Thus price is a critical component of the marketing mix. Price often is used as a competitive tool; in fact, extremely intense price competition sometimes leads to price wars. Airlines such as Northwest, Continental, and Southwest have touched off air-fare price wars that caused some larger, higher-cost airlines to go bankrupt or lose millions of dollars.

Price also helps establish a product's image. For instance, if the makers of Halston tried to sell that perfume in a one-gallon jug for $3.95, consumers probably would not buy it because the price would destroy the image of Halston.

Developing and maintaining an effective marketing mix is a major requirement for having a strong marketing strategy. Thus, as indicated in Figure 1.7, a considerable portion of this text (Chapters 7 through 17) focuses on the concepts, decisions, and activities associated with the components of the marketing mix.

Management of Marketing Activities

Managing marketing activities involves planning, organizing, implementing, and controlling. Marketing planning is a systematic process that focuses on assessing opportunities and resources, determining marketing objectives, developing a marketing strategy, and developing plans for implementation and control. Planning determines when and how marketing activities will be performed and who is to perform them. It forces marketing managers to think ahead, to establish objectives, and to consider future marketing activities. Effective planning also reduces or eliminates daily crises.

Organizing marketing activities involves developing the internal structure of the marketing unit. This structure is the key to directing marketing activities. The marketing unit can be organized by functions, products, regions, or types of customers. An organization may use one of these forms or a combination of them.

Properly implementing marketing plans depends on coordinating marketing activities, motivating marketing personnel, and effectively communicating within the unit. Marketing managers must coordinate the activities of marketing personnel and integrate these activities both with those within other areas of the firm and with the marketing efforts of personnel in external organizations, such as advertising agencies and research firms. Marketing managers also must motivate marketing personnel. An organization's communication system must allow the marketing manager to communicate with high-level management, with managers of other functional areas within the firm, and with personnel involved in marketing activities both inside and outside the organization.

The marketing control process consists of establishing performance standards, evaluating actual performance by comparing it with established standards, and reducing the difference between desired and actual performance. An effective control process has four requirements. It should ensure that there is a rate of information flow that allows the marketing manager to detect quickly differences between actual and planned levels of performance. It must accurately monitor different kinds of activities and be flexible enough to accommodate changes. The control process must be economical so that its costs are low relative to the costs that would arise if there were no controls. Finally, the control process should be designed so that both managers and subordinates can understand it. To maintain effective marketing control, an organization needs to develop a comprehensive control process that evaluates marketing operations at regular intervals.

The Organization of This Book

Figure 1.6 is a map of the overall organization of this book. Chapter 2 discusses the marketing environment variables listed in the outer portion of Figure 1.6. We then focus on the center of the figure, analyzing markets, buyers, and marketing research (in Chapters 3, 4, 5, and 6, respectively). Chapters 7 through 17 explore the marketing mix variables, starting with the product variable and moving clockwise around Figure 1.6. Chapters 18 and 19 discuss strategic market planning, organization, implementation, and control. Chapters 20, 21, and 22 consider decisions and activities that are unique to industrial marketing, international marketing, and services and nonbusiness marketing, respectively. If, as you are reading, you wonder where the text is leading, look again at Figure 1.6.

Summary

Marketing consists of individual and organizational activities that facilitate and expedite satisfying exchange relationships in a dynamic environment through the creation, distribution, promotion, and pricing of goods, services, and ideas. Four conditions must exist for an exchange to occur: (1) participation by two or more individuals, groups, or organizations; (2) each party must have something of value the other party desires; (3) each party must be willing to give up what it has to receive the value item the other party holds; and (4) the parties to the exchange must be able to communicate with each other to make their somethings of value available. In an exchange, products are traded either for other products or for financial resources, such as cash or credit. Products can be goods, services, or ideas.

About half of each consumer dollar is spent on marketing activities. You should be aware of what marketing is because its activities permeate our lives. The activities are performed by business firms and also by nonbusiness organizations such as political, social, church, cultural, and civic groups. Moreover, marketing activities help business organizations generate profits, the lifeblood of a capitalist economy. Finally, the study of marketing will help you evaluate marketing activities.

The marketing concept is a management philosophy that affects all activities of a business organization. According to this philosophy, a business organization should try to satisfy customers' needs through a coordinated set of activities that, at the same time, allows the organization to achieve its goals. Customer satisfaction is the major objective of the marketing concept. The organization first must determine consumers' needs and then try to satisfy those needs through a coordinated set of activities. An organization achieves its own goals by satisfying customers. To make the marketing concept work, top management must accept it as an overall management philosophy. Implementing the marketing concept always requires an efficient information system and sometimes the restructuring of the organization.

Strategic marketing management attempts to facilitate and expedite exchanges effectively and efficiently. Marketing managers focus on four generic marketing management tasks to achieve set objectives: (1) market opportunity analysis, (2) target market selection, (3) marketing mix development, and (4) management of marketing activities.

Conducting a market opportunity analysis involves reviewing several organizational factors to identify internal characteristics. Primary factors that need consideration are organizational objectives, financial resources, managerial skills, organizational strengths, organizational weaknesses, and cost structures. In addition to performing an internal evaluation, the marketing manager needs to be aware of environmental forces. The marketing environment variables include political, legal, regulatory, societal, economic and competitive, and technological forces. The forces in the marketing environment affect a manager's strategic decisions in general ways. The environmental forces affect consumers' wants and needs, buyer reactions to the firm's marketing mix, and the extent to which a marketing manager can perform certain marketing activities. Marketers must recognize that dynamic environmental forces can create marketing opportunities as well as problems. They must be able to adjust marketing strategies to the rapid changes in the environment.

The development of a marketing strategy encompasses two steps: (1) selecting and analyzing a target market and (2) creating and maintaining an appropriate marketing mix. Target market selection is not only the foundation on which a marketing mix is developed; it is crucial to productive marketing efforts. Cost-benefit analysis as well as determination of available resources can determine whether entrance into a particular target market is a feasible alternative. The four variables that make up the marketing mix are product, price, promotion, and distribution. These components can be altered as they are affected by fluctuating environmental variables. Marketers research consumer wants in their effort to create want-satisfying products. To achieve customer satisfaction, products must be made accessible at the right time and place in the quantities desired—the distribution variable. The promotion variable applies to informing the target group about an organization and its products. Because price is important to the consumer, it is a critical component of the marketing mix. Developing and maintaining an effective marketing mix is the basis for having a strong marketing strategy. Within limits, a marketing manager can alter marketing mix variables as consumers' preferences and needs change.

The marketing management process includes planning, organizing, implementing, and controlling marketing activities. This systematic process focuses on assessing opportunities and resources, setting goals and objectives, developing strategic and tactical marketing plans, and establishing steps for implementation and control. Planning determines when, how, and who is to perform marketing activities. Organizing deals with internal structure, which can be defined by function, product, region, or type of customers. Implementing the plans depends on the coordination of marketing activities, the motivation of marketing personnel, and communication flow. To maintain control, performance standards are set, and actual performance is evaluated against standards at regular intervals; whatever difference exists between the two must be eliminated.

Important Terms

Marketing
Exchange
Product
Good
Service
Idea
Marketing concept
Production orientation
Sales orientation
Customer orientation
Marketing management
Marketing strategy
Marketing mix
Marketing environment
Political forces

Legal forces
Regulatory forces
Societal forces
Economic forces
Technological forces
Target market
Product variable
Distribution variable
Promotion variable
Price variable

Discussion and Review Questions

1. In what important ways does the definition of marketing used in this text differ from the other definitions given? How did you define marketing before you read this chapter?
2. Why should someone study marketing?
3. Discuss the basic elements of the marketing concept. Which businesses in your

area use this concept? In your opinion, have these businesses adopted the marketing concept? Why or why not?

4. Identify several business organizations in your area that obviously have not adopted the marketing concept. What characteristics of these organizations indicate nonacceptance of the marketing concept?

5. Describe the major components of a marketing strategy. What is the relationship among the components?

6. Identify the generic marketing management tasks.

7. What are the primary issues that marketing managers consider when conducting a market opportunity analysis?

8. What are the variables in the marketing environment? How much control does a marketing manager have over environmental variables?

9. Why is the selection of a target market such an important issue?

10. Why are the elements of the marketing mix known as variables?

11. What types of management activities are involved in the marketing management process?

12. What is the relationship between a marketing strategy and the generic marketing management tasks?

Cases

1.1   Levi Strauss and the 501 Jeans[24]

During the California Gold Rush, a young entrepreneur introduced what was to become one of the longest-living products in American history. Levi Strauss actually intended to sell dry goods to gold prospectors and California settlers in the 1850s. On Strauss's arrival in California, however, an old prospector told him, "Should'a brought pants. Pants don't wear worth a hoot up in the diggin's. Can't get a pair strong enough to last." So Strauss had a tailor turn his brown tent canvas into the first pairs of jeans ever made. And so begins the story of the Levi's 501 jeans, now worn by people of every social class in the United States and abroad.

As mentioned, the first Levi's jeans were made of brown canvas, and they had one back pocket and no belt loops. When Strauss ran out of the tent canvas, he made his jeans out of French cotton (called serge de Nîmes, later shortened to denim) and dyed them blue. The "blue" jeans had a button fly and shrank to fit the wearer after several washings. Word soon spread among the miners that Levi's jeans were quality pants, and Levi Strauss opened a shop in San Francisco to make his Levi's jeans. The company later added copper rivets to reinforce the pockets

24. Based on information from "Everyone Knows His First Name," Levi Strauss & Co., P.O. Box 7215, San Francisco, CA 94120; "Evolution of an American Classic: Levi's 501 Jeans," Levi Strauss & Co. press release, July 1986; "Man at His Best," *Esquire*, September 1986, p. 37; fact sheets on the 1985 and 1986 advertising campaigns, provided by Levi Strauss & Co. Marketing Department, San Francisco, 1986; "Big Ad Campaign Comes Up Winners," *Patterns*, January 1985, p. 1; "A Business Success, An Artistic Triumph," *Patterns*, January 1985, p. 3; "The Twenty-five Favorite TV Ads of 1987," *Adweek's Marketing Week*, Mar. 7, 1988, p. 13.

after miners complained that heavy gold nuggets ripped out the pockets. Strauss made other, minor alterations over the years in direct response to the needs of cowboys, students, and other Levi's jeans wearers. The jeans were assigned the lot number 501, which has stayed with the jeans over the years.

In 1873, Strauss added the trademark to the back pockets of his jeans; the trademark, in a pattern called a "double arcuate" and shaped roughly like the wings of a seagull in flight, has been used longer than any other American clothing trademark. Later, Strauss added to the rear waistband of the 501 jeans, another classic trademark, a leather guarantee patch showing two horses trying to pull apart a pair of copper-riveted pants.

The popularity of the 501 jeans spread with the advent of the dude ranches in the 1930s, and the jeans were soon available nationwide. During World War II, the government declared Levi's jeans "an essential industry," and only those people involved in the defense effort were allowed to purchase them. In the 1950s, the jeans became the uniform of American teenagers as they copied James Dean and Marlon Brando. Thus, Levi's 501 jeans have been and are being worn by just about everyone, from cowboys to soldiers, from hippies to yuppies. Webster's dictionary defines the word "Levi's," and a pair of Levi's jeans are displayed in the Smithsonian Institution in Washington, D.C. Although Levi Strauss & Co. now makes all kinds of clothing for men, women, and children and no longer sells dry goods, the company's 501 button-fly jeans are still its best-selling product, more than 135 years after the company began.

In 1971, Levi Strauss & Co. went public; that is, they decided to sell shares of the company to investors. The money obtained from sales of Levi stock helped the company pay for expanded product lines and increased sales efforts overseas. Despite the company's success on the public market, relatives of Levi Strauss's nephews wanted to regain control of their ancestor's company, and in 1985, the company bought back all its stock. Today Levi Strauss & Co. remains a private company in the hands of the Haas and Koshland families, relatives of the original Levi Strauss.

In 1984, sales of basic blue jeans fell for all producers. In an attempt to reverse that decline, Levi Strauss & Co. introduced an innovative new advertising campaign, the largest campaign for a single product in the history of the clothing industry. The key message of the campaign was that Levi's 501 jeans give the wearer a uniquely personal fit because only Levi's 501 jeans shrink to fit the wearer's body. The advertising spots featured "real" people, not actors, doing real, everyday things to a background of original blues (of course) music. In 1987 the Levi's jeans commercials created by Foote, Cone, and Belding were cited as the thirteenth most popular television commercial. The advertisements were successful in halting the declining sales of Levi's jeans; in fact, the blues campaign resulted in a 50 percent increase in the sales of 501 jeans. Many experts have attributed the revival of consumer interest in back-to-basic jeans to the Levi Strauss blues advertisements. The advertisements were also successful artistically: They won several awards, including a Clio (for excellence in advertising) and an award from the National Blues Foundation. One advertisement was recognized for its portrayal of a handicapped man. The blues campaign is still running, with the new advertisements still portraying real people in real-life street scenes and wearing 501 jeans that look very comfortable.

Levi Strauss & Co. continues to be a major force in the clothing industry after 135 years largely because it still applies the same high standards that Levi Strauss set in the 1850s. The company is responsive to the needs of people who buy the jeans, and it is willing to make changes and introduce new products to fulfill those consumers' needs. And a highly successful, creative advertising campaign and careful management certainly help keep the company running smoothly.

Questions for Discussion

1. What do you suppose might have been the effect on sales if Levi Strauss & Co. did everything as specified in the case except that it only ran its advertisements in *Business Week, Forbes,* and the *Journal of Marketing Research?*
2. Does Levi Strauss & Co. follow the marketing concept?
3. How have societal forces affected Levi Strauss & Co.'s marketing strategy?

1.2 RJR Nabisco[25]

Most of us are familiar with the red triangle trademark on packages of Nabisco cookies and crackers. That instant recognition can be attributed to RJR Nabisco's understanding of the marketing concept: The company realizes that it must carefully coordinate its activities to both satisfy consumers' needs and achieve its own objectives. Marketing was the key to success for the many different companies that made up R. J. Reynolds Industries and Nabisco Brands, Inc. before they were united under the name RJR Nabisco in 1985. In addition, strategic market planning is crucial to the success of the huge company, which had sales of $16 billion in 1986.

R. J. Reynolds bought Nabisco to take advantage of Nabisco's strengths and to minimize its own organizational weaknesses. After purchasing Nabisco, R. J. Reynolds had to rethink its marketing strategy to accommodate the diversity of all those different brands under one corporate banner. The company restructured to increase its efficiency. For example, it moved the Planters (peanuts) and Life Savers (candy) units into its tobacco division; this move led to more efficient distribution of those products because they are frequently sold in the same outlets. The company also sold its Heublein Inc. liquor division and Kentucky Fried Chicken to reduce the debt incurred from the purchase of Nabisco Brands, Inc. Now the company is involved in marketing its many diversified products, such as Winston, Salem, and Camel cigarettes; Oreo cookies; Planters peanuts; Ritz crackers; and Del Monte Corp. pineapples all over the United States and Canada and throughout the world.

Tobacco is still the main moneymaker for RJR Nabisco. The company's operating profit margin on tobacco products, after paying for equipment facilities and so on, was 27 percent in 1986. It costs the company a mere 17 cents to produce a pack of cigarettes, which it then sells to retailers for about 80 cents (state and federal

25. Based on information from Melvin J. Grayson, *27 Million Daily: The Story of Nabisco Brands* (Parsippany, NJ: Nabisco Brands, 1984); Kevin Maney, "Move Shows It's Not Giving Up Tobacco," *USA Today,* June 22, 1987, pp. 1, 2B; Bob Messenger, "The Leading 50 Prepared Food and Beverage Processors," *Prepared Foods,* July 1986, pp. 40–46; and the RJR Nabisco 1986 Annual Report.

government taxes eat up the rest of the retail price of a pack of cigarettes). RJR Nabisco's share of the market in 1985 was 32.4 percent, despite an overall decline in the domestic consumption of tobacco products. To meets its goal of being the low-cost producer, the company opened Tobaccoville, a $1 billion super modern production facility in North Carolina. The plant enabled the company to reduce its tobacco work force by nearly 20 percent, saving the company at least $60 million per year. Now operating at full capacity, the plant manufactures 110 billion cigarettes per year, one-fifth of the entire industry's production.

RJR Nabisco is leading many of the nation's food markets as well. Oreo cookies have been the number-one seller in the cookie market for more than 70 years. The company's crackers are still number one after many decades, and its nutritious cereals are rapidly gaining market share as consumers become more health conscious. RJR Nabisco plans to continue restructuring in this area, streamlining operations to reduce costs and even selling those units that do not fit efficiently into the RJR Nabisco family.

RJR Nabisco must constantly study and adjust its marketing mix to maintain and raise its profit margin. The company uses both research and development, and it is continuously developing new products and improving older ones to meet its target markets' needs and wants. Distribution is also important: The company tries to make its products available to distributors at low prices so savings can be passed on to the consumer. It has opened new facilities to ensure that enough of the products are available to consumers. RJR Nabisco vigorously promotes its products, and it plans to further increase its promotional expenditures. In 1987, Nabisco Brands was scheduled to spend $70 million to promote its cookies and crackers, with an emphasis on new products. Over the years, Nabisco promotions have been some of the most innovative and memorable within the industry. In addition, the company tries to keep its costs down so that it can keep the retail prices of its products low. Its many diverse products are targeted at equally diverse target markets, from most economical to fairly prestigious products.

It should be obvious then that marketing is very important to RJR Nabisco and to its continuing success. The company understands the importance of the marketing concept, and it uses strategic market planning to keep itself in line with its goals and in tune with its consumers' needs. Without marketing, the company could not be responsive to those needs, it could not make products available to customers, it could not make customers aware of new products, and it could not establish a reasonable pricing policy. Perhaps to RJR Nabisco, marketing is the cream in the middle of the Oreo cookie: There wouldn't be an Oreo without it.

Questions for Discussion

1. What is the RJR Nabisco marketing strategy as explained in this case?
2. What is RJR Nabisco's marketing mix?
3. How does RJR Nabisco follow the marketing concept?

2. The Marketing Environment

- ▶ To understand the importance of environmental scanning and analysis.
- ▶ To identify the types of political forces in the marketing environment.
- ▶ To understand how laws and their interpretation influence marketing practices.
- ▶ To determine how government regulations and self-regulatory agencies affect marketing activities.
- ▶ To identify social and ethical issues that marketers must deal with as they make decisions.
- ▶ To identify the tools firms use to compete.
- ▶ To understand how economic and competitive factors affect organizations' abilities to compete and customers' buying power and willingness to spend.
- ▶ To explore the effects of technological knowledge on society.
- ▶ To understand how technology can influence marketing activities.

*T*he movie "Wall Street" recently depicted illegal and unethical activities in the marketing of securities (see Figure 2.1). In addition, the news media frequently report Wall Street's unethical and often illegal scandals—bribes, questions about fairness and integrity, and insider trading. Insider trading occurs when someone with "inside" knowledge of events in a corporation uses it to purchase a company's stock before the public has access to that information.

The biggest insider-trading scandal on Wall Street surfaced when Dennis B. Levine, a merger specialist in the investment banking firm of Drexel Burnham Lambert, Inc., admitted that he stole confidential information and gave it to stock speculator Ivan Boesky. Levine and Boesky had agreed that Levine would provide Boesky with valuable insider information in exchange for up to 5 percent of the profits Boesky earned on the basis of that information. Assuming that the value of a company's stock would increase when news about its upcoming merger became public, Boesky successfully purchased stock in companies that were merger or acquisition targets. For example, Boesky purchased shares in Carnation, a leading marketer of consumer products, based on insider information that Nestlé was about to purchase Carnation. When that news became public, Boesky's shares in Carnation increased in value for more than a $28 million profit. In many cases the activities of Levine and Boesky were not only unethical but also illegal.

Recently probably no area of business has had its ethical standards questioned more than marketing activities in the securities and investment banking areas. Herbert A. Allen, Jr., President of Allen S. Company, Inc. states that investment bankers routinely trade confidential information. "A major disquieting factor

is the loss of confidentiality, well short of illegality. Important clients often find out inside information about other important clients." This is a clear violation of ethical standards found in the American Marketing Association Code of Ethics presented in Table 2.3. The current environment of caution and mistrust has led some clients to demand confidentiality and high standards, in writing, if necessary. The whole affair can only undermine the public's confidence in traders and brokers who are Wall Street's salespeople.

Both the industry as well as specific firms are developing codes of ethics and policies that forbid questionable insider-information exchanges. Wall Street's creativity, combined with new technology, has led to changes more rapid than regulators can oversee. While tougher sentencing and expanded enforcement may be one solution, ultimately it is firms in the financial industry that must restore public confidence. Success depends on clear, fair rules, rigorously applied and enforced.[1]

1. Based on information from William A. Schreyer, "Ethics and Wall Street," *American Way,* Sept. 1, 1987; Ford S. Worthy, "Wall Street's Spreading Scandal," *Fortune,* Dec. 22, 1986, p. 27; Joel Dressang, "Companies Get Serious About Ethics," *USA Today,* December 1986, p. 1–2B; James B. Stewart, "Insider-Trading Plot Unraveled as Profits Lured Copycat Buyers," *Wall Street Journal,* July 15, 1987, p. 1; Myron Magnet, "The Decline and Fall of Business Ethics," *Fortune,* Dec. 8, 1986, pp. 65–72; John Byrne, "Corporate Clients Feel Seduced and Abandoned," *Business Week,* Mar. 2, 1987, p. 34.

I NITIALLY, in this chapter we consider why it is critical to scan and analyze the environment. Next we discuss political forces, which are the foundation for government actions that influence marketing activities. Then we consider the effects of laws and regulatory actions on marketing activities. Next we describe the general societal forces in the marketing environment and focus on some of the social and ethical issues facing marketers. Then we explore several types of economic forces that influence firms' abilities to compete and consumers' willingness and ability to buy. We also consider the effects of general economic conditions: prosperity, recession, depression, and recovery. Finally, we analyze the major dimensions of the technological forces in the environment.

Examining and Dealing with the Marketing Environment

The **marketing environment** consists of external forces that directly or indirectly influence an organization's acquisition of inputs and generation of outputs. Examples of inputs include skilled personnel, financial resources, raw materials, and information. The outputs could be information (such as advertisements), packages, goods, services, or ideas. As indicated in Chapter 1 and as shown in Figure 1.6, we view the marketing environment as consisting of six categories of forces: political, legal, regulatory, societal, economic and competitive, and technological. Although there are numerous environmental factors, most fall into one of these six categories. Whether they fluctuate rapidly or slowly, environmental forces are always dynamic. For an organization, the changes in the marketing environment create uncertainty, threats, and opportunities. Although marketers cannot predict the environment with certainty, they must try to anticipate which technology will dominate, how consumer preferences will shift, and the changing political climate as well as the other marketing environment variables.

Although the future is not predictable, marketers can obtain appraisals of what is "most probable."[2] We do know with certainty that the dynamic environment will continue to modify the marketing strategies of companies. Marketing managers who fail to recognize environmental changes leave their organizations unprepared to capitalize on marketing opportunities or to cope with adverse environmental pressures. The inability to cope with an unfavorable environment can cause an organization's demise. For example, many banks in the southwest United States could not cope with depressed oil and real estate markets and so went out of business because creditors could not repay loans. Standard Oil (see Figure 2.2) recognizes the importance of diversifying its assets to survive and grow while oil prices remain unstable. Thus, monitoring the environment is crucial to an organization's survival and to the long-term achievement of its goals.

2. Gene R. Laczniak, and Robert F. Lusch, "Environment and Strategy in 1995: A Survey of High-Level Executives," *The Journal of Consumer Marketing*, Spring 1986, p. 28.

Environmental Scanning and Analysis

To monitor changes in the marketing environment effectively, marketers must engage in environmental scanning and analysis. **Environmental scanning** is the process of collecting information about the forces in the marketing environment. Scanning involves observation, perusal of secondary sources such as business, trade, and government publications, and marketing research efforts. It is important to gather useful information about the environment; however, managers must be careful not to gather so much information that sheer volume makes analysis impossible.

Environmental analysis is the process of assessing and interpreting the information gathered through scanning. A manager evaluates the information for accuracy, tries to resolve inconsistencies in the data, and assigns significance to the findings, if warranted. Through analysis, a marketing manager attempts to define current environmental changes and, if possible, to predict future changes. By evaluating these changes, a marketing manager should be able to determine possible threats and opportunities associated with environmental fluctuations. Knowledge of current and predicted environmental changes helps a marketing manager assess the performance of current marketing efforts and develop marketing strategies for the future.

Responding to Environmental Forces

Marketing managers can use two general approaches when responding to environmental forces. One approach views environmental forces as totally uncontrollable and difficult to predict and the organization as passive and reactive toward the environment. In this approach, the organization does not try to influence forces in

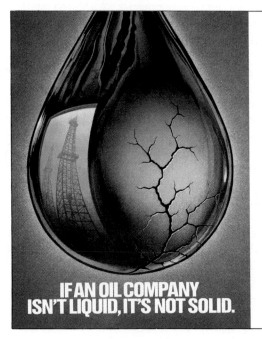

FIGURE 2.2

Standard Oil acknowledges the importance of diversifying its assets in the midst of unstable oil prices (SOURCE: The Standard Oil Company)

the marketing environment. Marketing managers attempt to adjust current marketing strategies to changes in the environment, and market opportunities discovered through environmental scanning and analysis are approached cautiously.

A second approach is to take an aggressive stance toward environmental forces.[3] Rather than viewing forces in the environment as totally uncontrollable, a practitioner of this proactive approach attempts to influence and shape environmental forces. For example, the NRA urges citizens to oppose gun control legislation (see Figure 2.3).

It may be possible to use economic, psychological, political, and public relations skills to gain access to or operate in a market blocked by traditional environmental constraints. Once the power structure or the other forces blocking a market opportunity are identified, marketers can assess the power of various parties and develop strategies to overcome environmental forces. Such strategies may be difficult to implement, but if successful, they could blur the distinction between environmental and controllable (marketing mix) variables.[4]

Management may try to influence environmental forces so as to create market opportunities or to extract greater benefits relative to costs from existing market opportunities. When using this approach, managers must recognize that there are limits on how much an environmental force can be influenced and that these limits

3. Carl P. Zeithaml and Valarie A. Zeithaml, "Environmental Management: Revising the Marketing Perspective," *Journal of Marketing,* Spring 1984, pp. 46–53.
4. Philip Kotler, "Megamarketing," *Harvard Business Review,* March–April 1986, pp. 117–124.

vary across environmental forces. The Application on page 45 illustrates how the advertising industry successfully lobbied for repeal of the Florida advertising tax six months after it became law. However, although an organization may be able to influence the shape of legislation through lobbying, it is quite unlikely that a single organization can significantly increase the national birthrate or move the economy from recession to prosperity!

We cannot generalize and say that one of these approaches to environmental response is superior to the other. For some organizations, the passive, reactive approach is most appropriate, but for other firms the aggressive approach leads to better performance. The selection of a particular approach is affected by an organization's managerial philosophies, objectives, financial resources, markets, and human skills and by the composition of the set of environmental forces within which the organization operates.

Politics and the Marketing Environment

Political and legal forces are closely interrelated aspects of the marketing environment. Legislation is enacted, legal decisions are interpreted by the courts, and regulatory agencies are created and operated, for the most part, by persons who occupy government positions.

When political officials view particular firms or industries favorably, they are less likely to create or enforce laws and regulations that are unfavorable to those business organizations. For example, political officials who believe that oil companies are making honest efforts to control pollution are unlikely to create and enforce highly restrictive pollution control laws. There is another reason why business organizations need to be concerned about making a favorable impression on political officials. As we point out in Chapter 3, governments are big buyers, and people who hold political office can influence how much a government purchases and from whom. Still another reason to seek political favor is that political officials can play key roles in helping organizations secure foreign markets. The Department of Commerce reports that only about 10 percent of American companies produce for export and that there are 18,000 American companies that have the ability but do not take advantage of the opportunity to export.[5]

Many marketers view political forces as beyond their control; therefore they simply try to adjust to conditions that arise from those forces. However, some firms attempt to influence political events by helping elect certain individuals to political offices. Much of this help is in the form of campaign contributions. Although laws restrict direct corporate contributions to campaign funds, corporate money is channeled into campaign funds as personal contributions of corporate executives or stockholders. Not only do such actions violate the spirit of the corporate campaign contribution laws, they are also unethical. A sizable contribution to a campaign fund may carry with it an implicit understanding that the elected official will perform political favors for the contributing firm.

It is not unusual for a corporation to contribute to the campaign funds of several candidates who seek the same position. Occasionally, it is so important to ensure

5. Stephen Brookes, "Winning the Global Market," *Europe,* August 1987, p. 21.

favorable treatment that certain businesses make direct illegal corporate contributions to campaign funds. Indeed, a former official of American Airlines admitted that the firm made illegal contributions of $55,000 from corporate funds, not to purchase political favors, but because executives feared what might happen if a contribution were not made. Governments can and do take actions aimed at specific industries or companies. Many markets concern themselves with the political environment primarily because of its strong influence on the legal forces with which they must deal.

Laws and Their Interpretation

In the United States, major changes in law usually come about slowly, and historically the changes have been linked to changes in public attitudes and ethics.[6] Even the enforcement of laws changes because the political and social environment is so dynamic. Since the passage of the landmark Sherman Act in 1890, a number of laws have been enacted that influence marketing decisions and activities. These laws affect pricing, advertising, personal selling, distribution, product development, and product warranty and repair policies. For purposes of analysis, laws that directly affect marketing practices can be divided into two categories: (1) procompetitive legislation and (2) consumer protection laws.

Procompetitive Legislation

Table 2.1 briefly describes several major procompetitive laws. **Procompetitive legislation** is enacted to preserve competition. As the Industrial Revolution gained momentum in the mid-1800s, many people were fascinated by new production techniques, the introduction of mass production, and the use of new equipment driven by new sources of power. Although the Industrial Revolution and the rapid growth in business enterprises may have had some beneficial effects on society in the long run, these changes were often devastating to individuals. Masses of workers toiled long, hard hours for little money under bad working conditions while a few industrialists amassed tremendous wealth. Eventually, public resentment in the United States became so strong that the Sherman Act was passed.

The Sherman Act The **Sherman Act** was passed in 1890 to prevent businesses from restraining trade and monopolizing markets. Section 1 of the act condemns "every contract, combination, or conspiracy in restraint of trade." Section 2 prohibits monopolizing or attempting to monopolize. Enforced by the Antitrust Division of the Department of Justice, the Sherman Act applies to firms operating in interstate commerce and to U.S. firms operating in foreign commerce. The Sherman Act was written in general terms, and the courts have not always interpreted it as its creators intended. For this reason, the second major procompetitive act, the **Clayton Act,** was passed in 1914. The Clayton Act prohibits price discrimination (section 2), tying and exclusive agreements (section 3), and the acquisition of stock in another corporation (section 7) "where the effect may be to substantially lessen

6. Barry Render, Richard Cottinberger, Ella P. Gardner, Stephen R. Ruth, and Linda Samuels, "Perspectives on Computer Ethics and Crime," *Business,* January–March 1986, p. 36.

competition or tend to create a monopoly." In addition, interlocking directorates are deemed unlawful under section 8. Sections 6 and 20 exempt farm cooperatives and labor organizations from antitrust laws.

The Federal Trade Commission (FTC) Act and the Wheeler-Lea Amendment   The Federal Trade Commission, established by the **Federal Trade Commission Act** (1914), today regulates the greatest number of marketing practices. Like the Clayton Act, the FTC Act was written to strengthen antimonopoly provisions of the Sherman Act. Whereas the Clayton Act prohibits specific practices, the FTC Act more broadly prohibits unfair methods of competition. This act also empowers the FTC to work with the Department of Justice to enforce the provisions of the Clayton Act. Later sections of this chapter discuss the FTC's regulatory activities.

The creators of the FTC Act, as did the authors of the Sherman Act, found that the courts did not always interpret the act as they had intended. In the Raladam case (1931), the Supreme Court held that a producer's misrepresentation of an obesity cure was not an unfair method of competition because the firm's action did

TABLE 2.1

Major federal procompetitive laws affecting marketing decisions

ACT	PURPOSES
Sherman Act (1890)	Prohibits contracts, combinations, or conspiracies to restrain trade; establishes as a misdemeanor monopolizing or attempting to monopolize
Clayton Act (1914)	Prohibits specific practices such as price discrimination, exclusive dealer arrangements, and stock acquisitions in which the effect may notably lessen competition or tend to create a monopoly
Federal Trade Commission Act (1914)	Created the Federal Trade Commission; also gives the FTC investigatory powers to be used in preventing unfair methods of competition
Robinson-Patman Act (1936)	Prohibits price discrimination that lessens competition among wholesalers or retailers; prohibits producers from giving disproportionate services or facilities to large buyers
Wheeler-Lea Act (1938)	Prohibits unfair and deceptive acts and practices regardless of whether competition is injured; places advertising of foods and drugs under the jurisdiction of the FTC
Celler-Kefauver Act (1950)	Prohibits any corporation engaged in commerce from acquiring the whole or any part of the stock or other share of the capital or assets of another corporation when the effect substantially lessens competition or tends to create a monopoly
Consumer Goods Pricing Act (1975)	Prohibits the use of price maintenance agreements among manufacturers and resellers in interstate commerce
Trademark Counterfeiting Act (1980)	Provides civil and criminal penalties against those who deal in counterfeit consumer goods or any counterfeit goods that can threaten health or safety

The Florida Advertising Tax

Government regulations and laws obviously influence the marketing environment. Nevertheless, businesses are not completely powerless, and they can be motivated to use all their marketing resources to protest what they believe are unfair laws or taxes. On July 1, 1987, the state of Florida instituted a 5 percent sales tax on services, including advertising. The tax proved so controversial, and the loss in local business so great, that state officials ultimately repealed the tax.

Because Florida is the nation's fastest growing state but ranks only forty-seventh in state and local taxes as a proportion of income, lawmakers had to raise additional funds to meet the needs of Florida's growing population. The state's constitution prohibits a state income tax and limits property taxes, so state legislators decided to expand the state's 5 percent sales tax to cover a variety of services, including legal services, pet care, and advertising. State officials expected to raise $761 million from the tax in 1988, with about $100 million of that coming from taxes on advertising. Although other states, including Hawaii, Iowa, New Mexico, and South Dakota, have a broad tax on services, Florida was the first state to tax national advertising. (Illinois and Texas rejected a similar tax in the same year.)

The advertising tax covered not only Florida newspapers, magazines, billboards and direct-mail advertising, television and radio stations, and cable systems but also national advertisers, based on the number of viewers or readers in Florida who saw the advertisement. The tax even covered advertising production costs.

A study by Wharton Econometric Forecasting Advocates at the University of Pennsylvania predicted dire consequences for Florida's economy if the state went ahead with the tax. The study forecasted that there would be an exodus of many members of the advertising industry and media from Florida, along with corresponding job losses within the advertising industry. The Wharton study further predicted less advertising in Florida, resulting in a decrease in production and consumption. Some businesses would raise prices and fees to continue operations, passing the cost of the tax to the consumer instead of to the service provider as officials had intended.

Many of the Wharton study's predictions were validated. Corporations, media organizations, and advertising agencies were naturally outraged and angered when the tax went into effect. Several national corporations, including Procter & Gamble and Kellogg Co., ended millions of dollars of Florida advertising, and many others threatened to follow suit. Other companies threatened to raise prices. To protest the tax, many associations and companies canceled conventions they had scheduled in Florida; such conventions bring the state's hotels and retailers billions of dollars every year.

In July 1987, the Florida Supreme Court upheld the constitutionality of the controversial tax. Nevertheless, opponents of the tax, including major advertisers and corporations, continued to campaign for its repeal. Antitax advertising and the complexity and confusion of administering the tax itself gradually turned Florida citizens against it. The Florida legislature repealed the tax on December 10, 1987, and voted to increase the state sales tax on goods by 1 percent to replace the revenues.

Florida's experiences will be a lesson to other states who consider levying a tax on services. Florida businesses and national advertisers were unhappy with the tax, and their lobbying efforts certainly helped sway public opinion against it. As a result, it will probably be a while before any state again attempts to tax advertising. As federal and state governments have to tighten their belts a few more notches, however, more of them will look at the largely untaxed service sector as a source of money.

SOURCES: Martha Brannigan, "Repeal of Florida 5% Service Tax Caps Controversy Other States Viewed Warily," *Wall Street Journal,* Dec. 11, 1987, p. 7; Jeanne DeQuine and Stephan Stern, "Fla. High Court Upholds Service Tax," *USA Today,* July 15, 1987, p. 3A; Alex Taylor III, "Why Florida Faces Tax Rebellion," *Fortune,* July 6, 1987, p. 82; Joe Agnew, "Advertisers and Media Gird Against Advertising Tax," *Marketing News,* June 19, 1987, pp. 1, 20; James Cox, "State Sees Advertisers Paying $100M," *USA Today,* June 23, 1987, p. 1B, 2B; and Sydney P. Freedberg, "Fate of Florida's Tax on Services May Make Others Go Slow," *Wall Street Journal,* Sept. 21, 1987, pp. 1, 8.

---

not injure competition.[7] This ruling—among others—spurred Congress in 1938 to enact the **Wheeler-Lea Act,** which amended section 5 of the FTC Act. Essentially, the Wheeler-Lea Act makes unfair and deceptive acts or practices unlawful, regardless of whether they injure competition. It specifically prohibits false advertising of foods, drugs, therapeutic devices, and cosmetics and provides penalties for violations and procedures for enforcement. ("False advertising" means an advertisement, other than labeling, that is misleading in any respect.)

The Robinson-Patman Act During the early 1930s, when the Depression was at its peak, the FTC was alarmed by the buying practices and lower prices of some chain stores. The commission reported to the Senate that many of the low prices that suppliers offered to chains could not be justified on the basis of cost savings arising from quantity purchases. Eventually, after several years of economic hardship, pressure from the FTC and popular political support for further legislation led to the enactment of the Robinson-Patman Act in 1936.

The **Robinson-Patman Act** is significant because it directly influences pricing policies. The major provisions of the Robinson-Patman Act include the following:

1. Price discrimination among different purchasers of commodities of like grade and quality is prohibited if the effect of such discrimination may lessen competition substantially or tend to create a monopoly.
2. Price differentials are legal if they can be justified as cost savings or as meeting competition in good faith. Price differentials per se are not illegal.

7. *Federal Trade Commission* v. *Raladam Company,* 283 U.S. 643, 1931.

3. Paying, receiving, or accepting anything of value as a commission, brokerage, or other compensation—except for actual services rendered—is prohibited.
4. It is unlawful to knowingly induce or receive discriminatory prices when prohibited by this law.
5. The furnishing of services or facilities to purchasers upon terms not accorded to all purchasers on proportionately equal terms is illegal.[8]

The Robinson-Patman Act deals only with discriminatory price differentials. Price differentials become discriminatory when one reseller, who is competing against other resellers, can acquire similar quantities of commodities of like grade and quality at lower prices than can other purchasers dealing with the same supplier. Such price differentials give that reseller an unfair advantage in the market.

Consumer Protection Legislation

The second category of regulatory laws, **consumer protection legislation,** is not a recent development. During the mid-1800s, lawmakers in many states enacted laws to prohibit the adulteration of food and drugs. However, consumer protection laws at the federal level mushroomed in the mid-1960s and early 1970s. A number of the federal laws are designed to provide consumer safety. For example, the food and drug acts were enacted to protect people from actual and potential physical injuries.

To help buyers become better informed, Congress has passed several laws concerning the disclosure of information. Some laws deal with information about specific products such as textiles, furs, cigarettes, and automobiles. Other laws focus on particular marketing activities—product development and testing, packaging, labeling, advertising, and consumer financing, for example.

Interpreting Laws

Many laws have the potential to influence marketing activities, but the actual effects of the laws are determined by how the marketers and the courts interpret the laws. At first glance, laws seem to be quite specific because they contain many complex clauses and subclauses. In reality, however, many laws and regulations are stated in vague terms that force marketers to rely on legal counsel rather than their own understanding and common sense. Because of this vagueness, an organization may operate in a legally questionable way to see how much it can get away with before it is prosecuted under the law. On the other hand, some marketers interpret regulations and statutes very conservatively to avoid violating a vague law.

If a company is charged with violating a law, courts must interpret the law to see if there was wrongdoing. This process can be quite lengthy. Occasionally, a firm may take action regarding the violation before the courts make their decision. Toshiba Corporation took internal action when one of its subsidiaries violated U.S. foreign trade laws by selling sensitive military technology to the Soviet Union.[9]

8. E. T. Grether, *Marketing and Public Policy* (Englewood Cliffs, N.J.: Prentice-Hall, 1966), pp. 60–61. Used by permission of the author.
9. These facts are from Christopher J. Chipello, "Matter of Honor: Japanese Top Managers Quick to Resign When Trouble Hits Firm," *The Wall Street Journal,* July 10, 1987, p. 19; David E. Sanger, "Toshiba Case Delays U.S. Contracts," *The New York Times,* June 2, 1987, pp. D1, D5; Clyde H. Farnsworth, "Toshiba, Norway Concern Assailed in Soviet Sale," *The New York Times,* May 1, 1987, p. D5; Joichi Aoi's (CEO of Toshiba) public apology to the American people, in *The Wall Street Journal,* July 20, 1987, p. 7.

Toshiba issued a formal apology to the American people when it was discovered that one of its subsidiaries, Toshiba Machine Company (TMC), was dealing with the Soviets. TMC reportedly sold the Soviets four milling machines that would permit Russia to manufacture ultraquiet propeller blades for submarines; the Soviet submarines would then be able to escape detection by the United States. Toshiba claimed that it had no knowledge of this unauthorized sale. However, because TMC was a subsidiary of Toshiba, the parent company took full responsibility. The top two executives of Toshiba resigned, the highest form of apology in the Japanese business world.

Toshiba took several actions to ensure that this kind of activity does not happen again within its corporation. The company increased security measures in all its companies and fired the president and three other board members of TMC who were responsible for the conduct of the TMC employees actually involved. It also authorized an investigation to find out all the facts concerning TMC's actions and to design methods to prevent such actions from occurring again. In addition, Toshiba fired all officers and employees who they found knowingly participated in the sale. It also appointed several senior company officials to TMC's board to make sure that TMC obeyed the laws and security alliances with Japan's allies.

As a further attempt to apologize to the United States and to re-establish a good relationship with America, Toshiba shifted much of its manufacturing to the United States, which greatly increased the number of American-built Toshiba products. Toshiba now employs thousands of Americans in twenty-one states.

The legal environment that a company operates within may have a big influence on its marketing strategy. Toshiba took many steps following the Soviet scandal to renew its marketing power within the United States. Only time will tell if the American people will forgive the Japanese company for its violation of an important trade law.

Although court rulings have a direct effect on businesses that are being tried for violations, they also have broader, less direct effects on other businesses. When marketers try to interpret laws in relation to specific marketing practices, they often analyze recent court decisions. By being aware of current court interpretations, marketers acquire a better understanding of what the law is intended to do and how the courts are likely to interpret the law in the future.

Regulatory Forces

Interpretation alone does not determine the effectiveness of laws; the level of enforcement by regulatory agencies is also significant. Some regulatory agencies are created and administered by government units; others are sponsored by non-governmental sources. Here we first discuss federal, state, and local government regulatory units and then examine self-regulation forces.

Federal Regulatory Agencies

Federal agencies influence many marketing activities, including product development, pricing, packaging, advertising, personal selling, distribution, and storage.

Regulatory units usually have the power to enforce specific laws and some discretion in establishing operating rules and drawing up regulations to guide certain types of industry practices. Because of this discretion and overlapping areas of responsibility, confusion or conflict as to which agencies have jurisdiction over specific types of marketing activities is common.

In recent years the federal government has attempted to deregulate some industries. Airline routes and fares are one well-known example. Deregulation in the airline industry is still controversial because certain studies show that service quality has gone down and accident rates have increased.

Since deregulation, marketing in the banking industry is a new ball game. Competition is more intense, and the customer is considered more important in developing strategies. Deregulation has allowed banks to offer new products because banks are not limited to traditional checking and savings accounts. The ability to offer new products and pricing means that the customer now has more choices.[10] On the negative side, there has been an increase in bank failures since deregulation.

The Federal Trade Commission (FTC) Of all the federal regulatory units, the Federal Trade Commission has the broadest powers to influence marketing activities. The **Federal Trade Commission** consists of five commissioners, each appointed for a term of seven years by the president of the United States with the consent of the Senate. Not more than three commissioners may be members of the same political party. Their terms of office are staggered to ensure continuity of experience in the judgment of cases. The FTC has many administrative duties under existing laws, but the policy underlying them all is the same: "To prevent the free enterprise system from being stifled or fettered by monopoly or anti-competitive practices and to provide the direct protection of consumers from unfair or deceptive trade practices."[11] For example, the FTC used its broad powers to rule that the Coca-Cola Company could not acquire Dr Pepper Co. and that PepsiCo Inc. could not buy the Seven-Up Company because these mergers were considered anticompetitive.[12]

One major function of the FTC is to enforce laws and regulatory guidelines falling under its jurisdiction. When it has reason to believe that a firm is violating a law, the commission issues a complaint stating that the business is in violation. If the company continues the questionable practice, the FTC can issue a cease and desist order, which is simply an order for the business to stop doing whatever caused the complaint in the first place. The firm can appeal to the federal courts to have the FTC order rescinded. However, the FTC can seek civil penalties in the courts with a maximum penalty of $10,000 a day for each violation if a cease and desist order is violated.

The FTC provides assistance and information to businesses so that they will know how to comply with laws. New marketing methods are evaluated every year. When general sets of guidelines are needed to improve business practices in a particular industry, the FTC sometimes encourages the firms within that industry to establish a set of trade practices voluntarily. The FTC may even sponsor a conference to bring together industry leaders and consumers for this purpose.

10. Nancy Arden-Ellson, "The New Four P's," *B&E Review,* Jan.–Mar. 1987, pp. 25–29.
11. "Your Federal Trade Commission" (Washington, D.C.: Federal Trade Commission, 1977), pp. 8–9.
12. Andrew Feenberg, "Hecks & Haas: Can Uncola 'Cowboys' Stay in the Saddle?" *Adweek,* August 1987, p. 8.

Although the FTC regulates a variety of business practices, it allocates a large portion of its resources to curbing false advertising, misleading pricing, and deceptive packaging and labeling.

Other Federal Regulatory Units The FTC has broad powers to regulate a variety of business practices. The powers of other regulatory units are limited to specific products, services, or business activities. For example, the Federal Communications Commission (FCC) licenses radio and television stations and develops and enforces regulations regarding their operations. In one case, the FCC revoked the license of WJIM-TV in Lansing, Michigan, for reasons of misrepresentation and fraud. Table 2.2 outlines the major areas of responsibility of seven federal agencies.

As marketing activities become more complex, some of the responsibilities of federal units overlap. When authority over a specific product or marketing practice cannot be assigned to a single federal unit, marketers must try to comply with many different regulations.

State and Local Regulatory Agencies

All states—as well as numerous towns and cities—have agencies that enforce laws and rules regarding marketing practices. State and local regulatory agencies try hard not to establish and enforce regulations that conflict with the actions of national regulatory agencies. State and local agencies enforce specific laws dealing with the production and/or sale of particular goods and services. Industries that are commonly regulated by state agencies include banking, savings and loan, insurance, utilities, and liquor.

Nongovernmental Regulatory Forces

In the absence of governmental regulatory forces and in an attempt to prevent government intervention, some businesses try to regulate themselves. Trade associations in a number of industries have developed self-regulatory programs. Even though these programs are not a direct outgrowth of laws, many are established as an indirect result of legal action or proposed legislation. That is, numerous self-regulatory programs are created to stop or stall the development of laws and governmental regulatory groups that would regulate marketing practices. Sometimes, these programs deal with ethical and social issues. For example, many firms in the cigarette industry agreed, through a code of ethics, not to advertise cigarettes to children and teen-agers.

Self-regulatory programs have several advantages over governmental laws and guidelines. They are usually less expensive to establish and implement, at least in comparison to government programs, and their guidelines are generally more realistic and operational. In addition, industry self-regulatory programs reduce the need to expand government bureaucracy.

Nongovernmental self-regulatory programs do have three limitations. When a trade association creates a set of industry guidelines, nonmember firms do not have to follow the guidelines. Many self-regulatory programs lack the tools or the authority to enforce guidelines. Finally, guidelines in self-regulatory programs often are less strict than those established by government agencies.

Better Business Bureaus The **Better Business Bureau,** perhaps the best-known nongovernmental regulatory group, is a local regulatory agency supported by local

AGENCY	MAJOR AREAS OF RESPONSIBILITY
Federal Trade Commission (FTC)	Enforces laws and guidelines regarding business practices; takes action to stop false and deceptive advertising and labeling
Food and Drug Administration (FDA)	Enforces laws and regulations to prevent distribution of adulterated or misbranded foods, drugs, medical devices, cosmetics, veterinary products, and particularly hazardous consumer products
Consumer Product Safety Commission	Ensures compliance with the Consumer Product Safety Act; protects the public from unreasonable risk of injury from any consumer product not covered by other regulatory agencies
Interstate Commerce Commission (ICC)	Regulates franchises, rates, and finances of interstate rail, bus, truck, and water carriers
Federal Communications Commission (FCC)	Regulates communication by wire, radio, and television in interstate and foreign commerce
Environmental Protection Agency (EPA)	Develops and enforces environmental protection standards and conducts research into the adverse effects of pollution
Federal Power Commission (FPC)	Regulates rates and sales of natural gas producers, thereby affecting the supply and price of gas available to consumers; also regulates wholesale rates for electricity and gas, pipeline construction, and U.S. imports and exports of natural gas and electricity

TABLE 2.2

Major federal regulatory agencies

businesses. Today there are more than 140 bureaus that help settle problems between consumers and specific business firms. The bureaus also act to preserve good business practices in a locality, although they usually do not have strong enforcement tools to use in dealing with firms that employ questionable practices. When a firm continues to violate what the Better Business Bureau believes to be good business practices, the bureau warns consumers through local newspapers that a particular business is operating unfairly.

National Advertising Review Board   The Council of Better Business Bureaus, a national organization, and three advertising trade organizations have created a self-regulatory unit called the **National Advertising Review Board** (NARB). In addition to screening national advertisements to check for honesty, the NARB processes complaints about deceptive advertisements. The National Advertising Division (NAD) of the Council of Better Business Bureaus serves as the investigative arm of the NARB. The following example describes a typical case handled by NAD/NARB:

> A spaghetti sauce, made to be extra thick, was demonstrated alongside a competitor's regular spaghetti sauce by pouring them through kitchen strainers. The NAD found that this was misleading because the competition also made extra thick sauce under the same brand name, a fact not disclosed in the advertising.[13]

13. Report of NARB Panel no. 34, p. 4.

The NARB has no official enforcement powers. However, if a firm refuses to comply with its decision, the NARB publicizes the questionable practice and files a complaint with the FTC.

Societal Forces

Societal forces comprise the structure and dynamics of individuals and groups and the issues with which they are concerned. The public becomes concerned about marketers' activities when the consequences of those activities are questionable. Even when marketers do a good job of satisfying society, letters of praise or positive evaluation rarely follow. Society expects marketers to provide a high standard of living and to protect the general quality of life that we enjoy. In this section we examine some of society's expectations, the vehicles used to express those expectations, and the problems and opportunities that marketers experience as they try to deal with society's often contradictory wishes.

Living Standards and Quality of Life

In our society, we want more than just the bare necessities. We want not only protection from the elements but comfort and a satisfactory lifestyle. Our food must be safe and readily available, in many varieties, and in easily prepared forms. We use our clothing to protect our bodies, but most of us want a variety of clothing for adornment and to project an "image" to others.

We have many other wants beyond the necessities of life. We want vehicles that provide rapid, safe, and efficient transportation. We desire communication systems that give us information from around the globe. We want sophisticated medical services that prolong our life and improve our physical appearance. And we expect our education to equip us to both acquire and enjoy a higher standard of living.

Our society's high material standard of living is not enough. We also desire a high degree of quality in our lives. We do not want to spend all our waking hours working. We also seek leisure time for recreation and relaxation. The quality of life is enhanced by leisure time, clean air and water, and unlittered earth, conservation of wildlife and natural resources, and security from radiation and poisonous substances. Figure 2.4 illustrates concern about the quality of our oceans.

Our society seeks a multitude of goods and services in addition to healthy environmental conditions. It expects business to provide many elements necessary for both a high standard of living and a satisfying quality of life. Since marketing activities are a vital part of the total business structure, marketers have a responsibility to help provide what societal members want and to minimize what they do not want.

Consumer Movement Forces

The **consumer movement** is a diverse group of independent individuals, groups, and organizations that attempts to protect the rights of consumers. The major issues of the consumer movement fall into three categories: environmental protection, product performance and safety, and information disclosure. The major forces of the consumer movement are individual consumer advocates, consumer organizations, consumer education, and consumer laws. Consumer advocates,

FIGURE 2.4

Many citizens are concerned about the quality of life in our oceans (SOURCE: Courtesy of the National Wildlife Federation)

We care about OCEANS

Join and Support the National Wildlife Federation and State Affiliates

such as Ralph Nader, take it on themselves to protect the rights of consumers. Recently, Nader released studies to indicate that there is a crisis in the quality of the drinking water in many cities. Consumer advocates band together into consumer organizations, either voluntarily or under government sponsorship. Some organizations operate nationally, whereas others are active at state and local levels. They inform and organize other consumers, help businesses develop consumer-oriented programs, and pressure lawmakers to enact consumer laws.

Educating consumers to make wiser purchasing decisions perhaps will be one of the most far-reaching aspects of the consumer movement. Consumer education is increasingly becoming a part of high school and college curricula and adult education programs.

Ethical Issues and Social Responsibility

Marketing ethics relate to a moral evaluation of decisions based on commonly accepted principles of behavior; this evaluation results in an action being judged right or wrong. Marketers should operate in accordance with sound moral philosophies based on ideals such as fairness, justice and trust.[14] Ethics pertain to

14. Donald P. Robin and R. Eric Reidenbach, "Social Responsibility, Ethics, and Marketing Strategy: Closing the Gap Between Concept and Application," *Journal of Marketing,* January 1987, p. 45.

more than what is legal; they provide mutual trust among individuals and businesses. Although marketers often act in their own self-interest, for relationships to continue, exchange must be grounded on confidence and trust. An ethical violation makes continued trust and marketing exchanges difficult, if not impossible.[15] Consider the following ethical issues.

Conflict of Interest Conflict of interest is a common ethical issue facing many marketers. It usually results from a marketer taking advantage of situations for personal and selfish interest rather than for the long-run interest of the business. When payments, gifts, or special favors are granted to get new business or maintain existing business, there is always some concern of a bribe. A *bribe* is anything given to improperly influence the outcome of a decision. Even when a bribe is given to benefit the organization, it is unethical, and it usually hurts the organization in the long run.

Fairness and Honesty Fairness and integrity in business have become major ethical issues in the last few years. Maintaining integrity and dignity in business decisions is achieved by developing trust, confidence, and reliance. Minimally, business persons are expected to follow all applicable laws and regulations. But beyond obeying the laws, business people are expected to not knowingly harm others through deception, misrepresentation, or coercion.

Communications Communications, particularly in the form of advertising, also poses ethical problems. False and misleading advertising, as well as misleading personal-selling tactics, leads some businesses astray, and it certainly angers consumers when they find out about it. Manipulating communications regarding the safety of products is an important issue. But ethics in communications is not limited to promotion activities. Lying is also a significant problem in the United States. A national poll conducted by the Roper Center for Public Opinion Research revealed that of those people sampled, 72 percent sometimes lie. The same poll also revealed that 54 percent of those surveyed believed people are less honest today than they were ten years ago.[16]

Organizational Relationships Relationships with customers and one's own organization create such ethical problems as maintaining confidentiality in personal relations, meeting obligations and responsibilities in mutual agreements, and avoiding undue pressure that may force others to behave unethically. Other problems are *plagiarism,* the taking of someone else's work and representing it as your own without the person's consent. Situations may differ among businesses, but there always seem to be opportunities for taking advantage of situations to maximize personal welfare in a way that hurts others or the organization.

One way to evaluate whether a specific behavior is acceptable is to ask other persons in the business if they approve of it. Or check to see if there is a specific company policy about the activity. If other persons in the business approve of the

---

15. Vernon R. Loucks, Jr., "A CEO looks at Ethics," *Business Horizons,* March–April 1987, p. 4.
16. CNN poll conducted by the Roper Center for Public Opinion Research, *U.S. News & World Report,* Feb. 23, 1987.

activity and it is customary within the industry, chances are the activity is ethical. A rule of thumb for ethical problems is that an ethical decision will withstand open discussion and survive untarnished. Openness is not the end-all solution to the ethics problem, but it does create trust and facilitate learning relationships.[17]

The factors that affect people's propensity to make ethical or unethical decisions are not fully understood. There is speculation that three general sets of factors influence the ethics of one's decisions:[18] First, individual factors such as values, knowledge, attitudes, and intentions are believed to influence a person's decisions. Second, opportunity resulting from the absence of professional codes of ethics, corporate policies regarding ethics, or punishment may encourage unethical decision making. Third, the values, attitudes, and behavior of significant others such as peers, supervisors, and top management affect the ethics of one's decisions.

It is hard for employees to determine what is acceptable behavior within a company if the company does not have uniform policies and standards. Without standards for behavior, employees will generally make ethical decisions based on their observations of how their peers and management behave. To encourage ethical behavior, top management should eliminate opportunities for unethical behavior and create and issue formal rules and cooperation procedures.

Codes of ethics formalize what the company expects of its employees. These codes eliminate opportunity for unethical behavior because employees know what is expected of them and the punishment if they do engage in such action.

Table 2.3 is the American Marketing Association Code of Ethics. The code does not cover every ethical issue, but it is a useful overview of what marketers believe are sound moral principles for ethical marketing activities. This code could be used to help structure an organization's code of ethics.

Social responsibility relates to how marketing decisions affect society as a whole and various groups and individuals within society. Firms are recognizing that social responsibility relates to daily decisions of marketers rather than abstract ideals. Recognition is growing among companies that for firms' survival and competitive advantage, the long-term value of conducting business in a socially responsible manner far outweighs short-term costs.[19] To preserve socially responsible behavior while accomplishing goals, organizations must monitor changes and trends in society's values. Also, marketers must develop control procedures to ensure that daily decisions do not damage their company's relations with the public. An organization's top management must assume some responsibility for the employees' conduct by establishing and enforcing policies.

Being socially responsible may be a noble and necessary endeavor, but it is not a simple one. To be socially responsible, marketers must confront certain major problems. When PepsiCo promoted corn chips on television with its Frito-Bandito theme, it greatly offended a group of Mexican-Americans, who put such pressure on the company that the ad campaign was dropped. Surely PepsiCo did not enter

17. Sir Adrian Cadbury, "Ethical Managers Make Their Own Rules," *Harvard Business Review,* September–October 1987, p. 33.

18. O. C. Ferrell and Larry G. Gresham, "A Contingency Framework for Understanding Ethical Decision-Making in Marketing," *Journal of Marketing,* Summer 1985, pp. 87–96.

19. Margaret A. Stroup, Ralph L. Newbert, and Jerry W. Anderson, Jr., "Doing Good, Doing Better: Two Views of Social Responsibility," *Business Horizons,* March–April 1987, p. 23.

Members of the American Marketing Association (AMA) are committed to ethical professional conduct. They have joined together in subscribing to this Code of Ethics embracing the following topics:

Responsibilities of the Marketer

Marketers must accept responsibility for the consequences of their activities and make every effort to ensure that their decisions, recommendations, and actions function to identify, serve, and satisfy all relevant publics: consumers, organizations and society. Marketers' professional conduct must be guided by:

1. The basic rule of professional ethics: not knowingly to do harm;
2. The adherence to all applicable laws and regulations;
3. The accurate representation of their education, training and experience; and
4. The active support, practice and promotion of this Code of Ethics.

Honesty and Fairness

Marketers shall uphold and advance the integrity, honor, and dignity of the marketing profession by:

1. Being honest in serving consumers, clients, employees, suppliers, distributors and the public;
2. Not knowingly participating in conflict of interest without prior notice to all parties involved; and

3. Establishing equitable fee schedules including the payment or receipt of usual, customary and/or legal compensation for marketing exchanges

Rights and Duties of Parties

Participants in the marketing exchange process should be able to expect that:

1. Products and services offered are safe and fit for their intended uses;
2. Communications about offered products and services are not deceptive;
3. All parties intend to discharge their obligations, financial and otherwise, in good faith; and
4. Appropriate internal methods exist for equitable adjustment and/or redress of grievances concerning purchases.

It is understood that the above would include, *but is not limited to,* the following responsibilities of the marketer:

In the area of product development and management:

Disclosure of all substantial risks associated with product or service usage

Identification of any product component substitution that might materially change the product or impact on the buyer's purchase decision

Identification of extra-cost added features

TABLE 2.3

Code of Ethics, American Marketing Association

into this campaign with the idea of perpetuating a stereotype; it just did not think through the social consequences of its promotional campaign.[20] Marketers must determine what society wants and then predict the long-run effects of their decisions, often by turning to specialists such as lawyers, doctors, and scientists. However, specialists do not necessarily agree with each other, and the fields in which they work can yield findings that undermine previously acceptable marketing decisions. Forty years ago, marketers promoted cigarettes as being good for one's health. Now, a few years after the discovery that cigarette smoking is linked to cancer, society's opinion about smoking is changing and businesses are confronted with a new social responsibility, such as giving customers a smoke-free atmosphere. Most major lodging companies allocate at least some of their rooms for nonsmokers, and most other businesses within the food, travel, and entertainment industries provide smoke-free environments.

20. Archie B. Carroll, "In Search of the Moral Managers," *Business Horizons,* March–April 1987, p. 11.

In the area of promotions:

Avoidance of false and misleading advertising

Rejection of high pressure manipulations, or misleading sales tactics

Avoidance of sales promotions that use deception or manipulation

In the area of distribution:

Not manipulating the availability of a product for purpose of exploitation

Not using coercion in the marketing channel

Not exerting undue influence over the resellers' choice to handle a product

In the area of pricing:

Not engaging in price fixing

Not practicing predatory pricing

Disclosing the full price associated with any purchase

In the area of marketing research:

Prohibiting selling or fund raising under the guise of conducting research

Maintaining research integrity by avoiding misrepresentation and omission of pertinent research data

Treating outside clients and suppliers fairly

Organizational Relationships

Marketers should be aware of how their behavior may influence or impact on the behavior of others in organizational relationships. They should not encourage or apply coercion to obtain unethical behavior in their relationships with others, such as employees, suppliers or customers.

1. Apply confidentiality and anonymity in professional relationships with regard to privileged information.
2. Meet their obligations and responsibilities in contracts and mutual agreements in a timely manner.
3. Avoid taking the work of others, in whole, or in part, and represent this work as their own or directly benefit from it without compensation or consent of the originator or owner.
4. Avoid manipulation to take advantage of situations to maximize personal welfare in a way that unfairly deprives or damages the organization or others.

Any AMA members found to be in violation of any provision of this Code of Ethics may have his or her Association membership suspended or revoked.

SOURCE: Reprinted by permission of the American Marketing Association.

TABLE 2.3
(continued)

Because society is made up of many diverse groups, finding out what "society" as a whole wants is difficult, if not impossible. In trying to satisfy the desires of one group, marketers may dissatisfy others. Moreover, costs are associated with many of the demands of society. Marketers must evaluate the extent to which members of society are willing to pay for what they want. For example, consumers may want more information regarding a product yet be unwilling to pay the costs that the firm sustains in providing the data. Thus, marketers who want to make socially responsible decisions may find the task difficult.

Economic and Competitive Forces

The economic and competitive forces in the marketing environment influence both marketers' and customers' decisions and activities. Here we explore the effects of broad economic and competitive forces, specifically, competition, buying power, willingness to spend, spending patterns, and general economic conditions.

Assessment of Competitive Forces

Few firms, if any, operate free of competition. Broadly speaking, all firms compete with each other for consumers' buying power. From a more practical viewpoint, however, a business generally views as **competition** those firms that market products similar to, or substitutable for, its products in the same geographic area. For example, a local supermarket manager views all grocery stores in town as competitors but almost never thinks of all other local or out-of-town stores as competitors. Several factors affect the strength—and thus the importance—of the competitive forces acting on a firm. Let us explore several of them.

Types of Competitive Structures   The number of firms that control the supply of a product may affect the strength of competition. When only one or a few firms control supply, competitive factors will exert a different sort of influence on marketing activities than when there are many competitors. Table 2.4 presents four general categories or models of competitive relationships.

A **monopoly** exists when a firm produces a product that has no close substitutes. The organization has complete control over the supply of the product. In this case, a single seller can erect barriers to potential competitors.

An **oligopoly** exists when a few sellers control the supply of a large proportion of a product. In this case, each seller must consider the reactions of other sellers to

TABLE 2.4

Selected characteristics of competitive structures

TYPE OF STRUCTURE	NUMBER OF COMPETITORS	EASE OF ENTRY INTO MARKET	PRODUCT	KNOWLEDGE OF MARKET	EXAMPLE
Monopoly	One	Many barriers	Almost no substitutes	Perfect	Dayton (Ohio) Power and Light (gas and electricity service)
Oligopoly	Few	Some barriers	Homogeneous or differentiated (real or perceived differences) products	Imperfect	Philip Morris (cigarettes)
Monopolistic competition	Many	Few barriers	Product differentiation with many substitutes	More knowledge than oligopoly; less than monopoly	Levi Strauss (jeans)
Perfect competition	Unlimited	No barriers	Homogeneous products	Perfect	Vegetable farm (sweet corn)

changes in marketing activities. Products facing oligopolistic competition may be homogeneous, such as aluminum, or differentiated, such as cigarettes and automobiles. Usually there are some barriers that make it difficult to enter the market and compete with oligopolies. Few companies or individuals could enter the oil refining or steel industries, for example, because of the tremendous financial resources that are necessary. Moreover, some industries require special technical or marketing skills that block the entry of many potential competitors.

Monopolistic competition exists when a firm with many potential competitors attempts to develop a differential marketing strategy to establish its own market share. For example, Levi's has established a differential advantage for its jeans through a well-known trademark, design, advertising, and a quality image. Although many competing brands of jeans are available, this firm has carved out its market share through use of a differential marketing strategy.

Perfect competition, if it existed at all, would entail a large number of sellers, no one of which could significantly influence price or supply. Products would be homogeneous, and there would be full knowledge of the market and easy entry into it. The closest thing to an example of perfect competition would be an unregulated agricultural market.

Few, if any, marketers operate in a structure of perfect competition. Perfect competition is an ideal at one end of the continuum, with monopoly at the other end. Most marketers function in a competitive environment that falls somewhere between these two extremes.

The Tools of Competition Another set of factors that influences the level of competition is the number and types of competitive tools competitors use. To survive, a firm uses one or several available competitive tools to deal with competitive economic forces. Once a firm has analyzed its particular competitive environment and decided which factors in that environment it can or must adjust to or influence, it can choose among the variables it can control to strengthen its competitive position.

Probably the first competitive tool that occurs to most of us is price. Recognizing this phenomenon, Bic Corp. produces disposable products that are similar to competing products but less expensive. There is, however, one major problem with using price as a competitive tool. Frequently competitors will either match or beat your price. This threat is one of the primary reasons for employing nonprice competitive tools that are based on the differentiation of market segments, product offering, promotion, distribution, or enterprise.[21] For example, PAM® Cooking Spray, in Figure 2.5, advertises that it is an ideal alternative to cooking oil, its major competitor.

By focusing on a specific market segment, a marketer sometimes gains a competitive advantage. As the Application on page 62 indicates, Apple Computer, Inc. has traditionally appealed more to the home market, whereas International Business Machines Corp. (IBM) has appealed to the office market. Apple and IBM have each attempted to gain a competitive edge by incorporating product features that make their brands, to some extent, distinctive. Firms use distinguishing promotional methods to compete, such as advertising and personal selling. Competing

21. Wroe Alderson, *Dynamic Marketing Behavior* (Homewood, Ill.: Irwin, 1965), pp. 195–197.

Apple Tries to Stay Ahead of IBM

The competition among producers of personal computers (PCs) is essentially a race to get the best, most innovative products to the marketplace. Marketers in this environment frequently have to assess their competitors' role when making marketing strategy decisions. If major competitors are changing their products, then a marketer may want to follow suit to remain competitive. Apple Computer, Inc. has introduced two new, faster personal computers, the Macintosh II and Macintosh SE, in anticipation of the introduction of a new PC by IBM, one of Apple's major competitors.

Apple's new computers are much faster and more powerful than its earlier models. The improved Macintosh uses a new chip, the powerful 68000 to run programs that previously were impossible to run on an Apple PC, including IBM-compatible programs and UNIX, a software package many scientists and engineers use. This compatibility feature illustrates computer manufacturers' new attitude of giving customers the features they want. Making Apple computers capable of running IBM software is Apple's effort at making the Macintosh compatible with IBM computers and thus more popular in the office, where Apple hopes to increase sales. Users of the new Apple can also add accessories to make their machines specialize in specific uses, such as engineering, accounting, or writing.

The new computers represent a big improvement over past models, but they also carry a much higher price tag: $3,900 for the Macintosh II. Company officials do not think the higher price will slow down buyers who want to step up to a more powerful computer. Apple wants to stay in the high-price end of the personal computer market to finance research for even faster, more sophisticated computers.

Although the new models can run currently available software, it will be several years before sufficient software is available to make full use of the increased speed and graphics of the new Macintoshes. Nevertheless, several software developers, including the software giants, Lotus and Microsoft, have already begun work on new programs for the Macintosh computers.

Even though Apple and IBM are major competitors, both companies realize that their competitor's computers have certain features that their own models do not. The Apple line has always been popular for its sophisticated color graphics, whereas the IBM machines have always been favored in offices. In the future, there will probably be more compatibility between the two companies' products, which no doubt will require that both Apple and IBM change marketing strategies.

SOURCES: Mark Lewyn, "Machines Get Faster, More Flexible," *USA Today,* Mar. 2, 1987, pp. 1B, 2B; Benton R. Schlender, "Calculated Move: Apple Computer Tries to Achieve Stability but Remain Creative," *Wall Street Journal,* July 16, 1987, pp. 1, 21; 1985 and 1986 Annual Reports for Apple Computers, Inc.

producers sometimes use different distribution channels to gain competitive advantage over each other. Merchants may compete by placing their outlets in locations that are convenient for a large number of shoppers.

Monitoring Competition   Marketers in an organization need to be aware of the actions of major competitors. They should monitor what competitors are currently doing and assess the changes that are occurring in competitive actions. By doing this, the specific strategy competitors are following, and how that strategy reacts with their own, can guide marketers and their operations as they seek to develop competitive advantages.[22] This aids marketers in making adjustments to current marketing strategies and in planning new ones. Information may come from direct observation or from sources such as salespeople, customers, trade publications, syndicated marketing research services, distributors, and marketing studies.

An organization also needs information about competitors that will allow its marketing managers to assess the performance of the firm's marketing efforts. Comparison of performance relative to competitors helps marketing managers recognize strengths and weaknesses in their own marketing strategies. Data about market shares, product movement, sales volume, and expenditure levels can be quite useful. However, accurate information regarding these issues often is difficult to obtain.

22. Ian Gordon, "Exit 'Marketing Concept'—Enter 'Competition Concept,' " *Business Quarterly,* Summer 1986, p. 30.

FIGURE 2.5
PAM® Cooking Spray competes with cooking oil (SOURCE: Boyle-Midway Household Products, Inc. PAM® is a registered trademark of Boyle-Midway Household Products, Inc.)

Consumer Demand and Spending Behavior

Marketers must understand the factors that determine whether, what, where, and when people buy. In Chapters 4 and 5 we look at behavioral factors underlying these choices. Here we focus on economic aspects of buying behavior. Specifically, we analyze buying power and consumers' willingness to purchase as well as their spending patterns.

Buying Power   One of the requirements for a market is that people have buying power. The strength of a person's **buying power** depends on both the size of the resources that give that individual the ability to purchase and the state of the economy. The resources that make up buying power are goods, services, and financial holdings. The state of the economy affects buying power because it influences price levels. During inflationary periods, when prices are rising, buying power decreases because more dollars are required to buy products. For example, products today cost almost three times as much as they did in 1967. Conversely, in periods of declining prices, the buying power of a given set of resources increases.

The major financial sources of buying power are income, credit, and wealth. From an individual's viewpoint, **income** is the amount of money received through wages, rents, investments, pensions, and subsidy payments for a given period, such as a month or a year. Normally, this money is used for three purposes: paying taxes, spending, and saving. The average annual family income in the United States is approximately $25,000. However, because of the differences in people's educational levels, abilities, occupations, and wealth, income is not equally distributed in this country (or in other countries). Income distribution is discussed further in Chapter 3.

Marketers are most interested in the amount of money that is left after taxes are paid. After-tax income is called **disposable income** and is used for spending or saving. Because disposable income is a ready source of buying power, the total amount available in our country is important to marketers. Several factors affect the size of total disposable income; one, of course, is the total amount of income. Total national income is affected by wage levels, rate of unemployment, interest rates, and dividend rates. These factors in turn affect the size of disposable income. Because disposable income is the income left after taxes are paid, the number of taxes and their amount directly affect the size of total disposable income. When taxes rise, disposable income declines; when taxes fall, disposable income increases.

Disposable income that is available for spending and saving after an individual has purchased the basic necessities of food, clothing, and shelter is called **discretionary income.** People use discretionary income to purchase entertainment, vacations, automobiles, education, pets and pet supplies, furniture, appliances, and so on. Changes in total discretionary income affect the sales of these products, especially of automobiles, furniture, large appliances, and other durable goods.

Credit transactions enable people to spend future income now or in the near future. Credit increases current buying power at the expense of future buying power. Several factors determine whether consumers use or forgo credit. First, credit must be available to consumers. Interest rates too affect consumers' decisions to use credit, especially for expensive purchases such as homes, appliances, and automobiles. When credit charges are high, consumers are more likely to delay buying expensive items. Credit usage also is affected by credit terms, such as the size of the down payment and the amount and number of monthly payments.

A person can have a high income and very little wealth. It is also feasible, but not likely, for a person to have great wealth but not much income. **Wealth** is the accumulation of past income, natural resources, and financial resources. It may exist in many forms, including cash, securities, savings accounts, jewelry, antiques, and real estate. Like income, wealth is unevenly distributed among people in this country. The significance of wealth to marketers is that as people become wealthier, they gain buying power in three ways: They can use their wealth for current purchases, to generate income, and to acquire large amounts of credit.

Marketers need to analyze buying power because of its tremendous impact on consumers' reactions to firms' marketing strategies. Marketing managers can use buying power analysis for many purposes, including evaluating opportunities in various markets, forecasting sales, establishing sales quotas, and budgeting marketing expenditures. Buying power information is available from government sources, trade associations, and research agencies.

One of the most current and comprehensive sources of buying power data is the *Sales and Marketing Management Survey of Buying Power,* published annually by *Sales and Marketing Management* magazine. As Table 2.5 shows, the *Survey of Buying Power* presents data for specific geographic areas, including states, counties, and most cities with populations in excess of forty thousand. The *Survey of Buying Power* also contains population and retail sales data for the same geographic areas.

The most direct indicators of buying power in the *Survey of Buying Power* are "effective buying income" (EBI) and "buying power index" (BPI). **Effective buying income** is similar to what we call disposable income; it includes salaries, wages, dividends, interest, profits, and rents, less federal, state, and local taxes. The **buying power index** is a weighted index consisting of population, effective buying income, and retail sales data.[23] The higher the index number, the greater the buying power. Like other indexes, the buying power index is most useful for comparative purposes. Marketers can use buying power indexes for a particular year to compare the buying power of one area with the buying power of another area, or they can analyze trends for a particular area by comparing the area's buying power indexes for several years.

Income, wealth, and credit equip consumers to purchase goods and services. Marketing managers should be aware of current levels and expected changes in buying power in their own markets because buying power directly affects the types and quantities of goods and services that consumers purchase, as we see later in our discussion of spending patterns. Just because consumers have buying power, however, does not mean that they will buy. Consumers must also be willing to use their buying power.

Consumers' Willingness to Spend People's **willingness to spend** is, to some degree, related to their ability to buy. That is, people are sometimes more willing to buy if they have the buying power. However, a number of other elements also influence willingness to spend. Some elements affect specific products; others influence spending in general. A product's absolute price and its price relative to the price of substitute products influence almost all of us. At times, the total dollar outlay for an item may seem too great, or consumers may know of a similar,

23. *Sales and Marketing Management 1987 Survey of Buying Power,* Oct. 26, 1987.

TABLE 2.5

S&MM's U.S. Metropolitan Area Projections

STATE S&MM METRO AREA COUNTY	EFFECTIVE BUYING INCOME				RETAIL SALES				BUYING POWER INDEX	
	TOTAL EBI ($000) 1991	% CHANGE 1986–1991	AVERAGE HOUSEHOLD EBI 1986	AVERAGE HOUSEHOLD EBI 1991	TOTAL RETAIL SALES ($000) 1991	% CHANGE 1986–1991	RETAIL SALES PER HOUSEHOLD 1986	RETAIL SALES PER HOUSEHOLD 1991	1986	1991
Utah										
Provo-Orem										
Utah	2,569,104	44.7	25,874	34,624	1,137,244	30.3	12,725	15,327	.0685	.0674
Salt Lake City–Ogden	16,345,369	56.6	30,695	43,951	7,904,538	45.7	15,953	21,254	.3718	.3906
Davis	2,481,967	57.4	31,165	42,866	1,107,406	54.7	14,145	19,126	.0559	.0603
Salt Lake	11,426,653	56.8	31,065	44,846	5,509,532	44.2	16,284	21,623	.2582	.2704
Weber	2,436,749	55.1	28,672	41,161	1,287,600	45.0	16,205	21,750	.0577	.0599
Total metro counties	18,914,473	54.9	29,885	42,400	9,041,782	43.6	15,411	20,269	.4403	.4580
Total state	24,069,852	54.9	29,362	41,679	11,656,038	44.2	15,275	20,184	.5650	.5891
Vermont										
Burlington	2,369,083	49.9	34,063	47,764	1,621,111	48.1	23,599	32,684	.0592	.0610
Chittenden	2,298,366	50.2	34,302	48,083	1,607,727	48.3	24,308	33,634	.0578	.0596
Grand Isle	70,717	39.6	28,137	39,287	13,384	23.3	6,031	7,436	.0014	.0014
Total metro counties	2,369,083	49.9	34,063	47,764	1,621,111	48.1	23,599	32,684	.0592	.0610
Total state	8,428,623	46.4	28,491	39,331	5,749,751	45.5	19,556	26,830	.2216	.2235

EBI = effective buying income.

SOURCE: "S&MM's U.S. Metropolitan Area Projections," *Sales & Marketing Management*, Oct. 26, 1987, p. 79.

substitutable item with a much lower price. The amount of satisfaction currently received or expected in the future from a product already owned may also influence consumers' desire to buy other products. Satisfaction depends not only on the quality of the functional performance of the currently owned product but on numerous psychological and social forces.

Factors that affect consumers' general willingness to spend are expectations about future employment, income levels, prices, family size, and general economic conditions. If people are unsure whether or how long they will be employed, willingness to buy ordinarily declines. Willingness to buy may increase if people are reasonably certain of higher incomes in the future. Expectations of rising prices in the near future may also increase the willingness to spend. For a given level of buying power, the larger the family, the greater the willingness to buy. One of the reasons for this relationship is that as the size of a family size increases, a greater number of dollars must be spent to provide the basic necessities of life to sustain the family members. Lastly, perceptions of future economic conditions influence willingness to buy.

Consumer Spending Patterns Marketers must be aware of the factors that influence consumers' ability and willingness to buy, but they should also analyze how consumers actually spend their disposable incomes. Marketers obtain this information by studying consumer spending patterns.

Consumer spending patterns indicate the relative proportions of annual family expenditures or the actual amount of money spent on certain kinds of goods and services. Families are usually categorized by one of several characteristics, including family income, age of the household head, geographic area, and family life cycle. There are two types of spending patterns: comprehensive and product-specific.

The percentages of family income allotted to annual expenditures for general classes of goods and services constitute **comprehensive spending patterns.** Comprehensive spending patterns or the data to develop them are available in government publications and in reports of the Conference Board. In Table 2.6, comprehensive spending patterns are classified by the life cycle of the family. Note the variation in expenditures between husband and wife families and single-parent families.

Product-specific spending patterns indicate the annual dollar amounts families spend for specific products within a general product class. Information sources used to construct product-specific spending patterns include government publications, the Conference Board, trade publications, and consumer surveys. Table 2.7 illustrates a product-specific spending pattern. Notice the differences between this type of spending pattern and the comprehensive ones. The products listed fall into one general product category, and the figures are stated in dollar amounts.

A marketer uses spending patterns to analyze general trends in the ways that families spend their incomes for various kinds of products. For example, a person who is considering opening a bakery might use the data in Table 2.7 to estimate the demand for various categories of bakery products. Analyses of spending patterns yield information that a marketer can use to gain perspective and background for decision making. However, spending patterns reflect only general trends and thus cannot be used as the only basis for making specific decisions.

HUSBAND AND WIFE FAMILIES

| ITEM | ALL CONSUMER UNITS | TOTAL HUSBAND AND WIFE FAMILIES | HUSBAND AND WIFE ONLY | HUSBAND AND WIFE WITH CHILDREN | | | OTHER HUSBAND AND WIFE FAMILIES | ONE PARENT, AT LEAST ONE CHILD UNDER 18 | SINGLE PERSON AND OTHER FAMILIES |
				OLDEST CHILD UNDER 6	OLDEST CHILD 6 TO 17	OLDEST CHILD 18 OR OVER			
Total expenditures	$17,144	$21,173	$17,959	$18,605	$23,054	$26,146	$23,993	$12,066	$11,417
Food	18.8%	18.7%	17.6%	17.1%	19.5%	19.9%	19.9%	22.8%	18.4%
Alcoholic beverages	1.6%	1.3%	1.6%	1.3%	1.2%	1.3%	1.2%	1.0%	2.7%
Housing	16.4%	15.4%	16.3%	19.5%	15.8%	11.8%	13.3%	20.0%	19.0%
Fuels, utilities, and public services	7.4%	7.3%	7.3%	6.9%	7.2%	7.4%	7.5%	9.2%	7.4%
House furnishings, equipment, and supplies	5.7%	5.8%	6.2%	7.3%	5.8%	4.3%	6.1%	5.5%	5.3%
Apparel	5.5%	5.5%	5.1%	5.0%	5.8%	5.7%	5.9%	7.0%	5.2%
Transportation	20.1%	20.7%	20.1%	20.9%	19.7%	23.0%	21.2%	16.0%	19.1%
Health care	4.4%	4.4%	5.8%	3.6%	3.7%	4.0%	4.2%	2.9%	4.3%
Entertainment	4.4%	4.5%	4.3%	4.3%	5.3%	4.1%	4.3%	3.9%	4.3%
Personal care	0.9%	0.9%	1.1%	0.6%	0.8%	1.0%	1.0%	0.8%	0.9%
Reading	0.7%	0.7%	0.8%	0.7%	0.6%	0.6%	0.6%	0.5%	0.8%
Education	1.3%	1.3%	0.7%	0.3%	1.5%	2.6%	1.1%	1.2%	1.2%
Tobacco and smoking supplies	1.0%	1.0%	1.0%	1.0%	1.0%	1.0%	1.2%	1.2%	1.1%
Miscellaneous	1.5%	1.5%	1.3%	1.5%	1.3%	1.5%	2.7%	1.4%	1.6%
Cash contributions	2.9%	2.9%	3.6%	1.5%	2.5%	3.6%	2.4%	1.5%	3.1%
Personal insurance and pensions	7.4%	8.0%	7.5%	8.5%	8.3%	8.4%	7.5%	5.0%	5.8%

SOURCE: U.S. Department of Labor, Bureau of Labor Statistics, *Consumer Expenditure Survey: Interview Survey, 1980–81*, Bulletin 2225, pp. 31–32.

General Economic Conditions

The overall state of the economy fluctuates in all countries. These changes in general economic conditions affect (and are affected by) the forces of supply and demand, buying power, willingness to buy, consumer expenditure levels, and the intensity of competitive behavior. Therefore, present-day economic conditions and changes in the economy have a broad impact on the success of organizations' marketing strategies.

Fluctuations in the U.S. economy follow a general pattern that is often referred to as the "business cycle." In the traditional view, the business cycle consists of four stages: prosperity, recession, depression, and recovery. To understand some of the effects of the general economic climate, let us explore certain characteristics of the four stages.

During **prosperity,** unemployment is low and aggregate income is relatively high. Assuming a low inflation rate, this combination causes buying power to be high. To the extent that the economic outlook remains prosperous, consumers generally are willing to buy. In the prosperity stage, marketers often expand their product mixes to take advantage of the increased buying power. They sometimes capture a larger market share by intensifying distribution and promotion efforts.

Because unemployment rises during a **recession,** total buying power declines. The pessimism that accompanies a recession often stifles both consumer and business spending. Because of decreased buying power, many consumers become more price and value conscious—they look for products that are basic and functional. For instance, people ordinarily reduce their consumption of the more expensive convenience foods and exert greater effort to save money by growing and preparing more of their own food. Individuals buy fewer durable goods and more repair and do-it-yourself products. During a recession, some firms make the mistake of drastically reducing their marketing efforts and thus damage their ability to survive. Obviously, marketers should consider some revision of their marketing activities during a recessionary period. Because consumers are more concerned about the functional value of products, a firm must focus its marketing research on determining precisely what product functions are important to buyers and then make certain that these functions are included in the firm's products. Promotional efforts should emphasize value and utility.

A **depression** is a period in which there is extremely high unemployment, wages are very low, total disposable income is at a minimum, and consumers lack confidence in the economy. The federal government has used both monetary and fiscal policies in an attempt to offset the effects of recession, depression, and inflation. Monetary policies are employed to control the money supply, which in turn influences spending, saving, and investment by both individuals and businesses. Through fiscal policies, the government can influence the amount of savings and expenditures by altering the tax structure and by changing the levels of government expenditures. Some experts believe that effective use of monetary and fiscal policies can eliminate depressions from the business cycle.

Recovery is the business cycle stage in which the economy moves from recession to prosperity. During this period, the high unemployment rate begins to decline, total disposable income increases, and the economic gloom that lessened consumers' willingness to buy subsides. Both the ability and the willingness to buy rise. Marketers face some problems during recovery. One is the difficulty of ascertaining how quickly prosperity will return. It can also be difficult to forecast the level of prosperity that will be attained. In the recovery stage, marketers should maintain as

TABLE 2.7

TABLE 2.7
Annual dollar expenditures for nonfrozen bakery products by various household incomes

	TOTAL	UNDER $5,000	$5,000– $10,000	$10,000– $15,000	$15,000– $20,000	$20,000– $25,000	$25,000– $35,000	$35,000– $50,000	$50,000 AND ABOVE
Households (millions)	70.0	12.5	12.5	10.2	8.7	8.0	10.7	5.4	2.1
Distribution of households	100.0%	17.9	17.9	14.5	12.4	11.4	15.3	7.7	3.1
Average household size	2.6	1.9	2.1	2.4	2.8	3.0	3.1	3.4	3.3
Distribution of persons	100.0%	13.0	14.7	13.4	13.5	13.0	18.6	10.0	3.9
Distribution of income	100.0%	2.5	7.4	10.2	12.2	14.3	25.4	17.8	10.2
Expenditures of dollars	AVERAGE								
Nonfrozen bakery products	144.79	98.01	112.89	117.98	151.22	165.77	192.42	215.82	210.64
White bread	40.64	31.68	33.81	37.66	41.99	48.22	49.42	50.62	44.26
Bread other than white	16.98	11.91	14.52	15.45	17.27	17.67	21.14	23.00	28.60
Fresh biscuits, rolls, etc.	17.55	9.51	11.37	13.14	19.13	20.57	24.43	33.40	29.55
Cakes and cupcakes	16.29	9.57	14.10	11.50	18.23	17.44	22.44	25.38	25.21
Cookies	19.52	12.31	13.62	14.95	19.87	22.71	29.16	29.99	29.78
Crackers	11.23	7.79	8.59	9.66	10.70	13.03	14.50	16.65	19.74
Bread and cracker products	2.11	1.06	1.25	1.70	2.19	2.51	2.42	5.16	4.14
Doughnuts, sweetrolls, etc.	15.81	11.46	11.58	10.59	15.76	18.48	22.78	24.72	23.62
Fresh pies and tarts	4.67	2.72	4.05	3.32	6.09	5.16	6.12	6.90	5.73

HOUSEHOLD INCOME

SOURCE: Consumer Research Center, *How Consumers Spend Their Money* (New York: Conference Board, 1984), pp. 20, 44. Used by permission.

much flexibility in their marketing strategies as possible to be able to make the needed adjustments as the economy moves from recession to prosperity.

Technological Forces

The impact of technology on society and businesses is a major factor in the success—or failure—of a business enterprise. Economic forces are related to technology because the pursuit and existence of technological information may affect income, taxation, prices, and consumers' willingness to spend. The effects of technology are broad in scope and today exert a tremendous influence on our lives.

The rapid technological growth of the last several decades is expected to continue through the 1990s. Areas that hold great technological promise include solid-state electronics, artificial intelligence, materials research, biotechnology, and geology. Current research is investigating new forms of chips and computers that are a hundred times faster than current models. Special artificial intelligence systems are presently being used in industry and medicine. These systems mimic human experts with astonishing precision. New "microscience" equipment allows scientists to explore the innermost structure of matter and to modify the basic elements of the periodic table.

Because these and other technological developments will have a definite impact on buyers' and marketers' decisions, we now define technology and consider several of its effects on society and marketers. We then discuss several factors that influence the adoption and use of technology.

Technology Defined The word "technology" brings to mind creations of progress such as computers, synthetic fibers, lasers, and heart transplants. Even though such items are outgrowths of technology, none *is* technology. **Technology** is the knowledge of how to accomplish tasks and goals;[24] often this knowledge comes from scientific research.

Technology is credited with providing mechanical, physical, and numerous other processes that let us achieve a high standard of living. Yet it is also blamed for pollution, unemployment, crime, and a number of other social and environmental problems. Technology itself is neither good nor bad. Its effects are determined largely by how it is applied. Technology has been used to improve health care so that people can live longer. In addition, although the potential effects of technology may be significant, the actual effects of certain types of technology are nonexistent unless the technology is used. For example, some technological knowledge that has come out of our space explorations has not yet been put to use.

Technology grows out of research performed by businesses, universities, and nonprofit organizations. For example, in Figure 2.6, Southwestern Bell explains how an employee developed a device that could determine whether a problem occurred in the telephone lines in the consumer's equipment. Much of this research—in fact, more than half of it—is paid for by the federal government, which supports investigations in a variety of areas, including health, arms, agriculture,

---

24. Herbert Simon, "Technology and Environment," *Management Science,* June 1973, p. 1110.

energy, and pollution. Because much federally funded research requires the use of specialized machinery, personnel, and facilities, a sizable proportion of this research is conducted by large business organizations that already possess the necessary specialized equipment and people.

The Impact of Technology

FIGURE 2.6
Southwestern Bell Corporation promotes its service orientation in an advertisement detailing the development of a technological device to improve service (SOURCE: Courtesy of Southwestern Bell Corporation)

Marketers must be aware of new developments in technology and their possible effects because technology can and does affect marketing activities in many different ways. Consumers' technological knowledge influences their desires for goods and services. To provide marketing mixes that satisfy consumers, marketers must be aware of these influences. Technological developments can put some people out of business while opening up new business opportunities to others. The introduction and general acceptance of synthetic fabrics drove some sheep raisers, cotton growers, and dry cleaners out of business. Yet this technology provided new market opportunities for synthetic fabric producers, clothing manufacturers, retail clothiers, and self-service laundries. Technology definitely affects the types of products that are offered to consumers. The following items are only a few of the many thousands of existing products that were not available to consumers twenty years ago:

It's called a "Smart Block." And it's the brainchild of Steve Weinert, an employee of our Southwestern Bell Telephone subsidiary.

What's so smart about it? Simply put, it lets us spot whether a problem is in our data lines or a customer's equipment. Electronically. From our own test centers.

Before Smart Block, our technicians had to rely on a most ancient invention— the wheel.

Every time a problem was reported, someone had to hop into a truck and head out to the customer's premises. Then check each data circuit. One by one.

The time saved increases the efficiency of our technicians and lowers operating costs. Of course, our customers are delighted too. The speedier diagnosis also helps their bottom line.

And Steve's invention is just beginning to gain momentum. We've licensed the invention to an independent company who manufactures and markets Smart Blocks. Now other phone companies across the country are sending in their orders.

Which is great. Because it means royalties rolling in for us.

Making the most of what we know best.

Southwestern Bell Corporation

This invention is helping us replace this invention.

Solar-powered pocket calculators	Calorie-reduced beer, wine, and pasta
Microwave ovens	NutraSweet
Antiskid automobile brake systems	Low-cost personal computers
Videotape recorders for home use	Small personal televisions (e.g., Sony
Super stain-resistant carpeting	Corp.'s Watchman)

The various ways technology affects marketing activities fall into two broad categories. It affects consumers and society in general, and it influences what, how, when, and where products are marketed.

The Effects of Technology on Society Technology determines how we satisfy our physiological needs. In various ways and to varying degrees, eating and drinking habits, sleeping patterns, sexual activities, and health care are all influenced by both existing technology and changes in technology. Technological developments have improved our standard of living, thus giving us more leisure time. Education, information, and entertainment have been improved through technology.

Nevertheless, technology can detract from the quality of life through undesirable side effects such as unemployment, polluted air and water, and other health hazards. Some people believe that further applications of technology can soften or eliminate these undesirable side effects; other people argue that the best way to improve the quality of our lives is to reduce the use of technology.

The Impact of Technology on Marketing Activities Technology affects the types of products that marketers can offer. Technological improvements in production processes and materials sometimes result in more durable, less expensive products. Because of technological changes in communications, marketers now can reach large masses of people through a variety of media more efficiently.

Technological advances in transportation enable consumers to travel farther and more often to shop at a larger number of stores. Changes in transportation also have affected the producers' ability to get products to retailers and wholesalers. The ability of present-day manufacturers of relatively lightweight products to reach any of their dealers within twenty-four hours (via air freight) would astound their counterparts of fifty years ago.

Adoption and Use of Technology

Through a procedure known as **technology assessment,** managers try to foresee the effects of new products and processes on their firm's operation, on other business organizations, and on society in general. With the information gained through a technology assessment, management tries to estimate whether the benefits of using a specific kind of technology outweigh the costs to the firm and to society generally. The degree to which a business is technologically based also will influence how its management responds to technology. Firms whose products and product changes are outgrowths of recent technology are very much concerned with gathering and using technological information.

Although technology may exist that could radically improve a firm's products or other parts of the marketing mix, the firm may not apply the technology as long as its competitors do not attempt to use it. In addition, the extent to which a firm can protect inventions that arise from research influences its use of technology. How secure a product is from imitation depends on how easily the product can be copied without violating its patent. If new products and processes cannot be protected through patents, a firm is less likely to market them and make the benefits of its research available to competitors.

How a firm uses (or does not use) technology is important for its long-run survival. A firm that makes the wrong decisions may well lose out to its competitors. Poor decisions may also affect a firm's profits by requiring expensive corrective actions. Poor decisions about technological forces may even drive a firm out of business.

Summary

The marketing environment is made up of constantly changing environmental forces that marketing managers must monitor to secure organizational survival. To monitor the changes in these forces, marketers can practice environmental scanning and analysis, which involve observation and information gathering. By gathering useful information and making accurate observations, marketing managers should be able to predict opportunities and threats associated with environmental fluctuation. Marketing management may assume either a passive, reactive approach or an active, aggressive approach in responding to these environmental fluctuations. There is no best method of response; the choice depends on an organization's structure and needs and on the composition of the environmental forces that affect it. The marketing environment contains political, legal, regulatory, societal, economic and competitive, and technological forces that marketers must understand to operate successfully. Political and legal forces are closely interrelated aspects of the marketing environment. The atmosphere in which legal and regulatory forces are developed and implemented is strongly shaped by political forces. The current political outlook of lawmakers is reflected in legislation or the lack of it.

Federal legislation covers all major areas of marketing activities and can be divided into two categories: procompetitive legislation and consumer protection laws. Beginning with very broad procompetitive legislation or laws enacted to preserve competition such as the Sherman Act, these laws gradually have focused more directly on specific marketing practices. The apparent vagueness of the Sherman Act let the courts apply its provisions to a variety of situations that had the common characteristic of being harmful to competition. Subsequent legislation, such as the Clayton Act, the Federal Trade Commission Act, the Wheeler-Lea Act, and the Robinson-Patman Act, were directed more toward specific practices. Awareness of laws alone is not enough; marketers must also consider court interpretation of the laws.

Regulatory agencies exert considerable force on marketing practices. Often these agencies generate regulatory guidelines that carry considerable weight in the marketplace. For example, the FTC has been active in several areas, including the monitoring and regulation of advertising practices. Marketers must not overlook state and local laws and regulatory agencies when considering the legal forces in the marketing environment.

Industry self-regulation is another source of concern for marketers. However, marketers view this type of regulation more favorably than government action because they have more opportunity to participate in the creation of the guidelines. Self-regulatory groups provide a more operational and often a less expensive regulatory structure. However, they generally cannot enforce compliance as effectively as government agencies.

Marketers are subjected to a variety of societal forces that express what society does and does not want. Members of our society want a high standard of living and a high quality of life. People expect business organizations to help them obtain what they want. As they attempt to provide what society wants, marketers must also avoid transgressions that society does not desire—faulty and unsafe products, misleading and unsupported warranties, deceptive packages and labels, misleading advertisements, fraudulent selling practices, or unfair and exploitative prices. In trying to be socially responsible, marketers experience two general problems. It is difficult, if not impossible, to determine what society as a whole wants because its various groups have diverse and often contradictory desires. Marketers also have a tough job attempting to estimate their decisions' long-run effects on society.

The economic factors that can strongly influence marketing decisions and activities are competitive forces, buying power, willingness to spend, spending patterns, and general economic conditions. Although all business organizations compete for consumers' dollars, a business usually views its competitors as the businesses in its geographic area that market products similar to, or substitutable for, its own products. Several factors influence the intensity of competition in a firm's environment, including the type of competitive structure in which a firm operates and the kinds of competitive tools the organizations within that particular industry use.

Consumer demand is affected by consumers' buying power and willingness to purchase. Consumers' goods, services, and financial holdings make up their buying power, that is, their ability to purchase. The financial sources of buying power are income, credit, and wealth. Just because consumers have buying power, however, does not mean that they will use it; they also must be willing to spend. Factors that affect the willingness to spend are the product's price, the level of satisfaction that is obtained from currently used products, family size, and expectations about future employment, income, prices, and general economic conditions.

The general economic conditions in our country affect the forces of supply and demand, buying power, the willingness to buy, consumer expenditure levels, and the intensity of competitive behavior. The overall state of the economy fluctuates in a general pattern known as a business cycle. The stages of the business cycle are prosperity, recession, depression, and recovery.

Technology is the knowledge of how to accomplish tasks and goals. Technological knowledge grows out of research—much of it paid for by the federal government—performed by businesses and nonprofit organizations such as universities. Technology today exerts a tremendous influence on our lives, including our work, recreation, eating and drinking, sleep, and sexual behavior.

As with all other aspects of our society, marketing decisions and activities are affected by technology. Product development, packaging, promotion, prices, and distribution systems are all influenced directly by technology. Not all businesses, however, are affected the same way or to the same degree. Several factors determine how much and in what way a particular business will make use of technology, including the firm's ability to use it, consumers' ability and willingness to buy technologically improved products, the firm's perception of the long-run effects of applying technology, the extent to which the firm is technologically based, the degree to which technology is used as a competitive tool, and the extent to which the business can protect technological applications through patents.

Important Terms

Marketing environment
Environmental scanning
Environmental analysis
Procompetitive legislation
Sherman Act
Clayton Act
Federal Trade Commission Act
Wheeler-Lea Act
Robinson-Patman Act
Consumer protection legislation
Federal Trade Commission (FTC)
Better Business Bureau
National Advertising Review Board (NARB)
Societal forces
Consumer movement
Marketing ethics
Social responsibility
Competition
Monopoly
Oligopoly
Monopolistic competition
Perfect competition
Buying power
Income

Disposable income
Discretionary income
Wealth
Effective buying income
Buying power index
Willingness to spend
Consumer spending patterns
Comprehensive spending patterns
Product-specific spending patterns
Prosperity
Recession
Depression
Recovery
Technology
Technology assessment

Discussion and Review Questions

1. How are political forces related to legal and governmental regulatory forces?
2. Describe marketers' attempts to influence political forces.
3. What types of procompetitive legislation directly affect marketing practices?
4. What was the major objective of most procompetitive laws? Do these laws generally accomplish this objective? Why or why not?
5. What are the major provisions of the Robinson-Patman Act? Which marketing mix decisions are influenced directly by this act?
6. What types of problems do marketers experience as they try to interpret legislation?

7. What are the goals of the Federal Trade Commission? List the ways the FTC affects marketing activities. Do you think a single regulatory agency should have such broad jurisdiction over so many marketing practices? Why or why not?

8. Name several nongovernmental regulatory forces. Do you feel that self-regulation is more or less effective than governmental regulatory agencies? Why?

9. How does society expect marketers to handle social responsibility and ethical matters?

10. Describe the consumer movement. Analyze some active consumer forces in your area.

11. Define income, disposable income, and discretionary income. How does each type of income affect consumer buying power?

12. How is consumer buying power affected by wealth and consumer credit?

13. How is buying power measured? Why should it be evaluated?

14. What factors influence a consumer's willingness to buy?

15. In what ways can each of the business cycle stages affect consumers' reactions to marketing strategies?

16. What business cycle stage are we experiencing currently? How is this stage affecting business firms in your area?

17. What does the term *technology* mean to you?

18. How does technology affect you as a member of society? Do the benefits of technology outweigh its costs and dangers?

19. Discuss the impact of technology on marketing activities.

20. What factors determine whether a business organization adopts and uses technology?

Cases

2.1 Alcohol and Tobacco Advertising[25]

Advertisements for all alcohol products may soon be banished from radio, television, and print if consumer groups and the federal government have their way. Even billboards may be prohibited from displaying advertisements for cigarettes and liquor. Alcohol and tobacco companies spend large amounts of money marketing their products: tobacco companies are among the top five advertisers nationally in newspapers, billboards, and magazines, spending $2 billion annually. But like all companies trying to market their products, alcohol and tobacco firms must be responsive to the political, legal, and social forces in the marketing environment.

25. Based on information from Camille P. Schuster and Christine Pacelli Powell, "Comparison of Cigarette and Alcohol Advertising Controversies," *Journal of Advertising*, 1987, pp. 26–33; Steven W. Colford, "Tobacco Ad Foes Press Fight," *Advertising Age*, Feb. 23, 1987, p. 12; Julie Franz, "AAF Sounds Alarm to Fight Ad-ban Plans," *Advertising Age*, June 23, 1986, p. 4; Joe Agnew, "Alcohol, Tobacco Marketers Battle New Ad Restraints," *Marketing News*, Jan. 30, 1987, pp. 1,12; Steven W. Colford, "Tobacco Ad Ban Seen Unlikely," *Advertising Age*, Apr. 13, 1987, p. 36.

These forces include the federal government, consumer movement groups, religious groups, and the medical profession. All these groups want all advertising of tobacco and alcohol products banned, as a means of reducing consumption of these "harmful" products. The efforts of these pro-ban groups are fueled by public concern over diseases caused by smoking and by increased traffic fatalities caused by drunk driving. The groups are also concerned about the general health of the nation; they say smoking and drinking have certainly proven harmful to many. These groups believe that present advertising campaigns do not sufficiently inform consumers about the dangers associated with the consumption of alcohol and cigarettes, and they believe that a total ban on such advertising is the only solution. The pro-ban groups were successful in getting a bill introduced into the House of Representatives in 1987 to ban tobacco advertising altogether; the groups would like to see a similar bill to eliminate the advertising of beer, wine, and liquor.

Similar public pressure led to the prohibition of tobacco advertising from television and radio in 1971; all other tobacco advertising is regulated by the federal government, with some self-regulation by the tobacco industry. The government requires that a health-hazard warning be placed on all cigarette packs and prohibits advertising targeted at children, schools, and universities. Presently the alcohol industry is policing itself by not advertising hard liquor on television and by running advertisements promoting safety and moderation. You never see a beer or wine commercial in which people actually drink the product; they seem to spend all sixty seconds of the spot just enjoying the company they are in or admiring the product's clarity, color, or beauty!

Obviously, tobacco and alcohol marketers are not pleased with the prospect of an advertising ban, and they are aggressively responding to these environmental forces by lobbying in Congress, appearing at congressional hearings on the subject, and running advertisements to combat the negative publicity. The marketers have as one weapon the results of a study by R. S. Weinberg and Associates, which showed that advertising expenditures for alcohol beverages between 1947 and 1983 had no significant relationship to the total consumption of beer, wine, and distilled spirits or to the industry as a whole. Other studies have corroborated the results of the Weinberg study. Similar studies were conducted after cigarette advertisements were banned from television: The studies showed that cigarette smoking actually increased after the ban went into effect.

One particularly touchy aspect of this battle for the right to advertise alcohol and tobacco products is the First Amendment to the Constitution, which guarantees free speech without prior censorship. The marketers do not want their right to free commercial speech restricted, and they do not believe that the government can constitutionally ban their First Amendment rights. They believe that it is wrong to take away an industry's right to free speech because certain groups do not like the products that industry manufactures. Many of those who are against an advertising ban on alcohol and tobacco products are also concerned that such a ban would set a dangerous precedent, whereby in the future there may be bans even on products that have not been shown to be harmful.

Tobacco and alcohol producers also point to the fact that they are concerned about their responsibilities as advertisers. Both industries have spent portions of their advertising budgets running advertisements advocating safety and moderation. For example, RJR Nabisco's advertisements aimed at teen-agers asked, "Does smoking really make you look more grown up?" and Joseph E. Seagram & Sons, Inc. has run anti-drunk driving advertising for decades. Other alcohol and tobacco product marketers are following suit, at least in part to stave off federal legislation. Radio and television stations and journals are also running antidrinking and anti-smoking public service announcements alongside those paid advertisements promoting the use of alcohol and tobacco products.

There is no obvious solution to this controversy. Compromise does not seem to be a possibility because neither side seems willing to concede anything at this time. If the consumer groups involved are not immediately successful in getting their desired ban on this class of advertising, they will not give up. But then, neither will the producers of these products. Part of the complexity of this issue lies in the constitutionality of such a ban: whether the government has the authority to prohibit the right to commercial free speech, weighed against the necessity of protecting its citizens against products that may be harmful. This controversy will continue to be in the news during the next few years; the ultimate outcome will certainly affect the way products are advertised in this country.

Questions for Discussion

1. Which of the two general approaches discussed in the text are marketing managers in the alcohol and tobacco markets following in their response to environmental forces?
2. In view of the results of research on expenditures for alcohol and tobacco advertisements, what would you logically conclude about your advertising budget if you wanted to increase sales of alcohol or tobacco products?
3. Do you think that the manufacturers and advertisers of alcohol and tobacco products are acting in an ethical, socially responsible manner?
4. What impact do you think the Surgeon General's finding that cigarette smoking is as addictive as a number of illegal drugs will have on the tobacco companies' ability to advertise?

2.2 Nestlé and the Marketing of Infant Formulas[26]

Nestlé Company, Inc.'s most famous products may be chocolates, but the Swiss-based company markets many products, including an infant formula to substitute for human breast milk. Nestlé concentrated on marketing this formula in Third World countries because of their rising birthrate. The company received much public criticism and suffered a boycott as a result of its aggressive marketing of that formula.

26. Based on information from "Nestlé's Infant Formula: The Consequences of Spurning the Public Image," in *Marketing Mistakes,* 3rd ed., Robert F. Hartley (ed.) (Columbus, Ohio: Grid Publishing Co., 1986), pp. 47–61; "The Dilemma of Third World Nutrition: Nestlé and the Role of Infant Formula," a report prepared for Nestlé S.A. by Maggie McComas, Geoffrey Fookes, and George Taucher, Nestlé S.A., 1983; "Nestlé and the Role of Infant Formula in Developing Countries: The Resolution of a Conflict," a series of reports, articles, and press releases provided by Nestlé Coordination Center for Nutrition, 1984; and the 1983 Nestlé Annual Report.

Throughout the 1970s, several health and consumer groups (U.S. and European) charged that the aggressive marketing of infant formulas by Nestlé and other companies was contributing to the high infant death rate in Third World nations. These critics singled out Nestlé because it held the largest share of the infant formula market in those countries (more than 40 percent). These groups were not questioning the product itself; infant formula can be a valuable source of nutrition for Third World infants who are unable to receive their mothers' milk. Rather, these critics questioned Nestlé's marketing of the formula in areas where consumers often have poor sanitation, receive little or no health care, and are largely illiterate. As a result, many consumers misused the infant formula. The formula was often mixed with contaminated water, put in unsterile containers or bottles, or excessively diluted. These practices increased the infant mortality rate.

Nestlé was also criticized for aggressively promoting the formula in these countries. The company used many forms of advertising including radio, billboards, vans with loudspeakers, and direct customer contact. Perhaps the most controversial charge involved Nestlé's use of "milk nurses." These were nurses, nutritionists, and midwives employed by Nestlé to visit mothers and give out free product samples. Critics charged that these milk nurses were actually saleswomen and were taking advantage of the naiveté of Third World mothers because a nurse's uniform holds credibility with Third World consumers. Critics also charged that Nestlé's advertising encouraged mothers to stop breast feeding by portraying it as primitive and inconvenient. Nestlé directed its promotional efforts to physicians and other health care personnel in addition to consumers.

In 1977 consumer groups began to boycott all Nestlé products, including its coffee and chocolates. Other groups joined the boycott, and it spread to nine countries by 1982. Nestlé treated the boycott as a public relations problem at first: They did not change their behavior, but they tried to convince people that they were socially responsible. After five years of boycotts, declining profits, and a tarnished reputation, the company recognized that it had more serious problems.

Nestlé worked with the World Health Organization (WHO), United Nations International Children's Emergency Fund (UNICEF), and consumer groups to establish a Code of Marketing of Breastmilk Substitutes for all marketers of the product. In 1984, Nestlé agreed to approve and support the code. By following the code, Nestlé agreed to stop several marketing practices, including advertising infant formula to the general public, using milk nurses, and distributing free samples (except in special circumstances). The company said it would clearly state on labels and educational materials the dangers involved in using infant formulas incorrectly, and that breast feeding is always preferable to using a formula. On its own initiative, Nestlé formed the Nestlé Infant Formula Audit Commission, a panel of medical experts, clergy, and civic leaders led by former Secretary of State Edmund Muskie, to monitor its performance in following the code. Most groups dropped their boycott against the company after it took these positive steps.

Nestlé estimated that it lost close to $40 million as a result of the boycott, and it may take Nestlé many years to recover from the loss in public faith. The company will have to carefully monitor its future activities to ensure that they do not adversely affect society or take advantage of any one group in particular. Society today expects businesses to act in an ethical and socially responsible manner.

Questions for Discussion

1. What were the key ethics and social responsibility issues in the case of Nestlé's marketing of infant formula?
2. Why did Nestlé have a special social responsibility in selling infant formulas to Third World countries?
3. The boycott of Nestlé's products, not just formula, resulted in sales losses. Did Nestlé handle this problem correctly?
4. If a firm that you worked for developed an infant formula, what would be the major ethical issues in deciding to market the formula in underdeveloped countries?

3. Target Markets: Segmentation and Evaluation

O B J E C T I V E S

- ▶ To understand the definition of a market.
- ▶ To find out what types of markets exist.
- ▶ To learn how firms identify target markets.
- ▶ To gain an understanding of market potential.
- ▶ To understand the definition of a company sales forecast.
- ▶ To become familiar with sales forecasting methods.

W*hen does a customer* for Cover Girl cosmetics begin to think of herself as a "cover woman" instead? After she passes 30, says the Noxell Corporation, maker of Cover Girl makeup, Noxzema Skin Cream, and other skin-care products. To appeal to the growing market segment of customers older than 30—who often develop sensitive skin after that age—the company has recently introduced Clarion, a line of fragrance-free, hypoallergenic cosmetics (see Figure 3.1). So far Clarion is a hit. Industry analysts are predicting that Clarion's sales will reach $70 million this year, which may give first-place Noxell a 30 percent share of the mass market beauty business.

Noxell tried before—with less success—to market to mature cosmetics users. Raintree, a Noxell moisturizing lotion introduced several years ago, failed to appeal to its target market. And when the company extended its Cover Girl line to include Moisture Wear and Replenishing makeup, promoted by long-time Cover Girl model Jennifer O'Neill, many customers past their twenties were reluctant to purchase products with the youthful Cover Girl image.

This time, the company seems to have a winner, partly because of innovative in-store marketing in the drugstores and supermarkets where Clarion is sold. The makeup is displayed with an interactive computer system that asks a customer questions about her coloring and skin condition. When the customer answers by pressing buttons, the computer recommends the most appropriate Clarion products, coded and organized to simplify makeup selection even further. In effect, by serving as "salesperson" in an impersonal setting, the computer encourages the customer to feel confident about her choices and buy additional products.

FIGURE 3.1

Noxell aims at cus-
tomers older than 30
(SOURCE: Courtesy of
Noxell Corporation)

Acknowledging that some customers will shy away from Clarion's price tag—about 25 percent higher than most Cover Girl products—the company developed a new Extremely Gentle line: fragrance-free, sensitivity-tested cosmetics to be marketed under the Cover Girl name at Cover Girl prices. Noxell says it has no plans to produce a truly expensive line for department store distribution. Instead, the company will continue to sell all its products through mass merchandisers, marketing to women who choose makeup based on price, convenience, and self-service. In response to growing demand, by next year Noxell plans to offer an inexpensive ($7) treatment for aging skin; currently such products run from $60 to $100 an ounce in upscale retail stores.

Renowned for its attention to marketing detail, Noxell usually spends 20 percent of its sales on advertising, more than either of its closest competitors, Revlon, Inc. and Maybelline Co. Cover Girl advertising alone accounts for $50 million annually. Noxell will continue to promote the clean, healthy good looks first associated with Cover Girl in 1961, but now the company hopes the image of all-American beauty will carry over to the new Clarion line, even as Jennifer, Cheryl, Cybill, and millions of other lesser known cover girls move gracefully into middle age.[1]

A COMPANY such as Noxell identifies or singles out groups of customers (women younger than 30 and women older than 30 in Noxell's case) for its products and directs some or all of its marketing activities at those groups. It develops and maintains a marketing mix consisting of a product, a distribution system, promotion, and price that effectively meets customers' needs.

In this chapter we initially discuss the characteristics of a market and the major types of markets. Then we examine two approaches to selecting target markets. Next we consider the major issues associated with market measurement and evaluation. Finally, we describe the primary sales forecasting techniques.

What Are Markets?

The word *market* has a number of meanings. People sometimes use the word to refer to a specific location where products are bought and sold. A large geographic area may also be called a market. Sometimes the word refers to the relationship between the demand and supply of a specific product, as in the question, "How is the market for diamonds?" At times "market" is used to mean the act of selling something.

As used in this book, a **market** is an aggregate of people who, as individuals or as organizations, have needs for products in a product class and who have the ability, willingness, and authority to purchase such products. In general use, "market" sometimes refers to the total population—or mass market—that buys products in general. However, our definition is more specific; it refers to persons seeking products in a specific product category. Obviously, there are many different markets in our complex economy. In this section we identify and describe several general groups of markets.

Requirements of a Market

For an aggregate of people to be a market, it must meet the following four requirements:

1. The people must need or desire a particular product. If they do not, then that aggregate is not a market.
2. The people in the group must have the ability to purchase the product. Ability

1. Based on information from Dottie Enrico, "Noxell to Market Line Under Cover Girl Name," *Adweek's Marketing Week,* July 6, 1987, p. 5; "Discs Define Beauty," *Marketing Communications,* July 1987, p. 41; Faye Rice, "Making Millions on Women over 30," *Fortune,* May 25, 1987, p. 75; Pat Sloan, "Noxell Ups Pressure on Maybelline," *Advertising Age,* May 11, 1987, p. 3.

to purchase is a function of their buying power, which consists of resources such as money, goods, and services that can be traded in an exchange situation.

3. The people in the aggregate must be willing to use their buying power.
4. Individuals in the group must have the authority to buy the specific products.

Individuals can have the desire, the buying power, and the willingness to purchase certain products but may not be authorized to do so. For example, young teenagers may have the desire, the money, and the willingness to buy liquor, but a liquor producer does not consider them a market because teenagers are prohibited by law or social custom from buying alcoholic beverages. An aggregate of people that lacks any one of the four requirements thus does not constitute a market.

Types of Markets

Markets fall into one of two categories: consumer markets and organizational or industrial markets. These categories are based on the characteristics of the individuals and groups that make up a specific market and the purposes for which they buy products. A **consumer market** consists of purchasers and/or individuals in their households who intend to consume or benefit from the purchased products and who do not buy products for the main purpose of making a profit. Each of us belongs to numerous consumer markets. The millions of individuals with the ability, willingness, and authority to buy make up a multitude of consumer markets for such products as housing, food, clothing, vehicles, personal services, appliances, furniture, and recreational equipment. In Chapter 4 we discuss consumer markets in detail.

An **organizational or industrial market** consists of individuals or groups who purchase a specific kind of product for one of three purposes: resale, direct use in producing other products, or use in general daily operations. For example, a lamp producer who buys electrical wire to use in the production of lamps is a part of the industrial market for electrical wire. This same firm purchases dust mops to clean its office areas. Although the mops are not used in the direct production of lamps, they are used in the operations of the firm; thus this manufacturer is part of the industrial market for dust mops. The four categories of organizational or industrial markets—producer, reseller, government, and institutional—are discussed in Chapter 5.

FIGURE 3.2
Total market approach

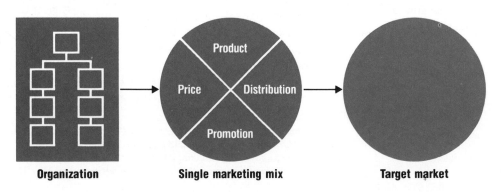

Organization   **Single marketing mix**   **Target market**

Selecting Target Markets

In Chapter 1 we said that a marketing strategy has two components: (1) the selection of the organization's target market and (2) the creation and maintenance of a marketing mix that satisfies the market's needs for a specific product. Regardless of what general types of markets a firm focuses on, marketing management must select the firm's target markets. We now examine two general approaches to identifying target markets: total market and market segmentation.

Total or Undifferentiated Market Approach

An organization sometimes defines the total market for a particular product as its target market. When a company designs a single marketing mix and directs it at an entire market for a particular product, it is using a **total market** (or **undifferentiated**) **approach.** Notice in Figure 3.2 that the organization is aiming a single marketing mix at the total market for the product. This approach assumes that individual customers in the target market for a specific kind of product have similar needs and, therefore, that the organization can satisfy most customers with a single marketing mix. This single marketing mix consists of one type of product with no (or very little) variation, one price, a promotional program aimed at everyone, and one distribution system to reach all customers in the total market. Products that can be marketed successfully with the total market approach include staple food items such as sugar and salt, certain kinds of farm produce, and some other products that most customers think of as homogeneous (no different from any other product of the same type). Morton's table salt, for instance, is aimed at the total market. One marketing mix can satisfy most consumers of this product.

The total market approach can be effective under two conditions. First, a large proportion of customers in the total market must have similar needs for the product. A marketer who uses a single marketing mix for a total market of customers with a variety of needs will find that the marketing mix satisfies very few people. Anyone could predict that a "universal shoe" that "fits everyone" would satisfy very few customers' needs for shoes because it would not fit most people. Second, the organization must be able to develop and maintain a single marketing mix that satisfies customers' needs. The company must be able to identify a set of product needs that are common to most customers in a total market, and it must have the resources and managerial skills to reach a sizable portion of that market. If customers' needs are dissimilar or if the organization is unable to develop and maintain a satisfying marketing mix, then a total market approach is likely to fail.

Companies that take the total market approach frequently attempt to use promotional efforts to differentiate their own products from competitors' products. They hope to establish in customers' minds that their products are superior and preferable to competing brands. This strategy is called **product differentiation** because a marketer tries to differentiate the product, in consumers' minds, from competitive brands.[2] Premium Saltines are promoted as The All Goodness Family

---

2. Wendell R. Smith, "Product Differentiation and Market Segmentation as Alternative Marketing Strategies," *Journal of Marketing,* July 1956, pp. 3–4.

Cracker. The reclosable bags that help keep the crackers fresh are promoted to differentiate the product.

A marketer who uses product differentiation rarely designs a product that is very different physically from other brands. After all, consumers have relatively similar needs for the product. Because the product actually is not much different from competing brands, marketers rely heavily on promotional efforts to emphasize one or several small differences. Unleaded gasoline, for example, has a broad appeal. Millions of consumers need and use it. Yet most unleaded gasolines are not much different physically from other unleaded gasolines, so oil companies differentiate their unleaded gasolines from competing brands by promoting greater mileage, additives, or economy. The effectiveness of product differentiation is determined largely by whether the features used to distinguish one brand from another are credible and important to a large number of customers in the total market.

Although customers' needs for some products, such as staple food items, may be similar, there are a multitude of products for which customers' needs are decidedly different. In these cases, a company should use the market segmentation approach.

Market Segmentation Approach

Markets made up of individuals with diverse product needs are called **heterogeneous markets.** Not everyone wants the same type of car, house, furniture, or clothes. If you were to ask fifty people what type of home each person would like to have, you probably would receive fifty different answers, many of them quite distinct. The automobile market is another example of a heterogeneous market. Some individuals want a car that is economical, some see a car as a status symbol, and still others seek an automobile that is roomy and comfortable for travel. For such heterogeneous markets, the market segmentation approach is appropriate.

As Figure 3.3 shows, **market segmentation** is the process of dividing a total market into market groups consisting of people who have relatively similar product needs. The purpose is to design a marketing mix (or mixes) that more precisely matches the needs of individuals in a selected segment (or segments). Market segments arise from the segmentation process. A **market segment** is a group of individuals, groups, or organizations who share one or more similar characteristics that cause them to have relatively similar product needs.

FIGURE 3.3

Market segmentation approach

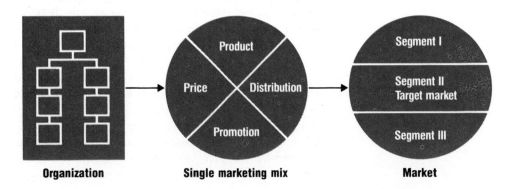

Organization   Single marketing mix   Market

FIGURE 3.4
Cross pen advertise-
ment (SOURCE: Cross
Pens)

The principal rationale for using the segmentation approach is that in a hetero-geneous market, an organization is better able to develop a marketing mix that satisfies a relatively homogeneous portion of a total market than it is to design a marketing mix that meets the product needs of all people. The segmentation approach differs from the total approach because it aims one marketing mix at one segment of a total market rather than directing a single marketing mix at a total market.

The market segmentation approach is widely used. We therefore analyze several of its most important features, including types of market segmentation strategies, conditions required for effective segmentation, selection of segmentation variables, and types of variables used to segment consumer and industrial markets.

Market Segmentation Strategies

There are two major segmentation strategies: the concentration strategy and the multisegment strategy.

Concentration Strategy   When an organization directs its marketing efforts to-ward a single market segment through one marketing mix, it is following a **concentration strategy.** This strategy is used, for example, by Cross Co., which concentrates on only the gift segment of the writing instrument market (see Figure 3.4).

The concentration strategy has advantages and disadvantages. A primary advan-tage is that it allows a firm to specialize. By concentrating all marketing efforts on a single segment, the firm has an opportunity to analyze the characteristics and needs of a distinct customer group. The firm can then direct all its efforts toward satisfy-ing that group's needs. A firm can generate a large sales volume by reaching a single segment. In addition, concentrating on a single segment allows a firm with restricted resources to compete with much larger organizations. However, speciali-zation can also be a disadvantage because the firm puts all its eggs in one basket. If a company's sales depend on a single segment and that segment's demand for the

FIGURE 3.5
Multisegment strategy

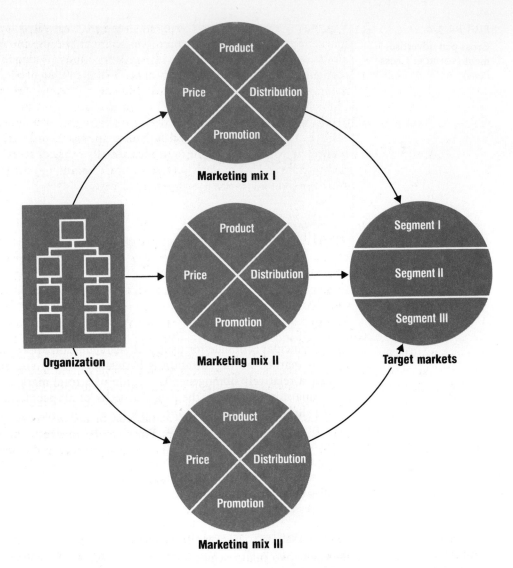

Marketing mix I

Marketing mix II

Marketing mix III

Organization

Target markets

product declines, then the company's financial strength also declines. Moreover, when a firm penetrates one segment and becomes well entrenched, its popularity may keep it from moving into other segments. For example, in the automobile market, Ferrari would have trouble moving into the economy car segment, whereas Volkswagen would have difficulty entering the luxury car segment.

Multisegment Strategy   After a firm uses a concentration strategy successfully in one market segment, it sometimes focuses on several segments. With a **multisegment strategy** (see Figure 3.5), an organization directs its marketing efforts at two or more segments by developing a marketing mix for each selected segment. For example, designer fragrances have traditionally been aimed at one segment: women. However, Halston Enterprises, Inc. markets designer fragrances for men as well as women. The marketing mixes used for a multisegment strategy may vary as to product differences, distribution methods, promotion methods, and prices.

A business using the multisegment strategy can usually increase its sales in a total market by focusing on more than one segment because the firm's mixes are being aimed at more people. A firm with excess production capacity may find the multisegment approach advantageous because the sale of products to additional segments may absorb excess capacity. However, because the multisegment strategy often requires a greater number of production processes, materials, and skills, production costs may be higher than with the concentration strategy. Keep in mind also that a firm using the multisegment approach ordinarily experiences higher marketing costs. Because the approach usually requires several different promotion plans and distribution methods, the costs of planning, organizing, implementing, and controlling marketing activities increase.

Conditions for Effective Segmentation

Whether a firm uses the concentration or the multisegment approach, five conditions must exist for market segmentation to be effective. First, a company must find out whether consumers' needs for the product are heterogeneous. If they are not, there is little need to segment the market. Second, the segments must be identifiable and divisible. The company must find some basis for effectively separating individuals in a total market into groups, each of which has a relatively uniform need for the product. Third, the total market should be divided in such a way that the segments can be compared with respect to estimated sales potential, costs, and profits. Fourth, at least one segment must have enough profit potential to justify developing and maintaining a special marketing mix. Finally, the firm must be able to reach the chosen segment with a particular marketing mix.

Some market segments may be difficult or impossible to reach because of legal, social, or distribution constraints. For instance, marketers of rock music recordings or jeans are not permitted to sell to a large market in the Soviet Union because of political and trade restrictions. For similar reasons, the strong demand in the United States for Cuban cigars is not met.

Choosing Segmentation Variables

Segmentation variables are the dimensions or characteristics of individuals, groups, or organizations that are used for dividing a total market into segments. For example, location, age, sex, or rate of product usage can be used for segmentation purposes. Here we discuss how marketers determine a single segmentation variable; later in the chapter we examine multivariable segmentation.

Several factors are considered in selecting a segmentation variable. The segmentation variable should be related to customers' needs for, uses of, or behavior toward the product. That is, people's needs, uses, and actions should vary according to the chosen segmentation characteristic. Automobile producers use income as one means of segmenting the automobile market, but they do not use religion because one person's automobile needs are not much different from those of persons of other religions. In addition, for individuals or organizations in a total market to be classified accurately, the segmentation variable must be measurable. For example, age, location, and sex are measurable because such information can be obtained through observation or questioning. But trying to divide a market on the basis of intelligence is extremely difficult because this characteristic is harder to measure accurately.

FIGURE 3.6
Segmentation variables
for consumer markets

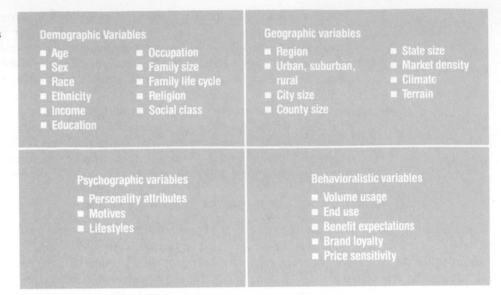

Choosing a segmentation variable is a critical step in segmenting a market. Selecting an inappropriate variable limits the chances of developing a successful strategy. So that you can gain a better understanding of possible segmentation variables, we now consider the major types of variables in more detail.

Variables for Segmenting Consumer Markets

A marketer who uses a segmentation strategy to reach a consumer market can select one or several variables from a broad assortment of possible ones. As shown in Figure 3.6, segmentation variables can be grouped into four categories: (1) demographic, (2) geographic, (3) psychographic, and (4) behavioralistic.

Demographic Variables A demographer studies aggregate population characteristics such as the distribution of age and sex, fertility rates, migration patterns, and mortality rates. Marketers typically consider a broader range of socioeconomic characteristics as demographic variables. Demographic characteristics that marketers commonly use to segment markets include age, sex, race, ethnicity, income, education, occupation, family size, family life cycle, religion, and social class. Marketers use demographic characteristics frequently because they are closely related to customers' product needs and purchasing behavior and they can be readily measured.

Because age is often used for segmentation purposes, marketers need to be aware of the distribution of age and how that distribution is changing. Figure 3.7 shows the proportion of the U.S. population in various age groups for 1985 and projections for 2000. All age groups (except the 5 to 13 group) that include persons now 34 years or younger are expected to decrease, and all other age categories are expected to increase. In 1970, the average age of a U.S. citizen was 27.9 and it is currently about 32; it is projected that the average age will be 35.5 in the year 2000.

Consider the types of markets that are segmented according to age. Examples include clothing, toys, automobiles, and diet foods. Figure 3.8 shows a possible segmentation scheme for the toy market. Notice that with the exception of the twelve-to-adult segment, the age ranges that define the segments are relatively narrow because children's needs for toys change rapidly. A toy that entertains children at age two rarely interests them at age five.

A firm's resources and capabilities affect the number and size of segment ranges used. The type of product and the degree of variation in consumers' needs also dictate the number and size of segment categories for a particular firm's marketing approach. For example, the number and size of the segments in Figure 3.8 may be appropriate for dividing the toy market, but clearly the same age ranges would not be satisfactory for segmenting the market for dairy products.

Gender is commonly used to segment a number of markets, including clothes, soft drinks, nonprescription medications, deodorants, magazines, soaps, and even cigarettes. The product in Figure 3.9 is definitely aimed at women. The *1980 U.S. Census of Population* indicated that there are about six million more females than males in the United States. Females represent 51.3 percent of the total population.

Various markets are divided on the basis of income. Beginning in 1950, real

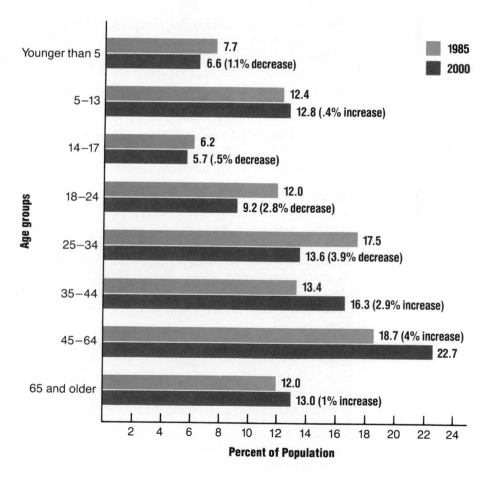

FIGURE 3.7

U.S. age distribution and projected changes (SOURCE: *Projections of the Population of the United States, by Age, Sex and Race 1983 to 2080,* U.S. Department of Commerce, Bureau of the Census, May 1984, p. 8)

FIGURE 3.8
Segmentation of the
toy market

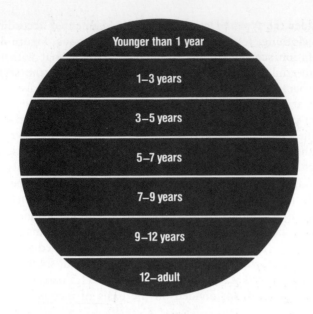

family income rose steadily for thirty years, almost doubling during that time. Figure 3.10 shows the distributions of annual family income for 1975, 1980, and 1985. In 1975, about one-third (33.2 percent) of the families earned incomes of less than $10,000, whereas in 1980 only about one out of five (18.9 percent) had incomes below $10,000. Approximately 14 percent of the families in 1975 earned more than $25,000 annually; by 1985, more than 55 percent did.

Income is often used to divide markets because it strongly influences people's product needs. It affects their ability to buy (discussed in Chapter 2) and their aspirations for a certain style of living. Examples of product markets segmented by income include housing, furniture, clothing, automobiles, food, and certain kinds of sporting goods.

Ethnicity too is used to segment markets for goods such as food, music, and clothing and for services such as banking and insurance. A striking example of the importance of ethnicity as a segmentation variable is the U.S. Hispanic population. Made up of people with Mexican, Cuban, Puerto Rican, and Central and South American heritage, this ethnic group is growing six times faster than the general population. The Hispanic population is concentrated in nine states, as Table 3.1 indicates. If it continues to grow at its current rate, it will be the largest ethnic group in the country by the year 2020.

The product needs of a household also vary according to marital status and the presence and age of children. These characteristics can be combined into a single variable, sometimes called the family life cycle. Housing, appliances, food, automobiles, and boats are a few of the numerous product markets sometimes segmented by family life cycle stages. The family life cycle has been broken down in several different ways, including the following:

1. Young
   a. Single without children
   b. Married without children
   c. Single with children
   d. Married with children

2. Middle-aged
   a. Single without children
   b. Married without children
   c. Single with children
   d. Married with children
   e. Single without dependent children
   f. Married without dependent children
3. Older
   a. Single
   b. Married[3]

The number of single-person households has increased from 17 percent in 1970 to about 25 percent in the mid-1980s. The "typical" American family of two adults (with one being the breadwinner) and two children makes up only 6 percent of all U.S. households. Almost 60 percent of all adult women work outside the home. Of these women, 40 percent have children younger than 6. Over two-thirds of all adults are married. However, people are waiting longer to get married and are having fewer children. About half of all families do not have children younger than 18.

People of the same age may have diverse product needs because they are in different stages of the family life cycle. Persons in a particular life cycle stage may have very specific needs that can be satisfied by precisely designed marketing mixes. Young, educated single adults may desire small but well-appointed apartments or

3. Adapted with permission from Patrick E. Murphy and William A. Staples, "A Modernized Family Life Cycle," *Journal of Consumer Research,* 6 (June), Table 2, p. 16.

FIGURE 3.9
Revlon's Charlie cosmetics and fragrances are aimed at women younger than 30 years of age (SOURCE: Courtesy of Revlon, Inc.)

FIGURE 3.10

Distribution of annual
family income for
1975, 1980, and 1985
(unadjusted dollars)
(SOURCE: "Money In-
come and Poverty
Status of Families and
Persons in the United
States: 1986," *Current
Population Reports,*
U.S. Department of
Commerce, Bureau of
the Census, July 1987,
p. 11)

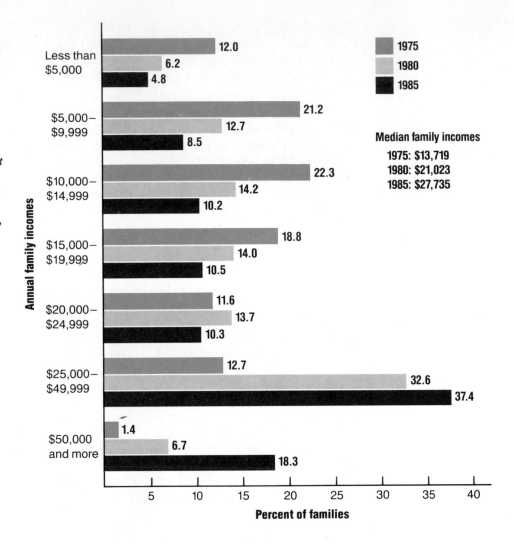

condominiums; many can afford expensive clothing, stereo systems, and appliances such as microwave ovens. Divorced women with children may be seeking life insurance. A middle-aged couple, with children no longer at home, has more discretionary income for entertainment, expensive restaurants, and travel.

We discussed only a few of the many demographic variables. Publishers of encyclopedias and dictionaries use education level to segment markets; brewers sometimes aim their products at broad occupational categories. Producers of cosmetics and hair-care products sometimes segment markets based on race. Certain types of foods and clothing are directed toward people of specific religious sects.

Geographic Variables   Geographic variables—climate, terrain, natural resources, population density, and subcultural values—also influence consumer product needs. Markets may be divided into regions because one or more geographic variables cause customers to differ from one region to another. A company that markets products to a national market might divide the United States into the following regions: Pacific, Southwest, Central, Midwest, Southeast, Middle Atlantic, and New England. A firm operating in one or several states might regionalize its market by counties, cities, zip code areas, or other units. See the Application on page 99 for related details.

Marketers sometimes segment on the basis of state populations, and they use population figures in estimating demand. Between 1970 and 1980, the U.S. population grew by 11.4 percent, but the population in all geographic areas did not grow proportionally. The South and the West increased significantly, while the Midwest and East experienced only minor gains. However, New York, Rhode Island, and the District of Columbia lost population. The map in Figure 3.11 indicates the projected population growth (or loss) of each state between 1980 and 2000. Note that the heaviest growth will be in Florida and the western states. Nine states and the District of Columbia are expected to decline in population. For segmentation and market analysis purposes, marketers must be aware of both current population patterns and projected changes in these patterns.

City size can be an important segmentation variable. Some marketers want to focus their efforts on cities of a certain size. For example, a certain franchised restaurant organization will not locate in cities of less than 200,000 people because it takes at least that many people to generate enough sales volume to provide the profit potential for a successful operation. Other firms seek opportunities in smaller towns. Initially, Wal-Mart Stores, Inc., a rapidly growing discount chain now with a thousand stores in twenty-three states, would locate only in towns with less than 25,000 people.

Because cities often cut across political boundaries, the U.S. Census Bureau developed a system to classify metropolitan areas (any area with a city of at least 50,000 or with an urbanized area of at least 50,000 and a total metropolitan population of at least 100,000). Metropolitan areas are categorized as one of the following: a metropolitan statistical area (MSA), a primary metropolitan statistical area (PMSA), or a consolidated metropolitan statistical area (CMSA). An MSA is an urbanized area encircled by nonmetropolitan counties and neither socially nor

TABLE 3.1

Nine states that contain 85 percent of U.S. Hispanics

STATE	1970	1980	PERCENT OF 1980 HISPANICS IN USA
California	2,369,292	4,544,331	31.1
Texas	1,840,648	2,985,824	20.4
New York	1,351,982	1,659,300	11.4
Florida	405,036	858,158	5.9
Illinois	393,204	635,602	4.4
New Jersey	288,488	491,883	3.4
New Mexico	308,340	477,222	3.3
Arizona	264,770	440,701	3.0
Colorado	225,506	339,717	2.3

SOURCE: U.S. Census Bureau.

economically dependent on any other metropolitan area. A metropolitan area within a complex of at least one million inhabitants can elect to be named a PMSA. A CMSA is a metropolitan area of at least one million consisting of two or more PMSAs. CMSAs total twenty-three, including one in Puerto Rico (see Figure 3.12). The five largest CMSAs, New York, Los Angeles, Chicago, Philadelphia, and San Francisco, account for 20 percent of the U.S. population. The federal government provides a considerable amount of socioeconomic information about MSAs, PMSAs, and CMSAs that is useful for market analysis and segmentation purposes.

Market density refers to the number of potential customers within a unit of land area, such as a square mile. Although market density is related generally to population density, the correlation is not exact. For example, in two different geographic

FIGURE 3.11

Projected U.S. population growth in 1980–2000 (percent) (SOURCE: U.S. Census Bureau)

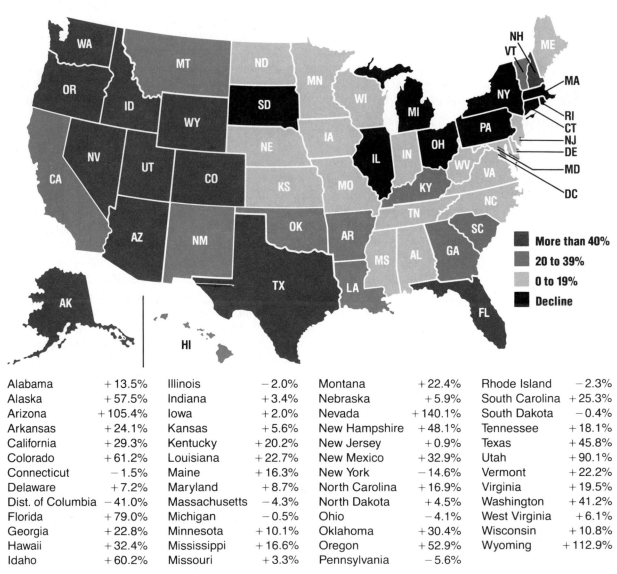

Alabama	+13.5%	Illinois	−2.0%	Montana	+22.4%	Rhode Island	−2.3%
Alaska	+57.5%	Indiana	+3.4%	Nebraska	+5.9%	South Carolina	+25.3%
Arizona	+105.4%	Iowa	+2.0%	Nevada	+140.1%	South Dakota	−0.4%
Arkansas	+24.1%	Kansas	+5.6%	New Hampshire	+48.1%	Tennessee	+18.1%
California	+29.3%	Kentucky	+20.2%	New Jersey	+0.9%	Texas	+45.8%
Colorado	+61.2%	Louisiana	+22.7%	New Mexico	+32.9%	Utah	+90.1%
Connecticut	−1.5%	Maine	+16.3%	New York	−14.6%	Vermont	+22.2%
Delaware	+7.2%	Maryland	+8.7%	North Carolina	+16.9%	Virginia	+19.5%
Dist. of Columbia	−41.0%	Massachusetts	−4.3%	North Dakota	+4.5%	Washington	+41.2%
Florida	+79.0%	Michigan	−0.5%	Ohio	−4.1%	West Virginia	+6.1%
Georgia	+22.8%	Minnesota	+10.1%	Oklahoma	+30.4%	Wisconsin	+10.8%
Hawaii	+32.4%	Mississippi	+16.6%	Oregon	+52.9%	Wyoming	+112.9%
Idaho	+60.2%	Missouri	+3.3%	Pennsylvania	−5.6%		

Regional Marketing

True or false: Despite America's melting pot heritage, modern Americans are fairly homogeneous and have similar tastes in foods and consumer products. False, say proponents of regional marketing, the marketing approach that calls for tailoring products and sales programs to geographic subcultures. Regional marketers point to such success stories as Campbell Soup Company's two nacho-cheese products: the zippy jalapeno soup developed just for markets in the West and the Southwest and the original, milder version for everybody else. Although many national consumer-product companies still hesitate to scrap tried-and-true standardized marketing programs, a growing number of other organizations now firmly believe that competitive advantage lies in catering to local and regional preferences.

Those preferences can be marked. Sociological and market studies show, for example, that westerners accept new products and technologies more readily than other groups of Americans and are more likely to buy energy-efficient imported sports cars, high-tech products, and exercise equipment. Southerners, on the other hand, prefer a slower-paced, social way of life and are more apt to center their activities on home, church, and family. Northeasterners lead all other groups in reading, watching television, and movie attendance. Midwesterners, many of whom are of Germanic stock, value hard work and prefer dependability to glamour. In the Mountain states—the only region where men outnumber women—oatmeal sells better than bubble bath. Here, even city dwellers are likely to identify with the outdoor life by purchasing pickup trucks.

So how do companies go about incorporating these varied likes and dislikes into effective regional marketing programs? Campbell Soup, whose shift to regionalization has changed the very structure of the company, now assigns as much as 15 percent of its advertising budget to its twenty-two regional staffs, who can then tie Campbell promotions to local interests and community events. Bowing to regional preferences, household-products manufacturer Lever Brothers recently introduced its new heavy-duty Surf detergent in liquid form in the Northeast and in powdered form in the South. At Denny's, a nationwide restaurant chain based in California, the menu varies from region to region in accordance with customer surveys and the offerings of local competitors. Denny's patrons can order catfish in the Sunbelt and the Midwest, for example, and bagels and cream cheese in Hawaii, Florida, and the Northeast.

Automobile makers too have recognized differences in purchase patterns in various parts of the country. Chevrolet recently created six regional districts, and Oldsmobile is experimenting with diverting advertising funds to regional dealer organizations. Most automobile makers position their model lines differently in different markets. Full-sized cars sell well in Florida, but drivers in the wintry Northeast seek cars with front-wheel drive. In Texas, trucks outsell all other vehicles. California car buyers look for performance first; thus Chevrolet's Cavalier, advertised nationally as a family vehicle, is marketed in California as a sporty, exciting car.

Regional marketing is not without its disadvantages, of course, especially when it comes to efficiency. Separate regional promotions can cost two to three times as much as a single national campaign. National companies also risk strong competition from well-established regional firms and may find that product image becomes blurred when different messages are sent to different regional market segments.

SOURCES: Christine Dugas, "Marketing's New Look," *Business Week,* Jan. 26, 1987, pp. 64–69; Brad Edmondson, "Chili Recipes," *American Demographics,* April 1987, p. 22; Brad Edmondson, "From Dixie to Detroit," *American Demographics,* January 1987, pp. 26–30; Rebecca Fannin, "Hit the Road, Jack," *Marketing & Media Decisions,* July 1987, pp. 118–121; Alix Freedman, "National Firms Find That Selling to Local Tastes Is Costly, Complex," *The Wall Street Journal,* Feb. 9, 1987, p. 17; Laurie Freeman, "P&G Hops on Regional Trend," *Advertising Age,* Apr. 20, 1987, p. 1; Peter Oberlink, "Regional Marketing Starts Taking Hold," *Adweek,* Apr. 6, 1987, p. 36.

markets of approximately equal size and population, the market density for denture cleaners might be much higher in one area than in another if one area contains a significantly greater proportion of older people. That low-density markets often require different sales, advertising, and distribution activities than high-density markets explains why market density is used as a segmentation variable.

Climate is commonly used as a geographic segmentation variable because it has such a broad impact on people's behavior and product needs. The many product markets affected by climate include air conditioning and heating equipment, clothing, yard tools, sports equipment, and building materials.

Psychographic Variables   Many psychographic factors could be used to segment markets, but the three most common are personality characteristics, motives, and lifestyles. A psychographic dimension can be used by itself to segment a market, or it can be combined with other types of segmentation variables.

Examples of personality characteristics used to segment markets are gregariousness, compulsiveness, competitiveness, extroversion, introversion, ambitiousness, and aggressiveness. Personality characteristics are useful when a product is similar to many competing products and consumers' needs are not affected significantly by other segmentation variables.

When attempting to segment a market according to personality characteristic, marketers face two major problems. First, personality characteristics are difficult, if not impossible, to measure accurately. Existing personality tests were developed for clinical use, not for segmentation purposes. Second, even though it seems reasonable that personality characteristics affect buyers' actions, research has yielded little evidence to support this assumption.

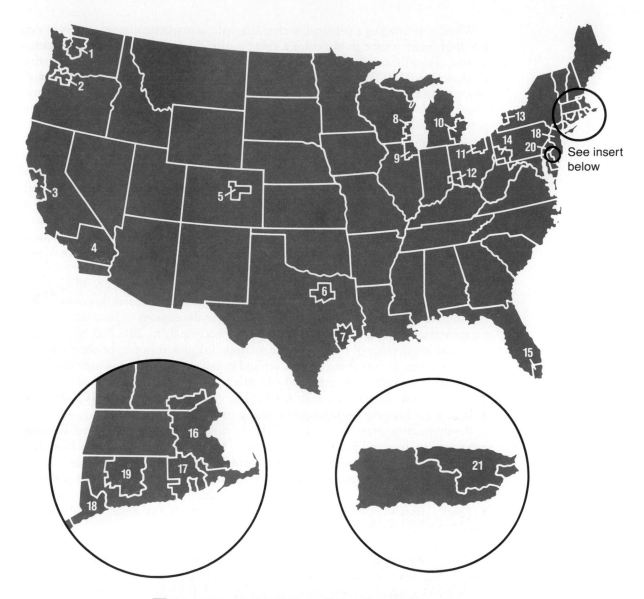

Consolidated Metropolitan Statistical Area (CMSA)

FIGURE 3.12

Consolidated metropolitan statistical areas and projected growth (SOURCE: U.S. Census Bureau)

1 Seattle—Tacoma
2 Portland—Vancouver
3 San Francisco—Oakland—San Jose
4 Los Angeles—Anaheim—Riverside
5 Denver—Boulder
6 Dallas—Fort Worth
7 Houston—Galveston—Brazoria
8 Milwaukee—Racine
9 Chicago—Gary—Lake County
10 Detroit—Ann Arbor
11 Cleveland—Akron—Lorain

12 Cincinnati—Hamilton
13 Buffalo—Niagara Falls
14 Pittsburgh—Beaver Valley
15 Miami—Fort Lauderdale
16 Boston—Lawrence—Salem
17 Providence—Pawtucket—Fall River
18 New York—Northern New Jersey— Long Island (Part)
19 Hartford—New Britain—Middletown
20 Philadelphia—Wilmington—Trenton
21 San Juan — Caguas

When appealing to a personality characteristic, a marketer almost always selects one that many people in our culture value positively. Individuals with this characteristic, as well as those who would like to have it, may be influenced to buy that marketer's brand. For example, a brand may be promoted as "not for everyone" but for those who are "independent," "strong-minded," or "outgoing." Marketers who take this approach do not worry about measuring how many people have the positively valued characteristic because they assume that a sizable proportion of people in the target market either have it or want to have it.

A motive is an internal energizing force that moves an individual toward a goal. To some degree, motives influence what people buy. Despite the difficulty of measuring them, motives are occasionally used to divide markets. Product durability, economy, convenience, and status are all motives that may affect the types of products purchased and the choice of stores in which they are bought. When a market is segmented according to a motive, it is divided on the basis of consumers' reasons for making a purchase. For example, one motive for the purchase of soft drinks in nonreturnable containers is convenience.

Lifestyle analysis provides a broad view of buyers because it encompasses numerous characteristics related to people's activities, interests, and opinions. Table 3.2 illustrates factors that are a part of the major dimensions of lifestyle. Lifestyle segmentation divides individuals into groups according to how they spend their time, the importance of things in their surroundings (their homes or their jobs, for example), their beliefs about themselves and broad issues, and some socioeconomic characteristics such as income and education.[4] Obviously, the manner in which people live affects their product needs. The Application on page 103 discusses several ways lifestyle segmentation is being used.

Psychographic dimensions can effectively divide a market. However, their use has been limited, and probably will continue to be, for several reasons. First, they are more difficult than other types of segmentation variables to measure accurately. Second, the relationships among psychographic variables and consumers' needs are

4. Joseph T. Plummer, "The Concept and Application of Life Style Segmentation," *Journal of Marketing,* January 1974, p. 33.

TABLE 3.2

Lifestyle dimensions

ACTIVITIES	INTERESTS	OPINIONS
Work	Family	Themselves
Hobbies	Home	Social issues
Social events	Job	Politics
Vacation	Community	Business
Entertainment	Recreation	Economics
Club membership	Fashion	Education
Community	Food	Products
Shopping	Media	Future
Sports	Achievements	Culture

SOURCE: Adapted from Joseph Plummer, "The Concept and Application of Life Style Segmentation," *Journal of Marketing,* January 1974, p. 34.

Lifestyle Segmentation: A Slice of Life

Through lifestyle segmentation, an organization can attract customers by demonstrating that its products fit with customers' activities, interests, or opinions. Changing lifestyles have been credited with the 65 percent rise in sales of light trucks during the past ten years, compared to an increase of just 10 percent for cars. When the Japanese introduced compact pickups to the U.S. market in the early 1980s, Americans who previously had bought subcompact cars found the small trucks roomier and less expensive than cars. American automobile makers quickly began marketing their own light trucks and vans as "second vehicles" for families and outdoors enthusiasts, and today about 600,000 buyers each year make the switch from cars to trucks.

Lifestyle segmentation also has made its way into the banking business. Specialized marketing is not new to the industry; years of strict banking regulations have in effect already segmented financial institutions along lines of geography, function, and product. Now, however, banks are reaching out to targeted groups through shared clubs, recreational activities, and special events. One approach to family oriented markets is cross-merchandising bank services with local photographers because families are the prime customers for photographs. Banks in university communities emphasize services to students. Valley Bank of Nevada recently completed a credit card arrangement with the Good Sam Club—a nationwide recreational vehicle owners' club—and gained immediate access to a market of 450,000 creditworthy adults.

The potential of lifestyle segmentation is quite broad, according to lifestyle marketers. For example, newspaper readers have been classified by one market research organization into such groups as Vanguards, upscale professional women who read newspapers thoroughly; New Breed Workers, younger men who judge a newspaper by its sports and entertainment coverage; and Senior Solid Conservatives, long-time corporate employees active in community affairs and interested in local news. A newspaper aware of its readers' lifestyles could plan layouts, editorial content, and circulation drives with greater insight and effectiveness. Advertisers also would benefit. Knowing, for instance, that in certain markets readers of the sports pages were heavier consumers of sports equipment than fans in other markets, marketers could allocate advertising dollars accordingly.

Not all marketers have jumped on the lifestyle bandwagon, which now includes such market research systems as Lifestyle Monitor, Values and Lifestyles Program (VALS), and List of Values (LOV). Humans are too complex, say some experts, to be stereotyped as baby boomers, achievers, or senior citizens. These experts suggest that lifestyle segmentation should take into account the everchanging nature of values and lifestyles. In addition, reliable analyses should acknowledge that adult behavior is sometimes determined by childhood experiences or cultural norms that marketers cannot easily measure. Some marketing professionals agree that lifestyle segmentation can be more useful than simple demographic divisions. But without allowance for variation and change, they add, a lifestyle category becomes just another pigeonhole.

SOURCES: Ernest Dichter, "Whose Lifestyle Is It Anyway?" *Psychology and Marketing* (New York: Wiley, 1986), pp. 151–163; M. K. Guzda, "Lifestyle Segmentation," *Editor and Publisher,* June 9, 1984, pp. 16–17; Lynn R. Kahle, Sharon E. Beatty, and Pamela Homer, "Alternative Measurement Approaches to Consumer Values," *Journal of Consumer Research,* December 1986, pp. 405–409; "Lifestyle Roulette," *American Demographics,* April 1987, p. 24; Chester A. Swenson, "Effective Use of Lifestyle Marketing," *The Bankers Magazine,* July–August 1986, pp. 19–22; James B. Treece, "Why All Those City Folks Are Buying Pickups," *Business Weekly,* July 13, 1987, pp. 102–103.

sometimes obscure and unproven. Third, segments that result from psychographic segmentation may not be reachable. For example, a marketer may determine that highly compulsive individuals want a certain type of clothing. However, no specific stores or specific media vehicles—such as television or radio programs, newspapers, or magazines—appeal precisely to this group and this group alone.

Behavioralistic Variables   Marketers can divide a market on the basis of a characteristic of the consumer's behavior toward the product. These characteristics commonly involve some aspect of product use. Thus, a total market may be divided into users and nonusers. Users may then be classified as heavy, moderate, or light. To satisfy a specific group, such as heavy users, a marketer may have to create a distinctive product, set special prices, and initiate special promotion and distribution activities.

How customers use or apply the product may also be a basis for segmenting the market. To satisfy customers who use a product in a certain way, some feature— say, packaging, size, texture, or color—may have to be designed precisely to make the product easier to use, safer, or more convenient. In addition, special distribution, promotion, or pricing activities may have to be created.

Another product-related characteristic is the benefit that consumers expect from the product. **Benefit segmentation** is the division of a market according to the benefits that customers want from the product. Although most segmentation variables imply a purported relationship between the variable and customers' needs, benefit segmentation is different in that the benefits the customers seek *are* their product needs. That is, individuals are segmented directly according to their needs. By determining the benefits that consumers want, marketers may be able to divide people into groups that are seeking certain sets of benefits.

The effectiveness of benefit segmentation depends on several conditions. The benefits people seek must be identifiable. Using these benefits, marketers must be able to group people into recognizable segments, and one or more of the resulting segments must be accessible to the firm's marketing efforts.

As this brief discussion shows, consumer markets can be divided according to

FIGURE 3.13

Single-variable seg-
mentation

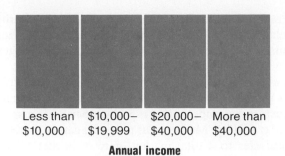

Less than $10,000 $10,000–$19,999 $20,000–$40,000   More than $40,000

Annual income

A marketer must evaluate the sales potential in possible target markets as well as in the target markets that the firm currently serves. Moreover, a marketing manager must determine the proportion of this potential that the firm can capture relative to its objectives, resources, and managerial skills. The marketer must ponder the question, "To what extent can our company tap this market if the potential is there?"

Demand can be measured along several dimensions, including product level, competitive level, geographic area, and time.[5] With respect to product level, demand can be estimated for specific product items (such as frozen orange juice) or for a product line (such as frozen foods). The competitive level specifies whether sales are being measured for one firm or for an entire industry. A manager must also decide the geographic area to be included in an evaluation of demand. For

5. Philip Kotler, *Marketing Management: Analysis, Planning, and Control,* 6th ed. (Englewood Cliffs, N.J.: Prentice-Hall, 1988), p. 257.

FIGURE 3.14

Multivariable segmentation

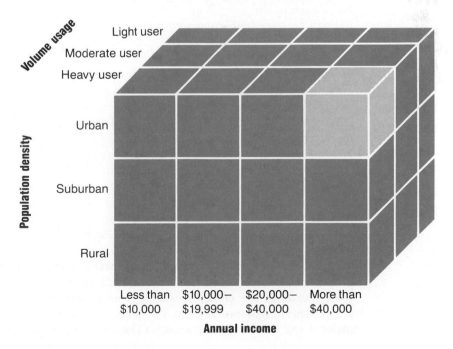

Chapter 3   TARGET MARKETS: SEGMENTATION AND EVALUATION   107

example, demand could be measured for a neighborhood, town, county, state, or nation. In relation to time, demand measurements can be short range (one year or less), medium range (one to five years), or long range (longer than five years).

Market and Company Sales Potentials

Market sales potential refers to the amount of a product that would be purchased by specific customer groups within a specified period at a specific level of industry-wide marketing activity. Market sales potential can be stated in terms of dollars or units and can refer to a total market or to a market segment. When analyzing market sales potential, it is important to specify a time frame and to indicate the relevant level of industry marketing activities.

Note here that marketers have to assume a certain general level of marketing effort in the industry when they estimate market sales potential. The specific level of marketing effort varies, of course, from one firm to another, but the sum of all firms' marketing activities equals industry marketing efforts. A marketing manager also must consider whether and to what extent industry marketing efforts will change.

Company sales potential is the amount of a product that an organization could sell during a specified period. Several general factors influence a company's sales potential. First, the market sales potential places absolute limits on the size of the company's sales potential. Second, the intensity of industrywide marketing activities has an indirect but definite effect on the company sales potential. Those activities have a direct bearing on the size of the market sales potential. When Texas Instruments advertises calculators, for example, it indirectly promotes calculators in general; it may, in fact, help sell competitors' calculators. Third, the intensity and effectiveness of a company's marketing activities in proportion to the total industry's marketing efforts affect the size of the company's sales potential. If a company is spending twice as much as any of its competitors on marketing efforts, and if each dollar spent is more effective in generating sales, the firm's sales potential will be quite high compared with its competitors'.

There are two general approaches to measuring company sales potential: breakdown and buildup. In the **breakdown approach,** the marketing manager initially develops a general economic forecast for a specific time period. The market sales potential is estimated on the basis of this economic forecast. The company sales potential then is derived from the general economic forecast and the estimate of market sales potential. Thus this is called the breakdown approach because the marketer starts with broad, comprehensive estimates of general economic activity and finishes with an estimate of a single firm's sales of a specific product.

In the **buildup approach,** an analyst begins by estimating how much of a product a potential buyer in a specific geographic area, such as a sales territory, will purchase in a given period. Then the analyst multiplies that amount by the total number of potential buyers in that area. The analyst performs the same calculation for each geographic area in which the firm sells products and then adds the totals for each area to calculate the market potential. To determine the company sales potential, the analyst must estimate, by specific levels of marketing activities, the proportion of the total market potential that the firm can obtain.

For example, the marketing manager of a regional paper company with three competitors might estimate the company sales potential for bulk gift wrapping paper using the buildup approach. The manager might determine that each of sixty-six paper buyers in a single sales territory purchases an average of 10 rolls annually. Thus for that sales territory, the market potential is 660 rolls annually. The analyst follows the same procedure in each of the firm's other nineteen sales territories and then totals the sales potential for each sales territory. Assume that this total market potential is 18,255 rolls of paper (the quantity expected to be sold by all four paper companies). Then the marketing manager would estimate the company sales potential by ascertaining what percentage of the estimated 18,255 rolls the firm could sell, assuming a certain level of marketing effort. The marketing manager might develop several company sales potentials, based on several levels of marketing effort.

Notice that regardless of whether marketers use the breakdown or buildup approach, they depend heavily on sales estimates. To get a clearer idea of how these estimates are derived, let us explore sales forecasting.

Developing Company Sales Forecasts

A **company sales forecast** is the amount of a product that the company actually expects to sell during a specific period at a specified level of marketing activities. When analyzing sales potential, marketers consider what sales amounts are possible at various levels of marketing activities, assuming that certain environmental conditions will exist. However, when marketers develop a sales forecast they concentrate on what the actual sales will be at a certain level of marketing effort.

Many operating units use the company sales forecast for planning, organizing, implementing, and controlling their activities. Managers use sales forecasts when purchasing raw materials, scheduling production, securing financial resources, considering plant or equipment purchases, hiring personnel, and planning inventory levels. The success of numerous activities depends on the accuracy of the company sales forecast.

A sales forecast must be time specific. As indicated earlier, sales estimates' ranges can be short (one year or less), medium (one to five years), or long (longer than five years). The length of time chosen for the sales forecast depends on what the forecast will be used for, how stable the market is, and the firm's objectives and resources.

To forecast company sales, a marketer can choose from a number of forecasting methods. Some forecasting methods are rather arbitrary; others are more scientific, complex, and time consuming. The method(s) that a firm uses depend on costs involved, type of product, characteristics of the market, time span of the forecast, purposes for which the forecast is used, stability of the historical sales data, availability of required information, and forecasters' expertise and experience.[6] For purposes of analysis, common forecasting techniques can be grouped into five categories: executive judgment, surveys, time series analysis, correlation methods, and market tests. We now explore each technique.

Executive Judgment At times, a company forecasts sales primarily on the basis of **executive judgment,** which is the intuition of one or more executives. This approach is highly unscientific, but it is expedient and inexpensive. Executive judgment may work reasonably well when product demand is relatively stable and the

6. David Hurwood, Elliott S. Grossman, and Earl Bailey, *Sales Forecasting* (New York: Conference Board, 1978), p. 2.

forecaster has years of market-related **experience. However,** because intuition is swayed most heavily by recent experience, **the forecast** may be overoptimistic or overpessimistic. Another drawback to intuition **is that the** forecaster has **only past** experience as a guide for deciding where **to go in the** future.

Surveys   A second way to predict sales is to **question** customers, sales personnel, or **experts** regarding their expectations about future purchases.

Customer Surveys   Through a **customer forecasting survey,** marketers can ask customers what types and quantities of products they intend to buy during a specific period. This approach may be useful to a business that has relatively few customers. For example, a transistor producer with fewer than two hundred potential buyers could conduct a customer survey. PepsiCo, though, has millions of customers and **cannot** feasibly use a customer survey to forecast future sales.

Customer surveys have several drawbacks. Customers must be able and willing to make accurate estimates of future product requirements. Although industrial buyers can sometimes estimate their anticipated purchases accurately from historical buying data and their own sales forecasts, many customers cannot make such estimates. For a variety of reasons, customers may not want to participate in a survey. Occasionally, a few respondents give answers that they know are incorrect, making survey results inaccurate. In addition, customer surveys reflect buying intentions, not actual purchases. Customers' intentions may not be well formulated, and even when potential purchasers have definite buying intentions, they do not necessarily follow through on them. Finally, customer surveys consume much time and money.

Sales-force Surveys   In a **sales-force forecasting survey,** members of the firm's sales force are asked to estimate the anticipated sales in their territories for a specified period of time. The forecaster combines these territorial estimates to arrive at a tentative forecast.

Let us trace this process in one manufacturing organization, Ex-Cell-O Corporation, which manufactures machine tools. Machine tools usually are sold through open proposals. These bids are submitted to specific customers for certain types of products. The data in the proposals go into the firm's marketing information system. When the forecast is being prepared, each salesperson receives a summary of his or her proposals, reviews this summary, updates it as needed, and then prepares the forecast for his or her territory for the next five quarters. The sales representatives then send their forecasts to regional managers, who review them and make necessary refinements. The regional managers send the forecasts to the marketing staff at corporate headquarters, where the forecasts are processed. The new forecast is transmitted to Ex-Cell-O's eight manufacturing plants to aid in production and inventory control.[7]

A marketer may survey the sales staff for several reasons, the most important being that the sales staff is closer to customers on a daily basis than are other company personnel and therefore should know more about customers' future product needs. Moreover, when sales representatives assist in developing the forecast, they are more likely to work toward its achievement. Another benefit of this

7. Ibid., pp. 40–41.

method is that forecasts can be prepared for single territories, for divisions consisting of several territories, for regions made up of multiple divisions, and then for the total geographic market. This method readily provides sales forecasts from the smallest geographic sales unit to the largest.

Despite these benefits, a sales-force survey has certain limitations. Salespeople can be too optimistic or pessimistic because of recent experiences. Their estimates may be either inflated or low. In addition, salespeople tend to underestimate the sales potential in their territories when they believe that their sales goals will be determined by their forecasts. Finally, salespeople usually dislike paperwork because it consumes time that could be spent selling. If the preparation of a territorial sales forecast is time consuming, the sales staff may do an inadequate job on it.

Nonetheless, sales-force surveys can be effective under certain conditions. If, for instance, the salespeople as a group are accurate—or at least consistent—estimators, the overestimates and underestimates should counterbalance each other. If the aggregate forecast is consistently over or under actual sales, then the marketer who develops the final forecast can make the necessary adjustments. Assuming the survey is well administered, the sales force can really believe that it is making a definite contribution to developing reasonable sales goals. Alternatively, the sales force can be assured that its forecasts are not used to set sales quotas.

Expert Surveys In an **expert forecasting survey,** a company uses experts to help prepare the sales forecast. These experts are usually economists, management consultants, advertising executives, college professors, or other persons outside the firm who have much experience in a specific market. Drawing on their experience and their analysis of available information about the company and the market, these experts prepare and present their forecasts or attempt to answer questions regarding a forecast.

The use of experts is expedient and relatively inexpensive. However, because they work outside the firm, experts may not be as motivated as company personnel to do an effective job.

Time Series Analysis **Time series analysis** is a technique in which the forecaster, using the firm's historical sales data, tries to discover a pattern or patterns in the firm's sales volume over time. If a pattern is uncovered, it can be used to forecast sales. This forecasting method assumes that the past sales pattern will continue in the future. The accuracy, and thus the usefulness, of time series analysis depends heavily on the validity of this assumption.

In a time series analysis, a forecaster usually performs four types of analysis: trend, cycle, seasonal, and random factor.[8] **Trend analysis** focuses on aggregate sales data, such as a company's annual sales figures, from a period of many years to determine whether annual sales are generally rising, falling, or staying about the same. Through **cycle analysis** a forecaster analyzes sales figures (often monthly sales data) over a period of three to five years to ascertain whether sales fluctuate in a consistent, periodic manner. When performing **seasonal analysis,** the analyst studies daily, weekly, or monthly sales figures to evaluate the degree to which seasonal factors such as climate and holiday activities influence the firm's sales.

8. Kenneth E. Marino, *Forecasting Sales and Planning Profits* (Chicago: Probus Publishing, 1986), p. 155.

Random factor analysis is an attempt to attribute erratic sales variations to random, nonrecurrent events such as a regional power failure, a natural disaster, or the death of a president of the United States. After performing each of these analyses, the forecaster combines the results to develop the sales forecast.

Time series analysis is an effective forecasting method for products with reasonably stable demand, but it is not useful for products with highly erratic demand. Joseph E. Seagram & Sons, Inc., an importer and producer of liquor and wines, uses several types of time series analyses for forecasting and has found them quite accurate. For example, Seagram's forecasts of industry sales volume have proved correct within ±1.5 percent, and the firm's company sales forecasts have been accurate within ±2 percent. Time series analysis is not always so dependable.[9]

Correlation Methods   Like time series analysis, correlation methods are based on historical sales data. When **correlation methods** are used, the forecaster attempts to find a relationship between past sales and one or more variables such as population, per capita income, or gross national product. To determine whether a correlation exists, the analyst uses regression analysis, which analyzes the statistical relationships among changes in past sales and changes in one or more variables. The objective of regression analysis is a mathematical formula that accurately describes a relationship between the firm's sales and one or more variables; however, the formula indicates only an associational relationship, not cause and effect. Once an accurate formula has been established, the forecaster plugs the necessary information into the formula to derive the sales forecast.

Correlation methods are useful when a precise relationship can be established. However, a forecaster seldom finds a perfect correlation. In addition, this method can be used only when the available historical sales data are extensive. Ordinarily, then, correlation techniques are useless for forecasting the sales of new products.

Market Tests   A **market test** consists of making a product available to buyers in one or more test areas and measuring purchases and consumer responses to distribution, promotion, and price. Even though test areas are often cities with populations of 200,000 to 500,000, test sites can be larger metropolitan areas or towns with populations of 50,000 to 200,000. A market test provides information about consumers' actual purchases rather than about their intended purchases. In addition, purchase volume can be evaluated in relation to the intensity of other marketing activities—advertising, in-store promotions, pricing, packaging, distribution, and the like. On the basis of customer response in test areas, forecasters can estimate product sales for larger geographic units.

When considering the use of a market test, a marketer must weigh the advantages and disadvantages. A market test is an effective tool for forecasting the sales of new products or the sales of existing products in new geographic areas because it does not require historical sales data. The test gives the forecaster information about customers' real actions rather than intended or estimated behavior. A market test also gives a marketer an opportunity to test various elements of the marketing mix. But these tests are often time consuming and expensive. In addition, a marketer cannot be certain that the consumer response during a market test represents the total market response or that such a response will continue in the future.

9. David Hurwood, Elliott S. Grossman, and Earl Bailey, *Sales Forecasting* (New York: Conference Board, 1978), p. 61.

Using Multiple Forecasting Methods

Although some businesses depend on a single sales forecasting method, most firms use several techniques. At Rockwell International Corp., for example, division managers are encouraged to use multiple forecasting methods and are even sent manuals describing numerous sales forecasting methods.[10] A firm is sometimes forced to use several methods when it markets diverse product lines, but even for a single product line several forecasts may be needed, especially when the product is sold in different market segments. For example, a producer of automobile tires may use one technique for forecasting new car tire sales and another to forecast the sales of replacement tires. Variation in the length of the needed forecasts may require the use of several forecast methods. A firm that uses one method for a short-range forecast may find it inappropriate for long-range forecasting. Sometimes a marketer verifies the results of one method by using one or several other methods and comparing results.

Summary

A market is an aggregate of people who, as individuals or as organizations, have needs for products in a product class and who have the ability, willingness, and authority to purchase such products. Two types of markets are consumer markets and organizational or industrial markets. A consumer market consists of purchasers and/or persons in their households who intend to consume or to benefit from the purchased products. An organizational or industrial market consists of persons and groups who purchase a specific kind of product for resale, direct use in producing other products, or use in day-to-day operations. Four major categories of organizational markets are producer, reseller, government, and institutional.

Marketers use two general approaches to identify their target markets: the total market and the market segmentation approaches. A firm using a total market approach designs a single marketing mix and directs it at an entire market for a particular product. The total market approach can be effective under two conditions: a large proportion of individuals in the total market must have similar needs for the product, and the organization must be able to develop and maintain a single marketing mix to satisfy the needs.

Companies taking the total market approach frequently use a product differentiation strategy. One type of product is aimed at the total market to establish in customers' minds that their product is superior to competing brands.

The market segmentation approach divides the total market into groups consisting of people who have similar product needs. The purpose is to design a marketing mix (or mixes) that more precisely matches the needs of persons in a selected segment (or segments). There are two major types of market segmentation strategies. In the concentration strategy, the organization directs its marketing efforts toward a single market segment through one marketing mix. In the multisegment strategy, the organization develops different marketing mixes for two or more segments.

Certain conditions must exist for market segmentation to be effective. First, consumers' needs for the product should be heterogeneous. Second, the segments of the market should be identifiable and divisible. Third, the total market should be

10. Ibid., p. 216.

divided in such a way that the segments can be compared with respect to estimated sales potential, costs, and profits. Fourth, at least one segment must have enough profit potential to justify developing and maintaining a special marketing mix for that segment. Fifth, the firm must be able to reach the chosen segment with a particular marketing mix.

A segmentation variable is the basis for dividing a total market into segments. The segmentation variable should be related to customers' needs for, uses of, or behavior toward the product. Segmentation variables for consumer markets can be grouped into four categories: demographic, geographic, psychographic, and behavioralistic. Segmentation variables for industrial and reseller markets include geographic factors, type of organization, customer size, and product use. Besides selecting the appropriate segmentation variable, a marketer also must decide how many variables to use.

A marketer must be able to evaluate the sales potential in possible target markets as well as in target markets that the firm currently serves. There are two general approaches to measuring company sales potential: the breakdown and the buildup approaches. Several methods are used to forecast company sales: executive judgment, surveys, time series analysis, correlation, and market tests.

Important Terms

Market
Consumer market
Organizational or industrial market
Total (or undifferentiated) market approach
Product differentiation
Heterogeneous markets
Market segmentation
Market segment
Concentration strategy
Multisegment strategy
Segmentation variables
Market density
Benefit segmentation
Single-variable segmentation
Multivariable segmentation

Market sales potential
Company sales potential
Breakdown approach
Buildup approach
Company sales forecast
Executive judgment
Customer forecasting survey
Sales-force forecasting survey
Expert forecasting survey
Time series analysis
Trend analysis
Cycle analysis
Seasonal analysis
Random factor analysis
Correlation methods
Market test

Discussion and Review Questions

1. What is a market? What are its requirements?
2. In your local area, is there a group of people with unsatisfied product needs who represent a market? Could this market be reached by a business organization? Why or why not?
3. Identify and describe two major types of markets. Give examples of each type.

4. What is the total market approach? Under what conditions is it most useful? Describe a present market situation in which a firm is using a total market approach. Is the business successful? Why or why not?

5. Explain the basic characteristics of the product differentiation strategy. What companies are currently using this approach? Is it working for them? Why or why not?

6. What is the market segmentation approach? Describe the basic conditions required for effective segmentation. Identify several firms that use the segmentation approach.

7. List the differences between the concentration and the multisegment strategies. Describe the advantages and disadvantages of each strategy.

8. When choosing a segmentation variable, what major factors should marketers consider?

9. Identify and describe four major categories of variables that can be used to segment consumer markets. Give examples of product markets that are segmented by variables in each category.

10. What dimensions are used to segment industrial or organizational markets?

11. How do marketers decide whether to use single- or multivariable segmentation? Identify examples of product markets that are divided through multivariable segmentation.

12. Why is a marketer concerned about sales potential when trying to find a target market?

13. Describe the relationship between market sales potential and company sales potential.

14. What is a company sales forecast and why is it important?

15. Identify five major types of sales forecasting methods.

16. What are the advantages and disadvantages of using executive judgment as a sales forecasting technique?

17. Explain three types of surveys used for sales forecasting. Compare their benefits and limitations.

18. Compare and contrast correlation forecasting methods with time series analysis.

19. Under what conditions are market tests useful for sales forecasting? Discuss the advantages and disadvantages of market tests.

Cases

3.1 Kinder-Care Segments Child-Care Market[11]

Kinder-Care Learning Centers operates 1,100 day-care facilities in forty-two states and two Canadian provinces. Founded in Montgomery, Alabama, in 1969, the

11. Based on information from William Dunn, "Kinder-Care Sets Its Sites," *American Demographics,* May 1985, pp. 20–21; Peter Hall, "Bringing Child Care Back into Focus," *Financial World,* Oct. 17, 1984, pp. 29–30; David Wiessler with Jeannye Thornton, "Who'll Watch the Kids? Working Parents Worry," *U.S. News and World Report,* June 27, 1983, pp. 67–68; Pete Engardio, "Kinder-Care Will Mind Your Money, Too," *Business Week,* June 9, 1986, pp. 34–35.

publicly owned chain cares for about 100,000 children daily. Kinder-Care provides a full day of child care for preschoolers and afterschool programs for children younger than 13. Its overall goal is to provide educationally stimulating programs of uniform quality in clean, secure surroundings.

Including Kinder-Care, about 30,000 day-care centers are now operating within the United States. Although most child-care providers are small, single-unit operations, Kinder-Care competes with La Petite Academy (385 units) and DayBridge Learning Centers (150 units). Other enterprises with multiple units include Children's World, Mary Moppet's Day Care Schools, and Gerber Products. Locally, these proprietary child-care operations face competition from religious institutions, charitable groups, and other nonprofit organizations. In addition, such businesses as Polaroid Corp. in Cambridge, Massachusetts, are beginning to address the need for child care by funding referral services that help employees find day care, by subsidizing part of child-care costs, or by providing day-care centers at company headquarters.

Kinder-Care uses demographic and geographic characteristics as variables for segmenting markets. The company's primary target is the young, two-career couple with children and a combined annual income of $20,000 or more. Kinder-Care usually avoids sites near apartments, which often attract singles, or near older neighborhoods with few children, preferring to place its Learning Centers near new housing developments, where both husbands and wives are likely to be working to meet mortgage payments. Similarly, Kinder-Care looks not only for regions of population growth, such as the West Coast and the Southwest, but for areas growing in income, educational levels, and number of working class families.

Last year Kinder-Care invested $75 million in additional child-care centers. The company believes that the potential for its services will increase because the entire child-care industry now serves only 20 percent of children younger than 5, with more than 50 percent of all mothers working outside the home. By 1990, marketers expect that two-thirds of all mothers with children age 6 or younger will have jobs. In addition, many parents now distrust in-home providers because of recent child abuse cases; approximately 95 percent of reported cases have occurred in such facilities. Thus Kinder-Care anticipates that parents will be more likely to use larger, commercial facilities such as theirs.

Kinder-Care is diversifying into other forms of family services as well. Last year Kinder-Care, which has operated the Kinder Life Insurance Company since 1981, acquired a second insurance company and a savings and loan association. The company now hopes to offer its day-care customers a complete package of financial services. Kinder-Care recently bought into a company that operates centers for tutoring school-age children, and Kinder-Care also hopes to open in two or three years day-care facilities for elderly persons.

Questions for Discussion

1. Which types of segmentation variables is Kinder-Care using? Is multivariable segmentation appropriate for Kinder-Care? Explain your answer.
2. The number of single-parent households with children is sizable and increasing. Assess Kinder-Care's decision to not direct its marketing efforts toward these households.
3. If you were asked to develop a long-range estimate of national demand for child-care services, what factors would you consider?

3.2 Sales Forecasting at Bay State Machine Company

Bay State Machine Company is a medium-sized producer of portable rigs that are used in drilling oil or water wells. Bay State manufactures several standardized models and also custom-designs rigs. Although Bay State began as a small machine shop in 1918, for more than forty years its primary business activities have focused on building high-quality portable drilling rigs. Bay State's sales force of thirty-six is managed by three regional sales managers and a national sales director.

For a number of years, Bay State managers have used several types of sales forecasting techniques, including sales-force surveys, correlation methods, executive judgments, and expert opinions. Table 3.3 shows the annual sales forecasts arrived at with each method for the last ten years, along with actual sales figures for each year.

Bay State managers recently have begun to question whether it is really necessary to use four different sales forecasting methods, given that the costs associated with each method have been escalating, especially during the last few years.

Questions for Discussion

1. How does Bay State management benefit from using several sales forecasting techniques?
2. Given Bay State's experience over the last ten years, which sales forecasting method should be used if the managers decide to rely on a single method? Explain your answer, and be sure to enumerate the major advantages and disadvantages of the method that you recommend.
3. Which combination of sales forecasting methods should Bay State management use if multiple methods are employed? Why?

TABLE 3.3

Bay State's actual and forecasted sales (in millions of dollars)

YEAR	ACTUAL ANNUAL SALES	SALES FORECASTS			
		SALES-FORCE SURVEY	CORRELATION METHOD	EXECUTIVE JUDGMENT	EXPERT OPINION
10	42.0	41.1	44.5	37.2	44.1
9	46.2	43.9	48.0	50.4	46.6
8	54.3	52.7	51.0	53.9	58.1
7	57.8	56.6	56.1	54.0	61.3
6	72.4	70.2	77.5	81.9	75.3
5	98.7	93.7	100.1	107.9	99.7
4	114.0	111.9	107.1	113.0	122.0
3	131.8	129.1	127.8	120.7	133.1
2	152.9	148.3	160.5	170.1	159.0
Last year	184.4	180.2	195.4	175.0	189.9

4. Consumer Buying Behavior

► To understand the types of decision behaviors consumers use when making purchases.

► To become aware of the stages of the consumer buying decision process.

► To explore how demographic and situational factors may affect the consumer buying decision process.

► To examine how psychological factors influence the consumer buying decision process.

► To become familiar with the social influences that may affect the consumer buying decision process.

W*ho is in line* at the supermarket these days? More men than ever before, that's who.

According to a recent report sponsored by Campbell Soup Company and *People* magazine, male shoppers now account for 40 percent of all food purchases. About 37 percent of the men sampled in the Campbell survey say that they shop for food more often than they did a few years ago. Most surveyed expect to do even more shopping in the future. Other surveys present similar findings.

Demographers say the evolving purchasing patterns are related to several factors: higher divorce rates, postponed marriages, changing sex roles within the family, and the increase in the number of working women. Some men shop out of necessity; according to census records, 7.5 million men now live alone, and another 2 million head families without wives. Other men shop by choice, either because they enjoy shopping and cooking or they believe in sharing household chores with their spouses.

The popular notion of male shoppers as inexperienced, impulsive, and disorganized is largely an inaccurate stereotype, say researchers. Although some studies have shown that men are somewhat less likely than women to make a shopping list, use coupons, or comparison-shop, their purchasing habits appear to be linked more to age and marital status than to gender. Young single male shoppers, for example, buy more convenience foods and health and beauty aids than do men in other groups, and they also tend to shop as needed, without much advance planning. Men 55 and older, on the other hand, are more apt to buy food basics, shop in the daytime, and hold businesslike attitudes toward shopping. Affluent

FIGURE 4.1

More men are shopping than ever before (SOURCE: OSCAR MAYER and the OSCAR MAYER RHOMBOID are registered trademarks of Oscar Mayer Food Corporation)

working couples may shop together or separately, often in the evenings; these husbands and wives both are attracted to unusual and expensive items, such as upscale frozen dinners.

As a result of the changes in men's purchasing patterns, astute marketers now consider men an important "new" market segment (see Figure 4.1). General Foods Corp., for one, is directing commercials at men. Its "Shortcuts" series offers tips on food preparation, such as choosing cuts of meat or preparing dinner in a skillet. Campbell Soup has added men to its consumer testing panels, and such products as Maxwell House coffee, Sure deodorant, Nutri-Grain cereal, and Planters peanuts are now advertised in male-oriented *Sports Illustrated*. On the retail end, food stores hoping to attract male customers are using a variety of strategies, such as product demonstrations during evening shopping hours, printed purchasing guides, posted diagrams of store layout, and newspaper advertisements that emphasize shopping ease and convenience.[1]

1. Based on information from Eileen B. Brill, "Super Marketers Pursue the New Consumers," *Advertising Age,* Oct. 13, 1986, p. S-4; Priscilla Donegan, "The Myth of the Male Shopper," *Progressive Grocer,* May 1986, pp. 36–38; Ronald D. Michman, "The Male Queue at the Checkout Counter," *Business Horizons,* May–June 1986, pp. 51–55; Eileen Prescott, "New Men," *American Demographics,* August 1983, p. 16.

B OTH MEN'S AND WOMEN'S roles have changed, leading to many changes in their buying behavior. Being able to recognize and adjust to changes in customers' purchasing behavior is required if firms are to provide customer satisfaction. A firm's ability to establish and maintain satisfying exchange relationships requires an understanding of buying behavior. **Buying behavior** is the decision processes and acts of people involved in buying and using products.[2] **Consumer buying behavior** refers to the buying behavior of ultimate consumers, those persons who purchase products for personal or household use, not for business purposes. Marketers should analyze buying behavior for several reasons. First, buyers' reactions to a firm's marketing strategy have great impact on the firm's success. Second, as indicated in Chapter 1, the marketing concept stresses that a firm should create a marketing mix that satisfies customers. To find out what satisfies buyers, marketers must examine the main influences on what, where, when, and how consumers buy. Third, by gaining a better understanding of the factors that affect buyer behavior, marketers are in a better position to predict how consumers will respond to marketing strategies.

Marketers may attempt to understand and influence buying behavior, but they cannot control it. Even though some critics credit them with the ability to manipulate buyers, marketers have neither the powers nor the knowledge to do so. Their knowledge of behavior comes from what psychologists, social psychologists, and sociologists know about human behavior in general. Even if marketers wanted to manipulate buyers, the lack of laws and principles in the behavioral sciences would prevent them from doing so.

In this chapter we initially examine the types of decision making that consumers use. Next we analyze the major stages of the consumer buying decision process. Finally, we explain several factors believed to influence the consumer buying decision process.

Types of Consumer Decision Behavior

As we analyze buyer behavior, we will think of buyers as decision makers. Consumers usually have the general objective of creating and maintaining a collection of goods and services that provides current and future satisfaction. To accomplish this objective, buyers make many purchasing decisions. For example, an average adult must make several decisions daily regarding food, clothing, shelter, medical care, education, recreation, or transportation. As they make these decisions, buyers use different decision making behaviors.

Although the types of consumer decision making vary considerably, they can be classified into one of three broad categories: routine response behavior, limited decision making, and extensive decision making.[3] A consumer uses **routine response behavior** when buying frequently purchased, low-cost items that require

2. James F. Engel and Roger D. Blackwell, *Consumer Behavior* (Hinsdale, Ill.: Dryden Press, 1986), p. 5.
3. John A. Howard and Jagdish N. Sheth, *The Theory of Buyer Behavior* (New York: Wiley, 1969), pp. 27–28.

very little search and decision effort. These items are sometimes called low-involvement products. When buying them, a consumer may prefer a particular brand, but he or she is familiar with several brands in the product class and views more than one as being acceptable. The products that are bought through routine response behavior are purchased quickly with very little mental effort. Most buyers, for example, do not stand at the detergent shelf pondering the detergents for twenty minutes. Instead, they walk by, grab a box, and proceed down the aisle.

Limited decision making is used for products that are purchased occasionally and when a buyer needs to acquire information about an unfamiliar brand in a familiar product category. This type of decision making requires a moderate amount of time for information gathering and deliberation.

A consumer uses **extensive decision making** when purchasing an unfamiliar expensive product or an infrequently bought item. This process is the most complex type of consumer decision making behavior. A buyer uses many criteria for evaluating alternative brands and spends much time seeking information and deciding on the purchase.

The type of decision making that individuals use when buying a specific product does not necessarily remain constant. In some instances, the first time we buy a certain kind of product we might use extensive decision making and then limited decision making for subsequent purchases of that product. Also, when a routinely purchased, formerly satisfying brand no longer satisfies, we may use limited or extensive decision processes to switch to a new brand.

The Consumer Buying Decision Process

As defined earlier, a major part of buying behavior is the decision process used in making purchases. Figure 4.2 is a simplified model of the **consumer buying decision process** and shows the five major factors believed to affect this process: problem recognition, information search, evaluation of alternatives, purchase, and post-purchase evaluation. Before we examine each stage, consider these important points. First, the actual act of purchasing is only one stage in the process, and the process is initiated several stages prior to the actual purchase. Second, even though for discussion purposes we indicate that a purchase occurs, not all decision processes lead to a purchase; the individual may terminate the process during any stage. Finally, not all consumer decisions always include all five stages. Persons engaged in extensive decision making usually employ all stages of this decision process, whereas those engaged in limited decision making and routine response behavior may omit some stages.

Problem Recognition

Problem recognition occurs when a buyer becomes aware that there is a difference between a desired state and an actual condition. For example, a consumer may want an automobile that is reliable. When her car will not start in the morning for the third time in a week, she may recognize that a difference exists between the desired state—a reliable car—and the actual condition—a car that refuses to start.

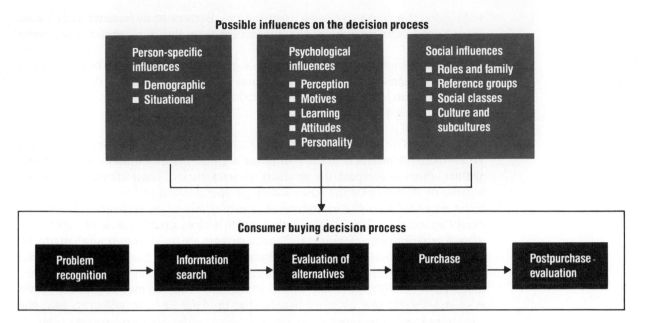

Possible influences on the decision process

Person-specific influences	Psychological influences	Social influences
■ Demographic ■ Situational	■ Perception ■ Motives ■ Learning ■ Attitudes ■ Personality	■ Roles and family ■ Reference groups ■ Social classes ■ Culture and subcultures

Consumer buying decision process

Problem recognition → Information search → Evaluation of alternatives → Purchase → Postpurchase evaluation

FIGURE 4.2

Consumer buying decision process and possible influences on the process

Sometimes a person has a problem or need but is unaware of it. Marketers use sales personnel, advertising, and packaging to help trigger the recognition of such needs or problems. The speed of consumer problem recognition can be rather slow or quite rapid.

Information Search

After becoming aware of the problem or need, the consumer (if continuing the decision process) searches for information. Information search can focus on availability of brands, product features, seller characteristics, warranties, operating instructions, prices, and the like. The duration and intensity of search efforts depend on the consumer's experience in purchasing the product and the importance of the purchase to the consumer. If the woman with the unreliable car moves into the information search stage, she is likely to engage in a rather lengthy search. However, if she is buying a blouse, her information search stage will probably be shorter.

When seeking information, a consumer may turn to one or several major sources. One primary source of information is experience. Direct experience with a product can provide selected kinds of needed information that a consumer may not be able to acquire in other ways. Marketers sometimes attempt to help customers experience products through free samples, demonstrations, and temporary use, such as a test drive of an automobile. Personal contacts—friends, relatives, and associates—can also be sources of information. Because they tend to trust and respect these sources, consumers view them as credible. A third category of information sources is called marketer-dominated sources, which include salespersons, advertising, packaging, and displays. These sources typically do not require the consumer to expend much effort to receive the information. Finally, buyers can use public sources of information, such as government reports, news presentations, and reports from product-testing organizations. Because of its factual and unbiased nature, consumers frequently view information from public sources as being quite credible.

A successful information search yields a group of brands that a buyer views as possible alternatives. This group of products is sometimes called the buyer's evoked set. For example, an evoked set of imported station wagons might include Peugeot, Mercedes-Benz, and Volvo.

Evaluation of Alternatives

To evaluate the products in the evoked set, a consumer establishes a set of criteria against which to compare the products' characteristics. These criteria are characteristics or features that the buyer wants (or does not want). For example, one car buyer might want a red car, whereas another might have no preference about color except an intense dislike of red. The buyer also assigns a certain level of importance to each criterion; some features and characteristics are more important than others. Using the criteria and considering the importance of each one, a buyer rates and eventually ranks the brands in the evoked set. Evaluation may yield no brand that the buyer is willing to purchase, in which case further search may be required. If the evaluation yields one or more brands that the consumer is willing to buy, the consumer is ready to move on to the next stage of the decision process.

Purchase

The consumer selects the product or brand to be bought during the purchase stage. The choice is based on the outcome of the previous evaluation stage and on other dimensions. Product availability may influence which brand is purchased. For example, if the brand that ranked the highest during evaluation is not available, the buyer may purchase another acceptable brand. During this stage, the consumer determines from which seller she or he will buy the product. The choice of the seller may influence the final product selection, as might the terms of sale that, if they are negotiable, are determined during the purchase decision stage. Issues such as price, delivery, warranties, maintenance agreements, installation, and credit arrangements are discussed and settled. Finally, the actual act of purchase occurs during this stage, unless of course the consumer terminates the buying decision process prior to purchase.

Postpurchase Evaluation

After purchase, a buyer will begin evaluating the product. Shortly after an expensive product has been bought, postpurchase evaluation may result in **cognitive dissonance,** which is dissatisfaction that occurs because the buyer questions whether he or she should have purchased the product at all or would have been better off purchasing another brand that was evaluated very favorably. A consumer who feels cognitive dissonance may attempt to return the product or may seek positive information about it to justify that choice.

As the product is used, the consumer evaluates it to determine if its actual performance meets expected levels. Many of the criteria used in the evaluation of alternatives stage are used during postpurchase evaluation. The outcome of this stage is either satisfaction or dissatisfaction, which feeds back to other stages of the decision process and influences subsequent purchases.

As Figure 4.2 shows, there are three major categories of factors that are believed to influence the consumer buying decision process: person-specific, psychological, and social. The remainder of this chapter focuses on these factors that may affect the consumer buying decision process. Although we discuss each major factor separately, keep in mind that their effects on the consumer decision process are interrelated.

Buying Decision Process: Person-Specific Influences

A **person-specific factor** is one that is unique to a particular individual. Numerous person-specific characteristics can affect purchasing decisions. In this section we consider two categories of person-specific factors: demographic and situational.

Demographic Factors

Demographic factors are individual characteristics such as age, sex, race, ethnicity, income, family, life cycle state, and occupation. (These and other characteristics are discussed in Chapter 3 as possible variables for segmentation purposes.) Demographic factors can influence who is involved in family decision making. For example, findings of a study several years ago indicated that husbands and wives without children make more joint decisions than do husbands and wives with children.[4] Demographic attributes may influence the speed at which a person moves through the consumer buying decision process. Also, behavior during a specific stage of the decision process is partially determined by demographic factors. For example, during the information stage, a person's age and income may affect the number and types of information sources used and the amount of time devoted to seeking information.

Demographic factors also affect the extent to which a person uses products in a specific product category. For example, the singles demographic group, which is growing rapidly in the United States, accounts for 12.5 percent of consumer spending. Yet singles account for 15 percent of total vacation expenditures, 15.5 percent of expenditures for eating away from home, 15.5 percent of car sales, and 20 percent of alcohol sales.[5] Brand preferences, store choice, and timing of purchases are other areas influenced by selected demographic factors. Consider, for example, how differences in occupation result in variations in product needs.

A college professor may earn almost as much income annually as a plumber does. Yet these incomes will be spent quite differently because the product needs that arise from these two occupations vary considerably. Both occupations require the purchase of work clothes. Yet a professor and a plumber purchase quite different types of clothes, and the types of vehicles they drive surely will vary to some extent. What and where they eat for lunch are likely to be different. Finally, the "tools" that they purchase and use in their work clearly are not the same.

4. Pierre Filiatrault and J. R. Brent Ritchie, "Joint Purchase Decisions: A Comparison of Influence Structure in Family and Couple Decision-Making Units," *Journal of Consumer Research,* Sept. 1980, p. 139.
5. Gay Jerrey, "Y & R Study: New Life to Singles," *Advertising Age,* Oct. 4, 1982, p. 14.

Many demographic factors lead to variations in consumer buying behavior. These factors are very closely associated with people's needs, product expectations, and behavior toward products.

Situational Factors

Situational factors are the set of circumstances or conditions that exist when a consumer is making a purchase decision. Sometimes a consumer engages in buying decision making as a result of an unexpected situation. For example, a person may be buying an airline ticket hurriedly to spend the last few days with a relative who is terminally ill. Or a situation may arise that causes a person to lengthen or terminate the buying decision process. A consumer who is considering the purchase of a personal computer, for example, may be laid off during the evaluation of alternatives stage. The job loss would certainly slow the buying decision process and might cause the person to reject the purchase entirely. However, if the same person experienced a different circumstance, say a 20 percent raise in salary, then the buying decision process might be completed more quickly than if no pay increase had been received.

Situational factors can influence a consumer's actions during any stage of the buying decision process and in a variety of ways. If there is little time for selecting and purchasing a product, a person may make a quick choice and purchase a brand that is readily available. Uncertainty about future marital status may influence a consumer's purchases. A couple who is experiencing marital difficulties will probably delay the purchase of durable goods. A single person who is contemplating marriage also might delay buying durables such as appliances and furniture. People who believe that the supply of necessary products is sharply limited are more likely to make a purchase. For example, people have purchased and hoarded gasoline and toilet paper when these products were believed to be in short supply. When a product is viewed as a necessity and it shows signs of malfunctioning, a consumer is more likely to consider making a purchase. These and other situational factors can change rapidly, and the effects on purchase decisions can arise or subside quickly.

Buying Decision Process: Psychological Influences

Psychological influences operating within individuals partly determine people's general behavior and thus influence their behavior as consumers. The primary psychological influences on consumer behavior are (1) perception, (2) motives, (3) learning, (4) attitudes, and (5) personality. Even though these behavioral factors operate internally, later in this chapter we see that they are very much affected by social forces outside the individual.

Perception

In Figure 4.3, are the horsemen riding to the left or to the right? It could be either way depending on how the riders are perceived. Different people perceive the same thing at the same time in different ways. Similarly, the same individual at different times may perceive the same item in a number of ways.

Perception is the process of selecting, organizing, and interpreting information inputs to produce meaning. A person receives information through the senses:

sight, taste, hearing, smell, and touch. **Information inputs** are the sensations received through sense organs. When we hear an advertisement, see a friend, smell polluted air or water, or touch a product, we receive information inputs.

As the definition indicates, perception is a three-step process. Although we receive numerous pieces of information at once, only a few of them reach awareness. We select some inputs and ignore many others because we do not have the ability to be conscious of all inputs at one time. (The Application on page 129, dealing with subliminal influence, focuses on whether and how people might be affected by some inputs that do not reach conscious awareness.) This phenomenon is sometimes called **selective exposure** because we select inputs that are to be exposed to our awareness. If you are concentrating on this paragraph, you probably are not aware that people or cars are outside making noise, that the light is on, or that you are touching this book. Even though you are receiving these inputs, you ignore them until they are mentioned.

There are several reasons why some types of information reach awareness while others do not. An input is more likely to reach awareness if it relates to an anticipated event. Stuckey's, a chain of roadside snack-food stores, uses a series of billboards to encourage travelers to anticipate seeing a Stuckey's store. Even though some motorists may not stop, there is a good chance that they will at least notice the store. A person also is likely to let an input reach consciousness if the information helps satisfy current needs. For example, you are more likely to notice food commercials when you are hungry. Conversely, if you have just eaten a large pizza and you hear a Burger King commercial, there is a good chance that the advertisement will not reach your awareness. Finally, if the intensity of an input changes significantly, the input is more likely to reach awareness. When a store manager reduces a price slightly, we may not notice because the change is not significant, but if the manager cuts the price in half, we are much more likely to recognize the reduction.

FIGURE 4.3

Are the horsemen riding to the left or to the right? (SOURCE: © 1988 M. C. Escher % Cordon Art— Baarn—Holland)

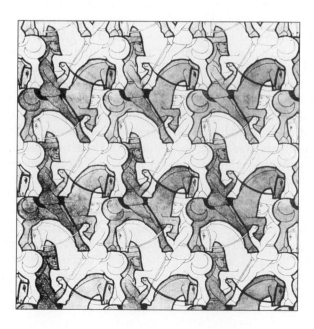

The selective nature of perception leads to two other conditions: selective distortion and selective retention. **Selective distortion** is changing or twisting currently received information. This condition can occur when a person receives information inconsistent with personal feelings or beliefs. For example, upon seeing an advertisement promoting a brand that he or she dislikes, a person may distort the information to make it more consistent with prior views. This distortion substantially lessens the effect of the advertisement on the individual. In the **selective retention** phenomenon, a person remembers information inputs that support personal feelings and beliefs and forgets inputs that do not. After hearing a sales presentation and leaving the store, a customer may forget many of the selling points if they contradict prior beliefs.

The information inputs that do reach awareness are not received in an organized form. To produce meaning, an individual must organize them. Ordinarily, this organizing is done rapidly. How a person organizes information affects the meaning obtained. For example, depending on how you organize the input in Figure 4.3, you could perceive one of two different forms.

As Figure 4.3 illustrates, an individual can organize inputs in more than one way and obtain more than one meaning. Thus, interpretation—the third step in the perceptual process—is needed to reduce mental confusion. A person bases interpretation on what is familiar. For this reason, a manufacturer that changes a package design faces a major problem: People look for the product in the old, familiar package, and they might not recognize it in the new one.

Several years ago, Du Pont test-marketed in several cities a new package design for one of its established automobile polishes. Sales declined significantly because consumers interpreted a different container to mean a different polish. They did not interpret the product as the same polish in a container with a new package design. Unless a package change is accompanied by a promotional program that makes people aware of the change, a firm may lose sales.

Not only does one form perceptions of packages, products, brands, and organizations, a buyer also has a self-perception. That perception is called the person's **self-concept** or self-image. Some behavioral scientists believe that the self-concept is a combination of the actual self-concept and the ideal self-concept. The actual self-concept is how a person actually perceives himself or herself, and the ideal self-concept is the way he or she would like to be perceived. One's self-concept is a function of experiences and hereditary traits, so an individual changes self-concept over time.

It is reasonable to believe that a person's self-concept affects purchase decisions and consumption behavior. The results of some studies suggest that buyers purchase products that reflect and enhance their self-concepts.

Although marketers cannot control people's perceptions, they often try to influence them. Several problems may arise from this attempt. First, a consumer's perceptual process may operate in such a way that a seller's information never reaches that person. For example, a consumer may block out a store clerk's sales pitch. Second, a buyer may receive a seller's information and perceive it differently than was intended. For example, when a toothpaste producer states in an advertisement that "35 percent of the people who use this toothpaste have fewer cavities," a customer could take the statement to mean that 65 percent of the people who use the product have more cavities. Third, a buyer who perceives information inputs that are inconsistent with prior beliefs is likely to forget the information quickly.

Subliminal Influence

Can subliminal appeals really alter behavior? Most psychologists are skeptical. But supporters of subliminal techniques claim that messages aimed at the subconscious can indeed influence people to not only refrain from stealing but to lose weight, stop smoking, deal with stress, and perhaps buy products. The key, say most subliminalists, is a predisposition to certain behavior on the part of the person receiving the message. That is, to be effective the tape must provide reinforcement for what the person basically wants to do anyway.

In theory, subliminal messages can be communicated several ways. One approach is to present visual stimuli at very brief intervals. The most famous use of visual subliminals was in the 1950s in a New Jersey movie theater; concession sales reportedly increased after the messages "Drink Coca-Cola" and "Eat popcorn" were flashed repeatedly on the screen during the feature film. Another form of subliminal communication is suggestiveness, which is used in pictures or advertisements that mean one thing on a superficial level but convey a deeper message as well. A third, more questionable form of subliminal stimulation is *embedding,* the concealing of sexual imagery in various products or advertisements to appeal to consumers' subconscious sex drives.

Of greatest current interest to retailers is subaudible stimulation. Developers of auditory subliminals point out that tapes may improve productivity and workplace safety, but most retailers using subliminal systems are concerned chiefly with shoplifting, which accounts for annual losses exceeding $1 billion. Most shoppers are accustomed to hearing piped-in music as they browse through merchandise. In some stores, however, customers are hearing more than they realize. The music is mixed with subliminal suggestions: antitheft directives broadcast just below the level of awareness. Although the effectiveness of such ultrasoft messages as "Don't steal," "Be honest," and "We arrest shoplifters" is difficult to measure, companies that market these computerized systems claim their clients can reduce shoplifting by anywhere from 3 to 80 percent.

Observers estimate that more than one thousand supermarkets, discount houses, clothing stores, and general merchandise chains are now broadcasting antitheft messages under cover of canned music. According to tape distributors, retailers are using auditory subliminal systems because they are easy to operate, pay for themselves quickly, and cost less than prosecution of shoplifters after the fact.

The focus of numerous scientific studies, subliminal communication is often criticized by researchers, who say a stimulus so weak that it does not reach conscious awareness is unlikely to change behavior. Even the marketers of subaudible subliminal systems concede the importance of other factors in customer behavior. Theft rates, for example, are influenced also by a store's overall level of customer service, management's attention to record keeping, and the mix of full- and part-time employees (part-time workers are less likely to be alert for shoplifters). Still, auditory subliminals may turn into big business, if enough stores use them to demonstrate their effectiveness. For now, makers of subliminal materials cannot guarantee that the tapes will work, but, they say, no one has proved conclusively that they will not either.

SOURCES: Sid C. Dudley, "Subliminal Advertising: What Is the Controversy About?", *Akron Business and Economic Review,* Summer 1987, pp. 6–18; Mark McLaughlin, "Subliminal Tapes Urge Shoppers to Heed the Warning Sounds…," *New England Business,* Feb. 2, 1987, pp. 36–37; John Ross, "Shop Talk Takes on a New Twist," *Mother Jones,* November–December 1985, p. 8; "Subliminal Messages: Subtle Crime Stoppers," *Chain Store Age Executive,* July 1986, p. 85; Bob Tripi, "Subliminals: Putting Your Mind to It," *Houston Chronicle,* Oct. 5, 1986, sec. 7, p. 5.

Thus if a salesperson tells a prospective car buyer about a highly favorable EPA mileage rating but the customer does not believe it, the customer probably will not retain the information very long.

It is obvious that how and what consumers perceive strongly affect their behavior toward products, prices, package designs, salespeople, stores, advertisements, and manufacturers. With good reason, then, marketers often concern themselves with how consumers perceive their organizations and products. As Figure 4.4 illustrates, organizations sometimes attempt to change customers' perceptions of products. In this advertisement, the Potato Board is saying that the potato should be perceived as nutritious food containing many of the vitamins and minerals that people need.

Motives and Motivation Research

A **motive** is an internal energizing force that orients a person's activities toward a goal. A buyer's actions at any time are affected by a set of motives rather than by just one motive. At a single point in time, some motives in the set are stronger than others, but the strengths of motives vary from one time to another. For example, a person's motives toward having a cup of coffee are much stronger right after waking up than just before going to bed.

Motives can reduce or build tension. When motives drive us toward our goals, they reduce tension. But if some motives impel us toward one goal while other motives pull us toward a different goal, tension may increase because we cannot accomplish either goal.

Many different motives influence buying behavior at once. For example, a person buying a sofa might be attracted by several characteristics, such as durability, economy, and styling. If a marketer appeals to customers by emphasizing only one attractive characteristic, the effort may fail to generate a satisfactory sales level.

Motives that influence where a person purchases products on a regular basis are called **patronage motives.** A buyer may shop at a specific store because of such patronage motives as price, service, location, honesty, product variety, or friendliness of salespeople. To capitalize on patronage motives, a marketer should try to determine why regular customers patronize a store and then emphasize these characteristics in the store's marketing mix.

Motivation research lets marketers analyze the major motives that influence consumers to buy or not buy their products. Motives, which often operate at a subconscious level, are difficult to measure. Because people ordinarily do not know what motivates them, marketers cannot simply ask them about their motives. Most motivation research relies on interviews or projective techniques.

When researchers study motives through interviews, they may use depth interviews, group interviews, or a combination of the two. In a **depth interview,** the researcher tries to get the subject to talk freely about anything to create an informal atmosphere. The researcher may ask general, nondirected questions and then probe the subject's answers by asking for clarification. A depth interview may last for several hours. In a **group interview,** the interviewer—through leadership that is not highly structured—tries to generate discussion about one or several topics among the six to twelve people in the group. Through what is said in the discussion, the interviewer attempts to uncover people's motives relating to some issue such as the use of a product. The researcher usually cannot probe as deeply in a group interview as in a depth interview. To determine the subconscious motives reflected in the interviews, motivation researchers must be extremely well trained in clinical psychology. Their skill in uncovering subconscious motives from what is said in an interview determines the effectiveness of their research. Both depth and group interview techniques can yield a variety of information. For example, they might discover why customers do not like prunes or why they select desserts high in calories.

FIGURE 4.4
Advertisement aimed at changing buyers' perceptions (SOURCE: The Potato Board, Denver, CO)

Projective techniques are tests in which subjects are asked to perform specific tasks for particular purposes while in fact they are being evaluated for other purposes. Such tests are based on the assumption that subjects unconsciously will "project" their motives as they perform the required tasks. Researchers who are trained in projective techniques can analyze the materials a subject produces and can make predictions about the subject's subconscious motives. Some common types of projective techniques are word-association tests, sentence-completion tests, and balloon tests.

Motivation research techniques can be reasonably effective. They are, however, far from perfect. Marketers who want to research people's motives should obtain the services of professional psychologists who are skilled in the methods of motivation research.

Learning

Learning consists of changes in a person's behavior that are caused by information and experience. Variations in behavior that result from psychological conditions such as hunger, fatigue, physical growth, or deterioration are not considered learning. Learning refers to the effects of direct and indirect experiences on future behavior.

The response to a person's behavior strongly influences the learning process. If an individual's actions bring about rewarding or satisfying results, the person may behave the same way in a subsequent, similar situation. However, when behavior leads to unsatisfying outcomes, a person is likely to behave differently in future situations. For example, when a consumer buys a specific brand of candy bar and likes it, that person is more likely to buy the same brand the next time. In fact, he or she will probably continue to purchase that brand until it no longer provides satisfaction. When the effects of the behavior are no longer satisfying, the person will switch to a different brand perhaps, or stop eating candy bars altogether!

For a firm to market products successfully, it must help consumers learn about them. Consumers learn about products directly by experiencing them. As noted earlier, many marketers try to provide consumers with direct experiences before the consumers purchase products. Consumer learning is also affected by experiencing products indirectly through information from salespersons, advertisements, friends, and relatives. Through sales personnel and advertisements, marketers provide information before (and sometimes after) purchases to influence what consumers learn and to create a more favorable attitude toward the products.

Although marketers may attempt to influence what a consumer learns, their attempts are seldom fully successful. Marketers experience problems attracting and holding consumers' attention, providing consumers with the kinds of information that are important for making purchase decisions, and convincing them to try the product.

Attitudes

An **attitude** consists of knowledge and positive or negative feelings about an object. We sometimes say that a person has a "positive attitude," but that statement is incomplete; it has no meaning until we know what the positive attitude relates to. The objects toward which we hold attitudes may be tangible or intangible, living or nonliving. For example, we have attitudes about sex, religion, and politics, just as we do about flowers and beer.

An individual learns attitudes through experience and interaction with other people. Just as attitudes are learned, they can also be changed. However, an individual's attitudes remain generally stable and do not change from moment to moment. Likewise, at any one time, a person's attitudes do not all have equal impact; some are stronger than others.

Consumer attitudes toward a firm and its products greatly influence the success or failure of the firm's marketing strategy. When consumers have strong negative attitudes about one or more aspects of a firm's marketing practices, they may not only stop using the firm's product but may also implore their relatives and friends to do the same. Because attitudes can play such an important part in determining consumer behavior, marketers should measure consumer attitudes toward such dimensions as prices, package designs, brand names, advertisements, salespeople, repair services, store locations, and features of existing or proposed products.

There are several available methods marketers can use to measure consumer attitudes. One of the simplest ways is to question people directly. An attitude researcher for a watch manufacturer, for example, might ask respondents what they think about the styling and design of the firm's new digital watch. Projective techniques used in motivation research can also be employed to measure attitudes. Marketers sometimes use attitude scales to evaluate attitudes. An **attitude scale** usually consists of a series of adjectives, phrases, or sentences about an object. Subjects are asked to indicate the intensity of their feelings toward the object by reacting to the adjectives, phrases, or sentences in a certain way. For example, if a marketer were measuring people's attitudes toward cable television, respondents might be asked to state the degree to which they agree or disagree with a number of statements, such as "Cable television is too expensive." The several computer-assisted analytic approaches currently being developed hold great promise for future attitude research. However, a discussion of these analytic approaches is beyond the scope of this text.

A marketer can gather many types of information by researching attitudes. One food processor researched dog owners' attitudes toward their dogs and dog foods and found that dog owners could be categorized into three attitudinal groups. One group viewed their dogs as performing a utilitarian function, such as protecting the family or household, playing with children, or herding farm animals. These consumers wanted a low-priced, nutritious dog food; they were not interested in a wide variety of flavors. People in the second group were quite fond of their dogs and treated them as companions and family members. These buyers were willing to pay a relatively high price for dog food and wanted many types and flavors so that their dogs would not get bored. Persons in the third group had negative feelings and, in fact, were found to hate their dogs. These customers wanted the cheapest dog food that they could buy and were not concerned with nutrition, flavor, or variety. Because this research determined that other firms were serving these three groups quite effectively, the processor decided not to enter the dog food market after all.

When marketers determine that a significant number of consumers have strong negative attitudes toward an aspect of a marketing mix, they may try to change consumer attitudes to make them more favorable. This task is generally long, expensive, and difficult and may require extensive promotional efforts. When they first entered the U.S. motorcycle market, Honda discovered that many people in this country had negative attitudes toward motorcyclists, believing that most motorcycle riders were thugs or hoodlums. Honda also determined that people associated motorcyclists with such negative images as crime, black leather jackets, and knives. Knowing this, Honda was able to develop and launch a massive advertising campaign with the general theme "You meet the nicest people on a Honda." Although this campaign required considerable effort, time, and money, Honda became a leader in the U.S. motorcycle market. In the same vein, both business and nonbusiness organizations try to change people's attitudes about many things, from health and safety to product prices and features.

Personality

One personality may not be as noticeable as another, but everyone does have one. **Personality** is an internal structure in which both experience and behavior are related in an orderly way. The manner in which these traits are organized within each individual makes each of us unique. Our uniqueness arises from heredity and our experiences.

Personalities typically are described as having one or more characteristics such as compulsiveness, ambitiousness, gregariousness, dogmatism, authoritarianism, introversion, extroversion, aggressiveness, and competitiveness. Marketing researchers attempt to find relationships among such characteristics and buying behavior. Even though a few relationships among several personality characteristics and buyer behavior have been determined, the results of many studies have been inconclusive. Nevertheless, some marketers believe that a person's personality does influence the types and brands of products purchased. For example, the type of clothing, jewelry, or automobile that a person buys may reflect one or more personality characteristics.

At times, marketers aim advertising campaigns at general types of personalities. In doing so, they use positively valued personality characteristics such as gregariousness, independence, or competitiveness. Products promoted this way include beer, soft drinks, cigarettes, and sometimes clothing. In Figure 4.5, for example, Hathaway is appealing to the personality characteristics of individualism and a sense of well-being.

Buying Decision Process: Social Influences

So far we have examined the person-specific and the psychological forces that can influence the consumer buying decision process. Now we consider how other people influence buying decisions. The forces that other people exert on buying behavior are called **social influences**. As Figure 4.2 shows, they can be grouped into four major areas: (1) roles and family influences, (2) reference groups, (3) social classes, and (4) culture and subcultures.

Roles and Family Influences

All of us occupy positions within groups, organizations, and institutions. Associated with each position is a **role**—a set of actions and activities that a person in a particular position is supposed to perform, based on the expectations of both the individual and surrounding persons. For example, even though family roles have changed a good deal, traditionally a married male parent has held two positions in

Bob Costas, the man in the Hathaway shirt.

Network Television and Radio Sportscaster.

His specialty: fast, accurate information. His audience: fanatical. So Bob Costas counts on Hathaway to know the score. In basic white or an exacting stripe, he trusts Hathaway for fabric patterns that match precisely and neckwear that will be the perfect complement. These assurances cost a little more, but better quality always does. Bob Costas knows nobody else makes a shirt the "Hathaway."

Hathaway 150 *Years* - Est. 1837

the family: husband and father. The behaviors and activities that make up a man's role as father are determined by the expectations that he, his wife, and his children have regarding the behavior of a father.

Because people occupy numerous positions, they also have many roles. The male in our example not only performs the roles of husband and father but may perform the roles of plant supervisor, church deacon, Little League coach, and student in an evening college class. Thus there are several sets of expectations placed on each person's behavior.

An individual's roles influence both general behavior and buying behavior. The demands of a person's many roles may be inconsistent and confusing. To illustrate, assume that the father we have been discussing is thinking about buying a boat. His wife wants him to buy it next year. His fourteen-year-old daughter is hoping for a high-powered skiing boat. His eighteen-year-old son wants a sailboat. His fellow deacons are casually suggesting that he increase his monetary contribution to the church. Several classmates at the college are urging him to buy a specific brand of boat. A coworker indicates that he should buy a different brand, one known for high performance. Thus, an individual's buying behavior is partially affected by the input and opinions of significant others (family and friends).

Family roles relate directly to purchase decisions. The male head of household is likely to be involved heavily in the purchase of products such as liquor and tobacco. And although female roles have changed, women still make buying decisions related to many household items, including health-care products, laundry supplies, paper products, and foods. Children are making many purchase decisions and more heavily influencing numerous household purchase decisions that traditionally were made by only the husbands and wives (see the Application on page 137). Husband and wife participate jointly in the purchase of a variety of products, especially durable goods. When two or more family members participate in a purchase, their roles may dictate that each is responsible for performing certain tasks: initiating the idea, gathering information, deciding whether to buy the product, or selecting the specific brand. The particular tasks performed depend on the types of products being considered.

Marketers need to be aware of how roles affect buying behavior. To develop a marketing mix that precisely meets the needs of the target market, marketers must know not only who does the actual buying but what other roles influence the purchase. Because sex roles are changing so rapidly in our country, marketers must ensure when using data that the information is current and accurate.

Reference-Group Influence

A group is a **reference group** when an individual identifies with the group so much that he or she takes on many of the values, attitudes, or behaviors of group members. The person who sees a group as a reference group may or may not know the actual size of the group. Most people have several reference groups, such as families, fraternities, civic organizations, and professional groups like the American Medical Association.

A group can be a negative reference group for an individual. Someone may have been a part of a specific group at one time but later rejected the group's values and members. Also, one can specifically take action to avoid a particular group.[6] However, in this discussion we refer to reference groups as those that the individual involved views positively.

A reference group may be a point of comparison and a source of information for an individual. A customer's behavior may change to be more in line with the actions and beliefs of group members. For example, a person might stop buying one brand of cold medication and switch to another on the advice of members of the reference group. Similarly, an individual may seek information from the reference group about one or more factors affecting a purchase decision, such as where to buy a certain product.

The degree to which a reference group affects a purchase decision depends on an individual's susceptibility to reference-group influence and the strength of involvement with the group. In addition, reference-group influence may affect the purchase decision, the brand decision, or both. For example, the purchase decision for frozen prepared dinners is affected by reference-group influence, but the brand decision for this product is not. Generally, the more conspicuous a product is, the more likely the brand decision will be influenced by reference groups.

6. Henry Assael, *Consumer Behavior and Marketing Action* (Boston: Kent Publishing Company, 1987), p. 369.

Children's Changing Roles Alter Their Buying Behavior

In some ways they are a marketer's dream. They have billions of dollars in discretionary income—and spend most of it. Although their individual purchases are small, they buy regularly, often in response to peer pressure. They are heavily influenced by the hours of television advertising they see each week. And, as a result of today's smaller families and the increase in the number of two-income households, they have more to say about family purchase decisions than ever before.

"They" are children, of course, a group whose spending habits are attracting the attention of more and more marketers. One recent study estimates that the thirty million U.S. children 4 to 12 years old receive about $4.7 billion annually from allowances, gifts, and odd jobs. Of that amount, they spend a total of $4.2 billion each year on snacks ($1.4 billion), toys and games ($1.1 billion), movies and sports ($771 million), video games ($766 million), and gifts ($164 million), engaging in some 280 independent purchase transactions annually. Children thirteen to nineteen account for even greater yearly expenditures: $30.5 billion of their own money.

But children's financial muscle does not end there. Researchers estimate that children directly influence more than $40 billion in adult purchases each year. A Nickelodeon/*USA Today*/Yankelovich Youth Monitor study found that children are extremely aware of brands and have considerable input into their parents' selections of apparel, cereal, snacks, cars, videocassette recorders, televisions, and personal computers. Many children are involved in actual household purchasing, especially food; in a recent Teenage Research study, half the teen girls surveyed reported shopping for groceries at least once a week. Recognizing this indirect purchasing power that children have, a growing number of marketers are approaching the youths directly. The National Dairy Board, for example, now airs milk commercials with youth appeal, and Procter & Gamble has developed a Crest for Kids toothpaste.

How did children acquire such buying clout? Researchers point to several factors. As the number of working couples and single-parent households increased, many parents shifted certain household responsibilities onto children's shoulders. Thrust into adult roles, children have ended up with more influence over the family's purchases, and they also tend to spend increased amounts of money themselves. In addition, many older, professional couples have fewer children. These parents can afford to lavish more on their children, including extra spending money for such items as Fisher-Price Toys' $225 children's camcorder and the My First Sony line of electronics gear for children. The bandwagon effect is yet another factor: when one marketer begins to focus on children, competitors follow suit, encouraging even more children's purchases. McDonald's Corp., for example, has aimed advertisements for its hamburgers, meal kits, and parties at children for years; now Hardee's Food Systems, Inc. and Wendy's International Inc. are doing the same.

Astute marketers realize that children actually represent three markets: current consumers, influential consumers, and future buyers. Because children are steadily developing brand awareness and product preferences that someday will translate into purchasing decisions, even companies not selling youth products per se are beginning to pay attention to children. Marketers are overcoming their traditional reluctance to sell directly to children, realizing that, out there somewhere, tomorrow's big-ticket customer is playing video games today.

SOURCES: "Children Come of Age as Consumers," *Marketing News,* Dec. 4, 1987, p. 6; Kim Foltz, "Kids as Consumers: Teaching Our Children Well," *Adweek,* Nov. 30, 1987, p. 40; Ellen Graham, "Children's Hour," *The Wall Street Journal,* Jan. 19, 1988, p. 1; James U. McNeal, *Children as Consumers* (Lexington, Mass.: Lexington Books, 1987); Noreen O'Leary, "Study Portrays Children as Complex, Savvy Media Mavens," *Adweek,* Nov. 30, 1987, p. 42.

A marketer sometimes tries to use reference-group influence in advertisements by suggesting that people in a specific group buy a product and are highly satisfied with it. In this type of appeal, the advertiser hopes that many people use the suggested group as a reference group and buy (or react more favorably to) the product. Whether or not this kind of advertising will be successful depends on three factors: how effectively the advertisement communicates the message, the type of product, and the individual's susceptibility to reference-group influence.

Social Classes

Within all societies, people rank others into higher and lower social positions of respect. This ranking results in social classes. A **social class** is an open group of individuals who have similar social rank. A class is referred to as "open" because people can move into and out of it. The criteria used to group people into classes vary from one society to another. In our society, we use many factors, including occupation, education, income, wealth, religion, race, ethnic group, and possessions. A person who is ranking someone does not necessarily apply all of a society's criteria. The number and the importance of the factors chosen depend on the characteristics of the individual being ranked and the values of the person who is doing the ranking.

To some degree, persons within social classes develop and assume common patterns of behavior. They may have similar attitudes, values, language patterns, and possessions. Social class influences many aspects of our lives. For example, it affects our chances of having children and their chances of surviving infancy. It influences our occupation, religion, childhood training, and educational attainment. Because social class affects so many aspects of a person's life, it also influences buying decisions.

The analyses of social class commonly divide people in our country into three to seven categories. The Coleman-Rainwater classification divides people into the following seven categories:[7]

1. UPPER AMERICANS
   a. *Upper-upper* (0.3 percent): The "capital S society" world of inherited wealth, aristocratic names
   b. *Lower-upper* (1.2 percent): The newer social elite, drawn from current professional, corporate leadership
   c. *Upper-middle* (12.5 percent): The rest of college graduate managers and professionals; lifestyle centers on private clubs, causes, and the arts
2. MIDDLE AMERICANS
   a. *Middle class* (32 percent): Average pay white-collar workers and their blue-collar friends; live on "the better side of town," try to "do the proper things"
   b. *Working class* (38 percent): Average pay blue-collar workers; lead "working class life style" whatever the income, school background, and job
3. LOWER AMERICANS
   a. *Lower class* (9 percent): Working, not on welfare; living standard is just above poverty
   b. *Lower-lower class* (7 percent): On welfare, visibly poverty stricken; often has no steady employment

Coleman suggests that for purposes of consumer analysis and mass marketing, the consuming public be divided into the four major status groups shown in Table 4.1, but he cautions marketers to remember that there is considerable diversity in people's life situations within each status group.

Social class determines to some extent the type, quality, and quantity of products that a person buys and uses. Social class also affects an individual's shopping patterns and the types of stores patronized. Advertisements, such as the one in Figure 4.6, sometimes are based on an appeal to a specific social class.

Culture and Subcultures

Culture is everything in our surroundings that is made by human beings. It consists of tangible items such as foods, furniture, buildings, clothing, and tools and intangible concepts such as education, welfare, and laws. Culture also includes the values and broad range of behaviors that are acceptable within a specific society. The concepts, values, and behavior that make up a culture are learned and passed on from one generation to the next.

Cultural influences have broad effects on buying behavior because they permeate our daily lives. Our culture determines what we wear and eat, where we reside and travel. It broadly affects how we buy and use products, and it influences our satisfaction from them. For example, in our culture, the problem of time scarcity is increasing because of the increase in the number of females who work and the current emphasis we place on physical and mental self-development. Many people do time-saving shopping and buy time-saving products to cope with this scarcity.[8]

7. Richard P. Coleman, "The Continuing Significance of Social Class in Marketing," *Journal of Consumer Research,* December 1983, p. 267.
8. Leonard L. Berry, "The Time Sharing Consumer," *Journal of Retailing,* Winter 1979, p. 69.

TABLE 4.1

Social class behavioral and purchasing characteristics

CLASS (% OF POPULATION)	BEHAVIORAL TRAITS	BUYING CHARACTERISTICS
Upper (14); includes upper-upper, lower-upper, uppermiddle	Income varies among the groups, but goals are the same Various lifestyles: preppy, conventional, intellectual, etc. Neighborhood and prestigious schooling important	Prize quality merchandise Favor prestigious brands Products purchased must reflect good taste Invest in art Spend money on travel, theater, books, and tennis, golf, and swimming clubs
Middle (32)	Often in management Considered white collar Prize good schools Desire an attractive home in a nice, well-maintained neighborhood Often emulate the upper class Enjoy travel and physical activity Often very involved in children's school and sports activities	Like fashionable items Consult experts via books, articles, etc. before purchasing Will spend for experiences they consider worthwhile for their children (e.g., ski trips, college education) Tour packages; weekend trips Attractive home furnishings
Working (38)	Emphasis on family, especially for economic and emotional supports (e.g., job opportunity tips, help in times of trouble) Blue collar Earn good incomes Enjoy mechanical items and recreational activities Enjoy leisure time after working hard	Buy vehicles and equipment related to recreation, camping, and selected sports Strong sense of value Will shop for best bargains at off-price and discount stores Automotive equipment for making repairs Enjoy local travel; recreational parks
Lower (16)	Often down and out through no fault of their own (e.g., layoffs, company takeovers) Can include individuals on welfare; the homeless Often have strong religious beliefs May be forced to live in less desirable neighborhoods In spite of their problems, often goodhearted toward others	Most products purchased are for survival Ability to convert good discards into usable items Enjoyment of everyday activities when possible

SOURCE: Adapted with permission from Richard P. Coleman, "The Continuing Significance of Social Class to Marketing," *Journal of Consumer Research*, 1983, 10 (December), pp. 265–280, with data from J. Paul Peter and Jerry C. Olson, *Consumer Behavior: Marketing Strategy Perspective* (Homewood, Ill.: Irwin, 1987), p. 433.

FIGURE 4.6

Product aimed at
specific social class
(SOURCE: Brainstorms
Advertising/Ft.
Lauderdale, FL)

Because culture, to some degree, determines how products are purchased and used, it in turn affects the development, promotion, distribution, and pricing of products. Food marketers, for example, have had to make a multitude of changes in their marketing efforts. Thirty years ago most families in our culture ate at least two meals a day together, and the mother devoted four to six hours a day to preparing those meals. Today, more than 60 percent of the women in the 25 to 54 age group are employed outside the home, and average family incomes have risen considerably. These two changes have led to changes in the national per capita consumption of certain foods.

When U.S. marketers sell products in other countries, they often see the tremendous impact that culture has on the purchase and use of products. International marketers find that people in other regions of the world have different attitudes, values, and needs, which in turn call for different methods of doing business as well as different types of marketing mixes. Some international marketers fail because they do not or cannot adjust to cultural differences. The effect of culture on international marketing programs is discussed in greater detail in Chapter 22.

On the basis of geographic regions or human characteristics, such as age or ethnic background, a culture can be divided into **subcultures.** In our country, we have a number of different subcultures: West Coast, teen-age, and German, for example. Within subcultures there are even greater similarities in people's attitudes, values, and actions than within the broader culture. Relative to other subcultures, individuals in a certain subculture may have stronger preferences for certain types of clothing, furniture, or foods. For example, there is a greater per capita consumption of rice among southerners than among New Englanders or midwesterners.

Marketers must recognize that even though their operations are confined to the United States, to one state, or even to one city, subcultural differences may dictate considerable variations in what, how, and when people buy. To deal effectively with these differences, marketers may have to alter their product, promotion, distribution systems, or price to satisfy members of particular subcultures.

Understanding Consumer Behavior

Many marketers try to understand buyer behavior so that they can give consumers greater satisfaction. Yet there is still a certain amount of customer dissatisfaction. Some marketers have not adopted the marketing concept, so they are not consumer oriented and do not regard customer satisfaction as a primary objective. Also, because the tools for analyzing consumer behavior are imprecise, marketers may not be able to determine accurately what is highly satisfying to buyers. Finally, even if marketers know what increases consumer satisfaction, they may not be able to provide it.

Understanding consumer behavior is an important task for marketers. Even though consumer behavior research has not provided all the knowledge that marketers need, progress has been made during the last twenty years and is likely to continue in the next twenty years. Not only will refinements in research methods yield more information about consumer behavior, but the pressure of an increasingly competitive business environment will increase marketers' needs for a greater understanding of consumer decision processes.

Summary

Buyers' reactions to a firm's marketing strategy or strategies have great impact on the firm's success. Understanding buying behavior is thus essential for creating a marketing mix that satisfies customers.

Consumer buying behavior refers to the behavior of ultimate consumers—those who purchase products for personal or household use, not for business purposes. The three types of consumer decision making are (1) routine response decision making, used for frequently purchased, low-cost items that require very little search and decision effort; (2) limited decision making, used for products that are purchased occasionally or when a buyer needs to acquire information about an unfamiliar brand in a familiar product category; and (3) extensive decision making, used for purchasing an unfamiliar expensive product or an infrequently bought item.

The five parts of the consumer buying decision process are problem recognition, information search, evaluation of alternatives, purchase, and postpurchase evaluation. Problem recognition occurs when a buyer becomes aware that there is a difference between a desired state and an actual condition. Consumers search for information about such factors as availability of brands, product features, seller characteristics, warranties, and prices. To evaluate alternatives, the consumer establishes criteria based on the information search and uses them to compare product characteristics. When the consumer buys the product, the purchase is completed. After the purchase, the buyer uses postpurchase evaluation to assess the product. The buyer may experience cognitive dissonance, which is dissatisfaction because the buyer questions whether the purchase should have been made at all.

The consumer buying decision process can be affected by three categories of factors: person-specific, psychological, and social. A person-specific factor is one unique to a particular individual. Two categories of person-specific factors are demographic factors, such as age, sex, race, and nationality, and situational factors, which are the set of circumstances or conditions that exist when a consumer is making a purchase decision.

Psychological influences are perception, motives, learning, attitudes, and personality. Perception is the process by which an individual selects, organizes, and interprets information inputs to create meaning. Motives are internal energizing forces that orient a person's activities toward personal goals; they sometimes are researched through interviews and projective techniques. Learning consists of changes in one's behavior that are caused by information and experience. An attitude consists of knowledge and positive or negative feelings about an object. Personality is an internal structure in which experience and behavior are related in an orderly way.

The main social influences on consumer behavior are roles and family influences, reference groups, social classes, and cultural and subcultural forces. A role is a set of actions and activities that a person in a particular position is supposed to perform. A reference group is a group with which an individual identifies so much that the person takes on the values, attitudes, and behaviors of group members. A social class is an open aggregate of people with similar social rank. Culture is everything in our surroundings that is made by human beings. A culture consists of several subcultures. Both cultural and subcultural forces influence people's buying behavior.

Important Terms

Buying behavior
Consumer buying behavior
Routine response behavior
Limited decision making
Extensive decision making
Consumer buying decision process
Cognitive dissonance
Person-specific factor
Demographic factors
Situational factors
Psychological influences
Perception
Information inputs

Selective exposure
Selective distortion
Selective retention
Self-concept
Motive
Patronage motives
Depth interview
Group interview
Projective techniques
Learning
Attitude
Attitude scale
Personality

Social influences
Role
Reference group
Social class

Culture
Subcultures

Discussion and Review Questions

1. Why do we think of consumers as decision makers when we analyze buyer behavior?
2. What are the types of decision making consumers use?
3. What are the major stages in the consumer buying decision process? Are all these stages used in all consumer purchase decisions?
4. How do person-specific influences affect the consumer buying decision process?
5. How does perception influence buyer behavior?
6. How do motives influence a person's buying decisions?
7. What is the role of learning in a consumer's purchasing decision process?
8. How do marketers attempt to shape consumers' learning?
9. Why are marketers concerned about consumer attitudes?
10. How do roles affect a person's buying behavior?
11. Describe reference groups. How do they influence buying behavior?
12. In what ways does social class affect a person's purchase decisions?
13. What is culture? How does it affect a person's buying behavior?
14. Describe your own subculture. Identify buying behavior that is unique to your subculture.

Cases

4.1 First Bank & Trust

First Bank & Trust is located in a medium-sized city. In total deposits, First Bank is third among the six banks in the trade area. Top-level managers of First Bank are not happy about being number three. They want to attract new accounts and have placed much of the responsibility for attaining this goal on Sandra Stinson, vice president of marketing.

To develop a strategy to attract new customer accounts, Stinson, with the help of an independent research company, conducted a telephone survey of residents in the trade area. The group of respondents included both First Bank customers and customers at other banks. The survey focused on (1) residents' attitudes regarding general features of the banks in the area and (2) residents' attitudes regarding the relative importance of several characteristics when selecting a bank. Table 4.2 shows the percentage of respondents who answered with various banks' names when questioned about several general features such as size and strength. Responses regarding the importance of certain characteristics when selecting a bank are in Table 4.3.

GENERAL FEATURES	AMER-ICAN STATE BANK	CITI-ZENS BANK	CAPI-TAL BANK	CITY NATIONAL BANK	FIRST BANK & TRUST	GUARANTY NATIONAL BANK	OTHER	DON'T KNOW	TOTAL
Largest bank	17.0	0.4	1.4	3.2	7.0	59.8	0.4	10.8	100.0
Strongest bank	18.0	1.0	1.6	3.8	5.8	37.4	0.4	32.0	100.0
Bank with most convenient locations	14.2	2.4	7.2	11.2	15.2	33.2	2.2	14.4	100.0
Most progressive bank	19.0	2.6	3.0	2.8	8.2	41.0	0.6	22.8	100.0
Bank catering to the young	24.0	19.8	6.6	3.0	10.6	12.0	0.8	23.2	100.0
Bank for everyone	10.6	2.0	1.4	3.0	6.0	20.0	4.2	52.8	100.0

TABLE 4.2

Percent of responses regarding general bank characteristics

Questions for Discussion

1. Will the information in Tables 4.2 and 4.3 be useful to Stinson in her efforts to attract new customers? What additional information does she need? Why?
2. Which data in Tables 4.2 and 4.3 are most important for developing a strategy to attract new accounts? Why?
3. On the basis of these findings, what recommendations might Stinson make?

4.2 Beef Industry Council Tries to Change Attitudes[9]

Once a staple in the American diet, beef has lost favor with many health-conscious consumers in recent years. Between 1975 and 1985, per capita consumption of beef dropped by 33 percent as Americans turned increasingly to chicken and fish. At 78.8 pounds per person, poultry consumption this year is expected to top beef purchases (by 5 pounds) for the first time ever. But the beef industry is now fighting back, spending $29 million dollars this year to persuade consumers that red meat, trimmed of excess fat, can be just as lean and nutritious as white meat.

9. Based on information from Cathy Cohn, John Morse, and Patrick Geoghegan, "More Cash, More Pizzazz Could Spell Relief for Beef," *Supermarket News,* Jan. 19, 1987, pp. 12–13; Patrick Geoghegan, "$21 Million Earmarked to End Beef Sales Slump," *Supermarket News,* Nov. 17, 1986, p. 1; Annetta Miller, "And Now, Designer Beef," *Newsweek,* Mar. 10, 1986, p. 57; Annetta Miller, "A Sizzling Food Fight," *Newsweek,* Apr. 20, 1987, p. 56; Eileen Norris, "Beef Council Leans on Point-of-Purchase," *Advertising Age,* Aug. 15, 1985, p. 32.

BANK FEATURES	VERY IMPORTANT	SOMEWHAT IMPORTANT	NOT IMPORTANT	DON'T KNOW	TOTAL
Convenient to home	76.0	14.8	9.2	0.0	100.0
Convenient to work	46.4	21.8	31.6	0.2	100.0
New building	11.0	15.4	72.8	0.8	100.0
Travel department	8.8	17.6	67.2	6.4	100.0
Financial counseling	37.4	28.6	31.4	2.6	100.0
Financial strength	66.2	16.8	12.4	4.6	100.0
Weekend banking services	37.2	24.6	37.2	1.0	100.0
Evening banking hours	48.4	29.6	21.8	0.2	100.0
Drive-in windows	59.0	23.8	16.6	0.6	100.0
Bank credit card	31.6	22.8	43.8	1.8	100.0
Free checking accounts	56.2	19.8	22.8	1.2	100.0
Gives premiums such as stamps or gifts	14.6	15.6	68.8	1.0	100.0
Ease in acquiring loans	44.4	26.4	26.8	2.4	100.0
Twenty-four-hour cash machines	25.6	19.8	47.8	6.8	100.0

TABLE 4.3

Percent of responses regarding the importance of selected bank characteristics

Administered by the Beef Industry Council, this year's promotional effort follows the successful "Beef Gives Strength" point-of-purchase campaign, which helped raise beef sales 16 percent in participating stores several years ago. The new campaign, "Real Food for Real People," features spokespersons James Garner and Cybill Shepherd in television, radio, and print advertisements. In one advertisement, for example, Shepherd muses that the craving for a hamburger must be a basic human instinct. The advertisements coincide with in-store promotions that stress beef's flavor and versatility. The campaign also extends the industry's popular Nutri-Facts program, a series of consumer brochures and placards that emphasize beef cuts containing less than 200 calories and provide information about beef's fat, cholesterol, sodium, and protein contents.

The beef industry is aiming most of its current marketing efforts toward two market segments in particular: consumers who have active lifestyles and those who consider themselves health-conscious. A recent survey found that these two groups together make up 50 percent of the market and are the consumers least likely to eat beef. (The three other groups identified—meat lovers, creative cooks, and price-driven consumers—have positive attitudes toward beef and continue to buy it, according to the survey.) Consumers who seldom or never buy beef are usually between the ages of 25 and 54, have above-average levels of education, earn at least $30,000 annually, and are likely to hold professional, technical, or managerial positions. Because other groups observe and sometimes try to imitate these consumers, the beef industry considers their attitudes critical and is directing 80 percent of the campaign's first-year budget at them.

To boost demand for beef in individual stores, retailers are supplementing the industrywide promotion with marketing efforts of their own. For example, during the past five years, most major retailers have successfully reduced the fat trim on beef cuts from one-half to one-quarter inch. Some meat experts believe that eventually one-eighth inch will be standard. The ninety-store P&C Food Market chain based in Syracuse, New York, sells convenience to its shoppers via smaller beef packages for smaller households, precut beef for stir-fry cooking, and prestuffed meats and peppers. In its meat departments, P&C also has tested informational videos, which are accompanied by beef recipes and other printed materials for shoppers to take home. The company reports that beef sales remain stable.

The industry also is counting on technology to help meet the demand for new tastes. The Agriculture Department's new category for light beef—which is at least 25 percent leaner than standard cuts and can be advertised by brand name—has already brought several new beef products to market. One of the first, Key Lite, produced by Texas-based Chianina Lite Beef, Inc., is said to taste as good as choice grade beef, with 36 percent fewer calories. Ranchers in several western states are experimenting with low-cholesterol beef, produced without chemicals. Last year Colorado rancher Mel Coleman shipped 20,000 head of "all-natural" cattle raised on pesticide-free corn and alfalfa. Marketed as Coleman Natural Beef, the meat is produced without hormones, growth stimulants, or antibiotics and is available in New York, California, Texas, Colorado, and Massachusetts.

Although meat retailers acknowledge that brand-name and natural beef products may reassure skeptical consumers, resulting in consumer brand loyalty and higher sales for packers, they also point out that the new cuts are usually more expensive than standard beef, which may drive other consumers away. Some retailers believe that the prices of branded beef will drop as sales build.

Questions for Discussion

1. Is it feasible for the Beef Industry Council to change buyers' attitudes toward the consumption of beef? Explain your answer.
2. Assess the Beef Industry Council's decision to focus on the two market segments: active lifestyle and health-conscious.
3. Will the higher price of branded beef reduce the demand for it among those people in the Beef Industry Council's current target markets?

5. Organizational Markets and Buying Behavior

O B J E C T I V E S

▶ To become aware of the various types of organizational markets.

▶ To identify the major characteristics of organizational buyers and transactions.

▶ To understand several attributes of organizational or industrial demand.

▶ To become familiar with the major components of a buying center.

▶ To understand the major stages of the organizational buying decision process and the factors that affect this process.

*I*t *is 180 times sweeter* than sugar, but taste is not the only thing remarkable about NutraSweet® brand sweetener (see Figure 5.1).

Consider, for example, that the low-calorie product was developed by the pharmaceutical house, G. D. Searle & Co., which had no previous experience with sweeteners. Yet once the new sweetener was available commercially, its impact on the diet soft-drink industry was so powerful that it has become the only sweetener used in 90 percent of all diet drinks. To top it off, now The NutraSweet Company says its product will soon help dieters take the calories out of cakes and cookies. Little wonder that—after only seven years on the market—annual sales of Nutra-Sweet exceed $700 million, with no slowdown in sight.

Known generically as aspartame, NutraSweet is contained in hundreds of products worldwide. In the United States, NutraSweet has been approved by the Food and Drug Administration and is used as an ingredient in more than 500 products, many of which are soft drinks. The number of new products containing NutraSweet brand sweetener has almost doubled in the last two years alone. Manufacturers of cold breakfast cereals, powdered soft drinks, sweetened seltzers, hot beverages, gelatin products, and laxatives have been using the sweetener for some time, and a tabletop version of NutraSweet is marketed under the brand name EQUAL®. As a result of recent FDA approval, NutraSweet is now available in several new food and beverage categories as well. For example, the sweetener is used by The Coca-Cola Company and General Foods Corporation in a variety of beverages and desserts. Warner-Lambert Company now adds NutraSweet to its breath mints, and the product is included in Lipton ready-to-drink teas.

In addition, the NutraSweet Company (now a subsidiary of Monsanto) is awaiting regulatory approval so it can incorporate NutraSweet brand sweetener into commercially baked goods and mixes. Until recently, NutraSweet tended to break down under the high heat of baking. But now the Company says it has come up with a method of encapsulating the sweetener, so that its sweetening properties can be released just at the end of baking. By using bulking agents currently available as well as those which may be developed in the future that can duplicate sugar's volume and texture in baked goods, the market for both NutraSweet brand sweetener and commercially prepared baked goods may increase dramatically.

Though executives of The NutraSweet Company like to point out the inherent market appeal of their low-calorie sweetener, they also say that hard work on several fronts is responsible for much of the product's success. For instance, the firm has established a food-applications department to help beverage companies and other customers develop product formulations using NutraSweet. A regulatory affairs staff works with industrial customers and government agencies. A scientific affairs group answers inquiries and monitors health and safety issues. Dietitians handle consumer questions from 9 A.M. to 3 P.M. on a special toll-free telephone line. The Company has also used advertising and various promotional activities to increase consumer awareness of the product.

True, the Company will have to stay on its marketing toes. Its U.S. patent on aspartame runs out in 1992 (the Canadian patent has already expired), and both Pfizer and Johnson & Johnson are currently working on sweeteners of their own. Still, the number of potential uses for NutraSweet appears almost endless.[1]

T HE WIDESPREAD USE of NutraSweet sweetener is partly due to the NutraSweet organization's use of effective marketing efforts. NutraSweet is an example of a company that serves organizational markets; it does not deal with consumers directly. An organizational market is defined in Chapter 3 as consisting of individuals or groups that purchase a specific type of product for resale, for use in producing other products, or for use in day-to-day operations. In this chapter we look closer at organizational markets and organizational buying decision processes. We first discuss the various kinds of organizational markets and the types of buyers that make up these markets. Next we explore several dimensions of organizational buying, including the attributes of organizational transactions, the characteristics and concerns of organizational buyers, the methods of organizational buying, and the characteristics of demand for products sold to organizational purchasers. Finally, we examine organizational buying decisions by considering who makes organizational purchases and how the decisions are made.

Types of Organizational Buyers

In Chapter 3 we identify four major kinds of organizational markets: producer, reseller, government, and institutional. The following section discusses the characteristics of the customers that make up these markets.

Producer Markets Individuals and business organizations that purchase products for the purpose of making a profit by using them to produce other products or by using them in their

---

1. Based on information from "Company Welcomes New Aspartame Uses," *Journal of Commerce,* Dec. 1, 1986, p. 10A; Gary A. Hemphill, "NutraSweet: A Swirl of Success," *Beverage Industry,* June 1986, pp. 28–29; Kate Mahar, "Sweeteners' Quest for Stability Goes On," *Beverage Industry,* June 1987, p. 1; "Making 'Lite' of Frozen Desserts," *Prepared Foods,* August 1987, p. 150; Wendy Wall, "Monsanto's NutraSweet Unit Is Seeking Approval to Use Baked-Goods Sweetener," *The Wall Street Journal,* Oct. 23, 1987, p. 32.

operations are classified as **producer markets.** Producer markets include buyers of raw materials as well as purchasers of semifinished and finished items used to produce other products. For example, grocery stores and supermarkets are part of the producer markets for numerous support products such as paper bags, counters, scanners, and floor care products. Farmers are part of the producer markets for farm machinery, fertilizer, seed, and livestock. A broad array of industries make up producer markets, including, besides agriculture, forestry, fisheries, mining, construction, transportation, communications, and utilities. As the data in Table 5.1 indicate, the number of business units in national producer markets is enormous.

Manufacturers are geographically concentrated. More than half are located in only seven states: New York, California, Pennsylvania, Illinois, Ohio, New Jersey, and Michigan. This concentration sometimes enables an industrial marketer to serve customers more efficiently. Within certain states, production in only a few industries may account for a sizable proportion of total industrial output.

Reseller Markets

Reseller markets consist of intermediaries, such as wholesalers and retailers, who buy finished goods and resell them to make a profit. (Wholesalers and retailers are discussed in Chapters 10 and 11.) Other than making minor alterations, resellers do not change the physical characteristics of the products they handle. With the exception of items that producers sell directly to consumers, all products sold to consumer markets are first sold to reseller markets.

Wholesalers purchase products for resale to retailers, to other wholesalers, and to producers, governments, and institutions. Of the 337,943 wholesalers in the United States, a large percentage are located in New York, California, Illinois, Texas, Ohio, Pennsylvania, and New Jersey.[2] Although some expensive, highly technical products are sold directly to end users, many products are sold through wholesalers who, in turn, sell products to other firms in the distribution system. Thus wholesalers are very important in helping a producer's product be accepted by users. Wholesalers often carry a huge number of products, perhaps as many as 250,000 items. When inventories are vast, the reordering of products normally is automated and the wholesaler's initial purchase decisions are made by professional buyers and buying committees.

2. *Statistical Abstract of the United States,* 1988, p. 745.

TABLE 5.1

Number of firms in industry groups

INDUSTRY	NUMBER OF FIRMS
Agriculture, forestry, fishing	3,524,000
Mining	251,000
Construction	1,758,000
Manufacturing	622,000
Transportation, public utilities	721,000
Finance, insurance, real estate	2,272,000
Services	6,220,000

SOURCE: *Statistical Abstract of the United States,* 1988, p. 496.

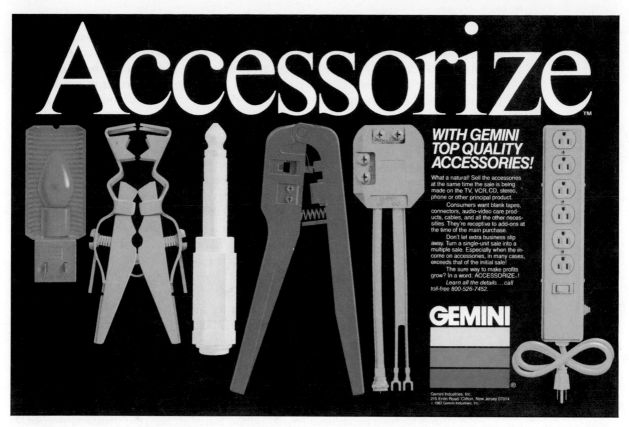

FIGURE 5.2

Promotion of accessory items aimed at electronics resellers (SOURCE: Gemini Industries, Inc.)

Retailers purchase products and resell them to final consumers. There are approximately 1,330,000 retailers in the United States. They employ about sixteen million people and generate close to $1 trillion in annual sales.[3] Some retailers carry a large number of items. Drugstores, for example, may stock up to 12,000 items, and some supermarkets may handle as many as 20,000 different products. In small family owned retail stores, the owner frequently makes purchasing decisions. Large department stores have one or more employees in each department who are responsible for buying products for that department. For chain stores, a buyer or buying committee in the central office frequently decides whether a product will be available in the firm's stores. But, for most products, local store management makes the actual buying decisions for its particular store.

When making purchase decisions, resellers consider several factors. They evaluate the level of demand for a product to determine in what quantity and at what prices the product can be resold. They assess the amount of space required to handle a product relative to its potential profit. Retailers, for example, sometimes evaluate products on the basis of sales per square foot of selling area. Often, customers depend on a reseller to have a product when they need it, so a reseller typically evaluates a supplier's ability to provide adequate quantities when and where needed. Resellers also consider the ease of placing orders and the availability of technical assistance and training programs from the producer. (The Gemini

3. Ibid, p. 739.

advertisement in Figure 5.2 is aimed at resellers and addresses profitability.) More broadly, when resellers consider the purchase of a product not previously carried, they try to determine whether the product competes with or complements products the firm is currently handling. These types of concerns distinguish reseller markets from other markets. Markets dealing with reseller markets must recognize these needs and be able to serve them.

Government Markets

Federal, state, county, and local governments make up **government markets.** They spend billions of dollars annually for a variety of goods and services to support their internal operations and to provide citizens with such products as highways, education, water, national defense, and energy. For example, in 1985, the federal government spent more than $240 billion on defense, about $14 billion on health, and about $13 billion on education.[4] Governmental expenditures annually account for about 20 percent of this country's gross national product.

In addition to the federal government, there are 50 state governments, 3,042 county governments, and 83,166 other local governments.[5] The amount spent by federal, state, and local units during the last thirty years has increased rapidly because the total number of government units and the services they provide have both increased. In addition, the costs of providing these services have increased. In Table 5.2, notice that the federal government spends more than half of the total amount spent by all governments.

The types and quantities of products government markets purchase reflect societal demands on various government agencies. As citizens' needs for government services change, so does the demand for products by government markets. Because government agencies spend public funds to buy the products needed to provide services, they are accountable to the public. This accountability explains their relatively complex set of buying procedures. Some firms do not even try to sell to government buyers because they do not want to deal with so much red tape. However, many marketers learn to deal efficiently with government procedures and do not find them a stumbling block. For certain products, such as defense-related items, the government may be the only customer. The U.S. Government Printing Office publishes and distributes several documents explaining buying procedures and describing the types of products various federal agencies purchase.

Government purchases are made through bids or negotiated contracts. To make a sale under the bid system, a firm must appear on a list of qualified bidders. When a government unit wants to buy, it sends out a detailed description of the products to qualified bidders. Businesses that wish to sell such products submit bids. The government unit usually is required to accept the lowest acceptable bid.

When buying nonstandard or highly complex products, a government unit often uses a negotiated contract. Under this procedure, the government unit selects only a few firms and then negotiates specifications and terms; it eventually awards the contract to one of the negotiating firms. Most large defense-related purchases are made through negotiated contracts.

Although government markets can have complicated requirements, they can also be very lucrative. When the Postal Service, Social Security Administration, and

4. *Statistical Abstract of the United States,* 1988, p. 258.
5. Ibid, p. 256.

TABLE 5.2

Annual expenditures by government units for selected years (in billions of dollars)

YEAR	TOTAL GOVERNMENT EXPENDITURES	FEDERAL GOVERNMENT EXPENDITURES	STATE AND LOCAL EXPENDITURES
1960	151	90	61
1970	333	185	148
1975	560	292	268
1980	959	526	432
1981	1,110	625	485
1983	1,351	786	565
1985	1,581	799	782

SOURCE: *Statistical Abstract of the United States*, 1988, p. 258.

other government agencies modernize obsolete computer systems, successful bidders can gain a billion dollars over the life of a contract, usually five years or more. Some firms have established separate departments to facilitate marketing to government units.

Institutional Markets

Organizations that seek to achieve other than normal business goals, such as profit, market share, or return on investment, constitute **institutional markets.** Members of institutional markets include churches, some hospitals, civic clubs, fraternities, sororities, charitable organizations, and foundations. Institutions purchase millions of dollars' worth of products annually to provide goods, services, and ideas to congregations, students, patients, club members, and others. Because institutions often have different goals and fewer resources than other types of organizations, marketers may use special marketing activities to serve these markets.

Dimensions of Organizational Buying

Having gained an understanding of the different types of organizational customers, we need to consider several dimensions of organizational buying. Now we examine several characteristics of organizational transactions. Then we discuss several attributes of organizational buyers and some of their primary concerns when making purchase decisions. Next we consider methods of organizational buying and the major types of purchases. We conclude the section with a discussion of how the demand for industrial products differs from the demand for consumer products.

Characteristics of Organizational or Industrial Transactions

Organizational or industrial transactions differ from consumer sales in several ways. Orders by organizational buyers tend to be much larger than individual consumer sales. Suppliers often must sell their products in large quantities to make profits; they therefore prefer not to sell to customers who place small orders.

Organizational purchases are generally negotiated less frequently than are consumer sales. Some purchases involve large, expensive items, such as capital equipment, that are used for a number of years. Other products, such as raw materials and component items, are used continuously in production and may have to be supplied frequently. However, the contract regarding the terms of sale and supply for these items is likely to be a long-term agreement, requiring negotiations, for example, every third year.

In addition to infrequent sales negotiations, long negotiating periods may be needed to complete organizational sales. Purchasing decisions are often made by a committee, orders are frequently large and expensive, and products may be custom-built. There is a good chance that several people or departments in the purchasing organization will be involved. One department might express a need for a product, a second department might develop its specifications, a third might stipulate the maximum amount to be spent, and a fourth might actually place the order.

One practice unique to organizational sales is **reciprocity,** an arrangement in which two organizations agree to buy from each other. Reciprocal agreements that threaten competition are illegal. The Federal Trade Commission and the Justice Department take action to stop reciprocal practices judged to be anticompetitive. However, a considerable amount of "innocent" reciprocal dealing occurs among small businesses, especially in the service industries. Some larger corporations engage in informal reciprocity to a lesser extent.[6] Because reciprocity forces or strongly influences purchasing agents to deal only with certain suppliers, its use can lower morale among agents and lead to less than optimal purchases.

Attributes of Organizational Buyers

We usually think of organizational or industrial buyers as being more rational than ultimate consumers in their purchasing behavior because, compared with ultimate consumers, organizational buyers are informed about the products they purchase or they seek more information before purchasing. This assumption is not unfounded. To make purchasing decisions that fulfill an organization's needs, organizational buyers demand detailed information about products' functional features and technical specifications.

Marketers may try to appeal to the assumed rationality of organizational buyers. Despite the assumption of rational behavior, however, personal goals still influence organizational buying behavior. Most organizational purchasing agents seek the psychological satisfaction that comes with organizational advancement and financial rewards. Agents who consistently exhibit rational organizational buying behavior are likely to attain these personal goals because they are performing their jobs in ways that help their firms achieve organizational objectives. Suppose, though, that an organizational buyer develops a close friendship with a certain supplier. If the buyer values friendship more than organizational promotion or financial rewards, he or she may behave irrationally from the firm's point of view. Dealing exclusively with that supplier regardless of better prices, product qualities, or services from competitors may indicate an unhealthy alliance between the buyer and seller.

6. E. Robert Finney, "Reciprocity: Gone but Not Forgotten," *Journal of Marketing,* January 1978, p. 55.

Primary Concerns of Organizational Buyers

Organizational customers consider various factors when they make purchasing decisions. Many of their primary considerations relate to quality level, service, or price.

Most organizational customers try to achieve and maintain a specific level of quality in the products they offer to their target markets. To accomplish this goal, they often buy their products on the basis of a set of expressed characteristics, commonly called *specifications*. Thus, an organizational buyer evaluates the quality of the products being considered to determine whether they meet specifications.

Meeting specifications is extremely important to organizational customers. Amoco's advertisement in Figure 5.3 details polypropylene's uses and properties so that a potential customer can more adequately evaluate the product relative to required specifications. If a product fails to meet specifications and its use results in a final product that malfunctions for the ultimate consumer, the organizational customer may become disenchanted with the product and switch to a different supplier. On the other hand, organizational customers are ordinarily cautious about buying products that exceed specifications because such products frequently cost more and thus increase an organization's production costs.

Service is also important to organizational buyers. The services offered by suppliers directly and indirectly influence organizational customers' costs, sales, and

FIGURE 5.3

Applications promoted to organizational buyers (SOURCE: Amoco Chemical Company)

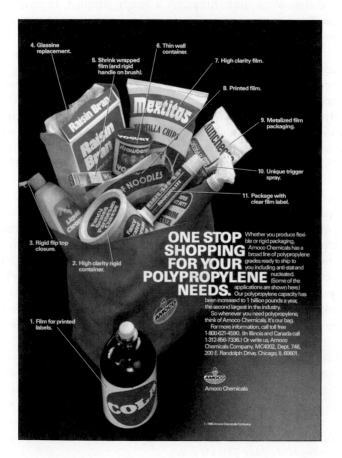

profits. When tangible goods are the same or quite similar—as is the case with most raw materials—the goods may be sold at the same price in the same kind of containers and may have the same specifications. Under such conditions the mix of supplier services is likely to be the major avenue by which an organizational marketer can gain a competitive advantage. Specific services vary in importance, but those commonly desired include market information, inventory maintenance, on-time delivery, repair services and replacement parts, and credit. Organizational buyers are likely to need technical product information, data regarding demand, information about general economic conditions, or supply and delivery information. Maintaining an inventory is critical because it helps make products accessible when an organizational buyer needs them and reduces the buyer's inventory requirements and costs. On-time delivery is crucial to organizational buyers because it is usually their responsibility to have the products available and ready for use when needed. By providing reliable, on-time delivery, organizational marketers enable customers to carry less safety stock, thus reducing the customers' costs. Organizational purchasers of machinery are especially concerned about obtaining repair services and replacement parts quickly because inoperable equipment is costly.

Availability of credit can improve an organizational customer's cash flow and reduce the peaks and valleys of capital requirements, which, in turn, lower the firm's cost of capital. Although a single supplier cannot provide every possible service to its organizational customers, a marketing-oriented supplier strives to create the service mix that best satisfies the target market.

Price is obviously important to an organizational customer because it influences operating costs and costs of goods sold, and these costs affect the customer's selling price and profit margin. When purchasing capital equipment, an industrial buyer views the price as the amount of investment necessary to obtain a certain level of return or savings. Thus, an organizational purchaser is likely to compare the price of a machine with the value of the benefits that the machine will yield. For example, the automated inserting systems advertised in Figure 5.4 are being promoted on the basis of speed, efficiency, and control. An organizational buyer does not compare alternative products strictly by price; other factors, such as product quality and supplier services, are also important elements of the purchase decision. A study of more than one hundred business and medical equipment markets (including copying and data processing) found that the most important factors in user selection of equipment involved customer service, including equipment reliability, quality of performance, ease of operation, field service response time, and cost of service.[7] As indicated in the Application on page 161, Merck & Co., Inc., a pharmaceutical manufacturer, has changed its marketing efforts to better serve organizational markets.

Methods of Organizational Buying

Although no two organizational buyers go about their jobs in the same way, most use one or more of the following purchase methods: *description, inspection, sampling,* or *negotiation.* When the products being purchased are commonly standardized according to certain characteristics (e.g., size, shape, weight, and color) and

7. Dick Berry, "Industrial Marketers Use 'Secret Weapon' Consumer Services for Marketing Success," *Marketing News,* May 1, 1981. p. 8.

are normally graded using such standards, an organizational buyer may be able to purchase simply by describing or specifying quantity, grade, and other attributes. Agricultural commodities often fall into this category. Purchases through description are especially common between a buyer and seller who have established an ongoing relationship built on trust.

Certain products—large industrial equipment, used vehicles, and buildings, for example—have unique characteristics and may vary regarding their condition. A particular used truck might have a bad transmission. Thus, organizational buyers of such products must base their purchase decisions on inspection.

In buying based on sampling, a sample of the product is taken from the lot and evaluated. It is assumed that the characteristics of this sample represent the entire lot. This method may be appropriate when the product is highly homogeneous—grain, for example—and examination of the entire lot is not technically or economically feasible.

Some industrial purchasing relies on negotiated contracts. In certain instances an organizational buyer describes exactly what is needed and then asks sellers to submit bids. The buyer may take the most attractive bids and negotiate with those suppliers. In other cases, the buyer may not be able to identify specifically what is to be purchased but can provide only a general description, as might be the case for a special piece of custom-made equipment. A buyer and seller might negotiate a contract that specifies a base price and contains provisions for the payment of additional costs and fees. These contracts are most likely to be used for one-time projects such as buildings and capital equipment.

Types of Organizational Purchases

Most organizational purchases are one of three types: new-task purchase, modified rebuy purchase, or straight rebuy purchase. In a **new-task purchase,** an organization makes an initial purchase of an item to be used to perform a new job or to solve a new problem. A new-task purchase may require the development of product specifications, vendor specifications, and procedures for future purchases of that product. To make the initial purchase, the organizational buyer usually needs much information. A new-task purchase is important to a supplier because if the organizational buyer is satisfied with the product, the supplier may be able to sell the buyer large quantities of the product for a period of years.

In a **modified rebuy purchase,** a new-task purchase is changed the second or third time it is ordered or the requirements associated with a straight rebuy purchase are modified. For example, an organizational buyer might seek faster delivery, lower prices, or a different quality level of product specifications. A modified rebuy situation may cause regular suppliers to become more aggressive and competitive to keep the account. Other competing suppliers may have the opportunity to obtain the business.

A **straight rebuy purchase** occurs when a buyer purchases the same products routinely under approximately the same terms of sale. Buyers require little information for these routine purchase decisions. The buyer tends to use familiar suppliers that have provided satisfactory service and products in the past. These suppliers try to set up automatic reordering systems to make reordering easy and convenient for organizational buyers. A supplier may even monitor the organizational buyer's inventory and indicate to the buyer what needs to be ordered.

Demand for Industrial Products

Products sold to organizational customers are called industrial products. The demand for these products is referred to as industrial demand. Unlike consumer demand, industrial demand is (1) derived, (2) inelastic, (3) joint, and (4) more fluctuating. As we discuss each of these characteristics, remember that the demand for different types of industrial products varies.

Derived Demand The demand for industrial products is **derived demand** because organizational customers purchase products to be used directly or indirectly in the production of goods and services to satisfy consumers' needs. Therefore the demand for industrial products derives from the demand for consumer products. In the long run, no industrial demand is totally unrelated to the demand for consumer goods.

The derived nature of industrial demand is usually multilevel. Industrial sellers at different levels are affected by a change in consumer demand for a particular product. For example, a few years ago, fiber makers were turning out large quantities of doubleknits. When consumers stopped buying doubleknits, the demand for equipment used in manufacturing doubleknits also dropped. Therefore factors

Merck Serves Changing Organizational Markets

Ten years ago, explains an executive at Merck & Co., Inc., the New Jersey-based pharmaceutical firm, the company's strategy for marketing and distributing its products was fairly simple. By directing most of its promotional efforts at physicians—who generated product demand by writing prescriptions—Merck could boost sales to its real customers, the pharmacists, either directly or through wholesalers. Even in hospitals, physicians were still Merck's primary target market because they made most of the pharmaceutical purchasing decisions.

But in today's health-care environment, say Merck officials, a different marketing approach is called for, largely because the industry is scrambling to contain costs and thus involving more groups in the purchasing process. For example, Merck now communicates not only with doctors but with insurers and government administrators, who pay most of the country's medical bills and are directly concerned with the efficiency of providers. In addition, Merck markets to the new providers—health maintenance organizations, preferred provider organizations, and ambulatory care centers—that have emerged as direct competitors of hospitals and private physicians. The company also promotes its products to pharmacists, whose input has become more important with the proliferation of brand-name, generic, and imported pharmaceuticals. Merck has even addressed a few patients directly and expects to do more of this in the future.

Merck's marketing objective, in short, is now twofold: to communicate to a wide variety of customer groups and to get out the message that its products are safe, effective, *and* economical. Merck, named "most admired corporation" by *Fortune* magazine last year, achieves this objective through painstaking market research, market segmentation, and careful allocation of promotional resources. The company also studies the relationships between its pharmaceuticals and other aspects of treatment so that each product can be marketed as part of a treatment "system."

Consider, for example, the launching several years ago of Merck's injectable antibiotic Mefoxin, intended for use in hospitals. Because of the fact that hospital pharmacies spend more on antibiotics than any other single group of drugs, Merck knew that hospital cost-cutters would be scrutinizing Mefoxin very closely. The company also knew that hospitals would be sensitive to the issue of antibiotic overuse. Merck therefore promoted Mefoxin only for the most difficult infections, those infections that would not respond to other, less expensive medications. The company also showed that Mefoxin could save hospitals money by providing the same results as two or three other drugs given in combination. With this marketing approach, hospitals around the country accepted Mefoxin, and use of the product has increased.

Merck's latest product offering is the new anticholesterol drug Mevacor, which won FDA approval less than a year after the company's initial application. A similar Merck product, Zocor, may be on the market soon. Merck has used seminars and symposiums to present Mevacor to influential cardiologists and internists, and Merck's sales force has called on nearly 100,000 other physicians around the country. The company may also run consumer advertisements to build awareness of the dangers of high cholesterol levels. Although the company does not refer to Mevacor and Zocor as miracle drugs, financial analysts seem to think they are; annual sales of the two products are predicted to reach $1 billion within five years.

SOURCES: Edward C. Baig, "America's Most Admired Corporations," *Fortune*, Jan. 19, 1987, pp. 18–19; John A. Byrne, "The Miracle Company," *Business Week*, Oct. 19, 1987, pp. 84–88; E. F. McCabe, "Merck Responds to Market Changes," *Management Review*, January 1987, pp. 56–59.

influencing consumer buying of doubleknit fabrics affected fiber makers, equipment manufacturers, and other suppliers. Changes in derived demand are the result of a chain reaction. When consumer demand for a product changes, a wave is set in motion that affects the demand for all firms involved in the production of that consumer product.

Inelastic Demand   The demand for many industrial products at the industry level is **inelastic demand,** which simply means that a price increase or decrease will not significantly affect demand for the item. Because many industrial products contain a great many parts, price increases that affect only one or two parts of the product may yield only a slightly higher per-unit production cost. Of course, when a sizable price increase for a component represents a large proportion of the product's cost, then demand may become more elastic because the price increase in the component causes the price at the consumer level to rise sharply.

The inelasticity characteristic applies only to market or industry demand for the industrial product, not to the demand for an individual supplier. Suppose, for example, that a sparkplug producer increases the price of sparkplugs sold to small-engine manufacturers but its competitors continue to maintain their same lower prices. The sparkplug company probably would experience reduced sales because most small-engine producers would switch to lower-priced brands. A specific firm is quite vulnerable to elastic demand, even though industry demand for a particular product is inelastic.

Joint Demand   The demand for certain industrial products, especially raw materials and components, is affected by joint demand. **Joint demand** occurs when two or more items are used in combination to produce a product. For example, a firm that manufactures axes needs the same number of ax handles as it does ax blades; these two products are demanded jointly. If the supplier of ax handles cannot furnish the required number of handles and the ax producer cannot obtain them elsewhere, the producer will stop buying ax blades.

Understanding the effects of joint demand is particularly important for a marketer selling multiple, jointly demanded items. Such a marketer must realize that when a customer begins purchasing one of the jointly demanded items, a good opportunity exists for selling other related products. Similarly, when customers purchase a number of jointly demanded products, the producer must exercise extreme caution to avoid shortages of any item because such shortages jeopardize the marketer's sales of all the jointly demanded products.

Demand Fluctuations The demand for industrial products may fluctuate enormously because it is derived demand. In general, when particular consumer products are in high demand, producers of those products buy large quantities of raw materials and components to ensure that long-run production requirements can be met. In addition, these producers may expand their production capacity, which entails the acquisition of capital goods.

A fall in the demand for certain consumer goods works in the same way to significantly reduce the demand for industrial products used to produce those goods. In fact, under such conditions, a marketer's sales of certain products may come to a short-run standstill. When consumer demand is low, industrial customers cut their purchases of raw materials and components and stop purchasing equipment and machinery, even for replacement purposes.

A marketer of industrial products may notice substantial changes in demand when its customers change their inventory policies, perhaps because of expectations about future demand. For example, if several dishwasher manufacturers who buy timers from one producer increase their inventory of timers from a two-week to a one-month supply, the timer producer will have a significant immediate increase in demand.

Sometimes, price changes can lead to surprising short-run changes in demand. A price increase for an industrial item may initially cause organizational customers to buy more of the item because they expect the price to rise further. Similarly, demand for an industrial product may be significantly lower following a price cut because buyers are waiting for further price reductions. Fluctuations in demand can be significant in industries in which price changes occur frequently.

Organizational Buying Decisions

Organizational (or industrial) **buying behavior** refers to the purchase behavior of producers, resellers, government units, and institutions. Although several of the same factors that influence consumer buying behavior (discussed in Chapter 4) also influence organizational buying behavior, a number of factors are unique to the latter. This section discusses who participates in making organizational purchase decisions by analyzing the buying center. Then we focus on the stages of the buying decision process and the factors that affect it.

The Buying Center Relatively few organizational purchase decisions are made by just one person; they are made through a buying center. Typically, the **buying center** consists of individuals who participate in the purchase decision process. These individuals include users, influencers, buyers, deciders, and gatekeepers.[8] One person may perform several of these roles. These participants share some goals and risks associated with their decisions.

Users are the organization members who actually use the product being acquired. They frequently initiate the purchase process and/or generate the specifications for the purchase. After the purchase, they also evaluate the product's performance relative to the specifications. Influencers have a definite impact on the purchase decision process. Often they are technical personnel, such as engineers, who help develop the specifications and evaluate alternative products. Technical personnel are especially important influencers when the products being considered involve new, advanced technology.

Buyers are responsible for selecting suppliers and actually negotiating the terms of purchase. They may also become involved in developing specifications. Buyers are sometimes called purchasing agents or purchasing managers. Their choices of vendors and products are heavily influenced by persons occupying other roles in the buying center, especially for new-task purchases. For straight rebuy purchases, the buyer plays a major role in the selection of vendors and in negotiations with them. Deciders actually choose the products and vendors. Although buyers may be the deciders, it is not unusual for different people to occupy these roles. For routinely purchased items, buyers usually are the deciders. However, a buyer may not be authorized to make purchases that exceed a certain dollar limit, in which case higher-level management personnel are the deciders. Gatekeepers, such as secretaries and technical personnel, control the flow of information to and among the persons who occupy the other roles in the buying center. Buyers who deal directly with vendors also may be gatekeepers because they can control the flow of information. The flow of information from supplier sales representatives to users and influencers often is controlled by personnel in the purchasing department.

The number and structure of an organization's buying centers are affected by the organization's size and market position, by the volume and types of products being purchased, and by the firm's overall managerial philosophy regarding exactly who should be involved in purchase decisions. A marketer attempting to sell to an organizational customer should determine who is in the buying center, the types of decisions each individual makes, and which individuals are the most influential in the decision process. Because in some instances many people make up the buying center, marketers cannot contact all participants; instead, they must be certain to contact a few of the most influential individuals in the buying center.

Stages of the Organizational Buying Decision Process

The right side of Figure 5.5 shows the stages of the organizational buying decision process. In the first stage, one or more individuals in the organization recognize that a problem or need exists. Problem recognition may arise under a variety of circumstances, for instance, when a machine malfunctions or a firm is modifying an existing product or introducing a new one. Individuals in the buying center, such as users, influencers, or buyers, may be involved in problem recognition, but it may be stimulated by external sources, such as sales representatives.

8. Frederick E. Webster, Jr. and Yoram Wind, *Organizational Buying Behavior* (Englewood Cliffs, N.J.: Prentice-Hall, 1972), pp. 78–80.

The development of product specifications (the second stage) requires organizational participants to assess the problem or need and determine what will be necessary to satisfy it. During this stage, users and influencers, such as technical personnel and engineers, often provide information and advice used in developing product specifications. By assessing and describing needs, the organization should be able to establish product specifications.

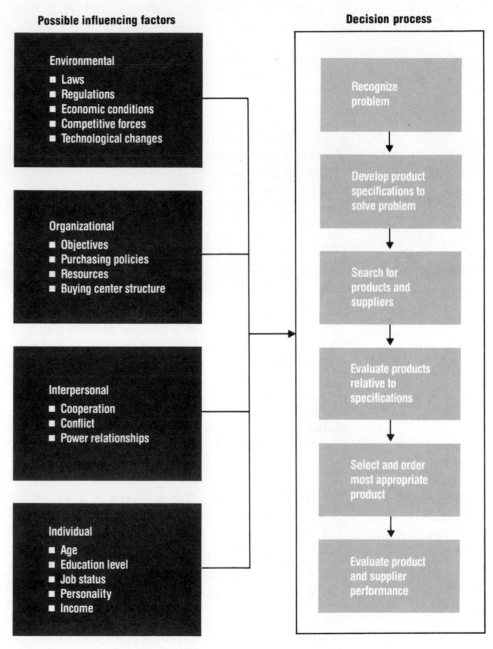

FIGURE 5.5

Organizational buying decision process and factors that may influence the process (SOURCE: Adapted from Frederick Webster and Yoram Wind, *Organizational Buying Behavior*, 1972, pp. 33–37. Adapted by permission of Prentice-Hall, Englewood Cliffs, N.J.)

Possible influencing factors

Environmental
- Laws
- Regulations
- Economic conditions
- Competitive forces
- Technological changes

Organizational
- Objectives
- Purchasing policies
- Resources
- Buying center structure

Interpersonal
- Cooperation
- Conflict
- Power relationships

Individual
- Age
- Education level
- Job status
- Personality
- Income

Decision process

Recognize problem

Develop product specifications to solve problem

Search for products and suppliers

Evaluate products relative to specifications

Select and order most appropriate product

Evaluate product and supplier performance

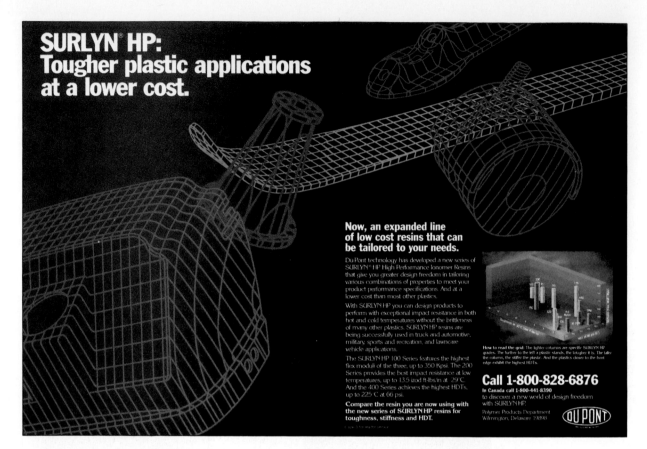

FIGURE 5.6

Promotion of source of low-cost resins (SOURCE: Courtesy of DuPont)

Searching for possible products to solve the problem and locating suppliers is the third stage in the decision process. Search activities may involve looking in company files and trade directories, contacting suppliers for information, soliciting proposals from known vendors, and examining catalogs and trade publications. The industrial advertisement in Figure 5.6 is an example of information available in trade publications. Some vendors may not be viewed as acceptable because they are not large enough to supply the needed quantities, and others may have poor records of delivery and service.

If all goes well, the search stage will result in a list of several alternative products and suppliers. The fourth stage is evaluating the products on the list to determine which ones (if any) meet the product specifications developed in the second stage. Also, during this stage various suppliers are evaluated based on multiple criteria such as price, service, and ability to deliver.

The results of the deliberations and assessments in the fourth stage are used during the fifth stage to select the product to be purchased and the supplier from whom to buy it. In some cases the buyer may decide to buy from several suppliers, and in other cases only one supplier is selected, which is known as sole sourcing. The Application on page 167 provides details about sole sourcing. In this stage the product is actually ordered. Specific details regarding terms, credit arrangements, delivery dates and methods, and technical assistance are worked out during this

Sole Sourcing

Sole sourcing, or purchasing all of an item from a single vendor, was once considered an arrangement to avoid. At best, most buyers regarded sole sourcing as a necessary evil, to be used only when product specifications were inflexible, other suppliers were too far away, or the product simply wasn't available from any other firm.

Even today, the practice is discouraged in many large organizations. Firms that contract with the federal government, for example, are required to have several sources for each item. Some purchasing managers maintain that a policy of sole sourcing leaves firms vulnerable to supply disruptions. Given the possibilities of strikes, shortages, or business closings, these companies find greater security and flexibility having multiple vendors. Other buyers believe that they are more likely to obtain fair prices and consistent quality when suppliers must compete for their business.

Despite these arguments, however, sole sourcing is becoming increasingly popular. About 43 percent of the purchasing managers recently sampled reported that their firms are doing more sole sourcing than in the past, and 52 percent said they expected to do more of it in the future. Some of the current sole-sourcing contracts are hefty: For example, Rockwell International Corp.'s automotive division in Troy, Michigan, recently signed a $350 million agreement with Ford Motor Company to produce all of the medium and heavy rear axles used in Ford trucks.

Firms using sole sourcing say the policy offers advantages for buyers and vendors alike, especially when it comes to quality control and cost reduction. With a single supplier, a buyer can spend more time communicating problems and needs and therefore is more likely to receive products exactly as ordered, with fewer rejected shipments and less reworking. Though the buyer must provide the vendor with reliable forecasting, the vendor may reciprocate with valuable feedback, such as suggestions for design modifications that could improve quality and prevent problems. A buyer may also end up with lower prices when the vendor can pass along savings from economies of scale and higher-volume freight discounts.

At the same time, say proponents of sole sourcing, the arrangement provides operating stability for the vendor. Because the sole-source supplier knows far in advance how much product the buyer needs and when the product is needed, the vendor can purchase materials and schedule production more efficiently. With the assurance of steady future sales, a vendor also has more freedom to invest in technological development, which can boost product quality and reduce costs further. In some cases a vendor may even decide to narrow its product line to focus its energies on the specific products needed by the buyer. The supplier may also work with the buyer to develop new products.

The key to successful sole sourcing, of course, is good communication between buyer and vendor. Both sides must be committed to the policy and must be willing to invest the time necessary for improving the flow of information. Although experts advise buyers and vendors to evaluate potential partners carefully and to get all aspects of the arrangement in writing, they say that sole sourcing can definitely pay off in higher product quality, timely deliveries, and lower prices.

SOURCES: Susan Avery, "Single Sourcing: The Risks Aren't As Bad As They Seem," *Purchasing,* July 16, 1987, p. 33; Mark Treleven, "Single Sourcing: A Management Tool for the Quality Supplier," *Journal of Purchasing and Materials Management,* Spring 1987, pp. 19–24; "Sole-Sourcing Reduces Costs, Improves Quality and Delivery," *Purchasing,* Oct. 9, 1986, pp. 20–21; and Thomas F. Wallace, "Sole Sourcing Doesn't Have To Be As Scary As It Sounds," *Purchasing,* Aug. 21, 1986, p. 35.

stage. During the sixth stage, the product's performance is evaluated. Actual performance is compared to specifications. Sometimes, it is determined that although the product met the specifications, its performance did not adequately satisfy the problem or need recognized in the first stage, in which case product specifications must be adjusted. In addition, during the sixth stage the supplier's performance is evaluated, and if it is found to be unacceptable, the organizational purchaser seeks corrective action from the supplier or searches for a new supplier. The results of the evaluation in this stage become feedback for the other stages and influence future organizational purchase decisions.

This organizational buying decision process is used in its entirety primarily for new-task purchases. Several of the stages, but not necessarily all, are used for modified rebuy and straight rebuy situations.

Influences on Organizational Buying

As Figure 5.5 shows, four major categories of factors appear to influence organizational buying decisions: environmental, organizational, interpersonal, and individual.

Environmental factors are uncontrollable forces such as laws, regulatory actions and guidelines, activities of interest groups, inflation, competitors' actions, and technological changes. These forces generate a considerable amount of uncertainty for an organization, which can make individuals in the buying center rather apprehensive about certain types of purchases. Changes in one or more environmental forces can create new purchasing opportunities and make yesterday's purchase decisions look terrible.

Organizational factors include the buying organization's objectives, purchasing policies, and resources as well as the size and composition of its buying center. An organization may have certain buying policies to which buying center participants must conform. For instance, a firm's policies may mandate long-term contracts, perhaps longer than most sellers desire. The nature of an organization's financial resources may require special credit arrangements. Any of these conditions could affect the firm's purchase decision processes.

The interpersonal factors are the relationships among the people in the buying center. The use of power and the level of conflict among buying center participants, for example, influence organizational buying decisions. Certain persons in the buying center may be better communicators than others and may thus be more convincing. These interpersonal dynamics frequently are hidden, making them difficult for marketers to assess.

Individual factors are the personal characteristics of individuals in the buying center, such as age, education, personality, position in the organization, and income. How influential these factors are varies according to the buying situation, the type of product being purchased, and whether the purchase is new-task, modified rebuy, or straight rebuy. The negotiating styles of people vary within an organization and from one organization to another. To be effective, a marketer must know customers well enough to be aware of these individual factors and the effects they may have on purchase decisions.

Summary

This chapter initially focuses on the various types of organizational markets. Organizational markets consist of producers, resellers, governments, and institutions that purchase a specific kind of product for resale, for direct use in producing other products, or for use in day-to-day operations. Producer markets consist of individuals and business organizations that purchase products for the purpose of making a profit by using them to produce other products or by using them in their operations. Reseller markets consist of intermediaries who buy finished products and resell them for the purpose of making a profit. Government markets consist of federal, state, and local governments. These government units spend billions of dollars annually for a variety of goods and services to support their internal operations and to give citizens such products as highways, education, health protection, water, waste disposal, national defense, fire and police protection, and energy. Institutional markets consist of organizations that seek to achieve other than normal business goals such as profit, market share, or return on investment. Institutions purchase millions of dollars' worth of products annually to provide goods, services, and ideas to congregations, students, patients, club members, and others.

Organizational customers are usually viewed as being more rational than ultimate consumers and as more likely to seek information about a product's features and technical specifications. When purchasing products, organizational customers are concerned especially about quality, service, and price. Quality is important because it directly affects the quality of products the buyer's firm produces. Because services can have such a direct influence on a firm's costs, sales, and profits, such things as market information, on-time delivery, and availability of parts can be crucial to an organizational buyer. Although an organizational customer does not depend solely on price to decide which products to buy, price is of prime concern because it directly influences a firm's profitability.

Organizational transactions differ from consumer transactions in several ways. The orders tend to be considerably larger. Negotiations occur less frequently but are often lengthy when they do occur. Organizational transactions sometimes involve more than one person or one department in the purchasing organization.

Organizational buyers use several purchasing methods, including description, inspection, sampling, and negotiation. Most purchases are one of three types: new-task, modified rebuy, or straight rebuy.

Industrial demand differs from consumer demand along several dimensions. Industrial demand derives from the demand for consumer products. At the industry level, industrial demand is inelastic; if the price of an industrial item changes, demand for the product will not change as much proportionally. In some cases, an industrial product is demanded jointly with another product. The demand for industrial products can fluctuate widely.

Organizational buying behavior refers to the purchase behavior of producers, resellers, government units, and institutions. Organizational purchase decisions are made through a buying center—a group of several people with multiple roles in the organization, such as users, influencers, buyers, deciders, and gatekeepers. Users are those in the organization who actually use the product. Influencers help develop the specifications and evaluate alternative products for possible use. Buyers are responsible for selecting the suppliers and negotiating the terms of the purchases. Deciders choose the products and vendors. Gatekeepers control the flow of information to and among persons who occupy the other roles in the buying center.

Stages of the organizational buying decision process are problem recognition, the establishment of product specifications to solve the problem, the search for products and suppliers, evaluation of products relative to specifications, selection and ordering of the most appropriate product, and evaluation of the product's and the supplier's performance. Four categories of factors influence organizational buying decisions: environmental, organizational, interpersonal, and individual.

Important Terms

Producer markets
Reseller markets
Government markets
Institutional markets
Reciprocity
New-task purchase
Modified rebuy purchase

Straight rebuy purchase
Derived demand
Inelastic demand
Joint demand
Organizational buying behavior
Buying center

Discussion and Review Questions

1. Identify and describe four major types of organizational markets. Give examples of each type.
2. Regarding purchasing behavior, why are organizational buyers generally considered more rational than ultimate consumers?
3. What are the primary concerns of organizational buyers?
4. List several characteristics that differentiate organizational transactions from consumer sales.
5. What are the commonly used methods of organizational buying?

6. Why do buyers involved in a straight rebuy purchase require so much less information than in a new-task purchase?
7. How does industrial demand differ from consumer demand?
8. What are the major components of a buying center?
9. Identify the stages of the organizational buying decision process. How is this decision process used when making straight rebuys?
10. How do environmental, organizational, interpersonal, and individual factors affect organizational purchases?

Cases

5.1 Eberhard Faber Markets Low-Tech Products to Organizational Markets[9]

Eberhard Faber Inc., originator of the familiar yellow pencil, has been producing wood-cased pencils since 1849. Today the privately owned Pennsylvania-based firm and its dozen or so U.S. competitors turn out two billion pencils annually, totaling $100 million in sales. Eberhard Faber maintains a 10 percent share of this domestic market. The company's sales of pencils, pens, erasers, and rubber bands are increasing in Third World countries, but recent sales in the United States have been essentially static, largely because of our high literacy rate. As a result, Eberhard Faber's U.S. pencil sales account for less than 20 percent of its worldwide sales of $40 million, and company earnings have declined over the past five years.

When the pencil market became particularly competitive in the early 1980s, Eberhard Faber's top management concluded that the key to greater domestic profitability was marketing, a philosophy never before followed in the firm's history. At first the firm made some marketing blunders, company head Eberhard Faber IV now concedes. For example, after producing pencils in bright yellow for nearly a century, the company decided to introduce a natural-looking pencil: bare cedar wood covered with a coat of clear lacquer. Eberhard Faber projected a 15 percent market share for the new product, predicting that the current fashion for naturalness would carry over to the pencil market. But pencil dealers avoided the new product in droves, preferring to stick with a proven seller, so the company was forced to scale down its projections. (About 80 percent of all pencils sold are still in the traditional yellow.)

Another strategic miscalculation involved the company's redoubled efforts in art supplies, a market that yields greater profit margins than the highly competitive office products market. Because Eberhard Faber's Design markers were already successful, the company acquired several art supply firms, such as NSM, maker of leather portfolios. At the same time, however, the company began to neglect the commercial office products field that accounted for two-thirds of its total sales. In this market, which includes sales to corporations under private labels as well as the

---

9. Based on information from James Braham, "Ho-Hum: How Do You Peddle a Low-Tech Product?" *Industry Week,* June 9, 1986, pp. 53–56; Alix M. Freedman, "The Next Thing You Know, They'll Change the Coke Formula," *The Wall Street Journal,* June 27, 1985, p. E33; Al Urbanski, "Eberhard Faber," *Sales & Marketing Management,* November 1986, pp. 44–47.

Eberhard Faber name, the firm found itself gaining a reputation for noncompetitive pricing and sluggish new-product development, despite the consistently good quality and service it offered.

Deciding that professional marketing expertise was needed, chief executive officer Faber brought in a new president, Frank McHugh of Ampad Corp. (formerly American Pad & Paper), who in turn hired the company's first marketing director, Gordon Haight, formerly of Hallmark Cards. Together, McHugh and Haight have revamped every aspect of the company's ineffective marketing operation, beginning with the sales force, which had dwindled by one-third. To build sales among office product wholesalers, they increased the advertising budget, created new promotional programs, and redesigned the company's catalogs and order sheets. They developed new products, such as five-sided erasers in stylish colors. With commodity products such as rubber bands, they market quality and price. Nearly every product package has been updated. Office products distributors say such moves have definitely improved the company's image.

Moreover, in accordance with the aggressive new-product development policy McHugh and Haight established, the company now positions every new item with at least some overlap in each of three target markets: commercial and office products, art supplies, and gift items. Although commercial sales remain the backbone of the company, Haight now foresees the most growth in the consumer novelty and gift market, a new area for the company. Many of these products are aimed at teenagers. For example, the company has developed Wiff scented markers, Glocil fluorescent pencils, and Chameleon heat-sensitive pencils, which change colors at a touch. Desk Pals are pencil sets with a Teddy Bear theme. Other gift pencils read "It's a boy!" or "It's a girl!" Still on the drawing board are consumer products that will tie in with the growing use of personal computers. The short life cycle inherent in these new Eberhard Faber items—about eighteen months for the Desk Pals, for example—contrasts sharply with the staying power of the company's traditional products.

Today, Eberhard Faber IV acknowledges that the current marketing outlook at Eberhard Faber Inc. represents a radical change in company philosophy. Other long-standing company policies have changed as well. To improve profitability, for example, all pencil and marker manufacturing has been moved to Mexico, although Faber himself opposed such a step for years. (The Pennsylvania plant will continue to produce erasers, rubber bands, and pencil lead.)

Industry observers are divided on Eberhard Faber's new marketing stance. They applaud the company's aggressiveness in office products, but they also emphasize the importance of habit in pencil-and-eraser purchases. As a rule, they point out, the pencil business is not an industry given to fads.

Questions for Discussion

1. What types of organizational markets (as classified in this chapter) purchase the products Eberhard Faber makes?
2. Most purchases of Eberhard Faber's products would be of what type: new-task, modified rebuy, or straight rebuy? Why?
3. Why were Eberhard Faber's "natural looking" pencils less than successful?
4. Evaluate Eberhard Faber's changes in its marketing efforts.

5.2 IBM Serves Organizational Customers[10]

International Business Machines Corp. (IBM) is the premier manufacturer, marketer, and service company within the computer industry. The company employs 400,000 people and last year had gross revenues of about $50 billion. Since 1980, IBM has invested $28 billion in land, buildings, equipment, and research and development. The company plans to invest an additional $56 billion by 1990.

IBM makes one of every four mainframe computers sold in the United States. It is this dominance of the mainframe market that led IBM to its number-one position. Mainframes give the company a solid customer base and are high-profit products; one analyst estimates that IBM's gross margins on its mainframes are about 80 percent. Although the personal computer is becoming a mainstay of the office, mainframes are still the hub of large computer operations for financial (banking and insurance), factory (computer-aided design and manufacturing), and scientific and engineering applications. As IBM's customers prosper, they continue to request more powerful systems to accommodate new needs.

In response to this demand, IBM recently introduced a new family of fifth-generation mainframes, the Sierra computers, available in several versions and from about $1 million to $11.5 million. The new Sierra model 600, six large computers linked in a single system, is IBM's most powerful machine ever. By targeting the Sierras at scientific research and engineering users, IBM hopes to increase its competitiveness and reinforce its dominance of the mainframe market.

Other IBM customers, however, say that what they need most are solutions, not more hardware. They are asking IBM to help them increase productivity with the computers they already have, and they want the company to improve the ability of its machines to communicate with each other, from mainframes to desktops.

Buyers have also requested additional applications software. Accordingly, IBM has stepped up its software development efforts. The company is also retraining its marketing force—expanded from 23,000 to 28,000—and is organizing sales personnel along industry lines so that expertise can be directed to customers in specific businesses. IBM intends to place new emphasis on customer assistance and to provide the networking and communications solutions its organizational customers want.

Questions for Discussion

1. What types of organizations buy large mainframe computers such as those in the Sierra family?
2. The purchase of a large computer is what type of organizational purchase?
3. What types of people make up IBM customers' buying centers?
4. What are IBM customers' major concerns when purchasing a large computer?

10. Based on information from Frank Barbetta, "IBM Debuts Two Sierras," *Electronic News,* Feb. 18, 1985, pp. 1, 8; Jeff Moad, "Price/Performance Upgrades in Sierra Called 'Moderate,'" *Electronic News,* Feb. 18, 1985, p. 8; "High Sierra," *The Economist,* Feb. 16, 1985, p. 68; Carol J. Loomis, "IBM's Big Blues: A Legend Tries to Remake Itself," *Fortune,* Jan. 19, 1987, pp. 34–36; Hank Gilman, "IBM Unveils 2 Computers in Sierra Line," *Wall Street Journal,* Jan. 27, 1987, p. 2; Paul B. Carroll and Hank Gilman, "IBM, Beset by Rivals, Seeks to Assure Major Customers on Networks, Software," *Wall Street Journal,* Feb. 4, 1987, p. 1B.

6. Marketing Research and Information Systems

O B J E C T I V E S

- ▶ To understand the relationship between research and information systems in marketing decision making.
- ▶ To distinguish between research and intuition in solving marketing problems.
- ▶ To learn five basic steps for conducting a marketing research project.
- ▶ To understand the fundamental methods of gathering data for marketing research.
- ▶ To understand questionnaire construction, sampling, and the design of experiments.
- ▶ To gain insights about ethical concerns in marketing research.

*T*oday *marketing managers* are using highly innovative marketing research projects to develop a customer orientation. New technology and changes in media viewership gave Illinois Bell Telephone Co. an opportunity to test whether advertising would increase local telephone usage and if so, for what types of households the advertising would have the most effective appeal.

N. W. Ayer, an advertising agency in Chicago, created new television advertising for Illinois Bell that demonstrated the advantages of making more local calls. Two campaigns were run at the same time: Phone first[SM], emphasizing the efficiency and time-management benefits of telephoning, and Just call[SM], stressing the emotional benefits of telephoning (see Figure 6.1).

A study was designed by The Test Marketing Group, Chicago, to determine whether the television advertisements using these two campaigns increased local telephone use (as measured by number of calls made) in private households and the extent of any increase and to determine the types of households in which the advertisements were most effective. Two matched panels of about six hundred cable television households each were established, based on demographic information acquired from a telephone survey. Before the start of the advertising campaigns, both panels were first monitored for 13 weeks to determine each household's baseline number of local phone calls. The test period then ran for 38 weeks immediately following the baseline monitoring period. One panel received both of Illinois Bell's local-use advertising campaigns on their cable television; the other panel received no local-use cable television advertising. Bell monitored telephone use for every household in each panel for the duration of the test.

The advertising campaigns did indeed increase local telephone use. Calls were up 7 percent among the panel that received advertising as compared to the panel that received no advertising. Households reporting annual incomes of $40,000 or more responded most strongly to advertising: Calls among this group were up 25 percent.

This research illustrates that a highly structured marketing research study can provide valuable data to help managers make important marketing decisions. Based on this study, Illinois Bell could launch a large-scale advertising campaign aimed at increasing telephone usage.[1]

M ARKETING RESEARCH and systematic information gathering increase the probability of successful marketing. In fact, the failure of companies, and even entire industries, has been attributed to a lack of marketing research.[2] The conventional wisdom about the evaluation and use of marketing

1. Based on information from James Dodge, Ray Lewis, and Marshall H. Zandell, "Illinois Bell Finds That Targetable TV Research Is the Right Number," *Marketing News,* Jan. 4, 1988, p. 8.
2. Bernie Whalen, "An Executive Charges: Marketing Research Killed Salesmanship," *Marketing News,* Mar. 15, 1985, p. 1.

research by marketing managers suggests that in the future managers will use marketing research appropriately in the decision environment to reduce uncertainty and to make decisions better than the ones they would make in the absence of relevant research.[3] Research findings are essential in planning and developing marketing strategies. Information about target markets provides vital input in planning the marketing mix and controlling marketing activities. It is no secret that companies can use information technology as a key to gaining an advantage over the competition.[4] In short, the marketing concept—the marketing philosophy of customer orientation—can be implemented better when adequate information about customers is available.

Marketing research and information systems provide the insight for carrying out the marketing concept. Without adequate information and research, the marketing concept cannot be effectively implemented. With the intense competition in today's marketplace, it is not wise to develop a product and then look for a market where it can be profitably sold. Marketing research and marketing information systems that provide objective information help firms avoid the assumptions and misunderstanding that could lead to poor marketing performance. Implementing the marketing concept through effective marketing intelligence enhances a firm's ability to compete successfully in both the United States and other parts of the world. Marketing intelligence is an absolute necessity when a firm is entering foreign markets for the first time. In Figure 6.2, National Decision Systems focuses on its ability to segment customers, evaluate sites, and provide market analysis and other services that allow companies such as Merrill Lynch, Wells Fargo, and Citicorp to provide good marketing.

This chapter focuses on the approaches to and processes of gathering information needed for marketing decisions. It distinguishes between managing information within an organization (a marketing information system) and conducting marketing research projects. We discuss the role of marketing research in decision making and problem solving and compare it with intuition. Next we examine individual steps in the marketing research process. We look at sampling and experimentation as approaches to reducing error in gathering information. The three major methods of obtaining data are described. Finally, ethical concerns in marketing research are examined.

Defining Marketing Research and Marketing Information Systems

Marketing intelligence is a broad term that includes all data available for marketing decisions. **Marketing research,** a part of marketing intelligence, involves specific inquiries into problems. Its purpose is to guide marketing decisions, and it does this by gathering information not available to decision makers. Market research is conducted on a special-project basis, and research methods are adapted to the

3. Hanjoon Lee, Frank Acits, and Ralph L. Day, "Evaluation and Use of Marketing Research by Decision Makers: A Behavioral Simulation," *Journal of Marketing Research*, May 1987, p. 187.
4. Brandt Allen, "Make Information Services Pay Its Way," *Harvard Business Review,* January–February 1987, p. 57.

problems studied and changes in the environment. The American Marketing Association defines marketing research as

> the function which links the consumer, customer, and public to the marketer through information—information used to identify and define marketing opportunities and problems; generate, refine, and evaluate marketing actions; monitor marketing performance; and improve understanding of marketing as a process.
>
> Marketing Research specifies the information required to address these issues; designs the method for collecting information; manages and implements the data collection process; analyzes the results; and communicates the findings and their implications.[5]

Dr Pepper Co. is an example of marketing research conducted on a special-project basis. Dr Pepper's market share had been sliding by the 1980s. Research indicated that Dr Pepper drinkers were "inner-directed" people who followed their own values rather than the values of others. This consumer profile was in conflict with the early 1980s advertising theme "Be a Pepper," so the company dropped that theme in favor of a more individualistic one: "Hold out for the out of the ordinary."[6]

A **marketing information system (MIS)** is the framework for the day-to-day managing and structuring of information gathered regularly from sources both

5. "New Marketing Research Definition Approved," *Marketing News,* Jan. 2, 1987, p. 1.
6. Ronald Alsop, "Dr Pepper Is Bubbling Again After Its 'Be a Pepper' Setback," *Wall Street Journal,* Sept. 26, 1985, p. 33.

FIGURE 6.2

Marketing research is useful to identify target markets (SOURCE: National Decision Systems)

Part I AN ANALYSIS OF MARKET OPPORTUNITIES

FIGURE 6.3

An organization's
marketing information
system

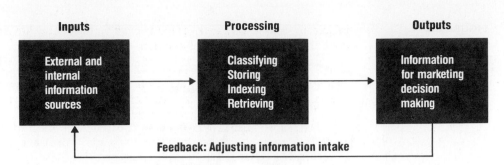

inside and outside an organization. As such, an MIS provides a continuous flow of information about prices, advertising expenditures, sales, competition, and distribution expenses. When information systems have been strategically created and focused by a superior business strategy and then institutionalized throughout an organization, their value is continually enhanced. They have the power to distance marketers from competitors by leaps and bounds.[7] Figure 6.3 illustrates the chief components of an MIS.

MIS inputs include those information sources inside and outside the firm assumed useful for future decision making. Processing information involves classifying information and developing categories for meaningful storage and retrieval. Marketing decision makers determine which information is useful for making decisions. These data make up the outputs shown in Figure 6.2. Finally, feedback enables those who are responsible for gathering internal and external data systematically to adjust the information intake.

Nabisco Brands, Inc. handles 235,000 consumer contacts each year, usually inquiries about product usage, nutrition, and ingredients. This consumer feedback is computerized and available on demand throughout Nabisco's operating divisions.

Regular reports of sales by product or market categories, data on inventory levels, and records of salespersons' activities are all examples of information flows. In the MIS, the means of gathering data receive less attention than do the procedures for expediting the flow of information. The main focus of the system is on data storage and retrieval, as well as on computer capabilities and management's information requirements.

Radisson, for example, places evaluation cards in rooms urging customers to report both positive and negative aspects of their stay. This information provides a continuous flow of data that can be used to evaluate the firm's ongoing operations and its individual units. In addition, it leads to timely corrective actions. Figure 6.4 is an example of the questionnaire Radisson uses to determine the overall level of customer satisfaction.

Whereas an MIS provides a continuous data input for an organization, marketing research is an information gathering process for specific situations. Nonrecurring decisions that deal with the dynamics of the marketing environment often call for a data search structured according to the problem and decision. Marketing research is usually characterized by in-depth analyses of major problems or issues.

---

7. Andrea Dunham, "Information Systems Are the Key to Managing Future Business Needs," *Marketing News,* May 23, 1986, p. 11.

FIGURE 6.4

An evaluation card
used by Radisson
(SOURCE: Radisson
Hotel Corporation)

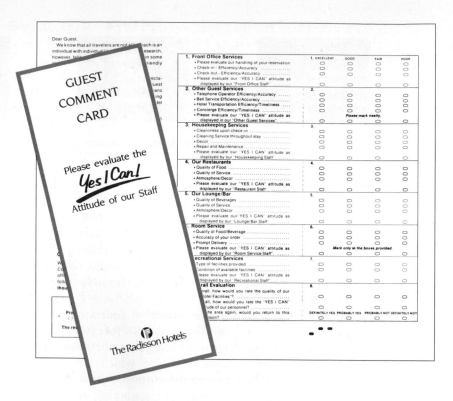

Often, the needed information is available only from sources outside an organization's formal channels of information. An organization may want to know something about its competitors or may want to gain an objective, unbiased understanding of its own customers. Such information needs may require an independent investigation by a marketing research firm. However, data brought into the organization through marketing research do become part of its **marketing databank,** a file of data collected through both the MIS and marketing research projects.

The marketing databank permits researchers to retrieve information that is useful for addressing problems quite different from those that prompted the original data collection. For example, the Miles Laboratories databank contained information that people were not overeating as much as in the past. The result was a change in the Alka-Seltzer slogan from one that stressed relief from overeating to "For the symptoms of stress that come with success." Often, a research study developed for one purpose will be very useful for developing a research method or indicating problems in researching a particular topic. For example, research may show that in consumer surveys respondents most frequently select a pink bar of soap as their favorite, even though pink is rarely a top-selling color. Such knowledge permits those interested in marketing soap to be cautious when interpreting research findings. Thus marketers should make sure that data from marketing research and the MIS are classified and stored in the databank so that the information's usefulness for future marketing decision making can be identified.

Databanks vary widely from one organization to another. In a small organization, the databank can simply be a large notebook, but in many organizations a computer storage and retrieval system is needed to handle the large volume of data. Figure 6.5 illustrates how marketing decision makers combine research findings with data from an MIS to develop a databank. Although many organizations do not use the term *databank*, they still have some system for storing information for later use. Smaller organizations may not use the terms *MIS* and *marketing research*, but they usually do perform these marketing activities.

After a marketing information system—of whatever size and complexity—has been established, information needs to be related to marketing planning. The following section discusses how marketers use marketing information, experience, and judgment in making decisions.

Information Needs and Decision Making

The real value of marketing research and the systematic gathering of information that supports it is measured by improvements in a marketer's ability to make decisions. For example, marketing research has guided the marketing and advertising of Mercedes-Benz automobiles since 1965. Before 1965, the company knew nothing about its buyers, and marketing was a hip-shot affair. Research indicated that Mercedes customers had little in common with buyers of other luxury models. Mercedes buyers wanted a car with distinct quality, engineering, design, and performance values.[8] In Figure 6.6, InfoScan advertises that it can provide specific information about consumers who purchase particular products.

8. "Research Played Role in Launch of Baby Benz," *Marketing News*, Jan. 4, 1985, p. 20.

FIGURE 6.5

Combining marketing research and the marketing information system

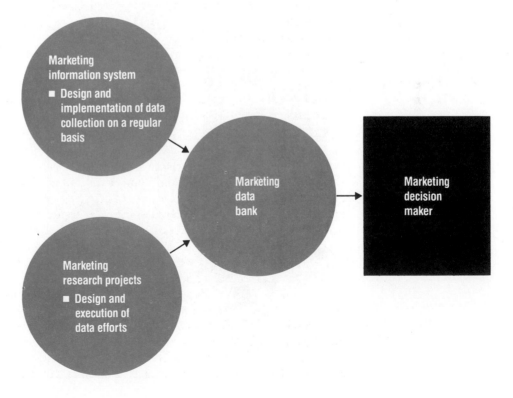

Research and information systems provide the organization with customer feedback. Without feedback, a marketer cannot understand the dynamics of the marketplace. The role of marketing information in decision making is increasing as managers recognize its benefits. For example, Japanese managers, who put much more faith in information they get directly from wholesalers and retailers in the distribution channels, are now beginning to realize the importance of consumer surveys and scientific methods of marketing research as they begin to look for ways to diversify their companies.[9]

Although uncertainty is inherent to decision making, research can make the process more objective and systematic. The increase in marketing research activities represents a transition from intuitive to scientific problem solving. In relying on **intuition,** marketing managers do not look for any information other than personal knowledge or experience. However, in **scientific decision making,** managers take an orderly and logical approach to gathering information. They seek facts on a systematic basis; they apply methods other than trial and error or generalization from experience. Consider the approach to scientific decision making that Information Resources, Inc. used. Its use of research to link sales and advertising is described in the Application on page 183.

9. Johny K. Johansson and Ikujiro Nonaha, "Market Research the Japanese Way," *Harvard Business Review,* May–June 1987, pp. 16–22.

FIGURE 6.6

InfoScan provides specific consumer purchase data (SOURCE: Information Resources, Inc.)

Using Research to Link Advertising to Sales

Researchers not only collect research data, they also analyze and interpret what they find. Today, in this world of rapidly changing technology, researchers are always finding faster ways of obtaining and analyzing more accurate data. Information Resources Inc. (IRI) has developed a method for relating consumer exposure to television advertising to sales of the advertised products.

IRI links television program viewing data from BehaviorScan microcomputers placed in 10,000 households in several cities. In these sample households, the microcomputers record when the television set is on and which station is on and then send this information to IRI's central data collection office. When members of a sample household go grocery shopping, they present an identification card at the checkout stand; the checker records the purchases by scanner and the data are automatically sent to IRI.

This research produces single-source data. In other words, it lets researchers track the behavior of individual households from the television set to the checkout counter. The data IRI provide enable marketers to assess the effectiveness of their advertising by determining whether viewers saw a particular advertisement and whether the advertisement led the viewer to buy the product. In addition, IRI can measure the frequency of advertisement exposures needed to increase sales while integrating other factors, such as promotion activity and brand loyalty. This information lets advertisers target their advertising messages to viewers who frequently use their products and target programs that heavy users of competitive products watch, to increase support for their brand. The BehaviorScan system gives marketers a major alternative to buying television shows that are based on broad demographic data.

Although this method provides accurate data quickly, it still has a few drawbacks. The scanning services do not know if viewers are actually watching the television set when it is on. Furthermore, the sample households receive compensation for their participation, and they may react in unusual ways because they know they are sending a message to advertisers. Nevertheless, a majority of marketers feel that the IRI service is a quick and reliable way of obtaining data they can analyze and interpret, leading to better marketing decisions.

The BehaviorScan system is already providing some useful information. In a test of twelve products, an increase in advertising led to significantly better sales for only four of the products. IRI noticed that Kraft's Velveeta Shells & Cheese Dinners improved in sales and market share position, but only to a certain point. Among the four products that did respond, consumers who saw more of the product did seem to buy more of the product; however, Velveeta seemed to reach a threshold at six to ten advertisements a year. Such

Despite the obvious value of formal research, marketing decisions often are made in its absence. It is true that relatively minor problems requiring immediate attention can and should be handled on the basis of personal judgment and common sense. But limited research is valuable when it appears that complete data are not needed for good decisions and would be too expensive in relation to the data's usefulness to decision makers. As the number of solutions to a problem, the expected economic or social payoffs, and the possible risks multiply, the use of full-scale research in planning becomes more desirable and rewarding.

We are not suggesting here that intuition has little or no value. Successful decisions blend both research and intuition. Statistics, mathematics, and logic are tools that contribute to problem solving and provide information that decreases the uncertainty of predictions based on limited experience. However, these tools do not necessarily produce all the answers, or even the right ones. Consider one extreme example. A marketing research study conducted for Xerox Corporation in the late 1950s indicated that there was a very limited market for an automatic photocopier. Xerox management judged that the researchers had drawn the wrong conclusions from the study and decided to launch the product anyway. That product, the Xerox 914 copier, was an instant success. An immediate backlog of orders developed, and the rest is sales history.

Thus a proper blend of research and intuition is required for making a correct decision. Table 6.1 distinguishes between the roles of research and intuition in decision making.

The Marketing Research Process

Marketers determine when research is needed and design projects to give decision makers useful information. They must develop practical and understandable procedures to guide the research and provide a framework for its conduct. Marketers approach marketing research logically to maintain the control necessary for obtaining accurate data. The difference between good research and bad depends on input, which includes effective control over the entire marketing research process.

The five major steps in Figure 6.7 should be thought of as an overall approach to conducting research rather than as a rigid set of rules to be followed in each project. When they plan research projects, marketers must think about each of the steps and how they can best be tailored to fit a particular problem.

TABLE 6.1

Distinction between
research and intuition
in marketing decision
making

	RESEARCH	INTUITION
Nature	Formal planning, predicting based on scientific approach	Preference based on personal feelings
Methods	Logic, systematic methods, statistical inference	Experience and demonstration
Contributions	General hypotheses for making predictions, classifying relevant variables, carrying out systematic description and classification	Minor problems solved quickly through consideration of experience, practical consequences

**Defining and
Locating Problems**

Initially, marketers focus their attention on how best to discover the nature and boundaries of a problem. This **problem definition** is the first step toward finding a solution or launching a research study. The problem definition stage should occupy researchers and decision makers until they are very clear about what they want from the research and how they will use it.[10] Fuzzy, inconclusive studies are a waste of time and money.

The first sign of a problem is usually a departure from some normal function, such as conflicts between or failures in attaining objectives. If a corporation's objective is a 12 percent return on investment and the current return is 6 percent, this discrepancy should be a warning flag. It is a symptom that something inside or outside the organization has blocked the attainment of the desired goal or that the goal could be unrealistic. Decreasing sales, increasing expenses, or decreasing profits are also broad indications of problems. To get at the specific causes of the problem through research, however, marketers must define the problem and its scope in a way that goes beneath its superficial symptoms.

The interaction between the marketing manager and the marketing researcher should result in a clearly defined problem. Depending on the abilities of the manager and the marketing researcher, various methods may be used to help define problems. Traditionally the problem formulation process has been assumed to be a subjective, creative process. Today, however, more objective and systematic approaches are being used. For example, the delphi method for problem definition consists of a series of interviews with a panel of experts. With repeated interviews,

FIGURE 6.7

The five steps of the
marketing research
process

10. Bruce R. Dreisbach, "Marketing: The Key to Successful Research Management," *Marketing News,* Jan. 4, 1985, p. 3.

the range of responses converges toward a "correct" definition of the problem.[11] This method introduces structure as well as objectivity into the process of problem definition.

The research objective specifies the information required to achieve the research purpose. Deciding how to refine a broad, indefinite problem into a clearly defined and researchable statement is a prerequisite for the next step in planning the research: developing the type of hypothesis that best fits the problem.

Developing Hypotheses

The objective statement of a marketing research project should include hypotheses drawn from both previous research and expected research findings. A **hypothesis** is a guess or assumption about a certain problem or set of circumstances. It is based on all the insight and knowledge available about the problem from previous research studies and other sources. As information is gathered, a researcher can test the hypothesis. Sometimes several hypotheses are developed during the actual study; the hypotheses that are accepted or rejected become the study's chief conclusions.

Collecting Data

Two types of data are available to marketing researchers. **Primary data** are observed and recorded or collected directly from respondents. **Secondary data** are compiled inside or outside the organization for some purpose other than the current investigation. Secondary data include general reports supplied to an enterprise by various data services. Such reports might concern market shares, retail inventory levels, and consumers' purchasing behavior. Figure 6.8 illustrates how primary and secondary sources differ. Secondary data are usually already available in private or public reports or have been collected and stored by the organization itself. Primary data must be gathered by observing phenomena or surveying respondents.

The nature and type of the hypothesis being tested determine the choice of a general data gathering approach: exploratory, descriptive, or causal investigations. When more information about the problem is needed and the tentative hypothesis must be made more specific, marketers conduct **exploratory studies.** For instance, a review of information in the organization's databank or a review of publicly available data may be helpful. By questioning knowledgeable people inside and outside the organization, marketers may get additional insight into the problem. An advantage of the exploratory approach is that it permits marketers to conduct mini-studies with a very restricted database.

Descriptive studies are undertaken when marketers recognize that they must understand the characteristics of certain phenomena to solve a particular problem. For example, Nielsen provides a cable audience profile service that assists in determining cable television viewership by market (see Figure 6.9). Marketers may plan to conduct surveys of consumers' education, occupation, or age; they may find out how many consumers purchased Ford Escorts last month; or they may determine how many adults between the ages of eighteen and thirty drink coffee at least three times a week.

11. Raymond E. Taylor, "Using the Delphi Method to Define Marketing Problems," *Business,* October–December 1984, p. 17.

FIGURE 6.8
Approaches to collecting data

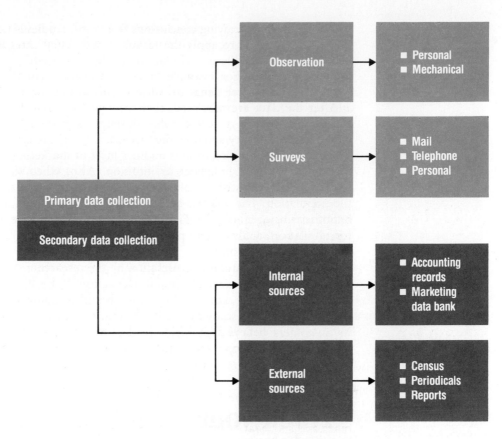

Descriptive studies may call for statistical analysis and predictive tools. A researcher trying to find out how many people will vote for a certain political candidate, for example, may have to use sampling, questionnaires, computer tabulations, and estimates of error to predict the correct answer. Descriptive studies generally require much prior knowledge and assume that the problem is clearly defined. The marketers' major task is to find adequate methods for collecting and measuring data.

Hypotheses about causal relationships require a more complex approach than a descriptive study. In **causal studies,** it is assumed that a particular variable X is the cause of the variable Y. Marketers must plan the research so that the data collected prove or disprove that X causes Y. To do so, marketers must try to hold constant all variables except X and Y. For example, to find out whether premiums increase the number of new accounts in a savings and loan association, marketers must try to keep all variables constant except premiums and new accounts.

**Interpreting
Research Findings**

After collecting data to test their hypotheses, marketers interpret the research findings. Interpretation is easier if marketers carefully plan their data analysis methods early in the research process. They should also allow for continual evaluation of the data during the entire collection period. They can then gain valuable insight into areas that ought to be probed during the formal interpretation.

The first step in drawing conclusions from most studies is tabulation of the data. If marketers intend to apply the results to individual categories of the things or people being studied, cross-tabulation may be quite useful, especially in tabulating joint occurrences. For example, a cross-tabulation could show how men and women differ in some behavior, such as purchasing automobile tires.

After the data are tabulated, they must be analyzed. **Statistical interpretation** focuses on what is typical or what deviates from the average. It indicates how widely responses vary and how they are distributed in relation to the variable being measured. This interpretation is another facet of marketing research that calls for marketers to apply judgment or intuition. Also, when they interpret statistics, marketers rely on estimates of expected error or deviation from the true values of the population. The analysis of data may lead researchers to accept or reject the hypothesis being studied. In Figure 6.10, computer software packager SPSS allows for tabulation, analysis, and preparation of reports, maps, and charts to assist in marketing research projects.

Studies require careful interpretation by the researcher. If the results of a study are valid, the decision maker should take action; if it is discovered that a question has been incorrectly worded, the results should be ignored.

For example, if a study by an electric utility company reveals that 50 percent of its customers believe that meter readers are "friendly," is that good, bad, or indifferent? Two important benchmarks help interpret the finding: how the 50

FIGURE 6.9

Profiling the audience of cable television is a descriptive study (SOURCE: Nielsen Media Research)

Track your audience with CAP.

Nielsen's Cable Audience Profile (CAP) is the answer to your audience research quest. Through CAP you can determine a cable network's delivery on your system, compare this performance to other systems and obtain important local demographic data. Call your Nielsen representative at (212)708-7719.

CABLE AUDIENCE PROFILE
Information with Integrity

Nielsen Media Research

a company of The Dun & Bradstreet Corporation   Reader Service Number 12   Visit the Nielsen booth at the CAB conference.

FIGURE 6.10

SPSS software for tabulation and analysis of data (Copyright © 1988, SPSS, Inc.)

percent figure compares to competitors' and how it compares to a previous time period. The point is that managers must understand the research results and relate the results to a context that permits effective decision making.[12]

Reporting Research Findings

The final step in the marketing research process is preparing a report of the research findings. Before writing the report, the marketer must take a clear, objective look at the findings to see how well the gathered facts answer the fundamental research question posed in the beginning. In most cases, it is extremely doubtful that the study will provide everything needed to answer the research question. Thus a lack of completeness and the reasons for it probably will have to be pointed out in the report.[13]

Usually, results are communicated in a formal written report. Marketers must allow time for the writing task when they plan and schedule the project. Because the purpose of the report is to communicate with the decision makers who will use the research findings, researchers also should decide beforehand how much detail and supporting data to include in their report. Often they will give their summary and recommendation first, especially if decision makers do not have time to study how the results were obtained. A technical report does allow its users to analyze

12. Michael J. Olivette, "Marketing Research in the Electric Utility Industry," *Marketing News,* Jan. 2, 1987, p. 13.
13. George E. Breen and Albert B. Blankenship, "How to Present a Research Report That Gets Action," *Marketing Times*, March–April 1983, p. 33.

data and interpret recommendations because it describes the research methods and procedures and the most important data gathered.

A survey of top corporate executives indicated that they have a low opinion of marketing research reports. Their chief complaints were the impracticality of results and the inefficiency of research reports (inefficient in the sense of the executive time needed to read them). Specifically, executives stated that (1) researchers are captivated by techniques and often fit the problem to a favored technique and (2) researchers prefer complex studies, language, and reports to simple ones.[14] Obviously, the researcher must recognize the needs and expectations of the report user and adapt to them.

When marketing decision makers have a firm grasp of research methods and procedures, they are better able to integrate reported findings and personal experience. If marketers can spot limitations in research from reading the report, then personal experience assumes additional importance in the decision-making process. The inability of some marketers to understand basic statistical assumptions and data gathering procedures causes them to misuse research findings. Thus report writers should understand the backgrounds and research abilities of those who will use the report to make decisions. Providing adequate explanations in understandable language makes it easier for decision makers to apply the findings and consequently diminishes the likelihood that a report will be misused or ignored entirely. Communicating with potential research users prior to writing a report can help the researcher provide information that will, in fact, improve decision making.

Now that we have looked briefly at the factors to consider in planning a research project, let us explore—in general terms—how marketers design research procedures to fit particular problems. The next section discusses how to collect data that will fulfill the design.

Designing the Research

That marketers must be able to design research procedures and produce reliable and valid data may seem obvious. However, reliability and validity have precise meanings for researchers. A research technique has **reliability** if it produces almost identical results in successive repeated trials. But a reliable technique is not necessarily valid. To have **validity,** the method must measure what it is supposed to measure, not something else. A valid research method provides data that can be used to test the hypothesis being investigated.

Now that we have introduced the basic aims of research, we are ready to examine some of the main concepts of designing research.

Sampling

By systematically choosing a limited number of units to represent the characteristics of a total population, marketers can project the reactions of a total market or

14. Joseph H. Rabin, "Top Executives Have Low Opinion of Marketing Research, Marketers' Role in Strategic Planning," *Marketing News,* Oct. 16, 1981, p. 3.

market segment from the reactions of the sample. The objective of **sampling** in marketing research therefore is to select representative units from a total population. Figure 6.11 shows that a failure to select the correct sample can lead to disastrous results. Sampling procedures must be used in studying human behavior as well as in estimating the likelihood of events not connected directly with an activity. For one thing, it would be almost impossible to investigate all members of a population because the time and resources available for research are limited.

A **population,** or "universe," is made up of all elements, units, or individuals that are of interest to researchers for a specific study. For example, if a Gallup poll is designed to predict the results of a presidential election, all registered voters in the United States would constitute the population. A representative national sample of several thousand registered voters would be selected in the Gallup poll to project the probable voting outcome.

Random Sampling   In simple **random sampling,** all the units in a population have an equal chance of appearing in the sample. Random sampling is basic probability sampling. The various events that can occur have an equal or known chance of taking place. For example, a specific card from a deck should have a 1/52 probability of being drawn at any one time. Similarly, if each student at a university or college were given a sequential number and these numbers were mixed up in a large basket, each student's number would have a known probability of being selected.

FIGURE 6.11

Selecting the wrong sample can make survey results useless (SOURCE: Courtesy of Survey Sampling, Inc. Copyright 1988, Survey Sampling, Inc.)

Sample units are ordinarily chosen by selecting from a table of random numbers statistically generated so that each digit, zero through nine, will have an equal probability of occurring in each position in the sequence. The sequentially numbered elements of a population are sampled randomly by selecting the units whose numbers appear in the table of random numbers.

Stratified Sampling   In **stratified sampling,** the population of interest is divided into groups according to a common characteristic or attribute, and then a probability sample is conducted within each group. The stratified sample may reduce some of the error that could occur in a simple random sample. By ensuring that each major group or segment of the population receives its proportionate share of sample units, investigators avoid including too many or too few sample units from each strata. Usually, samples are stratified when researchers believe that there may be variations among different types of respondents. For example, many political opinion surveys are stratified by sex, race, and age.

Area Sampling   **Area sampling** involves two stages: (1) selecting a probability sample of geographic areas such as blocks, census tracts, or census enumeration districts and (2) selecting units or individuals within the selected geographic areas for the sample. This approach is a variation of stratified sampling, with the geographic areas serving as the segments, or primary units, used in sampling. To select the units or individuals within the geographic areas, researchers may choose every nth house or unit, or random selection procedures may be used to pick out a given number of units or individuals from a total listing within the selected geographic areas. Area sampling may be used when a complete list of the population is not available.

Quota Sampling   **Quota sampling** is different from other forms of sampling in that it is judgmental. That is, the final choice of respondents is left to the interviewers. A study of consumers who wear eyeglasses, for example, may be conducted by interviewing any person who wears eyeglasses. In quota sampling, there are some controls—usually limited to two or three variables such as age, sex, and education—over the selection of respondents. The controls attempt to ensure that representative categories of respondents are interviewed.

   Quota samples are unique because they are not probability samples; not everyone has an equal chance of being selected. Therefore, sampling error cannot be measured statistically. Judgmental samples are used most often in exploratory research, when hypotheses are being developed. Often, a small judgmental sample will not be projected to the total population, although the findings may provide valuable insights into a problem. Quota samples are useful when people with some unusual characteristic are found and questioned about the topic of interest. A probability sample to find people allergic to cats would be highly inefficient.

Experimentation

Finding out which variable or variables caused an event to occur may be difficult unless researchers adopt an experimental approach, which is used to investigate relationships. **Experimentation** involves maintaining as constants those factors that are related to or may affect the variables under investigation so that the effects of

FIGURE 6.12

Relationship between
independent and de-
pendent variables

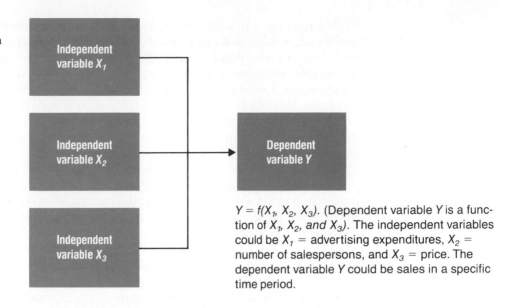

$Y = f(X_1, X_2, X_3)$. (Dependent variable Y is a function of X_1, X_2, and X_3). The independent variables could be X_1 = advertising expenditures, X_2 = number of salespersons, and X_3 = price. The dependent variable Y could be sales in a specific time period.

the experimental variables may be measured. For instance, when Coca-Cola Company taste tests a new cola formula, all variables should be held constant except the formula of the beverage. **Marketing experimentation** is a set of rules and procedures data gathering is organized under to expedite analysis and interpretation.

In the experimental approach, an **independent variable** (a variable not influenced by or dependent on other variables) is usually manipulated and changes are measured in a **dependent variable** (a variable contingent on, or restricted to, one or a set of values assumed by the independent variable). Figure 6.12 shows the relationship between these variables. For example, when a book publisher sets the price of a new dictionary, it may want to estimate the number of dictionaries that could be sold at various prices. The dependent variable would be sales, and the independent variable would be price. Researchers would design the experiment so that other independent variables that might influence sales—such as advertising, distribution, and variation of the product—would be controlled. Experiments may be conducted in the laboratory or in the field; each research setting has advantages and disadvantages.

Laboratory Settings Participants or respondents in marketing experiments are often invited to a central location to react or respond to experimental stimuli. In such an isolated setting it is possible to control independent variables that might influence the outcome of an experiment. The features of laboratory settings might include a taste kitchen, video equipment, slide projectors, tape recorders, one-way mirrors, central telephone banks, and interview rooms. In an experiment to determine the influence of price (independent variable) on sales of dictionaries (dependent variable), respondents would be invited to a laboratory—a room with table, chairs, and sample dictionaries—before the dictionary was available in stores. The dictionary would be placed on a table with competitors' dictionaries. Analysts would then question respondents about their reactions to the dictionaries at various prices.

One problem with a laboratory setting is its isolation from the real world. It is simply not possible to duplicate all the conditions that affect choices in the market-place. On the other hand, by controlling variables that cannot be controlled in the real world, laboratory simulations can focus on variables that marketers think may be significant for the success of a marketing strategy. Market Facts, Inc., a leading marketing research firm, reported that test market laboratories are being used more frequently today. Of the largest consumer goods and services companies surveyed by the firm, 37 percent reported using test market laboratories in the preceding year.[15]

Field Settings   The experimental approach also can be used in field or survey research. Market Facts reported that 36 percent of major consumer goods and services companies use controlled store testing.[16] This procedure tests consumer reaction to new products or product modification in the store under usual shopping conditions. Field settings give the marketer an opportunity to obtain a more direct test of marketing decisions than laboratory settings.

There are several limitations to field experiments. Field experiments can be influenced or biased by inadvertent events such as weather or major economic news. Carryover effects of field experiments are impossible to avoid. What respondents have been asked to do in one time period will influence what they do in the next time period. For example, evaluating competing advertisements may influence attempts to obtain objective evaluations of new proposals for a firm's future advertising. Respondent cooperation may be difficult because respondents do not understand what role they play in the experiment. Finally, only a small number of variables can be controlled in field experiments. It is impossible, for example, to control competitors' advertising or their attempts to influence the outcome of the experiment. Tactics that competitors can use to thwart field test marketing efforts include couponing, temporary price discounting, and the use of point-of-purchase materials.

Experimentation is used in marketing research design to improve hypothesis testing. However, whether experiments are conducted in the laboratory or in the field, many assumptions must be made to limit the number of factors and isolate causes. Marketing decision makers must recognize that assumptions may diminish the reliability of the research findings. For example, viewing proposed advertisements on a videocassette recorder in a laboratory is different from watching the advertisements on television at home.

Simulated test markets for new products can use an experimental approach. For example, one marketing research company, BehaviorScan, brought a new dimension to experimental research by combining cable television, supermarket scanners, and computers. The company tracks every commercial its panelists watch and every purchase they make in a supermarket or drugstore. This procedure permits a projection of the impact of advertising on new product purchases by various consumer groups.[17]

---

15. Based on a survey conducted by Market Facts, Inc., Apr. 28, 1983.
16. Ibid.
17. James S. Figuia, "Simulated Test Markets Are an Oasis in an Era of Marketing Research Which Doesn't Deliver," *Marketing News,* Jan. 20. 1984, p. 3.

Gathering Research Data

As mentioned in our discussion of collecting data, the two types of data available to marketing researchers are primary and secondary. Primary data are observed and recorded or collected directly from respondents; secondary data are compiled inside or outside the organization for some purpose other than the current investigation. Firsthand information obtained to test a hypothesis is primary data, for example, survey results of consumer attitudes toward Coca-Cola's Diet Coke. Secondary data may be internal accounting records and other information stored in the company's marketing databank or information collected by such external organizations as the Census Bureau and trade associations.

Most marketing research investigations use a combination of primary and secondary data sources. A thorough search of internal records and past studies is particularly useful in determining which additional data should be gathered by primary collection methods such as surveys or observation.

Survey Methods

Survey methods include interviews by mail or telephone and personal interviews. Selection of an interviewing method depends on the nature of the problem, the data needed to test the hypothesis, and the resources, such as funding and personnel, that are available to the researcher. Table 6.2 summarizes and compares the advantages of the various methods. Researchers must know exactly what type of information is needed to test the hypothesis and what type of information can be obtained through interviewing. Table 6.3 lists the most frequently used consumer survey techniques. The data are based on a survey of large American consumer goods and services companies. Gathering information by survey methods is becoming increasingly difficult because respondent rates are declining "across the board." There is also an indication that people with higher incomes and education are most likely to respond. Problems include difficulty in hiring qualified interviewers and respondents' reluctance to participate in surveys owing to overly long questionnaires, dull topics, and time pressures.[18] Also there is a fear of crime, which results in respondents' failure to trust interviewers.

Mail Surveys In mail surveys, questionnaires are sent to respondents who are encouraged to complete and return them. This type of survey is used most often when the individuals chosen for questioning are spread over a wide area and funds for the survey are limited. A mail survey is the least expensive survey method as long as the response rate is high enough to produce reliable results. The main disadvantages of this method are the possibility that the response rate may be low or that the results may be misleading if respondents are significantly different from the population being sampled.

There is usually a high response rate when respondents have some motivation to return the questionnaire. They might be regular customers, organization members,

18. Martha Farnsworth Riche, "Who Says Yes?" *American Demographics*, February 1987, p. 8; George Gallup Jr., "Survey Research: Current Problems and Future Opportunities," *Journal of Consumer Marketing*, Winter 1988, pp. 27–29.

or hard-to-interview respondents who have an interest in the topic. Some techniques that have been useful in achieving a 50 to 70 percent response rate include (1) giving advance notification (postal card, letter, mailgram, or phone call) prior to mailing the actual questionnaire package; (2) using a questionnaire package that is personalized; (3) letting respondents know the benefits of filling out the questionnaire, making it easy for them to complete, offering them a monetary incentive, and including a self-addressed stamped envelope; (4) sending a follow-up letter two to three weeks after mailing the questionnaire; and (5) making the results of the survey available to the respondents upon request.[19]

Although these techniques have proved useful in increasing response rates, they may introduce sample-composition bias, which results when those responding to a survey differ in some important respect from those not responding to the survey. In other words, response-enhancing techniques may alienate some portion of the sample and appeal to another, causing the results to be nonrepresentative of the

TABLE 6.2

Comparison of the three basic survey methods

19. Milton M. Pressley, "Try These Tips to Get 50% to 70% Response Rate from Mail Surveys of Commercial Populations," *Marketing News*, Jan. 21, 1983, p. 16.

	MAIL SURVEYS	TELEPHONE SURVEYS	PERSONAL INTERVIEW SURVEYS
Economy	Potentially the lowest cost per interview if there is an adequate return rate; increased postage rates are raising costs	Avoids interviewers' travel expenses; less expensive than in-home interviews; most common survey method	In-home interviewing is the most expensive interviewing method; shopping mall, focus-group interviewing may lower costs
Flexibility	Inflexible; questionnaire must be short, easy for respondents to complete; no probing questions; may take more time to implement than other survey methods	Flexible because interviewers can ask probing questions, encourage respondents to answer questions; rapport may be gained, but observations are impossible	Most flexible method; respondents can react to visual materials, help fill out questionnaire; because observation is possible, demographic data are more accurate; in-depth probes are possible
Interviewer bias	Interviewer bias eliminated; questionnaires can be returned anonymously	Some anonymity; may be hard to develop trust among respondents	Refusals may be decreased by interviewers' rapport-building efforts; interviewers' personal attributes may bias respondents
Sampling and respondents' cooperation	Obtaining a complete mailing list is difficult; nonresponse is a major disadvantage	Sample must be limited to respondents with telephones and listed numbers; busy signals, no answers, and nonresponse—including refusals—are problems	Not-at-homes are more difficult to deal with; focus-group, shopping mall interviewing may overcome these problems

TABLE 6.3

Changes in the frequency of use of survey research techniques

	1978	1983	1987	1987 vs. 1983
Central WATS	90%	91%	98%	+7
Shopping mall intercepts	89%	90%	86%	−4
Focus groups	87%	90%	98%	+8
Mail panel	53%	57%	67%	10
Custom mail	46%	33%	43%	+10
Purchase diary	46%	48%	37%	−11
Door-to-door	61%	47%	39%	−8
Trade surveys	33%	39%	40%	+1
Local telephone	67%	61%	*	*
Scanner panel	*	*	39%	*
Average number named	5.7	5.6	5.5	

* Not measured.

SOURCE: *Practices, Trends and Expectations for the Market Research Industry 1987*, Market Facts, Inc., April 29, 1987, p. 23.

population of interest.[20] Perhaps as a result of these problems and the others discussed earlier, firms surveyed in Table 6.2 spent less than 5 percent of their research funds for direct mail surveys.

Premiums or incentives used to encourage respondents to return questionnaires have been effective in developing panels of respondents who are interviewed repeatedly by mail. Mail panels, which are selected to represent a market or market segment, are especially useful for evaluating new products, providing general information about consumers, and providing records of consumers' purchases. As Table 6.3 indicates, 67 percent of the companies surveyed used consumer mail panels, but these panels represented a major budget share for less than 15 percent of the companies. It is interesting that 37 percent of the sample used consumer purchase diaries. (These surveys are similar to mail panels, but consumers only keep track of purchases.) Consumer mail panels and consumer purchase diaries are much more widely used than direct mail surveys, but they do have shortcomings. Research indicates that the people who take the time to fill out a consumer diary have higher income and are more educated than the general population. If researchers include less-educated consumers in the panel, they must risk poorer response rates.[21]

Telephone Surveys In telephone surveys, respondents' answers to a questionnaire are recorded by interviewers. A telephone survey has some advantages over a mail survey. The rate of response is higher because it takes less effort to answer the telephone and talk than to fill out a questionnaire and return it. If there are enough

20. Charles D. Parker and Kevin F. McCrohan, "Increasing Mail Survey Response Rates: A Discussion of Methods and Induced Bias," in *Marketing: Theories and Concepts for an Era of Change,* John Summey, R. Viswanathan, Ronald Taylor, and Karen Glynn, eds. (Southern Marketing Association, 1983), pp. 254–256.
21. Martha Farnsworth Riche, "Who Says Yes?", *American Demographics,* February 1987, p. 8.

interviewers, telephone surveys can be conducted very quickly. Thus they can be used by political candidates or organizations seeking an immediate reaction to an event. In addition, this survey technique permits interviewers to gain rapport with respondents and ask probing questions.

WATS (Wide Area Telecommunications Service) significantly reduces the expense of long-distance telephone interviewing. The data in Table 6.3 show that virtually all the surveyed firms used telephone interviewing. Computer-assisted telephone interviewing permits an integration of questionnaire, data collection, and tabulations and provides data to aid decision makers in the shortest time possible.

In computer-assisted telephone interviewing, the paper questionnaire is replaced by a video screen or a cathode ray tube (CRT). Responses are entered on a terminal keyboard, or the interviewer can use a light pen (a pen-shaped flashlight) to record a response on a light-sensitive screen. On the most advanced devices, the interviewer uses a finger to touch the responses on a touch-sensitive CRT. Open-ended responses can be typed on the keyboard or recorded with paper and pencil.

CRT interviewing saves time and facilitates monitoring the progress of interviews. Entry functions are largely eliminated; the computer determines which question to display on the CRT, skipping irrelevant questions. Because data are available as soon as they are entered into the system, cumbersome hand computations are eliminated and interim results can be quickly retrieved. With some systems, a microcomputer may be taken to off-site locations for use in data analysis. Some suppliers claim that CRT telephone interviewing—including hardware, software, and operation costs—is less expensive than conventional paper and pencil methods.[22]

Telephone interviews have disadvantages, however. They are limited to oral communication; visual aids or observation cannot be included. Interpretation of results must make adjustments for subjects who are not at home or who do not have telephones. Many households are excluded from telephone directories by choice (unlisted numbers) or because the residents moved after the directory was published. If households with unlisted numbers are systematically excluded, the resulting sample will be somewhat older, more rural, more white, more educated, more retired, and more white-collar than the universe of households with telephone service.[23]

These findings have serious implications for the use of telephone samples in conducting surveys. Some adjustment must be made for groups of respondents that may be undersampled because of a smaller-than-average incidence of telephone listings. Nondirectory telephone samples can overcome such bias. Various methods are available, including random-digit dialing (adding random numbers to the telephone prefix) and plus-one telephone sampling (adding one to the last digit of a number in the directory). These methods make it feasible to dial any working number, whether it is or is not listed in a directory.

Telephone surveys, like mail and personal interview surveys, are sometimes used to develop panels of respondents who can be interviewed repeatedly to measure changes in attitudes or behavior. Use of these telephone panels is increasing.

Personal Interview Surveys Traditionally, marketing researchers have favored the face-to-face interview, primarily because of its flexibility. Various audiovisual aids—pictures, products, diagrams, or prerecorded advertising copy—can be incorporated into a personal interview. Rapport gained through direct interaction usually permits more in-depth interviewing, including probes, follow-up questions, or psychological tests. In addition, because face-to-face interviews can be longer, they can yield more information. Finally, respondents can be selected more carefully, and reasons for nonresponse can be explored. Quick Test Opinion Centers (see Figure 6.13) advertises its focus group interviewing, one-on-one interviewing, mall intercept interviewing, and other personal interviewing services.

Shopping Mall Intercept Interviews In the past, most personal interviews, which were based on random sampling or prearranged appointments, were conducted in the respondent's home. Today, the nature of personal interviews has changed. As Table 6.3 indicates, most personal interviews are conducted in shopping malls. The technique consists of interviewing a percentage of persons passing by certain "intercept" points in a mall. Although there are many variations of this technique, Table 6.3 indicates that shopping mall intercept interviewing is the third most popular survey technique used today, next only to WATS interviewing. Not only did 86 percent of the major consumer goods and services companies use this technique, but almost half reported that shopping mall intercept interviewing was their major expenditure on survey research.

As with any face-to-face interviewing method, mall intercept interviewing has many advantages. The interviewer is in a position to recognize and react to respondents' nonverbal indications of confusion. Respondents can be shown product prototypes, videotapes of commercials, story boards, and the like, and reactions can be sought. The mall environment lets the researcher deal with complex situations, such as those requiring taste tests, by ensuring that all the respondents are reacting to the same product, which can be prepared and monitored from the mall test kitchen or some other facility. Lower cost, greater control, and the ability to conduct tests requiring bulky equipment are the major reasons for the popularity of this survey method.[24]

Research indicates that given a comparable sample of respondents, shopping mall intercept interviewing is a suitable substitute for more traditional telephone interviewing.[25] In addition, there seem to be no significant differences in the completeness of consumer responses between telephone interviewing and shopping mall intercept interviewing. For questions dealing with socially desirable behavior, shopping mall intercept respondents appear to be more honest about their past behavior.[26]

On-site computer interviewing consists of respondents completing a self-administered questionnaire displayed on a computer monitor. General Motors Corp. used this technique to ask passersby at automobile shows their opinions about the Chevrolet Astro Van. After analyzing the data, GM learned that most of the eight hundred respondents did not like the placement of the fuel filler in the middle of the side body panel.[27]

Focus-Group Interview   The object of a focus-group interview is to observe group interaction when members are exposed to an idea or concept. Often, these interviews are conducted informally, without a structured questionnaire. Consumer attitudes, behavior, lifestyles, needs, and desires can be explored in a flexible and creative manner through focus-group interviews. Researchers approach consumers without preconceived notions. Questions are open-ended and stimulate consumers to answer in their own words. Researchers who hear something they do not fully understand or something unexpected and interesting can probe for insights into deeper thoughts and feelings that explain consumer behavior.[28] Table 6.3 indicates that 98 percent of the firms surveyed used focus-group interviewing, and less than 10 percent of the firms spent the major share of their budgets on this technique.

In-Home Interviews   Although in-home (door-to-door) interviews represent less than 10 percent of the budget spent on surveys, 39 percent of the largest consumer companies use this technique. Because it may be desirable to eliminate group influence, in-depth interviews offer a real advantage when thoroughness of self-

24. Roger Gates and Paul J. Soloman, "Research Using the Mall Intercept: State of the Art," *Journal of Advertising Research,* August–September 1982, pp. 47–48.
25. Alan J. Bush and A. Parasuraman, "Mall Intercept Versus Telephone-Interviewing Environment," *Journal of Advertising Research,* April–May 1985, p. 42.
26. Alan J. Bush and Joseph F. Hair, Jr., "An Assessment of the Mall Intercept as a Data Collecting Method," *Journal of Marketing Research,* May 1985, p. 162.
27. Bernie Whalen, "On-Site Computer Interviewing Yields Research Data Instantly," *Marketing News,* Nov. 9, 1984, p. 1.
28. NFO Research Inc., Advertisement, *Marketing News,* Jan. 21, 1983, p. 20.

disclosure is important. In a long-depth interview of forty-five to ninety minutes, respondents can be probed to reveal their real motivations, feelings, behaviors, and aspirations. In-depth interviews permit the discovery of emotional "hot buttons" that provide psychological insights.[29]

Coca-Cola failed to investigate consumers' emotional attachment to its existing product before launching New Coke. The company only conducted superficial taste tests with 200,000 people in shopping malls, asking, "Do you like it or don't you?" In-depth interviews might have revealed that even if the new formula tasted better, many people might still be suspicious of it.[30]

Questionnaire Construction A carefully constructed questionnaire is essential to the success of a survey. First, questions must be designed to elicit information that meets the study's data requirements. Questions must be clear, easy to understand, and directed toward a definable objective. Until that objective has been defined, researchers should not attempt to develop a questionnaire because the composition of the questions depends on the nature of the objective and the detail demanded. One common mistake in questionnaire construction is to ask questions that interest the researchers but do not provide information that helps decide whether to accept or reject a hypothesis. Finally, the most important rule is to maintain an unbiased, objective approach in composing questions.

Several kinds of questions can be included: open-ended, dichotomous, and multiple-choice. Following are examples of each kind of question:

OPEN-ENDED QUESTION
What is your general opinion of the American Express Optima Card?

_____

_____

_____

DICHOTOMOUS QUESTION
Do you presently have an American Express Optima Card?

Yes   _____
No   _____

MULTIPLE-CHOICE QUESTION
What age group are you in?

Under 20   _____
20–29   _____
30–39   _____
40–49   _____
50–59   _____
60 and over   _____

29. Hal Sokolow, "In-Depth Interviews Increasing in Importance," *Marketing News,* Sept. 13, 1985, p. 26.
30. Mitchell J. Shields, "Coke's Research Fizzles: Fails to Factor in Consumer Loyalty," *Adweek,* July 15, 1985, p. 8.

TABLE 6.4

A series of questions
designed to overcome
the objectionable na-
ture of a subject

Problem

Have you ever shoplifted anything?
  1 no
  2 yes

Revision

As you know, there is now a great deal of community concern about shoplifting and how to handle it. Some people believe it is a serious problem, but others believe it is not. How about yourself? How serious a problem do you think shoplifting is in our community?
  1 serious
  2 moderate
  3 slight
  4 not at all

During the past few years do you think the frequency of shoplifting has increased, stayed about the same, or decreased in this community?
  1 increased
  2 stayed about the same
  3 decreased

When you were a teenager, did you personally know anyone who took something from a store without paying for it?
  1 no
  2 yes

How about yourself? Did you ever consider taking anything from a store without paying for it?
  1 no
  2 yes

(If yes) Did you actually take it?
  1 no
  2 yes

SOURCE: Don A. Dillman, *Mail and Telephone Surveys: The Total Design Method* (New York: Wiley, 1978), p. 107. Used by permission.

Researchers must be very careful about questions that a person might consider too personal or that might result in a respondent's admitting to activities that other people are likely to condemn. Questions of this type should be worded in such a way as to make them less offensive. For example, Table 6.4 shows how a series of questions can be designed to overcome the potentially objectionable nature of a question about shoplifting. Even though this approach does not guarantee truthful responses, it should improve their probability of occurring. Note that the series of questions in Table 6.4 asks about the importance of shoplifting as a crime. These questions are designed to measure beliefs or behavior both indirectly and directly.

For persons in special markets likely to own or have access to a personal computer (e.g., executives, scientists, engineers), questionnaires may be programmed on a diskette and the diskettes delivered through the mail. This technique may cost less than a telephone interview and eliminate bias by simplifying flow patterns in answering questions. The respondent sees less clutter on the screen than on a printed questionnaire; also, the respondents' attention may peak owing to the novelty of the approach.

Observation Methods

Various methods other than surveys can be used to collect primary data. In using the **observation method,** researchers record respondents' overt behavior, taking note of physical conditions and events. Direct contact with respondents is avoided; instead, their actions are examined and noted systematically. For example, researchers might use observation methods to answer the question, "How long does the average McDonald's restaurant customer have to wait in line before being served?"

Observation methods can be used to control such retail store factors as inventory, spoilage, and breakage. Observation may also be combined with interviews. For example, during personal interviews, the condition of a respondent's home or other possessions may be observed and recorded, and demographic information such as race, approximate age, and sex can be confirmed by direct observation.

Data gathered through observation sometimes can be biased if the respondent is aware of the observation process. The Application on page 204 describes one approach for eliminating bias in observation. An observer can be placed in a natural market environment, such as a grocery store, without biasing or influencing shoppers' actions. However, if the presence of a human observer is likely to bias the outcome or if human sensory abilities are inadequate, mechanical means may be used to record behavior. **Mechanical observation devices** include cameras, recorders, counting machines, and equipment to record physiological changes in individuals. For instance, an audiometer is used to record the station to which a television or radio receiver is tuned. Similarly, a special camera can be used to record eye movements of respondents looking at an advertisement; the sequence of reading and the parts of the advertisement that receive greatest attention can be detected. Electric scanners in supermarkets are mechanical observation devices that provide an exciting opportunity for marketing research. Scanner technology can provide accurate data on sales and consumers' purchase patterns. Some supermarket chains are now selling scanner data to marketing researchers.[31]

Observation methods, as are survey methods, are used to test hypotheses, discover problems, or provide a continuous flow of information into a databank. Observation is straightforward and avoids a central problem of survey methods, motivating respondents to state their true feelings or opinions. However, observation tends to be descriptive. When it is the only method of data collection, it may not provide insights into causal relationships. Another limitation is that analyses based on observation are subject to the biases and limitations of the observer or the mechanical device.

Secondary Data Collection

In addition to or instead of collecting primary data, marketers may use available reports and other information to study a marketing problem. An organization's marketing databank may contain information about past marketing activities, such as sales records and research reports, that can be used to test hypotheses and pinpoint problems.

Secondary data also are found in periodicals, government publications, and unpublished sources. Periodicals such as *Business Week, Sales and Marketing Management,* and *Industrial Marketing* print general information that is helpful for

31. Fitzhugh L. Carr, "Scanners in Marketing Research: Paradise (Almost)," *Marketing News,* Jan. 4, 1985, pp. 1, 15.

Systematic Observation—An Effective Way to Gather Research Data

Although survey methods usually work quite well as a way of obtaining primary data, the answers they provide do not always relate to actual behavior; people may exaggerate, attempt to please, or even lie when they participate in a survey. Systematic observation is one way to overcome these problems. In the observation method, researchers record respondents' overt behavior but avoid any direct contact with the respondents.

Observation has several advantages, but it also presents two problems. First is *selective perception:* Most people have a highly selective perception, and what they really see depends on their background. Socialization determines how people look at the world, and their value systems tell them how to interpret what they see. The second problem is *nonrepresentative behavior.* With observational techniques there is a tendency to think that the observed behavior is representative of the total population. However, this is not necessarily true because the observed behavior may be an isolated incident and not representative of normal behavior.

Researchers have developed a method to overcome these problems by using a computerized data collector in a controlled research design. Step 1 in this process is developing a code. The code consists of categories of behavior that help researchers describe a complex series of behaviors. Step 2 is constructing a design or set of instructions that tells the researcher how to gather data. This design helps the researcher control extraneous variations in observed behavior.

Step 3 is the actual collecting of data through the use of a hand-held, battery-powered data collector and analyzer, which helps researchers obtain data that effectively measures behavior. Step 4 is quantifying the results, letting the researcher calculate ratios between groups of behaviors as well as generating minimum, maximum, and average times for each behavior. Researchers may also conduct further analysis to compare behaviors using this research design.

This formalized, four-step observation method is an effective research tool, and it eliminates many of the disadvantages of survey methods.

SOURCE: Daniel T. Seymour, "Seeing Is Believing with Systematic Observation," *Marketing News,* Aug. 28, 1987, p. 36.

defining problems and developing hypotheses. *Survey of Buying Power,* the annual supplement to *Sales and Marketing Management,* contains sales data for major industries on a county-by-county basis. Many marketers consult federal government publications such as the *Census of Business,* the *Census of Agriculture,* and the *Census of Populations* available from the Superintendent of Documents in

Washington, D.C. Table 6.5 summarizes the major external sources of secondary data, excluding syndicated services.

Syndicated data services collect general information that is sold to clients. Their information is available only to subscribers. American Research Bureau (ARB) furnishes television stations and media buyers with estimates of the number of viewers at specific times. Selling Areas Marketing, Inc. (SAMI) furnishes monthly information that describes market shares for specific types of manufacturers. The A. C. Nielsen Company Retail Index gathers data about products primarily sold through food stores and drugstores. This information includes total sales in a product category, sales of clients' own brands, and sales of important competing brands. The Market Research Corporation of America (MRCA) collects data through a national panel of consumers to provide information about purchases. MRCA maintains data on sales by brands classified by age, race, sex, education, occupation, and family size.

Similar organizations operate at the local level. Market Search, a marketing research company in Indianapolis, for example, offers Indyindex. This monthly

TABLE 6.5
Guide to external sources of secondary data

Trade journals	Virtually every industry or type of business has a trade journal. These journals give a feel for the industry—its size, degree of competition, range of companies involved, and problems. To find trade journals in the field of interest, check *Ulrich's,* a reference book that lists American and foreign periodicals by subject.
Trade associations	Almost every industry, product category, and profession has its own association. Depending on the strength of each group, they often conduct research, publish journals, conduct training sessions, and hold conventions. A call or a letter to the association may yield information not available in published sources. To find out which associations serve which industries, check the *Encyclopedia of Associations.*
International sources	Periodical indexes, such as the *F&S Index International,* are particularly useful for overseas product or company information. More general sources include the *United Nations Statistical Yearbook* and the *International Labour Organization's Yearbook of Labour Statistics.*
Government	The federal government, through its various departments and agencies, collects, analyzes, and publishes statistics on practically everything. Government documents also have their own set of indexes: the *Monthly Catalog.* Other useful indexes for government-generated information are the *American Statistical Index* and the *Congressional Information Service.*
Books in Print (BIP)	*BIP* is a two-volume reference book found in most libraries. All books issued by U.S. publishers and currently in print are listed by subject, title, and author.
Periodical indexes	The library's reference section contains indexes on virtually every discipline. The *Business Periodicals Index,* for example, indexes each article in all major business periodicals.
Computerized literature-retrieval databases	Literature-retrieval databases are periodical indexes stored in a computer. Books and dissertations are also included. Key words (such as the name of a subject) are used to search a database and generate references.

omnibus study for small Indianapolis businesses contains information gleaned from three hundred consumer telephone interviews about product preferences, prices, stores, and other marketing topics. Small businesses use this research information to plan their marketing activities.[32]

Another type of secondary data available for a fee involves demographic analysis. Companies that specialize in demographic databanks have the special knowledge and computer systems to work with the very complex U.S. Census databank. As a result, they are able to respond to specialized requests that the Census Bureau cannot or will not handle. Such information may be valuable in tracking demographic changes that have implications for consumer behavior.[33]

Internal sources of information can contribute tremendously to research. An organization's accounting records are an excellent source of data, but, strangely enough, they are often overlooked. The large volume of data an accounting department collects does not automatically flow to the marketing area. As a result, detailed information about costs, sales, customer accounts, or profits by product category may not be part of the MIS. This condition is especially true in organizations that do not store marketing information on a systematic basis. As pointed out early in this chapter, such information—collected systematically and continuously through a carefully constructed marketing information system—is essential to the success of marketing efforts.

Marketing Research Ethics

Clearly, marketing research and information systems are vital to marketing decision making. Today, managers in all types of organizations are recognizing the need for more and better information. One final area of marketing research practice must not go unmentioned. It is imperative that marketers establish acceptable standards of education and ethics. Too often, respondents are unfairly manipulated, and research clients are not told about flaws in data. Attempts to stamp out shoddy practices and establish generally acceptable procedures for conducting research will enhance the professional image of marketing researchers.

One common practice that hurts the image of marketing research is called "sugging" (an acronym for "selling under the guise of marketing research"). A leading European marketing research association (ESOMAR) is attempting to get research companies and marketing research firms worldwide to adopt codes and policies prohibiting this practice. Germany has passed a law that prohibits companies from calling people in their homes for any reason. Research firms want to avoid similar legislation in other countries.[34]

Because so many parties are involved in the marketing research process, developing shared ethical concern is difficult. The relationships among respondents who cooperate and share information, subcontractors such as interviewing companies, marketing research agencies that manage projects, and organizations that use the

32. "Marketing Research Briefs," *Marketing News,* Jan. 21, 1983, p. 5.
33. Ronald L. Vaughn, "Demographic Data Banks: A New Management Resource," *Business Horizons,* November–December 1984, pp. 38–42.
34. Lynn Colemar, "ESOMAR Hits Selling Disguised as Research," *Marketing News,* Jan. 4, 1988, p. 1.

data, are interdependent and complex. Ethical conflict typically occurs because the parties involved in the marketing research process often have different objectives. For example, the organization that uses the data tends to be result-oriented, and success is often based on performance rather than following a set of standards. On the other hand, a data gathering subcontractor is evaluated based on ability to follow a specific set of standards or rules. The relationships among all participants in marketing research must be understood so that decision making becomes ethical. Without clear understanding and agreement, including mutual adoption of standards, ethical conflict will lead to mistrust and questionable research results.[35] For example, because A. C. Nielsen's people meter registered consistently lower television ratings than the old diary rating system, in 1987 ABC and CBS refused to accept this new innovative method of determining ratings. The two networks use ratings for their sales and programming decisions, and lower ratings mean less revenue (see Case 6.2 for more details).

Most studies of ethics in marketing research have focused on either delineating responsibilities of researchers to clients and respondents or exploring whether certain marketing research practices are perceived as ethical or unethical. Research integrity, fair treatment of outside clients, and research confidentiality are the top three ethical issues in marketing research. A survey revealed that 61 percent of the surveyed market researchers perceived many opportunities to engage in unethical behavior within an organization.[36] Opportunity and the perceived behavior of peers and superiors are major determinants of ethical behavior.[37] There is limited agreement on the uniformity of marketing research, and companies perform these techniques differently. On the other hand, general codes of marketing research ethics, statements on respondents' rights, and principles of appropriate conduct are available. The American Marketing Association and the Marketing Research Association both have codes to promote marketing research ethics. Improving marketing research ethics helps ensure that data inputs are accurate and useful for marketing decisions.

Summary

Marketing research and information systems are essential to an organization's planning and strategy development. The marketing concept cannot be implemented without information about buyers. As acceptance of the marketing concept in planning efforts has increased, higher levels of management have begun using marketing research.

Marketing research is the design and execution of specific inquiries to yield results for making marketing decisions. The marketing information system (MIS) is a framework for the day-to-day managing and structuring of information regularly

35. O. C. Ferrell and Steven J. Skinner, "Ethical Behavior and Bureaucratic Structure in Marketing Research Organizations," *Journal of Marketing Research*, February 1988, pp. 103–104.

36. Shelby D. Hunt, Lawrence B. Chonko, and James B. Wilcox, "Ethical Problems of Marketing Researchers," *Journal of Marketing Research*, August 1984, pp. 309–324.

37. O. C. Ferrell and Larry Gresham, "A Contingency Framework of Ethical Decision Making," *Journal of Marketing*, Summer 1985, p. 89.

gathered from sources both inside and outside an organization. Marketing research usually is characterized by in-depth analysis of a problem, whereas the MIS focuses on data storage, retrieval, and classification.

Research and information systems are scientific approaches to decision making in marketing. Intuitive decisions are made on the basis of past experience and personal bias. Scientific decision making is an orderly, logical, and systematic approach. Minor, nonrecurring problems can be handled successfully by intuition. As the number of alternative solutions, payoffs, and risks multiply, the use of research becomes more desirable and rewarding.

The five basic steps of planning marketing research are (1) defining the problems, (2) developing hypotheses, (3) collecting data, (4) interpreting research findings, and (5) reporting the findings. A problem must be stated clearly for marketers to develop a hypothesis, which is a guess or assumption about that problem or set of circumstances. To test the accuracy of hypotheses and to gather data, researchers may use exploratory, descriptive, or causal studies. To apply research to decision making, marketers must interpret and report their findings properly.

Research design involves establishing procedures for obtaining reliable and valid marketing data. A study is valid if it measures what it is supposed to measure. Reliable studies can be repeated with approximately the same results obtained.

Sampling is a method of selecting representative units from a total population. Four basic sampling designs for marketing research are random, stratified, area, and quota sampling. The first three sampling methods are based on statistical probability; that is, sample units have a known or equal chance of being chosen. Quota sampling depends on judgmental selection.

Experimentation is a procedure for organizing data to increase the validity and reliability of research findings. Experimentation focuses on controlling some variables and manipulating others to determine cause-and-effect relationships. Laboratory settings give marketers maximum control over influential factors. Field settings are preferred when marketers want experimentation to take place in natural surroundings.

The three basic methods for obtaining data are surveys, observation, and secondary sources. The three types of surveys—personal interview, telephone, and mail—gather data through interviews or by having respondents fill out questionnaires. Questionnaires are instruments used to obtain information from respondents and to record observations; they should be unbiased and objective.

Attempts to stamp out shoddy practices and to establish generally acceptable procedures for conducting research are enhancing the professional image of marketing researchers. A need exists to develop shared ethical concern by all parties involved in the marketing research process. Also eliminating opportunity will reduce the frequency of unethical activities in marketing research.

Important Terms

Marketing research	Intuition
Marketing information system (MIS)	Scientific decision making
Marketing databank	Problem definition

Hypothesis
Primary data
Secondary data
Exploratory studies
Descriptive studies
Causal studies
Statistical interpretation
Reliability
Validity
Sampling
Population
Random sampling
Stratified sampling
Area sampling
Quota sampling
Experimentation
Marketing experimentation

Independent variable
Dependent variable
Survey methods
Observation method
Mechanical observation devices
Syndicated data services

Discussion and Review Questions

1. How do the benefits of decisions guided by marketing research compare with those of intuitive decision making? How do marketing decision makers know when it will be worthwhile to conduct research?
2. Give specific examples of situations in which intuitive decision making would probably be more appropriate than marketing research.
3. What is the MIS likely to include in a small organization? Do all organizations have a marketing databank?
4. In what ways do marketing research and the MIS overlap?
5. What is the difference between defining a research problem and developing a hypothesis?
6. *Nonresponse* is the inability or refusal of some respondents to cooperate in a survey. What are some ways to decrease nonresponse in personal door-to-door surveys?
7. Make some suggestions for encouraging respondents to cooperate in mail surveys.
8. If a survey of all homes with listed telephone numbers is conducted, what sampling design should be used?
9. List some problems of conducting a laboratory experiment on respondents' reactions to the taste of different brands of beer. How would these problems differ from those of a field study of beer taste preferences?
10. Give some examples of marketing problems that could be solved through information gained from observation.
11. What are the major limitations of using secondary data to solve marketing problems?
12. What are the major ethical concerns when coordinating a marketing research project involving different organizations?

Cases

6.1 Lady Indian Basketball[38]

Benny Hollis, Athletic Director at Northeast Louisiana University (NLU), was very interested in the results of a survey he had just received. The research had been conducted by his staff in response to his request for information about the women's basketball program at the university. Although the team was becoming very successful, growth in fan attendance was lagging behind. Hollis hoped that the results of a survey to find out what type of person attends women's basketball games might be used to develop a better program for marketing the sport at NLU.

The Lady Indians were gaining much success. They were undefeated in the 1982–83 season in Southland Conference play. In the same season they were ranked among the top twenty teams in the nation in four of the eight team-statistics categories compiled by the NCAA, and they were third in the nation in scoring. However, Hollis was not sure that they had been adequately marketed to the relevant groups of fans who might be attracted. This was true not only at NLU, but also around the country as women's sports were just beginning to grow.

Hollis believed the greatest return for the cost, at that time, was to be found in the promotion of women's basketball. The quality of competition and the level of interest had increased to the point that if the sport were effectively marketed, it could have a significant impact on university athletic income. Additionally, most conferences, including the Southland Conference, had now incorporated women's programs into their conference structures, thus enhancing image and interest. Most of these changes had occurred in just the past three to five years.

It was also apparent to Hollis that there was tremendous room for attendance growth in women's basketball. For instance, the average attendance for all NCAA Division I women's basketball games (excluding doubleheaders with men) was only 555—up 9.25 percent over the previous year. Yet, a few teams did better: Louisiana Tech (located 30 miles from NLU), Iowa, and Southern California averaged 5,285, 3,381, and 3,159, respectively, during their seasons. NLU averaged only 2,441 at home for the season. However, as recently as five years before, a crowd of 200 was considered good.

Although the potential for increased attendance appeared to be present, Hollis realized that women's basketball had to be properly marketed. Before an effective marketing plan could be developed, however, the market for women's basketball had to be defined and selected. Then a marketing program could be assembled to attract this target market. Thus the Sports Information Department planned a survey aimed at learning some things about women's collegiate basketball fans to help establish appropriate marketing strategies.

A questionnaire was developed to administer to patrons at one of the well-attended games during the season (see Figure 6.14). The single-page, two-sided questionnaire was designed to obtain general demographic information as well as to gauge what attracts women's fans to the game.

---

38. This case was prepared by David Loudon, C. W. McConkey, and Maynard M. Dolecheck, all of Northeast Louisiana University. Copyright © 1986 by David Loudon, C. W. McConkey, and Maynard M. Dolecheck. Reprinted with permission.

FIGURE 6.14
Women's college basketball survey

Dear Fan:
 To learn more about the growing interest in WOMEN'S college basketball please help us by completing this questionnaire. It will take you less than 10 minutes to complete.----THANK YOU.

SECTION 1
 For EACH of the statements below, CIRCLE the Number that best describes how much you AGREE with that statement. Please give careful thought to each of the statements.

		Strongly Disagree	Disagree	Neither	Agree	Strongly Agree	
1.	WOMEN'S basketball should be the preliminary game to the MEN'S game so the fans can view two games for a single admission............................	1	2	3	4	5	(5)
2.	Sufficient tax dollars should be spent on athletics to produce a winning program............................	1	2	3	4	5	(6)
3.	WOMEN'S basketball is more entertaining than MEN'S basketball because it displays more finesse than physical dominance.......................	1	2	3	4	5	(7)
4.	I select basketball games to attend based on the reputation and ranking of the visiting team.........................	1	2	3	4	5	(8)
5.	WOMEN'S basketball is one of the best entertainment values available.........	1	2	3	4	5	(9)
6.	I attend WOMEN'S basketball because of the urging of my spouse or children...	1	2	3	4	5	(10)
7.	I usually attend WOMEN'S basketball games with a friend or neighbor........	1	2	3	4	5	(11)
8.	I am personally acquainted with one or more players in tonight's game........	1	2	3	4	5	(12)
9.	I would be inclined to attend more WOMEN'S basketball games when my team is ranked nationally.....................	1	2	3	4	5	(13)
10.	I listen to the away games on the radio when I am unable to attend......	1	2	3	4	5	(14)
11.	I enjoy participation in recreational activity..................................	1	2	3	4	5	(15)
12.	Special event nights (such as T-shirt night) are important to my attending WOMEN'S basketball.....................	1	2	3	4	5	(16)
13.	Quality education is more important for WOMEN athletes because of the lack of professional sports opportunities.	1	2	3	4	5	(17)
14.	A successful athletic program is important for a positive University image in the community...................	1	2	3	4	5	(18)

SECTION 2
 Please supply the following information by either filling in the blanks or circling the number of the appropriate reply:

1. SEX: 1. Male 2. Female (18) 2. MARITAL STATUS: 1. Single   (19)
                                                     2. Married

3. NUMBER OF CHILDREN: 0 1 2 3 4 5 or more   (20)

4. THE AGE OF MY YOUNGEST CHILD IS ____.   (21-22)

5. EDUCATION (highest level of education attained):   (23)
    1. Grade   2. High   3. Vo-Tech   4. Attended   5. College
       School   School   College   Graduate

6. MY AGE IS ____. (23-24)   7. RACE: 1. Black 2. White 3. Other   (25)

8. EMPLOYMENT STATUS: (26)
    1. Retired   2. Home-maker   3. Self-employed
    4. Employed (not self)   5. Student

FIGURE 6.14
(Continued)

```
 9. I have attended the following universities:                    (27)
    1. NLU   2. TECH   3. OTHER

10. I am a graduate of the following university:                   (28)
    1. NLU   2. TECH   3. OTHER


11. My children have attended the following universities:         (29)
    1. NLU   2. TECH   3. OTHER

12. Circle all of the following that describe you:          (30-35)
    1. College Athletic Club        2. College Alumni Association Member
    Member                          4. Country/Tennis Club Member
    3. Civic Club Member            6. Union Member
    5. Fitness Club Member

13. How many miles have you traveled to see tonight's game?       (36)
    1. 10 or less   2. 11-20   3. 21-50   4. More than 50

14. How many WOMEN'S basketball games will you attend
    this season? ___.                                         (37-38)

15. How many MEN'S basketball games will you attend this
    season? ___.                                              (39-40)

16. My interest in WOMEN'S basketball started when I was exposed via (41)
    1. Newspaper   2. T.V.
    3. Radio       4. Game Attendance   5. Discussion of friends

17. For sports information, I depend on: (Rank the following
    based on frequency of use--1 most used thru 8 least used)  (42-49)
    ____ KTVE-TV     (42)    ____ Ouachita Citizen     (46)
    ____ KNOE-TV     (43)    ____ Ruston News Leader    (47)
    ____ KARD-TV     (44)    ____ Monroe News-Star World (48)
    ____ KNLU        (45)    ____ Word of Mouth         (49)

18. Which radio format do you listen to most often?              (50)
    1. Country   2. Soft Rock   3. Hard Rock   4. Easy Listening

19. Other than basketball, which WOMEN'S sport would you most
    enjoy viewing?                                                (51)
    1. Softball   2. Tennis   3. Swimming   4. Track   5. Volleyball

20. Do you plan to attend the NLU vs TECH MEN'S basketball game
    on Feb. 9?                                                    (52)
    1. Yes   2. No   3. Undecided

21. Which team are you "rooting" for tonight? 1. TECH   2. NLU   (53)
```

```
WE NEED YOUR HELP ! ! ! !
WOULD YOU BE WILLING TO SPEND 15-30 MINUTES TO COMPLETE AN IN-
DEPTH QUESTIONNAIRE, CONCERNING COLLEGE ATHLETICS? IF SO, PLEASE
PRINT YOUR NAME AND ADDRESS BELOW. THOSE SELECTED WILL BE MAILED
A QUESTIONNAIRE (NO ONE WILL CALL). UPON COMPLETION AND RETURN OF
THE QUESTIONNAIRE YOU WILL RECEIVE A COUPON WORTH $10.00 OFF THE
PURCHASE PRICE OF EACH 1984-1985 NLU WOMEN'S BASKETBALL SEASON
TICKET AS AN EXPRESSION OF OUR APPRECIATION.
```

```
NAME: _____
ADDRESS: _____
         _____
```

```
PLEASE PASS THE COMPLETED QUESTIONNAIRE TO THE END OF THE ROW FOR
COLLECTION AS INSTRUCTED BY THE PUBLIC ADDRESS ANNOUNCER----THANK YOU.
```

The questionnaire was distributed at the home game between the NLU women and Louisiana Tech University. Almost everyone entering the arena was offered a questionnaire to complete for usher pickup at half time. To assure maximum participation, a pencil was supplied with each questionnaire. A total of 2,200 questionnaires were distributed and 717 were returned. Questionnaires completed by half time were collected by ushers; those not completed by half time could be deposited in boxes provided at all exits.

The questionnaires were tabulated, and findings were significant. Many of the fans were devoted solely to the women's game, and two-thirds of those respondents believed their game was more entertaining because it displays more finesse than physical dominance. Women's fans also tended to be older and female and were more likely to be white. In the fan's mind, the product is not just the sport of women's basketball. It includes elements such as uniforms, music, half-time entertainment, cheerleading, concessions, schedules, and so on.

The results indicate that most women's basketball fans consider the games to be one of the best entertainment values available. Also, special events and premiums such as T-shirt giveaways had little value in boosting game attendance. This was particularly true of nonstudents.

The study also found that getting people to attend a few games is the key to continued attendance. The entire marketing program could be geared to inducing people to attend a couple of games to overcome any misperceptions about the sport. As Hollis evaluated the responses, he now had the challenging job of interpreting their meaning for the future marketing direction of the Lady Indian basketball program.

Questions for Discussion

1. Evaluate the research project conducted to improve attendance at Lady Indian basketball games.
2. What type of basketball fan would have been likely to fill out the questionnaire? What can be said about the nonrespondents?
3. Suggest a marketing strategy for Hollis based on the results of the Lady Indian survey.

6.2   Nielsen's People Meter[39]

Traditionally, the survey methods used to collect data for marketing research have been mail, telephone, or personal interview. However, A. C. Nielsen Company pioneered the use of a microwave computerized rating system to measure national television audiences.

39. Based on information from Roland Soong, "The Statistical Reliability of People Meter Ratings," *Journal of Advertising Research,* February–March 1988, p. 56; "People Meters to Be Sole Tool for '87 Nielsen TV Ratings," *Marketing News,* Jan. 30, 1987, p. 1; Verne Gay, "Networks Zap Debut of Meters," *Advertising Age,* Sept. 7, 1987, pp. 1, 56; Brian Donlon, "TV Rating Rivals Tune in New Device," *USA Today,* Sept. 16, 1987, pp. 1B, 2B.

The so-called people meter transmits demographic information overnight on what television shows people are watching, the number of households that are watching the shows, and which family members are watching. The data are recorded automatically when household members press buttons on the meter. The people meter replaces the old National Audience Composition (NAC) diary used for the past thirty years.

The people meter initially was placed in two thousand homes in 1987. The device enables Nielsen monitors to record second-by-second viewing choices of up to eight household members, with the viewers using remote control keyboards to record their program selection. The people meter is the state of the art in electronic measuring equipment, undergoing extensive testing and analysis before its introduction. Nielsen officials believe that the people meter far more accurately determines national audience composition than the old NAC diary, and it can more quickly give advertisers information about the television shows their target market is watching, enabling them to reach that target market with their commercials. A study published by Roland Soong in a 1988 issue of the *Journal of Advertising Research* concludes that ". . . the people meter sample is considerably more reliable than a diary sample with the same total number of households."

Even though the people meter is a faster and more accurate way of measuring audience composition than was the NAC diary, it has its critics. The introduction of the people meter caused much concern among the networks, and all three major networks have expressed doubt that the people meter is more accurate than the diary. In 1987, both ABC and CBS requested that Nielsen continue to use the NAC diary for that year. The two networks also based their sales and programming decisions solely on the NAC during that period. But ABC became so disgusted with "declining standards" that it canceled its contract with Nielsen early in the year; ABC felt that the diary sample results were not as accurate because Nielsen had most of its resources tied up with the people meter. CBS also canceled its contract with Nielsen, and both CBS and ABC refused to buy the people meter data. CBS signed a contract with AGB, Nielsen's major competitor, to use its people meter instead. NBC also voiced its displeasure with the people meter. NBC agreed to use the device, but it questioned the meter's reliability.

Nielsen's and AGB's people meters have registered consistently lower ratings than the old diary system, leading to confusion and controversy throughout the industry. The networks are unhappy because the higher the rating for a program, the more they can charge for commercial time during that program. The lower ratings could mean significant losses of revenue for the networks.

To protect themselves against possible revenue losses from people meter ratings, the networks raised prices for commercial time 15 to 25 percent in 1987. Advertisers get "make-good" time, or free-advertisement time, from a network when the ratings for a show it sponsors fall below the guidelines of the original purchase contract. The result of this make-good time is higher price tags for advertisers.

In fact, some industry analysts believed that this increased cost of prime-time advertising might squeeze out many smaller companies with small advertising budgets. These companies will then have to decide whether they can even afford network television advertising.

Even though the networks do not like the people meter, advertisers like its faster, and, ideally, more accurate information. A computer records the show a person is viewing, so the system does not depend on a person's memory, as did the diary. In addition, the people meter provides more information about the viewer, such as age, sex, income, education, and ethnic background: The user simply pushes a designated button to give Nielsen personal background information.

Despite the networks' feelings about the people meter, there is no doubt that the meter will have a profound effect on the television industry. Networks are carefully watching the people meter ratings to see how the results will affect the way companies use television advertising.

Questions for Discussion

1. What are the advantages and disadvantages of Nielsen's people meter compared with its old diary survey method?
2. Why do you think that Nielsen switched from the NAC diary to the people meter?
3. Does the people meter collect primary or secondary data? Why?

Part I   *S T R A T E G I C   C A S E*

Stew Leonard's: The World's Largest Dairy Store

Stew Leonard's is the top-grossing, highest-volume food store in the world (see Figure 1). Built on the philosophy that the customer is king, Stew Leonard's offers food shoppers low prices, high product quality, excellent customer service, and a festive, Disney-like atmosphere. The Norwalk, Connecticut, store draws 100,000 shoppers a week, some from as far away as Massachusetts, Rhode Island, Pennsylvania, and New York. Annual sales total $100 million.

Milkman and entrepreneur Stewart Leonard opened his store in 1969 after the state of Connecticut decided to route a highway through the small dairy he had inherited from his father. The original Stew Leonard's offered only eight products, but customers were attracted to the dairy store by the prices and Leonard's showmanship and marketing flair. Today, twenty-six expansions later, family owned Stew Leonard's is a 110,000-square foot complex built around a highly automated milk-processing operation. The store continues to offer a narrow product mix— about 750 items, as compared to the 15,000 items conventional supermarkets stock. Nevertheless, Stew Leonard's sells in such volume that the store's per square foot sales of $2,700 recently earned the business a spot in the Guinness Book of World Records.

Each year Stew Leonard's customers buy 10 million quarts of milk, 1 million pints of cream, 100 tons of cottage cheese, 2.9 million quarts of orange juice, and more than 500,000 pounds of butter. They also walk out with 1,040 tons of ground beef, 1,820 tons of Perdue poultry products, and 520 tons of fixings from the store's salad bar. According to the Food Marketing Institute, the bake shop

Stew Leonard's daughter, Beth, operates sells twenty times more baked goods than any other in-store bakery in the country—almost 3 million muffins, more than 500,000 pies, and 348 tons of freshly baked chocolate chip cookies annually. In addition, the store sells 2,000 pounds of pistachio nuts a week, which is 1 percent of the country's entire pistachio crop.

Customer Orientation

Stew Leonard's low prices—about 10 to 25 percent lower than prices at stores in a five-mile radius—are partly responsible for the store's popularity, but even more important is the store's responsiveness to customers. Indeed, the store opened in response to requests from Leonard's former milk route customers. Today, customer demand continues to dictate what products the store carries. Although Stew Leonard's may test-market as many as 10,000 different products in a year, an item must sell 1,000 units weekly to remain in inventory. Thus the store carries only the best-selling brands of such items as cereal, yogurt, and peanut butter. Stew Leonard's also emphasizes product quality. Because of its enormous sales volume, the store can buy by the truckload directly from producers, passing along the savings and freshness to customers. Stew Leonard's also has the leverage to order house brands made to its own specifications.

Stew Leonard's strong customer orientation is reflected in the two rules carved in a huge, three-ton granite boulder just outside the door. Rule 1 states that "the customer is always right." Rule 2 says, "If the customer is ever wrong, reread Rule 1." Customer service is the top priority at Stew Leonard's. To eliminate long waits at check-out time, the Leonards have equipped the store with twenty-five cash registers. Should any line back up to more than three customers, a store employee immediately passes out free ice cream or snacks to waiting customers. The Leonards also actively solicit ideas from their customers, both to keep up with trends (such as Chinese cooking) and to improve service. About once a month, focus groups of customers are invited to critique the store's products and policies—and management listens. For example, Stew Leonard's began to sell strawberries loose, instead of packaged. The store's profit margin on strawberries decreased, but sales increased tenfold, the store was able to get a better deal from the supplier, and ultimately profits on strawberries were higher.

Stew Leonard's also acts promptly on the hundred-odd messages dropped into the store's suggestion box each day. When the Leonards followed one customer's suggestion that English muffins be displayed near bacon and eggs, muffin sales increased 50 percent. Another customer reported that he would have bought deli roast beef on special if the hard rolls had not been located clear across the store at the bakery. Leonard moved some rolls near the deli counter; sales of both rolls and deli roast beef doubled.

At Stew Leonard's, nothing is too good for a customer. When a woman complained to Leonard the day after Thanksgiving that her turkey had been too dry, he immediately handed her a $20 turkey free of charge, knowing that her week-in, week-out business means much more to the store than the price of a single turkey. Leonard also had high praise for the new courtesy booth employee who surprised a distraught customer with $50 in gift certificates after the customer was unable to find her missing sterling silver pen. Leonard's oft-repeated slogan gets the point across to all employees: "*S*atisfy the customer; *T*eamwork gets it done; *E*xcellence makes it better; *W*ow makes it fun!"

The "Wow!" is a reminder of Leonard's deeply held conviction that a food retailer must give customers a pleasant and memorable shopping experience if the store is to remain competitive. Hence Stew Leonard's is full of surprises reminiscent of Leonard's hero, Walt Disney. In the parking lot, for example, is "The Little Farm," a collection of one hundred live cows, goats, chickens, sheep, and geese. Inside the store, employees dressed as farm animals and cartoon characters roam the aisles, passing out balloons to children and telling shoppers about store specials. Installed above display cases along the store's single twisting aisle are larger-than-life musical robots, such as a huge banjo-playing dog and a cow singing nursery rhymes with a farmer. Purchases totaling more than $100 set off electronic mooing at the cash registers.

Building Customer Loyalty

The Leonards also enhance the appeal of their products by bringing store functions out front, where customers can watch. The milk-processing plant (so highly automated that a tank truck's load of raw milk can be pasteurized and packaged in one day by just four employees) is enclosed in glass; customers see 150 half-gallon cartons of milk per minute moving along a conveyor belt. A plastic cow's head affixed to the front wall of the dairy plant moos when customers press a button. Butchers and fish cutters slice and package in full view of shoppers, and in the deli department an employee uses a special in-store demonstration oven to make pizza. Throughout the store, employees hand out samples of everything from gazpacho to cupcakes, in accordance with the Leonards' observation that sales quadruple when samples are available.

FIGURE I

Stew Leonard's dairy store (SOURCE: Richard Lung)

Because of all this, Stew Leonard's satisfied customers often take it on themselves to tell others about the store. The Leonards are fond of reminding their staff, "Lower the price; sell the best; word of mouth will do the rest." Several years ago a customer presented Leonard with a snapshot of herself standing in front of the Kremlin in Moscow, holding a Stew Leonard's plastic shopping bag. When Leonard posted the picture on the store's bulletin board, other customers began following suit. Today, an entire wall in the store is covered with more than seven thousand photos of customers at locations around the world—the Matterhorn, the Great Wall of China, the Egyptian pyramids, the North Pole, and the floor of the Pacific Ocean—each customer holding one of the 250,000 bags Stew Leonard's gives away each year. Such practices build customer loyalty, say the Leonards, and inspire customers to pass the word to friends.

Employee Motivation

Although Stew Leonard has had no formal management training (he studied dairy manufacturing at the University of Connecticut), numerous groups of Japanese and American executives have toured the store to observe his management style firsthand. In fact, many Japanese management policies parallel the techniques Leonard has developed instinctively. For example, at Stew Leonard's, the five hundred employees, or "team members," regard themselves as one big family. The Leonards make a point of knowing each employee by name. Because the Leonards believe that productive employees motivate each other, they prefer to hire by referrals from the staff. As a result, about 55 percent of the employees have at least one other relative working in the store, including more than two hundred who are younger than 21. Leonard's own family is heavily involved in the business; Leonard's wife Marianne, their four children, and several other relatives work there. Recently Stew Jr. was named president of the company when Stew Sr. moved up to chairman.

The Leonards recognize that only when employees are happy and satisfied can they help produce satisfied customers. A nonunion operation, Stew Leonard's offers employee benefits on the scale of a large corporation. In addition, the Leonards encourage initiative by giving employees public recognition for their ideas. The Leonards look for "a good attitude" in potential employees and tell their team members, "If you're training the person under you to do your job better than you do, you're valuable to the company and will be promoted." About one hundred of the employees currently working at the store have graduated from Dale Carnegie courses conducted in-house. Outstanding employees also are rewarded with plaques, dinners, gift certificates, recognition in the company newsletter and (for managers) profit sharing. On the store's walls are framed pictures of employees of the month and team members whose suggestions have saved the organization money. Leonard's own efforts earned him a Presidential Award for Entrepreneurial Achievement, presented recently in a White House ceremony. He was also named Connecticut's Small Business Advocate of the Year by the U.S. Small Business Administration, and Stew Leonard's is featured in the book *A Passion for Excellence* as one of the best-run companies in America.

Because the Leonards have always been more interested in being best than in being biggest, until recently they kept Stew Leonard's a single-store operation.

Having developed all available space on the original site, the Leonards opened a second store in Danbury, Connecticut. The new Stew Leonard's—a two-story, 272,000-square foot facility on a 44-acre site—employs about four hundred persons and includes all the features of the Norwalk store, plus a garden center and parking for eight hundred cars.

Questions for Discussion

1. Has Stew Leonard's adopted the philosophy of the marketing concept? Explain your answer.
2. In what ways does Stew Leonard's demonstrate a strong customer orientation?
3. What types of marketing research does Stew Leonard's use?
4. How does Stew Leonard's understanding of customer needs contribute to the firm's success?

SOURCES: Katharine Davis Fishman, "The Disney World of Supermarkets," *New York Magazine,* Mar. 11, 1985; Joanne Kaufman, "In the Moo: Shopping at Stew Leonard's," *The Wall Street Journal,* Sept. 17, 1987, p. 26; Margaret Mahar, "Supermarketer," *Success!,* March 1986, pp. 50–53; Gail Perrin, "Stew Leonard's Superstore," *The Boston Globe,* Sept. 17, 1986, pp. 29–30; Stew Leonard's Fact Sheet, B. L. Ochman Public Relations, New York; "Stew Leonard's Launches a New Invasion," *Progressive Grocer,* May 1986, p. 18.

II. Product Decisions

We now are prepared to analyze the decisions and activities associated with developing and maintaining effective marketing mixes. In Parts II through V we focus on the major components of the marketing mix: product, distribution, promotion, and price. Specifically, in Part II we explore the product ingredient of the marketing mix. Chapter 7 introduces basic concepts and relationships that must be understood to make effective product decisions. Branding, packaging, and labeling are also discussed in this chapter. In Chapter 8 we analyze a variety of dimensions regarding product management, such as the ways that a firm can be organized to manage products, the development and positioning of products, product modification, and phasing out products.

7. Product Concepts

7. Product Decisions

OBJECTIVES

- ▶ To learn how marketers define products.
- ▶ To understand how to classify products.
- ▶ To see how product mix and product line policies are developed.
- ▶ To develop an understanding of the concept of product life cycle.
- ▶ To grasp the basic product identification concepts as they relate to branding, packaging, and labeling.

*W*hen British publishing executive David Collischon and his wife Lesley decided several years ago to set up a home-based mail-order business to sell Filofax loose-leaf binders, they expected to earn enough for a nice vacation—and not much more. After all, the six-ring leather notebooks with specialized inserts had changed little since their introduction in 1910, and sales had always been small. To the Collischons's surprise, however, the binders became extremely popular, with turnover rising from $160,000 in 1980 to almost $11 million last year. The Collischons eventually bought the company, and today Filofax organizers remain hot items among bankers, lawyers, and executives on both sides of the Atlantic and in Tokyo.

The basic Filofax cover, which now comes in over 120 different versions, sells for $160 on average (see Figure 7.1). It can hold address pages, diaries, maps, memo sheets, data information, and a host of other inserts. The inserts were given a clean, updated look by Collischon and a large part of the Filofax appeal is the purchasers' ability to customize the system. The company produces 16 different diaries and over 300 other printed forms costing $2 to $5 each, including logs for expenses, bridge games, recipes, birdwatching, and even windsurfing. Diane Keaton, one of many celebrity Filofax users, is credited with inventing an insert for holding money. Because the inserts are printed only in English, Japanese buyers consult the best-selling *Filofax Manual* for tips on using the inserts most effectively.

In addition to order and efficiency, Filofax promises to confer status on its users. When the Collischons took control, the organizers were marketed mostly in a few British stationery shops. The new owners changed all that, moving Filofax into upscale department stores such as Harrod's, and, in the United States,

FIGURE 7.1

The Filofax organizer
(SOURCE: Filofax)

Bloomingdale's, Saks Fifth Avenue, and Neiman-Marcus. There, ostrich-skin versions of Filofax sell for $580, while the top of the line is a $1700 crocodile-skin model. (A low-budget Filofax is bound in vinyl and retails for $25.) Although Collischon maintains that Filofax never advertises, the company benefits from highly publicized marketing ploys such as the promotion for the limited edition of two hundred Filofaxes bound in reindeer leather salvaged from an eighteenth-century shipwreck.

The loose leaf concept was invented by an American and consisted in the early days of technical data sheets for engineers and scientists. Norman & Hill, the company responsible for originating the Filofax system, imported some of these papers into the United Kingdom, but were soon to originate their own unique organizer, which they called Filofax, with general and expendable inserts appealing to a much wider market.

Today, Filofax plc sells its upscale organizers in over 3,000 retail outlets worldwide and plans to expand its U.S. distribution into further specialty boutiques and selected stationery shops.

To critics of "Filomania," who charge that overexposure will damage the product's snob appeal, the company believes that quality and innovation will maintain the Filofax image.[1]

1. Based on information from Joseph Connolly, "Marshalling My Phalanx of Fax," *The London Times,* Apr. 12, 1986, p. 8f; Steve Lohr, "Organizing Pays Off at Filofax," *The New York Times,* Apr. 8, 1987, p. D1; Mark Maremont, "The Little Black Book Becomes a Mania," *Business Week,* Apr. 20, 1987, p. 82.

PRODUCTS SUCH AS THOSE of Filofax are among a firm's most important and visible contacts with buyers. If a company's products do not meet buyers' desires and needs, the company will fail unless it makes adjustments. Developing a successful product requires knowledge of fundamental marketing and product concepts. The product is an important variable in the marketing mix, and other variables (promotion, distribution, and price) must be coordinated with product decisions.

The concepts and definitions that we discuss first in this chapter help clarify what a product is and how buyers view products. Product planners must consider what other products their company offers in the marketplace. Thus an examination of the concepts of product mix and product line help us understand product planning. However, a product is not created in a vacuum, nor does it exist in one, so we must look at the stages of product life cycles. Each life cycle stage generally requires a specific marketing strategy, assumes a certain competitive environment, and has its own profit pattern. Finally, because branding and packaging are vital components of a product—in fact, they help create the product—we explore these topics, along with labeling, an important informational device.

What Is a Product?

A **product** is everything, both favorable and unfavorable, that one receives in an exchange. It is a complexity of tangible and intangible attributes including functional, social, and psychological utilities or benefits.[2] A product can be an idea, a service, a good, or any combination of these three. This definition includes supporting services that go with goods, such as installation, guarantees, product information, and promises of repair or maintenance. (Chapter 21 is a detailed discussion of marketing services.) Goods are tangible and have form utility. Services are intangible and provide facilitating or direct benefits. Ideas provide psychological stimulation that helps us solve problems or adjust to our environment.

When buyers purchase a product, they actually are buying the benefits and satisfaction they think the product will provide. A sports car is purchased for excitement and fun, not merely for transportation. Buyers purchase services—education, health care—on the basis of promises of satisfaction. Promises, with the images and appearances of symbols, help consumers make judgments about tangible and intangible products.[3] Often symbols and cues are used to make intangible products more tangible or real to the consumer. Exxon Corporation has used a tiger for many years to communicate the chemical ingredients that produce power in its gasoline. Although gasoline is itself tangible, the average consumer may have difficulty judging its performance. Merrill Lynch & Co., Inc. uses a bull to symbolize its investment philosophy. The type of cue depends on the type of benefit to be stressed, regardless of the product or service being provided.[4]

---

2. Part of this definition is adapted from James D. Scott, Martin R. Warshaw, and James R. Taylor, *Introduction to Marketing Management,* 5th ed. (Homewood, Ill.: Irwin, 1985), p. 215.
3. Theodore Levitt, "Marketing Intangible Products and Product Intangibles," *Harvard Business Review,* May–June 1981, pp. 94–102.
4. Kathleen A. Krentler and Joseph P. Guiltinan, "Strategies for Tangibilizing Retail Services: An Assessment," *Journal of the Academy of Marketing Science,* Fall 1984, p. 90.

Classifying Products

Products fall into one of two general categories, depending on the buyers' intentions. Products purchased to satisfy personal and family needs are **consumer products.** Those bought for use in a firm's operations or to make other products are **industrial products.** Consumers buy products to satisfy their personal wants, whereas industrial buyers seek to satisfy the goals of their organizations. Thus the buyer's intent—or the ultimate use of the product—determines whether an item is classified as a consumer or an industrial product.

The same item can be both a consumer product and an industrial product. For example, an electric light bulb is a consumer product if it is used in someone's home and an industrial product if it is purchased either to become part of another product or to light an assembly line. After a product is classified as either a consumer or an industrial product, it can be categorized further. In this section we examine the characteristics of these subcategories and explore the marketing activities associated with some of them.

Why do we need to know about product classifications? The primary reason is that classes of products are aimed at particular target markets, and this affects distribution, promotion, and pricing decisions. Industrial products, for example, usually require less advertising than consumer products do. Also, the types of marketing activities and efforts needed differ among the classes of consumer or industrial products. In short, the entire marketing mix can be affected by how a product is classified.

Classification of Consumer Products

Although there are several approaches to classifying consumer products, the traditional and most widely accepted approach consists of four categories: convenience, shopping, specialty, and unsought products. This approach is based primarily on characteristics of buyers' purchasing behavior. One problem associated with the approach is that not all buyers behave the same way when purchasing a specific type of product. Thus a single product can fit into all four categories. To minimize this problem, marketers think in terms of how buyers *generally* behave when purchasing a specific item. In addition, they recognize that a product may fall into more than one category and that the "correct" classification can be determined only by considering a particular firm's intended target market. With these thoughts in mind, let us examine the four traditional categories of consumer products.

Convenience Products **Convenience products** are relatively inexpensive, frequently purchased items for which buyers want to exert only minimal purchasing effort, such as bread, gasoline, newspapers, soft drinks, and chewing gum. The buyer spends little time either planning the purchase of a convenience item or comparing available brands or sellers. Even a buyer who prefers a specific brand will readily choose a substitute if the preferred brand is not conveniently available.

Classifying a specific product as a convenience product has several implications for a firm's marketing strategy. A convenience product normally is marketed through many retail outlets. Because sellers experience high inventory turnover of a convenience item, per-unit gross margins can be relatively low. Producers of convenience products such as Lay's potato chips and Crest toothpaste can expect little promotional effort at the retail level and thus must provide it themselves in the

FIGURE 7.2

Example of a shopping product (SOURCE: Toshiba America, Inc. Consumer Products Business Sector)

form of product advertising. Packaging is an important element of the marketing mix. The package may have to sell the product because many convenience items are available only on a self-service basis at the retail level.

Shopping Products   **Shopping products** are items for which buyers are willing to expend considerable effort planning and making the purchase. Buyers allocate much time for comparing stores and brands with respect to prices, product features, qualities, services, and perhaps warranties. Appliances, upholstered furniture, men's suits, bicycles, and stereos are examples of shopping products. Figure 7.2 shows a shopping product, a compact disc player. These products are expected to last a fairly long time and thus are purchased less frequently than convenience items. Even though shopping products are more expensive than convenience products, few buyers of shopping products are particularly brand loyal.

To market a shopping product effectively, a marketer considers several key issues. Shopping products require fewer retail outlets than convenience products do. Because shopping products are purchased less frequently, inventory turnover is lower and middlemen expect to receive higher gross margins. Although large sums of money may be required to advertise shopping products, an even larger percentage of resources is likely to be used for personal selling. Usually, a producer and the middlemen expect some cooperation from one another with respect to providing parts and repair services and performing promotional activities.

Specialty Products **Specialty products** possess one or more unique characteristics, and a significant group of buyers is willing to expend considerable purchasing effort to obtain them. Buyers actually plan the purchase of a specialty product; they know exactly what they want and will not accept a substitute. An example of a specialty product is a Jaguar automobile. When searching for specialty products, buyers do not compare alternatives; they are concerned primarily with finding an outlet that has a preselected product available.

That an item is a specialty product can affect a firm's marketing efforts several ways. Specialty products are often distributed through a limited number of retail outlets. Like shopping goods, they are purchased infrequently, causing lower inventory turnover and thus requiring relatively high gross margins.

Unsought Products **Unsought products** are purchased because of a sudden problem that needs to be solved or when aggressive selling is used to obtain a sale that otherwise would not take place. In general, the consumer does not think of buying these products regularly. Emergency automobile repairs and cemetery plots are classic examples of unsought products. Life insurance and encyclopedias, in contrast, are examples of products that need aggressive personal selling. The salesperson must try to make consumers aware of benefits that can be derived from buying such products.

Industrial Products

Industrial products are purchased to produce other products or for use in a firm's operations. Purchases of industrial products are based on an organization's goals and objectives. Usually, the functional aspects of the product are much more important than the psychological rewards sometimes associated with consumer products. On the basis of their characteristics and intended uses, industrial products can be classified into seven categories: raw materials, major equipment, accessory equipment, component parts, process materials, consumable supplies, and industrial services.[5]

Raw Materials **Raw materials** are the basic materials that actually become part of a physical product. They are obtained from mines, farms, forests, oceans, and recycled solid wastes. Other than the processing required for transporting and physically handling the products, raw materials have not been processed when a firm buys them. Raw materials are usually bought and sold according to grades and specifications. Purchasers frequently buy raw materials in relatively large quantities.

Major Equipment **Major equipment** includes large tools and machines used for production purposes, such as lathes, cranes, and stamping machines. Usually, major equipment is expensive and intended to be used in a production process for a considerable length of time. Some major equipment is custom-made to perform specific functions for a particular organization, but other items are standardized products that perform one or several tasks for many types of organizations. Because major equipment is so expensive, purchase decisions often are made by high-

5. Robert W. Haas, *Industrial Marketing Management*, 3rd ed. (Boston: Kent Publishing Company, 1986), pp. 15–25.

level management. Marketers of major equipment frequently must provide a variety of services, including installation, training, repair and maintenance assistance, and even aid in financing the purchase.

Accessory Equipment   **Accessory equipment** does not become a part of the final physical product but is used in production or office activities. Examples include typewriters, fractional-horsepower motors, calculators, and tools such as those in Figure 7.3. Compared to the cost of major equipment, accessory items are usually much cheaper; purchased routinely, with less negotiation; and treated as expense items, rather than as capital items, because they are not expected to be used as long. Accessory products are standardized items that generally can be used in several aspects of a firm's operations. More outlets are required for accessory equipment than for major equipment, but sellers do not have to provide the multitude of services expected of major equipment marketers.

Component Parts   **Component parts** become a part of the physical product and are either finished items ready for assembly or products that need little processing before assembly. Although they become part of a larger product, component parts often can be identified and distinguished easily. Spark plugs, tires, clocks, and switches are all component parts of the automobile. Buyers purchase such items

FIGURE 7.3

Example of accessory equipment (SOURCE: Rogers Tool Works, Inc.)

according to their own specifications or industry standards. They expect the parts to be of specified quality and delivered on time so that production is not slowed or stopped. Producers that are primarily assemblers, such as most lawn mower manufacturers, depend heavily on the suppliers of component parts.

Process Materials   **Process materials** are used directly in the production of other products. Unlike component parts, however, process materials are not readily identifiable. For example, Reichhold Chemicals, Inc., markets a treated fiber product: a phenolic-resin, sheet-molding compound. This material is used by a major aircraft manufacturer in the production of flight deck instrument panels and cabin interiors. Although the material is not identifiable in the finished panels and interiors, it retards burning, smoke, and formation of toxic gas if molded components are subjected to fire or high temperatures. As with component parts, process materials are purchased according to industry standards or the purchaser's specifications.

Consumable Supplies   **Consumable supplies** facilitate production and operations, but they do not become part of the finished product, for example, paper, pencils, oils, cleaning agents, and paints. Because such supplies are standardized items used in a variety of situations they are purchased by many different types of organizations. Usually, consumable supplies are sold through numerous outlets and are purchased routinely. To ensure that consumable supplies are available when

FIGURE 7.4
Johnson & Johnson's product line (SOURCE: Johnson & Johnson)

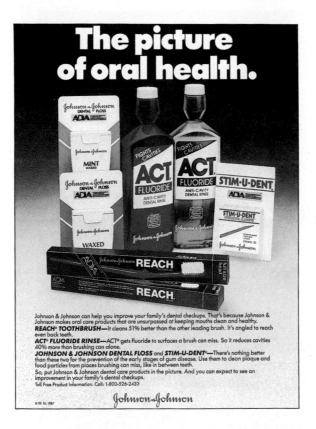

needed, buyers frequently deal with more than one seller. Because supplies can be divided into three categories—maintenance, repair, and operating (or overhaul) supplies—they are sometimes called **MRO items.**

Industrial Services **Industrial services** are the intangible products that many organizations use in their operations, including financial products, legal services, marketing research services, and janitorial services. Purchasers must decide whether to provide their own services internally or obtain them outside the organization. This decision depends greatly on the costs associated with each alternative and how frequently the services are needed.

Product Mix and Product Line

Marketers must understand the relationships among all of an organization's products if they are to coordinate the marketing of the total group of products. The following concepts help describe the relationships among an organization's products. A **product item** is a specific version of a product that can be designated as a distinct offering among an organization's products. A **product line** includes a group of closely related product items that are considered a unit because of marketing, technical, or end-use considerations. Marketers must understand buyers' goals if they hope to come up with the optimum product line. Figure 7.4 illustrates the product line of Johnson & Johnson. Specific product items in a product line usually reflect the desires of different target markets or the different needs of consumers.

A **product mix** is the composite or total group of products that an organization makes available to customers. All the products that Gerber Products Co. manufactures make up that firm's product mix.

A product mix has several dimensions. The **depth** of a product mix is measured by the number of different products offered in each product line. The **width** of the product mix is measured by the number of product lines a company offers. Figure 7.5 illustrates these concepts by showing the width of the product mix (number of product lines) and the depth of each product line (number of items in each product line) for selected Procter & Gamble products. Procter & Gamble is known for using differential branding, packaging, and consumer advertising to promote individual items in its detergent product line. Tide, Bold, Gain, Bonus, Dash, Cheer, Oxydol, and Duz—all Procter & Gamble detergents—share the same distribution channels and similar manufacturing facilities. Yet each is promoted as distinctive, and this claimed uniqueness adds depth to the product line.

Product Life Cycles

Products are like living organisms: They are born, they live, and they die. A new product is introduced into the marketplace; it grows; and when it loses appeal, it is terminated. Remember that our definition of a product focuses on both tangible and intangible attributes. Thus the total product might not be just a good but also the ideas and services attached to it. Packaging, branding, and labeling techniques alter or help create products. And just as biological cycles progress through growth and decline, so do the life cycles of products. However, product life cycles can be modified by marketers. (The marketing strategies for different life cycle stages are discussed in Chapter 8.)

As Figure 7.6 shows, a **product life cycle** has four major stages: (1) introduction, (2) growth, (3) maturity, and (4) decline. As a product moves through its cycle, the strategies relating to competition, promotion, distribution, pricing, and market information must be periodically evaluated and possibly changed. Astute marketing managers use the life cycle concept to make sure that the introduction, alteration, and termination of a product are timed and executed properly. By understanding the typical life cycle pattern, marketers can, in theory at least, maintain profitable products and drop unprofitable ones.

Introduction

The **introduction stage** of the life cycle begins at a product's first appearance in the marketplace, when sales are zero and profits are negative. Profits are below zero because initial revenues are low at the same time that the firm usually must cover large expenses for promotion and distribution. Notice in Figure 7.6 how sales should move upward from zero, and profits should move from below zero. In this stage, it is important to communicate product benefits to buyers. Very few new products represent major inventions because of cost: Developing and introducing a new product can cost $100 million or even more. The failure rate for new products is quite high, ranging from 33 to 90 percent, depending on the industry and how product failure is defined. For example, L'Oréal introduced the first hairstyling mousse; in less than a year the company had forty direct competitors. California Cooler marketed the first combination of wine and fruit juices but today is up

FIGURE 7.5

The concepts of width of product mix and product line depth applied to selected Procter & Gamble products.

Detergents	Toothpaste	Bar soap	Deodorants	Disposable diapers	Coffee
Ivory Snow 1930	Gleem 1952	Ivory 1879	Secret 1956	Pampers 1961	Folger's 1963
Dreft 1933	Crest 1955	Camay 1927	Sure 1972	Luvs 1976	Instant Folger's 1963
Tide 1946		Lava 1928			High Point
Joy 1949		Kirk's 1930			Instant 1975
Cheer 1950		Zest 1952			Folger's Flaked
Oxydol 1952		Safeguard 1963			Coffee 1977
Dash 1954		Coast 1974			
Cascade 1955					
Duz 1956					
Ivory Liquid 1957					
Gain 1966					
Dawn 1972					
Era 1972					
Bold 3 1976					
Solo 1979					

Product line depth ↕

Product mix width ↔

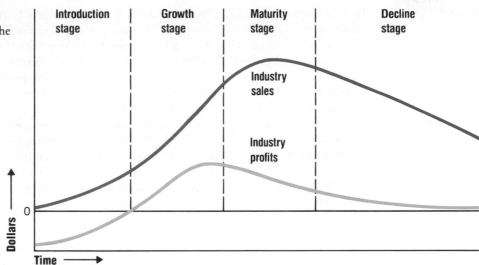

FIGURE 7.6

The four stages of the product life cycle

| Introduction stage | Growth stage | Maturity stage | Decline stage |

Industry sales

Industry profits

Dollars

Time

against approximately forty other companies for the wine cooler business.[6] More typically, product introductions involve a new packaged convenience food, a new automobile model, or a new fashion in clothing rather than a major product innovation.

During the introduction stage, potential buyers must be made aware of the product's features, uses, and advantages. Two difficulties may arise at this point. There may be only a few sellers with the resources, technological knowledge, and marketing know-how to launch the product successfully. And initially a high product price may be required to recoup expensive marketing research or development costs. Given these difficulties, it is not surprising that many products never get beyond the introduction stage.

Growth

During the **growth stage,** sales rise rapidly and profits reach a peak and then start to decline (see Figure 7.6). The growth stage is critical to a product's survival because competitive reactions to the product's success during this period will affect the product's life expectancy. Profits decline late in the growth stage as more firms enter the market, driving prices down and creating the need for heavy promotional expenses. At this point a typical marketing strategy encourages strong brand loyalty and competes with aggressive emulators of the product. During the growth stage, an enterprise tries to strengthen its market share by identifying the product's benefits and emphasizing them to develop a competitive niche.

Aggressive promotional pricing including price cuts is typical during the growth stage. Today, the VCR industry in the United States is in the growth stage. Many competitors have entered the market. By adjusting their prices competitively, firms such as Panasonic and RCA Corp. are able to maintain their market lead during the growth stage. They thus extend the life expectancy of their product far beyond that of marginal competitors.

6. Carrie Gottlieb, "Products of the Year," *Fortune,* Sept. 9, 1985, p. 107.

Maturity

During the **maturity stage,** the sales curve peaks and starts to decline and profits continue to decline (see Figure 7.6). This stage is characterized by severe competition as many brands enter the market. Competitors emphasize improvements and differences in their versions of the product. As a result, during the maturity stage weaker competitors are squeezed out or lose interest in the product. For example, many brands of personal computers will perish as the personal computer moves through the maturity stage.

During the maturity phase, those producers who remain in the market must make fresh promotional and distribution efforts; advertising and dealer-oriented promotions are typical during this stage of the product life cycle. Also, as the product reaches maturity, buyers' knowledge of it reaches a high level. Consumers of the product are now no longer inexperienced generalists but experienced specialists. As buyers change, the benefits they seek change, for instance, from full service to low price.[7]

Decline

During the **decline stage,** sales fall rapidly (see Figure 7.6). New technology or a new social trend may cause product sales to take a sharp turn downward. When this happens, the marketer considers pruning items from the product line to eliminate those not returning a profit. Also at this time, the marketer may cut promotion efforts, eliminate marginal distributors, and, finally, plan to phase out the product.

Because most enterprises have a product mix consisting of multiple products, a firm's destiny is rarely tied to one product. A composite of life cycle patterns is formed when various products in the mix are at different cycle stages. As one product is declining, other products are in the introduction, growth, or maturity stage. Marketers must deal with the dual problem of prolonging the life of existing products and introducing new products to meet organizational sales goals. For example, General Mills, Inc. has prolonged the product life cycle of Bisquick prepared biscuit mix by materially improving the product since it was introduced in the mid-1930s. But General Mills has also continued to introduce new products, such as Betty Crocker's Pop Secret. Pop Secret is shelf-stable microwave popcorn. The new product competes against Pillsbury's and Orville Redenbacher's microwave popping corn but has twice the advertising budget of the competition.[8] The microwave brands, which account for approximately one-third of the unpopped popcorn market, are the fastest-growing market segment. Today, one-half of all households in the United States have a microwave oven, versus 19 percent in 1980.[9] General Mills differentiates its brand and its appeal to consumers by promoting that Pop Secret will pop in microwave ovens of any wattage; the competition works best in high-wattage ovens. We examine approaches to developing new products and managing products in their various life cycle stages in the next chapter.

7. E. Steward De Bruicker and Gregory L. Summe, "Make Sure Your Customers Keep Coming Back," *Harvard Business Review,* January–February 1985, p. 92.
8. Janet Neiman, "General Mills Pops Big-Buck Budget," *Adweek,* Nov. 11, 1985, p. 82.
9. "Microwaves Spur Frozen Food Sales," *Duns Business Month,* July 1985, p. 24.

Branding

Marketers must make many product decisions associated with branding, such as brands, brand names, brand marks, trademarks, and trade names. A **brand** is a name, term, symbol, design, or a combination thereof that identifies a seller's products and differentiates them from competitors' products.[10] A **brand name** is that part of a brand which can be spoken—including letters, words, and numbers—such as 7-Up. A brand name is often a product's only distinguishing characteristic. Without the brand name, a firm could not identify its products. To consumers, brand names are as fundamental as the product itself. Brand names simplify shopping, guarantee quality, and allow self-expression.[11] The element of a brand that cannot be spoken, often a symbol or design, is called a **brand mark**. An example is the inscribed anchor on Anchor Hocking Corp. glassware. A **trademark** is a legal designation indicating that the owner has exclusive use of a brand or a part of a brand and that others are prohibited by law from using it. In the United States, to protect a brand name or brand mark, an organization must register it as a trademark with the U.S. Patent Office. Finally, a **trade name** is the legal name of an organization, such as Ford Motor Company or Safeway Stores, Inc., rather than the name of a specific product.

Benefits of Branding   As we just noted, branding can give both buyers and sellers benefits. Brands aid buyers by identifying specific products that they do and do not like, which in turn facilitates the purchase of items that satisfy individual needs. Without brands, product selection would be rather random because buyers could not be assured that what they purchased was the preferred item. A brand also helps buyers evaluate the quality of products, especially when people lack the ability to judge a product's characteristics. That is, a brand may symbolize a certain quality level to a purchaser, and in turn the person lets that perception of quality represent the quality of the item.

As an example, a car buyer associates certain quality levels with the automobile brands Plymouth, Ford, and Chevrolet. Although a buyer may go through a ritual of slamming doors, kicking tires, and starting the engine to judge a car's quality, this behavior provides most people with little information. Actually, the brand name is among the main indicators of quality to the prospective car buyer.

Another benefit a brand can provide is the psychological reward that comes from owning a brand that symbolizes status. Certain brands of watches (Rolex), automobiles (Mercedes-Benz), and shoes (Allen-Edmonds and Nichols), for example, fall into this category.

Sellers benefit from branding because each firm's brands identify its products, which facilitates repeat purchasing by consumers. To the extent that buyers become loyal to a specific brand, the firm's market share for that product achieves a

---

10. Adapted from Committee on Definitions, *Marketing Definitions: A Glossary of Marketing Terms* (Chicago: American Marketing Association, 1960), p. 8. Used by permission.
11. James U. McNeal and Linda Zeren, "Brand Name Selection for Consumer Products," *MSU Business Topics,* Spring 1981, p. 35.

certain level of stability. A stable market share allows a firm to use its resources more efficiently. When a firm develops some degree of customer loyalty to a brand, it can charge a premium price for the product. The producer of Bayer aspirin enjoys this position. Branding also helps an organization introduce a new product that carries the name of one or more of its existing products because buyers are already familiar with the firm's existing brands. For example, Coca-Cola is testing a variety of new soft drink flavors such as Vanilla Coke, Lemon Coke, Chocolate Coke, Cream Coke, and a berry-flavored Coke. Carrying the Coke name would give these potential new products quicker recognition and trial in the marketplace than would an unfamiliar brand name.[12] Finally, branding facilitates promotional efforts because the promotion of each branded product indirectly promotes all other products that are similarly branded.

Types of Brands

Two categories of brands are manufacturer and private distributor. **Manufacturer brands** are initiated by producers and ensure that producers are identified with their products at the point of purchase, for example, Green Giant, Sylvania Electric Products Inc., and Exxon. A manufacturer brand usually requires a producer to become involved with distribution, promotion, and, to some extent, pricing decisions. Brand loyalty is created by promotion, quality control, and guarantees; it is a valuable asset to a manufacturer. The producer tries to stimulate demand for the product, which tends to encourage middlemen to make the product available.

Private distributor brands, or **private brands,** are initiated and owned by resellers (marketing organizations that buy products for the purpose of reselling them). The major characteristic of private brands is that manufacturers are not identified on the products. Retailers and wholesalers use private distributor brands to develop more efficient promotion, to generate higher gross margins, and to improve store images. Private distributor brands give retailers or wholesalers freedom to purchase products of a specified quality at the lowest cost without disclosing the identity of the manufacturer.

Wholesaler brands include IGA (Independent Grocers' Alliance) and Topmost (General Grocer). Familiar retailer brand names include Kenmore (Sears, Roebuck) and Penncraft (J. C. Penney Company, Inc.). Many successful private brands are distributed nationally. The Sears Die-Hard battery is at least as well known as most manufacturer brands. The private-brand tires sold by such stores as K mart and Montgomery Ward and Co., Inc. are manufactured by major tire companies: Firestone Tire and Rubber Co., B. F. Goodrich Co., Goodyear Tire and Rubber Company, Uniroyal, and others. Sometimes retailers with successful distributor brands start manufacturing their own products in the hope of increasing profits and gaining even more control over their products.

Competition between manufacturer brands and private distributor brands (sometimes called "the battle of the brands") is becoming more intense in several major product categories. Private distributor brands now account for approximately 25 percent of all retail sales and are expected to increase to 30 percent by the early 1990s.[13]

---

12. "Coke Testing Tastes for Everyone," *Adweek,* Nov. 11, 1985, p. 85.
13. Penelope Ody, "The Growth in Private Brands," *Retail and Distribution Management,* May–June 1987, p. 10.

Developing multiple manufacturer brands and distribution systems has been an effective means of combating the increased competition from private brands. Holiday Inns Inc. has effectively developed several different brand names appealing to varying lifestyles and needs. Traditionally, lodging was categorized as budget, midscale, and upscale. Now more categories are recognized and appealed to, for example, all-suite, extended stay, and residence hotels. Holiday Inns has expanded into four types of lodging: Hampton Inns, budget; Embassy Suites, all-suite; Residence Inn, apartments; and Crown Plaza, upscale.[14] By developing a new brand name, manufacturers can adjust various elements of the marketing mix to appeal to a different target market. For example, Scott Paper has developed lower-priced brands of paper towels; it has tailored its new products to a target market that tends to purchase private brands.

It is difficult for manufacturers to ignore the market opportunities to be gained by producing private distributor brands. Usually, if a manufacturer refuses to produce a private brand, a competing manufacturer will get the business. Also, the production of private distributor brands allows the manufacturer to use excess capacity during periods when its own brands are at nonpeak production. The final decision about whether to produce a private or a manufacturer brand depends on an enterprise's resources, production capabilities, and goals.

| Selecting and Protecting a Brand | Marketers should consider a variety of issues when they select a brand name. The name should be easy for customers to say, spell, and recall (including foreign buyers, if the firm intends to market its products in other countries). Short, one-syllable names such as Cheer often satisfy this requirement. If possible, the brand name should suggest in a positive way the product's uses and special characteristics; negative or offensive references should be avoided. For example, a deodorant spray against underarm body odor should not be called Sweat. Instead, it should be branded with a name that connotes freshness, dryness, or perhaps long-lasting protection, as do Ban, Arrid, and Ice Blue Secret. The name should be descriptive of the product's major benefits. In a recent survey of large, consumer goods producers, almost 60 percent of the respondents reported that the latter issue is a major criterion in brand-name selection.[15] |

If a marketer intends to use a brand for a product line, it must be designed to be compatible with all products in the line. The manufacturer of Hotpoint products (a brand originally used on kitchen ranges) may have had some misgivings about the name when it introduced Hotpoint room air conditioners. Finally, a brand should be designed so that it can be used and recognized in all of the various types of media.

To protect the firm's exclusive rights to a brand, the company should be certain that the selected brand is not likely to be considered an infringement on any existing brand already registered with the U.S. Patent Office. This task may be complex because infringement is determined by the courts, whose decisions are based on whether a brand causes consumers to be confused, mistaken, or deceived

14. "A Variety of Lodging 'Brands' Enables Holiday Inns to Cater to Independent-Minded People," *Marketing News,* Oct. 25, 1985, p. 29.
15. James U. McNeal and Linda Zeren, "Brand Name Selection for Consumer Products," *MSU Business Topics,* Spring 1981, p. 37.

about the source of the product.[16] In recent years, the producers of such brands as Ultra Brite, Tylenol, Scrabble, Tic Tac, and Playboy have brought infringement charges against competing brands. Coca-Cola, with a trademark research department of twenty-five people, files between forty and sixty suits annually to protect its brands.[17]

The marketer should also design a brand that can be protected easily through registration. Because of their designs, some brands can be legally infringed upon more easily than others. Although registration protects trademarks domestically for twenty years and can be renewed indefinitely, a firm should develop a system that ensures that its trademarks will be renewed as needed. If possible, a marketer must guard against allowing a brand name to become a generic term used to refer to a general product category. Generic terms cannot be protected as exclusive brand names. For example, names such as cellophane, linoleum, and shredded wheat—all brand names at one time—eventually were declared generic terms that refer to product classes; thus they no longer could be protected.

To keep a brand name from becoming a generic term, the firm should spell the name with a capital letter and use it as an adjective to modify the name of the general product class, as in Kool-Aid Brand Soft Drink Mix, shown in Figure 7.7.[18] Including the word "brand" just after the brand name is also helpful. An organization can deal with this problem directly by advertising that its brand is a trademark and should not be used generically. The firm can also indicate that the brand is trademarked with the symbol ®, as Kool-Aid has done and as shown in Figure 7.7.

A U.S. firm that tries to protect a brand in a foreign country frequently encounters problems. In many foreign countries, brand registration is not possible; the first firm to use a brand in such a country has the rights to it. In some instances, a U.S. company actually has had to buy its own brand rights from a firm in a foreign country because the foreign firm was the first user in that country. In Italy (one of the world's biggest producers of counterfeit brands), one can purchase fake Cartier watches, Marlboro cigarettes, and Levi's jeans (the fake Levi's do not fade). None of the products are made by the U.S. firms that own these brands. But not all the fake merchandise is manufactured in foreign countries; roughly 20 percent of the bogus merchandise is made in the United States. The Counterfeit Intelligence Bureau in London estimates that roughly $60 billion in annual world trade involves counterfeit merchandise.[19]

Branding Policies

In attempting to establish branding policies, the first decision to be made is whether the firm should brand its products at all. When an organization's product is homogeneous and similar to competitors' products, it may be difficult to brand. Raw materials, such as coal, sand, and farm produce, are hard to brand because of the homogeneity of such products and their physical characteristics.

16. George Miaoulis and Nancy D'Amato, "Consumer Confusion and Trademark Infringement," *Journal of Marketing,* April 1978, pp. 48–49.
17. Frank Delano, "Keeping Your Trade Name or Trademark Out of Court," *Harvard Business Review,* March–April 1982, p. 73.
18. "Trademark Stylesheet," U.S. Trademark Association, no. 1A.
19. Thomas C. O'Donnell and Elizabeth Weiner, "The Counterfeit Trade," *Business Week,* Dec. 16, 1985, pp. 64–68, 72.

Some marketers of products that traditionally have been branded have embarked on a policy of not branding, often called generic branding. A **generic brand** indicates only the product category (such as aluminum foil) and does not include the company name or other identifying terms. Many supermarkets are selling generic brands at prices lower than their comparable branded items. Purchasers of generic-branded grocery items tend to be concentrated in middle income, large households that are price conscious and predisposed to select regularly low-priced alternatives, as opposed to temporarily lower-priced products. Much of the growth in generic grocery brand sales has thus been at the expense of private distributor brands.[20] It was estimated recently that generic brands represented 10 percent of all grocery sales.[21]

Assuming that a firm chooses to brand its products, marketers may opt for one or more of the following four branding policies: individual, overall family, line family, and brand-extension branding. **Individual branding** is a policy of naming each product differently. A major advantage of individual branding is that when an organization introduces a poor product, the negative images associated with it do not contaminate the company's other products. An individual branding policy may

20. Martha R. McEnally and Jon M. Hawes, "The Market for Generic Brand Grocery Products: A Review and Extension," *Journal of Marketing,* Winter 1984, pp. 75–83.
21. "Metamorphosis: Now They're with Names, Colorful Labels," *Marketing News,* Apr. 30, 1985, p. 1.

also facilitate market segmentation when a firm wishes to enter many segments of the same market. Separate, unrelated names can be used, and each brand can be aimed at a specific segment. As mentioned, Procter & Gamble relies on an individual branding policy for its line of detergents, which includes Tide, Bold, Dash, Cheer, and Oxydol.

In **overall family branding,** all of a firm's products are branded with the same name or at least part of the name, such as Sealtest and General Electric. In some cases, a company's name is combined with other words to brand items. Arm & Hammer uses its name on all its products along with a generic description of the product, such as Arm & Hammer Heavy Duty Detergent, Arm & Hammer Pure Baking Soda, and Arm & Hammer Carpet Deodorizer.[22] Unlike individual branding, overall family branding means that the promotion of one item with the family brand promotes the firm's other products.

Sometimes an organization uses family branding only for products within a line rather than for all its products. This policy is called **line family branding.** The same brand is used within a line, but the firm does not use the same name for a product in a different line. Colgate-Palmolive Co., for example, produces a line of cleaning products including a cleanser, a powdered detergent, and a liquid cleaner, all of which carry the name Ajax. Colgate also produces several brands of toothpaste, none of which carry the Ajax brand.

Brand-extension branding occurs when a firm uses one of its existing brand names as part of a brand for an improved or new product that is usually in the same product category as the existing brand. The makers of Arrid deodorant eventually extended the name Arrid to Arrid Extra-Dry and Arrid Double-X. There is one major difference between line family branding and brand-extension branding. With line family branding, all products in the line carry the same name, but with brand-extension branding, this is not the case. The producer of Arrid deodorant, for example, also makes other brands of deodorants.

An organization's marketers are not limited to a single branding policy. Instead, branding policy is influenced by the number of products and product lines the firm produces, the characteristics of its target markets, the number and types of competing products available, and the size of the firm's resources. Anheuser-Busch, Inc., for example, uses both individual and brand-extension branding. Most of the brands are individual brands; however, the Michelob Light brand is an extension of the Michelob brand.

Brand Licensing

A more recent trend in branding strategies involves the licensing of trademarks. Companies allow approved manufacturers to use their trademark on other products for a licensing fee. Royalties may be as low as 2 percent of wholesale revenues or better than 10 percent. As recently as 1980, only a few firms such as Playboy Enterprises, Inc. licensed their corporate trademarks. Today, licensing is a multibillion dollar business and growing. (See the Application on page 241 for additional details and examples of brand licensing.) Harley-Davidson Motor Co., Inc. has authorized use of its name on such unrelated products as cologne, wine coolers, gold rings, and polo shirts. Coca-Cola, however, has moved into licensing in hopes

22. Gerald Schoenfeld, "Line Extensions: Milking a Name for All It's Worth," *Adweek,* Nov. 18, 1985, pp. 44, 46.

The Growth of Brand Licensing

Thanks to licensing, consumers have been treated to everything from Spuds MacKenzie beach towels to Michael Jackson dolls and Minnie Mouse watches. Today, however, the real growth in licensing is not in celebrity or cartoon character marketing but in corporate, or brand, licensing. Products bearing licensed trademarks and brand names outsold all other licensing categories in last year's $54.3 billion market for licensed goods, bringing in $15.2 billion, or 28 percent of total sales.

Although brand licensing once meant simply sticking the corporate logo on drinking glasses or T-shirts to boost brand awareness, more and more companies are using licensing to extend their brands into completely new product categories. Adidas, for example, put its name on a new line of men's toiletries produced by Chicago-based Beecham Cosmetics; Sears, Roebuck has introduced McKids, children's sportswear licensed by McDonald's Corp. Generally, a company licensing its name receives from the licensee royalties from 4 to 8.5 percent of wholesale sales, plus a minimum guarantee. The licensee is responsible for all manufacturing, selling, and advertising functions. If the combination flops, the licensee bears the costs. But if it works, the licensee makes a profit and the licenser gets to move into new product areas without the usual outlay for new-product development.

In fact, although royalties can be a secondary source of income, most companies do not enter into brand licensing just for the money. Instead, they find that brand licensing lets them enter new distribution and advertising channels, reach new markets, and increase sales of their primary products. Trademark protection was a factor in Coca-Cola's decision to put its name on Murjani International's apparel line, now considered one of the most successful licensing arrangements. Similarly, motor home maker Winnebago Industries licensed a line of tents, air mattresses, and other camping gear to keep its name from becoming a generic term for "recreational vehicle." The licensing royalties contribute to Winnebago's overall revenues, and the program also keeps the company name before younger consumers who may someday move up from sleeping bags to motor homes.

Companies considering corporate licensing, however, should be aware of potential pitfalls, say licensing experts. For a licensee, the renting of a famous name means, in effect, that the manufacturer gives up its own corporate identity. In addition, licensing arrangements can fizzle because of poor timing, inappropriate distribution channels, or mismatch of product and name. A licenser should be particularly careful that the quality of the licensed product is satisfactory; otherwise, the company's reputation and core business are at risk.

For companies taking the licensing plunge, growth categories in the next few years will include food—such as Hershey's chocolate milk and Hiram

of protecting its trademark. The Coca-Cola name appears or is scheduled to appear on products in fourteen different product areas, including glassware, radios, trucks, and clothing.[23] The major advantages of licensing include extra revenues, little cost, free publicity, new images, and trademark protection. The major disadvantages include a lack of manufacturing control, which could hurt the company's name, and bombarding consumers with too many unrelated products bearing the same name.

Packaging

Packaging involves the development of a container and a graphic design for a product. A package can be a vital part of a product. It can make the product more versatile, safer, or easier to use. As can a brand name, a package can influence customers' attitudes toward a product, which in turn affects their purchase decisions. For example, several producers of jellies, sauces, and catsups have packaged their products in squeezable containers to make use and storage more convenient (see Figure 7.8).

Buyers' impressions of a product, formed at the point of purchase or during use, are significantly influenced by package characteristics. In this section we examine the major functions of packaging and consider several major packaging decisions. We also analyze the role of the package in a market strategy.

Packaging Functions   Effective packaging involves more than simply putting products in containers and covering them with wrappers. Packaging materials serve several primary functions. First, they protect the product or maintain its functional form. Product tampering recently has become a problem for marketers of many types of products, and several packaging techniques are being used to counter the problem. Fluids such as milk, orange juice, and hair spray need packages that preserve and protect them;

23. Frank E. James, "I'll Wear the Coke Pants Tonight; They Go Well with My Harley-Davidson Ring," *Wall Street Journal,* June 6, 1985, p. 31.

the packaging should effectively reduce damage that could affect the product's usefulness and increase costs. Another function of packaging is to offer the convenience that consumers often look for. For example, aseptic packages, individual-sized boxes or plastic bags that contain liquids, have had the strongest appeal among children and young adults who have active lifestyles. Juice manufacturers have benefited greatly from this packaging development. Formerly, their target market was 25–54-year-olds; the convenience of the package makes the product more appealing to a much younger market. For example, when Ocean Spray Cranberries, Inc. introduced its cranberry juice in aseptic packaging, sales rose 20 percent.[24] The size or shape of a package may relate to the product's storage, convenience of use, or replacement rate. Small, single-serving cans of vegetables, for instance, may prevent waste and facilitate storage. A third function of packaging is to promote a product by communicating its features, uses, benefits, and image.

Major Packaging Considerations

Marketers must consider many factors as they develop packages. Obviously, one major consideration is cost. Although a variety of packaging materials, processes, and designs are available, some are rather expensive. In recent years buyers have

24. "Knowing a Drink by Its Cover," *American Demographics,* April 1985, p. 16.

FIGURE 7.8

Squeezable packaging makes the use and storage of products more convenient (SOURCE: Courtesy of Eastman Chemical Products, Inc.)

shown a willingness to pay more for improved packaging, but there are limits. Marketers should try to determine through research just how much customers are willing to pay for packages.

Marketers must also decide whether to package the product singly or in multiple units. Multiple packaging is likely to increase demand because it increases the amount of the product available at the point of consumption (in one's home, for example). However, multiple packaging is not appropriate for infrequently used products because buyers do not like to tie up their dollars or store these products for a long time. Multiple packaging *can,* however, make products easier to handle and store (such as the six-packs used for soft drinks); and special price offers, such as a two-for-one sale, are facilitated through multiple packaging. In addition, multiple packaging may increase consumer acceptance of a product by encouraging the buyer to try it several times. On the other hand, because they must buy several units, customers may hesitate to try the product the first time.

Marketers should consider how much continuity among an organization's package designs is desirable. No continuity may be the best policy, especially if a firm's products are unrelated or aimed at vastly different target markets. To promote an overall company image, a firm may decide that all packages are to be similar or include one major element of the design. This approach is called **family packaging.** Sometimes this approach is used only for lines of products, as with Campbell's soups, Weight Watchers' foods, and Planters nuts.

A package's promotional role should be considered; will it be used to attract customers' attention and encourage them to examine the product? Through verbal and nonverbal symbols, the package can inform potential buyers about the product's content, features, uses, advantages, and hazards. A firm can create desirable images and associations by its choice of color, design, shape, and texture. Many cosmetics manufacturers, for example, design their packages to create impressions of richness, luxury, and exclusiveness. A package may perform a promotional function when it is designed to be safer or more convenient to use if such characteristics help stimulate demand. (The Application on page 247 explores issues about making packages more appealing to customers.)

To develop a package that has a definite promotional value, a designer must consider size, shape, texture, color, and graphics. Beyond the obvious limitation that the package must be large enough to hold the product, a package can be designed to appear taller or shorter. Thin vertical lines, for example, make a package look taller; wide horizontal stripes make it look shorter. In some cases a marketer may want a package to appear taller because many people perceive something that is taller as being larger.

The shape of the package can help communicate a particular message. Research and successful promotions have led marketers to stereotype the sexes and so they offer men packages with angular shapes and wood or burlap textures. Women's packages, on the other hand, have rounded, curved shapes and soft, fuzzy textures.

Colors on packages are often chosen to attract attention. People associate certain feelings and connotations with specific colors. Red, for example, is linked with fire, blood, danger, and anger; yellow suggests sunlight, caution, warmth, and vitality; blue can imply coldness, sky, water, and sadness.[25] When selecting packaging

---

25. James U. McNeal, *Consumer Behavior: An Integrative Approach* (Boston: Little, Brown, 1982), pp. 221–222.

colors, marketers must first decide whether a particular color will evoke positive or negative feelings when it is used with a specific type of product. Rarely, for example, do processors package meat or bread in green materials because customers may associate green with mold. A sunburn ointment is more likely to appear in a soothing blue package than in a fiery red one. Marketers must also decide whether a specific target market will respond favorably or unfavorably to a particular color. Cosmetics for women are much more likely to be sold in pastel packaging than are personal-care products for men. Packages designed to appeal to young children often use primary colors and bold designs.

Packaging and Marketing Strategy

Packaging can be a major component of a marketing strategy. A unique cap or closure, a better box or wrapper, or a more convenient container size may give a firm a competitive advantage. Packaging of consumer products is extremely important at the point of sale. Manufacturers of beer, detergents, and most packaged foods spend a great deal of money to research consumers' reactions to packages. For established brands, marketers should evaluate and change package designs to keep them stylish and up-to-date looking. As Figure 7.9 shows, Procter & Gamble has changed the Ivory Bar Soap package several times to give this century-old product a contemporary look.

FIGURE 7.9

Changes in the Ivory bar soap package since 1898 (SOURCE: Reproduced with permission from the Procter & Gamble Company)

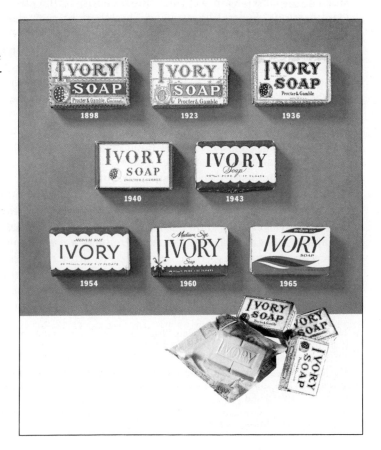

As package designs improve, it becomes harder for any one product to dominate because of packaging. For example, Stouffer Food Corp. decided to package its frozen foods in orange boxes so that they would visually dominate the frozen food section where they compete.[26] As competitors have developed more eye-catching packaging, Stouffer's advantage has eroded. The typical large store stocks fifteen thousand items, so the product that stands out is more likely to be purchased. Today skilled artists and package designers, who have experience in marketing research, test packaging to see what sells well, not just what is aesthetically appealing.[27]

Packaging must also take into account the needs of middlemen. Resellers (wholesalers and retailers) consider whether a package facilitates the transporting, storing, and handling of the product. In some cases, resellers refuse to carry certain products because their packages are too cumbersome.

Labeling

Labeling too is an important dimension related to packaging, for both promotional and informational reasons and legal perspectives. The Food and Drug Administration and the Consumer Product Safety Commission can require that products be labeled or marked with warnings, instructions, certifications, and manufacturer's identifications. Federal laws require disclosure of such data as textile identifications, potential hazards, and nutritional information. Del Monte Corp. introduced nutritional labeling before it was required by federal law. In this case, the eventual legal requirement worked to the advantage of the marketer. Consumers responded favorably to the nutritional information, and Del Monte gained a competitive edge over manufacturers who did not disclose nutritional values. Yet, despite the fact that consumers have responded favorably to the inclusion of this type of information on labels, there is little evidence that they actually use it. In fact, research results have been mixed—several studies indicate that consumers do not use nutritional information, whereas other studies indicate that the information is useful.[28] Labels also can be used to promote a manufacturer's other products or to encourage proper use of products and therefore greater satisfaction with them.

Color and eye-catching graphics on labels overcome the jumble of words—known to designers as "mouse print"—that have been added to satisfy government regulations. Because so many similar products are available, an attention-getting device, or "silent salesperson," is needed to attract interest. As one of the most visible parts of a product, the label is an important element in the marketing mix.

26. Bill Abrams and David P. Garino, "Package Design Gains Stature as Visual Competition Grows," *Wall Street Journal*, Aug. 6, 1981, p. 25.
27. Ibid.
28. Jeffrey W. Totten, "The Effect of Nutrition Information on Brand Rating—An Extension," in *Marketing Comes of Age*, David M. Klein and Allen E. Smith, eds. (Southern Marketing Association, 1984), pp. 48–50 and Jim L. Grimm and James B. Spalding, Jr., "Shoppers' Perceptions and Use of Nutritional Label Information," in *Marketing: Theories and Concepts for an Era of Change* (Southern Marketing Association, 1983).

Product Enhancement Through Package Design

Modern packaging owes a lot to the familiar Quaker Oats box. Originally developed in the 1800s as an alternative to unsanitary open barrels, the heavy paper container was the first package produced in four colors, the first to include cooking instructions, the first to appear in sample sizes, and the first to make possible attention-getting displays. Today, competition for the consumer's attention is keener than ever. The modern supermarket stocks about 17,000 items, with 2,200 new products appearing every year. For package designers, the challenge is to convey a powerful marketing message through a mere container—and to exactly the right customers. These days, designers are trying to reach those customers in several ways.

For one thing, package graphics—colors, pictures, and lettering—are becoming more sophisticated. To make a package stand out on the shelf, designers are using ideas once considered risky or very unconventional. Minute Maid's black containers, for example, were once the exception, but now black packaging is popular. The revamped black label bottles for Heinz's line of wine vinegars won a packaging award and helped boost sales of the product as much as 50 percent in some markets. "In" colors are also used in cosmetics packaging to attract style-conscious customers. Sometimes graphics are used to overcome consumer resistance to product advances. In the case of Farm Best aseptically packaged milk—fresh milk in vacuum-packed, airproof boxes for liquids, which does not require refrigeration—the carton was redesigned to show a peaceful country scene and a banner with the words "freshly packed," a phrase with health appeal.

Package structures too are being revamped for serviceability and style. The original waxed-paper cup for Yoplait yogurt leaked, contributing to product deterioration. But when General Mills, Inc. took over the Yoplait product, developed a plastic package, and promoted the yogurt aggressively, sales of Yoplait outstripped even Cheerios, the company's leading brand. Customers also like such easy-open, easy-hold containers as Liquid Tide's plastic bottle with built-in spout and measuring cup. Consumer demand prompted Welch Foods to introduce a line of jellies and marmalades in squeezable containers that children could manage, once technology made the new containers possible; now a wide range of products are sold in squeezable packaging. Aseptic packs are being used for dozens of fruit juices, flavored drinks, and other liquids, and ground coffee is now available in foil "bricks" for extra freshness. Concerns over tampering have produced additional structural changes, such as overwrap and vacuum seals.

The real impetus behind many packaging innovations, however, is customer convenience. Single-serving frozen foods, pump-style toothpaste, and liquid detergents are all packaged for the customer who wants to save time. In toiletries and beauty aids, convenience packaging often means portability, such as travel sizes of deodorant and styling mousse, complete kits of coordinated eye shadow and blusher, and nail polish pens for touchups on the go. The microwave oven, itself a convenience item, has revolutionized convenience packaging. By its very popularity, the microwave has increased the number of convenience foods available. Packaging materials and printed cooking instructions have also been adjusted for the microwave's requirements.

Convenience packaging can mean higher costs for manufacturers and consumers alike. A sample-size aerosol can of spray deodorant, for example, costs almost as much to produce and fill as a standard canister, and the retail price of a 4.1-ounce pump of toothpaste is about the same as a 6.4-ounce tube. Manufacturers believe, however, that small packages may attract first-time customers who might not buy a larger, more expensive size. For their part, busy consumers seem willing to pay extra for convenience containers, provided that perceived product value balances the added cost.

SOURCES: Kate Bertrand, "Convenient and Portable Packaging Pays," *Advertising Age,* Feb. 20, 1986, p. 16; Michael Gershman, "Packaging's Role in Remarketing," *Management Review,* May 1987, pp. 41–45; Mitch Head, "An Ounce of Prevention Against Tampering," *Progressive Grocer,* February 1986, pp. 17–18; David Kalish, "New Rules in the Package-Design Game," *Adweek,* Oct. 6, 1986, p. 34; Lori Kesler, "Successful Packages Turn Medium into Message," *Advertising Age,* Oct. 13, 1986, pp. S2–3.

Other Product-Related Characteristics

When developing products, marketers make many decisions. Some of these decisions involve the physical characteristics of the product; others focus on less tangible supportive services that are very much a part of the total product.

Physical Characteristics of the Product

A major question that arises during product development is how much quality to build into the product. A major dimension of quality is durability. Higher quality often calls for better materials and more expensive processing, which increase production costs and, ultimately, the product's price. In determining the specific level of quality, a marketer must know or ascertain approximately what price the target market views as acceptable. In addition, a marketer usually tries to set a level for a specific product that is consistent with the firm's other products that carry a similar brand. Obviously, the quality of competing brands is a consideration.

A product's physical features require careful consideration by marketers. The prime basis for decisions about the physical features should be the desires of target market members. If marketers do not know what physical features people in the target market want in a product, it will be an accident if the product is satisfactory. Even a firm whose existing products have been designed to satisfy target market desires should assess these desires periodically to determine whether they have changed enough to require alterations to such features as textures, colors, or sizes. (Product modification is discussed in Chapter 8.)

Supportive Product-Related Services

All products, whether they are goods or not, possess intangible qualities: "When prospective customers can't experience the product in advance, they are asked to buy what are essentially promises—promises of satisfaction. Even tangible, testable, feelable, smellable products are, before they're bought, largely just promises." [29] Here we briefly discuss three product-related services: warranties, repairs and replacements, and credit. There are of course many other product-related services and product intangibles.

The type of warranty a firm provides can be a critical issue for buyers, especially when expensive, technically complex products such as appliances are involved. A **warranty** specifies what the producer will do if the product malfunctions. In recent years, government actions have required a warrantor to state more simply and specifically the terms and conditions under which the firm will take action. Because warranties must be more precise today, marketers are using them more vigorously as tools to give their brands a competitive advantage.

A marketer must be concerned with establishing a system to provide replacement parts and repair services. This support service is especially important for expensive, complex products that buyers expect to last a long time. Although the producer may provide these services directly to buyers, it is more common for the producer to provide such services through regional service centers or middlemen. Regardless of how services are provided, it is important to customers that they be performed quickly and correctly.

Finally, a firm must sometimes provide credit services to customers. Even though doing so places financial burdens on an organization, it can yield several benefits. Providing credit services can help a firm obtain and maintain a stable market share. Many major oil companies, for example, have competed effectively against gasoline discounters by providing credit services. For marketers of relatively expensive items, offering credit services enables a larger number of people to buy the product, thus enlarging the market for the item. Another reason for offering credit services is to earn interest income from customers. The types of credit services offered depend on the characteristics of target market members, the firm's financial resources, the type of products sold, and the types of credit services competitors offer.

Summary

A product is much more than a physical object or a service rendered. It includes everything that a customer receives in an exchange. It is a complex set of tangible and intangible attributes, including functional, social, and psychological utilities or benefits. When buyers purchase a product, they actually are buying the benefits and satisfaction they think the product will provide.

Products fall into one of two general categories: consumer products and industrial products. Consumer products satisfy personal and family needs. Industrial products are purchased for use in a firm's operations or to make other products. Consumer products can be subdivided into convenience, shopping, specialty, and

29. Theodore Levitt, "Marketing Intangible Products and Product Intangibles," *Harvard Business Review,* May–June 1981, p. 96.

unsought products. Industrial products can be divided into raw materials, major equipment, accessory equipment, component parts, process materials, consumable supplies, and industrial services.

The product mix is the composite or total group of products that an organization makes available. The product line is a related group of products within the product mix. Product lines are based on marketing, technical, or end-use considerations. The product item within the product line is a unique offering.

The product life cycle describes how product items in an industry move through (1) introduction, (2) growth, (3) maturity, and (4) decline. The life cycle concept is used to evaluate product strategy and adjust the marketing strategy to particular situations. The sales curve is at zero at introduction, rises at an increasing rate during growth, peaks at maturity, and then declines. Profits peak toward the end of the growth stage of the product life cycle. The life expectancy of a product is based on buyers' wants, the availability of competing products, and other environmental conditions. Products move through various stages of their life cycles according to saturation of market potential. Some enterprises have a composite of life cycle patterns for various products. A major marketing task is to manage existing products and develop new products to keep the overall sales performance at a desired level.

A brand is a name, term, symbol, design, or a combination thereof that identifies a seller's products and differentiates them from competitors' products. Branding can benefit both marketers and customers. A manufacturer brand is initiated by a producer and makes it possible for producers to be identified with their products at the point of purchase. A private distributor brand is initiated and owned by a reseller. When selecting a brand, a marketer should choose one that is easy to say, spell, and recall and that alludes to the product's uses, benefits, or special characteristics. Major branding policies are individual branding, overall family branding, line family branding, and brand-extension branding.

Packaging offers protection, economy, convenience, and promotion. When developing a package, marketers must consider packaging costs relative to the needs of target market members. Other considerations include both whether to use multiple packaging and family packaging and how to design the package so that it is an effective promotional tool. Labeling is used on packages to provide instructions, information about the contents, certifications, and manufacturer identifications. Labels can perform both informational and promotional functions.

When creating products, marketers must take into account other product-related considerations, such as physical characteristics and less tangible supportive services. Specific physical product characteristics that require attention are the level of quality, product features, textures, colors, and sizes. Supportive services that may be viewed as part of the total product include warranties, repairs and replacements, and credit services.

Important Terms

Product	Convenience products
Consumer products	Shopping products
Industrial products	Specialty products

Unsought products
Raw materials
Major equipment
Accessory equipment
Component parts
Process materials
Consumable supplies
MRO items
Industrial services
Product item
Product line
Product mix
Depth (of product mix)
Width (of product mix)
Product life cycle
Introduction stage
Growth stage
Maturity stage

Decline stage
Brand
Brand name
Brand mark
Trademark
Trade name
Manufacturer brands
Private distributor brands
Generic brand
Individual branding
Overall family branding
Line family branding
Brand-extension branding
Family packaging
Labeling
Warranty

Discussion and Review Questions

1. List the tangible and intangible attributes of a bottle of mouthwash. Compare the benefits of mouthwash with those of an intangible product, such as life insurance.
2. A product has been referred to as a "psychological bundle of satisfaction." Is this a good definition of a product? Why or why not?
3. Is a roll of shag carpeting in a store a consumer product or an industrial product? Defend your answer.
4. How do convenience products and shopping products differ? What are the distinguishing characteristics of each type of product?
5. Would a stereo tape deck that sells for $869 be a convenience, shopping, or specialty product?
6. In the category of industrial products, how do component parts differ from process materials?
7. How does an organization's product mix relate to its development of a product line? When should an enterprise add depth to its product lines rather than width to its product mix?
8. How do industry profits change as a product moves through the four stages of its life cycle?
9. What is the relationship between the concepts of product mix and product life cycle?
10. What is the difference between a brand and a brand name? Compare and contrast the terms *brand mark* and *trademark*.
11. How does branding benefit an organization?
12. What are the distinguishing characteristics of private distributor brands?
13. Given the competition between private distributor brands and manufacturer brands, should manufacturers be concerned about the increasing popularity of

private distributor brands? How should manufacturers fight back in the brand battle? At what point should a manufacturer make private brands?

14. The brand name Xerox is sometimes used generically to refer to photocopying machines. How can Xerox Corporation protect this brand name?
15. Identify and explain the four major branding policies and give examples of each. Can a firm use more than one policy at a time? Explain your answer.
16. Describe the functions that a package can perform. Which function is most important? Why?
17. Why is the determination of a product's quality level an important decision? What major factors affect this decision?

Cases

7.1   Nike's Product Line Development[30]

In 1972, with forty-five employees, Nike Inc. began producing running shoes. Sales for that year were $1.96 million. More than a decade later, Nike's worldwide sales totaled $920 million, and the corporation employed more than four thousand workers. Nike capitalized on the jogging and running crazes that swept the country in the 1970s and early 1980s, when the number of active runners jumped from five million to forty million in just ten years. As running became the number-one fitness hobby, production and selling reached a frantic level for the athletic shoe and clothing company. Nike became well-known for light-weight shoes that provided exceptional durability and special injury-reduction design features.

What Nike failed to anticipate, however, was the flattening and ultimate downturn in the running shoe market. By the mid-1980s, the number of runners was declining. Runners and other people who wanted exercise pursued swimming, weightlifting, aerobics, bicycling, tennis, racquetball, and soccer. Nike had misread consumer demand and buyers' attitudes, and the company found itself overstocked with running shoes and underdeveloped with respect to new products.

Changes in fitness activities also led to a decline in the use of running shoes for casual wear; court and aerobics shoes became fashionable instead. One industry analyst estimated that at least 70 percent of the shoes designed for basketball and aerobics exercise were being used for street wear. Reebok, one of Nike's newest competitors, made the most of this trend. In addition to providing comfort and performance, Reebok shoes came in brilliant colors, soft leather, and interesting styles. Reebok sales increased from $66 million in 1984 to $307 million in 1985, while Nike's aerobics shoes and clothes were plagued by quality problems.

Nike evaluated its products in light of the changing market, laid off 10 percent of its work force to cut expenses, and over an eighteen-month period reduced its

30. Based on information from 1985 Nike *Annual Report;* Lois Therrien and Amy Borrus, "Reeboks: How Far Can a Fad Run?", *Business Week,* Feb. 24, 1986, pp. 89–90; Lynn Strongin Dodds, "Heading Back on the Fast Track," *Financial World,* Aug. 21–Sept. 3, 1985, pp. 90–91; Mike Tharp, "Nike Recoups Laurels in the Sportswear Market," *Wall Street Journal,* Mar. 19, 1986, p. 6; Brian Lowry, "Nike Tries on Street Socks," *Advertising Age,* Mar. 24, 1986; Barbara Lee, "Nike's Run for the Money," *Savvy,* May 1986, p. 24.

inventory from 22 million pairs of shoes to less than 10 million pairs. Now, Nike is taking a functional approach to product development: meeting athletes' needs instead of attempting to meet fashion demands with new colors and styles, as many of Nike's competitors are doing. The company intends to maintain its 50 percent share of the running shoe market while providing products that meet consumers' increasingly diverse fitness requirements. Nike leads the industry in sports shoe technology, spending $8 million to $10 million each year researching shoes for specific sports. Nike's strategy calls for each new product to

Provide functional innovation and unique design
Be driven by the marketing concept
Be developed around and with athletes
Lead to other successful new products

One of Nike's biggest successes has been the Air Jordan line of basketball shoes, named for Chicago Bulls NBA star Michael Jordan. First marketed two years ago, Air Jordans generated more than $100 million in orders in a six-month period and helped keep Nike at the top in basketball shoe sales. Other recent Nike offerings include the John McEnroe line of tennis apparel; clothing for weight training, aerobics, and cross-country skiing; and a complete line of aerobics shoes for men and women. For the $700 million running shoe market segment, Nike introduced the Sock Racer, a lightweight shoe for serious runners; the Sock Trainer, a training shoe with broader appeal than the Racer; and the new Street Socks line, a casual, lower-priced version of the Racer.

Nike also predicts that walking will become an increasingly popular activity. According to the Census Bureau, 50 million to 80 million Americans walk for exercise. Following almost four years of research, last year Nike brought out its EXW walking shoe, accompanied by a print and outdoor advertising campaign and company-sponsored walking events.

As a cost-control measure, Nike cut back on the number of athletic stars signed as product endorsers. At one time the company had as many as 130 NBA players under contract; Nike's roster now has about forty big-name athletes. Similarly, the company's Athletic West track and field club now numbers only fifty members. However, with Alberto Salazar, Mary Decker Slaney, and other athletes endorsing Nike products, the club is considered the best in the United States. Nike intends to use these star athletes selectively, applying their endorsements to newly developed sports-specific lines rather than to the brand name Nike. By taking advantage of each athlete's individual personality and popularity, Nike plans to inject more creativity and subtlety into its advertising.

Although Nike has experienced losses in recent years, the company appears to have improved its understanding of consumers' athletic needs. Last year sales reached the $1 billion mark, one of the company's best years ever. Nike now provides a broad product line that appeals to many different sports enthusiasts, and the company continues to improve existing products, identify opportunities for new products, and manage its lines successfully.

Questions for Discussion

1. What stage of the product life cycle are Nike's running shoes in compared with the life cycle stage of the Air Jordan basketball shoes?

2. Evaluate Nike's decision to produce shoes catering to the athlete's needs, as opposed to Reebok, whose initial strategy was to produce fashionable, colorful shoes.
3. Evaluate and categorize the depth and width of Nike's product lines.

7.2 Disney Expands Its Product Mix[31]

Following the death of founder Walt Disney in 1966, the Walt Disney Company appeared to lose its creative edge. As other studios diversified into television, cable, and video, Disney seemed content with its huge library of feature films and animated classics. The company turned out only three or four new movies a year, largely unimaginative box office bombs. Disney also pulled out of television after twenty-nine years of network programming. By the mid-1980s, Disney was depending on its theme parks and real estate development for about 75 percent of its revenues.

Today, however, Disney is intent on recapturing—and building on—the old Disney magic. The Disney name, culture, movies, and library are the company's biggest resources, say company executives, and Disney's plan is to rejuvenate old assets and develop new ones. For example, while continuing its traditional appeal to family markets, Disney has begun turning out products for adult audiences as well, including such recent films as "Ruthless People," "Adventures in Babysitting," "Outrageous Fortune," and "Down and Out in Beverly Hills." The company is releasing both old and new programs for television syndication and testing new promotional and licensing projects for existing Disney products. In addition, the Disney theme park has been exported. In Japan, the Tokyo Disneyland is expected to attract eleven million visitors this year, and a Disneyland is scheduled to open near Paris in the early 1990s. Disney's overall strategy is to channel the company's revived creativity into improved theme parks, to use the parks to generate interest in Disney films, and to promote both parks and merchandise through the Disney television shows.

Disney received its new lease on life a few years ago, when threats of a corporate takeover prompted the company to replace its top executives. The new management team—headed by Michael D. Eisner, former president of Paramount Pictures—moved quickly to tap the resources of the Disney television and film library. About two hundred Disney movies and cartoon packages are now available on videocassette, and other classic films, such as "Snow White," will be rereleased every five years instead of every seven years. The studio plans to release one new

31. Based on information from Pamela Ellis-Simon, "Hi Ho, Hi Ho," *Marketing and Media Decisions,* September 1986, pp. 52–54; Stephen J. Sansweet, "Disney Co. Cartoons Are Going to China in Commercial Foray," *The Wall Street Journal,* Oct. 23, 1986, p. 19; Dudley Clendinen, "Disney's Mouse of Marketing," *The New York Times,* Nov. 22, 1986, p. 41-L; Andrea Gabor and Steve L. Hawkins, "Of Mice and Money in the Magic Kingdom," *U.S. News and World Report,* Dec. 22, 1986, pp. 44–46; Ronald Grover, "Disney's Magic," *Business Week,* Mar. 9, 1987, pp. 62–65; Marcy Magiera, "Disney Tries Retailing," *Advertising Age,* June 1, 1987, p. 80; Myron Magnet, "Putting Magic Back in the Magic Kingdom," *Fortune,* Jan. 5, 1987, p. 65; Raymond Roel, "Disney's Marketing Touch," *Direct Marketing,* January 1987, pp. 50–53.

animated movie for children every eighteen months and, through Disney's Touchstone Pictures division, about a dozen adult films a year.

Disney is back on the small screen too. The *Disney Sunday Movie,* hosted each week by Eisner, returned to network television after a two-year absence. The company also produces the comedy show *Golden Girls,* along with two top-rated Saturday morning cartoon shows. Following the lead of other studios, Disney has moved into television syndication by marketing packages of feature movies, old cartoons, and *Wonderful World of Disney* shows. New shows are being produced for syndication as well, including a game show, a business news program, and movie reviews by Gene Siskel and Roger Ebert. In an otherwise flat cable television market, the number of subscribers to the family oriented Disney Channel jumped 27 percent last year, to almost 3.2 million. The channel now offers twenty-four-hour features and more original programming—upward of 35 percent—than any other pay service. Disney has even signed an agreement with the Chinese government to air a weekly television series starring Mickey Mouse and Donald Duck, and the company may license the Chinese to produce Disney merchandise.

At home too, marketing of Disney characters is receiving considerable emphasis. Mickey, Donald, and the others visited hospital wards and marched in parades in a 120-city tour. Early this year, Snow White and all the dwarfs made a special appearance on the floor of the New York Stock Exchange to promote the celebration of Snow White's fiftieth birthday. Minnie Mouse now has a trendy new look and appears on clothing and watches and in a fashion doll line. Disney is also working with toy companies to develop such new characters as Fluppy Dogs and Wuzzles, both of which will be sold in stores and featured in television shows. In addition, the company recently opened its first nontourist retail outlet. Located in a California shopping mall, the Disney Store carries both licensed products and exclusive theme park merchandise. Disney plans to test up to eight stores next year. If successful, the concept will be expanded into a national chain.

Disney's revitalized market presence has been credited with boosting attendance at the Disney theme parks, up 8 percent last year. In Florida, Disney is planning several new hotels and a movie studio/tour attraction as well as a fifty-acre water park and additions to Disney World. The company is also considering a series of regional centers that would combine restaurants and shopping with evening entertainment. Disney plans to finance these developments by spinning off both its Arvida real estate unit and the Epcot Center in Orlando. At the same time, Disney intends eventually to reduce the company's financial dependence on parks and hotels. Disney's strategy is to triple the proportion of company profits from movies and television (currently 13 percent) and to acquire such distribution outlets as movie theaters, television stations, and record companies.

Questions for Discussion

1. Disney's product mix consists of many products. Does Disney have product lines? If so, what are they?
2. Disney labels many of its new movies for adults as Touchstone Productions. With a well-known name like Disney, why does the company not use the Disney name?
3. Do the products in the Disney product mix have product life cycles? Explain your answer.

8. Developing and Managing Products

O B J E C T I V E S

- ▶ To develop an awareness of organizational alternatives for managing products.
- ▶ To understand the importance and role of product development in the marketing mix.
- ▶ To become aware of how existing products can be modified.
- ▶ To learn how product deletion can be used to improve product mixes.
- ▶ To gain insight into how businesses develop a product idea into a commercial product.
- ▶ To acquire knowledge about product positioning and the management of products during the various stages of the products' life cycles.

*F*or *Polaroid Corp.,* the problem wasn't that people had lost interest in taking pictures; they were simply taking fewer *instant* pictures. Annual sales of all instant cameras dropped steadily, from nine million in 1978 to only three million two years ago, as more and more amateur photographers chose 35mm and single-reflex lens cameras for better picture quality and cheaper film.

But Polaroid decided to dig in. The company conducted extensive market research among camera users and last year introduced the Spectra, a high-tech instant camera that produces higher-quality prints (see Figure 8.1). Priced from $150 to $200, Spectra was an instant hit, selling 800,000 units in its first nine months on the market. Thanks largely to Spectra, Polaroid almost tripled its earnings last year (to $103.5 million) and is selling more Polaroid film and other camera products as well.

Although Polaroid now has the instant-photography market to itself—following Kodak's court-ordered departure from that market because of patent violations—many observers say Spectra has succeeded on its own merits. New technology enables Spectra to take sharper pictures with truer colors. Its rectangular prints, about 15 percent larger than other instant pictures, resemble prints from 35mm cameras in shape and size. Furthermore, reprints of Spectra photos, available through Polaroid's special laser reprint service, are better than reprints from other Polaroid films; Polaroid hopes this advantage will figure in consumers' initial purchase decisions.

Acknowledging, however, that demand for new camera models typically drops off after two years or so, Polaroid is looking ahead to the next revolution in

FIGURE 8.1

Advertisement for
Polaroid (SOURCE:
Courtesy of Polaroid)

photography: the electronic still camera, which stores images on magnetic disks instead of film. Kodak Company, Sony Corp., Matsushita Electric Industrial Co., Ltd., and others are also working on their own electronic cameras, although so far the prototypes have produced only poor-quality pictures. Polaroid believes that an electronic camera incorporating instant-film technology will ultimately produce the best pictures, and it hopes to have a consumer version on the market within five to ten years.

Polaroid is also courting industrial photographic customers, who account for about 40 percent of the company's sales. Polaroid's newest commercial product is FreezeFrame, a device that can freeze, store, and print instant photographs or slides from videotape. FreezeFrame's biggest appeal is to broadcasters, magazine publishers, and advertising agencies. Other potential applications include medical diagnostics, surveillance, and archival fields. In addition, Polaroid's expanding magnetics division is working on high-density information storage systems, particularly a new floppy disk for personal computers that will hold more than twice as many characters as a personal computer hard disk.

Until some of its other new products reach the marketplace, Polaroid is counting on the continued popularity of the Spectra and is already extending the Spectra line. The Onyx, a more expensive ($280 to $350) version introduced recently, includes a smoked plastic top that lets the user see into the camera works. Polaroid says it plans to add telephoto lens capability and will also market a lower-priced Spectra in the near future.[1]

To COMPETE EFFECTIVELY and achieve its goals, an organization such as Polaroid must be able to adjust its product mix in response to changes in buyers' preferences. A firm often must modify existing products, introduce new products, or eliminate products that were at one time successful, perhaps only a few years ago. These adjustments and the way a firm is organized to make them are facets of product management.

This chapter examines how enterprises are organized to develop and manage products. We look at several ways to improve a product mix, including product modification, product deletion, and new-product development. We also examine product positioning: how marketers decide where a product should fit into the field of competing products and which benefits to emphasize. Finally, we consider several decisions that must be made to manage a product through its life cycle.

Organizing to Manage Products

A firm must often manage a complex set of products and/or markets. It frequently finds that the functional form of organization businesses traditionally use does not fit its needs. In the functional form, managers specialize in business functions such as advertising, sales, and distribution. A manager—or a group of managers—must find an organizational approach that accomplishes the tasks necessary to develop and manage products. Alternatives to functional organization include the product manager approach, the market manager approach, and a combination approach.

A **product manager** holds a staff position in a multiproduct company in which the number of products makes it difficult to use other organizational forms. Product managers are responsible for a product, a product line, or several distinct products that make up an interrelated group. A **brand manager** is a type of product manager, responsible for a single brand. General Foods Corp., for example, has one brand manager for Maxim coffee and one for Maxwell House coffee. A product or brand manager operates cross-functionally to coordinate the activities, information, and strategies involved in marketing an assigned product. Product managers plan marketing activities to achieve objectives by coordinating a mix of

1. Based on information from Gail Bronson, "Watching the Wrong Birdie," *Forbes,* Apr. 28, 1986, p. 96; Brian Dumaine, "How Polaroid Flashed Back," *Fortune,* Feb. 16, 1987, pp. 72–73; Carol Hall, "Instant Gratification," *Marketing & Media Decisions,* March 1987, pp. 28–29; Lisa E. Phillips, "Polaroid Reveals Image of New High-Tech Gear," *Advertising Age,* May 25, 1987, p. 62; Polaroid Corporation, *Annual Report,* 1986.

distribution, promotion (especially sales promotion and advertising), and price. The areas they must consider include packaging, branding, and the coordination of research and development, engineering, and production. Marketing research enables product managers to understand consumers and find target markets. The product or brand manager form of organization is used by many large, multiple-product companies in the consumer package goods business.[2]

A **market manager** is responsible for managing the marketing activities that serve a particular group or class of customers. This organizational approach is especially useful when a firm uses different types of marketing activities to provide products to diverse customer groups. For example, a firm might have one market manager for industrial markets and another for consumer markets. These broad market categories might be broken down into more limited market responsibilities.

A **venture team** is designed to create entirely new products that may be aimed at new markets. Unlike a product or a market manager, a venture team is responsible for all aspects of a product's development: research and development, production and engineering, finance and accounting, and marketing. Venture teams work outside established divisions to create inventive approaches to new products and markets. As a result of this flexibility, new products can be developed to take advantage of opportunities in highly segmented markets.

The members of a venture team come from different functional areas of an organization. When the commercial potential of a new product has been demonstrated, the members may return to their functional areas, or they may join a new or existing division to manage the product. The new product may be turned over to an existing division, a market manager, or a product manager.[3] A venture department is a separate department or division formed to find, develop, and commercialize promising new-product or new-business areas.[4] Innovative organizational forms such as venture teams are necessary for many companies, especially well-established firms operating primarily in mature markets. These companies must take a dual approach to marketing organization: They must accommodate the management of mature products and also encourage the development of new products.[5]

Managing the Product Mix

To provide products that satisfy target markets and achieve the organization's objectives, a marketer must develop, alter, and maintain an effective product mix (although seldom can the same product mix be effective for long). An organization's product mix may need several types of adjustments. Because customers' product preferences and attitudes change, their desire for a product may dwindle.

2. Thomas J. Cosse and John E. Swan, "Strategic Marketing Planning by Product Managers—Room for Improvement?", *Journal of Marketing,* Summer 1983, pp. 92–102.
3. Richard M. Hill and James D. Hlavacek, "The Venture Team: A New Concept in Marketing Organization," *Journal of Marketing,* July 1972, p. 49.
4. Dan T. Dunn, Jr., "Venture Groups Redefined," *Akron Business and Economic Review,* Fall 1980, pp. 7–11.
5. Roger C. Bennett and Robert G. Cooper, "The Product Life Cycle Trap," *Business Horizons,* September–October 1984, pp. 7–16.

People's fashion preferences obviously change quite often, but individuals' preferences and attitudes change with respect to almost all products.

In some cases a firm needs to alter its product mix to adjust to competition. A marketer may have to delete a product from the mix because one or more competitors dominate the market for that product. Similarly, an organization may have to introduce a new product or modify an existing one to compete more effectively. A marketer may expand the firm's product mix to take advantage of excess marketing and production capacity.

Regardless of why a product mix is altered, the product mix must be managed. In strategic market planning, the management of the product mix is often referred to as the portfolio approach. The **product portfolio approach** attempts to create specific marketing strategies to achieve a balanced mix of products that will produce maximum long-run profits. In a portfolio analysis, the most time-consuming task is collecting data about the items in the portfolio and their performance along selected dimensions. This evaluation requires hard data from company records (for instance, sales and profitability) and from outside sources (for instance, market share and industry growth). However, management's judgment is a key element of the portfolio approach.[6]

The product portfolio concept is a useful framework for managing the marketing mix. We examine product portfolio models in Chapter 18 in the discussion of strategic market planning. Here we look into three major ways to improve a product mix: modifying an existing product, deleting a product, and developing a new product.

Modifying Existing Products

Product modification is changing one or more of a product's characteristics. It is most likely to be used in the maturity stage of the product life cycle to give a brand a competitive advantage. Altering a product mix this way entails less risk than developing a new product.

Product modification can effectively improve a firm's product mix under certain conditions. First, the product must be modifiable. Second, existing customers must be able to perceive that a modification has been made (assuming that the modified item is still aimed at them). Third, the modification should make the product more consistent with customers' desires so that it provides greater satisfaction. There are three major ways to modify products: quality modifications, functional modifications, and style modifications.

Quality Modifications **Quality modifications** are changes that relate to a product's dependability and durability. They usually are executed by altering the materials or production process used. Reducing a product's quality may allow an organization to lower the price and direct the item at a larger target market.

Increasing the quality of a product may give a firm an advantage over competing brands. In fact, some experts claim that quality improvement is a major means of successfully competing with foreign marketers.[7] Higher quality may enable a firm

6. Yoram Wind and Vijay Mahajan, "Designing Product and Business Portfolios," *Harvard Business Review,* January–February 1981, p. 163.
7. Frank S. Leonard and W. Earl Sasser, "The Incline of Quality," *Harvard Business Review,* September–October 1982, p. 171.

FIGURE 8.2

Black & Decker functionally modified its iron by adding a safety feature (SOURCE: The Black & Decker Corporation)

to charge a higher price by creating customer loyalty and by lowering customer sensitivity to price. On the other hand, higher quality may require the use of more expensive components, less standardized production processes, and other manufacturing and management techniques that force a firm to charge higher prices.[8]

Functional Modifications Changes that affect a product's versatility, effectiveness, convenience, or safety are called **functional modifications;** they usually require that the product be redesigned. Typical product categories in which there have been considerable functional modifications include office and farm equipment, vacuum cleaners, and small appliances. Black & Decker Corporation, for example, made its iron safer by adding an automatic shut-off feature, as Figure 8.2 shows. Functional modifications can make a product useful to more people, which enlarges its market. This type of change can place a product in a favorable competitive position by providing benefits competing items do not offer. Functional modifications can also help an organization achieve and maintain a progressive image. Finally, functional modifications sometimes are made to reduce the possibility of product liability claims (see the Application on page 263).

8. Lynn W. Phillips, Dae R. Chang, and Robert D. Buzzell, "Product Quality, Cost Position and Business Performance: A Test of Some Key Hypotheses," *Journal of Marketing,* Spring 1983, pp. 26–43.

Product Liability: A Threat to Producers

To what extent are companies responsible for the safety of their products? Consider this recent product liability case. When the driver of a 1976 Ford Mercury Cougar accelerated to 100 miles per hour, a tire exploded. In the resulting crash, the driver was killed and his passenger was seriously injured. The lawsuit that followed charged Ford Motor Company and the Goodyear Tire & Rubber Company—manufacturer of the tires—with selling a defective product. Although the car's owner's manual warned explicitly against driving the car more than 90 miles per hour, the court ruled for the plaintiff. The judge's reasoning? Given that some drivers would inevitably ignore Ford's recommendation, the manufacturer should have equipped the car with tires that would stand up to the 105 mile per hour speeds the car was capable of. In other words, the manufacturer was found liable even though its product had not been used as intended.

The Ford case is not an isolated instance, and product liability is an issue of growing concern to U.S. companies. Although accurate figures are difficult to obtain, experts say that both the number of liability suits and the average amount of settlements are increasing. According to one study, the number of $1 million awards has quadrupled in less than ten years. Insurance premiums are climbing, and many manufacturers of potentially hazardous products calculate that their liabilities could run more than their insurance coverage—or even their corporate assets.

In the face of such enormous risk, some companies have dropped certain product lines entirely. Last year, product liability considerations forced G. D. Searle & Co. to withdraw its Copper 7 and Tatum T intrauterine contraceptive devices from the U.S. market, despite the company's general reputation for safety. The number of firms producing the seven vaccines most states require for school-age children has dwindled to three: Merck & Co., Inc., Lederle Laboratories, and Connaught Laboratories. The production of football helmets is now dominated by just two companies, Bike Athletic Co. and Riddell, both subsidiaries of large corporations that can afford the costly liability insurance premiums. Riddell recently appealed a $12 million judgment in the case of a high school player who broke his neck during a game; the court held that the company's helmets should have carried warnings against butting opponents.

Other companies have turned to "preventive law." That is, they are attempting to minimize liabilities by anticipating and correcting as many product design problems as possible. When defects cannot be corrected, companies often issue warnings and caution distributors to limit sales of the products in question to qualified users. Helene Curtis Industries and Cosmair successfully defended themselves against a plaintiff whose scalp was burned when a nonbeautician, ignoring printed instructions, applied two incompat-

Style Modifications   **Style modifications** change the sensory appeal of a product by altering its taste, texture, sound, smell, or visual characteristics. Because a buyer's purchase decision is affected by how a product looks, smells, tastes, feels, or sounds, a style modification may have a definite impact on purchases. For years automobile makers (see the example in Figure 8.3) have relied on style modifications.

   Through style modifications, a firm can differentiate its product from competing brands and thus gain a sizable market share. The major drawback in using style modifications is that their value is determined subjectively. Although a firm may strive to improve the product's style, customers may actually find the modified product less appealing.

Deleting Products

Generally, a product cannot indefinitely satisfy target market customers and contribute to achieving an organization's overall goals. To maintain an effective product mix, a firm has to get rid of some products, just as it has to modify existing products or introduce new ones. This pruning process is called **product deletion.** A weak product is a drain on potential profitability. In addition, too much of a marketer's time and resources are spent trying to revive the product, which in turn reduces the time and resources available for modifying other products or developing new ones. Shorter production runs, which can increase per-unit production costs, may be required for a marginal product. Finally, when a weak product causes unfavorable impressions among customers, the negative ideas may rub off onto some of the firm's other products.

   Most organizations find it difficult to delete a product. It was probably a difficult decision for IBM to drop the PCjr and admit that it had failed in the low end of the personal computer market. A decision to drop a product may be opposed by management and other employees who feel the product is necessary in the product mix. Salespeople who still have some loyal customers are especially upset when a product is dropped. Considerable resources and effort are sometimes spent trying to change the product's marketing mix to improve its sales and thus avoid having to abandon the item.

Some organizations drop weak products only after they have become heavy financial burdens. A better approach is some form of systematic review in which each product is evaluated periodically to determine its impact on the overall effectiveness of the firm's product mix. Such a review should analyze a product's contribution to the firm's sales for a given period. It should include estimates of future sales, costs, and profits associated with the product and a consideration of whether changes should be made in the marketing strategy to improve the product's performance. A systematic review enables an organization to improve product performance and to ascertain when to delete products, thus maximizing the effectiveness of the product mix.

There are several alternatives for deleting a product, but basically it can be phased out, run out, or dropped immediately (see Figure 8.4). A phase-out approach lets the product decline without a change in the marketing strategy. No attempt is made to give the product new life. A runout policy exploits any strengths left in the product. By increasing marketing efforts in core markets or by eliminating some marketing expenditures such as advertising, the product may provide a

FIGURE 8.3

Automobile makers use style modification (SOURCE: Volvo North America Corporation)

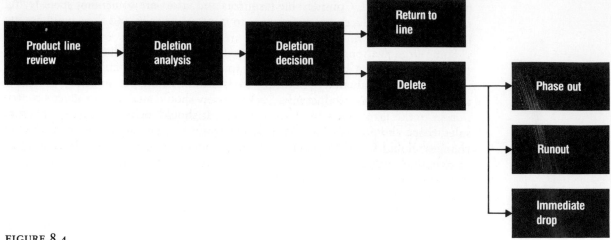

FIGURE 8.4
Product deletion process (SOURCE: Martin L. Bell, *Marketing: Concepts and Strategy,* 3rd ed., p. 267. Copyright © 1979, Houghton Mifflin Company. Used by permission)

sudden spurt of profits. This approach is often used for technologically obsolete products, such as calculators, computers, and cassette recorders. Often the price is reduced to get a sales spurt before the product inventory is depleted. An immediate-drop decision results in sudden termination of an unprofitable product. This strategy is appropriate when losses are too great to prolong the life of a product.

Developing New Products

Developing and introducing new products is frequently expensive and risky. Thousands of new products are introduced annually. Depending on how it is defined, the failure rate for new products is from 33 to 90 percent. Although it is sometimes reported that up to 90 percent of new products fail, a recent study of industrial and consumer-oriented firms indicated that only 33 percent of the new products actually introduced to the marketplace fail. This same study, conducted by the Conference Board, reported that medium- and large-sized firms obtain 15 percent of their sales volume from new products introduced in the last five years. Lack of research is the leading cause of new-product failure. The Code-A-Phone company points out in Figure 8.5 that it spends considerable time and money researching its markets to determine customer needs. Other often-cited causes are technical problems in design or production and errors in timing the product's introduction.[9]

New-product development is evidently risky, but so is failure to introduce new products. For example, Those Characters from Cleveland (TCFC), a division of American Greetings that produces toys, has in the past successfully introduced Strawberry Shortcake and the Care Bears. But TCFC has had no recent new-product introduction and has lost share to products such as Tonka's Pound Puppies. To regain market share, TCFC put much of its marketing strength behind a new product called the Popple. A Popple is a stuffed fur animal that folds into its

9. David Hopkins, "Survey Finds 67% of New Products Succeed," *Marketing News,* Feb. 8, 1980. p. 1.

own pouch; children can make the Popple's arms, legs, and tail disappear easily. To market this product, American Greetings chose Mattel. The firms spent $10 million in advertising this new product's introduction. Popples also were supported with a television special and a syndicated cartoon series. With this costly new product, American Greetings had the opportunity to regain its share of the $10 billion toy and game market.[10] On the other hand, a product failure could have left the company further behind the competition.

The term *new product* can have several meanings. A genuinely new product—such as Crest or the VCR once were—offers innovative benefits. But products that are different and distinctly better are often viewed as new. The following items (listed in no particular order) have been named as the best product innovations of the last twenty-five years: disposable lighters, Post-it note pads, Polaroid cameras, the birth control pill, the water pik, felt-tip pens, seat belts, disposable razors, quartz watches, and contact lenses.[11] For our purposes, a new product is one that a given firm has not marketed previously, although similar products may have been available from other organizations. For example, Advil was one of the first new nonaspirin pain relievers marketed over the counter since Tylenol was introduced in 1955. The drug was formerly available by prescription only, but as an over-the-counter drug it was a new product.

10. Pamela Sherrid, "The Making of a Popple," *Fortune,* Dec. 16, 1985, pp. 174–178.
11. Ellen Brown, "Our Best Innovations of 25 Years," *USA Today,* Mar. 1, 1985, p. D-1.

FIGURE 8.5

The importance of customer research in product development (SOURCE: Code-A-Phone)

There's a place for companies that ignore the market.

Some of the most venerable names in American business were folding in the late fifties, just as we were getting under way. So for thirty years we've made it a practice to find out what the customer wants before we produce it. Continually researching the market is time-consuming and expensive, and anyone who hasn't been around for a while might try to take a shortcut. But you don't have to go along for the ride.

CODE·A·PHONE

Portland, Oregon

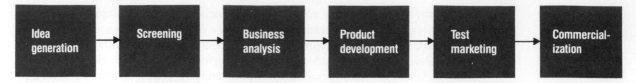

FIGURE 8.6

Phases of new-product development

Before a product is introduced, it goes through the six phases of **new-product development** shown in Figure 8.6: (1) idea generation, (2) screening, (3) business analysis, (4) product development, (5) test marketing, and (6) commercialization. A product can be dropped, and many are, at any stage of development.

Idea Generation   Businesses and other organizations seek product ideas that will help them achieve their objectives. This activity is **idea generation.** The difficulty of the task is illustrated by the fact that only a few ideas are good enough to be commercially successful. Although some organizations get their ideas almost by chance, firms that are trying to maximize product mix effectiveness usually develop systematic approaches for generating new product ideas. At the heart of innovation is a purposeful, focused effort to identify new ways to serve a market. Unexpected occurrences, incongruities, new needs, industry and market changes, and demographic changes all may indicate new opportunities.[12]

New product ideas can come from several sources. They may come from internal sources—marketing managers, researchers, engineers, or other organizational personnel. For example, the idea for 3M Post-its adhesive-backed yellow notes came from an employee. As a church choir member, he used slips of paper for marking songs in his hymnal. Because the pieces of paper would fall out, he suggested an adhesive-backed note.[13]

New product ideas may also arise from sources outside the firm—competitors, advertising agencies, management consultants, private research organizations, and customers. For example, customers or users developed 67 percent of the machines used in the semiconductor industry. The Pillsbury Bake-Off, a recipe contest, has generated several recipes that Pillsbury Company has commercialized.[14]

Brainstorming and incentives or rewards for good ideas are typical intrafirm devices used to encourage the development of ideas. Sometimes, potential buyers of a product are questioned in depth to discover what attributes would appeal to them.

Screening Ideas   In the process of **screening ideas,** those with the greatest potential are selected for further development. Those that do not match a firm's objectives or that have a limited potential are rejected. Screening product ideas involves a general assessment of the organization's resources. Through forecasting techniques, an early projection of economic payoffs is made. The firm's overall ability

12. Peter F. Drucker, "The Discipline of Innovation," *Harvard Business Review*, May–June 1985, pp. 67–68.
13. Lawrence Ingrassia, "By Improving Scotch Paper, 3M Gets New Product Winner," *Wall Street Journal*, Mar. 31, 1983, p. 27.
14. Eric von Hippel, "Get New Products from Customers," *Harvard Business Review*, March–April 1982, p. 118.

to produce and market the product is analyzed. Other aspects of an idea that should be weighed are the nature and wants of buyers, the competition, and environmental factors. The largest number of new product ideas are rejected during this phase of the development process.

At times, a checklist of new-product requirements is used when making screening decisions. It encourages evaluators to be systematic, thereby reducing the possibility that they might overlook some fact. The type of formal research described in Chapter 6 may be needed if a critical checklist factor remains unclear. To screen ideas properly, testing product concepts may be necessary; a product concept and its benefits can be described or shown to consumers. Several product concepts may be tested to determine which might appeal most to a particular target market.

Business Analysis **Business analysis** provides a tentative sketch of a product's compatibility with the marketplace, including its probable profitability. Compatibility factors include the company's manufacturing and marketing capabilities, its financial resources, and its management's attitude toward the product.[15] During a business analysis, evaluators ask such questions as the following:

1. Does the product fit in with the organization's existing product mix?
2. Is demand strong enough to justify entering the market? Will the demand endure?
3. How will the introduction and marketing of this product affect the firm's sales, costs, and profits?
4. What types of environmental and competitive changes can be expected, and how will these changes affect the product's future sales, costs, and profits?
5. Are the organization's research, development, engineering, and production capabilities adequate?
6. If new facilities must be constructed to manufacture the product, how quickly can they be built? (If it is possible to use existing facilities, the product idea usually has a better chance of survival.)
7. Is the necessary financing for development and commercialization on hand or obtainable at terms consistent with a favorable return on investment?

During business analysis, firms seek information about the market. A poll of consumers, together with secondary data, supply information for estimating potential sales, costs, and profits. A research budget should explore the financial objectives and related financial considerations for the new product.

Product Development **Product development** is a stage in creating new products that moves the product from concept to test stage and also involves the development of other elements of the marketing mix (promotion, distribution, and price).

In the development phase, the company must first find out if it is technically feasible to produce the product and if the product can be produced at costs low enough so that the final price is reasonable. If a product idea makes it to the development point, it is then transformed into a model. To test its acceptability, the idea or concept is converted into a prototype or working model. The prototype should reveal tangible and intangible attributes associated with the product in

15. Fritz A. Schumacher, "Successful New Product Ideas Require Right Marketing, Financial 'Fit', Corporate 'Champion'," *Marketing News*, Oct. 16, 1981, p. 1.

consumers' minds. The product's design, mechanical features, and intangible aspects must be linked to wants in the marketplace. The development phase of a new product is frequently lengthy and expensive; thus a relatively small number of product ideas are put into development.

However, the development stage is not restricted to mechanical or production aspects of the product. The various ingredients that will make up the marketing mix must also be tested. Management must, for example, review copyrights, preliminary advertising copy, packaging, and labeling to see if there are any legal problems. Management must also plan for personal selling and distribution. The aim is to ensure the effective integration of all marketing mix elements.

Test Marketing   **Test marketing** is a limited introduction of a product in areas chosen to represent the intended market. Its aim is to determine the reactions of probable buyers. Test marketing is *not* an extension of the screening and development stages; it is a sample launching of the entire marketing mix. Test marketing should be conducted only after the product has gone through development and after initial plans regarding the other marketing mix variables have been made.

Companies of all sizes use test marketing to minimize the risk of product failure. The test marketing for Slice is discussed in the Application on page 273. The dangers of introducing an untested product include undercutting already profitable products and, should the new product fail, loss of credibility with distributors and customers. Consider Ocean Spray Cranberries, Inc. and its development of a liquid concentrate juice that requires no refrigeration and costs 10 percent less than frozen concentrate and 30 percent less than bottled drinks. Concerned that this new entry would takes sales from its existing line, Ocean Spray conducted a five-city test; the company's sales rose 15 percent after the new concentrate was introduced. Ocean Spray therefore proceeded to introduce the product with a $10 million advertising campaign.[16]

Test marketing provides several benefits. It lets marketers expose a product in a natural marketing environment to obtain a measure of its sales performance. While the product is being marketed in a limited area, it is possible to identify weaknesses in the product or in other parts of the marketing mix. Marketers can experiment with variations in advertising, price, and packaging in different test areas and can measure the extent of brand awareness, brand switching, and repeat purchases that result from alterations in the marketing mix.

A product weakness discovered after a nationwide introduction can be expensive to correct. Moreover, if initial reactions among consumers are negative, marketers may not be able to convince consumers to retry the product. Thus making adjustments after test marketing can be crucial to the success of a new product.

Selection of appropriate test areas is a major influence on the accuracy of test-marketing results. Table 8.1 lists some of the most popular test-market cities. The criteria used for choosing test cities depend on the product's characteristics, the target market's characteristics, and the organization's objectives and resources. Even though the selection criteria will vary from one firm to another, the general issues the questions in Table 8.2 raise can be useful when assessing a potential test market.

16. Barbara Buell, "How Ocean Spray Keeps Reinventing the Cranberry," *Business Week,* Dec. 2, 1985, p. 142.

TABLE 8.1

Popular test markets
for new products

Akron	Fresno	Portland, Maine
Albany-Schenectady-Troy	Grand Rapids-Kalamazoo-Battle Creek	Portland, Oregon
Albuquerque		Poughkeepsie
Ann Arbor	Green Bay-Appleton, Wisconsin	Providence, Rhode Island
Atlanta	Greensboro-Winston-Salem-High Point, North Carolina	Quad Cities: Rock Island & Moline, Illinois, Davenport & Bettendorf, Iowa (Davenport-Rock Island-Moline metro market)
Augusta, Georgia	Greenville-Spartanburg, South Carolina–Asheville, North Carolina	
Austin		
Bakersfield, California		
Baltimore-Washington, D.C.		
Bangor, Maine	Harrisburg	Raleigh-Durham
Baton Rouge	Hartford, Connecticut	Reading, Pennsylvania
Beaumont-Port Arthur, Texas	Houston	Reno-Carson City
Binghamton, New York	Huntsville, Alabama	Roanoke-Lynchburg
Birmingham-Anniston, Alabama	Indianapolis	Rochester, New York
Boise	Jacksonville, Florida	Rockford, Illinois
Boston	Kansas City, Missouri	Sacramento-Stockton
Buffalo	Knoxville	St. Louis
Canton, Ohio	Lansing	Salem, Oregon
Cedar Rapids-Waterloo, Iowa	Las Vegas	Salinas-Monterey
Charleston, South Carolina	Lexington, Kentucky	Salt Lake City
Charleston, West Virginia	Lincoln, Nebraska	San Antonio
Charlotte, North Carolina	Little Rock	San Diego
Chattanooga, Tennessee	Los Angeles	San Francisco-Oakland
Chicago	Louisville	Savannah
Cincinnati	Lubbock, Texas	Seattle-Tacoma
Cleveland	Macon, Georgia	Shreveport
Colorado Springs	Madison	Sioux Falls, South Dakota
Columbia, South Carolina	Memphis	South Bend-Elkhart, Indiana
Columbus, Georgia	Miami	Spokane
Columbus, Ohio	Milwaukee	Springfield, Massachusetts
Corpus Christi	Minneapolis-St. Paul	Springfield, Missouri
Dallas-Fort Worth	Modesto	Springfield-Decatur-Champaign, Illinois
Dayton	Nashville	
Denver-Boulder	New Haven, Connecticut	Syracuse
Des Moines	New Orleans	Tallahassee
Detroit	Newport News	Tampa-St. Petersburg
Duluth-Superior, Minnesota	New York	Toledo
El Paso	Oklahoma City	Topeka
Erie, Pennsylvania	Omaha-Council Bluffs	Tucson
Eugene, Oregon	Orlando-Daytona Beach	Tulsa
Evansville, Indiana	Pensacola	West Palm Beach
Flint, Michigan	Peoria	Wichita-Hutchinson, Kansas
Fort Lauderdale	Philadelphia	Youngstown, Ohio
Fort Smith, Arkansas	Phoenix	
Fort Wayne, Indiana	Pittsburgh	

SOURCE: "The Nation's Most Popular Test Markets," *Sales and Marketing Management*, March 1987, p. 70.

Test marketing is not without risks, however. Not only is it expensive, but a firm's competitors may try to interfere. A competitor may try to "jam" the test program by increasing advertising or promotions, lowering prices, and offering special incentives, all to combat the recognition and purchase of a new brand. Any such devices can invalidate test results. Sometimes too, competitors copy the product in the testing stage and rush to introduce a similar product. Schick, for example, introduced a double-bladed razor less than six months after the Gillette Company brought out Trac II. It is therefore desirable to move quickly and commercialize as soon as possible after testing.

Because of these risks, many companies are using alternative methods to gauge consumer preferences. One such method is simulated test marketing. Consumers at shopping centers are typically asked to view an advertisement for a new product and given a free sample to take home. These consumers are subsequently interviewed over the phone and asked to rate the product. Scanner-based test marketing is another, more sophisticated version of the traditional test-marketing method.[17] (Chapter 6 discusses this type of testing.) The major advantage of simulated test marketing is lower cost. Some marketing research firms, such as A. C. Nielsen Company, offer test-marketing services to help provide independent assessment of products.

Commercialization During **commercialization**, plans for full-scale manufacturing and marketing must be refined and settled, and budgets for the project must be prepared. Early in the commercialization phase, marketing management analyzes the results of test marketing to find out what changes in the marketing mix are needed before the product is introduced. The results of test marketing may tell the

17. Eleanor Johnson Tracy, "Testing Time for Test Marketing," *Fortune*, Oct. 29, 1984, pp. 75–76.

TABLE 8.2

Questions to consider when choosing test markets

1. Is the area typical of planned distribution outlets?
2. Is the city relatively isolated from other cities?
3. What local media are available, and are they cooperative?
4. Does the area have a dominant television station? Does it have multiple newspapers, magazines, and radio stations?
5. Does the city contain a diversified cross section of ages, religions, and cultural/societal preferences?
6. Are the purchasing habits atypical?
7. Is the city's per capita income typical?
8. Does the city have a good record as a test city?
9. Would testing efforts be easily "jammed" by competitors?
10. Does the city have stable year-round sales?
11. Are retailers who will cooperate available?
12. Are research and audit services available?
13. Is the area free from unusual influences, such as one industry's dominance or heavy tourist traffic?

SOURCE: Adapted from "A Checklist for Selecting Test Markets," copyright 1982 *Sales and Marketing Management*. Used by permission.

Test Marketing Slice

When PepsiCo became dissatisfied several years ago with the weak showing of its lemon-lime Teem against 7Up and Sprite, it began to develop the soft drink eventually marketed as Slice. Because consumers obviously liked products with certain elements removed (calories and caffeine, for example), Pepsi reasoned that they might also like a product to which something of value—fruit juice—had been added. Settling on a 10 percent juice formulation (based on market findings that consumers notice levels of "10 percent" or more), Pepsi researchers worked for months to solve recurring problems of cloudiness, discoloration, and inconsistency. Finally, the new product was ready in regular and diet versions for test-group sampling.

Unfortunately, the test groups found little to distinguish the new product's taste from that of 7Up or Sprite. They were not excited about yet another lemon-lime drink, even one that tasted good. Additional research showed, however, that panelists thought *all* lemon-lime soft drinks contained fruit juice. When the new drink was presented as a unique product—the only one with the added value of real juice—it was chosen by an overwhelming majority of the panelists. Building on this idea ("We Got The Juice"), Pepsi quickly developed the Slice brand name, packaging, and promotional support, and prepared to test market the product.

Nationwide, the lemon-lime category accounted for 12.7 percent of all soft-drink sales. For a true test of its appeal, Slice was introduced into three markets with varying levels of demand for lemon-lime drinks: Milwaukee and most of Wisconsin, a highly developed market for lemon-lime; Tulsa, an average market; and Phoenix, a below-average market. From the outset, Pepsi positioned Slice head-to-head against 7Up and Sprite, with visuals and copy emphasizing the uniqueness of Slice's fruit content. After three months, Slice had captured 3.5 to 4.5 percent of soft-drink sales in those markets, exceeding Pepsi's expectations. Furthermore, Diet Slice also made an unexpectedly strong showing: 50 percent of total Slice sales, compared to 25 to 35 percent for most diet versions. Following successful testing in the strong West Coast lemon-lime market, Pepsi started distributing Slice nationally.

While lemon-lime Slice was still being tested, Pepsi prepared to go after the orange-flavored-drink market, the third-largest soft-drink segment after colas and lemon-lime drinks. Mandarin Orange Slice was introduced simultaneously in two strong orange-drink markets: Phoenix, where Slice was by now an established brand, and Hartford, an entirely new market for Slice. Because Mandarin Orange Slice did equally well in both markets—and because Coca-Cola was about to launch an orange juice-based Minute Maid soft drink—Pepsi proceeded quickly with national distribution of Mandarin Orange. Apple Slice and Cherry Cola Slice soon followed, without market testing.

Today Slice is a $1 billion soft drink, accounting for 3 to 4 percent of all soft-drink sales. Diet and regular versions are available in about 80 percent of the U.S. markets, and Mandarin Orange is the top seller in its flavor category. Industry observers credit Pepsi with creating an entirely new product category in the crowded soft-drink market. Although Pepsi's original objective was to make Slice the number-one lemon-lime soft drink, the company now has an ambitious new goal: to push Slice right into the top three soft-drink trademarks, just behind Pepsi and Coca-Cola.

SOURCES: Tim Davis, "Slicing the Market," *Marketing & Media Decisions,* Winter 1986, pp. 23–26; Jennifer Lawrence, "Testing Juices Up Slice's Performance," *Advertising Age,* Aug. 24, 1987, p. S-2; PepsiCo., Inc., *1986 Annual Report,* pp. 8–10.

marketers, for example, to change one or more of the product's physical attributes, to modify the distribution plans to include more retail outlets, to alter promotional efforts, or to change the product's price.

The organization gears up for production during the commercialization phase. This may require sizable capital expenditures for plant and equipment, and the firm also may need to hire additional personnel.

The product is introduced into the market during commercialization. During product introduction, marketers often spend enormous sums of money for such promotional efforts as advertising, personal selling, and sales promotion. These expenses, together with capital expenditures, can make commercialization extremely costly; such expenditures may not be recovered for several years. For example, when Liquid Cascade was introduced (see Figure 8.7), large expenditures were necessary to communicate product attributes.

Commercialization is significantly easier when customers accept the product rapidly. There is a better chance of this occurring if marketers can make customers aware of a product's benefits. The following stages of the **product adoption process** are generally recognized as those that buyers go through in accepting a product:

1. *Awareness.* The buyer becomes aware of the product.
2. *Interest.* The buyer seeks information and is receptive to learning about the product.
3. *Evaluation.* The buyer considers the product's benefits and determines whether to try it.
4. *Trial.* The buyer examines, tests, or tries the product to determine its usefulness.
5. *Adoption.* The buyer purchases the product and can be expected to use it to solve problems.[18]

This adoption model has several implications for the commercialization phase. First, promotion should be used to create widespread awareness of the product and its benefits. Samples or simulated trials should be arranged to help buyers make initial purchase decisions. At the same time, marketers should emphasize quality

18. Adapted from *Diffusion of Innovations* by Everett M. Rogers (New York: Macmillan Publishing Co., 1962), pp. 81–86.

control and provide solid guarantees to reinforce buyer opinion during the evaluation stage. Finally, production and physical distribution must be linked to patterns of adoption and repeat purchases. (The product adoption process is also discussed in Chapter 13.)

Products are not usually introduced nationwide overnight. Most products are introduced in stages, starting in a set of geographic areas and gradually expanding into adjacent areas. It may take several years to market the product nationally. Sometimes, the test cities are used as initial marketing areas, with the introduction being a natural extension of test marketing. For example, a product test-marketed in Sacramento, Denver, Dallas, St. Louis, and Atlanta, as the map in Figure 8.8 shows, could be introduced first in those cities. After the stage 1 introduction is complete, stage 2 could include market coverage of the states in which the test cities are located. In stage 3, marketing efforts could be extended into adjacent states. All remaining states would then be covered in stage 4. Gradual product introductions do not always occur state by state, however; other geographic combinations are used as well.

Gradual product introduction is popular for several reasons. It reduces the risks of introducing a new product. If the product fails, the firm will experience smaller losses when the item has been introduced in only a few geographic areas than when it has been marketed nationally. Furthermore, it is usually impossible for a company to introduce a product nationwide overnight because the system of wholesalers and retailers necessary to distribute a product cannot be established that

FIGURE 8.7

Communication of product attributes during commercialization (SOURCE: Reproduced with permission from the Procter & Gamble Company)

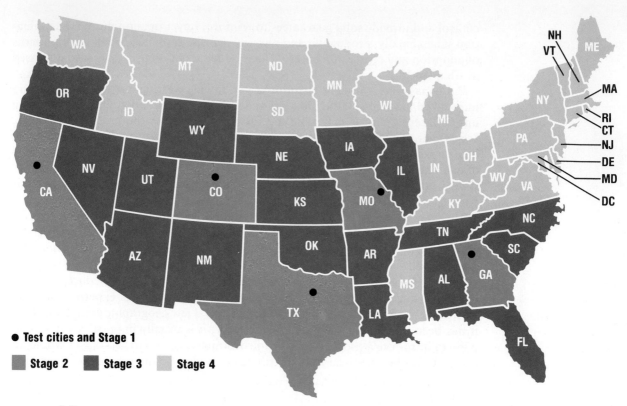

Test cities and Stage 1

Stage 2 **Stage 3** **Stage 4**

FIGURE 8.8

Stages of expansion into a national market during commercialization (SOURCE: Adapted from *Business: An Involvement Approach,* by Herbert G. Hicks, William M. Pride, and James D. Powell. Copyright © 1975 by McGraw-Hill. Used with permission of McGraw-Hill Book Company)

quickly. The development of a distribution network may take considerable time. Keep in mind also that the number of units needed to satisfy the national demand for a successful product can be enormous, and a firm usually cannot produce the required quantities in a short time.

Despite the good reasons for introducing a product gradually, marketers realize that this approach creates some competitive problems. A gradual introduction allows competitors to observe what a firm is doing and to monitor results, just as the firm's own marketers are doing. If competitors see that the newly introduced product is successful, they may enter the same target market quickly with similar products. Also, as a product is introduced region by region, competitors may expand their marketing efforts to offset promotion of the new product.

Product Positioning

The term **product positioning** refers to the decisions and activities intended to create and maintain a firm's product concept in customers' minds. When marketers introduce a product, they attempt to position it so that it seems to possess the characteristics the target market most desires. This projected image is crucial. *Product position* is the customers' concept of the product's attributes relative to their concept of competitive brands. For example, Crest is positioned as a fluoride toothpaste that fights cavities and Close-Up is positioned as a whitening toothpaste that enhances the user's sex appeal.

Product positioning is a part of a natural progression when market segmentation is used. Segmentation lets the firm aim a given brand at a portion of the total market. Effective product positioning helps serve a specific market segment by creating an appropriate concept in the minds of customers in that market segment.

A firm can position a product to compete head-on with another brand, as Pepsi has done against Coca-Cola, or to avoid competition, as 7Up has done relative to other soft-drink producers. Head-to-head competition may be a marketer's positioning objective if the product's performance characteristics are at least equal to competitive brands and if the product is lower priced. Head-to-head positioning may be appropriate even when the price is higher if the product's performance characteristics are superior. Conversely, positioning to avoid competition may be best when the product's performance characteristics are not significantly different from competing brands. Also, positioning a brand to avoid competition may be appropriate when that brand has unique characteristics that are important to buyers.

Avoiding competition is critical when a firm introduces a brand into a market in which it already has one or more brands. In this situation, marketers usually want to avoid cannibalizing sales of their existing brands, unless the new brand generates substantially larger profits. When Coca-Cola reintroduced Tab, it attempted to position the cola so as to minimize the adverse effects on Diet Coke's sales. Tab was positioned as the diet drink containing calcium—catering specifically to a female target market.

If a product has been planned properly, its attributes and its brand image will give it the distinct appeal needed. Style, shape, construction, quality of work, color—all elements of the product component of the marketing mix—help create the image and the appeal. If they can easily identify the benefits, then of course buyers are more likely to purchase the product. When the new product does not offer some preferred attributes, there is room for another new product or for repositioning an existing product. Ramada Inns, Inc., has been experiencing this dilemma currently. Ramada is the third largest lodging chain in the world, yet it is saddled with many run-down units and an increasingly downscale image. Management is now attempting to buy back many franchise units and either renovate or sell the inns. The sale of some locations will provide capital for renovation of others. Ramada ultimately will be repositioned as a finer, more exclusive lodging.[19]

Managing Products After Commercialization

Most new products start off slowly and seldom generate enough sales to produce profits immediately. As buyers learn about the product, marketers should be alert for product weakness and make corrections quickly, to prevent the early demise of the product. Marketing strategy should be designed to attract the segment that is most interested and has the fewest objections. If any of these factors need to be adjusted, this action too must be taken quickly to sustain demand. As the sales curve moves upward and the breakeven point is reached, the growth stage begins.

19. Stewart Toy, "Ramada: Searching for a Touch of Class," *Business Week*, Dec. 16, 1985, pp. 85–86.

Marketing Strategy in the Growth Stage

As sales increase, management must support the momentum by adjusting the marketing strategy. The goal is to establish the product's position and to fortify it by encouraging brand loyalty. As profits increase, the organization must brace itself for the entrance of aggressive competitors who may make specialized appeals to selected market segments.

During the growth stage, product offerings may have to be expanded. To achieve greater penetration of an overall market, more intense use of segmentation may be required, which necessitates developing product variations to satisfy the needs of people in several different market segments. Marketers should analyze the product position regarding competing products and correct weak or omitted attributes. Quality, functional, or style modifications may be required.

Gaps in the marketing channels should be filled during the growth period. It may be easier to obtain new distribution outlets once product acceptance has been established. Sometimes marketers tend to move from an exclusive or selective exposure to a more intensive network of dealers to achieve greater market penetration. Marketers must also make sure that the physical distribution system is running efficiently and delivering supplies to distributors before their inventories are exhausted. Because competition increases during the growth period, service adjustments and prompt credit for defective products are important marketing tools.

Advertising expenditures may be lowered slightly from the high level of the introductory stage but still be quite substantial. As sales increase, promotion costs should drop as a percentage of total sales. A falling ratio between promotion expenditures and sales should contribute significantly to increased profits. The advertising messages should stress brand benefits. Coupons and samples may be used to increase market share.

After recovering development costs, a business may be able to lower prices. As sales volume increases, efficiencies in production can result in lower costs. These savings may be passed on to buyers. If demand remains strong and there are few competitive threats, prices tend to remain stable. Providing price cuts are possible, they can facilitate price competition and discourage new competitors from entering the market. For example, when compact disc players were introduced several years ago, they sported a $1,000 price tag. Primarily because of the price, the product was positioned as a "toy for audiophiles," a very small market segment. To generate mass market demand, compact disc player manufacturers dropped their prices to $400 or less, and the cost of discs dropped from $22 to $14. The price is now at a point where the margin is low but the turnover is high. Recently, worldwide annual sales reached approximately $1.3 billion, triple the volume of the previous year. That figure is projected to double in the next several years.[20]

Marketing Strategy for Mature Products

Because many products are in the maturity stage of their life cycles, marketers must deal with these products and be prepared to improve the marketing mix constantly. During maturity, the competitive situation stabilizes and some of the weaker competitors drop out. It has been suggested that as a product matures, its customers

20. Brian Dumaine, "The Compact Disc's Drive to Become King of Audio," *Fortune,* July 8, 1985, pp. 104–107.

FIGURE 8.9

Product with expanded uses (SOURCE: Courtesy of Kornhauser & Calene, Inc.)

become more experienced and specialized (at least for industrial products). As these customers gain knowledge, the benefits they seek may change as well. Thus new marketing strategies may be needed.[21]

Marketers may need to alter the product's quality or otherwise modify the product. A product may be rejuvenated through different packaging, new models, or style changes. Sales and market share may be maintained or strengthened by developing new uses for the product. The makers of Arm & Hammer have developed many new uses for its baking soda to increase demand (see Figure 8.9).

During the maturity stage of the cycle, marketers actively encourage dealers to support the product. Dealers may be offered promotional assistance in lowering their inventory costs. In general, marketers go to great effort to serve dealers and provide incentives for selling the manufacturer's brand, partly because private brands are a threat at this time. As we discuss in Chapter 7, private brands are both an opportunity and a threat to manufacturers, who may be able to sell their products through recognized private brand names as well as their own. However, private brands frequently undermine manufacturers' brands. If manufacturers refuse to sell to private-brand dealers, their competitors usually take advantage of this opportunity.

21. F. Stewart DeBruicker and Gregory L. Summe, "Make Sure Your Customers Keep Coming Back," *Harvard Business Review,* January–February 1985, pp. 92–98.

Moderate and sometimes large advertising expenditures are necessary during the maturity stage to maintain market share. Advertising messages focus on differentiating a brand from many numerous competitors. Sales promotion efforts aimed at customers are used. Promotional allowances are used to maintain or increase a brand's shelf space.

There is a greater mixture of pricing strategies used during the maturity stage. In some cases, strong price competition occurs and price wars may break out. On the other hand, firms may compete in ways other than through price. Marketers develop price flexibility to differentiate offerings in product lines. Markdowns and price incentives are more common, but price increases are likely to occur if distribution and production costs increase.

Marketing Strategy for Declining Products

As a product's sales curve turns downward, profits are continuing to fall. A business can justify maintaining a product as long as it contributes to profits or enhances the overall effectiveness of a product mix. In this stage, marketers must determine when to eliminate the product. Usually a declining product has lost its distinctiveness because similar competing products have been introduced. Competition engenders increased substitution and brand switching as buyers become insensitive to minor product differences. For these reasons, marketers do little to change a product's style, design, or other attributes during its decline. New technology, product substitutes, or environmental considerations may also indicate that the time has come to delete a product.

During a product's decline, outlets with strong sales volumes are maintained and unprofitable outlets are weeded out. An entire marketing channel may be eliminated if it does not contribute adequately to profits. Sometimes a new marketing channel, such as a factory outlet, will be used to liquidate remaining inventory of an obsolete product. As sales decline, the product becomes more obscure, but loyal buyers seek out dealers who carry it.

Advertising expenditures are at a minimum. Advertising of special offers may slow the rate of decline. Sales promotions, such as coupons and premiums, may temporarily regain buyers' attention. As the product continues to decline, the sales staff shifts its emphasis to more profitable products.

That a product returns a profit may be more important to a firm than maintaining a certain market share through repricing. To squeeze out all possible remaining profits, marketers may maintain the price despite declining sales and competitive pressures. Prices may even be increased as costs rise if a loyal core market still wants the product. In other situations, the price may be cut to reduce existing inventory so that the product can be deleted. Severe price reductions may be required if a new product is making an existing product obsolete.

Summary

Developing and managing products is critical to an organization's survival and growth. The organizational approaches available to product management all share common activities, functions, and decisions necessary to guide a product through its life cycle. Product managers coordinate marketing efforts for the product in all markets. Market managers focus on products for specific markets. A venture team is sometimes used to develop new products. Members of the venture team come from different functional areas within the organization and are responsible for all aspects of a product's development.

To maximize the effectiveness of a product mix, an organization usually has to alter its mix through modification of existing products, deletion of a product, or new-product development. Product modification is changing one or more of a product's characteristics. This approach to altering a product mix can be effective when the product is modifiable, when customers can perceive the change, and when customers want the modification. Products' quality, function, or style can be changed.

To maintain an effective product mix, a firm has to eliminate weak products. Although a firm's personnel may oppose product deletion, weak products are unprofitable, consume too much time and effort, may require shorter production runs, and can create an unfavorable impression of the firm's other products. A product mix should be systematically reviewed to determine when to delete products. Products to be deleted can be phased out, run out, or dropped immediately.

The six phases of new-product development are generating ideas, screening to determine which ideas to develop, expanding an idea through business analysis, developing a product into a demonstrable concept, test marketing, and commercialization. The decision to enter the commercialization or introduction phase means that full-scale production of the product begins and a complete marketing strategy is developed. The process that buyers go through in accepting a product includes awareness, interest, evaluation, trial, and adoption.

As a product moves through its life cycle, marketing strategies may require continual adaptation. In the growth stage, it is important to develop brand loyalty and a market position. In the maturity stage, a product may be modified or new market segments may be developed to rejuvenate its sales. A product that is declining may be maintained as long as it makes a contribution to profits or enhances the product mix.

Important Terms

Product manager
Brand manager
Market manager
Venture team
Product portfolio approach
Product modification
Quality modifications
Functional modifications
Style modifications
Product deletion
New-product development
Idea generation
Screening ideas
Business analysis

Product development
Test marketing
Commercialization
Product adoption process
Product positioning

Discussion and Review Questions

1. What organizational alternatives are available to a firm with two product lines having four product items in each line?
2. When is it more appropriate to use a product manager than a market manager? When might an alternative or combined approach be used?
3. What type of organization might use a venture team to develop new products? What are the advantages and disadvantages of such a team?
4. Do small firms that manufacture one or two products need to be concerned about developing and managing products? Why or why not?
5. Why is product development a cross-functional activity within an organization? That is, why must finance, engineering, manufacturing, and other functional areas be involved?
6. Develop information sources for new product ideas for the automobile industry.
7. Some firms believe that they can omit test marketing. What are some advantages and disadvantages of test marketing?
8. Under what conditions is product modification appropriate for changing a product mix? How does a quality modification differ from a functional modification? Can an organization make one modification without making the other?
9. Give several reasons why an organization might be unable to eliminate an unprofitable product.

Cases

8.1 Introduction of New Products at Hershey Foods Corp.[22]

For years, Hershey's position at the top of the U.S. candy market was secure. Following the policy of founder Milton Hershey, the Pennsylvania chocolate maker let its high-quality products promote themselves; the company did not even advertise nationally until 1970. In the late 1960s, however, rival candy maker Mars Inc. caught up with Hershey, surpassing Hershey's market share by as much as 14 percent at one point in the 1970s. To combat Mars's gains, and to cushion itself against wild price fluctuations in the cocoa bean and sugar markets, Hershey began to diversify into noncandy product lines and to step up new-product introductions.

In 1979, Hershey acquired Friendly Ice Cream Corp., a chain of ice cream shops and family restaurants in the Northeast and Midwest. The Friendly units, which now number 835, contributed 25 percent of Hershey's $2.2 billion in sales last year. The Friendly chain provides outlets for such Hershey products as Reese's Peanut Butter Cups and Reese's Pieces, used in Friendly ice cream desserts and take-home pints. In addition, the Friendly acquisition will facilitate Hershey's entry

22. Based on information from Kimberley Carpenter, "Candy May Be Dandy, but Confectioners Want a Sweeter Bottom Line," *Business Week*, Oct. 6, 1986, p. 66; Judann Dagnoli, "Hershey Seeks Edge in Luden Buy," *Advertising Age*, Sept. 22, 1986, p. 113; Lynn Strongin Dodds, "Sweetening Up the Bottom Line," *Financial World*, Aug. 29, 1986, pp. 14–15; "Hershey and Advertising," Hershey Foods Corp. Fact Sheet; Steve Lawrence, "Bar Wars: Hershey Bites Mars," *Fortune*, July 8, 1985, pp. 52–54; Janet Novack, "The High-Profit Candy Habit," *Forbes*, June 29, 1987, p. 76; "R&D Profile: Hershey's," *Food Processing*, August 1986, pp. 21–22.

into the ice cream novelty market should Hershey decide to introduce a mass-marketed ice cream snack on the order of the Nestlé Company Inc.'s Quik bar or Mars's DoveBar. Sales of all ice cream novelties have been climbing steadily for the past five years and are expected to reach more than $3 billion by 1990.

Hershey has also become the leader in the pasta industry, holding a 17 percent market share. Hershey sells five brands of pasta regionally in forty states; brands include San Giorgio, Skinner, and American Beauty, purchased two years ago from the Pillsbury Company. Pasta sales accounted for 9 percent of revenues and 3 percent of profits last year.

Candy is of course Hershey's mainstay, contributing 66 percent of last year's sales. Per capita consumption of candy and other snack foods is rising, despite Americans' current preoccupation with diet and fitness. Because Hershey's research shows that customers seldom buy the same candy bar twice in a row, the company keeps a broad range of products on the market by adapting existing candies and introducing new ones.

Many of Hershey's new products are aimed at candy customers over eighteen, who consume 55 percent of all candy sold and are prime targets for premium candy products. Hershey developed the Golden Almond and Golden Pecan lines, for example, from a premium box-candy product. These milk chocolate bars weigh 3.2 ounces, contain whole instead of chopped nuts, and sell for more than $1. Several years ago Hershey introduced its Big Blocks, thicker, chewier versions of such favorites as Hershey Milk Chocolate and Hershey Almond, which cost 50 cents and appeal especially to adult males. Two new smaller bars developed for adult tastes also have been selling well: Take Five, a chocolate-covered wafer and peanut cream bar, and Skor, a toffee bar with a chocolate coating. By appealing to adult women, Hershey hopes to build sales among children as well, calculating that their tastes are initially influenced by their mothers' tastes.

Ideas for new products at Hershey's come from many sources but are usually channeled through New Product Planning, a group that is the liaison between Research and Marketing personnel. In many cases, Hershey's Marketing Division first identifies consumer needs; the New Product Planning Group explores possibilities for filling those needs; and a third section, the Product Development Group, designs prototypes for further testing. When granola snacks became popular a few years ago, for example, Hershey's product development groups came up with New Trail granola bars to compete with products from the Quaker Oats Co. and General Mills, Inc. Some new-product prototypes originate in the Hershey kitchens as a part of food-preparation research. Yet another branch, the Food Science and Technology Group, conducts basic research into ingredient technology.

After a decade of new-product introduction and aggressive marketing, Hershey now trails Mars by one percentage point in supermarket sales (36 to 35 percent) and slightly more at newsstand and candy counters (38.5 to 31.5 percent). Still, Hershey foresees continued growth in the chocolate and candy business and seems satisfied with its present rate of diversification. Although cocoa beans (which sold for $2.60 a pound in 1977) are now below $1, Hershey's continues to reduce its vulnerability to price swings; only 45 percent of its products are 70 percent or more chocolate, compared to 80 percent of its candy in the early 1960s. The company's latest offering, Grand Slam, is a chocolate-covered bar of caramel, roasted peanuts, and crisped rice, expected to do well against Quaker Oats' Granola Dipps. And some observers believe that Hershey's recent acquisition of the Dietrich Corp.—maker of Luden's cough drops, 5th Avenue candy bars, and Mellomints—may put Hershey back at the top of the candy industry. Luden's holds 12 percent of the cough drop market, a category Mars investigated last year and declined to enter.

Questions for Discussion

1. Why has Hershey diversified into products with less chocolate or not made from chocolate?
2. Identify the departments in the Hershey organization and the roles they play in developing new products.
3. Unlike some of its competitors, Hershey generally has not diversified from treats or snack foods, except for its pasta products. Assess Hershey's approach to product diversification.
4. Has Hershey's program of new-product introductions been effective?

8.2 Saab's Product Positioning[23]

Saab-Scania, a "transport technology" company based in Sweden, was formed in 1969 from the merger of Saab, maker of cars and aircraft, and Scania-Vabis, a thriving truck producer. Through technological cooperation among the company's car, aircraft, and truck and bus divisions, the company is now known today as a small specialist manufacturer, offering distinctive products based on high-tech innovation. Sales have increased by an average of 18 percent a year for the last five years, with the Scania truck division contributing most to sales, about 43 percent. The company spends an average of 13 percent of its sales on product development, production methods, new equipment, and research and development.

Last year, Saab automobile sales in the United States were up 20 percent over the previous year (up 38 percent in Europe). Just after the merger, however, cars were the company's weakest products, weak in both sales and performance. A poor competitor and not well-known outside Sweden, the early Saab automobile was called "a homely, underpowered car that only a troll could love." According to Robert Sinclair, president of Saab-Scania of America, the car was "out of touch with the market." The company also had trouble recruiting dealers in top markets.

In 1977, however, Saab evaluated and improved its automobile lines to increase profits and reduce debt. Engineers were allowed to experiment, with few constraints—except that the end product was to offer high performance and quality. The result was that Saab became the first to introduce a turbo-charged engine, in

23. Based on information from Gay Jervey, "Saab Steers Into Import-Car Mainstream," *Advertising Age*, Oct. 3, 1983, p. 4; Bernie Whalen, "Tiny Saab Drives Up Profits with Market Niche Strategy Repositioning," *Marketing News*, Mar. 16, 1984, p. 14; "Saab Hitches Its Star to the Yuppie Market," *Business Week*, Nov. 19, 1984, p. 62; Louis Richman, "Saab-Scania Kicks into High Gear," *Fortune*, Nov. 26, 1984, p. 105; John A. Russell, "Saab Is Racing Because Boss Likes It," *Automotive News*, July 28, 1986, p. 48; Jules Arbose, "How Saab's Car Boom Took Management by Surprise," *International Management*, September 1986, pp. 30–32; John A. Russell, "Saab-Scania Sees Continued Growth by Staying on Course," *Automotive News*, Oct. 13, 1986, p. 2; Stephen D. Moore, "Saab-Scania's Truck Division Supports Swedish Firm's Higher-Tech Endeavors," *Wall Street Journal*, Dec. 24, 1986, p. 14.

which fuel and air were mixed under high pressure for additional power. Next, Saab abandoned the car's ten-year-old design and developed the sleeker line of 900 models. Then, having built a technologically and aerodynamically superior product, Saab pioneered such safety features as seat belts, crumple zones, and gas tanks positioned above rear axles to prevent explosion during collisions.

In addition, to support a high-value market position, Saab included an impressive list of standard equipment on the 900 series: air conditioning, five-speed or automatic transmission, sun roof, alloy wheels and radial tires, electric door locks and outside mirrors, electrically heated front seats, quartz clocks, tachometer, bronze-tinted glass, rear-window defogger, power steering, and front and rear power disk brakes. The turbo version also included an AM/FM stereo radio and cassette player with four speakers, a graphic equalizer, and a retractable antenna.

These innovations, developed jointly with Lancia, enabled Saab to move its cars strategically into a small but growing and profitable market niche: the luxury sports segment. To increase consumer awareness of the 900 series and the new 9000 models, marketers have positioned the Saab car as a luxurious, high-performance automobile that competes directly with BMW and Volvo in the $13,000 to $20,000 price range.

As a result, according to a company executive, Saab has become the car of the yuppies, especially in the important North American market. Today's Saab owners are typically thirty to forty years old, well-educated (96 percent are college graduates and 40 percent have attended graduate school), with incomes from $50,000 to $80,000. Saab takes great pride in its ability to provide this upscale segment with effective service. Sales personnel thoroughly explain the car's operations and introduce the buyer to the service manager. Saab also follows up on each sale with a questionnaire about dealer performance, a thank-you from the company's president, and a Saab coffee mug and key ring. As a result of the strong service and product quality, brand loyalty is high. About 75 percent of current owners say they plan to buy another Saab automobile. Many Saab buyers belong to owners' clubs, attending annual meetings and picnics to discuss their cars.

What Saab did not expect, in fact, was the car's enormous success in North America, where the company sold 39,000 models last year. The company's successful positioning of its automobiles has created a new problem: how to meet increased consumer demand. Saab is currently producing about 120,000 cars a year—all of which are sold months in advance—and plans to increase that number to 150,000 by the end of next year. Company officials feel that sales can go as high as 1 percent of the total U.S. automobile market before the car begins to lose its exclusivity. Saab's American success shows how a small automobile maker can develop expertise, position its product carefully, and meet consumer requirements in one of the most intensely competitive product markets in the United States.

Questions for Discussion

1. How has Saab positioned its 900 series relative to other import automobiles (for example, Volvo, BMW, Mercedes-Benz)?
2. In what way should Saab's new-product development support its current market image or position?
3. As a product manager for Saab, would you support a redesign of the 900 model to make it more stylistically competitive with other foreign imports?

Procter & Gamble's Product Management

Procter & Gamble, the company founded in Cincinnati, Ohio, by candlemaker William Procter and soapmaker James Gamble, has been described as the world's foremost marketer of packaged consumer goods. For more than 150 years, the founders' policy of selling quality products for premium prices has served the company well. Procter & Gamble estimates that its products currently account for about 25 percent of all U.S. sales in the thirty-eight product categories in which the company competes. In thirty-three of those categories, Procter & Gamble products are among the top three brands; in nineteen categories, Procter & Gamble brands lead the market outright. Total sales last year exceeded $16 billion.

In recent years, however, Procter & Gamble has suffered from maturing markets and intensified competition. Three years ago the company posted its first decline in annual earnings in more than three decades, after losing market share in its core businesses: disposable diapers, toothpaste, and detergents. Although performance in several product categories has improved since then, Procter & Gamble is still struggling to regain its former profitability. In the process, the company is experimenting with new ways of developing and marketing its products.

Traditionally, the longevity of Procter & Gamble brands has affected the company's success. In contrast to competing brands, many of which fade from the marketplace within twenty years, Procter & Gamble products often sell briskly for generations. Pampers diapers, for example, were launched in 1961; Crest toothpaste, in 1955; Tide laundry detergent, in 1946. Ivory soap, the brand that built Procter & Gamble's national reputation, has been around since 1879 (the product itself was actually introduced in 1878, as "Procter & Gamble's White Soap").

Brand Management at Procter & Gamble

The staying power of Procter & Gamble brands has rested largely on the company's system of brand management, a marketing approach Procter & Gamble pioneered more than fifty years ago. The brand management concept was originally proposed by Neil McElroy, a young Procter & Gamble advertising manager who was dissatisfied with sales of Camay, the bar soap Procter & Gamble introduced in 1926. In a now-famous memo dated May 13, 1931, McElroy argued that Camay would never live up to its potential as long as the energies of the company's marketing and sales managers were divided between Camay and Ivory. What Camay (and every other Procter & Gamble product) needed, insisted McElroy, was the undivided attention of one person, with full responsibility for the marketing of that product. The "brand man" would be supported by an assistant and a marketing team, with additional help from a group monitoring product sales in the field. In other words, each Procter & Gamble brand would be managed as an individual business, in competition with other Procter & Gamble "businesses." By letting Procter & Gamble products compete with each other this way, McElroy believed that total sales would go up and the company would grow.

McElroy (who eventually became chairman of the board) won over Procter & Gamble's top executives. The company has been organized around the brand management system ever since, and through the years, nearly every major packaged-goods manufacturer in the United States has borrowed the concept. At present, Procter & Gamble has about one hundred brand managers, most of whom handle a single brand, or a brand and its extensions (Crest and Tartar Control Crest, for example). Brand managers are responsible for building market share for their respective products and are considered the company's experts on those products, each of which may generate annual sales of $100 million. Brand managers work with teams of three or four people to develop marketing strategies for their products, including promotion and packaging plans. Using their powers of persuasion—they have no formal authority over any department in the company—the brand managers draw on the resources of the company's sales, manufacturing, marketing research, and finance departments. Although brand managers are ultimately accountable to several superiors and usually must have the approval of a divisional vice president for funding, their role in the company is pivotal. Rivalry among brand management teams is fierce, and a successful brand manager can move up the corporate ladder quickly.

Changing Market Conditions

Despite the system's effectiveness in the past, however, some industry analysts believe that brand management is outmoded—or at least inadequate—in today's marketplace. For one thing, they say, consumers have changed. Today Procter & Gamble must sell its soaps, toothpastes, and diapers to not just a mass market of housewives but to a heterogeneous mix of working couples, singles, male shoppers, and the elderly. These consumers are less likely to have similar tastes or to respond to the standardized national advertising Procter & Gamble used for so many years. Moreover, today's consumers are much less loyal to brands than their predecessors, preferring to shop by price—never Procter & Gamble's point of emphasis—by buying generic products and taking advantage of coupons and other sales promotions. In some areas of the country, consumers favor regional labels. Southern coffee drinkers, for example, are as likely to buy a regional brand of coffee that offers strong taste or chicory flavor as they are to purchase Procter & Gamble's Folger's brand.

Also, the brand management system may have made it more difficult for Procter & Gamble to cope with the rapid proliferation of new products in today's market. Renowned for the thoroughness of its research, Procter & Gamble has always chosen to work for years, if necessary, to ensure high product quality. Brand managers' proposals are subject to approval by several layers of marketing hierarchy, and the company's research staff has sometimes found it difficult even to gain a hearing for new products. In contrast, competitors have been getting new products to market quickly, leaving Procter & Gamble to catch up. For example, while Procter & Gamble was still testing reclosable tabs on its Pampers diapers, Kimberly-Clark was already gaining market share with its refastenable Huggies. In another situation, Procter & Gamble was preoccupied with development of Tartar Control Crest and responded only belatedly to Colgate's move into toothpaste gels and pump dispensers.

Other marketing problems have arisen from the growing independence of Procter & Gamble's wholesalers and retailers. In the past, few retailers had the technology to monitor accurately what their customers were buying; to know what to stock, they relied largely on manufacturers' market surveys. Thus Procter & Gamble, producer of numerous popular brands, could (and did) exercise great control over wholesalers and retailers. The company could restrict quantities of discounted brands, for example, or insist that stores carry all sizes of a product if they wanted any at all during special promotions. But mergers in the food industry are now leading to a consolidation of power held by fewer wholesalers and retailers. One study estimates that 9 percent of all grocery outlets will account for 50 percent of all grocery sales by 1990. Now that they have sophisticated computer systems that can calculate product handling costs and update inventory instantaneously, large retailers no longer have to allot prominent brands shelf space. Retailers do not have to feel compelled to acquiesce to every marketing policy handed down from above.

Changes in Procter & Gamble's Product Management

Faced with today's complex marketing environment, therefore, Procter & Gamble has been reexamining its traditional approach to brand management and product development. One of the company's recent innovations was the formation of more than fifty "business teams," product development groups that cut across departmental and divisional lines. Originally instituted to boost the company's manufacturing productivity, business teams are now widely used in brand marketing to speed up decision making and prevent costly mistakes. For example, when Procter & Gamble developed new Ultra Pampers, a business team was responsible for getting the product to market in half the time usually required. Another business team came up with the drip-proof cap for Liquid Tide, Procter & Gamble's most popular new detergent brand in fifteen years. Still another team is credited with turning around Pringle's Potato Chips. Sales went up after the team developed new flavors, changed the product's double canister to a single container, and shifted the advertising focus from package to taste.

In some product groups, Procter & Gamble now is placing related brands under a category brand manager, who decides where the company should place its resources for the group as a whole. Procter & Gamble's dishwashing liquids—Joy, Dawn, Ivory, and others—are now supervised by a category brand manager, who has reduced manufacturing and packaging costs by making the soaps' containers and formulations more alike. The company has also formed new-brand groups, which study possible extensions of existing brands. Although the brand manager still plays an important role, company insiders say the job has been expanded; the brand manager is becoming something of a general manager, visiting manufacturing plants, calculating costs, and performing other nonmarketing functions.

Another change for Procter & Gamble is its new approach to wholesalers and retailers. The company has clarified the wording of its contracts and has started offering extended credit and greater promotional flexibility. Procter & Gamble also is adjusting its pricing structure to allow retailers greater profit margins. Some products have been redesigned to cut distributors' handling costs. For example, the teardrop-shaped bottle originally used for Ivory shampoo has been replaced with a squarer container that takes up less space and saves about 29 cents a case. Tide powdered detergent has been reformulated so that the same amount of detergent for the same number of washes now fits into a smaller box.

Procter & Gamble believes, however, that, as in the past, the most promising route to renewed profitability is new-product development. The company employs a research staff of six thousand and spends almost $500 million annually researching new products and improving old ones. The company's soap and detergent businesses still account for about 25 percent of research expenditures, but Procter & Gamble has been pushing into new areas as well, particularly in health care, where research has been supported by acquisitions. In the past five years, Procter & Gamble purchased Norwich Eaton Pharmaceuticals, Richardson-Vicks, and part of G. D. Searle, adding to its roster of brand names such well-known over-the-counter products as Pepto-Bismol stomach remedy, Oil of Olay facial moisturizer, and Vicks cough and cold medicines. Eventually, Procter & Gamble is expected to expand into hair-care and skin-care products. In the area of ethical drugs, the company hopes to incorporate its prescription mouthwash, Peridex, into Scope or Crest (or sell it without a prescription) and may eventually market its new drug Didronel as a treatment for osteoporosis.

Procter & Gamble also has great hopes for its new fat substitute, olestra. Now under scrutiny by the Food and Drug Administration, olestra is said to look, act, and taste like a fat, without any of the calories of fat. Procter & Gamble says olestra may be useful in reducing cholesterol levels as well. If the FDA approves olestra, Procter & Gamble may launch the product in some of its own brands, such as Crisco and Puritan cooking oil, and later license it to other businesses. Once regulatory and marketing problems have been worked out, sales of olestra could reach $1.5 billion in ten years.

Questions for Discussion

1. What was Procter & Gamble's original rationale for establishing a brand management approach for marketing its products?
2. Why has Procter & Gamble experienced difficulty competing in several core product categories recently?
3. To be more competitive, how has Procter & Gamble changed the manner in which it manages products?

SOURCES: Clare Ansberry, "P&G Posts $324 Million Quarterly Loss," *The Wall Street Journal,* Aug. 11, 1987, p. 12; Laurie Freeman, "Extraordinary Means to Meet Basic Needs," *Advertising Age,* Aug. 20, 1987, p. 102; Laurie Freeman, "The House That Ivory Built," *Advertising Age,* Aug. 20, 1987, p. 4; Jennifer Pendleton, "Dealing with No. 1," *Advertising Age,* Aug. 20, 1987, pp. 122–123; Bill Saporito, "Procter & Gamble's Comeback Plan," *Fortune,* Feb. 4, 1985, p. 30; Zachary Schiller, "Procter & Gamble Goes on a Health Kick," *Business Week,* June 29, 1987, pp. 90–92; Julie Solomon and Carol Hymowitz, "Team Strategy," *The Wall Street Journal,* Aug. 11, 1987, p. 1; Joseph Winski, "One Brand, One Manager," *Advertising Age,* Aug. 20, 1987, p. 86.

III. Distribution Decisions

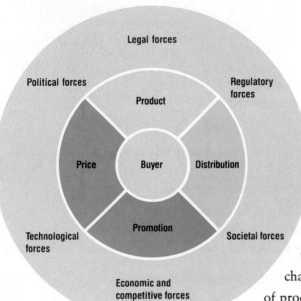

Providing customers with satisfying products is important but not enough for successful marketing strategies. These products also must be available in adequate quantities in accessible locations at the times when customers desire them. The chapters in Part III deal with the distribution of products and the marketing channels and institutions that provide the structure for making products available. In Chapter 9 we discuss the structure and functions of marketing channels and present an overview of institutions that make up marketing channels. In Chapter 10 we analyze the types of wholesalers and their functions. In Chapter 11 we focus on retailing and retailers. Specifically, we examine the types of retailers and their roles and functions in marketing channels. Finally, in Chapter 12 we analyze the decisions and activities associated with the physical distribution of products, such as order processing, materials handling, warehousing, inventory management, and transportation.

9. Marketing Channels

O B J E C T I V E S

- ▶ To understand the marketing channel concept and the types of marketing intermediaries in the channel.
- ▶ To discuss the justification of channel members.
- ▶ To examine the structure and function of the channel system.
- ▶ To explore the power dimensions of channels, especially the concepts of cooperation, conflict, and leadership.

*R*eebok *executives* do not like to hear their stylish athletic shoes called "footwear for yuppies." They contend that Reebok shoes appeal to diverse market segments, especially now that the company offers basketball and children's shoes for the under-18 set and walking shoes for older consumers not interested in aerobics or running (see Figure 9.1). The executives also point out that through recent acquisitions they have added hiking boots, dress and casual shoes, and high-performance athletic footwear to their product lines, all of which should attract new and varied groups of customers.

Still, despite its emphasis on new markets, Reebok plans few changes in the upscale retailing network that helped push sales to $1 billion annually, ahead of all other sports shoe marketers. Reebok shoes, which are priced from $27 to $85, will continue to be sold only in better specialty, sporting goods, and department stores, in accordance with the company's view that consumers judge the quality of the brand by the quality of its distribution.

In the past few years, the Canton, Massachusetts-based company has imposed quotas on the number of its distributors (and the number of shoes supplied to stores), partly out of necessity. At times the unexpected demand for Reeboks exceeded supply, and the company could barely keep up with orders from the dealers it already had. These fulfillment problems seem to be under control now, but the company is still selective about its accounts. At present, Reebok shoes are available in about five thousand retail stores in the United States.

Reebok has already anticipated that walking shoes will be the next fitness-related fad, replacing aerobics shoes the same way its brightly colored, soft leather

FIGURE 9.1

Advertisement for
Reebok (SOURCE: Re-
printed by permission
of Reebok Interna-
tional Ltd.)

exercise footwear supplanted conventional running gear. Through product diversification and careful market research, Reebok hopes to avoid the distribution problems that befell Nike several years ago, when Nike misjudged the strength of the
aerobics shoe craze and was forced to unload huge inventories of running shoes
through discount stores.

Reebok will attempt to avoid mass merchandisers by giving its affluent,
fashion-conscious customers the quality products they want, when they want them.
Market surveys show that 70 to 80 percent of all sport shoes are purchased for
street wear, not for any sort of athletic activities. But Reebok intends to market to
consumer lifestyles. By being choosy about its distribution outlets, Reebok believes
its target markets will perceive Reebok shoes as everyday footwear that is nevertheless a little extraordinary.[1]

1. Based on information from Leslie Helm, "Reebok's Recent Blisters Seem to Be Healing," *Business
Week,* Aug. 3, 1987, p. 62; Mary Rowland, "Keep on Walking," *Working Woman,* May 1987, pp. 87–
88; Jean Sherman, "No Pain, No Gain," *Working Woman,* May 1987, p. 92; Aimee L. Stern, "Reebok:
In for the Distance," *Business Month,* August 1987, pp. 22–25; Lois Therrien, "Reebok: How Far Can
a Fad Run?", *Business Week,* Feb. 28, 1986, pp. 89–90; Carl Weinschenk, "Setting the Pace," *Marketing & Media Decisions,* Winter 1986, pp. 34–36.

REEBOK CAREFULLY CONTROLS the structure of its marketing channels to ensure that its products maintain the right image and are readily available to Reebok's target markets. What marketing channels to select is one of the most critical decisions in the development of a marketing strategy. This chapter presents the concepts used to describe and analyze marketing channels. We first discuss the main types of channels and their structures and then explain the need for intermediaries and analyze the functions these people perform. Next we outline several forms of channel integration. We explore how marketers determine the appropriate intensity of market coverage for a product and how they consider a number of factors when selecting suitable channels of distribution. Finally, after examining behavioral patterns within marketing channels, we look at several legal issues that affect channel management.

The Structures and Types of Marketing Channels

A **channel of distribution** (sometimes called a **marketing channel**) is a group of individuals and organizations that direct the flow of products from producers to customers. The customer should be the ultimate driver of all marketing channel activities. Buyers' desires and behavior are therefore the impo tant concerns of channel members.

Most, but not all, channels of distribution have marketing intermediaries. A **marketing intermediary**, or middleman, is a go-between who links producers and customers. Marketing intermediaries perform the activities described in Table 9.1. There are two major types of marketing intermediaries: merchants and functional middlemen (agents and brokers). **Merchants** take title to products and resell them, whereas **functional middlemen** do not take title.

TABLE 9.1

Marketing channel activities that intermediaries perform

CATEGORY OF MARKETING ACTIVITIES	POSSIBLE ACTIVITIES REQUIRED
Marketing information	Analyze information such as sales data; perform or commission marketing research studies
Marketing management	Establish objectives; plan activities; manage and coordinate financing, personnel, and risk taking; evaluate and control channel activities
Facilitating exchange	Choose product assortments that match the needs of buyers
Promotion	Set promotional objectives, coordinate advertising, personal selling, sales promotion, publicity, and packaging
Price	Establish pricing policies and terms of sales
Physical distribution	Manage transportation, warehousing, materials handling, inventory control, and communication

Both retailers and wholesalers are intermediaries. **Retailers** purchase products for the purpose of reselling them to ultimate consumers. **Merchant wholesalers** resell products to other wholesalers and to retailers. **Functional wholesalers,** such as agents and brokers, expedite exchanges among producers and resellers and are compensated by fees or commissions. For purposes of discussion in this chapter, all wholesalers are considered merchant middlemen unless otherwise specified.

Channel members share certain significant characteristics. Each member has different responsibilities within the overall structure of the distribution system, but mutual profit and success can be attained only if channel members cooperate in delivering products to the market.

Although channel decisions need not precede other marketing decisions, they do exercise a powerful influence on the rest of the marketing mix. Channel decisions are critical because they determine a product's market presence and buyers' accessibility to the product. Their strategic significance is further heightened by their inherent long-term commitments. It is much easier, for example, to change prices or packaging than distribution systems.

Availability benefits the total product. Marketing channel members make products available at the right time, in the right place, and in the right quantity by providing such product-enhancing functions as transportation and storage. Although consumers do not see the distribution of a product, they value product availability that channels of distribution make possible. Days Inns of America, Inc. made a location decision to build budget motels along interstate highways from the Northeast and the lower Ohio valley to Orlando, Florida, home of Walt Disney World. Today the Days Inn motels in Orlando are the largest provider of lodging in the area.[2] Now the company has a new distribution strategy designed to push development through the Sun Belt and the remaining parts of the North. Because motels basically deliver a service, making this service available at particular locations is a crucial distribution decision, with long-run consequences.

Because the marketing channel most appropriate for one product may be less suitable for another product, many different distribution paths have been developed in most countries. The links in any channel, however, are the merchants (including producers) and agents who oversee the movement of products through that channel. Although there are many various marketing channels, they can be classified generally as channels for consumer products or channels for industrial products.

Channels for Consumer Products

Figure 9.2 illustrates several channels used in the distribution of consumer products. In addition to these steps, a manufacturer may use sales branches or sales offices (discussed in Chapter 10).

Channel A describes the direct movement of goods from producer to consumers. Customers who harvest their own fruit from commercial orchards or buy cookware from door-to-door salespeople are acquiring products through a direct channel. A producer that sells products directly from its factory to end users and ultimate consumers is using a direct marketing channel. Although this channel is the simplest, it is not necessarily the cheapest or the most efficient method of distribution.

2. "Days Inns: Looking for a Berth in a Crowded National Field," *Business Week,* Oct. 31, 1983, p. 70.

FIGURE 9.2

Typical marketing
channels for consumer
products

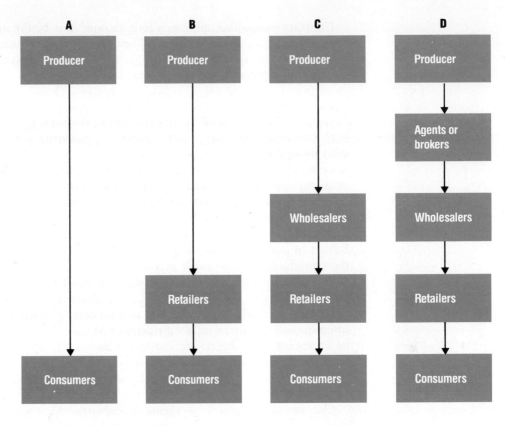

Channel B—producer to retailers to consumers—is often used by large retailers who can buy in quantity from a manufacturer. Such retailers as J. C. Penney Company, Inc., K mart Corporation, and Sears, Roebuck, for example, sell clothing, stereos, and many other products that they have purchased directly from the producers. Automobiles are also commonly sold through this type of marketing channel.

Channel C—producer to wholesalers to retailers to consumers—is a long-standing distribution pattern, especially for consumer goods. It is a very practical option for a producer that sells to hundreds of thousands of consumers through thousands of retailers. It is difficult for a single producer to do business directly with thousands of retailers. For example, consider the number of retailers that market Wrigley's chewing gum. It would be extremely difficult, if not impossible, for Wrigley's to deal directly with all the retailers that sell its brand of gum. Manufacturers of tobacco products, some home appliances, hardware, and many convenience goods sell their products to wholesalers, who then sell to retailers, who in turn do business with individual consumers.

Channel D—producer to agents to wholesalers to retailers to consumers—is frequently used for products intended for mass distribution, such as processed food. To place its cracker line in specific retail outlets, for example, a food processor may hire an agent (or a food broker) to sell the crackers to wholesalers. The wholesalers then sell the crackers to supermarkets, vending machine operators, and other retail outlets.

Contrary to popular opinion, a long channel may be the most efficient distribution channel for consumer goods. When several channel intermediaries are available to perform specialized functions, costs may be lower than if one channel member is responsible for all the functions.

Channels for Industrial Products

Figure 9.3 shows four of the most common channels for industrial products. As with consumer products, manufacturers of industrial products sometimes work with more than one level of wholesalers.

Channel E illustrates the direct channel for industrial products. In contrast to consumer goods, many industrial products—especially expensive equipment such as steam generators, aircraft, and computers—are sold directly to the buyers. The direct channel is most feasible for many manufacturers of industrial goods because they have fewer customers, and those customers are often clustered geographically. Buyers of complex industrial products also can receive technical assistance from the manufacturer more easily in a direct channel.

If a particular line of industrial products is aimed at a large number of customers, the manufacturer may use a marketing channel that includes industrial distributors, merchants who take title to products (channel F). Mitsubishi Aircraft International Corporation, a subsidiary of Mitsubishi Heavy Industries, Ltd., sells its Diamond I jets directly to corporate buyers (channel E). Mitsubishi fork lift trucks and other construction products, on the other hand, are sold through industrial distributors. Building materials, operating supplies, and air conditioning equipment are frequently channeled through industrial distributors.

Channel G—producer to agents to industrial buyers—is often used when a manufacturer without its own marketing department needs market information, when the firm is too small to field its own sales force, or when the firm wants to

FIGURE 9.3

Typical marketing channels for industrial products

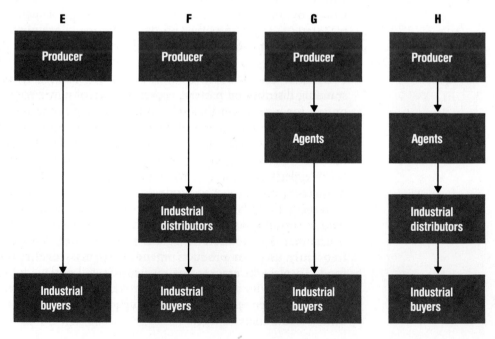

introduce a new product or enter a new market without using its own salespeople. A large soybean producer, for example, might use an agent to sell its product to animal food processors.

Channel H is a variation of channel G—producer to agents to industrial distributors to industrial buyers. A manufacturer without a sales force may use this channel if its industrial users purchase products in small quantities or if the users must be resupplied frequently and therefore need access to decentralized inventories. Japanese manufacturers of electronic components work through export agents, who sell to industrial distributors serving small producers or dealers in the United States. Chapter 20 presents more information about marketing channels for industrial products.

Multiple Marketing Channels

To reach diverse target markets, a manufacturer may use several marketing channels simultaneously, with each channel involving a different group of intermediaries. A manufacturer uses multiple channels, for example, when the same product is directed to both consumers and industrial customers. When Del Monte Corp. markets catsup for household use, the catsup is sold to supermarkets through grocery wholesalers or, in some cases, directly to the retailers, whereas catsup for restaurant or institutional use follows a different distribution channel. Xerox Corporation markets its products through both a worldwide network of Xerox stores and a direct sales force. In some instances, a producer may use **dual distribution,** or the use of two or more marketing channels for distributing the same products to the same target market. An umbrella manufacturer may sell large quantities of umbrellas directly to big retail chains and also market the same brand of umbrellas to wholesalers who in turn sell to smaller retailers. Dual distribution can cause dissatisfaction among wholesalers and smaller retailers.

Justifications for Intermediaries

Even if producers and buyers are located in the same city, there are costs associated with exchanges. As Figure 9.4 shows, if five buyers purchase the products of five producers, twenty-five transactions are needed for the buyers to obtain their products. If one intermediary serves both producers and buyers, the number of transactions can be reduced to ten. Intermediaries become specialists in facilitating exchanges. They provide valuable assistance because of their access to, and control over, important resources for the proper functioning of the marketing channel.

Nevertheless, the press, consumers, public officials, and other marketers freely criticize wholesalers. Table 9.2 indicates that in a recent national survey of the general public, 74 percent believed that "wholesalers frequently make profits which significantly increase prices that consumers pay." The critics accuse wholesalers of being inefficient and parasitic. Consumers often are obsessed with making the distribution channel as short as possible, assuming that the fewer the intermediaries, the lower the price. Because suggestions to eliminate them come from both ends of the marketing channel, wholesalers must be careful to perform only those marketing activities that are truly desirable. To survive, they must be more efficient and more service oriented than alternative marketing institutions.

Critics who suggest that eliminating wholesalers would lower prices for consumers do not recognize that this would not do away with the need for the services wholesalers provide. Other institutions would have to perform those services, and consumers would still have to pay for the services. In addition, all producers would have to deal directly with retailers or consumers, meaning that every producer would have to keep voluminous records and hire enough personnel to deal with every customer. Even in a direct channel, consumers might end up paying a great deal more for products because prices would reflect the costs of inefficient producers' operations.

To illustrate the efficient service that wholesalers provide, assume that all wholesalers were eliminated. Because there are more than 1.3 million retail stores, a widely purchased consumer product—say candy—would require an extraordinary number of sales contacts, possibly more than a million, to maintain the current level of product exposure. For example, Mars, Inc. would have to deliver its candy, purchase and service thousands of vending machines, establish warehouses all over the country, and maintain fleets of trucks. Selling and distribution costs for candy would skyrocket. Instead of a few contacts with food brokers, large retail organizations, and various merchant wholesalers, candy manufacturers would face thousands of expensive contacts with and shipments to smaller retailers. Such an

FIGURE 9.4

Efficiency in exchanges provided by an intermediary

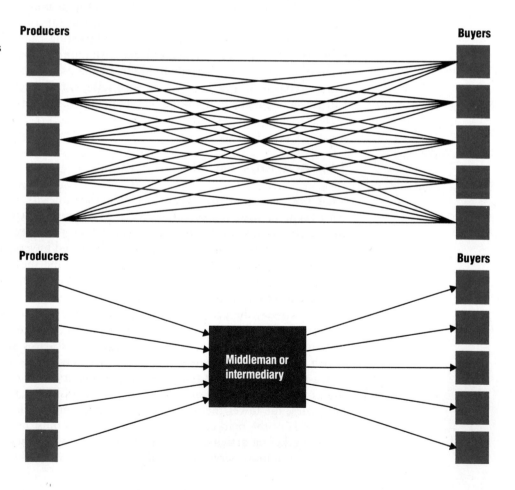

Statement: Wholesalers frequently make high profits, which significantly
increase prices that consumers pay.

	TOTAL %	MALE %	FEMALE %
Strongly agree	35.5	33	38
Somewhat agree	38	40	36
Neither agree nor disagree	16	14	18
Somewhat disagree	8	9	7
Strongly disagree	2.5	4	1

SOURCE: © O. C. Ferrell and William M. Pride, National multistage area probability sample of 2,045 households, 1985.

operation would be highly inefficient, and its costs would be passed on to consumers. Candy bars would cost more, and they would be harder to find. Wholesalers are more efficient and less expensive not only for manufacturers but for consumers.

Functions of Intermediaries

Before we examine the functions of intermediaries in some detail, we should note that a distribution network helps overcome two major distribution problems. Consider a firm that manufactures jeans. The company specializes in the goods it can produce most efficiently, denim clothing. To make jeans the most economical way possible, the producer turns out 100,000 pairs of jeans each day. Few persons, however, want to buy 100,000 pairs of jeans. Thus the quantity of jeans the company can produce efficiently is more than the average customer wants. We call this a *discrepancy in quantity*.

An **assortment** is a combination of products put together to provide benefits. A consumer creates and holds an assortment. The set of products made available to customers is an organization's assortment. Most consumers want a broad assortment of products. In addition to jeans, a consumer wants to buy shoes, food, a car, a stereo, soft drinks, and many other products. Yet our jeans manufacturer has a narrow assortment because it makes only jeans (and perhaps a few other denim clothes). There is a *discrepancy in assortment* because a consumer wants a broad assortment but an individual manufacturer produces a narrow assortment.

Quantity and assortment discrepancies are resolved through the sorting activities of intermediaries in a marketing channel. **Sorting activities** are functions that allow channel members to divide roles and separate tasks. Sorting activities, as Figure 9.5 shows, may be grouped into four main tasks: sorting out, accumulation, allocation, and assorting products.[3]

3. Wroe Alderson, *Marketing Behavior and Executive Action* (Homewood, Ill.: Irwin, 1957), pp. 201–211.

FIGURE 9.5

Sorting activities conducted by intermediaries

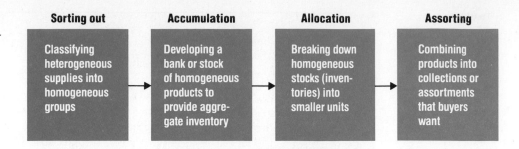

Sorting out	Accumulation	Allocation	Assorting
Classifying heterogeneous supplies into homogeneous groups	Developing a bank or stock of homogeneous products to provide aggregate inventory	Breaking down homogeneous stocks (inventories) into smaller units	Combining products into collections or assortments that buyers want

Sorting Out

Sorting out, the first step in developing an assortment, is separating conglomerates of heterogeneous products into relatively uniform, homogeneous groups based on product characteristics such as size, shape, weight, or color. Sorting out is especially common in the marketing of agricultural products and other raw materials, which vary widely in size, grade, and quality and would be largely unusable in an undifferentiated mass. A tomato crop, for example, must be sorted into tomatoes suitable for canning, those for making tomato juice, and those for sale in retail food stores.

Sorting out for specific products is performed according to a set of predetermined standards. The sorter must know how many classifications to use and the criteria for each classification and usually provide for a group of miscellaneous leftovers as well. Certain product characteristics can be categorized more easily than others; appearance and size of agricultural products are more readily apparent than flavor or nutritional content, for instance. Because the overall quality of a crop or supply of raw material most likely will vary from year to year or from region to region, classifications must be somewhat flexible.

Changing consumer needs and new manufacturing techniques influence the sorting-out process. If sorting out results in manufactured goods with minor defects, these damaged or irregular products are often marketed at lower prices through factory outlet stores, which are growing in consumer popularity. Improved processing also permits the use of materials that might have been culled previously, such as the paper and aluminum now being recycled. In some industries, producers have stopped using natural materials because the manufacturing process demands the greater uniformity possible only with synthetic materials.

Sorting out thus helps alleviate discrepancies in assortment by making relatively homogeneous products available for the next step, accumulation.

Accumulation

Accumulation is the development of a bank or inventory of homogeneous products that have similar production or demand requirements. Farmers who grow relatively small quantities of tomatoes, for example, transport their sorted tomatoes to central collection points, where tomatoes are accumulated in large lots for movement into the next level of the channel.

Combining many small groups of similar products into larger groups serves several purposes. Products move through subsequent marketing channels more economically in large quantities because transportation rates are lower for bulk loads. In addition, accumulation gives buyers a steady supply of products in large volumes. If Del Monte had to frequently purchase small amounts of tomatoes from individual farmers, the company's tomato products would be produced much less efficiently. Instead, Del Monte buys bulk loads of tomatoes through brokers, thus maintaining a continuous supply of uniform-quality materials for processing. Accumulation lets producers continuously use up stocks and replenish them, thus minimizing losses from interruptions in the supply of materials.

For both buyer and seller, accumulation also alleviates some of the problems associated with price fluctuations and highly seasonal materials. Buyers may obtain large-volume purchases at lower prices because sellers are anxious to dispose of perishable goods; purchasing agents may accumulate stocks of materials in anticipation of price hikes. In other cases, sellers may receive higher prices because they enter into long-term supply contracts with producers or they agree to store accumulated materials until the producer is ready for them.

Accumulation thus relieves discrepancies in quantity. It enables intermediaries to build up specialized inventories and allocate products according to customers' needs.

Allocation

Allocation is the breaking down of large homogeneous inventories into smaller lots. This process, which addresses discrepancies in quantity, enables wholesalers to buy efficiently in truckloads or carloads and then apportion products by cases to other channel members. A food wholesaler, for instance, serves as a depot, allocating products according to market demand. The wholesaler may divide a single truckload of Del Monte canned tomatoes among several retail food stores.

Because supply and demand are seldom in perfect balance, allocation is influenced by several factors (and can sometimes resemble rationing). At times price is the overriding consideration: The highest bidder, or perhaps the buyer placing the largest order, is allocated most of the stock. At other times an intermediary gives preference to customers whose loyalty has been established or to those whose businesses show the most growth potential. In still other cases, products are allocated through compromise and negotiation.

Depending on the product, allocation may begin with the manufacturer and continue through several levels of intermediaries, including retailers. Allocation ends when the ultimate user selects the desired quantity of a particular product from the assortment of products available.

Assorting

Assorting is the process of combining products into collections or assortments that buyers want to have available in one place. Assorting eliminates discrepancies in assortment by grouping products in ways that satisfy buyers. The same food wholesaler supplying supermarkets with Del Monte tomato products may also buy canned goods from competing food processors so that grocery stores can choose from a wide assortment of canned fruits and vegetables.

Buyers want an assortment of products at one location because of some task they want to perform or some problem they want solved. A buyer looking for a variety of products, all serving different purposes, requires a broad assortment from which to choose; a buyer with more precise needs or interests will seek out a narrower, but deeper, product assortment.

Assorting is especially important to retailers, who strive to create assortments that match the demands of consumers who patronize their stores. Although no single customer is likely to buy one of everything in the store, a retailer must anticipate the probability of purchase and provide a satisfactory range of product choices. The risk involved is greater for some retailers than for others. For example, supermarkets purchase staple foods repeatedly, and these items can be stocked with little risk. But clothing retailers who misjudge consumer demand for "hot" fashion items can lose money if their assortments contain too few (or too many) of these products. Discrepancies in assortment reappear, in fact, when retailers fail to keep pace with shifts in consumer attitudes. New specialists—such as retail outlets for computer products—may even enter the market to provide assortments existing retailers do not offer.

Channel Integration

Channel functions may be transferred among intermediaries and to producers and even customers. This section examines how channel members can either combine and control most activities or pass them on to another channel member. Remember, though, that the channel member cannot eliminate functions; unless buyers themselves perform the functions, they must pay for the labor and resources needed for the functions to be performed. The statement that "you can eliminate middlemen but you can't eliminate their functions" is a universally accepted principle of marketing.

Many marketing channels are determined by consensus. Producers and intermediaries coordinate their efforts for mutual benefit. Some marketing channels, however, are organized and controlled by a single leader, which can be a producer, a wholesaler, or a retailer. The channel leader may establish channel policies and coordinate the development of the marketing mix. Sears, for example, is a channel leader for several of the many products it sells.

The various links or stages of the channel may be combined under the management of a channel leader either horizontally or vertically. Integration may stabilize supply, reduce costs, and increase coordination of channel members.

Vertical Channel Integration

Combining two or more stages of the channel under one management is **vertical channel integration.** One member of a marketing channel may purchase the operations of another member or simply perform the functions of the other member, eliminating the need for that intermediary as a separate entity. Total vertical integration encompasses all functions from production to ultimate buyer; it is exemplified by oil companies that own oil wells, pipelines, refineries, terminals, and service stations.

Whereas members of conventional channel systems work independently and seldom cooperate, participants in vertical channel integration coordinate their efforts to reach a desired target market. This more progressive approach to distribution enables channel members to regard other members as extensions of their own operations. At one end of an integrated channel, for example, a manufacturer might provide advertising and training assistance, and the retailer at the other end would buy the manufacturer's products in quantity and actively promote them.

FIGURE 9.6

Promotion of corpo-
rate VMS (SOURCE:
Gucci)

During the past few decades, integration has been successfully institutionalized in marketing channels called vertical marketing systems (VMS). A **vertical marketing system (VMS)** is a marketing channel in which a single channel member coordinates or manages channel activities to achieve efficient, low-cost distribution aimed at satisfying target market customers. Because efforts of individual channel members are combined in a VMS, marketing activities can be coordinated for maximum effectiveness and economy, without duplication of services. Vertical marketing systems are also competitive, accounting for a growing share of retail sales in consumer goods.

Most vertical marketing systems today take one of three forms: corporate, administered, or contractual. The *corporate* VMS combines successive channel stages from producers to consumers under a single ownership. For example, manufacturer Gucci (see Figure 9.6) established a corporate VMS by opening its own retail outlets to market fashions, leather goods, shoes, and accessories. Food chains that own processing plants and large retailers that purchase wholesaling and production facilities are other examples of corporate VMSs. Figure 9.7 contrasts a conventional marketing channel with a VMS, which consolidates marketing functions and institutions.

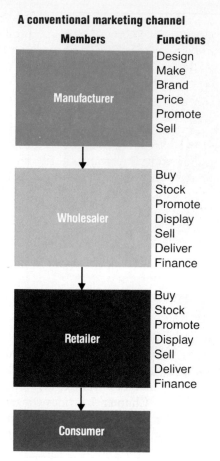

A conventional marketing channel

Members	Functions
Manufacturer	Design Make Brand Price Promote Sell
Wholesaler	Buy Stock Promote Display Sell Deliver Finance
Retailer	Buy Stock Promote Display Sell Deliver Finance
Consumer	

A vertical marketing system

Members	Functions
Manufacturer	Design Make Brand Price Promote Buy Stock Display Sell Deliver Finance
Wholesaler	
Retailer	
Consumer	

In an *administered* VMS, channel members are independent, but a high level of interorganizational management is achieved by informal coordination. Members of an administered VMS may agree, for example, to adopt uniform accounting and ordering procedures and to cooperate in promotional activities. Although individual channel members maintain their autonomy, as in conventional marketing channels, one (or more) members dominate the administered VMS, so that distribution decisions take into account the system as a whole. Because of its size and power as a retailer, Sears, Roebuck exercises a strong influence over the independent manufacturers in its marketing channels, as do Kellogg Co. (cereal) and Magnavox (television and other electronic products).

Under a *contractual* VMS, the most popular form of vertical marketing system, interorganizational relationships are formalized through contracts. Channel members are linked by legal agreements that spell out each member's rights and obligations. Franchise organizations such as McDonald's and Kentucky Fried Chicken are contractual VMSs. Other contractual VMSs include wholesaler-sponsored groups such as IGA (Independent Grocers' Alliance) stores, in which independent retailers band together under the contractual leadership of a wholesaler. Retailer-sponsored cooperatives, which own and operate their own wholesalers, are a third type of contractual VMS.

Horizontal Channel Integration	Combining institutions at the same level of operation under one management constitutes **horizontal channel integration.** An organization may integrate horizontally by merging with other organizations or by adding units (retail stores, for example) at one channel level. The Sharper Image, originally a mail order retailer, has opened a number of retail stores (see the Application on page 309). Horizontal integration may enable a firm to generate sufficient sales revenue to integrate vertically as well.

Although horizontal integration permits efficiencies and economies of scale in purchasing, market research, advertising, and specialized personnel, it is not always the most effective method of improving distribution. Problems of "bigness" often follow, resulting in decreased flexibility, difficulties in coordination, and the need for additional market research and large-scale planning. Unless distribution functions for the various units can be performed more efficiently under unified management than under the previously separate managements, horizontal integration will not reduce costs or improve the competitive position of the integrating firm.

Intensity of Market Coverage

Characteristics of the product and the target market determine the kind of coverage a product should get, that is, the number and kinds of outlets in which it is sold. To achieve the desired intensity of market coverage, distribution must correspond to the behavior patterns of buyers. Chapter 5 divides consumer products into three categories—convenience products, shopping products, and specialty products—according to how consumers make purchases. Consumers view products as to replacement rate, product adjustment (services), duration of consumption, searching time necessary for finding the product, and similar factors.[4] These variables directly affect the intensity of market coverage.

Three major levels of market coverage are intensive, selective, and exclusive distribution. In **intensive distribution,** all available outlets are used for distributing a product. In **selective distribution,** only some available outlets in an area are chosen to distribute a product. In **exclusive distribution,** only one outlet is used in a relatively large geographic area.

Intensive Distribution	Intensive distribution is appropriate for convenience products such as bread, chewing gum, beer, and newspapers. To consumers, availability means a store located nearby and minimum time necessary to search for the product at the store. Sales may have a direct relationship to availability. The successful sale of bread and milk at service stations or of gasoline at convenience grocery stores has shown that the availability of these products is more important than the nature of the outlet. Convenience products have a high replacement rate and require almost no service; to meet these demands, intensive distribution is necessary, and multiple channels may be used to sell through all possible outlets.

4. Leo Aspinwall, "The Marketing Characteristics of Goods," in *Four Marketing Theories* (Boulder: University of Colorado Press, 1961), pp. 27–32.

Consumer packaged products rely on intensive distribution. Intensive distribution is one of Procter & Gamble's key strengths. It is fairly easy for this company to formulate marketing strategies for many of its products (soaps, detergents, food and juice products, and personal-care products) because consumers want availability provided quickly and intensively.

Selective Distribution

Selective distribution is appropriate for shopping products. Durable goods such as typewriters and stereos usually fall into this category. Such products are more expensive than convenience goods. Consumers are willing to spend greater searching time visiting several retail outlets to compare prices, designs, styles, and other features.

Selective distribution is desirable when a special effort—such as customer service from a channel member—is important. Shopping products require differentiation at the point of purchase. To motivate retailers to provide adequate presale service, selective distribution and company-owned stores are often used. Many industrial products are sold on a selective basis to maintain a certain degree of control over the distribution process. For example, agricultural herbicides (chemicals that kill weeds) are distributed on a selective basis because dealers must offer services to buyers, such as instructions about how to apply the herbicides safely or the option of having the dealer apply the herbicide. Mariner's outboard motors are sold by dealers on a selective basis.

Exclusive Distribution

Exclusive distribution is suitable for products that are purchased rather infrequently, consumed over a long period of time, or require service or information to fit them to buyers' needs. Exclusive distribution is used often as an incentive to sellers when only a limited market is available for products. For example, automobiles such as the Rolls-Royce (see Figure 9.8) are sold on an exclusive basis. Customers often seek out the product, but specialized promotion is needed occasionally. For example, a Rolls-Royce motorcar dealer in Houston, Texas, mailed 30,000 letters to individuals with incomes over $100,000 in order to make this select potential target market aware of his product offering.

Selection of Distribution Channels

The process of selecting appropriate distribution channels for a product is often complex, for a variety of reasons. Producers must choose specific intermediaries carefully, evaluating their sales and profit levels, performance records, other products carried, clientele, availability, and so forth. But producers must also examine other factors that influence distribution channel selection, including organizational objectives and resources, market characteristics, buyer behavior, product attributes, and environmental forces. The Application on page 313 provides examples of channel selections made by several organizations including Esprit, Vivitar, and Xerox.

The Sharper Image Uses Horizontal Integration

Desktop massagers, pocket-size microrecorders, computers that play three-handed bridge—such high-tech gadgets and conveniences are what The Sharper Image, a California-based mail-order firm, is all about. Founded ten years ago, the company began with a direct mail advertisement for a $69 jogger's watch. The Sharper Image now mails three million catalogs a month worldwide and has annual sales exceeding $100 million.

But The Sharper Image, along with most other catalog companies, is experiencing market saturation. Studies show that less than one-third of the population actually buys from the ten billion catalogs that firms send out each year, and overlap of mailing lists can run as high as 30 percent. Overexposure to mail-order appeals may even turn off some established catalog buyers: In one three-year period in the early 1980s, The Sharper Image's growth rate dropped from 143 percent to 30 percent.

The Sharper Image and other catalog firms believe the solution to the problem is to open retail outlets that will attract new customers who simply prefer stores to catalogs. In the past five years, The Sharper Image has opened thirty stores, most located in or near shopping centers or financial districts in markets where its catalog sales are strongest. Every item in The Sharper Image stores has appeared in the catalog during the previous three months. When an item is dropped from the catalog, it goes on sale in the stores. The stores also provide the same services as the catalogs: one-year guarantees, thirty-day returns, matching of advertised prices, and gift certificates for frequent buyers. The unique thing about the stores is the hands-on experience with the merchandise. Customers in The Sharper Image stores are encouraged to operate the CD players, relax in the massage chairs, and check out the talking scales, aided by salespeople trained to demonstrate each item.

For any mail-order firm, the shift from running a catalog operation to becoming a conventional retailer can be tricky. For example, when it was just a mail-order operation, The Sharper Image required little inventory or working capital because the company could buy merchandise on deferred credit and pay for it with cash sales. The Sharper Image catalog itself was the largest expenditure. Now, however, the company must invest in real estate and inventory for each store while competing with other retail stores. With stores scattered across the country, the firm no longer has the luxury of testing small markets to see what sells.

The Sharper Image appears to have made the transition successfully, with in-store sales now accounting for 52 percent of the company's revenues. Still, industry observers say that the company may have to adjust its marketing mix to keep its stores and catalogs from taking business away from each other. Overlaps in store trading areas have already pulled down same-store sales in certain units. Other stores are finding it difficult to maintain high sales levels once the grand opening hoopla dies down. And if The Sharper Image continues to target the same group of affluent consumers for both stores and mailings, overall business may suffer. Similar firms try to reach different customer groups by emphasizing different products; so far, The Sharper Image has not done so.

SOURCES: Regina Eisman, "Sharper Image's Retail Outlets Bring Catalog to Life," *Merchandising,* January 1986, p. 30; "ES & SD Hones POS System," *Chain Store Age Executive,* September 1987, p. 80; A. E. Hardie, "Cataloguers Move Up from Mail," *The New York Times,* Aug. 17, 1986, p. 12F; Ralph King, Jr., "Richard Thalheimer's Toy Chest," *Forbes,* Feb. 10, 1986, p. 80; "Of Our Time," *The New Yorker,* Jan. 12, 1987, pp. 22–23; The Sharper Image catalog, October 1987; "Up and Down Wall Street," *Barron's,* Apr. 27, 1987, p. 1.

Organizational Objectives and Resources

A producer must consider what it is trying to accomplish in the marketplace and what resources can be brought to bear on the task. A company's objectives may be broad, such as higher profits, increased market share, greater responsiveness to customers, or narrow, such as replacing an intermediary who has left the channel. The organization may possess sufficient financial and marketing clout to control its distribution channels, by engaging in direct marketing, for example, or by operating its own trucking fleet. On the other hand, an organization may have no interest in performing distribution services or may be forced by lack of resources and experience to depend on middlemen.

The company must also evaluate the effectiveness of past distribution relationships and methods in light of its current goals. One firm might decide to maintain its basic channel structure but add members for increased coverage in new territories. Another company might alter its distribution channel so as to provide same-day delivery on all orders. When selecting distribution channels, organizational factors and objectives are important considerations.

Market Characteristics

Beyond the basic division between consumer markets and industrial markets, several market variables influence the design of distribution channels. Geography is one factor; in most cases, the greater the distance between the producer and its markets, distribution through intermediaries is less expensive than direct sales. A related consideration is market density. If customers tend to be clustered in several locations, the producer may be able to eliminate middlemen. Transportation, storage, communication, and negotiation are specific functions performed more efficiently in high-density markets. Market size—measured by number of potential customers in a consumer or industrial market—is yet another variable. Direct sales may be effective if a producer has relatively few buyers for a product, but for larger markets the services of middlemen may be required.[5]

Buyer Behavior

Buyer behavior is a crucial consideration when selecting distribution channels. To be able to match intermediaries with customers, the producer must have specific,

5. Bert Rosenbloom, *Marketing Channels: A Management View* (Hinsdale, Ill.: Dryden, 1987), p. 160.

current information about who are buying the product and when and where they are buying it.[6] How customers buy is important as well. A manufacturer might find direct selling economically feasible for large-volume sales but inappropriate for small orders.

The producer must also understand how buyer specifications vary according to whether buyers perceive products as convenience, shopping, or specialty items (see Chapter 7). Customers for chewing gum, for example, are likely to buy the product frequently (even impulsively) from a variety of outlets. Buyers of home computers, however, carefully evaluate product features, dealers, prices, and postsale services. Buying patterns influence the selection of channels.

Buyers may be reached most effectively when producers use creativity in opening up new distribution channels. The Hanes Company, manufacturer of L'eggs pantyhose, concluded that hosiery customers would be attracted to a product they could buy conveniently while grocery shopping. As a result of L'eggs' innovative strategy, supermarkets are now included in the distribution channels for several brands of women's hosiery.

6. Ibid., p. 161.

FIGURE 9.8

Product sold through exclusive distribution (SOURCE: Reprinted by permission of Rolls-Royce Motor Cars Inc.)

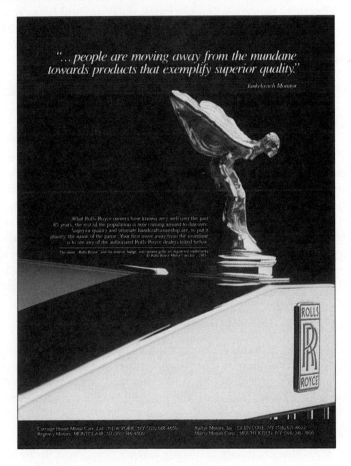

Product Attributes   Another variable in the selection of distribution channels is the product itself. Because producers of complex industrial products must often provide technical services to buyers both before and after the sale, these products are usually shipped directly to buyers. Perishable or highly fashionable consumer products with short shelf lives are also marketed through short channels. In other cases, distribution patterns are influenced by the product's value; the lower the price per unit, the longer the distribution chain. Additional factors to consider are the weight, bulkiness, and relative ease of handling the products. Producers may find wholesalers and retailers reluctant to carry items that create storage or display problems.[7]

Environmental Forces   Finally, producers making decisions about distribution channels must consider forces in the total marketing environment, that is, such issues as competition, ecology, economic conditions, technology, society, and law. Technology, for example, has made possible electronic scanners, computerized inventory systems, telemarketing, and teleshopping devices, all of which are changing present distribution systems and making it more difficult for technologically unsophisticated firms to remain competitive. Changing family patterns and the emergence of important minority consumer groups are necessitating new distribution methods for reaching market segments, sometimes resulting in nontraditional approaches that increase competitive pressures. Interest rates, inflation, and other economic variables affect members of distribution channels at every level. Environmental forces are numerous and complex and must be considered if distribution efforts are to be appropriate, efficient, and effective.

Behavior of Channel Members

The marketing channel is a social system with its own conventions and behavior patterns. Each channel member performs a different role in the system and agrees (implicitly or explicitly) to accept certain rights, responsibilities, rewards, and sanctions for nonconformity. And each channel member expects certain things of every other channel member. Retailers expect wholesalers to maintain adequate inventories and deliver goods on time. Wholesalers expect retailers to honor payment agreements and keep them informed of inventory needs. In this section we discuss several issues related to channel member behavior, including cooperation, conflict, and leadership. Marketers need to understand these behavioral issues to make effective channel decisions.

Channel Cooperation   There must be channel cooperation if each member is to gain something from other members.[8] Without cooperation, neither overall channel goals nor member goals can be realized. Policies must be developed that support all essential channel members; otherwise, failure of one link in the chain could destroy the channel.

---

7. Ibid., p. 254–255.
8. Wroe Alderson, *Dynamic Marketing Behavior* (Homewood, Ill.: Irwin, 1965), p. 239.

Channel Choices and Changes

In the fashion business, most better-quality clothing manufacturers market their products through department stores or specialty shops. Currently, however, the system is being challenged by a number of apparel makers, including Esprit, L. A. Gear, Murjani International, Guess?, and Cherokee. Dissatisfied with the performance of big retailers, these firms are opening their own outlets to gain greater control over the display and merchandising of their product lines. Although the producer-owned shops compete directly with department stores, the manufacturers insist that they are not out to undermine the big chains; they simply do not want their labels stuffed on racks with competing lines. In the long run, they say, the distinctive image created by distribution diversity will boost sales through both marketing channels.

It is a high-risk approach, but the distribution strategy of Esprit and other apparel firms demonstrates that when it comes to getting products into the hands of end users, all marketing channels are not created equal. The channel that works for product A may not work for product B, and a distribution system appropriate five years ago may be outmoded in today's marketplace. In other words, effective marketing demands continuous reevaluation of existing distribution channels, with adjustments made when necessary.

Some manufacturers find that existing distribution systems no longer meet market needs. A substantial loss in earnings, for example, made photographic equipment producer Vivitar aware of its tardiness in responding to consumer demand. After researching consumer needs in various markets, the company moved aggressively to open up new avenues of distribution and to supply distributors with the right product lines for their particular customers. Now Vivitar cameras, lens, and camera kits are available in several versions and price ranges through independent retailers, mail-order houses, department stores, mass marketers, drugstores, and armed services exchanges.

In other cases, marketing channels are changed as a matter of economy. Xerox—a firm that climbed to the top of the $10 billion copier business through the efforts of more than four thousand sales reps—decided that it might attract more doctors, lawyers, accountants, and other small-business customers by augmenting its direct sales force with retail stores. Over a three-year period, Xerox opened fifty-four stores, each selling Xerox products, computers made by other firms, and office supplies. Xerox soon found, however, that overhead and marketing costs ate into profits. Concluding that its products could be sold more efficiently through third-party retailers who would assume these operating expenses, Xerox scrapped its original plan, selling off most of its stores to a group of investors.

Since then, Xerox has made further changes in its channel structure. Before, the general copier-duplicator sales force was supported by specialists who sold printing systems, office systems, information processing systems,

There are several ways to improve channel cooperation. A marketing channel should consider itself a unified system, competing with other systems. This way, individual members will be less likely to take actions that would create disadvantages for other members. Similarly, channel members should agree to direct their efforts toward a common target market so that channel roles can be structured for maximum market effectiveness, which in turn can help members achieve their individual objectives. In addition, producers and intermediaries can perform reciprocal services. Miller Brewing Company, for example, licensed Carling O'Keefe, Ltd., Canada's fastest-growing brewer, to open up new markets in Canada for Miller beer. After just four months on the market, Miller products accounted for 9 percent of Canadian beer consumption. Because Canada restricts the importation of beer, the licensing agreement was the best way for Miller to enter this market; for its part, Carling O'Keefe was able to increase dramatically its market share.[9]

Channel Conflict

Although all channel members work toward the same general goal—distributing products profitably and efficiently—members may sometimes disagree about the best methods for accomplishing this goal. Each channel member wants to maximize its own profits while maintaining as much autonomy as possible. But if this self-interest creates misunderstanding about role expectations, the end result is frustration and conflict for the whole channel. For individual organizations to function together in a single social system, each channel member must clearly communicate and understand role differentiation.

Because channel integration and coordination are achieved through role behavior, channel conflict often results from role deviance or malfunction, either real or perceived. That is, members of the channel expect any given member of the channel to conduct itself in a certain way and to make a certain contribution to the total system. Wholesalers expect producers to take care of quality control and production scheduling, and they expect retailers to market products effectively. Both producers and retailers expect wholesalers to provide coordination, functional services, and communication. But if members do not meet role expectations—if wholesalers or producers fail to deliver products on time or the producers' pricing policies cut into the margins of downstream channel members, for example—there may be conflict.

9. John J. Cunon, "Beer Stocks with Yeasty Promise," *Fortune*, Oct. 17, 1983, p. 180.

At times, a channel member merely perceiving that another member is blocking goal attainment will cause tension and dissatisfaction. Adolph Coors Co., for instance, contends that for maximum taste retention its beer should be refrigerated at all times. To ensure that their products are shipped under the proper refrigeration, Coors exerts tight control over both the number of distributors that sell its beer and the territories those distributors can serve. In one instance, before Coors had selected distributors for Missouri, Coors beer was being shipped in that state by a distributor apparently more interested in boosting sales than in maintaining quality control. Coors expressed its displeasure publicly and encouraged consumers to boycott Coors products until the company could guarantee proper distribution.[10]

Channel conflicts also arise when dealers overemphasize competing products or diversify into product lines traditionally handled by other, more specialized intermediaries. In some cases, conflict develops because producers attempt to increase efficiency by circumventing intermediaries, as is happening in marketing channels for microcomputer software. Many software-only stores are establishing direct relationships with software producers, bypassing wholesale distributors altogether. Some dishonest retailers are also pirating software, or making unauthorized copies, thus cheating other channel members out of their due compensation. The ensuing suspicion and lack of trust are contributing to mounting tensions in software marketing channels.[11]

A manufacturer embroiled in channel conflict may ship late (or not at all), withdraw financing, use promotion to build consumer brand loyalty, and operate or franchise its own retail outlets. To retaliate, a retailer may develop store brands, refuse to stock certain items, focus its buying power on one supplier or group of suppliers, and attempt to strengthen its position in the marketing channel. Although there is no single method for resolving conflict in every situation, an atmosphere of cooperation can be re-established if two conditions are met. First, the role of each channel member must be specified. To minimize misunderstanding, all members must be able to expect unambiguous, agreed-on levels of performance from each other. Second, channel members must institute certain measures of channel coordination, which requires leadership and the benevolent exercise of control.[12]

Channel Leadership

Effective marketing channels depend on channel leadership. Channel leadership may be assumed by producers, retailers, or wholesalers. To assume leadership, a channel member must want to influence and direct overall channel performance. In addition, to achieve desired objectives, the leader must possess **channel power,** which is the ability to influence another channel member's goal achievement. As

10. Robert E. Weigand, "Policing the Marketing Channel—It May Get Easier," in *Contemporary Issues in Marketing Channels*, Robert F. Lusch and Paul H. Zinszer, eds. (Norman: University of Oklahoma Press, 1979), pp. 105–109.

11. Lanny J. Ryan, Gaye C. Dawson, and Thomas Galek, "New Distribution Channels for Microcomputer Software," *Business*, October–December 1985, pp. 21–22.

12. Adel I. El-Ansary, "Perspectives on Channel System Performance," in *Contemporary Issues in Marketing Channels*, Robert F. Lusch and Paul H. Zinszer, eds. (Norman: University of Oklahoma Press, 1979), p. 50.

Figure 9.9 shows, the channel leader derives power from two economic sources and five noneconomic sources of power including reward, expert, referent, legitimate, and coercive power. A channel leader gains reward power by providing financial benefits. Expert power exists when other channel members believe that the leader provides special expertise required for the channel to function properly. Referent power occurs when other members strongly identify with and emulate the leader. Legitimate power is based on a superior-subordinate relationship. Coercive power is a function of the leader's ability to punish other channel members.[13]

In the United States, producers assume the leadership role in many marketing channels. A manufacturer—whose large-scale production efficiency demands increasing sales volume—may exercise power by giving channel members financing, business advice, ordering assistance, advertising, and support materials. Because Tide, Bold, Bounty, Pampers, and other Procter & Gamble products are popular with consumers, Procter & Gamble has been able to structure channel policy and exert considerable control over the marketing of its products for many years. Many retailers have even allocated the most desirable position on their store shelves to Procter & Gamble products. Procter & Gamble has exercised coercive power as well, however, by restricting the supplies of its products under certain circumstances.[14] Coercion causes dealer dissatisfaction that is stronger than any impact from rewards, so the use of coercive power can be a major cause of channel conflict.[15]

Retailers can also function as channel leaders, and with the rise of national chain stores and private-label merchandise they are doing so increasingly. Small retailers as well may share in the leadership role when they command particular consumer respect and patronage in local or regional markets. Among large retailers, K mart, J. C. Penney, and Kroger base their channel leadership on wide public exposure to and consumer confidence in their products. They control many brands and sometimes replace uncooperative producers. As the channel leader in the marketing of its private-label power tools, paints, tires, motor oil, batteries, and appliances, Sears exercises two types of power. First, Sears' high-volume sales enable the company to offer profit reward to producers that supply the private-label goods; second, its marketing expertise means that many of the producers depend on Sears to perform all marketing activities.

Wholesalers assume channel leadership roles as well, although they were more powerful decades ago when most manufacturers and retailers were small, underfinanced, and widely scattered. Today, wholesaler leaders may form voluntary chains with several retailers to whom they provide bulk buying or management services or who market their own brands. In return, the retailers shift most of their purchasing to the wholesaler leader. The Independent Grocers' Alliance (IGA) is one of the best-known wholesaler leaders in the United States. IGA's power is based on the expert advertising, pricing, and purchasing knowledge it makes available to independent business owners. Other wholesaler leaders might also help retailers with store layouts, accounting, and inventory control.

13. Ronald D. Michman and Stanley D. Sibley, *Marketing Channels and Strategies* (Columbus, Ohio: Grid Publishing Co., 1980), pp. 412–417.
14. Bill Saporito, "Procter & Gamble's Comeback Plan," *Fortune*, Feb. 4, 1985, pp. 30–35.
15. John F. Gaski and John R. Nevin, "The Differential Effects of Exercised and Unexercised Power Sources in a Marketing Channel," *Journal of Marketing Research*, July 1985, p. 139.

FIGURE 9.9

Determinants of channel leadership (SOURCE: Ronald D. Michman and Stanley D. Sibley, *Marketing Channels and Strategies,* 2nd ed., Grid Publishing, Inc. Columbus, Ohio, 1980, p. 413.)

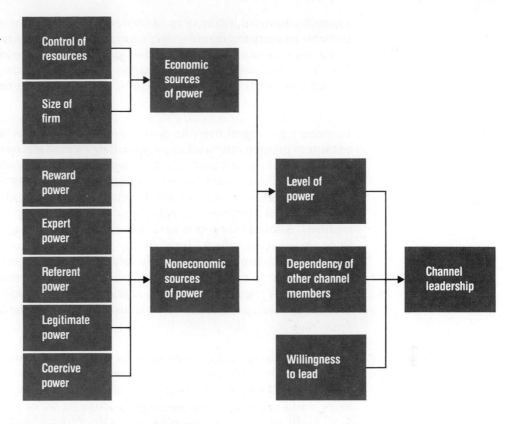

Legal Issues in Channel Management

The multitude of federal, state, and local laws governing channel management are based on the general principle that the public is best served when competition and free trade are protected. Under the authority of such federal legislation as the Sherman Antitrust Act, the Clayton Act, the Federal Trade Commission Act, the Robinson-Patman Act, and the Celler-Kefauver Act, the courts and regulatory agencies determine under what circumstances channel management practices violate this underlying principle and must be restricted and when these practices may be permitted. Although channel managers are not expected to be legal experts, they should be aware that attempts to control distribution functions may have legal repercussions. The following practices are among those frequently subject to legal restraint.

Dual Distribution   A producer that distributes the same product through two or more different channel structures, or sells the same or similar products through different channels under different brand names, is engaging in dual distribution.[16] The courts do not consider this common practice illegal when it promotes competition. For example,

---

16. Bert Rosenbloom, *Marketing Channels: A Management View* (Hinsdale, Ill.: Dryden Press, 1987), p. 91.

a manufacturer can legally open its own retail outlets where no other retailers are available to carry the manufacturer's products. But the courts view as a threat to competition a manufacturer who uses company-owned outlets to dominate or drive out of business independent retailers or distributors who handle its products. In such cases, dual distribution is held to be a violation of the law.

Restricted Sales Territories

To tighten its control over the distribution of its products, a manufacturer may attempt to prohibit intermediaries from selling its products outside designated sales territories. The intermediaries themselves often favor this practice because they can thereby avoid competition for the producer's brands within their own territories.

In recent years the courts have adopted conflicting positions with respect to restricted sales territories, a policy that for years many companies followed routinely. Although the courts have deemed restricted sales territories a restraint of trade among intermediaries handling the same brands (except for small or newly established companies), the courts have also stated that exclusive territories can actually promote competition among dealers handling different brands. At present, the producer's intent in establishing restricted territories and the overall effect of doing so on the market must be evaluated for each case individually.

Tying Contracts

When a supplier (usually a manufacturer or franchisor) furnishes a product to a channel member stipulating that the channel member must purchase other products as well, a **tying contract** exists.[17] Suppliers may institute tying arrangements to move weaker products along with more popular items, or a franchisor may tie the purchase of equipment and supplies to the sale of franchises, justifying the policy as necessary for quality control and protection of the franchisor's reputation.

A related practice is full-line forcing, in which a supplier requires that channel members purchase the supplier's entire line to obtain any of the products. Manufacturers sometimes use full-line forcing to ensure that intermediaries accept new products and that a suitable range of products is available to customers.

The courts accept tying contracts when the supplier alone can provide products of a certain quality, when the intermediary is free to carry competing products as well, and when a company has just entered the market. Most other tying contracts are considered illegal.

Exclusive Dealing

When a manufacturer forbids an intermediary to carry products of competing manufacturers, the arrangement is called **exclusive dealing.** A manufacturer receives considerable market protection in an exclusive dealing arrangement and may cut off shipments to an intermediary who violates such an agreement.

The legality of an exclusive dealing contract is generally determined by the application of three tests. If the exclusive dealing blocks competitors from as much as 10 percent of the market, if the sales revenue involved is sizable, and if the manufacturer is much larger (and thus more intimidating) than the dealer, the arrangement is considered anticompetitive.[18] If, on the other hand, dealers and

17. Ibid., p. 98.
18. Ibid., pp. 92–93.

customers in a given market have access to similar products, or if the exclusive dealing contract strengthens an otherwise weak competitor, the arrangement is allowed.

Refusal to Deal　　　For nearly seventy years the courts have held that producers have the right to choose the channel members with whom they will do business (and the right not to choose others). Within existing distribution channels, however, suppliers may not refuse to deal with wholesalers or dealers for resisting policies that are anticompetitive or in restraint of trade. Suppliers are further prohibited from organizing some channel members in refusal-to-deal actions against other members who choose not to comply with illegal policies.[19]

Summary

A channel of distribution, or marketing channel, is a group of individuals and organizations that direct the flow of products from producers to customers. In most channels of distribution, producers and customers are linked by marketing intermediaries, called merchants if they take title to products and functional middlemen if they do not take title. Channel structure reflects the division of responsibilities among members.

Channels of distribution are broadly classified as channels for consumer products or channels for industrial products. Within these two broad categories, different marketing channels are used for different products. Although some consumer goods move directly from producer to consumers, consumer product channels that include wholesalers and retailers are usually more economical and efficient. Industrial goods move directly from producer to end users more frequently than do consumer goods. Channels for industrial products may also include agents and/or industrial distributors. Most producers have dual or multiple channels so that the distribution system can be adjusted for various target markets.

Although intermediaries can be eliminated, their functions are vital and cannot be eliminated; these activities must be performed by someone in the marketing channel or passed on to customers. Because intermediaries serve both producers and buyers, they reduce the total number of transactions that would otherwise be needed to move products from producer to ultimate users. Intermediaries' specialized functions also help keep down costs. To survive, however, wholesalers must provide services more efficiently than alternative marketing institutions.

Intermediaries perform sorting activities essential to the development of product assortments. Through the basic tasks of sorting out, accumulating, allocating, and assorting products for buyers, intermediaries resolve discrepancies in quantity and assortment. The number and characteristics of intermediaries are determined by the assortments and by the expertise needed to perform distribution activities.

Integration of marketing channels brings various activities under the management of one channel member. Vertical integration combines two or more stages of

19. Ibid., pp. 96–97.

the channel under one management. Horizontal integration combines institutions at the same level of channel operation under a single management. The vertical marketing system is managed centrally and controlled for the mutual benefit of all channel members. Vertical marketing systems may be corporate, administered, or contractual.

A marketing channel is managed so that products receive appropriate market coverage. Intensive distribution strives to make a product available to all possible dealers. Selective distribution screens dealers to select those most qualified to expose a product properly. Exclusive distribution usually gives one dealer exclusive rights to sell a product in a large geographic area.

When selecting distribution channels for products, manufacturers evaluate potential channel members carefully. Producers also consider the organization's objectives and available resources; the location, density, and size of a market; buyers' behavior in the target market; characteristics of the product; and outside forces in the marketing environment.

A marketing channel is a social system in which individuals and organizations are linked by a common goal: the profitable and efficient distribution of goods and services. The positions or roles of channel members are associated with rights, responsibilities, rewards, and sanctions for nonconformity. Channels function most efficiently when members cooperate, but role deviance can lead to channel conflict. Effective marketing channels are usually a result of channel leadership.

Channel leaders have the ability to facilitate or hinder the attainment of other members' goals, and they derive this power from authority, coercion, rewards, referents, or expertise. Producers are in an excellent position to structure channel policy and to use technical expertise and consumer acceptance to influence other channel members. Retailers gain channel control through consumer confidence, wide product mixes, and intimate knowledge of consumers. Wholesalers become channel leaders when they have expertise other channel members value and coordinate functions to match supply with demand.

Federal, state, and local laws regulate channel management to protect competition and free trade. The courts may prohibit or permit a given practice depending on whether it violates this underlying principle. The Sherman Act, the Clayton Act, the Federal Trade Commission Act, the Robinson-Patman Act, and the Celler-Kefauver Act are important pieces of federal legislation applicable to distribution practices. The channel management practices frequently subject to legal restraint include dual distribution, restricted sales territories, tying contracts, exclusive dealing, and refusal to deal. When these practices strengthen weak competitors or increase competition among dealers, they may be permitted; in most other cases they are considered illegal.

Important Terms

Channel of distribution
Marketing channel
Marketing intermediary
Merchants

Functional middlemen
Retailers
Merchant wholesalers
Functional wholesalers

Dual distribution
Assortment
Sorting activities
Sorting out
Accumulation
Allocation
Assorting
Vertical channel integration
Vertical marketing system (VMS)
Horizontal channel integration
Intensive distribution

Selective distribution
Exclusive distribution
Channel power
Tying contract
Exclusive dealing

Discussion and Review Questions

1. Compare and contrast the four major types of marketing channels for consumer products. Through which type of channel is each one of the following products most likely to be distributed: (a) new automobiles, (b) saltine crackers, (c) cut-your-own Christmas trees, (d) new textbooks, (e) a sofa, (f) soft drinks?
2. "Shorter channels are usually a more direct means of distribution and therefore are more efficient." Comment on this statement.
3. Describe an industrial distributor. What types of products are marketed through industrial distributors?
4. Under what conditions is a producer most likely to use more than one marketing channel?
5. List several of the reasons that consumers often blame intermediaries for distribution inefficiencies.
6. How do the major functions intermediaries perform help resolve the discrepancies in assortment and quantity?
7. How does the number of intermediaries in the channel relate to the assortments retailers need?
8. Can one channel member perform all channel functions?
9. Identify and explain the major factors that influence decision makers' selection of marketing channels.
10. Name and describe firms that use (a) vertical integration and (b) horizontal integration in their marketing channels.
11. Explain the major characteristics of each of the three types of vertical marketing systems (VMSs).
12. Explain the differences among intensive, selective, and exclusive methods of distribution.
13. "Channel cooperation requires that members support the overall channel goals to achieve individual goals." Comment on this statement.
14. How do power bases within the channel influence the selection of the channel leader?
15. Under what conditions are tying contracts, exclusive dealing, and dual distribution judged illegal?

Cases

9.1 Marketing Channels for California Cooler[20]

When California Cooler was introduced commercially in the early 1980s, the low-alcohol mixture of white wine and fruit juice was in a category by itself. Since then, as many as 150 cooler brands, both wine- and malt-based, have been jostling for a share of the cooler market, but California Cooler remains near the top, second only to E&J Gallo Winery's Bartles & Jaymes. In 1986 California Cooler accounted for about 18 percent of the $1.7 billion cooler market; total sales of its citrus, orange, tropical fruit, and peach flavors were estimated at thirteen million cases.

For the past several years, California Cooler has been owned by Brown-Forman Beverage Company, producer of such brands as Southern Comfort and Jack Daniel's Tennessee Whiskey. The product originated in the 1970s on a California beach, when Michael Crete stirred up chablis and citrus juice in plastic tubs as an alternative to cold beer for his volleyball-playing friends. The cooler was the hit of the party, and during the next few years Crete kept experimenting with the formula, taking note of rising consumer interest in nonalcoholic and low-alcohol beverages such as Perrier water and wine. Convinced that his cooler had marketplace potential, Crete—then working as a beer and wine distributor—began to give his wine customers bottled samples. The customers asked for more, and by 1981 Crete decided to go into cooler production full-time.

Crete and a pal from high school, Stuart Bewley, each put up $5,000 to start the business. Operating first out of an abandoned migrant farm workers' camp and later from a vacant wine warehouse in Lodi, California, the two did everything themselves: mixing, bottling, capping, and labeling. Initially, they also handled distribution, supplying their accounts from the back of Bewley's 1953 pickup.

After five months, with their wine cooler sales totaling seven hundred cases, demand was beginning to exceed the fledgling company's modest production rate. Crete and Bewley hired one employee, paying him in stock, and decided to broaden their distribution network. Despite California Cooler's wine content, Crete and Bewley found beer wholesalers more receptive to the new product than wine distributors. For one thing, from the outset Crete and Bewley followed standard beer marketing practice by using foil-wrapped 12.7-ounce bottles (which resembled imported beers), four-pack cartons, and twenty-four-bottle cases. In addition, the cooler—clearly intended as a leisure-time beverage, not as a drink to be sipped with meals—was directed primarily to beer and soft-drink consumers, not to wine drinkers. Furthermore, the cooler sold better when chilled, and most wine distributors declined to work in the refrigerated cases ("cold boxes") where the beer wholesalers were predominant.

Eventually, several Adolph Coors Co. distributors agreed to carry California Cooler, and in 1982 sales zoomed to eighty thousand cases. Distributors liked

20. Based on information from Brown-Forman Inc., *1987 Annual Report*, pp. 8–10; "The Concoction That's Raising Spirits in the Wine Industry," *Business Week*, Oct. 8, 1984, p. 182; Harvey M. Lederman, "Cooler Success Freezes Out Most Competitors," *Advertising Age*, Oct. 6, 1986, p. S-1; Paula Schnorbus, "Cool(ers) and the Gang," *Marketing & Media Decisions*, May 1987, pp. 127–128; Richard Street, "How They Became Kings of Coolers," *Nation's Business*, October 1985, p. 68.

California Cooler because it could be warehoused and handled right alongside beer and required only some rearranging of products in the cold boxes. In addition, the new beverage, priced at just less than $1 a bottle and seldom discounted, offered distributors healthy profits. Whereas most beer lines earned California distributors margins of 20 to 22 percent, California Cooler yielded returns much closer to the 33 percent typical of wine products. California Cooler sold briskly and soon developed a following, although at that point the product had been advertised only through in-store displays and by word of mouth.

The use of outside distribution enabled Crete and Bewley to move their wine cooler into mass markets that otherwise would have been out of reach. The California distributors who handled the cooler serviced various establishments, from family owned liquor outlets to giant chain stores. After one year in outside distribution, California Cooler reached $1.4 million (180,000 gallons) in sales, and it was available throughout the state. The next year, after the company entered distribution in Texas and Arizona, sales were up to $26 million wholesale. Within two more years, California Cooler was being handled by a network of five hundred beer wholesalers and being distributed in forty-nine states.

The success of California Cooler did not go unnoticed in the wine industry, where recent sales had been flat and no new product had been introduced for years. Competing wine coolers quickly appeared on the market, including Bartles & Jaymes, Sun Country (Canandaigua Wine Co.), and Seagram's Coolers. (Sales volume of all coolers jumped 1900 percent within the first two years after the product was introduced.) Retailers finally accepted coolers as a permanent category, allocating the products more space on shelves, on floors, and in cold boxes. At the same time, however, retailers became more selective about the brands they carried, sometimes limiting their stock to the top five or six coolers plus one or two regional brands. The ensuing struggle for market share led producers to cut prices even more and to engage in heavy promotional spending.

By 1985, certain weaknesses in California Cooler's wholesale network became evident, particularly in comparison with Gallo's powerful distribution system. For example, although the beer distributors that carried California Cooler visited retailers frequently, their territories were smaller than those of wine distributors and frequently overlapped. A retailer might be contacted by a single Gallo distributor with one price but by several beer wholesalers, each quoting different prices. In addition, California Cooler's competitors could field larger, more experienced sales forces. California Cooler's sales volume continued to increase, but the cooler consistently lost market share. In 1986, California Cooler was forced into second place by Bartles & Jaymes.

Today, although acknowledging Gallo's marketing strength, Brown-Forman (which paid Crete and Bewley more than $55 million plus a percentage of future sales) insists that it has distribution muscle of its own. Brown-Forman recently reorganized and consolidated its sales territories for greater efficiency and strength in the distribution of all its products, including California Cooler. Predicting continued growth in the cooler market, Brown-Forman plans to position California Cooler as a year-round beverage instead of a hot-weather drink and will try to broaden the age segment targeted for the cooler. The company notes further that coolers now account for 25 percent of all wine products consumed in the United States and are beginning to enter foreign markets.

Questions for Discussion

1. When establishing marketing channels for a product such as California Cooler, what important factors must be considered?
2. Why did Crete and Bewley select beer distributors to be part of the marketing channel for California Cooler?
3. Is California Cooler being distributed through intensive, selective, or exclusive distribution?

9.2 Channel Selection for Cincinnati Microwave's Escort and Passport Radar Detectors[21]

For the past ten years, motorists with a penchant for exceeding posted speed limits have been beating a mail order path to the door of Cincinnati Microwave, maker of the Escort radar detector, a device that alerts speeding drivers to police radar signals up to four miles away.

The Escort came into being when electrical engineers James Jaeger and Michael Valentine analyzed the workings of a radar detector Jaeger had just purchased and saw how the model could be improved. The two fast-car buffs first offered their idea to Electrolert Inc., maker of the Fuzzbuster, the best-selling detector at that time. When Electrolert was uninterested, Valentine and Jaeger formed a partnership to manufacture their own detectors. Working out of Jaeger's basement on money Valentine's father had loaned them, the two entrepreneurs used sophisticated heterodyne technology to produce a detector with a microwave system to amplify and filter incoming signals, thereby increasing the detector's range and reducing the false alarms common in other models.

To attract an upscale clientele, Jaeger and Valentine introduced the Escort at $245, a price almost twice that of competing models. They also decided to sell the product exclusively by mail. The fledgling company could not afford retail distribution, and direct marketing would minimize risk because the detectors could be manufactured as orders arrived and need not be shipped until customers' checks or credit-card payments had cleared. In addition, mail order distribution would enable Jaeger and Valentine to expand the company without tying up borrowed capital in extensive inventory.

Jaeger and Valentine published a toll-free telephone number in *Road & Track* and *Motor Trend* and took turns answering the phone. At first orders trickled in at the rate of 250 or so per month. By the end of the first year Cincinnati Microwave had sold about 1800 units. Then *Car & Driver* magazine published results of

21. Based on information from Warren Brown, "Radar Detector Maker Thrives Despite Attacks," *Washington Post,* June 1, 1986, p. F1+; "Microwave Learning from Its Mistakes," *Cincinnati Enquirer,* Aug. 10, 1987, p. D6; "Microwave to Transfer Subsidiary's Product," *Cincinnati Business Courier,* March 8, 1987, p. 9; Michele Morris, "Dollar Signs on a Radar Screen," *Financial World,* Aug. 22-Sept. 4, 1984, pp. 80–81; "Radar's Foe," *Barron's,* Dec. 23, 1985, pp. 35–36+; Michael Rogers, "Speed Bumps Ahead for Cincinnati Microwave," *Fortune,* Apr. 28, 1986, p. 84; "Sales Drop Signals Problems for Cincinnati Microwave," *Cincinnati Enquirer,* Aug. 10, 1987, p. D1; Jolie B. Solomon, "Learning to Manage," *Wall Street Journal,* May 20, 1985, pp. 38C–40C; and Barry Stavro, "A License to Speed," *Forbes,* Sept. 10, 1984, p. 94+.

comparison tests on radar detectors, calling the Escort the most reliable and sensitive model on the market. The magazine also exposed the fraudulent claims of a competing firm whose entry was merely an Escort with a different exterior. Escort sales took off. Within six months Cincinnati Microwave was swamped with more than 1400 orders every month; at one point the company was 33 weeks behind in filling orders.

After a year of rapid growth, Cincinnati Microwave regained control of operations by expanding production, computerizing many functions, and hiring more personnel. (During one period the company was adding ten to twenty new employees per week.) Four years after its founding, Cincinnati Microwave's revenues had risen from $2.1 million to $57.1 million. During the start-up period Jaeger was in charge of production and Valentine handled marketing. Following disagreements over strategy, however, Jaeger bought out Valentine and his father, took the company public, and began to delegate management functions to other executives.

Meanwhile, with Escort sales still climbing, Cincinnati Microwave introduced the Passport, a detector one-fourth the size of the Escort. Priced at $295, the Passport offered the same capabilities as the Escort but was pocket-size and thus easier to transfer from car to car. Eventually the Passport replaced the Escort as the best-selling detector, and today the Escort and Passport together account for about 40 percent of the radar detector industry's $400 million in annual sales.

Since its founding the company has opened one retail outlet (at its Cincinnati, Ohio, headquarters) in an effort to attract truckers, a market segment sometimes difficult to reach through direct marketing. Mail order, however, continues to account for most of the company's business. A sales staff of thirty-five fields the 9000 calls that come in weekly. Most orders are shipped the next day. Cincinnati Microwave tries to hold the line on prices, choosing to increase its profit margins (about 20 percent after taxes) by reducing production costs instead. About 42 percent of Cincinnati Microwave's customers are repeat buyers, and customer service has been an important factor in the company's mail order success.

Cincinnati Microwave expects the demand for radar detectors to level off in a few years, and increased competition from low-priced radar detectors, including some Japanese models, already has slowed the company's growth. Accordingly, the company has begun to broaden its product mix and has even sent 25,000 Escort buyers an 18-page mail order catalog featuring Escort luggage. Also, Cincinnati Microwave purchased Wilson Microwave Systems Inc., a Nevada producer of satellite television receivers. But sales of the dishes dropped when pay-cable services began to scramble their signals; Cincinnati Microwave recently sold the operation. Cincinnati Microwave's latest product is the Guardian, an auto ignition interlock system designed to keep intoxicated drivers from starting their cars.

Questions for Discussion

1. Why did Cincinnati Microwave select a direct distribution channel for its radar detectors?
2. What are the advantages and disadvantages of using a direct channel of distribution for products such as radar detectors?
3. Evaluate Cincinnati Microwave's decision to open a retail outlet to serve truckers.

10. Wholesaling

O B J E C T I V E S

- ► To understand the nature of wholesaling in the marketing channel.
- ► To learn about wholesalers' activities.
- ► To understand how wholesalers are classified.
- ► To examine organizations that facilitate wholesaling.
- ► To explore changing patterns in wholesaling.

O*ne hundred companies,* fifty, ten—even the most seasoned observers of the food wholesaling industry disagree about how many wholesaling firms are likely to survive into the next century, given current trends toward consolidation. But one food wholesaler that clearly intends to be around in the year 2000 is Fleming Companies, Inc., an Oklahoma City distributor serving more than 4,500 food retailers in thirty-five states.

Fleming's annual $9 billion in sales make it the second-largest food wholesaler in the United States, just behind Minneapolis-based Super Valu Stores. Fleming attributes 60 percent of its growth in the past ten years to the acquisition of other wholesale firms, a policy that has boosted Fleming's buying power, provided economies of scale, and allowed the company to spread fixed costs. But with fewer than three hundred food wholesalers now remaining, Fleming is pursuing additional growth strategies to prepare for the day when acquisitions inevitably cease.

One such strategy is to increase productivity in its thirty-six distribution facilities (twenty-three full-line grocery houses, five general merchandise warehouses, five food-service operations, and three refrigerated warehouses; see Figure 10.1). Fleming uses engineered work standards against which warehouse employees measure their own performances to improve efficiency up to 40 percent. Where feasible, Fleming also uses mechanization to boost productivity, measured in tons moved per hour. For example, the company has experimented with computer-operated loading systems, and in the company's 400,000-square foot Oklahoma City warehouse, about 80 percent of all cases travel by conveyor belt.

Another of Fleming's growth strategies is to increase market share by offering a high level of customer service. Fleming has long assisted its retail buyers with store planning and development, financial and insurance services, consumer services, printing, advertising, and merchandising. Fleming was also one of the first wholesalers to track electronically the direct product profit of selected grocery items. Such information ultimately helps retailers determine which products are handled most economically. In addition, for years Fleming has provided an extensive line of private labels, including IGA, True Value (TV), and Piggly Wiggly, to give retailers a competitive tool against national brands.

Today, such retailer support services are being expanded, say company officials. For example, Fleming is developing a computerized program to give retailers demographic information by zip code for use in market segmentation. In addition, Fleming has established a Sales Training Institute covering topics such as electronic retail systems and retail counseling to equip its sales and service representatives to meet retailers' needs more effectively.[1]

I N THIS CHAPTER we focus on wholesaling activities (such as those performed by Fleming) within a marketing channel, viewing wholesaling as all exchanges among organizations and individuals in marketing channels, except transactions with ultimate consumers. First we examine the importance of wholesalers and their functions, noting the services they render to producers and retailers alike. Then we classify various types of wholesalers and facilitating organizations. Finally, we explore changing patterns in wholesaling.

The Nature and Importance of Wholesaling

Wholesaling includes all transactions in which the purchaser intends to use the product for resale, for use in making other products, or for general business operations. It does not include exchanges with ultimate consumers. Wholesaling establishments are engaged primarily in selling products directly to industrial, reseller, government, and institutional users.

A **wholesaler** is an individual or organization that facilitates and expedites exchanges that are primarily wholesale transactions. Although a wholesaler may occasionally engage in retail transactions (which are sales to ultimate consumers), it usually engages in wholesale transactions. There are more than 337,943 wholesaling establishments in the United States. Wholesale sales increased from $144 billion in 1960 to $1,159 billion in 1982, a 705 percent increase.[2] Retail sales, in comparison, rose from $216 billion in 1960 to $1,452 billion in 1986, almost a 700 percent increase.[3] Profits of wholesalers have also increased more rapidly than those of retail chain stores.[4]

Wholesalers perform marketing activities, such as transportation, storage, and information gathering, that are necessary to expedite exchanges. They provide marketing activities for organizations above and below them in the marketing channel. Most of the marketing functions we discuss in Chapter 1 can be performed by wholesalers.

1. Based on information from David Merrefield, "Efficiency Stressed at Fleming Depots," *Supermarket News,* May 12, 1986, pp. 1, 3A; David Merrefield, "Food-Field Growth Gets Fleming Focus," *Supermarket News,* May 5, 1986, pp. 1, 1A; David Merrefield, "Serve Bigger Units, Bolster Small Ones," *Supermarket News,* May 19, 1986, pp. 1, 4A; Patricia Natschke and David Merrefield, "Fleming's Best Deal?" *Supermarket News,* July 27, 1987, pp. 1, 10, 46; Vartanig G. Vartan, "Hopes for Food Wholesalers," *The New York Times,* Oct. 14, 1986, p. D12; Elliot Zwiebach, "Fleming's Focus," *Supermarket News,* Jan. 12, 1987, pp. 1, 8–9.
2. *Statistical Abstract of the United States,* 1988, p. 745.
3. Ibid., p. 512.
4. Walter H. Heller, "Business Outlook," *Progressive Grocer,* June 1983, p. 17.

The Activities of Wholesalers

More than 50 percent of all products are exchanged, or their exchange is negotiated, through wholesaling institutions. Of course, it is important to remember that the distribution of all goods requires wholesaling activities, whether a wholesaling institution is or is not involved. Table 10.1 lists major activities wholesalers perform. The activities are not mutually exclusive; individual wholesalers may perform more or fewer activities than Table 10.1 shows.

Services for Producers

Producers have a distinct advantage when they use wholesalers. Wholesalers perform specialized accumulation and allocation functions for a number of products, thus allowing producers to concentrate on developing and manufacturing quality products to match consumers' wants.

Wholesalers provide other services to producers as well. By selling a manufacturer's products to retailers and other customers and by initiating sales contacts with the manufacturer, wholesalers serve as an extension of the producer's sales force. Wholesalers also provide four forms of financial assistance. They often pay the costs of transporting goods; they reduce a producer's warehousing expenses by holding goods in inventory; they assume the losses from buyers who turn out to be poor credit risks; and when they buy a producer's entire output and pay promptly or in cash, they are a source of working capital. In addition, wholesalers are conduits for information within the marketing channel, keeping manufacturers informed about market developments and passing along the manufacturers' promotional plans to other middlemen in the channel.

Ideally, many producers would like more direct interaction with retailers. Wholesalers, however, usually have closer contact with retailers because of their strategic positioning in the marketing channel. For this reason, many producers have chosen to control promotion and influence the pricing of products and shifted transportation, warehousing, and financing functions to wholesalers.

Services for Retailers

In most cases, wholesalers specialize in selling. Wholesalers help their retailer customers select inventory. In industries where obtaining supplies is important, skilled buying is essential. A wholesaler who buys is a specialist in understanding market conditions and an expert at negotiating final purchases. The customer's buyer can thus avoid the responsibility of looking for and coordinating supply sources. Moreover, if the wholesaler makes purchases for several different buyers, expenses can be shared by all customers. Another advantage is that a manufacturer's salespersons can offer retailers only a few products at a time, but independent wholesalers have a wide range of products available.

By buying in large quantities and delivering to customers in smaller lots, a wholesaler can perform physical distribution activities—for example, transportation, materials handling, inventory planning, communication, and warehousing—more efficiently and can provide more service than a producer or retailer could with its own physical distribution system. As Figure 10.2 shows, Southland Distribution Center promises retailers to have most of the products in stock and to deliver them quickly. Furthermore, wholesalers can provide quick and frequent delivery even when demand fluctuates. They are experienced in providing the

TABLE 10.1

Major wholesaling
activities

ACTIVITY	DESCRIPTION
Wholesale management	Planning, organizing, staffing, and controlling wholesaling operations
Planning and negotiating supplies	Serving as the purchasing agent for customers by negotiating supplies
Promotion	Providing an outside (field) sales force and inside sales, advertising, sales promotion, and publicity
Warehousing and product handling	Receiving, storing and stockkeeping, order processing, packaging, shipping outgoing orders, and materials handling
Transportation	Arranging local and long-distance shipments
Inventory control and data processing	Controlling physical inventory, bookkeeping, recording transactions, keeping records for financial analysis
Security	Safeguarding merchandise
Pricing	Developing prices and price quotations on value-added basis
Financing and budgeting	Extending credit, borrowing, making capital investments, and forecasting cash flow
Management and merchandising assistance to clients	Supplying information about markets and products and providing advisory services to assist customers in their sales efforts

fastest delivery at the lowest cost because they provide time and place utility, which lets the producer and the wholesalers' customers avoid risks associated with holding large product inventories.

Because they carry products for many customers, wholesalers can maintain a wide product line at a relatively low cost. For example, a small Chrysler-Plymouth dealer in the Midwest discovered that it was cheaper to let wholesale suppliers provide automobile parts than to maintain a parts inventory at the dealership. Often wholesalers can perform storage and warehousing activities more efficiently, permitting retailers to concentrate on other marketing activities. When wholesalers provide storage and warehousing they generally take on the ownership function as well, an arrangement that frees retailers' and producers' capital for other purposes.

Classifying Wholesalers

Many types of wholesalers meet the different needs of producers and retailers. In addition, new institutions and establishments develop in response to producers and

FIGURE 10.2
Wholesaler promotes
the services it provides
to retailers (SOURCE:
The Southland Corpo-
ration)

retail organizations that want to take over wholesaling functions. Wholesalers adjust their activities as the contours of the marketing environment change.

Wholesalers are classified along several dimensions. Whether a wholesaler is owned by the producer influences how it is classified. They are also grouped as to whether they take title to (actually own) the products they handle. The range of services provided is another criterion used for classification. Finally, wholesalers are classified according to the breadth and depth of their product lines. Using these dimensions, we discuss three general categories or types of wholesaling establishments: (1) merchant wholesalers, (2) agents and brokers, (3) manufacturers' sales branches and offices.

Merchant Wholesalers

Merchant wholesalers are wholesalers that take title to goods and assume risk. These independently owned businesses, which make up about two-thirds of all wholesale establishments, generally buy and resell products to industrial or retail customers. A producer is likely to use merchant wholesalers when selling directly to customers would be economically unfeasible. From the producer's point of view, merchant wholesalers are also valuable for providing market coverage, making sales contacts, storing inventory, handling orders, collecting market information, and furnishing customer support.[5] Some merchant wholesalers are even involved in

5. Bert Rosenbloom, *Marketing Channels: A Management View* (Hinsdale, Ill.: Dryden Press, 1987), p. 63.

branding, packaging, and coordinating the marketing strategy of the products they carry. Certified Grocers of California, Ltd. is a typical merchant wholesaler.

During the past thirty years, merchant wholesalers have expanded their share of the wholesale market, despite stiff competition from other types of middlemen. Presently they account for slightly more than half (58 percent) of all wholesale revenues.[6] As a rule, merchant wholesalers for industrial products are better established and earn higher profits than consumer goods merchant wholesalers that usually deal in products of lower unit value and face more competition from other middlemen. Industrial products wholesalers also are more likely to have selective distribution arrangements with manufacturers because of the technical nature of many industrial products.

Merchant wholesalers go by many various names, including wholesaler, jobber, distributor, assembler, exporter, and importer.[7] They fall into one of two broad categories: full-service and limited-service. **Full-service wholesalers** are middlemen who offer the widest possible range of wholesaling functions. Their customers rely on them for product availability, suitable assortments, bulk-breaking, financial assistance, and technical advice and service.[8] **Limited-service wholesalers** are middlemen who provide only some marketing services and specialize in a few functions; producers perform the remaining functions, or the functions are passed on to customers or other middlemen. Figure 10.3 illustrates the different types of merchant wholesalers.

Full-Service Merchant Wholesalers Full-service wholesalers make numerous marketing services available to interested customers. Many large grocery wholesal-

6. *Census of Wholesale Trade,* May 1985, p. 207.
7. Bert Rosenbloom, *Marketing Channels: A Management View* (Hinsdale, Ill.: Dryden Press, 1987), p. 34.
8. Ibid., p. 63.

FIGURE 10.3

Types of merchant wholesalers

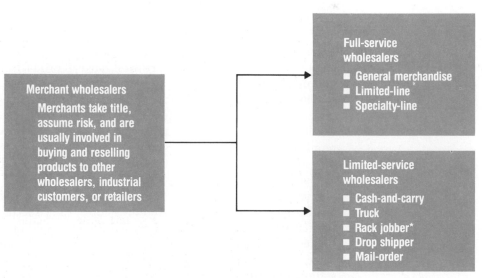

*Rack jobbers, in many cases, provide such a large number of services that they can be classified as full-service, specialty-line wholesalers.

ers, for example, help retailers with store design, site selection, personnel training, financing, merchandising, advertising, coupon redemption, and scanning. Although full-service wholesalers often earn higher gross margins than other wholesalers, their operating expenses are also higher because they perform a wider range of functions.

Full-service merchant wholesalers may handle either consumer products or industrial products and are categorized as general merchandise, limited-line, or specialty-line wholesalers.

General Merchandise Wholesalers **General merchandise wholesalers** are middlemen who carry a very wide product mix but offer limited depth within the product lines. They deal in such products as drugs, hardware, nonperishable foods, cosmetics, detergents, and tobacco. General merchandise wholesalers develop strong, mutually beneficial relationships with the neighborhood grocery stores, hardware and appliance shops, and local department stores that are their typical customers. The small retailers often obtain everything they need from these wholesalers; the wholesale firms, in turn, can count on these regular customers to buy all or most of their inventory. General merchandise wholesalers for industrial customers provide supplies and accessories and are sometimes called *industrial distributors* or *mill supply houses*.

Limited-Line Wholesalers **Limited-line wholesalers** are wholesalers who carry only a few product lines, such as groceries, lighting fixtures, or oil well drilling equipment, but offer an extensive assortment of products within those lines. They provide a range of services similar to those of full-service merchandise wholesalers. Limited-line wholesalers for industrial goods serve relatively large geographic areas and provide technical expertise; in consumer goods, they supply single- or limited-line retailers. Leading Edge Products, Inc., for example, is a limited-line wholesaler of computer equipment and supplies. The company markets printers, modems, screens, and its own private-label computer disks to the retailers who serve home- and office-computer users.

Specialty-Line Wholesalers Of all the wholesalers, **specialty-line wholesalers** are the middlemen who carry the narrowest range of products, usually a single product line or a few items within a product line. For example, wholesalers that carry shellfish or other food delicacies are specialty-line wholesalers. These wholesalers understand the specialized requirements of the ultimate buyers and offer customers detailed product knowledge and depth of choice. To provide sales assistance to retailers, specialty wholesalers may set up displays and arrange merchandise. In industrial markets, specialty wholesalers often are better able than manufacturers to give customers technical advice and service.

Rack jobbers are specialty-line wholesalers who own and maintain their own display racks in supermarkets and drugstores. They specialize in nonfood items—particularly branded, widely advertised products sold on a self-serve basis—that the retailers themselves prefer not to order and stock because of risk or inconvenience. Health and beauty aids, toys, books, magazines, hardware, housewares, and stationery are typical products rack jobbers handle. The jobbers send out delivery persons to set up displays, mark merchandise, stock shelves, and keep billing and inventory records; retailers need only furnish the space. Although most rack job-

TABLE 10.2

Various services that
limited-service mer-
chant wholesalers
provide

	CASH AND CARRY	TRUCK	DROP SHIPPER[a]	MAIL ORDER
Physical possession of merchandise	Yes	Yes	No	Yes
Personal sales calls on customers	No	Yes	No	No
Information about market conditions	No	Some	Yes	Yes
Advice to customers	No	Some	Yes	No
Stocking and maintenance of merchandise in customers' stores	No	No	No	No
Credit to customers	No	Some	Yes	Some
Delivery of merchandise to customers	No	Yes	No	No

[a] Also called *desk jobber*.

bers operate on consignment and take back any unsold products, some do not provide this full-service financing. Those who require cash payments from retailers at the time the shelves are stocked are sometimes viewed as limited-service wholesalers.

Limited-Service Merchant Wholesalers Limited-service merchant wholesalers take title to merchandise but perform fewer marketing functions than full-service wholesalers. In many cases they do not deliver merchandise, grant credit, provide marketing information, store inventory, or plan ahead for customers' future needs. Because they offer only restricted services, limited-service wholesalers are compensated with lower rates and thus earn smaller profit margins than full-service wholesalers.

Although certain types of limited-service wholesalers are few in number (and are not even categorized separately by the Census Bureau), they are important in the distribution of such products as specialty foods, perishable items, construction materials, and coal. In this section we discuss the specific functions of four typical limited-service wholesalers: cash-and-carry wholesalers, truck wholesalers, drop shippers, and mail-order wholesalers. (Table 10.2 is a summary of the services these wholesalers provide.)

Cash-and-Carry Wholesalers **Cash-and-carry wholesalers** are middlemen whose customers—usually small retailers and small industrial firms—will pay cash and furnish transportation or pay extra to have products delivered. In some cases, full-service wholesalers set up cash-and-carry departments because they cannot otherwise supply small retailers profitably. Cash-and-carry middlemen usually handle a limited line of products with a high turnover rate, such as groceries, building materials, electrical supplies, or office supplies.

Metro Cash and Carry, for example, operates a huge wholesale grocery outlet in Hillside, Illinois. Metro caters to small grocery, gas station, and convenience store owners who use the wholesaler as a source of stock for their own store shelves. To buy from Metro, customers must be business owners. They load products into flatbed carts, push them down eleven-foot aisles, and pay in cash or by check. The cash-only rule eliminates the need for a credit department, and transportation by customers eliminates the need for delivery persons and equipment.[9]

Cash-and-carry wholesaling developed after 1920 when independent retailers began experiencing competitive pressure from the large chain stores then emerging. Today cash-and-carry wholesaling offers wholesaler and customers alike advantages. The wholesaler has no expenditures for outside salespersons, marketing, research, promotion, credit, or delivery, and the customer benefits from lower prices and immediate access to products. Many small retailers whose accounts were refused by other wholesalers have survived through the services of cash-and-carry wholesalers.

Truck Wholesalers   **Truck wholesalers,** sometimes called truck jobbers or wagon jobbers, are middlemen who transport a limited line of products directly to customers for on-the-spot inspection and selection. These wholesalers are often small operators who own and drive their own trucks. Usually, truck wholesalers have regular routes and call on retailers and institutions to determine their needs.

Truck wholesalers play an important part in supplying small grocery stores with perishables such as fruits and vegetables, which other wholesalers often choose not to carry. They may also sell meat, potato chips, supplies for service stations, and tobacco products. Although truck wholesalers perform selling, promotional, and transportation functions, they are generally classified as limited-service wholesalers because they do not extend credit. As a result of their low-volume sales and wide range of customer services, their operating costs are high.

Drop Shippers   **Drop shippers,** also known as desk jobbers or carlot wholesalers, are intermediaries who take title to goods and negotiate sales but never take actual possession of products. They forward orders from retailers, industrial buyers, or other wholesalers to manufacturers and then arrange for carload shipments of items to be delivered directly from producers to customers. The drop shipper assumes responsibility for the products during the entire transaction, including the costs of any unsold goods.

Drop shippers are most commonly used in large-volume purchases of bulky goods, such as coal, coke, oil, chemicals, lumber, and building materials. Because these products, which are usually sold in carload quantities, are expensive to handle and ship relative to their unit value, extra loading and unloading is an added (and unnecessary) expense. One trend in this form of wholesaling is the use of more drop shipping from manufacturers to supermarkets. A drop shipment eliminates warehousing and deferred deliveries to the stores, and large supermarkets can sell entire truckloads of products rapidly enough to make drop shipping profitable.[10]

9. Eileen Norris, "Wholesaler Cashes in on Desire to Cut Costs," *Advertising Age,* Apr. 18, 1985, p. 32.
10. "Drop-Shipping Grows to Save Depot Costs," *Supermarket News,* Apr. 1, 1985, pp. 1, 17.

Because drop shippers incur no inventory costs and provide only minimal promotional assistance, they have lower operating costs and can pass along some of the savings to their customers. In some cases drop shippers do offer planning services, credit, and personal selling.

Mail-Order Wholesalers **Mail-order wholesalers** are middlemen who use catalogs instead of sales forces to sell products to retail, industrial, and institutional buyers. A convenient and effective method of selling small items to customers in remote areas, mail order enables buyers to send in their orders and receive shipments through United Parcel Service, the U.S. Postal Service, or common carriers. Wholesalers can thus generate sales in locations that otherwise would be unprofitable to service.

Wholesale mail-order houses generally feature cosmetics, specialty foods, hardware, sporting goods, business and office supplies, and automotive parts. They usually require payment in cash or by credit card, and they give discounts for large orders. Mail-order wholesalers hold goods in inventory and offer some planning services but seldom provide assistance with promotional efforts.

Agents and Brokers

Agents and brokers (see Figure 10.4) negotiate purchases and expedite sales but do not take title to products. They are **functional middlemen,** intermediaries who perform a limited number of marketing activities in exchange for a commission, generally 2 to 7 percent of a product's selling price. **Agents** are middlemen who represent buyers or sellers on a permanent basis. **Brokers** are middlemen that either buyers or sellers employ temporarily. Together, agents and brokers account for 10.6 percent of the total sales volume of all wholesalers.[11]

11. *Census of Wholesale Trade,* May 1985, p. 207.

FIGURE 10.4

Types of agents and brokers

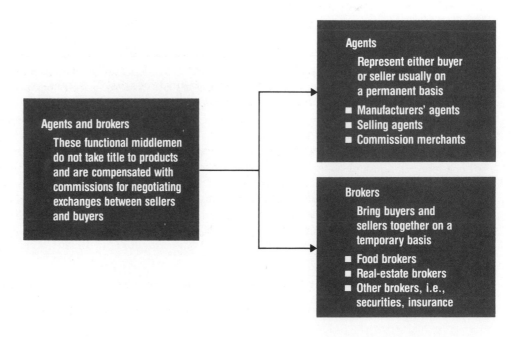

Although agents and brokers perform even fewer functions than limited-service wholesalers, they are usually specialists in particular products or types of customers and can provide valuable sales expertise. They know their markets well and often form long-lasting associations with their customers. Agents and brokers enable manufacturers to expand sales even when resources are limited, to benefit from the services of a trained sales force, and to hold personal selling costs to a predetermined percentage of sales.[12] However, despite the advantages they offer, agents and brokers are facing increased competition from merchant wholesalers, manufacturers' sales branches and offices, and direct sales efforts.

Here we look at three types of agents: manufacturers' agents, selling agents, and commission merchants. We also examine the brokers' role in bringing about exchanges between buyers and sellers. Table 10.3 summarizes these services.

Manufacturers' Agents **Manufacturers' agents**—who account for more than half of all agent wholesalers—are independent middlemen who represent two or more sellers and usually offer customers complete product lines. They sell and take orders year-round, much the same way a manufacturer's sales office does. Restricted to a particular territory, a manufacturers' agent handles noncompeting and complementary products. The relationship between the agent and each manufacturer is governed by written agreements explicitly outlining territories, selling price, order handling, and terms of sale relating to delivery, service, and warranties. Manufacturers' agents are commonly used in the sale of apparel and accessories, machinery and equipment, iron, steel, furniture, automotive products, electrical goods, and certain food items.

Although most manufacturers' agents run small establishments, their employees are professional, highly skilled salespersons. The agents' major advantages, in fact,

12. Edwin E. Bobrow, "Suddenly, An Urge to Boost Their Potential," *Sales & Marketing Management,* June 1982, Special Report.

TABLE 10.3

Various services agents and brokers provide

	BROKERS	MANUFACTURERS' AGENTS	SELLING AGENTS	COMMISSION MERCHANTS
Physical possession of merchandise	No	Some	No	Yes
Long-term relationship with buyers or sellers	Some	Yes	Yes	Yes
Representation of competing product lines	Yes	No	No	Yes
Limited geographic territory	No	Yes	No	No
Credit to customers	No	No	Yes	Some
Delivery of merchandise to customers	No	Some	Yes	Yes

are their wide range of contacts and strong customer relationships. These middle-men help large producers minimize the costs of developing new sales territories and adjust sales strategies for different products in different locations. Agents are also useful to small producers that cannot afford outside sales forces of their own because the producers incur no costs until the agents have actually sold something. By concentrating on a limited number of products, agents can exert an aggressive sales effort that would be impossible with any other distribution method except producer-owned sales branches and offices. In addition, agents are able to spread operating expenses among noncompeting products and thus can offer each manufacturer lower prices for services rendered.

The chief disadvantage of using agents is the higher commission rate (usually 10 to 15 percent) they charge for new-product sales. When sales of a new product begin to build, total selling costs go up, and producers sometimes transfer the selling function to in-house sales representatives. For this reason agents try to avoid depending on a single product line; most work for more than one manufacturer at a time. The Application on page 341 explores how large retailers' pressure to buy direct is a threat to manufacturers' agents.

Manufacturers' agents have little or no control over producers' pricing and marketing policies. They do not extend credit, and they may not be able to provide technical advice. They do occasionally store and transport products, assist with planning, and provide promotional support. Some agents help retailers advertise and maintain a service organization. The more services offered, the higher the agent's commission.

Selling Agents **Selling agents** are middlemen who market either all of a specified product line or a manufacturer's entire output. They perform every wholesaling activity except take title to products. Selling agents usually assume the sales function for several producers at a time and often are used in place of a marketing department. In contrast to other agent wholesalers, selling agents generally have no territorial limits and have complete authority over prices, promotion, and distribution. They play a key role in the advertising, marketing research, and credit policies of the sellers they represent, sometimes even offering advice on product development and packaging.

Selling agents, who account for about 1 percent of all wholesale trade, are used most often by small producers or by manufacturers who find it difficult to maintain a marketing department because of seasonal production or other factors. A producer having financial problems may also engage a selling agent, thereby relinquishing some control of the business but possibly gaining working capital.

To avoid conflicts of interest, selling agents represent noncompeting product lines. The agents play an important part in the distribution of coal and textiles, and they also sometimes handle canned foods, household furnishings, clothing, lumber, and metal products. In these industries, competitive pressures increase the importance of marketing relative to production, and the selling agent is a source of essential marketing and financial expertise.

Commission Merchants **Commission merchants** are agents who receive goods on consignment from local sellers and negotiate sales in large central markets. Most often found in agricultural marketing, commission merchants take possession of truckload quantities of commodities, arrange for any necessary grading or storage, and transport the commodities to auction or markets where they are sold. When sales have been completed, an agent deducts a commission plus the expense of making the sale and then turns over the profits to the producer.

Sometimes called factor merchants, these agents may have broad powers regarding prices and terms of sale, and they specialize in obtaining the best price possible under market conditions. Commission merchants offer planning assistance and sometimes extend credit, but they do not usually provide promotional support. Because commission merchants deal in large volumes and do not have to market their services aggressively, their costs are usually low. Their services are most useful to small producers who must get products to buyers but choose not to field a sales force or accompany the goods to market themselves. In addition to farm products, commission merchants may handle textiles, art, furniture, or seafood products.

Businesses—including farms—that use commission merchants have little control over pricing, although the seller can specify a minimum price and generally supervise the agent's actions by checking the commodity prices published regularly in newspapers. Large producers, however, must maintain closer contact with the market and therefore have limited need for commission merchants.

Brokers Brokers seek out buyers or sellers and help negotiate exchanges. In other words, brokers' primary purpose is to bring buyers and sellers together. Thus brokers perform fewer functions than other intermediaries. They are not involved in financing or physical possession, they have no authority to set prices, and they assume almost no risks. Instead, they offer their customers specialized knowledge of a particular commodity and a network of established contacts.

Brokers are especially useful to sellers of certain types of products who market those products only occasionally. Sellers of insurance, seasonal food products, financial securities, real estate, some kinds of machinery, and even ships may lack knowledge of potential buyers. A broker can furnish this information. The party who engages the broker's services—usually the seller—pays the broker's commission when the transaction is completed.

In the food industry—where brokers are most commonly found—**food brokers** are intermediaries who sell food and general merchandise items to retailer-owned and merchant wholesalers, grocery chains, industrial buyers, and food processors. Food brokers enable buyers and sellers to adjust to fluctuating market conditions, and the brokers provide assistance in grading, negotiating, and inspecting foods (in some cases they store and deliver products). Because of the seasonal nature of food production, the association between food broker and producer is temporary. Many mutually beneficial broker-producer relationships, however, are resumed year after year. Because food brokers provide a range of services on a somewhat permanent basis and operate in specific geographic territories, they can more accurately be described as manufacturers' agents. Several of the issues food brokers face are discussed in the Application on page 344.

| Manufacturers' Sales Branches and Offices | Sometimes called manufacturers' wholesalers, manufacturers' sales branches and offices resemble merchant wholesalers' operations. According to the *Census of Wholesale Trade*, these producer-owned middlemen account for about 9 percent of |

Buying Direct: A Threat to Manufacturers' Agents and Reps

About 100,000 persons across the country are employed as manufacturers' agents, according to the Manufacturers' Agents National Association—and these days many of the agents are worried. Recent action by a few large retailers to bypass agents and buy directly from producers has alarmed many agents, who see the move as a threat to their livelihood.

Most of the controversy has centered on Wal-Mart Stores, Inc., the Arkansas-based mass merchandiser. Although Wal-Mart officials do not acknowledge the policy publicly, agents who once sold regularly to the discount chain now find themselves unwelcome in Wal-Mart offices because Wal-Mart buyers are doing more and more of their business only with suppliers' top sales executives. Manufacturers of housewares, automotive supplies, and health and beauty aids all report that Wal-Mart has threatened to buy from other producers if firms refuse to sell direct.

Similar policies are in effect at Lowe's Companies, Inc., the nation's largest retailer of do-it-yourself building supplies, and at Builders Square, a home improvement chain owned by K mart Corporation. These retailers—which, like Wal-Mart, emphasize low prices—maintain that the no-middleman approach cuts costs. Manufacturers can charge less, they say, because they spend less on sales commissions, and the retailers' savings can then be passed on to customers. Builders Square also finds that with direct buying purchasing can be handled by fewer buyers, who can find out about new products at trade shows instead of through numerous sales calls.

Manufacturers' agents counter, however, that their commissions are a lower percentage of product cost than the expense of hiring, training, and compensating an in-house sales staff. A large independent agency may be able to furnish many more representatives than a single company could afford to hire on its own. Agents also argue that independent representatives are more highly motivated and thus cover more accounts and provide better service than company salespeople. The Organization of Manufacturers Representatives (OMR)—a group now conducting a public information campaign about the rights of producers to choose their own marketing methods—notes that the average independent rep outsells a company salesperson by 68 percent, according to U.S. Chamber of Commerce estimates. If manufacturers' agents were not more efficient and cost-effective in the first place, says OMR, they would not be used as widely as they are.

Manufacturers have responded in several ways to the demands of Wal-Mart and other no-rep retailers. Some flatly refuse to comply. So far Lee Pharmaceuticals has managed to avoid replacing its beauty aids reps despite Wal-Mart's two requests for direct sales. Some firms send their own executives along with the reps and even continue to pay the reps' commissions for a time, particularly where the reps have exclusive contracts to sell in certain territories. Some manufacturers insist on keeping the reps but offer to add extra customer services. And, of course, some producers are forced to go along.

Given Wal-Mart's powerful marketplace presence (it is now the second largest discounter in the country), manufacturers' reps fear that direct selling may become a trend. Although some manufacturers have contemplated legal action based on provisions of the Robinson-Patman Act, litigation is unlikely. Instead, reps will probably work to publicize their position through clients and trade associations. For now, however, the controversy will continue to grow.

SOURCES: Karen Blumenthal, "A Few Big Retailers Rebuff Middlemen," *The Wall Street Journal*, Oct. 21, 1986, p. 6; Arthur Bragg, "Wal-Mart's War on Reps," *Sales and Marketing Management*, March 1987, pp. 41–43; "Reps Riled Over Wal-Mart Ban," *DM*, January 1987, p. 12.

---

wholesale establishments and generate approximately one-third (31 percent) of all wholesale sales.[13]

Sales branches are manufacturer-owned middlemen selling products and providing support services for the manufacturer's sales force, especially in locations where large customers are concentrated and demand is high. They offer credit, deliver goods, give promotional assistance, and furnish other services. In many cases they carry inventory (although this practice often duplicates the functions of other channel members and is now declining). Customers include retailers, industrial buyers, and other wholesalers. Branch operations are common in the electrical supplies (Westinghouse Electrical Corp.), plumbing (Crane Co. and American Standard), lumber, and automotive parts industries.

Sales offices are manufacturer-owned operations that provide services normally associated with agents. As are sales branches, they are located away from manufacturing plants, but unlike branches, they carry no inventory. A manufacturer's sales offices or branches may sell products that enhance its own product line. For example, Hiram Walker, Inc., a liquor producer, imports wine from Spain to increase the number of products that its sales offices can offer wholesalers. United States Tobacco Company imports Borkum Riff smoking tobacco from Sweden to add variety to its chewing tobacco and snuff lines.

Manufacturers may set up sales branches or sales offices so they can reach their customers more effectively by performing wholesaling functions themselves. In other cases the specialized wholesaling services manufacturers need are not available through existing middlemen. In some situations, however, the manufacturer may bypass its wholesaling organization entirely—if, for example, the producer decides to serve large retailer customers directly. One major distiller bottles private-label bourbon for California supermarkets and separates this operation completely from the company's sales office, which serves other retailers.

13. *Census of Wholesale Trade*, May 1985, p. 207.

Facilitating Agencies

The total marketing channel is more than a chain linking the producer, intermediary, and buyer. **Facilitating agencies**—transportation companies, insurance companies, advertising agencies, marketing research agencies, and financial institutions—may perform activities that enhance channel functions. Note, however, that any of the functions these facilitating agencies perform may be taken over by the regular marketing intermediaries in the marketing channel (producers, wholesalers, and retailers).

The basic difference between channel members and facilitating agencies is that members perform the negotiating functions (buying, selling, and transferring title), whereas facilitating agencies do not.[14] In other words, facilitating agencies assist in the operation of the channel but do not sell products. The channel manager may view the facilitating agency as a subcontractor to whom various distribution tasks can be farmed out according to the principle of specialization and division of labor.[15] Channel members (producers, wholesalers, or retailers) may rely on facilitating agencies because they believe that these independent businesses will perform various activities more efficiently and more effectively than they themselves could. Facilitating agencies are functional specialists performing special tasks for channel members without getting involved in directing or controlling channel decisions. The following sections describe ways facilitating agencies provide assistance in expediting the flow of products through marketing channels.

Public Warehouses

Public warehouses are storage facilities available for a fee. Producers, retailers, and wholesalers may rent space in a warehouse instead of constructing their own facilities or using a merchant wholesaler's storage services. Many warehouses also order, deliver, collect accounts, and maintain display rooms where potential buyers can inspect products.

To use goods as collateral for a loan, a channel member may place products in a bonded warehouse. If it is too impractical or expensive to physically transfer goods into a warehouse, the channel member may arrange for a field public warehouser to verify that goods are in the member's own facilities and then issue receipts for lenders.[16] Under this arrangement, the channel member retains possession of the products but the warehouser has control. Many field public warehousers know where their clients can borrow working capital and are sometimes able to arrange low-cost loans.

Finance Companies

Wholesalers and retailers may be able to obtain financing by transferring ownership of products to a sales finance company, bank, or savings and loan association while retaining physical possession of the goods. Often called "floor planning," this form of financing enables wholesalers and retailers—especially automobile and applicance dealers—to offer a greater selection of products for

14. Bert Rosenbloom, *Marketing Channels: A Management View* (Hinsdale, Ill.: Dryden Press, 1987), p. 61.
15. Ibid.
16. Ibid., p. 62.

Issues Facing Food Brokers

By definition, the broker is the party in the middle—the intermediary between the buyer and the seller. To stay competitive, brokers must satisfy both the manufacturers whose products they sell and the wholesalers and retailers who are the brokers' customers, all while earning a fair profit for themselves. Brokering is thus something of a balancing act, and—not surprisingly—when various channel members view the broker's role differently, problems can arise.

One hotly debated issue among brokers and food retailers, for example, is how much brokers should assist retailers with shelving and store layout. Some retailers maintain that because display has a direct effect on product sales, resetting shelves should be part of the broker's job. With hundreds of new-product introductions annually, they say, broker assistance in developing store schematics is essential. Brokers argue, on the other hand, that time spent resetting shelves is time taken away from selling the manufacturer's products. They point out that resetting, originally introduced as an extra service to retailers, can consume as much as 25 percent of a broker's time. Some brokerage firms have established departments devoted entirely to placing products on shelves. This practice shifts the cost of resetting from the retailer to the broker, whose commissions must remain the same, and small brokerage firms find it difficult to compete.

On the positive side, however, sixteen grocery product marketers, including Nabisco Brands, Inc., California & Hawaiian Sugar, Coca-Cola Foods, and Star-Kist Foods, recently participated in a high-tech enterprise designed to improve relations between producers and brokers. Called NeoProbe, the project is a computerized compilation of food broker responses to questions about producers' strategies, policies, and sales personnel. The producers can use the database to find out how brokers rate their companies and identify areas for improvement. As a result of NeoProbe's findings, for example, James River-Dixie Marathon has begun developing a computerized retail shelf allocation program for brokers, Coca-Cola Foods changed its commission policy, and SCM Durkee Famous Foods revamped its sales manager training program to include more courses on broker operations.

The consultants who devised NeoProbe are encouraged by the high response rate and the improvements that followed. A second NeoProbe now in the works will give producers a similar opportunity to rate brokers. Participants believe that the program helps reinforce the idea that producers and brokers are a team working for mutual success.

SOURCES: Thayer C. Taylor, "The Food Industry's High-Tech Marriage Counselor," *Sales & Marketing Management,* July 1986, pp. 52–54; Elliot Zwiebach, "Lucky Execs Stress Cooperation Among Wholesalers and Retailers," *Supermarket News,* June 1, 1987, p. 6; Elliot Zwieback, "Retailers Want Broker Help in Store Resets," *Supermarket News,* Apr. 20, 1987, p. 1.

customers and thus increase sales. When a product is sold, the dealer may have to pay off the loan immediately. The products financed through floor plans are usually well-known, sell relatively easily, and present little risk.

Factors perform other financing functions. Factors are organizations that provide clients with working capital by buying their accounts receivable. Most factors minimize their own risks by specializing in particular industries, the better to evaluate individual channel members within those industries. Factors usually lend money for a longer time than banks. They may help clients improve their credit and collection policies and may also provide management expertise.

| Transportation Companies | Rail, truck, air, and other carriers are facilitating organizations that help manufacturers and retailers transport products. Each form of transportation has its own advantages.[17] Railroads ship large volumes of bulky goods at low cost; in fact, a "unit train" is the cheapest form of overland transportation for ore, grain, or other commodities. Air transport is relatively expensive but often preferred for shipping high-value or perishable goods. Trucks, which usually carry short-haul, high-value goods, now carry more and more products because factories are moving closer to their markets. As a result of technological advances, pipelines now transport powdered solids and fluidized solid materials as well as petroleum and natural gas. |

Transportation companies sometimes take over the functions of other middlemen. Because of the ease and speed of using air transportation for certain types of products, for example, air freight companies can eliminate the need of maintaining large inventories and branch warehouses.[18] In other cases, freight forwarders perform accumulation functions by combining less-than-full shipments into full loads and passing on the savings to customers—perhaps charging a carload rate rather than a less-than-carload rate.

| Trade Shows and Trade Marts | Trade shows and trade marts enable manufacturers or wholesalers to exhibit products to potential buyers and thus help the selling and buying functions. **Trade shows** are industry exhibitions that offer both selling and nonselling benefits.[19] On the selling side, trade shows let vendors identify prospects; gain access to key decision makers in current or potential customer companies; disseminate facts about their products, services, and personnel; and actually sell products and service current accounts through contacts at the show. The nonselling benefits include opportunities to maintain the company image with competitors, customers, and the industry; gather information about competitors' products and prices; and identify potential channel members.[20] Trade shows have a positive influence on other important marketing variables, including maintaining or enhancing company morale, product testing, and product evaluation. |

Trade shows can permit direct buyer-seller interaction and may eliminate the need for agents. For example, more than 35,000 graphic arts company owners and

---

17. George Fisk, *Marketing Systems* (New York: Harper & Row, 1967), pp. 609–610.
18. Ibid., p. 610.
19. Thomas V. Bonoma, "Get More Out of Your Trade Shows," *Harvard Business Review*, January–February 1983, pp. 75–83.
20. Bert Rosenbloom, *Marketing Channels: A Management View* (Hinsdale, Ill.: Dryden Press, 1987), p. 185.

managers convene every fall in Chicago to attend the McCormick Place Graphic Expo.[21] Companies exhibit at trade shows because of the high concentration of prospective buyers for their products. Studies show that it takes on average 5.1 sales calls to close an industrial sale but less than 1 sales call (0.8) to close a trade show lead. The explanation for the latter figure is that more than half of the customers who purchase a product based on information gained at a trade show order the product by mail or by phone after the show. When customers use these more impersonal methods to gather information, the need for major sales calls to provide such information is eliminated.[22]

Trade marts are relatively permanent facilities that firms can rent to exhibit products year-round. At these marts, such products as furniture, home decorating supplies, toys, clothing, and gift items are sold to wholesalers and retailers. In the United States, trade marts are located in several major cities, including New York, Chicago, Dallas, High Point (North Carolina), Atlanta, and Los Angeles. In Dallas, the Dallas Market Center, the Dallas Trade Mart, the Homefurnishing Mart, the World Trade Center, the Decorative Center, Market Hall, Info Mart, and the Apparel Mart are housed in six buildings designed specifically for the convenience of professional buyers. The Stiffel Company (see Figure 10.5) has permanent showrooms in trade marts located in Dallas, High Point, and New York.

Changing Patterns in Wholesaling

The distinction between wholesaling activities that any business can perform and the traditional wholesaling establishment is somewhat blurred. Manufacturers, retailers, and facilitating organizations perform wholesaling functions to bridge the gap between manufacturers and consumers. As pointed out, wholesaling functions can be shifted or shared but not eliminated; they have to be performed by someone or by some institution.

Wholesalers Gain More Power

New marketing methods that offer more service, lower prices, or both have triggered a move away from traditional retail or wholesale establishments. New stores such as discount warehouses and superstores are flourishing. As a result, in the food industry the lines of demarcation between wholesalers and retailers are not as sharp as they once were. Several large grocery wholesalers are now operating or planning large retail outlets; Super Valu Stores, Inc., Wetterau, and Fleming are large wholesalers expanding into the retail store business.[23] This trend has sparked a controversy about wholesalers positioning themselves in direct competition with their retail customers.[24] Wholesalers argue that their retail stores are not intended to break independent retailers but are a means of increasing volume.

21. *Official Show Directory*, Graphic Expo 81, September 1981, p. 9.
22. Richard K. Swandby and Jonathan M. Cox, "Trade Show Trends: Exhibiting Growth Paces Economic Strengths," *Business Marketing*, May 1985, p. 50.
23. Patricia Natschke, "Not Meant as Threat to Any Independent," *Supermarket News*, Sept. 24, 1984, p. 1.
24. Ted C. Wetterau, "A Case for Consolidation," *Progressive Grocer*, March 1985, p. 17.

The wholesale industry, as are most major industries, including retailing, is also experiencing a great number of mergers. The underlying forces influencing firms to consolidate or combine at the wholesale level seem to be economic conditions that create price-sensitive buyers and new advances in materials handling and communication technology.[25] Many retailers consequently have fewer supply choices. It is claimed that conflict of interest occurs when wholesalers become dominant in a market through mergers with other wholesalers and purchases or openings of retail outlets. Nevertheless, the trend toward more mergers and consolidations in wholesaling appears to be advancing.[26]

New Types of Wholesalers

The nature of future types of wholesaling establishments will depend on both the changing mix of activities that retailers and producers perform and wholesalers' innovative efforts to develop efficiency in the marketing channel.[27] The trend toward larger retailers—superstores and the like—will provide opportunities to as well as threaten wholesaling establishments. Opportunities will develop from the expanded product lines of these mass merchandisers. A merchant wholesaler of

25. "Trends Are Changing Grocery Wholesaling," *Supermarket News,* Mar. 18, 1985, pp. 1, 24.
26. David Merrefield, "Says Wholesaler Mergers Harm Independents," *Supermarket News,* Aug. 27, 1984, p. 1.
27. Bruce Mallen, "Functional Spin-Off: A Key to Anticipating Change in Distribution Structure," *Journal of Marketing,* July 1973, p. 22.

FIGURE 10.5

Stiffel lamps are shown in showrooms in three trade marts (SOURCE: The Stiffel Company)

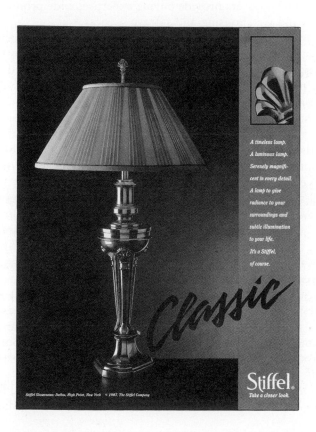

groceries, for instance, may want to add other low-cost, high-volume products that are sold in superstores. On the other hand, some limited-function merchant wholesalers may not be needed. The volume of sales may eliminate the need for rack jobbers, for example, who usually handle slow-moving products that are purchased in limited quantities. The future of independent wholesalers, agents, and brokers depends on their ability to delineate markets and provided desired services.

Summary

Wholesaling includes all transactions in which the purchaser intends to use the product for resale, for use in making other products, or for general business operations. It does *not* include exchanges with the ultimate consumers. Wholesalers are individuals or organizations that facilitate and expedite primarily wholesale transactions.

The Census Bureau counts more than 337,000 wholesaling establishments in the United States. Their sales volume is significantly higher than that of retail establishments. More than half of all goods are exchanged through wholesalers, although the distribution of any product requires that someone must perform wholesaling activities whether a wholesaling institution is or is not involved. For producers, wholesalers perform specialized accumulation and allocation functions for a number of products, letting the producers concentrate on manufacturing products. For retailers, wholesalers provide buying expertise, wide product lines, efficient distribution, and warehousing and storage services.

Various types of wholesalers serve different market segments. How a wholesaler is classified depends on whether the wholesaler is owned by a producer, whether it takes title to products, the range of services it provides, and the breadth and depth of its product lines. The three general categories of wholesalers are merchant wholesalers, agents and brokers, and manufacturers' sales branches and offices.

Merchant wholesalers are independently owned businesses that take title to goods and assume risk; they make up about two-thirds of all wholesale firms. They are either full-service wholesalers offering the widest possible range of wholesaling functions or limited-service wholesalers providing only some marketing services and specializing in a few functions.

Full-service merchant wholesalers include general-merchandise wholesalers, which offer a wide but relatively shallow product mix; limited-line wholesalers, which offer extensive assortments in a few product lines; and specialty-line wholesalers, which offer great depth in a single product line or in a few items within a line. Rack jobbers are specialty-line wholesalers that own and service display racks in supermarkets and drugstores.

There are four types of limited-service merchant wholesalers. Cash-and-carry wholesalers sell to small businesses, require payment in cash, and do not deliver. Truck wholesalers sell a limited line of products from their own trucks directly to customers. Drop shippers own goods and negotiate sales but never take possession of products. Mail-order wholesalers sell to retail, industrial, and institutional buyers through direct mail catalogs.

Agents and brokers, sometimes called functional middlemen, negotiate purchases and expedite sales but do not take title to products. They are usually specialists and provide valuable sales expertise. Agents represent buyers or sellers on a permanent basis. Manufacturers' agents offer customers the complete product lines of two or more sellers; selling agents market a complete product line or a producer's entire output and perform every wholesaling function except taking title to products; commission merchants receive goods on consignment from local sellers and negotiate sales in large central markets. Brokers, such as food brokers, negotiate exchanges between buyers and sellers on a temporary basis.

Manufacturers' sales branches and offices are vertically integrated units owned by manufacturers. Branches sell products and provide support services for the manufacturer's sales force in a given location. Sales offices carry no inventory and function much as agents do.

Facilitating agencies do not buy, sell, or take title but perform certain wholesaling functions. They include public warehouses, finance companies, transportation companies, and trade shows and trade marts. In some instances, these organizations eliminate the need for a wholesaling establishment.

As producers, retailers, and other institutions take over certain wholesaling functions, traditional wholesalers may become direct competitors of their suppliers and retail customers. The future of wholesaling establishments will depend on the changing activities of retailers and producers and on the innovative efforts of wholesalers to increase efficiency in the marketing channel.

Important Terms

Wholesaling	Agents
Wholesalers	Brokers
Merchant wholesalers	Manufacturers' agents
Full-service wholesalers	Selling agents
Limited-service wholesalers	Commission merchants
General merchandise wholesalers	Food brokers
Limited-line wholesalers	Sales branches
Specialty-line wholesalers	Sales offices
Rack jobbers	Facilitating agencies
Cash-and-carry wholesalers	Public warehouses
Truck wholesalers	Trade shows
Drop shippers	Trade marts
Mail-order wholesalers	
Functional middlemen	

Discussion and Review Questions

1. Is there a distinction between wholesalers and wholesaling? If so, what is it?
2. Why do wholesaling establishments (excluding retailers' wholesaling activities) have a sales volume greater than that of retailers?
3. Would it be appropriate for a wholesaler to stock both interior wall paint and office supplies? Under what circumstances would this product mix be logical?

4. What services do wholesalers provide to producers and retailers?
5. Drop shippers take title to products but do not accept physical possession. Commission merchants take physical possession of products but do not accept title. Defend the logic of classifying drop shippers as wholesale merchants and commission merchants as agents.
6. What are the advantages of using agents to replace merchant wholesalers? What are the disadvantages?
7. What, if any, are the differences in the marketing functions manufacturers' agents and selling agents perform?
8. Why are manufacturers' sales offices and branches classified as wholesalers? Which independent wholesalers are replaced by manufacturers' sales branches? Which independent wholesalers are replaced by manufacturers' sales offices?
9. "Public warehouses are really wholesale establishments." Comment on this statement.
10. Discuss the role of facilitating organizations. Identify three facilitating organizations and explain how each type performs this role.
11. Is there a trend toward bypassing wholesalers? What environmental variables favor direct distribution by manufacturers?

Cases

10.1 Anheuser-Busch and Its Wholesalers[28]

St. Louis-based Anheuser-Busch, Inc. is the world's largest brewing company. Last year Anheuser-Busch increased its market share to 38 percent of total brewing industry sales, producing more than one out of every three beers sold in the United States. Its products include Budweiser, Michelob, Natural Light, Michelob Light, Bud Light, and Michelob Classic Dark. Brewery sales last year were $6.39 billion.

In the United States and the Caribbean, Anheuser-Busch distributes its beers through a network of approximately 960 independently owned wholesalers and 10 company-owned wholesale operations—a distribution system considered the strongest in the brewing industry. Anheuser-Busch's independent wholesalers employ approximately 30,000 people, more than 18,000 of whom work in direct beer marketing positions. (One Anheuser-Busch distributor is Frank Sinatra, who owns Somerset Distributing in California.) Company-owned distributorships employ about 1,600 people. Wholesalers handle volumes of 870 barrels to 1.1 million barrels annually.

Anheuser-Busch's effective distribution system is bolstered by a variety of cooperative arrangements with wholesalers. For example, the company tries to make certain that its beers are sold to wholesalers FOB (free on board) from the "least cost" brewery. That is, the wholesaler must supply or pay for transportation

28. Based on information from Anheuser-Busch Cos., Inc., *Annual Report,* 1986; Anheuser-Busch Cos., Inc., *Fact Book,* 1986–87; Anheuser-Busch, Inc. Distribution Fact Sheet, 1984; Michael Oneal, "Anheuser-Busch: The Scandal May Be Small Beer After All," *Business Week,* May 11, 1987, pp. 72–73; Patricia Sellers, "How Busch Wins in a Doggy Market," *Fortune,* June 22, 1987, pp. 99–100.

from the brewery that can provide the product at the lowest shipping cost. But if a product must be shipped at a higher cost—perhaps because the nearest brewery does not produce a specific package—Anheuser-Busch compensates the wholesaler for the difference in cost. The company's Traffic Department also helps wholesalers arrange transportation. Twenty years ago, Anheuser-Busch introduced its Wholesaler Equity Program, recently expanded to give distributors exclusive territories where permitted by law. A Wholesaler Advisory Panel of a cross section of wholesalers and top company managers meets regularly to discuss and act on industry issues.

In addition, the ten distributorships in the company's Wholesale Operations Division serve as a testing ground for programs that are then made available to independent wholesalers. In one case, the company developed computer software to help wholesalers make the most of retail shelf space. Anheuser-Busch wholesalers can also get group discounts on computers, trucks, and insurance and can take company courses ranging from Draught Beer Basics to Dynamics of Business Reading. To build morale among wholesalers, Anheuser-Busch puts top executives in charge of its biggest-volume states (president August Busch III handles California personally). Every three years, the company throws a Las Vegas–style wholesalers' convention, with appearances by such stars as Paul Newman, Gene Kelly, Bob Hope, and Lou Rawls.

Anheuser-Busch's most-evident support for its distributors is its backing of special promotions: sporting events, college parties, rodeos, and festivals. The company may pay as much as half the cost for these events, in cooperation with local wholesalers. To improve sales of Michelob Light, for example, a local New York distributor decided to hold a Michelob Light Concentration Day. On that day, only Michelob Light was delivered to retailers. Tuxedo-clad representatives from St. Louis headquarters rode the trucks, accompanied by two Playboy Playmates with free photos for retailers. The distributorship sold 21,000 cases of Michelob Light in one day (instead of the normal twenty days), and Anheuser-Busch is now staging Concentration Days in other cities.

The company has helped support everything from Chicago's Lithuanian festival to the Iron Man Triathlon in Hawaii. Just before Coors moved into the New York–New Jersey market, Anheuser-Busch supplied its wholesalers with a three-hundred-page "Coors Defense Plan," along with funding for promotional events that might have attracted Coors sponsorship. Coors was unable to reach an agreement with any major beer wholesalers and had to distribute instead through a soft-drink bottler.

For distributors, however, the price of such generous corporate support is unquestioned loyalty. Anheuser-Busch asks more of its wholesalers than any other brewer. Each year all distributors are requested to contribute ideas for local promotions—one for every brand. Furthermore, although the distributors are independent business owners, technically free to sell whatever they choose, Anheuser-Busch takes a dim view of wholesalers who decide to carry a competing product. When a Florida distributorship added Heineken and Amstel Light to its line, twenty-two Anheuser-Busch field managers swarmed in and rode the company's trucks for a week, and the distributor and his general manager were summoned to St. Louis for a meeting with top management.

Anheuser-Busch defends its policies, maintaining that the company will not allow "greedy" wholesalers to jeopardize market share. And although Anheuser-

Busch has a firm first-place lead over all other brewers, the company is taking no chances. Anheuser-Busch has launched several nonbeer beverages in recent years, including L.A. (low-alcohol beer), Dewey Stevens (a low-calorie wine cooler aimed at women), and Zeltzer Seltzer (a flavored sparkling water). So far these products have not been marketed aggressively, and they may never be highly profitable. But with rival brewers entering these new markets, Anheuser-Busch wants to be able to supply its distributors with competing products. Along with its share of the market, say Anheuser-Busch executives, the company intends to maintain its share of the wholesalers.

Questions for Discussion

1. Are Anheuser-Busch's wholesalers merchant wholesalers? Explain your answer. Are they full-service or limited-service wholesalers? Why?
2. Why does Anheuser-Busch give its wholesale distributors so much support?
3. Why has Anheuser-Busch introduced nonbeer products? Evaluate this practice.

10.2   Ralston Purina[29]

Ralston Purina Company, founded in 1894 and headquartered in St. Louis, is the largest producer of dry dog foods and dry and soft-moist cat foods in the world. The company also produces canned seafood, specialty foods, and branded and private-label cereals. Last year Ralston Purina acquired its first nonfood business, the Eveready and Energizer lines of household batteries, and is now the world's largest manufacturer of dry cell battery products. Since 1984, the company has operated Continental Baking Company, the largest wholesale producer of fresh bakery products in the United States. A major producer of isolated soy protein, Ralston Purina also produces commercial livestock and poultry feed for international markets.

Ralston's Grocery Product Group comprises pet foods and consumer foods. Last year Ralston Purina held 27 percent of the $5.4 billion U.S. pet food market, with its Purina Dog Chow, Chuck Wagon, Butcher's Blend, Purina Cat Chow, Tender Vittles, Happy Cat, Puppy Chow, Happy Kitten, Happy Dog, and Hearty Chews brands. The Grocery Product Group also manufactures and sells Chex cereals, crackers, and cookies. Ralston's grocery products are marketed primarily in the United States, through direct sales forces, to grocery chains, wholesalers, industrial buyers, and other retailers. Another product within Ralston's grocery category is Chicken of the Sea tuna, which is sold primarily to grocery stores in the United States through a network of independent food brokers.

Ralston views its newly acquired Eveready Battery Company, which holds a 60 percent share of the U.S. battery market, as diversification into a product line

29. Based on information from Ralston Purina Company, *Annual Report,* 1983, 1984, 1985, 1986; Robert Johnson, "Ralston's Proposed Battery Acquisition Complements Its Lines, Bolsters Defenses," *Wall Street Journal,* Apr. 9, 1986, p. 27; Michael J. McCarthy and Paul Hemp, "Ralston to Sell U.S. Feed Line to Unit of BP," *Wall Street Journal,* July 11, 1986, p. 4; Kenneth Dreyfack and James R. Norman, "Ralston Looks Like Top Dog in the Fight For Gaines," *Business Week,* Oct. 6, 1986, pp. 36–37.

closely related to grocery products but less seasonal and less price sensitive. Because batteries are often sold in supermarkets, Ralston expects its marketing experience with other consumer grocery products to be applicable. Eveready operates forty-three plants worldwide serving 125 countries, and Ralston plans extensive distribution through grocery stores, mass merchandising, and other outlets.

Through its Continental Baking Company, Ralston operates forty-seven bakeries nationwide; fresh products are delivered daily to major retailers on more than seven thousand individual routes. This extensive network is part of the vertically integrated distribution channel of Continental, which owns and controls sales branches or offices. Continental's bread products include Wonder and Home Pride breads, Beefsteak rye breads, English muffins, Italian breads, and dinner rolls. The Breakfast Bake Shop line encompasses a wide range of sweet rolls and donuts, and the Hostess line of snack cakes includes Twinkies, Ding Dongs, Sno Balls, Suzy Q, and Choco-diles brands as well as cupcakes and fruit pies.

For more than ninety years Ralston Purina has been the industry leader in producing high-quality feeds for swine, poultry, dairy and beef cattle, horses, and other animals. Although Ralston sold its U.S. animal feed business last year, the company continues to operate fifty-eight facilities in fourteen countries. Its agricultural products include Chow brand formula feeds, poultry products, and animal health products, which are distributed primarily through a network of more than 3,200 dealers outside the United States. The dealers act as industrial distributors, taking title to products, assuming risk, and directing local marketing efforts aimed at agricultural buyers. Ralston competes with other large feed manufacturers, cooperatives and single-owner establishments, and government feed companies in other countries.

Ralston Purina markets its food protein and industrial polymer products chiefly through direct sales forces in the United States and through brokers and distributors in international markets. This dual distribution approach illustrates the necessity of matching the marketing channel with the environment. A direct vertically integrated marketing channel is most effective in the United States, where Ralston Purina has expertise and direct access. To reach international markets, on the other hand, Ralston needs the expertise and local contacts that brokers and other intermediaries familiar with individual countries can best provide.

Questions for Discussion

1. Why does Ralston Purina use so many diverse marketing intermediaries to distribute its many products?
2. Why is a direct sales force used for most grocery products but food brokers are used for tuna products?
3. How does Continental Baking's vertically integrated distribution system differ from other distribution networks at Ralston Purina?

11. Retailing

OBJECTIVES

▶ To understand the purpose and function of retailers in the marketing channel.

▶ To classify retail stores.

▶ To understand nonstore retailing and franchising.

▶ To examine types of planned shopping centers.

▶ To learn about strategic issues in retailing, including the wheel of retailing hypothesis.

*S*omewhere in the world, two new green and white Benetton stores will open their doors today. Two others opened yesterday, and if the Italian sportswear manufacturer keeps up its present rate of growth, two more will open tomorrow, and two more the day after. With four thousand stores in sixty countries, including six hundred in the United States, family run Benetton is nicknamed the "McDonald's of fashion." But the fifteen- to thirty-year-olds in Benetton's target market continue to snap up the company's brightly colored knitwear, and with the help of high-tech manufacturing and distribution systems, Benetton plans to intensify its presence in old and new markets alike (see Figure 11.1).

Although Benetton is now the largest knitwear manufacturer and consumer of virgin wool in the world, the company's beginnings were modest. In the mid-1950s, Luciano Benetton decided to try to sell the striking sweaters his younger sister Giuliana knitted for family and friends in her spare time. Sales of Giuliana's creations took off; in 1965 Benetton was incorporated, with Luciano heading the company, Giuliana the chief designer, and brothers Gilberto and Carlo in charge of finance and production, respectively. The first factory was built that same year, and when the Benettons hit on the idea of selling their products through small, exclusive retail outlets, the prototype Benetton store was born.

Benetton owes much of its rapid rise to the skillful marketing of color—lots of colors. Designed to let the merchandise speak for itself, the bright, uncluttered Benetton shops pull in customers with distinctive window displays that highlight two or three basic colors. Inside, floor-to-ceiling chrome shelves are stacked with stylish clothing in a wide range of vivid hues. Benetton itself owns only a

FIGURE 11.1

Advertisement for
Benetton (SOURCE:
Benetton)

handful of the stores; most are franchised to individual owners, who pay no franchise fees but simply agree to buy all their merchandise from Benetton and uphold the established image.

Benetton also owes its success to production techniques that allow for quick response to market trends and fads that may appear midseason. Instead of manufacturing clothing lines several months in advance, as is common practice within the fashion industry, Benetton uses a "just-in-time" system of production. Individual Benetton stores evaluate trends, decide which styles and colors to reorder, and relay the information to Italy. There, Benetton factories—mostly small, independent subcontractors—quickly dye untreated gray wool knitwear in the specified colors, resulting in order turnaround time of only two to six weeks. Computerized inventory control ties the whole system together. Thus, by letting consumer demand determine product offerings, Benetton cuts the inventory and production costs associated with product variety, minimizes its fashion risk, and stabilizes its operation while increasing its flexibility.

Although Benetton is most closely identified with sweaters, its collections also include shirts and jeans (last year the company bought a North Carolina factory to accommodate U.S. demand for cotton and denim products). Benetton is also experimenting with T-shirts, sunglasses, watches, cosmetics, and perfume and has opened a number of Benetton 012 stores to carry children's wear. In addition, the company plans to open a new chain of Sisley stores, which will offer sophisticated, higher quality clothing in a more traditional setting.[1]

BENETTON IS SUCCESSFUL because it offers products that customers want and uses effective marketing efforts. Marketing methods that satisfy consumers serve well as the guiding philosophy of retailing. Retailers are an important link in the marketing channel because they are both marketers and customers for producers and wholesalers. They perform many marketing activities, such as buying, selling, grading, risk taking, and developing information about consumers' wants. Of all marketers, retailers are the most visible to ultimate consumers. They are in a strategic position to gain feedback from consumers and to pass ideas along to producers and intermediaries in the marketing channel. Retailing is an extraordinarily dynamic area of marketing.

In this chapter we examine the nature of retailing and its importance in providing goods and services to consumers. We discuss the major types of retail stores—department stores, mass merchandisers, and specialty retailers—and describe several forms of nonstore retailing. We also look at franchising, a retailing form that continues to grow in popularity. Following a discussion of planned shopping centers, we present several strategic issues in retailing: location, product assortment, customer services, atmospherics, store image, scrambled merchandising, and the wheel of retailing.

The Nature of Retailing

Retailing includes all transactions in which the buyer intends to consume the product through personal, family, or household use. The buyers in retail transactions are ultimate consumers. A **retailer** is an organization in which most of its sales are retail transactions. Although most retailers' sales are to consumers, some nonretail transactions do occur with other businesses. Retailing activities usually take place in a store or in a service establishment, but telephone selling, vending machines, and mail-order catalogs enable retail exchanges to occur outside stores.

It is fairly common knowledge that retailing is important to the national economy. The *Statistical Abstract of the United States* indicates that approximately

1. Based on information from Stephen Battaglio, "Benetton Matures with Sisley Shops," *Adweek's Marketing Week,* Sept. 22, 1986, p. 4; Rose Brady, "McSweater: The Benetton-ing of America," *Working Woman,* May 1986, pp. 114–116; Andrea Lee, "Being Everywhere," *The New Yorker,* Nov. 10, 1986, pp. 53–54; William C. Symonds, "Benetton Is Betting on More of Everything," *Business Week,* Mar. 23, 1987, p. 93.

1,330,000 retailers are operating in the United States.[2] This number has been relatively constant for the past twenty years, but sales volume has increased more than four times, implying that the average size of stores has increased. Most personal income is spent in retail stores, and nearly one out of every seven persons employed in the United States works in a retail store.

By providing assortments of products that match consumers' wants, retailers create place, time, and possession utilities. They move products from wholesalers or producers to a location accessible to consumers (place utility). They make inventories or product stocks available when consumers want them (time utility). And they facilitate the transfer of ownership or use of a product to consumers (possession utility).

In the case of services such as hair styling, dry cleaning, and automotive repair, retailers themselves develop most of the product utilities. The services of such retailers provide aspects of form utility associated with the production process. Retailers of services usually have more direct contact with consumers and more opportunity to alter the product in the marketing mix. Compared with physical goods, the unique aspects of services are that (1) their intangible nature makes consumers' choices more difficult; (2) the retailer and the product are inseparable, which tends to localize service retailing and give consumers fewer choices; (3) the perishability of services prevents storage and increases the risk associated with the retail operation; and (4) the heterogeneity of the delivery process makes delivery hard to standardize and quality control difficult.[3] (See Chapter 21 for more details about the marketing of services.)

The production process cannot be performed uniformly for each transaction in service retailing. For example, each cavity that a dentist fills requires a minor adjustment in approach, and every haircut requires a personal touch. A pleasant, trusting relationship between customer and retailer is necessary to overcome the customer's anxiety regarding the lack of uniform standards and thus to maintain the customer's confidence. Personal trust and mutual respect are critical to success when providing retail services.[4]

The depth and width of the product mixes retailers develop vary considerably. The type of store (discussed later in this chapter) affects the breadth and width of its product mix. As Figure 11.2 illustrates, a specialty store has a single product line but considerable depth in that line. For example, Godiva chocolate stores and Fannie May Candy Shops carry only one line of products but many items within that line. In contrast, discount stores may have a wide product mix (such as housewares, automotive services, apparel, and food). Department stores may have a wide product mix with different product line depths. Nevertheless, it is usually difficult to maintain a wide and deep product mix because of the inventories required. In addition, some producers prefer to distribute through retailers who offer less variety so that their products get more exposure and less impact from competitors' influence.

2. *Statistical Abstract of the United States,* 1988, p. 739.
3. A. Parasuraman, Valarie A. Zeithaml, Leonard L. Berry, "A Conceptual Model of Service Quality and Its Implications for Future Research," *Journal of Marketing,* Fall 1985, p. 42.
4. Kathleen A. Krentler and Joseph P. Guiltinan, "Strategies for Tangibilizing Retail Services: An Assessment," *Journal of the Academy of Marketing Science,* Fall 1984, pp. 89–90.

FIGURE 11.2

Relationship between merchandise breadth and depth for a typical discount store, department store, and specialty store (SOURCE: Robert F. Hartley, *Retailing: Challenge and Opportunity,* 3rd ed., p. 118. Copyright © 1984 by Houghton Mifflin Company. Used by permission)

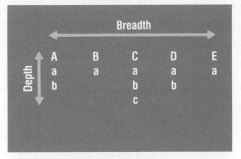

Discount store

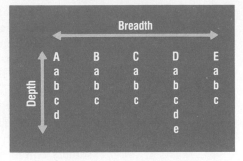

Department store

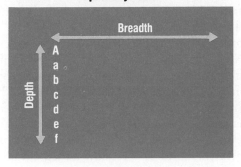

Specialty store

With the capital letters representing number or breadth of product lines, and the small letters depicting the choices in any one product line, it can be seen that discount stores are wide and shallow in merchandise assortment. Specialty stores, at the other extreme, have few product lines, but much more depth in the few they carry. The typical department store falls between these two extremes, having a broad assortment with many merchandise lines and medium depth in each line.

Consumers with different tastes, and with the ability and willingness to purchase, support a variety of retail establishments. The American retail markets are splintered, causing many retailers to create broad product assortments and target their products to many market segments. It is up to the retailer to determine what makes target consumers shop in one store rather than another. J. C. Penney is an excellent example of a store that has been very active in using marketing research to plan and position itself as a leading retailer. Marketing research helps J. C. Penney determine its overall image, decide which magazines to advertise in, and learn which items in a department will sell.[5]

Major Types of Retail Stores

Retail stores try to provide product mixes to match consumers' shopping preferences. Figure 11.2 illustrates how the width of the product mix and the depth of product lines are affected by the types of stores. These factors are important in classifying different types of stores, yet there is generally much variation among stores of a particular type. In this section we examine the types of retail stores that account for most retail sales: department stores, mass merchandisers, and specialty retailers.

5. "Retailers Taking a Closer Look at Customers," *Chain Store Age Executive,* October 1984, p. 21.

Department Stores   Department stores are large retail organizations employing at least twenty-five people and characterized by wide product mixes. To facilitate marketing efforts and internal management in these stores, related product lines are organized into separate departments, such as cosmetics, housewares, apparel, home furnishings, and appliances. Each department functions much as a self-contained business, and the buyers for individual departments are fairly autonomous.

Department stores are distinctly service oriented. Their total product includes credit, delivery, personal assistance, merchandise returns, and a pleasant atmosphere. Although some so-called department stores are actually large, departmentalized specialty stores, most department stores are shopping stores. That is, consumers compare products' price, quality, and service at one store with those at competing stores. Along with large discount stores, department stores are often considered the retailing leaders in a community and are found in most communities with a population of more than 10,000 people.

Today, conventional department stores—R. H. Macy and Co., Hudson's, Bloomingdale's, Marshall Field, Bullock's, and others—obtain 75 percent of their sales from apparel and cosmetics.[6] (Table 11.1 lists the top ten department store chains that focus mainly on apparel and cosmetics, ranked by sales volume.) Other products these stores carry include gift items, accessories, and luggage.

General merchandise department stores (not included in Table 11.1) carry a larger number of product lines. To attract additional customers, many general merchandise department stores have recently added automotive, recreational, and sports equipment departments as well as services such as insurance, hair care, travel advice, and income tax preparation. In some cases, space for these specialized services is leased out, with the proprietors managing their own operations and paying rent to the department stores.

Corporate chain department stores generate tremendous sales volume, which gives them considerable control over a wide range of the products they sell. J. C. Penney, Sears, Roebuck, and Montgomery Ward, for example, have many more store units and far greater sales volume than certain conventional department store units that usually operate regionally. Sears has been very successful in both integrating marketing activities and owning or controlling production. Consumers' loyalty and trusted private store brands make Sears extremely powerful regarding channel leadership and competitive status. Chain stores have high name recognition and advertise through many forms of media.

Although corporate chain department stores are relatively strong, many other types of department stores have encountered problems in recent years. Their overhead and operating expenses (about 35 percent of sales) are higher than those of most other retailers, partly because of the variety of services they offer. Too, population growth is now centered in the suburbs; to stay close to their customers, many downtown department stores have been forced to open branch stores in outlying shopping centers and malls. In addition, department stores face competition from a growing number of specialty and discount retailers that cater to specific market segments.

In answer to these challenges, downtown department stores are often taking the lead in urban redevelopment projects designed to stimulate downtown business activity. Offering broad product assortments, the stores are working to attract both

6. "The Future of Retailing," *Retailweek,* Mar. 1, 1981, p. 27.

tourists and downtown office workers and lower-income groups who live near central business districts. Suburban department stores are targeting market segments, trimming their overall product mixes, displaying merchandise in boutique settings, and sometimes expanding their budget-priced lines to ease the competitive pressure from specialty and discount stores. To attract and hold customers, some department stores are adding, rather than reducing, services. Macy's and Neiman-Marcus, for example, offer personal shopping services to interested customers.[7]

Mass Merchandisers

Mass merchandisers are retailers that generally offer fewer customer services than department stores and emphasize lower prices, high turnover, and large sales volumes. They usually have a wider—and sometimes shallower—product mix than department stores. They are less likely than department stores to reorder sold-out sizes and styles.

Mass merchandising operations are characterized by one-story, low-cost facilities; self-serve shopping; central check-out counters; and multiple purchases.[8] Mass merchandisers appeal to large heterogeneous target markets, especially price-conscious consumers. With their relatively low operating costs, mass merchandisers project an image of efficiency and economy. These operations include discount stores, supermarkets, superstores, warehouse/wholesale clubs, and warehouse and catalog showrooms.

Discount Stores **Discount stores** are self-service, general merchandise outlets that regularly offer brand-name merchandise at low prices. Discounters accept lower margins than conventional retailers in exchange for high sales volume. To keep turnover high, they carry a wide but carefully selected assortment of products,

7. Leonard L. Berry and Larry G. Gresham, "Relationship Retailing: Transforming Customers into Clients," *Business Horizons,* November–December 1986, pp. 44–45.
8. J. Barry Mason and Morris L. Mayer, *Modern Retailing: Theory and Practice* (Plano, Tex.: Business Publications, 1987), pp. 59–60.

TABLE 11.1

Top ten U.S. department stores focusing on apparel and cosmetics, ranked by sales

RANK	DEPARTMENT STORE	1987 ESTIMATED SALES (MILLIONS)
1	Federated Department Stores	$11,300
2	May Department Stores Co.	10,800
3	Dayton-Hudson Corp.	10,630
4	R. H. Macy & Co., Inc.	4,652
5	Allied	4,573
6	Carter Hawley Hale Stores, Inc.	2,650
7	Batus Inc.	2,578
8	Dillard	2,200
9	Mercantile	2,160
10	Ames	2,040

SOURCE: Reprinted by permission of *Chain Store Age Executive,* August 1987, pp. 11–12.

from appliances to housewares to clothing. Toys, automotive services, garden supplies, and sports equipment are also offered at major discount establishments. Often, a food supermarket is operated as a department within a discount store.

Table 11.2 lists the top ten discount stores in the United States. Many of the discounters, such as Wal-Mart, which is in second place, are regional organizations. Most operate in large, no-frills, 50,000- to 80,000-square-feet facilities, often in low-rent areas. Some discount retailers, including Wal-Mart, focus on rural and small-town markets, where competition is weaker and customer loyalty high.[9]

Discount retailing developed on a large scale in the early 1950s, when postwar production began to catch up with consumer demand for appliances, home furnishings, and other hard goods. Discount stores in those days were often cash-only operations in warehouse districts, offering goods at savings of 20 to 30 percent over conventional retailers. Through the years, facing increased competition from department stores and other discount stores, discounters generally have improved store services, atmosphere, and location, boosting prices and sometimes blurring the distinction between discount houses and department stores. For example, K mart developed a new program for handling customer complaints at the store level. Research shows that more than half of all complaints handled to the customer's satisfaction result in strong customer loyalty. K mart hopes to improve customer relations and strengthen its image in the market by placing greater emphasis on service and customer satisfaction.[10]

Other discounters continue to focus on price alone. D. S. Revco, Inc., an Ohio-based discount drugstore chain with 1,630 stores, tries to keep its prices consistently low and never runs sales. The company believes it attracts customers by

9. Sarah Peterson, "How Small-Town Retailers Make the Big Money," *U.S. News & World Report*, Dec. 2, 1985, p. 62.
10. Molly Brauer, "K mart Shapes Policy to Settle Complaints," *Houston Chronicle*, Oct. 21, 1985, p. F1.

TABLE 11.2

Top ten discount stores (by retail sales)

RANK	CHAIN	1987 ESTIMATED SALES (MILLIONS)
1	K mart Corporation	$25,626
2	Wal-Mart Stores, Inc.	15,957
3	Zayre Corp.	6,185
4	Toys "Я" Us, Inc.	3,825
5	Service Merchandise Co., Inc.	2,900
6	Best Products Co., Inc.	2,065
7	Rose's	1,370
8	Jamesway	700
9	Dollar General	588
10	Family Dollar Stores Inc.	560

SOURCE: *The Value Line Investment Survey*, 12th ed., Mar. 4, 1988, pp. 1631–1713. © Value Line Investment Survey; used by permission of Value Line, Inc.

TABLE 11.3

Top ten food chains (ranked by sales volume)

COMPANY	1986 SALES (MILLIONS)
1. Safeway Stores, Inc.	$20,311
2. Kroger Co.	17,123
3. American Stores Co.	14,021
4. Winn-Dixie Stores, Inc.	8,225
5. Southland Corporation	8,039
6. The Great Atlantic and Pacific Tea Company (A & P), Inc.	7,835
7. Lucky Stores, Inc.	6,441
8. Supermarkets General Corporation	5,508
9. Albertson's, Inc.	5,380
10. The Stop & Shop Companies, Inc.	3,872

SOURCE: Reprinted by permission of *Chain Store Age Executive*, August 1987, pp. 11–12.

maintaining its image as a discount outlet.[11] Another successful discount retailer, New York-based 47th Street Photo, sells cameras and electronic products out of small, crowded stores that offer few customer services. Competing solely on price, the company keeps overhead low and receives price breaks from manufacturers for its large-volume orders.[12]

Generally, however, many better-known discount houses have assumed the characteristics of department stores. As discounters upgrade their merchandise and facilities and provide more customer services, their risks and operating expenses increase. In recent years, rising costs have forced several discount chains that could no longer price competitively to close.

Supermarkets Supermarkets are large, self-service stores that carry a complete line of food products as well as some nonfood products, such as cosmetics and nonprescription drugs. A supermarket has minimum annual sales of $2 million, according to the Food Marketing Institute. Supermarkets are arranged in departments for maximum efficiency in product stocking and handling, with central check-out facilities. They have lower prices than smaller neighborhood grocery stores. Although they usually provide free parking and may cash checks, most supermarkets offer minimal customer services. They may be independently owned but more often are part of a chain operation. Table 11.3 lists the top ten food chains, including nonsupermarket chains.

Supermarkets, the first mass merchandisers, originated more than fifty years ago, when most food retailers were still small, limited-line organizations. Responding to competitive pressures from chain food stores, certain independent food retailers began combining broad assortments of food products with low-price, self-service operations. Three factors made the high-volume experiment a success: the price-

11. "Revco Focuses on Discounts," *Product Marketing,* April 1983, p. 32.
12. John Merwin, "The Source," *Forbes,* Apr. 9, 1984, pp. 74–78.

consciousness of Depression-era consumers; improved packaging and refrigeration technologies; and the widespread use of automobiles, which enabled the stores to attract many customers who formerly had patronized neighborhood stores. Within a few years, the supermarket became the dominant form of food retailing.

Today, consumers make more than three-quarters of all their grocery purchases in the 37,000 supermarkets currently in operation. Even so, the supermarkets' total share of the food market is declining because consumers now have widely varying food preferences and buying habits, and in most communities they can choose from among a number of competing supermarkets, convenience stores, discount stores, and specialty food stores. American consumers also are eating more and more meals away from home. To remain competitive, some supermarkets are cutting back on services, emphasizing low prices, and using sales promotion methods such as games or coupons. Other supermarkets, reducing their prices and services even further, have converted to discount and/or warehouse retailing. Still other supermarkets have taken the opposite approach, dramatically expanding both services and product mixes.

Supermarkets are also attempting to increase their efficiency and economy with technological changes. For example, many supermarkets are replacing the cash registers at their check-out counters with electronic scanners, which identify and record purchases via bar codes on each product. These detailed sales data let management maintain inventories on each item, identify buying patterns, and improve store and shelf layouts.[13] Regardless of the technology used, supermarkets must be operated efficiently because net profits after taxes are usually less than 1 percent of sales.

Superstores Superstores—which originated in Europe but are fairly new to U.S. markets—are giant retail outlets that carry not only all food and nonfood products ordinarily found in supermarkets but most consumer products purchased routinely. In addition to a complete food line, superstores offer such product lines as housewares, hardware, small appliances, clothing, personal-care products, garden products, and tires—in all, about four times as many items as supermarkets. Services available at superstores include laundry and dry cleaning, automotive repair, check cashing, bill paying, and snack bars.

Superstores combine features of discount houses and supermarkets. To cut handling and inventory costs, they use sophisticated operating techniques and often tall, visible shelving to display entire assortments of products. Most superstores contain about 30,000 square feet (compared to 18,000 square feet in supermarkets), although some are as large as 100,000 square feet. Their sales volume is two to three times that of supermarkets, partly because they locate near good transportation networks that help generate the in-store traffic needed for profitability.

Consumers are most attracted to superstores by the lower prices and one-stop shopping feature, so food retailers have started handling general merchandise because gross margin and net profit are higher on those items than on food items. Several supermarket chains have added supersized units or enlarged existing stores and product mixes. But superstores require large investments, stringent cost con-

13. J. Barry Mason and Morris L. Mayer, *Modern Retailing: Theory and Practice* (Plano, Tex.: Business Publications, 1987), p. 181.

trols, appropriate facilities, and managers who can coordinate broad product assortments. Conventional supermarkets, hampered by economic uncertainty and lack of space for physical expansion, find it difficult to compete effectively with superstores.

Warehouse/Wholesale Clubs   The newest form of mass merchandising is the **warehouse/wholesale club,** a large-scale, members-only selling operation that combines cash-and-carry wholesaling features with discount retailing. Small business owners account for about 60 percent of a typical warehouse club's sales. (Thus a warehouse/wholesale club could be viewed as a wholesaler.) For a small fee (usually about $25), small retailers may purchase products at wholesale prices for business use or for resale. Warehouse clubs also sell to ultimate consumers who are affiliated with government agencies, credit unions, schools, hospitals, and banks. Instead of paying a membership fee, individual consumers pay about 5 percent more on each item than do retailers.

Sometimes called buying clubs, warehouse clubs offer the same types of products as discount stores but in a limited range of sizes and styles. Whereas most discount stores carry forty thousand items, a warehouse club handles only four thousand to five thousand different products, usually acknowledged brand leaders.[14] But because their product lines are shallow and sales volumes high, warehouse clubs can offer a broad range of merchandise, including nonperishable foods, beverages, books, appliances, housewares, automotive parts, hardware, clothing, furniture, and sundries.

To keep their prices 20 to 40 percent lower than those of supermarkets and discount stores, warehouse clubs provide few services. They do not generally advertise, except through direct mail. Their facilities are often located in industrial parks and feature concrete floors and aisles wide enough for forklifts. Merchandise is stacked on pallets or displayed on pipe racks. All payments must be in cash, and customers must transport purchases themselves.

Still, warehouse clubs appeal to many price-conscious consumers and small retailers who may be unable to obtain wholesaling services from larger distributors. The sales volume of most warehouse clubs is four to five times that of a typical department store. With stock turning over at the average rate of eighteen times a year, warehouse clubs sell their goods before manufacturers' payment periods are up, virtually eliminating the need for capital.[15]

The warehouse club concept, which is expected to spread widely during the next few years, was pioneered in the United States in the late 1970s by the Price Company, which now has twenty-five Price Club outlets. Other warehouse club chains include Costco Wholesale Clubs, Sam's Wholesale Clubs (owned by Wal-Mart Stores), and BJ's Warehouse Club (owned by the Zayre Corporation). As competition increases, the clubs may begin to offer more services. The Price Club, for example, tested an in-store pharmacy, optical department, and gas station in its San Diego store,[16] and Dallas-based American Wholesale Club emphasizes luxury goods such as better-quality clothing, jewelry, and gift items.[17]

14. Ibid., pp. 65–66.
15. Ibid., p. 66.
16. Jay L. Johnson, "Keeping Up with the Wholesale Clubs," *DM,* July 1987, p. 78.
17. Renee M. Covino, "American Wholesale Leans Toward Luxuries," *DM,* February 1987, p. 52.

Warehouse and Catalog Showrooms   The **warehouse showroom** is a retail facility with five basic characteristics: (1) large, low-cost building, (2) use of warehouse materials handling technology, (3) use of vertical merchandise display space, (4) a large on-premises inventory, and (5) minimum services.

Although some superstores and discount supermarkets have used warehouse retailing, most of the best-known showrooms are operated by large furniture retailers. Wickes Furniture and Levitz Furniture Corporation brought sophisticated mass merchandising to the highly fragmented furniture industry. These high-volume, low-overhead operations stress less personnel and services. Lower costs are possible because some marketing functions have been shifted to consumers, who must transport, finance, and perhaps store merchandise. Most consumers carry away their purchases in the manufacturer's carton, although the stores will deliver for a fee.

In the **catalog showroom,** one item of each product is on display, often in a locked case, and remaining inventory is stored out of the buyer's reach. Using catalogs that have been mailed to their homes or are on counters in the store, customers order products by phone or in person. Clerks fill the orders from the warehouse area, and products are presented in the manufacturer's carton. In contrast to traditional catalog retailers, which offer no discounts and require that customers wait for delivery, catalog showrooms regularly sell below list price and often provide goods immediately.

Catalog showrooms usually sell jewelry, luggage, photographic equipment, toys, small appliances and housewares, sporting goods, and power tools. They advertise extensively and carry established brands and models that are not likely to be discontinued. Because catalog showrooms have higher product turnover, fewer losses through shoplifting, and lower labor costs than department stores, they are able to feature lower prices. They offer minimal services, however. Their locations are not always convenient, and customers may have to stand in line to examine items or place orders. Still, such showrooms appear to be one of the fastest-growing areas of retailing, despite competition from discounters and wholesale clubs. Service Merchandise, Best Products, and Consumer Distributing are three of the largest catalog showroom retailers.

Specialty Retailers

In contrast to department stores and mass merchandisers, which offer broad product mixes, specialty retailers emphasize the narrowness and depth of their product lines. Despite their name, specialty retailers do not sell specialty items (except when the specialty goods complement the overall product mix). Instead, these retailers offer substantial assortments in a few product lines. In this section we examine two types of specialty stores: traditional specialty retailers and off-price retailers.

Traditional Specialty Retailers   **Traditional specialty retailers** are stores carrying a narrow product mix with deep product lines. They are sometimes called limited-line retailers; if they carry unusual depth in one main product category, they may be referred to as single-line retailers.

Shopping goods such as apparel, jewelry, sporting goods, art supplies, fabrics, computers, and pet supplies are commonly sold through specialty retailers. For example, the Foot Locker, owned by Kinney Shoe Corp., specializes in a product mix of running shoes, tennis shoes, and other types of athletic footwear. The Gap,

Radio Shack, Hickory Farms, and The Limited are other retailers that offer limited product lines but great depth within those lines.

Although the number of chain specialty stores is increasing, most specialty stores are independently owned. Specialty stores occupy about two-thirds of the space in most shopping centers and malls and account for 40 to 50 percent of all general merchandise sales.[18] Florists, bakery shops, and book stores are among the small, independent specialty retailers that appeal to local target markets, although these stores can, of course, be owned and managed by large corporations. Even if this kind of retailer adds a few supporting product lines, the store may still be classified as a specialty store.

Traditional specialty stores attempt to provide a unique store image, especially when they cannot compete directly with the prices of large retailers.[19] By capitalizing on fashion, service, personnel, atmosphere, location, and social class, specialty retailers can position themselves strategically to attract customers in specific market segments. Irresistibles, a chain of women's apparel stores in New England, targets professional women who purchase higher-priced clothing and accessories. To maintain a store image that will appeal to these customers, Irresistibles is willing to pay higher rent in exchange for desirable locations.[20]

Because they are usually small, specialty stores' costs may be high in proportion to sales, and to satisfy customers they may have to carry some products with low turnover rates. On the other hand, they sometimes obtain lower prices from suppliers because they buy limited lines of merchandise in large quantities. Successful specialty stores understand their customer types and know what products to carry, thus reducing the risk of unsold merchandise. They usually offer better selections and more sales expertise than department stores, their main competitors. They may even become exclusive dealers in their markets for certain products.

Through specialty stores, small business owners can provide unique services to match consumers' varied desires. For consumers dissatisfied with the impersonal nature of large retailers, the close, personal contact of a small specialty store can be a welcome change.

Off-Price Retailers   **Off-price retailers** are stores that buy manufacturers' seconds, overruns, returns, and off-season production runs at below-wholesale prices for resale to consumers at deep discounts. Unlike true discount stores, which pay regular wholesale prices for their goods and usually carry second-line brand names, off-price retailers offer limited lines of national-brand and designer merchandise, usually clothing, shoes, or housewares. The number of off-price retailers has grown rapidly since the mid-1980s and now includes such major chains as T. J. Maxx, Hit or Miss, Dress Barn, and Marshall's.[21]

Off-price stores charge 20 to 50 percent less than department stores for comparable merchandise but offer few customer services. They often feature community

18. Barry Berman and Joel Evans, *Retail Management: A Strategic Approach* (New York: Macmillan, 1986), p. 99.
19. Leonard Berry, "Retail Positioning Strategies for the 1980s," *Business Horizons,* November–December 1982, p. 45.
20. "Location Is Everything," *Chain Store Age Executive,* January 1986, pp. 41–42.
21. Barry Berman and Joel Evans, *Retail Management: A Strategic Approach* (New York: Macmillan, 1986), p. 107.

dressing rooms, central check-out counters, and no credit, returns, or exchanges. Off-price stores may or may not sell goods with original labels intact (Filene's Basement Stores do, Loehmann's outlets do not). Some, such as Marshall's and Burlington Coat Factory, sell family clothing in a supermarket format.[22] Off-price stores turn over their inventory nine to twelve times a year, about three times as often as traditional specialty stores. They compete with department stores for the same customers: price-conscious members of relatively affluent suburban households who are knowledgeable about brand names.

To ensure a regular flow of merchandise into their stores, off-price retailers must establish long-term relationships with suppliers who can provide large quantities of goods at reduced prices. Manufacturers may approach the retailers with samples, discontinued products, or items that have not sold well; or the retailers may seek out producers, offering to pay cash for goods produced during the manufacturers' off-season. Although manufacturers benefit from such arrangements, they also risk alienating their specialty and department store customers.[23] Department stores tolerate off-price stores as long as they do not advertise brand names, limit their merchandise to lower-quality items, and are located away from the department stores. (In fact, such off-price chains as T. H. Mandy, J. Brannam, and Loehmann's are owned by full-price, traditional retailers.) But when off-price retailers are able to obtain large stocks of in-season, top-quality merchandise—as many do—tension builds between department stores and manufacturers.

Still, the increase of off-price retailing is expected to continue. In a growing number of communities, manufacturer-owned factory outlets and off-price stores have grouped together in off-price malls and shopping districts. Combined, these two forms of discount retailers now account for 13 percent of all retail sales.[24]

Nonstore Retailing and Direct Marketing

Nonstore retailing is the selling of goods or services outside the confines of a retail facility. This form of retailing accounts for an increasing percentage of sales and includes personal sales methods, such as in-home retailing and telephone retailing, and nonpersonal sales methods, such as automatic vending and mail-order retailing (which includes catalog retailing).

Certain nonstore retailing methods are in the category of **direct marketing,** the use of nonpersonal media to introduce products to consumers, who then purchase the products by mail or telephone. In the case of telephone orders, salespersons may be required to complete the sales. Telephone, mail-order, and catalog retailing are all examples of direct marketing, as are sales generated by coupons, direct mail, and toll-free 800 numbers.[25]

22. J. Barry Mason and Morris L. Mayer, *Modern Retailing: Theory and Practice* (Plano, Tex.: Business Publications, 1987), p. 486.
23. Barry Berman and Joel Evans, *Retail Management: A Strategic Approach* (New York: Macmillan, 1986), p. 99.
24. "Now It's Chic to Shop Cheap," *U.S. News & World Report,* Sept. 22, 1986, pp. 70–71.
25. M. E. Ziegenhagen, "Let's Stop 'Diluting' Direct Marketing," *Business Marketing,* February 1986, pp. 88–89.

In-Home Retailing

In-home retailing is selling via personal contacts with consumers in their own homes. Organizations such as Avon, Electrolux, and Fuller Brush Company send representatives to the homes of preselected prospects. Products such as *World Book Encyclopedia,* Kirby vacuum cleaners, and Mary Kay cosmetics are also sold to consumers in their homes.

Traditionally, in-home retailing relied on a random door-to-door approach. Some companies (such as World Book and Kirby, both divisions of Scott & Fetzer Co.) now use a more efficient approach. Prospects are first reached by phone or mail or intercepted in shopping malls or at fairs. These initial contacts are limited to a brief introduction and the setting of appointments. Salespeople then go to customers' homes to make their sales presentations.[26] Several large retailers, such as J. C. Penney, offer in-home decorating services. Consultants are invited by consumers and sell a line of home furnishings not otherwise available in the department stores.[27] Consumers find in-home selling of rugs, draperies, and home improvements helpful because these products must be coordinated with existing home interiors.

Some in-home selling, however, is still undertaken without information about sales prospects. Door-to-door selling without a prearranged appointment is a tiny proportion of total retail sales, probably less than 1 percent. Because it has so often been associated with unscrupulous and fraudulent techniques, door-to-door selling is illegal in some communities. Generally, this technique is regarded unfavorably because so many door-to-door salespersons are undertrained and poorly supervised. A big disadvantage of door-to-door selling is the large expenditure, effort, and time it demands. Sales commissions are usually 25 to 50 percent (or more) of the retail price; as a result, consumers often pay more than a product is worth. Door-to-door selling is used most often when a product is unsought and thus consumers will not make a special effort to go to a store to purchase it, such as encyclopedias. Avon and Fuller Brush, two successful and respected companies, have used door-to-door selling very effectively.

A variation of in-home retailing is the home demonstration or party plan, which such companies as Tupperware, Stanley Home Products, and Mary Kay Cosmetics use successfully. One consumer acts as host and invites a number of friends to view merchandise at his or her home, where a salesperson is on hand to demonstrate the products. The home demonstration is more efficient for the sales representative than contacting each prospect door-to-door, and the congenial atmosphere partly overcomes consumers' suspicions and encourages them to buy. Home demonstrations also meet the buyers' needs for convenience and personal service. Commissions and selling costs make this form of retailing expensive, however. Additionally, successful party-plan selling requires networks of friends and neighbors who have time to attend such social gatherings as well as large numbers of effective salespersons. With increasing numbers of household members now holding full-time jobs, both prospects and sales representatives are harder to recruit. The growth of interactive telephone-computer home shopping may also cut into party-plan sales.

26. Bill Saporito, "A Door-To-Door Bell Ringer," *Fortune,* Dec. 10, 1984, pp. 83–84.
27. Barry Berman and Joel Evans, *Retail Management: A Strategic Approach* (New York: Macmillan, 1986), p. 111.

Telephone Retailing and Telemarketing

A growing number of organizations—IBM, Merrill Lynch, Allstate, Avis, Ford, Quaker Oats, Time, and American Express, to name a few—are using the telephone to increase the effectiveness of traditional marketing methods. Telemarketing can generate sales leads, improve customer service, speed up collection of past-due accounts, raise funds for nonprofit groups, and gather market data.[28]

The most familiar form of telemarketing is **telephone retailing,** which is direct selling of goods and services by telephone based on either a cold canvass of the telephone directory or a prescreened list of prospective clients. (In some areas, certain telephone numbers are listed with an asterisk to indicate those people who consider sales solicitations a nuisance and do not want to be bothered.) In some cases, telephone retailing uses advertising that encourages consumers to initiate a call or to request information about placing an order. Although this type of retailing is only a small part of total retail sales, its use is growing. According to AT&T, U.S. companies spent $13.6 billion in one recent year on telemarketing phone calls and equipment (phones, lines, and computers). Telephone Marketing Resources, a telemarketing firm, estimates telephone sales of goods and services at $75 billion annually (the figure includes business-to-consumer sales *and* business-to-business sales).[29] Research indicates that telephone retailing is most successful when combined with other marketing strategies, such as direct mail or advertising in newspapers, radio, and television. (Additional uses of telemarketing are explored in the Application on page 371.)

Automatic Vending

Automatic vending makes use of machines and accounts for less than 2 percent of all retail sales. Approximately six million vending units generate about $15 billion in retail sales annually. It is significant that although vending retail sales increased rapidly in the 1970s, the sales trend in the 1980s has been relatively flat. Vending items that show a slight decline include milk, bottled cold drinks, cigarettes, cigars, ice cream, and canned hot foods. On the other hand, canned cold drinks and some nonfood items have increased in sales volume.[30]

Vending machine locations and the percentage of sales each generates are as follows:[31]

Plants and factories	36.4	Government facilities	6.5
Public locations (e.g., stores)	20.2	Hospitals and nursing homes	5.4
Offices	10.0	Primary and secondary schools	4.2
Colleges and universities	8.2	Others	9.4

Video game machines provide an entertainment service, and many banks now offer machines that dispense cash or offer other services, but these uses of vending machines are not reported in total vending sales volume.

Automatic vending is one of the most impersonal forms of retailing. Small, standardized, routinely purchased products (chewing gum, soft drinks, coffee) can be sold in machines because consumers usually buy them at the nearest available

28. Kenneth C. Schneider, "Telemarketing as a Promotional Tool—Its Effects and Side Effects," *The Journal of Consumer Marketing,* Winter 1985, pp. 29–39.
29. Joel Dreyfuss, "Reach Out and Sell Something," *Fortune,* Nov. 26, 1984, pp. 127–128.
30. *Vending Times,* "V/T Census of the Industry," July 1984, pp. 216, 244.
31. Ibid.

New Uses for Telemarketing

The dead grass did it—brought telemarketing to Scott's Lawn Care Products, that is. Several years ago, Scott's realized that its mail-based system of answering requests for gardening advice was not working. The information often reached customers too late, after their ailing lawns and gardens had already died, and because Scott's entire product line was covered by warranties, the company was having to pay substantial sums to disgruntled customers. But now that Scott's has a toll-free number for immediate customer assistance, the company is handling more than 100,000 calls annually. Scott's saves on warranty costs and maintains customer loyalty, and because telephone representatives inform callers of the nearest Scott's dealer, the company sells more gardening products as well.

Scott's is just one example of the growing number of organizations that are adding telemarketing to their promotional efforts. Telemarketing revenues multiplied sixteen times in the last decade and now account for 46 percent of all direct marketing sales. Companies are using telephone systems for promotion, order processing, sales support, customer service, and account management. Some marketing executives say that telemarketing's potential is limited only by the imagination of its users.

Performing arts organizations, for instance, now use telemarketing for subscription sales, fund-raising, or both purposes. About half of all new subscriptions to the New York Philharmonic come through the Philharmonic's in-house telemarketing staff, who emphasize service rather than sales by helping potential subscribers choose seats and performance dates. Often knowledgeable themselves about classical music and opera, telemarketing personnel also field customer complaints and help assess the effectiveness of other promotional efforts. The San Francisco Opera, which does not use telemarketing for subscription sales, finds telemarketing an effective tool for fund-raising: They raised $500,000 by telephone in one recent six-month period. In Santa Fe, the opera box office personnel solicit subscription renewals through a combination of in-house telemarketing and direct mail campaigns.

Such combinations may prove to be the most effective use of telemarketing. When New York-based Citicorp was about to launch a second-mortgage loan program in the Baltimore area, the bank initiated a telemarketing campaign to introduce prospects to both the new product and the Citicorp name. Citicorp tested several promotion mixes—mail only, mail plus telemarketing, mail plus telemarketing plus print advertisements—and found that the most effective combination incorporated direct mail (the basic loan application, an 800 number, and a coupon for more information), outbound telemarketing, and a newspaper advertising campaign. Citicorp executives say that this mix increased the number of Citicorp's accounts 15 percent, compared with direct

location. Machines in areas of heavy traffic provide efficient and continuous services to consumers. The elimination of sales personnel and the small amount of space necessary for vending machines give this retailing method some advantages over stores. The advantages are partly offset by the expense of the frequent servicing and repair needed.

Mail-order Retailing

Mail-order retailing is a form of selling by description because buyers usually do not see the actual product until it arrives in the mail. Sellers contact buyers through direct mail, catalogs, television, radio, magazines, and newspapers. A wide assortment of products such as records, books, and clothing are sold to consumers through the mail. Placing mail orders by telephone is increasingly common. The advantages of mail-order selling include efficiency and convenience. Mail-order houses can be located in remote lower-cost areas and forgo the expenses of store fixtures. Eliminating personal selling efforts and store operations may result in tremendous savings that can be passed along to consumers in the form of lower prices. On the other hand, mail-order retailing is inflexible, provides limited service, and is more appropriate for specialty products than for convenience products.

Catalog retailing is a specific type of direct marketing conducted by retailers. Orders may be delivered by mail, or customers may pick them up. Although in-store visits result in some catalog orders, most are placed by mail or telephone. Figure 11.3 promotes L. L. Bean, an organization that has marketed clothing, footwear, sports equipment, and home furnishings through catalog retailing for more than seventy-five years.

General Foods created Thomas Garroway, Ltd., a mail-order service providing gourmet pasta, cheese, coffee, and similar items. General Foods chose the fictitious British name to give the company a classier image. Other packaged-goods manufacturers involved in catalog retailing include Procter & Gamble, Hanes, Nestlé, Thomas J. Lipton, Sunkist, R. J. Reynolds, and Whitman Chocolates.[32] These catalog retailers are able to reach many two-income families who have more money and less time for special shopping. Catalog sales have been growing 50 to 100 percent faster than annual retail sales over the past five years. About 4,000 catalogs are in circulation. Industry estimates place direct mail sales of general merchandise and related goods at $30 billion and total catalog sales at about $40 billion.[33]

32. Ronald Alsop, "Food Giants Take to Mails to Push Fancy Product Lines," *Wall Street Journal,* Feb. 28, 1985, p. 85.
33. "The Sale Is in the Mail," *Chain Store Age Executive,* March 1984, pp. 44, 49, 51, 54.

Franchising

Franchising is an arrangement whereby a supplier, or franchisor, grants a dealer, or franchisee, the right to sell products in exchange for some type of consideration. For example, the franchisor may receive some percentage of total sales in exchange for furnishing equipment, buildings, management know-how, and marketing assistance to the franchisee. Additionally, the franchisee must agree to operate according to the franchisor's rules (see Figure 11.4).

Franchised health clubs, exterminators, restaurants, and campgrounds abound. There are also franchised tax preparers and travel agencies. The real estate industry is experiencing rapid growth in franchising. Also expected to join the franchising ranks in large numbers are hair salons, tanning salons, and professionals such as dentists and lawyers.[34] In fact, franchising has been one of retailing's major growth areas during the past twenty years. During this period, many organizations such as McDonald's Corporation, Holiday Inns, Inc., Kentucky Fried Chicken, and Pizza Hut restaurants have emerged as major competitive forces in their respective industries.

34. Franchising types and examples are adapted from Robert F. Hartley, *Retailing: Challenge and Opportunity,* 3rd ed. Copyright © 1984 Houghton Mifflin Company. Adapted with permission.

FIGURE 11.3

Promotion of L. L. Bean, a catalog retailing organization (SOURCE: Courtesy L. L. Bean, Inc.)

Three basic types of franchising arrangements have been developed.[35] A producer may franchise a number of stores to sell a particular brand of product. One of the oldest franchising arrangements, this method prevails in the areas of passenger cars and trucks, farm equipment, shoes, paint, earth-moving equipment, and petroleum. Virtually all new cars and trucks are sold through franchised dealers, and an estimated 90 percent of all gasoline is sold through franchised independent retail service stations. Table 11.4 illustrates selected franchising industries, ranked by 1985 sales and projected sales for 1990.

A producer may franchise wholesalers to sell to retailers. This arrangement is most common in the soft-drink industry. Most national producers of soft-drink syrups—Coca-Cola, Dr Pepper, Pepsi-Cola, 7Up, Royal Crown—franchise independent bottlers who then serve retailers.

Sometimes, rather than franchising a complete product, a franchisor provides brand names, techniques, procedures, or other services. The franchisor may perform some manufacturing and wholesaling functions, but its major contribution is a carefully developed, and controlled, marketing strategy. This is the most common type of franchise today. There are many examples, including Holiday Inn, McDonald's, Dairy Queen, Avis, Hertz, Kentucky Fried Chicken, and H & R Block.

35. "Franchising—Opening the Doors to Expansion," *Retailweek,* Feb. 1, 1981, p. 29.

Franchising continues to grow rapidly. The Department of Commerce indicates that franchise establishments did about $116 billion in sales in 1969. By 1980 sales had increased to approximately $338 billion. The number of new franchises or new businesses entering the franchising arena is increasing by about 9 percent each year. The current trends of franchising growth will probably continue at approximately the same rate.

The expansion of the franchise system to many industries highlights the benefits of central management control and coordinated marketing efforts for franchise members. The advantages for franchisees are tremendous. They are entrepreneurs who invest their own money and must perform at a high level to protect their investment. (Table 11.5 shows the level of initial investment for the most expensive and the least expensive franchises.) But unlike most entrepreneurs, they go into business under the protective wing of a company with a proven track record. Still, as with all businesses, franchising does pose risks. Many franchisees have gone out of business as a result of poor management, minimal marketing research, poor marketing planning, or overexpansion.

Planned Shopping Centers

The planned shopping center is constructed by private owners to contain a complementary mix of stores that provides one-stop shopping for family and household needs. Although shopping centers may vary, the principle of a coordinated, complementary mix of stores that generates consumer traffic is a key factor.

TABLE 11.4

Selected franchising industries and projected growth

| BUSINESS CATEGORY | SALES (IN MILLIONS) | | ANNUAL GROWTH (%) |
	1985	1990	
Restaurants (all types)	$ 48,926	$ 86,109	12.0
Retailing (nonfood)	18,790	33,560	12.3
Hotels/motels/campgrounds	14,631	22,511	9.0
Convenience stores	12,309	19,377	9.5
Business services	12,076	21,282	12.0
Automotive products and services	10,604	15,944	8.5
Food retailing (other than convenience stores)	10,370	14,544	7.0
Rental services (automobile/truck)	5,282	8,900	11.0
Construction and home services	3,720	9,255	20.0
Recreation/entertainment/travel	1,840	6,573	29.0
Total	$138,548	$238,055	11.5%

SOURCE: Meg Whittemore, "Franchising's Future," *Nation's Business*, February 1986, p. 49. Original source: The Nesbitt Group.

10 MOST EXPENSIVE FRANCHISES		10 LEAST EXPENSIVE FRANCHISES	
COMPANY	START-UP COST AND FRANCHISE FEE	COMPANY	START-UP COST AND FRANCHISE FEE
1. Hampton Inn	$2.3 million	1. Packy the Shipper	$995
2. Quality Inns Intl.	$1.9 million	2. Novus Windshield Repair	$2,000
3. Econo Lodge	$1.8 million	3. Sunshine Polishing Systems	$2,675
4. Hardee's	$433,000	4. Coverall	$4,200
5. Roy Rogers	$396,000	5. Stork News	$5,000
6. McDonald's	$363,000	6. Chem-Dry	$9,000
7. Ponderosa Steakhouse	$342,000	7. Coustic Glo	$11,250
8. Jack-in-the-Box	$331,000	8. Jani-King	$13,500
9. Round Table Pizza	$322,000	9. Duraclean	$16,800
10. Super 8 Motels	$320,000	10. Video Data Services	$16,950

TABLE 11.5

The ten most expensive and the ten least expensive franchises

SOURCE: *USA Today,* Feb. 11, 1988, p. 8B. Copyright *USA Today.* Reprinted with permission.

Shopping centers are planned, coordinated, and promoted to appeal to heterogeneous groups of consumers. The shopping center management ensures an environment that is comfortable and conveniently set up to serve consumers with a variety of needs. Parking facilities, landscaping, and special events create an overall atmosphere that attracts consumers.

Neighborhood Shopping Centers

Neighborhood shopping centers usually consist of several small convenience and specialty stores such as small grocery stores, drugstores, gas stations, and fast-food restaurants. They serve consumers who live less than ten minutes' driving time from the center. Many of these retailers consider their target markets to be consumers who live within a two- to three-mile radius of their stores. Because most purchases are based on convenience or personal contact, the coordination of selling efforts within a neighborhood shopping center usually is limited. Product mixes are usually held to essential products, and the depth of the product lines tends to be limited. Convenience stores are most successful when they are closer to the consumer than, for example, supermarkets. The best strategy for neighborhood centers is to locate along travel patterns that allow the center to intercept the greatest number of potential consumers before they reach a regional shopping center.[36]

Community Shopping Centers

Community shopping centers include one or two department stores and some specialty stores, as well as convenience stores. They serve a larger geographic area and draw consumers who are looking for shopping and specialty products that are not available in neighborhood shopping centers. Consumers drive longer distances

36. Franklin S. Houston and John Stanton, "Evaluating Retail Trade Areas for Convenience Stores," *Journal of Retailing,* Spring 1984, p. 135.

to community shopping centers than to neighborhood shopping centers. The community shopping center is carefully planned and coordinated to attract shoppers. Special events such as art exhibits, automobile shows, and sidewalk sales are used to stimulate traffic. The overall management of a community shopping center looks for tenants that complement the center's total assortment of products. There are wide product mixes and deep product lines.

Regional Shopping Centers

Regional shopping centers usually have the largest department stores, the widest product mix, and the deepest product lines of all shopping centers (see Figure 11.5). They carry most products found in a downtown shopping district. The success of regional shopping centers has led downtown retailers to adopt defensive measures. For example, downtown retailers have modernized their stores and increased parking facilities. Intracity expressways and improved public transportation have helped many downtown shopping districts remain competitive.

With 150,000 or more consumers in their target market, regional shopping centers must have well-coordinated management and marketing activities. Because of the expense of leasing space in regional shopping centers, tenants are more likely to be national chain stores than small independents. These large centers usually advertise, have special events, furnish transportation to some consumer groups, and carefully select the mix of stores. West Edmonton Mall in Edmonton, Canada,

FIGURE 11.5

Advertisement promoting a regional shopping center in an urban area (SOURCE: Trumbull Shopping Park)

is one of the largest shopping malls in the world, with 828 stores, including 50 shoe stores, 8 department stores, and 135 eating places. The shopping center features a 438-foot-long lake with submarines, dolphins, and a Spanish galleon. The mall also features a twelve-story roller coaster and a large skating rink.[37]

Intermarket patronage, or "outshopping," is important to regional shopping centers. Outshoppers are those who will forgo the convenience of hometown shopping and travel to out-of-town markets to purchase products. Studies indicate that frequent outshoppers have higher incomes and education, are more likely to own a home, have a negative attitude toward local shopping conditions, are shopping innovators, use more credit, shop less by catalog, and are more physically fit than those who shop locally.[38]

Nontraditional Shopping Centers

Two new types of discount malls or shopping centers are emerging that differ significantly from traditional shopping centers. The factory outlet mall features discount and factory outlet stores carrying traditional manufacturer brands, such as Van Heusen, Levi Strauss, Munsingwear, Healthtex, and Wrangler. Manufacturers own these stores and must exert particular effort to avoid conflicting with traditional retailers of their products. Manufacturers claim that their stores are in noncompetitive locations, and indeed most factory outlet malls are located outside metropolitan areas. Not all factory outlets stock closeouts and irregulars, but almost all seek to avoid comparison with discount houses. The factory outlet mall attracts customers because of lower prices for quality and major brand names.

The factory outlet mall operates in much the same way as the regional shopping center and probably draws traffic from a larger shopping radius. Promotional activity is at the heart of these new shopping centers. Craft shows, contests, and special events attract a great deal of traffic.

Another nontraditional shopping center is the miniwarehouse mall. These loosely planned centers sell space to retailers, who operate what are essentially retail stores out of warehouse bays. The developers of the miniwarehouse mall may also sell space to wholesalers or even to light manufacturers who maintain retail facilities in their warehouse bays. Some of these miniwarehouses are located in high-traffic areas and provide ample customer parking as well as display windows that can be seen from the street. Home improvement materials, specialty foods, pet supplies, and garden and yard supplies are often sold in these malls.

Unlike the traditional shopping center, the miniwarehouse mall usually does not have a coordinated promotional program and store mix. These nontraditional shopping centers come closest to a neighborhood or community shopping center.

Strategic Issues in Retailing

Consumers often have vague reasons for making a retail purchase. Whereas most industrial purchases are based on economic planning and necessity, consumer

---

37. Lou Ziegler, "Canadian Mall: Wonder Under a Roof," *USA Today,* Jan. 3, 1986, p. 1.
38. Jon M. Hawes and James R. Lumpkin, "Understanding the Outshopper," *Journal of the Academy of Marketing Science,* Fall 1984, pp. 200–217.

purchases often result from social influences and psychological factors. Because consumers shop for a variety of reasons—to search for specific items, to escape boredom, or to learn about something new—retailers must do more than simply fill space with merchandise; they must make desired products available, create stimulating environments for shopping, and develop marketing strategies that increase store patronage. In this section we discuss how store location, product assortment, customer services, atmospherics, store image, scrambled merchandising, and the wheel of retailing affect these retailing objectives.

Location

Location, the least flexible of the strategic retailing issues, is one of the most important because location dictates the limited geographic trading area from which a store must draw its customers. Retailers must evaluate potential locations carefully, especially retailers of services and retailers that rely on heavy customer traffic for business. Once retailers select a trading area (urban, suburban, or rural) and the type of retail location desired (free-standing store, unplanned business district, or planned shopping center), they must analyze specific sites within that trading area and type of retail location by considering several factors.[39]

First, relative ease of movement to and from the site is important, including pedestrian and vehicular traffic, parking, and transportation. Most retailers prefer sites with high pedestrian traffic, although preliminary site investigations often include a pedestrian count to determine how many of the passers-by are truly prospective customers. Similarly, the nature of the area's vehicular traffic is analyzed. Certain retailers, such as service stations and convenience stores, depend on large numbers of driving customers but try to avoid overly congested locations. In addition, parking space must be adequate for projected demand, and transportation networks (major thoroughfares and public transit) must be able to accommodate customers and delivery vehicles.

Retailers then evaluate the characteristics of the site itself: the types of stores in the area; the size, shape, and visibility of the lot or building under consideration; and the rental, leasing, or ownership terms under which the building may be occupied. Retailers also look for compatibility with nearby retailers because stores that complement each other draw more customers for everyone. Despite its off-price approach to selling, Bookstop, Inc., a twelve-store chain of discount bookstores in Texas, favors outlets in specialty-strip shopping centers, especially in older neighborhoods. There, typical cotenants include gourmet food stores, movie theaters, and small restaurants, whose patrons are also likely to be interested in books.[40] The Application on page 381 has examples of other factors that influence specific marketers' decisions about site selection.

Product Assortment

The product assortments retailers develop vary considerably in depth and width. As discussed, retail stores are often classified according to their product assortment. Conversely, a store's type affects the breadth and depth of the store's product mix. Research on retail chain stores indicates that the level of inventory has a

39. Barry Berman and Joel Evans, *Retail Management: A Strategic Approach* (New York: Macmillan, 1986), pp. 228–238.
40. Gary F. Perkinson, "The Biggest Little Bookstore in Texas," *DM*, May 1987, p. 138.

strong impact on each store's performance. Managers must ensure that individual store units stock an adequate product assortment, inventory shortages are minimized, and any unbalanced inventories are corrected as quickly as possible.[41]

Issues of product assortment are often a matter of what and how much to carry. When retailers decide what should be included in their product assortments, they consider the assortment's (1) purpose, (2) status, and (3) completeness.[42] *Purpose* relates to how well an assortment satisfies consumers and at the same time furthers the retailer's goals. *Status* identifies by rank the relative importance of each product in an assortment. For example, motor oil might have low status in a store that sells convenience foods. An assortment is *complete* when it includes the products necessary to satisfy a store's customers; it is incomplete when some products are missing. An assortment of convenience foods must include milk to be complete because most consumers expect to be able to buy milk when purchasing other food products. New products are added to (and declining products are deleted from) an assortment when they meet (or fail to meet) the retailer's standards of purpose, status, and completeness.

The retailer also considers the quality of the products to be offered. The store may limit its assortments to expensive, high-quality goods for upper-income market segments; it may stock cheap, low-quality products for low-income buyers; or it may try to attract several market segments by offering a range of quality within its total product assortment.

How much to include in an assortment depends on the needs of the retailer's target market. A discount store's customers expect a wide and shallow product mix, whereas specialty-store shoppers prefer narrow and deep assortments. If a retailer can increase sales by increasing product variety, the assortment may be enlarged. If a broader product mix ties up too much floor space or creates storage problems, however, the retailer may stock only the products that generate the greatest sales. Other factors that affect product assortment decisions are the investment risks involved, demands on personnel, store image, and inventory control procedures.[43]

Customer Services

Retailers provide services to attract and hold customers and thereby increase sales and profits. Services various types of retailers offer include delivery, credit, returns and exchanges, gift wrapping, extended store hours, sales assistance, and repairs. Because some services cost more than others, retailers must balance the expense of providing a given service against the revenues it generates, although this factor can be difficult to measure. Sometimes services that are only marginally profitable must be retained for competitive reasons or to maintain the store's image.

Full-service retailers—those that provide a complete range of customer services—are most common among specialty stores. The products are often expensive,

41. Richard Hise, J. Patrick Kelly, Myron Gable, and James B. McDonald, "Factors Affecting the Performance of Individual Chain Store Units: An Empirical Analysis," *Journal of Retailing,* Summer 1983, p. 37.

42. C. Glenn Walters and Blaise J. Bergiel, *Marketing Channels,* 2nd ed. (Glenview, Ill.: Scott, Foresman, 1982), p. 205.

43. Barry Berman and Joel Evans, *Retail Management: A Strategic Approach* (New York: Macmillan, 1986), p. 297.

APPLICATION

Site Location: A Crucial Retail Strategy Component

Luck and good timing have much to do with retail success, according to Oklahoma supermarket operator Bill Johnson. In just ten years, Johnson's three Muskogee food stores have captured an amazing 50 percent market share in a community once dominated by chains. The real credit, however, goes to Johnson's inside-out market understanding and careful site selection. As do most effective retailers, Johnson knows that the right location can mean the difference between business success and a ho-hum operation—or even failure.

Good location is a combination of factors, including proximity to target markets, appropriate facilities, accessibility, and nearness to suppliers. In Johnson's case, the crucial consideration was positioning stores for maximum coverage of the community (population forty thousand) with minimum overlap of trading areas. Johnson's first supermarket, which opened across the street from a now defunct chain operation, is in the commercial section of west Muskogee and pulls customers from surrounding towns. A second supermarket serves middle- and upper-income residential areas in southeast Muskogee. Johnson's newest store, a fifty thousand square foot food warehouse unique to the area, is near a highway network and a regional mall in north Muskogee. The three sites together draw more than thirty thousand customers weekly, and Johnson foresees Muskogee evolving into a regional trading center with plenty of traffic to support all three units.

Although Johnson's stores serve a middle-sized market, the same principle of avoiding store overlap can apply to rural operations. A host of national companies found suburban markets saturated and now choose small-town locations, citing the advantages of less competition, lower operating costs, and greater customer loyalty. Just for their rural locations, both Pay Less Drug Stores and Longs Drug Stores recently designed units with less floor space and smaller inventory than their standard stores. Sears too hopes to generate additional sales by opening downsized outlets in towns previously served only by catalog. Wal-Mart, the pioneer among rural-based chain stores, grew into the nation's second largest discounter by serving communities with populations less than twenty thousand.

At the other end of the scale, a growing number of commercial ventures are expanding into inner-city districts that are undergoing economic revival, or "gentrification." Targeting both long-time urban residents and recently arrived young professionals, chain stores and independent retailers alike are opening new units in previously underserved areas. For example, now that Super Fresh Food Market operates a store in Philadelphia's South Street section, residents who used to shop in the suburbs are buying in the neighborhood. Similarly, the two Walgreens drugstores that opened recently in

high-quality or technologically sophisticated items that require intensive personal selling, and customers expect considerable assistance.[44] These stores may offer restaurants, valet parking, and personal shopping consultants. Limited-service retailers provide some nonessential services but not others; most department stores fall into this category. Self-service retailers, such as supermarkets, discount stores, gasoline stations, and warehouse showrooms, shift many functions to their customers. However, self-service retailers usually offer lower prices, carry staple items that consumers buy frequently, and arrange products so that self-selection is not difficult.

Atmospherics

The term **atmospherics** describes the physical elements in a store's design that appeal to consumers' emotions and encourage them to buy. Exterior and interior characteristics, layout, and displays all contribute to a store's atmosphere. Department stores, restaurants, hotels, service stations, and shops combine these elements in different ways to create specific atmospheres that may be perceived as warm, fresh, functional, exciting, or depressing. The new Heritage interior design used in Kentucky Fried Chicken's Colonel's Classic restaurants conveys the warmth and charm of an old family home (see Figure 11.6).

Exterior atmospheric elements include the appearance of the storefront, display windows, store entrances, and degree of traffic congestion. Exterior atmospherics are particularly important to new customers, who tend to judge an unfamiliar store by its outside appearance and may not enter the store if they feel intimidated by the building or unduly inconvenienced by parking arrangements. Because consumers form general impressions of shopping centers and business districts, the businesses and neighborhoods surrounding a store will affect how buyers perceive the atmosphere of a store.

44. J. Barry Mason and Morris L. Mayer, *Modern Retailing: Theory and Practice* (Plano, Tex.: Business Publications, 1987), p. 623.

Interior atmospheric elements include aesthetic considerations such as lighting, wall and floor coverings, dressing facilities, and store fixtures. Interior sensory elements also contribute to atmosphere. Color, for example, can attract shoppers to a retail display. One study indicates that subjects in a furniture store may be physically drawn to bright, warm colors such as yellow or red and may sit closer to walls with those colors. At the same time, however, subjects may consider these warm colors less attractive and less pleasant than cool colors such as blue and green. Therefore, an effective color combination might be warm colors for a store's exterior or for display cases, with cool colors creating a pleasant environment near the products themselves.[45] Sound is another important sensory component of atmosphere and may consist of silence, soft music, or even noisiness. Scent may be relevant as well; within a store, the odor of perfume suggests an image different from that suggested by the smell of prepared food.

A store's layout—width of aisles, traffic flow, arrangement of departments, grouping of products, and placement of cash registers—is yet another determinant of atmosphere.[46] Closely related to store layout is the element of crowding, which

45. Joseph A. Bellizzi and Ayn E. Crowley, "The Effects of Color in Store Design," *Journal of Retailing,* Spring 1983, pp. 21–25.

46. Barry Berman and Joel Evans, *Retail Management: A Strategic Approach* (New York: Macmillan, 1986), pp. 371–376.

FIGURE 11.6

Interior design at Colonel's Classic restaurants (SOURCE: Kentucky Fried Chicken Corporation)

consists of two components: physical density and perceived crowding.[47] A crowded store may restrict exploratory shopping, impede mobility, and decrease shopping efficiency. In such a setting, buyers may rely more on familiar brands and disregard low-priority items.[48]

Once the exterior and interior characteristics and store layout have been determined, displays are added. Displays enhance the store's atmosphere and give customers information about products. When displays carry out a storewide theme, during the Christmas season, for example, they attract customers' attention and generate sales, as do displays that present several related products in a group, or ensemble. Interior displays of products stacked or hanging neatly on racks produce one kind of atmosphere; marked-down items dumped together on a sale table produce a different kind.

Retailers must determine the atmosphere the target market seeks and then adjust atmospheric variables to encourage the desired awareness and action in consumers. Discount department stores must not seem too exclusive and expensive; high-fashion boutiques may find an atmosphere of luxury and novelty most appropriate. To appeal to multiple market segments, a retailer may create different atmospheres for different operations within the store; for example, the discount basement, the sports department, and the women's shoe department may each have a unique atmosphere.

Store Image

To attract customers, a retail store must project an image—a functional and psychological picture in the consumer's mind—that is acceptable to its target market. A store's image depends heavily on atmospherics but is also linked to its reputation for integrity, the number and variety of services offered, location, merchandise assortments, pricing policies, promotional activities, and community involvement.

Characteristics of the target market—social class, lifestyle, income level, and past buying behavior—also help form store image. How consumers perceive the store can be a major determinant of store patronage. Consumers from lower social classes tend to patronize small, high-margin, high-service food stores and prefer small, friendly, high-interest loan companies over large, impersonal banks. Affluent consumers look for exclusive, high-quality establishments that offer prestige products and labels. For example, Tiffany & Company has an image that attracts customers seeking expensive jewelry such as that in Figure 11.7.

Retailers should be aware of the multiple factors that contribute to store image and recognize that perceptions of image vary from customer to customer. One study found that high-frequency shoppers, low-frequency shoppers, and noncustomers each perceive Sears differently. The study suggested that the Sears' management should pay attention to "difficulty in finding items" and "friendliness" when trying to get low-frequency shoppers to shop more often.[49]

Retailers must differentiate themselves, of course, by carefully selecting their market segments and projecting images that appeal to specific markets. But they

---

47. Gilbert D. Harrell and Michael D. Hutt, "Crowding in Retail Stores," *MSU Business Topics,* Winter 1976, p. 34.
48. Ibid.
49. Gerald Albaun, Roger Best, and Del Hawkins, "Retailing Strategy for Customer Growth and New Customer Attraction," *Journal of Business Research,* March 1980, p. 7.

Tiffany flowers. A lyrical mosaic of lapis and black jade inlaid in eighteen karat gold. Choker, bracelet and earclips from the Tiffany Allures Collection.

TIFFANY & CO.

NEW YORK LONDON BEVERLY HILLS CHICAGO DALLAS HOUSTON BOSTON ATLANTA SAN FRANCISCO 800-526-0649

must not overlook the possibility that the use of several marketing strategies simultaneously may create a "multifaceted" image, one that may attract new customers and increase sales among existing customers.[50] K mart, for example, recently remodeled many of its stores to strengthen its image as the leading national low-priced discount chain. At the same time, K mart is introducing several better-quality lines of children's clothing, which will be displayed separately in "Children's World" settings with racks and fixtures more like those in specialty and department stores. K mart hopes that the move will give customers the value they expect from a discount store, along with the color and fashion they see in higher-priced stores.[51]

Scrambled Merchandising

Scrambled merchandising is adding unrelated products and product lines, particularly fast-moving items that can be sold in volume, to an existing product mix. For example, a convenience store might start selling lawn fertilizer. Retailers who adopt the practice hope to (1) convert their stores into one-stop shopping centers, (2) generate more traffic, (3) realize higher profit margins, and/or (4) increase impulse purchases.

50. Ibid.
51. "Upscale Look for K mart Kids' Departments," *DM*, May 1987, p. 24.

There are benefits from scrambling merchandise, but merchants who do so must deal with diverse marketing channels and may reduce their own buying, selling, and servicing expertise. Scrambled merchandising can also blur a store's image in consumers' minds, making it more difficult for a retailer to succeed in today's highly competitive, saturated markets. Finally, scrambled merchandising intensifies competition among traditionally distinct types of stores and forces suppliers to adjust distribution systems so that new channel members can be accommodated.

The Wheel of Retailing

As new types of retail businesses come into being, they attempt to fill niches in the dynamic environment of retailing. One hypothesis regarding the evolution and development of new types of retail stores is the **wheel of retailing,** which holds that new retailers often enter the marketplace with low prices, margins, and status. The new competitors' low prices are usually the result of innovative cost-cutting procedures, and they soon attract imitators. Gradually, as these businesses attempt to broaden their customer base and increase sales, their operations and facilities become more elaborate and more expensive. They may move to more desirable locations, begin to carry higher-quality merchandise, or add customer services. Eventually, they emerge at the high end of the price/cost/service scales, competing with newer discount retailers following the same evolutionary process.[52]

For example, supermarkets have undergone many changes since their introduction in 1921. Initially, they provided limited services in exchange for lower food prices. However, over time they developed a variety of new services, including delicatessens, free coffee, gourmet food sections, and children's play areas. Now, supermarkets are being challenged by superstores, which offer more product choices than the original supermarkets and have undercut supermarket prices.

Figure 11.8 illustrates the wheel of retailing for department stores and discount houses. Department stores such as Sears started out as high-volume, low-cost merchants competing with general stores and other small retailers; discount houses developed later, in response to the rising expenses of services in department stores. Many discount houses now appear to be following the wheel of retailing by offering more services, better locations, quality inventories, and, therefore, higher prices. Some discount houses are almost indistinguishable from department stores.

The wheel of retailing, as are most hypotheses, may not be applicable in every case. For example, the hypothesis does not adequately explain the development of convenience stores, specialty stores, department store branches, and vending machine operations. Another major weakness of the theory is that it does not predict what retailing innovations will develop, or when. Still, the hypothesis works reasonably well in industrialized, expanding economies.

Summary

Retailing includes all transactions in which the buyer intends to consume the product through personal, family, or household use. Retailers, which are organizations that sell products primarily through retail transactions, are important links in

52. Stanley C. Hollander, "The Wheel of Retailing," *Journal of Marketing*, July 1960, p. 37.

FIGURE 11.8

The wheel of retailing, which explains the origin and evolution of new types of retail stores (SOURCE: Adapted from Robert F. Hartley, *Retailing: Challenge and Opportunity,* 3rd ed., p. 42. Copyright © 1984 by Houghton Mifflin Company. Used by permission)

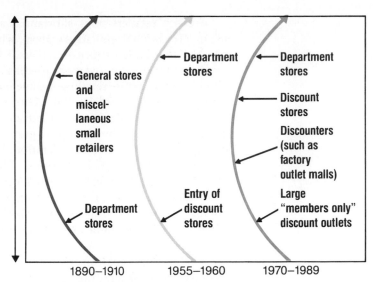

If the "wheel" is considered to be turning slowly in the direction of the arrow, then the department stores around 1900 and the discounters later can be viewed as coming on the scene at the low end of the wheel. As it turns slowly, they move with it, becoming higher-price operations, and at the same time leaving room for lower-price firms to gain entry at the low end of the wheel.

the marketing channel because they are customers for wholesalers and producers. Of all marketers, they are the most visible to ultimate consumers. Most retailing occurs inside stores or service establishments, but retail exchanges may also occur outside stores through telephone selling, vending machines, and mail-order catalogs. Retail institutions provide utilities of place, time, and possession. In the case of services, retailers develop most of the product's form utility as well. To target their products to many market segments, retailers create product assortments that vary greatly in width and depth.

Retail stores are usually classified according to width of product mix and depth of product lines. The major types of retail stores are department stores, mass merchandisers, and specialty stores.

Department stores are large retail organizations characterized by wide product mixes in considerable depth for most product lines. Their product lines are organized into separate departments that function much as self-contained businesses. These stores employ at least twenty-five people.

Mass merchandisers generally offer fewer customer services than department stores and emphasize lower prices, high turnover, and large sales volumes. This type of retailer includes discount stores (self-service, low-price general merchandise outlets), supermarkets (large, self-service food stores that also carry some nonfood products), superstores (giant retail outlets that carry all products found in supermarkets and most consumer products purchased on a routine basis), warehouse/wholesale clubs (large-scale, members-only discount operations), and warehouse and catalog showrooms (low-cost operations characterized by warehouse methods of materials handling and display, large inventories, and minimum services).

Specialty retailers offer substantial assortments in a few product lines. They include traditional specialty retailers, which carry narrow product mixes with deep product lines, and off-price retailers, which sell brand-name manufacturers' seconds and production overruns to consumers at deep discounts.

Forms of nonstore retailing include in-home selling, telephone selling, automatic vending, and mail-order selling. Direct marketing is a type of nonstore retailing that uses nonpersonal media to introduce products to customers. Franchising is an arrangement whereby a supplier grants a dealer the right to sell products in exchange for some type of consideration. Planned shopping centers' environment is a complementary mix of retail stores. The centers include neighborhood, community, regional, and nontraditional shopping centers.

To increase sales and store patronage, retailers must consider several strategic issues. Location determines the trading area from which a store must draw its customers and should be evaluated carefully. The width, depth, and quality of the product assortment should satisfy the retailer's target market customers. Customer services may draw patrons to a store, but increased sales must be balanced against the costs of providing the services. Atmospherics are the physical elements of a store's design that can be adjusted to appeal to consumers' emotions so they will be encouraged to buy. Store image, which various consumers perceive differently, is associated with atmosphere but also includes location, products offered, customer services, prices, promotion, and the store's overall reputation. Scrambled merchandising adds unrelated product lines to an existing product mix and is being used by a growing number of stores to generate sales.

The wheel of retailing hypothesis holds that new retail institutions develop as low-status, low-margin, low-price operators. As they increase service and prices, they become vulnerable to newer institutions, which enter and repeat the cycle. However, the wheel of retailing hypothesis may not apply in every case. It also cannot predict what retailing innovations will develop, or when.

Important Terms

Retailing
Retailer
Department stores
Mass merchandisers
Discount stores
Supermarkets
Superstores
Warehouse/wholesale clubs
Warehouse showroom
Catalog showroom
Traditional specialty retailers
Off-price retailers
Nonstore retailing
Direct marketing
In-home retailing
Telephone retailing

Automatic vending
Mail-order retailing
Catalog retailing
Franchising
Neighborhood shopping centers
Community shopping centers
Regional shopping centers
Atmospherics
Scrambled merchandising
Wheel of retailing

Discussion and Review Questions

1. What are the major differences between discount houses and department stores?
2. How does a superstore differ from a supermarket?
3. Should a warehouse/wholesale club be classified as a wholesaler or as a retailer?
4. In what ways are traditional specialty stores and off-price retailers similar? How do they differ?
5. Evaluate the following statement: "Direct marketing and nonstore retailing are about the same thing."
6. Why is door-to-door selling a form of retailing? Some consumers feel that direct mail orders skip the retailer. Is this true?
7. If you were to open a retail business, would you prefer to open an independent store or to own a store under a franchise arrangement? Explain your answer.
8. Describe the three major types of shopping centers. Give examples of each type in your area.
9. What major issues should be considered when determining a retail site location?
10. How does atmosphere add value to products sold in a store? How important is atmospherics for convenience stores?
11. How should one determine the best retail store atmosphere?
12. Discuss the major factors that help determine a retail store's image.
13. Is it possible for a single retail store to have an overall image that appeals to sophisticated shoppers, extravagant ones, and bargain hunters? Why or why not?
14. In what ways does the use of scrambled merchandising influence a store's image?

Cases

11.1 Mrs. Fields Cookies[53]

To drum up customers for her fledgling cookie shop, entrepreneur Debbi Fields spent her first day in business giving away freshly baked chocolate chip cookies to pedestrians outside her small Palo Alto, California, store. The strategy worked; customers followed her into the shop, and by the end of the day she had made $75. Today—ten years later—Mrs. Fields Cookies operates nearly five hundred retail outlets located in thirty-seven states and five other countries. Sales last year were $87 million, up from $72.6 million two years ago.

The current fad for gourmet cookies and other snacks has given rise to about three thousand cookie companies in the United States, including Famous Amos

53. Based on information from "Blue Chip Cookies Puts Stock in Quality," *Chain Store Age Executive*, November 1987, pp. 190–191; Nancy Rivera Brooks, "To Entrepreneur, Success Tastes Sweet," *Los Angeles Times*, Sept. 4, 1986, sec. IV, p. 1; Mark Lewyn, "Executive Tales, Told by the Book," *USA Today*, Oct. 12, 1987, pp. 1–2B; Tom Richman, "Mrs. Fields' Secret Ingredient," *Inc.*, October 1987, pp. 65–67.

Chocolate Chip Cookie Co., Blue Chip Cookies, the Great American Chocolate Chip Cookie, and numerous regional and local firms, but Mrs. Fields Cookies is the largest. Unlike many multiunit retailers, however, Mrs. Fields has not franchised any of its operations. Instead, using an innovative and sophisticated management information system, the company maintains direct control over its widely dispersed outlets and keeps its 4,500 store employees motivated and productive.

Designed by Randy Fields, Debbi's husband, the company's computer network provides a constant flow of information between every store manager and corporate headquarters at Park City, Utah. The machines themselves are ordinary. Each Mrs. Fields store has a Tandy personal computer hooked up to Park City's IBM minicomputer, with a computer modem for transmitting daily store reports. The company uses the everyday computer technology to achieve two objectives unusual for most cookie retailers. First, by automating (and thus speeding up) routine tasks, the system frees store managers from time-consuming paperwork and administrative chores. Second, because the interactive software encodes Fields' enthusiastic, people-first management style, the system projects her presence into each store and enables managers to duplicate the high quality standards and effective selling that first made her a success.

For example, at the start of every business day, using the Day Planner software, a store manager examines that store's performance for the three previous weeks and calculates how many customers will be needed and how many cookies must be sold that day if the manager is to meet sales projections. (Actual sales goals are set hour by hour because Fields set hourly sales goals when she was managing her original store.) The computer also helps the manager schedule that day's cookie baking to meet sales demand and yet have minimum leftovers. Although the manager could make these calculations personally if necessary, the computer saves valuable time. Then, throughout the day, the manager enters sales figures into the computer (the company is beginning to equip its stores with cash registers that transmit this information automatically to the computer). The computer, in turn, adjusts hourly projections and offers selling advice if customer count or total sales drop below predicted levels.

The computer assists with other managerial activities as well. It helps the manager determine how many employees to schedule for the upcoming two-week period, based on sales projections and Fields' own mixing and baking times. With a special series of interview questions, it evaluates prospective employees and initiates the paperwork with Park City when the manager makes the final hiring decision. By asking the manager questions, the system also troubleshoots when equipment malfunctions, and it generates a repair request and alerts Park City to pay the bill when repair services are required. In short, because the computer reorganizes and makes accessible the information managers provide about their own operations, every store manager is equipped to make better day-to-day decisions.

From the corporate perspective, the system lets the company maintain tight control of its retail outlets and reduce conventional hierarchy. Although the company does have area, district, and regional managers, the responsibility for monitoring the stores' daily reports and weekly inventory reports lies with seven store controllers in Park City, who make sure the reports tally with sales figures. In case of discrepancies, the controllers go whenever possible to the source of the problem, even if that means going down, not up, the chain of command. Thus with store controllers tracking the routine figures, the company's executives are free to deal with the exceptions—the differences between expected outcome and actual outcome. They can concentrate on people, not numbers, just as Fields wants them to.

Moreover, as a result of the company's lean management structure, Fields maintains the personal contact with her store managers she believes is essential to product quality. She visits stores regularly; last year she flew nearly 350,000 miles. Her managers also communicate with her electronically, through computer messages that she and her staff answer within forty-eight hours. For urgent matters, or whenever Fields wants managers to actually hear her voice, messages are sent and received by electronic PhoneMail. In the electronic sense, Debbi Fields is in all her stores at once.

Mrs. Fields Cookies began to automate its operations when its second store opened in 1978, starting with standard clerical chores and data entry, and the network has developed along with the company. Today Mrs. Fields spends about one-half of 1 percent of sales on data processing, buying only equipment that will pay for itself in two years or less. Two important principles keep the company's technology manageable. First, the firm maintains a single database so that all users have equal access and data have to be entered only once. Second, machines are delegated to perform any tasks they are capable of performing. The company plans, for example, to shift routine ordering functions to store computers. By comparing a store's weekly inventory report with projected sales, the computer should be able to determine the supplies needed, generate an order (with a copy on the screen for the manager to confirm or correct), match the invoice for supplies received with the original order, and issue a check to the supplier. Clerks then would be responsible for handling the exceptions. Eventually, the company hopes even to handle many of the exceptions electronically, by designing the system to monitor past decisions and apply them to situations at hand.

Questions for Discussion

1. Most entrepreneurs such as those at Mrs. Fields would have franchised the individual retail outlets instead of owning and managing them directly. How are the corporate-level managers able to effectively manage more than five hundred retail outlets?
2. Top management at Mrs. Fields focuses on what types of issues?
3. How is the computer system used to aid in-store managers?

11.2 The Home Depot, Inc.[54]

Atlanta-based Home Depot, Inc. operates retail warehouse stores, selling a wide assortment of building materials and home improvement products primarily to the do-it-yourself and home remodeling markets. Stores are located in sixteen markets in Georgia, Florida, Louisiana, Alabama, Arizona, Texas, and California.

54. Based on information from Home Depot *Annual Reports*, 1983, 1984, 1985, 1986; Philip Bolton, "Building Growth in the South: The Home Depot Story," *The Southern Banker*, January 1986, pp. 24–27; "Home Depot Cuts Plan for 5 Stores, Sets Sale," *Wall Street Journal*, Feb. 4, 1986, p. 19; "Retailers Plan Expansion as Stores Thrive in Duval," *Florida Times Union & Jacksonville Journal*, Oct. 12, 1986, p. F-1; Standard and Poor, *Standard NYSE Stock Reports*, vol. 53, no. 201, sec. 11.

Home Depot's extraordinary success since its founding in 1978 is a result of innovative merchandising concepts, thorough training of store personnel, and broad inventory selection. Extensive marketing research helps the company determine which geographic markets to enter and where to locate stores within those markets. Home Depot also consistently educates customers to "do it themselves" and motivates its sales staff to serve customers well.

Home Depot's commitment to customer service has helped make it the fastest-growing home improvement chain in the United States. In the period 1983 to 1985, Home Depot tripled the number of its stores and revenues increased 740 percent. Late last year a total of fifty-six stores were in operation, with sales of $700 million. Home Depot's long-term strategy is twofold: to penetrate further the markets where its reputation is established and its stores are operating at capacity, and eventually to become a national chain by entering new markets. Expansion plans call for several new stores, depending on the suitability of available locations. Because of competition and a weakened economy in some of its Sunbelt locations, Home Depot has dropped its plans to open five stores in Detroit and will concentrate instead on improving operations in its existing markets.

The idea for a chain of do-it-yourself warehouse home improvement stores was developed by Bernard Marcus and Arthur Blank, who were CEO and chief financial officer, respectively, of Handy Dan, another home improvement company. After leaving Handy Dan, Marcus and Blank used their managerial experience in home improvement retailing to put together financing and then open the Home Depot stores.

Home Depot stores have about 65,000 to more than 100,000 square feet of enclosed selling space, with an additional 4,000 to 10,000 square feet of outdoor space. Home Depot carries a complete line of home building merchandise—about 25,000 items—enough to build an entire house from scratch and landscape its grounds. The chain also sells all the tools necessary for the job and usually leads the industry in offering merchandise at the lowest possible prices.

Home Depot views every homeowner as a potential customer for do-it-yourself home improvement, regardless of age, background, economic status, or location. With wide selection and proper instruction, the company believes, any homeowner can learn to do his or her own projects and repairs, large or small. Home Depot's sales force is trained to provide expert advice to customers on how to complete projects, including which tools and materials to buy. In addition, stores offer clinics in such projects as wallpapering, electrical wiring, cabinetry, and plumbing. Home Depot's philosophy is that customers should be able to say, "I learned to do it at Home Depot, and I did it myself."

Although Home Depot originally had most of its markets to itself, now other corporate chains have opened competing stores in the markets Home Depot helped develop. Home Depot has found that it must respond to retail trends and competitors that were formerly nonexistent. But the experienced management team that made Home Depot the leading do-it-yourself retailer considers the company to be in a good position to meet this competition head-on. Home Depot has equipped its stores with computer systems to provide more efficient service, track sales, control inventory, and reduce operating costs; it has trained a new corps of personnel to keep pace with store expansion; and it has altered merchandising and operations where appropriate for its markets. Home Depot believes that these changes will enhance the company's already strong customer base, high visibility, excellent reputation, and sound financial position.

Questions for Discussion

1. What type of image and position does Home Depot hold in the retail marketplace?
2. How should Home Depot compete with emerging imitators that now challenge the company in some markets?
3. What can Home Depot do to continue its relationship with its customers once they have learned how to do home do-it-yourself projects? What should Home Depot do if competitors offer limited service at lower prices?
4. Should Home Depot continue store expansion at its current rate?

12. Physical Distribution

O B J E C T I V E S

- ▶ To understand how physical distribution activities are integrated into marketing channels and overall marketing strategies.
- ▶ To examine three important physical distribution objectives: customer service, total distribution costs, and cost trade-offs.
- ▶ To learn how efficient order processing facilitates product flow.
- ▶ To illustrate how materials handling is a part of physical distribution activities.
- ▶ To learn how warehousing facilitates the storage and movement functions in physical distribution.
- ▶ To become aware of how inventory management is conducted to develop and maintain adequate assortments of products for target markets.
- ▶ To gain insight into how transportation modes, which bridge the producer-customer gap, are selected and coordinated.

Retailing wizard Sam Walton recalls that it was not always easy to obtain stock for his Wal-Mart stores (see Figure 12.1). Back in the 1960s, the first retail outlets of the Bentonville, Arkansas, company were located in rural, out-of-the-way communities, and distributors often found it more feasible to service Wal-Mart's urban competitors instead. Thus, according to Walton, Wal-Mart's only real alternative was to build a company-owned warehouse so that the firm could buy in volume and store goods until they were needed. The plan worked, of course, and today—thanks to its eleven state of the art distribution centers—Wal-Mart keeps merchandise moving efficiently into 1,023 stores in a twenty-three-state area.

More than 75 percent of Wal-Mart's entire inventory is shipped from its own huge warehouses, each of which can deliver goods daily to about 150 stores. The average Wal-Mart distribution center ships and receives 240,000 cases of merchandise each day, stocking about nine thousand staple items year-round and two thousand other items seasonally. In many cases the merchandise is ordered from suppliers by direct computer hookups between Wal-Mart's central data processing center in Bentonville and the vendors' computers. Wal-Mart estimates that electronic ordering reduces processing time three to five days. When the merchandise is received at the distribution centers, a computer assigns a destination to each pallet; each pallet is then marked, moved from the unloading docks by forklift, and sent to either storage or an order assembly site. Meanwhile, goods pulled for shipment to individual Wal-Mart stores are speeded by conveyor belt to holding lanes high above the floor, where the merchandise moves into a single merge lane for final sorting before being shipped.

FIGURE 12.1
A Wal-Mart store
(SOURCE: Courtesy of
Wal-Mart Stores, Inc.)

New distribution technology has made the Wal-Mart network more efficient than ever. For example, optical scanning systems and bar code labeling are now standard at all distribution centers. When orders for merchandise are received from Wal-Mart stores, a computer generates bar code labels, which give order fillers the necessary information and also serve as address labels. Laser scanners then guide the labeled cartons into the correct shipping lanes. A final laser scan just before loading ensures greater accuracy in shipping. Once the goods arrive at a Wal-Mart store, stock crews use hand-held laser scanners to unload and process the merchandise. What used to be "paperwork" is now electronic work, and goods move from freight dock to store shelf up to 60 percent faster than before. The final step, scheduled for completion soon, is a satellite communications system linking distribution centers with most Wal-Mart outlets, enabling each store to notify Wal-Mart's general offices of merchandise received—within moments of arrival.

Not surprisingly, Wal-Mart's distribution costs—3 percent of sales—are about half the costs of most chain stores. Now trailing Sears, K mart, and J. C. Penney in total sales, Wal-Mart's goal is to boost last year's $12 billion in sales to

$30 billion by 1990. Accordingly, within the next three years Wal-Mart plans to cluster even more stores around the distribution centers and to double its total distribution space to about ten million square feet.[1]

W AL-MART'S USE of well-managed physical distribution activities coupled with the latest technologically advanced equipment has helped it become a very large and highly successful retail leader. Physical distribution deals with the integration of the movement and handling of goods and the processing of orders, activities necessary to provide a level of service that will satisfy customers. As implied in Chapter 9, the physical movement of products is costly. Physical distribution creates time and place utility, which maximizes the value of products by delivering them when and where they are wanted.

This chapter describes how marketing decisions are related to physical distribution. After considering basic physical distribution concepts, we outline the major objectives of physical distribution. We then examine each major distribution function: order processing, materials handling, warehousing, inventory management, and transportation. We close the chapter with a discussion of marketing strategy considerations in physical distribution. When reading this chapter, keep in mind how important customer service is to physical distribution and how physical distribution is related to marketing channels.

The Importance of Physical Distribution

Physical distribution is a set of activities, including order processing, materials handling, warehousing, inventory management, and transportation, used in the movement of products from producers to consumers and end users. Planning an effective physical distribution system can be a significant decision in developing an overall marketing strategy. A company that places the right goods in the right place, at the right time, in the right quantity, and with the right support services is able to sell more than competitors who fail to accomplish these goals.[2] Physical distribution is an important variable in a marketing strategy because it can decrease costs and increase customer satisfaction (see Figure 12.2). In fact, speed of delivery, along with services and dependability, is often as important to buyers as cost.

Physical distribution activities should be integrated with marketing channel decisions. The marketing channel is a group of interrelated organizations that directs products to customers; physical distribution deals with physical movement and inventory holding (storing and tracking inventory until it is needed) both within and among intermediaries. Often, one channel member will arrange the movement

1. Based on information from Toni Apgar, "The Cash Machine," *Marketing & Media Decisions,* March 1987, pp. 79–80; Howard Rudnitsky, "Play It Again, Sam," *Forbes,* Aug. 10, 1987, p. 48; *Wal-Mart 1987 Annual Report,* pp. 8–10; "Wal-Mart Computers Talk to Vendors," *Chain Store Age Executive,* January 1985, p. 20; "Wal-Mart Distribution Centers Blend of High Tech, Skilled Personnel," *Wal-Mart World,* July 1986, pp. 12–13.
2. Thomas Foster, "Bowing Down to the Beancounters," *Distribution,* Sept. 1983, p. 5.

of goods for all channel members involved in exchanges. For example, a packing company ships fresh California cherries and strawberries (often by air) to remote markets on a routine basis. Frequently, buyers are found while the fruit is in transit.

The physical distribution system is often adjusted to meet the unique needs of a channel member. For example, a construction equipment dealer who keeps a low inventory of replacement parts requires the fastest and most dependable service when parts not in stock are needed. In such a case, the physical distribution cost may be a minor consideration when compared with service, dependability, and timeliness.

Physical Distribution Objectives

For most companies, the main objective of physical distribution is to decrease costs while increasing service. In the real world, however, few distribution systems manage to achieve these goals in equal measure. Because the large inventories and rapid transportation essential to high levels of customer service drive up costs and reduced inventories and slower, cheaper transportation methods cause customer dissatisfaction, effective physical distribution managers strive for a reasonable bal-

FIGURE 12.2

Advertisement for a national distribution center (SOURCE: Walker & Associates/ Memphis Chamber of Commerce)

ance among service, costs, and resources. The managers determine a level of customer service that is acceptable, yet realistic; they develop a "system" outlook of figuring total distribution costs; and they trade higher costs at one stage of distribution for savings in another. In this section we examine these three performance objectives more closely.

Customer Service

In varying degrees, all organizations attempt to satisfy customer needs and wants through a set of activities known collectively as *customer service*. Many companies maintain, in fact, that service to the customer is their top priority. Clearly, without customers, profit is not possible; service may be as important in attracting customers and building sales as the cost or quality of the organization's products.

Customers require a variety of services. At the most basic level, they need fair prices, acceptable product quality, and dependable deliveries.[3] Customers seeking a higher level of customer service may also want sizable inventories, efficient order processing, availability of emergency shipments, progress reports, postsale services, prompt replacement of defective items, and warranties. Because service needs vary from customer to customer, companies must analyze—and adapt to—customer preferences. Attention to customer needs and preferences is crucial to increasing sales and obtaining repeat sales. A company's failure to provide the desired level of service may mean the loss of customers.

Companies must also examine the service levels competitors offer and match those standards, at least when the costs of providing the services can be balanced by the sales generated. Companies may step up their efforts to identify the causes of customer complaints, for example, or institute corrective measures for billing and shipping errors. In extremely competitive businesses, such as the packaged food industry, firms may concentrate on product availability. To compete effectively, food processors may strive for inventory levels and order-processing speeds that are considered unnecessary and too costly in other industries.[4]

Services are provided most effectively when service standards are developed and stated in terms that are specific, measurable, and appropriate for the product: "98 percent of all orders filled within forty-eight hours," for example. Standards should be communicated clearly to both customers and employees and rigorously enforced. In many cases it is necessary to maintain a policy of minimum order sizes to ensure that transactions are profitable; that is, special service charges are added to orders smaller than a specified quantity. Also spelled out in many service policies are delivery times and provisions for backordering, returning goods, and obtaining emergency shipments. The overall objective of any service policy should be to improve customer service just to the point at which increased sales will be negated by increased distribution costs.

Total Distribution Costs

Although physical distribution managers try to minimize the costs of each element in the system—order processing, materials handling, inventory, warehousing, and

3. Carl M. Guelzo, *Introduction to Logistics Management* (Englewood Cliffs, N.J.: Prentice-Hall, 1986), p. 32.
4. Charles A. Taff, *Management of Physical Distribution and Transportation* (Homewood, Ill.: Irwin, 1984), p. 250.

transportation—decreasing costs in one area often increases costs in another area. By using a total cost approach to physical distribution, however, managers are able to view the distribution system as a whole, not as a collection of unrelated activities. The emphasis shifts from lowering the separate costs of individual functions to minimizing the total cost of the entire distribution system.

The total cost approach calls for analyzing the costs of all possible distribution alternatives, even those considered too impractical or expensive in and of themselves. Total cost analyses weigh inventory levels against warehousing expenses, materials handling costs against various modes of transportation, and all distribution costs against customer service standards. The costs of potential sales losses from lower performance levels are also considered. In many cases, accounting procedures and statistical methods can be used to figure total costs. Where hundreds of combinations of distribution variables are possible, computer simulations may be helpful. In no case is a distribution system's lowest total cost the result of using a combination of the cheapest functions; instead, it is the lowest overall cost compatible with the company's stated service objectives.

Cost Trade-Offs

A distribution system that attempts to provide a specific level of customer service for the lowest possible total cost must use cost trade-offs to resolve conflicts about resource allocations. That is, higher costs in one area of the distribution system must be offset by lower costs in another area if the total system is to remain cost effective.

Trade-offs are strategic decisions to combine (and recombine) resources for greatest cost-effectiveness. When distribution managers regard the system as a network of interlocking functions, trade-offs become useful tools in a unified distribution strategy. Trade-offs are apparent in the distribution strategy of Swedish furniture retailer IKEA, whose stylish, ready-to-assemble goods are now available in this country (see Case 12.1). Because IKEA management decided to test the U.S. market before committing resources to additional warehouse facilities here, inventory for the two U.S. IKEA stores was shipped from Sweden, with some support from distribution centers in Canada. But the six- to eight-week shipping times created huge backlogs of out-of-stock items. Rather than jeopardize sales levels, IKEA has chosen to trade higher warehousing costs for improved customer service and will move into a national warehouse and distribution complex in Philadelphia soon.[5]

Order Processing

Order processing—the first stage in a physical distribution system—is the receipt and transmission of sales order information. Although management sometimes overlooks the importance of this set of activities, efficient order processing facilitates product flow. When carried out quickly and accurately, order processing contributes to customer satisfaction, repeat orders, and increased profits.

5. Pat Corwin, "The Vikings Are Back—With Furniture," *DM,* April 1987, p. 52, and Jennifer Lin, "IKEA's U.S. Translation," *Stores,* April 1986, p. 60.

Generally, there are three main tasks to order processing: order entry, order handling, and order delivery.[6] Order entry begins when customers or salespersons place purchase orders by mail, telephone, or computer. In some companies, sales service representatives receive and enter orders personally and also handle complaints, prepare progress reports, and forward sales order information.[7]

The next task, order handling, involves several activities. Once an order has been entered, it is transmitted to the warehouse, where the availability of the product is verified, and to the credit department, where prices, terms, and the customer's credit rating are checked. If the credit department approves the purchase, the warehouse is instructed to begin filling the order. If the requested product is not in stock, a production order is sent to the factory or the customer is offered a substitute item.

When the order has been filled and packed for shipment, the warehouse schedules pickup with an appropriate carrier. If the customer is willing to pay for rush service, premium transportation is used. An invoice is sent to the customer, inventory records are adjusted, and order delivery is carried out.

Order processing can be manual or electronic, depending on which method provides the greatest speed and accuracy within cost limits. Manual processing suffices for a small volume of orders and is more flexible in special situations; electronic processing is more practical for a large volume of orders and lets a company integrate order processing, production planning, inventory, accounting, and transportation planning into a total information system.[8] Wal-Mart stores and about three hundred of its suppliers now use electronic order-processing networks. Instead of sending paper purchase orders—which take five to ten days to reach their destination and then must be keyed into a supplier's system—Wal-Mart transmits purchase orders directly from its central data processing center to a participating vendor's computer. (All but a few of the vendors use a standard format Wal-Mart developed.) The operation cuts three to five days from the order cycle and eliminates the need for the vendor to rekey information. Electronic order processing also reduces the amount of inventory Wal-Mart must carry.[9]

Materials Handling

Materials handling, or physical handling of products, is important in efficient warehouse operations as well as in transportation from points of production to points of consumption. The characteristics of the product itself often determine how it will be handled. For example, bulk liquids and gases have unique characteristics that determine how they can be moved and stored.

Materials handling procedures and techniques should increase the usable capacity of a warehouse, reduce the number of times a good is handled, and improve

6. Carl M. Guelzo, *Introduction to Logistics Management* (Englewood Cliffs, N.J.: Prentice-Hall, 1986), pp. 35–36.
7. Charles A. Taff, *Management of Physical Distribution and Transportation* (Homewood, Ill.: Irwin, 1984), p. 240.
8. Ibid., p. 244.
9. "Wal-Mart Computers Talk to Vendors," *Chain Store Age Executive,* January 1985, p. 20.

service to customers and increase their satisfaction with the product. Packaging, loading, and movement systems must be coordinated to maximize cost reduction and customer satisfaction.

Chapter 7 notes that the protective functions of packaging are important considerations in product development. Good decisions about packaging materials and methods make possible the most efficient physical handling; most companies use packaging consultants or specialists to accomplish this important task.

Materials handling equipment is used in the design of handling systems. **Unit loading** is grouping one or more boxes on a pallet or skid; it permits movement of efficient loads by mechanical means such as forklifts, trucks, or conveyor systems. The next-sized load in materials handling is the container, discussed later in the chapter. Containers are usually eight feet wide, eight feet high, and ten, twenty, twenty-five, or forty feet long. Containerization has revolutionized physical distribution by broadening the capabilities of our transportation system, enabling shippers to transport a wider range of cargoes quickly and reliably and at stable costs. Not only is containerization energy efficient, it decreases the need for elaborate security measures and cuts down on losses and damage.

Warehousing

Warehousing, the design and operation of facilities for storing and moving goods, is an important physical distribution function. Warehousing provides time utility by enabling firms to compensate for dissimilar production and consumption rates. That is, when mass production creates a greater stock of goods than can be sold immediately, companies may warehouse the surplus goods until customers are ready to buy. Warehousing also helps stabilize the prices and availability of seasonal items. Here we describe warehouses' basic functions and the different types of warehouses available. We also examine the distribution center concept, a special warehouse operation designed so that goods can be moved rapidly.

Warehousing Functions

Warehousing is not limited simply to storage of goods; warehouses also provide valuable bulk-breaking and bulk-making services. When warehouses receive goods by carloads or truckloads, they break down the shipments into smaller quantities for individual customers; when goods arrive in small lots, the warehouses assemble the lots into bulk loads that can be shipped out more economically.[10] Here are the basic distribution functions a warehouse performs:

1. *Receives goods.* The merchandise is accepted, whether delivered from an adjacent factory or transported from a distance, and the warehouse assumes responsibility for it.
2. *Identifies goods.* The appropriate stockkeeping units are recorded, along with the quantity of each item received. The item may be marked with a physical code, tag, or other label, or it may be identified by an item code (a code on the carrier or container) or by physical properties.

10. Carl M. Guelzo, *Introduction to Logistics Management* (Englewood Cliffs, N.J.: Prentice-Hall, 1986), p. 102.

3. *Sorts goods.* The merchandise is sorted for storage in appropriate areas.
4. *Dispatches goods to storage.* The merchandise is put away for later retrieval when necessary.
5. *Holds goods.* The merchandise is kept in storage and properly protected until needed.
6. *Recalls, selects, or picks goods.* Items customers have ordered are efficiently retrieved from storage and readied for the next step.
7. *Marshals the shipment.* The items making up a single shipment are brought together and checked for completeness or explainable omissions. Order records are prepared or modified as necessary.
8. *Dispatches the shipment.* The consolidated order is packaged suitably and directed to the right transport vehicle. Necessary shipping and accounting documents are prepared.[11]

Types of Warehouses

A company's choice of warehouse facilities is an important strategic consideration. By using the right warehouse, a company may be able to reduce transportation and inventory costs or improve its service to customers; the wrong warehouse may drain company resources. In addition to deciding how many facilities to operate and where to locate them, a company must determine which type of warehouse will be most appropriate. Warehouses fall into two general categories, private and public. In many cases a combination of private and public facilities provides the most flexible approach to warehousing.

Private Warehouses   A **private warehouse** is operated by a company for the purpose of distributing its own products. Private warehouses are usually leased or purchased when a firm believes its warehouse needs in given geographic markets are so substantial and so stable that it can make a long-term commitment to fixed facilities. They are also appropriate for firms that require special handling and storage features and want to control the design and operation of the warehouse.

The largest users of private warehouses are retail chain stores.[12] Retailers such as Sears, Roebuck, Radio Shack, and even Burger King often find it economical to integrate the warehousing function with purchasing for and distribution to their retail outlets. When sales volumes are fairly stable, ownership and control of a private warehouse may provide benefits such as property appreciation. Private warehouses experience fixed costs, however, such as insurance, taxes, maintenance, and debt expense. When owned by organizations, the warehouses allow little flexibility when firms wish to move inventories to more strategic locations. Before tying up capital in a private warehouse or entering into a long-term lease, a firm should consider its resources, the level of its expertise in warehouse management, and the role of the warehouse in the firm's overall marketing strategy.

Public Warehouses   **Public warehouses** rent storage space and related physical distribution facilities to other firms and sometimes provide distribution services such as receiving and unloading products, inspecting, reshipping, filling orders,

---

11. Adapted from *Physical Distribution Systems* by John F. Magee. Copyright 1967 McGraw-Hill, Inc.
12. James C. Johnson and Donald F. Wood, *Contemporary Physical Distribution & Logistics*, 2nd ed. (Tulsa: PenWell Publishing Company, 1982), p. 356.

financing, displaying products, and coordinating shipments. They are especially useful to firms with seasonal production or low-volume storage needs, companies with inventories that must be maintained in many locations, firms that are testing or entering new markets, and business operations that own private warehouses but occasionally require additional storage space. Public warehouses can also serve as collection points during product-recall programs. Private warehouses have fixed costs, but public warehouses' costs are variable (and often lower) because users rent space and purchase warehousing services only as needed.

Some public warehouses, such as farm commodity warehouses and refrigerated warehouses, serve specific market segments rather than several different industries.[13] They have developed specialized warehousing services for their customers, including more efficient materials handling, better use of space, computer systems, temperature and humidity control, and the ability to hold large inventories.

In addition, many public warehouses furnish security for products that are being used as collateral for loans, a service that can be provided at either the warehouse or the site of the owner's inventory. A **field public warehouse** is a warehouse established by a public warehouse at the owner's inventory location. The warehouser becomes the custodian of the products and issues a receipt that can be used as collateral for a loan. Public warehouses can also provide **bonded storage,** a warehousing arrangement under which imported or taxable products are not released unless the owners of the products have paid U.S. customs duties, taxes, or other fees. Bonded warehouses enable firms to defer tax payments on such items until the products are delivered to customers.

The Distribution Center   A **distribution center** is a large, centralized warehouse that receives goods from factories and suppliers, regroups them into orders, and ships them out to customers quickly, with the focus being on active movement of goods rather than passive storage.[14] Distribution centers are specially designed for the rapid flow of products. They are usually one-story buildings (to eliminate elevators) and have good access to transportation networks, such as major highways. Many distribution centers are highly automated, with computer-directed robots, forklifts, and hoists collecting and moving products to loading docks. Although some public warehouses offer such specialized services, most distribution centers are privately owned. They serve customers in regional markets and in some cases function as consolidation points for a company's branch warehouses.

Distribution centers offer several benefits. First is improved customer service. Distribution centers ensure product availability by maintaining full product lines. The speed of their operations cuts delivery time to a minimum. In addition, distribution centers reduce costs. Instead of having to make many smaller shipments to scattered warehouses and customers, factories can ship large quantities of goods directly to distribution centers at bulk-load rates, which lowers transportation costs, and rapid turnover of inventory reduces the need for warehouses and cuts storage costs. Some distribution centers also facilitate production by receiving and consolidating raw materials and providing final assembly for some products.

13. "Warehousing Trends: Service Moves to Center Stage," *Traffic Management,* October 1984, pp. 88–90.
14. Carl M. Guelzo, *Introduction to Logistics Management* (Englewood Cliffs, N.J.: Prentice-Hall, 1986), p. 102.

Inventory Management

Inventory management involves developing and maintaining adequate assortments of products to meet customers' needs. Because a firm's investment in inventory usually represents 30 to 50 percent of its total assets, inventory decisions have a significant impact on physical distribution costs and the level of customer service provided. When too few products are carried in inventory, the result is **stockouts,** or shortages of products, which cause brand switching, lower sales, and loss of customers. But when too many products (or too many slow-moving products) are carried, costs increase, as do the risks of product obsolescence, pilferage, and damage. The objective of inventory management therefore is to minimize inventory costs while maintaining an adequate supply of goods.

There are three types of inventory costs. *Carrying costs* are holding costs; they include expenditures for storage space and materials handling, financing, insurance, taxes, and losses from spoilage of goods. *Replenishment costs* are related to the purchase of merchandise. The price of goods, handling charges, and expenses for order processing contribute to replenishment costs. *Stockout costs* include sales lost when demand for goods exceeds supply on hand and the clerical and processing expenses of backordering. All costs of obtaining and maintaining inventory must be controlled if profit goals are to be achieved.

Inventory managers deal with two issues of particular importance: They must know when to reorder and how much merchandise to order. The **reorder point** is the inventory level that signals that more inventory should be ordered. Three factors determine the reorder point: the anticipated time between the date an order is placed and the date the goods are received and made ready for resale to customers; the rate at which a product is sold or used up; and the quantity of **safety stock** on hand, or inventory needed to prevent stockouts. The optimum level of safety stock depends on the general demand and the standard of customer service to be provided. If a firm is to avoid shortages without tying up too much capital in inventory, some systematic method for determining reorder points is essential.

The inventory manager faces several trade-offs when reordering merchandise. Large safety stocks ensure product availability and thus improve the level of customer service, and they lower order-processing costs because orders are placed less frequently. Small safety stocks, on the other hand, cause frequent reorders and higher order-processing costs but lower the overall cost of carrying inventory. (Figure 12.3 illustrates two order systems involving different order quantities but the same level of safety stocks. Figure 12.3(a) indicates inventory levels for a given demand of infrequent orders; Figure 12.3(b) illustrates levels needed to fill frequent orders at the same demand.)

To quantify this trade-off between carrying costs and order-processing costs, a model for an **economic order quantity (EOQ)** has been developed (see Figure 12.4), which specifies the order size that minimizes the total cost of ordering and carrying inventory.[15] The fundamental relationships underlying the widely accepted EOQ model are the basis of many inventory control systems. Keep in mind, however,

15. The EOQ formula for the optimal order quantity is $EOQ = \sqrt{2DR/I}$, where EOQ = optimum average order size, D = total demand, R = cost of processing an order, and I = cost of maintaining one unit of inventory per year. For a more complete description of EOQ methods and terminology, see Frank S. McLaughlin and Robert C. Pickardt, *Quantitative Techniques for Management Decisions* (Boston: Houghton Mifflin, 1978), pp. 104–119.

FIGURE 12.3

Effects of order size on an inventory system

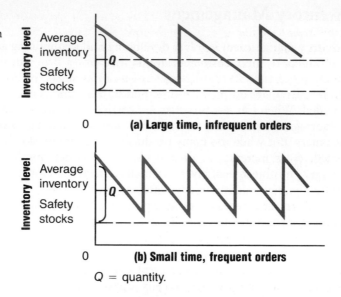

Q = quantity.

that the objective of minimum total inventory cost must be balanced against the customer service level necessary for maximum profits. Therefore, because increased costs of carrying inventory are usually associated with a higher level of customer service, the order quantity will often lie to the right of the optimal point in the figure, leading to a higher total cost for ordering and carrying larger inventory.

When management miscalculates reorder points or order quantities, inventory problems develop. Warning signs include an inventory that grows at a faster rate than sales, surplus or obsolete inventory, customer deliveries that are consistently late or lead times that are too long, inventory that represents a growing percentage of assets, and large inventory adjustments or write-offs.[16] However, there are several tools for improving inventory control. From a technical standpoint, an inventory system can be planned so that the number of products sold and the number of products in stock is determined at certain checkpoints. The control may be as simple as tearing off a code number from each product sold so that the correct sizes, colors, and models can be tabulated and reordered. A sizable amount of technologically advanced electronic equipment (see Figure 12.5) is available to aid in inventory management. In many larger stores, cash registers connected to central computer systems instantaneously update inventory and sales records. For continuous, automatic updating of inventory records, some firms use pressure-sensitive circuits installed under ordinary industrial shelving to weigh inventory, convert the weight to units, and display any inventory changes on a video screen or computer printout.

Various management techniques have also been used successfully to improve inventory management. The "just-in-time" concept, widely used in Japan, calls for companies to maintain low inventory levels and purchase products and materials in small amounts, just at the time they are needed for production. Just-in-time depends on a high level of coordination between producers and suppliers, but the technique enables companies to eliminate waste and reduce inventory costs

16. "Watch for These Red Flags," *Traffic Management*, January 1983, p. 8.

significantly. (Related issues are discussed in the Application on page 411.) Another inventory management technique, the 80/20 rule, holds that fast-moving products should generate a higher level of customer service than slow-moving products, on the theory that 20 percent of the items account for 80 percent of the sales. Thus an inventory manager attempts to keep an adequate supply of fast-selling items and a minimal supply of the slower-moving products.

Transportation

Transportation creates time and place utility for a firm's products. Because product availability and timely deliveries are so dependent on transportation functions, a firm's choice of transportation has a direct effect on customer service. A firm may even build its distribution and marketing strategy around a unique transportation system if the on-time deliveries that system ensures will give the firm a competitive edge. In this section we consider the principal modes of transportation, the criteria firms use to select one transportation mode over another, and several methods of coordinating transportation services.

Transportation Modes

As Figure 12.6 indicates, there are five major **transportation modes** or methods of moving goods: railways, motor vehicles, inland waterways, airways, and pipelines. Each mode offers unique advantages; many companies have adopted physical handling procedures that facilitate the use of two or more modes in combination. Table 12.1 illustrates typical transportation modes for various products.

Railways Railways carry heavy, bulky freight that must be shipped overland for long distances. Railways commonly haul minerals, sand, lumber, pulp, chemicals,

FIGURE 12.4

Economic order quantity model

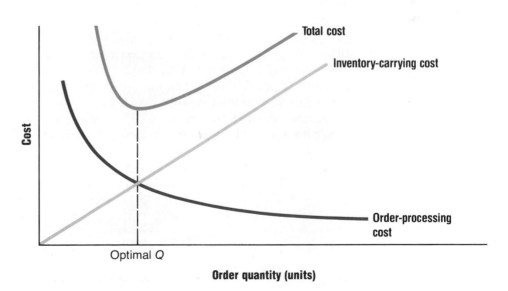

and farm products as well as low-value manufactured goods and an increasing number of automobiles. Railways are especially efficient for transporting full carloads, which require less handling—and can therefore be shipped at lower rates—than less-than-carload quantities. Many firms locate their factories or warehouses near major rail lines or on spur lines for convenient loading and unloading.

Although railways haul more intercity freight than any other mode of transportation, accounting for more than one-third of all cargo ton-miles carried, their share of the transportation market has steadily declined in recent years. High fixed costs, rail car shortages during peak periods, poor maintenance of tracks and equipment, and increased competition from other, faster carriers, especially trucks, have plagued railroad companies and cut into profits.

To improve customer service, railroads have turned to a variety of innovations. Several years ago, Railbox, a nationwide pool of 25,000 general-service box cars, was formed; the cars belong to no single rail company and can be dispatched around the country wherever cars are in short supply. Rail yards are also speeding up the formation of outbound trains by using optical scanners to read coded labels on the sides of cars, which helps sort cars by destination. Other special services include unit trains, which carry a single commodity from point of origin to destination and bypass classification yards; run-through trains, which also run nonstop but carry more than one product; and minitrains, which run often and are therefore useful in just-in-time inventory systems.

FIGURE 12.5

Promotion of electronic inventory management equipment (SOURCE: TEC America, Inc.)

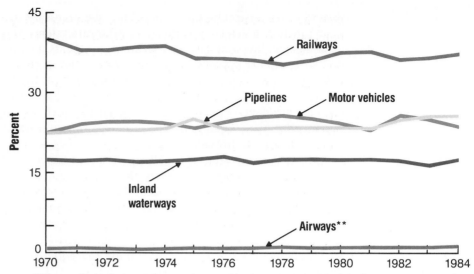

*A ton-mile is the movement of 1 ton (2,000 pounds) of freight for the distance of 1 mile.
**Airways represent less than 1% intercity traffic.

Motor Vehicles Motor vehicles provide the most flexible schedules and routes of all major transportation modes because they can go almost anywhere. Trucks usually haul small shipments of high-value goods over short distances, especially within cities, where they predominate. Because trucks have a unique ability to move goods directly from factory or warehouse to customer, they are often used in conjunction with other forms of transport that cannot provide door-to-door deliveries.

The Interstate Commerce Commission (ICC) classifies motor vehicles (along with other transportation firms) as common, contract, private, or exempt carriers.[17] Common carriers are legally obligated to serve all customers who request

17. Donald F. Wood and James C. Johnson, *Contemporary Transportation* (Tulsa: Petroleum Publishing Co., 1980), pp. 113–116.

TABLE 12.1

Typical transportation modes for various products

RAILWAYS	MOTOR VEHICLES	WATERWAYS	PIPELINES	AIRWAYS
Coal	Clothing	Petroleum	Oil	Flowers
Grain	Paper goods	Chemicals	Processed	Perishable
Chemicals	Computers	Iron ore	coal	food
Lumber	Books	Bauxite	Natural gas	Instruments
Automobiles	Fresh fruit	Grain	Water	Emergency
Iron, steel	Livestock		Chemicals	parts
				Overnight mail

their services, assuming the carriers have the necessary equipment. Contract carriers function much as private transportation systems and haul freight only for customers with whom they have written agreements. Private carriers are company-owned transport systems; although they are not economically regulated by the ICC, they are subject to safety regulations and prohibited from carrying other companies' products. Exempt carriers are freight haulers in any category who are carrying products exempted from regulation, such as unprocessed agricultural goods. As in many other industries, brokers bring together those wanting transport services and those providing them.

Although motor vehicles usually travel much faster than trains, they are somewhat more vulnerable to bad weather, and their services are more expensive. Trucks are also subject to the size and weight restrictions of the products they carry. In addition, motor carriers, especially common carriers, are sometimes criticized for high levels of loss and damage to freight and for delays from rehandling small shipments. In response, the trucking industry is turning to computerized tracking of shipments and developing new equipment to speed up loading and unloading.[18]

Inland Waterways   Water transportation is the cheapest method of shipping heavy, low-value, nonperishable goods such as ore, coal, grain, sand, and petroleum products. Water carriers offer considerable capacity. Towboat-propelled barges that travel along inland rivers, canals, and navigation systems can haul at least ten times the weight of one rail car, and deep-draft vessels operating within the Great Lakes-St. Lawrence Seaway system can carry up to 65,000 tons.[19]

Many markets are accessible to water, however, only with supplementary rail or truck transport. Furthermore, water transport is extremely slow and sometimes comes to a standstill during freezing weather. Companies that depend on water may ship their entire inventory during the summer and then store it for winter use. Flooding can also be hazardous. Nevertheless, because water transportation is extremely fuel efficient, its volume is expected to double by the year 2000.[20]

Airways   Air transportation is the fastest and most expensive form of shipping. It is used most often for perishable goods; for high-value, low-bulk items; and for products that must be delivered quickly over long distances, such as emergency shipments. The capacity of air transport is limited only by the capacity of individual aircraft: Medium-range jets can haul about 40,000 pounds of freight, and some new jet cargo planes equipped to carry containers can accommodate more than 200,000 pounds. Most air carriers transport a combination of passengers, freight, and mail.[21] The Application on page 415 focuses on related issues.

Although air transport accounts for less than 1 percent of total ton-miles carried, its importance as a mode of transportation is growing. Despite its expense, air

18. Carl M. Guelzo, *Introduction to Logistics Management* (Englewood Cliffs, N.J.: Prentice-Hall, 1986), pp. 50–52.

19. Donald F. Wood and James C. Johnson, *Contemporary Transportation* (Tulsa: Petroleum Publishing Co., 1980), pp. 290, 303.

20. Ibid., p. 289.

21. Charles A. Taff, *Management of Physical Distribution and Transportation* (Homewood, Ill.: Irwin, 1984), p. 126.

Just-In-Time Inventory Control

These days, more and more U.S. manufacturers are getting the hang of just-in-time, the Japanese system of supplying parts to the production line only as they are needed; there is no expensive backup inventory. Now, say distribution experts, just-in-time techniques are attracting the notice of retail firms as well. Large retailers, out to cut handling and warehousing costs, are incorporating just-in-time principles into their inventory control and replenishment systems. As a result, they are realizing savings from the increased efficiency and gaining a competitive edge.

One firm now using just-in-time is Walgreen Laboratories, a subsidiary of the Walgreen drugstore chain. Walgreen works with its vendors months in advance to project needs and plan delivery dates. For example, Continental Glass & Plastic receives Walgreen's order for health and beauty aids containers about six months ahead of time. One month ahead of projected delivery, a firm delivery date is agreed on. The plan, which allows a three-day margin on either side of the specified date, is a modified version of just-in-time. According to Continental officials, it is a great improvement over the haphazard scheduling of the old days.

Just-in-time also has become an integral part of Wal-Mart's distribution strategy, thanks to the discount chain's advanced distribution technology. Wal-Mart's 1,023 stores receive shipments five times weekly, on average. In addition to improving inventory control generally, the stores are using just-in-time to maintain 100 percent in-stock levels for best-selling items. Speedy, accurate shipments are possible by a combination of computerized merchandise reordering, bar codes and optical scanning systems in Wal-Mart's eleven distribution centers, and hand-held laser scanning in all Wal-Mart stores. The newest development in the company's just-in-time system is the Wal-Mart Satellite Network, which lets individual stores match deliveries against shipments and transmit "paperwork" electronically to Wal-Mart's general offices.

A third company using just-in-time is Benetton, supplier of colorful sportswear to four thousand Benetton stores around the world. Instead of filling their stockrooms with goods months before the goods are actually needed, Benetton franchisees order the items and colors they want at the time they want them—several times during a fashion season, if necessary. The orders are relayed instantly to Benetton headquarters via a sophisticated information system. Then, computerized manufacturing systems in the Benetton factories turn out the garments as specified. Shipments reach Benetton stores in two to six weeks. Because the just-in-time system provides such flexibility, Benetton can react quickly to trends and fads. In addition, the company can offer a wide variety of styles and colors without tying up large sums of capital in inventory.

> Although retail just-in-time is not yet widespread, distribution experts predict big changes ahead for most stores, which now are usually limited to accepting products only as suppliers make them available. Eventually, say analysts, retailers will push suppliers into modernizing their production methods so that stores can order goods as they need them, instead of months ahead of time.
>
> SOURCES: "American-Style Just-in-Time, Retail-Tailored," *Stores,* May 1986, p. 58; Steven P. Galante, "Distributors Bow to Demands of 'Just-in-Time' Delivery," *The Wall Street Journal,* June 30, 1986, p. 25; Howard Rudnitsky, "Play It Again, Sam," *Forbes,* Aug. 10, 1987, p. 48; William C. Symonds and Amy Dunkin, "Benetton Is Betting on More of Everything," *Business Week,* Mar. 23, 1987, p. 93; "Wal-Mart: On A Roll," *DM,* July 1987, p. 14; Wal-Mart, *1987 Annual Report,* pp. 9–10; Alan Zakon and Richard W. Winger, "Consumer Draw," *Management Review,* April 1987, pp. 20–27.

transit can reduce warehousing and packaging costs and also losses from theft and damage, thus helping lower total costs. The truck transportation needed for pickup and final delivery adds to cost and transit time.

Pipelines   Pipelines, the most automated transportation mode, usually belong to the shipper and carry the shipper's products. Most pipelines carry petroleum products or chemicals; slurry pipelines have been developed to carry pulverized coal, grain, or wood chips suspended in water. Despite the limited accessibility of their fixed routes, pipeline use accounts for about one-fourth of all intercity ton-miles.

Pipelines move products slowly but continuously and at relatively low cost. They are a reliable mode of transportation and ensure low product damage and theft. However, their contents are subject to as much as 1 percent shrinkage, usually from evaporation, and products must be shipped in minimum quantities of 25,000 barrels for efficient pipeline operation.[22]

Transportation Selection Criteria

Marketers select a transportation mode on the bases of costs, transit time (speed), reliability, capability, accessibility, security, and traceability.[23] Table 12.2 summarizes various cost and performance considerations that help determine the selection of transportation modes. It is important to remember that these relationships are approximations and that the choice of a transportation mode involves many trade-offs.

Costs   Marketers compare alternative modes of transportation to determine whether the benefits from a more expensive mode are worth the higher costs. More expensive air freight, such as UPS Next Day Air Services (Figure 12.7), provide many benefits, such as high speed, reliability, security, and traceability, but at

22. Carl M. Guelzo, *Introduction to Logistics Management* (Englewood Cliffs, N.J.: Prentice-Hall, 1986), p. 53.
23. John J. Coyle, Edward Bardi, and C. John Langley, Jr., *The Management of Business Logistics* (St. Paul: West, 1988), pp. 327–329.

higher costs relative to other transportation modes. When speed is less important, marketers desire lower costs. For example, bicycles are often shipped by rail because an unassembled bicycle can be shipped more than a thousand miles on a train for as little as $3.60. Bicycle wholesalers plan their purchases far enough in advance to be able to capitalize on this cost advantage.

Generally, marketers have been able to cut expenses and increase efficiency since the deregulation of transportation in the late 1970s and early 1980s. Railroads, airlines, trucks, barges, and pipeline companies all have become more competitive and more responsive to customers' needs. Surveys reveal that in recent years transportation costs per hundredweight and as a percentage of sales have declined, now averaging $33.45 per hundredweight, or 7.5 percent of sales. This figure varies by industry, of course; electrical machinery, textiles, and instruments have transportation costs of only 3 or 4 percent of sales, whereas lumber products, chemicals, and food have transportation costs close to 15 percent of sales.

Transit Time Transit time is the total time a carrier has possession of goods, including the time required for pickup and delivery, handling, and movement between the points of origin and destination. Closely related to transit time is frequency, or number of shipments per day. Transit time obviously affects a marketer's ability to provide service, but there are some less obvious implications as well. A shipper can take advantage of transit time to process orders for goods enroute, a capability especially important to agricultural and raw materials shippers. Some railroads also let carloads already in transit be redirected, for maximum flexibility in selecting markets. For example, a carload of peaches may be shipped to a closer destination if the fruit is in danger of ripening too quickly.

Reliability The total reliability of a transportation mode is determined by the consistency of service provided. Marketers must be able to count on their carriers to deliver goods on time and in an acceptable condition. Along with transit time, reliability affects a marketer's inventory costs, including sales lost when merchandise is not available. Unreliable transportation necessitates higher inventory levels so that stockouts will be avoided. Reliable delivery service, on the other hand, enables customers to carry smaller inventories, at lower cost. To maintain desired levels of inventory, Wal-Mart ships more than three-quarters of its stock through its own distribution network, which includes 11 distribution centers, 750 com-

TABLE 12.2
Ranking of transportation modes by selection criteria, highest to lowest

	COST	TRANSIT TIME	RELIABILITY	CAPABILITY	ACCESSIBILITY	SECURITY	TRACEABILITY
MOST	Air	Water	Pipeline	Water	Truck	Pipeline	Air
	Truck	Rail	Truck	Rail	Rail	Water	Truck
	Rail	Pipeline	Rail	Truck	Air	Rail	Rail
	Pipeline	Truck	Air	Air	Water	Air	Water
LEAST	Water	Air	Water	Pipeline	Pipeline	Truck	Pipeline

SOURCE: Certain of this information has been adapted from J. L. Heskett, Robert Ivie, and J. Nicholas Glaskowsky, *Business Logistics* (New York: Ronald Press, 1973). Used by permission.

pany-owned tractors, and 5,000 trailers. On average, every Wal-Mart store can count on five shipments of merchandise per week.[24]

Capability   Capability is the ability of a transportation mode to provide the appropriate equipment and conditions for moving specific kinds of goods. For example, many products must be shipped under controlled temperature and humidity. Other products, such as liquids or gases, require special equipment or facilities for shipment. In the railroad industry, a shipper with unusual transport needs can consult the *Official Railway Equipment Register,* which lists the various types of cars and equipment each railroad owns. The shipper can then judge which railroad company has the greatest capability for handling its products.[25]

Accessibility   A carrier's ability to move goods over a specific route or network (rail lines, waterways, or truck routes) is the measure of its accessibility. For example, marketers evaluating transportation modes for reaching Great Falls,

24. Wal-Mart Stores, Inc., *1987 Annual Report,* p. 9.
25. Donald F. Wood and James C. Johnson, *Contemporary Transportation* (Tulsa: Petroleum Publishing Co., 1980), p. 437.

FIGURE 12.7
Promotion of UPS
Next Day Air services
(SOURCE: Copyright,
United Parcel Service
of America, Inc. Used
with permission)

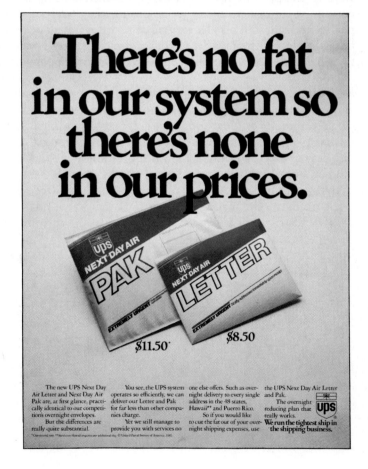

UPS Competes for More of the Overnight Air Services Market

The $6 billion overnight delivery business—ten years ago a booming new industry with room for everyone—is harder to break into these days. Currently, at least eight air express companies offer next-day delivery of small packages to about 95 percent of all U.S. addresses. In some regional markets, as many as eighteen firms compete for the overnight trade. Nevertheless, the company with the big brown trucks, United Parcel Service, is taking to the skies in a big way. Hoping to close in on market leader Federal Express, UPS is aggressively expanding its five-year-old air express service, adding planes, adopting new technology, and fine-tuning the efficiency of its operations.

The company's efficiency is already legendary. Since its early messenger service days in Seattle eighty years ago, UPS has worked hard to give its customers speed, accuracy, and economy. The company's 152,000 employees are held to exacting standards of efficiency. Drivers are instructed, for example, to walk briskly to a customer's door at the rate of three paces per second; sorters at the company's regional package-sorting hubs must handle more than 1,100 parcels per hour, with no more than one mistake per 2,500 packages. UPS management insists that such precision is essential, pointing out that the cost of inefficiency must ultimately be passed on to the customer. The strategy seems to have worked. Although UPS never discounts prices, its ground rates have increased only 6.5 percent since 1982 and its air rates have not increased at all.

In fact, cost is the biggest reason that UPS has always performed most operations manually, unlike Federal Express and other high-tech air express companies. UPS is the most profitable of all the transportation companies, with net earnings of $700 million, but the company traditionally has felt that expensive gadgetry would not be worth the money. But in the competitive environment of today's overnight delivery market, that is all changing. Responding to customer demands, UPS now plans to improve both air and ground operations by installing bar coding, electronic scanners, and shipment tracing. Computerized tracking systems will be added to many UPS trucks, and the company is also working on a kind of computerized clipboard for UPS drivers, which could transfer a day's transactions to a central computer electronically, including customer signatures.

On a more conventional level, UPS is adding to its fleet of 100 planes. Although UPS's market share is far behind that of Federal Express (15 percent to 57 percent), UPS controls a total of 258 aircraft, compared with Federal Express' 155. Furthermore, its overnight business is growing 30 percent annually. Some of UPS's recent purchases are Boeing package freighters, reputedly the quietest planes ever produced; they should be about one-third cheaper to operate than the present UPS fleet. In addition, UPS is enlarging its

Louisville air hub and has plans to build regional air hubs on the East and West Coasts. The company will also spend $35 million this year in television commercials for its air express service, its first advertising campaign ever.

Will there be enough packages to go around for everyone who would like to deliver them? Considering the crowded competitive state of the air express business, it is doubtful. Clearly, however, the "tightest ship in the shipping business" absolutely, positively plans to be a strong competitor.

SOURCES: Brian Dumaine, "Turbulence Hits the Air Couriers," *Fortune,* July 21, 1986, pp. 101–102; Dean Foust and Resa King, "Why Federal Express Has Overnight Anxiety," *Business Week,* Nov. 9, 1987, p. 62; Carol Hall, "High Fliers," *Marketing & Media Decisions,* August 1986, pp. 137–142; Lisa Harrington, "RPS Goes After the Top Dog," *Traffic Management,* May 1986, pp. 58–59; Lisa Harrington, "Sky Wars," *Traffic Management,* November 1986, pp. 38–41; Kenneth Labich, "Big Changes at Big Brown," *Fortune,* Jan. 18, 1988, pp. 56–58; Daniel Machalaba, "Up to Speed," *The Wall Street Journal,* Apr. 22, 1986, p. 1; "UPS Aims to Be Shipping's High-Technology Leader," *Purchasing,* Dec. 11, 1986, p. 49.

Montana, would realistically consider rail lines, truck routes, and scheduled airline service but would certainly eliminate water-borne carriers because Great Falls is inaccessible by water.

Some carriers differentiate themselves by servicing areas their competitors do not. After deregulation, for instance, many large railroad companies sold off or abandoned unprofitable routes, making rail service inaccessible to shippers located on spur lines. Some shippers were forced to buy their own truck fleets just to get their products to market. In recent years, however, small, short-line railroad companies have started buying up track and creating networks of low-cost feeder lines to reach those underserved markets. Small shippers are regaining access to rail service, and the short-line companies are profiting.[26]

Security A transportation mode's security is measured by the physical condition of goods upon delivery. A firm does not incur costs directly when goods are lost or damaged because the common carrier is usually held liable. Nevertheless, poor service and lack of security indirectly lead to increased costs and lower profits for the firm because damaged or lost goods are not available for immediate sale or use.

Security problems vary considerably among transportation companies and geographic regions. In the Northeast, for example, truck hijacking is a rapidly growing crime. According to the Federal Bureau of Investigation (FBI), approximately 19,000 truck tractors and 47,000 trailers are listed as stolen each year.[27] However, all transportation modes have security problems, and marketers must evaluate the relative risk of each mode.

Traceability Traceability is the relative ease with which a shipment can be located and transferred (or found if lost). Quick traceability is a convenience that some firms value highly. Shippers have learned that the tracing of shipments, along

26. Gary Slutsker, "Working on the Railroads," *Forbes,* Mar. 24, 1986, p. 126.
27. "Stop Thief," *Traffic Management,* June 1983, p. 84.

with prompt invoicing and processing of claims, increase customer loyalty and improve a firm's image in the marketplace.[28] Federal Express, for example, relies on computer systems to process and track the 600,000 packages it receives every night. At each stage of processing, from pickup to delivery, the location of every package is logged into the company's central computer in Memphis, Tennessee. If Federal Express is unable to track down a package within thirty minutes of a customer's query, the customer is charged nothing for the shipment.[29]

Coordinating Transportation Services

To take advantage of the benefits various types of carriers offer, and to compensate for their deficiencies, marketers often must combine and coordinate two or more modes of transportation. In recent years, **intermodal transportation,** as this integrated approach is sometimes called, has become easier because of several developments within the transportation industry.

One such innovation is **containerization,** the practice of consolidating many items into a single large container that is sealed at its point of origin and opened at its destination. (Certain other aspects of containers are discussed in the earlier materials handling section.) Containers can be conveniently stacked and sorted as units at the point of loading; because individual items are not handled in transit, containerization adds great efficiency and security to shipping. Several kinds of containerized shipping are available, all of which combine the flexibility of trucking with the low cost or speed of other forms of transport: piggyback (shipping that combines truck trailers and railway flatcars), fishyback (truck trailers and water carriers), and birdyback (truck trailers and air carriers). As transportation costs increase, containerization is becoming more popular. Piggyback loadings, for example, have been estimated as costing 25 to 40 percent less than all-highway transport and now make up 12 to 13 percent of total rail business.[30]

Specialized agencies known as **freight forwarders** provide other forms of transport coordination. These firms combine shipments from several organizations into efficient lot sizes. Small loads (less than five hundred pounds) are much more expensive to ship than full carloads or truckloads and frequently must be consolidated. Therefore, the freight forwarder accumulates small loads from various shippers, buys transport space from carriers, and arranges for the goods to be delivered to their respective buyers. The freight forwarder's profits come from the margin between the higher, less-than-carload rates charged to each shipper and the lower carload rates the agency pays. Because large shipments require less handling, the use of a freight forwarder can speed transit time. Freight forwarders can also determine the most efficient carriers and routes and are useful for facilitating shipments of goods to foreign markets.

One other transportation innovation is the development of **megacarriers,** which are freight transportation companies that provide several methods of shipment, such as rail, truck, and air service. Several railroads, such as CSX, illustrated in Figure 12.8, have acquired truck and barge lines, and air carriers have increased their ground transportation services. This increase in transportation alternatives

---

28. Thomas A. Foster and Joseph V. Barks, "Here Comes the Best," *Distribution,* September 1984, p. 25.
29. Brian Dumaine, "Turbulence Hits the Air Couriers," *Fortune,* July 21, 1986, pp. 101–102.
30. "Intermodalism: It's Your Move," *Inbound Traffic,* April 1985, pp. 16–22.

Another One Of Our Trains Arrives At The Station.

If you think we're just a railroad, take another look.

We're a lot more. We're Sea-Land, one of the largest container ship lines on earth, serving 76 ports in 64 countries.

We're also trucks. Barges. Pipelines. Energy resources. Fiber optics. Resorts and property development. And, of course, the railroad. And we're developing new technology to make it all work together.

We're CSX, the first true global transporter. If you've never heard of one before, it's because there's never been one before. This is a company on the move.

CSX
The Company
That Puts Things
In Motion.
Transportation/Energy/Properties/Technology

FIGURE 12.8

CSX is a megacarrier (SOURCE: Copyright 1987 CSX Corporation)

has led concurrently to a greater customer service orientation among carriers; for example, many megacarriers now offer warehousing, consulting, and personal leasing services.[31]

Strategic Issues in Physical Distribution

The physical distribution functions discussed in this chapter—order processing, materials handling, warehousing, inventory management, and transportation—account for about half of all marketing costs. Moreover, these functions have a significant impact on customer service and satisfaction, which are of prime importance to marketers. Effective marketers therefore accept considerable responsibility for the design and control of the physical distribution system. They work to ensure that the organization's overall marketing strategy is enhanced by physical distribution, with its dual objectives of decreasing costs while increasing customer service.

The strategic importance of physical distribution is evident in every element of the marketing mix. Product design and packaging must allow for efficient stacking, storage, and transport; decisions to differentiate products by size, color, and style

31. Joseph Barks, "Do Megacarriers Have You Covered—Or Smothered?", *Distribution*, March 1984, p. 10.

must take into account the additional demands that will be placed on warehousing and shipping facilities. Competitive pricing may depend on the firm's ability to provide reliable delivery or emergency shipments of replacement parts; a firm trying to lower its inventory costs may offer quantity discounts to encourage large purchases. Promotional campaigns must be coordinated with distribution functions so that advertised products will be available to buyers; order-processing departments must be able to handle additional sales order information efficiently. Distribution planners must take into consideration warehousing and transportation costs, which may influence, for example, the firm's policy on stockouts or its choice to centralize (or decentralize) its inventory.

No single distribution system is ideal for all situations, of course, and any given system must be evaluated continually and adapted as necessary. For example, pressures to adjust service levels or reduce costs may lead to totally restructuring the marketing channel relationships; changes in transportation, warehousing, materials handling, and inventory may affect speed of delivery, reliability, and economy of service. Marketing strategists must consider customers' changing needs and preferences and recognize that changes in any one of the major distribution functions will affect all the other functions. Consumer-oriented marketers analyze the characteristics of their target markets and then design distribution systems to provide products at acceptable costs.

Summary

Physical distribution is a set of activities, including order processing, materials handling, warehousing, inventory management, and transportation, used to move products from producers to consumers or end users. An effective physical distribution system can be an important component of an overall marketing strategy because it can decrease costs and increase customer satisfaction. Physical distribution activities should be integrated with marketing channel decisions and should be adjusted, if necessary, to meet the unique needs of a channel member. For most firms, physical distribution accounts for about one-fifth of a product's retail price.

The main objective of physical distribution is to decrease costs while increasing customer service. To this end, physical distribution managers strive to balance service, distribution costs, and resources. Customer service is important because customers are ultimately the source of all profits. Companies must adapt to customers' needs and preferences, offer service comparable to or better than their competitors, and develop and communicate desirable customer service policies. Costs of providing service are minimized most effectively through the total cost approach, which evaluates the costs of the system as a whole rather than as a collection of separate activities. Cost trade-offs must often be used to offset higher costs in one area of distribution with lower costs in another area.

Order processing, the first stage in a physical distribution system, is the receipt and transmission of sales order information. Order processing consists of three main tasks: order entry, order handling, and order delivery. Order entry is placing purchase orders from customers or salespersons by mail, telephone, or computer. Order handling involves checking customer credit, verifying product availability, and preparing products for shipping. Order delivery is provided by the carrier most suitable for a desired level of customer service. Order processing may be done manually or electronically, depending on which method gives the greatest speed and accuracy within cost limits.

Materials handling, or the physical handling of products, is an important element of physical distribution. Packaging, loading, and movement systems must be coordinated to take into account both cost reduction and customer requirements. Basic handling systems include unit loading on pallets or skids, movement by mechanical devices, and containerization.

Warehousing involves the design and operation of facilities for storing and moving goods. In addition to storage of goods, warehousing provides bulk-breaking and bulk-making functions. Private warehouses are owned and operated by a company for the purpose of distributing its own products. Public warehouses are business organizations that rent storage space and related physical distribution facilities to other firms. Public warehouses may furnish security for products that are being used as collateral for loans by establishing field warehouses. They may also provide bonded storage for companies wishing to defer tax payments on imported or taxable products. Distribution centers are large, centralized warehouses specially designed for the rapid movement of goods to customers. In many cases, a combination of private and public facilities is the most flexible approach to warehousing.

The objective of inventory management is to minimize inventory costs while maintaining a supply of goods adequate for customers' needs. All inventory costs—carrying, replenishment, and stockout costs—must be controlled if profit goals are to be met. To avoid stockouts without tying up too much capital in inventory, a firm must have a systematic method for determining a reorder point, the inventory level at which more inventory is ordered. The trade-offs between the costs of carrying larger average safety stocks and the costs of frequent orders can be quantified in the economic order quantity (EOQ) model. Inventory problems may take the form of surplus inventory, late deliveries, write-offs, and inventory that is too large in proportion to sales or assets. Methods for improving inventory management include systems for determining the number of products sold and in stock and management techniques such as just-in-time and the 80/20 rule.

Transportation creates time and place utility for a firm's products and has a direct effect on customer service. The five major modes of transporting goods among cities in the United States are railways, motor vehicles, inland waterways, airways, and pipelines. Marketers evaluate transportation modes regarding costs, transit time (speed), reliability, capability, accessibility, security, and traceability; final selection of a transportation mode involves many trade-offs. Intermodal transportation allows marketers to combine the advantages of two or more modes of transport; it is facilitated by containerization, the practice of consolidating many items into a single sealed container for transport by piggyback, fishyback, or birdyback; freight forwarders, who coordinate transport by combining small shipments from several organizations into efficient lot sizes; and megacarriers, freight transportation companies that offer several methods of shipment.

Physical distribution functions account for about half of all marketing costs and have a significant impact on customer satisfaction. Therefore, effective marketers are actively involved in the design and control of physical distribution systems. Physical distribution affects every element of the marketing mix: product, price, promotion, and distribution. To give their customers products at acceptable prices, marketers first consider consumers' changing needs and any changes within the major distribution functions. They then adapt existing physical distribution systems as needed for greater effectiveness.

Important Terms

Physical distribution
Order processing
Materials handling
Unit loading
Warehousing
Private warehouse
Public warehouses
Field public warehouse
Bonded storage
Distribution center
Stockouts

Reorder point
Safety stock
Economic order quantity (EOQ)
Transportation modes
Intermodal transportation
Containerization
Freight forwarders
Megacarriers

Discussion and Review Questions

1. Discuss the cost and service trade-offs in developing a physical distribution system.
2. What factors must physical distribution managers consider when developing a customer service mix?
3. Why should physical distribution managers develop service standards?
4. What is the advantage of using a total distribution cost approach?
5. What are the main tasks involved in order processing?
6. Discuss the advantages of using an electronic order-processing system. Which types of organizations are most likely to utilize electronic order processing?
7. How does a product's package affect materials handling procedures and techniques?
8. What is containerization? Discuss the major benefits of containerization.
9. Explain the major differences between private and public warehouses. What is a field public warehouse?
10. Under what circumstances should a firm use a private warehouse instead of a public one?
11. The focus of distribution centers is on active movement of goods. Discuss how distribution centers are designed for the rapid flow of products.
12. Describe the costs associated with inventory management.
13. Explain the trade-offs that inventory managers face when reordering merchandise.
14. How can managers improve inventory control? Give specific examples of techniques.
15. Compare the five major transportation modes as to costs, transit time, reliability, capability, accessibility, security, and traceability.

16. What is transit time, and how does it affect physical distribution decisions?
17. Discuss the ways marketers can combine or coordinate two or more modes of transportation. What is the advantage of doing this?
18. Identify the types of containerized shipping available to physical distribution managers.
19. Discuss how the four elements of the marketing mix affect physical distribution strategy.

Cases

12.1 IKEA Uses High-Tech Physical Distribution[32]

IKEA, one of Europe's largest furniture retailers, has set its sights on the huge U.S. market. Two years ago, the Swedish firm made its debut in this country with a two-story, six-acre store just outside Philadelphia. Last year a second store opened near Washington, D.C., bringing IKEA's worldwide total to seventy-five stores in nineteen countries, including nine stores in Canada. Sales in 1986 were $1.7 billion.

The clean Scandinavian styling and bright colors of IKEA's ready-to-assemble furniture and decorating accessories were an immediate success with American shoppers. Do-it-yourself furniture, however, is nothing new. British-based Conran introduced European design to American mass markets several years before IKEA arrived, and several other firms that sell Scandinavian furniture, both assembled and knocked down, have been located within the United States since the 1960s. What sets IKEA apart, besides its low prices, is its transnational distribution system. Both benefits are possible partly because of IKEA's innovative flat-pack technology (see Figure 12.9).

About 95 percent of IKEA's 14,000 product offerings are sold knocked-down in flat boxes, which lowers customers' prices by saving storage space and lowering the company's shipping costs. IKEA's central warehouse in Amhult, Sweden, is staffed by just three people using computerized forklifts and thirteen robots. At a command from the keyboard operator, a forklift glides down the aisles of the two-hundred-yard-long building to locate the designated pallets and bring them to the robots. The robots then follow magnetic strips in the floor to deliver the pallets to the shipping dock. Once the products reach an IKEA store, they are held (still boxed) in a self-serve warehouse adjoining the store's showrooms. After shoppers browse through the showrooms and examine IKEA's glossy catalog, they push supermarket-style carts into the self-serve area, pull their boxed selections from bins and shelves, and proceed to the check-out line. The customers themselves transport most purchases home, although delivery service for such heavy items as sofas and cabinets is available for a fee.

32. Based on information from Eugene Carlson, "How a Major Swedish Retailer Chose a Beachhead in the U.S.," *The Wall Street Journal*, Apr. 7, 1987, p. 37; Kimberley Carpenter, "Help Yourself," *Working Woman*, August 1986, p. 56; Pat Corwin, "The Vikings Are Back—With Furniture," *DM*, April 1987, p. 52; Mary Krienke, "IKEA = Simple Good Taste," *Stores*, April 1986, pp. 56–59; Jennifer Lin, "IKEA's U.S. Translation," *Stores*, April 1986, p. 60; Kevin Maney, "Customers Flood USA IKEA Outlets," *USA Today*, Nov. 4, 1986, sec. B, p. 1; Carolyn Pfaff, "IKEA: The Supermarket of Furniture Stores," *Adweek*, May 3, 1986, p. 26.

FIGURE 12.9

An IKEA furniture store (SOURCE: Paul Conklin)

IKEA is continually experimenting with ways to flat-pack more product per box. Whereas fully assembled bentwood chairs, for example, are usually shipped six to a pallet, IKEA engineers have figured out how to pack in twenty-eight chairs unassembled. And by farming out its in-house designs to the most efficient manufacturers and suppliers it can find, IKEA cuts costs even further. IKEA's "creative sourcing" might mean that a Polish windowmaker supplies wooden parts for tables; a shirt manufacturer, seat covers; and a third supplier, screws and bolts. IKEA passes its savings on to customers. On average, its retail prices are 50 percent lower than those of its competitors.

Philadelphia shoppers took to the IKEA system quickly, so quickly in fact that at first the Pennsylvania store was almost overwhelmed. During the four-day grand opening, 130,000 shoppers made their way through the store's stylish room settings. Sales for the first three months totaled $8 million, up $2 million from initial projections. Since then, crowds have leveled off at about 30,000 people a week; the Virginia store draws about 15,000 people on a typical weekend.

But success has not been without problems. First, both U.S. stores are too small. Inadequate warehouse space and loading platforms have necessitated a night shift just to replenish the stock. Second, demand has routinely exceeded supply in some product categories. At one point two years ago, the Philadelphia store had a backlog of fifteen thousand requests for out-of-stock items. IKEA maintains two distribution centers in Canada to service their stores there, but most of the stock for the two U.S. stores comes from the main warehouse in Sweden, spending six to eight weeks in transit. The stockouts are troublesome because many of IKEA's product designs are modular: If one piece is unavailable, sales of the other pieces are delayed. Too, IKEA is concerned about first-time shoppers who find an item out of stock and never return for a second visit.

Although they acknowledge that stockouts are irritating to customers, IKEA managers plan to move gradually and deliberately to solve the company's supply problems. A multimillion-dollar distribution center in the United States is still several years away. In the meantime, IKEA has leased a 400,000-square-foot warehouse complex in Philadelphia, which will open early next year. The company also intends to use a greater number of domestic suppliers. At present Canadian manufacturers provide some of the products for the U.S. stores (and about 20 percent of the items in Canadian stores), and a few of IKEA's sofas are now manufactured in Knoxville, Tennessee. Another possibility for avoiding distribution delays is the purchase of a private shipping line. Although IKEA offers mail-order service in Europe (and, in fact, started out as a mail-order furniture company), the company has no current plans to establish a mail-order business in the United States, despite a deluge of requests from customers.

Instead, IKEA's long-range U.S. strategy calls for as many as sixty new stores over the next 25 years, supported by five regional distribution and marketing systems. For now, IKEA is concentrating on the east coast and will probably open its next store in Boston, Baltimore, or suburban New York.

Questions for Discussion

1. What actions has IKEA taken to reduce its physical distribution problems?
2. Explain how IKEA's physical distribution system influences other parts of this organization's marketing strategies.
3. In the future, what types of physical distribution problems must IKEA resolve with respect to its U.S. stores?

12.2 Competition Among the Air Express Courier Services[33]

On a typical night, about 600,000 packages arriving at Federal Express' Memphis superhub will be unloaded, coded, sorted, and reloaded within two hours. Then, thanks to the hub's twenty miles of conveyor belts, sixty airplanes, and three thousand night-shift workers, those packages will be delivered to their destinations by 10:30 A.M. the next day. Delivering packages faster than anyone else is Federal's objective, and its integrated distribution system has brought the company 40 to 50 percent of the U.S. overnight delivery market.

The air express business is an industry Federal Express created. Although the rapid growth that characterized many express delivery firms in the 1970s and early

33. Based on information from Felecia Stratton, "Yes, There Is Life Beyond Federal Express," *Inbound Logistics*, January 1986, pp. 11–13; Betsy Haggerty, "A Smart Shopper's Guide to Expedited Delivery Services," *Inbound Logistics*, January 1986, pp. 15–16; Jim Curley, "Long Night's Journey into Day: How Your Package Gets from There to Here," *Inbound Logistics*, January 1986, pp. 19–23; Michael R. Pashall, "Bar Codes for Tracking Orders Instantly," *Modern Materials Handling*, March 1986, p. 69; Dean Foust and Resa King, "Why Federal Express Has Overnight Anxiety," *Business Week*, Nov. 9, 1987, p. 62; Dean Foust and Resa King, "Federal Express Delivers A Price Shock," *Business Week*, Mar. 30, 1987, pp. 31–32; Marie Morelli, "Revitalized Federal Express Delivers," *USA Today*, Oct. 7, 1987, p. 3B; Brian Dumaine, "Turbulence Hits the Air Couriers," *Fortune*, July 21, 1986, pp. 101–102.

TABLE 12.3

Domestic air cargo shipments by competitor, 1985–1986 (thousands of shipments)

COMPETITOR	1985	1986	PERCENT CHANGE 85/86
Federal Express	121,795	157,270	29.1
Emery Worldwide	11,207	11,349	1.3
Airborne Freight Corp.	19,277	26,699	38.5
Purolator Courier	13,314	16,931	27.2
UPS-Air	69,845	93,038	33.2
Burlington Northern	3,202	2,556	−20.2
CF AirFreight	1,476	1,797	21.7
Profit Systems[a]	634	718	13.2
Flying Tiger Retail[b]	883	676	−23.4
Sub Total	241,633	311,034	28.7
Other Competitors	90,637	87,015	− 4.0
Total Market	332,270	398,049	19.8

[a]For fiscal year ended in June. Excludes Puerto Rico traffic.
[b]Excludes business tendered by forwarders.

SOURCE: *The Domestic Air Cargo Trends Report*, The Colography Group, Inc., Marietta, Georgia, July 1987. Reprinted by permission of The Colography Group, Inc.

1980s has slowed, the domestic air express business continues to grow at a yearly rate of 15 to 20 percent, with annual sales now totaling more than $6 billion. Federal Express still outdistances all other air carriers in both number of shipments, as Table 12.3 shows, and revenue (more than $3.2 billion). The growth of the air cargo market has also increased combined truck and air operations for all major competitors providing those services.

Transportation experts point out that more than half of all domestic weight is *not* shipped by express systems. When transportation managers decide not to use air delivery, they usually choose highway carriers, which take longer but often charge cheaper rates for many products. They also use rail service, as evidenced by the 45 percent increase in rail express cargo Amtrak reported for one recent twelve-month period. The number of options available to the professional buyer of delivery services is staggering; before contracting for air express service, a physical distribution manager must determine the company's needs and how air cargo delivery fits into the company's marketing strategies.

Price is one consideration. Most small-package delivery services are fairly expensive; Federal Express, for example, charges $14 for overnight delivery of a five-pound package. Some of the recent slowdown in the air express industry has been attributed to cost-cutting by organizational customers. In other cases, speed and dependability may be more important than price; often, reliability is the most important factor in the final decision.

Firms choosing air express delivery may also be influenced by the special services various carriers offer. Federal Express labels packages with bar codes for greater sorting accuracy, and both Federal Express and United Parcel Service offer on-site computerized tracking of packages. United Parcel Service also is expanding its on-call service, heretofore a strength of Federal Express. Although most air cargo companies offered volume discounts in the past, price-cutting is now intense. To win price breaks, customers are consolidating their business among a few carriers; Airborne Freight, for example, recently undercut Federal Express' prices up to 84 percent to obtain a three-year contract from IBM.

Physical distribution managers find that the best way to determine a carrier's performance is to test it with noncritical deliveries. Companies may select two or three carriers or ship on a case-by-case basis. And overnight service continues to attract distribution managers for several reasons. First, freight that moves quickly is handled less and therefore less subject to damage or theft. Second, overnight delivery of repair parts or other inventory items decreases the need for costly warehouse stockpiling. Finally, companies know that they can rely on fast delivery and are reluctant to risk another delivery method.

Inbound Logistics, a magazine for transportation and purchasing professionals, called sixteen small-package delivery carriers and told representatives that it

TABLE 12.4

A buyer's guide to expedited deliveries

CARRIER	RATES[a]				SERVICE NOTES
	OVERNIGHT		2ND DAY	OTHER	
Airborne	$48		N/A	N/A	Door-to-door Delivery by 10:30 A.M.
Air Express International (AEI)	55		$40	N/A	Door-to-door Delivery between 9 A.M. and 5 P.M.
Amtrak	N/A		16	N/A	No guaranteed time-definite service, except as noted in train schedule No pickup or delivery service
Associated Air Freight	48		38	N/A	Door-to-door Noon delivery on overnight service
Burlington Northern Air Freight	44		44	N/A	Door-to-door A.M. delivery usual, but not guaranteed
CF AirFreight	40.66 (by noon)	38.63 (by 5 P.M.)	N/A	24.40 (3 days)	Door-to-door
DHL	49		N/A	N/A	Door-to-door Delivery by noon
Emery Worldwide	48 (before 10 A.M.)	45 (P.M.)	22	N/A	Door-to-door 2nd day delivery before 5 P.M.
Federal Express	45		20.50	N/A	Door-to-door Overnight delivery by 10:30 A.M. 2nd day delivery before 5 P.M.

wanted to have a ten-pound package of printing materials delivered from the Sears Tower in downtown Chicago to its offices at 1 Penn Plaza, New York City. Table 12.4 shows the quoted rates based on mileage (approximately eight hundred miles), weight, and delivery time.

Questions for Discussion

1. Discuss the criteria you would use for selecting a carrier for the ten-pound package of printing materials.
2. Which of the carriers in Table 12.4 would you select to deliver the ten-pound package of printing material from the Sears Tower to 1 Penn Plaza?
3. Assume that the ten-pound package was not needed until the second day. Defend your choice of a carrier for this service. Assume that the ten-pound package of printing materials is absolutely necessary and highly critical for a meeting in four days. Which service would you select? Defend your selection.

TABLE 12.4
(continued)

CARRIER	RATES[a] OVERNIGHT	2ND DAY	OTHER	SERVICE NOTES
Greyhound	N/A	$26.90[b]	$13.45 (2–3 day)	Terminal-to-terminal Door-to-door extra charge Bus takes less than 24 hours
Pilot Air Freight	$40	35	62.79 (5 day LTL)	Door-to-door Overnight and 2nd day deliveries before 5 P.M. LTL is minimum rate
Purolator Courier	45	20	N/A	Door-to-door Overnight delivery before noon 2nd day delivery by 5 P.M.
Roadway	N/A	N/A	3.44 (3 days)	Door-to-door Deliveries for regular customers only, therefore exact rate not available Base rate same as UPS
Trailways	N/A	11.10	N/A	Terminal-to-terminal Door-to-door extra charge
United Parcel Service	21	11.50	3.44 (3–4 days)	Door-to-door Delivery before 5 P.M.
U.S. Postal Service Express Mail	13.15	N/A	N/A	Door-to-door Delivery before 5 P.M.

[a]Rates based on a 10-lb package, delivered approximately 800 miles.
[b]Must pay higher rate for time-definite 2nd day service.

SOURCE: Betsy Haggerty, "A Smart Shopper's Guide to Expedited Delivery Services," *Inbound Logistics,* January 1986, p. 18. Used by permission.

7-Eleven Stores

The retail convenience store originated more than forty years ago, when Dallas-based Southland Corporation opened the first 7-Eleven stores. Today, Southland continues to dominate the convenience store industry. Of the 76,000 convenience stores now operating in the United States and Canada, 8,200 are 7-Eleven outlets. Neighborhood 7-Elevens pull in eight million customers a day in forty-one states, the District of Columbia, and five Canadian provinces. More than half of all Americans live within two miles of 7-Eleven's familiar red and green sign. Taken together, 7-Eleven stores ring up sales of $7 billion a year, selling more tobacco products, beer, and coffee to go than any other retailer in the United States. Southland is also the country's largest independent retailer of gasoline: Self-serve gasoline—available at about 3,600 7-Eleven outlets—accounts for more than $1.75 billion in sales each year. Until recently, 7-Eleven was a leader in sales of adult magazines as well; Southland lost $13.5 million to $15.5 million in annual sales when it stopped carrying *Playboy, Penthouse,* and *Forum* two years ago.

Although Southland has opened about 3,500 new 7-Eleven stores since 1978, the corporation is strongly committed to what it considers "real growth," that is, increasing sales and earnings in all its units. But competitive pressures are building in the convenience store business. The total number of convenience stores has doubled since 1981, driving per-store sales averages down. Southland operates more than twice as many outlets as Circle K, its nearest competitor, but in recent years Southland has trailed Circle K in both earnings growth and profit margins. Southland is also competing with oil companies for convenience store customers. Industry figures show that major oil companies now own more than 10,000 convenience stores, including at least seven of the top twenty convenience chains. In addition, convenience stores in general represent a bigger investment than ever before. Convenience chains often invest $500,000 to $1 million in a single new store and spend additional millions remodeling older units and expanding product lines.

Southland's New Distribution Strategies

To meet these challenges, Southland is adjusting its distribution system, retailing strategy, and product mix for the 7-Eleven stores. The firm has backed off, for example, from its costly venture into vertical integration. In the late 1960s, Southland decided that, given the difficulty of getting outside suppliers to service the 7-Eleven stores, the company could supply much of its own merchandise more efficiently. Over the years the company accumulated a variety of manufacturing operations, including a food laboratory and snack food processor; Southland Dairies, one of the country's largest dairy processors; Chief Auto Parts, a 465-store chain; Reddy Ice, world's largest producer of crushed ice; and half interest in Citgo Petroleum Corp., the refiner that supplies gasoline to 7-Eleven pumps. Two years ago Southland formed MovieQuik, a videotape distributorship that provides rental movies for 7-Eleven stores. Now, however, several of these operations are up for sale, and Southland is investigating less capital-intensive avenues of distribution.

One possibility is joint ventures with suppliers. In an experimental arrangement with Mobil Oil, several 7-Eleven stores recently leased retail property from Mobil, paying the oil firm a percentage of sales. A successful partnership with an oil company could help improve Southland's shrinking margins on gasoline sales, even if Southland follows through on its plans to retain part ownership in Citgo. Joint ventures with fast-food vendors appear even more promising. Whereas gross margins on gasoline are usually less than 9 percent, margins on fast foods run as high as 50 percent and more. Thus Southland has been test marketing Hardee's hamburgers, fries, and breakfast biscuits in several Midwestern 7-Eleven outlets. Some observers speculated initially that the branded fast foods might cut into sales of 7-Eleven's own deli lines, but Southland reported that sales of 7-Eleven sandwiches, hot dogs, coffee, Slurpees, and fountain drinks went up across the board. Pleased with the test results, Southland added other stores to the Hardee's program and announced plans for similar arrangements with Church's Fried Chicken and Rocky Rococo's Pizza Corp.

Expanding the Customer Base

Ventures with fast-food distributors may help increase profit margins, but such innovations may yield another benefit as well: increased store traffic. Southland is trying various strategies to attract new customers, particularly now that growth is slowing in 7-Eleven's traditional customer base: blue-collar men between 18 and 43 who stop in about three times a week for coffee, sandwiches, or beer. Southland would like to bring in more young professionals and persons older than 55, people who seldom shop at 7-Eleven. The company is even more interested in increasing its sales to women, who currently form less than a third of the chain's customers.

Accordingly, Southland is trying to spruce up its image. Recently the company spent $175 million to remodel older stores and add new fixtures for videocassettes and other services. The company also is closing down outlets in marginal locations, leaving a base of competitive, productive stores. Since the early 1980s, about 90 percent of all new 7-Eleven stores have been built on corner sites, which are more visible, more accessible, and more likely to generate gasoline sales, an important consideration given that one-third of 7-Eleven's gas customers buy something else while in the store. In addition, Southland has worked to clean up 7-Eleven's reputation for poor security by revising cash control policies, adding more outside lighting, and requiring stores to remove window clutter for greater visibility.

In line with market research showing that women are more bargain conscious than men, Southland also has embarked on a drastic price-cutting program in its most competitive markets. Traditionally, few convenience chains have attempted to compete head-on with grocery store prices. According to a recent study by the National Association of Convenience Stores, nongasoline margins at convenience stores usually average about 32 percent, compared with the 20 to 22 percent supermarket markups. Typically, a 7-Eleven might sell a bottle of aspirin for $2.95, up from $1.99 at the neighborhood supermarket, or Pampers disposable diapers for $4.49, compared with $4.27 at the grocery store.

Currently, however, 7-Elevens in Florida, Texas, and parts of Arizona are advertising some of the best buys in town on selected items. Backed by a television campaign featuring the slogan "Now even good prices come easy," Dallas 7-Eleven stores are offering soft drinks in two-liter bottles for $1.39, down from $1.80

elsewhere; a twelve-pack of beer is selling for $5.79, compared with $6.15 at other stores. Some Houston 7-Elevens sell single packs of cigarettes for $1.25, about 14 cents a pack less than at other convenience chains. Milk and eggs also are going at discounted prices in some markets.

Response to Southland's price-cutting policy has been mixed. National Convenience Stores Inc., operator of Stop N Go stores, has matched some, but not all, of 7-Eleven's prices. Circle K Corp., the country's second largest convenience store chain, lowered prices initially but raised them again when profit margins suffered. Most convenience store retailers believe that small outlets can never match the high-volume sales of large grocery stores and thus should not try to offer supermarket prices. Even if discounting should produce market gains, the retailers point out, the increased traffic may not offset the lower gross margins. To attract women and other new customers, say Southland's competitors, convenience stores should concentrate on offering cleaner, brighter stores and wider product selection to reduce shopping time.

Managing the Product Mix Efficiently

The convenience store's strongest selling point, in short, may still be convenience: easy access, short check-out lines, and long store hours. Despite its current emphasis on low prices, Southland has not overlooked the importance of store efficiency, and the company has thoroughly researched the techniques of convenience retailing. Company stores are governed by a procedures manual that spells out everything from handling cash to making sandwiches. (7-Eleven franchisees, who run about one-third of the chain's stores, have more freedom to adjust their store operations to local needs.) To look clean and modern, to control customer traffic, and to make products more accessible, company-managed stores also are required to follow a detailed diagram for merchandise display. Equally important to productivity and efficiency is managing information. Southland is outfitting its retail network with two-way data transmission systems so that management can find out quickly and accurately which products are selling well, what inventory levels are low, and which stores are operating at maximum efficiency.

Southland also sees a close connection between store productivity and the number and types of products offered. The company carefully monitors its product line for attractiveness and profitability and searches constantly for promising new products. Southland particularly looks for convenience items that appeal to impulse, can be bought with cash and carried home, guarantee an adequate profit per square foot used, and require minimal storage, display space, and employee support. During the past several years, 7-Eleven has introduced Danish pastries, fountain soft drinks, fresh fruits, burritos, juices, deli sandwiches, baked goods, and video games, all of which have been very successful. 7-Eleven also continues to promote established products with good sales potential, such as its Slurpee frozen carbonated drink. Hoping to attract lake-bound fishermen to his store, one enterprising Michigan 7-Eleven franchisee even added earthworms to his product mix. He keeps the earthworms in a small refrigerator near the check-out counter; the franchisee sells about 350 to 400 dozen worms a week and finds that the sportsmen often buy sandwiches, soft drinks, and beer as well.

To increase its market share, 7-Eleven is now including a line of customer services in its product mix. For example, video players and cassettes can now be rented in about 6,500 7-Eleven stores. The rental service has increased 7-Eleven's profits by bringing customers into the store twice (first to rent the tape and then to return it) and by generating add-on sales of other products. In addition, 7-Eleven has tested the sale of airline tickets and home delivery of telephone grocery orders ($10 minimum). Customers in some stores can purchase travelers' checks and state lottery tickets; ticketing for shows and sports events may soon follow.

Southland may even become a major player in interstate electronic consumer banking. The company was one of the first retailers to test in-store automatic teller machines (ATMs) and now has agreements to place ATMs in 3,800 convenience stores. The cash machines will accept credit cards from several banks. Southland also is issuing its own Citgo credit cards for use at 7-Eleven gas pumps—which now bear the Citgo brand name—and inside 7-Eleven stores.

Questions for Discussion

1. How has 7-Eleven designed its product mixes at the store level to attract customers?
2. Southland is especially interested in attracting certain customer groups to its stores. What steps are being taken to attract these special groups?
3. Why would fast-food chains such as Hardee's or Kentucky Fried Chicken want to sell its products through 7-Eleven stores?
4. Evaluate Southland's recent decision to use a price-cutting strategy on selected products.

SOURCES: Southland Corporation, *Annual Reports*, 1982, 1984, 1985; Marketing presentation handout from Southland Corporation, Nov. 4, 1983; Anne Reifenberg, "Citgo Pursues Aggressive Strategy," *Dallas Morning News*, Apr. 6, 1986, pp. H-1, 5; "Southland 7-Eleven Stores Drop Playboy, Penthouse," *The Wall Street Journal*, Apr. 11, 1986, p. 13; *1985 Moody's Industrial Manual*, vol. 2, pp. 3544–3556; "7-Eleven Stores: Next Stop, Home?", *Newsweek*, May 12, 1986, p. 64; Tom Bayer, "Fast (Food) Sales for Southland," *Advertising Age*, Aug. 8, 1986, p. 4; Lisa Gubernick, "Stores for Our Times," *Forbes*, Nov. 3, 1986, pp. 40–42; Gene G. Marcial, "The Crowd Gathering at 7-Eleven," *Business Week*, Dec. 15, 1986, p. 92; "Why the C-Store Image Race Could Lead to a 'Shakeout,'" *National Petroleum News*, September 1987, pp. 38–42; Dennis Cauchon, "Southland to Sell Assets to Keep 7-11s," *USA Today*, July 7, 1987, p. 2B; Lisa Gubernick, "Thank Heaven for 7-Eleven," *Forbes*, Mar. 23, 1987, p. 52; Karen Blumenthal, "Convenience Stores Try Cutting Prices . . . ," *The Wall Street Journal*, July 3, 1987, p. 15E; "MovieQuik: Southland's Newest Star," *Chain Store Age Executive*, June 1987, pp. 38–39; "Southwest to Sell Tickets Through Teller Machines," *The Wall Street Journal*, Oct. 17, 1986, p. 19; Candace Talmadge, "7-Eleven, King of Convenience Stores . . . ," *Adweek*, Aug. 3, 1987, p. 32; Don Smith, "C-Store Security," *National Petroleum News*, April 1987, pp. 38–43; Winston Williams, "Southland's Quest for Glamour," *The New York Times*, Mar. 16, 1986, p. L1; John Holusha, "Convenience Pays at 7-Eleven," *The New York Times*, July 13, 1987, p. D1.

IV. Promotion Decisions

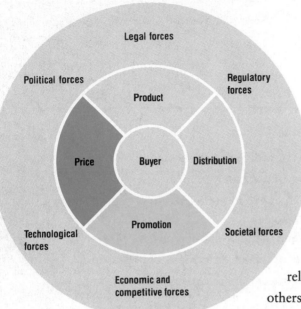

Part IV deals with communicating with target market members. A specific marketing mix cannot satisfy people in a particular target market unless they are aware of the product and where to find it. Some promotion decisions and activities are related to a specific marketing mix, whereas others, broader in scope, focus on the promotion of the whole organization. Chapter 13 presents an overview of promotion. We describe the communication process and the major promotion methods that can be included in promotion mixes. In Chapter 14, we analyze the major steps required to develop an advertising campaign, and we explain what publicity is and how it can be used. Chapter 15 deals with the management of personal selling and the role it can play in a firm's promotion mix. This chapter also explores the general characteristics of sales promotion and sales promotion techniques.

13. Promotion: An Overview

OBJECTIVES

- ▶ To understand the role of promotion in the marketing mix.
- ▶ To examine the process of communication.
- ▶ To understand the product adoption process and its implications for promotional efforts.
- ▶ To gain an understanding of the promotion mix.
- ▶ To acquire an overview of the major methods of promotion.
- ▶ To explore factors that affect the choice of promotional methods.

O*rganizations use* various promotional approaches to communicate with target markets, as the following four examples illustrate:

Spiegel, Inc. has developed an advertising campaign emphasizing that you can shop with Spiegel's catalog everywhere. The overall objective is to communicate that products can be purchased easily and leisurely through the Spiegel catalog. In the print campaign, products available at Spiegel's are pictured in nontraditional places. For example, a patent leather pump shoe is shown in the refrigerator with copy reading "Thanks to Spiegel, any place you can read can also be a convenient place to shop" (see Figure 13.1). The campaign has two goals: to give Spiegel a contemporary fashionable image and encourage catalog sales via direct response from customers. Catalog order cards are included as bound-in response cards in magazine advertisements.

Walt Disney Productions successfully used publicity to celebrate the fifteenth anniversary of the Walt Disney World Theme Park. Events were scheduled that would draw national attention, such as parades, fireworks, concerts, parties, and a press conference. These activities took place over a four-day period and cost $8 million, but the result was more than one thousand hours of live satellite television broadcasting the celebration. Disney successfully gained "free" press coverage by creating an extravaganza that had public interest and identification.

General Motors Corp. developed a joint sales promotion with Procter & Gamble to increase awareness of its Beretta and Corsica automobiles and its pickup trucks. General Motors gave away $9 million worth of cars and trucks through mock keys available in Procter & Gamble products. Consumers would

The Garolini Pump.
Now Available In Kitchens.

Thanks to Spiegel, anyplace you like to read can also be a convenient place to shop. Our Spring Catalog includes the latest designs from Ralph Lauren, Calvin Klein, Adrienne Vittadini, Liz Claiborne and others. To receive your copy for just $3, simply call (toll-free) 1-800-345-4500 and ask for catalog 757.

Spiegel

bring the keys in to General Motors dealers to see if they had won a new GM product. Through GM's association with Procter & Gamble, Chevrolet was able to get point-of-purchase displays into supermarkets, which is important because women form the fastest-growing new car market. In return for their participation, Procter & Gamble customers were given the opportunity to win a GM product; Procter & Gamble's consumer goods sales during this period rose notably.

IBM's sales success in the computer industry is attributed partly to the superior skills of its sales personnel in selling and meeting the product application needs of individual customers and specific industries. IBM sales recruits have technical backgrounds, good communication skills, and 3.5 or better college grade averages. New sales reps are sent to a highly competitive training program in which each rep is helped to determine personal performance objectives. Other criteria are specified for the reps in such areas as customer satisfaction and territory and marketing management. Sales reps are trained to maintain and troubleshoot accounts, using every available company resource. The worst mistake a sales representative can make, says a former IBM salesman, is to lose an account to a competitor. IBM provides strong support for its sales force.[1]

A CTIVITIES BY THESE various organizations can all be viewed as promotional activities.

This chapter looks at the general dimensions of promotion. Initially we consider the role of promotion. Then, to understand how promotion works, we analyze the meaning and process of communication and the product adoption process. The remainder of the chapter discusses the major types of promotional methods and the factors that influence an organization's decision to use specific methods.

The Role of Promotion

When people think about promotion, they frequently take one of two extreme positions. They may believe that the field of marketing consists entirely of promotional activities such as advertising because it is such a highly visible part of our everyday lives. People who take the other extreme see promotional activities as unnecessary and thus wasteful. They perceive that promotion costs (especially advertising) are high—sometimes excessively so—and believe these costs drive prices higher. For example, thirty seconds of commercial air time for Super Bowl XXII cost $650,000. Neither opinion is correct.

The role of **promotion** is to communicate with individuals, groups, or organizations to directly or indirectly facilitate exchanges by informing and persuading one or more of the audiences to accept an organization's products. For instance, Nike recruited tennis professional John McEnroe to promote a tennis apparel line; Joan Benoit, marathon runner, to endorse the more traditional running shoe; and Chicago Bull, Michael Jordan, to promote the Air Jordan line of basketball shoes. Nike felt the best way to support sagging sales was to offer a more widely promoted product line that targeted specific audiences by using readily identifiable athletic endorsers to communicate the message.[2] To facilitate exchanges directly, marketers communicate with selected audiences about a firm and/or its goods, services, and ideas. Federal Express's audience was looking for a solution to their personal business problems—developing the market for high priority shipping. Focusing directly on its customers' real needs, Federal Express came up with a

1. Based on information from Kim Kinter, "Spiegel Mixes Images for Catalogue," *Adweek's Marketing Week*, Jan. 4, 1988, p. 16; Aaron Sugarman, "New Product Rollouts," *Incentive Marketing*, July 1987, pp. 23–26, 52; "Parties for Fun and Profit: Event Marketing Can Pack A Powerful Punch," *Incentive Marketing*, December 1986, pp. 14, 83; "The IBM Salesperson Is King," *Sales and Marketing Management*, Dec. 3, 1984, p. 39.
2. Ruth Stroud, "Nike Weighing Ad, Promo Budget Cuts," *Advertising Age*, Jan. 21, 1985, p. 6; "Nike Unit's Sole Goal Will be New Products," *Advertising Age*, Feb. 11, 1985, p. 86.

highly successful message to its target market: "When it absolutely, positively, has to be there overnight."[3] Marketers indirectly facilitate exchanges by focusing communication about company activities and products on interest groups (such as environmental and consumer groups), current and potential investors, regulatory agencies, and society in general. Consider the Application on page 441, which examines the impact of cause-related marketing.

Viewed from this wider perspective, promotion can play a comprehensive communication role. Some promotional activities can be directed toward helping a company justify its existence and maintain positive, healthy relationships between itself and various groups in the marketing environment. Philip Morris Companies Inc. (see Figure 13.2) sponsors the Next Wave Festival to show its support of innovation and artistic spirit, not to directly sell its products (Miller beer, General Foods products, cigarettes, etc.).

Although a firm can direct a single type of communication—such as an advertisement—toward numerous audiences, marketers often design a communication precisely for a specific audience. A firm frequently communicates several different

FIGURE 13.2

Philip Morris Companies Inc. supports the Fifth Annual Next Wave Festival because it believes that innovation is the key to success

3. Carl Williams, "The Challenge of Retail Marketing at Federal Express," *The Journal of Services Marketing,* Summer 1987, p. 26.

FIGURE 13.3

Information flows into
and out of an organi-
zation

messages concurrently, each to a different group. For example, McDonald's Corp. may direct one communication toward customers for its Big Mac, a second message toward investors about the firm's stable growth, and a third communication toward society in general regarding the company's social awareness in supporting Ronald McDonald Houses.

To gain maximum benefit from promotional efforts, marketers must make every effort to be sure communications are properly planned, implemented, coordinated, and controlled. Effective promotional activities are based on information from the marketing environment (see Figure 13.3). How effectively marketers can use promotion to maintain positive relationships considering environmental forces depends largely on the quantity and quality of information an organization takes in. For example, pizza companies want to communicate effectively with customers to influence them to buy their products. To do so, they must have data about customers and about the kinds of information customers use in making decisions when buying pizza. Thus, to successfully communicate with selected audiences, Domino's collected information to determine that pizza consumers wanted quick delivery; now Domino's guarantees a thirty-minute delivery time.

Because the basic role of promotion is to communicate, we should analyze what communication is and how the communication process works.

Promotion and the Communication Process

Communication can be viewed as the transmission of information. Information is form or pattern used to communicate ideas and concepts. Thus the sending and receiving of form is communication. According to this description, we communicate with you when you perceive the following symbols:

在工廠吾人製造化粧品，在商店吾人銷售希望。[4]

We encounter a problem, however, because this view of communication does not consider the meaningfulness of the pattern that is transmitted.

For promotional purposes, a more useful approach is to define **communication** as a sharing of meaning.[5] Implicit in this definition is the notion of transmission of information because sharing necessitates transmission. More important, whatever

4. In case you do not read Chinese, this says, "In the factory we make cosmetics, and in the store we sell hope." Prepared by Chih Kang Wang.
5. Terence A. Shimp and M. Wayne Delozier, *Promotion Management and Marketing Communication* (Hinsdale, Ill.: Dryden Press, 1986), pp. 25–26.

is shared must, to some degree, have a common meaning for the individuals involved. Obviously, if we describe communication in these terms, we are not communicating with those who read English only when we transmit Chinese symbols because these symbols are not meaningful to such readers. Because this second approach to understanding communication is more comprehensive and realistic, we shall view communication as a sharing of meaning.

As Figure 13.4 shows, communication begins with a source. A **source** is a person, group, or organization that has a meaning it intends and attempts to share with a receiver or an audience. For example, a source could be a salesperson who wishes to communicate a sales message or an organization that wants to send a message to thousands of consumers through an advertisement.

To transmit meaning, a source must place the meaning into a series of signs that represent ideas. This is called the **coding process** or *encoding*. The coding process requires a source to convert the meaning into a series of signs that represent ideas or concepts. For example, there have been some notable problems in translating English advertisements into Spanish for the U.S. Hispanic market segment. A beer advertisement with the tag line "Suéltate" was supposed to mean "Let go!" but invited Hispanics to "Get diarrhea!" An airline advertisement intended to entice Hispanics to fly first class on leather seats invited them to fly naked.[6]

When coding meaning into a message, a source must take into account certain characteristics of the receiver or audience. First, to share meaning most easily, the source should use signs that are familiar to the receiver or audience. Marketers who understand this fact realize how important it is to know their target market and to make sure that an advertisement, for example, is written in language that the target market can understand. If the maker of Visine eye freshener advertises to a general adult audience that the product contains tetrahydrocycline, the company may fail to share the meaning. Most of the people in the audience most likely do not know what tetrahydrocycline will do for eyes. In fact, some adults may worry about using a potentially harmful chemical in their eyes. It is important that people understand the language in advertisements. For example, when DuPont used a chemical to make its new line of carpet resilient to spotting, it did not discuss the name of the chemical, just the name of the carpet—Stainmaster.

Second, when coding a meaning, a source should attempt to use signs that the receiver or audience uses for referring to the concepts the source intends. Marketers

6. Carlos E. Garcia, "Hispanic Market Is Accessible If Research Is Designed Correctly," *Marketing News*, Jan. 4, 1988, p. 46.

FIGURE 13.4

The communication process

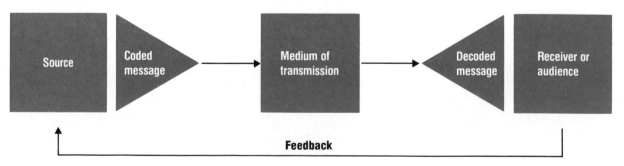

Cause-Related Marketing: A Unique Form of Promotion

One form of promotion that has gained in popularity during the last few years is cause-related marketing, which uses different methods of promotion to increase sales: philanthropy, fund raisers, and publicity linked to a worthy social cause. This strategy requires an organization's customers to first purchase a product; the organization then makes a contribution to the worthy cause. Varadarajan and Menon, in a recent article published in the *Journal of Marketing,* defined cause-related marketing as "the process of formulating and implementing marketing activities that are characterized by an offer from the firm to contribute a specified amount to a designated cause when customers engage in revenue providing exchanges that satisfy organizational and individual objectives."

Cause-related marketing has two basic goals: to generate goodwill and revenues for the marketing organization and to help worthy causes by linking fund-raising for a particular cause to the purchase of the organization's products and/or services. For example, American Express used direct mail and advertising to encourage its credit card holders to charge more often so they would help rebuild the Statue of Liberty. General Foods Corp. sponsored the Tang March Across America for Mothers Against Drunk Driving (MADD) in 1985. The giant food manufacturer put 47 million coupons in newspapers across the nation and pledged to donate 10 cents for every coupon actually redeemed up to $100,000. When the results of the campaign came in, the redemption rate for those coupons was 13 percent, considerably above normal. It seems then that cause-related marketing does help a company increase its revenues.

If the public sees cause-related marketing as a goodwill tactic, ideally positive publicity will develop. If cause-related marketing is viewed as a ploy, the technique may lead to negative publicity.

Cause-related marketing raises questions for businesses using this technique. If corporations examine their philanthropic budgets and see only modest returns, they may use cause-related marketing exclusively and do away with traditional giving. Because the public has a vague perception of philanthropy, owing primarily to its intangible nature, this tactic could cause confusion. In addition, corporations could make philanthropic decisions based solely on marketing potential, without any thought to the value of the cause.

Cause-related marketing also poses problems for fund raisers. If a charitable organization decides to use cause-related marketing, it could be viewed as exploiting its supporters, essentially compromising its integrity because donors become consumers in cause-related marketing. In addition, to ensure financial gains, some voluntary organizations might change their program philosophies or their objectives to meet those of the sponsoring company.

Moreover, if an organization's cause is strongly identified with a corporation, the public may believe the cause has sold out to the company and decrease their support for the organization.

Cause-related marketing is successful, but it has created much controversy in the philanthropic community. This method of promotion faces an uncertain future as it comes under scrutiny from an increasing number of critics.

SOURCES: P. "Rajan" Varadarajan and Anil Menon, "Cause-Related Marketing: A Coalignment of Marketing Strategy and Corporate Philanthropy," *Journal of Marketing,* July 1988, pp. 58–74; Kevin T. Higgins, "Cause-Related Marketing: Does It Pass the Bottom-Line Test?", *Marketing News,* May 9, 1986, pp. 1, 8; Maurice G. Gurin, "Cause-Related Marketing in Question," *Advertising Age,* July 27, 1987, p. S-16; Patrick McGeehan, "Visa, Kodak Big Winners in Olympics," *Advertising Age,* Feb. 1, 1988, pp. 1, 74.

generally should avoid signs that can have several meanings for an audience. A national advertiser of soft drinks, for example, should avoid using the word *soda* as a general term for soft drinks. Although in some parts of the United States *soda* is taken to mean *soft drink,* in other regions it may evoke other concepts in receivers' minds—bicarbonate of soda, an ice cream drink, or something that one mixes with Scotch whisky, for example.

To share a coded meaning with the receiver or audience, a source must select and use a medium of transmission. A **medium of transmission** carries the coded message from the source to the receiver or audience. Transmission media include ink on paper, vibrations of air waves produced by vocal cords, chalk marks on a chalkboard, and electronically produced vibrations of air waves—in radio and television signals, for example.

When a source chooses an inappropriate medium of transmission, several problems may arise, and marketers should be especially careful to avoid them. A coded message may reach some receivers, but not the right ones. For example, suppose a community theater spends most of its advertising dollars on radio advertisements. If theatergoers depend mainly on newspapers for information about local drama, then the theater will not reach its intended target audience. Also, coded messages may reach intended receivers in an incomplete form because the intensity of the transmission is weak. For example, a marketer may choose a printing method that reproduces an advertisement so poorly that people cannot read it. If the advertisement is barely legible, the audience will form an impression of poor quality and may associate it with the product or company.

A **receiver,** or audience—another major component of the communication process—is the individual, group, or organization that decodes a coded message. An audience is two or more receivers who decode a message. In the **decoding process,** signs are converted into concepts and ideas.

Seldom does a receiver decode exactly the same meaning that a source coded. When the result of decoding is different from what was coded, **noise** exists. Noise has many sources and may affect any or all parts of the communication process. When a source selects a medium of transmission through which an audience does not expect to receive a message, noise is likely to occur. Noise sometimes arises within the medium of transmission itself. Radio static, faulty printing processes, and laryngitis are sources of noise. Interference on viewers' television sets during a commercial is noise and lessens the impact of the advertisement. Suppose the source uses a sign that is unfamiliar to the receiver or that has a different meaning from the one the source intended. In either case, noise will occur during decoding. Noise also may originate in the receiver. As Chapter 4 discusses, a receiver may be unaware of a coded message because his or her perceptual processes block it out.

The receiver's response to a message is **feedback** to the source. The source usually expects and normally receives feedback, although it may not be immediate. During feedback, the receiver or audience is the source of a message that is directed toward the original source, which then becomes a receiver. Feedback is coded, sent through a medium of transmission, and is decoded by the receiver, the source of the original communication. It makes sense, then, to think about communication as a circular process.

During face-to-face communication, such as a personal selling situation or product sampling, both verbal and nonverbal feedback can be immediate. Campbell's Soup developed mall shopper exhibits at which customers could sample its Special Request line of soups, which have one-third less salt, and receive a nutritional facts booklet. The promotion started in January (National Soup Month) 1988. Campbell's projected that 9 million mall shoppers would be exposed to its mall exhibits, with 300,000 sampling the soup. Research has shown that when consumers are exposed to a product through sampling, their intent to buy increases. In addition, Campbell's collects response information from the customer through informal questioning. Campbell's could get relevant product information that could enable it to alter the product or packaging from this direct consumer interaction.[7] This instant feedback lets communicators adjust their messages quickly to improve the effectiveness of their communication. For example, when a salesperson realizes through feedback that a customer does not understand a sales presentation, the salesperson adapts the presentation to make it more meaningful to the customer. In interpersonal communication, feedback occurs through talking, touching, smiling, nodding, eye movements, and other body movements and postures.

When mass communication such as advertising is used, feedback is often slow and difficult to recognize. For example, if Disney World increased advertising to increase the number of visitors, it might be six to eighteen months before the firm could recognize the effects of the increased expenditures. Although it is harder to recognize, feedback does exist for mass communication. Advertisers, for example, obtain feedback in the form of changes in sales volume and in consumers' attitudes and product awareness levels. When PepsiCo, Inc. bought Taco Bell in 1978, its restaurants were often confused with cheap-looking taco stands, and some potential customers were offended by the company logo: a Mexican dozing under a large sombrero. PepsiCo redesigned the stores, keeping the arch windows and red tile roofs that customers liked but redesigning the sign to display a large bell, the stores' new company logo. All these changes were reflected in advertising. These actions produced notable results in three years, with the average store volume growing 50 percent.[8]

7. Amy Gross, "Now Playing: Video Marketing," *Adweek's Marketing Week,* Jan. 18, 1988, pp. 8–9.
8. "Taco Bell Wants to Take a Bite Out of Burgers," *Business Week,* Aug. 4, 1986, p. 63.

Each communication channel has a limit regarding the volume of information it can handle effectively. This limit, called **channel capacity,** is determined by the least efficient component of the communication process. Think about communications that depend on vocal speech. An individual source can talk only so fast, and there is a limit to how much a receiver can take in aurally. Beyond that point additional coded messages cannot be decoded; thus meaning cannot be shared. Although a radio announcer can read several hundred words a minute, a one-minute advertising message should not exceed 150 words because most announcers cannot articulate the words into understandable messages at a rate beyond 150 words per minute. This figure is the limit for both source and receiver, and marketers should keep this in mind when developing radio commercials. At times, a firm creates a television advertisement that contains several types of visual materials and several forms of audio messages, all transmitted to viewers at the same time. Such communication may not be totally effective because receivers cannot decode all the messages concurrently.

Now that we have explored the basic communication process, we consider more specifically how promotion is used to influence individuals, groups, or organizations to accept or adopt a firm's products. Although we introduced the product adoption process in Chapter 8, we explore it more fully in the following section to gain a better understanding of the conditions under which promotion occurs.

Promotion and the Product Adoption Process

Marketers do not promote simply to inform, educate, and entertain; they communicate to facilitate satisfying exchanges. One long-run purpose of promotion is to influence and encourage buyers to accept or adopt goods, services, and ideas. At times, an advertisement may be informative or entertaining, yet it may fail to get the audience to purchase the product. For example, Pizza Hut introduced an advertising campaign using comedian Rich Hall, who appeared as an apostle of pizza roaming the United States in a large recreational vehicle called the Mobile Institute for Pizza Studies. He wanted to determine why people like Pizza Hut pizza. The television spots were entertaining and clever but did little to increase awareness of Pizza Hut or stimulate sales. Chiat Day, the advertising agency that developed the campaign, was released; the new agency, BBD&O, developed a simpler product-focused campaign that had a more significant impact on sales.[9] The ultimate effectiveness of promotion is determined by the degree to which it affects product adoption among potential buyers or increases the frequency of current buyers' purchases.

To establish realistic expectations about what promotion can do, one should not view product adoption as a one-step process. Rarely can a single promotional activity cause an individual to buy a previously unfamiliar product. The acceptance of a product is a multistep process.

Although there are several ways to look at the **product adoption process,** one common approach is to view it as a five-stage technique: awareness, interest,

9. Adweek's Sixth Annual Badvertising Awards, "Slices of Life," *Adweek's Marketing Week,* Jan. 11, 1988, p. 13.

evaluation, trial, and adoption.[10] In the awareness stage, individuals become aware that the product exists, but they have little information about it and are not concerned about getting more. They enter the interest stage when they are motivated to get information about the product's features, uses, advantages, disadvantages, price, or location. During the evaluation stage, individuals consider whether the product will satisfy certain criteria that are critical for meeting their specific needs. In the trial stage, they use or experience the product for the first time, possibly by purchasing a small quantity, by taking advantage of a free sample or demonstration, or by borrowing the product from someone. Procter & Gamble developed a major breakthrough in sampling. The company created a technique for attaching a free sample of a Downy Fabric Softener sheet to its newspaper free-standing inserts. The sample lets the consumers try the product free of charge.[11] During this stage, potential adopters determine the usefulness of the product under the specific conditions for which they need it.

Individuals move into the adoption stage at the point when they choose that specific product when they need a product of that general type. Do not assume, however, that because a person enters the adoption process she or he eventually will adopt the new product. Rejection may occur at any stage, including adoption. Both product adoption and product rejection can be temporary or permanent.

For the most part, people respond to different information sources at different stages of the adoption process. Mass communication sources are often effective for moving large numbers of people into the awareness stage. Producers of consumer goods commonly use massive advertising campaigns when introducing new products. They do so to create product awareness as quickly as possible within a large portion of the target market. For example, through advertisements such as the one shown in Figure 13.5, Starrett tries to create awareness that it produces the best tape measures.

Because people in the interest stage are seeking information, mass communications may also be effective then. During the evaluation stage, individuals often seek information, opinions, and reinforcement from personal sources—relatives, friends, and associates. In the trial stage, individuals depend on salespersons for information about how to use the product properly to get the most out of it. After Harley-Davidson Motor Co., Inc. experienced a sales slump, the company's marketers decided to take an innovative step in the motorcycle market: letting potential customers testdrive Harley-Davidson motorcycles. Traditionally, motorcycle companies have not encouraged or promoted testdrives because of the dangers of theft and accident liability. Harley-Davidson started slowly promoting demonstration rides, introducing them nationwide during a three-year period. Harley-Davidson's market share increased 25 percent. The effective movement of customers to the trial stage of the product adoption process dramatically increased sales.[12]

Friends and peers may also be important sources during the trial stage. By the time the adoption stage has been reached, both personal communication from sales personnel and mass communication through advertisements may be required. Even

10. Many of the ideas in this section are drawn from Everett M. Rogers, *Diffusion of Innovations* (New York: Free Press, 1962), pp. 81–86, 98–102.
11. Russ Bowman, "Sampling Via FSIs," *Marketing and Media Decisions,* January 1988, p. 84.
12. Doris Walsh, "You Meet the Nicest People on a Harley," *American Demographics,* July 1985, p. 18.

FIGURE 13.5

Starrett uses promotion to develop awareness of its precision-made tape measures (SOURCE: Courtesy of the L. S. Starrett Company)

though the particular stage of the adoption process may influence the types of information sources consumers use, marketers must remember that other factors, such as the product's characteristics, price, uses, and the characteristics of customers, also affect the types of information sources that buyers desire. For example, when Polaroid Corp. introduced its new Impulse instant camera, "low price" was chosen as the key variable to promote.[13]

Because people in different stages of the adoption process often will require different types of information, marketers designing a promotional campaign must determine what stage of the adoption process a particular target audience is in before they can develop the message. Potential adopters in the interest stage will need different information than people who have already reached the trial stage.

When an organization introduces a new product, people do not all begin the adoption process at the same time, and they do not move through the process at the same speed. Of those people who eventually adopt the product, some enter the adoption process rather quickly, whereas others start considerably later. (And for most products there is a group of nonadopters who never begin the process.)

The amount of time people take to adopt a new product can be used to classify them into the five major adopter categories: innovators, early adopters, early majority, late majority, and laggards.[14] Figure 13.6 illustrates each adopter category and the percentage of total adopters that it typically represents. **Innovators** are the

---

13. "Polaroid to Introduce New Instant Camera," *Adweek's Marketing Week,* Jan. 11, 1988, p. 3.
14. Everett M. Rogers, *Diffusion of Innovations* (New York: Free Press, 1962), pp. 247–250.

first to adopt a new product. They enjoy trying new products and tend to be venturesome, rash, and daring. **Early adopters** choose new products carefully and are viewed as "the people to check with" by persons in the remaining adopter categories. Persons in the **early majority** adopt just prior to the average person; they are deliberate and cautious in trying new products. **Late majority** people, who are quite skeptical of new products, eventually adopt new products because of economic necessity or social pressure. **Laggards,** the last to adopt a new product, are oriented toward the past. They are suspicious of new products, and when they finally adopt the innovation, it already may have been replaced by a newer product. When developing promotional efforts, a marketer should bear in mind that persons in different adopter categories often need different forms of communication and different types of information.

Now, to gain a better understanding of how promotion is used to move people closer to the acceptance of goods, services, and ideas, we analyze the major promotional methods available to an organization.

The Promotion Mix

Several types of promotional methods can be used to communicate with individuals, groups, and organizations. When an organization combines specific ingredients to promote a particular product, that combination constitutes the promotion mix for that product. In this section we analyze the major ingredients of a promotion mix. We also examine the primary factors that influence an organization to include specific ingredients in the promotion mix for a specific product.

Promotion Mix Ingredients

The four possible ingredients of a **promotion mix** are advertising, personal selling, publicity, and sales promotion (see Figure 13.7). For some products, firms use all four ingredients; for other products, only two or three are necessary. At this point we consider some general characteristics of each promotion mix ingredient. In Chapters 14 and 15 we analyze the promotion mix in more detail.

FIGURE 13.6

Distribution of product adopter categories (SOURCE: Reprinted with permission of Macmillan, Inc. From *Diffusion of Innovations*. Third Edition, by Everett M. Rogers. Copyright © 1983 by The Free Press, a Division of Macmillan, Inc.)

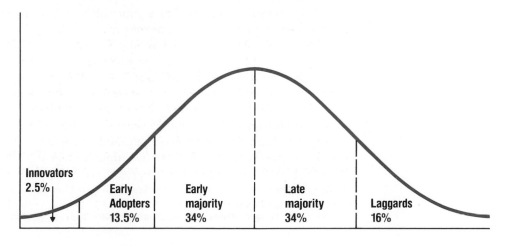

FIGURE 13.7

Possible ingredients for
an organization's pro-
motion mix

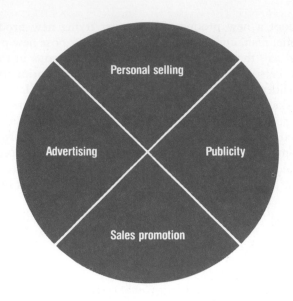

Advertising   **Advertising** is a paid form of nonpersonal communication about an organization and/or its products that is transmitted to a target audience through a mass medium. Individuals and organizations use advertising to promote goods, services, ideas, issues, and people. The Application on page 449 shows how cable television operators use advertising to try to boost ratings. Some of the mass media commonly selected to transmit advertising are television, radio, newspapers, magazines, direct mail, mass transit vehicles, outdoor displays, handbills, catalogs, and directories. Being a highly flexible promotional method, advertising offers the options of reaching an extremely large target audience or focusing on a small, precisely defined segment of the population. For example, the advertisement shown in Figure 13.8 is for a rare George III mahogany chair aimed at a very small target market. Steuben Glass ran an elegant advertisement showing a limited-edition crystal bowl engraved with tulips. In small type, the advertisement discreetly listed the artist's name, the bowl's diameter, and the price, $35,000.[15]

Advertising offers several benefits. It can be an extremely cost-efficient promotional method because it can reach a vast number of people at a low cost per person. For example, the cost of a four-color, one-page advertisement in *Time* magazine is $120,130. Because the magazine reaches 4.6 million subscribers, the cost of reaching 1,000 subscribers is only $26.12. Gerber Products Company used magazine advertising to expand into a new market area that represents only 4 percent of all households in the United States. The company decided to expand its products for babies by offering a new line of products called First Foods Fruits and Vegetables—a 100 percent natural line of foods meant for earlier feeding. To reach the target audience of households defined as women 18 to 34 with children younger than 2, Gerber advertised in magazines such as *American Baby, Mothers Today, People, Parents,* and *Redbook,* among others.[16] Advertising lets the user

15. Ronald Alsop, "Companies Pitch Elite Brands to Less Elite Target Audience," *The Wall Street Journal,* Nov. 6, 1986, p. 33.
16. "The Four Percent Solution," *Inside Print,* January 1988, pp. 97–98.

Cable Television Promotes Itself

Cable television originally began as a way of enhancing poor broadcast signal reception, but it has turned into the entertainment medium of the future. In the first half of the 1980s, cable's growth was phenomenal, limited only by how fast cable companies could install their systems. By 1987, the companies had reached more than 42 million subscribers, up from 17.6 million in 1980. Dozens of new cable networks appeared on the air as cable continued to expand. Cable television advertising revenues increased at the same time: They reached $1.4 billion in 1987, compared to just $50 million in 1980. An estimated 48 percent of all households in the United States now receive cable television.

As the cable industry matured in the second half of the 1980s, its incredible growth rate slowed. Most cities had access to one or more cable systems, and the only growth opportunity left for cable operators was to reach those households that resisted subscribing to cable. Moreover, the industry was deregulated on January 1, 1987, and although many cable operators increased the number of channels in their service, most raised their subscriber fees as well. Before deregulation, cable operators did not need to spend much on promotion, but deregulation, combined with an aging industry, meant operators had to advertise and promote their services to make the public aware of them.

Thus cable television operators have entered the era of self-promotion. To this end, almost all cable services have increased consumer print advertising to raise their ratings. In addition, local cable operators have promoted themselves more heavily since the deregulation of the cable television industry in 1987; the industry no longer depends on viewers to find shows by themselves.

United Cable Television (based in Denver) launched a particularly aggressive promotion campaign. The company invited more than 100,000 television viewers to play *The $500,000 Cable Network Challenge* in 1987. Game players had to match cable television shows with the proper cable networks to receive a $5 prize and an entry into the bigger sweepstakes. The game was a bit complicated so as to encourage viewers to look up shows in a printed listing of programs, or even better, watch them. UCT's objective was to educate subscribers, along with the nonsubscribers it wanted to attract, about cable television.

Viacom International offered Milwaukee residents a thirty-day free trial of its basic cable package to encourage more residents to sign up. Other cable operators and the cable networks engaged in similar promotion programs to pull in new viewers and keep old ones from canceling. In April of each year, many cable networks and operators join forces during National Cable Month to barrage the public with newspaper and billboard, direct mail, and on-air cable network advertisements. The cable television industry is following the lead of network and independent stations by promoting itself through advertising to increase its ratings.

SOURCES: Laura Landro, "As Cable-TV Networks Proliferate, Newcomers Face Stiff Competition," *The Wall Street Journal,* July 23, 1987, p. 29; Wayne Walley, "Industry Pushing Its New Image to the Public," *Advertising Age,* Mar. 20, 1987, pp. S-1, S-4; Lori Kesler, "MSO Challenges Viewers' Programming Savvy," *Advertising Age,* Mar. 30, 1987, p. S-12; Mark N. Vamos and Sandra D. Atchison, "Cable TV, Older and Wiser, Looks Like a Good Bet Again," *Business Week,* July 22, 1985, pp. 126–127.

repeat the message a number of times. In addition, advertising a product a certain way can add to its value. The visibility that an organization gains from advertising enhances the firm's public image.

Advertising also has several disadvantages. Even though its cost per person reached may be low, its absolute dollar outlay can be extremely high. The cost can limit, and sometimes preclude, its use in a promotion mix. Moreover, advertising rarely provides rapid feedback. Measuring its effect on sales is difficult, and it ordinarily has less persuasive impact on customers than personal selling.

Personal Selling   **Personal selling** is informing customers and persuading them to purchase products through personal communication in an exchange situation. The phrase *purchase products* should be interpreted broadly to encompass the acceptance of ideas and issues.

Personal selling has both advantages and limitations when compared with advertising. Advertising is paid, nonpersonal communication aimed at a relatively large target audience, but personal selling is aimed at one or several individuals. Reaching one person through personal selling costs considerably more than it does through advertising, but personal selling efforts often have greater impact on customers. Remember too that personal selling provides immediate feedback, which allows marketers to adjust their message to improve communication. It also helps them determine and respond to customers' needs for information.

Telemarketing is another form of personal selling, accounting for 46 percent of all direct marketing purchases. Highly trained telemarketing account executives do everything face to face that salespeople do, except they do it over the phone. They take over all the functions involved in a sale—including the selling. This saves the company money because the account executive can make as many as thirty sales calls in one day.[17] The benefits of telemarketing are its low costs and ability to instantly reach the potential customer. The key to telemarketing is to recruit and train the right sales people. If salespeople are ineffective in the field, they will continue to be ineffective behind a telemarketing console. Citicorp has successfully used telemarketing to help create awareness of new products and expand awareness beyond its traditional market.[18]

17. Merril Tutton, "Segmenting a National Account," *Business Horizons,* January–February 1987, p. 65.
18. Ernan Roman, "Telemarketing: The Newest Member of the Media Mix," *Marketing Communications,* June 1987, pp. 72–74.

When a salesperson and customer meet face to face, both individuals typically use several types of interpersonal communication. Obviously, the predominating communication form is language—both speech and writing. In addition, a salesperson and customer frequently use **kinesic communication,** or body language, by moving their heads, eyes, arms, hands, legs, or torsos. Winking, head nodding, hand gestures, and arm motions are forms of kinesic communication. A good salesperson can often evaluate a prospect's interest in a product or presentation by watching for eye contact and head nodding. **Proxemic communication,** a less obvious form of communication used in personal selling situations, occurs when either party varies the physical distance that separates the two parties. When a customer backs away from a salesperson, for example, that individual may be saying that he or she is not interested in the product or may be expressing dislike for the salesperson. Touching, or **tactile communication,** can also be a form of communication, although it is not as popular in the United States as it is in many other countries. Handshaking is a common form of tactile communication in our country.

Publicity   **Publicity** is nonpersonal communication in news story form, regarding an organization and/or its products, that is transmitted through a mass medium at no charge. Examples of publicity include magazine, newspaper, radio, and television news stories about new retail stores, new products, or personnel changes in an

FIGURE 13.8
British advertisement aimed at a small target market in England (SOURCE: Sotheby's, London)

organization. Although an organization does not pay for the mass medium, publicity should never be viewed as free communication. There are clear costs associated with preparing news releases and encouraging media personnel to broadcast or print them. A firm that uses publicity regularly must have employees to perform these activities or obtain the services of a public relations firm or an advertising agency. Either way, the firm bears the costs of the activities. Although both advertising and publicity are transmitted through mass communication, they differ in that the sponsor does not pay the media costs for publicity and is not identified. The communication is presented as a news story.

Publicity must be planned and implemented so that it is compatible with, and supportive of, other elements in the promotion mix. Publicity cannot always be controlled to the extent that other elements of the promotion mix can be. For example, Southland Corporation, owners and operators of 7-Eleven stores, experienced the impact of negative publicity. The firm was charged with an Internal Revenue Service violation and fined $10,000, even though the findings of the investigation showed that this action was the result of one ex-employee acting alone. The owners of Southland want to restore a more family image despite the negative publicity from the tax violation as well as criticism they have received for selling pornographic magazines and for continuing their support of developing a Texas lottery.[19]

Sales Promotion **Sales promotion** is an activity and/or material that acts as a direct inducement, offering added value or incentive for the product, to resellers, salespersons, or consumers.[20] Do not confuse the term *sales promotion* with *promotion;* sales promotion is but a part of the more comprehensive area of promotion, encompassing efforts other than personal selling, advertising, and publicity. Currently, marketers spend about one and one-half times as much on sales promotion as they do on advertising. Sales promotion appears to be growing in use more than advertising. In some companies, such as The Quaker Oats Co., the marketing budget is split into 75 percent for sales promotion and 25 percent for advertising. Predictions through the end of the decade show advertising growing 7 to 10 percent, whereas sales promotion is projected to grow 12 to 15 percent.[21]

Frequently marketers use sales promotion to improve the effectiveness of other promotion mix ingredients, especially advertising and personal selling. (Although such use is not common, sales promotion can be used as the primary promotion vehicle.) Marketers design sales promotion to produce immediate, short-run sales increases. For example, Hardee's successfully marketed a premium item in 1987 that not only increased dessert sales but had a significant impact on store sales in participating markets. Hardee's sold a series of California Raisins (two-inch-high plastic figures) for 99 cents each with any dessert purchase. There were four raisins available (a different one for each week of the month) to promote Hardee's Cinnamon 'n' Raisin biscuits. Hardee's was able to use a readily identifiable character—developed to support the raisin industry—to promote its own products. Recipro-

19. Joseph Weber, "7-Eleven Wants Out of the Glare," *Business Week*, July 20, 1987, p. 78.
20. This definition is adapted from John F. Luick and William L. Ziegler, *Sales Promotion and Modern Merchandising* (New York: McGraw-Hill, 1968), p. 4. Copyright © 1968 McGraw-Hill, Inc. Used with permission of McGraw-Hill Book Company.
21. Russ Bowman, "Sales Promotion—The Year in Review: Part II," *Marketing and Media Decisions*, July 1987, pp. 152–154.

FIGURE 13.9

Ralston Purina developed a "free cash" consumer sales promotion to stimulate sales of its Almond Delight cereal (SOURCE: Ralston Purina Company)

cally, the raisin industry benefited from the relationship through Hardee's massive media campaign, which gave greater exposure to their industry's spokescharacter.

If a company uses advertising or personal selling, it generally uses them either continuously or cyclically. However, a marketer's use of sales promotion devices is usually irregular. The airline industry is more aggressively using sales promotion. Recent promotions have included triple mileage awards for flying round trip between January 1 and March 31. American Airlines, Delta Airlines, Continental Airlines, and Eastern Airlines are using this tactic to boost usage in a traditionally lower-use period and to create loyalty to their airlines in particular for the entire year.[22]

Sales promotion methods fall into one of two groups, depending on the intended audience. **Consumer sales promotion methods** are directed toward consumers; coupons, free samples, demonstrations, and contests are typical. For example, Figure 13.9 shows a promotion Ralson Purina developed for its Almond Delight cereal. Each box offered free U.S. cash or reproductions of historic U.S. currency. Sales promotion methods that focus on wholesalers, retailers, and salespersons are called **trade sales promotion methods.** They are devised to encourage resellers to carry and aggressively market a specific product. Examples include sales contests, free merchandise, and displays.

22. Christine Donahue, "American Enters Triple-Mileage War," *Adweek's Marketing Week*, Jan. 4, 1988, p. 3.

Having discussed the basic components that can be included in an organization's promotion mix, we must now ask what factors and conditions affect the selection of the promotional methods that a specific organization uses in its promotion mix for a particular product.

Selecting Promotion Mix Ingredients

Marketers vary the composition of promotion mixes for many reasons. Although all four ingredients can be included in a promotion mix, frequently a marketer uses fewer than four. In addition, many firms that market multiple product lines use several promotion mixes simultaneously.

An organization's promotion mix (or mixes) is not an unchanging part of the marketing mix. Marketers can and do change the composition of their promotion mixes. The specific promotion mix ingredients employed and the intensity at which they are used depend on a variety of factors, including the organization's promotional resources, objectives, and policies; characteristics of the target market; characteristics of the product; and cost and availability of promotional methods.

Promotional Resources, Objectives, and Policies The quality of an organization's promotional resources affects the number and relative intensity of promotional methods that can be included in a promotion mix. If a company's promotional budget is extremely limited, the firm is likely to rely on personal selling because it is easier to measure a salesperson's contribution to sales than to measure advertising's contribution. A business must have a sizable promotional budget if it is to use regional or national advertising and sales promotion activities. Organizations with extensive promotional resources usually can include more ingredients in their promotion mixes. However, that they have more promotional dollars does not imply that they necessarily will use a greater number of promotional methods.

An organization's promotional objectives also influence the types of promotion used. If a company's objective is to create mass awareness of a new convenience good, its promotion mix is likely to be heavily oriented toward advertising, sales promotion, and possibly publicity. If a company hopes to educate consumers about the features of durable goods such as home appliances, its promotion mix may consist of a moderate amount of advertising, possibly some sales promotion efforts designed to attract customers to retail stores, and a great deal of personal selling because this method is an excellent way to inform customers about these types of products. If a firm's objective is to produce immediate sales of consumer nondurables, the promotion mix probably will depend heavily on advertising and sales promotion efforts.

Another element that marketers should consider when they plan a promotion mix is whether to use a push policy or a pull policy. With a **push policy,** the producer promotes the product only to the next institution down the marketing channel. For instance, in a marketing channel with wholesalers and retailers, the producer promotes to the wholesaler because in this case the wholesaler is the channel member just below the producer (see Figure 13.10). Each channel member in turn promotes to the next channel member. A push policy usually relies heavily on personal selling. Sometimes, sales promotion and advertising are used in conjunction with personal selling to push the products down through the channel.

As Figure 13.10 shows, a firm that uses a **pull policy** promotes directly to consumers with the intention of developing a strong consumer demand for the

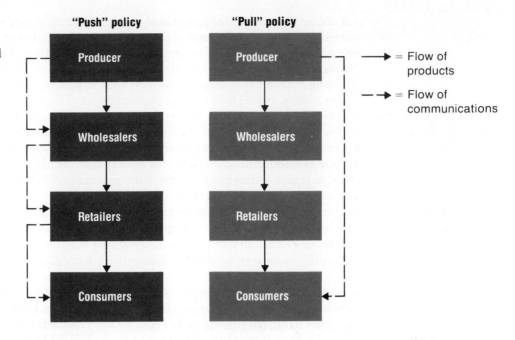

FIGURE 13.10

Comparison of push and pull promotional policies

"Push" policy

Producer → Wholesalers → Retailers → Consumers

"Pull" policy

Producer → Wholesalers → Retailers → Consumers

→ = Flow of products

⤍ = Flow of communications

products. This is done through advertising, point-of-purchase materials and packaging that helps manufacturers build and maintain market share.[23] Given strong consumer demand, consumers will seek the products in retail stores; recognizing the demand, retailers will in turn go to wholesalers or the producer to buy the products. The policy is thus intended to "pull" the goods down through the channel by creating demand at the consumer level.

The sellers of toys use the pull strategy. A New York toy analyst states, "Toys are not sold, toys are bought. If the peer group wants the product, it will sell."[24] To stimulate intensive consumer demand, an organization ordinarily must place heavy emphasis on advertising and sometimes on sales promotion. When a major food company recently used a pull policy to introduce a new brand of flaked coffee, it advertised extensively and told consumers to ask for the product at their favorite stores.

Characteristics of the Target Market The size, geographic distribution, and socioeconomic characteristics of an organization's target market also help dictate the ingredients included in a product's promotion mix. Market size determines, to some degree, the promotion mix composition. If the size is quite limited, the promotion mix will probably emphasize personal selling, which can be quite effective for reaching small numbers of people. Organizations that sell to small industrial markets and firms that market their products through only a few wholesalers frequently emphasize personal selling as the major component of their promotion mixes. When markets for a product consist of millions of customers, organizations

23. Alvin A. Achenbaum and F. Kent Mitchel, "Pulling Away from Push Marketing," *Harvard Business Review,* May–June 1987, p. 38.
24. Jolie Solomon, "Boys and Girls Each Have Their Own Toys (and Firms Still Pitch Them That Way)," *Wall Street Journal,* Dec. 24, 1986, p. 13.

use advertising and sales promotion because these methods can reach masses of people at a low cost per person. For example, Nestlé Company Inc. is attempting to reach consumers through a nontraditional vehicle. They advertise their Alpine White Chocolate bar in the introduction of the home video version of "Dirty Dancing." Diet Pepsi successfully used this same technique on the "Top Gun" videocassette. Nestlé feels that the characteristics of the buyers of "Dirty Dancing" parallel those of its target market for the Alpine White Chocolate bar.[25]

The geographic distribution of a firm's customers can affect the combination of promotional methods used. Personal selling is more feasible if a company's customers are concentrated in a small area than if they are dispersed across a vast geographic region. Advertising may be more practical when the company's customers are numerous and dispersed.

The distribution of a target market's socioeconomic characteristics, such as age, income, or education, may dictate the types of promotional techniques that a marketer selects. For example, personal selling may be much more successful than print advertisements for communicating with less-educated people.

Characteristics of the Product Generally, promotion mixes for industrial products concentrate heavily on personal selling. For promoting consumer goods, on the other hand, advertising plays a major role. Treat this generalization cautiously, however. Industrial goods producers do use some advertising to promote goods. Advertisements for computers, road building equipment, and aircraft are not altogether uncommon, and trade-type sales promotion occasionally is used to promote industrial goods. Personal selling is used extensively for consumer durables such as home appliances, automobiles, and houses, and consumer convenience items are promoted mainly through advertising and sales promotion. Publicity appears in promotion mixes for both industrial goods and consumer goods.

Marketers of highly seasonal products are often forced to emphasize advertising, and possibly sales promotion, because off-season sales will not support an extensive year-round sales force. Although many toy producers have sales forces to sell to resellers, a number of these companies depend to a large extent on advertising to promote their products.

A product's price also influences the composition of the promotion mix. High-priced products call for more personal selling. Because consumers associate greater risk with the purchase of an expensive product, they usually want the advice of a salesperson. Few of us, for example, would be willing to purchase a major appliance such as a freezer from a self-service establishment. For low-priced convenience items, marketers use advertising rather than personal selling at the retail level. The profit margins on many of these items are too low to justify the use of salespersons, and most customers do not need advice from sales personnel when buying such products.

The stage of the product life cycle also enters into marketers' decisions regarding an effective promotion mix. In the introduction stage, considerable advertising may be necessary for both industrial and consumer products to produce widespread awareness among potential users. For many products, personal selling and sales promotion are also used during this stage. For consumer nondurables, the growth

25. " 'Dirty Dancing' Takes 'Top Gun'—Diet Pepsi Route," *Adweek's Marketing Week,* Jan. 4, 1988, p. 45.

The cure for Athlete's | Foot and a half. *Bob Lanier*

You are looking at the actual size of this Athlete's Foot. Imagine the actual size of the itching and burning. Only one cure fits these feet: Tinactin. It's the #1 recommended brand by professionals: doctors, pharmacists and the owner of this size 19 shoe, former All Star basketball player Bob Lanier. And with daily use, the itching and burning may never come back. Athlete's Foot this big needs the biggest cure on two feet: Tinactin.

fast actin' **Tinactin**

The Professionals' Cure for Athlete's Foot.

FIGURE 13.11

Advertisement for a personal product (SOURCE: Copyright © 1987 Schering Corporation. All rights reserved)

and maturity stages necessitate a heavy emphasis on advertising. Industrial products, on the other hand, often require a concentration of personal selling and some sales promotion efforts during these stages. In the decline stage, marketers usually decrease their promotional activities, especially advertising. Promotional efforts in the decline stage often center on personal selling and sales promotion efforts.

Another factor affecting the composition of the promotion mix is intensity of market coverage. When a product is marketed through intensive distribution, the firm depends strongly on advertising. Sales promotion can also play a major role in the promotion of such products. A number of convenience products, such as lotions, cereals, cake mixes, and coffee, are promoted through samples, coupons, and cash refunds.

Where marketers have opted for selective distribution, marketing mixes vary considerably as to type and amount of promotional methods. Items distributed through exclusive distribution frequently demand more personal selling and less advertising. Expensive watches, furs, and high-quality furniture are typical products promoted heavily through personal selling.

How a product is used affects the combination of promotional methods. Manufacturers of highly personal products such as nonprescription contraceptives, menstrual products, and hemorrhoid medications depend heavily on advertising for promotion because many users do not like to talk with salespersons about such products. The makers of personal products such as Tinactin, an athlete's foot remedy (see Figure 13.11), rely heavily on advertising as a promotional method. In another example, Sterling Drugs, Inc., manufacturer of Midol, set up a toll-free number for customers to call for recorded messages from doctors discussing common problems associated with menstruation. In the print advertising, consumers are urged to send for free samples; from these addresses, Sterling Drugs is collecting information so it can develop a direct mail list that will target a group that has tried its product. The 800 number was promoted with newspaper free-standing inserts and positions the company as the "Menstrual Specialist."[26] An organization attempting to promote such highly personal products through door-to-door selling would probably fail badly.

Cost and Availability of Promotional Methods The costs of promotional methods are major factors to analyze when developing a promotion mix. National advertising and sales promotion efforts require large expenditures. However, if the efforts are effective in reaching extremely large numbers of people, the cost per individual reached may be quite small, possibly a few pennies per person. Not all forms of advertising are expensive, however. Many small, local businesses advertise their products through local newspapers, magazines, radio and television stations, and outdoor and transit signs.

Another consideration that marketers must explore when formulating a promotion mix is the availability of promotional techniques. Despite the tremendous number of media vehicles in the United States, a firm may find that no available advertising medium effectively reaches a certain market. For example, a stockbroker may discover that no advertising media precisely reach the holders and potential buyers of Boston Celtic stock. The problem of media availability becomes even more pronounced when marketers try to advertise in foreign countries. Some media, such as television, simply may not be available. Other media that are available may not be open to certain types of advertisements. For example, in West Germany, advertisers are prohibited from making brand comparisons on television commercials. There are limits on other promotional methods as well. A firm may wish to increase the size of its sales force but be unable to find qualified personnel. In addition, some state laws prohibit the use of certain types of sales promotion activities, such as contests. Those techniques are thus "unavailable" in those locales.

Summary

The primary role of promotion is to communicate with individuals, groups, or organizations in the environment to directly or indirectly facilitate exchanges.

Communication is a sharing of meaning. The communication process involves several steps. First, the source translates the meaning into code, a process known as coding or encoding. The source must use signs that are familiar to the receiver or audience and should attempt to employ signs that the receiver or audience uses for referring to the concepts or ideas being promoted. The coded message is sent through a medium of transmission to the receiver or audience. The receiver or

26. "Midol Sets Up 800 Number," *Adweek's Marketing Week,* Jan. 18, 1988, p. 51.

audience then decodes the message, and usually the receiver supplies feedback to the source. When the decoded message differs from the message that was encoded, a condition called noise exists.

The long-run purpose of promotion is to influence and encourage customers to accept or adopt goods, services, and ideas. The product adoption process consists of five stages. In the awareness stage, individuals become aware of the product. Next, people move into the interest stage when they seek more information about the product. In the evaluation stage, individuals decide whether the product will meet certain criteria that are critical for satisfying their needs. During the fourth stage, the trial stage, the individual actually tries the product. In the adoption stage, the individual decides to use the product on a regular basis. Rejection of the product may occur at any stage.

The promotion mix for a product may include four major promotional methods: advertising, personal selling, publicity, and sales promotion. Advertising is a paid form of nonpersonal communication about an organization and/or its products that is transmitted to a target audience through a mass medium. Personal selling is a process of informing customers and persuading them to purchase products through personal communication in an exchange situation. Publicity is nonpersonal communication in news story form, regarding an organization and/or its products, that is transmitted through a mass medium at no charge. Sales promotion is an activity and/or material that acts as a direct inducement, offering added value to or incentive for the product, to resellers, salespersons, or consumers.

There are several major determinants of what promotional methods to include in a promotion mix for a product: the organization's promotional resources, objectives, and policies; the characteristics of the target market; the characteristics of the product; and the cost and availability of promotional methods.

Important Terms

Promotion
Communication
Source
Coding process
Medium of transmission
Receiver
Decoding process
Noise
Feedback
Channel capacity
Product adoption process
Innovators
Early adopters
Early majority
Late majority
Laggards
Promotion mix

Advertising
Personal selling
Telemarketing
Kinesic communication
Proxemic communication
Tactile communication
Publicity
Sales promotion
Consumer sales promotion methods
Trade sales promotion methods
Push policy
Pull policy

Discussion and Review Questions

1. What is the major task of promotion? Do firms ever use promotion to accomplish this task and fail? If so, give several examples.
2. What is communication? Describe the communication process. Is it possible to communicate without using all the elements in the communication process? If so, which ones can be omitted?
3. Identify several causes of noise. How can a source reduce noise?
4. Describe the product adoption process. Under certain circumstances, is it possible for a person to omit one or more of the stages in adopting a new product? Explain your answer.
5. Describe a product that many persons are in the process of adopting. Have you begun the adoption process for this product? If so, what stage have you reached?
6. Identify and briefly describe the four major promotional methods that can be included in an organization's promotion mix. How does publicity differ from advertising?
7. What forms of interpersonal communication other than language can be used in personal selling?
8. Explain the difference between promotional efforts used with a pull policy and those used with a push policy. Under what conditions should each policy be used?
9. How do market characteristics determine the promotional methods to include in a promotion mix? Assume that a company is planning to promote a cereal to both adults and children. Along what major dimensions would these two promotional efforts have to be different?
10. How can a product's characteristics influence the composition of its promotion mix?
11. Evaluate the following statement: "Appropriate advertising media are always available if a company can afford them."

Cases

13.1 Delta's Promotion Decisions[27]

Promotion should help support a company's image and maintain positive relationships among the company and various interest groups within the company's marketing environment. Nevertheless, sometimes there are unique circumstances under which the best promotion is no promotion at all. In 1987, Delta Airlines decided not to modify its promotion programs to offset negative publicity surrounding

27. Based on information from Clare Ansberry, "Forgive or Forget: Firms Face Decision Whether to Apologize for Their Mistakes," *Wall Street Journal*, Nov. 24, 1987, p. 29; Candace Talmadge, "Delta Nixes Ads to Help Defuse Image Problem," *Adweek*, July 20, 1987, p. 6; Wayne Beissert, "FAA's Delta Probe to Focus on 'Human Factors,'" *USA Today*, July 17, 1987, p. 3A; "Delta Procedures Met and Exceeded FAA Requirements," Delta press release, Sept. 18, 1987; "Delta Again Recognized for Passenger Satisfaction," Delta press release, Oct. 12, 1987.

several Delta pilot errors and near-accidents. In the space of one month, July 1987, a Delta pilot inadvertently shut off the plane's engines; another pilot landed in the wrong city; still another Delta pilot landed on the wrong runway (where another jet was taking off); and a Delta plane narrowly avoided a midair collision with another jet. The press openly wondered what had gone wrong at Delta, the nation's fourth largest airline and one that has always held high safety ratings.

The Federal Aviation Administration (FAA) conducted an investigation into Delta's incidents to find out just what had gone wrong. The FAA investigation examined not only mechanical problems but such factors as pilot behavior, crew coordination, and cockpit discipline. The FAA decided that Delta was in general compliance with FAA regulations and did not assess any fines for violations. The FAA report did recommend, however, that Delta increase its emphasis on training and cockpit management guidance.

Delta immediately reacted to the incidents by forming an oversight committee of pilots to conduct an internal audit and a safety-review team to determine what caused the pilot mishaps. As a result of this internal investigation, Delta had already increased training activities and monitoring of cockpit instruction and standards before the FAA filed its report in September 1987.

At the time of the incidents, Delta elected to not issue any form of apology to the public. The company did send out letters to its frequent flyers, but it heavily emphasized Delta's safety record rather than specifically address the pilot errors. Delta's management was wary of introducing a new promotion program to combat the negative publicity surrounding the incidents, believing that such a program would be very difficult to implement because these incidents were so uncharacteristic of Delta's generally safe performance. The company also believed that it would be hard to explain to the public in an advertising campaign the reasons for these mishaps. Moreover, any attempt to reshape the story might be regarded as unethical. Delta may have also thought that an apology would only reinforce the negative publicity surrounding its accidents, whereas a program focusing on the positive aspects of Delta would be a more reasonable approach.

Delta decided to continue to emphasize its outstanding service record and introduced a new advertising campaign, "We love to fly and it shows," with that in mind. In October, Delta announced that it had logged the fewest number of consumer complaints (per 100,000 passengers flown) among the leading airlines for the first nine months of 1987. In fact, of the leading airlines, Delta has received the fewest complaints every year since 1974.

Other companies faced with negative publicity in the 1980s also struggled with the decision of whether to apologize to the public in a promotion campaign. In 1987, Chrysler Corp. chairman Lee Iacocca apologized to American consumers after two Chrysler officials were charged with tampering with several car odometers so that consumers would believe the cars were new. Earlier that same year, Toshiba Corporation's top officials resigned (the ultimate form of apology for Japanese officials) after learning that one of the company's subsidiaries had illegally sold sensitive technology to the Soviet Union. However, several years earlier, Union Carbide Corp. decided not to issue an apology to combat negative publicity after two thousand people died from a gas leak at its Bhopal, India, plant. Union Carbide officials believed that an apology was not enough and instead chose to help the victims of the leak by establishing a $1 million relief fund.

1. What was the potential impact of negative publicity on Delta's sales and revenues during 1987?
2. Delta decided not to directly address negative publicity in the news media. Evaluate this decision.
3. Recommend a promotional strategy to gain a positive company image for Delta's future.

13.2 Technology Affects Marketing: Home Shopping Network[28]

Technology continually changes the way marketers carry out their jobs. The year 1985 saw the birth of an entire new method of promotion, home shopping. The Home Shopping Network offers consumers a chance to shop without ever leaving that comfortable chair in front of the television. The new network lets consumers view discounted (usually closed-out) merchandise, and often the products are demonstrated. Buyers can then call a toll-free number and order the merchandise, which is then shipped to them.

The original Home Shopping Network (HSN) was actually born in the 1970s, when two radio station owners decided to sell products over the air themselves. In July 1985, HSN went national (via cable television) twenty-four hours a day. The network sold primarily closed-out electronics, appliances, clothing, and jewelry at very low prices. In its first nine months, the network sold $107 million worth of merchandise and showed a profit of $11 million. As a result of this phenomenal success, the company introduced another network in 1987, Innovations in Living, which offered more brand-name items, including General Electric and Pierre Cardin. The company also began manufacturing its own products to sell over the air.

Here is how home shopping works. HSN hosts demonstrate the product (a sort of vicarious testdrive) and extol its virtues while a toll-free number flashes on the screen. The hosts really push their merchandise hard, reminiscent of the old patent medicine salespersons. Customers can order the product only while it is being shown, usually for three to five minutes. Quantities are limited, and the product may be offered on the air only once. Customers call and charge the product on their credit cards; the product is usually shipped within forty-eight hours. Most products include standard warranties and may be returned with no questions asked. The typical customer places fifteen orders per year, at an average price of $32.

HSN already faces stiff competition; Telshop, Crazy Eddie, and J. C. Penney's now offer similar cable home shopping networks. Sears began offering some of its merchandise through the QVC network in 1986. Other networks are scheduled to go on line in the next few years, encouraged by the success of the Home Shopping

28. Based on information from Holly Klokis, "Cable TV: A Retail Alternative?", *Chain Store Executive,* August 1986, pp. 11, 12, 14; Joe Agnew, "Home Shopping: TV's Hit of the Season," *Marketing News,* Mar. 13, 1987, pp. 1, 20; Julia Reed, "Hitting Up the Public Where It Lives," *U.S. News & World Report,* Dec. 8, 1986, pp. 60, 61; Michael Kaplan, "Shoppers Tune in National Cable Network," *Advertising Age,* Mar. 6, 1986, p. 35; Gail DeGeorge, "Viewers Start Tuning Out Home Shopping," *Business Week,* Mar. 30, 1987, p. 30.

Network. Not all the networks are as widespread as HSN, but the competition among the networks for cable time is growing intense. HSN already reaches about 8 million households; the company recently bought fourteen UHF stations, which will allow it to reach nearly 25 million more households. By contrast, QVC was available to 7.6 million cable subscribers in 1987. The networks generally pay a 5 percent commission to the local cable companies on all local and cable sales made within their area.

Most of the networks offer contests and games to keep viewers from turning the dial. QVC offers viewers a chance to win a $25,000 weekly cash jackpot. Both home shopping networks offer "Spendable Kash" to regular customers to keep them calling in orders. All the networks use these promotional devices to hook viewers on home shopping.

Although the home shopping network is really a new form of promotion, it does use aspects of personal selling, publicity, and sales promotion. The seller and the buyer are not face to face; however, the home shopping network hosts who sell products maintain a sense of one-on-one communication with each viewer. The hosts use both kinesic and verbal communication to convince each viewer that the particular product they are demonstrating is a great buy. Home shopping networks also provide publicity for a company's products. The networks inform viewers about the benefits of various products, although the companies themselves do not always pay for this service. The networks use sales promotion when they demonstrate products and conduct contests to generate sales.

Cable analysts say it is possible that home shopping network sales will exceed $1 billion in the next few years. Viewers keep tuning in, lured by the contests and the entertainment (most networks have at least one celebrity host). Some analysts wonder, however, if the network will last that long: They say home shopping is merely a fad. Some consumers say that they are bored with home shopping and that their demand for gadgets is filled after a few buys. Other customers prefer going to the store to shop rather than buying by telephone. One thing is certain: customers are tuning in, and HSN is making much money with its new method of promoting merchandise.

Questions for Discussion

1. How does the Home Shopping Network demonstrate the role of promotion in marketing?
2. How does the Home Shopping Network use the four ingredients of the promotion mix to sell products?
3. What characteristics of the target market might be causing the Home Shopping Network acceptance problems?

14. Advertising and Publicity

- ▶ To explore the uses of advertising.
- ▶ To become aware of the major steps involved in developing an advertising campaign.
- ▶ To find out who is responsible for developing advertising campaigns.
- ▶ To gain an understanding of publicity.
- ▶ To analyze how publicity can be used.

M*ore companies* are using advertising and publicity associated with sports to build product loyalty and improve image because featuring leading sports personalities in advertising campaigns is an effective way to target specific customers and receive instant attention. Through its corporate sponsorship of the Iditarod dog sled race across Alaska, Timberland Co. gained favorable publicity. Only seconds after leading the Washington Redskins to victory in Super Bowl XXII, quarterback Doug Williams received $50,000 for smiling into a camera and saying "I am going to Disney World." Disney also persuaded Magic Johnson of basketball's Los Angeles Lakers and Frank Viola of baseball's Minnesota Twins to say the same words after their teams won the league championships. Chicago Bears' Jim McMahon and William "Refrigerator" Perry are two very popular sports personalities who have been featured advertising specific products.

When advertising results from running television spots in sporting events do not meet sales expectations, companies turn to sponsoring sporting events and teams to get more out of their advertising dollars. The popularity of using sports as an advertising vehicle increased after the 1984 Olympic Games in Los Angeles because the Games were a huge media hit and increased the profits of those organizations that promoted them. Many marketers, including Federal Express, 3M, Coca-Cola, and Visa, paid $10 million to $15 million to sponsor the 1988 Winter Olympics. Visa promotes its support of the Olympics and encourages the purchase of Travelers Checks by offering a donation to the U.S. Olympic Team for each purchase. In one survey, one-third of the respondents indicated they would buy a brand because of Olympic sponsorship. In 1987, U.S. companies

FIGURE 14.1

Nabisco uses sponsorship of the Championships of Golf to advertise its products and stimulate publicity (SOURCE: Courtesy of RJR Nabisco)

spent about $1.4 billion sponsoring sports events, four times the amount spent in 1983.

Although using sports as a promotional tool is not a new idea, companies are creatively featuring sports in more ways than they have in the past. They are pouring sponsorship money into entire teams and events, not just personal endorsements by sports stars. Sponsoring an entire team is safer than sponsoring an individual sports star, whose reputation (and thus the firm's) may be tarnished by the use of drugs or some other transgression. Organizations today sponsor everything from golf and tennis to professional beach volleyball. Even sponsorship of municipal events such as Duncan's Yo-Yolympics enhances a company's image and raises product awareness while providing athletic events for a community that otherwise would not have benefited from these opportunities.

Companies realize that sports advertising is a good way to reach target markets during leisure time. Procter & Gamble spends $5 million to sponsor its

Tide, Crisco, and Folger's racing cars because 43 percent of the racing circuit followers are women. Volvo officials believe publicity from their $3 million tennis sponsorship budget is worth $25 million in media advertising. When a firm is able to get its name into the mass media without purchasing airtime it results in positive positioning (in most instances). A message is presented without the commercial overtones. Nabisco sponsors the Championships of Golf, which not only determines the best PGA Tour professional but also provides $2 million for the support of charity (see Figure 14.1).

The use of sports advertising and publicity is definitely on the rise. Companies using these promotional methods have found that even though the technique can be expensive, the benefits to the company, including motivated employees, goodwill, and brand loyalty, are worth the expense.[1]

S PORTS ADVERTISING AND PUBLICITY can be highly visible promotional efforts that contribute to the effectiveness of marketing strategies. This chapter explores many dimensions of advertising and publicity. Our discussion initially focuses on how advertising is used; then we consider the major steps involved in developing an advertising campaign. Next we describe who is responsible for developing advertising campaigns. As we analyze publicity, we compare its characteristics with those of advertising and explore the different forms it may take. Then we consider how publicity is used and what is required for an effective publicity program. Finally, we discuss negative publicity and some problems associated with the use of publicity.

The Nature of Advertising

Advertising permeates our daily lives. At times people view it positively; at other times they avoid it by taping a television program and then zapping over the commercials with the fast forward button of their video cassette recorder. Some advertising informs, persuades, or entertains us; some of it bores, even insults, us. For example, Sure deodorant's advertisement introducing its new Desert Spice scent received one of *Adweek*'s annual Badvertising Awards because of its absur-

1. Based on information from Skip Wollenberg, "Super Bowl Champs Stand to Win Super Ad Contracts," *Ann Arbor News,* Feb. 4, 1988, p. B11; Timothy S. Mescon and Donna J. Tilson, "Corporate Philanthropy: A Strategic Approach to the Bottom Line," *California Management Review,* Winter 1987, pp. 49–59; Bill Gloede, "Paying for the Golden Rings," *Sports, Inc.,* Jan. 18, 1988, pp. 44–45; Michael Oneal and Peter Finch with Joan O.C. Hamilton and Keith Hammonds, "Nothing Sells Like Sports," *Business Week,* Aug. 31, 1987, pp. 48–53; Donna M. Lynn, "If the Shoe Fits," *Public Relations Journal,* February 1987, pp. 16–20, 43; Kevin Maney, "Game Plan: Firms Race to Be Sponsors," *USA Today,* Oct. 1, 1987, pp. 1A, 2A; Patrick McGeehan, "Visa, Kodak Big Winners in Olympics," *Advertising Age,* Feb. 1, 1988, pp. 1, 74.

dity. The advertisement showed cactus plants and rocks in place of the deodorant stick in a Sure container.[2]

As defined in Chapter 13, **advertising** is a paid form of nonpersonal communication that is transmitted through mass media such as television, radio, newspapers, magazines, direct mail, mass transit vehicles, and outdoor displays. An organization can use advertising to reach a variety of audiences ranging from small, precise groups such as the stamp collectors of Idaho to extremely large audiences such as all athletic shoe purchasers in the United States.

When they think of major advertisers, most people immediately mention business organizations. However, many types of organizations—including governments, churches, universities, civic groups, and charitable organizations—take advantage of advertising. In 1986, for example, the U.S. government was the twenty-ninth largest advertiser in the country, spending more than $306 million.[3] So even though we analyze advertising in the context of business organizations here, remember that much of what we say applies to all types of organizations.

Marketers sometimes give advertising more credit than it deserves. This attitude causes them to use advertising when they should not. For example, Ryan's Family Steak House, a budget-priced chain of steak houses featuring a multi-item megabar that offers soups, salads, vegetables, chicken, seafood, breads, and desserts, does not use any advertising. Bryan Elliott, a food industry analyst, states, "Advertising is necessary when the product or service cannot be differentiated on its own merit. What Ryan's is selling is clearly differentiated. Why advertise when you have people lined up out the door?"[4] Although Ryan's has an ideal situation now, its customer base could decline, in which case it would have to consider whether advertising could generate sales.

There are conditions under which advertising can work effectively for an organization. The questions in Table 14.1 raise some general points that a marketer should consider when trying to decide whether advertising could be an effective ingredient in a product's promotion mix. However, this list is certainly not all-inclusive; numerous factors influence whether and how much advertising should be used.

The Uses of Advertising

Individuals and organizations use advertising in a variety of ways and for many reasons, as we describe in this section.

To Promote Products and Organizations

Advertising is used to promote a great many things. For example, it is used to promote goods, services, ideas, images, issues, and people. Depending on what is being promoted, advertising can be classified as institutional or product advertising. **Institutional advertising** promotes organizational images, ideas, or political issues. Seagram's advertising promotes the idea that drinking and driving do not

2. Adweek's Sixth Annual Badvertising Awards, *Adweek's Marketing Week*, Jan. 11, 1988, p. 17.
3. "100 Leading National Advertisers by Rank," *Advertising Age*, Sept. 24, 1987, p. 1.
4. Jim Osterman, "Ryan's Steak House Refuses to Advertise," *Adweek's Marketing Week*, Jan. 4, 1988, p. 43.

mix. Seagram's goal is to create and develop the image of its being socially responsible. **Product advertising** promotes goods and services. Business, government, and private nonbusiness organizations use the technique to promote the uses, features, images, and benefits of their products. For example, when Neutrogena, manufacturer of skin cleansers, introduced its first shampoo, it was not only trying to create awareness of its new product, it was trying to educate the public about its use: periodically for two weeks to remove build-up caused by regular shampoo. Neutrogena's shampoo was not to be adopted as the customer's primary shampoo.

TABLE 14.1

Some issues to consider when deciding whether to use advertising

1. **Does the product possess unique, important features?**

   Although homogeneous products such as cigarettes, gasoline, and beer have been advertised successfully, they usually require considerably more effort and expense than other products. On the other hand, products that are differentiated on physical rather than psychological dimensions are much easier to advertise. Even so, "being different" is rarely enough. The advertisability of product features is enhanced when buyers believe that those unique features are important and useful.

2. **Are "hidden qualities" important to buyers?**

   If by viewing, feeling, tasting, or smelling the product buyers can learn all there is to know about the product and its benefits, advertising will have less chance of increasing demand. Conversely, if not all product benefits are apparent to consumers on inspection and use of the product, advertising has more of a story to tell, and the probability that it can be profitably used increases. The "hidden quality" of vitamin C in oranges once helped explain why Sunkist oranges could be advertised effectively whereas the advertising of lettuce has been a failure.

3. **Is the general demand trend for the product favorable?**

   If the generic product category is experiencing a long-term decline, it is less likely that advertising can be used successfully for a particular brand within the category.

4. **Is the market potential for the product adequate?**

   Advertising can be effective only when there are sufficient actual or prospective users of the brand in the target market.

5. **Is the competitive environment favorable?**

   The size and marketing strength of competitors and their brand shares and loyalty will greatly affect the possible success of an advertising campaign. For example, a marketing effort to compete successfully against Kodak film, Morton salt, or Campbell's soups would demand much more than simply advertising.

6. **Are general economic conditions favorable for marketing the product?**

   The effects of an advertising program and the sale of all products are influenced by the overall state of the economy and by specific business conditions. For example, it is much easier to advertise and sell luxury leisure products (stereos, sailboats, recreation vehicles) when disposable income is high.

7. **Is the organization able and willing to spend the money required to launch an advertising campaign?**

   As a general rule, if the organization is unable or unwilling to undertake an advertising expenditure that as a percentage of the total amount spent in the product category is at least equal to the market share it desires, advertising is less likely to be effective.

8. **Does the firm possess sufficient marketing expertise to market the product?**

   The successful marketing of any product involves a complex mixture of product and buyer research, product development, packaging, pricing, financial management, promotion, and distribution. Weakness in any area of marketing is an obstacle to the successful use of advertising.

SOURCE: Adapted from Charles H. Patti, "Evaluating the Role of Advertising," *Journal of Advertising,* Fall 1977, pp. 32–33. Used by permission.

By advertising Neutrogena Shampoo this way, the company's target market was *all* shampoo users, even those devoted to competitors' products.

To Stimulate Primary and Selective Demand

Product advertising often stimulates demand directly. When a specific firm is the first to introduce a revolutionary innovation, the marketer tries to stimulate primary demand through pioneer advertising. Primary demand is demand for the product category, not for a specific brand. **Pioneer advertising** informs people about a product: what it is, what it does, how it can be used, and where it can be purchased. Because pioneer advertising is used in the introductory stage of the product life cycle when there are no competitive brands, it neither emphasizes the brand name nor compares brands. The first company to introduce the compact disc player, for instance, initially tried to stimulate primary demand by emphasizing the benefits of the product in general rather than the benefits of its brand. Product advertising is also sometimes used to stimulate primary demand for an established product. At times, an industry trade group, rather than a single firm, sponsors advertisements to stimulate primary demand. In Figure 14.2, for example, the Sugar Association addresses the benefits of its product to stimulate primary demand.

An advertiser uses competitive advertising to build selective demand, which is demand for a specific brand. **Competitive advertising** points out a brand's uses, features, and advantages that benefit consumers and that may not be available in competing brands. Because many manufacturers currently sell "long-life" batteries, Eveready's advertisements say that its Energizer batteries "last longer than all the rest." To combat the Energizer, Duracell introduced "freshness dating," whereby there is an expiration date on the battery itself (see Figure 14.3). Duracell promotes that it offers the freshest battery and that no other brand is dated for freshness.

An increasingly popular form of competitive advertising is **comparative advertising,** in which two or more specified brands are compared on the basis of one or more product attributes. Both the sponsored brand and one or more competitive brands are identified in a comparative advertisement. This type of advertising is prevalent among manufacturers of toothpastes, aspirin, tires, automobiles, and a multitude of other products.

To Offset Competitors' Advertising

When marketers advertise to offset or lessen the effects of a competitor's promotional program, they are using **defensive advertising.** Although defensive advertising does not necessarily increase a company's sales or market share, it may prevent a loss in sales or market share. For example, AT&T used defensive advertising to encourage customers to trust AT&T telephones and long distance service rather than risking poor performance from its competitors. Defensive advertising is used most often by firms in extremely competitive consumer product markets.

FIGURE 14.3

Duracell competes with Eveready Energizer batteries by using freshness dating (SOURCE: Courtesy of Duracell Inc., Bethel, CT)

One of these tells you it's fresh without having to shuck it.

To Make Salespersons More Effective	Business organizations that allot a significant proportion of their promotional effort to personal selling often use advertising to improve the effectiveness of sales personnel. Advertising created specifically to support personal selling activities tries to presell buyers by informing them about a product's uses, features, and benefits and by encouraging them to contact local dealers or sales representatives. This form of advertising helps salespeople find good sales prospects. Advertising is often designed to support personal selling efforts for industrial products, insurance, and consumer durables such as automobiles and major household appliances. For example, advertising may get a prospective buyer to visit a showroom, but usually a salesperson plays a key role in closing the sale.
To Increase the Uses of a Product	The absolute demand for any product is limited. Persons in a market will consume only so much of a particular product. Because of the absolute limit on demand and competitive conditions, marketers can increase sales of a specific product in a defined geographic market only to a certain point. To increase sales beyond this point, they must either enlarge the geographic market and sell to more people or develop and promote a larger number of uses for the product. If a firm's advertising convinces buyers to use its products in more ways, then the sales of its products increase. For example, a National Institutes of Health's report on a study of the impact of aspirin on heart attacks in men revealed that one aspirin a day may lower the incidence of heart attacks in healthy men. Aspirin manufacturers responded quickly with advertisements promoting this research finding. Currently, nonaspirin Tylenol holds the number-one spot among pain relievers, with 30 percent of the $2.2 billion market. Aspirin manufacturers, hoping to overtake Tylenol and other nonaspirin products as a result of this research finding, had developed specific advertisements that addressed the heart attack issue. Bayer had planned to devote a significant portion of its overall advertising budget to heart attack prevention.[5] But shortly after the Institutes of Health report was released, the FDA stopped advertisers from promoting the daily benefit of aspirin in lowering heart attacks until more definitive research could be conducted. When promoting new uses, an advertiser attempts to increase the demand for its own brand without increasing the demand for competing brands.
To Remind and Reinforce Customers	Marketers sometimes use **reminder advertising** to let consumers know that an established brand is still around and that it has certain uses, characteristics, and benefits. Crest reminds users that its toothpaste is still the best one for preventing cavities. **Reinforcement advertising** tries to assure current users that they have made the right choice and tells them how to get the most satisfaction from the product. Both reminder and reinforcement advertising are used to prevent a loss in sales or market share. AT&T's advertising tells customers that its services are "the right choice."
To Reduce Sales Fluctuations	The demand for many products varies from month to month because of such factors as climate, holidays, seasons, and customs. A business, however, cannot

5. Scott Hume, "Aspirin Cashes In," *Advertising Age*, Feb. 1, 1988, pp. 1, 76.

operate at peak efficiency when sales fluctuate rapidly. Changes in sales volume translate into changes in the production or inventory, personnel, and financial resources required. To the extent that marketers can generate sales during slow periods, they can smooth out the fluctuations. When advertising reduces fluctuations, a manager can use the firm's resources more efficiently.

Advertising is often designed to stimulate sales during sales slumps. For example, advertisements promoting price reductions of lawn-care equipment or air conditioners can increase sales during fall and winter months. On occasion, a business organization advertises that customers will get better service by coming in on certain days rather than others. For example, one business advertised that customers could get better optical services Tuesdays through Fridays. During peak sales periods, a marketer may refrain from advertising to prevent overstimulation of sales to the point that the firm cannot handle all the demand. For example, coupons for the delivery of pizza are often valid only Monday through Thursday, not Friday through Sunday, which are the peak delivery times.

A firm's use of advertising depends on the firm's objectives, resources, and environmental forces. The degree to which advertising accomplishes the marketer's goals depends in large part on the advertising campaign.

Developing an Advertising Campaign

Several steps are required in developing an advertising campaign. The number of steps and the exact order in which they are carried out may vary according to an organization's resources, the nature of its product, and the types of target markets or audience to be reached. However, as Figure 14.4 indicates, the major steps in the creation of an advertising campaign are (1) identifying and analyzing the advertising target, (2) defining the advertising objectives, (3) creating the advertising platform, (4) determining the advertising appropriation, (5) developing the media plan, (6) creating the advertising message, (7) executing the campaign, and (8) evaluating the effectiveness of the advertising. These general guidelines for developing an advertising campaign are appropriate for all types of organizations.

Identifying and Analyzing the Advertising Target

A basic question that marketers must answer as they begin to develop an advertising campaign is: "Whom are we trying to reach with our message?" The **advertising target** is the group of people toward which advertisements are aimed. Identifying and analyzing the advertising target is critical because the other steps in developing the campaign are based on this. Because companies are becoming more interested in understanding their customers or target markets, a number of research ventures into this area have developed. By reviewing a group of consumers' television viewing patterns and grocery purchases, Campbell's Soup discovered an interesting fact: Viewers of *All My Children* buy 46 percent more V8 than the average consumers. In response, Campbell promotes V8 vegetable juice on *All My Children.* The company's approach is to go after the most likely target audience.[6] The advertising target often includes everyone in a firm's target market. Marketers may,

6. Felix Kessler, "High Tech Shocks in Ad Research," *Fortune,* July 7, 1986, pp. 58, 59.

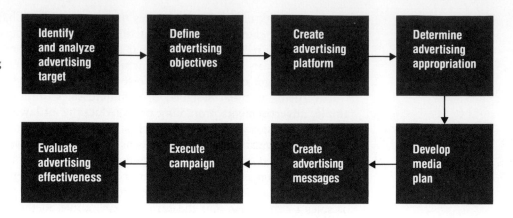

however, seize some opportunities to slant a campaign at only a portion of the target market. The Application on page 475 reveals how the Seven-Up Corporation is positioning Cherry 7-Up to primarily appeal to the 13- to 24-year-old group.

Advertisers analyze advertising targets to develop an information base for a campaign. Information commonly needed includes the location and geographic distribution of the target group; the distribution of age, income, race, sex, and education; and consumer attitudes regarding the purchase and use of both the advertiser's products and competing products. The exact kinds of information that an organization will find useful depend on the type of product being advertised, the characteristics of the advertising target, and the type and amount of competition.

Generally the more that advertisers know about the advertising target, the more able they are to develop an effective advertising campaign. When the advertising target is not precisely identified and properly analyzed, the campaign has less chance of success.

Defining the Advertising Objectives

The advertiser's next step is to consider what the firm hopes to accomplish with the campaign. Because advertising objectives guide campaign development, advertisers should define their objectives carefully to make certain that the campaign will accomplish what they desire. Advertising campaigns based on poorly defined objectives are seldom successful.

Advertising objectives should be stated clearly and precisely and in measurable terms. Precision and measurability let advertisers evaluate advertising success—to judge whether or how well the objectives have been accomplished after the campaign has been completed. Imagine that an advertiser sets the following vague objective: "The objective of our campaign is to increase sales." If this advertiser's sales increase by $1, has the objective been achieved? Without a reference point, no one knows whether the campaign was successful.

Advertising objectives should contain benchmarks giving the current condition or position of the firm. For example, companies that purchased sponsorships in the 1988 Olympics may have wondered how effective those sponsorships were. A poll that *Advertising Age* conducted showed that Olympic sponsorships paid off. Greater than 50 percent of those surveyed could recall if a particular company was

Cherry 7-Up Targeted at Youth Market

Advertisers must aim their message at a specific target market if the message is to be effective. Seven-Up Corporation, producer of the "uncola," traditionally targeted its products and advertising to older generations, but declining sales led the company to change its strategy in 1987. The company targeted its most recent advertising campaign, for Cherry 7-Up, to the 13 to 24 age group. Because research has determined that this age group consumes nearly half of all soft drinks, the change in target market could mean a substantial increase in the sales of 7-Up. Company officials at Seven-Up (now a part of the Dr Pepper Company) hope that Cherry 7-Up will improve the image of its other uncola products as well. "Cherry 7-Up will establish definite inroads into the youth market, and also will favorably impact the images of our other brands," said president and chief operating officer of Seven-Up James J. Harford.

The introduction of Cherry 7-Up and its sugar-free version marks the first time Seven-Up has deviated from its lemon-lime formulation. Nevertheless, the two new drinks still fit into the uncola category that differentiates Seven-Up products from the many colas and cherry colas present in the market today.

The advertising campaign for Cherry 7-Up features the tag "Isn't it cool in pink?" Pink is obviously the dominant color in these advertisements. The television commercials are black and white except for prominent pink articles such as suspenders, earrings, and, of course, Cherry 7-Up itself, which are in color. Seven-Up chose pink as the primary color of the campaign partly because it is a favorite fashion color of the target market and partly because of its eye appeal.

The advertisements are slice-of-life ads, focusing on the lifestyles of the target market. They show teen-agers in their natural surroundings, experiencing things teen-agers typically experience, such as breaking up with a girlfriend. The campaign also tries to bring to the pink theme certain qualities that teen-agers want, such as self-assurance, popularity, and independence. The television spots use light rock music and electronic musical effects known as "pink noise" to appeal to the target market. The spots also run during the target market's favorite programs: *Miami Vice, The Cosby Show, Moonlighting,* and *Family Ties*.

The new campaign is further supported by a "Cool in Pink" merchandise catalog offering Cherry 7-Up clothes and accessories, including Cherry 7-Up T-shirts and sweatshirts, pink sunglasses, shoelaces and headbands, gumball machines, neon signs, and Cherry 7-Up watches, which Seven-Up hopes fashion-conscious teen-agers will find "cool." Radio commercials and a sampling program additionally support the new campaign.

Seven-Up has increased profits with Cherry 7-Up. The new drinks have already captured 2 percent of the soft-drink market. The company objective is for Cherry 7-Up to carry at least 25 percent of all Seven-Up sales. Advertising is the tool the company will use to reach its target market to achieve that objective.

SOURCES: Jeannette Walls, "Cherry Soda a Fountain of Profits for Seven-Up Co.," *USA Today,* Oct. 27, 1987, p. 1B; "7UP 'in the Pink' with Rollout of Cherry-Flavored Regular, Diet," *Beverage Industry,* January 1987, p. 53; Jeffry Scott, "7UP Beefs Up Ad Spending to Reclaim No. 1 Status," *Adweek,* Mar. 23, 1987, p. 16A; Michael Weiss, "Seven-Up to Debut New Ad Campaign," *The Dallas Morning News,* Feb. 23, 1987, p. 23; Candace Talmadge, "7UP Campaign Gets Younger Look," *Adweek,* Feb. 23, 1987, p. 6; "Watch Out Cherry Cola, Here Comes 7UP," *Slidell, Louisiana, Sentry-News,* Feb. 25, 1987, p. 8; "Bottlers Hot for Cherry 7UP," *Beverage Industry,* March 1987, p. 18; "7UP Targets Youth Market," *Beverage Industry,* April 1987, p. 23.

---

an Olympic sponsor or supplier.[7] If the major sponsors had a goal of achieving more than 30 percent recall, then they reached the benchmarks with the Olympic sponsorships. They also should indicate how far and in what direction an advertiser wishes to move from these benchmarks. The advertiser should state the current sales level (the benchmark) and the amount of sales increase that is sought through advertising. Assuming that average monthly sales are $450,000, this advertiser might set the following objective: "Our primary advertising objective is to increase average monthly sales from $450,000 to $540,000."

Although this revised example may appear precise and clear, it is not. An advertising objective also should specify the time allotted for its achievement. By placing an objective into a time frame, advertisers know exactly how long they have to accomplish their objective. They also know when they should begin to evaluate the effectiveness of the campaign. To make our objective specific as to time, the advertiser could state, "Our primary advertising objective is to increase average monthly sales from $450,000 to $540,000 within twelve months."

Advertising objectives usually are stated in terms of either sales or communication. When an advertiser defines objectives by sales, the objectives focus on raising absolute dollar sales, increasing sales by a certain percentage, or increasing the firm's market share.

Even though an advertiser's long-run goal is to increase sales, not all campaigns are designed to produce immediate sales. Some campaigns are aimed at increasing product or brand awareness, at making consumers' attitudes more favorable, or at increasing consumers' knowledge of a product's features. These objectives are stated in terms of communication. When Apple Computer, Inc., for example, introduced home computers, its initial campaign did not focus on sales but created brand awareness and educated consumers about the features and uses of home computers. A specific communication objective might be to increase product feature awareness from 0 to 40 percent in the target market by the end of six months.

7. Patrick McGeehan, "Visa, Kodak Big Winners in Olympics," *Advertising Age,* Feb. 1, 1988, pp. 1, 74.

Creating the	Before launching a political campaign, party leaders meet and develop a political
Advertising	
Platform	

Creating the Advertising Platform

Before launching a political campaign, party leaders meet and develop a political platform, which states the major issues on which the party will base its campaign. Similar to a political platform, an **advertising platform** consists of the basic issues or selling points that an advertiser wishes to include in the advertising campaign. For example, a Suzuki print advertisement for its RM 125 and 250 models promotes the fact that this dirt bike has quicker, crisper throttle response for fast acceleration; new rear disk brakes to make split-second stopping quicker and more certain; improved cornering stability; and an extra rigid frame to minimize vibration.[8] A single advertisement in an advertising campaign may contain one or several issues in the platform. Although the platform contains the basic issues, it does not indicate how they should be presented.

A marketer's advertising platform should consist of issues that are important to consumers. One of the best ways to determine what those issues are is to survey consumers to learn what they consider most important in the selection and use of the product involved. The selling features must not only be important to consumers; if possible, they should also be features that competitive products do not have. The safety of their money is important to bank customers, yet they believe that virtually all banks are equally safe. Thus the advertising platform for a specific bank should not emphasize safety; the marketer should look for other selling features that are important to bank customers and not available at competing banks such as extended hours and higher interest rates on savings.

Research—although it is the most effective method for determining the issues of an advertising platform—is expensive. As a result, the advertising platform is most commonly based on the opinions of personnel within the firm and of individuals in the advertising agency, if an agency is used. This trial-and-error approach generally leads to some successes and some failures.

Because the advertising platform is a base on which to build the message, marketers should analyze this stage carefully. For example, a Chrysler Motors' advertising campaign was based on the theme "If you want to know who builds the best, see who backs them best." The focus of that campaign was the seven-year, seventy-thousand-mile warranties offered on Chrysler cars. A campaign can be perfect as to the selection and analysis of its advertising target, the statement of its objectives, its media strategy, and the form of its message. But the campaign will still fail miserably if the advertisements communicate information that consumers do not consider important when they select and use the product.

Determining the Advertising Appropriation

The **advertising appropriation** is the total amount of money that a marketer allocates for advertising for a specific time period. It is hard to decide how much to spend on advertising for a month, three months, a year, or several years because there is no way to measure what the precise effects of spending a certain amount of money on advertising will be.

Many factors affect a firm's decision about how much to appropriate for advertising. The geographic size of the market and the distribution of buyers within the market have a great bearing on this decision. As Table 14.2 shows, both the type of product advertised and a firm's sales volume relative to competitors' sales volumes

---

8. Mark Dolliver, "What's New Portfolio," *Adweek's Marketing Week*, Jan. 4, 1988, p. 31.

also play a part in determining what proportion of a firm's revenue is spent on advertising. Advertising appropriations for industrial products are usually quite small relative to the sales of the products. Consumer convenience items such as soft drinks, razors, soaps, drugs, and cosmetics generally have large advertising appropriations.

Of the many techniques used to determine the advertising appropriation, one of the most logical is the **objective and task approach.** Using this approach, marketers initially determine the objectives that a campaign is to achieve and then attempt to list the tasks required to accomplish them. Once the tasks have been identified, their costs are added to arrive at the amount of the total appropriation. This approach has one main problem: Marketers usually find it hard to estimate the level of effort needed to achieve certain objectives. A coffee marketer, for example, might find it extremely difficult to determine how much to increase national television advertising to raise a brand's market share from 8 to 12 percent. Because of this problem, advertisers do not widely use the objective and task approach.

TABLE 14.2

Sales volume and advertising expenditures for selected national advertisers (in millions of dollars)

PRIMARY BUSINESS	RANK (TOP 100)	COMPANY	ADVERTISING EXPENDITURES	SALES	ADVERTISING AS % OF SALES
Automotive	5	General Motors Corp.	839,000	102,814,000	.8
	6	Ford Motor Corp.	648,500	62,716,000	1.0
	20	Chrysler Corp.	426,000	22,586,000	1.9
	40	Toyota Motor Sales Co.	208,877	36,754,000	.6
	41	Honda Motor Co.	205,082	19,016,000	1.1
	47	Nissan Motor Corp.	180,136	25,918,000	.7
	52	Goodyear Tire & Rubber Co.	161,858	9,103,000	1.8
	54	Mazda Motor Corp.	156,846	10,100,000	1.6
	56	Volkswagen A.G.	152,211	29,100,000	.5
Electronics and office equipment	25	General Electric	354,250	35,210,000	1.0
	31	International Business Machines	295,498	51,250,000	.6
	33	Tandy Corp.	262,161	3,036,000	8.6
	34	Eastman Kodak Co.	255,586	11,550,000	2.2
	92	Xerox Corp.	92,732	12,929,000	.7
Food	4	RJR Nabisco Brands	935,036	15,975,000	5.9
	8	McDonald's Corp.	592,000	4,280,000	13.8
	11	General Mills	551,561	5,189,000	10.6
	16	Pillsbury Co.	494,877	6,128,000	8.1
	17	Ralston Purina Co.	478,031	5,515,000	8.7
	19	Kraft Inc.	437,952	8,742,000	5.0
	23	Kellogg Co.	374,142	3,341,000	11.2

The **percent of sales approach** is a more widely used technique. Marketers simply multiply a firm's past sales plus a factor for planned sales growth or declines by a standard percentage that is based on both what the firm traditionally spends on advertising and what the industry averages. For example, from the data in Table 14.2 and from experience, a large food processing firm might determine its total advertising appropriation by multiplying the past year's sales by 6.7 percent (the average for the sixteen food processors shown in Table 14.2). This approach has one major disadvantage. Because the approach is based on the incorrect assumption that sales create advertising, rather than that advertising creates sales, a marketer who uses this approach and experiences declining sales will reduce the amount spent on advertising. But the reduction may, in fact, cause a further decline in sales. Although illogical, this technique is widely accepted because it is easy to use and less disruptive competitively. It stabilizes a firm's market share within an industry. Also, in times of declining sales, many firms increase the percentage of their contribution to advertising to reverse the decline.

TABLE 14.2
(continued)

PRIMARY BUSINESS	RANK (TOP 100)	COMPANY	ADVERTISING EXPENDITURES	SALES	ADVERTISING AS % OF SALES
	28	Quaker Oats Co.	309,239	3,671,000	8.4
	30	Nestlé S.A.	305,451	21,900,000	1.4
	32	Sara Lee Corp.	271,623	9,155,000	3.0
	39	H. J. Heinz Co.	217,483	4,639,000	4.7
	42	Campbell Soup Co.	204,233	4,379,000	4.7
	51	IC Industries	165,199	4,222,000	3.9
	68	CPC International	121,956	4,549,000	2.7
	80	Hershey Foods Corp.	111,335	2,170,000	5.1
	81	Wendy's International	110,011	1,140,000	9.7
Retail	3	Sears, Roebuck & Co.	1,004,708	44,281,000	2.3
	9	K Mart Corp.	590,350	23,812,000	2.5
	15	J.C. Penney Co.	496,241	14,740,000	3.4
	88	Zale Corp.	99,106	1,061,000	9.3
Toiletries and cosmetics	57	Revlon Group	149,255	2,600,000	5.7
	62	Gillette Co.	129,574	2,818,000	4.6
	69	Cosmair Inc.	120,410	725,000	16.6
	73	Beecham Group PLC	115,877	3,342,000	3.5
	79	Noxell Corp.	112,110	439,000	25.5
Wine, beer, and liquor	7	Anheuser-Busch Cos.	643,522	8,402,000	7.7
	61	Adolph Coors Co.	130,609	1,314,000	9.9
	63	Stroh Brewery Co.	128,690	1,499,000	8.6
	71	E & J Gallo Winery	116,716	N/A	N/A
	91	Seagram Co. Ltd.	94,932	3,346,000	2.8

SOURCE: Adapted with permission from "100 Leading National Advertisers with U.S. Sales," *Advertising Age,* Sept. 24, 1987, p. 1. Reprinted with permission from *Advertising Age,* Sept. 24, 1987. Copyright Crain Communications Inc. All rights reserved.

Marketers usually are concerned about the type and intensity of their competitors' advertising. Another way to arrive at the advertising appropriation is the **competition-matching approach.** Marketers who follow this approach try to match their major competitors' appropriations in terms of absolute dollars or to allocate the same percentage of sales for advertising as their competitors do. Although a wise marketer should be aware of what competitors spend on advertising, this technique should not be used by itself because a firm's competitors probably have different advertising objectives and different resources available for advertising. Many companies and advertising agencies engage in quarterly competitive spending reviews, comparing competitors' dollar expenditures in print, radio, and television to their own spending levels. Competitive tracking of this nature occurs at both the national and regional levels.

At times, marketers use the **arbitrary approach,** in which a high-level executive in the firm states how much can be spent on advertising for a certain time period. The arbitrary approach often leads to underspending or overspending. Although it is not a scientific budgeting technique, it is expedient!

Establishing the advertising appropriation is critically important. If it is set too low, the campaign cannot achieve its full potential for stimulating demand. When too much money is appropriated for advertising, overspending occurs, and financial resources are wasted. In some situations, television advertising campaigns that are too long or backed by too many dollars may cause *wear out:* The consumer is bombarded with the message at too high a frequency and as a result is alienated by the advertisement and not persuaded to purchase the product.

Developing the Media Plan

As Table 14.3 shows, advertisers spend tremendous amounts of money on advertising media. These amounts have grown rapidly during the past two decades. To derive the maximum results from media expenditures, a marketer must develop an effective media plan. A **media plan** sets forth the exact media vehicles to be used (specific magazines, television stations, newspapers, and so forth) and the dates and times that the advertisements will appear. To formulate a media plan, the planner

TABLE 14.3

Total advertising expenditures (in millions)

	1970	1975	1980	1985	1987 (est)
Newspapers	$ 5,704	$ 8,234	$14,794	$25,170	$ 28,541
Magazines	1,292	1,539	3,279	5,341	5,777
Television	3,596	5,263	11,366	20,738	24,388
Radio	1,308	1,980	3,777	6,490	7,242
Outdoor	234	335	600	945	1,068
Direct mail	2,766	4,124	7,596	15,500	18,755
Business press	740	919	1,674	2,375	2,594
Miscellaneous	3,910	5,558	10,767	18,159	20,936
Total	19,550	27,952	53,853	94,718	109,301

SOURCE: DDB Needham, *Worldwide Media Trends,* 1987 Edition.

selects the media for a campaign and draws up a time schedule for each medium. The media planner's primary goal is to reach the largest number of persons in the advertising target per dollar spent on media. In addition, a secondary goal is to achieve the appropriate message reach and frequency for the target audience while staying within the budget.

Media planners begin by making rather broad decisions; eventually, however, they must make very specific choices. A planner first must decide which kinds of media to use; the major kinds are radio, television, newspapers, magazines, direct mail, outdoor displays, and mass transit vehicles. After making the general media decision, the planner selects specific subclasses within each medium. Gerber Products Company, a baby food producer, might use young women's magazines or daytime, family, and late night television.

Media planners take many factors into account as they devise a media plan. They analyze the location and demographic characteristics of people in the advertising target because the various media appeal to particular demographic groups in particular locations. For example, there are radio stations especially for teen-agers, magazines for men in the 18 to 34 age group, and television programs aimed at adults. Media planners also should consider the sizes and types of audiences specific media reach. Several data services collect and periodically publish information about the circulations and audiences of various media.

The cost of media is an important but troublesome consideration. Planners try to obtain the best coverage possible for each dollar spent, yet there is no accurate way of comparing the cost and impact of a television commercial with the cost and impact of a newspaper advertisement.

The content of the message sometimes affects the choice of media. Print media can be used more effectively than broadcast media to present many issues or numerous details. The maker of Grey Poupon, a zesty brown mustard, found an interesting way to increase sales of its product with print advertisements. Recipes were developed using Grey Poupon. John McDaniels, creative director at the advertising agency Lowe-Marschalk at that time, said, "We knew name recognition was high and . . . we wanted to link the name to broader groups of foods that would be used for other occasions." The advertisements mentioned a particular recipe and invited readers to send away for a complete recipe book. Response to the four-color print advertisements was overwhelming, with ten thousand requests processed in the first month. Use of the print medium lets Grey Poupon target a particular audience. Included in the print buy were *Bon Appetit, The Cook's Magazine, Gourmet,* and *Food & Wine.*[9] If an advertiser wants to promote beautiful colors, patterns, or textures, media that offer high-quality color reproduction— magazines or television—should be used instead of newspapers. For example, food can look extremely appetizing and delicious in a full-color magazine advertisement, but it might look far less so in black and white. Compare the black and white and color versions of the advertisement in Figure 14.5.

The information in Table 14.3 indicates that each medium is used quite differently than the others and that the pattern of media usage has changed over the years. For example, the proportion of total media dollars spent on magazines has declined slowly but steadily since 1970. Part of the reason for the decline in magazine advertising sales is the extensive growth in the number and types of

9. "Ad Mustard," *Inside Print,* January 1988, pp. 94, 96.

FIGURE 14.5

Comparison of black and white and color advertisements (SOURCE: Courtesy Oneida Ltd., All Rights Reserved)

magazines available. Magazines are now very targeted in their appeal because of all the specialty areas they cover. Therefore it is more expensive to reach the mass marketplace through targeted magazines, and readership of more popular, general magazines is down because of specialty magazine subscribership. This variation in usage arises from the characteristics, advantages, and disadvantages (such as the ones listed in Table 14.4) of the major mass media used for advertising. Given the variety of vehicles within each medium, media planners must deal with a vast number of alternatives, and the multitude of factors that affect media rates obviously add to the complexity of media planning. A **cost comparison indicator** lets an advertiser compare the costs of several vehicles within a specific medium (such as two radio stations) regarding the number of persons reached by each vehicle. For example, the "milline rate" is the cost comparison indicator for newspapers; it shows the cost of exposing a million persons to a space equal to one agate line.[10] A Detroit advertiser that can afford to use only one local newspaper probably will compare the milline rates of the *Detroit Free Press* and the *Detroit News* to determine whether there are cost differences relative to their circulations.

The development of the media plan is another crucial step in the creation of an advertising campaign. The effectiveness of the plan determines the number of

10. An agate line is one column wide and the height of the smallest type normally used in classified newspaper advertisements. There are fourteen agate lines in one column inch.

TABLE 14.4

Characteristics, advantages, and disadvantages of major advertising media

MEDIUM	TYPES	UNIT OF SALE	FACTORS AFFECTING RATES	COST COMPARISON INDICATOR	ADVANTAGES	DISADVANTAGES
Newspaper	Morning Evening Sunday Sunday supplement Weekly Special	Agate lines Column inches Counted words Printed lines	Volume and frequency discounts Number of colors Position charges for preferred and guaranteed positions Circulation level	Milline rate = cost per agate line × 1,000,000 divided by circulation	Almost everyone reads a newspaper; purchased to be read; national geographic flexibility; short lead time; frequent publication; favorable for cooperative advertising; merchandising services	Not selective for socioeconomic groups; short life; limited reproduction capabilities; large advertising volume limits exposure to any one advertisement
Magazine	Consumer Farm Business	Pages Partial pages Column inches	Circulation level Cost of publishing Type of audience Volume discounts Frequency discounts Size of advertisement Position of advertisement (covers) Number of colors Regional issues	Cost per thousand (CPM) = cost per page × 1,000 divided by circulation	Socioeconomic selectivity; good reproduction; long life; prestige; geographic selectivity when regional issues are available; read in leisurely manner	High absolute dollar cost; long lead time

TABLE 14.4
(continued)

MEDIUM	TYPES	UNIT OF SALE	FACTORS AFFECTING RATES	COST COMPARISON INDICATOR	ADVANTAGES	DIS-ADVANTAGES
Direct mail	Letters Catalogs Price lists Calendars Brochures Coupons Circulars Newsletters Postcards Booklets Broadsides Samplers	Not applicable	Cost of mailing lists Postage Production costs	Cost per contact	Little wasted circulation; highly selective; circulation controlled by advertiser; few distractions; personal; stimulates actions; use of novelty; relatively easy to measure performance; hidden from competitors	Expensive; no editorial matter to attract readers; considered junk mail by many; criticized as invasion of privacy
Radio	AM FM	Programs: sole sponsor, co-sponsor, participative sponsor Spots: 5, 10, 20, 30, 60 seconds	Time of day Audience size Length of spot or program Volume and frequency discounts	Cost per thousand (CPM) = cost per minute × 1,000 divided by audience size	Highly mobile; low-cost broadcast medium; message can be quickly changed; can reach a large audience; geographic selectivity; socioeconomic selectivity	Provides only audio message; has lost prestige; short life of message; listeners' attention limited because of other activities while listening

Medium	Types	How sold	Factors affecting rates	Cost basis	Advantages	Disadvantages
Television	Network Local CATV	Programs: sole sponsor, co-sponsor, participative sponsor Spots: 5, 10, 15, 30, 60 seconds	Time of day Length of program Length of spot Volume and frequency discounts Audience size	Cost per thousand (CPM) = cost per minute × 1,000 divided by audience size	Reaches large audience; low cost per exposure; uses audio and video; highly visible; high prestige; geographic and socioeconomic selectivity	High-dollar costs; highly perishable message; size of audience not guaranteed; amount of prime time limited
Inside transit	Buses Subways	Full, half, and quarter showings are sold on a monthly basis	Number of riders Multiple-month discounts Production costs Position	Cost per thousand riders	Low cost; "captive" audience; geographic selectivity	Does not reach many professional persons; does not secure quick results
Outside transit	Buses Taxicabs	Full, half, and quarter showings; space also rented on per-unit basis	Number of advertisements Position Size	Cost per thousand exposures	Low cost; geographic selectivity; reaches broad, diverse audience	Lacks socioeconomic selectivity; does not have high impact on readers
Outdoor	Papered posters Painted displays Spectaculars	Papered posters: sold on monthly basis in multiples called "showings" Painted displays and spectaculars: sold on per-unit basis	Length of time purchased Land rental Cost of production Intensity of traffic Frequency and continuity discounts Location	No standard indicator	Allows for repetition; low cost; message can be placed close to the point of sale; geographic selectivity; operable 24 hours a day	Message must be short and simple; no socioeconomic selectivity; seldom attracts readers' full attention; criticized for being traffic hazard and blight on countryside

SOURCE: Some of the information in this table is from S. Watson Dunn and Arnold M. Barban, *Advertising: Its Role in Modern Marketing*, 6th ed. (Hinsdale, Ill.: Dryden Press, 1986); and Anthony F. McGann and J. Thomas Russell, *Advertising Media* (Homewood, Ill.: Irwin, 1981).

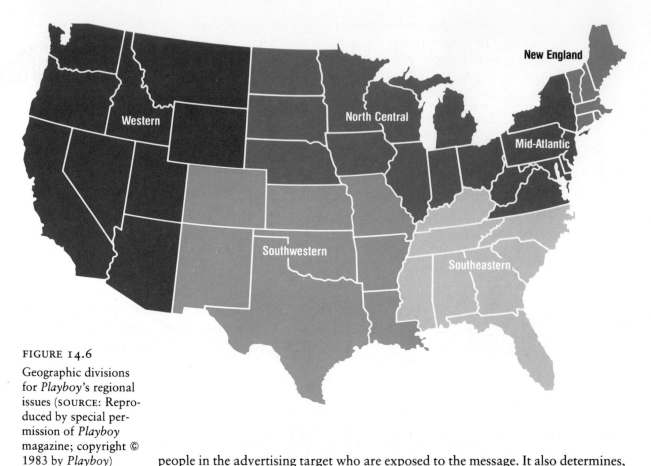

FIGURE 14.6

Geographic divisions for *Playboy*'s regional issues (SOURCE: Reproduced by special permission of *Playboy* magazine; copyright © 1983 by *Playboy*)

people in the advertising target who are exposed to the message. It also determines, to some degree, the effects of the message on those individuals. Media planning is a complex task that requires thorough analysis of the advertising target.

Creating the Advertising Message

The basic content and form of an advertising message are a function of several factors. The product's features, uses, and benefits affect the message's content. Characteristics of the people in the advertising target—their sex, age, education, race, income, occupation, and other attributes—influence both the content and form. When Crest promotes its toothpaste to children, the company emphasizes the importance of daily brushing and cavity control. When Crest is marketed to adults, the tartar and plaque issues are discussed. To communicate effectively, an advertiser must use words, symbols, and illustrations that are meaningful, familiar, and attractive to those persons who make up the advertising target.

The objectives and platform of an advertising campaign affect the content and form of its messages. If a firm's advertising objectives involve large sales increases, for example, the message demands hard-hitting, high-impact language and symbols. When campaign objectives aim at increasing brand awareness, the message may use much repetition of the brand name and words and illustrations associated with it. The advertising platform consists of the basic issues or selling features to be stressed in the campaign; it is the foundation on which campaign messages are built.

The choice of media obviously influences the content and form of the message. Effective outdoor displays and short broadcast spot announcements require concise, simple messages. Magazine and newspaper advertisements can include much detail and long explanations. Because several different kinds of media offer geographic selectivity, a precise message content can be tailored to a particular geographic section of the advertising target. Some magazine publishers produce **regional issues.** For a particular issue, the advertisements and editorial content of copies appearing in one geographic area differ from those appearing in other areas. As Figure 14.6 shows, *Playboy* publishes six regional issues. A clothing manufacturer that advertises in *Playboy* might decide to use one message in the western region and another in the rest of the nation. In addition, a company may choose to advertise in only a few regions. Such geographic selectivity lets a firm use the same message in different regions at different times.

Figure 14.7 identifies the basic components of a print advertising message. The messages for most advertisements depend on the use of copy and artwork. Let us examine these two elements in more detail.

Copy   Copy is the verbal portion of an advertisement. It includes headlines, subheadlines, body copy, and the signature (see Figure 14.7). When preparing advertising copy, marketers attempt to move readers through a persuasive sequence called AIDA: attention, interest, desire, and action. Not all copy need be this extensive, however.

FIGURE 14.7

Basic elements of a print advertisement (SOURCE: Del Monte Corporation)

DDB NEEDHAM WORLDWIDE
Advertising

RADIO • TELEVISION AS RECORDED SCRIPT	

CLIENT:	HERSHEY	TITLE:	"Zoom" Vers. 1 Rev
PRODUCT:	Syrup	CODE #:	HUSY 6191
JOB #:	HSSY-65196	LENGTH:	:30
MEDIUM:	TV	AS RECORDED DATE:	11/7/86

VIDEO	AUDIO
	(MUSIC THROUGHOUT.)
OPEN ON MS OF GIRL SITTING ON BED, TALKING ON TELEPHONE.	MOM (V/O): Jennifer--would you like some milk? JENNIFER: Okay. MOM: And Hershey's Syrup?
GIRL JUMPS OFF BED. PHONE RECEIVER REMAINS HANGING SUSPENDED IN AIR AND AS GIRL RACES OUT ALL THE THINGS IN HER ROOM ARE BLOWN AROUND.	
CUT TO BOY WATCHING TELEVISION. BOY TURNS TO CAMERA.	MOM: Jim--want some milk? JIM: Sure Mom. MOM: And Hershey's Syrup?
BOY JUMPS UP AND LEAVES FRAME, EVERYTHING IN ROOM IS BLOWN AROUND, INCLUDING THE MAN ON THE TV PROGRAM.	
CUT TO HERSHEY'S SYRUP BEING POURED INTO GLASS OF MILK.	ANNCR.: As good as milk is, the rich
CUT TO HERSHEY'S SYRUP BEING STIRRED UP FROM BOTTOM OF GLASS OF MILK. CAMERA MOVES UP TO TOP OF GLASS, SPOON IS TAKEN OUT.	chocolately taste of Hershey's Syrup makes it even better. Just ask your kids.
CUT TO BOY ON DIVING BOARD AT POOL. HE JUMPS, DOES A CANNONBALL INTO WATER. HE POPS BACK OUT OF WATER, BACK ONTO BOARD AND RACES AROUND POOL AND OUT OF FRAME.	MOM: Michael--how 'bout some milk-- and Hershey's Syrup?
CUT TO PRODUCT SHOT--GLASS OF MILK, SQUEEZE BOTTLE OF HERSHEY'S, AND CAN OF HERSHEY'S. (SUPER: "Hershey's Syrup makes good things even better.") WHITE MILK IN GLASS CHANGES TO CHOCOLATE MILK INSTANTLY.	ANNCR. .Hershey's syrup makes good things-- even better.
FADE TO BLACK.	

DDB NEEDHAM WORLDWIDE INC. 437 MADISON AVENUE. NEW YORK, NY 10022 (212) 415-2000 TELEX. 127453 CABLE. DDBNEEDHAM NEW YORK. ADELAIDE · AMSTERDAM · AUCKLAND · BALTIMORE · BANGKOK · BARCELONA · BRISBANE · BRUSSELS · CHICAGO · DENVER · DETROIT · DUNEDIN · DUSSELDORF · HAMBURG · HONG KONG · HONOLULU · KUALA LUMPUR · LISBON · LONDON · LOS ANGELES · MADRID · MELBOURNE · MEXICO CITY · MILAN · MONTREAL · MUNICH · NEW YORK · PARIS · PERTH · SAN FRANCISCO · SINGAPORE · STOCKHOLM · SYDNEY · TAIPEI · TOKYO · TORONTO · VIENNA · WASHINGTON, D.C. · WELLINGTON · ZURICH

The headline is critical because often it is the only part of the copy that people read. It should attract readers' attention and create enough interest to make them want to read the body copy. The subheadline, if there is one, links the headline to the body copy. It sometimes helps explain the headline.

Body copy for most advertisements consists of an introductory statement or paragraph, several explanatory paragraphs, and a closing paragraph. Some copywriters adopt a pattern or set of guidelines to develop body copy systematically: (1) identify a specific desire or problem of consumers, (2) suggest the good or service as the best way to satisfy that desire or solve that problem, (3) state the advantages and benefits of the product, (4) indicate why the advertised product is the best for the buyer's particular situation, (5) substantiate the claims and advantages, and (6) ask the buyer for action.[11]

The signature identifies the sponsor of the advertisement. It may contain several elements, including the firm's trademark, name, and address. The signature should be designed to be attractive, legible, distinctive, and easy to identify in a variety of sizes.

11. James E. Littlefield and C. A. Kirkpatrick, *Advertising Mass Communication in Marketing* (Boston: Houghton Mifflin, 1970), p. 178.

FIGURE 14.9

Final storyboard
(SOURCE: Created by
DDB Needham
Worldwide for
Hershey Chocolate
USA)

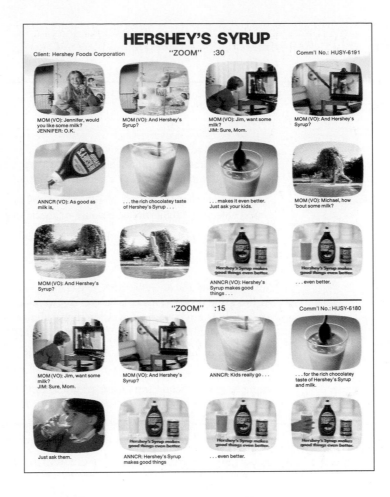

Because radio listeners often are mentally not fully "tuned in," radio copy should be informal and conversational to attract listeners' attention, resulting in greater impact. The radio message is highly perishable. Thus radio copy should consist of short, familiar terms. Its length should not require a rate of speech exceeding approximately two and one-half words per second.

In television copy, the audio material must not overpower the visual material and vice versa. However, a television message should make optimal use of its visual portion. As Figure 14.8 illustrates, copy for a television commercial is initially written in parallel script form. The video is described in the left column and the audio in the right column. When the parallel script is approved, the copywriter and artist combine the copy with the visual material through use of a **storyboard** (see Figure 14.9), which depicts a series of miniature television screens to show the sequence of major scenes in the commercial. Beneath each screen is a description of the audio portion that is to be used with the video message shown. Technical personnel use the storyboard as a blueprint when they produce the commercial.

Artwork **Artwork** consists of the illustration and layout of the advertisement (see Figure 14.7). Although **illustrations** are often photographs, they also can be drawings, graphs, charts, and tables. A vibrant photograph in a newspaper's business

TABLE 14.5
Illustration techniques
for advertisements

ILLUSTRATION TECHNIQUE	DESCRIPTION
Product alone	Simplest method; advantageous when appearance is important, when identification is important, when trying to keep a brand name or package in the public eye, or when selling through mail order
Emphasis on special features	Shows and emphasizes special details or features as well as advantages; used when product is unique because of special features
Product in setting	Shows what can be done with product; people, surroundings, or environment hint at what product can do; often used in food advertisements
Product in use	Puts action into the advertisement; can remind readers of benefits gained from using product; must be careful not to make visual cliché; should not include anything in illustration that will divert attention from product; used to direct readers' eyes toward product
Product being tested	Uses test to dramatize product's uses and benefits versus competing products
Results of product's use	Emphasizes satisfaction from using product; can liven up dull product; useful when nothing new can be said
Dramatizing headline	Appeal of illustration dramatizes headline; can emphasize appeal but dangerous to use illustrations that do not correlate with headlines
Dramatizing situation	Presents problem situation or shows situation in which problem has been resolved
Comparison	Compares product with "something" established; the something must be positive and familiar to audience
Contrast	Shows difference between two products or two ideas or differences in effects between use and nonuse; before-and-after format is a commonly used contrast technique
Diagrams, charts, and graphs	Used to communicate complex information quickly; may make presentations more interesting
Phantom effects	X-ray or internal view; can see inside product; helpful to explain concealed or internal mechanism
Symbolic	Symbols used to represent abstract ideas that are difficult to illustrate; effective if readers understand symbol; must be positive correlation between symbol and idea
Testimonials	Actually shows the testifier; should use famous person or someone to whom audience can relate

SOURCE: Dorothy Cohen, *Advertising* (New York: Wiley, 1972), pp. 458–464; and S. Watson Dunn and Arnold M. Barban, *Advertising: Its Role in Modern Marketing,* 6th ed. (Hinsdale, Ill.: Dryden Press, 1986), pp. 497–498.

section, an important trade journal, or a major news magazine can say much about a company's personality to customers, employees, and investors.[12] Illustrations are used to attract attention, to encourage the audience to read or listen to the copy, to communicate an idea quickly, or to communicate an idea that is difficult to put into words.[13] Advertisers use a variety of illustration techniques, which are identified and described in Table 14.5.

The **layout** of an advertisement is the physical arrangement of the illustration, headline, subheadline, body copy, and signature. The arrangement of these parts in Figure 14.7 is only one possible layout. These same elements could be positioned in many ways. The final layout is the end result of several stages of layout preparation. As it moves through these stages, the layout helps people involved in developing the advertising campaign exchange ideas. It also provides instructions for production personnel.

Executing the Campaign

The execution of an advertising campaign requires an extensive amount of planning and coordination. Regardless of whether an organization uses an advertising agency, many people and firms are involved in the execution of a campaign. Production companies, research organizations, media firms, printers, photoengravers, and commercial artists are just a few of the people and organizations that contribute to a campaign.

Implementation requires detailed schedules to ensure that various phases of the work are done on time. Advertising management personnel must evaluate the quality of the work and take corrective action when necessary. In some instances, changes have to be made during the campaign so it more effectively meets campaign objectives.

Evaluating the Effectiveness of the Advertising

Today the United States does more advertising testing than any other country or region in the world.[14] There are a variety of reasons for testing the effectiveness of advertising, including measuring achievement of advertising objectives; assessing the effectiveness of copy, illustrations, or layouts; or evaluating certain media.

Advertising can be evaluated before, during, and after the campaign. Evaluations performed before the campaign begins are called **pretests** and usually attempt to evaluate the effectiveness of one or more elements of the message. To pretest advertisements, marketers sometimes use a **consumer jury,** a number of persons who are actual or potential buyers of the advertised product. Jurors are asked to judge one or several dimensions of two or more advertisements. Such tests are based on the belief that consumers are more likely than advertising experts to know what will influence them.

To measure advertising effectiveness during a campaign, marketers usually take advantage of "inquiries." In the initial stages of a campaign, an advertiser may use

12. Kevin Foley, "A Good Photo Is Worth 1,000 Bad Ones," *Marketing News,* Dec. 5, 1986, p. 12.
13. S. Watson Dunn and Arnold M. Barban, *Advertising: Its Role in Modern Marketing,* 6th ed. (Hinsdale, Ill.: Dryden Press, 1986), p. 493.
14. Joseph L. Plummer, "The Role of Copy Research in Multinational Advertising," *Journal of Advertising Research,* October–November 1986, pp. 11–12.

several advertisements simultaneously, each containing a coupon or a form requesting information. The advertiser records the number of coupons that are returned from each type of advertisement. If an advertiser receives 78,528 coupons from advertisement A, 37,072 coupons from advertisement B, and 47,932 coupons from advertisement C, advertisement A is judged superior to advertisements B and C.

Evaluation of advertising effectiveness after the campaign is called a **posttest.** Advertising objectives often indicate what kind of posttest will be appropriate. If an advertiser sets objectives in terms of communication—product awareness, brand awareness, or attitude change—then the posttest should measure changes in one or more of these dimensions. Advertisers sometimes use consumer surveys or experiments to evaluate a campaign based on communication objectives. These methods are costly, however.

For campaign objectives that are stated in terms of sales, advertisers should determine the change in sales or market share that can be attributed to the campaign. Unfortunately, changes in sales or market share that result from advertising cannot be measured precisely; many factors independent of advertisements affect a firm's sales and market share. Competitive actions, government actions, changes in economic conditions, consumer preferences, and weather are only a few factors that might enhance or diminish a company's sales or market share. However, by using data about past and current sales and advertising expenditures, an advertiser can make gross estimates of the effects of a campaign on sales or market share.

Because consumer surveys and experiments are so expensive, and because it is so difficult to determine the direct effects of advertising on sales, many advertisers evaluate print advertisements according to the degree to which consumers can remember them. The posttest methods based on memory include recognition and recall tests. Such tests usually are performed by research organizations through consumer surveys. If a **recognition test** is used, individual respondents are shown the actual advertisement and asked whether they recognize it. If they do, the interviewer asks additional questions to determine how much of the advertisement each respondent read. When recall is evaluated, the respondents are not shown the actual advertisement but instead are asked about what they have seen or heard recently.

Recall can be measured through either unaided recall or aided recall methods. In an **unaided recall test,** subjects are asked to identify advertisements that they have seen recently but are not shown any clues to stimulate their memory. A similar procedure is used with an **aided recall test,** except that respondents are shown a list of products, brands, company names, or trademarks to jog their memories. Several research organizations, including Daniel Starch and Gallup & Robinson, provide syndicated research services regarding recognition and recall of advertisements. As discussed in Chapter 6, researchers are also using a sophisticated technique called single-source data. With this technique, individuals' behaviors are tracked from television sets to the check-out counter. Monitors are placed in preselected homes, and microcomputers record when the television set is on and which station is being viewed. At the supermarket check-out, the individual in the sample household presents an identification card. The checker records the purchases by scanner, and the data are sent to the research facility. This technique is bringing more insight into people's buying patterns than ever before.

The major justification for using recognition and recall methods is that individuals are more likely to buy a product if they can remember an advertisement about it than if they cannot. That individuals remember an advertisement, however, does not mean they will actually buy the product or brand advertised. Evidence shows that the more "likable" an advertisement is, the more persuasive it will be with consumers. People who enjoy an advertisement are twice as likely to be convinced that the advertised brand is best. Of about 16 percent of those who liked an advertisement, a significant number increased their preference for the brand, whereas only about 8 percent who were neutral about the advertisement felt more favorable toward it as a result of the advertisement.

Charming advertisements, however, are by no means absolutely necessary. Advertising experts cite the Wisk's "ring around the collar" and Mr. Whipple's "don't squeeze the Charmin" campaigns as classic examples of grating advertisements that have nonetheless helped sell those brands for many years.[15]

Who Develops the Advertising Campaign?

An advertising campaign may be handled by an (1) individual or a few persons within the firm, (2) advertising department within the organization, or (3) advertising agency.

In very small firms, one or two individuals are responsible for advertising (and many other activities as well). Usually these individuals depend heavily on personnel at local newspapers and broadcast stations for copywriting, artwork, and advice about scheduling media.

In certain types of large businesses—especially in larger retail organizations—advertising departments create and implement advertising campaigns. Depending on the size of the advertising program, an advertising department may consist of a few multiskilled persons or a sizable number of specialists such as copywriters, artists, media buyers, and technical production coordinators. An advertising department sometimes obtains the services of independent research organizations and also hires free-lance specialists when they are needed for a particular project.

When an organization uses an advertising agency, the firm and the agency usually develop the advertising campaign jointly. How much each party participates in the campaign's total development depends on the working relationship between the firm and the agency. Ordinarily a firm relies on the agency for copywriting, artwork, technical production, and formulation of the media plan.

An advertising agency can assist a business in several ways. An agency, especially a larger one, supplies the firm with the services of highly skilled specialists such as copywriters, artists, media experts, researchers, legal advisers, and production coordinators. Agency personnel often have had broad experience in advertising and are usually more objective than the firm's employees about an organization's products.

Because the agency traditionally receives most of its compensation from a 15 percent commission the media pay, a firm can obtain some agency services at a low

15. Ronald Alsop, "TV Ads That Are Likeable Get Plus Ratings for Persuasiveness," *The Wall Street Journal*, Feb. 20, 1986, p. 21.

or moderate cost. For example, if an agency contracts for $400,000 of television time for a firm, it receives a commission of $60,000 from the television station. Although the traditional compensation method for agencies is changing and now includes other factors, the media commission still offsets some costs of using an agency.

Now that we have explored advertising as a potential promotion mix ingredient, let us consider a related ingredient, publicity.

Publicity

As indicated in Chapter 13, **publicity** is communication in news story form, regarding an organization and/or its products, that is transmitted through a mass medium at no charge. Publicity can be presented through a variety of vehicles, several of which we examine in this section.

Within an organization, publicity is sometimes viewed as part of public relations—a larger, more comprehensive communication function. **Public relations** is a broad set of communication activities used to create and maintain favorable relations between the organization and its publics: customers, employees, stockholders, government officials, and society in general.

Publicity and Advertising Compared

Although publicity and advertising both depend on mass media, they differ in several respects. Whereas advertising messages tend to be informative or persuasive, publicity is mainly just informative. Advertisements sometimes are designed to have an immediate impact on sales; publicity messages are more subdued. Publicity releases do not identify sponsors as their sources; advertisements do.

When advertising is used, the sponsor pays for the media time or space. For publicity, an organization does not pay for the use of time or space; communications through publicity usually are included as part of a program or a print story. Advertisements usually are separated from the broadcast programs or editorial portions of print media so that the audience or readers can easily recognize (or ignore) them. Publicity may have greater credibility than advertising among consumers because as a news story it may appear more objective. Finally, a firm can use advertising to repeat the same messages or issues as many times as desired; publicity is generally not subject to repetition.

Kinds of Publicity

There are several types of publicity mechanisms.[16] The most common is the **news release,** which is usually a single page of typewritten copy containing fewer than three hundred words. A news release also gives the firm's or agency's name, its address and phone number, and the contact person. Automobile companies often use news releases to introduce new products. Figure 14.10 is an example of a news release. A **feature article** is a longer manuscript (up to three thousand words) that usually is prepared for a specific publication. A **captioned photograph** is a photo-

16. Richard E. Stanley, *Promotion* (Englewood Cliffs, N.J., Prentice-Hall, 1982), pp. 245–246.

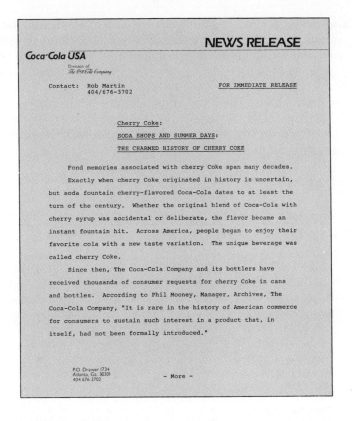

graph with a brief description that explains the picture's content. Captioned photographs are especially effective for illustrating a new or improved product with highly visible features.

There are several other kinds of publicity. A **press conference** is a meeting used to announce major news events. Media personnel are invited to a news conference and usually are supplied with written materials and photographs. In addition, letters to the editor and editorials sometimes are prepared and sent to newspapers and magazine publishers. However, newspaper editors frequently allocate space on their editorial pages to local writers and national columnists. Finally, films and tapes may be distributed to broadcast stations in the hope that they will be aired.

A marketer's choice of specific types of publicity depends on considerations that include the type of information being transmitted, the characteristics of the target audience, the receptivity of media personnel, the importance of the item to the public, and the amount of information needing to be presented.

Sometimes, a marketer uses a single type of publicity in a promotion mix. In other cases, a marketer may use a variety of publicity mechanisms, with publicity being the primary ingredient in the promotion mix.

Uses of Publicity

Publicity has a number of uses. It can be used to make people aware of a firm's products, brands, or activities; to maintain a certain level of positive public visibility; and to enhance a particular image, such as innovativeness or progressiveness. It also can be used to overcome negative images. Some firms use publicity for a single purpose, whereas others use it for several purposes. Companies can include a multitude of specific issues in publicity releases (see Table 14.6).

Requirements of a Publicity Program

For maximum benefit, a firm should create and maintain a systematic, continuous publicity program. A single individual or department—within the organization or from its advertising agency or public relations firm—should be responsible for managing the program.

TABLE 14.6

Possible issues for publicity releases

Marketing developments
New products
New uses for old products
Research developments
Changes of marketing personnel
Large orders received
Successful bids
Awards of contracts
Special events

Company policies
New guarantees
Changes in credit terms
Changes in distribution policies
Changes in service policies
Changes in prices

News of general interest
Annual election of officers
Meetings of the board of directors
Anniversaries of the organization
Anniversaries of an invention
Anniversaries of the senior officers
Holidays that can be tied to the organization's activities
Annual banquets and picnics
Special weeks, such as Clean-up Week
Founders' Day
Conferences and special meetings
Open house to the community
Athletic events
Awards of merit to employees
Laying of cornerstone
Opening of an exhibition

Reports on current developments
Reports of experiments
Reports on industry conditions
Company progress reports
Employment, production, and sales statistics
Reports on new discoveries
Tax reports
Speeches by principals
Analyses of economic conditions
Employment gains
Financial statements
Organization appointments
Opening of new markets

Personalities—names are news
Visits by famous persons
Accomplishments of individuals
Winners of company contests
Employees' and officers' advancements
Interviews with company officials
Company employees serving as judges for contests
Interviews with employees

Slogans, symbols, endorsements
Company's slogan—its history and development
A tie-in of company activities with slogans
Creation of a slogan
The company's trademark
The company's name plate
Product endorsements

SOURCE: Albert Wesley Frey, ed., *Marketing Handbook*, 2nd ed. (New York: Ronald Press), pp. 19–35. Copyright © 1965. Reprinted by permission of John Wiley & Sons, Inc.

It is important to establish and maintain good working relationships with media personnel. Personal contact with editors, reporters, and other news personnel is often necessary because without their input it is difficult to determine exactly how to design an organization's publicity program so as to facilitate the work of media news people. For example, when Tom Monaghan, owner of Domino's Pizza, offered to adopt three orphaned bear cubs, *The Detroit Free Press* and *Ann Arbor News* gave the subject front-page coverage, generating positive publicity for Monaghan and Domino's.[17] Domino's has worked to maintain ongoing good relations with the media.

Media personnel reject a great deal of publicity material because it is not newsworthy or because it is poorly written. If a firm hopes to have an effective publicity program, it must do its best to avoid these flaws. Guidelines and checklists are sometimes helpful in achieving these goals.

Finally, a firm has to evaluate its publicity efforts. Usually, the effectiveness of publicity is measured by the number of releases actually published or broadcast. To monitor print media and determine which releases are published and how often, an organization can hire a clipping service, a firm that clips and sends published news releases to client companies. To measure the effectiveness of television publicity, a firm can enclose a card with its publicity releases and request that the station record its name and the dates when the news item is broadcast, but station personnel do not always comply. Some television and radio tracking services also exist but are extremely costly.

Dealing with Unfavorable Publicity

Up to this point we have discussed publicity as a planned promotion-mix ingredient. However, firms may have to deal with unfavorable publicity regarding an unsafe product, an accident, the actions of a dishonest employee, or some other negative event. The Application on page 499 shows the tactics McNeilab, Inc. used to salvage the Tylenol brand after the occurrences of the tampering incidences.

The negative impact of unfavorable publicity can be quick and dramatic. A single negative event that produces unfavorable publicity can wipe out a firm's favorable image and destroy consumer attitudes that took years to build through promotional efforts. To protect an organization's image, it is important to avoid unfavorable publicity, or at least to lessen its effects. First and foremost, the organization can directly reduce negative incidents and events through safety programs, inspections, and effective quality control procedures. But because firms obviously cannot eliminate all negative occurrences, it is important that they establish policies and procedures for the news coverage of such events. These policies should be designated to lessen negative impact. Audi of America used a print campaign that focused on newspapers to minimize the impact of negative publicity toward its Audi 5000 (see Figure 14.11). The company believed that it needed to react to a *60 Minutes* investigative report that blamed Audi for the sudden acceleration problem its 5000 was experiencing. Audi's advertisement did not apologize for the occurrence because it did not admit negligence. Instead, the copy discussed the car's engineering, presented test results, and dealt directly with issues raised on *60*

17. Bob Campbell, "Monaghan Offers a Home for Orphaned Cubs," *Ann Arbor News,* Apr. 5, 1988, p. 1.

FIGURE 14.11

Audi used print advertising to ease consumers' fears regarding sudden acceleration (SOURCE: Courtesy of Audi)

The facts about unintended acceleration.

What Is Unintended Acceleration? Sudden or unintended acceleration is a phenomenon that reportedly occurs in cars with automatic transmissions, when the driver starts the engine and then shifts out of park into either drive or reverse.

The scenario goes like this: Suddenly the engine starts to race and the car surges forward or backward. Drivers involved in this situation report that braking fails to bring the surging car under control.

According to a leading financial publication, the National Highway Traffic Safety Administration has been investigating reports of unintended acceleration in over 60 million cars...among them cars made by Volvo, General Motors, Ford, American Motors, Nissan and Toyota, as well as Audi. For some months we at Audi have been conducting our own intensive investigation.

We believe you are entitled to know what we've discovered.

What Makes It Happen? Audi conducted thorough on-site inspections of Audi 5000 cars involved in incidents of unintended acceleration. Our investigators interviewed not only drivers, but passengers and observers as well. What we found is as consistent as it is puzzling.

In no case was there any technical malfunction, either in the vehicle or its systems, that could explain unintended acceleration along with brake loss.

For example, tests on cars where brake failure was cited showed that both brakes and brake lights were operating normally after the incident.

Moreover, in none of the examinations was it possible to duplicate the sudden surging motion drivers had described. Our investigators were, in fact, unable to find any evidence of related mechanical failure.

What Is Audi Doing About It? Audi has long been known for its commitment to safety...the safety of our owners as well as of the general public. So we've put in place a comprehensive program to help drivers avoid unintended acceleration...whatever its cause.

We're attacking the issue in three ways.

First: Audi will ask owners of 1978 through 1986 Audi 5000 vehicles equipped with automatic transmissions to bring their cars to their dealers for modification. An electromechanical system known as the Automatic Shift Lock will be installed free of charge in the gear-selector mechanism.

What the Automatic Shift Lock does is to allow the driver to shift out of park into drive or reverse *only when the brake pedal is depressed.*

Second: Audi realizes that safe driving requires driver education to support intelligent car design. So we're stepping up our efforts to educate owners. We've produced video tapes (you can see them at your Audi dealers), plus audio tapes, both designed to remind new and current owners, as well as secondary drivers, of certain fundamentals. We remind you that safe driving depends on a thorough knowledge of the features and operating procedures of your car. We remind you that all cars are different, and that it is in your own best interest to keep those operating differences in mind.

And we give you specific driving tips. For example, experts recommend that you start your car *only* when it is in park, never in neutral.

Third: Audi will continue to monitor the issue, and we will continue to work closely with government agencies to help solve the issue of unintended acceleration.

What Can You Do About Unintended Acceleration? First: Be sure you're familiar with the information in your owner's manual on starting procedures.

Make sure your seating position puts you comfortably in reach of all controls.

Be sure that anyone else who drives your car is familiar with its recommended starting and operating procedures before you let them take the wheel.

And when your dealer asks you to come in for modification, be sure to respond.

Experts offer some practical advice to Audi drivers if unintended acceleration ever does occur.

Turn off the ignition, but don't pull the key out, or the steering wheel will lock. Stopping the engine is the most effective move you can make.

Ever since the first Audi rolled off the assembly line, we've endeavored to build motorcars that set a worldwide standard for excellence in engineering.

Audi is committed to building quality performance automobiles and stands behind each and every one.

And that commitment doesn't end when you walk out of the showroom.

If you or anyone you know becomes involved in an incident of unintended acceleration in an Audi, report it to Audi Consumer Services, P.O. Box 3951, Troy, Michigan 48007-3951.

Or call us at (313) 362-6950.

Be sure to do it at once, so that we can investigate the incident promptly.

If you have any additional questions or would like further information on unintended acceleration, write to us at the address listed above.

Audi of America

Minutes. Audi chose newspapers because it wanted to get its message out quickly to combat the negative publicity *60 Minutes* created and to target its audience specifically by going into the *Wall Street Journal* and newsweeklies that would reach its target market.[18]

In most cases, organizations should expedite news coverage of negative events rather than trying to discourage or block it; the facts are more likely to be reported accurately. If news coverage is discouraged, there is a chance that rumors and misinformation will be passed along. An unfavorable event can easily balloon into a scandal or a tragedy. It could even result in public panic.

Six Flags, a theme amusement park, established a set of policies and procedures to be used when a negative event occurs. The policies are aimed at helping news personnel get into the park quickly and providing them with as much information as possible. Not only does this approach tend to lessen the effects of negative events, it enables the organization to maintain positive relationships with media personnel. Such relationships are essential if news personnel are to cooperate with a firm and broadcast favorable news stories about an organization.

18. Warren Berger, "Crisis Advertising," *Inside Print,* January 1988, pp. 40, 44.

Tylenol on the Rebound from Tampering Problems

McNeilab, Inc. (a subsidiary of Johnson & Johnson) introduced Tylenol in 1961, and the aspirin substitute proved highly profitable for the company. By 1982, Tylenol was the number-one pain reliever, with 35 percent of that market. Then disaster struck. On September 30, 1982, multiple deaths in the Chicago area were traced to cyanide-laced Extra-Strength Tylenol capsules. And again, in 1986, cyanide-laced Tylenol capsules were blamed for the death of a New York woman. In both cases, Johnson & Johnson immediately took action to deal with the problem.

After the first incident in 1982, Johnson & Johnson spent $100 million to buy back Tylenol products from retailers and consumers. The company closely monitored public opinion on the Tylenol incident to determine its course of action. Surveys found that 94 percent of all adults in the nation knew about the Tylenol incident, although 90 percent believed that it was not McNeilab's fault. Of those surveyed, 93 percent felt that the tragedy might have occurred in any over-the-counter capsule brand, and 90 percent realized that only capsules were involved. McNeil and Johnson & Johnson decided to relaunch the tarnished product.

After the Chicago incident, the federal government required that manufacturers package all over-the-counter medicines in tamper-resistant packages. McNeil repackaged Tylenol with glued-end flaps, a plastic-neck seal, and an inner-foil seal, with a label instructing consumers, "Do not use if safety seals are broken." Although the government required only one of the three preventative measures, McNeil did not want to take any chances. The company launched a massive production and distribution effort to make the newly packaged product available in as short a time as possible.

At the same time, to rebuild consumer confidence in Tylenol products, Johnson & Johnson implemented an intensive promotional program on television and in print to encourage consumers to "Continue to trust Tylenol." Newspaper advertisements offered consumers a $2.50 coupon to replace products they might have thrown out when the tampering incident came to light. Consumers could also call a toll-free number to receive the coupon.

Thus, within sixty days, Johnson & Johnson and McNeil had relaunched Tylenol. Within six months, Tylenol's market share rose to 27 percent, and within one year, the medicine had nearly recaptured its previous market share. Although the company spent $100 million to save the brand, the brand saved was one that grossed more than $500 million in annual sales.

When the second tampering incident occurred in 1986, Johnson & Johnson knew what to do. In addition to recalling and replacing Tylenol capsules, which this time cost $130 million, Johnson & Johnson suspended production of all over-the-counter medicines in capsules, although they accounted for 30 percent of Tylenol sales. The company asked consumers to trade their capsules for caplets, oval-shaped tablets created after the 1982 incident as an alternative to capsules. The company felt that any tampering of the caplets would result in a visible change in appearance. Johnson & Johnson also offered $100,000 for information that might lead to the arrest of anyone involved with the tampering.

Johnson & Johnson's actions were quick, well-publicized, and influential: Many companies quickly assessed their own vulnerability to potential tampering, along with the public's perception of their vulnerability. Johnson & Johnson made every effort to show strong sensitivity and concern toward consumers, not just in words but in actions. Although Tylenol's share is now less than 30 percent, the decline is as much due to the introduction of ibuprofen products (such as Advil and Nuprin) as it is to the cyanide incidents.

SOURCES: "The 100 Leading National Advertisers," 1987 ed., *Advertising Age*, Sept. 24, 1987, pp. 120–121; "Tylenol Firm Abandoning All Capsules," *Houston Post*, Feb. 18, 1986, p. 1; "Johnson & Johnson Reincarnates a Brand," *Sales and Marketing Management*, Jan. 16, 1984, p. 63; Rebecca Fannin, "Diary of an Amazing Comeback," *Marketing & Media Decisions*, Spring 1983, pp. 129–134; "The Rise—and Fall?" *Advertising Age*, Oct. 11, 1982, p. 78; Thomas Moore, "The Fight to Save Tylenol," *Fortune*, Nov. 29, 1982, pp. 44–49.

Limitations in Using Publicity

That media do not charge for transmitting publicity is a double-edged sword. Although it provides a financial advantage, it brings with it several limitations. Media personnel must believe that messages are newsworthy if they are to be published or broadcast. That means that messages must be timely, interesting, and accurate. Many communications simply do not qualify. Time and effort may be necessary to convince media personnel of the news value of publicity releases.

Although marketers usually encourage media personnel to air a publicity release at a certain time, they control neither the content nor the timing of the communication. Media personnel alter the length and content of publicity releases to fit publishers' or broadcasters' requirements. They may delete the parts of the message that are most important—at least from the firm's perspective. Media personnel generally use publicity releases in time slots or positions that are most convenient for them; thus the messages are frequently presented at times or in locations that do not effectively reach the audiences an organization hopes to reach. Despite its drawbacks, though, properly managed publicity offers significant benefits to an organization.

Summary

Advertising is a paid form of nonpersonal communication that is transmitted to consumers through mass media such as television, radio, newspapers, magazines, direct mail, mass transit vehicles, and outdoor displays. Both nonbusiness and business organizations use advertising.

Organizations use advertising in many ways. Institutional advertising promotes organizations' images and ideas as well as political issues and candidates. Product advertising focuses on uses, features, images, and benefits of goods and services. To make people aware of a new or innovative product's existence, uses, and benefits, marketers use pioneer advertising in the introductory stage to stimulate primary demand for a general product category. Marketers switch to competitive advertising to increase selective demand by promoting a particular brand's uses, features, and advantages.

Advertising sometimes is used to lessen the impact of a competitor's promotional program. It is sometimes designed to make the sales force more effective. To increase market penetration, an advertiser sometimes focuses a campaign on promoting an increased number of uses for the product. Some advertisements for an established product remind consumers that the product is still around and that it has certain characteristics and uses. Marketers may try to assure users of a particular brand that they are using the best brand. Marketers also use advertising to smooth out fluctuations in sales.

Although marketers may vary in how they develop advertising campaigns, they should follow a general pattern. First, they must identify and analyze the advertising target. Second, they should establish what they want the campaign to accomplish by defining the advertising objectives. The next step is to create the advertising platform, which contains the basic issues to be presented in the campaign. Next, the advertiser must decide how much money is to be spent on the campaign. Fifth, the marketer must develop the media plan by selecting and scheduling the media to be used in the campaign. In the sixth stage, the advertiser uses copy and artwork to create the message. Finally, the advertiser must devise one or more methods for evaluating the effectiveness of the advertisements.

Advertising campaigns can be developed by personnel within the firm or in conjunction with advertising agencies. When a campaign is created by the firm's personnel, it may be developed by only a few people, or it may be the product of an advertising department within the firm. The use of an advertising agency may be advantageous to a firm because an agency can provide highly skilled, objective specialists with broad experience in the advertising field at low to moderate costs to the firm.

Publicity is communication in news story form, regarding an organization and/or its products, that is transmitted through a mass medium at no charge. Usually publicity is part of the larger, more comprehensive communication function of public relations. Publicity is mainly informative and usually more subdued than advertising. There are many types of publicity, including news releases, feature articles, captioned photographs, press conferences, editorials, films, and tapes. Marketers can use one or more of these forms to achieve a variety of objectives. To have an effective publicity program, someone—either in the organization or the firm's agency—must be responsible for creating and maintaining systematic and continuous publicity efforts.

An organization should avoid negative publicity by reducing the number of negative events that result in unfavorable publicity. To diminish the impact of unfavorable publicity, an organization should institute policies and procedures for properly handling news personnel when negative events do occur. Problems that surround the use of publicity include reluctance of media personnel to print or air releases and lack of control over the timing and content of messages.

Important Terms

Advertising
Institutional advertising
Product advertising
Pioneer advertising
Competitive advertising
Comparative advertising
Defensive advertising
Reminder advertising
Reinforcement advertising
Advertising target
Advertising platform
Advertising appropriation
Objective and task approach
Percent of sales approach
Competition-matching approach
Arbitrary approach
Media plan
Cost comparison indicator
Regional issues

Copy
Storyboard
Artwork
Illustrations
Layout
Pretests
Consumer jury
Posttest
Recognition test
Unaided recall test
Aided recall test
Publicity
Public relations
News release
Feature article
Captioned photograph
Press conference

Discussion and Review Questions

1. What is the difference between institutional and product advertising?
2. When should advertising be used to stimulate primary demand? When should advertising be used to stimulate selective demand?
3. How can advertising be used as a competitive tactic?
4. Describe the relationship between advertising and personal selling.
5. How does a marketer use advertising to promote year-round sales stability?
6. What are the major steps in creating an advertising campaign?
7. What is an advertising target? How does a marketer analyze the target audience after it has been identified?
8. Why is it necessary to define advertising objectives?
9. What is an advertising platform, and how is it used?
10. What factors affect the size of an advertising budget? What techniques are used to determine this budget?
11. Describe the steps required in developing a media plan.
12. What is the role of copy in an advertising message?
13. How is artwork used in the development of an advertising message?
14. What role does an advertising agency play in developing an advertising campaign?
15. Discuss several ways to posttest the effectiveness of advertising.
16. What is publicity? How does it differ from advertising?
17. Identify and describe the major types of publicity.
18. How do organizations use publicity? Give several examples of publicity releases that you observed recently in local media.

19. How should an organization handle negative publicity? Identify a recent example of a firm that received negative publicity. Did the firm deal with it effectively?
20. Explain the problems and limitations associated with using publicity. How can some of these limitations be minimized?

Cases

14.1   McDonald's Advertising[19]

Most people around the world are familiar with the golden arches of McDonald's. But the huge fast-food chain, along with its competitors, is now under fire to divulge the contents of its food. Consumer advocates frequently accuse the company of serving food with poor nutritional value; now the federal government as well wants to know what is in McDonald's food.

McDonald's turned to defensive advertising to combat both the effects of these charges and competitive nutritional promotion by other fast-food companies. In response to a request in 1986 from the attorneys general of California, New York, and Texas, the company released a booklet listing the ingredients for all its menu items. In 1987, McDonald's budgeted more than $12 million for an advertising platform emphasizing the nutritional value of its McDLTs, Chicken McNuggets, and all its other famous selections. This campaign attempted to position McDonald's as a company that cares about its customers' nutritional concerns, especially their fears about the sodium and cholesterol levels in McDonald's food.

There were several purposes behind this campaign strategy. Advertisements were designed not only to stimulate primary and selective demand but to lessen the effects of consumer advocates' charges and Arby's, Burger King's, and other fast-food giants' nutritional advertising. The advertisements also reminded and reinforced for those who already eat at McDonald's that not only is McDonald's fast food fast, it has sound nutritional value. The advertisements particularly tried to reduce consumers' fears about the fat and sodium levels in McDonald's foods.

McDonald's media plan relied heavily on the print media, where it could more effectively deal with the details of the nutritional issue. Some magazines ran two-page advertisements: the first page contained a general message about nutrition, and the second page ran more detailed nutritional information on eight different subjects. Other advertisements were only one page long. All the advertisements were targeted to both a general audience and health-conscious consumers, appearing in such journals as *Ladies' Home Journal, TV Guide, Ebony, Reader's Digest, American Health, Prevention,* and the *New England Journal of Medicine.*

Simple illustrations and catchy slogans got the nutritional message across to the consumer. Slogans such as "Eat your calcium" and "We're getting a handle on

19. Based on information from Robert Johnson, "Fast-Food Chains Draw Criticism for Marketing Fare as Nutritional," *Wall Street Journal,* Apr. 6, 1987, p. 23; Scott Hume, "McDonald's Heavy in Print for Nutrition," *Advertising Age,* Jan. 19, 1987, pp. 2, 90; Fran Brock, "McDonald's, States to Discuss Disagreement over Ads," *Adweek,* May 25, 1987, p. 6; Robert Johnson, "Three States Charge McDonald's Ads on its Foods' Nutrition Are Deceptive," *Wall Street Journal,* Apr. 27, 1987, p. 22; Jim Osterman, "Fast-Food Chains Try Meal Deals to Boost Sagging Sales," *Adweek,* Apr. 13, 1987, p. 53.

nutrition" caught the reader's attention. One advertisement showed a bottle of milk, a container of beef, and a potato; another advertisement pointed out that there is real milk in that famous McDonald's milkshake and lean beef in the hamburgers. McDonald's also promoted its then new packaged salads with commercials and newspaper coupons. At the same time, McDonald's reduced prices on selected menu items to bring in more customers.

Although the company said it went to great pains to ensure that the 1987 advertisements were accurate, they still generated much controversy among consumer advocates, health experts, and federal and state governments. California, New York, and Texas state governments asked McDonald's to stop running the advertisements because they allegedly contained misleading and inaccurate information about the nutritional value of McDonald's meals. The consumer groups were particularly concerned about those advertisements that said that McDonald's had reduced the salt content in its entire menu and that its milkshakes contain real milk and no preservatives; the groups believed these advertisements contained only part of the story. There was also much discussion about passing a law that would require all fast-food restaurants to list all the ingredients of all fast-food products on the package.

McDonald's will have to continue using defensive advertising, although probably with another platform, to combat the negative publicity arising from the nutritional controversy. It is somewhat ironic that a nutritional advertising platform intended to reduce the impact of negative publicity about the nutritional value of McDonald's food actually generated more negative publicity for the company. It is certain that other fast-food chains will capitalize on the negative publicity facing McDonald's, but those companies too will have to be careful, lest the controversy engulf them. The entire industry could be adversely affected if in fact it does become law that all fast-food items must include a listing of all ingredients.

Questions for Discussion

1. What are the marketing considerations in promoting the nutritional value of McDonald's foods?
2. What supposedly makes the advertising in this case deceptive?
3. If you were the chief executive officer at McDonald's, what would you do if it were necessary to make McDonald's socially responsible but still meet your marketing objectives?

14.2   Dr Pepper Changes Its Advertising Campaign[20]

To the soda fountain customers of Morrison's Drug Store in Waco, Texas, in the 1880s, the new drink tasted distinctly different. Charlie Alderton, a Morrison

20. Based on information from *Clockdial* (Dr Pepper news magazine), January–February 1987; *Clockdial*, October–December 1986; *Clockdial*, Centennial Issue 1985; Candace Talmadge, "Dr Pepper Orders New Creative," *Adweek*, Apr. 20, 1987, pp. 1, 6; Barbara Lippert, "Cult Pepper Worship: Just What the Doctor Ordered," *Adweek*, Jan. 13, 1986, p. 21; Tom Bayer, "Aspartame, Ads Back Diet Dr Pepper," *Advertising Age*, Sept. 22, 1986, p. 12; Jennifer Lawrence, "Dr Pepper Rx: Product Ads," *Advertising Age*, Apr. 20, 1987, pp. 3, 93.

employee, invented the tasty soft drink made from twenty-three different flavors. He called it Dr Pepper. The new drink caught on quickly among local residents. Today, Dr Pepper has 7 percent of the United States soft-drink market, and it is distributed worldwide. In 1985, The Dr Pepper Company showed profits of $60.6 million.

It is unlikely that Dr Pepper would be so popular without some form of promotion (see Figure 14.12). Advertising has made the difference. Dr Pepper has had a variety of advertising campaigns in its one-hundred-year history; the fact that some of its earlier advertising gimmicks (buttons, signs, and matchbook covers) are now valuable collectors' items is a measure of how successful these campaigns were. The Dr Pepper Company understands how important advertising is to its success and so continues to make it a top priority for increasing sales. In 1987, the company budgeted $35 million for advertising regular and diet Dr Pepper, up 15 percent from the 1986 budget.

The company realizes that the key to its success is professional advertising that cuts through the clutter of advertising its competitors generate, three of whom push twenty-four brands in the cola category alone to the same target market as Dr

Pepper. Dr Pepper has to stand out on a national scale with competitive advertising to reach the people it wants with a message they will remember. In the 1950s, it was Frosty, a friendly St. Bernard dog, who attracted children to Dr Pepper; in the 1960s, adults were told about the friendly "Pepper-upper." In the 1970s, Dr Pepper became the "most original soft drink ever," and late in that decade, everyone was encouraged to "Be a Pepper." "I'm a Pepper," "Wouldn't you like to be a Pepper, too?" and "Hold out for the out of the ordinary" continued into the 1980s. Dr Pepper switched themes, from "Taste for originality" to "Just what the Dr ordered," but the idea that it is fun to "Be a Pepper" did not change.

The previous advertising themes were aimed at only the 13- to 34-year-old target market, but now Dr Pepper acts as if there are only two market segments: those who drink Dr Pepper, and those who do not. All television viewers have seen the heavy doses of advertisements reminding us that Dr Pepper is still alive and well and the reinforcement advertisements that say it is right to set ourselves apart from ordinary things and ordinary people by drinking Dr Pepper. This reinforces the idea of a narrow market segment defined not just by age but by attitude. The cola giants, by contrast, use a mass appeal that defines the market in much broader terms.

The 1987 Diet Dr Pepper campaign told diet cola seekers to "throw your diet a curve" with Diet Dr Pepper. The advertisements capitalized on the popular idea of searching for relationships through the "personal ads," suggesting that one way to find the soft drink to answer your dreams is to take out a personals advertisement in the newspaper classifieds. One television spot showed a beautiful woman who wanted to spice up her life, with the copy from her personal advertisement rolling up the screen. Dr Pepper is of course the answer to her advertisement. To make certain the diet-soda spots were seen by the target market, they were run during shows the target market watches, such as *General Hospital* and *Moonlighting*. The Dr Pepper Company also planned a sweepstakes promotion to accompany the campaign called "Desperately Seeking Diet Dr Pepper."

Dr Pepper simultaneously ran its regular Dr Pepper campaign on the same media, but with a slightly different message. The regular Pepper commercials, with advertisements similar to the earlier "Be a Pepper" campaign, used popular music and upbeat people to catch the attention of the target market and convince them that Dr Pepper is indeed "just what the Dr ordered." These spots were more product oriented than the earlier campaigns in an effort to get consumers to ask for Dr Pepper by name, instead of just whatever soft drink is on sale. The spots were aimed at both the 13- to 34-year-old core soft-drink market and consumers older than 35.

Although the 1987 campaigns for Dr Pepper were new creative concepts, the basic platform remained the same. The new advertisements continued to highlight the idea that Dr Pepper is different, bold, one of a kind. Pepper drinkers continued to be portrayed as being as unusual as the product they love. The key idea is that Pepper drinkers see themselves as normal; it is everyone else who is different. Thus the campaign looked at the world through the eyes of a Pepper drinker, who sees that world as backward, two-dimensional, and monotone.

The Dr Pepper Company thinks the dual campaigns are great. The campaigns answered advertising analysts' concerns that Dr Pepper is not aiming enough of its message at the 35-and-older market, and the new spots focused more on the product (whereas competitive colas ran lifestyle-oriented campaigns). However, analysts wonder if the two campaigns will confuse viewers with their different messages, or even make some viewers angry. Some viewers might see the Diet Dr Pepper spots as insulting; others may take offense at the double meaning of personals classified advertisements and switch brands as a result. Analysts also wonder if the Dr Pepper Company had enough in its advertising budget to make both its diet and regular campaigns visible over the "noise" of the competition.

Questions for Discussion

1. Based on the information in this case, assess whether Dr Pepper's advertising objectives were stated in terms of sales or communication.
2. What are the primary issues in Dr Pepper's advertising platform?
3. In general, do you believe that this campaign was successful?

15. Personal Selling and Sales Promotion

OBJECTIVES

▶ To understand the major purposes of personal selling.

▶ To learn the basic steps in the personal selling process.

▶ To identify the types of sales force personnel.

▶ To gain insight into sales management decisions and activities such as setting objectives for and determining size of the sales force; recruiting, selecting, training, compensating, and motivating salespeople; creating sales territories; and routing, scheduling, and controlling sales personnel.

▶ To become aware of what sales promotion activities are and how they can be used.

▶ To become familiar with specific sales promotion methods used.

*I*n *1906,* Alfred Fuller went door to door selling the household brushes he made in his basement. Before long, he had an army of Fuller Brush people knocking on doors all over the country. Fuller's salespeople are masters of personal selling. The Fuller selling technique involved nonstop talking and free samples. Alfred Fuller believed that if a salesperson could get inside a potential customer's door, he or she could make a sale. He also felt that a belief in one's own ability to succeed was important in closing a sale. Today, the Fuller Brush Company has become a leader in door-to-door sales and one of the most highly regarded manufacturers of household supplies in the country. In 1968 the firm was purchased by Sara Lee Corporation, and it derives 50 percent of its income from sales in Mexico.

There are now about 20,000 Fuller Brush sales representatives, down from 30,000 of the late 1960s. Today's Fuller Brush man, however, is likely to be a woman—80 percent of Fuller's sales force are now women. Ninety percent of the company's sales force is part time.

Although Fuller representatives still sell door to door, they usually call ahead to set up a time and date for making their sales presentation. Representatives generally do not sell over the telephone to new clients. Instead, the first call is spent telling the customer about the Fuller Brush Company. Crime-induced fear of strangers has decreased the effectiveness of the cold sales call.

Fuller representatives maintain a low-key sales approach. Most favor a soft-sell approach because of the high quality of Fuller Brush products. Company representatives try to visit customers twice a month. Many salespeople leave

FIGURE 15.1

Advertisement for
Fuller Brush (SOURCE:
Fuller Brush/L. C. Wil-
liams and Associates,
Inc.)

catalogs so that the customers will have an opportunity to decide for themselves what they want to purchase (see Figure 15.1).

Fuller has cut its prices since 1984 and often discounts the price of popular products to regular customers. The company has expanded its product line to include kitchen utensils and gardening tools, in addition to the traditional grooming products, brushes and cleaning products. Despite the expansion of the product line, Fuller does not advertise nationally. The company believes that advertising is unnecessary because customers already know about its products; however, commissions to salespeople have been increased to increase sales.

Fuller is suffering from a problem common to other door-to-door marketing companies: a shrinking customer base. More women work outside the home, so it is often difficult for a Fuller representative to catch customers at home. To overcome this problem, Fuller recently distributed its first nationwide mail-order catalog.

Despite the shortcomings of door-to-door selling, well over half of Fuller's revenues still come from home sales. The company hopes that its mail-order catalog will boost sales even higher by introducing its products to a wider clientele. Less than 1 percent of all salespeople work door-to-door today, despite the fact that the public believes this sales approach to be more common. And Fuller Brush still offers customers the traditional free sample.[1]

M OST PERSONAL SELLING TODAY requires highly trained individuals who strategically select customers with problems or needs that their products directly address. Personal selling is becoming more professional and sophisticated as it leans further toward consulting with and advising customers. In a number of business organizations, sales personnel are among the highest-paid employees. As many salespeople become familiar with their firm's total marketing and company operations, they move up rapidly into managerial positions. Many of today's high-level executives, such as those at Kodak Company, Chrysler Corp., and IBM, began their careers in sales.

As indicated in Chapter 13, personal selling and sales promotion are two possible ingredients in a promotion mix. Personal selling is the most widely used. Sometimes it is a company's sole promotional tool. Generally, it is used in conjunction with other promotion-mix ingredients. Occasionally, personal selling plays only a minor role in an organization's total promotional activities.

This chapter focuses on personal selling and sales promotion. Our discussion considers the purposes of personal selling, its basic steps, the types of individuals who make up a sales force and how they are selected, and the major sales management decisions and activities. We also examine several characteristics of sales promotion efforts. Then we look at the reasons for using sales promotion and at the sales promotion methods available for use in a promotion mix.

The Nature of Personal Selling

Personal selling is a process of informing customers and persuading them to purchase products through personal communication in an exchange situation. Personal selling gives marketers the greatest freedom to adjust a message to satisfy customers' information needs. In comparison with other promotion methods, personal selling is the most precise, enabling marketers to focus on the most promising sales prospects. Other promotion-mix ingredients are aimed at groups of people, some of whom may not be prospective customers. A major disadvantage of personal selling is its cost: It generally is the most expensive ingredient in the promotion mix. Personal selling costs are increasing faster than advertising costs.

1. Based on information from "Fuller Brush Man Uses Soft Sell, Humor to Boost Sales," *Marketing News,* Jan. 18, 1988, p. 3; "Brushing Up at Fuller," *Newsweek,* Sept. 7, 1987, p. 44; Kerry Hannon, "A Foot in the Door," *Forbes,* Oct. 20, 1986, pp. 134–136; Gerald Carson, "The Fuller Brush Man," *American Heritage,* Aug.–Sept. 1986, pp. 26–31; Harvey Shore, "Brush Strokes: The Life and Thought of Alfred C. Fuller (1885–1973)," *Business Quarterly,* Spring 1986, pp. 16–17.

Business organizations spend more money on personal selling than on any other promotion mix ingredient. Millions of people earn their livings through personal selling. Women are increasingly becoming involved in personal sales. Women began moving extensively into the selling field when they recognized the intrinsic and extrinsic rewards involved. A selling career offers high income, a great deal of freedom, a high level of training, and a high level of job satisfaction.[2] Unfortunately, consumers often view personal selling negatively. The results of a study of college marketing students examining their thoughts toward personal selling showed that approximately 25 percent thought directly of door-to-door selling. In addition, 59 percent of all students surveyed had a negative impression of personal selling. Major corporations, professional sales associations, and academic institutions are directing efforts at changing the negative stereotypes of salespeople.[3]

Personal selling goals vary from one firm to another. However, they usually involve finding prospects, convincing prospects to buy, and keeping customers satisfied. Identifying potential buyers who are interested in an organization's products is critical.

Generally, salespeople need to be aware of their competitors. They need to monitor new products being developed, and they should be aware of all competitors' sales activity in their sales territory. Salespeople must highlight an advantage of their product when their competitors' products do not offer that specific advantage.[4] Later in this chapter we discuss this issue in more detail.

Finding prospects is important. Because most prospects seek information before they make a purchase, salespersons must ascertain prospects' informational needs and then provide the relevant information. To do so, sales personnel must be well trained regarding both their products and the selling process in general.

Few businesses survive solely on profits from one-sale customers. For long-run survival most marketers depend on repeat sales. A company has to keep its customers satisfied to obtain repeat purchases. Also, satisfied customers help attract new ones by telling potential customers about the organization and its products.

Even though the whole organization is responsible for providing customer satisfaction, much of the burden falls on salespeople. As Figure 15.2 indicates, Olin Chemicals tries to make the salesperson's job easier by providing preliminary information on Olin's products and encouraging potential customers to call the salesperson for more information. The salesperson is almost always closer to customers than anyone else in the company. The sales force often provides buyers with information and service after the sale. Such activities let a salesperson generate additional sales while evaluating the strengths and weaknesses of the company's products and other marketing mix ingredients. These observations are helpful in developing and maintaining a marketing mix that better satisfies both customers and the firm.

A salesperson may be involved with achieving one or several of these general goals. In some organizations, there are individuals whose sole job is to find prospects. This information is relayed to salespeople, who contact the prospects. After

2. Myron Gable and B. J. Reed, "The Current Status of Women in Professional Selling," *Journal of Personal Selling and Sales Management*, May 1987, pp. 33–39.
3. William A. Weeks and Darrel D. Muehing, "Students' Perceptions of Personal Selling," *Industrial Marketing Management*, May 1987, pp. 145–151.
4. "Getting Ahead and Staying Ahead as the Competition Heats Up," *Agency Sales Magazine*, June 1987, pp. 38–42.

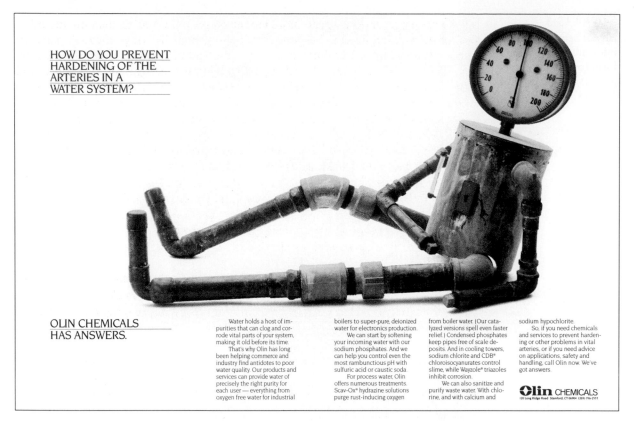

FIGURE 15.2

Olin Chemicals created an advertisement to encourage potential customers to contact a salesperson to answer questions (SOURCE: Courtesy of Olin Corporation)

the sale, these same salespeople may do the follow-up work, or a third group of employees may have the job of maintaining customer satisfaction. In many smaller organizations, a single person handles all these functions. Regardless of how many groups are involved, several major sales tasks must be performed to achieve these general goals.

Elements of the Personal Selling Process

The exact activities involved in the selling process vary among salespersons and differ for particular selling situations. No two salespersons use exactly the same selling methods. However, many salespersons—either consciously or unconsciously—move through a general selling process as they sell products. This process consists of seven elements, or steps: prospecting and evaluating, preparing, approaching the customer, making the presentation, overcoming objections, closing, and following up.

Prospecting and Evaluating

Developing a list of potential customers is called **prospecting**. A salesperson seeks the names of prospects from such sources as the company's sales records, referrals, trade shows, newspaper announcements (of marriages, births, deaths, and so on),

FIGURE 15.3

Advertisement with an information request form to identify prospects (SOURCE: Alitalia Airlines)

public records, telephone directories, trade association directories, and many others. Sales personnel also use responses from advertisements that encourage interested persons to send in an information request form (see Figure 15.3). Seminars and meetings also can produce good leads. Seminars may be geared to attract particular types of clients, such as attorneys, accountants, and specific business persons.

After developing the prospect list, a salesperson evaluates whether each prospect is able, willing, and authorized to buy the product. On the basis of this evaluation, some prospects may be deleted, and others are deemed acceptable and ranked relative to their desirability or potential.

Preparing

Before contacting acceptable prospects, a salesperson should find and analyze information regarding each prospect's specific product needs, current use of brands, feelings about available brands, and personal characteristics. A salesperson uses this information when selecting an approach and putting together a sales presentation. A salesperson with more information about a prospect is better equipped to develop an approach and presentation that precisely communicates with the prospect.

Xerox developed an automated sales process that lets a salesperson sit at a workstation to do homework for complex sales situations. The salesperson uses the computer/workstation to assist in proposals, prospecting, and preparing. Xerox discovered that half the salesperson's time was taken up by sales-inhibiting activities, such as looking for forms or gathering information. In fact, salespeople were drowning in an ocean of paperwork. Preparing an order required five to thirteen forms, and one-third of all orders were rejected because of mistakes on the forms. By 1989, Xerox had four thousand of its salespersons on workstations that facilitated most paperwork in a few hours a day. Workstations link the salesperson throughout the company without a piece of paper having to be touched.[5]

Approaching the Customer

The **approach**—the manner in which a salesperson contacts a potential customer— is a critical step in the sales process. The prospect's first impression of the salesperson may be a lasting one, with long-run consequences.

One type of approach is based on referrals. The salesperson approaches the prospect and explains that an acquaintance, an associate, or a relative has suggested the call. The salesperson who uses the cold canvass method calls on potential customers without their prior consent. Repeat contact is another common approach; when making the contact, the salesperson mentions a prior meeting. The exact type of approach depends on the salesperson's preferences, the product being sold, the firm's resources, and the characteristics of the prospect.

Making the Presentation

During the sales presentation, the salesperson must attract and hold the prospect's attention to stimulate interest and stir up a desire for the product. The salesperson should have the prospect touch, hold, or actually use the product. If possible, the salesperson should demonstrate the product and get the prospect more involved with it to stimulate greater interest. Audiovisual materials may be used to enhance the presentation. Such material can include overhead projectors, cassette players, televisions, and VCRs. In Figure 15.4, Vanport International promotes its line of presentation audiovisual equipment targeted at salespeople.

During the presentation, the salesperson must not only talk but listen. The sales presentation gives the salesperson the greatest opportunity to determine the prospect's specific needs by listening to questions and comments and observing responses. Even though the salesperson has planned the presentation in advance, she or he must be able to adjust the message to meet the prospect's information needs.

Overcoming Objections

One of the best ways to overcome a prospect's objections is to anticipate and counter them before the prospect has an opportunity to raise them. However, this approach can be risky. The salesperson may mention some objections that the prospect would not have raised. If possible, the salesperson should handle objections when they arise. They also can be dealt with at the end of the presentation.

5. Thayer C. Taylor, "Xerox: Who Says You Can't Be Big and Fast?" *Sales & Marketing Management,* November 1987, pp. 62–65.

FIGURE 15.4

Vanport International's line of audiovisual equipment is targeted toward salespeople for improving presentation effectiveness (SOURCE: Vanport International)

An effective salesperson usually seeks out a prospect's objections so as to answer them. If they are not apparent, the salesperson cannot deal with them, and they may keep the prospect from buying.

Closing

Closing is the element in the selling process whereby the salesperson asks the prospect to buy the product or products. During the presentation, the salesperson may use a "trial close" by asking questions that assume the prospect will buy the product. For example, the salesperson might ask the potential customer about financial terms, desired colors or sizes, delivery arrangements, or the quantity to be purchased. The reactions to such questions usually indicate how close the prospect is to buying. A trial close lets prospects indirectly respond that they will buy the product without having to say those sometimes difficult words, "I'll take it."

A salesperson should try to close at several points during the presentation because the prospect may be ready to buy. One closing strategy involves asking the potential customer to take a try-out order. The sales representative should either guarantee a refund if the customer is not satisfied or make the order a free offer.[6] Often an attempt to close the sale will result in objections. Thus closing can be an important stimulus that uncovers hidden objections.

6. John Nemec, "Do You Have Grand Finales?" *American Salesman*, June 1987, pp. 3–6.

Following Up After a successful closing, the salesperson must follow up the sale. In the follow-up stage, the salesperson should determine whether the order was delivered on time and installed properly, if installation was required. The salesperson should contact the customer to learn what problems or questions have arisen regarding the product. The follow-up stage also can be used to determine customers' future product needs.

Types of Salespersons

To intelligently develop a sales force, a marketing manager must decide what kind of salesperson will sell the firm's products most effectively. Most business organizations use several different kinds of sales personnel. Based on the functions they perform, salespersons can be classified into three groups: order getters, order takers, and support personnel. One salesperson can, and often does, perform all three functions.

Order Getters To obtain orders, a salesperson must inform prospects and persuade them to buy the product. The **order getters'** job is to increase the firm's sales by selling to new customers and by increasing sales to present customers. This task sometimes is called creative selling. It requires that salespeople recognize potential buyers' needs and then give them the necessary information. Order-getting activities sometimes are divided into two categories: current customer sales and new-business sales.

Current Customer Sales Sales personnel who concentrate on current customers call on people and organizations that have purchased products from the firm at least once. These salespeople seek more sales from existing customers by following up previous sales. Current customers can also be sources of leads for new prospects.

New-Business Sales Business organizations depend on sales to new customers, at least to some degree. New-business sales personnel locate prospects and convert them to buyers. Salespersons in many industries help to generate new business, but industries that depend in large part on new-customer sales are real estate, insurance, appliances, heavy industrial machinery, and automobiles.

US Sprint, a long distance telephone company, attempted to gain new business by encouraging potential customers to call and talk with sales representatives. The program tied in with the twenty-third Winter Olympics and offered a toll-free number that provided news from ABC about the Winter Olympics. The calls ran through Sprint's fiber-optic lines, allowing callers to sample the service. After receiving the Olympics information, callers were requested to stay on the line to talk with a Sprint sales representative. Customers who stayed on the line were probably pleased with the quality of Sprint service and had an interest in obtaining more information.[7]

7. "Sprint in Hotline Promotion for Olympics," *Adweek's Marketing Week*, Feb. 1, 1988, p. 3.

Order Takers

Taking orders is a repetitive task that salespersons perform to perpetuate long-lasting, satisfying relationships with customers. **Order takers** seek repeat sales. One of their major objectives is to be absolutely certain that customers have sufficient product quantities where and when they are needed. There are two groups of order takers: inside order takers and field order takers.

Inside Order Takers   In many businesses, inside order takers, who work in sales offices, receive orders by mail and telephone. Certain producers, wholesalers, and even retailers have sales personnel who sell from within the firm rather than in the field. That does not mean that inside order takers never communicate with customers face to face. Salespeople in retail stores, for example, are classified as inside order takers.

Mid-Continent Bottlers, a Des Moines soft-drink distributor, traditionally sold beverages to retailers off its trucks. Sometimes, the brands a retailer needed were not on the truck. The rising cost of fuel forced Mid-Continent to switch to inside order takers. Today, the bottler telephones 75 percent of its accounts to determine what the retailers need; then the beverages are loaded and delivered. The use of inside order takers has helped Mid-Continent significantly reduce costs.[8]

Field Order Takers   Salespersons who travel to customers are referred to as "outside," or "field," order takers. Often a customer and a field order taker develop an interdependent relationship: The buyer depends on the salesperson to take orders periodically (and sometimes to deliver them), and the salesperson counts on the buyer to purchase a certain quantity of products periodically.

Field or inside order takers should not be thought of as passive functionaries who simply record orders in a machinelike manner. Order takers generate the bulk of many organizations' total sales.

Support Personnel

Support personnel facilitate the selling function but usually are not involved only with making sales. They are engaged primarily in marketing industrial products. They are active in locating prospects, educating customers, building goodwill, and providing service after the sale. Although there are many kinds of sales support personnel, the three most common are missionary, trade, and technical.

Missionary Salespersons   **Missionary salespersons,** who usually are employed by manufacturers, assist the producer's customers in selling to their own customers. A missionary salesperson may call on retailers to inform and persuade them to buy the manufacturer's products. If the call is successful, the retailers purchase the products from wholesalers, who are the producer's customers. Manufacturers of medical supplies and pharmaceutical products often use missionary salespersons to promote their products to physicians, hospitals, and retail druggists.

Trade Salespersons   **Trade salespersons** are not strictly support personnel because they usually perform the order-taking function as well. However, they direct much of their efforts toward helping customers, especially retail stores, promote the

---

8. "Mid-Continent Keeps Costs Bottled Up," *Sales and Marketing Management Portfolio,* 1982, p. 7.

product. They are likely to restock shelves, obtain more shelf space, set up displays, provide in-store demonstrations, and distribute samples to store customers. Food producers and processors commonly employ trade salespersons.

Technical Salespersons **Technical salespersons** give technical assistance to the organization's current customers. They advise customers on product characteristics and applications, system designs, and installation procedures. Because this job is often highly technical, the salesperson usually needs to have formal training in one of the physical sciences or in engineering. Technical sales personnel often sell technical industrial products such as computers, heavy equipment, and steel.

When hiring sales personnel, marketers seldom restrict themselves to a single category because most firms require different types. Several factors dictate how many of each type of salesperson a particular firm should have. A product's uses, characteristics, complexity, and price influence the kind of sales personnel used, as do the number of customers and their characteristics. The kinds of marketing channels and the intensity and type of advertising also have an impact on the selection of sales personnel.

Management of the Sales Force

The sales force is directly responsible for generating an organization's primary input: sales revenue. Thus in many cases the effectiveness of sales-force management determines a firm's success. Without adequate sales revenue, a business cannot survive long. A firm's reputation is often determined by the ethical conduct of the sales force. The Application on page 521 explores some of the ethical considerations in the management of the sales force.

Our discussion of sales management explores nine general areas, each of which requires numerous decisions and activities. The specific areas analyzed are (1) establishing sales-force objectives, (2) determining sales-force size, (3) recruiting and selecting salespeople, (4) training sales personnel, (5) compensating salespeople, (6) motivating salespeople, (7) creating sales territories, (8) routing and scheduling salespeople, and (9) controlling and evaluating sales-force performance.

| Establishing Sales-Force Objectives | To manage a sales force effectively, a sales manager must develop sales objectives. Sales objectives should be stated in precise, measurable terms and should specify the time period and the geographic areas involved. |

To manage a sales force effectively, a sales manager must develop sales objectives. Sales objectives should be stated in precise, measurable terms and should specify the time period and the geographic areas involved.

Sales objectives usually state goals for both the total sales force and each salesperson. Objectives for the entire force are normally stated according to sales volume, market share, or profit. Volume objectives refer to a quantity of dollars or sales units. For example, the objective for an electric drill producer's sales force might be to sell $10 million worth of drills annually or 600,000 drills annually. When sales goals are stated in terms of market share, they ordinarily call for an increase in the proportion of the firm's sales relative to the total number of products sold by all businesses in that particular industry. When sales objectives are based on profit, they are usually stated in terms of dollar amounts or return on investment.

Sales objectives for individual salespersons commonly are stated in terms of dollar or unit sales volume. Other bases used for individual sales objectives include average order size, average number of calls per time period, and the ratio of orders to calls.

Sales objectives tell salespersons what they are expected to accomplish during a specified time period. They give the sales force direction and purpose and serve as performance standards for the evaluation and control of sales personnel.

Determining Sales-Force Size

Deciding how many salespersons to use is important because it influences the company's ability to generate sales and profits. In addition, the size of the sales force affects the compensation methods used, salespersons' morale, and overall sales-force management. Sales-force size must be adjusted from time to time because a firm's marketing plans change, as do markets and forces in the marketing environment. One danger is to cut back the size of the sales force to increase profits. The sales organization can lose its strength and resiliency, inhibiting it from rebounding when growth rebounds or buoyant market conditions prevail. The organization that loses capacity from cutbacks may not have the energy to accelerate.[9] There are several methods for determining the optimal size of the sales force. Two analytical techniques are the equalized workload method and the incremental productivity method.

Equalized Workload Method[10]   The **equalized workload method** lets a marketing manager base the sales-force size on the condition that every salesperson is assigned a roughly equal set of accounts in terms of the total amount of sales time and effort needed. Marketers must answer several questions if they are considering this method. First, can the manager divide the customers into groups based on size of purchases? Second, is it possible to determine the number of sales calls required to service various account sizes adequately? Third, what is the annual average number of calls per salesperson?

To determine sales-force size through the equalized workload method, a marketing manager must (1) multiply the number of customers in each size group by the number of sales calls that are required annually to serve those groups effectively, (2) add the products, and (3) divide this sum by the average number of calls made annually by each salesperson.

As a hypothetical case, assume that a company divides its customers into two size groups. It has three hundred class A customers who each require twenty sales calls annually, and nine hundred class B customers who require twelve sales calls annually. The firm's average salesperson makes six hundred calls annually. In this case, sales-force size is determined as follows:

$$\frac{300\ (20)\ +\ 900\ (12)}{600} = 28$$

9. A. J. Magrath, "Are You Overdoing 'Lean and Mean'?" *Sales and Marketing Management*, January 1988, pp. 46–53.
10. This method, developed by Walter J. Talley, is described in "How to Design Sales Territories," *Journal of Marketing*, January 1961, pp. 7–13.

Ethics in Personal Selling

A salesperson usually has several goals, such as finding prospects, convincing prospects to buy, and keeping customers satisfied after the sale. In addition, salespersons usually have to find out what a prospect needs to know and give the prospect this information before a sale can be made. A common problem in the personal selling process is ethics—judgments about right and wrong conduct in selling behavior.

Insider trading scandals on Wall Street in the 1980s focused public attention on business ethics. Every aspect of our society, from politics to religion to sports, has had its share of ethics problems, which the media have carefully publicized. The public often calls salespeople unethical because they assume that sales personnel pressure consumers to purchase unwanted products. And some research suggests that ethical considerations are sometimes not important to sales managers and sales representatives.

Studies indicate that salespeople are three to four times more likely to be dishonest about their background when applying for a new job. This dishonesty includes lying about education, past achievements, and why they left their last job; it may also involve coverups about theft. Salespeople are prone to embellish their products and tend to exaggerate their achievements when they are selling themselves, which may partly explain why they lie when applying for a new job. An executive search firm reports that for the past twenty years, 45 percent of all sales applicants have lied about their past salaries and job responsibilities, 30 percent about their educational backgrounds, and 5 percent have had something to hide, such as fake documentation (for example, a bogus driver's license).

People now seeking first-time sales jobs will find that ethics has a big impact on their search, and on their success. Many corporations are changing their hiring practices to reflect current ethical concerns. Applicants are now more thoroughly screened than in the past, and résumés are meticulously checked for accuracy. Once they have landed jobs, newly hired salespeople may still have to take a course in business ethics.

At one time or another, most salespeople face ethical conflicts in their jobs. A sales representative must decide whether to tell a customer the truth and possibly lose that customer's business, or somehow mislead the customer to appease him or her. Failure to instruct salespeople about what to do in such situations leads to their being unable to deal with the situations when they arise. And worse, sales personnel who are untrained and confused about what action to take when facing an ethical dilemma often experience high levels of job-related frustration, anxiety, and stress. These characteristics may lead to other problems, such as increased employee turnover and low job performance.

Many times the problem of ethics has a snowball effect. Once a salesperson stops telling the truth to a customer, it becomes increasingly difficult to tell the truth later. If the customer learns of the falsehoods, the sales representative loses all credibility in the eyes of that customer, as well as with that customer's associates and friends. This leads to customer dissatisfaction, negative publicity, and possibly less sales and profits for the firm.

The problem of ethics frequently surfaces in personal selling. The manner in which a salesperson deals with this problem can have far-reaching consequences for the individual, the firm, and society.

SOURCES: Paul Hawken, "Truth or Consequences," *Inc.*, August 1987, pp. 48–52; Arthur Bragg, "Ethics in Selling, Honest!" *Sales and Marketing Management,* May 1987, pp. 42–44; Alan J. Dubinsky, "Studying Field Salespeople's Ethical Problems: An Approach for Designing Company Policies," in *Marketing Ethics Guidelines for Managers,* Gene R. Laczniak and Patrick E. Murphy, eds. (Lexington, Mass: D. C. Heath, 1985); Patrick E. Murphy and Gene R. Laczniak, "Marketing Ethics: A Review with Implications," in *Review of Marketing,* Ben M. Enis and Kenneth J. Roering, eds. (Chicago: American Marketing, 1981), pp. 251–266; Liz Murphy, "Did Your Salesman Lie to Get His Job?" *Sales and Marketing Management,* November 1987, pp. 54–58.

The manager who opts for this technique is confronted with several problems. Estimating the number of sales calls that are required to service an account is difficult because, regardless of their size, individual customers have different problems and different needs. Moreover, a salesperson's workload depends not only on the number of sales calls but on travel time between customers and the amount of time spent with each account. Although these factors help determine the average annual number of sales calls per salesperson, there may be marked variations between the average and the actual number of calls that a specific salesperson can make.

Incremental Productivity Method As a firm adds salespersons within a geographic market, total sales normally increase. However, total selling costs increase as well. According to the **incremental productivity method,** a marketer should continue to increase the sales force as long as the additional sales increases are greater than the additional selling-cost increases. The optimal sales-force size lets the firm obtain the greatest operating margin.[11]

The incremental productivity method has several limitations. Its users must be able to estimate accurately how much sales will rise when a salesperson is added. They must also estimate the incremental selling costs. This method's effectiveness depends on management's ability to develop accurate estimates.

Marketers seldom depend on one technique to determine sales-force size. Although they may use one or several analytical methods, marketing managers usually temper their decisions with a good deal of subjective judgment.

11. Walter J. Semlow developed this method; a more detailed analysis of it is in "How Many Salesmen Do You Need?", *Harvard Business Review,* May–June 1959, pp. 126–132.

Recruiting and Selecting Salespeople

To create and maintain an effective sales force, a sales manager must recruit the right type of salespeople. The cost of hiring, training, and retaining a salesperson is soaring; currently, costs can reach $100,000 or more.[12] **Recruiting** is a process by which the sales manager develops a list of applicants for sales positions.

To ensure that the recruiting process produces a usable list, a sales manager should establish a set of required qualifications before beginning to recruit. For example, as Figure 15.5 illustrates, The Prudential promotes its intent to hire aggressive, intelligent, and ambitious salespeople to market its insurance and investment products. Although for years marketers have attempted to enumerate a set of traits that characterize effective salespeople, there is currently no such set of generally accepted characteristics. Therefore a sales manager must develop a set tailored to the sales tasks in a particular company. Two activities can help establish this set of requirements. The sales manager should prepare a job description that lists the specific tasks salespersons are to perform. The manager also should analyze the characteristics of the firm's successful salespersons, as well as those of ineffective sales personnel. There are several reasons why people fail in sales. First,

12. Phil Faris, "No More Winging It," *Sales and Marketing Management,* August 1986, p. 88.

FIGURE 15.5

The Prudential seeks aggressive, intelligent sales representatives to market its products (SOURCE: The Prudential Insurance Company of America)

many persons are unable to plan their daily activities in an efficient and organized manner. Other shortcomings are an inability to control personal attitudes, failure to continually grow and learn through training, lack of self-discipline, failure to develop goals, procrastination, inability to cope with rejection, not concentrating 100 percent on the prospect, and lack of creativity in approach and presentation.[13] From the job description and the analysis of traits, the sales manager should be able to develop a set of specific requirements and be aware of potential weaknesses that could lead to failure.

A sales manager usually recruits applicants from several sources: departments within the firm, other firms, employment agencies, educational institutions, respondents to advertisements, and individuals recommended by current employees. The specific sources a sales manager uses depend on the type of salesperson required and the manager's experiences with particular sources.

The process of hiring a sales force varies tremendously from one company to another. One technique used to determine whether potential candidates will be good salespeople is an assessment center. Assessment centers are intense training environments that place candidates in realistic problem settings in which they must give priorities to their activities, make decisions, and act on their decisions. Candidates are judged by experienced managers or trained observers. Assessment centers have proved valuable in selecting good salespeople.[14]

Sales management should design a selection procedure that specifically satisfies the company's needs. The process should include enough steps to yield the information needed for making accurate selection decisions. However, because each step incurs a certain expense, there should be no more steps than necessary. The stages of the selection process should be sequenced so that the more expensive steps, such as physical examination, are near the end. Fewer people will then move through the higher-cost stages.

Recruitment and selection of salespeople are not one-time decisions. The market and marketing environment change, as do an organization's objectives, resources, and marketing strategies. Maintaining the proper mix of salespeople thus requires the firm's sales management's continued decision making.

Recruitment should not be sporadic; it should be a continuous activity aimed at reaching the best applicants. The selection process should systematically and effectively match applicants' characteristics and needs with the requirements of specific selling tasks. Finally, the selection process should ensure that new sales personnel are available where and when they are needed.

Training Sales Personnel

Both new and experienced salespersons require sales training, even though the types of training may vary considerably. A good number of organizations have formal training programs; others depend on on-the-job training. Some systematic training programs are quite extensive; others are rather short and rudimentary. Regardless of whether the training program is complex or simple, its developers must consider the following questions.

13. Tim Conner, "Why People Fail," *American Statesman*, June 1987, pp. 25–29.
14. Patrick C. Fleenor, "Selling and Sales Management in Action: Assessment Center Selection of Sales Representatives," *Journal of Personal Selling and Sales Management*, May 1987, pp. 57–59.

Who Should Be Trained and Who Does the Training? Training programs can be aimed at newly hired salespeople, at experienced salespersons, or at both groups. Ordinarily, new sales personnel require comprehensive training, whereas experienced personnel need both refresher courses regarding established products and training that provides new-product information. Training programs can be directed at the entire sales force or at one segment of it.

Sales managers as well as other salespeople often get involved in giving sales training. Such training may occur daily, on the job, or periodically in sales meetings. Salespeople sometimes receive training from technical specialists within their own organizations. Also, there are a number of individuals and organizations that sell special sales training programs. Some of these programs consist of actual teaching sessions; others take the form of books and manuals or computerized instructional materials.

Where and When Should the Training Occur? Sales training may be performed in the field, at educational institutions, in company facilities, or in several of these locations. In some firms, new employees receive most of their training, or at least a substantial portion of it, before being assigned to a specific sales position. Other business organizations put new recruits into the field immediately. After a brief period, the new salespersons begin their formal training. Training programs for new personnel can be as short as several days or as long as three years or more.

Sales training for experienced personnel often is scheduled during a period when sales activities are not too demanding. It is not reasonable to interrupt sales efforts during peak selling periods. Usually, sales training meetings for experienced salespeople are short but intense training efforts. Depending on the size and geographic distribution of the sales force, the training may occur at a single national site or be conducted regionally. Because training of experienced salespeople is commonly a recurring effort, a firm's sales management must determine the frequency, sequencing, and duration of these activities.

What Should Be Taught? A sales training program can concentrate on the company, on products, or on selling methods. Training programs often cover all three areas. Training for experienced company salespersons usually emphasizes product information, although salespeople also must be informed about new selling techniques and any changes in company plans, policies, and procedures.

An increasingly popular area for training is international marketing. Here several key factors should be addressed. When selling in a foreign country, salespeople should attempt to understand any existing cultural barriers. There are several areas the salesperson must acknowledge. First, salespeople should understand that their foreign counterparts may conduct business differently than what is done in their own country. There should be extensive research into the business protocol of the country they plan to do business with. Correct titles and local etiquette should be observed.[15] In addition, new selling techniques may be necessary.

How Should the Information Be Taught? Many teaching methods and materials are appropriate for sales training programs. Lectures, films, texts, manuals, cases,

15. Brian H. Flynn, "Homing In on Foreign Sales Customs," *Business Marketing*, June 1987, pp. 90–92.

programmed learning devices, audio- and videocassettes, demonstrations, simulation exercises, and on-the-job training can all be effective. The methods and materials used in a particular sales training program depend on the type and number of trainees, the program's content and complexity, the length of the training program, the size of the training budget, the location, the number of teachers, and the teachers' preferences for methods and materials.

Compensating Salespeople

To develop and maintain a highly productive sales force, a business must formulate and administer a compensation plan that attracts, motivates, and holds the most effective individuals. A compensation plan should give sales management the desired level of control and provide sales personnel with an acceptable level of freedom, income, and incentive. The sales compensation program should be flexible, equitable, easy to administer, and easy to understand. Good compensation programs facilitate and encourage proper treatment of customers.

Even though these requirements appear to be logical and easily satisfied, it is actually quite difficult to incorporate them all into a simple program. Some of them will be satisfied, and others will not. There have been studies to evaluate the impact of financial incentives on sales performance. Results show that generally there are five responses that can occur. For money-sensitive individuals, an increase in incentives will generally increase their sales efforts, and a decrease in financial rewards will decrease their selling efforts. Unresponsive salespeople will sell at the same level regardless of the incentive. Leisure-sensitive salespeople generally work less when the incentive system is implemented. Income satisfiers generally adjust their performance to match their income goal. Understanding potential reactions and analyzing the personalities of the sales force will give management a way to evaluate whether an incentive program might work.[16] Therefore, in formulating a compensation plan, sales management must strive for a proper balance among these factors.

The developer of a compensation program must determine the general level of compensation required and the most desirable method of calculating it. In analyzing the required compensation level, sales management tries to ascertain a salesperson's value to the company on the basis of the tasks and responsibilities associated with the sales position. The sales manager may consider a number of factors, including salaries of other types of personnel in the firm, competitors' compensation plans, costs of sales-force turnover, and the size of nonsalary selling expenses.

Sales compensation programs usually reimburse salespersons for their selling expenses, provide a certain number of fringe benefits, and deliver the required compensation level. To do that, a firm may use one or more of three basic compensation methods: straight salary, straight commission, or a combination of salary and commission. In a **straight salary compensation plan,** salespeople are paid a specified amount per time period. This sum remains the same until they receive a pay increase or decrease. In a **straight commission compensation plan,** salespeople's compensation is determined solely by the amount of their sales for a given time period. A commission may be based on a single percentage of sales or on a sliding scale involving several sales levels and percentage rates. In a **combination**

16. Rene Y. Darmon, "The Impact of Incentive Compensation on the Salesperson's Work Habits: An Economic Model," *Journal of Personal Selling & Sales Management,* May 1987, pp. 21–32.

compensation plan, salespeople are paid a fixed salary and a commission based on sales volume. Some combination programs require a salesperson to exceed a certain sales level before earning a commission; other combination plans are designed so that a commission is paid for any level of sales.

For example, traditionally department stores paid salespeople a straight salary. But now combination compensation plans are becoming popular. R. H. Macy & Co., Inc. is offering commissions (averaging 6 to 8 percent) to a large segment of its sales force. Now the salespeople are more attentive to a customer's presence and needs, and the practice has attracted older, more experienced salespeople, who tend to be in short supply. Dayton-Hudson Corp. tested a program called "Performance Plus." Management teams consisting of buyers and sales managers were developed, with each team spending approximately 50 percent of their time on the sales floor. The ratio of part-time employees to full-time employees was cut to approximately 1:3, and a bonus system was designed for employees who performed well. There was significant sales growth in test stores as a result of the program.[17]

Table 15.1 lists the major characteristics of each sales-force compensation method. Notice that the combination method is most popular. Some methods are especially well suited for certain selling situations. When selecting a compensation method, sales management weighs the advantages and disadvantages shown in Table 15.1.

Proper administration of the sales-force compensation program is crucial for developing high morale and productivity among sales personnel. A good salesperson is very marketable in the workplace. Today successful sales managers are switching industries on a regular basis. Basic knowledge and skills related to sales management are in demand, and sometimes new insights can be gained from different work experiences. For example, Charles of the Ritz Group, Ltd. hired a sales and promotion manager for its skin sun-care product line away from Joseph E. Seagram & Sons, Inc., a leading distilled spirits company.[18] To maintain an effective compensation program, sales management should periodically review and evaluate the plan and make necessary adjustments.

Motivating Salespeople

A sales manager should develop a systematic approach for motivating salespersons to obtain high productivity. Motivating should not be viewed as a sporadic activity reserved for periods of sales decline. Effective sales-force motivation is achieved through an organized set of activities performed continuously by the company's sales management. Scheduled sales meetings can motivate salespeople. Periodic sales meetings have four main functions: recognizing and reinforcing performing salespeople, sharing sales techniques that are working, focusing employees' efforts on matching the corporate goals and evaluating their progress toward achieving these goals, and teaching the sales staff about new products and services.[19]

17. Aimee Stern, "Commissions Catch on at Department Stores," *Adweek's Marketing Week*, Feb. 1, 1988, p. 5.
18. Martin Everett, "Would It Pay You to Switch Industries?" *Sales & Marketing Management*, January 1988, pp. 32–36.
19. Terese Hudson, "Holding Meetings Sharpens Employees Sales Skills," *Savings Institutions*, July 1987, pp. 109–111.

Although financial compensation is important, a motivational program must also satisfy nonfinancial needs. Sales personnel, like other people, join organizations to satisfy personal needs and achieve personal goals. A sales manager must become aware of personnel's motives and goals and then must attempt to create an organizational climate that lets sales personnel satisfy their personal needs.

TABLE 15.1

Characteristics of sales-force compensation methods

COMPENSATION METHOD	FREQUENCY OF USE (%)[a]	WHEN ESPECIALLY USEFUL	ADVANTAGES	DISADVANTAGES
Straight salary	17.4	Compensating new salespersons; firm moves into new sales territories that require developmental work; salespersons need to perform many nonselling activities	Gives salesperson maximum amount of security; gives sales manager large amount of control over salespersons; easy to administer; yields more predictable selling expenses	Provides no incentive; necessitates closer supervision of salespersons' activities; during sales declines, selling expenses remain at same level
Straight commission	6.5	Highly aggressive selling is required; nonselling tasks are minimized; company cannot closely control sales-force activities	Provides maximum amount of incentive; by increasing commission rate, sales managers can encourage salespersons to sell certain items; selling expenses relate directly to sales resources	Salespersons have little financial security; sales manager has minimum control over sales force; may cause salespeople to give inadequate service to smaller accounts; selling costs less predictable
Combination	76.1	Sales territories have relatively similar sales potentials; firm wishes to provide incentive but still control sales-force activities	Provides certain level of financial security; provides some incentive; selling expenses fluctuate with sales revenue	Selling expenses less predictable; may be difficult to administer

[a]The figures are computed from "Alternative Sales Compensation and Incentive Plans," *Sales and Marketing Management*, Feb. 17, 1986, p. 57. *Note:* The percentage for Combination includes compensation methods that involved any combination of salary, commission, or bonus.

SOURCE: Based on the *Harvard Business Review* article "How to Pay Your Sales Force" by John P. Steinbrink (July/August 1978).

A sales manager can use a variety of positive motivational incentives other than
financial compensation. For example, enjoyable working conditions, power and
authority, job security, and an opportunity to excel are effective motivators. Salespeople can be motivated by businesses' taking an interest in making their job more
productive and efficient. For example, Honeywell Information Systems developed a
computerized sales support system that has increased sales productivity 31 percent
and dropped sales-force attrition 40 percent in the first year's use. These systems
can track leads and provide customer profiles and competitor data. Computer
graphics packages help salespeople analyze and illustrate complex information for
customers.[20]

Sales contests and other devices that provide an opportunity to earn additional
rewards can be effective motivators as well. Some companies find that their incentive programs are one of the most powerful motivating tools marketing managers
can use to achieve corporate goals (see Figure 15.6). Properly designed, an incentive program can pay for itself many times over. A plan's success depends on the
quality of the marketing objectives that determine the rules and quota systems. For
an incentive system to be successful, the marketing objectives must be accepted by

20. Dan Woog, "Taking Sales High Tech," *High Tech Marketing,* May 1987, pp. 17–22.

participants and prove effective in the marketplace. Companies that are new to incentive campaigns can benefit from the expertise of an incentive company that can track employee performance as well as operate fulfillment programs.[21] Some organizations also use negative motivational measures: financial penalties, demotions, even terminations.

Creating Sales Territories

The effectiveness of a sales force that must travel to its customers is influenced, to some degree, by sales management's decisions regarding sales territories. Sales managers deciding on territories must consider size, shape, routing, and scheduling.

Size of Territory   Sales managers usually try to create territories that have similar sales potentials or that require about the same amount of work. If territories have equal sales potentials, they will almost always be unequal in geographic size. The salespersons who get the larger territories will have to work longer and harder to generate a certain sales volume. When a sales manager attempts to create territories that require equal amounts of work, sales potentials for those territories will often vary. If sales personnel are partially or fully compensated through commissions, they will have unequal income potentials. Rather than relying on a single approach, many sales managers try to balance territorial workloads and earning potentials by using differential commission rates. Although a sales manager seeks equity when developing and maintaining sales territories, some inequities will always prevail.

Shape of Territory   Several factors enter into designing the shape of sales territories. First, sales managers must construct the territories so that sales potentials can be measured. Thus sales territories often consist of several geographic units for which market data are obtainable, such as census tracts, cities, counties, or states. Second, a territory's shape should help the sales force provide the best possible customer coverage. Third, the territories should be designed to minimize selling costs. Fourth, the territory shapes should take into account the density and distribution of customers. And finally, the territory shapes may have to reflect topographical features.

Sales territories seldom form symmetrical patterns. However, sales managers often use geometric shapes as general patterns for sales territories. Circles, rectangles, wedges, and cloverleaves are a few patterns used in designing sales territories.

Routing and Scheduling Salespeople

Someone must route and schedule sales calls in the field. That person must consider the sequence in which customers are called on, the specific roads or transportation schedules to be used, the number of calls to be made in a given period, and what time of day the calls will occur. In some firms, salespeople plan their own routes and schedules with little or no assistance from the sales manager; in other organizations, the sales manager draws up the routes and schedules. No matter who plans the routing and scheduling, the major goals should be to minimize salespersons' nonselling time (the time spent traveling and waiting) and maximize their selling

---

21. Maria Conte, "Marketing Your Market," *Business Marketing*, April 1987, pp. 92–97.

time. The planners should try to achieve these goals in a way that also holds a salesperson's travel and lodging costs to a minimum.

The geographic size and shape of a sales territory are the most important factors affecting routing and scheduling. Next are the number and distribution of customers within the territory, followed by the frequency and duration of sales calls. Finally, the availability of roads and public transportation and the location of the salesperson's home base vis-à-vis customers' locations dictate possible routes and schedules.

Controlling and Evaluating Sales-Force Performance

To control and evaluate sales-force activities properly, sales management needs information. A sales manager cannot observe the field sales force daily so the manager relies on call reports, customer feedback, and invoices. Call reports identify the customers called on and present detailed information about interaction with those clients. Traveling sales personnel often must file work schedules indicating where they plan to be during specific future time periods.

The dimensions used to measure a salesperson's performance are determined largely by sales objectives. These objectives are normally set by the sales manager. If an individual's sales objective is stated in terms of sales volume, then that person should be evaluated on the basis of sales volume generated. Even though a salesperson may be assigned a major objective, he or she ordinarily is expected to achieve several related objectives as well. Thus salespeople often are judged along several dimensions. Sales managers evaluate many performance indicators, including average number of calls per day, average sales per customer, actual sales relative to sales potential, number of new-customer orders, average cost per call, and average gross profit per customer.

To evaluate a salesperson, a sales manager may compare one or more of these dimensions with a predetermined performance standard. However, sales management commonly compares one salesperson's performance with the performance of other employees operating under similar selling conditions or compares current performance with past performance. Sometimes, management judges factors that have less direct bearing on sales performance, such as personal appearance, knowledge of the product, and competitors.

After evaluating salespeople, sales managers must take any needed corrective action because it is their job to improve the performance of the sales force. They may have to adjust performance standards, provide additional sales training, or try other motivational methods. Corrective action may demand comprehensive changes in the sales force.

Technical industries, such as the chemical field, are monitoring their sales forces and increasing productivity through the use of laptop (portable) computers. Part of the reason for the increasing use of computers in chemical sales is a response to customers' greater technical sophistication. Product information, including price, product specifications, and availability, could help salespeople be more valuable. Some companies that have provided their sales forces with laptops expect a 15 to 20 percent increase in their sales.[22]

22. Robert Martinott, "The Traveling Salesman Goes High Tech," *Chemical Week,* June 10, 1987, pp. 22–24.

Obviously, effective management of sales activities is crucial to an organization's survival. These activities help generate the revenues that a firm uses to acquire its resources.

The Nature of Sales Promotion

As defined earlier, **sales promotion** is an activity and/or material that acts as a direct inducement, offering added value or incentive for the product, to resellers, salespersons, or consumers.[23] It encompasses all promotional activities and materials other than personal selling, advertising, and publicity. Many sales promotion activities are noncyclical and are designed to produce immediate, short-run effects. For example, cents-off coupons and consumer contests have relatively short deadlines so that consumers must act quickly. There has been growth in sales promotion recently because of a short-term orientation by management and advertisers' inability to measure the effects or impact of general media advertising.[24]

An organization often uses sales promotion activities in concert with other promotional efforts to facilitate personal selling, advertising, or both. For example, people may have to go to a store to enter a consumer contest. This facilitates personal selling by drawing people into the establishment. To improve the effectiveness of advertisements, point-of-purchase displays often are designed to include pictures, symbols, and messages that appear in advertisements.

Sales promotion efforts are not always secondary to other promotion-mix ingredients. Companies sometimes use advertising and personal selling to support sales promotion activities. For example, marketers frequently use advertising to promote trading stamps, cents-off offers, contests, free samples, and premiums. Manufacturers' sales personnel occasionally administer sales contests for wholesale or retail salespersons. In any case, the most effective sales promotion efforts are highly interrelated with other promotional activities. Decisions regarding sales promotion therefore often affect advertising and personal selling decisions, and vice versa.

Sales Promotion Objectives

Marketers use sales promotion for a variety of reasons. A single sales promotion activity may be employed to achieve one or several objectives, or several sales promotion activities may be required to accomplish a single goal or set of goals. For example, Japanese electronics firms are reducing their advertising budgets and increasing their sales promotion spending in response to slow sales and the fluctuating foreign exchange rate. In 1988, Sony Corp. reduced its advertising budget by 10 percent and launched its first major sales promotion: offering buyers of Sony products discounts on American Airlines tickets. The promotion's objectives were

23. John F. Luick and William L. Ziegler, *Sales Promotion and Modern Merchandising* (New York: McGraw-Hill, 1968); and Don E. Schultz and William A. Robinson, *Sales Promotion Management* (Chicago: Crain Books, 1982).
24. Don E. Schultz, "Above or Below the Line?—Growth of Sales Promotion in the United States," *International Journal of Advertising*, Vol. 6, No. 1, 1987, pp. 17–27.

to boost sales in the slower summer months and reverse the sales decline.[25] Marketers use sales promotion to achieve the following objectives:

1. To identify and attract new customers
2. To introduce a new product
3. To increase the total number of users for an established brand
4. To encourage greater usage among current customers
5. To educate consumers regarding product improvements
6. To bring more customers into retail stores
7. To stabilize a fluctuating sales pattern
8. To increase reseller inventories
9. To combat or offset competitors' marketing efforts
10. To obtain more and better shelf space and displays[26]

Some of these objectives are designed specifically to stimulate resellers' demand and effectiveness; some are directed at increasing consumer demand; and others focus on both resellers and consumers. Sales promotion is effective for both offensive and defensive purposes. Whatever its use, the marketer should be certain that the sales promotion objectives are consistent with the organization's overall objectives as well as its marketing and promotion objectives.

Sales Promotion Methods

Most sales promotion methods can be grouped into two categories: consumer sales promotion and trade sales promotion. **Consumer sales promotion techniques** encourage or stimulate consumers to patronize a specific retail store or to try and/or purchase a particular product. Consumer sales promotion techniques can be used to draw people into particular retail stores, to introduce new products, or to promote established products. **Trade sales promotion methods** stimulate wholesalers and retailers to carry a producer's products and to market these products aggressively. Most trade sales promotion techniques offer resellers incentives—money, merchandise, gifts, or promotional assistance—to purchase products or perform certain activities.

Marketers consider a number of factors before deciding which sales promotion method(s) to use. The objectives of the effort are of primary concern. Marketers must weigh product characteristics—size, weight, costs, durability, uses, features, and hazards—and target market characteristics—age, sex, income, location, density, usage rate, and shopping patterns—before choosing a sales promotion method. How the product is distributed and the number and types of resellers may determine the type of method used. Finally, the competitive environment and legal forces influence the selection of sales promotion methods.

To understand sales promotion, we need to examine several sales promotion techniques. Our analysis divides the major sales promotion methods into four

25. Lisa A. Phillips and Sara E. Stern, "Electronics Ad Dollars Down—Japanese Companies Show Effects of Yen," *Advertising Age*, June 1, 1987, pp. 4, 82.
26. Richard E. Stanley, *Promotion: Advertising, Publicity, Personal Selling, and Sales Promotion* (Englewood Cliffs, N.J.: Prentice-Hall, 1982), pp. 304–305.

categories: (1) sales promotion methods used by retailers, (2) new-product sales promotion techniques, (3) sales promotion methods for established products, and (4) sales promotion methods aimed at resellers.[27]

Sales Promotion Methods Used by Retailers

There are four broad categories of sales promotion methods that retailers use: retailer coupons, demonstrations, trading stamps, and point-of-purchase displays.

Retailer Coupons   **Retailer coupons** usually take the form of cents-off coupons distributed through advertisements or handouts and redeemable only at specific stores. They are especially useful when price is a primary motivation for consumers' purchasing behavior. For example, Lincoln (see Figure 15.7) promotes its apple juice through cents-off coupons. Because of the significant price savings, customers loyal to another product might be encouraged to try Lincoln apple juice.

Retailer coupons bring customers into a particular store and build sales volume for a specific brand. Competitive counteroffers can significantly reduce the effectiveness of retailer coupons, however. Given their emphasis on price, coupons may undercut customer loyalty to a retailer.

27. Much of the information in the descriptions of the sales promotion techniques is from *Sales Promotion and Modern Merchandising,* by John F. Luick and William L. Ziegler. Copyright © 1968 by McGraw-Hill, Inc. Used with permission of McGraw-Hill Book Company.

FIGURE 15.7

Lincoln uses cents-off coupons to promote its apple juice (SOURCE: Sundor Brands)

Demonstrations **Demonstrations** are excellent attention getters. Manufacturers often use them temporarily either to encourage trial use and purchase of the product or to actually show how the product works. Because labor costs can be extremely high, demonstrations are not used widely. They can, however, be highly effective for promoting certain types of products, such as appliances, for example, extrusion pasta machines and microconvection ovens.

Trading Stamps **Trading stamps** are dispensed in proportion to the amount of a consumer's purchase and can be accumulated and redeemed for goods. Retailers use trading stamps to attract consumers to specific stores. In addition, they can increase sales of specific items when purchasers of those items receive extra stamps. Stamps are attractive to consumers as long as they do not drive up the price of goods. They are effective for many types of retailers.

Point-of-Purchase Displays **Point-of-purchase (POP) materials** include such items as outside signs, window displays, counter pieces, display racks, and self-service cartons. New innovations in POP displays include sniff-teasers, which give off a product's aroma in the store as consumers walk within a radius of four feet, and computerized interactive displays, which ask a series of multiple-choice questions and then release information on a screen to help consumers make a product decision.[28] These items, which are frequently provided by producers, attract attention, inform customers, and encourage retailers to carry particular products. A retailer is likely to use point-of-purchase materials if they are attractive, informative, well-constructed, and in harmony with the store. With 66 percent of all purchases resulting from in-store decisions, POP materials can help sustain incremental sales if the brands' essential components—brand name, positioning, and visual image—are the basis of the POP display.[29]

New-Product Sales Promotion Techniques

Several sales promotion methods can be used to promote new products. Three of the most common techniques are free samples, coupons, and money refunds.

Free Samples Marketers use **free samples** for several reasons: to stimulate trial of a product, to increase sales volume in early stages of the product's life cycle, or to obtain desirable distribution. The sampling program should be planned as a total event, not merely a giveaway.[30]

In designing a free sample, marketers should consider certain factors, such as the seasonality of the product, the characteristics of the market, and prior advertising. Free samples are not appropriate for mature products and slow-turnover products.

Sampling is the most expensive of all sales promotion methods. Production and distribution through such channels as mail delivery, door-to-door delivery, in-store distribution, and on-package distribution entail very high costs.

Coupons **Coupons** are used to stimulate trial of a new or established product, to increase sales volume quickly, to attract repeat purchasers, or to introduce new

---

28. Joe Agnew, "P-O-P Displays Are Becoming a Matter of Consumer Convenience," *Marketing News*, Oct. 9, 1987, p. 14.
29. Ibid., p. 16.
30. "Sampling Accelerates Adoption of New Products," *Marketing News*, Sept. 11, 1987, p. 21.

package sizes or features. Coupons usually reduce the purchase price of an item. For example, a cereal manufacturer might use a 20-cent coupon to promote a new type of cereal. The savings may be deducted from the purchase price or offered as cash. For best results, coupons should be easy to recognize and state the offer clearly. The nature of the product (seasonality, maturity, frequency of purchase, and the like) is the prime consideration in setting up a coupon promotion. Coupons have two disadvantages: fraud or misredemption is possible, and the redemption period can be quite lengthy. Approximately 80 percent of all households and more than two thousand manufacturers use coupons. The approximate redemption rate is 3.6 percent, with 10 to 15 percent of the coupons accepted being misredemptions. Coupons are distributed through free-standing inserts (FSIs), print advertising, direct mail, and in stores. Determination of the proper vehicle to use should consider strategies and objectives, cost redemption, availability, circulation, and exclusivity. Historically, FSIs have been the dominant vehicle for coupons.[31] A technique many grocers use to encourage customers to redeem coupons at their store is to offer double and sometimes triple coupon redemption.

Companies are now targeting specific consumers who use a competitor's product. Targeting nonusers through database systems gets coupons to nonusers, unlike free-standing inserts, which cover a broader segment of the population. General Motors Corp. targets competitors' customers with coupons. The company is testing a $500 gift certificate premium for use toward the purchase of a General Motors car. The rebate will be earmarked for consumers who have indicated that they plan to buy a non-GM vehicle in the next three to six months.[32] The Application on page 537 discusses the future of coupons.

Money Refunds With **money refunds,** consumers submit proof of purchase and are mailed a specific amount of money. Usually, manufacturers demand multiple purchases of the product before a consumer can qualify for a refund. For example, Panasonic marketed a line of VHS tapes that featured a $1 rebate per tape, for up to twelve purchases. A customer had to send in a proof of purchase from inside each tape package and the sales receipt. This method, used primarily to promote trial use of a product, is relatively low in cost. Nevertheless, because money refunds sometimes generate a low response rate, they have limited impact on sales.

Sales Promotion Devices for Established Products

Sales promotion devices for established products are usually aimed at providing additional value for the customer who purchases the item. Four methods commonly used to promote sales of established products are premiums, cents-off offers, consumer contests, and consumer sweepstakes.

Premiums **Premiums** are items offered free or at a minimum cost as a bonus for purchasing a product. They can attract competitors' customers, introduce different sizes of established products, add variety to other promotional efforts, and stimu-

31. Donna Campanella, "Sales Promotion: Couponmania," *Marketing and Media Decisions,* June 1987, pp. 118–122.
32. Nancy Zeldis, "Targeted Coupons Hit Non-Users," *Advertising Age,* Apr. 27, 1987, p. S26.

Future of Coupons as a Promotion Technique

Coupons are one of the most popular techniques used to promote the sales of a new product. Even though coupons' redemption rate is relatively low (one of every twenty-seven coupons is actually redeemed), manufacturers are extensively using them. Clipping coupons is popular these days, with an estimated 80 percent of all households actually using them. In 1986, manufacturers distributed approximately 203 billion coupons; some experts estimate that coupon distribution could reach 375 billion by 1990.

There are several advantages to using coupons. Print advertisements with coupons are often more effective than nonpromotional advertising for generating brand awareness. Generally, the larger the coupon's cash offer, the better the recognition generated. Another advantage is that coupons are a good way to reward present users of the product, win back former users, and encourage purchases in larger quantities. Coupons also let manufacturers determine whether the coupons reached the target market because they get the coupons back.

Despite the advantages of coupons, many manufactures feel that they are not that effective. Some companies, such as Colgate-Palmolive Co. and General Foods Corp., have cut back the number of coupons they offer. Colgate's redemption rate of coupons dropped 10 to 15 percent in 1985 compared to 1984; company officials believe that saturation of the marketplace with coupons was the primary reason. Similarly, General Foods distributed fewer coupons in 1987 than it did in 1986 because it believes that coupons are not as effective as advertising. Other companies are following this belief and reducing their emphasis on coupons as a promotion technique.

Some experts believe that coupons have lost some of their value because so many manufacturers are offering them. They say that manufacturers have trained consumers not to buy without some incentive, whether it be a coupon, a rebate, or a refund. In addition, there has been a general decline in brand loyalty among heavy coupon users. Studies have shown that about 75 percent of coupons are redeemed by people who already use the brand on the coupon. Another problem with the use of coupons is that stores often do not have enough of the item indicated on the coupon in stock, which can lead to bad customer feelings toward both the store and product.

Although the use of coupons as a sales promotion technique will continue to grow in the next few years, there is developing concern among marketers that could ultimately lead to a decrease in the not too distant future. Coupons will probably continue to be used as a major sales promotion component to stimulate trial of new products. Also, coupons will be used to increase the frequency of purchase for established products that have sluggish sales. On the other hand, successful established products may be reducing their profits if 75 percent of the coupons are redeemed by brand-loyal customers. An

late loyalty. Inventiveness is necessary because if an offer is to stand out and achieve meaningful redemptions, the premium must be matched to both the target audience and the brand's image.[33] To be effective, premiums must be easily recognizable and desirable. General Foods believes that for a premium item to work it must be related to the product and carefully tied in to the marketing plan. For example, Sanka advertisements promoted a fifty-five-minute video tape by Rita Moreno on fitness walking. The video was marketed at $14.95 with one Sanka proof of purchase. Sanka was seeking to enhance its image of being health conscious.[34] Premiums usually are distributed through retail outlets or the mail, but they may also be placed on or in packages.

J&B Scotch made an incredible premium offer. Consumers who bought a $12 bottle of J&B were entitled, free of charge, to select a watch, credit card radio, or movie videocassette; the retail values of the products were $20 to $50. How can a company afford premiums? Companies depend on *slippage,* the percentage of consumers who buy a product but never follow through on the redemption offer. In this case, the company required that consumers soak off the J&B label and return it to the company with a proof of purchase. The company took a risk that few consumers would soak the label off the premium product prior to emptying the bottle. And if they did, by that time the offer would be forgotten. By using this strategy, companies are getting the benefit of incremental sales without having to pay for redemption.[35]

Cents-Off Offers When a **cents-off offer** is used, buyers receive a certain amount off the regular price shown on the label or package. This method can be a strong incentive for trying the product, stimulate product sales, yield short-lived sales increases, and promote products in off-seasons. It is an easy method to control and is used frequently. However, it reduces the price to customers who would buy at the regular price, and frequent use of cents-off offers may cheapen a product's image. In addition, the method often requires special handling by retailers.

33. Gerrie Anthea, "Sales Promotion: Putting Up the Premium," *Marketing* (U.K.), Apr. 16, 1987.
34. Amy Gross, "Now Playing: Video Marketing," *Adweek's Marketing Week,* Jan. 18, 1988, pp. 8–9.
35. Richard Edel, "No End in Sight to Promotion's Upward Spiral," *Advertising Age,* Mar. 23, 1987, pp. S1–S10.

Consumer Contests In **consumer contests,** individuals compete for prizes based on their analytical or creative skill. This method generates traffic at the retail level. Contestants are usually more involved in consumer contests than they are in sweepstakes (discussed in the following section), even though the total participation may be lower. Contests may be used in conjunction with other sales promotion methods, such as coupons.

Consumer Sweepstakes The entrants in a **consumer sweepstakes** submit their names for inclusion in a drawing for prizes. Sweepstakes are used to stimulate sales and, as with contests, are sometimes teamed with other sales promotion methods. Sweepstakes are used more often than consumer contests, and they tend to attract a greater number of participants. The cost of a sweepstakes (about $3 per one thousand entrants) is considerably less than the cost of a contest.[36]

Successful sweepstakes can generate widespread interest and short-term increases in sales or market share. For example, Levi Strauss & Co. attracted 1.75 million entries in a two-week sweepstakes; the Benson & Hedges sweepstakes generated 5 million participants; and Cracker Jacks sponsored a $6 million sweepstakes that helped the firm increase sales 25 percent in one year.[37] Sweepstakes are, however, prohibited in some states.

Sales Promotion Methods Aimed at Resellers

Producers use sales promotion methods to encourage resellers to carry their products and promote them effectively. The methods include buy-back allowances, buying allowances, counts and recounts, free merchandise, merchandise allowances, cooperative advertising, dealer listings, premium or push money, sales contests, and dealer loaders.

Buy-Back Allowances A **buy-back allowance** is a certain sum of money given to a purchaser for each unit bought after an initial deal is over. This method is a secondary incentive in which the total amount of money that buyers can receive is proportional to their purchases during an initial trade deal such as a coupon offer. Buy-back allowances encourage cooperation during an initial sales promotion effort and stimulate repurchase afterward. The main drawback of this method is its expense.

Buying Allowances A **buying allowance** is a temporary price reduction to resellers for purchasing specified quantities of a product. A soap producer, for example, might give retailers $1 for each case of soap purchased. Such offers may be an incentive to handle a new product, achieve a temporary price reduction, or stimulate the purchase of an item in larger than normal quantities. The buying allowance, which takes the form of money, yields profits to resellers and is simple and straightforward to use. There are no restrictions on how resellers use the money, which increases the method's effectiveness.

36. Eileen Norris, "Everyone Will Grab at a Chance to Win," *Advertising Age*, Aug. 22, 1983, p. M-10.
37. Franklynn Peterson and Judi Kesselman-Turkel, "Catching Customers with Sweepstakes," *Fortune*, Feb. 8, 1982, pp. 84–87.

Counts and Recounts   The **count and recount** promotion method is based on the payment of a specific amount of money for each product unit moved from a reseller's warehouse in a given time period. Units of a product are counted at the start of the promotion and again at the end to determine how many have moved from the warehouse. This method can reduce retail stockouts by moving inventory out of warehouses and can also clear distribution channels of obsolete products or packages and reduce warehouse inventories.

The count and recount method might benefit a producer by reducing resellers' inventories, making resellers more likely to place new orders. However, this method is often difficult to administer and may not appeal to resellers who have small warehouses.

Free Merchandise   **Free merchandise** is sometimes offered to resellers who purchase a stated quantity of the same or different products. Occasionally, free merchandise is used as payment for allowances provided through other sales promotion methods. To avoid handling and bookkeeping problems, the giving of free merchandise usually is accomplished by reducing the invoice.

Merchandise Allowances   A **merchandise allowance** is a manufacturer's agreement to pay resellers certain amounts of money for providing special promotional efforts, such as advertising or displays. Before paying retailers, manufacturers usually verify their performance. Manufacturers hope that the retailers' additional promotional efforts will yield substantial sales increases.

This method is best suited to high-volume, high-profit, easily handled products. One major problem with using merchandise allowances is that some retailers perform their activities at a minimally acceptable level simply to obtain the allowances.

Cooperative Advertising   **Cooperative advertising** is an arrangement whereby a manufacturer agrees to pay a certain amount of a retailer's media costs for advertising the manufacturer's products. The amount allowed usually is based on the quantities purchased. Before payment is made, a retailer must show proof that advertisements did appear. These payments give retailers additional funds for advertising. They can, however, put a severe burden on the producer's advertising budget. Some retailers exploit cooperative advertising programs by crowding too many products into one advertisement. Surprisingly, though, not all available cooperative advertising dollars are used. Some retailers cannot afford to advertise. Others can afford it but do not want to advertise. Still others actually do advertising that qualifies for an allowance but are not willing to do the paperwork necessary for receiving reimbursement from producers.[38]

Dealer Listings   A **dealer listing** is an advertisement that promotes a product and identifies the names of participating retailers who sell the product. Dealer listings can influence retailers to carry the product, build traffic at the retail level, and encourage consumers to buy the product at participating dealers.

38. Ed Crimmins, "A Co-op Myth: It Is a Tragedy That Stores Don't Spend All Their Accruals," *Sales and Marketing Management*, Feb. 7, 1983, pp. 72–73.

Premium or Push Money   **Premium** or **push money** is used to push a line of goods by providing additional compensation to salespeople. It is appropriate when personal selling is an important part of the marketing effort; it is not effective for promoting products that are sold through self-service. This method helps a manufacturer obtain commitment from the sales force, but it can be very expensive.

Sales Contests   A **sales contest** is designed to motivate distributors, retailers, and sales personnel by recognizing outstanding achievements. The Colt Car Co., importer of Japanese-made Mitsubishi cars into the United Kingdom, designed a sales contest for dealers. An incentive trip for two to Barbados was offered for dealers who went 10 to 12 percent over existing sales figures. Approximately 50 percent of the dealers met their sales goals and won the trip.[39] To be effective, this method must be equitable for all salespersons involved. One advantage to this method is that it can achieve participation at all levels of distribution. However, results are temporary, and prizes are usually expensive.

Dealer Loaders   A **dealer loader** is a gift given to a retailer who purchases a specified quantity of merchandise. Often, dealer loaders are used to obtain special display efforts from retailers by offering essential display parts as premiums. A manufacturer, for example, might design a display that includes a sterling silver tray as a major component and give the tray to the retailer. Marketers use dealer loaders to obtain new distributors and push larger quantities of goods.

Summary

Personal selling is the process of informing customers and persuading them to purchase products through personal communication in an exchange situation. The three general purposes of personal selling are finding prospects, convincing them to buy, and keeping customers satisfied. The selling process consists of prospecting and evaluating potential customers, preparing and approaching the customer, making the presentation, overcoming objections, closing, and following up.

In developing a sales force, marketing managers must consider which types of salespersons will sell the firm's products most effectively. The three classifications of salespersons are order getters, order takers, and support personnel. Order getters inform prospects and persuade them to buy. Order-getting activities are divided into two categories: those aimed at current customer sales and those aimed at new-business sales. Order takers seek repeat sales and fall into two categories: inside order takers and field order takers. Sales support personnel facilitate the selling function, but their duties usually extend beyond making sales. The three types of support personnel are missionary, trade, and technical salespersons.

The effectiveness of sales-force management is an important determinant of a firm's success because the sales force is directly responsible for generating an organization's primary input: sales revenue. Major decision areas and activities sales

39. Gillian Upton, "Sales Promotion: Getting Results Barbados Style," *Marketing* (U.K.), Apr. 16, 1987, pp. 37–40.

managers focus on are establishing sales objectives, determining sales-force size, recruiting and selecting salespeople, training sales personnel, compensating salespeople, motivating salespeople, creating sales territories, routing and scheduling salespeople, and controlling and evaluating the sales force.

Sales objectives should be stated in precise, measurable terms and specify the time period and the geographic areas involved. The size of the sales force must be adjusted from time to time because a firm's marketing plans change, as do markets and forces in the marketing environment. Two techniques that sometimes are used to determine the size of the sales force are the equalized workload method and the incremental productivity method.

Recruiting and selecting salespeople involves attracting and choosing the right type of salesperson to maintain an effective sales force. When developing a training program, one must consider a variety of dimensions, such as who should be trained, where and when the training should occur, what should be taught, and how the information should be presented. Compensation of salespeople involves formulating and administrating a compensation plan that attracts, motivates, and holds the right types of salesperson for the firm. Motivation of salespeople should allow the firm to attain high productivity. Creating sales territories, another aspect of sales-force management, focuses on such factors as size, shape, routing, and scheduling. To control and evaluate sales-force performance, the sales manager must use information obtained through salespersons' call reports, customer feedback, and invoices.

Sales promotion is an activity and/or material that acts as a direct inducement, offering added value or incentive for the product, to resellers, salespersons, or consumers. Marketers use sales promotion to identify and attract new customers, to introduce a new product, and to increase reseller inventories. Sales promotion techniques fall into two general categories: consumer and trade. Consumer sales promotion methods encourage consumers to trade at specific stores or to try and/or buy a specific product. Trade sales promotion techniques stimulate resellers to handle a manufacturer's products and market these products aggressively.

Important Terms

Personal selling
Prospecting
Approach
Closing
Order getters
Order takers
Support personnel
Missionary salespersons
Trade salespersons
Technical salespersons
Equalized workload method
Incremental productivity method
Recruiting

Straight salary compensation plan
Straight commission compensation
   plan
Combination compensation plan
Sales promotion
Consumer sales promotion techniques
Trade sales promotion methods
Retailer coupons
Demonstrations
Trading stamps
Point-of-purchase (POP) materials
Free samples
Coupons

Money refunds
Premiums
Cents-off offer
Consumer contests
Consumer sweepstakes
Buy-back allowance
Buying allowance
Count and recount
Free merchandise
Merchandise allowance

Cooperative advertising
Dealer listing
Premium or push money
Sales contest
Dealer loader

Discussion and Review Questions

1. What is personal selling? How does personal selling differ from other types of promotional activities?
2. What are the primary purposes of personal selling?
3. Identify the elements of the personal selling process. Must a salesperson include all these elements when selling a product to a customer? Why or why not?
4. How does a salesperson find and evaluate prospects? Do you consider any of these methods questionable ethically?
5. Are order getters more aggressive or creative than order takers? Why or why not?
6. What are the similarities and differences between the equalized workload method and the incremental productivity method for determining sales-force size? Can marketers in a new firm use either method to determine the size of the initial sales force? Why or why not?
7. Identify several characteristics of effective sales objectives.
8. How should a sales manager establish criteria for selecting sales personnel? What are the general characteristics of a good salesperson?
9. What major issues or questions should be considered when developing a training program for the sales force?
10. Explain the major advantages and disadvantages of the three basic methods of compensating sales personnel. In general, which method do you most prefer? Why?
11. What major factors should be taken into account when designing the shape of a sales territory?
12. How does a sales manager—who cannot be with each salesperson in the field on a daily basis—control the performance of sales personnel?
13. What is sales promotion? Why is it used?
14. For each of the following, identify and describe three techniques and give several examples: (a) sales promotion methods for retail establishments, (b) new-product sales promotion techniques, (c) sales promotion devices for established products, and (d) sales promotion methods aimed at resellers.
15. What types of sales promotion methods have you observed or experienced recently?

Cases

15.1 Avon Revises Its Direct Sales Strategy[40]

Avon Products, Inc. is one of the most recognized direct sales organizations; many women have been approached at least once by their neighborhood Avon representative. However, the number-three cosmetics company has had its problems of late and so is revamping its strategy.

The one-hundred-year-old company has always depended on its huge sales representative force, which at one time numbered 425,000. For ninety years the company followed two rules: keep adding sales representatives and keep making their territories smaller. The saleswomen went door to door demonstrating and selling cosmetics, jewelry, and gifts to friends and neighbors. Then, in the 1980s, in droves women began working outside the home, reducing Avon's pool of representatives 35 percent and leaving no customers at home when the reps rang the doorbells. Avon's profits fell sharply, losses rose, and employee morale hit an all-time low.

At the same time, Avon faced stiff competition from mass merchandisers and direct mail catalogs, which had upgraded their cosmetic lines and offered designer selections. The company was further hampered because the compensation it offered its reps was not on par with that similar direct sales firms offered.

Avon had to act fast to save itself. In 1984, the company adopted a five-year plan that began with the firing of four hundred managers and the elimination of several thousand positions. The new chairman of the board brought in a management team with a fresh outlook to tackle the problem of declining profits. First, the team had to identify what Avon customers wanted, and they had to figure out how to make the sales force more productive, not bigger. They stopped approaching potential customers as if all were high school educated wives of blue-collar workers, with two or three children, and a household income of less than $30,000. Instead, they segmented territories into home, office, urban, and suburban selling areas.

The new "customer-driven" culture at Avon emphasizes the importance of door-to-door selling and the Avon sales representative. New applicants are given a written "success survey" that identifies high-potential sellers and matches them with high-potential territories. The survey segments reps by recognizing that people sell for different reasons, have different levels of sales volume that mean success to them, and want to spend different amounts of time in different selling environments. Avon then offered a free, progressive, modular training program to new recruits; before, the new recruits had to pay for their own training.

Avon also revamped its compensation program. The company now pays representatives a 10 to 50 percent commission on the sales volume for each two-week sales period. This replaces the old flat rate of 40 percent. For example, sales of $1,000 in a two-week period earn 50 percent commission, sales of $500 to $999 earn 45 percent, and so on. Avon also pays a 5 percent bonus, based on the sales of

40. Based on information from Julie A. Monahan, "Avon Calling for a Comeback," *Women's Wear Daily*, Mar. 27, 1987, pp. 37–38; Geoffrey Smith, "Avon Crawling," *Forbes*, Apr. 21, 1986, pp. 72–74; personal correspondence with Rolene Keller, public relations manager for Avon Products, Inc., May 5, 1987; Amy Dunkin, "Big Names Are Opening Doors for Avon," *Business Week*, June 1, 1987, pp. 96–97; James R. Russo, "An Inside Look at Avon," *Packaging*, March 1986, pp. 26–37.

new recruits, to the representatives who brought the recruits into the organization.

The company also offers nonmonetary awards to encourage its representatives to keep ringing doorbells, such as free training and assigning more profitable territories to more successful representatives. The company's reward system gives representatives increasing rewards and public recognition: the more you sell, the more you earn. Representatives may receive encouraging cards in the mail from the sales manager and praise at sales meetings. As sales volume increases, rewards increase; rewards include household items, jewelry, and trips to Hawaii. Representatives who sell $8,000 worth of products in a year become members of the President's Club, which in turn enables them to become eligible for other prizes of increasing value, including scholarships for family members. After selling $15,000 worth of products, representatives become members of the President's Club Honor Society and a reception is held in their honor.

Avon is creating more competitive cosmetics for its representatives to sell, upgrading its line to meet or beat the competition. The company wants to be more appealing to women in the workplace, who tend to use more cosmetics than women who work at home and who tend to have more money to spend on Avon products. The company has also revamped other products and introduced new ones to meet the needs of the Avon target market.

Today Avon has about 375,000 representatives. Earnings and profits are up, and the company is sending out feelers about entering the retail business. It has introduced its own designer products, including a fragrance called Deneuve, promoted by Catherine Deneuve herself. The number-three cosmetics company is definitely on the mend, and aiming for the number-one spot.

Questions for Discussion

1. How does Avon compensate its representatives?
2. How are Avon representatives motivated?
3. How has Avon's marketing philosophy changed, and how does that change affect Avon representatives?

15.2 Sperry & Hutchinson: Green Stamps and Gold Stamps[41]

The trading stamps your parents used to collect are coming back into fashion, with a few new twists. In the late 1960s approximately 75 percent of all supermarkets issued trading stamps, as did many gas stations. Trading stamps offered by companies such as Sperry & Hutchinson (S&H) were once a popular way to acquire household items, but they declined in popularity in the mid-1970s. Because of the oil embargo, service stations stopped issuing stamps; additionally, grocery stores

41. Based on information from Dianne Schneidman, "Trading Stamps Face Redemption as Viable Marketing Tool," *Marketing News*, Feb. 13, 1987, pp. 1, 28; Lynn G. Coleman, "Electronic Trading Stamps Successful in Test Market," *Marketing News*, June 19, 1987, p. 2. Karen Singer, "Trading Stamps: Promotional Relic Seeks Revival," *Adweek's Marketing Week*, Mar. 28, 1988, pp. 43, 46.

started discounting their products instead of offering stamps. Today S&H (marketers of Green Stamps), Quality Stamps, Inc., and Gold Bond are changing the image of the trading stamp, and retailers may once again offer them to encourage customers to shop at their stores.

Retailers used trading stamps as a consumer sales promotion technique for the better part of a century. Stamps were offered in proportion to the amount of a customer's purchase. Sometimes to increase sales of a specific product, extra stamps were given to customers who purchased that item. Customers saved their stamps in special books and redeemed the stamp-filled books for stereos, lamps, typewriters, and other household items listed in a catalog or displayed at a store. The stamps required long-term involvement and expense for the retailer, however, and retailers had to give out a large number of stamps. Eventually, retailers turned to more cost-efficient methods of sales promotion.

In the 1980s S&H experimented with different forms of trading stamps in an attempt to revive their use. S&H changed its Green Stamps into Green Seals to make them easier for customers (and retailers) to use. Customers had to lick fifty of the old stamps to get $5 worth of merchandise from the S&H catalog; now they need only one seal. This will encourage supermarkets and retailers to distribute stamps again because they will not have to give out as many. S&H also experimented with electronic Green Stamps. At a check-out computer terminal, a customer presents a personalized consumer card (similar to a credit card) and the computer registers how many stamps the customer has earned with each purchase. These credit cards could also function as check authorization cards or as video rental membership cards. Also under development is a redemption kiosk where consumers could debit their cards to order and purchase gifts. Results of surveys from Green Stamp tests have been positive.

S&H is targeting its stamps to the under-35 market because this group is not as familiar as their parents are with trading stamps and this group does most of the shopping today. To attract the attention of this market, S&H has updated both its catalog and promotion. S&H hired Arnell/Bickford Associates to update its image. S&H began using its full name—Sperry & Hutchinson—on its catalog, and, instead of taking traditional product photographs, began silhouetting items in its catalog. A new advertising theme was developed, "They Just Can't Be Licked." Items in the catalog were updated also: microwaves, videocassette recorders, exercise equipment, and more children's items are currently being offered. Gold Bond is even allowing consumers to trade their stamps for airline tickets.

Quality Stamps also changed its look, but not its form. The company changed the color of its stamps to an eye-catching blue and gold and introduced them with the slogan, "Worth Their Weight in Gold." Quality is also targeting its stamps to the under-35 market, using television advertising that features contemporary music and people.

The trading stamp companies are trying to make their stamps more attractive to both consumer and retailer. If the stamp companies can make their product more cost-efficient for retailers, the retailers will renew their distribution because Green Stamps (or seals) and Quality Stamps create consumer loyalty for that retailer. George Meredith, executive director of the association of Retail Marketing Services, sees this as an opportunity area, stating, "Retailers are showing more and more disaffection for some of the things they've been doing in discounts, things like double-coupon programs, which cost them a small fortune and don't really build any continuity or customer loyalty. So they are going to be ready for a program they perceive as working more effectively." Because of their new look and image, trading stamps may once again become a valuable promotional tool.

Questions for Discussion

1. Why did the use of Green Stamps decline in the 1970s?
2. Evaluate the benefits of a trading stamp program versus current promotional techniques used by grocers to increase sales (such as double coupon redemption and product discounts)?
3. Do you believe that trading stamps are a potentially strong sales promotion technique for the 1990s?

Part IV S T R A T E G I C C A S E

New Coke and Coke Classic

The Coca-Cola Company has been successfully selling syrup to bottling distributors and promoting its soft drink products for one hundred years. The Coca-Cola Company first considered changing its formula several years ago when researchers, while developing diet Coke, discovered a new cola formula. Secret taste tests at that time revealed that 61 percent of consumers preferred the blend of new Coke, compared with 39 percent supporting the original Coke. Whether to proceed and act on this finding was a marketing decision that developed as the company's growth slowed and Coke's dominant position eroded (see Figure 1). At least some of this erosion could be attributed to Coke's chief competitor, Pepsi-Cola. In 1972, Pepsi began its Pepsi Challenge, pitting the two colas against each other in blind taste tests. Pepsi's sales and market share increased while Coke's market share gradually declined. More recently, Coke has been losing ground to Pepsi in supermarkets, where 45 percent of all soft drinks are sold. Some industry watchers said that Coca-Cola neglected Coke in recent years in favor of diet drinks such as Tab, Fresca, and diet Coke, which contributed to Coke's market share decline.

When new Coke was discovered, Coke's president, Roberto C. Goizueta, perceived two options: "We could do nothing—put it on the shelf and forget we ever developed it. Or we could change the taste and give the world a new Coca-Cola."

Between 1981 and 1985, in twenty-five cities across the United States and Canada, Coke tested three or four new tastes on approximately 200,000 consumers. The new Coke flavors beat the old one even when old Coke was identified in the tests. The results were also positive when tested against Pepsi. Following these tests Coke began secret and serious preparations to introduce its new taste.

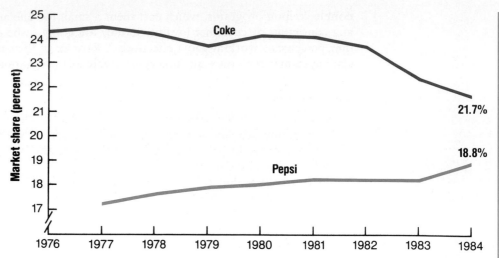

FIGURE I

Coke faced steadily declining market share in the early 1980s while Pepsi showed stable growth

Introduction of New Coke

On April 23, 1985, the company announced the introduction of the new Coke that would replace the old. The Coca-Cola Company brought back the "I'd Like to Buy the World a Coke," theme and produced a series of advertisements featuring Bill Cosby. One hundred fifty million persons tried new Coke; more than have tried any other new product in history. Coca-Cola was optimistic about sales and the fact that a large majority said they would buy it again.

For several weeks after the introduction of new Coke, sales were excellent, although complaints about the replacement of old Coke were immediate and strong (this was not anticipated). Shipments of new Coke to bottlers rose by the highest percentage in five years. Then suddenly—according to the head of the company's market research department—the mood of consumers changed. Bottlers, who are Coke's main contacts with consumers, were first to feel the heat. At a Dallas regional convention, they petitioned The Coca-Cola Company demanding a return to the old formula. The Atlanta office was besieged with a steady 1,500 calls a day requesting a return to the old Coke. Consumer groups, too, sprang up around the country and demanded a return to the old Coke through boycotts, write-ins, and call-ins. Perhaps the most publicity was received by Seattle's Gay Mullins and his Old Cola Drinkers of America. They crusaded against the new Coke with T-shirts, protests, banners, and posters; Mullins even threatened a class-action lawsuit against The Coca-Cola Company and a demonstration at Coke's stockholders meeting. Consumers referred to the new Coke as "furniture polish," "sewer water," and "two-day-old Pepsi." The popular consensus was that new Coke was sweeter and somewhat flatter. People stockpiled the old Coke, and some of these entrepreneurs sold it off at a premium price. Coca-Cola officials began to feel the heat and were finally forced to consider alternate plans of action. To many their decision seemed an easy and obvious one. Coke officials had two important meetings—one with distributors and bottlers for five of their largest markets and another with distributors and bottlers in Atlanta. At both meetings the decision was to bring back the old Coke.

Reintroduction of Old Coke "Coke Classic"

In July 1985 The Coca-Cola Company announced that it would bring back the original formula of Coke under the new name of Coke classic. The new Coke would still be available, and efforts would be made to maintain it as the company's flagship drink. Now The Coca-Cola Company was faced with the challenge of successfully handling two full-calorie colas nationally.

The Coca-Cola Company officials would admit no failure, but president Goizueta did state, "We knew some people were going to be unhappy, but we could never have predicted the depth of their unhappiness . . . you cannot quantify emotion." Another executive denied a widely held belief that the company brought out new Coke as part of a deliberate plot to create support for the older product and increase its sales. He admitted, "The passion for original Coke was something that just flat caught us by surprise. The simple fact is that all of the time and money and skill poured into consumer research on new Coke could not measure or reveal the depth of emotional attachment to the original Coke felt by so many people." He added, "Some critics will say Coca-Cola has made a marketing mistake. Some cynics say that we planned the whole thing. The truth is, we're not that dumb, and we're not that smart."

While admitting that eliminating the old Coke was a mistake, The Coca-Cola Company officials began looking at the two-cola strategy in a positive manner. They could see the market as notably larger for the combination of two cola brands than for either one alone. Those that tried new Coke in the first eleven weeks after its introduction amounted to more than double the number of usual Coke drinkers. And dedicated drinkers of old Coke could be relied on as its core market.

Consumers were probably confused enough with the initial replacement of the original Coke with new Coke. Then they were confronted with the return of the old Coke, complicated by its new name, Coca-Cola classic. Some questioned the validity of The Coca-Cola Company's market research, which had been criticized as incomplete and less than thorough.

The addition of product lines only complicated The Coca-Cola Company's relationship with retailers who already had limited soft-drink shelf space. The problem was that retailers were forced to accommodate two Cokes with the premium space that originally was used only for old Coke alone. Even a double display of Coke would not necessarily make up for the loss of sales on other, displaced soft drinks. In addition, many bottlers were equipped to bottle only one Coke syrup. To handle another soft drink increased costs, thus adding to the distribution problems fostered by retailers' limited shelf space. Indeed many bottlers chose to bottle and distribute only one cola flavor in an attempt to help reduce costs. Usually when this was the case, the bottlers chose Coca-Cola classic, which also reflected consumer demand. Indeed, in many markets in the United States, Coca-Cola classic began outselling new Coke by a margin of ten to one.

But the sales of new Coke were also affected by the big fountain customers. All fountain sales had accounted for 65 percent of Coca-Cola's sales (only 35 percent of its sales had come from supermarkets versus 50 percent for Pepsi). By owning approximately 60 percent of the fountain business in fast-food outlets and convenience stores alone, The Coca-Cola Company had been a powerhouse with the original Coke. Several months after new Coke's introduction, however, The Coca-Cola Company's big fountain customers began abandoning it. Marriott's Roy

FIGURE 2

Coke outspends Pepsi
by approximately 15
percent in advertising
its Cola brands
(SOURCE: Betsy Mor-
ris, "Coke vs. Pepsi:
Cola War Marches
On," *Wall Street Jour-
nal,* June 3, 1987,
p. 33. Data from
Furman Selz Mager
Dietz & Birney.)

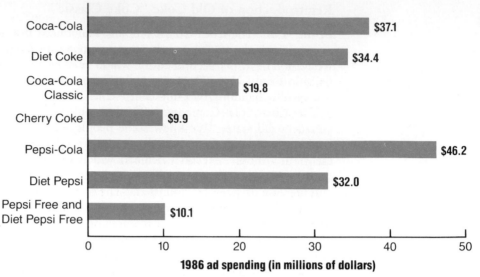

1986 ad spending (in millions of dollars)

Note: Does not include ad spending by bottlers.

Rogers restaurants and several of General Mills's Red Lobster Inns were two of the first to switch back to Coca-Cola classic. Several of Church's Fried Chicken restaurants in Alabama, Georgia, and Texas also switched back to Coca-Cola classic. Meanwhile, McDonald's, Hardee's, and Marriott's Big Boy restaurants announced that they too were dropping the new Coke in favor of Coca-Cola classic. This started a chain reaction among fountain customers who continued to follow suit.

Promotional Strategies

Before the introduction of new Coke, The Coca-Cola Company spent less on advertising than Pepsi-Cola. At the same time, however, The Coca-Cola Company and its Coca-Cola classic and new Coke received immense publicity in many trade magazines and in mass media of all kinds. This free publicity helped the company a great deal because it had not budgeted for the reintroduction of old Coke—officials thought it was gone from the product line.

Despite the accelerating decline in demand for new Coke, The Coca-Cola Company officials stated that they would still promote the new Coke formula as their primary brand. The promotional muscle was clearly behind new Coke in attempts to increase its growth. But because Coca-Cola classic notably outsold new Coke, the company retrenched from its original plans and scrapped its new Coke advertising campaign, which featured Bill Cosby. Next, promotions and advertising took a low-key umbrella approach to both Cokes: Neither one was advertised separately. Eight months after the reintroduction of the old Coke, The Coca-Cola Company announced a two-tier coadvertising campaign: one for new Coke and a separate campaign for Coca-Cola classic. New Coke was to go head-on versus Pepsi, with its own new slogan of "Catch The Wave." The advertisements would feature slick high-tech visual effects featuring Max Headroom, with overtones of surfing and fast-paced living. These advertisements gave new Coke an image and a personality and became the most popular campaign of that year. Coca-Cola classic was to have a slogan of "Red, White and You," focusing on Coca-Cola classic as a piece of the American landscape. The advertisements featured patriotic glimpses of "ordinary" Americans, athletes, and entertainers. This advertising strategy attempted to recognize two different segments of the market and zero in on each with an appeal targeting each market. In Figure 2 the advertising spending for Coca-Cola and Pepsi-Cola soft-drink products is shown by specific brand category.

Aided by these campaigns, Coke racked up growth rates higher than any soft drink, allowing its two colas to become number one in food stores replacing Pepsi. Table 1 illustrates the cost of retained impressions (a measure of advertising effectiveness) for Coca-Cola and its competitors 1986–1987.

There were, however, other reasons besides advertising for this growth. The Coca-Cola Company was living up to its promise and broadening its product offerings at a rapid pace. Diet Coke became the nation's number-three soft drink, and The Coca-Cola Company followed new Coke's introduction with cherry Coke, a juice-based Minute Maid soda, and diet cherry Coke. When president Goizueta became CEO, only one cola bore the famous name. Now a few years later seven colas were marketed under the Coca-Cola trademark. Add to these colas Sprite, Tab, sugar-free Sprite, caffeine-free Tab, Fresca, Hi-C, and Minute Maid sodas and it becomes obvious why The Coca-Cola Company is number one in the soft-drink industry.

Impact of Coke's Promotion on Market Share

By this time, market share results were in on soft-drink sales for the year in which new Coke was introduced. According to *Beverage Digest,* an industry trade journal, The Coca-Cola Company's share of the U.S. soft-drink market grew about 6 percent in 1985 to 39 percent, its strongest position in decades. Interestingly,

TABLE 1

Soft drink advertising in 1986–1987

	1987			1986
SOFT DRINKS	AVERAGE WEEKLY RETAINED IMPRESSIONS (MILLIONS)	AVERAGE WEEKLY TV MEDIA SPENDING (000)	COST PER 1000 RETAINED IMPRESSIONS	COST PER 1000 RETAINED IMPRESSIONS
Coca-Cola	76.2	$ 767.5	$10.07	$12.07
Pepsi-Cola	77.2	1,049.9	13.60	10.92
RC Cola	5.4	117.1	21.68	16.50
7-Up	27.2	694.8	25.54	27.36
Diet Pepsi	19.3	682.9	35.38	40.81
Diet Coke	15.3	682.3	44.59	29.31
Sprite	7.5	419.9	55.99	34.40
Slice	6.2	553.3	89.24	52.39

SOURCE: "America's Favorite Campaigns," *Adweek's Marketing Week,* Mar. 7, 1988, p. F.C. 26. Used by permission.

however, Pepsi-Cola grew 8 percent to hold a 27 percent share of the U.S. soft-drink market. But evidence points to much of Coke's growth resulting from the successful introduction of other new products, particularly cherry Coke. Another factor was consumers' fascination with the Coke saga. People were exposed to news programs, magazines, and radio disc jockeys discussing the Coke situation.

According to some bottlers' estimates, Coca-Cola classic outsold new Coke, which caught company executives by surprise. Coca-Cola classic was dominant, even in several Northern markets, where new Coke initially outsold the old. Reportedly, only in Detroit was new Coke outselling Coca-Cola classic. In other markets from New York through the South, into Texas, the midwest, and to California, old Coke was outselling new Coke anywhere from one and a half times to ten times to one. The old Coke was once again being hailed as the flagship brand, by bottlers first, and eventually the company itself.

The Coca-Cola Company's officials did not discuss the Coca-Cola classic-new Coke national sales ratio, but showed strategic progress by achieving the company's goal of reinforcing its position in the sugar-cola segment. The growth was attributed to the two colas and cherry Coke. The company claimed that one of every two colas and one of every three soft drinks consumed by Americans was a Coca-Cola branded product.

The Coca-Cola Company Remains Number One

The Coca-Cola Company now claimed to be the number-one marketer of sugar-cola under the Coca-Cola megabrand in food stores, never mind the entire soft-drink industry (see Table 2). It captured this for the first time in ten years with a 19.9 percent share versus Pepsi's 19.8 percent share in food stores. Of the Coke megabrand total, 16.6 percent was for Coca-Cola classic, 1.7 percent for new Coke, 1.1 percent for cherry Coke, and 0.5 percent for caffeine free Coke. But

TABLE 2

Ranking the brands
industry wide

RANK	BRAND	MARKET SHARE	
		1986	1985
1	Coke classic	18.9%	5.9
2	Pepsi	18.5	18.6
3	Diet Coke	7.1	6.0
4	Diet Pepsi	4.3	3.6
5	Dr Pepper	4.1	4.0
6	Sprite	3.6	3.7
7	7-Up	3.5	4.1
8	Mountain Dew	2.6	2.6
9	Coke	2.3	15.0
10	RC	1.7	1.7
10	Cherry Coke	1.7	1.7

SOURCE: Reprinted from *Beverage Digest*, Jan. 23, 1987, by permission of the publisher.

FIGURE 3

The Coca-Cola Company's market share dominance is shown relative to major competitors both domestically and internationally (SOURCE: Beverage Industry Annual Manual, 1987–1988.)

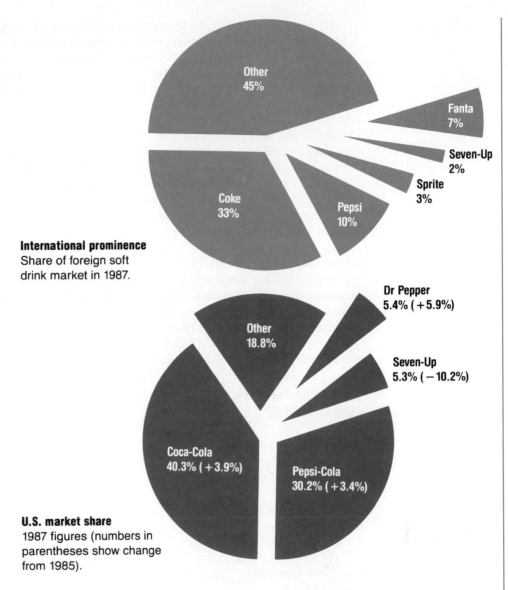

International prominence
Share of foreign soft drink market in 1987.

U.S. market share
1987 figures (numbers in parentheses show change from 1985).

unfortunately for Coke, Pepsi remained the largest *single* selling soft-drink brand in food stores. The company's total U.S. soft-drink market share, which also includes diet Coke, caffeine free Coke, caffeine free diet Coke, diet cherry Coke, Sprite, sugar-free Sprite, Fanta, Fresca, and Tab, has risen to about 40 percent compared with 30 percent for Pepsi (see Figure 3). This figure shows that Coke's international sales are nearly triple those of Pepsi's. Coca-Cola classic still outsells new Coke by about ten to one. Coke's 1987 television campaign in support of Coca-Cola classic was voted as the seventh favorite campaign of the year. Reminiscent of the 1971 campaign, "I'd Like to Teach the World to Sing," it focused on hope and peace.

In the last several years, Coke and Pepsi have gained up to three share points at the expense of others such as 7Up, Dr Pepper, Royal Crown, and others.

Recently, The Coca-Cola Company promoted a radio campaign, "Coke In The Morning." Set to a jingle, it aired heavily in major markets during morning drive time. Outdoor advertising, principally billboards, also supported the campaign. This campaign was developed for three reasons: (1) The Coca-Cola Company's research showed that consumption before 11 A.M. had increased sevenfold for ten years; (2) consumers are shifting from hot drinks to cold, sweet drinks; and (3) the number of working families who eat out or eat while driving has increased. Perhaps surprisingly, consumption of soft drinks today is even ahead of water.

The Coca-Cola Company meanwhile has not forgotten its number-three industry seller, diet Coke. In an effort to portray the Coke name with sophistication and style, actor Pierce Brosnan, from television's "Remington Steele," and Joely Richardson, Vanessa Redgrave's daughter, starred in a James Bond–style series of commercials. In the first, Brosnan is chased onto a train by Ninjas and relaxes with a diet Coke in the company of Richardson. The Coca-Cola Company was apparently not relaxing although 70 percent more diet Coke is sold than diet Pepsi in the total market, and 40 percent more diet Coke is sold in food stores than diet Pepsi.

In conclusion, some still remain convinced that to introduce the new Coke, remove the old Coke, and bring back the old Coke as Coca-Cola classic was a marketing or publicity stunt planned by The Coca-Cola Company. Most view the entire incident as a major blunder by a highly respected marketer. It was a blunder, however, that resulted in a "back-door" entrance to a two-cola strategy, which has not hurt The Coca-Cola Company, but has allowed it to continue to grow and prosper. The bottom line is that The Coca-Cola Company's overall market share increased, achieving one of its key promotional objectives. If there were any mistakes made, it was in the strategy it used to accomplish the transition to the two cola strategy. The Coca-Cola Company's products now include the following:

Coca-Cola classic
Coke
caffeine free Coke
diet Coke
caffeine free diet Coke
cherry Coke
diet cherry Coke
Tab
caffeine free Tab
Sprite
diet Sprite
Minute Maid Division: soft drinks and fruit juice beverages

The Coca-Cola Company has many soft drinks that are already among the leaders in the soft-drink industry. The company's expertise and power were shown in the successful adjustment from a marketing blunder to a coup.

Questions for Discussion

1. Why did new Coke fail as an improved replacement for old Coke?
2. Trace the promotional decisions of The Coca-Cola Company from the launch of new Coke in 1985 until today. What could the company do to improve its promotion?
3. Suggest a promotional strategy to improve new Coke's market share.

This case was contributed by James H. Kennedy, Angelina College.

SOURCES: Timothy K. Smith, "More Coke Sellers Consider a Return to Original Drink," *Wall Street Journal,* Apr. 11, 1986, p. 30(W), p. 13(E). Scott Kilman and Timothy K. Smith, "New Coke Gets Its Own Ad Campaign—And One More Chance to Find a Market" *Wall Street Journal,* Feb. 14, 1986; "Coke's 'Family' Sales Fly As New Coke Stumbles," *Advertising Age,* Jan. 27, 1986, pp. 1, 91; Scott Kilman, "Coke Posts Rise of 19% In Profit On Operations," *Wall Street Journal,* Feb. 20, 1986, p. 8; Scott Ticer, "Coca-Cola: A Flexible Highflier," *Business Week,* Oct. 5, 1987, p. 82; Nancy Giges, "Pepsi Rekindles Cola War," *Advertising Age,* May 4, 1987, pp. 3, 112; Thomas More, "He Put the Kick Back Into Coke," *Fortune,* Oct. 26, 1987, pp. 46–56; Jennifer Lawrence, "Cola Wars Move In-Store," *Advertising Age,* Nov. 9, 1987, p. 4; Patricia Winters, "Coke Eyes Sweet Role at Breakfast," *Advertising Age,* Nov. 2, 1987, p. 100; Laurel Wentz, "Brosnan Steals Coke's Heart," *Advertising Age,* Nov. 11, 1987, pp. 3, 72; Kevin Kelly and Scott Ticer, "The UnCola Company Gives Bottlers a Friendly Pepper-Upper," *Business Week,* Feb. 8, 1988, p. 94; "The 10 Favorite Campaigns," *Adweek's Marketing Week,* Mar. 7, 1988.

V. Pricing Decisions

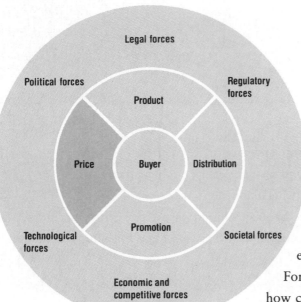

Obviously, for an organization to provide a satisfying marketing mix, the price must be considered, at least, to be acceptable by target market members. Pricing decisions can have numerous effects on other parts of the marketing mix. For example, a product's price can influence how customers perceive it, what types of marketing institutions are used in distributing the product, and how the product is promoted. In Chapter 16, we discuss the importance of price and look at some of the characteristics of price and nonprice competition. Then we examine the major factors that affect marketers' pricing decisions. Eight major stages used by marketers in establishing prices are discussed in Chapter 17.

16. Pricing Concepts

▶ To understand the nature and importance of price.

▶ To be aware of price and nonprice competition characteristics.

▶ To examine various pricing objectives.

▶ To explore key factors that may influence marketers' pricing decisions.

▶ To consider issues affecting the pricing of products for industrial markets.

Long-distance telephone companies waged price wars in the 1980s as deregulation permitted more than one hundred companies to compete for providing long-distance services. Long-distance services have been differentiated by rate reductions and a wide range of new services. For example, there were once just the two classes of message telephone services (MTS) and wide-area telecommunications services (WATS), but now there are five classes of long-distance service. In addition, some changes are related to the types of physical connections between a user and long-distance supplier. Most competitors now pay as much as AT&T pays for connections to local networks.

The three major long-distance carriers—AT&T, MCI Telecommunications Corp., and US Sprint Communications Co.—have largely completed their price and quality competition for residential customers. All three are now concentrating on the more profitable business segment. Since 1984, both MCI and US Sprint have lost most of their price advantages over AT&T as competition and the Federal Communications Commission have driven down long-distance rates by more than 30 percent. Growth in the residential market is slowing. MCI is attempting to make further inroads into the corporate market and diversify further into such market segments as toll-free calling and international telephone service. Increasing costs and dwindling long-distance rates continue to reduce MCI Communications Corp.'s profits. MCI's largest single expense, and one that continues to increase, is the cost of connecting to local telephone companies. MCI is now feeling more price competition from AT&T than at any time in its history.

US Sprint Communications Co. has spent billions on an advanced fiber-optic network and is a formidable competitor, pushing to move into MCI's second place in the industry (see Figure 16.1). However, losses by both companies have led to speculation that MCI and Sprint may merge to be more able to compete with AT&T. US Sprint's primary target is business customers, particularly midsized companies that can be lured away from AT&T. The underdogs are in a "me-too" competition to see who can offer the best volume discounts and free installation. Sprint gained two million customers with a charter customer 10 percent discount promotion, but AT&T remains the dominant force in the industry.

Most experts agree that deregulation of long-distance telephone service has lowered prices for consumers and businesses. Before deregulation, local telephone service was subsidized through excessive long-distance usage charges. Because of intense competition and cost-shifting, pricing long-distance services is much more competitive. Long-distance companies that historically competed on only a price basis will have to focus on nonprice variables in the future.[1]

Pricing is a crucial element in an organization's total marketing mix. In this chapter we initially focus on the nature of price and its importance to marketers. Then we consider some of the characteristics of price and nonprice competition. Next we explore the various types of pricing objectives that marketers may establish, and we examine in some detail the numerous factors that can influence pricing decisions. Finally, we discuss selected issues related to the pricing of products for industrial markets.

The Nature of Price

Price is probably the most flexible variable in the marketing mix. Marketers can usually adjust their prices more easily and more quickly than they can change any other marketing mix variable. Bear in mind, however, that under certain circumstances, the price variable may be relatively inflexible.

To a buyer, **price** is the value placed on what is exchanged. Something of value—usually purchasing power—is exchanged for satisfaction or utility. **Purchasing power** depends on a buyer's income, credit, and wealth. It is a mistake to believe that price is always money paid or some other financial consideration. In fact, trading of products—**barter**—is the oldest form of exchange. Money may or may not be involved.

Buyers' concern for and interest in price is related to their expectations about the satisfaction or utility associated with a product. To illustrate, one study indicates that 25 percent of all meat purchase decisions are based primarily on price.[2] Because buyers have limited resources, they must allocate their purchasing power to obtain the most desired products. Buyers must decide whether the utility gained in an exchange is worth the purchasing power sacrificed.

Almost anything of value—ideas, services, rights, and goods—can be assessed by a price because in our society the financial price is the measurement of value commonly used in exchanges. Thus a painting by Picasso may be valued, or priced, at $500,000. Financial price, then, quantifies value. It is the basis of most market exchanges.

1. Based on information from Richard Laermer, "Sales Promotion: Carriers Vie for Corporate Segments' Numbers," *Advertising Age,* Mar. 23, 1987, pp. 511–513; Pam Powers, "MCI Tries to Dig Out of Market Bog," *Network World,* Mar. 16, 1987, pp. 1, 38; Michael T. Hill, "Comparing Long Distance Costs," *Business Communications Review,* May–June 1987, pp. 14–19; William S. Reece, "Consumer Welfare Implications of Changes in Interstate Telephone Pricing," *Journal of Consumer Affairs,* Summer 1987, pp. 141–154.
2. "Yankelovich Says Effort to Up Consumption of Meat Must Focus on Life-Style Changes," *Frozen Food Age,* November 1983, p. 20.

Terms Used to Describe Price

Price is expressed in different terms for different exchanges. For instance, automobile insurance companies charge a *premium* for protection from the cost of injuries or repairs stemming from an automobile accident. An officer who stops you for speeding writes a ticket that requires you to pay a *fine*. If a lawyer defends you, a *fee* is charged, and if you use a railway or taxi, a *fare* is charged. A *toll* is charged for the use of bridges or turnpikes.

Rent is paid for the use of equipment or an apartment. A *commission* is remitted to an agent for the sale of real estate. *Dues* are paid for membership in a club or group. A *deposit* is made to hold or lay away merchandise. A *tip* helps pay waitresses or waiters for their services. *Interest* is charged for the loan that you obtain, and *taxes* are paid for government services. The value of many products is called *price*. Although price may be expressed in many different ways, it is important to remember that the purpose of this concept is to quantify and express the value of the items in a market exchange.

The Importance of Price to Marketers

As pointed out in Chapter 8, it can take a long time to develop a product. It takes time to plan promotion and to communicate benefits. Distribution usually requires a long-term commitment to dealers who will handle the product. Often, the only thing a marketer can change quickly to respond to changes in demand or to the actions of competitors is price.

Price is also a key element in the marketing mix because it relates directly to the generation of total revenue. The following equation is an important one for the entire organization:

$$\text{Profits} = \text{Total Revenues} - \text{Total Costs}$$
$$\text{or}$$
$$\text{Profits} = (\text{Prices} \times \text{Quantities Sold}) - \text{Total Costs}$$

Prices affect an organization's profits, which are its lifeblood for long-term survival. Price affects the profit equation several ways. It directly influences the equation because it is a major component. It has an indirect impact because it can be a major determinant of the quantities sold. Even more indirectly, price influences total costs through its impact on quantities sold.

Because price has a psychological impact on customers, marketers can use it symbolically. By raising a price, they can emphasize the quality of a product and try to increase the status associated with its ownership. By lowering a price, they can emphasize a bargain and attract customers who go out of their way—spending extra time and effort—to save a small amount. Price can have a strong effect on sales.

Price and Nonprice Competition

A product offering can compete on a price or nonprice basis. The choice will affect not only pricing decisions and activities but those associated with other marketing mix decision variables.

Price Competition

When **price competition** is used, a marketer emphasizes price as an issue and matches or beats the prices of competitors who are also emphasizing low prices (see the advertisement in Figure 16.2). A seller who competes based on price may change prices frequently or at least must be willing and able to do so. Whenever competitors change their prices, the seller must respond quickly and aggressively. Emerson, a manufacturer of consumer electronics, has manufactured no complete products since 1980. The company still designs its own products, but they are essentially copies of competitors' products with Emerson exteriors. Emerson's products are priced approximately 10 percent below the major, recognized brands such as General Electric and Sony but are priced above the "no name" brands. The combination of brand and price appeals to consumers and retailers. The company is able to keep its prices low partly because it avoids new products, instead letting major manufacturers develop, test, commercialize, and either succeed or fail with new ideas.[3]

Price competition gives a marketer flexibility. Prices can be altered to account for changes in the firm's costs or in demand for the product. If competitors try to gain market share by cutting prices, an organization competing on a price basis can

3. Laura A. Walbert, "Copycat," *Forbes,* May 19, 1987, pp. 92–93.

FIGURE 16.2

Car rental companies compete through market-specific price competition (SOURCE: © 1987 Alamo Rent A Car, Inc.)

react quickly to such competitive efforts. However, a major disadvantage of price competition is that competitors also have the flexibility to adjust their prices. Thus they can quickly match or beat an organization's price cuts. Furthermore, if a user of price competition is forced to raise prices, competing firms that are not under the same pressures may decide not to raise their prices. The Application on page 565 focuses on pricing in the automobile industry. Domestic automobile companies use many approaches in coping with price and product quality competition from imports.

Nonprice Competition

Nonprice competition occurs when a seller elects not to focus on price and instead emphasizes distinctive product features, service, product quality, promotion, packaging, or other factors to distinguish its product from competing brands. Thus nonprice competition is based on factors other than price. When the new management team of Heritage Kitchen Specialty Foods was brought on board, one of their first priorities was to redesign the packaging for Effie Marie's Rum Butter Cakes, a line of upscale gourmet cakes. Quality packaging is a key factor in successful marketing of gourmet foods, as they are higher priced, highly differentiated products. The Effie Marie box was redesigned to communicate the quality

FIGURE 16.3

Effie Marie's line of rum butter cakes needed a new package to communicate its upscale price. The lower box is the original package. The middle two pictures show the intermediary stages of potential packaging designs, and on top is the final package (SOURCE: Heritage Kitchens)

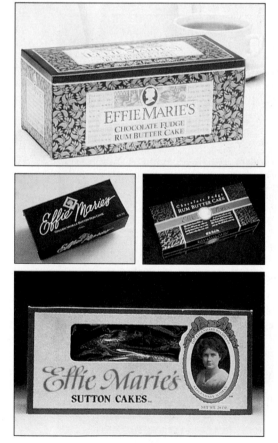

APPLICATION

How Domestic Compact Cars Are Priced

Of all cars sold in the United States today, 35 percent are imported compacts, of which Japanese imports account for 80 percent. As a result, price competition is the norm in today's automotive industry. Traditionally American automobile makers cannot compete with the Japanese and the Koreans, who have a definite cost advantage: Throughout most of the 1980s, the Japanese could sell their cars in the United States, even after paying $500 in tariffs and shipping costs, for less money. Moreover, when U.S. automobile makers put a new car into production, they try to break even in four or five years; the Japanese automobile makers set their breakeven point at eight years, allowing them to sell compacts for less.

To compete with the Japanese and Koreans in the long run, American car makers must cut production costs dramatically. They have tried to do this by reducing overhead and negotiating concessions from labor unions. Between 1987 and 1989 the rising value of the yen has increased the costs of importing Japanese and Korean cars, but the higher costs of American manufacturing, labor, and raw materials and the difference between the countries' tax structures means that Detroit has not recaptured the compact market.

Rather than basing the price of a car on true production costs and then adjusting the price to stay competitive, American car makers set the price of a car five years in advance. They conduct market research to understand the car's target market, determine what features to include, and settle on a price. American car makers try to make at least 10 percent profit on the sale of a car, but that margin depends on variables that are hypothetical at the point of price formulation: production costs, sales volume, and price competition. The total cost of the car includes both fixed and variable costs incurred through the manufacturing process. The sticker price covers the total cost plus the dealer's profit markup.

Because domestic car makers cannot beat their foreign competition, they are trying to join them in a number of ways. U.S. manufacturers are using cheaper foreign raw materials and components. General Motors has replaced some of its assembly lines with modular construction and is using intelligent robots to reduce labor costs. Ford is trying to redesign its cars with fewer components to reduce costs. Chrysler is taking similar steps to reduce its costs.

Another strategy American car manufacturers have adopted is buying compact cars from Japanese producers or building them in the United States using designs and components supplied by foreign partners. General Motors Corp. makes Chevrolet Novas and Toyota Tercels with Toyota at the New United Manufacturing Motor Inc. plant. Ford Motor Company has joined forces with Mazda near Detroit, and Chrysler Corp. has a joint venture with Mitsubishi called Diamond Star Motors in Normal, Illinois. Such compact car ventures help American manufacturers increase their competitive advantage, and they help foreign car makers who fear legislative measures might affect their imports into the United States.

SOURCES: William J. Hampton, "Why Image Counts: A Tale of Two Industries," *Business Week,* June 8, 1987, pp. 138–139; "More Power to Nissan," *The Economist,* Dec. 13, 1986, p. 77; Maralyn Edid, "A New Labor Era May Dawn at GM's Saturn," *Business Week,* July 22, 1985, pp. 65–66; "The All-American Small Car Is Fading," *Business Week,* Mar. 12, 1984, pp. 88–95; Amal Nag, "To Build a Small Car, GM Tries to Redesign Its Production System," *The Wall Street Journal,* May 14, 1984, pp. 1, 12; "Why Detroit Can't Cut Prices," *Business Week,* Mar. 1, 1982, pp. 110–111.

and price ($16) variables[4] (see Figure 16.3). Nonprice competition gives an organization the opportunity to increase its brand's unit sales through means other than changing the brand's price. One major advantage of nonprice competition is that a firm can build customer loyalty to its brand. If customers prefer a brand because of nonprice issues, they may not easily be lured away by competing firms and brands. Customers, whose primary attraction to a store is based on nonprice factors, are less likely to leave their regular store for a lower competitive price. Price is not the most durable factor from a standpoint of maintaining customer loyalty.[5] But when price is the primary reason why customers buy a particular brand, the competition can attract such customers through price cuts.

Nonprice competition is workable under the right conditions. A company must be able to distinguish its brand through unique product features, higher product quality, customer service, promotion, packaging, and the like. Buyers not only must be able to perceive these distinguishing characteristics but must view them as desirable. The distinguishing features that set a particular brand apart from its competitors should be difficult, if not impossible, for competitors to imitate. Finally, the organization must be able to promote extensively the distinguishing characteristics of the brand to establish its superiority and to set it apart from competitors in the minds of buyers.

Foreign firms put less emphasis on price than do their U.S. counterparts. Firms look for a competitive edge by concentrating on promotion, research and development, marketing research, and marketing channel considerations. In a study of pricing strategy, five foreign firms stated specifically that they emphasize research and development and technological superiority; competition based on price was seldom a major marketing consideration.[6] Figure 16.4 illustrates that Yamaha emphasizes technological excellence rather than price in its advertising.

A marketer attempting to compete on a nonprice basis cannot ignore competitors' prices, however. The firm must be aware of competitors' prices and will

4. Debbie Seman, "Effie Marie Sheds Her Dowdy Image," *Adweek's Marketing Week,* Jan. 11, 1988.
5. Michael J. O'Connor, "What Is the Logic of a Price War?" Arthur Andersen & Company, *International Trends in Retailing,* Spring 1986.
6. Saeed Samier, "Pricing in Marketing Strategies of U.S. and Foreign-Based Companies," *Journal of Business Research,* 1987, pp. 15–23.

probably price its brand near or slightly above competing brands. As an example, Curtis Mathes Corp. sells televisions and video recorders in a highly competitive market. The company charges a 30 percent price premium but is successful. The firm stresses service before and after the sale. Quality service lets the company set higher prices and distinguishes it from its competitors.[7] Price thus remains a crucial marketing mix component in situations that call for nonprice competition.

Pricing Objectives

Pricing objectives are overall goals that describe what the firm wants to achieve through its pricing efforts. Because pricing objectives influence decisions in most functional areas—including finance, accounting, and production—the objectives must be consistent with the organization's overall mission and purpose. Since deregulation, banks have become increasingly interested in pricing. Banks began to realize that with the increased competition, their products had to be priced to meet

7. Tom Peters, "More Expensive, But Worth It," *U.S. News & World Report,* Feb. 3, 1986, p. 54.

FIGURE 16.4
Yamaha practices non-price competition (SOURCE: Courtesy of Yamaha Music Corporation)

The Yamaha Piano:
because its 12,241 precision crafted parts
will stand the test of time.

From the Yamaha gallery of fine musical instruments.

⊕ YAMAHA

© 1987 Yamaha Music Corporation, USA • Piano Division • P.O. Box 6600 • Buena Park, California 90622

not only short-term profit goals but also the long-term strategic objectives.[8] Because of the many areas involved, a marketer often uses multiple pricing objectives. In this section we look at a few of the typical pricing objectives that firms might set for themselves.

Survival

A fundamental pricing objective is survival. Most organizations will tolerate difficulties such as short-run losses and internal upheaval if they are necessary for survival. Because price is such a flexible and convenient variable to adjust, sometimes it is used to increase sales volume to levels that match the organization's expenses. "Survival" pricing is the current price objective for much of the U.S. steel industry, which is attempting to meet or slightly undercut the price of the competition by pricing at or below the break-even point. But even with this short-term survival-level pricing, domestic steel producers are barely maintaining market share.[9]

Profit

Although businesses sometimes claim that their objective is to maximize profits for their owners, the objective of profit maximization is rarely operational because its achievement is difficult to measure. Apple Computer, Inc., for instance, is more concerned with long-range survival in the computer industry than with maximizing profits in the short run. The chairman of Apple claims that building good computers is the most important objective at the company.[10] As a result of the difficulty in measurement, profit objectives tend to be set at levels that the owners and top-level decision makers view as "satisfactory." Specific profit objectives may be stated in terms of actual dollar amounts or in terms of percentage change relative to the profits of a previous period.

Return on Investment

Pricing to attain a specified rate of return on the company's investment is a profit-related pricing objective. Although General Motors Corp. prices for profit objectives, actual earnings have fluctuated dramatically between 1980 and 1989. Most pricing objectives based on return on investment (ROI) are achieved by trial and error because not all cost and revenue data needed to project the return on investment are available when prices are set.

Market Share

Market share, which is a firm's sales in relation to total industry sales, is a very meaningful benchmark of success.[11] Many firms establish pricing objectives to maintain or increase market share. For example, a company's pricing objective might be to increase its market share from 22 to 28 percent within the next twelve months. In the advertisement shown in Figure 16.5, Fruit-of-the-Loom promotes its new lower price and discusses its quality and its tag line as America's number-one underwear producer in an effort to gain market share.

8. Robert P. Ford, "Pricing Operating Services," *Bankers Magazine*, May–June 1987.
9. Ray Hellstern, "A Pricing Strategy for the U.S. Steel Producer," *Akron Business and Economic Review*, Spring 1987, p. 46.
10. Peter Nulty, "Apple's Bid to Stay in the Big Time," *Fortune*, Feb. 7, 1983, p. 36.
11. Martin L. Bell, *Marketing: Concepts and Strategy*, 3rd ed. (Boston: Houghton Mifflin, 1979), p. 398.

FIGURE 16.5

Fruit-of-the-Loom promotes its new low price to gain market share (SOURCE: Fruit of the Loom, Inc.)

Maintaining or increasing market share need not depend on growth in industry sales. Remember that an organization can increase its market share even though sales for the total industry are decreasing. For example, in recent years Philip Morris has focused all marketing strategies on increasing its market share in the cigarette industry. With increased awareness of the negative health consequences of smoking, there is the potential for declining sales in the industry as a whole.[12] On the other hand, an organization's sales volume may, in fact, increase while its market share within the industry decreases, assuming that the overall market is growing.

Cash Flow

Some organizations set prices to recover cash as fast as possible. Financial managers are understandably interested in quickly recovering capital spent to develop products. This objective may have the support of the marketing manager, who anticipates a short product life cycle.

Although it may be acceptable in some situations, the use of cash flow and recovery as an objective oversimplifies the value of price in contributing to profits. A disadvantage of this pricing objective could be high prices, which might allow competitors with lower prices to gain a large share of the market.

12. "Why Cigarette Makers Are So Nervous," *Business Week*, Dec. 20, 1982, p. 55.

Status Quo

In some instances, an organization may be in a favorable position and, desiring nothing more, may set an objective of status quo. Status quo objectives can focus on several dimensions—maintaining a certain market share, meeting (but not beating) competitors' prices, achieving price stability, or maintaining a favorable public image. A status quo pricing objective can reduce a firm's risks by helping stabilize demand for its products. The use of status quo pricing objectives sometimes minimizes pricing as a competitive tool, which can lead to a climate of nonprice competition in an industry.

Product Quality

A company might have the objective of product quality leadership in the market. This goal normally dictates a high price to cover the high product quality and the high cost of research and development. For instance, as the advertisement in Figure 16.6 shows, Aston Martin positions its cars as extremely powerful, with high performance, and very exclusive (only thirty cars are available in the United States each year). The exclusivity implies a high price, even though the price is not addressed directly in the advertisement.

FIGURE 16.6

The Aston Martin Lagonda maintains a high price, consistent with its high-performance image (SOURCE: Aston Martin Lagonda Limited)

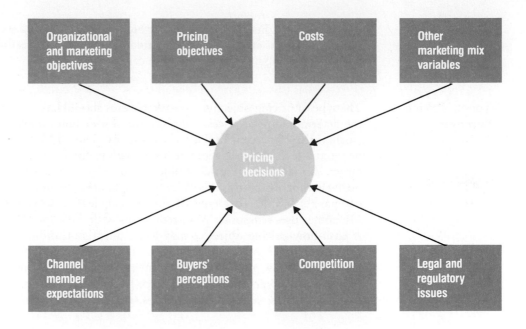

FIGURE 16.7

Factors that affect pricing decisions

Factors Affecting Pricing Decisions

Pricing decisions can be complex because of the number of details that must be considered. In addition, frequently there is considerable uncertainty regarding the reaction of buyers, channel members, competitors, and others. Most price-decision factors can be grouped into one of the eight categories shown in Figure 16.7. In this section we explore how each of these eight groups of factors enters into price decision making.

Organizational and Marketing Objectives

Marketers should set prices consistent with the organization's goals and mission. For example, a retailer trying to position itself as value oriented—meaning that for the prices charged, its products are above average in quality—may wish to set prices that are quite reasonable relative to product quality. In this case, a marketer would not want to set premium prices on products but would strive to price products in line with this overall organizational goal.

The firm's marketing objectives must also be considered. Decision makers should make pricing decisions that are compatible with the organization's marketing objectives. Say, for instance, that one of a producer's marketing objectives is to increase unit sales by 12 percent by the end of the next year. Assuming that buyers are price sensitive, a price increase or setting a price above the average market price would not be in line with the firm's sales objective. For example, Polaroid Corp. chose to focus on price when developing the marketing strategy for the introduction of the Impulse instant camera. The Impulse will complement the Spectra camera, a much higher priced product in the category. According to a Polaroid executive, "We re-motivated the whole field of instant photography with our

Chapter 16   PRICING CONCEPTS   571

Spectra camera. But the Spectra is our higher price entry and we feel there's a need for new products at a low cost." Polaroid has chosen price as the key variable in its advertising campaign for the Impulse camera.[13]

Types of Pricing Objectives

The type of pricing objectives a marketer uses should have considerable bearing on the determination of prices. An objective of a certain target return on investment (such as the 20 percent ROI after taxes set by General Motors) requires that prices be set at a level that will generate a sales volume high enough to yield the specified target. A market-share pricing objective usually causes a firm to price a product below competing brands of similar quality to attract competitors' customers to the company's brand. This type of pricing can lead to lower profits. A marketer sometimes uses temporary price reductions with the hope of gaining market share. A cash-flow pricing objective may cause an organization to set a relatively high price, which can place the product at a competitive disadvantage. On the other hand, a cash-flow pricing objective sometimes results in a long, sustained low price. However, this type of objective is more likely to be addressed by using temporary price reductions, such as sales, rebates, and special discounts.

Costs

Obviously, costs must be an issue when establishing price. A firm may temporarily sell products below cost to match competition, to generate cash flow, or even to increase market share, but in the long run it cannot survive by selling its products below cost. IBM used a unique pricing policy. The IBM System/360 mainframe computers were sold at little or no profit to lock new users into the system. IBM compensated with higher prices on larger systems aimed at industrial and corporate purchasers. The lower pricing tactic on certain computers keeps IBM's competition at a disadvantage and lets IBM sell peripheral and support equipment at the normal profit and pricing level.[14] Even when a firm has a high-volume business, it absolutely cannot survive if each item is sold slightly below what it costs. A marketer should be careful to analyze all costs so that they can be included in the total cost associated with a product. Most marketers view a product's cost as a minimum or floor below which the product cannot be priced. On the other hand, the high cost of producing a product line such as Waterford Crystal (see Figure 16.8) results in a quality that maintains high prices (value) and profit. We discuss cost analysis in more detail in the next chapter and in Chapter 19.

Other Marketing Mix Variables

All marketing mix variables are highly interrelated. Pricing decisions can influence decisions and activities associated with product, distribution, and promotion variables. A product's price frequently affects the demand for the item. A high price, for instance, may result in low unit sales, which in turn may lead to higher production costs per unit. Conversely, lower per-unit production costs may result from a low price. For many products, buyers associate better product quality with a high price and poorer product quality with a low price. This perceived price-quality rela-

13. "Polaroid to Introduce New Instant Camera," *Adweek's Marketing Week*, Jan. 11, 1988, p. 3.
14. Richard Thomas Dehamarter, "Square Pegs, and Round Holes, Big Bucks," *Datamation*, Oct. 1, 1986, pp. 52–60.

FIGURE 16.8

High production costs
mean high prices for
Waterford Crystal
(SOURCE: Waterford
Crystal)

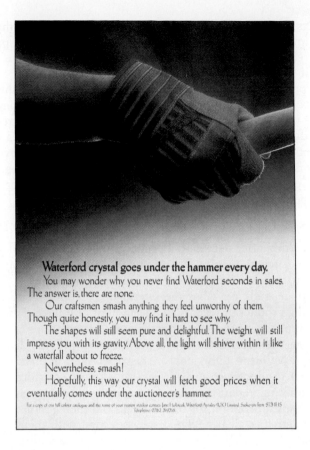

Waterford crystal goes under the hammer every day.

You may wonder why you never find Waterford seconds in sales.
The answer is, there are none.

Our craftsmen smash anything they feel unworthy of them.
Though quite honestly, you may find it hard to see why.

The shapes will still seem pure and delightful. The weight will still
impress you with its gravity. Above all, the light will shiver within it like
a waterfall about to freeze.

Nevertheless, smash!

Hopefully, this way our crystal will fetch good prices when it
eventually comes under the auctioneer's hammer.

For a copy of our full colour catalogue and the name of your nearest stockist contact: Jane Hubbock, Waterford Aynsley (UK) Limited, Stoke-on-Trent ST3 II IS
Telephone: 0782 269216

tionship influences customers' overall image of products or brands. The price sometimes determines the degree of status associated with ownership of the product.

Pricing decisions can influence the number of competing brands in a product
category. When a firm introduces a new product, sets a relatively high price, and
achieves high unit sales, competitors may be attracted to this product category. If a
firm uses a low price, the low profit margin may be unattractive to potential
competition.

The price of a product is linked to several dimensions of its distribution. Pre-
mium-priced products often are marketed through selective or exclusive distribution; lower-priced products in the same product category may be sold through
intensive distribution. For example, Cross pens are distributed through selective
distribution and Bic pens through intensive distribution. The manner in which a
product is stored and transported may also be associated with its price. When a
producer is developing the price of a product, the profit margins of marketing
channel members such as wholesalers and retailers must be considered. Channel
members must be adequately compensated for the functions they perform. Inade-
quately compensated channel members will withdraw from a marketing channel.

The way a product is promoted can be affected by its price. Bargain prices often
are included in advertisements, whereas premium prices are less likely to appear in
advertising messages. The issue of a premium price is sometimes included in advertisements for upscale items such as luxury cars or fine jewelry. Higher-priced

products are more likely to require personal selling efforts than lower-priced ones. For example, a customer may be willing to purchase an inexpensive watch in a self-service environment, yet that same person would hesitate to buy an expensive watch if it was available in the same store.

The price structure can affect a salesperson's relationship with customers. A complex pricing structure takes longer to explain to customers, is more likely to confuse the buyer, and may cause misunderstandings that result in long-term customer dissatisfaction. For example, the pricing structures of many airlines are complex and frequently confuse ticket sales agents and travelers alike.

Price is an important consideration in marketing planning, market analysis, and sales forecasting. It also is a major issue when assessing a brand's position relative to competing brands.

Channel Member Expectations

When making price decisions, a producer must consider what distribution channel members (such as wholesalers and retailers) expect. A channel member certainly expects to receive a profit for the functions it performs. The amount of profit expected depends on what the intermediary could make if it were handling a competing product instead. Also, the amount of time and the resources required to carry the product influence intermediaries' expectations.

Channel members often expect producers to provide discounts for large orders and quick payment. (Discounts are discussed later in this chapter.) At times, resellers expect producers to provide several support activities, such as sales training, service training, repair advisory service, cooperative advertising, sales promotions, and perhaps a program for returning unsold merchandise to the producer. These support activities clearly have costs associated with them. A producer must consider these costs when determining prices because failure to price the product so that the producer can provide some of these support activities may cause resellers to view the product less favorably.

Buyers' Perceptions

One important question that marketers should assess when making price decisions is "How important is the price to people in the target market?" The importance of price is not absolute; it can vary from market to market and from market segment to market segment. However, for a particular product, some buyers perceive the price to be more important than do other buyers. Members of one market segment may be more price sensitive than members in a different target market. Also, the importance of price to buyers will vary across different product categories. For example, price may be a more important factor in the purchase of gasoline than in the purchase of a pair of jeans because buyers may be more price sensitive to gasoline than they are to jeans.

For numerous products, buyers have a range of acceptable prices. In some cases this range is fairly narrow, but for other product categories there is a wider range. A marketer should become aware of the acceptable range of prices in the relevant product category. (This issue and related ones are discussed in more detail in the next chapter.)

Buyers' perceptions of a product relative to competing products may allow or encourage a firm to price the item at a price significantly different from those of competing products. If the product is viewed as being superior to most of the competition, a premium price may be feasible. Strong brand loyalty sometimes provides the opportunity to charge a premium price. When buyers have an unfavorable view of the product (assuming that they are not extremely negative), a lower price may be required to generate sales.

Competition

A marketer needs to remain aware of the prices competitors are charging. This information helps the firm adjust its prices relative to competitors' prices. This does not mean that a marketer necessarily will keep the price the same as competitors' prices; marketers may set a price above or below that of most competitors. Thus knowledge of the prices charged for competing brands is one important factor among several. The airline industry is strongly affected by competitors' pricing. Pricing is the airlines' principal competitive weapon; matching competitors' fares is an important strategy for survival in the industry.[15]

When adjusting prices, a marketer must assess how competitors will respond. Will competitors change their prices (some, in fact, may not), and if so, will they move their prices up or down? In Chapter 2 we describe several types of competitive market structures. The structure that characterizes the industry in which a firm participates affects flexibility of price setting. When an organization operates under conditions of a monopoly and is unregulated, the firm can set prices at whatever the market will bear. However, an organization may choose not to price the product at the highest possible level for fear of inviting government regulation or because the company wants to penetrate a market by using a lower price. If the monopoly is regulated, pricing flexibility normally is reduced, with the regulatory body letting the organization set prices that generate a reasonable, but definitely not excessive, return. A government-owned monopoly may price products below cost to make them accessible to people who otherwise could not afford them. Transit systems, for example, are sometimes operated this way. However, government-owned monopolies sometimes charge higher prices to control demand. In states with state-owned liquor stores, the price of liquor tends to be significantly higher than in states where liquor stores are not owned by a government body.

In an oligopoly there are high barriers to competitive entry into the industry, meaning that there are only a few sellers in that industry. Examples of oligopolistic industries are automobiles, mainframe computers, and steel. A firm in such industries can raise its price hoping that its competitors will do the same. When an organization cuts its price to gain a competitive edge, other firms also are likely to cut theirs, which means that very little is gained through price cuts in an oligopolistic market structure. Marketers obviously must remain aware of the competition's prices to be able to keep their prices in line.

There are numerous sellers with differentiated product offerings in a market structure characterized by monopolistic competition. The products are differentiated by physical characteristics, features, quality, and brand images. An organization may be able to use a price that differs from those of competitors because of its product's distinguishing characteristics. Nevertheless, firms engaged in a monopolistic competitive market structure are likely to practice nonprice competition, which was discussed earlier in this chapter.

15. Andrew T. Chalk and John A. Steiber, "Managing the Airlines in the 1990's," *Journal of Business Strategy*, Winter 1987, pp. 87–91.

Under conditions of perfect competition there are many sellers. Buyers view all sellers' products the same. All firms sell their products at the going market price, and buyers will not pay more than that. Thus for this type of market structure a marketer has no flexibility in setting prices.

Legal and Regulatory Issues

At times government action strongly influences marketers' pricing decisions. In an attempt to curb inflation, the federal government may invoke price controls, "freeze" prices at certain levels, or determine the rates at which prices can be increased. In some states, regulatory agencies set the prices of such products as insurance, liquor, dairy goods, and electricity.

Many regulations and laws have an effect on pricing decisions and activities. The Sherman Act prohibits conspiracies to control prices, and court interpretations of the act have ruled that price fixing among firms in an industry is illegal. Marketers not only must refrain from fixing prices, they must also develop independent pricing policies and set prices in ways that do not even suggest collusion. Both the Federal Trade Commission Act and the Wheeler-Lea Act prohibit deceptive pricing. In establishing prices, marketers must not deceive customers.

The Robinson-Patman Act has had a strong impact on pricing decisions. For various reasons, marketers may wish to sell the same type of product at different prices. Provisions in the Robinson-Patman Act, as well as those in the Clayton Act, limit the use of such price differentials. If price differentials tend to lessen or injure competition, they are considered discriminatory and are prohibited. Not all price differentials, however, are discriminatory. Marketers can use them for a product if any one of the following conditions is satisfied:

1. The price differentials do not injure or lessen competition.
2. The price differentials result from differences in the costs of selling to various customers.
3. The customers are not competitors.
4. The price differentials arise because the firm has had to cut its price to a particular buyer to meet competitors' prices.

Until 1975, manufacturers of consumer goods could set and enforce minimum retail prices for their products in some states. Now the Consumer Goods Pricing Act prohibits the use of price maintenance agreements among producers and resellers involved in interstate commerce.

Retailers and wholesalers in states that have effective unfair trade practices acts are limited in their use of pricing as a competitive tool. Because such acts place a "floor" under prices that retailers and wholesalers can regularly charge, marketers who compete on the basis of price must be aware of legal constraints on their competitors' pricing policies.

Pricing for Industrial Markets

Industrial or organizational markets consist of individuals and organizations that purchase products for resale, for use in their own operations or for producing other products. Quoting prices to this category of buyers is sometimes different from setting prices for consumers. Industrial purchasing has been experiencing much change because of economic uncertainty, sporadic supply shortages, and an increasing interest in service. Suppliers use various pricing approaches to gain market share; buyers must be aware of these approaches and determine their service, quality, and benefit considerations.[16]

Differences in the size of purchases, geographic factors, and transportation considerations require sellers to make adjustments in prices. Also, the rational purchase motives of industrial customers may limit the use of psychological and some promotional pricing policies.

Price Discounting

Producers commonly provide intermediaries with discounts off list prices. Although there are many types of discounts, they usually fall into one of five categories: trade, quantity, cash, seasonal discounts, and allowances.

Trade Discounts   A reduction off the list price given by a producer to a middleman for performing certain functions is called a **trade,** or **functional discount.** A trade discount usually is stated in terms of a percentage or series of percentages off the list price. Middlemen are given trade discounts as compensation for performing various functions such as selling, transporting, storing, final processing, and perhaps providing credit services. Although certain trade discounts are often a standard practice within an industry, discounts do vary considerably among industries.

Quantity Discounts   Deductions from list price that reflect the economies of purchasing in large quantities are called **quantity discounts.** Price quantity discounts are used to pass cost savings, through economies of scale, to the buyer. Cost savings usually occur in four areas. First, with fewer, larger orders, per-unit selling costs are reduced. Second, fixed costs, such as billing and sales contracts, remain the same—or even go down. Third, there are lower costs for raw materials because quantity discounts are often available to the seller. Fourth, longer production runs mean no increases in holding costs.[17] Finally, a large purchase may shift some of the storage, finance, and risk-taking functions to the buyer. Thus quantity discounts usually reflect legitimate reductions in costs.

Quantity discounts can be either cumulative or noncumulative. **Cumulative discounts** are quantity discounts aggregated over a stated period of time. Purchases of $10,000 in a three-month period, for example, might entitle the buyer to a 5 percent, or $500, rebate. Such discounts are supposed to reflect economies in selling and encourage the buyer to purchase from one seller. **Noncumulative discounts** are one-time reductions in prices based on the number of units purchased, the dollar size of the order, or the product mix purchased. As do cumulative discounts, these discounts should reflect some economies in selling or trade functions.

16. William B. Wagner, "The Changing Price Dimension in Purchasing," *European Journal of Marketing,* 1987, pp. 5–13.
17. James B. Wilcox, Roy D. Howell, Paul Kuzdrall, and Robert Britney, "Price Quantity Discounts: Some Implications for Buyers and Sellers," *Journal of Marketing,* July 1987, pp. 60–61.

Cash Discounts   A **cash discount**—price reduction—is given to a buyer for prompt payment or cash payment. Accounts receivable are an expense and a collection problem for many organizations. A policy to encourage prompt payment is a popular practice and sometimes a major concern in setting prices.

Discounts are based on cash payments or cash paid within a stated time. For example, "2/10 net 30" means that a 2 percent discount will be allowed if the account is paid within 10 days and that the balance is due within 30 days without a discount. If the account is not paid within 30 days, interest may be charged.

Seasonal Discounts   A price reduction to buyers who buy goods or services out of season is a **seasonal discount.** These discounts let the seller maintain steadier production during the year. For example, automobile rental agencies offer seasonal discounts in winter and early spring to encourage firms to use automobiles during the slow months of the automobile rental business.

Allowances   Another type of reduction from the list price is an **allowance**—a concession in price to achieve a desired goal. Trade-in allowances, for example, are price reductions given for turning in a used item when purchasing a new one. Allowances help give the buyer the ability to make the new purchase. This type of discount is popular in the aircraft industry. Another example is promotional allowances, which are price reductions granted to dealers for participating in advertising and sales support programs intended to increase sales of a particular item.

For example, because supermarkets focus on major brands first in their own price discount promotions, consumers often find that Dr Pepper is priced higher than Coca-Cola or Pepsi-Cola. This price disadvantage has hurt Dr Pepper's attempts to increase the market share of its soft drink in a nation of heavy cola drinkers. To overcome this price disadvantage, Dr Pepper is urging bottlers and retailers to establish new lower prices for its six-packs of ten-ounce bottles. The company offers a promotional allowance so that retailers and bottlers can retain their usual profit margins.[18]

Geographic Pricing   **Geographic pricing** involves reductions for transportation costs or other costs associated with the physical distance between the buyer and the seller. Prices may be quoted as being **F.O.B. (free-on-board) factory,** which is a price that excludes transportation charges and indicates a shipping point. F.O.B. factory indicates the price of the merchandise at the factory, before it is loaded onto the carrier vehicle. The buyer must pay for shipping. Although this is an easy way to price products, it is sometimes difficult for marketers to administer, especially when a firm has a wide product mix or when customers are dispersed widely. Because customers will want to know about the most economical method of shipping, the seller must keep posted on shipping rates.

To avoid the problems involved with charging different prices to each customer, **uniform geographic pricing,** sometimes called postage-stamp pricing, may be used. This type of pricing results in a fixed average cost of transportation. Gasoline, paper products, and office equipment often are priced on a uniform basis.

18. Al Urbanski, "Dr Pepper Heals Itself," *Sales and Marketing Management,* Mar. 14, 1983, pp. 33–36.

Zone prices are regional prices that take advantage of a uniform pricing system; prices are adjusted for major geographic zones as the transportation costs increase. For example, a Florida manufacturer's prices may be higher for buyers on the Pacific Coast and in Canada than for buyers in Georgia.

Base-point pricing is a geographic pricing policy that includes the price at the factory plus freight charges from the base point nearest the buyer. This approach to pricing has virtually been abandoned because its legal status has been questioned. The policy resulted in all buyers paying freight charges from one location, say Detroit or Pittsburgh, regardless of where the product was manufactured.

When the seller absorbs all or part of the actual freight costs, **freight absorption pricing** is being used. The seller might use this method because it wishes to do business with a particular customer or to get more business; more business will cause the average cost to fall and counterbalance the extra freight cost. This strategy is used to improve market penetration and to retain a hold in an increasingly competitive market.

Transfer Pricing

When one unit in a company sells a product to another unit, **transfer pricing** occurs. The price is determined by one of the following methods:

Actual full cost: calculated by dividing all fixed and variable expenses for a period into the number of units produced
Standard full cost: calculated on what it would cost to produce the goods at full plant capacity
Cost plus investment: calculated as full cost plus the cost of a portion of the selling unit's assets used for internal needs
Market-based cost: calculated at the market price less a small discount to reflect the lack of sales effort and other expenses

The choice of a method of transfer pricing depends on the company's management strategy and the nature of the units' interaction. The company might initially choose to determine price by the actual full cost method. But later price changes could result in a market-based method or another method the management of the company decides is best suited for its changed business situation.[19]

Price Discrimination

A policy of **price discrimination** results in different prices being charged to give a group of buyers a competitive advantage. Price differentiation becomes discriminatory when a seller gives one reseller or industrial buyer an advantage over competitors by providing products at a price lower than other similar customers can obtain. If customers are not in competition with each other, different prices may be charged legally. For example, a producer of a standard sporting-goods product reported the following retail pricing variation among major accounts for an item wholesaling for $100: Warehouse clubs, $120; discount houses, $150 to $160; middle-income department stores, $200 to $210; and upscale department stores and specialty stores, $225.[20]

19. Robert G. Eccles, "Control with Fairness in Transfer Pricing," *Harvard Business Review,* November–December 1983, pp. 149–161.
20. Isadore Barmash, "Trying to Sell Without Sales," *The New York Times,* May 3, 1987, p. E1.

Business Fliers Face Price Discrimination

Sellers give a particular group of buyers an advantage by charging them less than they charge their other customers. Sometimes, however, this price discrimination can work against a group of buyers. In this case, airlines are now charging business fliers higher fares to offset the discounted fares for regular passengers instituted in the mid-1980s.

The major airlines introduced these heavily discounted fares, as much as 80 percent off regular fares, to encourage people to fly. These fares entail restrictions that make it difficult for business travelers to take advantage of them: Travelers must reserve their tickets at least two days in advance, must pay at the time of reservation, and must stay over a Saturday night. Some fares are also nonrefundable. Most business travelers fly during the week and frequently change their travel plans, so they can seldom meet the requirements for the discounted fares. And with the deepest discounted tickets if they have a sudden change of plans, they cannot get a refund for their ticket.

All major airlines reported increased volume because of the lower fares; however, the increased volume was not enough to generate a profit. Because the profits have not been as great as expected, the airlines tried to make up that difference by increasing the fares on both first-class and coach seats, seats usually occupied by business travelers. The airlines say the reason they raised the fares was rising fuel prices and labor costs. But business travelers and corporations feel as if the airlines are making business travelers "pay" for the discounted fares.

Corporations are upset with the higher fares and thus are more thoroughly searching for lower fares. Several corporations have started booking their own flights to eliminate the expense of using travel agents and to ensure that they get the lowest possible fares. Other corporations are trying different tactics, such as purchasing tickets at bulk rates. The drawback to this strategy is that the company must pay for the tickets whether it uses them or not. Several corporations, including McDonald's and Quaker Oats Co., have formed coalitions to pressure airlines into offering corporate discounts for their employees. J.C. Penney negotiated one low fare for its employees flying between New York and Dallas in 1987 and 1988 when it was moving its corporate headquarters to Dallas.

Analysts say the airlines will continue to offer discount fares because they generate a huge volume of passengers. It also seems likely that airlines will continue to discriminate against business travelers by charging them higher prices in an attempt to recoup profits lost because of the cheaper fares.

SOURCES: Jonathan Dahl and Francis C. Brown III, "Business Fliers Face Higher Fares, as Airlines Try to Offset Discounts," *The Wall Street Journal*, Apr. 8, 1987, p. 28; James R. Healey, "Cheap Fares Change Our Flight Pattern," *USA Today*, Mar. 13, 1987, pp. B1, B2; Mark Rohner, "Agents Feeling the Squeeze," *USA Today*, July 14, 1987, p. 9A.

Price differentials are legal when they can be justified on the basis of cost savings, when they are used to meet competition in good faith, or when they do not damage competition. The Application on page 580 discusses price discrimination in the airline industry. The Robinson-Patman Act prohibits price discrimination that lessens competition among wholesalers and retailers, and it prohibits producers from giving disproportionate services to large buyers.

Table 16.1 shows the principal forms of price discrimination. For price discrimination to work, the following conditions are necessary: (1) the market must be segmentable; (2) the cost of segmenting should not exceed the extra revenue from price discrimination; (3) the practice should not breed customer ill will; (4) competition should not be able to steal the segment that is charged the higher price; and (5) the practice should not violate any applicable laws.

Summary

Price is the value placed on what is exchanged. The buyer exchanges purchasing power—which depends on the buyer's income, credit, and wealth—for satisfaction or utility. Price is not always money paid; barter, the trading of products, is the

TABLE 16.1

Principal forms of price discrimination

MAIN CLASSES	BASES OF DISCRIMINATION	EXAMPLES
Personal	Buyers' incomes	Income-based sliding scale for doctors' fees
	Buyers' earning power	Royalties paid for use of patented machines and processes
Group	Buyers' socioeconomic characteristics, such as age or sex	Children's haircuts, lower admission charges for individuals in uniform, senior citizen rates
	Buyers' location	Zone prices, in-state vs. out-of-state tuition, lower export prices (dumping)
	Buyers' status	Lower prices to new customers, quantity discounts to big buyers
	Use of product	Railroad rates, public utility rates
Product	Qualities of products	Relatively higher prices for deluxe models
	Labels on products	Lower prices of unbranded products
	Sizes of products	Relatively lower prices for larger sizes (the "giant economy" size)
	Peak and off-peak services	Lower prices for off-peak services; excursion rates in transportation, off-season rates at resorts, holiday and evening telephone rates

oldest form of exchange. Various terms are used to describe price, including *premium, tip, taxes, dues,* and *interest.* Price is a key element in the marketing mix because it relates directly to the generation of total revenue. The profit factor can be determined mathematically by multiplying price by quantity sold to get total revenues, and then subtracting total costs. Price is the only variable in the marketing mix that can quickly and easily be adjusted to respond to changes in the external environment.

A product offering can compete on either a price or nonprice basis. Price competition emphasizes price as the product differential. Prices fluctuate frequently, and price competition among sellers is aggressive. Price competition can be effective when products in a market are standardized and undifferentiated and demand is elastic. Nonprice competition emphasizes product differentiation through distinctive features, services, product quality, or other factors. Establishing brand loyalty by using nonprice competition works best when the product can be physically differentiated and the customer can recognize these distinguishing characteristics.

Pricing objectives are overall goals that describe the role of price in an organization's long-range plans. The broadest and most fundamental pricing objective is survival. Price is easily adjusted to increase sales volume or to combat competition so that the organization can stay alive. Profit objectives, which usually are stated in terms of sales dollar volume or percentage change, are normally set at a satisfactory level rather than at a level designed for profit maximization. A sales growth objective focuses on increasing the profit base by increasing sales volume. Pricing for return on investment (ROI) has a specified profit as its objective. A pricing objective to maintain or increase market share implies that market position is linked to success. Other types of pricing objectives include cash flow and recovery, status quo, and product quality.

A group of eight diverse factors enters into price decision making. The eight factors are organizational and marketing objectives, pricing objectives, costs, other marketing mix variables, channel member expectations, buyer perceptions, competition, and legal and regulatory issues. When setting prices, marketers should make decisions consistent with the organization's goals and mission. Pricing objectives (for example, an ROI target) heavily influence price-setting decisions. Most marketers view a product's cost as the floor below which a product cannot be priced. Due to the interrelation of the marketing mix variables, price can affect product, promotion, and distribution decisions. The revenue that channel members expect for the functions they perform must also be considered when making price decisions.

Buyers' perceptions of price vary. Some consumer segments are price sensitive, but others may not be; thus before determining price, a marketer needs to be aware of its importance to the target market. Knowledge of the prices charged for competing brands is essential for the firm to adjust its prices relative to those of competitors. Government regulations and legislation also strongly influence pricing decisions. Congress has passed several acts to enhance perfect competition in the marketplace. Moreover, the government has the power to invoke price controls to curb inflation.

Unlike consumers, industrial buyers purchase products for the purpose of using them in their own operations or for producing other products. When adjusting prices, industrial sellers take into consideration the size of the purchase, geographic factors, and transportation requirements. Producers commonly provide discounts off list prices to intermediaries. The categories of discounts include trade, quantity, cash or seasonal discounts, and allowances. A trade discount is a price reduction for performing such functions as storing, transporting, final processing, or providing credit services. If a middleman purchases in large enough quantities, the producer gives a quantity discount. Quantity discounts can be either cumulative or noncumulative. A cash discount is a price reduction for prompt payment or payment in cash. Buyers who buy goods or services out of season may be granted a seasonal discount. These discounts help the seller maintain a more consistent production schedule throughout the year. A final type of reduction from the list price is an allowance, such as a trade-in allowance.

Geographic pricing involves reductions for transportation costs or other costs associated with the physical distance between the buyer and the seller. A price quoted as F.O.B. factory means the buyer pays for shipping from the factory. This is the easiest way to price products, but it can be difficult for marketers to administer. When the seller charges a fixed average cost for transportation, this is known as uniform geographic pricing. Zone prices take advantage of a uniform pricing system adjusted for major geographic zones as the transportation costs increase. Base-point pricing is similar to zone pricing; prices are adjusted for shipping expenses incurred by the seller from the base point nearest the buyer. A seller who absorbs all or part of the freight costs is using freight absorption pricing.

With a price discrimination policy, different prices are charged to give a group of buyers a competitive advantage. Price differentials are legal only when they can be justified on the basis of cost savings, when they meet competition in good faith, or when they do not attempt to damage competition.

Important Terms

Price	Allowance
Purchasing power	Geographic pricing
Barter	F.O.B. (free on board) factory
Price competition	Uniform geographic pricing
Nonprice competition	Zone prices
Pricing objectives	Base-point pricing
Trade or functional discount	Freight absorption pricing
Quantity discounts	Transfer pricing
Cumulative discounts	Price discrimination
Noncumulative discounts	
Cash discount	
Seasonal discount	

Discussion and Review Questions

1. Why are pricing decisions so important to an organization?
2. Compare and contrast price and nonprice competition. Describe the conditions under which each form works best.

3. How does a pricing objective of sales growth and expansion differ from an objective to increase market share?
4. Why is it crucial that marketing objectives and pricing objectives be considered when making pricing decisions?
5. In what ways do other marketing mix variables affect pricing decisions?
6. What types of expectations may channel members have about producers' prices, and how do these expectations affect pricing decisions?
7. How do legal and regulatory forces influence pricing decisions?
8. Compare and contrast a trade discount and a quantity discount.
9. What is the purpose of using the term F.O.B.?
10. What is the difference between a price discount and price discrimination?

Cases

16.1 Pricing of Al Dente Pasta[21]

In 1981, Monique Deschaine started making gourmet pasta by hand in a friend's Ann Arbor, Michigan, restaurant after it closed for the night. She laid her pasta out to dry on the restaurant tables and had to rush to finish her pasta preparation before the restaurant opened the next day at 10 A.M. By 1988 her business, Al Dente, Inc., was a small growing company with annual sales of more than $200,000. Al Dente pasta has also achieved a national reputation through references in several national magazines, including *Atlantic Monthly* and *The Gourmet Retailer*.

Monique Deschaine started her pasta business making all the pasta herself, about 7 pounds at a time, on one small machine. She promoted her pasta by in-store demonstrations of specific recipes. Her hard work paid off, and today she leaves the pasta-making to four full-time employees in her own shop, while maintaining close supervision of all pasta-making. With a state-of-the-art Italian pasta machine, Al Dente can now press 100 pounds of linguine and spaghetti at a time, although the product is still hand-rolled and hand-sheeted. The company makes about 500 pounds of pasta each day, which is distributed in Chicago, Detroit, and on both coasts.

Deschaine insists on making Al Dente pasta with the freshest ingredients: 100 percent semolina flour moistened with hand-cracked eggs fresh from a nearby farm. Ingredients for different flavored pastas—egg, tomato, spinach, herb, and unusual flavors such as spicy sesame, blue corn, walnut, three pepper, and wild mushroom—are mixed right into the dough. Deschaine uses no salt, preservatives, or artificial additives. She refuses to compromise on quality: "Making perfect pasta is a painstaking step-by-step process. We pride ourselves on doing each step well, so that Al Dente pasta looks, cooks, and tastes right." The term *al dente* literally means "to the tooth" and refers to perfectly made and cooked pasta.

21. Based on information from Karen Grassmuck, "Pasta Point of No Return," *Ann Arbor News*, Jan. 17, 1988; Al Dente press releases 1987, 1988; telephone interview with Monique Deschaine, Mar. 21, 1988, and Apr. 7, 1988.

TABLE 16.2

Size and cost of selected brands of gourmet pasta

MANUFACTURER	OUNCE	COST	COST PER OUNCE
Gaston Dupré	8	$1.99	24.9¢
Pastamania	12	2.39	19.9¢
Contadina	9	2.29	25.4¢
Al Dente	12	2.99	24.9¢

Deschaine is faced with a very competitive market. When pricing her pasta, she found competitors' costs and the actual cost of doing business to be the key determining factors. The competitors' price determined the upper limit that could be charged for a gourmet pasta. At the same time she had a minimum price that she had to earn to stay in business. Distribution of the pasta occurs through both brokers and specialty food distributors. The brokers arrange for sales directly between Deschaine and retailers for 10 to 15 percent of the sales price—they do not warehouse any Al Dente pasta. Specialty food distributors warehouse the pasta and sell it to department, specialty, and gift stores as well as to independent grocers and some grocery chains. Specialty food distributors buy the pasta from Deschaine for $1.50 per bag and then mark up sales to retailers 25 percent. Retailers in turn are given a suggested retail price list, which recommends a 33 to 50 percent markup resulting in a selling price from $2.99 to $3.49 per 12-ounce bag.

Deschaine has found that her profit margin on $1.50 per bag is slim. She offers free display racks for all retailers (at a cost of $30). She pays for all shipping of the pasta by common carrier. In addition, distributors are given a 10 percent discount for trade shows, and, when a new distributor is found, a 10 percent discount may be offered to secure the relationship.

Although standard mass market pasta from Prince can be purchased for less than $1 (12- to 16-ounce bags), Deschaine's primary competition comes from gourmet producers such as Gaston Dupré, Pastamania, and Contadina (see Table 16.2). The market is stable in its pricing with competitors' striving for a psychological pricing advantage by offering smaller packaging than Al Dente's 12-ounce package.

Al Dente will not cut its quality to increase its profitability. When striving to increase profits, Deschaine either looks for a less expensive bag manufacturer or lower-cost labels or—most importantly—increase in sales volume, which results in greater economies of scale. Outsiders may think that a small business has extraordinary flexibility in its pricing: That usually is not the case, as many new entrants painfully find out each year.

Questions for Discussion

1. How has Al Dente been able to sell pasta at approximately three times the price of such common supermarket brands as Prince?
2. What are the advantages of using psychological pricing in selling gourmet pasta? How have the specified competitors addressed this issue?
3. What are the advantages and disadvantages of Al Dente's considering lowering its selling price?

16.2 Toys "Я" Us Competes Through Price[22]

Toys "Я" Us is leading the U.S. toy market with its chain of 271 warehouse-style toy supermarkets in thirty-one states. It has long been an innovator, in both its pricing policies and toy supermarket format. In 1987 it held a market share of nearly 16 percent of the $12.5 billion annual U.S. toy sales. Some analysts are predicting that the company may have a 40 percent share of an even bigger U.S. toy market by the 1990s. Toys "Я" Us earnings have increased 35 percent annually since 1978.

Toys "Я" Us brings customers into the store by discounting such baby-care products as strollers and disposable diapers below cost. The thinking is that once parents are in the store, they will spend the money they saved on the discounted baby goods on toys for Junior. Customers come to Toys "Я" Us planning to spend a certain amount of money rather than planning to buy a specific item; lower prices here do not mean lower profits.

Toys "Я" Us stores are usually located along commercial highways, well away from shopping malls, to keep down costs and prevent customers from being distracted by other toy sellers. Isolation from shopping malls also means that customers will load up their shopping carts because they do not have to lug their purchases through crowded malls.

The first store was opened in 1957 as the Children's Supermart (with the "r's" printed backward to encourage name recognition) and offered name-brand toys and baby goods below normal retail price. Today, it still offers name-brand toys at 20 to 50 percent below retail price. Each store has a full stock of more than eighteen thousand different toys and baby goods tracked by a computer system that almost eliminates stockouts. Managers don't place orders for toys, the toys just arrive on time, thus averting the Toys "Я" Us definition of a major disaster: not having a certain toy on display and ready to sell.

Toys "Я" Us sets its price for a particular item based on how much it thinks customers will pay for it, not on the manufacturer's price. The company then decides the price at which it is willing to purchase the toy from the manufacturer and negotiates fiercely with manufacturers to get the toy at that price. The company has a definite advantage in negotiations because it buys in such large volume. Toy manufacturers are also nice to Toys "Я" Us because the company is often a testing ground for new toys. Price is so important to the Toys "Я" Us strategy that even when demand for a toy is high and supplies are short, the company will not raise its price on the toy to make a quick profit.

Market share is Toys "Я" Us' main pricing objective, and for now it is the number-one toy store in the United States. The company says it is willing to cut prices even more to retain its number-one position. Other toy stores are scrambling to meet the competition from Toys "Я" Us; those that do not change their strategies wind up out of the toy market altogether. Most stores, such as K mart and

22. Based on information from David Owen, "Where Toys Come From," *Atlantic Monthly*, October 1986, pp. 64–78; Anthony Ramirez, "Can Anyone Compete with Toys "Я" Us?" *Fortune*, Oct. 28, 1985, pp. 71–72; Mark Maremont, Dori Jones Yang, and Amy Dunkin, "Toys "Я" Us Goes Overseas—and Finds that Toys "Я" Them, Too," *Business Week*, Jan. 26, 1987, pp. 71–72; Susan Scherreik, "Toys "Я" Profitable," *New Jersey Monthly*, October 1986, pp. 45–51; Jesus Sanchez, "Toymakers Make a Play for Market," *USA Today*, Feb. 10, 1987, pp. 1B–2B; Dan Dorfman, "Toys "Я" Us: Mattel Play?" *USA Today*, June 28, 1987, p. 2B.

Macy's, expand their toy lines only for the six-week Christmas season and bring customers in with sales. Although Toys "Я" Us never holds sales, it maintains its huge selection, stock, and discount prices year-round. Those customers who found good buys at Toys "Я" Us at Christmas now shop there for children's birthdays and other special days, when other retail stores have little from which to choose. Even new parents who drop in to Toys "Я" Us for discounted baby products tend to return for toys until their baby outgrows toys (at age 16 or so). Of course, then there are still sporting-goods-type "toys," such as basketballs and bicycles, suitable for older teens, young adults, and families of almost any age.

Some competitors have changed to the Toys "Я" Us supermarket-style stores and try to meet Toys "Я" Us prices year-round. Other stores are trying to get into the number-one position with nonprice competition, by offering educational and baby-sitting type services. However, Toys "Я" Us intends to rely on its nonprice attributes of convenience, selection and stock as well as price competition to hold its position against its imitators.

It has already expanded internationally to Britain, Germany, and Canada, with twenty-four stores. The company has plans for many other stores overseas—two hundred by 1990—to take advantage of the world toy market, which is nearly double that of the U.S. toy market. Additionally, it opened Kids "Я" Us in the United States, a chain of children's clothing stores similar to the toy stores.

Toys "Я" Us has customer loyalty behind it. Customers know they can find *the* toy that children want, at the best price, at Toys "Я" Us. If the toy cannot be found at Toys "Я" Us, it does not exist. And if the child does not like the toy after all, they can return it for a full refund with no questions asked.

Questions for Discussion

1. What are Toys "Я" Us' major pricing objectives?
2. Assess Toys "Я" Us' practice of not raising the prices of products that are scarce and in high demand.
3. A major disadvantage of using price competition is that competitors can match prices. Evaluate this potential problem for Toys "Я" Us.

17. Setting Prices

- ▶ To understand eight major stages that can be used to establish prices.
- ▶ To explore issues connected with selecting pricing objectives.
- ▶ To realize the importance of identifying the target market's evaluation of price.
- ▶ To gain insight into demand curves and the elasticity of demand.
- ▶ To examine the relationships among demand, costs, and profits.
- ▶ To gain insights into analyzing competitive prices.
- ▶ To learn about different types of pricing policies.
- ▶ To examine the major kinds of pricing methods.

Setting prices for hospital services is an important activity in today's highly competitive health-care industry. With many hospital beds empty, both hospitals and groups such as health maintenance organizations (HMOs) are now offering their services at competitive prices (see Figure 17.1). For example, AmeriNet in St. Louis, Missouri, buys services from hospitals and then acts as a middleman in developing products and pricing incentives for consumers. According to AmeriNet president, Joseph Mulroy, the organization has already purchased $750 million in products for its members and has signed several contracts for programs that its sales force markets, including (1) eating disorder clinics, (2) Alzheimer's disease programs, (3) educational programs via satellite, and (4) home health-care products. AmeriNet's large size enables it to offer competitive prices and quality products; hospitals like to cooperate with service providers such as AmeriNet so they can gain revenue through large and efficient transactions.

Pricing concepts and strategies help hospitals compete more effectively in a market in which it has become increasingly difficult to survive. Hospitals are experiencing what airlines experienced several years ago—intensive competition in a major service industry. Unfilled seats on an airplane are similar to unfilled hospital beds—unused capacity is an opportunity lost to the company. To determine the profitability of using various pricing structures, hospitals and HMOs analyze aspects of planning (the difference between planned and actual case volume), intensity (the difference between expected and actual case complexity), and payment (the difference between expected and actual case reimbursement). Studies are being conducted to determine the price elasticity of hospital-specific demand curves.

FIGURE 17.1

Blue Cross and Blue Shield Association promotes its HMO (SOURCE: HMO-USA, Sponsored by Blue Cross and Blue Shield Association)

(Demand curves and price elasticity are discussed in this chapter.) Hospitals may have to negotiate prices, reduce prices, and/or engage in price discrimination (discussed in Chapter 16) to be competitive. Health-care managers must have an extensive knowledge of pricing policies and systematic approaches to pricing.[1]

S ETTING PRICES OF PRODUCTS such as health-care services requires careful consideration of numerous issues. In this chapter we discuss eight stages of a process that marketers can use when setting prices. These stages are not rigid steps that all marketers must use; they are guidelines that provide a logical sequence for establishing prices. In some situations, there may be other stages that should be included in the price-setting process; in other situations, some of the stages may not be necessary.

1. Based on information from Sandy Lutz, "AmeriNet Develops New Products, Incentives," *Modern Healthcare,* June 5, 1987, pp. 191–192; Philip D. Benz, "Pricing Strategies for Hospital Services," *Computers in Healthcare,* June 6, 1987, pp. 24–26; Roger Feldman, "Is There a Competitive Market for Hospital Services?", *Journal of Health Economics,* September 1986, pp. 277–292; Navegh K. Malhotra, "Hospital Marketing in the Changing Health Care Environment," *Journal of Health Care Marketing,* September 1986, pp. 37–48.

Figure 17.2 identifies the eight stages that marketers can use when establishing prices. The first stage is to develop a pricing objective that is congruent with the organization's overall objectives and its marketing objectives. The second stage is to assess the target market's evaluation of price and its ability to purchase. Next, examine the nature and elasticity of demand. Stage 4—analysis of demand, cost, and profit relationships—is necessary for estimating the economic feasibility of alternative prices. Evaluation of competitors' prices (stage 5) helps determine the role of price in the marketing strategy. Competitors' prices and the marketing mix variables that they emphasize partly determine how important price will be to customers. Stage 6 is selecting a pricing policy—the guidelines for using price in the marketing mix. Stage 7 is selecting a method for calculating the price charged to customers. Stage 8, determining the final price, depends on environmental forces and marketers' understanding and use of a systematic approach to establishing prices.

Selection of Pricing Objectives

In Chapter 16 we explore the various types of pricing objectives. Selecting pricing objectives is an important task because pricing objectives are a foundation on which decisions related to other stages of pricing are based. Thus pricing objectives must be explicitly stated. As our opening example illustrates, the health-care industry is beginning to grasp this concept. The industry is now integrating pricing decisions into other health-care delivery decisions. Until recently, health-care marketers were among the least influential in pricing decisions, historically having had limited involvement in establishing price objectives and prices for services they were responsible for developing and promoting. As in all industries, health-care marketers currently participate in developing pricing objectives that are explicitly stated.[2] The

2. Ellen F. Goldman, "Marketing's Past Hurrah: The Integration of Pricing Decisions," *Administration Radiology*, July 1987, pp. 69–71.

FIGURE 17.2
Stages for establishing prices

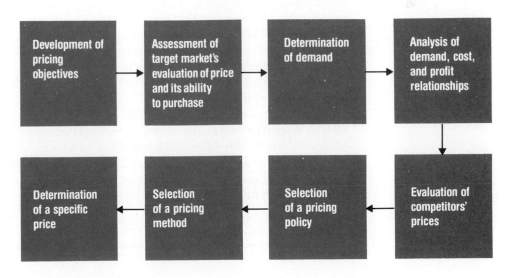

statement of pricing objectives should include the time period over which the objectives are to be accomplished.

Marketers must be certain that the pricing objectives they set are consistent with the organization's overall objectives and marketing objectives. Inconsistent objectives cause internal conflicts and confusion and can prevent the organization from achieving its overall goals. Furthermore, pricing objectives inconsistent with organizational and marketing objectives may cause marketers to make poor decisions associated with the other stages in the price-setting process.

Organizations normally have multiple pricing objectives, some short term and others long term. For example, the pricing objective of gaining market share is normally short term because it often requires the firm to price its product quite low relative to competitors' prices. For each product, an organization should have one or more pricing objectives. For the same product aimed at different market segments, marketers sometimes choose different pricing objectives. Over time, a marketer typically will alter pricing objectives.

Assessment of the Target Market's Evaluation of Price and Its Ability to Purchase

Although we generally assume that price is a significant issue for buyers, the importance of price depends on the type of product and the type of target market. For example, buyers, in general, are probably more sensitive to cigarette prices than to luggage prices. R. J. Reynolds introduced the first American low-priced cigarettes in Japan when trade barriers were lifted, making the Japanese market a target for increased U.S. importation. The cigarettes, called Islands, sell for approximately 10 percent less than most Japanese brands. The lower cigarette price gives Reynolds a major advantage over Japan Tobacco, Inc., which has 90 percent of all the market's cigarette sales. Another advantage is that 30 percent of all cigarettes and 40 percent of foreign cigarettes are sold through vending machines; smokers buying Islands need only two coins instead of the four that are required for Japanese brands.[3] By assessing the target market's evaluation of price, a marketer is in a better position to know how much emphasis to place on price. Information about the target market's price evaluation may also help a marketer determine how far above the competition a firm can set its prices.

As we point out in Chapter 3, the people who make up a market must have the ability to buy a product. Buyers must need a product, be willing to use their buying power, and have the authority (by law or social custom) to buy. Their ability to buy, as does their evaluation of price, has direct consequences for marketers. The ability to purchase involves such resources as money, credit, wealth, and other products that could be traded in an exchange. Understanding customers' purchasing power and knowing how important a product is to them in comparison with other products helps marketers correctly assess the target market's evaluation of price.

3. Christine Donahue, "Low Price Brand Launched in Japan," *Adweek's Marketing Week,* Feb. 1, 1988, p. 5.

FIGURE 17.3

Demand curve illus-
trating the price-quan-
tity relationship and
an increase in demand

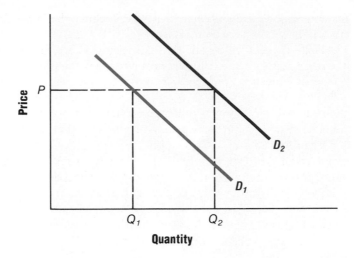

Determination of Demand

Determining the demand for a product is the responsibility of marketing managers
with the help of marketing researchers. Marketing research techniques yield estimates of sales potential or the quantity of a product that could be sold during a
specific period. (Chapter 3 describes such techniques as surveys, time series analyses, correlation methods, and market tests.) These estimates are helpful in establishing the relationship between a product's price and the quantity demanded.

The Demand Curve For most products, the quantity demanded goes up as the price goes down, and as
price goes up, the quantity demanded goes down. Thus there is an inverse relationship between price and quantity demanded. As long as the marketing environment
and buyers' needs, ability (purchasing power), willingness, and authority to buy
remain stable, this fundamental inverse relationship will continue.

Figure 17.3 illustrates the effect of one variable—price—on the quantity demanded. The classic **demand curve** (D_1) is a line sloping downward to the right,
showing that as price falls, quantity demanded will increase. Demand also depends
on other factors in the marketing mix, including product quality, promotion, and
distribution. An improvement in any of these factors may cause a shift to, say,
demand curve D_2. In such a case, an increased quantity (Q_2) will be sold at the
same price (P).

There are many types of demand and not all conform to the classic demand curve
shown in Figure 17.3. Prestige products such as selected perfumes, cosmetics, and
jewelry seem to sell better at high prices than at low ones. For example, the jewelry
shown in Figure 17.4 is known to be expensive and thus has a prestigious image. In
fact, these products are desirable partly because their expense makes their buyers
feel elite. If the price fell drastically and many people owned them, they would lose
some of their appeal.

The demand curve in Figure 17.5 shows the relationship between price and
quantity for prestige products. Demand is greater, not less, at higher prices. For a

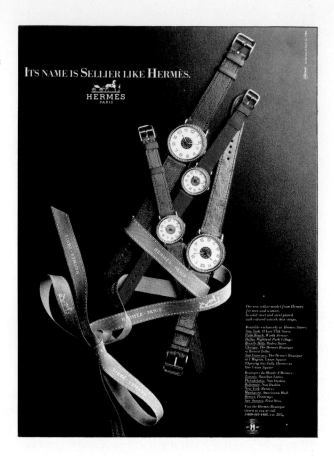

certain price range—from P_1 to P_2—the quantity demanded (Q_1) goes up to Q_2. After a point, however, raising the price backfires. If the price of a product goes too high, the quantity demanded goes down. The figure shows that if the price is raised from P_2 to P_3, quantity demanded goes back down from Q_2 to Q_1.

Demand Fluctuations

Changes in buyers' attitudes, other components of the marketing mix, and uncontrollable environmental factors can influence demand. The hotel industry has had a unique approach to demand fluctuations. Hotel rates tend to rise when the demand for the product is low subsequently causing the use of discounts, which confuses consumers. Now the hotel industry is recognizing the value and significant size of the demand for economical hotels. The Marriott and Sheraton Corporations are moving to expand that line of budget-priced hotels, reacting to consumer demand with an acceptable price.[4] Although demand can fluctuate unpredictably, some organizations have been able to anticipate change in demand by correlating demand for a specific product to demand for the total industry or to some other economic variable. If a brand maintains a fairly constant market share, its sales can be estimated as a percentage of industry sales.

4. Robert C. Lewis, "Customer-Based Hotel Pricing," *Cornell Hotel and Restaurant Administration Quarterly*, August 1986, pp. 18–21.

FIGURE 17.5

Demand curve illus-
trating the relationship
between price and
quantity for prestige
products

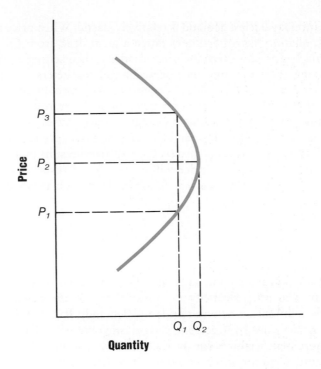

**Determining
Elasticity of
Demand**

To this point, we discussed how marketers identify the target market's evaluation
of price and its ability to purchase and examine demand to learn whether price is
related inversely or directly to quantity. The next stage in the process is to determine elasticity of demand. **Elasticity of demand** (see Figure 17.6) is the relative
responsiveness of changes in quantity demanded to changes in price. The percentage of change in quantity demanded caused by a percentage change in price is much
greater for elastic demand than for inelastic demand. For a product such as electricity, demand is relatively inelastic. When its price is increased, say from P_1 to P_2,
quantity demanded goes down only a little, from Q_1 to Q_2. For products such as

FIGURE 17.6

Elasticity of demand

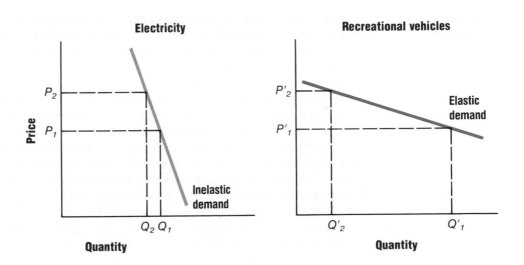

recreational vehicles, demand is relatively elastic. When price rises sharply, from P_1' to P_2', quantity demanded goes down a great deal, from Q_1' to Q_2'.

If marketers can determine **price elasticity,** then setting a price is much easier. By analyzing total revenues as prices change, marketers can determine whether a product is price elastic. Total revenue is price times quantity; thus 10,000 rolls of wallpaper sold in one year at a price of $10 per roll equals $100,000 of total revenue. If demand is *elastic,* a change in price causes an opposite change in total revenue—an increase in price will decrease total revenue, and a decrease in price will increase total revenue. An *inelastic* demand results in a parallel change in total revenue—an increase in price will increase total revenue, and a decrease in price will decrease total revenue. The following formula determines the price elasticity of demand:

$$\text{Price elasticity of demand} = \frac{\%\text{ change in quantity demanded}}{\%\text{ change in price}}$$

For example, if demand falls by 8 percent when a seller raises the price by 2 percent, the price elasticity of demand is -4 (the negative sign indicating the inverse relationship between price and demand). If demand falls by 2 percent when price is increased by 4 percent, then elasticity is $-\frac{1}{2}$. The less elastic the demand, the more beneficial it is for the seller to raise the price. Products without available substitutes and for which consumers perceive a strong need usually have inelastic demand.

Marketers cannot base prices solely on elasticity considerations. They must also examine the costs associated with different volumes and see what happens to profits.

Analysis of Demand, Cost, and Profit Relationships

Having looked at the role demand plays in setting prices and at various costs and their relationships, we now examine the relationships among demand, cost, and profit. To stay in business, a company has to set prices that cover all its costs. To help set prices, there are two approaches to understanding demand, cost, and profit relationships: marginal analysis and breakeven analysis. Before exploring these two approaches, let us identify several different types of costs.

Types of Costs

Costs are associated with the production of any good or service. To determine the costs of production, it is necessary to distinguish fixed costs from variable costs. **Fixed costs** do not vary with changes in the number of units produced or sold. The cost of renting a factory, for example, does not change because production increases from one shift to two shifts a day or because twice as much wallpaper is sold. Rent may go up, but not because the factory has doubled production or revenue. **Average fixed cost** is the fixed cost per unit produced and is calculated by dividing the fixed costs by the number of units produced.

Variable costs do vary directly with changes in the number of units produced or sold. The wages for a second shift and the cost of twice as much paper and dye are

1	2	3	4	5	6	7
QUANTITY	FIXED COST	AVERAGE FIXED COST (2) ÷ (1)	AVERAGE VARIABLE COST	AVERAGE TOTAL COST (3) + (4)	TOTAL COST (5) × (1)	MARGINAL COST
1	$40	$40.00	$20.00	$60.00	$ 60	
						$10
2	40	20.00	15.00	35.00	70	
						5
3	40	13.33	11.67	25.00	75	
						15
4	40	10.00	12.50	22.50	90	
						20
5	40	8.00	14.00	22.00	110	
						30
6	40	6.67	16.67	23.33	140	
						40
7	40	5.71	20.00	25.71	180	

TABLE 17.1

Costs and their relationships

extra costs that occur when production is doubled. Variable costs are usually constant per unit; that is, twice as many workers and twice as much material produces twice as many rolls of wallpaper. **Average variable cost,** the variable cost per unit produced, is calculated by dividing the variable costs by the number of units produced.

Total cost is the sum of fixed costs and variable costs times the quantity produced. **Marginal cost (MC)** is the extra cost a firm incurs when it produces one more unit of a product. The **average total cost** is the sum of the average fixed cost and the average variable cost. Table 17.1 illustrates various costs and their relationships. Notice that the average fixed cost declines as the output increases. The average variable cost follows a U shape, as does the average total cost. Because the average total cost continues to fall after the average variable cost begins to rise, its lowest point is at a higher level of output than that of the average variable cost. The average total cost is lowest at 5 units at a cost of $22, whereas the average variable cost is lowest at 3 units at a cost of $11.67. Marginal cost equals average total cost at the latter's lowest level, between 5 and 6 units of production. Average total cost decreases as long as the marginal cost is less than the average total cost, and it increases when marginal cost rises above average total cost.

Marginal Analysis

Marginal analysis is examining what happens when something is changed by one unit. **Marginal revenue (MR),** therefore, is the change in total revenue that occurs when a firm sells an additional unit of a product. Figure 17.7 depicts marginal revenue; Figure 17.8 shows the relationship between marginal cost and average cost.

Most firms in the United States face downward-sloping demand curves for their products. In other words, they must lower their prices to sell additional units. This

FIGURE 17.7

Typical marginal reve-
nue and average reve-
nue relationships

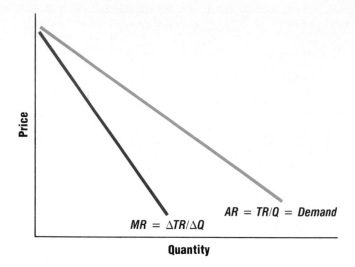

situation means that each additional product sold will provide the firm with less revenue than the previous unit sold. MR would then be less than average revenue, as Figure 17.7 shows. Eventually, MR will reach zero and the sale of additional units would merely hurt the firm.

However, before the firm can determine if a unit makes a profit, it must know its cost as well as its revenue because profit equals revenue minus cost. If MR is a unit's addition to revenue and MC is a unit's addition to cost, then MR minus MC tells us whether the unit is profitable or not. Table 17.2 illustrates the relationships between price, quantity sold, total revenue, marginal revenue, marginal cost, and total cost. It indicates where maximum profits are possible at various combinations of price and cost.

Profit is maximized where MC = MR (see Table 17.2). In this table MC = MR at four units. The best price is $37.50 and the profit is $60. Up to this point, the additional revenue generated from an extra unit of sale exceeds the additional total cost. Beyond this point, the additional cost of another unit sold exceeds the additional revenue generated, and profits decrease. If the price were based on minimum average total cost—$22 (Table 17.1)—it would result in less profit: only $52 (Table 17.2) for five units at a price of $32.40 versus $60 for four units at a price of $37.50.

FIGURE 17.8

Typical marginal cost and average cost relationships

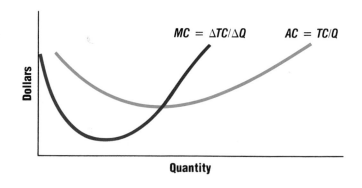

1	2	3	4	5	6	7
PRICE	QUANTITY SOLD	TOTAL REVENUE (1) × (2)	MARGINAL REVENUE	MARGINAL COST	TOTAL COST	PROFIT (3) − (6)
$57.00	1	$ 57	$57	$—	$ 60	− $ 3
55.00	2	110	53	10	70	40
40.00	3	120	10	5	75	45
37.50[a]	4	150	15	15	90	60
32.40	5	162	12	20	110	52
27.80	6	167	5	30	140	37
23.40	7	164	−3	40	180	24

[a]Boldface indicates best price-profit combination.

Graphically combining Figures 17.7 and 17.8 into Figure 17.9 shows that any unit for which MR exceeds MC is adding to a firm's profits, and any unit for which MC exceeds MR is subtracting from a firm's profits. The firm should therefore produce at the point where MR equals MC because this is the most profitable level of production.

This economic concept gives the false impression that pricing can be highly precise. If revenue (demand) and cost (supply) remained constant, then prices could be set for maximum profits. In practice, however, cost and revenue are constantly changing. The competitive tactics of other firms or government action can quickly undermine a firm's expectations of revenue. Thus the economic concept we discussed here is only a model from which to work. It offers little help in pricing new

FIGURE 17.9

Combining the marginal cost and marginal revenue concepts for optimum profit

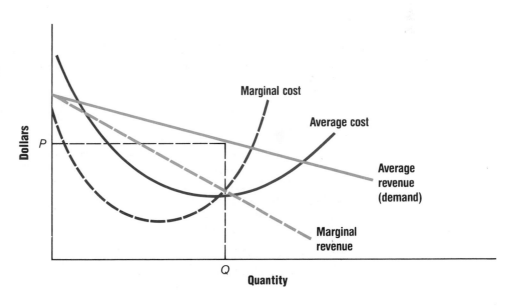

products before costs and revenues are established. On the other hand, in setting prices of existing products, especially in competitive situations, most marketers can benefit by understanding the relationship between marginal cost and marginal revenue.

Breakeven Analysis

The point at which costs of producing a product equal revenue made from selling the product is the **breakeven point.** If a wallpaper manufacturer has total annual costs of $100,000 and the same year it sells $100,000 worth of wallpaper, then the company has broken even.

Figure 17.10 illustrates the relationships of costs, revenue, profits, and losses involved in determining the breakeven point. Knowing the number of units necessary to break even is important in setting the price. If a product priced at $100 per unit has an average variable cost of $60 per unit, then the contribution to fixed costs is $40. If total fixed costs are $120,000, here is the way to determine the breakeven point in units:

$$\text{Breakeven point} = \frac{\text{fixed costs}}{\text{per unit contribution to fixed costs}}$$

$$= \frac{\text{fixed costs}}{\text{price} - \text{variable costs}}$$

$$= \frac{\$120,000}{\$40}$$

$$= 3,000 \text{ units}$$

To calculate the breakeven point in terms of dollar sales volume, multiply the breakeven point in units by the price per unit. In the preceding example, the breakeven point in terms of dollar sales volume is 3,000 (units) times $100, or $300,000.

FIGURE 17.10

Determining the breakeven point

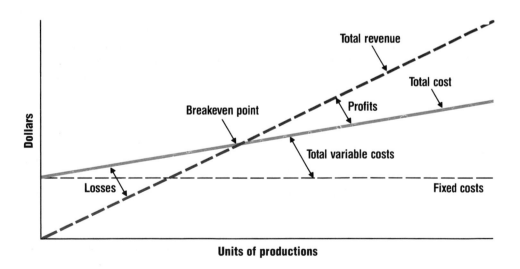

To use breakeven analysis effectively, a marketer should determine the break-even point for each of several alternative prices. This determination allows the marketer to compare the effects on total revenue, total costs, and the breakeven point for each price under consideration. Although this comparative analysis may not tell the marketer exactly what price to charge, it will identify highly undesirable price alternatives that should definitely be avoided.

Breakeven analysis is simple and straightforward. It does assume, however, that the quantity demanded is basically fixed (inelastic) and that the major task in setting prices is to recover costs. This analysis focuses more on how to break even than on how to achieve a pricing objective such as percentage of market share or return on investment. Marketing managers can use this concept to determine more accurately whether a product will achieve at least a breakeven volume. In other words, it is easier to answer the question "Will we sell at least the minimum volume necessary to break even?" than the question "What volume of sales will we expect to sell?"

Evaluation of Competitors' Prices

In most cases, marketers are in a better position to establish prices when they know the prices charged for competing brands. Learning competitors' prices may be a regular function of marketing research. Some grocery and department stores, for example, have full-time comparative shoppers who systematically collect data on prices. Companies may also purchase price lists, sometimes weekly, from syndicated marketing research services.

Becoming aware of competitors' prices is not always easy, especially in producer and reseller markets. Competitors' price lists are often closely guarded, and even if a marketer has access to price lists, they may not reflect the actual prices at which competitive products are sold because the actual prices may be established through negotiation.

Awareness of the prices that are charged for competing brands can be very important for a marketer. Marketers in an industry in which nonprice competition prevails need competitive price information to ensure that their organization's prices are the same as its competitors' prices. In some instances, an organization's prices are designed to be slightly above competitors' prices to give its products an exclusive image. Alternatively, another company may use price as a competitive tool and attempt to price its brand below competing brands. For example, American Express introduced the Optima credit card (discussed in the Application on page 603), which provides revolving credit, thus appealing to a different market segment than the American Express card. The annual membership fee is $15, and interest rate is 1.8 times the prime rate. The card is positioned as an economical alternative for cost-conscious consumers. American Express' pricing policy of tying the variable rate to the prime rate is attracting much attention and may succeed.[5]

5. Kathleen Hawk, "Plastic Warfare," *United States Banker,* June 1987, pp. 40–43.

Selection of a Pricing Policy

A **pricing policy** is a guiding philosophy or course of action designed to influence and determine pricing decisions. Pricing policies set guidelines for achieving pricing objectives. They are an important component of an overall marketing strategy. Generally, pricing policies should answer this recurring question: How will price be used as a variable in the marketing mix? This question may relate to (1) introduction of new products, (2) competitive situations, (3) government pricing regulations, (4) economic conditions, or (5) implementation of pricing objectives. Pricing policies help marketers solve the practical problems of etablishing prices. Let us examine the most common pricing policies.

Pioneer Pricing Policies

Pioneer pricing—setting the base price for a new product—is a necessary part of formulating a marketing strategy. The base price is easily adjusted (in the absence of government price controls), and its establishment is one of the most fundamental decisions in the marketing mix. The base price can be set high to recover development costs quickly or to provide a reference point for developing discount prices to different market segments.

When they set base prices, marketers also consider how quickly competitors will enter the market, whether they will mount a very strong campaign on entry, and the effect of their entry on the development of primary demand. If competitors will enter quickly, with considerable marketing force and with limited effect on the primary demand, then a firm may wish to adopt a base price that will discourage their entry.

Price Skimming   This pioneer approach provides the most flexible introductory base price. Demand tends to be inelastic in the introductory stage of the product life cycle. **Price skimming** is charging the highest possible price that buyers who most desire the product will pay.

Price skimming can provide several benefits, especially when a product is in the introductory stage of its life cycle. A skimming policy can generate much-needed initial cash flows to help offset sizable developmental costs. Kodak Company, for example, used a skimming introductory price for its disk camera to help defray large development costs. Price skimming protects the marketer from problems that arise when the price is set too low to cover costs. When a firm introduces a product, its production capacity may be limited. A skimming price can help keep demand consistent with a firm's production capabilities.

Penetration Price   A **penetration price** is a price below the prices of competing brands and is designed to penetrate a market and produce a larger unit sales volume. When introducing a product, a marketer sometimes uses a penetration price to gain a large market share quickly. Wrigley's, manufacturer of chewing gum, ran an outdoor billboard and poster campaign that promoted its then new five-stick pack of Doublemint for only 25 cents. This pricing and promotional test was developed to build awareness of the new Doublemint pack.[6] This approach places the marketer in a less flexible position than price skimming because it is

6. George Lazaras, "Wrigley Ventures Outdoors," *Adweek's Marketing Week,* Jan. 4, 1988, p. 17.

Optima Card Competes with Lower Interest Rates

When competing products in a particular market are more or less homogeneous, as is the case with bank credit cards, price is the key variable in an organization's marketing strategy. In such a market, a company may use price competition—meeting or beating competitors' prices. The American Express Company used this strategy to set the interest rate on its new Optima charge card.

In the early 1980s, interest rates rose dramatically, and Visa and MasterCard, the two giants in the bank credit card industry, raised their interest rates to 18 to 22 percent. When rates went down, however, the banks and the department stores kept the rates on their cards artificially high to increase profits. They were able to do this because they had no real competition. Holders of travel and entertainment cards such as American Express and Diner's Club must pay their balances in full each month, but holders of Visa or MasterCard can pay only a percentage of the balance each month.

In March 1987, American Express introduced the Optima card, its first revolving credit account (as with MasterCard and Visa, consumers can pay only a percentage of the balance each month). This card offered credit starting at an interest rate of 13.5 percent instead of the 18 to 22 percent Visa and MasterCard charged. However, American Express offered the Optima only to its current 24 million American Express card holders. The company says it can offer such a low interest rate on Optima because it is marketing only to American Express holders, and it already knows their credit history. Limiting the Optima offering to this group of people will help reduce the company's losses.

American Express had no spectacular marketing plans for introducing its new card. Promotion included an extensive direct mail campaign but not an expensive mass media campaign. Optima did receive some free publicity, thanks to Visa. A vice president from Visa sent a letter to banks that carried the Visa card, advising them of Optima's competitive threat. This letter suggested that these banks discontinue other American Express services. This incident caused a public uproar and generated much media attention.

One factor hindering Optima's success is a lack of acceptance by merchants; twice as many merchants now accept Visa and MasterCard as payment for goods and services than accept American Express. Nevertheless, as the Optima card gains acceptance and popularity among consumers, this hurdle can be overcome.

The Optima card is a significant new competitor in the bank credit card industry. Credit card offerers may finally lower their high interest rates, bringing the rates to near the market equilibrium level. Citicorp (one of the largest banks offering Visa and MasterCard) executives say it will be several years before Optima is a serious threat to the other bank cards. In the meantime, Optima's competitors must decide whether to lower their interest rates and decrease profits or lose some of their market share to Optima.

SOURCES: Janice Castro, "Charge of the Plastic Brigade," *Time,* Mar. 23, 1987, p. 52; Jonathan B. Levine and Christopher Farrell, "From American Express—Revolving Credit," *Business Week,* Mar. 23, 1987, p. 146; Phillip L. Zweig, "Citicorp Says Optima Card Will Need a Few Years to Challenge Bank Cards," *The Wall Street Journal,* Mar. 25, 1987, p. 36.

more difficult to raise a penetration price than to lower or discount a skimming price. It is not unusual for a firm to use a penetration price after having skimmed the market with a higher price.

Penetration pricing can be especially beneficial when marketers suspect that competitors could enter the market easily. First, if the penetration price lets one marketer gain a large market share quickly, competitors might be discouraged from entering the market. Second, entering the market may be less attractive to competitors when a penetration price is used because the lower per-unit price results in lower per-unit profit; this may cause competitors to view the market as not being especially lucrative. For example, as Figure 17.11 shows, Subaru uses penetration pricing for its Justy subcompact car.

In contrast, environmental conditions can make a penetration price less attractive to consumers. Private-label and generic-brand food products are promoted primarily on the basis of a penetration price advantage. However, their market share has been declining in recent years. An improving economy and easing food-price increases are two main reasons given for the decrease in the share of these lower-priced products. This example illustrates that penetration policy is not always effective in a dynamic environment.[7]

A penetration price is particularly appropriate when demand is highly elastic, meaning that target market members would purchase the product if it were priced at the penetration level but few would buy the item if it were priced higher. A marketer should consider using a penetration price when a lower price would result in longer production runs, increasing production significantly and reducing the firm's per-unit production costs.

Psychological Pricing

Psychological pricing encourages purchases based on emotional rather than rational responses. It is used most often at the retail level. Psychological pricing has limited use for industrial products.

Odd-Even Pricing   **Odd-even pricing** attempts to influence buyers' perceptions of the price or the product by ending the price with certain numbers. Odd pricing assumes that more of a product will be sold at $99.95 than at $100. Supposedly, customers will think, or at least tell friends, that the product is a bargain—not $100 mind you, but $99 plus a few insignificant pennies. Also, customers are

7. *Frozen Food Age,* November 1983, pp. 1, 32.

supposed to think that the store could have charged $100 but instead cut the price to the last cent, to $99.95. Some claim too that certain types of customers are more attracted by odd prices than by even ones. Odd prices seem to have little genuine effect on sales, except that they do force the cashier to use the cash register to make change. There are no substantial research findings that support the notion that odd prices produce greater sales. The daily newspaper is full of examples of odd prices. In fact, even prices are far more unusual today than odd prices.

Even prices are used to give a product an exclusive or upscale image. An even price supposedly will influence a customer to view the product as being a high-quality, premium brand. A shirt maker, for example, may print on a premium shirt package a suggested retail price of $32 instead of $31.95; the even price of the shirt is used to enhance its upscale image.

Customary Pricing In **customary pricing,** certain goods are priced primarily on the basis of tradition. Recent economic uncertainties have made most prices fluctuate fairly widely, but the classic example of the customary or traditional price is the candy bar. For scores of years, the price of a candy bar was 5 cents. A new candy bar would have had to be something very special to sell for more than a nickel. This price was so sacred that rather than change it, manufacturers increased or decreased the size of the candy bar itself as chocolate prices fluctuated. Now, of

course, the nickel candy bar has disappeared, probably forever. Yet most candy bars still sell at the same price. Thus customary pricing remains the standard for this market.

Prestige Pricing   In **prestige pricing,** prices are set at an artificially high level to provide prestige or a quality image. Pharmacists report that some consumers complain if a prescription does not cost enough. Apparently, some consumers associate a drug's price with its potency. For example, only 14 percent of the customers with new prescriptions eligible for generic substitutions actually took advantage of this cost saving and bought the generic drug.[8] Consumers may also associate quality in beer with high price. The beer industry caters to this perception, as evidenced by its jargon: popular (to mean inexpensive), premium (to mean higher priced), and super premium (to mean expensive).[9]

Prestige pricing is especially used when buyers associate a higher price with higher quality. Typical product categories in which selected products are prestige priced include perfumes, automobiles, liquor, and jewelry. If producers that use prestige pricing lowered their prices dramatically, it would be inconsistent with the perceived images of such products. In Figure 17.12, Cannondale presents its Black Lightning bike targeting a more upscale market. The bike is $800, and the price is subtly compared to that of the Porsche automobile, to denote the same quality.[10]

Price Lining   When an organization sets a limited number of prices for selected groups or lines of merchandise, it is using a form of psychological pricing called **price lining.** A retailer may have various styles and brands of men's shirts that sell for $15. Another line of shirts may sell for $22. Price lining simplifies consumers' decision making by holding constant one key variable in the final selection of style and brand within a line. In product line pricing, the company should look at the prices of the overall product line to ensure that the price of the new model lies within the range of existing prices for that line. Failure to consider the impact of the new model's price relative to the existing product line may change buyers' perceptions of all the models in the line.[11]

The basic assumption in price lining is that the demand is inelastic for various groups or sets of products. If the prices are attractive, customers will concentrate their purchases without responding to slight changes in price. Thus if a women's dress shop carries dresses priced at $85, $55, and $35, the store's management is indicating its belief that these are "good" prices and that a drop to, say, $83, $53, and $34 would not attract many more sales. The "space" between the prices of $55 and $35, however, can stir change in consumer response. With price lining, the demand curve looks like a series of steps, as shown in Figure 17.13.

8. Norman V. Carroll, Chamaporn Sciclhara, Jack E. Fincham, "Factors Affecting Market Acceptance of Generic Drug Products: An Examination of Inherent Risk, Price, and Maximum Allowable Cost Coverage," *Akron Business and Economic Review,* Spring 1987, p. 11.
9. Trish Hall, "Miller Seeks to Regain Niche as Envy of Beer Industry," *Wall Street Journal,* Dec. 3, 1986, p. 6.
10. Casey Davidson, "New Campaigns," *Adweek's Marketing Week,* Jan. 11, 1988, p. 16.
11. Kent B. Monroe, "Effect of Product Line Pricing Characteristics on Product Evaluation," *Journal of Consumer Research,* March 1987, p. 518.

Professional Pricing

Professional pricing is used by persons who have great skill or experience in a particular field or activity. Some professionals who provide such products as medical services feel that their fees (prices) should not relate directly to the time and involvement in specific cases; rather, a standard fee is charged regardless of the problems involved in performing the job. Some doctors' and lawyers' fees are prime examples: $35 for a checkup, $400 for an appendectomy, and $199 for a divorce. Other professionals set prices in other ways.

The concept of professional pricing carries with it the idea that professionals have an "ethical" responsibility not to overcharge unknowing customers. In some situations a seller can charge customers a high price and continue to sell many units of the product. Medicine offers several examples. If a diabetic requires one insulin treatment per day to survive, the individual will buy that treatment whether its price is $1 or $10. In fact, the patient surely would purchase the treatment even if the price went higher. In these situations sellers could charge exorbitant fees. Drug companies claim that despite their positions of strength in this regard, they charge "ethical" prices rather than what the market will bear.

Promotional Pricing

Price is an ingredient in the marketing mix, and it often is coordinated with promotion. The two variables sometimes are so interrelated that the pricing policy is promotion oriented.

FIGURE 17.13

Price lining

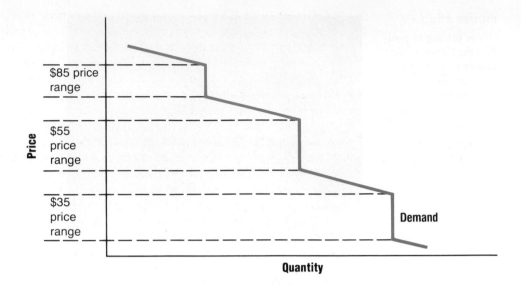

Price Leaders Sometimes a firm prices a few products below the usual markup or below cost. If some products are sold at less than cost, they are **price leaders;** management hopes that sales of regularly purchased merchandise will rise and increase sales volume and profits. This type of pricing is used most often in supermarkets and department stores to attract consumers by giving them an impression of low prices.

Special-Event Pricing To increase sales volume, many organizations coordinate price with advertising or sales promotion for seasonal or special situations. **Special-event pricing** involves advertised sales or price cutting to increase revenue or lower costs. For example, in Figure 17.14, Baldwin offers $125 off any anniversary sale piano during its 125th anniversary. If the pricing objective is survival, then special sales events may be designed to generate the necessary operating capital. Special-event pricing also entails coordination of production, scheduling, storage, and physical distribution. Whenever there is a sales lag, a special event may be launched.

Superficial Discounting **Superficial discounting,** sometimes called "Was-is pricing" in the trade, is fictitious comparative pricing, for example, "Was $259, is $199." The Federal Trade Commission and the Better Business Bureau discourage these deceptive markdowns. Legitimate discounts are not questioned, of course, but when a pricing policy gives only the illusion of a discount, it is unethical and in some states illegal.

As an example of superficial discounting, consider one large retailer that sells 93 percent of its power tools on sale with discounts ranging from 10 to 40 percent. The retailer's frequent special events or sales mean that the tools are sold at sale prices throughout most of the year. To combat such superficial discounting, Canada now requires retailers to post a base price for at least six months before discounting a product.

**Experience Curve
Pricing**

In **experience curve pricing,** a company fixes a low price that high-cost competitors cannot match and thus expands its market share. This practice is possible when a firm gains cumulative production experience and is able to reduce its manufacturing costs at a predictable rate through improved methods, materials, skills, and machinery. Texas Instruments used this strategy in marketing its calculators. The experience curve depicts the inverse relationship between production costs per unit and cumulative production quantity. To take advantage of the experience curve, a company must gain a dominant market share early in a product's life cycle. An early market share lead, with the greater cumulative production experience that it implies, will place a company further down the experience curve than its competitors. To avoid antitrust problems, companies must objectively examine the competitive structure of the market before and after implementing the experience curve strategy. The strategy should not be anticompetitive, and the company must have specific and accurate data that will be unshakable in a court of law. Under the proper conditions—a high probability of success, suitable precaution, sound legal counsel—the method is perfectly acceptable as a primary policy.[12]

12. Alan R. Beckenstein and H. Landis Gabel, "Experience Curve Pricing Strategy: The Next Target of Antitrust?" *Business Horizons,* September–October 1982, pp. 71–77.

FIGURE 17.14

Baldwin uses special event pricing during its 125th anniversary sale (SOURCE: Baldwin Piano and Organ Company)

Development of a Pricing Method

After selecting a pricing policy, a marketer must choose a **pricing method,** a mechanical procedure for setting prices on a regular basis. The pricing method structures the calculation of the actual price. The nature of a product, its sales volume, or the amount of product the organization carries will determine how prices are calculated. For example, a procedure for pricing the thousands of products in a supermarket must be more direct and simple than that for calculating the price of a new earth-moving machine manufactured by Caterpillar. Here we examine three types of market-oriented pricing methods: cost-oriented, demand-oriented, and competition-oriented pricing.

Cost-Oriented Pricing

In **cost-oriented pricing,** a dollar amount or percentage is added to the cost of a product. The method thus involves calculations of desired margins or profit margins. Cost-oriented pricing methods do not necessarily take into account the economic aspects of supply and demand, nor do they necessarily relate to a specific pricing policy or ensure the attainment of pricing objectives. They are, however, simple and easy to implement. Two common cost-oriented pricing methods are cost-plus and markup pricing.

Cost-Plus Pricing   In **cost-plus pricing,** the seller's costs are determined (usually during a project or after a project is completed) and then a specified dollar amount or percentage of the cost is added to the seller's cost to set the price. When production costs are unpredictable or production takes a long time, cost-plus pricing is appropriate. Custom-made equipment and commercial construction projects often are priced by this method. The government frequently uses such cost-oriented pricing in granting defense contracts. One pitfall for the buyer is that the seller may increase costs to establish a larger profit base. Also, some costs, such as overhead, may be difficult to determine.

In periods of rapid inflation, cost-plus pricing is popular, especially when the producer must use raw materials that are fluctuating in price. For industries in which cost-plus pricing is common and sellers have similar costs, price competition may not be especially intense.

Markup Pricing   A common pricing method among retailers is **markup pricing.** In markup pricing, a product's price is derived by adding a predetermined percentage of the cost, called *markup,* to the cost of the product. Although the percentage markup in a retail store varies from one category of goods to another (35 percent of cost for hardware items and 100 percent of cost for greeting cards, for example), the same percentage often is used to determine the price on items within a single product category, and the same or similar percentage markup may be standardized across an industry at the retail level. Using a rigid percentage markup for a specific product category reduces pricing to a routine task that can be performed quickly.

Markup can be stated as a percentage of the cost or as a percentage of the selling price. The following example illustrates how percentage markups are determined and points out the differences in the two methods. Assume that a retailer purchases a can of tuna at 45 cents, adds 15 cents to the cost, and then prices the tuna at 60 cents. Here are the figures:

$$\text{Markup as a percentage of cost} = \frac{\text{amount added to cost}}{\text{cost}}$$

$$= \frac{15}{45}$$

$$= 33.3\%$$

$$\text{Markup as a percentage of selling price} = \frac{\text{amount added to cost}}{\text{selling price}}$$

$$= \frac{15}{60}$$

$$= 25.0\%$$

Obviously, when discussing a percentage markup, it is important to know whether the markup is based on cost or selling price.

Markups usually reflect expectations about operating costs, risks, and stock turnovers. Wholesalers and manufacturers often suggest standard retail markups that are considered profitable. An average percentage markup on selling price may be as high as 75 percent or more for jewelry or as low as 20 percent for the textbook you are reading. To the extent that retailers use similar markups for the same product category, price competition is reduced. In addition, the use of rigid markups is convenient, which is the major reason that retailers—who face numerous pricing decisions—use this method.

Demand-Oriented Pricing

Rather than basing the price of a product on its cost, marketers sometimes use a pricing method based on the level of demand for the product: **demand-oriented pricing.** This method results in a high price when demand for the product is strong and a low price when demand is weak. AT&T uses demand-oriented pricing, as Figure 17.15 illustrates. To use this method, a marketer must be able to estimate the amounts of a product that consumers will demand at different prices. The marketer then chooses the price that generates the highest total revenue. Obviously, the effectiveness of this method depends on the marketer's ability to estimate demand accurately. The dry cleaning industry has experienced enormous growth in recent years, especially in the discount franchise segment. Industry analysts are concerned that the market is becoming saturated, but the discount chain operators, who offer their services 50 percent below the competition, believe they have discovered an entirely new market.[13]

A marketer sometimes uses a demand-oriented pricing method called **price differentiation** when the firm wants to use more than one price in the marketing of a specific product. Price differentiation can be based on such considerations as type of customer, type of distribution channel used, or the time of the purchase. Here

13. Richard Poe, "Franchise Facts: A Pressing Business," *Venture,* June 1987, pp. 24–25.

FIGURE 17.15
AT&T differentiates
its long-distance rates
for different times dur-
ing the day based on
demand (SOURCE:
AT&T)

are several examples. A twelve-ounce canned soft drink costs less from a supermarket than from a vending machine. Florida hotel accommodations are more expensive in the winter than in the summer. A homeowner pays more for air conditioner filters than does an apartment complex owner who purchases the same size filters in greater quantity. Christmas tree ornaments are usually cheaper on December 26 than on December 16.

For price differentiation to work properly, the marketer must be able to segment a market on the basis of different strengths of demand and then keep the segments separate enough so that segment members who buy at lower prices cannot then sell to buyers in segments that are charged a higher price. This isolation could be accomplished, for example, by selling to geographically separated segments.

Price differentiation is often facilitated in international marketing by the geographic distance between markets. For example, Matsushita Electric Co. sells deluxe cordless Panasonic telephones in Japan at eight times what cordless telephones of slightly lower quality sell for in the United States. When a Japanese trading company reimported the U.S. cordless telephones and sold them for $80 instead of the Japanese model at $657, consumers lined up to buy the cheaper telephone. To combat the reimportation, Matsushita bought up all the unsold made-for-export Panasonic telephones it could find to eliminate the obvious wide price differential.

(The major difference between the telephones was that the U.S. telephone had a range of forty meters and the Japanese telephone had a range of fifty meters, which is surprising, because the average Japanese home is much smaller than the average U.S. home.) For years, U.S. manufacturers have accused the Japanese of subsidizing foreign trade wars with high profits from their relatively closed home market.[14]

Also, price differentiation can be based on employment in a public service position. For example, USAIR, Inc., as well as most other airlines, permits 50 percent off each regular one-way or round-trip fare for all U.S. military personnel on active duty, leave, furlough, or a pass.

Compared with cost-oriented pricing, demand-oriented pricing places a firm in a better position to reach higher profit levels, assuming that buyers value the product at levels sufficiently above the product's cost. To use demand-oriented pricing, however, a marketer must be able to estimate demand at different price levels, which is frequently difficult to do accurately.

Competition-Oriented Pricing

In using **competition-oriented pricing,** an organization considers costs and revenue secondary to competitors' prices. The importance of this method increases if competing products are almost homogeneous and the organization is serving markets in which price is the key variable of the marketing strategy.

Amstrad (see the Application on page 614) uses competitive pricing. This company tries to always maintain the lowest price for electronic products.

Competition-oriented pricing should help attain a pricing objective to increase sales or market share. Competition-oriented pricing methods may be combined with cost approaches to arrive at price levels necessary for a profit.

Determination of a Specific Price

Pricing policies and methods should direct and structure the selection of a final price. If they are to do so, it is important for marketers to establish pricing objectives, to know something about the target market, and to determine demand, price elasticity, costs, and competitive factors. In addition to those economic factors, the role of price in the marketing mix will affect the final price.

Although we suggest a systematic approach to pricing, in practice prices often are finalized after only limited planning. Trial and error, rather than planning, may be used to set a price; then marketers determine whether revenue minus costs yields a profit. This approach to pricing is not recommended because it makes it much harder to discover pricing errors. If prices are based on both unrealistic pricing methods and unrealistic sales forecasts, price gimmickry may be a method used to sell products. This approach should be avoided because it can become permanent. The domestic car industry is a current example of how pricing incentives, such as cash rebates and discount financing, can become an essential and permanent part of pricing.[15]

14. "Frantic Cheap Phone Buy-Up Reveals a Lot About Japanese Marketing," *Ann Arbor News,* Feb. 14, 1988, p. C-9.
15. Ray Hellstern, "A Pricing Strategy for the U.S. Steel Producer," *Akron Business and Economic Review,* Spring 1987, p. 53.

Amstrad's Pricing Strategy

Amstrad Consumer Electronics, PLC is one of Europe's fastest-growing electronics companies. At one time, Amstrad was a tiny company that sold stereo systems and television sets. Today, the British company is one of Europe's top home computer marketers, with profits nearing $230 million. Amstrad's low-price, high-volume strategy has given its Asian-made stereos, compact-disc players, televisions, and home computers a large European market share.

One of the main reasons behind Amstrad's phenomenal growth is its competitive pricing strategy. The company's basic marketing philosophy is "Pile 'em high, and sell 'em cheap." For example, one of Amstrad's most successful products is a word processor with a built-in monitor, disk drive, and printer, eliminating the need for any attachments. It sells for $612 in England. The company often uses existing technology to come up with a product that the average consumer likes. In fact, appealing to the tastes and needs of the mass market seems to be one of Amstrad's specialties. It also contracts most of its manufacturing to Asian manufacturers, lowering Amstrad's costs and giving it much flexibility in the marketplace. Amstrad also has a flexible management team that is quick to discontinue products that have poor profit margins.

Amstrad first entered the lucrative U.S. computer market in 1985, but sales were not as high as expected. Although Amstrad's computers cost much less than those of its competitors, they were not compatible with the American standard IBM PC, a feature that is very important to many American computer shoppers. Sales picked up when the company reduced the price from $600 to $400.

Amstrad introduced its line of IBM-compatible personal computers to the American market in 1987. Some analysts feel Amstrad's IBM clone may cause waves in the home computer market because of its low price. Amstrad's PC costs about one-third less than an IBM PC, and it offers more power as well as optics for color graphics and enhanced storage capacity. Amstrad's IBM-compatible computers will retail for $899 to $1999, depending on options.

Analysts say that other business opportunities for Amstrad include office equipment, satellite dishes, and cellular telephones. Most analysts are optimistic about Amstrad's future, especially in European markets that have high growth potential for the next few years, even if Amstrad cannot substantially break into the American home computer market. The company plans to continue with its successful pile 'em high, sell 'em cheap strategy to increase market share all over the world.

SOURCES: Michael Skapinker, "The London Street Trader Who Would Like to Be As Big As Sony," *International Management*, September 1986, pp. 35–40; "An Upstart That IBM Can't Just Brush Off," *Business Week*, Sept. 15, 1986, p. 62; Steve Lohr, "Amstrad Plots a U.S. Invasion," *The New York Times*, Sept. 26, 1987, pp. 37–38.

In the absence of government price control, pricing remains a flexible and convenient way to adjust the marketing mix. In most situations, prices can be adjusted quickly—in a matter of minutes or over a few days. This flexibility and freedom do not characterize the other components of the marketing mix. Because so many complex issues are involved in establishing the right price, pricing is indeed as much an art as a science.

Summary

The eight stages in the process of establishing prices are (1) selecting pricing objectives; (2) assessing the target market's evaluation of price and its ability to purchase; (3) determining demand; (4) analyzing demand, cost, and profit relationships; (5) analyzing competitors' prices; (6) selecting a pricing policy; (7) developing a pricing method; and (8) determining a specific price.

The first stage, setting pricing objectives, is critical because the objectives form a foundation on which the decisions of subsequent stages are based. Organizations may use numerous pricing objectives. Some objectives are short term, others long term; different objectives are used for different products and market segments.

The second stage in establishing prices is an assessment of the target market's evaluation of price and its ability to purchase. This stage tells a marketer how much emphasis to place on price and may help the marketer determine how far above the competition the firm can set its prices. Understanding customers' purchasing power and knowing how important a product is to them in comparison with other products helps marketers correctly assess the target market's evaluation of price.

In the third stage, the organization must determine the demand for its product. The classic demand schedule shows an inverse relationship between price and quantity demanded; as the price of the product decreases, the demand increases, and vice versa. However, there is sometimes a direct positive relationship between price and quantity demanded, as in the case of prestige products, where demand increases as price increases. In setting prices, the organization must learn whether price is related to quantity inversely or directly. Next, elasticity of demand—the relative responsiveness of changes in quantity demanded to changes in price—must be determined. The percentage of change in quantity demanded caused by a percentage change in price is much greater for products with elastic demand than for products with inelastic demand. If demand is elastic, a change in price causes an opposite change in total revenue. Inelastic demand results in parallel change in total revenue when a product's price is changed.

The production of any product results in cost. Average fixed cost is the fixed cost per unit produced. Average variable cost is the variable cost per unit produced. Average total cost is the sum of average fixed cost and average variable cost times the quantity produced.

Analysis of demand, cost, and profit relationships, the fourth stage of the process, can be accomplished through marginal analysis or breakeven analysis. Marginal analysis combines the demand schedule with a firm's costs to develop an optimum price for maximum profit. This optimum price is the point at which marginal cost—the cost associated with producing one more unit of the product—equals marginal revenue. Marginal revenue is the change in total revenue that occurs when one additional unit of the product is sold. In reality, an organization's cost and revenue relationships are difficult to determine. Therefore, marginal analysis is only a model; it offers little help in pricing new products before costs and revenues are established.

The point at which the costs of producing a product equal the revenue made from selling the product is the breakeven point. Knowing the number of units necessary to break even is important in setting the price. To use breakeven analysis effectively, a marketer should determine the breakeven point for each of several alternative prices. This determination makes it possible to compare the effects on total revenue, total costs, and the breakeven point for each price under consideration. Breakeven analysis identifies undesirable price alternatives that should definitely be avoided. This approach assumes, however, that the quantity demanded is basically fixed and that the major task is to set prices to recover costs.

A marketer needs to be aware of the prices charged for competing brands. This allows a firm to keep its prices the same as competitors' prices when nonprice competition is used. If a company uses price as a competitive tool, it can price its brand below competing brands.

A pricing policy is a guiding philosophy or course of action designed to influence and determine pricing decisions. Pricing policies help marketers solve the practical problems of establishing prices. Two types of pioneer pricing policies are price skimming and penetration pricing. With price skimming, an organization charges the highest possible price that buyers who most desire the product will pay. This policy provides several benefits, especially when a product is in the introductory stage of its life cycle. Generating much-needed initial cash flows to help offset sizable development costs is one of the most important benefits. A penetration price is a lower price designed to penetrate the market and produce a larger unit sales volume.

Psychological pricing, another pricing policy, encourages purchases that are based on emotional rather than rational responses. It includes odd-even pricing, customary pricing, prestige pricing, and price lining. A third pricing policy, professional pricing, is used by people who have great skill or experience in a particular field. Promotional pricing, in which price is coordinated with promotion, is another type of pricing policy. Price leaders, special-event pricing, and superficial discounting are examples of promotional pricing. Experience curve pricing fixes a low price that high-cost competitors cannot match. Experience curve pricing is possible when experience reduces manufacturing costs at a predictable rate.

A pricing method is a mechanical procedure for assigning prices to specific products on a regular basis. Three types of pricing methods are cost-oriented, demand-oriented, and competition-oriented pricing. In using cost-oriented pricing, a firm determines price by adding a dollar amount or percentage to the cost of the product. Two common cost-oriented pricing methods are cost-plus and markup pricing. Demand-oriented pricing is based on the level of demand for the product. To use this method, a marketer must be able to estimate the amounts of a product that buyers will demand at different prices. Demand-oriented pricing results in a high price when demand for a product is strong and a low price when demand is weak. In the case of competition-oriented pricing, costs and revenues are secondary to competitors' prices. Competition-oriented pricing and cost approaches may be combined to arrive at price levels necessary for a profit.

Important Terms

Demand curve
Elasticity of demand
Price elasticity
Fixed costs
Average fixed cost
Variable costs
Average variable cost
Total cost
Marginal cost (MC)
Average total cost
Marginal revenue (MR)
Breakeven point
Pricing policy
Price skimming
Penetration price
Psychological pricing
Odd-even pricing

Customary pricing
Prestige pricing
Price lining
Professional pricing
Price leaders
Special-event pricing
Superficial discounting
Experience curve pricing
Pricing method
Cost-oriented pricing
Cost-plus pricing
Markup pricing
Demand-oriented pricing
Price differentiation
Competition-oriented pricing

Discussion and Review Questions

1. Identify the eight stages that make up the process of establishing prices.
2. Why do most demand curves demonstrate an inverse relationship between price and quantity?
3. List the characteristics of products that have inelastic demand. Give several examples of such products.
4. Explain why optimum profits should occur when marginal cost equals marginal revenue.
5. The Chambers Company has just gathered estimates for doing a breakeven analysis for a new product. Variable costs are $7 a unit. Additional plant will cost $48,000. The new product will be charged $18,000 a year for its share of general overhead. Advertising expenditures will be $80,000, and $55,000 will be spent on distribution. If the product sells for $12, what is the breakeven point in units? What is the breakeven point in dollar sales volume?
6. Why should a marketer be aware of competitors' prices?
7. For what type of products would a pioneer price-skimming policy be most appropriate? For what type of products would penetration pricing be more effective?
8. Why do consumers associate price with quality? When should prestige pricing be used?
9. Are price leaders a realistic approach to pricing?
10. What are the benefits of cost-oriented pricing?
11. Under what conditions is cost-plus pricing most appropriate?
12. If a retailer purchases a can of soup for 24 cents and sells it for 36 cents, what is the percentage markup on selling price?

Cases

17.1 Knockoff Fragrance Pricing[16]

To knockoff fragrance companies such as Parfums de Coeur, pricing is the key to the sweet smell of success. The company (its name translates to "perfumes of the heart") manufactures copies, or "impostures," of expensive designer perfumes and markets them to working women who cannot afford or who do not want to pay for expensive fragrances. For instance, the designer fragrance Opium perfume sells for about $190 per ounce, whereas Ninja, Parfums de Coeur's knockoff version of Opium, sells for $7.50 a bottle. The company also copies such hot smellers as Obsession and Giorgio. Nearly forty companies have joined the knockoff game; some companies are even knocking off the knockoffs!

Parfums de Coeur was started by former Charles of the Ritz executive Mark Laracy to fill a gap in the perfume market. Opium was the biggest seller in the department stores, with a prestige price to match its premium image. However, Laracy saw that there were no comparable scents sold in drugstores for women who did not wish to pay a premium price, say, $30 to $200, for a bottle of perfume. For men, the company markets Lancer, a knockoff of Polo.

Parfums de Coeur used comparative advertising to promote its products, with slogans saying, "If you like Opium [or Giorgio or some other fragrance], you'll love Ninja [or Primo, Turmoil, or Confess]." Yet, Parfums de Coeur is not really selling image: It sells price. The perfumes are distributed through drugstores and discount stores such as K mart and Wal-Mart (and through television advertisements).

Parfums de Coeur followed specific steps to establish the price of its perfumes. It sets its pricing objectives (primarily profit and market share) and assessed its target market's evaluation of price and ability to purchase the perfumes. Parfums de Coeur determined that this target market would be willing to purchase lower-priced fragrances that imitated the designer ones, and met this demand. It analyzed demand, cost, and profit relationships in its consideration of a pricing policy for the knockoff perfumes. It evaluated the prices of both the designer scents sold in department stores and the mass-market scents sold in drugstores. It finally determined that a penetration pricing policy would best generate a large market share quickly while reducing the impact of the designer's prestige pricing policies. Before setting the actual price of its product, the company also developed a method of setting prices based on demand and competition.

Actually, the low-priced knockoffs have not seriously reduced the market share of the designer fragrances they copy. Instead, they have cut into the sales of the less-expensive mass market brands, such as Jontue and Revlon. The women who buy those perfumes are trying out the copycat fragrances because of price and because they want to smell as if they had spent more on their scents.

The manufacturers of the designer fragrances are not exactly pleased with the copycat perfumes. Parfums de Coeur has been in court several times since it began

16. Based on information from Pat Sloan, "Knock-Offs Deliver Blows to Fragrance Market," *Advertising Age,* Mar. 2, 1987, p. S-14; Amy Dunkin, " 'Obsession' by Any Other Name Smells Sweetly," *Business Week,* June 1, 1987, p. 97; Kevin T. Higgins, "By Any Other Name Would Smell As Sweet— Imposture Line from Parfums de Coeur Striving to Knock Off Designer Brands, Literally and Figuratively," *Marketing News,* Jan. 17, 1986, pp. 1, 12.

to defend its right to copy designer fragrances. The manufacturer of Calvin Klein's Obsession has sued five of the knockoff companies for misuse of its trademark. However, scents cannot be patented, and most of the knockoff manufacturers print disclaimers on their packaging (right next to the name and trademark of the designer scent that it copies!). One designer company says that the use of the designer fragrance's trademark confuses consumers and damages the designer's name. The name-brand manufacturers are particularly concerned that consumers will never try the expensive designer fragrance if the knockoff they try is of poor quality. This issue is one the Supreme Court may have to decide, but meanwhile the controversy may be generating more sales for the knockoffs as consumers take time to stop and smell the knockoffs.

Questions for Discussion

1. Did Parfums de Coeur feel that the demand curve for perfume was elastic or inelastic? Why?
2. Evaluate Parfums de Coeur's choice of a penetration price policy versus other pricing policies available.
3. What might Parfums de Coeur's competitors, such as Jontue and Revlon, do to regain part of their lost market shares?

17.2   *Pricing at Chrysler*[17]

Chrysler Corp. experienced huge losses in the mid-1970s, and in 1979, the government bailed it out so it could avoid bankruptcy. Chrysler officials realized that one of its major problems was difficulty determining its pricing policies and that these policies needed to be changed if the company were to survive.

The company rebounded by finding several ways to compete successfully in the automobile industry. It experimented with various price rebates and discounts and eventually devised a price structure that compared favorably with that of its competitors. In addition, Chrysler enhanced the value of its product line by advertising its five-year, fifty-thousand-mile protection plan as the best in the car industry at the time.

In October 1980, Chrysler introduced its new K-car line for the 1981 model year. The basic models were priced to penetrate the market quickly, at $350 less than General Motors Corp.'s comparable basic X-car. Chrysler officials believed that the only way they could underprice GM and survive was to make up the difference on options. However, customers were not so interested in the models with options as they were with the lower-priced basic models. Fortunately, Chrysler noticed this trend early and began to produce more of the basic K-cars. Sales increased with the K-car holding more than 20 percent of the compact-car market.

In the mid-1980s, Chrysler introduced a $6.6 billion product development program to use the K-car engine, drive train, suspension parts, and other components

---

17. Based on information from Doug Carroll, "Chrysler Cuts Price on K-Cars," *USA Today,* Aug. 28, 1987, p. 1B; David J. Luck and O. C. Ferrell, *Marketing Strategy and Plans* (Englewood Cliffs, N.J.: Prentice-Hall, 1985), pp. 372–386; Lee Iacocca with William Novak, *Iacocca, An Autobiography* (New York: Bantam Books, 1984), pp. 267–268.

to produce most of its product mix. The basic K-cars, Reliant and Aries, were extended to create Chrysler Le Baron/Dodge 400, Chrysler E class/Dodge 600, Chrysler New Yorker, Dodge Daytona, Chrysler Laser, and Dodge Caravan/Plymouth Voyager minivan lines. Producing Chrysler's entire line of cars from one basic chassis design helped the company become profitable again because it greatly reduced production costs and eliminated the need for expensive retooling. In addition, the cost savings from this extension of the product line enabled Chrysler to keep the prices on its basic models consistently below those of comparable models from Ford Motor Company and GM. This technique, which illustrates how price objectives should be coordinated with other business decisions, has become a central part of Chrysler's marketing strategy.

By 1987, sales of the K-car were declining and the line was scheduled to be discontinued following the 1988 model year. However, Chrysler officials decided to cut the price on all the K-car models by more than $1,000. A similar price cut on Chrysler's subcompacts Dodge Omni and Horizon in 1986 greatly increased sales of these models, prompting company officials to continue to build those cars until 1991. Thus officials decided to see if a price cut would work the same way for the K-cars.

According to automobile industry analysts, the price cut on the K-car helped cure its poor sales figures. In addition, this move caused competition-oriented pricing on the part of Ford and GM as they lowered the prices on their comparable models. Chrysler can make almost as much money on the K-cars as before the price cut by offering fewer options and increasing volume.

Chrysler has become a strong company again after nearly falling into bankruptcy a few years ago. Sound management coupled with innovative pricing strategies has helped Chrysler regain its position as one of the giants of the automobile industry.

Questions for Discussion

1. How did Chrysler's pricing objectives affect its business decisions?
2. Why did Chrysler officials want to use a penetration-pricing policy on the K-car? Was this a good policy?
3. Why did Chrysler cut the price on K-cars? Do you think that Chrysler is using an experience curve pricing policy in this regard?

Part V   *S T R A T E G I C   C A S E*

Pricing Strategy at Texas Air

Early in 1987, Texas Air (a Houston-based holding company that owned Continental Airlines and New York Air) bought Eastern Airlines and the financially troubled People Express (which also owned Frontier Airlines). Texas Air merged Continental, New York Air, and People Express into one full-service, low-fare airline under the Continental banner, making Continental the third largest airline in the United States. Eastern remained an independent carrier, with most of its service limited to east of the Mississippi. As a result of these acquisitions, Texas

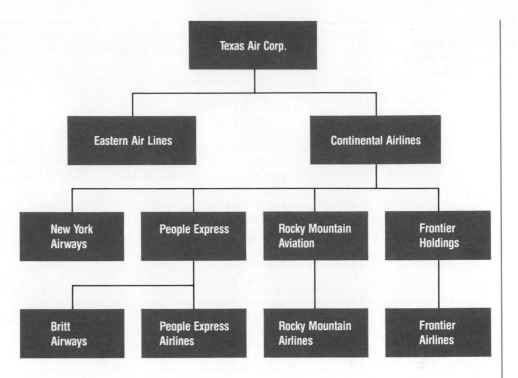

Air controlled the country's largest airline system, carrying 20 percent of the nation's airline passengers (see Figure 1).

Texas Air believes in giving its customers what they want, that is, the best possible service at the best possible price. The airline is committed to this low-price, high-value service and follows a cost-conscious, consumer-oriented philosophy to maintain it. Texas Air claims it follows this philosophy in the air and on the ground with friendly personnel, efficient baggage handling, convenient schedules and routes, tasty in-flight snacks and meals, and modern equipment. However, Texas Air spends less on meals than most airlines do. Of course, the passengers are the ultimate judges of the quality of the service. And, based on passenger complaints, Texas Air needs to improve in many areas; complaints include late departures, canceled flights, and dirty planes. In February 1988, the U.S. Department of Transportation evaluated fourteen major airlines for on-time arrivals: The department ranked Continental thirteenth and Eastern eleventh (see Table 1).

Texas Air keeps its costs down by using both large and small aircraft (smaller planes are more cost efficient on shorter routes) and by flying fuller airplanes (fuller airplanes have lower operating costs per passenger). It also pays its flight crews less than other airlines: Although Eastern Airlines is unionized, Continental is not. Eastern pays higher wages than Continental, but Continental's lower wages keep costs down for the entire holding company.

Texas Air's Pricing Philosophy

Even before deregulation of the airline industry, which analysts say lowered air fares 20 to 30 percent, the original Texas Airways (once referred to as Tinker Toy Airways and Treetop Airways) was a pioneer in cutting costs and setting low fares.

TABLE I

Percentage of flights arriving within fifteen minutes of scheduled time*

RANK	AIRLINE	PERCENTAGE
1	Pacific Southwest	90.6
2	American West	88.7
3	Southwest	88.5
4	American	80.8
5	Pan American	80.1
6	Alaska	76.9
7	Piedmont	75.0
8	USAir	74.8
9	Delta	73.6
10	United	73.2
11	Eastern	70.6
12	TWA	69.4
13	Continental	67.7
14	Northwest	61.7

* February 1988

SOURCE: Paulette Thomas, "Airlines Cutting Discount Fares in Some Areas," *Wall Street Journal*, Apr. 6, 1988. Reprinted with permission of *The Wall Street Journal*. © Dow Jones & Company, Inc. 1988. All rights reserved. Data from the U.S. Department of Transportation, February 1988.

Although Texas Airways (later Texas International Airways and finally Texas Air) was plagued with money problems from its very beginning, it has always maintained the cost-conscious philosophy that it still follows today. Two years before deregulation, the airline introduced Peanuts Fares to stimulate earnings. Peanuts Fares were discounted fares (50 percent off regular fares) whose purpose was to encourage more vacationers to fly instead of drive. The other airlines were unhappy about these first discount fares because they forced them to introduce their own discounted fares or lose market share.

Although Texas Air's primary pricing objective is to maintain the lowest price possible, the airline's managers realized that low costs and fares alone do not ensure success. If the company were to compete solely by price, passengers would continue to fly airlines offering full service as well as low fares, leaving empty seats on Texas Air flights. (One reason former no-frills airline People Express nearly went bankrupt was that full-service airlines reduced their fares to compete with People Express; thus passengers flew on the airlines that offered both low fares and full service. Only Texas Air's takeover of People Express prevented it from filing for bankruptcy.) Texas Air managers knew that they had to use nonprice competition to survive the air-fare wars.

Texas Air therefore consolidated and improved the reservations services of its many airlines into SystemOne Corp. and set up a better frequent flier program. It let Continental passengers apply the frequent flier mileage they had earned to Eastern Airline's Frequent Traveler Bonus Program. It merged all the programs into one frequent flier program, OnePass. When these services failed to attract enough passengers, Texas Air turned to massive discounting—a form of price competition—to fill those empty seats. It offered two-for-one introductory fares and an entire package of other discounted fares.

Texas Air introduced MaxSaver fares in 1987: These fares were discounted 80 percent off full-coach fares and 20 to 40 percent below Super Saver fares United, American, and other airlines offered. For example, as Table 2 indicates, a discount round trip between Chicago and Dallas on Continental was $188, the coach fare $650. To obtain MaxSaver fares, a passenger had to purchase a round-trip flight that included a Saturday night stop (for example, fly out on Thursday, fly home on Sunday). The MaxSaver fares were nonrefundable (up until this time most airline fares were refundable) and required two-days advance reservation and immediate purchase of the ticket. Other airlines matched Texas Air's fares but added even more restrictions to deter business travelers from using these low fares.

Texas Air Maintains Price Leadership

Texas Air set its fares low to increase its share of the U.S. market; however, it realized that its competitors would respond, and possibly undercut, its new low-fare structure. The other airlines did match but not beat the MaxSaver fares (see Table 2). Several times United and other airlines tried to raise their fares to their earlier rates, but Texas Air continued its low MaxSaver fares, so the other airlines had to continue to meet Texas Air's lower fares, at least for those flights in direct competition with Texas Air. To make a profit, the other airlines needed the higher

TABLE 2

Comparison of 1988 discount and coach fares of seven major airlines

AIRLINE	NEW YORK TO LOS ANGELES	CHICAGO TO DALLAS	LOS ANGELES TO HONOLULU	DALLAS TO ATLANTA	RESTRICTIONS
ROUND TRIP DIS-COUNT FARES					
Continental	$198	$188	$298	$178	Fly between April 18
Eastern	198	—	—	178	and June 15; start
American	198	188	298	178	trip between noon
Northwest	198	198	298	178	Monday and noon
United	198	198	298	178	Thursday and in-
TWA	198	198	298	178	clude a Saturday
Delta	198	198	298	178	stay
ROUND TRIP COACH FARES (NO RESTRIC-TIONS)					
Continental	$ 900	$650	$1,048	$590	
Eastern	900	620	—	640	
American	1,120	620	854	640	
Northwest	900	620	854	590	
United	1,120	620	854	590	
TWA	1,120	620	720	640	
Delta	1,120	620	854	640	

SOURCE: Air fares obtained directly from airlines, April 1988.

fares, to offset their high expenses. Texas Air thought it could make a profit on its low fares because company costs were the lowest in the U.S. airline industry. Continental and some subsidiaries have earned occasional quarterly profits over the years, but Eastern Airlines, with its higher costs, has been a loser, losing $181.7 million in 1987.

When Texas Air lost $466 million in 1987, the other airlines exerted pressure on the company to raise its fares and give up its position as price leader. In the spring of 1988, Texas Air's Continental unit led the industry in increasing full coach fares 12 to 18 percent. Most competitors, including American, United, TWA, Northwest, Delta, and of course Eastern Airlines, matched these higher prices. The variation in coach prices (Table 2) probably reflects the nature of competition in specific markets. Continental also made it much tougher for business travelers to purchase discount tickets. Middle-range discounts (discounts other than MaxSaver fares) were offered only to fliers who purchased tickets four to seven days in advance; the discounts also had a 25 percent cancellation penalty. Although these middle-range fares did not require travelers to stay over Saturday night, because business fliers often change plans on the spur of the moment, the four- to seven-day advance reservation requirement made it more difficult to get discounts. The International Airlines Passenger Association (mainly business fliers) charges that airlines are using business fliers to subsidize the highly competitive nonbusiness market.

The rising fares and more severe restrictions on Continental's discount fares created an uncertain future. In February 1988, Continental had the highest passenger complaint rate among all carriers, according to the Department of Transportation's monthly service record, and many—especially business travelers—avoided flying on Continental. Certain analysts believed that the airline had gained some loyalty from business fliers because its coach fares were lower than many competitors' fares. But with coach fares closer to competitors' prices, would business fliers go with carriers that had fewer perceived service problems? Although Texas Air had emerged as a price leader, it was less certain how this position would lead the company from losses to profits.

After increasing coach fares in the spring of 1988, both Continental and Eastern announced that they were reducing their even more restricted discount fares for travel between April and June. The MaxSaver fare between New York and Los Angeles, for example, was reduced from $248 to $198. As indicated in Table 2, all major airlines matched Texas Air units' new lower fares for the New York to Los Angeles route as well as some in other markets. These fare changes, along with the increases in business travelers' fares, seemed to be an attempt to fine-tune a highly complex pricing structure.

Despite these pricing skirmishes with its competitors, Texas Air was still losing market share. Other major carriers, such as American Airlines, experimented by raising some of their discount fares and tightening the restrictions. In the past, major airlines backed down on proposed price increases when Texas Air refused to go along with them. When a carrier the size of Texas Air refuses to match a price increase, it is difficult for other airlines to follow through with their plans. Texas Air has been considered the pricing leader in the industry, partly because of its low costs and size. However, the price increase enacted by American Airlines shows that several major airlines may be willing to raise fares independently of Texas Air.

The Impact of Pricing on Texas Air's Future

Some industry analysts believe that consumers may be willing to pay higher fares to fly with airlines that place greater emphasis on safety and service. This could lead to an industrywide two-tier pricing system for discount fares. The experts are worried that a full-scale fare war may break out. However, Texas Air has limited the availability of its discount fares by restricting them further.

Analysts are wondering how long Texas Air can continue to offer its low fares and stay in business. The airline industry is near saturation, but airlines are still scrambling to attract a few more passengers with the lowest fares they can afford. One airline, Braniff, went bankrupt by following the very same philosophy of expansion and ultralow fares to which Texas Air is now committed. However, Texas Air cannot keep its fares low forever. Its profits continue to drop, and it may have to re-examine its strategy if it continues to show such massive losses. Some consumers might wonder if lower fares and potential financial troubles mean less airplane maintenance and, ultimately, more dangerous flights.

Consumer concerns increased as a result of two events in April 1988. First, the FAA imposed a $823,000 fine against Eastern for safety-related violations. Only fourteen months earlier, Eastern paid $9.5 million for safety violations. Second, the Department of Transportation announced a financial probe of Texas Air, to determine if Texas Air is "fit, willing, and able" to carry commercial air traffic. However, the investigation concluded that Texas Air was financially fit and safe to fly. Moreover, Continental and Eastern continue to rank at the bottom for on-time arrivals. With other carriers matching almost all of Texas Air's prices with better performance and safety records, Texas Air could lose more market share. But for now, consumers definitely like the low fares, and record numbers are flying on Texas Air planes.

Questions for Discussion

1. How does Texas Air's pricing differ from that other airlines use?
2. List advantages and disadvantages of Texas Air's approach to pricing.
3. How should Texas Air use its price leadership position to improve profitability?

This case was prepared by O. C. Ferrell and Gwyneth M. Vaughn. It is provided as a basis for class discussion rather than an illustration of effective or ineffective organizational practices.

SOURCES: H. Josef Hebert, "FAA Fines Eastern, Plans New Probe," *The Detroit Free Press,* Apr. 14, 1988, p. 16A; "Do Airlines Put Money Where Your Mouth Is?" *Wall Street Journal,* Apr. 7, 1988, p. 27; Paulette Thomas, "Airlines Cutting Discount Fares in Some Areas," *Wall Street Journal,* Apr. 6, 1988, p. 23; Paulette Thomas and Jonathan Dahl, "Continental Air Triggers Increases in Fares Used by Business Travelers," *The Wall Street Journal,* Mar. 4, 1988, p. 23; Francis C. Brown III, "Texas Air Decision to Lift Fares Ensures Success of Some Boosts Planned by Others," *Wall Street Journal,* Sept. 14, 1987, p. 26; "Has Lorenzo Fired the First Salvo in a Fare War?" *Business Week,* Sept. 14, 1987, pp. 37–38; "Lorenzo Turns to Terra Firma," *Business Week,* Sept. 7, 1987, p. 34; Mike Sheridan, "Continental Says It Won't Match Rivals by Hiking Fares," *Houston Chronicle,* Sept. 1, 1987, pp. 1C, 7C; Jo Ellen Davis et al., "Continental: Full Planes May Not Mean Full Coffers," *Business Week,* Mar. 16, 1987, p. 37; James R. Healey, "Texas Air: Fare's Fair," *USA Today,* Mar. 2, 1987, p. 1B; Dana Ragen, "Reaching New Heights," *Continental,* February 1987, pp. 10–13; Candace Talmadge, "Dogfight Near for Air Giants?" *Adweek,* Feb. 23, 1987, pp. 1, 6; David Poulson, "Air-Fare Wars Bombarding the Trenches," *USA Today,* Feb. 6, 1987, p. 1B; Cecilia Preble, "People Express, New York Air Merging Under Continental Umbrella," *Aviation Week & Space Technology,* Jan. 19, 1987, pp. 32–33; Thomas G. Donlan, "Why People's Woes Won't Aid Its Rivals," *Barron's,* June 30, 1986, p. 28.

VI. Marketing Management

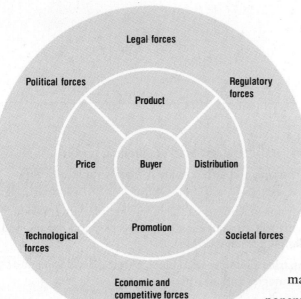

We have divided marketing into several sets of variables and have discussed the decisions and activities associated with each variable. By now, you should understand (1) how to analyze marketing opportunities, and (2) the components of the marketing mix. It is time to put all these components together in our discussion of marketing management issues. In Chapter 18 we discuss strategic market planning. Specifically, we focus on the planning process, the setting of marketing objectives, the assessment of opportunities and resources, and specific product/market matching approaches to strategic market planning. Chapter 19 deals with other marketing management issues including organization, implementation, and control. Approaches to organizing a marketing unit, issues regarding strategy implementation, and techniques for controlling marketing strategies are explored in this chapter.

18. Strategic Market Planning

▶ To provide an overview of the strategic market planning process.

▶ To define marketing planning and differentiate it from strategic market planning.

▶ To describe three major approaches to strategic market planning: product-portfolio analysis, the market attractiveness–business position model, and Profit Impact on Marketing Strategy (PIMS).

▶ To evaluate strategic market planning and relate it to the development of functional marketing strategies and activities.

Remington Products, Inc. of Bridgeport, Connecticut, markets electric shavers and other consumer products. In 1979, the company was in financial chaos. At that time, Remington Products emphasized high technology yet virtually ignored marketing. Retailers were reluctant to stock Remington products because they believed the company was unstable. Moreover, the company's distribution was characterized by long delays. As a result, sales and market share had been declining for several years. Enter Victor Kiam, an entrepreneur. Kiam became interested in Remington Products after using one of its shavers for the first time; he was so happy with the shave he got that he bought the company (see Figure 18.1).

Kiam brought to Remington an entrepreneurial spirit and an aggressive strategic marketing plan. His marketing objectives for the company were to increase profit and cash flow and increase market share in shavers. Kiam's strategy for meeting those objectives was to get employees to improve quality, cut the price of Remington's shavers, and launch an aggressive promotional campaign. Kiam offered employees new incentives and bonuses to increase productivity and quality; ultimately, the company's products achieved a near-zero defect rate. He cut the price of the shavers by more than one-third, which initially greatly decreased the company's profits. Nevertheless, the price cut gradually increased Remington shavers' market share over the next few years.

The heart of the aggressive marketing strategy involved television commercials featuring Kiam. Both Remington's advertising agency and Kiam felt that there was no one better qualified to promote the company's shavers than Kiam himself. The commercials also brought about another one of Kiam's innovative marketing

strategies: the no trade-in trade-in. If customers were not satisfied with the shave
they got from a Remington shaver, they could return the shaver for a full refund.
This plan was quite successful and firmly etched Remington as the shaver "that
shaves as close as a blade or your money back" into the minds of consumers. The
quality of Remington shavers was vital to the success of this campaign—if the
shavers had not been able to deliver as promised, the results would have been
disastrous.

Kiam implemented Remington's marketing strategy through good relations with retailers. He assured retailers that his new management team was going
to stabilize the company. The company promised retailers that orders would be
shipped within twenty-four hours of receipt. Remington also developed a unique
package for its shavers that made them difficult to steal. As a result of these
changes, retailers began to display Remington shavers on the sales floor instead of
behind locked glass cases. This move further boosted the company's sales.

Victor Kiam's zeal for entrepreneurship and his innovative strategic marketing plan revitalized Remington Products. In 1986 the company had sales of

nearly $180 million, up substantially from 1985. Despite his rather large part in Remington's comeback, Kiam gives the credit to his hard-working employees and high-quality product.[1]

S TRATEGIC PLANNING requires a general management orientation rather than a narrow functional orientation. Nevertheless, with market analysis becoming more important, in many companies the lead responsibility for formulating corporate strategy is increasingly being entrusted to the marketing department. The **corporate strategy** determines the means for utilizing resources in the areas of production, finance, research and development, personnel, and marketing to reach the organization's goals. Corporate strategy addresses the composition of the firm's distinct business operations and how the firm should divide business activities into manageable units.[2]

Corporate strategy planners are concerned with issues such as diversification, competition, differentiation, interrelationships among business units, and environmental issues. Differentiation can be a key idea in a corporate strategy. Kemmons Wilson, the founder of Holiday Inn Inc., is working to develop a new hotel chain called Wilson Inn. The chain will be positioned as a budget-priced hotel (rooms costing approximately $35), offering amenities associated with higher-priced hotels, such as microwave ovens, wet bars, and small refrigerators. Wilson's strategy is to locate his hotels close to the more expensive hotels that draw customers with their national reputations and advertising, and to create traffic from customers who switch over to the Wilson Inn. This corporate strategy differs considerably from that of Holiday Inn.[3]

Corporate strategic planning focuses on the decision making process that governs the overall direction of the corporation, including many marketing considerations. As we state in Chapter 1, a **marketing strategy** encompasses selecting and analyzing a target market and creating and maintaining an appropriate marketing mix. Unfortunately, sometimes corporate strategic planners have ignored the marketing concept and concerns such as segmentation, product positioning, and marketing research.[4]

This chapter looks closely at one portion of marketing management: planning. More specifically, there is a general overview of planning activities and approaches to strategic market planning. First, we provide an overview of the strategic market planning process, including the development of organizational goals, corporate strategy, and marketing objectives and strategy. We also examine organizational opportunities and resources as they relate to planning. We then look at approaches or methods used in product-portfolio analysis, the market attractiveness-business

1. Based on information from Marilyn Much, "Would You Buy a Shaver from This Man?" *Industry Week*, Aug. 24, 1987, pp. 37–38; Victor Kiam, "Remington's Marketing and Manufacturing Strategies," *Management Review*, February 1987, pp. 43–45; Jeff Bloch, "Wanna Buy a Kiam," *Forbes*, Feb. 24, 1986, p. 127.
2. Michael E. Porter, *Competitive Advantage* (New York: Free Press, 1985), p. 317.
3. Dean Foust, "Innkeepers Beware: Kemmons Wilson Is Checking In," *Business Week*, Feb. 1, 1988, pp. 79–80.
4. Yoram Wind, "Marketing and Corporate Strategy," *The Wharton Magazine*, Summer 1982, p. 38.

FIGURE 18.2

Products from Kraft's
strategic business units
(SOURCE: Courtesy of
Kraft)

position model, and Profit Impact on Marketing Strategy (PIMS). We conclude the
chapter by examining competitive strategies for marketing.

Strategic market planning should guide marketing strategy and marketing planning. Planning of marketing activities strongly affects the overall success of marketing efforts. Other aspects of the marketing management process—organizing, implementing, and controlling—are covered in Chapter 19.

Strategic Market Planning Defined

A **strategic market plan** takes into account not only marketing but all other functional areas of a business unit that must be coordinated, such as production,
finance, and personnel, as well as concern about the environment. The concept of
the strategic business unit is used to define areas for consideration in a specific
strategic market plan. Each **strategic business unit (SBU)** is a division, product line,
or other profit center within the parent company. For example, products from
Kraft's strategic business units are shown in Figure 18.2. They consist of dairy and
food service items, frozen pizza, as well as grocery products and other units such as
batteries. Each sells a distinct set of products and/or services to an identifiable
group of customers, and each is in competition with a well-defined set of competitors. In the context of the parent company, meaningful separation can be made of
an SBU's revenues, operating costs, investments, and strategic plans.

How a company conceives of its SBUs can have a direct impact on the nature of
the strategic market plans. If management fails to define the SBUs correctly, the
best planning available cannot undo the damage. Unfortunately, some firms use

familiar rationales for SBU boundaries, such as geography, old acquisition deals, and so on, that turn out to be very poor for strategic market planning purposes. For example, a manufacturer of plastic control devices had vaguely defined one SBU as a product supplier rather than as a unit that solved control problems of manufacturers in general.[5] By properly defining each SBU, planning and strategy development can be improved.

Thus a strategic market plan is *not* the same as a marketing plan; it is a plan of *all* aspects of an organization's strategy in the marketplace. A marketing plan, in contrast, deals primarily with implementing the market strategy as it relates to target markets and the marketing mix.[6]

The process of **strategic market planning** yields a marketing strategy that is the framework for a marketing plan. Through this process, an organization can develop marketing strategies that, when properly implemented and controlled, will contribute to achieving the organization's overall goals. To develop a marketing strategy, all aspects of an organization that interface with the marketplace must be considered.

Figure 18.3 shows the components of strategic market planning. The process is based on the establishment of an organization's overall goals, and it must stay within the bounds of the organization's opportunities and resources. When the firm has determined its overall goals and identified its resources, it can then assess its opportunities and develop corporate strategy. Thereafter, marketing objectives must be designed so their achievement will contribute to the corporate strategy and so they can be accomplished through efficient use of the organization's resources.

To reach its marketing objectives, an organization must develop a marketing strategy, or a set of marketing strategies, as shown in Figure 18.3. Usually, several marketing strategies are used simultaneously in an effort to achieve the firm's marketing objectives. The set of marketing strategies that are implemented and used at the same time is referred to as the organization's **marketing program.**

As we have mentioned before, to formulate a marketing strategy, the marketer identifies and analyzes the target market and develops a marketing mix to satisfy individuals in that market. *Marketing strategy is best formulated when it reflects the overall direction of the organization and is coordinated with all the firm's functional areas.*

As indicated in Figure 18.3, the strategic market planning process is based on an analysis of the environment, by which it is very much affected. Environmental forces can place constraints on an organization and possibly influence its overall goals. The amount and type of resources that a firm can acquire are also affected by forces in the environment. However, such forces do not always constrain or work against the firm; they can also create favorable opportunities that can be translated into overall organizational goals and marketing objectives. For example, in the mid-1980s oil prices plummeted, putting many small refineries and exploration companies out of business. This situation created an opportunity for the larger, better-leveraged oil companies to acquire oil rigs and drilling equipment at a fraction of original cost. The environmental situation of decreased oil prices created an

5. Daniel H. Gray, "Uses and Misuses of Strategic Planning," *Harvard Business Review,* January–February 1986, p. 92.
6. Derek F. Abell and John S. Hammond, *Strategic Market Planning* (Englewood Cliffs, N.J.: Prentice-Hall, 1979), p. 10.

FIGURE 18.3
Components of strate-
gic market planning

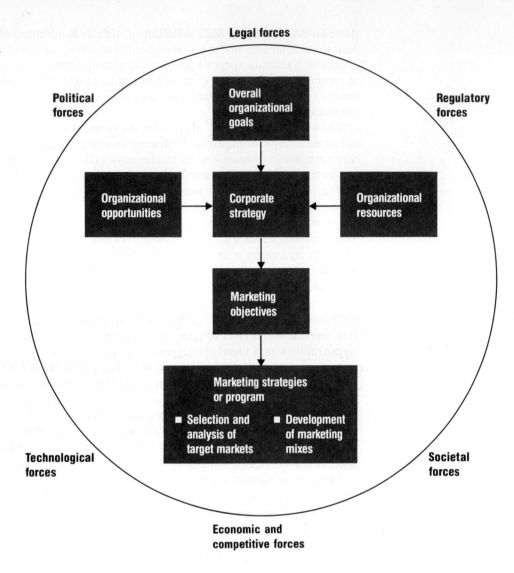

opportunity for select large oil companies to pick up valuable equipment at little
expense, relatively speaking.

Environmental variables affect the creation of a marketing strategy several ways.
When environmental variables affect an organization's overall goals, resources,
opportunities, or marketing objectives, they also affect the firm's marketing strategies, which are based on these factors. More directly, environmental forces influence the development of a marketing strategy through their impact on consumers' needs and desires. In addition, marketing mix decisions are influenced by a
variety of forces in the environment.

Competition, for instance, has an important impact on marketing mix decisions.
The organization must diagnose the marketing mix activities it performs, taking
into consideration competitors' marketing mix decisions, and develop some competitive advantage to support a strategy.

Next, we discuss the major components of strategic market planning.

Establishing Organizational Goals

A firm's organizational goals should direct its planning efforts. A company's overall goals may focus on one or several business activities. Goals specify ends or results that are sought. For example, a firm that is in serious financial trouble may be concerned solely with short-run results needed to stay in business. There always seems to be an airline or major retailer taking drastic action to stay in business due to cash shortages. On the other hand, some companies have more optimistic goals. Pacific Financial Companies' goal (see Figure 18.4) is to be in the top 1 percent of all money managers. A successful company, however, may want to sacrifice this year's profits for the long run and at the same time pursue other goals, such as finding new customers.

Organizational Opportunities and Resources

There are three major considerations in assessing opportunities and resources: market opportunity must be evaluated; environmental forces (discussed in Chapter 2) must be monitored; and the firm's capabilities should be understood. For example, Digital Equipment Corporation (DEC), a computer manufacturer, has become IBM's most formidable challenger, mainly through DEC's VAX minicomputer. However, IBM still holds a strong lead over DEC in personal computers and networks. Back in 1982, DEC developed its own personal computers, which were a flop. Yet DEC's ability to market computer networks is crucial for its continued growth, so instead of taking another shot at developing its own personal computer, DEC forged an alliance with Apple Computer, Inc. The two companies are developing communications and software that will enable Apple's Macintosh computers to work in networks connected to DEC's VAXs. DEC also plans to let IBM's PCs and the new Personal System/2s operate in DEC networks. This will give DEC nearly unlimited compatibility with any office or information system, which greatly enhances its ability to market products to add to existing systems. DEC is striving to carefully assess the opportunities and apply its resources to develop objectives and revise marketing strategies. All these activities are part of strategic market planning.[7]

Market Opportunity A **market opportunity** arises when the right combination of circumstances occurs at the right time to allow an organization to take action toward reaching a target market. For example, in reaction to the overwhelming growth in the all-natural, high-fiber cereal category, one sugar manufacturer observed a potential opportunity. The manufacturer knew that many of these products do not taste good, which meant that there was an opportunity to develop a new cereal topping. The manufacturer believed that there was a consumer market for a cereal sweetener made of raw cane sugar, wheat, and bran. The new topping was promoted as a "breakthrough for breakfast," available in a shaker canister. The product was positioned

---

7. Leslie Helm and John W. Verity, "DEC's New Plan: If You Can't Beat PCs, Join 'Em—To Each Other," *Business Week*, Feb. 1, 1988, pp. 83–84.

THE SWIFT. THE BRILLIANT. THE POWERFUL.

The Asset Managers of Pacific Financial Companies. Ranking in the top 1% of all fixed income managers for over a decade. Out-performing the Shearson Lehman Government/Corporate Index eight of the last ten years. Equity performance exceeding the Standard & Poor's 500 Index for the last five year period.

Using sophisticated analytic techniques wisely. Being sensitive to market trends. Capitalizing on evolving investment opportunities.

For bond management, equities, and real estate investments, talk to the Asset Managers from the Power of the Pacific.

They are inventive. Successful. For you.

PACIFIC FINANCIAL
COMPANIES
THE POWER OF THE PACIFIC

700 Newport Center Drive, Newport Beach, CA 92660
1-800-544-3660

FIGURE 18.4

Pacific Financial Companies achieve their goal of ranking in the top 1 percent of all money managers (SOURCE: Pacific Mutual Life Insurance Companies)

as a healthy, natural additive, one that will improve the taste of your favorite cereal.[8] An opportunity provides a favorable chance or opening for the firm to generate sales from identifiable markets. The term *strategic window* has been used to describe what are often only limited periods of optimum fit between the key requirements of a market and the particular capabilities of a firm competing in that market.[9]

For example, Procter & Gamble's Metamucil is currently marketed as a laxative. Yet a two-year study conducted for Procter & Gamble revealed that Metamucil safely reduced cholesterol levels by an average of 15 percent. Because of the public's growing concern and awareness of high cholesterol levels, Procter & Gamble was presented with a strategic window. As a result, the company petitioned the Food and Drug Administration to revise its listing of Metamucil's benefits to include cholesterol reduction.[10] The Procter & Gamble example illustrates that understanding the environment as well as the firm's ability to respond to a market opportunity are important considerations in strategic market planning.

Determinants of the attractiveness of market opportunity include market factors, such as size and growth rate, and other factors, such as competition; financial,

8. Robert McMath, "Old Favorites Find New Forms," *Adweek's Marketing Week*, Jan. 18, 1988, p. 17.
9. Derek F. Abell, "Strategic Windows," *Journal of Marketing*, July 1978, p. 21.
10. Laurie Freeman, "Metamucil Eyes New Claim," *Advertising Age*, Feb. 15, 1988, p. 3.

economic and technological factors; and social, legal, and political factors.[11] Because each industry and product are somewhat different, the factors that determine attractiveness tend to vary. Fruit of the Loom has taken an aggressive stance to become the market leader in men's and boys' underwear against Hanes Knit Products. Fruit of the Loom originally used Fruit of the Loom characters dressed as fruit and included an Inspector 12 to depict that their underwear is of extremely high quality. Hanes then promoted the fact that Fruit of the Loom underwear shrank more than their brand. Fruit of the Loom's market share began declining, so the company reviewed their product line and marketing strategy. Fruit of the Loom quickly came back with an advertising campaign promoting better fit. The company also recognized that there was a marketing opportunity in diversifying and providing men's fashion underwear, women's underwear, socks, and T-shirts and sweats featuring the Fruit of the Loom name, which has a 98 percent recognition rate. Fruit of the Loom increased their annual advertising budget by $3 million and changed their strategy by positioning themselves as an apparel company. In 1982, boys' and men's white underwear accounted for 80 percent of the company's revenue; today the new business segments account for more than 40 percent of revenue, and this segment is growing. Fruit of the Loom's ability to recognize and capitalize on marketing opportunities has made it a market leader in the category (see Figure 18.5).[12]

Market requirements relate to the customers' needs or desired benefits. The market requirement is satisfied by components of the marketing mix that provide buyers with these benefits. Of course, buyers' perceptions of what requirements fill their needs and provide the desired benefits determine the success of any marketing effort. Marketers must devise strategies to outperform the competition by determining product attributes that buyers use to select products. An attribute must be

11. Derek F. Abell and John S. Hammond, *Strategic Market Planning* (Englewood Cliffs, N.J.: Prentice-Hall, 1979), p. 213.
12. Michael Oneal, "Fruit of the Loom Escalates the Underwars," *Business Week*, Feb. 22, 1988, pp. 114, 118.

FIGURE 18.5
Fruit of the Loom market share of unit sales, men's and boys' versus Hanes underwear (SOURCE: Reprinted from February 22, 1988 issue of *Business Week* by special permission, copyright © 1988 by McGraw-Hill, Inc.)

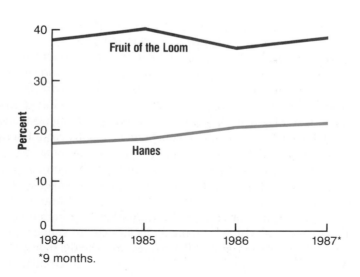

FIGURE 18.6

Lipton develops new products such as its Oriental Treasures Herbal Teas to appeal to different market segments (SOURCE: Courtesy Thomas J. Lipton, Inc.)

important and differentiating if it is to be useful in strategy development. Therefore, understanding buyer perceptions is the key to building a strategy based on important and differentiating attributes. For instance, Lipton (see Figure 18.6) has developed new products that appeal to varying market segments.

As we mention in Chapter 2, market requirements often change as competition offers new benefits to consumers. For example, Miller Brewing Company successfully segmented the beer-drinking market with the introduction of Miller Lite, the first successful light beer on the market. Miller Lite became the number-two beer behind Anheuser-Busch, Inc.'s Budweiser after its introduction, but then it grew only 1 percent in 1987, whereas Budweiser grew 3 percent and Bud Light increased 20.6 percent. To offset the declining market share from Lite, and Miller High Life, which is continuing to decline in volume, down approximately 14 percent in 1987, Miller is heavily promoting Genuine Draft, a beer touted to taste like draft beer. In addition, Miller has implemented a strategy of diversification, introducing Milwaukee's Best and Meister Brau as lower-priced brands. These two brands now account for 16.5 percent of Miller's output. But because of the lower margin on these products, Miller is changing its strategy to support premium brands, which provide a wider margin. Miller has test marketed a light version of Genuine Draft. Miller must act quickly to support a strategy to combat Anheuser-Busch, which holds a 39.7 percent market share.[13] Miller has differentiated its market into four categories: premium, conventional, light, and lower priced.

Environmental Monitoring

Environmental monitoring is seeking information about events and relationships in a company's outside environment, knowledge of which helps marketers identify opportunities and assists in planning.

Some corporations have derived substantial benefits from establishing an "environmental scanning (or monitoring) unit" within the strategic planning group or including line management in teams or committees to conduct environmental analysis.[14] Management is thus integrally involved in the process of environmental forecasting, and the likelihood of successfully integrating forecasting efforts into strategic market planning is considerably enhanced.[15] Results of forecasting research show that even simple quantitative forecasting techniques outperform the unstructured intuitive assessments of experts.[16]

Monitoring change in the environment is extremely important if a firm is to avoid crisis management. For example, an increasing number of Americans are becoming more and more health conscious, with a growing concern not only about calories but the amount of cholesterol and fat in their diet. Thus frozen yogurt chains have developed and expanded at an astounding rate. Frozen yogurt has the texture of ice cream yet only half the calories of premium ice creams. Major ice cream retail outlets such as Baskin Robbins and Dairy Queen have been monitoring the development of the yogurt chains, trying to determine if this is a fad or an ongoing demand among consumers. The major chains TCBY, Everything Yogurt, and Zack's Frozen Yogurt are independent organizations growing rapidly. Dairy Queen and Baskin Robbins are evaluating entrance into this market by gradually adding yogurt machines market by market or in limited test areas.[17] Lever Brothers Company monitors changing diet and eating habits to develop successful products (see Figure 18.7). New Promise sunflower oil and no-cholesterol spread are targeted for consumers who are concerned about their health.

An environmental change can suddenly alter a firm's opportunities or resources. Reformulated, more effective strategies may then be needed to guide marketing efforts. An environmental force such as technology can have far-reaching impact on diverse businesses. Because nearly every firm, including service firms, uses technology to provide buyers with benefits, it is imperative that organizations integrate technology considerations into their strategies. Companies do not have to be technology developers or leaders to benefit from technology change. Thus organizations must understand the position and role of technology in their strategies. This, however, does not necessarily mean that an organization should instantly respond

13. Michael Oneal, "Can A Marketing Man Make It Miller Time Again?" *Business Week,* Feb. 1, 1988, p. 26; Fran Brock, "High Life Turns to Low-key Approach," *Adweek,* Apr. 18, 1988, p. 6; Alix M. Freedman, "Miller Brewing to Test-Market New Light Beer," *Wall Street Journal,* Apr. 20, 1988, p. 24.
14. Liam Fahey, William K. King, and Vodake K. Naraganan, "Environmental Scanning and Forecasting in Strategic Planning—The State of the Art," *Long Range Planning,* February 1981, p. 38.
15. Ibid.
16. David M. Georgaff and Robert G. Mundick, "Managers Guide to Forecasting," *Harvard Business Review,* January–February 1986, p. 120.
17. Teresa Carson, "The Frozen Yogurt Race Is Red-Hot," *Business Week,* Mar. 7, 1988, p. 67.

to each technological development. Sometimes a firm is wise to not implement technological change too quickly if the change leads to a competitive disadvantage. General Motors Corp.'s decision to launch diesel engines in its automobiles before they were mechanically ready for the market proved to be a costly mistake.[18] The technologically inferior domestically produced diesel engine led to customer dissatisfaction and General Motors' great loss of customer loyalty. (The engines were converted gas engines—not "ground up" diesel engines. The stress from the extra compression caused mechanical difficulties, especially past 60,000 miles.) Environmental monitoring should identify new developments and determine the nature and rate of change.

Capabilities and Resources of the Firm

A firm's capabilities relate to distinctive competencies that it has developed to do something well and efficiently. For example, Citibank was one of the first banks to offer credit card services and promote this offering nationally. Now the bank card segment is too large for the current demand level, and competitors such as Citibank are trying to differentiate themselves from each other with free gifts, lower interest rates, waiver of annual fees, and identification with special interest groups. Citibank continues to be a leader by effectively distinguishing its products from those of its competitors.[19]

18. Alex Ben Block, "I've Put Everything on the Line," *Forbes,* Dec. 16, 1985, pp. 69, 70.
19. Patricia Winters, "Financial Services Marketing: Banks Play Trump Cards in Credit Fights," *Advertising Age,* Aug. 3, 1987, pp. S10–S12.

FIGURE 18.7
Lever Brothers Company monitors the environment to develop new products that relate to current health trends (SOURCE: Courtesy of Lever Brothers Company)

Create a new world where lightweight plastics can outfly metals.

Aerospace designers are limited by their materials, not their dreams.

At BASF, we looked at the design limitations of metals and saw the need for a radically new generation of materials. The result: strong, lightweight, carbon fiber reinforced plastics. These Advanced Composite Materials will enable future designs to carry more, faster, farther.

In one industry after another, from aerospace to automotive, our broad-based technologies help us create new worlds by seeing in new ways.

The Spirit of Innovation

BASF

FIGURE 18.8

BASF used its techno-
logical resources to de-
velop a new plastic
with uses in many in-
dustries (SOURCE:
BASF Corporation)

A company is likely to enjoy a differential advantage in an area where its competencies outmatch those of its potential competition.[20] Often a company may possess manufacturing or technical skills that are valuable in areas outside of its
traditional industry. For example, BASF (see Figure 18.8), known for its manufacturing and development of audio and video tapes, developed a new type of lightweight plastic that has uses in other industries.

Today marketing planners are especially concerned with resource constraints.
Due to shortages in energy and other scarce economic resources, strategic planning
options are often limited. On the other hand, planning to avoid shortages can
backfire. For example, early in the 1980s, 7-Eleven's parent company, the Southland Corporation, purchased Citgo Petroleum Corp. Southland's strategy was to
become more vertically integrated and avoid gasoline shortages. But Southland's
marketing research and environmental monitoring did not reveal that overcapacity
and falling demand would cause an oversupply and that the price of gasoline would
drop dramatically. The result was that Southland could have purchased gasoline
more cheaply on the spot market than refine it through Citgo. Yet the firm's
strategy has not been a complete failure. The purchase of Citgo has increased 7-
Eleven's gasoline sales, which in turn has drawn more customers into the stores,
increasing total sales and profits. Also, if there is ever again a gasoline shortage,
Southland will be prepared to weather the crisis.[21]

20. Philip Kotler, "Strategic Planning and the Marketing Process," *Business*, May–June 1980, pp. 6–7.
21. Steve Klinkerman, "Why Southland Won't Unload Its Albatross," *Business Week*, July 1, 1985,
p. 71.

Table 18.1 is a framework for viewing opportunities and resources in different planning periods. This framework suggests that individual firms face four distinct planning horizons, each constrained to a different degree in regard to resources, social concerns, and government regulations.[22] These constraints increase from the present to the intermediate long-range period, with resource constraints possibly declining thereafter as radically new technologies and resource applications become commercially available. Crucial to the usefulness of this framework is the ability to predict future technological developments or at least the likely direction of future breakthroughs. For example, the projected direction of technological innovation could, in effect, suggest the strategic horizons firms and industries face, in which case technological forecasting could be a crucial element in the strategic planning process.

Costs (resulting from various technology/resource combinations) and benefits must go through a series of modifications or extensions as constraints become more severe. As we have already pointed out, scarce resources are not always constraints; they may provide the impetus a firm needs to provide benefits at the most desirable cost. For example, Transamerica Corporation attempts to be a low-cost marketer by reducing costs because its products are closely related and because of operating efficiencies between complementary businesses the firm owns. Transamerica seeks to maximize the benefits of diversification and maintain a compatible mix of companies. This strategy permits the company to provide products (benefits) at resource/technology combinations (costs) to achieve industry leadership in service, reputation, innovation, and overall efficiency.

TABLE 18.1

Framework for viewing resource constraints and opportunities in different planning periods

22. This section is reprinted by permission from *Business* magazine. "Strategic Planning Under Resource Constraints," by Jacob Naor, September–October 1981, p. 17. Copyright © 1981 by the College of Business Administration, Georgia State University, Atlanta.

Present
(few or no resource constraints)
Current products (*benefits*) produced and supplied at currently feasible[a] technology/resource combinations (*costs*)

Intermediate/long-range horizon (extremely severe resource and social-governmental constraints)
Extensively modified products (*benefits*) that will be demanded at *costs* based on feasible[a] major modifications of current resource/technology combinations

Short/intermediate-range horizon (increasingly severe resource and social-governmental constraints)
Somewhat modified products (*benefits*) that will be demanded at *costs* based on feasible[a] extensions of current technology/resource combinations

Long-range horizon (resource constraints disappearing, continuing severe social-governmental constraints)
Products (*benefits*) that will be demanded at *costs* based on feasible[a] new resources/new technology combinations

a. Most advantageous to the corporation in terms of its long-run organizational goals.

SOURCE: Reprinted by permission from *Business* magazine, "Strategic Planning Under Resource Constraints," by Jacob Naor, September–October 1981, p. 18. Copyright 1981 by the College of Business Administration, Georgia State University, Atlanta.

Corporate Strategy

Corporate strategy defines the means and direction of reaching organizational goals. The resources of the corporation are matched with the opportunities and risks in the environment. Corporate strategy attempts to define the scope and role of the strategic business units of the firm that are coordinated to reach the ends desired. Xerox, for example, focuses on reprographics (photocopying, electronic printers), office systems, and work stations. The acquisition of Crum & Forster, a leading property and liability insurance company, represented a major change in the direction of Xerox and provided new opportunities and risks. Xerox does not engage in businesses to produce robots, automobiles, or earth-moving equipment because such products do not fit into the corporate strategy.

A corporate strategy determines not only the scope of the business but its resource deployment, competitive advantages, and overall coordination of production, finance, marketing, and other functional areas. For example, Black & Decker Mfg. Co.'s traditional corporate strategy has been to provide customized power tools for specialized markets. But many Japanese manufacturers are providing standardized products worldwide, taking a significant portion of Black & Decker's former market share. Black & Decker has responded by developing a global manufacturing and marketing strategy that has cut the number of production centers from eight to two and produces fewer specialized professional power tools. Black & Decker also acquired General Electric Co. small appliances and is now producing these home appliances under its own name. The firm hopes the diversification will compensate for the temporary flattening in the professional power tool market.[23] Competition, diversification, and the interrelationships among marketing, manufacturing, and financial considerations are corporate strategy concerns.

Marketing Objective

A **marketing objective** is a statement of what is to be accomplished through marketing activities. It specifies the results expected from marketing efforts. It should be expressed in clear, simple terms so that all marketing personnel understand exactly what they are to try to achieve. It should be written in such a way that its accomplishment can be measured accurately. If a company has an objective of increasing its market share by 12 percent, the firm should be able to measure changes in its market share accurately. A marketing objective should also indicate the time frame for accomplishing the objective. For example, a firm that sets an objective of introducing three new products should state the time period in which this is to be done.

A marketing manager who fails to set marketing objectives consistent with the firm's general goals will be less likely to accomplish the marketing objectives. Also, this action may work against the achievement of the firm's overall goals. Suppose a marketing manager sets an objective that requires greater use of consumer credit,

23. Christopher S. Eklund, "Why Black & Decker Is Cutting Itself Down to Size," *Business Week,* Nov. 25, 1985, pp. 42, 44.

but an overall goal of the firm is to reduce bad-debt loss: The two objectives probably will conflict.

Consider the corporate strategy of Transamerica Corporation: Transamerica should focus on key market segments related to primary businesses, including insurance and financial services, travel services, and the manufacturing of precision engineered products used in industry. "A key dimension of Transamerica is the value added to our operating companies from being part of a larger corporation."[24] This is obviously a corporate strategy because it indicates the overall thrust of the corporation. Now take a look at a marketing objective of the same corporation:

Achieve a significant market share in each segment of our businesses.[25]

It is evident that achieving a significant market share is a statement of what is to be accomplished through marketing activities. This marketing objective is clear and can be measured accurately once it is quantified. For example, to achieve a 25 percent market share in each segment of Transamerica's businesses in the next three years would explain exactly what is to be accomplished and when it is to be done. Also note that the corporate strategy and the marketing objective are consistent. Transamerica Corporation maintains a staff group to focus on strategic planning. Besides setting corporate goals, corporate strategy, and marketing objectives, Transamerica's planning actions encompass all the strategic market planning activities described in this chapter.

Marketing Strategy and Marketing Planning

Marketing strategy focuses on defining a target market and developing a marketing mix to gain long-run competitive and consumer advantages. (The Application on page 645 illustrates the impact of marketing strategy development on K mart's image and sales.) There is a degree of overlap between corporate strategy and marketing strategy. Marketing strategy is unique in that it has the responsibility to assess buyer needs and the firm's potential for gaining competitive advantage, both of which ultimately must guide the corporate mission.[26] In other words, marketing strategy guides the firm's direction in relationships between customers and competitors. The bottom line is that a marketing strategy must be consistent with consumer needs, perceptions, and beliefs. From the perspective of marketing strategy development, there must be actual assessment of buyer responses to strategic options. Marketing management, on the other hand, is more directly concerned with design and implementation of the marketing strategy.[27] Managing the sales force is a marketing management concern.

Marketing management is a process of planning, organizing, implementing, and controlling marketing activities to facilitate and expedite exchanges effectively and efficiently. "Effectively," an important dimension of our definition, is the degree

24. Transamerica *1982 Annual Report*, 1983, p. 5.
25. Ibid.
26. Yoram Wind and Thomas S. Robertson, "Marketing Strategy: New Directions for Theory and Research," *Journal of Marketing*, Spring 1983, p. 12.
27. Ibid.

K mart Changes Its Marketing Strategy

An organization must develop a marketing strategy to reach its marketing objectives. Occasionally, however, an organization may have to alter its strategy to meet changing organizational goals. K mart Corporation, the nation's second largest retailer, recently altered its corporate strategy by selling most of its domestic Kresge and Jupiter stores to the McCrory Corporation (which owns the TG&Y and Newberry chains). (The sale will not affect its Waldenbooks and Pay Less Drug Stores.) K mart wants to concentrate on improving the image of its namesake stores by increasing the variety and quality of goods sold in the stores. Barbara J. Palazzolo, K mart director of public relations, said, "The sale of the Kresge stores is a small move financially, but a big step symbolically. The sale of the Kresge and Jupiter stores tells we're narrowing in on a merchandising and marketing focus."

The Kresge and Jupiter stores were part of the K mart organization for many years. In fact, the company's name was S. S. Kresge Co. until 1977, when it was officially changed to K mart Corporation. However, Kresge and Jupiter are five-and-dime variety stores and do not fit in with K mart's new image; in particular the Kresge chain had been profitable but did not meet corporate growth plans. Nevertheless, K mart will continue to operate some sixty Kresge and Jupiter stores in the United States and Canada.

K mart's new marketing strategy focuses on new products and promotion. The company is upgrading the appearance of its stores in an attempt to regain middle-class customers (those whose incomes range from $15,000 to $60,000) lost to other retail stores. To appeal to these customers, the company is stocking its stores with higher quality goods and name-brand items, such as Samsonite and Black & Decker.

One of the most successful aspects of K mart's new multipart marketing strategy is its emphasis on clothing operations. The strategy includes advertising in high-fashion magazines such as *Vogue,* installing new fashion displays in its stores, and introducing its Jaclyn Smith line of women's clothing. K mart is also upgrading its men's apparel, especially outerwear, with the introduction of the Campus Sportswear line. These strategy changes have helped transform apparel into one of K mart's strongest sections. The company plans to increase its emphasis on apparel with more space in future K mart stores.

K mart is also adding banking services to its roster of activities. Forty-three stores already offer retail banking services, and the company plans to offer banking services in at least 150 more stores. K mart hopes the banking services will draw even more customers into the store, and perhaps the convenience of the service will encourage customers to purchase more items while they are in the store.

K mart has changed its corporate strategy and focused on its most profitable retail chain, the K mart stores. The corporation has partly implemented its new marketing strategy by focusing on a larger variety of goods in its flagship K mart stores.

SOURCES: Joe Agnew, "K mart Celebrates 25 Years with Revitalization of Marketing Strategy and Severing Its Kresge Roots," *Marketing News,* Apr. 24, 1987, pp. 1, 6; John Bussey, "K mart Is Set to Sell Many of Its Roots to Rapid-American Corp.'s McCrory," *Wall Street Journal,* Apr. 6, 1987, p. 28; Lebhar-Friedman, Inc., *Inside Retailing,* July 1987; Patricia Strand, "K mart Dresses Up Its Men's Wear," *Advertising Age,* Nov. 3, 1986, p. 28.

to which an exchange furthers an organization's objectives. "Efficiently" is the minimization of the resources that an organization must expend to achieve a specific level of desirable exchanges. Thus the purpose of the marketing management process is to facilitate highly desirable exchanges and to minimize as much as possible the costs of doing so.

As we noted at the start, this chapter deals with the planning part of the marketing management definition. So far, we have discussed strategic market planning. In this section we describe how the strategic plan is implemented. **Marketing planning** is a systematic process that involves assessing marketing opportunities and resources, determining marketing objectives, and developing a plan for implementation and control. A **marketing plan** includes the framework and entire set of activities to be performed; it is the written document or blueprint for implementing and controlling an organization's marketing activities. A firm should have a plan for each marketing strategy it develops. Because a firm's plans must be changed as forces in the firm and the environment change, marketing planning is a continuous process.

Because most organizations have existing plans and are engaged in ongoing activities, marketing managers must start with an organization's current situation and performance and then assess future marketing opportunities and constraints. The planning process calls for information about the difference, if any, between objectives and current performance. Probable performance in the future should be assessed; then the current marketing strategy can be altered or objectives changed if forecasted performance does not meet desired objectives in the next planning period. Figure 18.9 illustrates the **marketing planning cycle.** Note that marketing planning is a circular process. As the dotted feedback lines in the figure indicate, planning is not unidirectional. Feedback is used to coordinate and synchronize all stages of the planning cycle.

When formulating a marketing plan, a new enterprise or a firm with a new product does not have current performance to evaluate or an existing plan to revise. Therefore, its marketing planning centers on analyzing available resources and options to assess opportunities. Managers can then develop marketing objectives and a strategy. In addition, many firms recognize the need to include information systems in their plans so that they can have continuous feedback and keep their marketing activities oriented toward objectives. (Information systems are discussed in Chapter 6.)

To illustrate the marketing planning process, consider the decisions that went into the planning of the introduction of a national newspaper, *USA Today*. Table 18.2 lists several of the more important marketing decisions. Of course, to reach the objective, a detailed course of action was communicated throughout the organization. In short, specific marketing plans should do the following:

1. Specify expected results so that the organization can anticipate what its situation will be at the end of the current planning period
2. Identify the resources needed to carry out the planned activities so that a budget can be developed
3. Describe in sufficient detail the activities that are to take place so that responsibilities for implementation can be assigned
4. Provide for the monitoring of activities and results so that control can be exerted[28]

28. David J. Luck, O. C. Ferrell, and George Lucas, *Marketing Strategy and Plans,* 3rd ed. © 1989. Adapted by permission of Prentice-Hall, Inc., Englewood Cliffs, N.J.

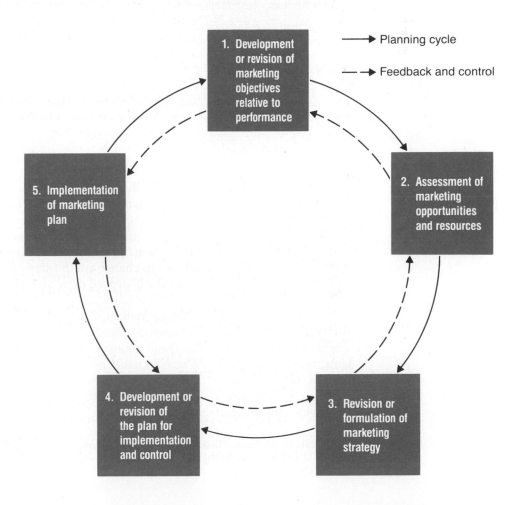

FIGURE 18.9

The marketing planning cycle

Objective: Achieve 1 million in circulation by reaching an upscale market, primarily of males who hold professional and managerial positions and who made at least one trip of 200 miles or more within the last year.

Opportunity: Paper tends to be a second newspaper purchase for readers. *USA Today* is not in competition directly with local papers, and it is not positioned against other national newspapers/magazines.

Market: Circulation within a 200-mile radius of 15 major markets, representing 54% of the U.S. population, including such cities as Chicago, Houston, New York, Los Angeles, and Denver.

Product: Superior graphic quality; appeal to the TV generation through short stories, a color weather map, and other contemporary features.

Price: Competitive.

Promotion: Pedestal-like vending machines with attention-grabbing design and a higher position than competitors to differentiate the paper and bring it closer to eye level. Outdoor advertising and some print advertising promotes the paper.

Distribution: Newsstand, vending machines in high-traffic locations, and direct mail.

Implementation and control: Personnel with experience in the newspaper business who can assist in developing a systematic approach for implementing the marketing strategy and design as well as an information system to monitor and control the results.

SOURCE: Kevin Higgins, "*USA Today* Nears Million Reader Mark," *Marketing News,* Apr. 15, 1983, pp. 1, 5. Reprinted by permission of the American Marketing Association.

The duration of marketing plans varies. Plans that cover a period of one year or less are called **short-range plans. Medium-range plans** usually encompass two to five years. Marketing plans that extend for more than five years are generally viewed as **long-range plans.** These plans can sometimes cover a period as long as twenty years. Marketing managers may have short-, medium-, and long-range plans all at the same time. Long-range plans are relatively rare. However, as the marketing environment continues to change and business decisions become more complex, profitability and survival will depend more and more on the development of long-range plans.[29]

The extent to which marketing managers develop and use plans also varies. Although planning provides numerous benefits, some managers do not use formal marketing plans because they spend almost all their time dealing with daily problems, many of which would be eliminated by adequate planning. However, planning is becoming more important to marketing managers, who realize that planning is necessary to develop, coordinate, and control marketing activities effectively and efficiently.

29. Ronald D. Michman, "Linking Futuristics with Marketing Planning, Forecasting, and Strategy," *Journal of Consumer Marketing,* Summer 1984, pp. 17–23.

Approaches to Strategic Market Planning

In recent years, marketing managers have developed target market/marketing mixes, sometimes called product/market matching approaches to strategic market planning. Because these approaches to planning are widely used today, let us focus briefly on three approaches that can be useful in structuring the overall strategic market plan. The Boston Consulting Group (BCG) product-portfolio analysis and the market attractiveness-business position model are popular approaches to strategic planning. The Profit Impact on Marketing Strategy (PIMS) project provides data to help direct strategic market planning efforts.

The Boston Consulting Group (BCG) Product-Portfolio Analysis

Product-portfolio analysis, the BCG approach, is based on the philosophy that a product's market growth rate and its relative market share are important considerations in determining its marketing strategy. All the firm's products should be integrated into a single, overall matrix and evaluated to determine appropriate strategies for individual SBUs and the overall portfolio strategies. Just as financial investors have different investments with varying risks and rates of return, firms have a range of products characterized by different market growth rates and relative market shares. However, a balanced product-portfolio matrix is the end result of a number of actions, not the result of the analysis alone. Portfolio models can be created based on present and projected market growth rate and proposed market share strategies (build share, maintain share, harvest share, or divest business). Managers can use these models to determine and classify each product's expected future cash contributions and future cash requirements.

Generally, managers who use a portfolio model must examine the competitive position of a product (or product line) and the opportunities for improving that product's contribution to profitability and cash flow.[30] The BCG analytical approach is more of a diagnostic tool than a guide for making strategy prescriptions. The Application on page 651 reviews Hasbro's successful product portfolio.

Figure 18.10, which is based on work by the BCG, enables the marketing manager to classify a firm's products into four basic types: stars, cash cows, dogs, and problem children.[31] Stars are products with a dominant share of the market and good prospects for growth; they generally generate a lot of cash, but they are used to finance growth, add capacity, and increase market share. Cash cows have a dominant share of the market but low prospects for growth; typically they generate more cash than is required to maintain market share. Dogs have a subordinate share of the market and low prospects for growth; these products are often found in mature markets. Problem children have a subordinate share of a growing market and generally require a large amount of cash to build share.

The growth-share matrix in Figure 18.10 can be expanded as in Figure 18.11 to show a firm's whole portfolio by providing for each product (1) its dollar sales volume, illustrated by the size of a circle on the matrix; (2) its market share relative

30. Joseph P. Guiltinan and Gordon W. Paul, *Marketing Management: Strategies and Programs* (New York: McGraw-Hill, 1982), p. 31.
31. George S. Day, "Diagnosing the Product Portfolio," *Journal of Marketing* (American Marketing Association), April 1977, pp. 30–31.

to competition, represented by the horizontal position of the product on the matrix, and (3) the growth rate of the market, indicated by the position of the product in the vertical direction. Figure 18.11 illustrates the growth-share matrix for Miller Brewing Company. As discussed earlier, Miller Lite grew only 1 percent in 1987, but it still has a high market share. Therefore it is a cash cow. Miller Genuine Draft

FIGURE 18.10

Illustrative growth-share matrix developed by the Boston Consulting Group (SOURCE: Adapted from "The Product Portfolio," Perspectives no. 66, The Boston Consulting Group, Inc., 1970. See also George Day, "Diagnosing the Product Portfolio," *Journal of Marketing,* April 1977, pp. 29–38)

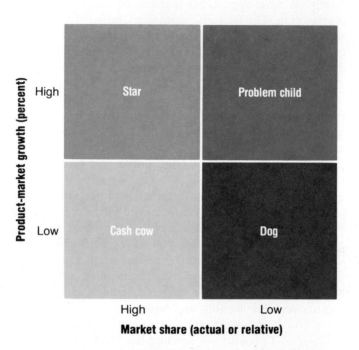

FIGURE 18.11

Illustrative growth-share matrix for Miller Brewing Company

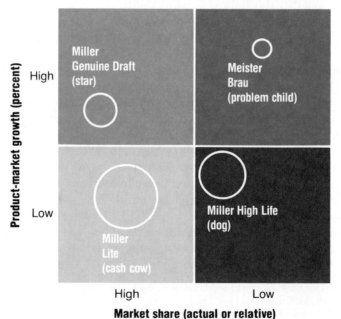

The area of each circle represents dollar sales of the product on the matrix.

Hasbro Finds Success with Balanced Product Portfolio

According to the product-portfolio analysis developed by the Boston Consulting Group, a product's market growth rate and its relative market share are important considerations in determining its marketing strategy. Thus marketing managers can create a portfolio model for a product based on its present and projected market growth rate and proposed market share strategies. In addition, organizations usually try to manage their product portfolios to achieve strategic objectives while at the same time minimizing risk and optimizing return. One company that has been successful at this is Hasbro, Inc.

Hasbro's products are among the leaders in the American toy industry. In fact, in 1987 they had thirty-four of the top one hundred products, including G.I. Joe, Jem, and the Transformers. Hasbro has firmly established itself as the worldwide leader in the toy industry, although the industry has not experienced much growth in the last few years.

The development of new products is a major factor behind Hasbro's success. The company balances its product portfolio among its major product categories. The development of new items helps Hasbro raise consumer interest and extend successful product lines. The introduction of new products for both adults and children, such as accessories for My Little Pony and the popular adult game A Question of Scruples, have further enhanced Hasbro's success.

The company attempts to manage its product portfolio to avoid depending on a single item or product line. For example, in 1982, the company earned $49 million from the sale of G.I. Joe products, 36 percent of the company's revenue that year. But chief executive Stephen Hassenfeld decided to invest G.I. Joe's profits into other toy ventures rather than depend on Joe's continued success, which ultimately depends on children's whims. Hasbro's philosophy has resulted in the development of one of the most extensive range of products in the industry, with a portfolio that includes Hasbro, Milton Bradley, and Playskool. These lines are the leaders in the industry's five major categories: infant and preschool products, games and puzzles, girls' toys and dolls, plush products, and boys' action toys.

Hasbro also relies on well-made products and extensive advertising to market its portfolio. Children (and the parents who buy the toys) have traditionally enjoyed Hasbro products because of their durability. The company illustrated its advertising savvy in the marketing of its Jem/Jerrica doll, who wears fashionable ("rad") clothes and sings in a rock band. The doll even got her own Saturday morning cartoon "video show." Hasbro currently employs three different agencies to advertise its products and plans to increase that number.

is a star because it is growing fast in market share in a new premium draft market but requires significant resources for continued growth. Miller High Life is a dog because it has lost 60 percent in market share since 1981 in a low-growth market. Milwaukee's Best is a problem child because it is gaining in market share but its low margin makes its role in the product portfolio uncertain.[32] Figure 18.12 suggests marketing strategies appropriate for each of the four basic types of products: cash cows, stars, dogs, and problem children.

The long-run health of the corporation depends on having some products that generate cash (and provide acceptable reported profits) and others that use cash to support growth. Among the indicators of overall health are the size and vulnerability of the cash cows, the prospects for the stars, if any, and the number of problem children and dogs. Particular attention must be paid to those products with large cash appetites. Unless the company has an abundant cash flow, it cannot afford to sponsor many such products at one time. If resources, including debt capacity, are spread too thin, the company simply will wind up with too many marginal products and suffer a reduced capacity to finance promising new product entries or acquisitions in the future.

Market Attractiveness– Business Position Model

The **market attractiveness–business position model,** illustrated in Figure 18.13, is a two-dimensional matrix. The vertical dimension, *market attractiveness,* includes all strengths and resources that relate to the market, such as seasonality, economies of scale, competitive intensity, industry sales, and the overall cost and feasibility of entering the market. The horizontal axis, *business position,* is a composite of factors such as sales, relative market share, research and development, price competitiveness, product quality, and market knowledge as they relate to the product in building market share. A slight variation of this matrix is called General Electric's Strategic Business Planning Grid because General Electric is credited for extending the product-portfolio planning tool to examine market attractiveness and business strength. The best situation is for a firm to have a strong business position in an attractive market.

32. Michael Oneal, "Can a Marketing Man Make It Miller Time Again," *Business Week,* Feb. 1, 1988, p. 21.

FIGURE 18.12

Characteristics and
strategies for the four
basic product types in
the growth-share ma-
trix (SOURCE: Con-
cepts in this figure
adapted from George
S. Day, "Diagnosing
the Product Portfolio,"
Journal of Marketing,
April 1977, pp. 30–31)

Product-market growth

High

Low

Market share

High   Low

Stars

Characteristics

- Market leaders
- Fast growing
- Substantial profits
- Require large investment to finance growth

Strategies

- Protect existing share
- Reinvest earnings in the form of price reductions, product improvements, providing better market coverage, production efficiency, etc.
- Obtain a large share of the new users

Problem children

Characteristics

- Rapid growth
- Poor profit margins
- Enormous demand for cash

Strategies

- Invest heavily to get a disproportionate share of new sales
- Buy existing market shares by acquiring competitors
- Divestment (see Dogs)
- Harvesting (see Dogs)
- Abandonment (see Dogs)
- Focus on a definable niche where dominance can be achieved

Cash cows

Characteristics

- Profitable products
- Generate more cash than needed to maintain market share

Strategies

- Maintain market dominance
- Invest in process improvements and technological leadership
- Maintain price leadership
- Use excess cash to support research and growth elsewhere in the company

Dogs

Characteristics

- Greatest number of products fall in this category
- Operate at a cost disadvantage
- Few opportunities for growth at a reasonable cost
- Markets are not growing; therefore, little new business

Strategies

- Focus on a specialized segment of the market that can be dominated and protected from competitive inroads
- Harvesting—cut back all support costs to a minimum level; supports cash flow over the product's remaining life
- Divestment—sale of a growing concern
- Abandonment—deletion from the product line

FIGURE 18.13

FIGURE 18.13
Market attractiveness–business position matrix (SOURCE: Adapted from Derek F. Abell and John S. Hammond, *Strategic Market Planning: Problems and Analytical Approaches,* © 1979, p. 213. Reprinted by permission of Prentice-Hall, Inc., Englewood Cliffs, N.J.)

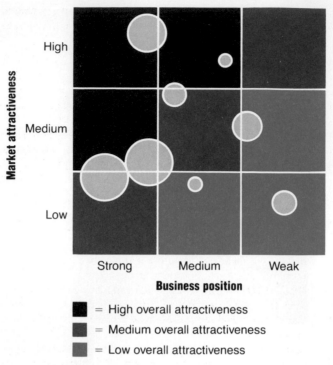

= High overall attractiveness

= Medium overall attractiveness

= Low overall attractiveness

The area of each circle represents the relative dollar sales on the matrix.

The upper left area in Figure 18.13 represents the opportunity for an invest/grow strategy, but the matrix does not indicate how to implement this strategy. The purpose of the model is to serve as a diagnostic tool to highlight SBUs that have an opportunity to grow or that should be divested or approached selectively. SBUs that occupy the invest/grow position can lose their position through faulty marketing strategies.

Decisions on resource allocation in regard to SBUs characterized by medium overall attractiveness should be arrived at on a basis relative to other SBUs that are either more attractive or less attractive. The lower right area of the matrix is a low-growth harvest/divest area. Harvesting is a gradual withdrawal of marketing resources on the assumption that sales will decline at a slow rate but profits will still be significant at a lower sales volume. Harvesting and divesting may be appropriate strategies for SBUs characterized by low overall attractiveness. For example, Westinghouse has decided to place less emphasis (harvest) on medium- and low-attractiveness sectors in utility businesses in favor of sectors with high overall attractiveness, such as services, cable television, robotics, and defense electronics.[33]

Profit Impact on Marketing Strategy (PIMS)

The Strategic Planning Institute (SPI) developed a databank of information on more than 1,700 products that members provide for the **Profit Impact on Marketing Strategy (PIMS)** research program. More than two hundred member firms of

33. "Operation Turnaround," *Business Week*, Dec. 5, 1983, p. 124.

the institute provide confidential information on successes, failures, and marginal products. Figure 18.14 shows a PIMS data form. The data are analyzed to provide reports for members on strategy.

Table 18.3 shows the types of information provided on each business in the PIMS data base. The results of PIMS include both diagnostic and prescriptive information to assist in analyzing marketing performance and formulating marketing strategies. The analysis focuses on options, problems, resources, and opportunities. The unit of observation in PIMS is an SBU.

The data on member firms' experiences have proved useful for evaluating current marketing strategies and examining alternatives. The following nine major strategic influences on profitability and net cash flow have been identified:

1. *Investment intensity.* Technology and the chosen way of doing business govern how much fixed capital and working capital are required to produce a dollar of sales or a dollar of value added in the business. Investment intensity generally produces a negative impact on percentage measures of profitability or net cash flow; i.e., businesses that are mechanized or automated or inventory-intensive generally show lower returns on investment and sales than businesses that are not.

2. *Productivity.* Businesses producing high value added per employee are more profitable than those with low value added per employee. (Definition: "value added" is the amount by which the firm increases the market value of raw materials and components it buys.)

3. *Market position.* A business's share of its served market (both absolute and relative to its three largest competitors) has a positive impact on its profit and net cash flow. (The "served market" is the specific segment of the total potential market—defined in terms of products, customers, or areas—in which the business actually competes.)

4. *Growth of the served market.* Growth is generally favorable to dollar measures of profit, indifferent to percent measures of profit, and negative to all measures of net cash flow.

5. *Quality of the products and/or services offered.* Quality, defined as the customers' evaluation of the business's product/service package as compared to that of competitors, has a generally favorable impact on all measures of financial performance.

6. *Innovation/differentiation.* Extensive actions taken by a business in the areas of new product introduction, R&D, marketing effort, and so on, generally produce a positive effect on its performance if that business has strong market position to begin with. Otherwise usually not.

7. *Vertical integration.* For businesses located in mature and stable markets, vertical integration (i.e., make rather than buy) generally impacts favorably on performance. In markets that are rapidly growing, declining, or otherwise changing, the opposite is true.

8. *Cost push.* The rates of increase of wages, salaries, and raw material prices, and the presence of a labor union, have complex impacts on profit and cash flow, depending on how the business is positioned to pass along the increase to its customers and/or absorb the higher costs internally.

9. *Current strategic effort.* The current direction of change of any of the above factors has effects on profit and cash flow that are frequently opposite to that of the factor itself. For example, having strong market share tends to increase net cash flow, but getting share drains cash while the business is making that effort.

Additionally, there is such a thing as being a good or a poor "operator." A good operator can improve the profitability of a strong strategic position or minimize the damage of a weak one; a poor operator does the opposite. The presence of a management team that functions as a good operator is therefore a favorable element of a business and produces a financial result greater than one would expect from the strategic position of the business alone.[34]

Significance of Strategic Market Planning Approaches

The Boston Consulting Group's portfolio analysis, the market attractiveness–business position model, and the Profit Impact on Marketing Strategy studies of the Strategic Planning Institute are planning tools only. They should not be viewed as strategic solutions but as diagnostic aids, which is all they are intended to be. The emphasis should be on making sound decisions using these analytical tools.[35]

34. *The PIMS Letter on Business Strategy No. 1* (Cambridge, Mass.: The Strategic Planning Institute, 1977), pp. 3–5. Reproduced by permission of the Strategic Planning Institute (PIMS Program), Cambridge, Massachusetts.
35. David W. Cravens, "Strategic Marketing's New Challenge," *Business Horizons,* March–April 1983, p. 19.

FIGURE 18.14

Sample page from PIMS data forms (SOURCE: PIMS Data Form reproduced by permission of the Strategic Planning Institute [PIMS Program], Cambridge, Massachusetts, 1979)

103: "LIFE CYCLE" STAGE OF PRODUCT CATEGORY

How would you describe the stage of development of the types of products or services sold by this business during the last three years? *(Check one)*

... Introductory Stage: Primary demand for product just starting to grow; products or services still unfamiliar to many potential users ☐ 1

... Growth Stage: Demand growing at 10% or more annually in real terms; technology or competitive structure still changing ☐ 2

... Maturity Stage: Products or services familiar to vast majority of prospective users; technology and competitive structure reasonably stable ☐ 3

... Decline Stage: Products viewed as commodities; weaker competitors beginning to exit ☐ 4

104: What was this business's first year of commercial sales? *(Check one)*

Prior to 1930	1930-1949	1950-1954	1955-1959	1960-1964	1965-1969	1970-1974	1975-
☐ 0	☐ 1	☐ 2	☐ 3	☐ 4	☐ 5	☐ 6	☐ 7

105: At the time this business first entered the market, was it... *(Check one)*

... One of the pioneers in first developing such products or services? ☐ 1

... An early follower of the pioneer(s) in a still growing, dynamic market? ☐ 2

... A later entrant into a more established market situation? ☐ 3

106-107: PATENTS AND TRADE SECRETS

Does this business benefit *to a significant degree* from patents, trade secrets, or other proprietary methods of production or operation...

106: Pertaining to products or services?   NO ☐ 0   YES ☐ 1   **107:** Pertaining to processes?   NO ☐ 0   YES ☐ 1

108: STANDARDIZATION OF PRODUCTS OR SERVICES

Are the products or services of this business... *(Check one)*

... More or less standardized for all customers? ☐ 0

... Designed or produced to order for individual customers? ☐ 1

109: FREQUENCY OF PRODUCT CHANGES

Is it typical practice for the business and its major competitors to change all or part of the line of products or services offered... *(Check one)*

... Annually (for example, annual model changes)? ☐ 1

... Seasonally? ☐ 2

... Periodically, but at intervals longer than one year? ☐ 3

... No regular, periodic pattern of change? ☐ 4

110: TECHNOLOGICAL CHANGE

Have there been *major* technological changes in the products offered by the business or its major competitors, or in methods of production, during the last 8 years? *(If in doubt about whether a change was "major," answer NO.)*   NO ☐ 0   YES ☐ 1

Characteristics of the business environment	Structure of the production process
Long-run growth rate of the market	Capital intensity (degree of automation, etc.)
Short-run growth rate of the market	Degree of vertical integration
Rate of inflation of selling price levels	Capacity utilization
Number and size of customers	Productivity of capital equipment
Purchase frequency and magnitude	Productivity of people
	Inventory levels
Competitive position of the business	
Share of the served market	**Discretionary budget allocations**
Share relative to largest competitors	R&D budgets
Product quality relative to competitors	Advertising and promotion budgets
Prices relative to competitors	Sales force expenditures
Pay scales relative to competitors	
Marketing efforts relative to competitors	**Strategic moves**
Pattern of market segmentation	Patterns of change in the controllable elements
Rate of new product introductions	above
	Operating results
	Profitability results
	Cash flow results
	Growth results

SOURCE: Reproduced by permission of the Strategic Planning Institute (PIMS Program), Cambridge, Mass.

TABLE 18.3

Types of information provided on each business in the PIMS database

The key to understanding the approaches to strategic market planning described in this chapter is recognition that strategic market planning takes into account all aspects of an organization's strategy in the marketplace. Whereas most of this book is about functional decisions and strategies of marketing as a part of business, this chapter focuses on the recognition that all functional strategies, including marketing, production, and finance, must be coordinated to reach organizational goals. Results of a survey, sponsored by the *Harvard Business Review,* of top industrial firms indicate that portfolio planning and other depersonalized planning techniques help managers strengthen their planning process and solve the problems of managing diversified industrial companies. However, the results also indicate that analytical techniques alone do not result in success. Management must blend this analysis with managerial judgment to deal with the reality of the existing situation.

One word of caution in regard to the use of portfolio approaches is necessary. The classification of SBUs into a specific portfolio position is dependent on four factors: (1) the operational definition of the matrix dimensions; (2) the rules used to divide a dimension into high and low categories; (3) the weighting of the variables used in composite dimensions, if composite dimensions are used; and (4) the specific model used.[36] In other words, changes in any of these four factors may well result in different classification for a single SBU.

There are other approaches to strategic market planning besides those discussed here. For example, for many years marketing planners have used the product life cycle discussed in Chapters 7 and 8. Many firms have their own approaches to

36. Yoram Wind, Vijay Mahajan, and Donald J. Swire, "An Empirical Comparison of Standardized Portfolio Models," *Journal of Marketing,* Spring 1983, pp. 89–99.

planning that incorporate, to varying degrees, some of the approaches that we have discussed. All strategic planning approaches have some similarity in that several of the components of strategic market planning outlined in Figure 18.3 (especially market/product relationships) are related to a plan of action for reaching objectives. The PIMS project makes a major contribution by providing data gathered from a broad range of companies to draw conclusions about strategic market planning.

The approaches presented here give you an overview of the most popular analytical methods used in strategic market planning. These approaches are supplements to, not substitutes for, the marketing manager's own judgment. The real test of each approach, or any integrated approach, is how well it helps management diagnose the firm's strengths and weaknesses and prescribe strategic actions for maintaining or improving performance. At many companies, management has moved strategic market planning to the top of its list of corporate priorities for the 1980s. The issues of product/market share definition, strategic information procurement, and organizational change will inevitably grow in importance as a result of increased use of strategic market planning concepts.[37]

Competitive Strategies for Marketing

After evaluating business operations and business performance, the next step in strategic planning is to determine future business directions and develop marketing strategies. A business may choose competitive strategies. Figure 18.15 shows competitive strategy on a product-market matrix. This matrix can be helpful in determining growth that can be implemented through marketing strategies.

Intense Growth

Intense growth can take place when current products and current markets have the potential for increasing sales. There are three main strategies for intense growth: market penetration, market development, and product development.

Market penetration is a strategy of increasing sales in current markets with current products. A fast-food chain, for instance, would probably attempt to increase its market share by increasing its advertising budget and the size of its marketing staff.

Market development is a strategy of increasing sales of current products in new markets. For example, a European aircraft manufacturer was able to enter the U.S. market by offering Eastern Airlines financing that Boeing could not match.

Product development is a strategy of increasing sales by improving present products or developing new products for current markets. Ski resorts are aggressively pursuing business through extensive product redevelopment. The $1.5 billion skiing market is not showing any growth, so owners are reacting by adding special children's slopes (complete with teepees, forts, and caves), Walt Disney characters on skis, family nights, and kids' nights. Many ski resorts have turned into entertainment resorts in an effort to increase their market share. Other resorts are

37. Ben M. Enis, "GE, PIMS, BCG and the PLC," *Business,* May–June 1980, pp. 17–18.

FIGURE 18.15

Competitive strategies
(From *Corporate
Strategy* by H. I. An-
soff, p. 109. Copyright
© 1965 by McGraw-
Hill Book Company)

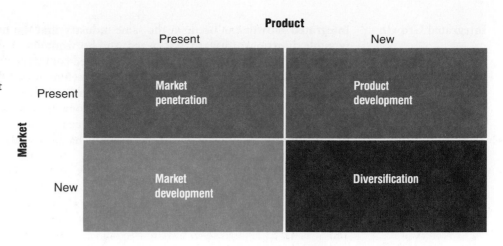

developing shopping areas and expensive boutiques, indoor tennis courts, gyms, and pools, and gourmet restaurants for the nonfamily market.[38]

Diversified Growth

Diversified growth occurs in three ways, depending on the technology of the new products and the nature of the new markets the firm enters. The three forms of diversification are horizontal, concentric, and conglomerate.

When new products that are not technologically related to current products are introduced to current markets, horizontal diversification occurs. An airline might diversify horizontally by starting or acquiring a chain of hotels at the destinations it serves. Walt Disney successfully diversified from a theme park giant to a box office hit maker. For years, Disney's operations were dominated by their theme park activities, but currently the film division is the fastest-growing segment of the company. Four years ago, Disney held 3 percent of the box office tickets; now they are second only to Paramount Pictures. Disney's films (many under the Touchstone nameplate) include "Big Business," "Good Morning Vietnam," "Three Men and a Baby," "Outrageous Fortune," "Down and Out in Beverly Hills," and "Raiders of the Lost Ark."[39]

In concentric diversification, the marketing and technology of new products are related to current products, but the new ones are introduced into new markets. For example, the advertisement in Figure 18.16 describes how Bell Atlantic is introducing its complex technologies into new markets. The advertisement explains to business how information technology can integrate a company's communication, computer, and data systems.

Conglomerate diversification occurs when new products are unrelated to current technology, products, or markets and are introduced to markets new to the firm. If an electronics company were to start a car rental business, the move would represent conglomerate diversification.

38. Mark Ivey, Corie Brown, and Alice Z. Cuneo, "Hi, I'm Goofy. Come Ski with Me," *Business Week,* Feb. 15, 1988, pp. 58, 60.
39. Ron Grover, "Michael Eisner's Hit Parade," *Business Week,* Feb. 1, 1988, p. 27.

Integrated Growth   **Integrated growth** can occur in the same industry that the firm is in and in three possible directions: forward, backward, and horizontally. A firm growing through forward integration takes ownership or increased control of its distribution system. For example, a shoe manufacturer might start selling its products through wholly owned retail outlets. In backward integration, a firm takes ownership or increased control of its supply systems. A newspaper company that buys a paper mill is integrating backward. Horizontal integration occurs when a firm takes ownership or control of some of its competitors. A hotel chain integrating horizontally might purchase a competing motel chain.

Summary

Strategic planning requires a general management orientation, rather than a narrow functional orientation. Corporate strategy determines the means for utilizing resources in the areas of production, finance, research and development, personnel, and marketing to reach the organization's goals. The concept of a strategic business unit (SBU) is used to define areas for consideration in a specific strategic market plan. Each SBU is a division, product line, or other profit center within its parent company. Each SBU sells a distinct set of products and/or services to an identifiable group of customers, and each is in competition with a well-defined set of competitors. In the context of the parent company, meaningful separation can be made of an SBU's revenues, operating costs, investments, and strategic plans. This chapter deals with strategic market planning and planning processes in marketing management.

When a marketing strategy—which is developed through strategic market planning—is implemented properly, it achieves the organization's marketing objectives; these objectives in turn contribute to accomplishing the organization's overall goals. Environmental forces are important in the strategic market planning process and very much affect it. These forces imply opportunities and threats that influence an organization's overall goals. The amount and type of resources that a firm can acquire are also affected by forces in the environment. However, such forces need not constrain or work against the firm; they may also create favorable opportunities that can be translated into overall organizational goals.

There are three major considerations in assessing opportunities and resources: market opportunity must be evaluated; environmental forces must be monitored; and the firm's capabilities should be understood. A market opportunity arises when the right combination of circumstances occurs at the right time to allow an organization to take action toward a target market. An opportunity provides a favorable chance or opening for the firm to generate sales from markets. Determinants of market opportunity include market size, market requirements, and the actions of other firms.

Environmental monitoring is seeking information about events and relationships in a company's outside environment, the knowledge of which assists marketers in planning. A firm's capabilities relate to distinctive competencies that it has developed to do something well and efficiently. A company is likely to enjoy a differential advantage in an area where its competencies outmatch those of its potential competition.

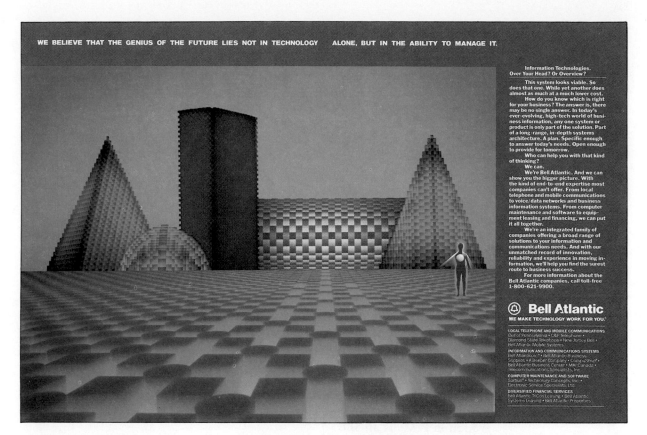

FIGURE 18.16

Bell Atlantic's concentric diversification—reaching out to new markets (SOURCE: Bell Atlantic/Pete Turner)

Corporate strategy defines the means and direction of reaching organizational goals. Marketing objectives are statements of what is to be accomplished through marketing activities. They should be expressed in clear, understandable, and measurable terms, and they must be consistent with an organization's overall goals. Marketing management is the process of planning, organizing, implementing, and controlling marketing activities to facilitate and expedite exchanges effectively and efficiently.

Marketing planning is a systematic process that involves assessing opportunities and resources, determining marketing objectives, developing a marketing strategy, and developing plans for implementation and control. A well-written plan clearly specifies when, how, and who is to perform marketing activities. Plans that cover one year or less are called short-range plans. Medium-range plans usually encompass two to five years, and plans that last for more than five years are long-range. Marketing planning has several benefits. Planning forces marketing managers to think ahead, to establish objectives, and to consider future marketing activities. Effective planning also reduces or eliminates daily crises.

In recent years, marketing managers have developed target market/marketing mixes, sometimes referred to as product/market matching approaches to strategic market planning. These approaches to planning are widely used today to structure the overall strategic market planning process. The Boston Consulting Group (BCG) product-portfolio analysis, the market attractiveness–business position model, and

Profit Impact on Marketing Strategy (PIMS) are popular approaches to strategic planning.

The BCG approach is based on the philosophy that a product's market growth rate and its market share are key factors influencing marketing strategy. All the firm's products should be integrated into a balanced product portfolio. Just as financial investors hold investments with varying risks and rates of return, firms have a variety of products. Managers can use portfolio models to classify products to determine each product's expected future cash contributions and future cash requirements. Generally, managers who use a portfolio model must examine the competitive position of a product (or product line) and the opportunities for improving that product's contribution to profitability and cash flow.

The market attractiveness–business position model is a two-dimensional matrix. The vertical dimension, *market attractiveness,* includes all the sources of strength and resources that relate to the market; competition, industry sales, and the cost of competing are among the sources. The horizontal axis, *business position,* measures sales, relative market share, research and development, and other factors that relate to building a market share for a product.

The Strategic Planning Institute (SPI) has developed a databank of information on more than 1,700 products that members report on for the PIMS (Profit Impact on Marketing Strategy) research program. More than two hundred members of the institute provide confidential information on successes, failures, and marginal products. The data are analyzed to provide reports for member firms on strategy. The results of PIMS include diagnostic and prescriptive information to assist in analyzing marketing performance and formulating marketing strategies. The analysis focuses on options, problems, resources, and opportunities. The unit of observation in PIMS is an SBU.

The real test of strategic planning is how well it helps in diagnosing a firm's strengths and weaknesses and improving performance. The approaches to strategic market planning covered in this chapter are supplements to, not substitutes for, the marketing manager's own judgment.

Competitive strategies that can be implemented through marketing include intense growth, diversified growth, and integrated growth. Intense growth includes market penetration, market development, or product development. Diversified growth includes horizontal, concentric, and conglomerate diversification. Integrated growth includes forward, backward, and horizontal integration.

Important Terms

Corporate strategy	Marketing objective
Marketing strategy	Marketing strategy
Strategic market plan	Marketing management
Strategic business unit (SBU)	Marketing planning
Strategic market planning	Marketing plan
Marketing program	Marketing planning cycle
Market opportunity	Short-range plans
Market requirements	Medium-range plans
Environmental monitoring	Long-range plans

Product-portfolio analysis
Market attractiveness–business
   position model
Profit Impact on Marketing
   Strategy (PIMS)

Intense growth
Diversified growth
Integrated growth

Discussion and Review Questions

1. Why should an organization develop a marketing strategy? What is the difference between strategic market planning and the strategy itself?
2. Identify the major components of strategic market planning, and explain how they are interrelated.
3. In what ways do environmental forces affect strategic market planning? Give specific examples.
4. Why is price flexibility important in implementing the marketing strategy?
5. What are some of the issues that must be considered in analyzing a firm's opportunities and resources? How do these issues affect marketing objectives and market strategy?
6. Why is market opportunity analysis necessary? What are determinants of market opportunity?
7. In relation to resource constraints, how can environmental monitoring affect a firm's long-term strategic market planning? Consider product costs and benefits affected by the environment.
8. What is marketing management, and why is it important to the survival of business organizations?
9. What benefits do marketing managers gain from planning? Is planning necessary for long-run survival? Why or why not?
10. How should an organization establish marketing objectives?
11. What are the major considerations in developing the product-portfolio grid? Define and explain the four basic types of products suggested by the Boston Consulting Group.
12. When should marketers consider using PIMS for strategic market planning?

Cases

18.1 Sigma Marketing Concepts[40]

Sigma Marketing Concepts is a publisher of high-quality, creatively designed promotional calendars. These calendars are sold directly to businesses for use as marketing tools. From 1985 to 1987, Sigma's sales volume grew nearly 200 percent. To ensure continued growth, Sigma reviewed its recent organizational changes and performance and from these findings developed long-range strategic plans and made several changes in its marketing program.

40. Based on information from Donald Sapit, Renee Mudd, and Warren Eldridge, Sigma Marketing Concepts, 1987.

Don Sapit, a mechanical engineer with an M.B.A., started Sigma in 1972. The company began as a small commercial printer, Sigma Press, Inc., located in Ottawa, Illinois. Even then its marketing strategy was oriented toward building a reputation for the most creative and highest quality printing within its forty-mile radius service area. Early on it became obvious that success in the printing industry requires specialization. Sigma's management noticed a gradual increase in demand for customized desk-pad calendars and perceived this demand as a possible strategic window with potential for expanding their business. After much discussion and investigation, the company management wrote a three-year corporate plan.

The corporate plan emphasized marketing, unique for a small printing firm. The marketing plan focused on exploiting the opportunities the desk-pad calendar presented. The marketing mix emphasized product and promotion. Sigma created desk-pad calendars that could be customized to meet various customer needs. Unusual designs, advertising messages, and creative photographic techniques were just a few alternatives available. For promotion, space advertising and direct mail were used. The advertising in sales and marketing-oriented publications created large numbers of inquiries but not sales. However, the direct mail, primarily to manufacturers, produced a much higher return on investment.

Sigma's sales of desk-pad calendars increased 40 percent per year between 1976 and 1980. However, this continued success soon overtaxed the company's production capacity. During 1979 and 1980, Sigma added a new large high-speed two-color press and purchased, redesigned, and rebuilt a specialized collating machine to further automate the calendar assembly. New marketing ideas were developed and implemented to complement the state of the art machinery. Improved direct mail techniques enabled the company to select prospects by SIC (Standard Industrial Classification number; government classification of business by industry) and sales volume. A toll-free phone line encouraged direct inquiries from interested parties. In most cases, the company responded by sending a sample calendar that contained advertising ideas related to the respondent's line of business. They followed up this sample with a personal phone call within eight to ten days.

Calendar sales continued to improve until, by 1983, they represented 40 percent of total sales and approximately 75 percent of net profit. Reorder rates were usually in the 90 percent range. In spite of the success of the calendars, Sapit was disturbed by printing industry trends toward a diminishing market and increased competition for the commercial segment, particularly in Sigma's local area of the Rust Belt. For some time Sigma's management had been considering selling the commercial portion of its business to become an exclusive marketer of custom-designed calendar products. The company found a buyer for the plant, equipment, and goodwill of the commercial portion of the business. Sigma and the buyer agreed to enter into a long-term contract under which the buyer would handle all calendar production for Sigma, using the same plant and staff that had handled production for the past 20 years.

This transaction freed Sigma management from the daily problems of production and plant management and made it possible to commit all Sigma's resources and efforts to creating and marketing new calendar products. Sapit wanted to move the business to the Sun Belt for the better weather, and more importantly, for the better business climate. In 1985, the corporate offices were moved to Jacksonville, Florida. Sapit's son Mike, a graduate of Illinois State University with a degree in graphic arts, also joined the company.

One of the first decisions the new organization made was to revise its target market to include blue chip, service-oriented companies. To more effectively attract these prospects, Sigma expanded its product line to include wall planners, pocket planners, and diaries. Each product was designed to allow Sigma to maintain its differential advantage of offering high advertising flexibility and creativity.

Other actions included developing an even more aggressive marketing program. Management researched and implemented new sophisticated techniques to help in selecting and contracting prospects in the target market. Prospects were chosen by SIC number, sales volume, and advertising budget. After choosing the prospects, direct mail and telemarketing efforts were effectively integrated. Key marketing executives were initially contacted by phone. Direct mail packages containing calendar samples and appropriate literature were then shipped via Federal Express or UPS. One week to ten days after mailing the package, Sigma made a follow-up phone call to determine interest, answer questions, and encourage orders.

At this date, results from the new marketing efforts are not conclusive, but they certainly appear to be favorable. Prime accounts such as Federal Express Corp., Nabisco Brands, Inc., Fidelity Investments, and Jacob Suchard Brach Candies have already been added to Sigma's list of satisfied customers.

Sigma Marketing Concepts continues to monitor and evaluate its internal and external environments. Sapit believes this practice contributes to Sigma's current level of success. The company has also installed a new computer system to coordinate and analyze operations, doubled the number of employees since the Jacksonville move, and recently completed construction of a new office building that will allow for years of future comfort and growth.

Questions for Discussion

1. Compare and contrast the need for long-range versus short-range marketing planning at Sigma Marketing Concepts.
2. Compare the changes in Sigma's marketing strategy from 1972 to 1989. What were the primary considerations for marketing strategy changes?
3. If you were Sigma's marketing consultant, what recommendation would you make for future strategic market planning?

18.2 Campbell's Soup[41]

Strategic market planning has always been an important part of the continuing success of the Campbell Soup Company. In 1987, the company, which is more than one hundred years old, held 66 percent of the $2 billion soup market. Cans of

41. Based on information from Darcy Reid Trick, "Food Giant's Recipe: Soup Up Business," *USA Today*, Feb. 5, 1987, p. B1; Christine Dugas et al., "Marketing's New Look: Campbell Leads a Revolution in the Way Consumer Products Are Sold," *Business Week*, Jan. 26, 1987, pp. 64–69; "Campbell to Sell Units," *Houston Chronicle*, Feb. 10, 1987, p. 2; James R. Russo, "Campbell Soup Company: 'Souperstar' of Innovation," *Packaging*, November 1985, pp. 29–34; Aimee Stern, "The New . . . Souped Up Campbell," *Marketing Communications*, February 1984, p. 34; Christopher S. Eklund, "Campbell Soup's Recipe for Growth: Offering Something for Every Palate," *Business Week*, Dec. 24, 1984, pp. 66–77; Campbell Soup Company Annual Reports, 1984, 1985; "Campbell Soup: Cooking Up a Separate Dish for Each Consumer Group," *Business Week*, Nov. 21, 1983, pp. 102–103.

Campbell's Soup can be found in no less than 93 percent of American homes! But Campbell's does much more than make soup these days. Since early 1980, the diverse consumer goods firm (it is composed of fifty-two strategic business units) has met the changing needs of consumers. Industry analysts have called Campbell's one of the fastest-growing companies today because it constantly monitors and evaluates its long- and short-term plans to stay in tune with what consumers want. The company's diverse product lines include Pepperidge Farm, LeMenu, Godiva chocolates, Mrs. Paul's seafood, Vlasic pickles, Swanson's frozen dinners, and Franco-American spaghetti products.

At one time, Campbell's was organized into only two product categories: canned goods and frozen foods. Current company president Gordon McGovern saw that this organization was not effective and transformed the company to one with a consumer-orientation approach, with new-product developments based on what consumers really want. The company reevaluated its corporate strategy, adding new product lines, streamlining operations, and increasing its emphasis on marketing. Campbell's responded to changes in family structure and eating habits and introduced new products accordingly, 482 of them since 1982. And it has changed its marketing focus, utilizing regional marketing instead of a broad national appeal.

The giant company altered its marketing strategy to take local tastes and customs into account, tailoring its products, distribution, and promotion for specific regions. For example, the company ran a Spanish commercial on a Hispanic radio station in California to promote its V8 cocktail juice. Campbell's feels that regional marketing is the key to reaching widely varied markets. The nation is breaking up according to demographic and regional lines, and regional marketing is the most cost-efficient strategy for dealing with the differences across these markets. The new marketing strategy also permits companies to handle regional (or even local) variations in competition, distribution, and consumer preferences.

Soup is still the cash cow for the Campbell Soup Company. The company sold four billion cans of its 127 varieties in 1986, accounting for 28 percent of the company's total sales. But the company will not let this cash cow rest: it introduced Gold Label Creamy Natural Soups and Chunky Fisherman's Chowder and expanded its line of Home Style Soups and Campbell's Quality Soup and Recipe Mix lines (both dry soups). Campbell's researchers are experimenting with frozen soups to be packaged in plastic bowls that could go from freezer to microwave to table. The company plans to enter the popular Oriental ramen soup market with its own version of ramen. And Campbell is spicing up some of its products to increase its market share in certain parts of the country: it made its nacho cheese soup a little spicier for Texans and Californians, and it plans to introduce a Creole soup to the South and a red bean soup for Hispanic regions.

Campbell's frozen foods have not been left out in the cold either. This business unit has grown because consumers want convenient, easy-to-prepare foods after a long day on the job. LeMenu dinners have been highly successful, and the company expanded the line with LeMenu Light Style dinners. These dinners are packaged in a round thermoset plastic plate with a plastic domed lid, to position them as a little classier than Campbell's Swanson frozen dinners. Sales of the less-expensive Swanson's line have dropped, which the company attributes to the old metal "TV dinner" tray; it is experimenting with a microwavable tray for the Swanson's dinners to appeal to customers' desires for convenience. The company recently introduced the L'Orient line of frozen oriental-styled dinners; they come complete with a tea bag.

Mrs. Paul's Kitchens is the market leader in the frozen seafood market. Like the other units of Campbell's, Mrs. Paul's is trying to give consumers what they want. The company is producing convenient seafood products that are nutritious, low in calories, microwavable, and relatively inexpensive, with a shift toward lighter, unbreaded, broiled seafood. To this end, the company has introduced a new product line called Light Seafood Entrees.

Vlasic pickles also lead the marketplace. Campbell's plans to develop new products for Vlasic and extend existing lines, improve product quality, and increase marketing expenditures. Vlasic's labels are color coded so customers can quickly identify their favorite products. Vlasic has also added new flavor variations.

The Pepperidge Farm unit was streamlined to make it more efficient and profitable. Products that had lagging sales (most notably its Star Wars cookies, which bombed) were discontinued, and some nonrelated businesses (such as gardening interests) were sold. Pepperidge Farms returned to the traditional product lines and quality that established its success from the beginning.

To succeed in today's marketplace, Campbell's had to alter its corporate strategy to determine the most efficient means of using resources in its production and marketing. Its new-product developments and product renovations illustrate that the company is aware of and understands consumer needs and preferences. By targeting its marketing efforts toward these needs and preferences, the company has dramatically raised its sales and profits. Campbell's management is now more concerned with long-term performance than with cost because it is secure enough with its long-range plans to know that technology for new packaging, product maturity, and increasing sales mean that mass volume production will lower its costs and ultimately raise its profits. Campbell Soup Company's reorganization of its corporate strategy has ensured that the firm will be able to take advantage of organizational opportunities and, in all probability, reach its organizational goals.

Questions for Discussion

1. Identify and evaluate the marketing strategies for each Campbell business unit presented in this case.
2. Classify each of Campbell's product lines according to the BCG product-portfolio analysis.
3. Do you think that Campbell's should consider harvesting its Swanson line? Should Campbell's then reintroduce this product line under a new name with new packaging? What are the advantages and disadvantages of this decision?

19. Organization, Implementation, and Control

O B J E C T I V E S

▶ To become aware of how the marketing unit fits in a firm's organizational structure.

▶ To become familiar with the ways of organizing a marketing unit.

▶ To examine several issues relating to the implementation of marketing strategies.

▶ To understand the control processes used in managing marketing strategies.

▶ To be aware of how cost and sales analyses can be used to evaluate the performance of marketing strategies.

▶ To become aware of the major components of a marketing audit.

*T*odd W. LeRoy and Michael L. Atkinson, financial consultants at Shearson Lehman Brothers, wanted to start a new business together. After several brainstorming sessions, they decided to start a chain of drive-through video-rental stores (see Figure 19.1). The stores are ultraconvenient, located in Fotomat-styled kiosks in suburban shopping center parking lots to take advantage of evening commuter traffic. The business can be expanded quickly because kiosks are inexpensive (they cost less than a full-sized video rental store because the rent and utilities are very cheap). The stores carry only hot new releases.

LeRoy and Atkinson franchised their business to finance fast growth. They incorporated in May 1986 as Associated Video Hut, Inc., and by the end of 1987, they had a dozen stores, called Video's 1st, in operation. The two businessmen plan to sell five thousand franchised video rental stores by the middle of 1990. The company markets the franchise idea to individuals who might want to buy only a single kiosk and buyers interested in three or more units. The biggest problem they foresee is not that the idea will not work but taking advantage of their head start to achieve national market strength before a competitor gets into the market with the same idea.

Originally LeRoy and Atkinson planned to develop their franchises by geographical regions. However, they changed their strategy to pursue a national marketing campaign because they found no advantages in a stepwise geographical strategy.

LeRoy and Atkinson set performance standards for their franchises based on a 1986 trade association survey that reported the average video store covers

FIGURE 19.1

Video's 1st drive-through video-rental kiosk (SOURCE: Video Huts)

2,089 square feet and stocks nearly 3,478 tapes, or 2,417 different titles. The survey also reported that the average video store rents only 185 tapes per day, or 5.3 percent of its stock. LeRoy and Atkinson believed that video stores pay too much in overhead to carry many tapes that customers do not rent very often. Furthermore, they believed that nearly 80 percent of people who go to video stores want to rent the latest releases.

Based on this market analysis, they decided that each of their drive-through kiosks would cover forty-eight square feet. Each kiosk carries only the thirty newest videos, about ten copies of each, so that every customer gets what he or she wants. Because the stores stock only new releases, LeRoy and Atkinson expect each franchise to rent 120 tapes, or 40 percent of its inventory, daily. If a store is unable to meet those objectives, the franchisee can literally pick up the kiosk and move it to a better location. Associated Video Huts receives a 7 percent weekly royalty on each franchise's gross revenues plus 1 percent for corporate and national advertising fees.

Although LeRoy and Atkinson are highly optimistic about the future of Associated Video Huts, some video industry analysts believe that their franchise business will not work because the video market is already saturated. However, LeRoy and Atkinson are enthusiastically implementing their marketing strategies, which they believe will establish Video's 1st as a highly successful franchise in the near future.[1]

T HIS CHAPTER focuses first on the marketing unit's position in the organization and the ways the unit itself can be organized. Then we examine several issues regarding the implementation of marketing strategies. Next, we consider the basic components of the process of control and discuss the use of cost and sales analyses to evaluate the effectiveness of marketing strategies. Finally, we describe a marketing audit.

Organizing Marketing Activities

The structure and relationships of a marketing unit, including lines of authority and responsibility that connect and coordinate individuals, strongly affect marketing activities. This section first looks at the place of marketing within an organization and examines the major alternatives available for organizing a marketing unit. Next it shows how marketing activities can be structured to fit into an organization so as to contribute to the accomplishment of overall objectives.

Company Organization: Centralization Versus Decentralization

The organizational structure that a company uses to connect and coordinate various activities has an important influence on success. Basic decisions relate to how various participants in the company will work together to make important decisions as well as coordinate, implement and control activities. Top managers create corporate strategies and coordinate lower levels. A **centralized organization** is one in which the top-level managers delegate very little authority to lower levels of the organization. In a **decentralized organization**, decision making authority is delegated as far down the chain of command as possible. A decision whether to maintain a centralized structure or a decentralized structure directly affects marketing in the organization.

A centralized organization attempts to originate major marketing decisions from top management down to lower levels of management. A decentralized structure gives marketing managers more opportunity for making key strategic decisions. IBM recently announced that it is decentralizing its management structure. Therefore marketing managers will have more opportunity to customize strategies for customers. On the other hand, Hewlett-Packard Co. and Minnesota Mining & Manufacturing are becoming more centralized by consolidating functions or

1. Reprinted with permission, *INC.* Magazine, February 1988. Copyright © 1988 by Inc. Publishing Company, 38 Commercial Wharf, Boston, MA 02110.

eliminating divisional managers.[2] Decentralization may provide innovation and an opportunity to be responsive to customers, but the decentralized company may be inefficient or appear to have a blurred marketing strategy when dealing with larger customers. A centralized organization avoids marketing staff confusion, marketing strategy vagueness, and autonomous decision makers who are out of control. Of course, overly centralized companies often become dependent on top management and respond too slowly to solve problems or to respond to new opportunities. Obviously, it is a difficult balancing act to determine the degree of centralization appropriate for a particular company.

Marketing's Place in an Organization

Because of a very dynamic marketing environment, the place of the marketing unit in the organization has been elevated during the past twenty-five years. The interest in the marketing unit developed because historically firms were focusing on research and development, design and engineering, and then turning their products over to manufacturing. Finally, the product was given to marketing to sell to the customer. These companies have found that if they use the marketing concept as a guiding philosophy, they will have a marketing unit closely coordinated with other functional areas, such as production, finance, and personnel.

For example, at Honda Motor Co., Ltd., the practice of all departments in the firm working together has been in effect for a long time, whereas at Chrysler Corp., the manufacturing group was not even on the product design committee until 1981. With rapid market segmentation forcing automobile companies to design cars even faster than in the past, coordination among engineering, production, marketing, and finance is essential.[3]

In a **marketing-oriented organization,** the focus is on finding out what buyers want and providing it in a manner that lets the organization achieve its objectives. As Figure 19.2 shows, the marketing manager in a marketing-oriented organization has a position equal to that of the financial, production, and personnel managers. This structure permits the marketing manager to participate in top-level decision making. Note too that the marketing manager is responsible for a variety of activities, several of which (sales forecasting and supervision and product planning) are under the jurisdiction of other functional managers in production- or sales-oriented firms.

Both the relationships between marketing and other functional areas (such as production, finance, and personnel) and marketing's importance to management depend heavily on the firm's basic orientation. Marketing encompasses the greatest number of business functions and occupies an important position when a firm is marketing oriented; it has a limited role when the firm views that the marketing role is selling products that the company makes. However, a marketing-oriented organization does not make a firm marketing oriented. The marketing orientation is not achieved simply by redrawing the organizational chart; management must also adopt and use the marketing orientation as a management philosophy.

2. Larry Reibstein, "IBM's Plan to Decentralize May Set a Trend—But Imitation Has a Price," *Wall Street Journal,* Feb. 19, 1988, p. 17.
3. John Bussey, "Manufacturers Strive to Slice Time Needed to Develop Products," *Wall Street Journal,* Feb. 23, 1988, p. 18.

FIGURE 19.2

Organizational chart of a marketing-oriented firm

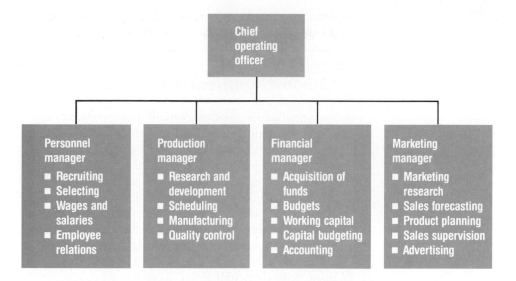

Major Alternatives for Organizing the Marketing Unit

How effectively a firm's marketing management can plan and implement marketing strategies depends on how the marketing unit is organized. Effective organizational planning can give a firm the competitive advantage. The organizational structure of a marketing department establishes the authority relationships among marketing personnel and specifies who is responsible for making certain decisions and performing particular activities. This internal structure provides the vehicle for directing marketing activities.

In organizing a marketing unit, managers divide the work into specific activities and delegate responsibility and authority for those activities to persons in various positions within the marketing unit. These positions include, for example, the sales manager, the research manager, and the advertising manager.

No single approach to organizing a marketing unit works equally well in all businesses. A marketing unit can be organized according to (1) functions, (2) products, (3) regions, or (4) types of customers. The best approach or approaches depend on the number and diversity of the firm's products, the characteristics and needs of the people in the target market, and many other factors.

Firms often use some combination of organization by functions, products, regions, or customer types. Product features may dictate that the marketing unit be structured by products, whereas customers' characteristics require that it be organized by geographic region or by types of customers. By using more than one type of organization, a flexible marketing unit can develop and implement marketing plans to match customers' needs precisely. To develop organizational plans that give a firm a competitive advantage, consider these four issues: (1) Which jobs or levels of jobs need to be added, deleted, or modified? For example, if new products are important to the success of the firm, marketers with strong product development skills should be added to the organization. (2) How should reporting relationships be structured to create a competitive advantage? This question is discussed further in the following descriptions of organizational structure. (3) Who should be assigned the primary responsibility for accomplishing work? Identifying primary

APPLICATION

Canon Organized for Success

An organization that markets diverse products may choose to organize its marketing units according to product groups. This helps the organization develop special marketing mixes for different products. One company that organizes by product group is Japan-based Canon Inc., the world's largest producer of copiers. The company also markets 35 mm cameras, photo and optical equipment, and other business machines in 130 countries. Copiers account for 41 percent of its sales; other business machines, 33 percent; photo and optical equipment, 26 percent. Each product group is responsible for its own marketing strategies and activities.

Canon's overall companywide strategy calls for faster product development, with particular emphasis on the office machines, and aggressive advertising. For example, Canon virtually created the market for personal copiers with advertisements featuring actor Jack Klugman. Before the introduction of Canon's machine, copiers were too big, expensive, and unreliable for low-volume users. Canon's personal copier uses small, easy to replace cartridges and still costs less than $1,000. The personal copier division thus became very profitable for Canon, with Canon copiers now holding 90 percent of the market.

One of Canon's goals is to be a leading multinational office-automation company, competing with Xerox Corporation and IBM in their own markets. The company has enjoyed success in this area largely because its powerful marketing strategy is centered around product group management. Furthermore, the company does not introduce a product unless it is sure the product will be successful. Canon likes to introduce new products when there is a change in the marketplace. Also, the company discourages competition with its low prices. As a result of aggressive marketing tactics, Canon now sells more copiers than Xerox, and it has gained in market share in typewriters against IBM.

In the future, Canon plans to develop product groups in telecommunications and computers. It also plans to develop business and communication software. By focusing on product development in these areas, the company hopes to integrate business machines and technology without sacrificing product quality.

Besides trying to reach its own marketing goals, Canon also wants to build cooperative strategies with other organizations that share similar goals and commitments. The company wants to incorporate cultural, sporting, and community activities as part of its promotional scheme. Canon's specialized product marketing has helped return the company to prosperous times.

SOURCES: Leslie Helm, "Canon: A Dream of Rivaling Big Blue," *Business Week*, May 13, 1985, pp. 98–99; *Canon, Inc. Annual Report*, 1986; *The Value Line Investment Survey* (New York: Value Line, 1987), pp. 1559, 1561.

responsibility explicitly is critical for effective performance appraisal and reward systems. (4) Should any committees or task forces be organized?[4]

Organizing by Functions   Some marketing departments are organized by general marketing functions, such as marketing research, product development, distribution, sales, advertising, and customer relations. The personnel who direct these functions report directly to the top-level marketing executive. This structure is fairly common because it works well for some businesses with centralized marketing operations, such as Mrs. Fields Cookies. In other firms, which tend to have decentralized marketing operations, functional organization can raise severe coordination problems. The functional approach may, however, suit a large centralized company whose products and customers are neither numerous nor diverse.

Organizing by Products   An organization that produces and markets diverse products may find the functional approach inadequate. The decisions and problems related to a single marketing function for one product may be quite different from those related to the same marketing function for another product. As a result, businesses that produce diverse products sometimes organize their marketing units according to product groups. In this type of organization, a product manager takes full responsibility for the marketing of a product or product group. For example, at Procter & Gamble, the product manager for Tide gains cooperation from the functional marketing managers. The product manager may also draw on the resources of specialized staff in the company. Organizing by product groups gives a firm the flexibility to develop special marketing mixes for different products such as Cheer, Bold, and Fab at Procter & Gamble. The Application on page 674 describes how Canon organizes its marketing units by product groups.

Organizing by Regions   A large company that markets products nationally (or internationally) may organize its marketing activities by geographic regions. All the regional marketing managers report directly to the executive marketing manager. Managers of marketing functions for each region report to their regional marketing manager. This form of organization is especially effective for a firm whose customers' characteristics and needs vary greatly from one region to another, such as with Komatsu, a Japanese construction equipment company that recently merged with Dresser Industries, a U.S. company in the same industry.

An organization with marketing managers for each separate region has a complete marketing staff at its headquarters to provide assistance and guidance to regional marketing managers. Pizza Hut, Inc. maintains a full marketing department in Wichita, Kansas, with regional offices having a regional marketing manager and regional marketing supervisors. However, not all firms organized by regions maintain a full marketing staff at their home offices. Companies that try to penetrate the national market intensively sometimes divide regions into subregions.

Organizing by Types of Customers   Sometimes the marketing unit is organized according to types of customers. This form of internal organization works well for a firm that has several groups of customers whose needs and problems differ

---

4. Dave Ulrich, "Strategic Human Resource Planning: Why and How?", *Human Resource Planning,* Vol. 10, No. 1, 1987, pp. 25–37.

significantly. For example, Bic Corp. may sell to large retail stores, wholesalers, and institutions. Retailers may want more rapid delivery of small shipments and more personal selling by the producer than do either wholesalers or institutional buyers. Because the marketing decisions and activities required for these two groups of customers differ considerably, the company may find it efficient to organize its marketing unit by types of customers.

In an organization with a marketing department broken down by customer group, the marketing manager for each group reports to the top-level marketing executive and directs most marketing activities for that group. A marketing manager directs all activities needed to market products to a specific customer group.

Implementing Marketing Activities

The planning and organizing functions provide purpose, direction, and structure for marketing activities. However, until marketing managers implement the marketing plan, exchanges cannot occur. Figure 19.3 illustrates an attempt by Mercedes-Benz Trucks to implement a customer-oriented marketing plan. Proper implementation of a marketing plan depends on the coordination of marketing

FIGURE 19.3

Mercedes-Benz Trucks try to implement a marketing plan through various coordinated programs (SOURCE: Mercedes-Benz Truck Company)

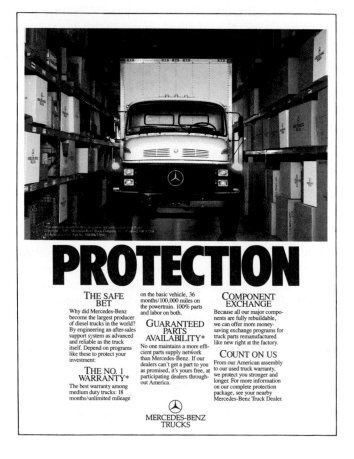

activities, the motivation of personnel who perform those activities, and effective communication within the marketing organization. According to former executives of the Pillsbury Company, upper management was so preoccupied with numbers and procedures that the business suffered because of the time spent developing plans. Each year, separate units spent the summer and fall revising a new five-year plan. One former executive said, "We were always planning—never executing." Obviously, implementation of plans is important to the success of any organization.[5] The Application on page 679 illustrates the need for marketing implementation at Kodak.

Coordinating Marketing Activities

Because of job specialization and differences related to marketing activities, marketing managers must synchronize individuals' actions to achieve marketing objectives. In addition, they must work closely with managers in research and development, production, finance, accounting, and personnel to see that marketing activities mesh with other functions of the firm. Marketing managers must coordinate the activities of marketing staff within the firm and integrate those activities with the marketing efforts of external organizations—advertising agencies, resellers (wholesalers and retailers), researchers, and shippers, among others. Marketing managers can improve coordination by making each employee aware of how one job relates to others and how each person's actions contribute to the achievement of marketing plans.

For example, General Motors Corp. operates a Vehicle Assessment Center in Warren, Michigan, for the sole purpose of analyzing and tearing down competitors' cars piece by piece. General Motors opened the center in 1983 to implement a strategy of improved product quality. GM has torn down BMWs, Hondas, Fords, Porsches, and so on. It has even brought in for inspection cars that are not available in the United States, such as the Nissan Cedric and Opel Senator. To illustrate how this research from the Vehicle Assessment Center is implemented, GM used 71 of the 110 new design ideas that came from the center on its 1988 fall line of cars. General Motors generally takes nonpatented ideas from competitors and develops them further on its own to provide a technologically advanced product.[6] The activities of this center must be coordinated with marketing to provide products that satisfy customer preferences.

Motivating Marketing Personnel

An important element in implementing the marketing plan is motivating marketing personnel to perform effectively. People work to satisfy physical, psychological, and social needs. To motivate marketing personnel, managers must therefore discover their employees' needs and then base their motivation methods on those needs. Additionally, rewards to individuals must be tied to organizational goals.

Consider the following example. Suppose a salesperson can sell product A or B to a particular customer, but not both products. Product A sells for $200,000 and has a contribution margin of $20,000. Product B sells for $60,000 and has a

5. Richard Gibson and Robert Johnson, "Why Pillsbury's Chief from the 70's Is Again Taking Firm's Helm," *Wall Street Journal*, Mar. 1, 1988, p. 25.
6. James Risen, " 'Spy Center' GM Gets Down to Its Competitors' Nuts and Bolts," *Ann Arbor News*, Mar. 9, 1988, pp. D7, D8.

contribution margin of $40,000. If the salesperson receives a commission of 3 percent of sales, he or she would obviously prefer to sell product A, even though the sale of product B contributes more to the firm's profits. If the salesperson's commission was based on contribution margin instead of sales, and the firm's goal was to maximize profits, both the firm and the salesperson would benefit more from the sale of product B.[7] By tying rewards to organizational goals, the firm thus encourages behavior that meets organizational goals.

In addition to tying rewards to organizational goals, managers must use different motivational tools to motivate individuals, based on an individual's value system. For example, some employees value recognition more than a slight pay increase. Managers can reward employees with money plus additional fringe benefits, prestige or recognition, and/or nonfinancial rewards such as job autonomy, skill variety, task significance, and increased feedback. A recent survey of Fortune 1000 companies found that "the majority of organizations feel that they get more for their money through non-cash awards, if given in addition to a basic compensation plan."[8]

Marketing managers can thus motivate marketing personnel to perform at a high level if they identify both organizational and employee goals, provide a means of goal attainment, and creatively reward goal attainment. It is also important that the plan to motivate employees be fair, ethical, and well understood by employees. Obviously, the degree to which a manager can motivate personnel has a major impact on the success of all marketing efforts.

To establish a level of excellence, a supervisor should become a role model for the unit. The message that average productivity is not acceptable should be communicated to all employees.[9] Highly motivated employees tend to be more productive, enhancing overall profitability. Two successful methods of employee motivation are job enrichment and implicit bargaining. **Job enrichment** gives employees a sense of autonomy and control over their work, with employees being encouraged to set their own goals. This program works best with employees who are bored with their job in its current state, when customer complaints and errors are high, when quality is low, and when turnover rates and absenteeism are excessive. **Implicit bargaining** recognizes the various needs of different employees and is based on the theory that there is no best way to motivate individuals. Managers give employees the most freedom with the fewest constraints. By cooperating with the needs of the business, employees see that their personal needs can be met.[10]

In general, companies can improve employee motivation by finding out what workers think and how they feel and determining what they want through an employee attitude survey, directly linking pay with performance, informing workers how their performance affects department and corporate results, and following through with appropriate compensation, promoting or implementing a flexible

7. The example is adapted from Edward B. Deakin and Michael W. Maher, *Cost Accounting,* 2nd ed. (Homewood, Ill.: Irwin, 1987), pp 838–839.

8. Jerry McAdams, "Rewarding Sales and Marketing Performance," *Management Review,* April 1987, p. 36.

9. "Peak Performance—It Can Be Learned. And Taught," *Management Solutions,* June 1986, pp. 26–27.

10. Charles Kahn, "New Views on Motivation," *Network World,* June 1, 1987, pp. 17, 19.

Kodak Implements a New Marketing Strategy

Proper implementation of a marketing plan is necessary for the plan to be successful. Eastman Kodak Co. implemented a new marketing plan designed to combat a negative image of being sluggish and too narrow in focus. The hundred-year-old company led the market for photographic products for many years, and photographers around the world use Kodak film. Nevertheless, heavy competition from Polaroid and Japanese companies such as Fuji and Nikon has eroded Kodak's market share. The amateur photography market has slowed to a growth rate of only 6 percent, from 15 percent in the past. Thus Kodak's photo business is in the mature stage and has little growth opportunity without product innovation. Moreover, the company lost a patent-infringement lawsuit Polaroid brought against it. Kodak management decided to make some changes and diversify into other areas in an effort to become more innovative.

Kodak first divided the company into autonomous units. It then tried to increase its share of traditional markets. The company bought Fox Photo, making Kodak the nation's largest wholesale photo finisher. It also brought out its own line of the popular "point-and-shoot" 35mm camera, which does everything except compose a picture and develop the final print. These actions expanded the market for Kodak's photographic paper, chemicals, and film. The company is constantly researching and developing new photographic products and recently introduced a new high-quality line of color film. The company also markets a disposable 110mm camera for people who seldom need a permanent camera.

Kodak is implementing marketing strategies beyond its traditional product lines. It now produces such diverse products as copy machines, printers, optical memory systems, and a digital medical imaging device. The company markets each of these products to portray Kodak as an innovative company. In 1988, the company purchased Sterling Drug for $5.1 billion in an effort to build a life sciences business. Kodak has also moved aggressively into publishing, industrial automation, and computers and has developed an advertising campaign that encourages businesses to recognize that the company is more than just a leader in photography.

Although Kodak is confident, it is unclear whether the company can find success with the fast-growing products it has introduced. Many analysts believe that Kodak will have to introduce a tremendous number of new products to do so; others have questioned the company's credibility in its new markets, particularly computers and copiers.

Kodak officials want their new marketing strategy to surprise people and make them rethink some of their perceptions about the company. Officials recognize that such a strategy may be risky, but they feel confident that they can handle the dangers. Kodak's implementation of the aggressive marketing

benefits program, and adopting a participative management approach.[11] Six characteristics are common to peak performers. Peak performers (1) have a sense of mission and know where they want to go in relation to where the company is going, (2) are results oriented, (3) are self-managers and self-starters, (4) are team builders and team players, (5) are able to correct their course if things do not go as planned, and (6) are adaptable to management's directive.[12]

Communicating Within the Marketing Unit

Without good communication, marketing managers cannot motivate personnel or coordinate their efforts. Marketing managers must be able to communicate with the firm's high-level management to ensure that marketing activities are consistent with the company's overall goals. Communication with top-level executives keeps marketing managers aware of the company's overall plans and achievements. It also guides what the marketing unit is to do and how its activities are to be integrated with those of other departments—such as finance, production, or personnel—with whose management the marketing manager must also communicate to coordinate marketing efforts. Marketing personnel must work with the production staff, for example, to help design products that customer groups want. To direct marketing activities, marketing managers must communicate with marketing personnel at the operations level, such as sales and advertising personnel, researchers, wholesalers, retailers, and package designers. Figure 19.4 illustrates an office automation program that helps in the management of communication activities.

To facilitate communication, marketing managers should establish an information system within the marketing unit. The information system should allow for easy communication among marketing managers, sales managers, and sales personnel. Marketers need an information system to support a variety of activities, such as planning, budgeting, sales analyses, performance evaluations, and the preparation of reports. An information system should also expedite communications with other departments in the organization and minimize destructive competition among departments for organizational resources.[13]

11. David C. Jones, "Motivation the Catalyst in Profit Formula," *National Underwriter,* July 13, 1987, pp. 10, 13.
12. "Peak Performance—It Can Be Learned. And Taught," *Management Solutions,* June 1986, pp. 26–27.
13. Robert E. Sweeney and Dan A. Boswell, "Obey 10 Commandments When Designing Marketing Info System," *Marketing News,* Apr. 16, 1982, p. 16.

Another useful method of enhancing communication within the marketing department and throughout the organization is internal marketing. Internal marketing is the process by which marketing and nonmarketing personnel understand and recognize the values of the marketing system and their place in it. This process involves top-management education and commitment, middle-management training and education, and staff-level commitment to customer service.[14] Figure 19.5 shows Chrysler's attempts to communicate a corporate credo of pride in marketing.

Controlling Marketing Activities

To achieve marketing objectives as well as general organizational objectives, marketing managers must effectively control marketing efforts. The **marketing control process** consists of establishing performance standards, evaluating actual performance by comparing it with established standards, and reducing the differences

14. Jeffrey P. Winter, "Getting Your House in Order with Internal Marketing: A Marketing Prerequisite," *Health Marketing Quarterly*, Fall 1987, p. 69.

FIGURE 19.4

Data General provides solutions to communicating (SOURCE: Advertisement developed by Data General Ltd. and Parks Advertising, London, England, in January 1986)

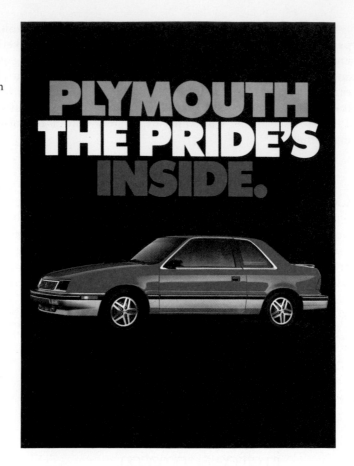

between desired and actual performance. Figure 19.6 illustrates the process. We discuss these steps in the control process and look at the major problems they involve. For example, Dunkin' Donuts has developed a program to control consistency throughout its franchises. Dunkin' Donuts controls the quality of operations in its franchised units by having franchisees attend Dunkin' Donuts University. Owners and managers of Dunkin' Donuts are required to pass a six-week training course, covering everything from customer relations and marketing to production including a test of making 140 dozen doughnuts in eight hours. As part of the test, an instructor randomly selects 6 of the 1,680 doughnuts made to make sure they weigh 12 to 13 ounces and measure 7¾ inches when stacked. The University was opened to guarantee uniformity in all aspects of the business operations throughout the 1,700 franchise units.[15]

Establishing Performance Standards

Planning and controlling are closely interrelated because plans include statements about what is to be accomplished. For purposes of control, these statements function as performance standards. A **performance standard** is an expected level of performance against which actual performance can be compared. Examples of

15. "Higher Education in Doughnuts," *The Ann Arbor News,* Mar. 9, 1988, p. B7.

performance standards might be the reduction of customers' complaints by 20 percent, a monthly sales quota of $150,000, or a 10 percent increase per month in new customer accounts. Performance standards are also given in the form of budget accounts; that is, marketers are expected to achieve a certain objective without spending more than a given amount of resources. As stated earlier, performance standards should be tied to organizational goals. Performance standards can relate to product quality. Figure 19.7 illustrates that Guhring strives for consistent quality.

Evaluating Actual Performance

To compare actual performance with performance standards, marketing managers must know what marketers within the company are doing and have information about the activities of external organizations that provide the firm with marketing assistance. (We discuss specific methods for assessing actual performance later in this chapter.) Information is required about the activities of marketing personnel at the operations level and at various marketing management levels. Most businesses obtain marketing assistance from one or more external individuals or organizations, such as advertising agencies, middlemen, marketing research firms, and consultants. To maximize benefits from external sources, a firm's marketing control process must monitor their activities. Although it may be difficult to obtain the necessary information, it is impossible to measure actual performance without it.

Records of actual performance are compared with performance standards to determine whether and how much of a discrepancy exists. For example, a salesperson's actual sales are compared with his or her sales quota (performance standard). If there is a significant negative discrepancy, the marketing manager takes corrective action.

FIGURE 19.6

The marketing control process

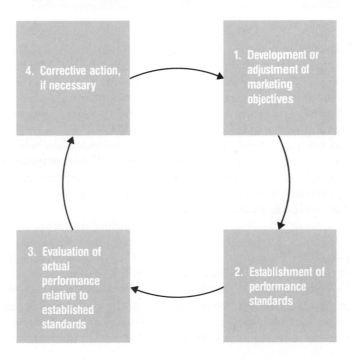

Taking Corrective Action

Marketing managers have several options for reducing a discrepancy between established performance standards and actual performance. They can take steps to improve actual performance, can reduce or totally change the performance standard, or do both. Changes in actual performance may require the marketing manager to use better methods of motivating marketing personnel or use more effective techniques for coordinating marketing efforts.

Sometimes, performance standards are unrealistic when they are written. In other cases, changes in the marketing environment make them unrealistic. For example, a firm's annual sales goal may become unrealistic if several aggressive competitors enter the firm's market. In fact, changes in the marketing environment may force managers to change their marketing strategy completely. For example, Goodyear Tire & Rubber Company shifted its corporate strategy in 1982. The company deemphasized tire sales to the point where tires became less than 50 percent of its business. The company focused instead on expanding its other businesses (rubber and plastics, automobile parts, and aerospace products, including blimps and radar). Goodyear also bought Celeron Corporation, an oil and gas company. Then oil prices dropped, and Goodyear was faced with falling stock prices and attempted takeover bids. Goodyear then completely reviewed its corporate strategies and subsequently sold Celeron and the aerospace division. Goodyear is now focusing on tire production, which now accounts for 74 percent of its sales.[16]

Requirements for an Effective Control Process

A marketing manager should consider several requirements in creating and maintaining effective control processes.[17] Effective control depends heavily on the quantity and quality of information available to the marketing manager and the speed at which it is received. The control process should be designed so that the flow of information is rapid enough to allow the marketing manager to quickly detect differences between actual and planned levels of performance. A single control procedure is not suitable for all types of marketing activities, and internal and environmental changes affect an organization's activities, so control procedures should be flexible enough to adjust to both varied activities and changes in the organization's situation. For the control process to be usable, its costs must be low relative to the costs that would arise if there were no controls. Finally, the control process should be designed so that both managers and subordinates can understand it.

Problems in Controlling Marketing Activities

When marketing managers attempt to control marketing activities, they frequently run into several problems. Often, the information required to control marketing activities is unavailable or is only available at a high cost. Even though marketing controls should be flexible enough to allow for environmental changes, the frequency, intensity, and unpredictability of such changes may hamper effective control. In addition, the time lag between marketing activities and their effects limits a marketing manager's ability to measure the effectiveness of marketing activities.

Consider the problems of demand fluctuation in the videogame industry. By failing to control the number of videogame products offered, firms such as Nintendo (70 percent of U.S. market share), Atari (16 percent of U.S. market share), and Sega (10 percent of U.S. market share) glutted the market with so many videogame titles that consumers were confused and disappointed with the numerous look-alike products. Companies are avoiding past mistakes by carefully analyzing the success of videogames and deleting older games that are no longer profitable. For example, in 1988, Nintendo withdrew eighteen of its thirty-six games to make room for new-product introductions. This careful analysis and control of product offerings has helped home videogames make a comeback from being a spectacular but short-lived fad of the early 1980s.[18]

Because marketing and other business activities overlap, marketing managers cannot determine the precise cost of marketing activities. Without an accurate measure of marketing costs, it is difficult to know if the effects of marketing activities are worth their expense. Finally, marketing control may be difficult because it is very hard to develop exact performance standards for marketing personnel.

16. Zachary Schiller and Roger Schreffler, "Goodyear Feels the Heat," *Business Week,* Mar. 7, 1988, pp. 26–28.
17. See Theo Haimann, William G. Scott, and Patrick E. Connor, *Management,* 5th ed. (Boston: Houghton Mifflin, 1985), pp. 478–492.
18. Jeffrey A. Tannenbaum, "Video Games Revive—and Makers Hope This Time the Fad Will Last," *Wall Street Journal,* Mar. 8, 1988, p. 35.

Methods of Evaluating Performance

There are specific methods for assessing and improving the effectiveness of a marketing strategy. A marketer should state, through plans and objectives, what a marketing strategy is supposed to accomplish. These statements should set forth performance standards, which usually are stated in terms of profits, sales, or costs. Actual performance must be measured in similar terms so that comparisons are possible. This section describes sales analysis and cost analysis, two general ways of evaluating the actual performance of marketing strategies.

Sales Analysis

Sales analysis uses sales figures to evaluate a firm's current performance. It is probably the most common method of evaluation because sales data partially reflect the target market's reactions to a marketing mix and often are readily available, at least in aggregate form.

Marketers use current sales data to monitor the impact of current marketing efforts. However, that information alone is not enough. To provide useful analyses, current sales data must be compared with forecasted sales, industry sales, specific competitors' sales, or the costs incurred to achieve the sales volume. For example, knowing that a variety store attained a $600,000 sales volume this year does not tell management whether the marketing strategy has been successful. However, if managers know that expected sales were $550,000, then they are in a better position to determine the effectiveness of the firm's marketing efforts. In addition, if they know that the marketing costs needed to achieve the $600,000 volume were 12 percent less than budgeted, they are in an even better position to analyze their marketing strategy precisely. Figure 19.8 is one example of a computer system that is a cost-effective tool for analyzing sales data.

Types of Sales Measurements   Although sales may be measured several ways, the fundamental unit of measurement is the sales transaction. A sales transaction results in a customer order for a specified quantity of an organization's product sold under specified terms by a particular salesperson or sales group on a certain date. Many organizations record these bits of information about their transactions. With such a record, a company can analyze sales in terms of dollar volume or market share.

Firms frequently use dollar volume sales analysis because the dollar is a common denominator of sales, costs, and profits. However, price increases and decreases affect total sales figures. For example, if a firm increased its prices 10 percent this year and its sales volume is 10 percent greater than last year, it has not experienced any increase in unit sales. A marketing manager who uses dollar volume analysis should factor out the effects of price changes.

A firm's market share is the firm's sales of a product stated as a percentage of industry sales of that product. For example, Coca-Cola at one time sold 40 percent of all the cola sold annually in this country and thus had a market share of 40 percent. Market share analysis lets a firm compare its marketing strategy with competitors' strategies.

The primary reason for using market share analysis is to estimate whether sales changes have resulted from the firm's marketing strategy or from uncontrollable environmental forces. When a company's sales volume declines but its share of the

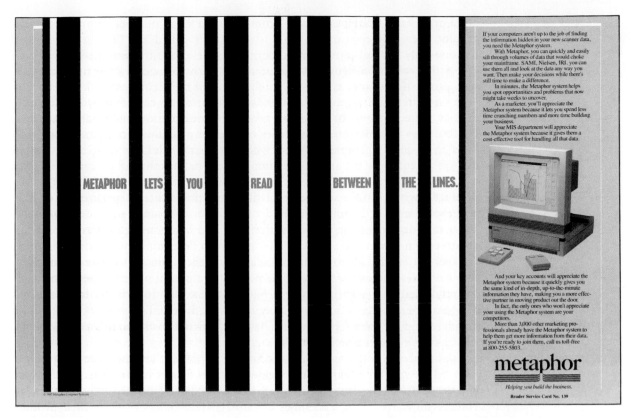

FIGURE 19.8

Metaphor is a computerized system for analyzing sales data (SOURCE: Metaphor Computer Systems, Inc.)

market stays the same, the marketer can assume that industry sales declined (because of some uncontrollable factors) and that this decline was reflected in the firm's sales. However, if the firm experiences a decline in both sales and market share, it should consider the possibility that its marketing strategy is not effective.

Even though market share analysis can be helpful in evaluating the performance of a marketing strategy, the user must interpret results cautiously. When attributing a sales decline to uncontrollable factors, a marketer must keep in mind that such factors do not affect all firms in the industry equally. Not all firms in an industry have the same objectives, and some firms change objectives from one year to the next. Changes in the objectives of one firm can affect the market shares of one or all firms in that industry. For example, if a competitor significantly increases promotional efforts or drastically reduces prices to increase market share, then a company could lose market share despite a well-designed marketing strategy. Within an industry, the entrance of new firms or the demise of established ones also affects a specific firm's market share, and market share analysts should attempt to account for these effects.

Bases for Sales Analysis   Whether it is based on sales volume or market share, sales analysis can be performed on aggregate sales figures or on disaggregated data. Aggregate sales analysis provides an overview of current sales. Although helpful, aggregate sales analysis is often insufficient because it does not bring to light sales variations within the aggregate. It is not uncommon for a marketer to find that a large proportion of aggregate sales comes from a small number of products, geographic areas, or customers. (This is sometimes called the "iceberg principle" because only a small part of an iceberg is visible above the water.) To find such disparities, total sales figures usually are broken down by geographic unit, salesperson, product, customer type, or a combination of these categories.

In sales analysis by geographic unit, sales data can be classified by city, county, district, state, country, or any other geographic designation for which a marketer collects sales information. Actual sales in a geographic unit can be compared with sales in a similar geographic unit, with last year's sales, or with an estimated market potential for the area. For example, if a firm finds that 18 percent of its sales are coming from an area that represents only 8 percent of the potential sales for the product, then it can be assumed that the marketing strategy is successful in that geographic unit.

Because of the cost associated with hiring and maintaining a sales force, businesses commonly analyze sales by salesperson to determine the contribution each salesperson makes. Performance standards for each salesperson are often set in terms of sales quotas for a given time period. Evaluation of actual performance is accomplished by comparing a salesperson's current sales to a preestablished quota or some other standard, such as last period's sales. If actual sales meet or exceed the standard and the sales representative has not incurred costs above those budgeted, that person's efforts are acceptable.

Sales analysis is often performed according to product group or specific product item. Marketers break down their aggregate sales figures by product to determine the proportion that each contributed to total sales. A firm usually sets a sales volume objective—and sometimes a market share objective—for each product item or product group, and sales analysis by product is the only way to measure such objectives. A marketer can compare the breakdown of current sales by product with those of previous years. In addition, within industries for which sales data by product are available, a firm's sales by product type can be compared with industry averages. To gain an accurate picture of where sales of specific products are occurring, marketers sometimes combine sales analysis by product with sales analysis by geographic area or salesperson.

Analyses based on customers are usually broken down by types of customers. Customers can be classified by the way they use a firm's products, their distribution level (producer, wholesaler, retailer), their size, the size of orders, or other characteristics. Sales analysis by customer type lets a firm ascertain whether its marketing resources are allocated in a way that achieves the greatest productivity. For example, sales analysis by type of customer may reveal that 60 percent of the sales force is serving a group that makes only 15 percent of total sales.

A considerable amount of information is needed for sales analyses, especially if disaggregated analyses are desired. The marketer must develop an operational system for collecting sales information; obviously, the effectiveness of the system for collecting sales information largely determines a firm's ability to develop useful sales analyses.

Marketing Cost Analysis

Although sales analysis is critical for evaluating the effectiveness of a marketing strategy, it gives only part of the picture. A marketing strategy that successfully generates sales may also be extremely costly. For example, as a result of the deregulation of the phone industry, AT&T, once the largest private employer in the United States, for the past several years has experienced significant losses. Although AT&T spun off profitable local phone companies, it recently lost nearly $1 billion a year. Chairman James E. Olson suggested that a strategy to increase sales to former subsidiaries would improve AT&T's profitability. Thus AT&T began to expand its sales by selling phones at cost to former AT&T divisions that were spun off as independent companies. These companies had been buying from outside vendors because of the significant cost differential. AT&T is building a cohesiveness among its internal organization and former divisions that operated as subsidiaries until deregulation. Through analysis of its product line, AT&T has reduced the number of phones in the line from fifty-four to twelve and cut costs further through foreign production.[19] By controlling and implementing a coordinated strategy, AT&T is becoming a more successful operator in the competitive telecommunications industry, even though initially this strategy may appear costly. To get a complete picture, a firm must know the marketing costs associated with using a given strategy to achieve a certain sales level.

Marketing cost analysis breaks down and classifies costs to determine which are associated with specific marketing activities. By comparing costs of previous marketing activities with results generated, a marketer can better allocate the firm's marketing resources in the future. Marketing cost analysis lets a firm evaluate the effectiveness of an ongoing or recent marketing strategy by comparing sales achieved and costs incurred. By pinpointing exactly where a firm is experiencing high costs, this form of analysis can help isolate profitable or unprofitable customer segments, products, or geographic areas. For example, the market share of Komatsu Ltd., a Japanese construction equipment manufacturer, was declining in the United States as a result of increasing prices because of the high yen value. Komatsu thus developed an equal joint venture with Dresser Industries, making it the second largest company in this industry. The joint venture with Dresser lets Komatsu shift a large amount of its final assembly to the United States in Dresser plants that had been running at 50 percent capacity. By using Dresser's unused capacity and existing U.S. plants, Komatsu avoids the start-up costs of new construction and can gain immediate manufacturing presence in the United States.[20] This cost-control tactic should enable Komatsu to more effectively use price as a marketing variable to compete with number-one Caterpillar Tractor Co. In some organizations, personnel in other functional areas—such as production or accounting—think that marketers are primarily concerned with generating sales regardless of the costs incurred. By conducting cost analyses, marketers can undercut this criticism and put themselves in a better position to demonstrate how marketing activities contribute to generating profits.

Determining Marketing Costs Frequently, the task of determining marketing costs is complex and difficult. Simply ascertaining the costs associated with marketing a product is rarely adequate. Marketers must usually determine the marketing

19. John J. Keller, Geoff Lewis, Todd Mason, Russell Mitchell, and Thane Peterson, "AT&T: The Making of a Comeback," *Business Week*, Jan. 18, 1988, pp. 56–62.
20. Kevin Kelly and Neil Gross, "A Weakened Komatsu Tries to Come Back Swinging," *Business Week*, Feb. 22, 1988, p. 48.

costs of serving specific geographic areas, market segments, or even specific customers.

A first step in determining the costs is to examine accounting records. Most accounting systems classify costs into accounts such as rent, salaries, office supplies, and utilities that are based on how the money was actually spent. Unfortunately, many of these accounts, called **natural accounts,** do not help explain what functions were performed through the expenditure of those funds. It does little good, for example, to know that $80,000 is spent for rent each year. The analyst has no way of knowing whether the money is spent for the rental of production, storage, or sales facilities. Therefore, marketing cost analysis usually requires that some of the costs in natural accounts be reclassified into **marketing function accounts.** Common marketing function accounts are transportation, storage, order processing, selling, advertising, sales promotional, marketing research, and customer credit.

In some instances a specific marketing cost is incurred to perform several functions. A packaging cost, for example, could be considered a production function, a distribution function, a promotional function, or all three. The marketing cost analyst must reclassify such costs across multiple functions.

Three broad categories are used in marketing cost analysis: direct costs, traceable common costs, and nontraceable common costs. **Direct costs** are directly attributable to the performance of marketing functions. For example, sales force salaries might be allocated to the cost of selling a specific product item, selling in a specific geographic area, or selling to a particular customer. **Traceable common costs** can be allocated indirectly, using one or several criteria, to the functions that they support. For example, if the firm spends $80,000 annually to rent space for production, storage, and selling, the rental costs of storage could be determined on the basis of cost per square foot used for storage. **Nontraceable common costs** cannot be assigned according to any logical criteria and thus are assignable only on an arbitrary basis. Interest, taxes, and the salaries of top management are nontraceable common costs.

The manner of dealing with these three categories of costs depends on whether the analyst uses a full-cost or a direct-cost approach. When a **full-cost approach** is used, cost analysis includes direct costs, traceable common costs, and nontraceable common costs. Proponents of this approach claim that if an accurate profit picture is desired, all costs must be included in the analysis. However, opponents point out that full costing does not yield actual costs because nontraceable common costs are determined by arbitrary criteria. With different criteria, the full-costing approach yields different results. A cost-conscious operating unit can be discouraged if numerous costs are assigned to it arbitrarily. To eliminate such problems, the **direct-cost approach** is used. It includes direct costs and traceable common costs but not nontraceable common costs. Opponents say that this approach is not accurate because it omits one cost category.

Methods of Marketing Cost Analysis   Marketers can use several methods to analyze costs. The methods vary in their precision. This section examines three cost analysis methods, beginning with the least precise.

Analysis of Natural Accounts   Marketers sometimes can perform a cost analysis by studying a firm's accounting records, or natural accounts. The precision of this method depends heavily on how detailed the firm's accounts are. For example, if accounting records contain separate accounts for production wages, sales-force wages, and executive salaries, the analysis can be more precise than if all wages and salaries are lumped into a single account. An analysis of natural accounts is more meaningful, and thus more useful, when current cost data can be compared with those of previous periods or with average cost figures for the entire industry. Cost analysis of natural accounts frequently treats costs as percentages of sales. The periodic use of cost-to-sales ratios lets a marketer ascertain cost fluctuations quickly.

Analysis of Functional Accounts   As indicated earlier, the analysis of natural accounts may not shed much light on the cost of marketing activities. In such cases, natural accounts must be reclassified into marketing function accounts as shown in the simplified example in Table 19.1. Note that a few natural accounts, such as advertising, can be reclassified easily into functional accounts because they do not have to be split across several accounts. For most of the natural accounts, however, marketers must develop criteria for assigning them to the various functional accounts. For example, the number of square feet of floor space used was the criterion for dividing the rental costs in Table 19.1 into functional accounts. Whether certain natural accounts are reclassified into functional accounts, and the criteria used to reclassify them, depend to some degree on whether the analyst is using direct costing or full costing. After natural accounts have been reclassified into functional accounts, the cost of each function is determined by summing the costs in each functional account. Thus Table 19.1 shows that the firm's cost of personal selling was $40,000.

Once the costs of these marketing functions have been determined, the analyst is ready to compare the resulting figures with budgeted costs, sales analysis data, cost data from earlier operating periods, or perhaps average industry cost figures, if available.

Cost Analysis by Product, Geographic Area, or Customer   Although marketers ordinarily get a more detailed picture of marketing costs by analyzing functional accounts than by analyzing natural accounts, some firms need an even more precise cost analysis. The need is especially great if the firms sell several types of products, sell in multiple geographic areas, or sell to a wide variety of customers. Activities vary in marketing different products in specific geographic locations to certain customer groups. Therefore the costs of these activities also vary. By allocating the functional costs to specific product groups, geographic areas, or customer groups, a marketer can find out which of these marketing entities are the most cost effective to serve. In Table 19.2, the functional costs derived in Table 19.1 are allocated to specific product categories. A similar type of analysis could be performed for geographic areas or for specific customer groups. The criteria used to allocate the functional accounts must be developed so as to yield results that are as accurate as possible. Use of faulty criteria is likely to yield inaccurate cost estimates that in turn lead to less effective control of marketing strategies. Marketers determine the marketing costs for various product categories, geographic areas, or customer groups and then compare them to sales. This analysis lets them evaluate the effectiveness of the firm's marketing strategy or strategies.

TABLE 19.1
Reclassification of natural accounts into functional accounts

PROFIT AND LOSS STATEMENT		FUNCTIONAL ACCOUNTS					
		ADVERTISING	PERSONAL SELLING	TRANSPORTATION	STORAGE	MARKETING RESEARCH	NON MARKETING
Sales	$250,000						
Cost of goods sold	45,000						
Gross profit	205,000						
Expenses (natural accounts)							
Rent	$ 14,000		$ 7,000		$6,000		$ 1,000
Salaries	72,000	$12,000	32,000	$7,000		$1,000	20,000
Supplies	4,000	1,500	1,000			1,000	500
Advertising	16,000	16,000					
Freight	4,000			2,000			2,000
Taxes	2,000				200		1,800
Insurance	1,000				600		400
Interest	3,000						3,000
Bad debts	6,000						6,000
Total	$122,000	$29,500	$40,000	$9,000	$6,800	$2,000	$34,700
Net profit	$ 83,000						

TABLE 19.2

Functional accounts
divided into product
group costs

FUNCTIONAL ACCOUNTS		PRODUCT GROUPS		
		A	B	C
Advertising	$29,500	$14,000	$ 8,000	$ 7,500
Personal selling	40,000	18,000	10,000	12,000
Transportation	9,000	5,000	2,000	2,000
Storage	6,800	1,800	2,000	3,000
Marketing research	2,000		1,000	1,000
Total	$87,300	$38,800	$23,000	$25,500

The Marketing Audit

A **marketing audit** is a systematic examination of the marketing group's objectives, strategies, organization, and performance. Its primary purpose is to identify weaknesses in ongoing marketing operations and plan the necessary improvements to correct these weaknesses. The marketing audit does not concern itself with the firm's marketing position because that is the purpose of the firm's marketing plan. Rather, the marketing audit evaluates how effectively the marketing organization performed its assigned functions.[21]

Like an accounting or financial audit, a marketing audit should be conducted regularly instead of only when performance control mechanisms show that the system is out of control. The marketing audit is not a control process to be used only during a crisis, although a business in trouble may use it to isolate problems and generate solutions.

A marketing audit may be specific and focus on one or a few marketing activities, or it may be comprehensive and encompass all of a company's marketing activities. Table 19.3 lists many possible dimensions of a marketing audit. An audit might deal with only a few of these areas, or it might include them all. Its scope depends on the costs involved, the target markets served, the structure of the marketing mix, and environmental conditions. The results of the audit can be used to reallocate marketing effort and to reexamine marketing opportunities.

The marketing audit should aid evaluation by doing the following:

1. Describe current activities and results related to sales, costs, prices, profits, and other performance feedback
2. Gather information about customers, competition, and environmental developments that may affect the marketing strategy
3. Explore opportunities and alternatives for improving the marketing strategy
4. Provide an overall database to be used in evaluating the attainment of organizational goals and marketing objectives

21. William A. Band, "A Marketing Audit Provides an Opportunity for Improvement," *Sales and Marketing Management in Canada*, March 1984, pp. 24–26.

TABLE 19.3

Dimensions of a
marketing audit

Part I. The Marketing Environment Audit

Macroenvironment

A. Economic-demographic

1. What does the company expect in the way of inflation, material shortages, unemployment, and credit availability in the short run, intermediate run, and long run?
2. What effect will forecasted trends in the size, age distribution, and regional distribution of population have on the business?

B. Technological

1. What major changes are occurring in product technology? In process technology?
2. What are the major generic substitutes that might replace this product?

C. Political-legal

1. What laws are being proposed that may affect marketing strategy and tactics?
2. What federal, state, and local agency actions should be watched? What is happening with pollution control, equal employment opportunity, product safety, advertising, price control, etc. that is relevant to marketing planning?

D. Cultural

1. What attitude is the public taking toward business and the types of products produced by the company?
2. What changes in consumer lifestyles and values have a bearing on the company's target markets and marketing methods?

E. Ecological

1. Will the cost and availability of natural resources directly affect the company?
2. Are there public concerns about the company's role in pollution and conservation? If so, what is the company's reaction?

Task Environment

A. Markets

1. What is happening to market size, growth, geographical distribution, and profits?
2. What are the major market segments and their expected rates of growth? Which are high opportunity and low opportunity segments?

B. Customers

1. How do current customers and prospects rate the company and its competitors on reputation, product quality, service, sales force, and price?
2. How do different classes of customers make their buying decisions?
3. What evolving needs and satisfactions are the buyers in this market seeking?

C. Competitors

1. Who are the major competitors? What are the objectives and strategy of each major competitor? What are their strengths and weaknesses? What are the sizes and trends in market shares?
2. What trends can be foreseen in future competition and substitutes for this product?

D. Distribution and dealers

1. What are the main trade channels bringing products to customers?
2. What are the efficiency levels and growth potentials of the different trade channels?

E. Suppliers

1. What is the outlook for the availability of key resources used in production?
2. What trends are occurring among suppliers in their patterns of selling?

F. Facilitators and marketing firms

1. What is the outlook for the cost and availability of transportation services?
2. What is the outlook for the cost and availability of warehousing facilities?
3. What is the outlook for the cost and availability of financial resources?
4. How effectively is the advertising agency performing? What trends are occurring in advertising agency services?

G. Publics

1. Where are the opportunity areas or problems for the company?
2. How is the company effectively dealing with publics?

TABLE 19.3

(continued)

Part II. Marketing Strategy Audit

A. Business mission

1. Is the business mission clearly focused with marketing terms and is it attainable?

B. Marketing objectives and goals

1. Are the corporate objectives clearly stated? Do they lead logically to the marketing objectives?
2. Are the marketing objectives stated clearly enough to guide marketing planning and subsequent performance measurement?
3. Are the marketing objectives appropriate, given the company's competitive position, resources, and opportunities? Is the appropriate strategic objective to build, hold, harvest, or terminate this business?

C. Strategy

1. What is the core marketing strategy for achieving the objectives? Is it sound?
2. Are the resources budgeted to accomplish the marketing objectives inadequate, adequate, or excessive?
3. Are the marketing resources allocated optimally to prime market segments, territories, and products?
4. Are the marketing resources allocated optimally to the major elements of the marketing mix, i.e., product quality, service, sales force, advertising, promotion, and distribution?

Part III. Marketing Organization Audit

A. Formal structure

1. Is there a high-level marketing officer with adequate authority and responsibility over those company activities that affect customer satisfaction?
2. Are the marketing responsibilities optimally structured along functional, product, end user, and territorial lines?

B. Functional efficiency

1. Are there good communication and working relations between marketing and sales?
2. Is the product-management system working effectively? Are the product managers able to plan profits or only sales volume?

3. Are there any groups in marketing that need more training, motivation, supervision, or evaluation?

C. Interface efficiency

1. Are there any problems between marketing and manufacturing, R&D, purchasing, finance, accounting, and legal that need attention?

Part IV. Marketing Systems Audit

A. Marketing information system

1. Is the marketing intelligence system producing accurate, sufficient, and timely information about developments in the marketplace?
2. Is marketing research being adequately used by company decision makers?

B. Marketing-planning system

1. Is the marketing-planning system well conceived and effective?
2. Is sales forecasting and market-potential measurement soundly carried out?
3. Are sales quotas set on a proper basis?

C. Marketing control system

1. Are the control procedures (monthly, quarterly, etc.) adequate to ensure that the annual-plan objectives are being achieved?
2. Is provision made to analyze periodically the profitability of different products, markets, territories, and channels of distribution?
3. Is provision made to examine and validate periodically various marketing costs?

D. New-product development system

1. Is the company well organized to gather, generate, and screen new product ideas?
2. Does the company do adequate concept research and business analysis before investing heavily in a new idea?
3. Does the company carry out adequate product and market testing before launching a new product?

Part V. Marketing-Productivity Audit

A. Profitability analysis

1. What is the profitability of the company's different products, served markets, territories, and channels of distribution?

(continued on next page)

TABLE 19.3
(continued)

2. Should the company enter, expand, contract, or withdraw from any business segments, and what would be the short- and long-run profit consequences?

B. Cost-effectiveness analysis
1. Do any marketing activities seem to have excessive costs? Are these costs valid? Can cost-reducing steps be taken?

Part VI. Marketing Function Audits

A. Products
1. What are the product line objectives? Are these objectives sound? Is the current product line meeting these objectives?
2. Are there particular products that should be phased out?
3. Are there new products that are worth adding?
4. Are any products able to benefit from quality, feature, or style improvements?

B. Price
1. What are the pricing objectives, policies, strategies, and procedures? Are prices set on sound cost, demand, and competitive criteria?
2. Do the customers see the company's prices as being in or out of line with the perceived value of its products?
3. Does the company use price promotions effectively?

C. Distribution
1. What are the distribution objectives and strategies?
2. Is there adequate market coverage and service?
3. How effective are the following channel members: distributors, manufacturers' reps, brokers, agents, etc.?

4. Should the company consider changing its distribution channels?

D. Advertising, sales promotion, and publicity
1. What are the organization's advertising objectives? Are they sound?
2. Is the right amount being spent on advertising? How is the budget determined?
3. Are the ad themes and copy effective? What do customers and the public think about the advertising?
4. Are the advertising media well chosen?
5. Is the internal advertising staff adequate?
6. Is the sales promotion budget adequate? Is there effective and sufficient use of sales promotion tools, such as samples, coupons, displays, and sales contests?
7. Is the publicity budget adequate? Is the public relations staff competent and creative?

E. Sales force
1. What are the organization's sales force objectives?
2. Is the sales force large enough to accomplish the company's objectives?
3. Is the sales force organized along the proper principle(s) of specialization (territory, market, product)? Are there enough (or too many) sales managers to guide the field sales reps?
4. Does the sales compensation level and structure provide adequate incentive and reward?
5. Does the sales force show high morale, ability, and effort?
6. Are the procedures adequate for setting quotas and evaluating performance?
7. How does the company's sales force compare to the sales forces of competitors?

SOURCE: Philip Kotler, *Marketing Management: Analysis, Planning, and Control*, 6th ed. © 1988, pp. 748–751. Adapted by permission of Prentice-Hall, Inc., Englewood Cliffs, N.J.

Marketing audits can be performed by people within a company or outside it. An internal auditor may be a top-level marketing executive, a companywide auditing committee, or a manager from another office or of another function. Although it is more expensive, an audit by outside consultants is usually more effective because external auditors have more objectivity, more time for the audit, and greater experience.

There is no single set of procedures for all marketing audits. Firms should adhere to several general guidelines. Audits are often based on a series of questionnaires that are administered to the firm's personnel. These questionnaires should be developed carefully to ensure that the audit focuses on the right issues. Auditors should develop and follow a step-by-step plan to guarantee that the audit is systematic. When interviewing company personnel, the auditors should strive to talk with a diverse group of people from many parts of the company. The auditor should become familiar with the product line, meet with headquarters staff, visit field organizations, interview customers, interview competitors, and analyze information for a report on the marketing environment.[22] To achieve adequate support, the auditors normally focus on the firm's top management initially and then move down through the organizational hierarchy. The auditor looks for different points of view within various departments of the organization or a mismatch between the customers' and company's perception of the product as signs of trouble in an organization.[23] The results of the audit should be set forth in a comprehensive written document.[24] The marketing audit report should include recommendations that will increase marketing productivity and determine the business's general direction.[25]

The marketing audit lets an organization change tactics or alter day-to-day activities as problems arise. For example, marketing auditors often wonder whether a change from budgeted sales activity is caused by general market conditions or is due to a change in the firm's market share. For example, in the audit of a consumer electronics firm, the goal was to determine why there was a 4,000-unit increase of actual sales over budgeted sales for a one-month period. Was this sales increase the result of an expanding market, increased market share, or some combination of both factors?

Examining the monthly budget projections, the auditor found that the firm's estimated market share was 20 percent. The projected industry sales were 80,000 units, of which the firm would sell 16,000. The firm actually sold 20,000 units. By examining sources of industry volume data such as trade journals, the marketing manager was able to ascertain where the gain in unit sales came from. Industry sales went up from 80,000 units to 83,333 units, and the firm's market share went up from 20 to 24 percent, as illustrated in Table 19.4. Of the 4,000-unit sales increase in company volume, a 667-unit increase, which is 20 percent of 3,333 units, is due to the increase in industry volume, holding market share constant. The

22. Ely S. Lurin, "Audit Determines the Weak Link in Marketing Chain," *Marketing News,* Sept. 12, 1986, pp. 35, 37.
23. Ibid.
24. Martin L. Bell, *Marketing: Concepts and Strategies,* 3rd ed. (Boston: Houghton Mifflin, 1979), p. 472.
25. Nathan D. King, "The Marketing Audit: An Extension of the Marketing Control Process," *Managerial Finance* (U.K.), 1985, pp. 23–26.

TABLE 19.4

Results of a marketing
audit showing industry
sales growth and the
firm's increased mar-
ket share

	INDUSTRY	FIRM
Current sales	83,333	20,000 (24%)
Projected sales	−80,000	−16,000 (20%)
Increase in sales	3,333	4,000 (4%)
Increase in industry sales	3,333	
Firm's projected market share (%)	×.20	
Increase from increased industry volume	667	
Current industry sales	83,333	
Increase in firm's market share (%)	×.04	
Increase from increased market share	3,333	
Increase from increased industry volume	667	
Increase from increased market share	+3,333	
Total increase in sales	4,000	

remaining unit sales increase of 3,333 units, which is 4 percent of 83,333 units, is due to the firm's increased market share. This indicates that the consumer electronics firm is achieving better than average sales volume change, which reflects favorably on the marketing department's performance.[26]

The concept of auditing implies an official examination of marketing activities. Many organizations audit their marketing activities informally. Any attempt to verify operating results and to compare them with standards can be considered an auditing activity. Many smaller firms probably would not use the word "*audit*," but they do perform auditing activities.

Several problems may arise in an audit of marketing activities. Marketing audits can be expensive in time and money. Selecting the auditors may be difficult because objective, qualified personnel may not be available. Marketing audits can also be extremely disruptive because employees sometimes fear comprehensive evaluations, especially by outsiders.

Summary

The organization of marketing activities involves the development of an internal structure for the marketing unit. The internal structure is the key to directing marketing activities. The marketing unit can be organized by (1) functions, (2) products, (3) regions, or (4) types of customers. An organization may use only one approach or a combination.

26. Adapted from Edward B. Deakin and Michael W. Maher, *Cost Accounting*, 2nd ed. (Homewood, Ill.: Irwin, 1987), pp. 840–841.

Implementation is an important part of the marketing management process. Proper implementation of marketing plans depends on the coordination of marketing activities, the motivation of marketing personnel, and effective communication within the unit. Marketing managers must coordinate the activities of marketing personnel and integrate these activities with those in other areas of the firm and with the marketing efforts of personnel in external organizations. Marketing managers also must motivate marketing personnel. An organization's communication system must allow the marketing manager to communicate with high-level management, with managers of other functional areas in the firm, and with personnel involved in marketing activities both inside and outside the organization.

The marketing control process consists of establishing performance standards, evaluating actual performance by comparing it with established standards, and reducing the difference between desired and actual performance. A performance standard is an expected level of performance against which actual performance can be compared. Performance standards are established in the planning process. In evaluating actual performance, marketing managers must know what marketers within the firm are doing and must have information about the activities of external organizations that provide the firm with marketing assistance. Then actual performance is compared with performance standards. Marketers must decide whether a discrepancy exists and, if so, whether it requires corrective action such as changing the performance standards or improving actual performance.

An effective control process has several requirements. First, it should be designed so that the flow of information is rapid enough to let the marketing manager quickly detect differences between actual and planned levels of performance. Second, a variety of control procedures must accurately monitor different kinds of activities. Third control procedures should be flexible enough to accommodate changes. Fourth, the control process must be economical so that its costs are low relative to the costs that would arise if there were no controls. Fifth, the control process should be designed so that both managers and subordinates are able to understand it.

To maintain effective marketing control, an organization needs to develop a comprehensive control process that evaluates its marketing operations at a given time. The control of marketing activities is not a simple task. Problems encountered include environmental changes that hamper effective control, time lags between marketing activities and their effects, and problems determining the costs of marketing activities. In addition to these, it may be difficult to develop performance standards.

Control of marketing strategy can be achieved through sales and cost analyses. For purposes of analysis, sales usually are measured in terms of either dollar volume or market share. For a sales analysis to be effective, it must compare current sales performance with forecasted company sales, industry sales, specific competitors' sales, or the costs incurred to generate the current sales volume. A sales analysis can be performed on the firm's total sales, or the total sales can be disaggregated and analyzed by product, geographic area, or customer group.

Marketing cost analysis involves an examination of accounting records and frequently a reclassification of natural accounts into marketing function accounts. Such an analysis is often difficult because there may be no logical, clear-cut way to allocate natural accounts into functional accounts. The analyst may choose either direct costing or full costing. Cost analysis can focus on (1) an aggregate cost analysis of natural accounts or functional accounts or (2) an analysis of functional accounts for products, geographic areas, or customer groups.

To control marketing strategies, it is sometimes necessary to audit marketing activities. Auditing is a systematic appraisal and review of activities in relation to objectives. A marketing audit attempts to identify what a marketing unit is doing, to evaluate the effectiveness of these activities, and to recommend future marketing activities.

Important Terms

Centralized organization
Decentralized organization
Marketing-oriented organization
Job enrichment
Implicit bargaining
Marketing control process
Performance standard
Sales analysis
Marketing cost analysis
Natural accounts
Marketing function accounts
Direct costs
Traceable common costs

Nontraceable common costs
Full-cost approach
Direct-cost approach
Marketing audit

Discussion and Review Questions

1. What determines marketing's place within an organization? Which type of organization is best suited to the marketing concept? Why?
2. What factors can be used to organize the internal aspects of a marketing unit? Discuss the benefits of each type of organization.
3. Why might an organization use multiple bases for organizing its marketing unit?
4. How does communication help in implementing marketing plans?
5. Why is motivation of marketing personnel important in implementing marketing plans?
6. What are the major steps of the marketing control process?
7. List and discuss the five requirements for an effective control process.
8. Discuss the major problems in controlling marketing activities.
9. What is a sales analysis? What makes it an effective control tool?
10. Identify and describe three cost analysis methods. Compare and contrast direct costing and full costing.
11. How is the marketing audit used to control marketing program performance?

Cases

19.1   Organizing Change at Beatrice[27]

Although Beatrice Foods Company has undergone many changes in the last few years, it is still one of the nation's leading food, beverage, and consumer products companies. Beatrice once followed a strategy of acquisition, but now it is turning to a cohesive marketing-driven orientation through two major reorganization efforts.

A few years ago, the company had 434 profit centers in 54 groups. It offered nine thousand products, but with less promotional backing than competitors used for their own products, and it had no long-term strategy for their future. In its first reorganization effort, Beatrice turned this loose aggregation of profit centers into a unified, directed marketing company. The company divided its business units into six operating groups and established its first corporate marketing department to oversee the planning and implementation of marketing efforts throughout the company. This restructuring into smaller numbers of larger units enabled Beatrice to implement national distribution and national advertising for its products. The six units were later reduced to four operating divisions: U.S. Food, Consumer Products, International Foods, and Avis/Other Operations.

The U.S. Food division has always been the cornerstone of Beatrice. It has 150 brands in ninety product categories, including grocery products, soft drinks, bottled water, meats, and dairy products. The Consumer Products division has operations in water treatment, luggage, lingerie, health and beauty aids, and fragrances. The International Foods division operates in thirty countries, selling food and grocery products. The Avis division owned Avis car rental, the nation's second largest car rental operation.

This reorganization greatly increased Beatrice's marketing clout; Beatrice is now the third largest advertiser in the United States. In one year, Beatrice spent $680 million on advertising and sales promotion to develop and maintain a leadership position in its highly competitive marketplace. Before this new corporate identity campaign, the Beatrice name was not widely recognized, although many of its products did have widespread national recognition. As a result of these marketing efforts, consumer awareness of the Beatrice name tripled, and consumers came to associate the name with quality and value. Beatrice was trying to enhance consumer awareness of Beatrice as a whole with the corporate identity program it used in packaging, advertising campaigns, and branding. Americans became used to seeing the red stripe logo and hearing "We're Beatrice, you've known us all along."

In 1985, the company went through more changes after it was bought out by a group of private investors. These investors studied the earlier reorganization plans,

27. Based on information from *Organizing Corporate Marketing* (New York: Conference Board, 1984), pp. 44–45; *Beatrice Annual Report*, 1985; Alan Karo, "Developing Corporate Identity," *Marketing & Media Decisions*, April 1984, pp. 98, 100, 102; Laura Konrad Jereski, "Beatrice Make-Over," *Marketing & Media Decisions*, May 1984, pp. 74–77; Ford S. Worthy, "Beatrice's Sell-Off Strategy," *Fortune*, June 23, 1986, pp. 44, 46, 49; Robert Johnson, "Beatrice Faces Tricky Task in Dismantling Its Empire," *Wall Street Journal*, Apr. 12, 1986, p. 12; Bob Messenger, "Marketing in the 80's: A Playground for the Giants," *Prepared Foods*, April 1986, pp. 46–50; Stephen Greenhouse, "Kelly Outlines His Ideas for Beatrice," *New York Times*, Nov. 28, 1985, p. D3; Christine Donahue, "Marketers Return to Product Testing," *Adweek*, May 4, 1987, p. 66.

conducted an audit, and then made sweeping changes of their own. They installed new control systems to keep Beatrice under tighter rein. The new CEO sold Avis immediately and made plans to sell off many other parts of the huge company, primarily from the Consumer Products division, to help the new investors pay off part of their purchase loans. That left food products as the core of Beatrice.

The investors' primary goal is to make what remains of Beatrice a financially worthwhile investment. Because Beatrice stock is no longer sold publicly, the company does not have to concern itself with short-term issues, such as stock prices and Wall Street investors, and can focus on long-range goals. That means more flexibility in implementing current strategy.

The company has also changed the slant of its marketing strategy: It dropped the corporate identity program and the red stripe and now puts those advertising dollars into specific brand advertising. The new CEO does not think that it is appropriate to spend money on image advertisements when the real job at Beatrice is to sell products. Beatrice must also concern itself with its competitors, who are increasing their own advertising expenditures. Beatrice must match them to maintain its market share and its cash flow so as to pay off its creditors.

Talent, especially in the management levels of planning and research, is looking for greener pastures, which will not help Beatrice continue as a leader in new-products introduction. Unfortunately, this is occurring at a time when the life cycle of consumer products grows shorter and the failure rate for new products is increasing.

Questions for Discussion

1. Beatrice has reorganized its divisions on what basis?
2. Why did Beatrice management reorganize?
3. Why did the new private investor group reorganize the old reorganization effort?
4. Although the overall long-term effects of Beatrice's strategy may be quite favorable, the company may face some adverse short-term effects. What are they?

19.2 TreeSweet Products Turns Sour[28]

TreeSweet Products Company, a regional producer of citrus juice beverages, changed its corporate strategy in an attempt to become a recognizable national company and join ranks with the top three juice producers: Minute Maid (Coca-Cola Company), Tropicana (Beatrice Foods Company), and Citrus Hill (Procter & Gamble).

28. Based on information from Tom Bayer, "TreeSweet Jumps into '86 Ripe for Growth," *Advertising Age,* Feb. 3, 1986, p. 58; Jon Berry, "TreeSweet Branches Out," *Adweek,* Dec. 16, 1985, pp. 1, 50; Judith Crown, "TreeSweet Bets Future on Aggressive Marketing Tactics," *Houston Chronicle,* Jan. 12, 1986, p. 5-1; Jo Ellen Davis, "A Juice Maker Squeezes Itself Dry," *Business Week,* Aug. 10, 1987, p. 42; Scott Clark, "TreeSweet Products Caught in Squeeze," *Houston Chronicle,* Aug. 9, 1987, pp. 5-1, 5-5.

To achieve this long-term goal, TreeSweet developed a multitiered corporate strategy. First, the company expanded its product line to offer blended fruit drinks, a variety of other fruit juices, juice-added soft drinks, and reduced-calorie juices. TreeSweet purchased the country's leading breakfast beverage, Awake, and Orange Plus from General Foods Corp., and it also bought Faygo Beverages, Inc., a small soft-drink maker. The company expanded its distribution channels, formerly limited to six states, to include half the country. In addition, TreeSweet arranged for H. J. Heinz to market its products to Heinz customers in the food service industry.

TreeSweet also changed many components of its marketing strategy. It spruced up its logo and package design to convey an image of higher quality. The new package, which emphasizes the TreeSweet company name, displays fruit hanging from a tree, instead of the smiling oranges that covered TreeSweet packages for many decades. To support all these changes, the company developed an aggressive advertising and promotional program. TreeSweet plastered 1,200 billboards with its new orange and blue logo in its major markets. TreeSweet also aggressively instituted major price cuts before its larger competitors did.

After a small spurt of growth, TreeSweet was in deep trouble. The cost of its expansion along with disappointing sales of the diet brands on which it had banked heavily left TreeSweet in a severe cash crunch. The company defaulted on a $32 million note to its previous owner and was forced to sell Faygo Beverages. It also laid off many employees, cut back its marketing budget, and watched its share of the orange juice market dive. After cutting back on advertising and other promotion in 1987, its market share dropped to 1.8 percent, compared to 4 percent in 1986.

TreeSweet's problems came about because its plans were simply too risky. The company did not take into account the realities of the juice business, and the vast resources of its large competitors proved too much for TreeSweet to overcome. The purchases from General Foods left TreeSweet with a debt-to-equity ratio of 56:1, making it tough for the company to finance any expansion of its major money maker, frozen orange juice.

Many industry observers believe that TreeSweet's problems resulted from the introduction of its line of reduced-calorie juices, TreeSweet Lite. The company committed several million dollars to developing the product, and it planned to back the line with a $40 million national marketing campaign. Yet, in its haste to beat its competitors to the market, the company took TreeSweet Lite national without any formal test marketing. The product was a failure, and this destroyed TreeSweet's plan to have a national presence.

Industry analysts feel that the concept of a diet-juice drink made sense for a calorie-conscious public. However, it seems that that diet concept does not apply to breakfast drinks; the public did not buy TreeSweet Lite because they prefer a juice that is fresh and natural, not one with fewer calories. As a result, sales of TreeSweet Lite were much lower than expected.

The cost of TreeSweet's acquisitions coupled with the disappointing sales of TreeSweet Lite left the company in financial straits. When its problems surfaced, the company halted all advertising and slashed its marketing spending and its payroll. Eventually, the five top officers of the company, including the president and the vice-president for marketing, were dismissed.

TreeSweet filed a lawsuit against its former owner, the Di Giorgio Corporation, claiming that many financial problems resulted from the seller's misrepresentations at the time of purchase. According to TreeSweet, it lost $3.9 million on contracts for frozen orange juice concentrate futures put in place by Di Giorgio. The company also claims it was forced to honor a contract with a grower to buy oranges it did not need.

The problems at TreeSweet illustrate the problems of implementing and controlling a marketing strategy. They also show the risks that a small company trying to compete with the giants in the consumer products industry must face.

Questions for Discussion

1. What are the implications of TreeSweet's having ineffective control of its marketing activities?
2. What problems did TreeSweet encounter in implementing its new marketing strategy?
3. Why did TreeSweet decide to implement a new marketing strategy?

Part VI   *S T R A T E G I C   C A S E*

Black & Decker Develops New Strategies

Black & Decker is one of the country's foremost producers of portable power tools, accessories, lawn mowers, and electric garden tools. Since purchasing General Electric's small-appliance business in 1984, Black & Decker is now a leading manufacturer of small household appliances. Black & Decker's annual sales are approximately $2 billion. Retailers and customers consistently give Black & Decker high marks for quality, good prices, and national brand-name status.

A New Corporate Strategy

Despite Black & Decker's successes, the Towson, Maryland, company recently revised its corporate strategy. During the 1980s, recession slowed sales of Black & Decker power tools, the company's most important product line. Meanwhile, Japanese manufacturers took advantage of the strong dollar to capture some of Black & Decker's domestic market share. With sales down, some Black & Decker plants were forced to operate at only 50 percent capacity. Black & Decker's overall profits also suffered because of its faltering McCulloch chain saw unit. The first major step in developing a new corporate strategy was to sell this strategic business unit.

Conditions continued to slide, and in 1985, Black & Decker posted a $158 million loss, its worst ever. Several chief executives were fired in an attempt to improve performance. Finally, Nolan D. Archibald, a marketing and operations specialist who had masterminded five corporate turnarounds, was hired away from Beatrice as president. In March 1986, the board of directors made Archibald chief executive, and he focused his energy on developing the new Black & Decker corporate strategy.

Under Archibald's direction, the strategy was to make Black & Decker an aggressive, customer-oriented company, one driven less by financial concerns and more by the needs of its target markets, both industrial and consumer. To cut down on overhead, Black & Decker streamlined its manufacturing operations around the world, closing six of twenty-five plants and eliminating two thousand jobs. Plants are now organized around the motor sizes of appliances and tools; there were more than one hundred sizes, but eventually they will be standardized to six.

Black & Decker's new corporate strategy changed not only the scope of the business (buying General Electric's appliance division and selling the McCulloch chain saw division) but also its resource deployment, competitive advantages, and overall coordination of production, finance, marketing, and other functional areas. Black & Decker traditionally made customized power tools for specialized markets (as evidenced by the more than one hundred different motor sizes). Japan's Makita Electric Works Ltd. took a portion of Black & Decker's market by providing standardized, competitively priced, quality markets worldwide. Black & Decker responded by standardizing its manufacturing and marketing worldwide as much as possible. The company bought General Electric's small appliances and power tools to diversify, to compensate for a flattening demand for professional tools and the loss of the chain saw division.

New Marketing Strategies

Black & Decker's unfocused approach to marketing contributed to its corporate troubles. For years, the company usually followed a simple marketing strategy: produce quality products and offer resellers year-end price cuts. Promotion was not emphasized in the marketing mix. Retailers complained that Black & Decker's promotional efforts were inadequate and failed to excite consumers. In some years, some distributors, disillusioned by the manufacturer's lack of promotional support, had even considered dropping the line. The poor communication between Black & Decker and its resellers stemmed partly from the company's preoccupation with finances. To save money, for example, Black & Decker combined its sales groups so that all accounts in a single territory—industrial, retail, and consumer— were managed alike, without regard to the different sales approaches required by various market segments. To improve its year-end balance sheet, Black & Decker routinely let inventory levels drop in September, leaving resellers short of products for the Christmas buying season.

Under its new strategy, Black & Decker created about ten distributor advisory councils to improve relations with its distributors. The councils have generated ideas for several new products, including a heavy-duty reciprocating power saw already in production. In addition, Black & Decker has established sales training programs for distributors and now sends out company representatives to call on customers jointly with distributors' salespeople. To introduce new product lines, the company has conducted regional seminars with key industrial wholesalers. Although admitting that changes in corporate attitudes occur slowly, Black & Decker officials say that the attempt to improve relationships with intermediaries is paying off. With distributors solidly behind Black & Decker products, the company expects the efforts of its own salespeople to be multiplied many times over.

The sales force itself is competing more effectively as a result of the new focus on marketing. In contrast to its past unfocused selling strategy, Black & Decker now has sales staff reorganized into industrial, consumer, national, and retail groups. Each sales force is formally trained in strategies for specific markets, the better to satisfy specialized customer needs. During the past five years, Black & Decker's sales have increased $700 million, despite stiff competition from foreign manufacturers. In a recent survey of industry experts, the company received high ratings for innovativeness in selling and for success in opening new accounts.

Industrial Markets

Two of the markets now receiving specialized attention from Black & Decker are the nation's manufacturing and construction (industrial) firms. With a 25 percent share of the $400 million manufacturing power tool business, Black & Decker dominates the market. But by assigning sales specialists to manufacturing and construction customers, Black & Decker hopes to strengthen further its name identification and demonstrate the importance of these two market segments.

Black & Decker is reinforcing the segmented sales approach with improved customer service to boost acceptance of its new Master Series line, targeted for manufacturing and construction customers. Master Series customers will be entitled to one year of free repairs, and the company will guarantee four-hour repair

service for any Master Series tool brought to an authorized service center. Loaner tools will be available in the interim, courtesy of Black & Decker's new policy of maintaining full spare-parts inventories at all times.

Consumer Markets

Given that to many consumers the Black & Decker name is synonymous with power tools, diversification into consumer housewares has presented the company with a completely different set of marketing challenges. First, by purchasing the General Electric line—about 150 products in all—Black & Decker has entered a crowded market that is largely mature. Only about 10 percent of small-appliance users buy new products in any given year; replacements, not initial purchases, account for most sales. Moreover, because competing products are much alike, appliance manufacturers have traditionally marketed to resellers on the basis of price instead of by advertising product features directly to consumers. As a result of price cutting, profits in the $8.3 billion industry have been low in recent years, less than 5 percent of sales. (Market leader General Electric cited lack of profitability as a major reason for selling to Black & Decker.)

Black & Decker has also faced the challenge of transferring consumer loyalty from the venerable General Electric brand name to its own label. Despite the success of Black & Decker's Dustbuster cordless vacuum cleaner (see Figure 1), the company's first venture into household appliances, Black & Decker had not been widely recognized as a housewares maker. Only 12 percent of the consumers in a recent survey listed Black & Decker as a small-appliance maker, whereas 92 percent named General Electric. According to another survey, most people think General Electric is still producing its line of toasters, irons, can openers, and other household appliances, a point of confusion compounded by the fact that General Electric continues to make audio products and microwave ovens.

Because of its low name recognition in housewares, Black & Decker decided to replace General Electric's logo over a period of three years, product by product, as allowed by the terms of sale. The company's marketing managers—some of which came from General Electric's marketing staff—organized the rebranding process into 140 steps, to be completed for each product over three months. Some products were manufactured in new colors, some were given extra features, and some were completely redesigned. Every product was marketed with a two-year warranty, twice as long as that offered by General Electric. First to be reintroduced under the Black & Decker name was a sleeker version of the Spacemaker appliances, a line of under-the-cabinet coffee makers, toaster ovens, and can openers. Last to be marketed were Black & Decker-brand irons, a crucial product line representing 25 percent of Black & Decker's small-appliance sales.

During the changeover, advertising generally displayed the Black & Decker name on products that had been reintroduced and the General Electric label remained on products not yet converted. Some advertisements included a combination of the two names. Black & Decker has also just completed a $100 million, three-year advertising campaign for its new line of household appliances, a promotional effort unprecedented in the small-appliance industry. The company is pouring additional millions into market research, product development, and improved distribution systems.

According to Black & Decker officials, the brand transition, now complete, went so smoothly that the original timetable was accelerated. Despite some initial share loss in certain categories—such as the iron market, where Sunbeam was first with models that shut off automatically—Black & Decker has continued to occupy General Electric's former position as market leader. Black & Decker has invested about $20 million to promote its housewares with retailers, although resellers must stock a specific number of Black & Decker models to qualify for certain discounts and promotional programs.

One reason for the new emphasis on promotion and advertising is the company's decision to eliminate rebates on all products. Rebates for Black & Decker kitchen and personal-care appliances ended last summer. Money-back incentives for lawn and garden products and all power tools will be phased out this year. Black & Decker officials say that manufacturers' rebates make little sense in an industry already squeezed by low profit margins. Moreover, many retailers consider the rebate system a nuisance. Market research shows that consumers too find rebates inconvenient and unnecessary, especially because 35 to 40 percent of all items subject to rebates are purchased as gifts. Even without rebates, the Spacemaker line has captured about 65 percent of the under-the-cabinet appliance business. Black & Decker's toaster ovens have garnered a 45 percent market share without rebates, and its automatic shut-off irons have also climbed to the top of the market without extra purchase incentives. Maintaining that customers prefer product superiority and innovation to rebates, Black & Decker intends to channel rebate dollars into advertising, research, and new-product development.

The Future

Looking into the future, Black & Decker plans innovative marketing strategies that will focus on new products while maintaining effective distribution, promotion, and pricing. A dozen new products each year is the goal of the company's tools division. In household products, Black & Decker is expected to keep pushing cordless appliances, a category popularized first by the Dustbuster and then by the Handymixer, Black & Decker's single-beater cordless kitchen mixer. Other new products in the works include a scaled-down food processor, a disposable travel iron, a home security system, a fire extinguisher, and a line of space heaters. Black & Decker has even licensed its trademark for a line of toy mixers, toasters, and irons, hoping that children who become aware of the Black & Decker label as youngsters will remain loyal to the brand as adults. Black & Decker has approval rights for packaging, advertising, and product quality and considers licensing toys a new avenue of distribution.

Questions for Discussion

1. Compare and contrast Black & Decker's corporate strategy and marketing strategy.
2. Due to intense competition, Black & Decker attempted to improve profits by purchasing General Electric's small appliance division. Discuss the success and future problems that Black & Decker will face implementing this competitive strategy.

3. How did Black & Decker use an improved organizational structure and improved implementation of marketing strategies to improve profits? How important are these areas to continued profits?

SOURCES: "Up and Down Wall Street," *Barron's,* Apr. 6, 1987, p. 1; Michael Abramowitz, "Black & Decker," *The Washington Post,* Feb. 17, 1986, p. 1; "B&D: Goodbye Rebates," *Marketing Week/Promote,* Apr. 18, 1987, p. 4; "B&D's New Line Hailed As Ultimate Power Tool," *Industrial Distribution,* August 1987, p. 9; "B&D, Stanley Head Diverse Hardware Brands," *Discount Store News,* Oct. 12, 1987, pp. 147–148; "Black & Decker Rebuilds," *Sales & Marketing Management,* June 1987, p. 49; "Black & Decker to Send Sales Specialists into Industrial and Construction Markets," *Industrial Distribution,* April 1987, p. 4; "Dennis Heiner's Vision," *HFD-Retailing Home Furnishings,* Nov. 10, 1986, p. 1; Christopher Eklund, "How Black & Decker Got Back in the Black," *Business Week,* July 13, 1987, p. 86; "How Black & Decker Forged a Winning Brand Transfer Strategy," *Business International,* July 20, 1987, p. 225; "Late Breaking News," *Hardware Age,* October 1987, p. 14; "Line of Black & Decker Toys Expected," *Baltimore Sun,* Feb. 11, 1987, p. G2; Bill Saporito, "Ganging Up on Black & Decker," *Fortune,* Dec. 23, 1985, pp. 63–64; Sara Stern, "Sunbeam, B&D Limit Rebate Plans," *Advertising Age,* Apr. 6, 1987, p. 3; "Today the Phone, Tomorrow the House," *The New York Times,* May 31, 1987, p. F19.

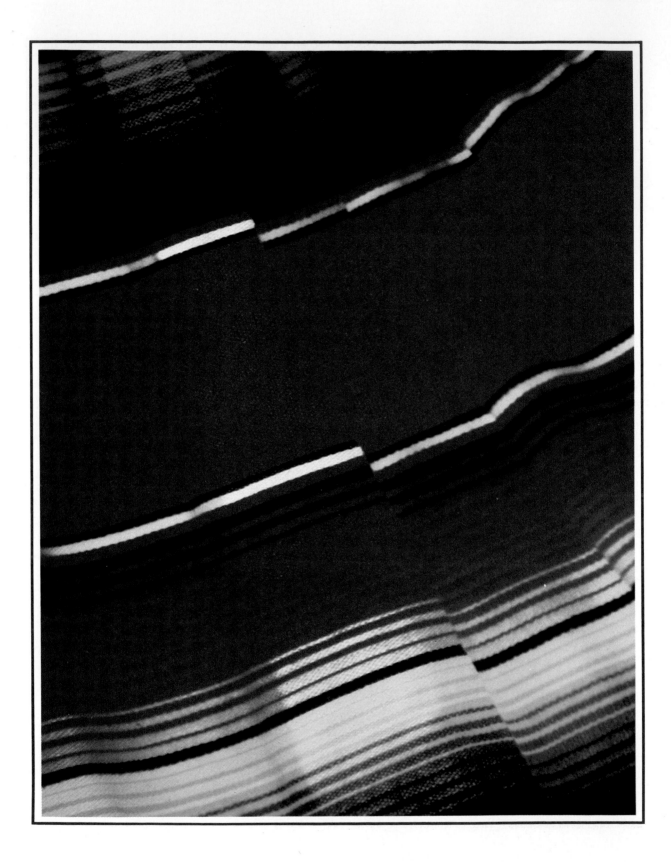

VII. Selected Applications

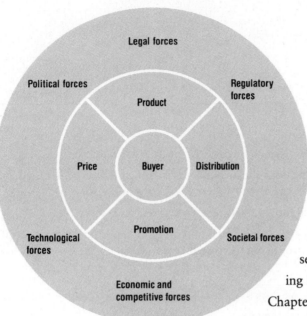

The remaining chapters in this book deal with strategic applications in industrial, services and nonbusiness, and international marketing. Emphasis is on the features and issues unique to each of these selected areas of marketing when formulating and implementing marketing strategies. Chapter 20 analyzes industrial marketing strategy development and discusses the decisions and activities that characterize industrial marketing. Chapter 21 explores selected aspects of services and nonbusiness marketing strategies. Chapter 22 focuses on the development and implementation of marketing strategies for foreign markets.

20. Industrial Marketing

O B J E C T I V E S

- ▶ To understand some unique characteristics of industrial marketing.
- ▶ To see how the demand for industrial products differs from the demand for consumer products.
- ▶ To learn how to select and analyze industrial target markets.
- ▶ To find out how industrial marketing mix components differ from the components in consumer product marketing mixes.

*T*he Boeing Co., the world's largest manufacturer of commercial jetliners, has dominated the civil aircraft industry for years (see Figure 20.1). But these days, even Boeing is finding the commercial aircraft business a buyer's market. Although about seven hundred airliners are produced annually by three companies alone—Boeing, McDonnell Douglas Corp., and Airbus Industrie, a European consortium—world demand for jet planes is estimated at only five hundred aircraft per year. Recession and the fierce competition among commercial carriers spawned by domestic deregulation have cut into airline profit margins, making it tougher for carriers to buy new planes. As a result, Boeing and other aircraft manufacturers are gearing up for a fight.

Boeing's most immediate threat is newcomer Airbus, a cooperative venture formed in 1969 by French, German, British, and Spanish interests. Although the 71-year-old Seattle giant ignored Airbus at first, Boeing's share of the world market has dropped from 70 percent to 50 percent in the last six years, largely because of the inroads Airbus has made. For example, Airbus has filled production capacity for its new 150-seat A320 plane through 1992 and will deliver the first A320s to customers this spring. Meanwhile, Boeing's competing plane, the 7J7, is still in the planning stage.

Boeing also has been forced to cut prices to remain competitive. On the strength of $14 billion in government backing, Airbus uses a pricing strategy so aggressive that Boeing and other manufacturers have filed official complaints with the current session of the General Agreement on Tariffs and Trade meeting in Geneva. Recently, to retain at least part of its business with long-time customer

FIGURE 20.1

Advertisement for
Boeing (SOURCE: The
Boeing Company)

American Airlines, Boeing agreed to leasing terms so liberal that its own sales policies were violated. In the end, American obtained fifteen planes from Boeing and twenty-five from Airbus.

Still, Boeing believes that its new 7J7 plane, now scheduled for production in 1992, will ultimately emerge victorious in the battle of the high-tech jetliners. Designed for efficiency and low cost of ownership, the 7J7 features the revolutionary propfan engine, a rear-mounted propellor estimated to burn 85 percent less fuel than the 727 and expected to make Airbus' conventional engines obsolete. A new aluminum-lithium alloy used in the wings and fuselage will reduce weight (and thus fuel consumption) even further. The 7J7 also eliminates forty-six miles of wiring and includes galleys, lavatories, and seats that can be positioned in the cabin according to customer specifications. In addition, recognizing that airlines must consider comfort as well as economy when purchasing aircraft, Boeing is including cordless entertainment systems and a screen in the back of each seat's headrest.

Now being fine-tuned to current market trends, the 7J7 is intended as the replacement for the 1200 or so Boeing 727s to be retired from service during the next fifteen years—a market with huge potential for aircraft manufacturers.[1]

T HE BOEING COMPANY is an industrial marketer facing stiff competition. To maintain its leadership in the commercial airliner market, it must develop effective industrial marketing strategies. Industrial marketers experience some problems similar to those of consumer product marketers and rely on basic marketing concepts and decisions. However, those concepts and decisions are applied in different ways that take into account the nature of industrial markets and products.

Industrial marketing is a set of activities directed toward facilitating and expediting exchanges involving industrial products and customers in industrial markets. As Chapter 3 discusses, an **industrial market** consists of individuals, groups, or organizations that purchase a specific kind of product for direct use in producing other products or for use in day-to-day operations. Industrial markets are made up of numerous types of customers, including commercial producers, governments, and institutions.

This chapter focuses on dimensions unique to developing marketing strategies for industrial products. Initially, we examine the selection and analysis of industrial target markets. Then we discuss the distinctive features of industrial marketing mixes.

The Nature of Industrial Marketing

As pointed out in Chapter 7, an **industrial product** differs from a consumer product in that it is purchased to be used directly or indirectly to produce other products or to be used in the operations of an organization. Industrial products fall into seven categories:

1. *Raw materials* actually become a part of a physical product. They are the basic materials delivered from mines, farms, forests, oceans, and recycled solid wastes.
2. *Major equipment* includes large tools and machines used for production.
3. Although it does not become a part of the product, *accessory equipment* consists of standardized items used in production and office activities.
4. *Component parts* become part of the physical product and are either finished items ready for assembly or products that need little processing before assembly.
5. *Process materials* are used directly in production, but, unlike component parts, are not readily identifiable.

1. Based on information from Frank Comes, "Widebody Wars: Airbus Decides 'To Go For the Kill,' " *Business Week*, July 6, 1987, pp. 80–81; Kenneth Labich, "Boeing Battles to Stay on Top," *Fortune*, Sept. 28, 1987, pp. 64–66; Nigel Moll, "Boeing," *Flying*, March 1987, pp. 28–39; Eileen White, "Boeing Now Gears Up to Block the Inroads of Airbus in Plane Sales," *Wall Street Journal*, Sept. 2, 1987, p. E1.

6. *Consumable supplies* facilitate a firm's production and operations but do not become an actual part of the finished product.
7. *Industrial services* are the intangible products that organizations use in their operations.

In addition to product differences, industrial marketing is considered unique for the following reasons: (1) the buyer's decision making process, (2) characteristics of the product market, and (3) the nature of environmental influences.[2] These differences influence the development and implementation of industrial marketing strategies.

Selection and Analysis of Industrial Target Markets

Marketing research is becoming more important in industrial marketing. Most of the marketing research techniques that we discuss in Chapter 6 can be applied to industrial marketing. In this section we focus on important and unique approaches to selecting and analyzing industrial target markets.

A considerable amount of information is available to industrial marketers regarding potential customers. Much of this information appears in government and industry publications; comparable data are not available regarding ultimate consumers. Even though industrial marketers may use different procedures to isolate and analyze target markets, most follow a similar pattern of (1) determining who potential customers are and how many there are, (2) locating where they are, and (3) estimating their purchase potential.[3]

Determining Who Potential Customers Are and How Many There Are

Much information about industrial customers is based on the **Standard Industrial Classification (SIC) system,** which the federal government developed to classify selected economic characteristics of industrial, commercial, financial, and service organizations. This system is administered by the Statistical Policy Division of the Office of Management and Budget. Table 20.1 shows how the SIC system can be used to categorize products. Various types of business activities are separated into lettered divisions, and each division is divided into numbered, two-digit major groups. For example, major group 22 includes all firms that manufacture textile mill products. Each major group is divided into three-digit-coded subgroups, and each subgroup is separated into detailed industry categories that are coded with four-digit numbers. In the most recent SIC Manual, there are 83 major groups, 596 subgroups, and 1005 detailed industry categories.[4] To categorize manufacturers in more detail, the *Census of Manufacturers* further subdivides manufacturers (Division D) into five- and seven-digit-coded groups. The fifth digit denotes the product class, and the sixth and seventh digits designate the specific product.

2. Edward F. Fern and James R. Brown, "The Industrial/Consumer Marketing Dichotomy: A Case of Insufficient Justification," *Journal of Marketing*, Spring 1984, pp. 168–177.
3. Robert W. Haas, *Industrial Marketing Management* (New York: Petrocelli Charter, 1976), pp. 37–48.
4. *1987 Standard Industrial Classification Manual*, Office of Management and Budget.

LEVEL	SIC CODE	DESCRIPTION
Division	D	Manufacturing
Major group	22	Textile mill products
Industry subgroup	225	Knitting mills
Detailed industry	2251	Women's full-length and knee-length hosiery
Product category	22513	Women's finished seamless hosiery
Product item	2251311	Misses' finished knee-length socks

SOURCES: *1987 Standard Industrial Classification Manual,* Office of Management and Budget; and *Census of Manufacturers 1982,* Bureau of the Census.

Much data are available for each SIC category through various government publications, such as *Census of Business, Census of Manufacturers,* and *County Business Patterns.* Table 20.2 shows types of information that can be obtained through government sources. Some data are available by state, county, and metropolitan area. Industrial market data also appear in such nongovernment sources as Dun & Bradstreet's *Market Identifiers, Sales and Marketing Management's Survey of Industrial Purchasing Power,* and other trade publications.

The SIC system is a ready-made tool that allows industrial marketers to divide industrial firms into market segments based mainly on the types of products produced or handled. Although the SIC system is a vehicle for segmentation, it must be used in conjunction with other types of data to enable a specific industrial marketer to determine exactly which customers it is possible to reach and their number.

In conjunction with the SIC system, input-output analysis can be used effectively. It is based on the assumption that the output or sales of one industry are the input or purchases of other industries. **Input-output data** report which types of industries purchase the products of a particular industry. A major source of national input-output data is the *Survey of Current Business,* published by the Office of Business Economics, U.S. Department of Commerce. These data are presented in matrix form, with eighty-three industries listed horizontally across the top of the table. To

TABLE 20.2

Types of government information available about industrial markets (based on SIC categories)

Value of industry shipments
Number of establishments
Number of employees
Exports as a percentage of shipments
Imports as a percentage of apparent consumption
Compound annual average rate of growth
Major producing areas

determine which industries purchase the output of a specified industry, simply read down the left column to the specified industry and then read across the horizontal row, which shows how much each of the eighty-three industries spends on the output of the specified industry. For example, sixty-two of the eighty-three industries purchase paints and allied products (industry number 30). However, the purchases of three industries (new construction, maintenance and repair construction, and motor vehicles and equipment) account for 54 percent of the total purchases of paint and allied products. Each of the remaining fifty-four industries buys less than 4.7 percent of the total.

After finding out which industries purchase the major portion of an industry's output, the next step is to determine the SIC numbers for those industries. Because firms are grouped differently in the input-output tables and the SIC system, ascertaining SIC numbers can be difficult. However, the Office of Business Economics does provide some limited conversion tables with the input-output data. These tables can assist industrial marketers in assigning SIC numbers to the industry categories used in the input-output analysis. For example, the motor vehicle and equipment industry, an industry that buys significant quantities of paint and allied products, can be converted into SIC categories 3711 and 3715.

After determining the SIC numbers of the industries that buy the firm's output, an industrial marketer is in a position to ascertain the number of firms that are potential buyers nationally, by state, and by county. Government publications such as the *Census of Business,* the *Census of Manufacturers,* and *County Business Patterns* report the number of establishments within SIC classifications, along with other types of data, such as those shown in Table 20.2. For manufacturing industries, *Sales and Marketing Management's Survey of Industrial Purchasing Power* contains state and county SIC information regarding the number and size of plants and shipment sizes. The *Survey of Industrial Purchasing Power,* unlike most government sources, is updated annually.

Locating Industrial Customers

At this point, an industrial marketer knows what types of industries purchase the kinds of products his or her firm produces as well as the number of establishments in those industries and certain other information. However, that marketer still has to find out the names and addresses of potential customers.

One approach to identifying and locating potential customers is to use state or commercial industrial directories, such as *Standard & Poor's Register* and Dun & Bradstreet's *Middle Market Directory* or *Million Dollar Directory.* These sources contain such information about a firm as its name, SIC number, address, phone number, and annual sales. By referring to one or more of these sources, an industrial marketer can isolate industrial customers that have SIC numbers, determine their locations, and thus develop lists of potential customers by city, county, and state.

A second approach, more expedient but also more expensive, is to use a commercial data company. Dun & Bradstreet, for example, can provide a list of firms that fall into a particular four-digit SIC group. For each firm on the list, Dun & Bradstreet identifies the name, location, sales volume, number of employees, type of products handled, names of chief executives, and other information.

Either approach can effectively identify and locate a group of potential industrial customers. However, an industrial marketer probably cannot pursue all firms on

FIGURE 20.2

Du Pont aims Antron
Precedent commercial
carpet at a benefit seg-
ment (SOURCE:
DUPONT)

the list. Because some firms have a greater purchase potential than others, the
marketer must determine which segment or segments to pursue.

In industrial marketing, situation-specific variables may be more relevant in
segmenting markets than are general customer characteristics. Industrial customers
concentrate on benefits sought; therefore, understanding end use of the product is
more important than the psychology of decisions or socioeconomic characteristics.
Segmenting by benefits rather than customer characteristics can provide insight
into the structure of the market and opportunities for new customers.[5] For example, as Figure 20.2 shows, Du Pont is aiming its Antron Precedent commercial
carpet at customers who are especially concerned about maintenance costs.

**Estimating Purchase
Potential**

To estimate the purchase potential of industrial customers or groups of customers,
an industrial marketer must find a relationship between the size of potential customers' purchases and a variable available in SIC data, such as number of employees. For example, a paint manufacturer might attempt to determine the average
number of gallons purchased by a specific type of potential industrial customer
relative to the number of persons employed. If the industrial marketer has no

5. Peter Doyle and John Saunders, "Market Segmentation and Positioning in Specialized Industrial
Markets," *Journal of Marketing*, Spring 1985, p. 25.

previous experience in this market segment, it will probably be necessary to survey a random sample of potential customers to establish a relationship between purchase sizes and numbers of persons employed. Once this relationship has been established, the relationship can be applied to potential customer segments to estimate their purchases. After deriving these estimates, the industrial marketer selects the customers to be included in the target market.

Despite their usefulness in isolating and analyzing industrial target markets, SIC data pose several problems for users. First, a few industries do not have specific SIC designations. Second, because a transfer of products from one establishment to another is counted as a part of total shipments, double counting may occur when products are shipped between two establishments within the same firm. Third, because the Census Bureau is prohibited from publishing data that would identify a specific business organization, some data—such as value of total shipments—may be understated. Finally, because SIC data are provided by government agencies, there is usually a significant lag between the time the data are collected and when that information becomes available.

Characteristics of Industrial Marketing Mixes

After selecting and analyzing a target market, an industrial marketer must create a marketing mix that will satisfy the customers in that target market. In many respects, the general concepts and methods involved in developing an industrial marketing mix are similar to those used in consumer product marketing. Here we focus on the features of industrial marketing mixes that differ from the marketing mixes for consumer products. We examine each of the four components in an industrial marketing mix: product, distribution, promotion, and price.

Product

After selecting a target market, management has to decide how to compete. Production-oriented managers fail to understand the need to develop a distinct appeal for their product to give it a competitive advantage. Positioning the product (discussed in Chapter 8) is necessary to successfully serve a market, whether consumer or industrial.[6] As indicated in the Application on page 721, 3M Company competes by providing innovative products that satisfy the needs of industrial customers.

Compared with consumer marketing mixes, the product ingredients of industrial marketing mixes often include a greater emphasis on services, both before and after sales. Services, including on-time delivery, quality control, custom design, and a nationwide parts distribution system, may be important components of the product.

Before making a sale, industrial marketers provide potential customers with technical advice regarding product specifications, installation, and application. Many industrial marketers depend heavily on long-term customer relationships that perpetuate sizable repeat purchases. Therefore industrial marketers also make

6. Ibid., p. 25.

Product Development at 3M

With a product mix of fifty thousand products ranging from computer disk-ettes to diaper tabs, 3M Company is admired for its innovative spirit. But 3M's encouragement of inventiveness is more than just management ideal-ism; because 3M sells primarily to industrial customers in mature markets, the Minnesota-based firm actually depends on new ideas to fuel its growth.

About 6.5 percent of the company's $8 billion in revenues goes to research and development—almost twice as much as in most other U.S. firms. In fact, one of 3M's stated goals is to derive 25 percent of its sales from products less than five years old, a goal the company has met in recent years. To stimulate new-product development, 3M lets its scientists and technicians spend up to 15 percent of their time working on any project of their choosing. Currently 3M is investing heavily in electronics research, particularly the development of optical disks for information management, a market that industry experts predict will be worth $1 billion or more by 1990.

In addition to coming up with new products, 3M is constantly on the lookout for new commercial applications for existing technologies. Recently, for example, a design engineer from Pontiac called up 3M's automotive products laboratory searching for a way to minimize the reflection of dash-board lights on car windshields. The 3M chemical engineer who took the call just happened to have a solution—a plastic film designed to be transparent only at a certain angle. Although this "light control film" had been developed almost twenty years earlier, the new application satisfied Pontiac's needs. Eventually 3M distributed the plastic film worldwide, with the chemical en-gineer spearheading the marketing program.

Innovativeness at 3M is not just limited to product development. The company also encourages and rewards good marketing ideas. One 3M mar-ket development manager in the automotive trades unit came up with an award-winning market information system that increased his unit's profits 50 percent. Because the system improved the accuracy of the unit's sales fore-casting and product planning, 3M was able to target and enter a newly emerging segment of the automotive repair market. Another marketing supervisor worked out a five-level career-development plan to improve the performance of salespeople in his packaging division, a system that is now a model for all company divisions. In distribution, 3M has introduced the Uniform Product Code throughout its operations. Besides saving the com-pany $16 million annually, the new bar coding provides greater accuracy and lower costs for 3M customers as well.

Officials at 3M point out that foreign competitors often have market ad-vantages that U.S. firms do not. Lower costs, for example, have put the Japanese ahead of 3M in the videotape and floppy disk markets. Innovation, on the other hand, often represents an unfilled niche—a different way to satisfy the needs of industrial and organizational customers. By continuing to emphasize new ways of doing things, 3M intends to be the company that fills that niche.

SOURCES: Marc Beauchamp, "A Sticky Business," *Forbes,* Jan. 26, 1987, p. 61; Bob Donath, "Inspiring the Marketing Troops to Greater Heights," *Business Marketing,* June 1986, pp. 158–159; Steven Greenhouse, "An Innovator Gets Down to Business," *The New York Times,* Oct. 12, 1986, sec. 3, p. F1; William Hoffer, "Spurs for Innovation," *Nation's Business,* June 1986, pp. 42–45; Patrick Houston, "How Jake Jacobson Is Lighting a Fire Under 3M," *Business Week,* July 21, 1986, pp. 106–107; Michael R. Pashall, "Four Success Stories—Bar Codes Made Them Happen," *Modern Materials Handling,* March 1986, pp. 66–69; "The Datamation 100," *Datamation,* June 15, 1987, p. 154.

a considerable effort to provide services after the sale. Because industrial customers depend heavily on having products available when needed, on-time delivery is another service included in the product component of many industrial marketing mixes. An industrial marketer unable to provide on-time delivery cannot expect the marketing mix to satisfy industrial customers. For example, the Bruck Plastics Company advertisement in Figure 20.3 promotes service, quality, and savings. Availability of parts must also be included in the product mixes of many industrial marketers because a lack of parts can result in costly production delays. The industrial marketer who includes availability of parts within the product component has a competitive advantage over a marketer who fails to offer this service. Customers whose average purchases are large often desire credit; thus some industrial marketers include credit services in their product mixes.

When planning and developing an industrial product mix, an industrial marketer of component parts and semifinished products must realize that a customer may decide to make the items instead of buying them. In some cases, then, industrial marketers compete not only with each other but with their own potential customers.

Industrial products frequently must conform to standard technical specifications industrial customers want. Thus industrial marketers tend to concentrate on product research directed at functional features rather than on marketing research.[7] This focus has led to some less than successful marketing mixes. For example, Steel Company of Canada (Stelco) sold trainloads of common nails to a market it did not really know. Its marketers did not know who bought Stelco nails, nor did they know for what applications the nails were used. Stelco introduced a revolutionary nail, an inexpensive spiral-threaded nail that is stronger than common nails, has more holding power, and is easier to drive. However, the new nails have not sold as well as management expected,[8] primarily because Stelco's research focused on nails rather than on customers' needs.

Because industrial products often are sold on the basis of specifications, rarely through self-service, the major consideration in package design is protection. There is less emphasis on the package as a promotional device.

7. Jon G. Udell, *Successful Marketing Strategies in American Industries* (Madison, Wis.: Mimir, 1972), pp. 48–49.
8. Peter M. Banting, "Unsuccessful Innovation in the Industrial Market," *Journal of Marketing,* January 1978, p. 100.

722   Part VII   SELECTED APPLICATIONS

Research on industrial customer complaints indicates that industrial buyers usually complain when they encounter problems with product quality or delivery time. On the other hand, consumers' complaints pertain to other problems. This type of buyer feedback allows industrial marketers to gauge marketing performance and provide satisfaction where possible. It is important that industrial marketers respond to valid complaints because the success of most industrial products depends on repeat purchases. Because buyer complaints serve a useful purpose, many industrial firms facilitate this feedback by providing customer service departments.[9]

If an industrial marketer is in a mature market, growth can come from attracting market share from another industrial marketer, or a firm can look at new applications or uses for its products. Wescon Products of Wichita, Kansas, is a maker of handtrucks and other handling devices, mainly for heavy industrial customers. In recent years, prospects for sales growth have been quite limited because heavy manufacturing has been on the decline in the United States. To compensate, the company developed a gadabout, a stylish handtruck that is useful in offices, and thereby made further growth in its handtruck business possible.[10]

9. Hiram C. Barksdale, Jr., Terry E. Powell, and Earnestine Hargrove, "Complaint Voicing by Industrial Buyers," *Industrial Marketing Management,* May 1984, pp. 93–99.
10. "Consider: Industrial Marketers Entering the Consumer Zone," *Marketing News,* Aug. 30, 1985, p. 1.

FIGURE 20.3

Industrial marketer promotes service, quality, and savings (SOURCE: Bruck Plastics Co.)

Distribution

The distribution ingredient in industrial marketing mixes differs from that of consumer products with respect to the types of channels used; the kinds of intermediaries available; and the transportation, storage, and inventory policies.

Distribution channels tend to be shorter for industrial products than for consumer products. Figure 20.4 shows four commonly used industrial channels. Other, less popular channels also may be available. Although **direct distribution channels,** in which products are sold directly from producers to users (see channel 1, Figure 20.4), are not used frequently in the distribution of consumer products, they are the most widely used for industrial products. More than half of all industrial products are sold through direct channels. Industrial buyers like to communicate directly with producers, especially when expensive or technically complex products are involved. In these circumstances, an industrial customer wants the technical assistance and personal assurances that only a producer can provide.

In channel 2 (Figure 20.4), a manufacturers' agent is employed. As described in Chapter 10, a **manufacturers' agent** or representative is an independent business person who sells complementary products of several producers in assigned territories and is compensated through commissions. A manufacturers' agent does not acquire title to the products and usually does not take possession. Acting as a salesperson on behalf of the producers, a manufacturers' agent has no latitude, or very little, in negotiating prices or sales terms.

Using manufacturers' agents can benefit an industrial marketer. These agents usually possess considerable technical and market information and have an established set of customers. For an industrial seller with highly seasonal demand, a manufacturers' agent can be an asset because the seller does not have to support a year-round sales force. That manufacturers' agents are paid on a commission basis also may be an economical alternative for a firm that has highly limited resources and cannot afford a full-time sales force.

Certainly, the use of manufacturers' agents is not problem-free. Even though straight commissions may be cheaper for an industrial seller, the seller may have little control over manufacturers' agents. Because of the compensation method, manufacturers' agents usually want to concentrate on their larger accounts. They are frequently reluctant to spend adequate time following up sales, to put forth special selling efforts, or to provide sellers with market information when such activities reduce the amount of productive selling time. Because they rarely maintain inventories, manufacturers' agents have a limited ability to quickly provide customers with parts or repair services.

Channel 3 in Figure 20.4 shows an **industrial distributor** between the producer and the customer. As are manufacturers' agents, industrial distributors are independent business organizations. However, they do take title to products, and they do carry inventories. Industrial distributors usually sell standardized items such as maintenance supplies, production tools, and small operating equipment. Some industrial distributors carry a wide variety of product lines; others specialize in one or a small number of lines. Industrial distributors can be most effectively used when a product has broad market appeal, is easily stocked and serviced, is sold in small quantities, and is needed rapidly to avoid high losses (as is a part for a machine in an assembly line).[11]

11. James D. Hlavacek and Tommy J. McCuistion, "Industrial Distributors: When, Who, and How?" *Harvard Business Review*, March–April 1983, p. 97.

FIGURE 20.4

Four major types of industrial marketing channels

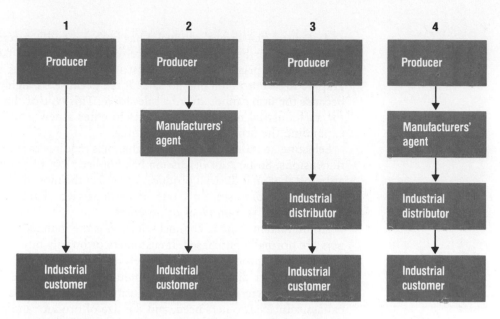

Industrial distributors offer sellers several advantages. They can perform the needed selling activities in local markets at relatively low cost to a manufacturer. They can reduce a producer's financial burden by providing their customers with credit services. And because industrial distributors usually maintain close relationships with their customers, they are aware of local needs and can pass on market information to producers. By holding adequate inventories in their local markets, industrial distributors reduce the producers' capital requirements.

Clark Equipment Company is an example of a company that has successfully turned its industrial distributors into a mass marketing organization to reach smaller industrial concerns. The first step was to downsize its materials handling systems products to fit anyone's needs. Next, distributors were trained to sell automated systems to smaller firms. To participate in the program, industrial distributors had to invest $150,000 to $200,000 in stock and send sales and service people for intensive training. Clark is relying on its industrial distributors to get closer to smaller customers so as to boost sales.[12] The Application on page 727 provides other examples of how producers and distributors are working together to improve marketing effectiveness.

There are, though, several disadvantages to using industrial distributors. Like manufacturers' agents, industrial distributors may be difficult to control because they are independent firms. They frequently stock competing brands, so an industrial seller cannot depend on them to sell a specific brand aggressively. Because industrial distributors maintain inventories—for which they sustain numerous expenses—they are less likely to handle items that are bulky, are slow sellers relative to profit margin, need specialized facilities, or require extraordinary selling efforts. In some cases, industrial distributors lack the technical knowledge necessary to sell and service certain industrial items.

12. "Clark 'Retails' Plant Automation Systems," *Sales and Marketing Management,* Apr. 1, 1985, p. 16.

As Figure 20.4 shows, channel 4 has both a manufacturers' agent and an industrial distributor between the producer and the industrial customer. This channel may be appropriate when the industrial marketer wishes to cover a large geographic area but maintains no sales force because of highly seasonal demand or because the firm cannot afford a sales force. This type of channel also can be useful for an industrial marketer that wants to enter a new geographic market without expanding the firm's existing sales force.

Selecting an industrial channel or channels requires careful analysis along several dimensions. So far, our discussion has implied that all channels are equally available and that an industrial producer can select the most desirable option. However, in a number of cases, only one or perhaps two channels are available for the distribution of certain types of products.

An important issue in channel selection is the manner in which particular products are normally purchased. If customers ordinarily buy certain types of products directly from producers, it is unlikely that channels with intermediaries will be effective. Other dimensions that should be considered are the product's cost and physical characteristics, the costs of using various channels, the amount of technical assistance customers need, and the size of product and parts inventory needed in local markets.

Physical distribution decisions regarding transportation, storage, and inventory control are especially important for industrial marketers. The continuity of most industrial buyer-seller relationships depends on the seller's having the right products available when and where the customer needs them. This requirement is so important that industrial marketers must sometimes make a considerable investment in order processing systems, materials handling equipment, warehousing facilities, and inventory control systems. Like marketers of consumer products, industrial marketers try to use the proper mix of these resources to minimize total physical distribution costs while maintaining a satisfactory level of service.

Promotion

The combination of promotional efforts used in industrial marketing mixes generally differs considerably from those used for consumer products, especially convenience goods. The differences are evident in both the emphasis on various promotion mix ingredients and the activities performed in connection with each promotion mix ingredient.

For several reasons, most industrial marketers rely on personal selling to a much greater extent than do consumer product marketers (except, perhaps, marketers of consumer durables). Because an industrial seller often has fewer customers, personal contact with each customer is more feasible. Some industrial products have technical features that are too numerous or too complex to explain through nonpersonal forms of promotion. Because industrial purchases frequently are high in dollar value and must be suited to the job and available where and when needed, industrial buyers want reinforcement and personal assurances from industrial sales personnel. Because industrial marketers depend on repeat purchases, sales personnel must follow up sales to make certain that customers know how to use the purchased items effectively, as well as to ensure that the products work properly.

As Table 20.3 illustrates, the average cost of an industrial sales call varies from industry to industry. Selling costs were defined as salaries, commissions, bonuses, and travel and entertainment expenses. The average cost of an industrial call is

Enhancing the Manufacturer-Distributor Relationship

How important is the partnership between producer and distributor? Consider the manufacturer that gave its distributors expensive merchandising materials that were "guaranteed" to increase sales. When a certain distributor's sales of the manufacturer's product remained flat quarter after quarter, a company sales representative came around at last to find out why. The sales rep found the materials gathering dust in the distributor's warehouse, unused. The distributor's explanation? The sales aids were quite complicated—and no one from the manufacturer had ever bothered to demonstrate how they fit into a sales presentation.

Obviously, this business arrangement was not much of a partnership. But many manufacturers do understand the importance of building solid relationships with distributors, who are a crucial link between producer and customer. Research indicates that more than three-fourths of all U.S. producers market their products through some form of intermediary, and often through industrial distributors specifically. Along with wholesalers, distributors account for more than $1.1 trillion in sales every year. And according to many industrial marketing managers, the distributor's role in U.S. business is expanding. As producers look for ways to contain their own rising marketing costs, more and more of the responsibility for sales prospecting, problem solving, and long-term service to end users is being shifted to the distributors.

So how can manufacturers improve these valuable working relationships? One way is to determine, and pay attention to, distributors' needs, through market research, field visits, or distributor meetings. Square D, manufacturer of electronics components, regularly gathers information about distributors' needs during its "counter days": Square D salespeople work with a distributor's customers from behind the distributor's own counter. Dayco Corporation's distributor council is a sounding board for the wholesalers of its rubber and plastics products. When the council recommends policy changes, the company eventually adopts many of them.

Another key is to communicate clearly—in both directions and at several levels—on issues ranging from performance problems to policy changes. Dayco and Du Pont both keep their distributors informed via newsletters, and Parker Hannifin Corporation is one of a growing number of manufacturers that send videotaped messages to distributors. Because ordering activities account for much of the contact between producer and distributor, effective partnerships pay special attention to communication between the manufacturer's order center and the distributor's purchasing department.

Manufacturers must also demonstrate lasting commitment to the relationship. Some do so by referring customer inquiries to distributors or by limiting the number of distributors in a given trading area. Lincoln Electric, maker of welding supplies, requires its sales trainees to become certified welders before they can be promoted to field positions, so that they will be of greater service to customers. In addition, research-oriented companies such as the Skil Corp., manufacturer of power tools, provide their distributors with long-range benefits by using technology to produce broader product lines at lower prices. In short, although good manufacturer-distributor relationships are based on years of effort, the improved performance, stable distribution networks, and satisfied customers that result make the effort clearly worthwhile.

SOURCES: Doug Harper, "Industrial R&D Seen Stimulating Distributor Sales," *Industrial Distribution,* April 1987, p. 46; James A. Narus and James C. Anderson, "Industrial Distributor Selling: The Roles of Outside and Inside Sales," *Industrial Marketing Management* (New York: Elsevier Science Publishing, 1986), pp. 55–62; James A. Narus and James C. Anderson, "Turn Your Industrial Distributors into Partners," *Harvard Business Review,* March–April 1986, pp. 66–71.

$229.70.[13] But keep in mind that some industrial sales are very large. A salesperson with Boeing, for instance, closed a sale with Delta Airlines for commercial aircraft worth $3 billion.[14] An average of only 350 aircraft are sold each year, though, resulting in sales of $105 billion. Usually aircraft salespeople work the hardest three to five years before a sale is made.[15]

Because of the escalating costs of advertising and personal selling, telemarketing, the creative use of the telephone to enhance the salesperson's function, is on the upswing. Some of the activities in telemarketing include toll-free 800 phone lines and data-terminal-assisted personal sales work stations that take orders, check stock and order status, and provide shipping and billing information.

Although not all industrial salespeople perform the same sales activities, they usually can be grouped into the following categories, as described in Chapter 15: technical, missionary, and trade or inside order takers. An inside order taker could effectively use telemarketing. Regardless of how sales personnel are classified, industrial selling activities differ from consumer sales efforts. Because industrial sellers frequently are asked for technical advice regarding product specifications and uses, they often need technical backgrounds and are more likely to have them than consumer sales personnel. Compared with typical buyer-seller relationships in consumer product sales, the interdependence that develops between industrial buyers and sellers is likely to be stronger, with sellers counting on buyers to purchase their particular products and buyers depending on sellers to provide information, products, and related services when and where needed. Although industrial salespeople do market their products aggressively, they almost never use hard-sell tactics because of their role as technical consultants and the interdependency between buyers and sellers.

Advertising is emphasized less in industrial sales than in consumer transactions. Some of the reasons given earlier for the importance of personal selling in industrial

13. Laboratory of Advertising Performance (LAP) Report #8052.3. McGraw-Hill Research.
14. Steve Sulerno, "The Close of the New Salesmanship," *PSA,* April 1985, p. 63.
15. "Aircraft Industry Emerging from Engineering Dominance," *Marketing News,* Aug. 2, 1985, p. 7.

TABLE 20.3

The average cost of an industrial sales call among selected industries

SIC#	INDUSTRY	NUMBER OF INDUSTRIAL COMPANIES REPORTING	AVERAGE DAILY NUMBER OF SALES CALLS PER SALESPERSON	AVERAGE COST OF INDUSTRIAL SALES CALL	AVERAGE DAILY SALES CALL COSTS[a] PER SALESPERSON
26	Paper and allied products	12	3.3	$263.70	$ 870.21
27	Printing and publishing	18	3.2	$148.60	$ 475.52
28	Chemicals and allied products	41	4.0	$155.20	$ 620.80
29	Petroleum and coal products	12	5.3	$ 99.10	$ 525.23
30	Rubber and miscellaneous plastics products	37	4.4	$129.30	$ 568.92
32	Stone, clay and glass products	18	4.3	$169.70	$ 729.71
33	Primary metal industries	15	3.9	$363.90	$1,419.21
34	Fabricated metal products	113	3.9	$186.10	$ 725.79
35	Machinery, except electrical	275	3.5	$257.30	$ 900.55
3573	Electronic computing equipment (computer hardware)	17	4.2	$452.60	$1,900.92
36	Electrical and electronic equipment	137	3.5	$238.40	$ 834.40
37	Transportation equipment	41	2.9	$255.90	$ 742.11
38	Instruments and related products	73	3.9	$209.50	$ 817.05
39	Miscellaneous manufacturing industries	16	3.8	$130.90	$ 497.42
50	Wholesale trade–durable goods	29	5.1	$139.80	$ 712.98
73	Business services	30	2.8	$227.20	$ 636.16

a. This cost is determined by multiplying the average daily number of calls per salesperson by the average cost per sales call for each industry.

SOURCE: Laboratory of Advertising Performance (LAP), Report #8052.3, McGraw-Hill Research, McGraw-Hill Publications Co., 1221 Avenue of the Americas, New York, N.Y. 10020. Reprinted by permission.

promotion mixes explain advertising's relative lack of importance. However, advertising often supplements personal selling efforts. Because the cost of an industrial sales call is high and continues to rise, advertisements that allow sales personnel to perform more efficiently and effectively are quite worthwhile for an industrial marketer. Advertising can make industrial customers aware of new products and brands; inform buyers about general product features, representatives, and organizations; and isolate promising prospects by providing inquiry forms or the addresses and phone numbers of company representatives. Mead Business Papers, as illustrated in Figure 20.5, solicits direct mail response from potential customers. To ensure that appropriate information is sent to a respondent, it is crucial that the inquiry be specific as to the type of information desired, the name of the company and respondent, the company's SIC number, and the size of the organization.

Because the demand for most industrial products is derived demand, marketers can sometimes stimulate demand for their products by stimulating consumer demand. Thus an industrial marketer occasionally sponsors an advertisement that promotes the products sold by that marketer's customers.

When selecting advertising media, industrial marketers primarily choose such print media as trade publications and direct mail; they seldom use broadcast media. Trade publications and direct mail reach precise groups of industrial customers and avoid wasted circulation. In addition, they are best suited for advertising messages that present numerous details and complex product information (which are frequently the types of messages that industrial advertisers wish to get across).

Compared with consumer product advertisements, industrial advertisements are usually less persuasive and more likely to contain a large amount of copy and numerous details. In contrast, marketers that advertise to reach ultimate consumers sometimes avoid extensive advertising copy because consumers are reluctant to read it. Industrial advertisers, however, believe that industrial purchasers that have any interest in their products will search for information and read long messages.

Sales promotion activities can play a significant role in industrial promotion mixes. They include such efforts as catalogs, trade shows, and trade-type sales promotion methods that include merchandise allowances, buy-back allowances, displays, sales contests, and other methods discussed in Chapter 15. Industrial marketers go to considerable effort and expense to provide catalogs that describe their products to customers. Customers refer to various sellers' catalogs to determine specifications, terms of sale, delivery times, and other information about products. Catalogs thus help buyers decide which suppliers to contact.

Trade shows can be effective vehicles for making many customer contacts in a short time. Although trade shows can be expensive, industrial marketers can use them for various purposes: to show and demonstrate new products, to find new customers, to take orders, to develop mailing lists, to promote the company image, and to find out what competitors are doing. Before exhibiting at trade shows, a firm must clearly specify its objectives. These objectives will influence the firm's choice of trade shows and the content of its exhibits.[16]

How industrial marketers use publicity in their promotion mixes may not be much different from the way that marketers of consumer products use it.

Price

Compared with consumer product marketers, industrial marketers face many more price constraints from legal and economic forces. As indicated in Chapter 2, the Robinson-Patman Act significantly influences producers' and wholesalers' pricing practices by regulating price differentials and the use of discounts. When the federal government invokes price controls, ordinarily the effect is to regulate industrial marketers' prices directly and to a greater extent than consumer product prices. With respect to economic forces, an individual industrial firm's demand is often highly elastic, requiring the firm's price to approximate competitors' prices. This condition often results in nonprice competition and a considerable amount of price stability.

Today's route to sustainable competitive advantage lies in offering the customer better value, even at a slightly higher price.[17] Customers are used to buying on the basis of price, which is visible and measurable, and producers are used to competing on the same basis, but a strategic advantage based on the total value delivered is

16. Joseph A. Bellizzi and Delilah J. Lipps, "Managerial Guidelines for Trade Show Effectiveness," *Industrial Marketing Management*, February 1984, pp. 49–52.
17. John L. Forbis and Nitin T. Mehta, "Value-Based Strategies for Industrial Products," *Business Horizons*, May–June 1981, p. 32.

In today's tight economy, you may have customers requesting the so-called bargain products. Cheaper versions of quality products you and they have been quite happy with. But suppose, in your efforts to service these budget-conscious customers, you sell them products of questionable quality. Who pays the price then?

You do.

You lose money on returns. You lose time and money on extra service. And, even worse, you risk losing the loyalty of the very same customers you were working so hard to please.

At 3M, we work hard to prevent that eventuality. Unlike other manufacturers, we don't use you and your customers as a test market.

Instead, we spend time and money up-front, building consistent quality into our products before we sell them.

Ask yourself. When was the last time you had a Post-it™ brand note returned, or a roll of Scotch™ brand Tape? We believe that kind of product integrity is something your customers won't mind paying for, in the long run.

Questions or comments? Write Commercial Office Supply Division/3M, 223-3S, 3M Center, St. Paul, MN 55144-1000.

If something doesn't work right, it's no bargain at any price.

FIGURE 20.6

3M promotes price relative to quality (SOURCE: 3M, Commercial Office Supply Division)

far less easy for competitors to duplicate.[18] Companies such as Caterpillar Tractor Co., Hewlett-Packard Co., and 3M have shown that a value-based strategy can effectively garner a commanding lead over competition. Such firms emphasize the highest-quality products at slightly higher prices. In Figure 20.6, 3M cautions resellers about the hazards of lower-priced imitations.

Although there are a variety of ways for determining prices of industrial products, the three most common are administered pricing, bid pricing, and negotiated pricing. With **administered pricing,** the seller determines the price (or series of prices) for a product, and the customer pays that specified price. Marketers who use this approach may employ a one-price policy in which all buyers pay the same price, or they may set a series of prices that are determined by one or more discounts. In some cases, list prices are posted on a price sheet or in a catalog. The list price is a beginning point from which trade, quantity, and cash discounts are deducted. Thus the actual (net) price an industrial customer pays is the list price less the discount(s). When a list price is used, an industrial marketer sometimes specifies the price in terms of list price times a multiplier. For example, the price of an item might be quoted as "list price $\times$ .78," which means the seller is discounting the item so that the buyer can purchase the product at 78 percent of the list price.

18. Ibid.

Simply changing the multiplier lets the seller revise prices without having to issue new catalogs or price sheets.

With **bid pricing,** prices are determined through sealed bids or open bids. When a buyer uses sealed bids, sellers are notified that they are to submit their bids by a certain date. Usually, the lowest bidder is awarded the contract, providing the buyer believes the firm is capable of supplying the specified products when and where needed. Under an open bidding approach, several but not all sellers are asked to submit bids. This differs from sealed bidding in that the amounts of the bids are made public. Finally, an industrial purchaser sometimes uses negotiated bids. Under this arrangement, the customer seeks bids from a number of sellers, screens the bids, and then negotiates the price and terms of sale with the most favorable bidders until a final transaction is consummated or until negotiations are terminated with all sellers.

Sometimes, a buyer will be seeking either component parts to be used in production for several years or custom-built equipment to be purchased currently and through future contracts. In such a circumstance, an industrial seller may submit an initial, less profitable bid to win "follow-on" (subsequent) contracts. The seller that wins the initial contract is often substantially favored in the competition for follow-on contracts. In such a bidding situation, an industrial marketer must determine how low the initial bid should be, the probability of winning a follow-on contract, and the combination of bid prices on both the initial and the follow-on contract that will yield an acceptable profit.[19]

For certain types of industrial markets, a seller's pricing component may have to allow for **negotiated pricing.** That is, even when there are stated list prices and discount structures, negotiations may determine the actual price an industrial customer pays. Negotiated pricing can benefit seller and buyer because price negotiations frequently lead to discussions of product specifications, applications, and perhaps product substitutions. Such negotiations may give the seller an opportunity to provide the customer with technical assistance and perhaps sell a product that better fits the customer's requirements; the final product choice might also be more profitable for the seller. The buyer benefits by gaining more information about the array of products and terms of sale available and may acquire a more suitable product at a lower price.

Some industrial marketers sell in markets in which only one of these general pricing approaches prevails. Such marketers can simplify the price components of their marketing mixes. However, a number of industrial marketers sell to a wide variety of industrial customers and must maintain considerable flexibility in pricing practices.

Summary

Industrial marketing is a set of activities directed at facilitating and expediting exchanges involving industrial products and customers in industrial markets. Industrial markets consist of producers, governments, or institutions that purchase a

19. Douglas G. Brooks, "Bidding for the Sake of Follow-On Contracts," *Journal of Marketing,* January 1978, p. 35.

specific kind of product for direct use in producing other products or for use in day-to-day operations.

Industrial marketers have a considerable amount of information available to them for use in planning their marketing strategies. Much of the available information is based on the Standard Industrial Classification (SIC) system developed by the federal government. This system categorizes businesses into major industry groups, industry subgroups, and detailed industry categories. The SIC system provides industrial marketers with information needed to identify market segments. It can best be used for this purpose in conjunction with other information, such as input-output data. After identifying target industries, the marketer can locate potential customers by using state or commercial industrial directories or by employing a commercial data company. The marketer then must estimate the potential purchases of industrial customers by finding a relationship between a potential customer's purchases and a variable available in published sources.

Like marketers of consumer products, an industrial marketer must develop a marketing mix that satisfies the needs of customers in the industrial target market. The product component frequently emphasizes services because they are often of primary interest to industrial customers. The marketer also must consider that the customer may elect to make the product rather than buy it. Industrial products must meet certain standard specifications that industrial users want.

The distribution of industrial products differs from that of consumer products in the types of channels used; the kinds of intermediaries available; and transportation, storage, and inventory policies. A direct distribution channel is common in industrial marketing. Also used are channels containing manufacturers' agents, industrial distributors, or both agents and distributors. Channels are chosen on the basis of availability, the typical mode of purchase for a product, and several other variables. The primary objective of the physical distribution of industrial products is to ensure that the right products are available when and where needed.

Personal selling is a primary ingredient of the promotional component in industrial marketing mixes. Sales personnel often act as technical advisers both before and after a sale. Advertising sometimes is used to supplement personal selling efforts. Industrial marketers generally use print advertisements containing more information but less persuasive content than consumer advertisements. Other promotional activities include catalogs and trade shows.

The price component for industrial marketing mixes is influenced by legal and economic forces to a greater extent than it is for consumer marketing mixes. Pricing may be affected by competitors' prices as well as by the type of customer who buys the product.

Important Terms

Industrial marketing
Industrial market
Industrial product
Standard Industrial Classification
  (SIC) system
Input-output data

Direct distribution channels
Manufacturers' agent
Industrial distributor
Administered pricing
Bid pricing
Negotiated pricing

Discussion and Review Questions

1. How do industrial products differ from consumer products?
2. What function does the SIC system help industrial marketers perform?
3. List some sources that an industrial marketer can use to determine the names and addresses of potential customers.
4. How do industrial marketing mixes differ from those of consumer products?
5. What are the major advantages and disadvantages of using industrial distributors?
6. Why do industrial marketers rely on personal selling more than consumer products marketers?
7. Why would an industrial marketer spend resources on advertising aimed at stimulating consumer demand?
8. Compare and contrast three methods for determining the price of industrial products.

Cases

20.1 Caterpillar Tractor Co.[20]

Caterpillar designs and manufactures heavy equipment multinationally in two product categories:

Earth-moving, construction, and materials handling machinery track and wheel tractors, track and wheel loaders, lift trucks, pipe layers, motor graders, asphalt and soil compactors, wheel tractor-scrapers, track and wheel excavators, backhoe loaders, track and wheel skidders, log loaders, tree harvesters, off-highway trucks, asphalt and concrete paving machines, asphalt plants, pavement profilers, and related parts and equipment

Engines for earth-moving and construction machines; on-highway trucks; locomotives; electric power generation systems; marine, petroleum, agricultural, industrial, and other applications; and related parts

For decades, the Illinois-based manufacturer remained profitable through a combination of technological advances, efficiency, and product quality. But in the early 1980s, falling oil prices, recession in Europe and the Third World, and a strong U.S. dollar cut into Caterpillar's earnings. Competition from independent distributors, especially Komatsu, the Japanese producer of heavy equipment, also eroded Caterpillar's market share. Finally, after having lost $1 billion since 1982, Caterpillar has been making money again as a result of currency exchange gains, higher sales, new-product introductions, and continued cost cutting. Figure 20.7 shows Caterpillar's worldwide sales broken down by end use.

20. Based on information from Caterpillar *Annual Reports*, 1984, 1985; Jack Willoughby, "Decision Time in Peoria," *Forbes*, Jan. 27, 1986, p. 36; Joseph Bohn, "Caterpillar's Engine Sales Help Firm Post 1985 Profit," *Automotive News*, Feb. 3, 1986, p. 12; Joseph Bohn, "Basic Machinery Market Softens as Foreign Competition Heats Up," *Business Marketing*, July 1986, p. 56; Barry Stavro, "Digging Out," *Forbes*, Nov. 3, 1986, pp. 127–128; John Merwin, "A Billion in Blunders," *Forbes*, Dec. 1, 1986, pp. 97–111; Alex Kotlowitz, "Weaker Dollar Isn't a Boon for Caterpillar," *Wall Street Journal*, Feb. 20, 1987, p. 6.

FIGURE 20.7

Worldwide dealer sales of Caterpillar machines and engines by major end use (SOURCE: Caterpillar *1985 Annual Report*)

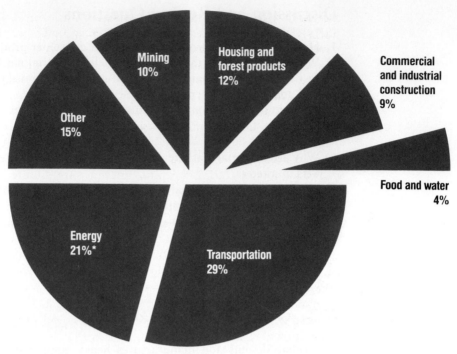

*Coal mining included under Energy.

Caterpillar's recent profits have resulted more from international than domestic transactions. In the United States, where Caterpillar has a 35 percent market share, the company has been negatively affected by slowdowns in the oil, natural gas, metals, and agricultural industries. Because industrial demand is derived from the demand for consumer products, decreases in consumer buying in these areas have decreased industrial sales. In addition, Komatsu and other Japanese competitors have undersold Caterpillar by as much as 10 to 15 percent while broadening their product lines. Negotiations for many industrial contracts are based on bid pricing, and the foreign competition has been able to bid lower than Caterpillar.

Caterpillar's domestic strategy has been to give the industrial buyer a quality product and superior service at a price slightly higher than the competition's. Caterpillar emphasizes the quality of its higher-priced products by focusing on long-term cost effectiveness. Recent record sales of truck engines have increased Caterpillar's profits, and the company has expanded its sales and marketing of small construction equipment, such as backhoe loaders. To cut production costs, Caterpillar has shifted many of the manufacturing and sourcing operations for these new, smaller machines to overseas. Increased highway spending, more commercial and industrial construction, and continued home building have accounted for most of Caterpillar's growth in the United States.

Internationally, Caterpillar has opened markets in Turkey, China, and Russia while increasing sales in existing markets: Canada, Australia, Italy, the United Kingdom, and France. Some important Third World markets have weakened. Once-large sales in the Middle East have declined because the oil recession has reduced government expenditures for construction projects, and in South Africa, industrial sales have fallen sharply because of the oil recession, high interest rates, and social unrest. Still, accelerated economic growth and government support for developmental projects have pushed up industrial sales in Australia. Sales have also increased in Canada as a result of strong economic growth and improved government attitudes toward business. Canadian industrial sales have been especially strong in the areas of housing and highway construction.

One of Caterpillar's most extensively developed industrial sales networks is in China, where sales have been increasing because of looser restrictions on the import of U.S. goods. Caterpillar China Limited, located in Hong Kong, makes direct sales to industrial buyers and provides end users with product support. With the increasing modernization of China, sales of transportation, mining, energy development, and agricultural equipment have increased dramatically. Caterpillar has also established an on-site service facility in China for one of the world's largest coal mines, where more than eighty Caterpillar machines are working.

Analysts predict that sales in the $8 billion construction equipment industry will be about the same as last year, or slightly lower. Caterpillar's strategy for the near future includes more cost cutting (15 percent during the next three years), a $1 billion investment in factory automation, and more overseas production and sourcing. Caterpillar plans to capture more of the available business with new products and marketing strategies and expects its high product quality and strong service orientation to differentiate the company from its competitors.

Questions for Discussion

1. Specify some characteristics of the industrial demand for Caterpillar products.
2. With increased competition from foreign competitors who charge less for their products, what strategy would you recommend that Caterpillar follow to maintain or increase its market share?
3. Describe Caterpillar's strengths or particular competencies as an industrial product manufacturer.
4. Would you suggest that Caterpillar divest any specific business categories? Evaluate international trends.

20.2 Navistar International: A Born-Again Industrial Marketer[21]

Navistar International Corporation, formerly known as International Harvester Company, is the country's largest manufacturer of medium- and heavy-duty trucks. After more than seventy years of producing trucks, Navistar leads Ford Motor Company, General Motors Corp., Isuzu Motors Ltd. and other truck manufacturers in sales of class 6, 7, and 8 vehicles, with a 26 percent share of the market.

21. Based on information from Kathleen Deveny, "Can the Man Who Saved Navistar Run It, Too?" *Business Week,* Mar. 9, 1987, p. 88; Bill Kelley, "Navistar Starts on the Road Back," *S&MM,* July 1986, pp. 49–51; Michael S. Lelyveld, "Navistar May Supply the Engines for Nissan's Mid-Sized Trucks," *Journal of Commerce,* June 5, 1987, p. 1A; Thomas Moore, "Old-Line Industry Shapes Up," *Fortune,* Apr. 27, 1987, p. 32; Brian S. Moskol, "It's Either Trucks or Bust," *Industry Week,* May 12, 1986, pp. 73–74; Barry Stavro, "A Surfeit of Equity," *Forbes,* Dec. 29, 1986, p. 62.

Today the Chicago-based firm has 15,000 employees, 850 dealers, and 6 plants in the United States and Canada.

But Navistar is far from complacent. Before its transformation from International Harvester into Navistar two years ago, the venerable company was teetering on the edge of bankruptcy. Despite record sales of $8.4 billion in 1979, the next four years were the worst in the company's long history as recession, aging physical plants, bloated corporate costs, and a bitter strike resulted in losses totaling $2.9 billion. The once-mighty International Harvester was forced to sell off its agricultural and construction equipment divisions, retaining only its profitable business in trucks, engines, and spare parts. In all, the troubled company dismissed more than 80,000 of its employees and closed 42 plants worldwide.

Several years and three financial reorganizations later, Navistar appears to be on its feet. Last year Navistar earned $1.7 million on sales of $3.4 billion, and with proceeds from last year's new stock issue, the company has retired some long-term debt and will now save $86 million a year in interest payments. In addition, dealers and customers have positively received the cosmetic name change. The purchase agreement under which Tenneco Inc. bought International Harvester's farm equipment business required the company to also sell its famous name, although legally the firm could use the Harvester name until 1990. The company decided to proceed early with the name change. The company now believes that its new name has helped play down the company's old agribusiness image and has reassured customers that the company still has the same vitality it had under its former name.

Now more aggressive and willing to take risks, Navistar intends to use the "customer-driven" marketing approach the firm took in its earlier, more prosperous days. Some industry observers say that Navistar has become noticeably more attuned to the market, perhaps because the company had to work so closely with dealers, customers, and suppliers to resolve its financial problems. These days communication is better between company executives and dealers. Advisory committees meet regularly to discuss objectives, advertising, financing, and new business. To keep abreast of the market, Navistar also has instituted programs to pinpoint emerging trends in the trucking industry and to apprise its manufacturing and engineering divisions of the customer needs the salespeople have identified.

In one pilot program, for example, a Navistar employee spends an entire day at the customer's place of business, studying the operation and working on site to improve the Navistar product. Another customer service innovation is the Fleet Charge, a credit card that lets fleet owners charge expenses for truck maintenance when the servicing is done through a nationwide network of participating dealers. Navistar's objective, say the company's top managers, is to be viewed not merely as a manufacturer but as a transportation service company—a provider of "lowest-cost ownership" in every way, including initial price, fuel efficiency, maintenance, and high resale value.

Despite the emphasis on service, purchase price remains an important factor in truck sales, which have fallen off for all truck companies in recent years. Deregulation has forced transportation companies to make more efficient use of existing equipment. The decline in heavy industries has also reduced the demand for freight haulers that, in turn, have less cash available for new vehicles. Some Navistar heavy-truck dealers have had to cut prices by as much as 40 percent, just to stay competitive. However, the dealers point out that the price cutting is industrywide, and they maintain that service will ultimately build customer loyalty.

To hold down costs, Navistar has dramatically improved productivity. Today raw materials move from inventory to finished product in 37 days, compared to 142 days in 1981, and the same employee who then produced six trucks a year now turns out twelve. The company is also working to improve relationships with suppliers and hopes to reduce total production costs 25 to 30 percent during the next five years. Its breakeven point dropped from 83,000 units five years ago to less than 60,000 last year.

Now structured as a holding company, Navistar intends eventually to acquire companies related to the corporation's core business. If all goes according to plan, in ten years up to half of Navistar's sales and earnings will come from businesses other than trucks and engines, which should provide some protection from cyclical fluctuations.

For now, however, Navistar will be learning the trucking business thoroughly and concentrating on market needs. In 1990, the company hopes to renew its contract with Ford for diesel engine sales, which bring in $300 million a year under the current contract. Navistar also has a five-year contract with Nissan Motor Company to distribute Nissan trucks in North America, and a new agreement calls for a project team to investigate the feasibility of putting Navistar engines into Nissan medium-weight trucks, to be sold under Navistar's International brand.

Questions for Discussion

1. What evidence is there that Navistar is attempting to adopt the marketing concept?
2. How have changes in the environment influenced Navistar's marketing strategies?
3. Is the demand for Navistar's large trucks derived demand? Explain your answer.
4. In what ways might Navistar's increases in productivity affect its marketing strategies?

21. Services and Nonbusiness Marketing

- ▶ To understand the nature and characteristics of services.
- ▶ To classify services.
- ▶ To understand the development of strategies for services.
- ▶ To explore the concept of marketing in nonbusiness situations.
- ▶ To understand the development of marketing strategies in nonbusiness organizations.
- ▶ To describe methods for controlling nonbusiness marketing activities.

*H*ealth-care providers, including dentists, are facing increased competition for patients, and many are turning to marketing to differentiate their services from those of competitors. Dentists once derived much of their income from filling cavities, but the widespread use of fluoridated water and toothpastes has dramatically decreased the incidence of tooth decay. At one time, dentists relied primarily on referrals from patients to attract new patients. But federal laws passed in the 1970s allowed dentists and other professionals to advertise for the first time (see Figure 21.1). Thus many dentists are now using marketing activities such as advertising and sales promotions to attract new business.

The American Dental Association defines marketing as a process designed to "meet the psychological needs of the patient." This definition is much more abstract than our definition of marketing in Chapter 1. Some dentists are improving their services to existing patients to get more patients by referral, and some are now offering services not commonly provided in the past, such as night and weekend services and screenings for cancer and gum disease. Still other dentists are advertising in the Yellow Pages, giving lectures, and holding open houses.

Dentists who use direct mail to solicit new patients mail brochures with information about their services and qualifications to prospective patients. Other dentists send their own newsletters or special patient-education brochures to newspapers and special groups to create or expand the image of their offices. Creating an image for an office can help the dentist reach people who have never heard of the office as well as impress current patients with the skills and range of services offered.

Some dental practices even use promotions such as free gifts or discounted initial examinations. One group of New Jersey dentists occasionally offers a free bike with a set of braces! Other dentists offer coffee and wine while patients are awaiting their turn in the chair. Some dentists even provide stereo headphones so patients can relax during the "ordeal" and then give the patients a rose or a hug when it is all over.

To bring in new patients, some dentists take advantage of the current health craze by offering nutritional products in addition to dental services for sale. These dentists hope that the increased emphasis on health will lead the patient to accept treatment and refer other patients.

Nearly half of all dentists now use some marketing techniques. Some practitioners, however, believe that advertising by dental professionals has lowered the overall image of the profession. Nevertheless, as long as there is an excess of dentists and a shortage of patients, dentists will probably continue to use marketing to make their services stand out from their competitors'.[1]

1. Based on information from Cathleen McGuigan, with Bob Cohn and Susan Katz, "A Free Bike with Your Braces," *Newsweek,* May 5, 1986; Paul Duke, Jr. and Albert R. Karr, "Dentists Step Up Services and Marketing as Competition Increases in Crowded Field," *Wall Street Journal,* Nov. 20, 1987, p. 29; Roger Levin, "Identity Crucial to Successful Marketing of Dental Practices," *Dentist,* November–December 1987, p. 38; Mark Harley, "Dentists Split on Advertising," *Dentist,* September–October 1987, pp. 31, 38; Roger Levin, "Specific Marketing Goals Pinpoint Helpful Statistics," *Dentists,* September–October 1987, pp. 36–37.

T HIS CHAPTER presents concepts that apply to marketing in organizations dealing primarily with services and nonbusiness activities. These two areas overlap in that most nonprofit marketing is concerned with services such as education, health care, and government. On the other hand, services marketing also involves for-profit areas such as finance, personal services, and professional services.

The chapter first discusses the growing importance of service industries in our economy. Second, it addresses the unique characteristics of services and the problems they present to marketers. Then, it presents various classification schemes that can help service marketers develop marketing strategies. Additionally, a variety of marketing mix considerations are discussed. Next, the chapter discusses nonbusiness marketing. We define nonbusiness marketing and then examine the development of nonbusiness marketing strategies and the control of nonbusiness marketing activities.

The Nature and Characteristics of Services

The product concept refers to a physical good, a service, an idea, or any combination of these three. As we mention in Chapter 7, all products, whether they are goods or not, possess a certain amount of intangibility. Goods are those tangible products that consumers can physically possess. A service is the result of applying human or mechanical efforts to people or objects. Services are intangible products involving a deed, a performance, or an effort that cannot be physically possessed.[2] We should note that few products can be classified as a pure good or a pure service. Consider, for example, an automobile. When consumers purchase a car, they take ownership of a physical item that provides transportation, but the warranty associated with the purchase is a service. When consumers rent a car, they purchase a transportation service that is provided through temporary use of an automobile. Most products, such as automobiles and automobile rentals, contain both tangible and intangible components. One component, however, will dominate, and it is this dominant component that leads to the classification of goods, services, and ideas.

Figure 21.2 illustrates the tangibility concept by placing a variety of products on a continuum of tangibility and intangibility. Tangible-dominant products are typically classified as goods, and intangible-dominant products are typically considered services. Thus, **services** are defined as intangible-dominant products that cannot be physically possessed.

Growth and Importance of Services

The increasing importance of services in the U.S. economy has led many people to call the United States the world's first service economy. The service industries, encompassing trade, communications, transportation, food and lodging, financial and medical services, education, government, and technical services, account for about 60 percent of the national income and three-fourths of the nonfarm jobs in the United States. In generating 44 million new jobs in the past thirty years, the

2. Leonard L. Berry, "Services Marketing Is Different," *Business Horizons,* May–June 1980, pp. 24–29.

| Goods (tangible) | | | | | | | | | | | Services (intangible) |

Bananas · Jewelry · Compact disc player · Automobiles/maintenance · Fast food restaurants · Airlines · Financial services · Tanning salons · Telephone services · Education

FIGURE 21.2

A continuum of product tangibility and intangibility

industries have absorbed most of the influx of women and minorities into the work force and fueled every recent economic recovery.[3]

One major catalyst to the growth in consumer services has been the general economic prosperity of the United States, which has led to a growth in financial services, travel, entertainment, and personal care. Lifestyle changes have similarly encouraged expansion of the service sector. In the past forty years, the number of women in the work force has more than doubled. With approximately 68 percent of the women between 18 and 34 now working, the need for child care, domestic services, and other time-saving services has increased. Consumers want to avoid tasks such as house cleaning, home maintenance, and tax preparation, so franchise operations, including Merry Maid, Chemlawn, and H & R Block, have experienced rapid growth. Americans are becoming more fitness and recreation oriented, so the demand for fitness and recreational facilities has escalated. Regarding demographics, the U.S. population is growing older, and this change has promoted tremendous expansion of health-care services. Finally, the number and complexity of goods needing servicing have increased demand for repair services.

Not only have consumer services grown in our economy; business services have prospered as well. Business or industrial services include repairs and maintenance, consulting, installation, equipment leasing, marketing research, advertising, temporary office personnel, and janitorial services. Expenditures for business and industrial services have grown even faster than expenditures for consumer services. This growth has been attributed to the increasingly complex, specialized, and competitive business environment. Large retailers such as Sears, Roebuck are successfully incorporating additional services into their retail stores. Providing additional services at one location is an excellent way to satisfy and keep customers who need and want more and more services. Sears operates its traditional department store but in addition offers optical services, financial services, automotive services, and so on. If customers enter a store for one service, they will be more likely to eventually shop at the store again or try another service the retailer provides.[4] Exposure for the service outlet incorporated into a major retail outlet such as Sears is exceptional, creating widespread awareness of the store's existence.

Characteristics of Services

The problems of service marketing are not the same as those of goods marketing. To understand these unique problems, it is first necessary to understand the distinguishing characteristics of services. Services have four basic characteristics:

3. James L. Heskett, "Lessons in the Service Sector," *Harvard Business Review*, March–April 1987, p. 118.
4. David Pottruck, "Building Company Loyalty and Retention Through Direct Marketing," *Journal of Services Marketing*, Fall 1987, p. 56.

(1) intangibility, (2) inseparability of production and consumption, (3) perishability, and (4) heterogeneity.[5] Table 21.1 summarizes these characteristics and the marketing problems they entail.

Intangibility stems from the fact that services are performances. They cannot be seen, touched, tasted, or smelled, nor can they be possessed. Intangibility also relates to the difficulty that consumers may have understanding service offerings.[6] Services have few tangible attributes, called **search qualities,** that can be viewed prior to purchase. When consumers cannot view a product in advance and examine its properties, they may not understand exactly what is being offered. And even when consumers gain sufficient knowledge about service offerings, they may not be able to evaluate the possible alternatives. On the other hand, services are rich in experience and credence qualities. **Experience qualities** are those qualities that can be assessed only after purchase and consumption (satisfaction, courtesy, and the like). **Credence qualities** are those qualities that cannot be assessed even after purchase and consumption.[7] An appendix operation is an example of a service high in credence qualities. How many consumers are knowledgeable enough to assess the quality of an appendectomy, even after it has been performed? In summary, it is difficult to go into a store, examine a service, purchase it, and take it home with you.

Related to intangibility is **inseparability** of production and consumption. Services are normally produced at the same time they are consumed. A medical exami-

5. Valarie A. Zeithaml, A. Parasuraman, and Leonard L. Berry, "Problems and Strategies in Services Marketing," *Journal of Marketing,* Spring 1985, pp. 33–46.
6. John E. G. Bateson, "Why We Need Service Marketing," in *Conceptual and Theoretical Developments in Marketing,* O. C. Ferrell, S. W. Brown, and C. W. Lamb, Jr., eds. (Chicago: American Marketing Association, 1979), pp. 131–146.
7. Valarie A. Zeithaml, "How Consumer Evaluation Processes Differ Between Goods and Services," in *Marketing of Services,* James H. Donnelly and William R. George, eds. (Chicago: American Marketing Association, 1981), pp. 186–190.

TABLE 21.1

Service characteristics and marketing problems

UNIQUE SERVICE FEATURES	RESULTING MARKETING PROBLEMS
Intangibility	Cannot be stored Cannot be protected through patents Cannot be readily displayed or communicated Prices are difficult to set
Inseparability	Consumer is involved in production Other consumers are involved in production Centralized mass production is difficult
Perishability	Services cannot be inventoried
Heterogeneity	Standardization and quality are difficult to control

SOURCE: Valarie A. Zeithaml, A. Parasuraman, Leonard L. Berry, "Problems and Strategies in Services Marketing," *Journal of Marketing,* Spring 1985, pp. 33–46. Used by permission of the American Marketing Association.

nation is an example of concurrent production and consumption. In fact, the doctor cannot possibly perform the service without the patient's presence, and the consumer is actually involved in the production process. With other services, such as air travel, many consumers are simultaneously involved in production. Because of high consumer involvement in most services, standardization and control are difficult to maintain.

Because production and consumption are simultaneous, services are also characterized by **perishability.** In other words, unused capacity in one time period cannot be stockpiled or inventoried for future time periods. Consider the airlines' seating-capacity dilemma. Each megacarrier maintains a sophisticated reservations system to juggle ticket prices and ensure maximum revenues for every flight. On a single day recently, Delta Air Lines, Inc. used its computer to make 79,000 fare changes, American Airlines, Inc. 106,000 fare changes, thus assuring these airlines maximum use of seats available on each flight.[8] This attempt to maximize profit on each flight has led to overbooking, which means airlines may sell tickets for more seats than are available to account for those people who may not actually take that flight. The airlines' dilemma illustrates how service perishability presents problems very different from the supply and demand problems encountered in the marketing of goods.[9] Unoccupied seats on an airline flight can not be stored for use on another flight that is booked to capacity.

Finally, because most services are labor intensive, they are susceptible to **heterogeneity.** People typically perform services, and people do not always perform consistently. There may be variation from one service to another within the same organization or variation in the service a single individual provides from day to day and from customer to customer. Thus standardization and quality are extremely difficult to control. But this fact may also lead to customizing services to meet customers' specific needs. Because of these factors, service marketers often face a dilemma: How does one provide efficient, standardized service at some acceptable level of quality while simultaneously treating each customer as a unique person? Giving "good service" is a major concern of all service organizations and it is often translated into more personalized service.[10]

Classification of Services

There is a general body of knowledge concerning the marketing of all products— the marketing concept, target markets, the four marketing mix components, and marketing strategy. However, during strategy development this general knowledge must be adjusted to the very wide diversity and the unique nature of products. Thus product classification schemes have been developed to help marketers in the development of a specific marketing strategy. All products, including services, can be

8. Kenneth Labich, "Winners in the Air Wars," *Fortune*, May 11, 1987, p. 68.
9. Leonard L. Berry, Valarie A. Zeithaml, and A. Parasuraman, "Responding to Demand Fluctuations: Key Challenge for Service Businesses," in *AMA Educators Proceedings*, Russell Belk et al., eds. (Chicago: American Marketing Association, 1984), pp. 231–234.
10. Carol F. Surprenant and Michael R. Solomon, "Predictability and Personalization in the Service Encounter," *Journal of Marketing*, April 1987, p. 86.

classified as consumer or industrial; durables or nondurables; and convenience, shopping, or specialty products.

Services are a very diverse group of products, and an organization may provide more than one kind. Services include car rentals, repairs, health care, barber shops, health spas, tanning salons, amusement parks, day care, domestic services, legal counsel, banking, insurance, air travel, education, business consulting, dry cleaning, and accounting. Nevertheless, services can be meaningfully analyzed by using a five-category classification scheme: (1) type of market, (2) degree of labor intensiveness, (3) degree of customer contact, (4) skill of service provider, and (5) goal of the service provider. Table 21.2 summarizes this scheme.

Services can be viewed in terms of the market or type of customer they serve—consumer or industrial. For example, Norfolk Southern (Figure 21.3) serves a $96 billion industry—pulp and paper. Norfolk Southern developed a transportation system specifically to help regional paper distribution for this industrial and consumer product. The implications of this distinction are very similar to those for all products and are not discussed here. A second way to classify services is by degree of labor intensiveness. Many services, such as repairs, education, and hair care, rely heavily on human labor. Other services, such as telecommunications, health spas, and public transportation, are more equipment intensive. The mutual fund industry relies on computer technologies to facilitate handling daily transactions. Use of computer technologies has enabled mutual fund companies to improve service and expand offerings. For example, Fidelity Investments has $80 billion in assets, more than two million customers, and offers twenty-four-hour service. Customers can

TABLE 21.2

Classification of services

CATEGORY	EXAMPLES
Type of market	
Consumer	Repairs, child care, legal counsel
Industrial	Consulting, lawn care, installation
Degree of labor intensiveness	
Labor-based	Repairs, education, hair cuts
Equipment-based	Telecommunications, health spas, public transportation
Degree of customer contact	
High contact	Health care, hotels, air travel
Low contact	Repairs, dry cleaning, postal service
Skill of the service provider	
Professional	Legal counsel, health care, accounting services
Nonprofessional	Air travel, dry cleaning, public transportation
Goal of the Service Provider	
Profit	Financial services, insurance, health care
Nonprofit	Health care, education, government

FIGURE 21.3

Norfolk Southern provides transportation services for pulp and paper manufacturers (SOURCE: Courtesy Norfolk Southern Corp.)

call anytime to check fund prices or move money between funds. The firm logs an average of 1,700 calls a night between midnight and 4:00 A.M.[11] For many mutual fund customers, the service they receive is just as important as the performance of their funds. The Application on page 752 explains how theme parks have used technology to improve service.

Labor (people-based) services are more susceptible to heterogeneity than are most equipment-based services. Marketers of people-based services must recognize that the service providers are often viewed as the service itself. Therefore, strategies relating to selecting, training, motivating, and controlling employees are extremely important.

The third way services can be classified is by customer contact. High-contact services include health care, hotels, real estate agencies, and restaurants; low-contact services include repairs, movie theaters, dry cleaning, and spectator sports.[12] Note that high-contact services generally involve actions directed toward individuals. Because these services are directed at people, the consumer must be

11. "The People's Choice: Mutual Funds," *Business Week,* Feb. 24, 1986, p. 56.
12. Christopher H. Lovelock, "Classifying Services to Gain Strategic Marketing Insights," *Journal of Marketing,* Summer 1983, p. 15.

present during production. Although it is sometimes possible for the service provider to go to the consumer, high-contact services typically require that the consumer go to the production facility. Thus the physical appearance of the facility may be a major component of the consumer's overall evaluation of the service. Because the consumer must be present during production of high-contact service, the process of production may be just as important as the final outcome of the production process. Low-contact service commonly involves actions directed at things. Consequently, the consumer is usually not required to be present during service delivery. The consumer's presence, however, may be required to initiate or terminate the service. The appearance of the production facilities and the interpersonal skills of actual service providers are thus not as critical in low-contact services as they are in high-contact services.[13]

Skill of the service provider is a fourth way to classify services. Professional services tend to be more complex and more highly regulated than nonprofessional services. In the case of legal counsel, for example, consumers often do not know what the actual service will involve or its cost until the service is completed because the final product is very situation specific. Additionally, attorneys are regulated by both the law and professional associations.

Finally, services can be classified according to the goal of the service provider—profit or nonprofit. The second half of this chapter examines nonbusiness marketing. Most nonbusiness organizations provide services rather than goods. An exception is the U.S. Postal Service's efforts to sell stamps to collectors, not for postal delivery (see Figure 21.4).

Developing Marketing Strategies for Services

Before we discuss the development of a marketing mix for service firms, we need to make one major point: The marketing concept is equally applicable to goods, services, and ideas. Thus service marketers, like goods marketers, must strive to provide a bundle of benefits that satisfies the needs of consumers.[14] Table 21.3 shows examples of approaches to consumer satisfaction for marketers of services.

The development phase, including defining target markets and finalizing a marketing mix, is a basic requirement of any marketing strategy. Following are seven areas to consider when developing a service marketing strategy:

1. Marketing should occur at all levels, from the marketing department to the point where the service is provided.
2. Allow flexibility in providing the service—when there is direct interaction with the customers, customize the service to their wants and needs.
3. Hire and maintain high-quality personnel and market your organization or service to them; often it is the people in a service organization who differentiate one organization from another.

13. Christopher H. Lovelock, *Services Marketing* (Englewood Cliffs, N.J.: Prentice-Hall, 1984), pp. 49–64.
14. Ben M. Enis and Kenneth J. Roering, "Services Marketing: Different Products, Similar Strategy," in *Marketing of Services,* J. H. Donnelly and W. R. George, eds. (Chicago: American Marketing Association, 1981), pp. 1–4.

4. Consider marketing to existing customers to increase their usage of the service or create loyalty to the service provider.
5. Quickly resolve any problems in providing the service, to avoid damaging a business's quality reputation.
6. Think high technology to provide improved services at a lower cost. Continually evaluate how to customize the service to the consumer's unique needs.
7. Brand your service to distinguish it from that of the competition. For example, instead of simply seeking a moving truck, a customer would seek a rental from U-Haul because of U-Haul's name recognition.[15]

In the following sections we discuss the marketing mix requirements for finalizing a services marketing strategy.

Product

Goods can be defined in terms of their physical attributes, but services cannot be because they are intangible. As we point out earlier in the chapter, it is often difficult for consumers to understand service offerings and to evaluate possible service alternatives. Increasingly, lawyers are looking to professional marketers of prepaid legal services to increase their business. Millions of Americans currently

15. Leonard Berry, "Big Ideas in Services Marketing," *Journal of Services Marketing,* Fall 1987, pp. 5–9. Used by permission.

FIGURE 21.4

The U.S. Postal Service provides collectors' stamps (a good) and postal delivery (a service) (SOURCE: Courtesy of United States Postal Service)

Are you still collecting the same old stuff?

Well, there's a lot of enjoyment in stamp collecting, too.
Stamps are a fascinating way to have an eyewitness view of America's past and present. New stamps are issued every few weeks that allow you to explore an almost endless variety of subjects.
With our new Locomotive

stamp booklet that's currently available at your post office, you can take a ride on five distinctly different trains that helped launch the railway age in America.
Come on. Hop aboard stamp collecting, the most popular hobby in the world. You'll be guaranteed a round-trip ticket of fun.

Available October 1.

Start something new with stamps.

U.S. Postal Service
© USPS 1987

SERVICE INDUSTRY	OUTCOME SOUGHT BY BUYER	TECHNICAL POSSIBILITIES	STRATEGIC POSSIBILITIES
Higher education	Educational attainment	Help professors to be effective teachers; offer tutoring	Admit better prepared students (or give them better preparation before entry for a fee)
Hospitals	Health	Instruct patients in how to manage their current problems and prevent others	Market preventive medicine services (weight loss, stress reduction, etc.)
Banks	Prosperity	Offer money management courses; provide management assistance to small businesses	Market expertise as well as money, probably by industry specialization
Plumbing repairs	Free flowing pipes	Provide consumers with instructions and supplies to prevent further clogs	Diversify (e.g., point-of-use water-purification systems)

TABLE 21.3

Examples of approaches to consumer satisfaction for marketers of services

SOURCE: Adapted from Betsy D. Gelb, "How Marketers of Intangibles Can Raise the Odds for Consumer Satisfaction," *Journal of Services Marketing*, Summer 1987, p. 15.

belong to prepaid legal plans. Most of these plans feature a toll-free number that connects subscribers with lawyers who give advice on a wide range of topics. This service is provided at a monthly rate for unlimited phone usage and insurance. By providing legal services almost as a packaged item available at a known cost per month and in an easy to use manner (simply dialing a toll-free number), customers are better able to understand the legal services.[16]

There may also be tangibles (such as facilities, employees, or communications) associated with a service. These tangible elements help form a part of the product and are often the only aspects of a service that can be viewed prior to purchase, which is why marketers must pay close attention to associated tangibles and make sure that they are consistent with the selected image of the service product.[17]

The service product is often equated with the service provider; for example, the teller or the beautician becomes the service a bank or a beauty parlor provides. Because consumers tend to view services in terms of the service personnel and because personnel are inconsistent in their behavior, it is imperative that marketers effectively select, train, motivate, and control contact people. Service marketers are selling long-term relationships as well as performance.

After testing many variables, the Strategic Planning Institute (SPI) in Cambridge, Massachusetts, developed an extensive database on the impact of various business

16. Al Urbanski, "Lawyers Go Mass Market," *Sales and Marketing Management*, August 1987, pp. 32–34.
17. G. Lynn Shostack, "Breaking Free from Product Marketing," *Journal of Marketing*, April 1977, pp. 73–80.

Promoting Theme Parks with High Technology

To appeal to an increasingly sophisticated public, many theme parks are introducing new attractions that make use of the latest technology. In 1986, 215 million visitors paid for entertainment at the nation's theme parks. The service-oriented parks work hard to keep these media-educated, computer-literate customers entertained enough to lure them back for a second or third visit; repeat customers are a large portion of their business. High technology and computers are making it easier, albeit more expensive, for the parks to capture the public's imaginations.

Among the new attractions is Universal Studio's "Miami Vice" outdoor stunt show. In this scenario, two big-city detectives (personifying Crockett and Tubbs) try to capture some evil drug smugglers. Fifteen minutes of high-speed water chases and the latest pyrotechnics are included.

Another attraction is Disneyland's $32 million Star Tours, which certainly entertains customers: It is a giant aircraft simulator complete with "Star Wars" film footage shown through the craft's windows. The simulator pitches and yaws to avoid the meteorites and laser blasts the passengers see through the windows. The stars and meteors whizzing by the pitching ship make the passengers feel as if they are actually speeding through the galaxy.

Interestingly, Star Tours can be transformed into an entirely different attraction by changing software and facades. Thus Disney can obtain several rides for the price of one.

Although such technology is expensive, it does give theme parks the ability to add to and upgrade attractions. In turn, it gives customers more reason to come back to the park another time. Industry analysts expect such flexible rides to become the future of theme parks. Soon, theme parks may offer interactive rides, which would let the passengers have some control over their ride experience via the use of buttons or levers. The technology for such rides is still a few years away, but the potential for customer satisfaction on interactive rides makes the wait for the technology worthwhile.

Partly because of the increased usage of computers, coupled with a demand for space-adventure films, customers expect more technologically sophisticated attractions. Industry officials believe that to be competitive in the future, they must invest in high-tech attractions now. Exciting attractions also help keep the parks fresh in the minds of their customers and keep those customers coming back. The parks use technology to provide mainly a service—the ultimate entertainment experience.

SOURCES: Johnathan B. Levine and Todd Mason, "The Force of George Lucas Is Now with Disney," *Business Week*, Mar. 9, 1987, p. 65; Nancy Jeffrey, "Joy Rides: Theme Parks Introduce More High-Tech Thrills and Chills," *Wall Street Journal*, July 2, 1987, p. 21; Stephen J. Sansweet, "Disney's 'Imagineers' Build Space Attraction Using High-Tech Gear," *Wall Street Journal*, Jan. 6, 1987, pp. 1, 16.

strategies on profits. The institute found that "relative perceived product quality" is the single most important factor in determining long-term profitability. The strength or weakness of service provided often affects consumers' perceptions of product quality. Of the companies in the SPI database, businesses that rate low on service lose market share at the rate of 2 percent a year and average a 1 percent return on sales. Companies that score high on service gain market share at the rate of 6 percent a year, average a 12 percent return on sales, and charge a significantly higher price.[18] These data indicate that firms having service-dominant products must score high on service quality.

Other product concepts discussed in Chapters 7 and 8 are also relevant here. Management must make decisions regarding the product mix, positioning, branding, and new-product development. Marketers can make better decisions if they analyze their service products as to complexity and variability. Complexity is determined by the number of steps required to perform the service, and variability is determined by the number of decisions required of service workers or the ability to customize.[19] An examination of the complete service delivery process, including the number of steps and the number of decisions, will enable marketers to plot their service products on a complexity/variability grid, such as the one in Figure 21.5. The position of a service on the grid will have implications for its positioning in the market. Furthermore, any alterations in the service delivery process that shift the position of the service on the complexity/variability grid will have an impact on the positioning of the service in the marketplace. Table 21.4 details the effects of such changes. When structuring the service delivery system, marketers should explicitly consider the firm's marketing goals and target market.

Promotion

As intangible-dominant products, services are not easily advertised. The intangible is difficult to depict in advertising, whether the medium is print, television, or radio. Service advertising should thus emphasize tangible cues that will help consumers understand and evaluate the service. The cues may be the physical facilities

18. Tom Peters, "More Expensive, But Worth It," *U.S. News and World Report,* Feb. 3, 1986, p. 54.
19. G. Lynn Shostack, 1985 American Marketing Association Faculty Consortium on Services Marketing, Texas A&M University, July 7–11.

FIGURE 21.5

Complexity/variability grid for medical services (SOURCE: Adapted from Lynn Shostack, 1985 American Marketing Association Faculty Consortium on Services Marketing, Texas A&M University, July 7–11)

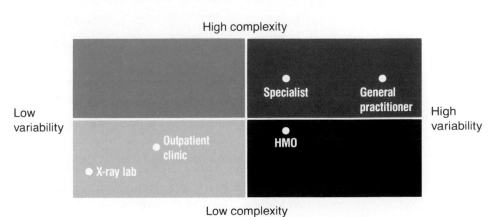

in which the service is performed or some relevant tangible object that symbolizes the service itself.[20] For example, restaurants may stress their physical facilities—clean, elegant, casual, and so on—to provide cues as to the quality or nature of the service. Insurance firms such as Allstate Insurance Co. and Travelers Corp. use objects as symbols to help consumers understand their services. Outstretched hands ("You're in good hands with Allstate") symbolize security, and the "Travelers Umbrella" suggests the protection Travelers' insurance plans provide (see Figure 21.6).

Employees in a service organization are an important secondary audience for service advertising. We have seen that variability in service quality, which arises from the labor-intensive nature of many services, is a problem for service marketers, and that consumers often associate the service with the service provider. Advertising can have a positive effect on customer contact personnel; it can shape employees' perceptions of the company, their jobs, and how management expects them to perform, and it can be a tool for motivating, educating, and communicating with employees.[21]

Personal selling is potentially powerful in services because this form of promotion lets consumers and salespeople interact. When consumers enter into a service transaction, they must, as a general rule, interact with service firm employees. Customer contact personnel can be trained to use this opportunity to reduce customer uncertainty, give reassurance, reduce dissonance, and promote the reputation of the organization.[22] Once again, this emphasizes the importance of properly managing contact personnel.

20. William R. George and Leonard L. Berry, "Guidelines for the Advertising of Services," *Business Horizons,* July–August 1981, pp. 52–56.
21. Ibid., pp. 55–70.
22. William R. George and J. Patrick Kelly, "The Promotion and Selling of Services," *Business,* July–September 1983, pp. 14–20.

TABLE 21.4

Effects of shifting positions on the complexity/variability grid

DOWNSHIFTING COMPLEXITY/ VARIABILITY	UPSHIFTING COMPLEXITY/ VARIABILITY
Standardizes the service	Increases costs
Requires strict operating controls	Indicates higher-margin/lower-volume strategy
Generally widens potential market	Personalizes the service
Lowers costs	Generally narrows potential market
Indicates lower-margin/higher-volume strategy	Makes quality more difficult to control
Can alienate existing markets	

SOURCE: Adapted from G. Lynn Shostack, 1985 American Marketing Association Faculty Consortium on Services Marketing, Texas A&M University, July 7–11, 1985.

FIGURE 21.6

The Travelers Insurance Company uses a tangible item—the umbrella—to communicate well-being and safety from daily change (SOURCE: Courtesy of The Travelers Companies)

Although consumer service firms have the opportunity to interact with actual customers and those potential customers who contact them, they have little opportunity to go out into the field and solicit business from all potential consumers. The very large number of potential customers and the high cost per sales call rule out such efforts. On the other hand, marketers of industrial services, like the marketers of industrial goods, are dealing with a much more limited target market and may find personal selling the most effective way of reaching customers.

Sales promotions, such as contests, are feasible for service firms, but other types of promotions are more difficult to implement. How do you display a service? How do you give a free sample without giving away the whole service? A visit to a health club or a free skiing lesson could possibly be considered a free sample to entice a consumer into purchasing a membership or taking lessons.

Although the role of publicity and the implementation of a publicity campaign do not differ significantly in the goods and services sectors, service marketers appear to rely on publicity much more than goods marketers do.[23] Consider, for example, the use of publicity by the provider of a "Fun in the Sun" cruise to

23. John M. Rathmell, *Marketing in the Services Sector* (Cambridge, Mass.: Winthrop, 1974), p. 100.

Mexico or Jamaica. The provider could use senior citizen groups to get the word out about the tour. Hospitals and other health-care providers use consumer education programs and health fairs as a major component in their promotion mix. In fact, certain segments of the service sector have made publicity their single communications medium.[24]

Consumers tend to value word-of-mouth communications more than company-sponsored communications. This preference is probably true for all products but especially for services because they are experiential in nature. For this reason, service firms should attempt to stimulate and to simulate word-of-mouth communications.[25] Word of mouth can be stimulated by encouraging consumers to tell their friends about satisfactory performance. Many firms, for instance, prominently display signs urging customers to tell their friends if they like the service and to tell the firm if they do not. Some service providers, such as hair stylists, give their regular customers discounts or free services for encouraging friends to come in for a haircut. Word of mouth can be simulated through communications messages that feature a testimonial, for example, television advertisements showing consumers who vouch for the benefits of a service a particular firm offers.

One final note should be made in regard to service promotion. The promotional activities of most professional service providers such as doctors, lawyers, and CPAs are severely restricted. Until recently, all these professionals were prohibited by law from advertising. Although restrictions have now been lifted, there are still many obstacles to be overcome. Not used to seeing professionals advertise, consumers may reject advertisements for those who do. Furthermore, professionals are not familiar with advertising and consequently do not always develop advertisements appropriate for their services. Increasingly, lawyers are being forced to consider professional services advertising because many potential clients do not know that they need legal services, there is an oversupply of lawyers, and there are more franchised law firms in shopping centers, causing a distinct change in the competition. Consumers want more information about legal services, and lawyers have a very poor public image.[26] On the other hand, physicians are more skeptical of the impact of advertising on their image and business. Many physicians are attempting to expand their customer base by promoting extended office hours, making house calls, consulting by telephone, and opening more offices.[27] Finally, the professions themselves exert pressure on their members to not advertise or promote because such activities are still viewed as highly unprofessional.

Price

Price plays both an economic and a psychological role in the service sector, just as it does with physical goods. However, the psychological role of price in respect to services is magnified somewhat because consumers must rely on price as the sole indicator of service quality when other quality indicators are absent. In its eco-

---

24. Ibid.

25. William R. George and J. Patrick Kelly, "The Promotion and Selling of Services," *Business*, July–September 1983, pp. 14–20; William R. George and Leonard L. Berry, "Guidelines for the Advertising of Services," *Business Horizons*, July–August 1981, pp. 55–70.

26. Doris C. Van Doren and Louise W. Smith, "Marketing in the Restructured Professional Services Field," *Journal of Services Marketing*, Summer 1987, pp. 69–70.

27. Joyce Jensen and Steve Larson, "Nation's Physicians Adding Healthcare Services, Marketing Their Practices to Attract New Patients," *Modern Healthcare*, July 16, 1987, pp. 49–50.

nomic role, price determines revenue and influences profits. Knowing the real costs of each service provided is vital to sound pricing decisions.[28]

As noted in Table 21.1, service intangibility may complicate the setting of prices. When pricing physical goods, management can look to the cost of production (direct and indirect materials, direct and indirect labor, and overhead) as an indicator of price. It is often difficult, however, to determine the cost of service provision and thus identify a minimum price. Price competition is severe in many service areas characterized by standardization. Usually price is not a key variable when marketing is first implemented in an organization. Once market segmentation and specialized services are directed to specific markets, specialized prices are set. Next comes comparative pricing as the service becomes fairly standardized. Price competition is quite common in legal services related to divorce and bankruptcy, in long-distance phone service, and in airline transportation.[29]

Many services, especially professional services, are very situation specific. Thus neither the service firm nor the consumer knows the extent of the service prior to production and consumption. Once again, because cost is not known beforehand, price is difficult to set. Despite the difficulties in determining cost, many service firms use cost-plus pricing. Others set prices according to the competition or market demand. For example, Curtis Mathes Corporation sells televisions and video recorders at up to a 30 percent price premium. Curtis Mathes is growing fast and its franchises are highly profitable because the company stands behind its products. Service before and after the sale is the key to the success of the Curtis Mathes pricing policy.[30]

Pricing of services can also help smooth fluctuations in demand. Given the perishability of service products, this is an important function. A higher price may be used to deter demand during peak periods, and a lower price may be used to stimulate demand during slack periods. For example, Domino's Pizza is the second largest pizza chain in the United States, but it is primarily known and differentiated by its delivery service: Delivery is guaranteed within thirty minutes after an order is received or the company provides a discount. And because pizza consumption tends to be seasonal, Domino's may offer two pizzas for the price of one to minimize sales declines during slow sales months.[31] Airlines rely heavily on price to help smooth their demand, as do many bars, movie theaters, and hotels.

Distribution

Almost by definition, service industries are limited to direct channels of distribution. Many services are produced and consumed simultaneously; for high-contact services in particular, service providers and consumers cannot be separated. With low-contact services, however, service facilities and service providers may be separated from retail outlets.[32] Dry cleaners, for example, generally maintain strategically located retail stores. These stores, which may be independent or corporate

---

28. James B. Ayers, "Lessons from Industry for Healthcare," *Administration Radiology,* July 1987, p. 53.
29. Stephen W. Brown, "New Patterns Are Emerging in Service Marketing Sector," *Marketing News,* June 7, 1985, p. 2.
30. Tom Peters, "More Expensive, But Worth It," *U.S. News and World Report,* Feb. 3, 1986, p. 54.
31. Raymond Seafin, "Domino's Pizza Takes 'Fresh' Angle," *Advertising Age,* Feb. 29, 1988, p. 34.
32. Richard B. Chase, "Where Does the Customer Fit in a Service Operation?", *Harvard Business Review,* November–December 1978, pp. 137–142.

owned, are simply drop-off centers. Consumers go to the retail store to initiate and terminate service, but the actual service is performed at a different location. The separation is possible because the service is directed toward the consumer's physical possessions and the consumer is not required to be present during delivery.

Other service industries are developing unique ways to distribute their services. Congruently, airlines, car rental companies, and hotels have long used intermediaries to make it more convenient for consumers to obtain their services. The intermediaries are the travel agencies who handle reservations. The two most important strategic concerns in financial services marketing are the application of technology and the use of electronic product delivery channels, such as automatic teller machines (ATMs) and electronic funds transfer systems, to provide customers with financial services in a more widespread and convenient manner.[33] Consumers no longer must go to their bank for routine transactions; they can now receive service from the closest ATM. Bank credit cards have enabled banks to extend their credit services to consumers over widely dispersed geographic areas through a nationwide network of intermediaries, namely, the retail merchants who assist consumers in applying for and using the cards.

In the service context, *distribution* is making services available to prospective users. *Marketing intermediaries* are the entities between the actual service provider and the consumer that make the service more available and more convenient to use.[34] The distribution of services is very closely related to product development. Indirect distribution of services may be made possible by a tangible representation or a facilitating good (for example, a bank credit card).[35]

Strategic Considerations

In developing strategies, the marketer must first understand the benefits the customer wishes to receive (translate features into benefits), understand how the marketer is perceived relative to the competition, and know what services consumers buy.[36] In other words, the marketer must develop the right service for the right people at the right price and at the right place. For example, in Figure 21.7, Avis, Inc. promotes its car rental services—Rapid Return, SuperValue Rates, bonus American Airlines AAdvantage miles, and an 800 number for making reservations.

The marketer must remember to communicate with consumers so they are aware of the need-satisfying services available to them. For example, Federal Express Corp. began offering its overnight delivery services in 1973, when many people believed that there was no need for this service. Today, the overnight delivery business generates more than $6 billion a year in revenues. To remain successful in the 1980s, Federal Express is focusing on five strategic objectives to help differentiate its services from those of the competition:

1. Improve service and further differentiate its products
2. Lower prices while enhancing value

33. Nigel A. L. Brooks, "Strategic Issues for Financial Services Marketing," *Journal of Services Marketing,* Summer 1987, p. 65.
34. James H. Donnelly, Jr., "Marketing Intermediaries in Channels of Distribution for Services," *Journal of Marketing,* January 1976, pp. 55–70.
35. Ibid.
36. Yoram Wind, "Financial Services: Increasing Your Marketing Productivity and Profitability," *Journal of Services Marketing,* Fall 1987, p. 8.

3. Get closer to the customer
4. Maximize its electronic and technological capability
5. Improve cash flow and financial returns[37]

Nevertheless, the unique characteristics of services create special problems for a marketing strategy.

One of the unique challenges service marketers face is matching supply and demand. We have seen that price can be used to help smooth demand for a service. There are other ways too that marketers can alter the marketing mix to deal with the problem of fluctuating demand. Through price incentives, advertising, and other promotional efforts, marketers can remind consumers of busy times and encourage them to come for service during slack periods. Additionally, the product itself can be altered to cope with fluctuating demand. Restaurants, for example, may change their menus, vary their lighting and decor, open or close the bar, and add or delete entertainment. A ski resort may install an Alpine slide to attract customers during summer months. Finally, distribution can be modified to reflect changes in demand. Theaters have traditionally offered matinees over the weekend

37. Carl Williams, "The Challenge of Retail Marketing at Federal Express," *Journal of Services Marketing*, Summer 1987, pp. 25–26.

TABLE 21.5

Strategies for coping
with fluctuations in de-
mand for services

MARKETING STRATEGIES	NONMARKETING STRATEGIES
Use differential pricing	Hire extra help/lay off employees
Alter product	Work employees overtime/part-time
Change distribution	Cross-train employees
Use promotional efforts	Use employees to perform nonvital tasks during slack times
	Subcontract work/seek subcontract work
	Slow the pace of work
	Turn away business

when demand is greater, and some libraries have mobile units that travel to different locations during slack periods.[38]

Before understanding such strategies, service marketers must first understand the pattern and determinants of demand. Does the level of demand follow a cycle? What are the causes of this cycle? Are the changes random?[39] The need to answer such questions is best illustrated through an example. Consider, for instance, an attempt to use price decreases to shift demand for public transportation to off-peak periods. Such an attempt would likely fail because of the cause of the cyclical demand for public transportation: employment hours. Employees have little control over working hours and are therefore unable to take advantage of pricing incentives.

Table 21.5 summarizes ways service firms may deal with the problem of fluctuating demand. Note that the strategies fall into two categories: marketing and nonmarketing strategies. Nonmarketing strategies essentially involve internal, employee-related actions.[40] They may be the only available alternatives when fluctuations in demand are random. For example, a strike may cause fluctuations in consumer demand for public transportation.

Nonbusiness Marketing

Nonbusiness marketing includes marketing activities conducted by individuals and organizations to achieve some goal other than ordinary business goals such as profit, market share, or return on investment. Nonbusiness marketing can be divided into two categories: nonprofit organization marketing and social marketing.

38. Christopher H. Lovelock, "Classifying Services to Gain Strategic Marketing Insights," *Journal of Marketing*, Summer 1983, pp. 279–289.
39. Ibid.
40. Leonard L. Berry, Valarie A. Zeithaml, and A. Parasuraman, "Responding to Demand Fluctuations: Key Challenge for Service Businesses," in *AMA Educators Proceedings*, Russell Belk et al., eds. (Chicago: American Marketing Association, 1984), pp. 231–234.

Nonprofit organization marketing is the application of marketing concepts and techniques to such organizations as hospitals and colleges. Social marketing is the development of programs designed to influence the acceptability of social ideas, such as contributing to the foundation for AIDS research.[41] Remember that earlier we broadly defined marketing as a set of individual and organizational activities aimed at facilitating and expediting satisfying exchanges in a dynamic environment through the creation, distribution, promotion, and pricing of goods, services, and ideas. Although most examples in this text involve business enterprises, this section examines the unique aspects of marketing in nonbusiness situations. Most of the previously discussed concepts and approaches to managing marketing activities apply to nonbusiness situations. Of special relevance is the material offered in the first half of this chapter because many nonbusiness organizations provide services.

As discussed in Chapter 1, an exchange situation exists when individuals, groups, or organizations possess something that they are willing to give up in an exchange. In nonbusiness marketing, obligations or rewards often are not clearly specified in advance. Additionally, the objects of the exchange may not be specified in financial terms. Usually, such exchanges are facilitated through **negotiation** (mutual discussion or communication of terms and methods) and **persuasion** (convincing and prevailing upon by argument). Acceptance of nonbusiness products is attained through constant efforts to further an organization's goals. Often negotiation and persuasion are conducted without reference to or awareness of the role that marketing plays in transactions. We are concerned with nonbusiness performance of marketing activities, whether the exchange is consummated or not.

Why Is Nonbusiness Marketing Different?

In this section we first examine the concept of nonbusiness marketing and see how organizational and individual goals determine whether an organization is a business or a nonbusiness. Next, we explore the overall objectives of nonbusiness organizations, their marketing objectives, and the development of their marketing strategies. Finally, we illustrate how an audit of marketing activities can promote marketing awareness in a nonbusiness organization.

Traditionally and mistakenly, people have not thought of nonbusiness exchange activities as marketing. Only organizations that attempt to make a profit—including those such as mutual insurance companies that seek profits by marketing services—have been viewed as the type that must perform marketing activities. But consider the following example. The University of Minnesota developed a comprehensive marketing program to fill the stands at women's basketball games. An essential feature of the plan is awareness-building advertisements to put people in the stands. The university depends on voluntary professional services and donated media time and space to reach the Minneapolis market. Viewing women's athletics as a viable form of family entertainment, the university is building a market by entering the competition for the entertainment dollar. Promotions have helped Minnesota boost average attendance at women's basketball games to about one thousand, but more than just advertising will be necessary to realize the goal of five

41. J. Whyte, "Organization, Person and Idea Marketing as Exchange," *Quarterly Review of Marketing* (U.K.), January 1985, pp. 25–30.

FIGURE 21.8

The Elm-Brook Humane Society (a nonprofit organization) creatively encourages pet adoption

thousand fans per game. The creator of the program hopes to develop a marketing campaign that can be applied generically to women's sports across the nation.[42]

Profit is a variable that only indirectly changes the nature of marketing activities. Many nonbusiness organizations strive for effective marketing activities. Charitable organizations and supporters of social causes are major nonbusiness marketers in this country. Political parties, unions, religious sects, and fraternal organizations also perform marketing activities, yet they are not considered businesses. Whereas the chief beneficiary of a business enterprise is whoever owns or holds stock in it, in theory the only beneficiaries of a nonbusiness organization are its clients, its members, or the public at large.

Nonbusinesses have a greater opportunity for creativity than most business organizations, but they are generally less productive and efficient because they are less directly accountable to an owner or ownership group. Organizations such as the Elm-Brook Humane Society in Figure 21.8 creatively encourage consumers to visit their organization and take home a pet. But trustees or board members of nonbusinesses are likely to have trouble judging performance when services can be provided only by trained professionals. It is harder for administrators to evaluate the performance of doctors, professors, or social workers than it is for sales managers to evaluate the performance of salespersons.

42. Kevin T. Higgins, "Gopher the Goal: Minnesota Marketers Donate Services, Media to Aid Women's Sports Program," *Marketing News,* Feb. 14, 1986, p. 1.

Nonbusinesses May Be Controversial

Nonbusiness organizations may have goals that some members of society do not accept. Opposing organizations may spring up to combat the success of a movement or social cause with which individuals disagree. Nonprofit groups such as Common Cause, the American Postal Workers Union, and Gun Owners of America spend lavishly on lobbying efforts to persuade Congress, the White House, and even the courts to support their interests, in part because acceptance of their aims is far from guaranteed.[43] Few people, however, oppose the basic goals of the American Cancer Society (to prevent cancer and treat victims) or the March of Dimes (to prevent birth defects).

The professional who manages marketing activities that promote the cause of a controversial group must make more value judgments about marketing the cause or organization than do marketers in most business enterprises. Also, the use of marketing by controversial groups may be called into question by various members of society.

Marketing as a field of study does not attempt to state what an organization's goals should be or to debate the issue of nonbusiness versus business goals. Marketing only attempts to provide a body of knowledge and concepts to help further an organization's goals. Individuals must decide whether they approve or disapprove of a particular organization's goal orientation. Most marketers would agree that profit and consumer satisfaction are appropriate goals for business enterprises, but there probably would be considerable disagreement about the goals of a controversial nonbusiness organization.

Nonbusiness Marketing Objectives

The basic aim of nonbusiness organizations is to obtain a desired response from a target market (public). The response could be a change in values, a financial contribution, the donation of services, or some other type of exchange. Nonbusiness marketing objectives are shaped by the nature of the exchange and the goals of the organization. For example, the Easter Seal telethon has raised more than $200 million since its inception in 1972; the telethon is Easter Seals' largest annual fund-raising event. Telethons have three specific marketing objectives: (1) raise funds to support programs, (2) plead a case on behalf of disabled people, and (3) inform the public about the organization's programs and services. Tactically, telethons have received support by presenting quality programs and services; generating extensive grassroots support; portraying disabled people in a positive and dignified way; developing national, regional and local support; and providing quality entertainment.[44] Figure 21.9 illustrates how the exchanges and the purpose of the organization can influence marketing objectives. (These objectives are used as examples and may or may not apply to specific organizations.)

Nonbusiness marketing objectives should state the rationale for an organization's existence. An organization that defines its marketing objective as providing a product can be left without a purpose if the product becomes obsolete. However, serving and adapting to the perceived needs and wants of a target public, or market, enhances an organization's chance to survive and achieve its goals.

---

43. "Lobbyists: Washington's 'Hidden Persuaders,'" *U.S. News and World Report,* Sept. 19, 1983, p. 63.
44. John Garrison, "Telethons—The Positive Story," *Fund Raising Management,* November, 1987, pp. 48–52.

FIGURE 21.9

Examples of marketing objectives for different types of exchanges (SOURCE: Philip Kotler, *Marketing for Nonprofit Organizations,* 2nd ed., © 1982, p. 38. Adapted by permission of Prentice-Hall, Inc., Englewood Cliffs, N.J.)

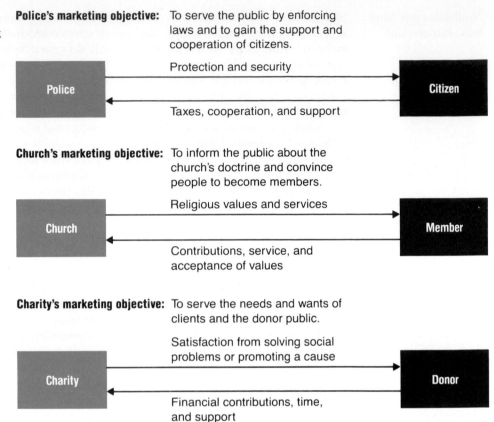

Police's marketing objective: To serve the public by enforcing laws and to gain the support and cooperation of citizens.

Police → Protection and security → Citizen
Police ← Taxes, cooperation, and support ← Citizen

Church's marketing objective: To inform the public about the church's doctrine and convince people to become members.

Church → Religious values and services → Member
Church ← Contributions, service, and acceptance of values ← Member

Charity's marketing objective: To serve the needs and wants of clients and the donor public.

Charity → Satisfaction from solving social problems or promoting a cause → Donor
Charity ← Financial contributions, time, and support ← Donor

Developing Nonbusiness Marketing Strategies

A marketing strategy encompasses (1) defining and analyzing a target market and (2) creating and maintaining a marketing mix. A nonbusiness organization may not think in terms of the needs, perceptions, or preferences of its market or public. It is very easy for an organization to assume that it knows what the public needs or wants. For example, an interest group may assume that it is only right to protect animals such as coyotes. But a group that is also concerned with the environment, ranchers, may view coyotes as a threat to their livestock and thus to their livelihood. Similarly, people who work for hospitals, welfare organizations, municipal transportation systems, and the like often assume that they have the technical competence to decide what services the public needs. However, hospitals often offend or frighten patients by failing to explain procedures; welfare organizations are sometimes patronizing; and city buses can be dirty and overcrowded. The Application on page 767 discusses a success story in marketing Indianapolis as a sports city. From such examples it is clear that success can be traced to a careful implementation of a marketing strategy.

Target Markets   We must revise the concept of target markets slightly to apply it to nonbusiness organizations. Whereas a business is supposed to have target groups that are potential purchasers of its product, a nonbusiness organization may attempt to serve many diverse groups. For our purposes, **target public** is broadly defined as a collective of individuals who have an interest in or concern about an organization, a product, or a social cause. It follows that the terms *target market* and *target public* are difficult to distinguish for many nonbusiness organizations. The Partnership for a Drug Free America has a target public of parents, adults, and concerned teen-agers. The target market for the advertisement is potential and current drug users. Once an organization is concerned about exchanging values or obtaining a response from the public, it views the public as a market.[45] For example, the Red Cross, to broaden its base of support, targets two markets with its direct mail: (1) prospects who have not previously donated to the Red Cross, costing 82 cents for every dollar raised, and (2) donor renewals, which cost only 9 cents per dollar raised.[46]

In nonbusiness organizations, direct consumers of the product are called **client publics** and indirect consumers are called **general publics**.[47] For example, the client public for a university is its student body, and its general public includes parents, alumni, and trustees. The client public usually receives most of the attention when an organization develops a marketing strategy. Techniques and approaches to segmenting and defining target markets are discussed in Chapter 3. These techniques apply also to nonbusiness target markets.

Table 21.6 exemplifies behavioral segmentation of the performing-arts market in a large urban area. By delineating markets for classical, country/folk, theater, pop, and recital art forms, arts administrators can provide more and better performances for defined audiences and develop new programs for unique market segments.[48] Notice that Table 21.6 indicates not only the types of performances attended but the types of performances that particular market segments are more likely not to attend. Arts administrators know, therefore, that the country/folk segment of the market is unlikely to attend musicals, plays, or performances of the symphony.

Developing a Marketing Mix

A marketing mix strategy limits alternatives and directs marketing activities toward achieving organizational goals. The strategy should outline or develop a blueprint for making decisions about product, distribution, promotion, and price. These decision variables should be blended to serve the target market.

A successful strategy requires careful delineation of a target market through marketing research and the development of a complete marketing mix. For example, many states have established agencies that use promotional methods to attract foreign investment for continued economic growth of the state. Some concrete examples include the following methods:

45. Philip Kotler, *Marketing for Nonprofit Organizations* (Englewood Cliffs, N.J.: Prentice-Hall, 1982), p. 37.
46. Eileen Norris, "Direct Marketing: Charities Step Up Solicitations," *Advertising Age,* July 27, 1987, pp. S4, S6.
47. Philip Kotler, *Marketing for Nonprofit Organizations* (Englewood Cliffs, N.J.: Prentice-Hall, 1982), p. 37.
48. John R. Nevin and S. Tamer Cavusgil, "Audience Segments for the Performing Arts," *Marketing of Services,* James H. Donnelly and William R. George, eds. (Chicago: American Marketing Association, 1981), p. 128.

TABLE 21.6

Art-form audience segments

MARKET SEGMENT	TYPE OF PERFORMANCE ATTENDED	TYPE OF PERFORMANCE NOT ATTENDED
Classical	Symphony Chamber music Opera Ballet	Experimental theater Rock Comedians
Country/folk	Country-western Folk/bluegrass Rock	Musicals Plays Symphony
Theater	Musicals Traditional plays Experimental theater	Rock Chamber music
Pop	Jazz Big bands Pop vocalist/group	Gospel
Recital	Instrumental recitals Solo vocal recitals	Musicals Pop

SOURCE: John R. Nevin and S. Tamer Cavusgil, "Audience Segments for the Performing Arts," *Marketing of Services,* James H. Donnelly and William R. George, eds. (Chicago: American Marketing Association, 1981), p. 127. Reprinted with permission of the publisher.

1. *Personal selling*—U.S. or foreign-based individuals directly contact potential investors.
2. *Sales promotion*—direct investment is encouraged through seminars and investment missions.
3. *Advertising*—printed and audiovisual promotional materials are used in foreign countries, along with advertisements in newspapers and magazines.
4. *Publicity*—the press is utilized systematically.

An examination of attempts by various southeastern states to attract foreign investment found that none of the states determined the wants and needs of potential investors. Instead, their selection of target markets was based on such factors as past investment levels and the feelings of state agency representatives. Another major problem was the agencies' failure to evaluate feedback from foreign investors regarding their states' promotional programs. Also, product was not emphasized as much as the promotion variable.[49]

The level of application for any given marketing mix variable may range from low to high (see Table 21.7), depending on the needs of the nonbusiness industry.[50]

49. Spero C. Peppas, "An Application of Marketing Theory to the Attraction of Foreign Investment," *A Spectrum of Contemporary Marketing Ideas,* John H. Summey, Blaise J. Bergiel, and Carol H. Anderson, eds. (Carbondale, Ill.: Southern Marketing Association, 1982), pp. 204–208.
50. Philip D. Cooper and George E. McIlvain, "Factors Influencing Marketing's Ability to Assist Non-Profit Organizations," *Evolving Marketing Thought for 1980, Proceedings of the Southern Marketing Association,* John H. Summey and Ronald D. Taylor, eds. (Nov. 19–22, 1980), p. 316.

Indianapolis Markets Itself as a Sports Capital

Many nonbusiness organizations use marketing activities to achieve their objectives. These activities may benefit several groups associated with the organization, including its clients, members, and the general public. Indianapolis, Indiana, has adopted a marketing strategy to position itself as the amateur sports capital of the United States.

Indianapolis experienced a 3.2 percent population growth between 1980 and 1985, one of the few cities in the economically plagued Midwest to grow. Nevertheless, city officials realized that to ensure further growth, Indianapolis needed a marketable position—and amateur sports seemed like a real winner.

In 1979, the city built the Indianapolis Sports Center, now the site of the annual U.S. Clay Court Tennis Championships. Market Square Arena (home of the Indiana Pacers), the Indiana University Natatorium, and the Track and Field Stadium were completed just in time for the 1982 National Sports Festival, the city's first major amateur athletic event. Indianapolis's success in hosting this event boosted its image and gave it the confidence to host future sporting events. The city permits the public to use many of these facilities when they are not scheduled for sporting events, thus increasing public support for the sports-oriented campaign. Of course, the city is also the home of the Indianapolis 500, the world's biggest professional automobile race, and the home-away-from-home for Bobby Knight's Hoosier (Indiana University) basketball team.

Several organizations in Indianapolis provided grants to help fund these facilities. The largest was the $25 million Lilly Endowment from Eli Lilly & Co., which enabled the $77 million Hoosier Dome to be completed in 1984. Actually, the city built the dome in hopes of attracting a professional football franchise, and eventually they succeeded in getting the Baltimore Colts to move to Indianapolis. The dome was also the site of the 1984 U.S. Olympic Basketball Exhibition Game, the 1985 NBA All-Star Game, the 1987 World Indoor Track and Field Championship, and many other amateur sporting events.

In 1987, Indianapolis received its biggest honor from the world of sports: It won the bid to host the Tenth Pan-American Games, the Western Hemisphere's equivalent of the Olympic Games and the second largest multisport event in the world. The city's numerous modern athletic facilities, and its performance in hosting other events, helped Indianapolis win the honor of hosting the games. The direct economic impact on Indianapolis from the Pan-American Games was an estimated $125 million spent in restaurants, hotels, shopping centers, and so on.

Sports, which began as a municipal development tool, has fueled tremendous growth in Indianapolis. The city's convention business is at an all-time high, and hotel occupancy has increased tremendously. Moreover, the downtown area of the city is in the midst of a revitalization boom because of all the surrounding sports-facility construction. More than twenty-six major downtown developments were opened between 1980 and 1985. Retail and residential construction is booming, and the city continues to grow.

Indianapolis has used a vigorous marketing strategy to promote itself as the amateur sports capital of the United States. These activities have greatly benefited the people of Indianapolis, both financially and in recognition and esteem in the eyes of the sporting world. Residents and natives take a greater pride in being from Indianapolis than ever before. What is next for the city they once called "hick town" and "India-no-place"? City officials are hoping to be the home of the Olympics at some future date.

SOURCES: Richard Kerin, "Marketing Indianapolis Sports and Statistics to Numb the Mind," *Sales and Marketing Management,* May 1987, pp. 45–47; Richard Edel, "Onetime 'Hick Town' Becomes International Star," *Advertising Age,* Apr. 20, 1987, pp. S-7, S-10, S-12; William Giese, "Hospitable Hoosiers Roll Out the Hype," *USA Today,* July 27, 1987, pp. 1A, 2A.

As Table 21.7 indicates, however, a marketing mix should always involve some decision about each of the four major elements: product, distribution, price, and promotion. For example, ethical and legal considerations tend to limit the use of promotional tools in the health-care industry. Keep in mind that Table 21.7 is based on a survey of nonbusiness organizations in one city; the marketing mix emphasis of similar organizations elsewhere can vary.

Product Nonbusiness organizations deal more often with ideas and services than with goods. Problems in developing a product configuration evolve when an organization fails to define what is being provided. What product does the Peace Corps provide? Its services include vocational training, health services, nutritional assistance, and community development. Ideas include international cooperation and the implementation of U.S. foreign policy. The Peace Corps product is more difficult to define than the average business product. As indicated in the first part of this chapter, services are intangible and therefore need special marketing efforts. The marketing of ideas and concepts is likewise more abstract than the marketing of tangibles, and it requires much effort to present benefits.

Distribution Nonbusiness products must be available before an exchange can take place. Marketers usually analyze distribution as it relates to decisions about product and promotion. Because most nonbusiness products are ideas and services, distribution decisions relate to how these ideas and services will be made available to clients. If the product is an idea, selecting the right media (the promotional strategy) to communicate the idea will facilitate distribution. The availability of services is closely related to product decisions. By nature, services consist of assistance, convenience, and availability. Availability is part of the total service (product). For example, making a product such as health services available calls for knowledge of such retailing concepts as site location analysis.

Most nonbusiness organizations in capitalist nations do not get involved in the physical distribution of goods. If goods must be moved, a facilitating agency such as the U.S. Postal Service or United Parcel Service may carry out the task. One exception is the U.S. Geological Survey, which arranges for sporting goods stores and other commercial outlets to sell its maps. Also, the Geological Survey has joined with another government office to sell colorful satellite images of the globe.[51]

Developing a channel of distribution to coordinate and facilitate the flow of nonbusiness products to clients is a necessary task, but in a nonbusiness setting the traditional concept of the marketing channel may need to be reviewed. The independent wholesalers available to a business enterprise do not exist in most nonbusiness situations. Instead, a very short channel—nonbusiness organization to client—is prevalent because production and consumption of ideas and services are often simultaneous.

51. Paul Harris, "Uncle Sam Discovers Marketing," *Sales and Marketing Management*, Mar. 14, 1983, p. 50.

TABLE 21.7

Marketing mix emphasis of nonbusinesses in a major Midwest city

NONBUSINESS INDUSTRY	LEVEL OF APPLICATION			
	PRODUCT	DISTRIBUTION	PRICE	PROMOTION
Health-care organizations	High	Medium-high	Low-medium	Low-medium
Educational facilities	High	Medium	Low-medium	High
Political organizations	High	Medium	Low-medium	High
Cultural organizations	Medium	Low-medium	High	Medium-high
Public service agencies	Medium-high	High	Low	Low-medium
Professional organizations	High	Low	Medium	Low-medium
Religious organizations	High	Medium	Low-medium	Low
Human services organizations	High	Low-medium	Low	Medium-high

SOURCE: Philip D. Cooper and George E. McIlvain, "Factors Influencing Marketing's Ability to Assist Non-Profit Organizations," *Evolving Marketing Thought for 1980, Proceedings of the Southern Marketing Association*, John H. Summey and Ronald D. Taylor, eds. (Nov. 19–22, 1980), p. 317. Used by permission.

FIGURE 21.10

An effective billboard
advertising Chicago's
Brookfield Zoo
(SOURCE: Brookfield
Zoo)

Promotion Making promotional decisions may be the first sign that nonbusiness
organizations are performing marketing activities. Nonbusiness organizations use
advertising and publicity to communicate with clients and the public, as Figure
21.10 illustrates for Chicago's Brookfield Zoo. Direct mail remains the primary
means of fund-raising for social services. Organizations such as the Red Cross and
Special Olympics use direct mail to reach their target markets. In addition to direct
mail, the Special Olympics uses telephone solicitation and television advertising.[52]
Although personal selling may be called something else, it too is used by many
nonbusiness organizations. Churches and charities rely on personal selling when
they send volunteers to recruit new members or request donations. The U.S. Army
uses personal selling when its recruiting officers attempt to convince men and
women to enlist. Special events to obtain funds, communicate ideas, or provide
services are sales promotion activities. Contests, entertainment, and prizes offered
to attract donations resemble the sales promotion activities of business enterprises.

The number of advertising agencies that are donating their time for public service announcements (PSAs) is increasing. The quality of print PSAs is improving
notably. Nonprofit groups are becoming increasingly interested in the impact of
advertising on their organizations, and they realize that second-rate PSAs can cause
a credibility loss.[53]

Religious advertising has changed drastically in recent years. For television,
religious advertisers increasingly are injecting slice of life themes into commercials
that might be confused with advertisements for Kodak Company, Pepsi-Cola, or

52. Eileen Norris, "Direct Marketing: Charities Step Up Solicitations," *Advertising Age,* July 27, 1987,
pp. S4, S6.
53. Meryl Davids, "Doing Well By Doing Good," *Public Relations Journal,* July 1987, pp. 17–21, 39.

Coca-Cola. In one advertisement for the Mormon Church, three muddy farm kids are having a water fight when their parents pull up in a truck. Instead of reprimanding the children, the father takes out his camera and snaps their picture. The commercial is capped by the message, "Don't let the magic pass you by." Most Mormon advertisements deal with family values; the church's name, in fact, is revealed only in the final three seconds. The Episcopal Church has run an advertisement featuring the line, "In the church started by a man who had six wives, forgiveness goes without saying." Behind the engaging attempt at humor, the real message emphasized that the Episcopal Church is concerned about forgiveness. Although some churches believe that personal contact is the best marketing tool, advertising seems to have helped many churches achieve their goals.[54]

Price   Although some marketing variables are easily adaptable to the nonprofit organization, not all nonprofit organizations are equally adaptable to marketing techniques. Product and promotion might require only low modification from the profit to the nonprofit sector, but pricing is generally quite different and the decision making more complex. The different pricing concepts the nonbusiness organization faces include pricing in user and donor markets. There are two types of monetary pricing: *fixed* and *variable*. Membership fees, such as the amount paid to become a friend of the Brookfield Zoo, represent a fixed approach to pricing, whereas zoo fund-raising activities that lead to a donation represent a variable pricing structure.[55]

The broadest definition of price (valuation) must be used to develop nonbusiness marketing strategy. Financial price, an exact dollar value, may or may not be charged for a nonbusiness product. Economists recognize the giving up of alternatives as a cost. **Opportunity cost** is the value of the benefit that is given up by selecting one alternative rather than another. This traditional economic view of price means that if a nonbusiness organization can convince someone to donate time to a cause or to change his or her behavior, then the alternatives given up are a cost to (or a price paid by) the individual.

This concept of price can be used to determine what price a new recruit pays to join the all-volunteer armed forces. The Air Force (see Figure 21.11) encourages recruits by stressing the job training and career development they will receive during their enlistment. The price is giving up both personal freedom (by submitting to military rules and regulations) and earning potential, if any, outside the armed service. In the armed forces' marketing strategy, price is not viewed as a major controllable aspect of the marketing mix, although a consideration of what the new recruit is giving up is programmed into product and promotion decisions. To counter the sacrifice, recruiting promotions stress military service as a challenging opportunity by which dedicated men and women can broaden their horizons and improve their prospects.

For other nonbusiness organizations, financial price is an important part of the marketing mix. Nonbusiness organizations today are raising money by upping the prices of their services or starting to charge for services if they have not done so before. They are using marketing research to determine what kinds of products

54. Ronald Alsop, "Advertisers Promote Religion in a Splashy . . . Style," *Wall Street Journal,* Nov. 21, 1985, p. 31.
55. Leyland F. Pitt and Russell Abratt, "Pricing in Non-Profit Organizations—A Framework and Conceptual Overview," *Quarterly Review of Marketing* (U.K.), Spring–Summer 1987, pp. 13–15.

people will pay for.[56] Pricing strategies of nonbusiness organizations often stress public and client welfare over equalization of costs and revenues. If additional funds are needed to cover costs, then donations, contributions, or grants may be solicited.

Controlling Nonbusiness Marketing Activities

To control marketing activities in nonbusiness organizations, managers use information obtained in the marketing audit to make sure that goals are achieved. Table 21.8 lists several helpful summary statistics. It should be obvious that the data in Table 21.8 are useful for both planning and control. Control is designed to identify what activities have occurred in conformity with the marketing strategy and to take corrective action where any deviations are found. The purpose of control is not only to point out errors and mistakes but to revise organizational goals and marketing objectives as necessary. Because of federal and state spending cuts, the need to encourage public support or donations is increasingly important. Many

56. Kelly Walker, "Not-for-Profit Profits," *Forbes*, Sept. 10, 1984, p. 165.

FIGURE 21.11

The U.S. Air Force compensates recruits for committing years of their lives to the Air Force with training and development programs (SOURCE: Courtesy of the Air Force)

Climb higher, faster in the Air Force.

As an Air Force officer your career will take off. You'll quickly get management experience that could take years to acquire in civilian industry.

As an Air Force second lieutenant, you'll manage people, projects and offices; you'll be in charge, making decisions, shouldering the responsibility. You'll belong to an organization dedicated to achievement, innovation and high technology.

And as an officer you'll have the satisfaction of knowing that your work makes a difference to the Air Force and to your country.

Find out if you qualify. See your Air Force recruiter or call toll-free 1-800-423-USAF (in California 1-800-232-USAF). Better yet, send your resume to HRS/RSAANE, Randolph AFB, TX 78150-5421.

Aim High. Be an Air Force Officer.

1. **Product mix offerings**
   A. Types of product or services
   B. Number of organizations offering the product or service

2. **Financial resources**
   A. Types of funding used
      1. Local grants
      2. State grants
      3. Federal grants
      4. Foundations
      5. Public solicitation
      6. Fees charged
   B. Number using each type of funding
   C. Number using combinations of funding sources

3. **Size**
   A. Budget (cash flows)

   B. Number of employees
      1. By organization
      2. Total industrywide
   C. Number of volunteers
      1. By organization
      2. Total industrywide
   D. Number of customers serviced
      1. By type of service
      2. By organization
      3. Total industrywide

4. **Facilities**
   A. Number and type
      1. By organization
      2. Total industrywide
   B. Location
      1. By address
      2. Zip code
      3. Census tract

SOURCE: Adapted from Philip D. Cooper and George E. McIlvain, "Factors Influencing Marketing's Ability to Assist Non-Profit Organizations," *Evolving Marketing Thought for 1980, Proceedings of the Southern Marketing Association,* John H. Summey and Ronald D. Taylor, eds. (Nov. 19–22, 1980), p. 315. Used by permission.

potential contributors decide which charities to support based on the amount of money actually used in charitable programs. Charities are more aggressively examining their own performance and effectiveness. For example, the Salvation Army contributes 86 cents out of every dollar it receives to the needy—employees are basically volunteers who work for almost nothing. Charities are making internal changes to increase their effectiveness, and many are hiring professional managers to help with strategic planning in developing short-term and long-range goals. Organizations such as the March of Dimes and the American Red Cross find changes harder to develop and implement because of their decentralized administration.[57]

To control nonbusiness marketing activities, managers must make a proper inventory of activities performed and prepare to adjust or correct deviations from standards. Knowing where and how to look for deviations and knowing what types of deviations to expect are especially important in nonbusiness situations. Because nonbusiness marketing activities may not be perceived as marketing, managers must clearly define what activity is being examined and how it should function.

It may be difficult to control nonbusiness marketing activities because it is often hard to determine whether goals are being achieved. A mental health center that wants to inform community members of its services may not be able to determine whether it is communicating with persons who need assistance. A growing case

57. Gwen Kinkead and Patricia A. Langan, "America's Best-Run Charities," *Fortune,* Nov. 9, 1987, pp. 145–50.

load does not guarantee that all needs have been met. Surveying to determine the percentage of the population that is aware of a mental health program can show whether the awareness objective has been achieved, but it fails to indicate what percentage of the persons with mental health problems has been assisted. The detection and correction of deviations from standards is certainly a major purpose of control, but standards must support the organization's overall goals. Managers can refine goals by examining the results that are being achieved and analyzing the ramifications of those results.

Techniques for controlling overall marketing performance must be compatible with the nature of an organization's operations. Obviously, it is necessary to control the marketing budget in most nonbusiness organizations, but budgetary control is not tied to profit and loss standards; responsible management of funds is the objective. Central control responsibility can facilitate orderly, efficient administration and planning. For example, Illinois Wesleyan University evaluates graduating students' progress to control and improve the quality of the educational product. The audit phase relies on questionnaires sent to students and their employers after graduation. The employer completes a questionnaire to indicate the student's progress; the student completes a questionnaire to indicate which additional concepts or skills were needed to perform duties. In addition, a number of faculty members interview certain employers and students to obtain information for control purposes. Results of the audit are used to develop corrective action if university standards have not been met. Corrective action might include an evaluation of the deficiency and a revision of the curriculum.

Summary

Services are intangible-dominant products that cannot be physically possessed—the result of applying human or mechanical efforts to people or objects. Services are a growing part of our economy, now accounting for approximately 60 percent of our gross national product and almost 50 percent of consumer expenditures.

Services have four distinguishing characteristics: (1) intangibility, (2) inseparability of production and consumption, (3) perishability, and (4) heterogeneity. Because services include a diverse group of industries, classification schemes are used to help marketers analyze their products and develop the most appropriate marketing mix. Services can be viewed as to (1) type of market, (2) degree of labor intensiveness, (3) degree of customer contact, (4) skill of the service provider, and (5) goal of the service provider.

When developing a marketing mix for services, several aspects deserve special consideration. Regarding product, service offerings are often difficult for consumers to understand and evaluate. The tangibles associated with a service may be the only visible aspect of the service, and marketers must manage these scarce tangibles with care. Because services are often viewed in terms of the providers, service firms must carefully select, train, motivate, and control employees. Service marketers are selling long-term relationships as well as performance.

Advertising services is problematic because of their intangibility. Advertising should stress the tangibles associated with the service or use some relevant tangible object. Customer contact personnel should be considered an important secondary audience for advertising. Personal selling is very powerful in service firms because customers must interact with personnel. Some forms of sales promotion, such as displays and free samples, are difficult to implement with services. The final component of the promotion mix, publicity, is vital to many service firms. Because customers value word-of-mouth communications, messages should attempt to stimulate or simulate word of mouth. Many professional service providers, however, are severely restricted in their use of promotional activities.

Price plays three major roles in service firms. It plays a psychological role by indicating quality and an economic role by determining revenues. Price is also a way to help smooth fluctuations in demand.

Service distribution channels are typically direct because of simultaneous production and consumption. However, innovative approaches such as drop-off centers, intermediaries, and electronic distribution are being developed.

Fluctuating demand is a major problem for most service firms. Marketing strategies (product, price, promotion, and distribution), as well as nonmarketing strategies (primarily internal, employee-based actions), can be used to deal with the problem. Before attempting to undertake any such strategies, however, service marketers must understand the patterns and determinants of demand.

Nonbusiness marketing includes marketing activities conducted by individuals and organizations to achieve some goal other than normal business goals. Nonbusiness marketing uses most concepts and approaches that are applied to business situations. An exchange situation exists when individuals, groups, or organizations possess something that they are willing to give up in an exchange.

The chief beneficiary of a business enterprise is whoever owns or holds stock in the business, but the beneficiary of a nonbusiness enterprise should be its clients, its members, or its public at large. The goals of a nonbusiness organization reflect its unique philosophy or mission. Some nonbusiness organizations have very controversial goals, but many organizations exist to further generally accepted social causes.

The marketing objective of nonbusiness organizations is to obtain a desired response from a target market. Developing a nonbusiness marketing strategy consists of defining and analyzing a target market and creating and maintaining a marketing mix. In nonbusiness marketing, the product is usually an idea or service. Distribution is not involved as much with the movement of goods as with the communication of ideas and the delivery of services, which results in a very short marketing channel. Promotion is very important in nonbusiness marketing; personal selling, sales promotion, advertising, and publicity are all used to communicate ideas and inform people about services. Price is more difficult to define in nonbusiness marketing because of opportunity costs and the difficulty of quantifying values exchanged.

It is important to control nonbusiness marketing strategies. Control is designed to identify what activities have occurred in conformity with marketing strategy and to take corrective actions where any deviations are found. The standards against which deviations are measured must support the overall goals of the nonbusiness organization.

Important Terms

Services
Intangibility
Search qualities
Experience qualities
Credence qualities
Inseparability
Perishability
Heterogeneity

Nonbusiness marketing
Negotiation
Persuasion
Target public
Client publics
General publics
Opportunity cost

Discussion and Review Questions

1. Identify and discuss the distinguishing characteristics of services. What problems do these characteristics present to marketers?
2. What is the significance of "tangibles" in service industries?
3. Analyze a house cleaning service in terms of the five classification schemes, and discuss the implications for marketing mix development.
4. How do search, experience, and credence properties affect the way consumers view and evaluate services?
5. Discuss the role of promotion in services marketing.
6. Analyze the demand for dry cleaning, and discuss ways to cope with fluctuating demand.
7. Compare and contrast the controversial aspects of nonbusiness versus business marketing.
8. Relate the concepts of product, distribution, promotion, and price to a marketing strategy aimed at preventing drug abuse.
9. What are the differences among clients, publics, and consumers? What is the difference between a target public and a target market?
10. What is the function of control in a nonbusiness marketing strategy?
11. Discuss the development of a marketing strategy for a university. What marketing decisions should be made in developing strategy?

Cases

21.1 Allegis Tries to Develop a Travel Service Company[58]

Allegis just might have been the ultimate travel service company, offering door-to-door service to its customers, literally. Previously known as United Airlines, Inc.,

58. Based on information from Clemens P. Work with Harwell Wells, "One Man's Dream Comes Down to Earth," *U.S. News & World Report*, June 22, 1987, pp. 44–45; Stratford P. Sherman, "The Trio That Humbled Allegis," *Fortune*, July 20, 1987, pp. 52–54, 58–59; James E. Ellis, "Allegis: Is a Name Change Enough for UAL?" *Business Week*, pp. 54–55, 58; commentary by Judith H. Dobrzynski, "Allegis Will Live On—In the Nightmares of CEO's," *Business Week*, June 29, 1987, p. 29; Joe Agnew, "Diversified Travel-Services' Giant Hopes Allegis Will Fly," *Marketing News*, Mar. 27, 1987, pp. 1, 11.

the company wanted to diversify yet remain in the travel business. The company already owned the Westin Hotel chain and Apollo Services, Inc., a computer reservations system. The company went on a spending spree, purchasing Hertz Corporation (rental cars) in 1985, the Pacific division of Pan American World Airways in 1986, and the Hilton International hotel chain in 1987. The entire group was named Allegis, to convey "the central corporate mission of service and guardianship for the domestic and worldwide traveler through its relation to the words 'allegiant,' meaning loyal or faithful, and 'aegis,' meaning protection and sponsorship." Allegis CEO Richard Ferris visualized Allegis customers flying to their destination on a United flight and driving their Hertz rental car to the nearest Westin or Hilton hotel for vacation or business. Naturally, customers would coordinate these activities through Covia Corp., the renamed Apollo Services.

The services Allegis offered were aimed primarily at a consumer market, especially business travelers. Allegis was equipment-based, with a high degree of customer contact. In fact, this customer contact was one of the company's easiest aspects to advertise to potential customers. Yet *poor* customer contact may drive customers away. The goal of the company was, without a doubt, profit. The services Allegis offered were intangible; they could not be seen or touched. Production and consumption are inseparable for airplane flights, car rentals, and hotel stays, and these services cannot be stockpiled for future use. Because of the intangible aspects of their services, marketing car rentals to air travel was not easy.

There were tangible aspects associated with Allegis that could be emphasized, such as airplanes, hotel rooms, automobiles, and the service personnel. Personal selling was also an important marketing tool because sales can be made, or lost forever, based on customer contact with reservations personnel, ticket agents, and hotel clerks. As the ultimate travel services company, Allegis also promoted the convenience of being able to book airline flights, car rentals, and hotel reservations through one reservation. The company further offered discount packages, tying all the services together for the consumer. The company spent $7 million in 1987 to inform the public about its new services and name. Allegis was to be positioned as a full-service travel company, not as an airline that offered additional services.

Unfortunately for CEO Richard Ferris, the Allegis dream of the total travel service company succumbed to the pressures of the marketplace, particularly Wall Street. Ferris had the support of Allegis managers and directors, but others were concerned that the huge corporation had simply become too big to control. Earnings for United Airlines were miserable and its costs continued to rise, although the other businesses in the Allegis hangar were doing fairly well. The market price of Allegis's stock dropped, a sure sign that Wall Street speculators did not think the long-range plans for the ultimate travel services company would be profitable. Enter Coniston Partners, an investment firm, which bought a 13 percent interest in the new company. When stock prices continued to drop, the partners forced out Ferris and had the directors of the company reevaluate their strategy.

The new strategy was to concentrate on the airline business. Hertz, Westin, and Hilton were targeted for sale. Finally, a decision was made to drop the Allegis name. The $7 million spent to promote the name did not create a successful, highly integrated travel service company. Today United is concerned mainly with offering airline services. Perhaps by concentrating on only one service, United may find the skies of Wall Street a bit friendlier.

1. Did Allegis have the characteristics needed to be classified as a service organization? Why?
2. Do you believe that Allegis followed the basic marketing concept of giving customers benefits that satisfy their needs? Why or why not?
3. Why did the diversification into hotel and rental cars fail?

21.2 Don't Mess with Texas![59]

In the first half of the 1980s, Texas taxpayers were paying $24 million a year for litter pickup along Texas roads and highways. Previous antilitter programs and promotional campaigns were unsuccessful in persuading Texans to "pitch in" instead of "pitching out" litter onto the roadside. A tight state budget in the middle of the decade forced the Texas Department of Highways and Public Transportation to take drastic action to reduce the amount of money spent to eliminate the trash problem.

In 1985, research by the Institute for Applied Research found that the primary Texas litterer was male, 18 to 34 years old, and more blue-collar than professional. Texas-based advertising agency Gurasich, Spence, Darilek and McClure, known for its innovative ideas, was asked to create a marketing campaign to reach this client public (whom the state labeled "Bubba") in an effort to reduce the state's expenditures for litter cleanup. Their tough goal: reduce litter 25 percent by August 31, 1986.

The agency realized that antilitter slogans that would stop people from other states dead in their tracks would not even slow down a Texan: They had to talk bold and tough to get Bubba's attention. "Don't mess with Texas," the campaign theme developed, would appeal to Texans' state pride, nationalism, and ego. Texans in general are quite proud of their state and their frontier heritage; Bubba in particular would probably sit up and listen to such an appeal.

When the campaign television and radio spots were planned, the agency chose Bubba's favorite stars to voice the message. Texas musicians Stevie Ray Vaughan, the Fabulous Thunderbirds, Johnny Dee and the Rocket 88s, and Johnny Rodriguez played the state's theme song, "The Eyes of Texas." Texas sports heroes Ed "Too Tall" Jones, Randy White, and Mike Scott set an example by picking up roadside litter in the commercials. Johnny Rodriguez also did his commercials in Spanish to reach the state's large Hispanic population. Both paid advertisements and public service announcements were used to get the Don't mess with Texas message across. To increase the impact, more advertisements were scheduled to run

59. Based on information from "Don't Mess with Texas: A Phenomenal Success," Gurasich, Spence, Darilek and McClure, Austin, Texas, 1987; "Campaign Gets 'Bubba's' to Quit Messin'," *Marketing News*, June 19, 1987, p. 16; "How to Talk Trash to Texans . . . Plus, the Antidote for Boring Advertising," Gurasich, Spence, Darilek and McClure, Austin, Texas, 1987; personal conversation with Nick Turnham, public affairs officer, Brazos County, Texas Department of Highways and Public Transportation, Bryan, Texas, June 25, 1987; press release issued by the State Department of Highways and Public Transportation, Sept. 22, 1986; Michael McCullar, "Trash on Roads Down 29% After Ads," *Austin American-Statesman*, Sept. 22, 1986, pp. A1, A8.

during the spring and summer months, when littering seemed to hit its peak. Some of the spots were so popular that radio listeners and television viewers called the stations and requested that they be run more often!

Other forms of promotion carried the message too. Bumper stickers, litter bags, and decals with the Don't mess with Texas message were distributed free for the asking. The message also appeared on highway road signs. Texas businesses, civic groups, and individuals sponsored the message on T-shirts, coffee cups, key chains, store windows, company trucks, billboards, and even grocery sacks. The state also held "The Great Texas Trash-Off" to encourage Texans to kick the littering habit for one day; sixteen thousand volunteers picked up trash along the roadsides. The trash-off is now an annual event.

The state has spent nearly $2 million on the campaign since it began in 1985. In 1986, the state again commissioned the Institute for Applied Research to survey the amount of litter on Texas roadsides. The researchers found that roadside litter had been reduced by 29 percent in less than one year! Deliberate littering dropped by 41 percent, and accidental littering (things blowing out of the back of pickup trucks, car windows, and so on) dropped 18 percent. The Institute for Applied Research, which has conducted similar litter surveys across the nation, cited the 29 percent drop in roadside litter in one year as the largest one-year reduction in litter it has *ever* measured. An awareness survey conducted during the same time found that 60 percent of Texans were familiar with the Don't mess with Texas message.

The Don't mess with Texas approach was incredibly effective in achieving its objective: to get young, blue-collar Texas men to stop throwing trash on the highway. The agency carefully defined its target and spoke directly to that target in words and gestures that group used every day. The slogan also made Texans feel better about their state and gave them a new rallying cry, perhaps one day to replace Remember the Alamo.

Texas has no plans to abandon the successful campaign in the near future; in fact, the campaign is being expanded. New spots are being created to appeal to a wider target public, not just Bubba. The spots still use popular Texas musicians and athletes, and cartoon figures have been added as well, to tell the state that "messin' with Texas is a big drag . . . it's mighty reckless to mess with Texas." Some of the advertisements also address litter on Texas beaches, rivers, and lakes. The message even appeared in two movies filmed in 1987. Not only was the "Don't mess with Texas" campaign successful in reducing litter, but it also generated "national" spirit in 1986, the year of the state's 150th birthday.

Questions for Discussion

1. How well did the state of Texas define and target its client publics?
2. How does this campaign differ from that usually expected of a for-profit business?
3. Do you see any potential problems with the continuation of the campaign?

22. International Marketing

O B J E C T I V E S

- ▶ To define the nature of international marketing.
- ▶ To describe the use of international marketing intelligence in understanding foreign markets and environments.
- ▶ To examine the potential of marketing mix standardization among nations.
- ▶ To describe adaptation of the international marketing mix when standardization is impossible.
- ▶ To look at ways of becoming involved in international marketing activities.

W*hen a price war* between number one and number three is squeezing number two—and none of the three can afford to call a truce—number two's best alternative may be stepped-up international marketing. At least, that is the strategy of British automobile maker Austin Rover Group, second-place competitor in the British domestic automobile market (behind market leader Ford and ahead of General Motors' Vauxhall). After building sales in Europe for several years, ARG recently entered the U.S. market with its new Sterling model, a joint venture with Honda Motor Co., Ltd. The company hopes that the Sterling will appeal to the growing segment of U.S. car buyers interested in high-performance, luxury imports such as Volvo, Mercedes-Benz, Saab, Audi, BMW, and Jaguar.

ARG has tried three times and failed to gain a foothold in the competitive U.S. market. This time, the company maintains that the repair problems and poor service that plagued its earlier Triumph and MG sports cars are things of the past. The Sterling, manufactured alongside the Honda Acura Legend, is the first ARG product to be designed and assembled with the latest computer-aided systems, robotics, and applied technology. Every car is test-driven twenty-five miles in Europe before being shipped to the United States. In addition, the car's styling is a departure from the austerity of many European imports. Standard options in the Sterling include leather upholstery, heated outside mirrors, an eight-speaker stereo system, and a trip computer. ARG sums up the Sterling as the best of two worlds: British image combined with Japanese quality (see Figure 22.1).

Mindful of past failures, ARG is leaving nothing to chance in the marketing of the Sterling. The company devoted two years to organizing its Miami-based

North American distribution system, finally selecting 152 dealers in 32 states out of 1,400 U.S. automobile dealers who requested the cars. Franchises were awarded on the basis of the dealership's facility size and location, reputation for customer service, and willingness to market the Sterling as a low-end luxury car. More than 60 percent of the Sterling franchises went to Cadillac and other domestic model dealerships; although exclusive display space for the Sterling has not been required of dealers thus far, Austin Rover believes that separate showrooms will follow as sales build.

The company also intends to offer exceptional customer service. Austin Rover provides one field service representative for every nine dealerships, a ratio among the highest in the industry. A 32,000-square-foot parts warehouse in Miami is designed to fill 95 percent of all parts requests overnight, with parts needed for all other requests shipped from England to arrive at dealerships within thirty-six hours. In addition, the best mechanic in every dealership is assigned to the Sterling and receives two weeks of specialized training in Miami. Sterling owners are also covered by an extensive emergency road service plan.

Austin Rover executives concede that the Sterling faces stiff competition in the United States, particularly given the company's dismal track record. But they are targeting specific niches, hoping that the Sterling will attract women car owners and buyers who are younger and better-educated but slightly less affluent than Cadillac owners. They insist that—at a starting price of $19,000—the Sterling is a unique blend of elegance and affordability.[1]

M ANAGEMENT of international marketing activities, such as those by the Austin Rover Group, requires an understanding of marketing variables and a grasp of the environmental complexities of foreign countries. In many cases, serving a foreign target market requires more than minor adjustments of marketing strategies. For example, Austin Rover has made numerous adjustments in its marketing efforts during the launch of the Sterling in the United States. There may also be many submarkets within a particular market that reflect different lifestyles and consumption behaviors. For instance, significant differences in consumption behaviors, media usage, and durable goods ownership have been found among French-speaking, bilingual, and English-speaking Canadian families.[2]

International marketing is marketing activities performed across national boundaries.[3] The planning and control of such marketing activities can differ significantly from marketing within national boundaries. This chapter looks closely at the unique features of international marketing and at the marketing mix adjustments businesses make when they cross national boundaries.

We begin by examining American firms' levels of commitment to and degree of involvement in international marketing. Then we analyze several examples to see why international marketing intelligence is necessary when a firm is moving beyond its domestic market. Next, we analyze marketing mix standardization and adaptation. Finally, we describe a number of ways of getting involved in international marketing.

International Marketing Involvement

Among the technological developments needed to support international marketing, worldwide transportation and communication systems are critical. Equally important is the ability to analyze different environments and determine market

1. Based on information from Laura Clark, "Sterling Name Nearly Settled; January Debut Set," *Automotive News,* Sept. 1, 1986, pp. 3, 37; Rebecca Fannin, "Sterling Goes for the Gold," *Marketing & Media Decisions,* February 1987, pp. 46–48; Richard Feast, "Rover 800 Debuts in England," *Automotive News,* July 21, 1986, p. 14; John A. Russell, "Sterling: Austin Rover's 'Future,' " *Automotive News,* Dec. 15, 1986, p. 24; Geoff Sundstrom, "Sterling Sales Forecast Boosted by 5000 Cars," *Automotive News,* July 21, 1986, p. 14.
2. Charles M. Schaninger, Jacques C. Bourgeois, W. Christian Buss, "French-English Canadian Subcultural Consumption Differences," *Journal of Marketing,* Spring 1985, p. 82.
3. Vern Terpstra, *International Marketing,* 4th ed. (Hinsdale, Ill.: Dryden Press, 1987), p. 4.

COMPANY	FOREIGN REVENUE (MILLIONS)	TOTAL REVENUE (MILLIONS)	FOREIGN REVENUE AS % OF TOTAL	FOREIGN OPERATING PROFIT (MILLIONS)	TOTAL OPERATING PROFIT (MILLIONS)	FOREIGN OPERATING PROFIT AS % OF TOTAL
Exxon	$50,337	$69,888	72.0%	$3,910[a]	$5,219[a]	74.9%
Mobil	27,388[b]	46,025[b]	59.5	1,858[a]	1,407[a]	132.1
IBM	25,888	51,250	50.5	3,184[a]	4,789[a]	66.5
Ford Motor	19,926	62,716	31.8	825[a]	3,285[a]	25.1
General Motors	19,837	102,814	19.3	−186[a]	2,945[a]	D-P
Texaco	15,494	31,613	49.0	1,170	1,187	98.6
Citicorp	10,940	23,496	46.6	522[a]	1,058[a]	49.3
EI du Pont de Nemours	9,955[c]	26,907	37.0	644[d]	1,791	36.0
Dow Chemical	5,948	11,113	53.5	684	1,285	53.2
Chevron	5,605	24,352	23.0	808[e]	1,055[e]	76.6

[a] Net income.
[b] Includes other income.
[c] Includes excise taxes.
[d] Operating income after taxes.
[e] Net income before corporate expenses.
D-P: Deficit over profit.

SOURCE: *Forbes,* July 27, 1987, p. 152. © Forbes Inc. 1987. Used by permission.

TABLE 22.1

Revenues and profits of the ten largest U.S. multinationals (in millions)

potentials in foreign countries. Before international marketing could achieve its current level of importance, enterprises with the necessary resources had to develop an interest in expanding their businesses beyond national boundaries. Global marketing strategies then developed to increase profits and the size and influence of firms.

Multinational Involvement

The term **multinational enterprise** refers to the organizational aspects of firms that have operations or subsidiaries located in many countries to achieve a common goal. Often the parent firm is based in one country, and the multinational company is developed by cultivating production, management, and marketing activities in other countries. Such petroleum firms as Exxon Corporation, Shell Oil Company, and Mobil Corporation are multinational companies that have worldwide operations. ITT Corporation (ITT) is a multinational giant with subsidiaries in many countries. ITT subsidiaries that operate on a multinational basis include its many telecommunications manufacturing units in various countries, Sheraton Corporation (an international hotel chain), and ITT World Communications (international communications services).

Table 22.1 lists ten U.S.-based multinationals that depend on foreign revenue for a significant proportion of their total operating profits. Look at the contribution of foreign profit as a percentage of total profit to see how important international involvement can be. The table indicates that Exxon, for instance, earned nearly 75 percent of its 1986 profits from foreign operations. Many of these firms could not operate at an acceptable profit without their foreign operations.

The level of involvement in international marketing covers a wide spectrum (see Figure 22.2). "Casual or accidental exporting" is the lowest level of commitment. "Active exporting" concentrates on selling activities to gain foreign market acceptance of existing products. "Full-scale international marketing involvement" means that top management recognizes the importance of developing international marketing strategies to achieve the firm's goals. "Globalization of markets" requires total commitment to international marketing; it embodies the view that the world is a single market.

Globalization Versus Customized Marketing Strategies

Only full-scale international marketing involvement and **globalization of markets** represent a full integration of international marketing into strategic market planning. Globalization of markets is to develop marketing strategies as if the entire world (or regions of it) were a single entity; standardized products are marketed the same way everywhere. Traditional full-scale international marketing involvement is based on products customized according to cultural, regional, and national differences. Marketing strategies are developed to serve specific target markets; from a practical standpoint, this means that to standardize the marketing mix, the strategy needs to group countries by social, cultural, technological, political, and economic similarities. A multinational enterprise is thus diversified to correspond to market differences. For example, until a few years ago, Black & Decker Mfg. Co. customized lighter electric drills for Americans, and its German subsidiary made higher-powered heavy-duty drills for Germans.

Nevertheless, for many years firms have attempted to standardize the marketing mix as much as possible. The economic and competitive payoffs for standardized marketing strategies are great. Brand name, product characteristics, packaging, and labeling are among the easiest marketing mix variables to standardize; media allocation, retail outlets, and price may be more difficult. In the end, the degree of similarity among environmental and market conditions determines the feasibility

FIGURE 22.2

Levels of involvement in international marketing (SOURCE: Vern Terpstra, *International Marketing*, 3rd ed., copyright © 1983. Used by permission of CBS College Publishing)

Casual or accidental exporting

Occasional, unsolicited foreign orders are received. There is no real commitment to international marketing.

Active exporting

This is an attempt to create sales without significant changes in the firm's products and overall operations. An active effort to find foreign markets for existing products is most typical.

Full-scale international marketing involvement

Markets across national boundaries are a consideration in the marketing strategy. International marketing activities are seen as a part of overall planning.

Globalization of markets

Companies try to operate as if the world were one large market, ignoring regional and national differences.

National or domestic orientation ◄————————————————————► **Global orientation**

of standardization. For example, Kodak Company, using a customized marketing strategy, has been able to claim the number-three spot in the European copier-duplicator market (IBM and Xerox Corporation are number one and two, respectively). Kodak did not assemble and ship an unmodified American product; the product was revamped for the European market. One adaptation was alteration in language keys on the control panel, and variable reduction capabilities were added because offices, factories, and government agencies throughout Europe handle a variety of paper sizes.[4] Kodak also tailored the entire sales, advertising, and support effort to the target market.

Some companies have changed from customizing products or standardizing products for a region of the world to offering globally standardized products that are advanced, functional, reliable, and low priced.[5] As we mentioned, a firm committed to the globalization of markets develops marketing strategies as if the entire world (or major regions of it) were a single entity; it sells the same things the same way everywhere.[6] Examples of globalized products are electrical equipment, western American clothing, movies, soft drinks, rock music, cosmetics, and toothpaste (see Figure 22.3). Sony televisions, Levi jeans, and American cigarette brands seem to make year-to-year gains in the world market. Even McDonald's seems to be widely accepted in markets throughout the world. Attempts are now being made to globalize industrial products such as computers, robots, and carbon filters and professional engineering products such as earth-moving equipment and communications equipment. But the question remains whether promotion, pricing, and distribution of these products can also be standardized. Nestlé Company Inc. has taken a global approach to new candy brands such as Alpine White with Almonds. Only recently has the company identified itself as a Swiss firm.

Many leading marketers, including Philip Kotler of Northwestern University, believe that for international marketing, most products must vary in quality, packaging, promotion, and distribution. Kotler believes that McDonald's was not successful in Germany until it began offering beer, and the company itself has recognized that Germans feel McDonald's eating style is too "plastic." An advertising campaign in Germany pointed out that "every culture's eating style has its little tricks" but suggested that even gourmets do not eat at fancy restaurants every day. The advertising offered McDonald's as an alternative to fine dining because the restaurant offers good food, inexpensive prices, and fast service. Thus McDonald's saw a need to reinforce a proper cultural image in the German environment.[7]

The debate will doubtless continue about which products, if any, can be standardized globally. As we point out, some firms, such as Black & Decker, have adopted globalized marketing strategies. For some products, such as soft drinks, a global marketing strategy, including advertising, seems to work well, but for others, such as beer, strategies must incorporate local, regional, and national differences.[8]

4. Joseph A. Lawton, "Kodak Penetrates the European Copier Market with Customized Marketing Strategy and Product Changes," *Marketing News,* Aug. 3, 1984, p. 1.
5. Theodore Levitt, "The Globalization of Markets," *Harvard Business Review,* May–June 1983, p. 92.
6. Ibid., p. 93.
7. Dagmar Mussey, "McDonald's Image Gets Polished in German Ads," *Advertising Age,* July 8, 1985, p. 36.
8. "Global Brands Need Local Ad Flavor," *Advertising Age,* Sept. 3, 1984, p. 26.

International Marketing Intelligence

Despite the debate over globalization of markets, most American firms perceive international markets as differing in some ways from domestic markets. International markets and possible marketing efforts can be analyzed based on many dimensions. Table 22.2 lists types of information international marketers need.

Gathering secondary data (see Table 22.3) should be the first step in analyzing a foreign market. Sources of information include U.S. government publications, financial services firms, international organizations such as the United Nations, governments of foreign countries, and international trade organizations. Depending on the source, secondary data can be misleading, however. The reliability, validity, and comparability of data from some countries are often problematic.

To overcome these shortcomings, marketers may need primary data to understand consumers' buying behavior in the country under investigation. After analyzing secondary and primary data, marketers should plan a marketing strategy. Finally, after market entry, review and control will result in decisions to withdraw from the foreign market, to continue to expand operations, or to consider additional foreign markets.

Demographic/physical environment
- Population size, growth, density
- Urban and rural distribution
- Climate and weather variations
- Shipping distance
- Product-significant demographics
- Physical distribution and communication network
- Natural resources

Political environment
- System of government
- Political stability and continuity
- Ideological orientation
- Government involvement in business
- Government involvement in communications
- Attitudes toward foreign business (trade restrictions, tariffs, nontariff barriers, bilateral trade agreements)
- National economic and developmental priorities

Economic environment
- Overall level of development
- Economic growth: GNP, industrial sector
- Role of foreign trade in the economy
- Currency, inflation rate, availability, controls, stability of exchange rate
- Balance of payments
- Per capita income and distribution
- Disposable income and expenditure patterns

Social/cultural environment
- Literacy rate, educational level
- Existence of middle class
- Similarities and differences in relation to home market
- Language and other cultural considerations

ANALYSIS OF INDUSTRY MARKET POTENTIAL

Market access
- Limitations on trade: tariff levels, quotas
- Documentation and import regulations
- Local standards, practices, and other nontariff barriers
- Patents and trademarks
- Preferential treaties
- Legal considerations: investment, taxation, repatriation, employment, code of laws

Product potential
- Customer needs and desires
- Local production, imports, consumption
- Exposure to and acceptance of product
- Availability of linking products
- Industry-specific key indicators of demand
- Attitudes toward products of foreign origin
- Competitive offerings
- Availability of intermediaries
- Regional and local transportation facilities
- Availability of manpower
- Conditions for local manufacture

ANALYSIS OF COMPANY SALES POTENTIAL

Sales volume forecasting
- Size and concentration of customer segments
- Projected consumption statistics
- Competitive pressures
- Expectations of local distributors/agents

Landed cost
- Costing method for exports
- Domestic distribution costs
- International freight and insurance
- Cost of product modification

Cost of internal distribution
- Tariffs and duties
- Value-added tax
- Local packaging and assembly
- Margins/commission allowed for the trade
- Local distribution and inventory costs
- Promotional expenditures

Other determinants of profitability
- Going price levels
- Competitive strengths and weaknesses
- Credit practices
- Current and projected exchange rates

SOURCE: Adapted from S. Tamer Cavusgil, "Guidelines for Export Market Research," *Business Horizons*, November–December 1985, pp. 30–31.

For foreign markets, marketers may need to adjust techniques of collecting primary data. Attitudes toward privacy, unwillingness to be interviewed, language differences, and low literacy rates can be serious research obstacles. In a bicultural country such as Canada, a national questionnaire that uses identical questions is impossible because of the cultural and language differences. In most areas of Africa, where the literacy rate is low, self-administered questionnaires would never work.

In many developing countries, purchasing behavior is based on unique symbols. It may be necessary to investigate basic patterns of social behavior, values, and attitudes to plan a final marketing strategy. Primary research should uncover significant cultural characteristics before a product is launched so that the marketing strategy is appropriate for the target market. Overall, the cost of obtaining international information may be higher than the cost of domestic research. This may occur because of the large number of foreign markets to be investigated, the distance between the marketer and the foreign market, unfamiliar cultural and marketing practices, language differences, or the scarcity and unreliability of published statistics.[9]

Environmental Forces in International Markets

A detailed analysis of the environment is an absolute necessity before a company enters foreign markets. If a marketing strategy is to be effective across national boundaries, the complexities of all the environments involved must be understood. In this section we see how the cultural, social, economic, technological, political, and legal forces in other countries differ from those in the United States. The Application on page 791 focuses on how the Soviet environment is changing and mentions a few environmental issues a marketer should know about when marketing to the Russians.

By moving from the analysis of individual behavior to the more abstract level of institutions, we can better understand foreign markets. Institutions serve as structures for achieving some necessary societal goals. For example, **social institutions** include family, education, religion, health, and recreational systems. **Economic institutions** are made up of producers, wholesalers, retailers, buyers, and other organizations that produce, distribute, and purchase products. **Political and legal institutions** include public agencies, laws, courts, legislatures, and government bureaus.

Cultural Forces

Concepts, values, and tangible items such as tools, buildings, and foods make up **culture.** Culture is passed on from one generation to another; in a way, it is the blueprint for acceptable behavior in a given society. When products are introduced into one nation from another, acceptance is far more likely if there are similarities between the two cultures. For example, when Johnson & Johnson tried to move its successful U.S. campaign for Affinity Shampoo to Spain, it did not understand the

---

9. Vern Terpstra, "Critical Mass and International Marketing Strategy," *Journal of the Academy of Marketing Science,* Summer 1983, pp. 269–282.

cultural differences between the two countries. Affinity was renamed Radiance and positioned as *the* shampoo for women older than 40, the same campaign as used in the United States. But Spain's culture treats age differently from America's. A woman's age in Spain is a closely guarded secret, especially if she is older than 40. According to the marketing director for Johnson & Johnson, "Nobody bought the product, fearing they would be identified with the age group it appealed to."

TABLE 22.3

Sources of secondary information for international marketing

TYPE OF INFORMATION	U.S. DEPARTMENT OF COMMERCE SOURCES	OTHER SOURCES
Foreign market information	Business America Foreign economic trends Overseas business reports International economic indicators	Business International Dun & Bradstreet International Chase World Information Corp. Stanford Research Institute International Trade Reporter Accounting firms Foreign trade organizations
Export market research	Country market sectoral surveys Global market surveys International market research	Market research firms Advertising agencies Publishing companies Trade associations Library of Congress section tracking
International statistics	Export statistics profile Customer service statistics	Predicasts U.S. foreign trade reports Foreign brokerage houses United Nations International Monetary Fund OECD, EEC, GATT
Overseas representatives	Customized export mailing list World traders data reports Agent/distributor service	Banks International Chambers of Commerce Consulting firms Direct telephone contact
Sales leads	Trade opportunities program Strategic and industrial product sales group Major export projects program Export information reference room	Banks International Chambers of Commerce Consulting firms State development agencies
Reference data on foreign markets	World traders data reports	Banks International Chambers of Commerce Consulting firms State development agencies Corporate information databases

SOURCES: S. Tamer Cavusgil, "Guidelines for Export Market Research," *Business Horizons,* November–December 1985, p. 32; Leonard M. Fuld, "How to Gather Foreign Intelligence Without Leaving Home," *Market News,* Jan. 4, 1988, pp. 24, 47. Data used by permission.

Marketing to the Soviets

What's this? Comrades experimenting with free enterprise, Soviet-Western joint ventures, Pizza Hut in Moscow? Change is in the air in the Soviet Union, more so than at any time since the Stalinist days of the 1920s. Western observers believe that under the leadership of Mikhail Gorbachev, the Soviets are embarking on fundamental economic reforms that ultimately may provide new marketing and investment opportunities for Western firms.

The dismal state of the Soviet economy is responsible for the shakeup, according to Soviet experts. With notable exceptions—the space program, for example—the country's outmoded industrial infrastructure compares unfavorably to that of the United States and Western Europe. Soviet goods are often poorly made and difficult to obtain. What Gorbachev proposes is to gradually shift some of the responsibility for running factories and business enterprises to the organizations themselves, away from centralized government control. As of this year, businesses are now allowed (within limits) to make deals and negotiate prices among themselves, distribute some of their profits or reinvest them, and bid for and order their own supplies. Moonlighting and small businesses such as beauty salons, watch repair shops, and private taxi services also have been legalized.

In addition, more than twenty government ministries and about seventy large state enterprises have been granted permission to bypass official channels and deal directly with foreign business organizations. To date, about 250 foreign firms have proposed joint ventures with the Soviets, including companies from Finland, Japan, Italy, and India. Among the thirty or so U.S. businesses now negotiating deals are Monsanto Company, Combustion Engineering, and SSMC, a division of Singer Company that hopes to produce half a million sewing machines a year in a factory near Minsk. PepsiCo, which has sold soft drinks to the Soviets for years, already operates eighteen plants in the U.S.S.R. and has signed a contract to build two Pizza Huts in Moscow. McDonald's Corp. may be close behind. Recently a popular news show on Soviet television aired a feature on the U.S. burger chain, praising McDonald's food and service.

Experienced trade negotiators point out that Westerners hoping to market to the Soviets should understand several things about their customers. To begin, because the Soviet bureaucracy is so complex, American firms should be prepared to negotiate with their Soviet counterparts for one to three years and to draw up contracts that are comprehensive and very specific. Legal assistance is essential for U.S. firms unfamiliar with Soviet negotiating procedures. In addition, each U.S. firm should designate a project manager to represent the company throughout all discussions because Soviets value continuity, and their own negotiators often work together for years. Too, in discussions of price, Americans should allow some leeway for later reduction.

Soviet organizations must usually obtain three prices on a given product before signing a contract and may bargain with several firms simultaneously to get the best deal.

Finally, Americans should demonstrate proper respect for protocol. Because the Soviets pay attention to age and rank, periodic visits from U.S. senior executives may help move things along. The Soviets prefer to do business with familiar organizations, and Western firms willing to back up product quality with good personal relationships are the ones most likely to gain additional Soviet business.

SOURCES: Richard I. Kirkland, "Russia: Where Gorbanomics Is Leading," *Fortune,* Sept. 28, 1987, pp. 82–84; Misha G. Knight, "The Russian Bear Turns Bullish on Trade," *Business Marketing,* April 1987, pp. 83–84; Roon Lewald, "Ivan Starts Learning the Capitalist Ropes," *Business Week,* Nov. 2, 1987, p. 154; "TV Advertising, Russian Style," *Forbes,* Sept. 7, 1987, pp. 107–108; "You Will Like Fast Food, Comrade," *Fortune,* Dec. 9, 1986, p. 9.

Nearly two years after its introduction, Radiance held only a 0.2 percent market share.[10]

The connotations associated with body motions, greetings, colors, numbers, shapes, sizes, and symbols vary considerably across cultures (Table 22.4 shows a few examples). For multinational marketers, these cultural differences have implications that pertain to product development, personal selling, advertising, packaging, and pricing.

A society's attitude toward the body also affects international marketers. The American custom of patting a child on the head would not be considered a sign of friendliness in the Orient, where the head is held sacred. And the illustration of feet is regarded as despicable in Thailand.

An international marketer also must know a country's customs regarding male-female social interaction. Advertising that is based on the togetherness of married life could backfire in Japan and Western Europe, where husbands and wives often lead separate lives. In Italy it is unacceptable for a salesman to call on someone's wife if the husband is not home. In Thailand, certain Listerine television commercials that portrayed boy-girl romantic relationships were unacceptable.

Social Forces

Marketing activities are primarily social in purpose; therefore they are structured by the institutions of family, religion, education, health, and recreation. In every nation, these social institutions can be identified. By finding major deviations in institutions among countries, marketers can gain insights into the adaptation of marketing strategy. Although football is a popular sport in the United States and a major opportunity for many television advertisers, soccer is the most popular television sport in Europe. Yet fan violence has caused major advertisers in the United Kingdom to have second thoughts about supporting such events with mil-

10. Laurel Wentz, "Local Laws Keep International Marketers Hopping," *Advertising Age,* July 11, 1985, p. 20.

TABLE 22.4
Sampling of cultural
variations

COUNTRY/ REGION	BODY MOTIONS	GREETINGS	COLORS	NUMBERS	SHAPES, SIZES, SYMBOLS
Japan	Pointing to one's own chest with a forefinger indicates one wants a bath. Pointing a forefinger to the nose indicates "me."	Bowing is the traditional form of greeting.	Positive colors are in muted shades. Combinations of black, dark gray, and white have negative overtones.	Positive numbers are 1, 3, 5, 8. Negative numbers are 4, 9.	Pine, bamboo, or plum patterns are positive. Cultural shapes such as Buddha-shaped jars should be avoided.
India	Kissing is considered offensive and not seen on television, in movies, or in public places.	The palms of the hands are placed together and the head is nodded for greeting. It is considered rude to touch a woman or shake hands.	Positive colors are bold colors such as green, red, yellow, or orange. Negative colors are black and white if they appear in relation to weddings.	To create brand awareness, numbers are often used as a brand name.	Animals such as parrots, elephants, tigers, or cheetahs are often used as brand names or on packaging. Sexually explicit symbols are avoided.
Europe	Raising only the index finger signifies a person wants two items. When counting on one's fingers, "one" is often indicated by thumb, "two" by thumb and forefinger.	It is acceptable to send flowers in thanks for a dinner invitation, but not roses (associated with sweethearts) or chrysanthemums (associated with funerals).	Generally, white and blue are considered positive. Black often has negative overtones.	The numbers 3 or 7 are usually positive. 13 is a negative number.	Circles are symbols of perfection. Hearts are considered favorably at Christmas time.
Latin America	General arm gestures are used for emphasis.	The traditional form of greeting is a hearty embrace followed by a friendly slap on the back.	Popular colors are generally bright or bold yellow, red, blue, or green.	Generally, 7 is a positive number. Negative numbers are 13, 14.	Religious symbols should be respected. Avoid national symbols such as flag colors.

TABLE 22.4
(continued)

COUNTRY/ REGION	BODY MOTIONS	GREETINGS	COLORS	NUMBERS	SHAPES, SIZES, SYMBOLS
Middle East	The raised eyebrow facial expression indicates "yes."	The word "no" must be mentioned three times before it is accepted.	Positive colors are brown, black, dark blues, and reds. Pink, violets, and yellows are not favored.	Positive numbers are 3, 7, 5, 9; 13, 15 are negative.	Round or square shapes are acceptable. Symbols of six-pointed star, raised thumb, or Koranic sayings are avoided.

SOURCE: James C. Simmons, "A Matter of Interpretation," *American Way*, April 1983, pp. 106–111; "Adapting Export Packaging to Cultural Differences," *Business America*, Dec. 3, 1979, pp. 3–7.

lions of advertising dollars. One advertising executive indicated that advertising on soccer matches is similar to placing advertisements in nude magazines in the United States.[11] The role of children in the family and a society's overall view of children also affect marketing activities. The use of cute, cereal-loving children in advertising for Kellogg's is illegal in France. In the Netherlands, children are banned from confectionery advertisements, and candymakers are required to place a little toothbrush symbol at the end of each confectionery spot.[12]

Economic Forces

Economic differences dictate many of the adjustments that must be made in marketing across national boundaries. The most prominent adjustments are caused by standards of living, availability of credit, discretionary buying power, income distribution, national resources, climate, and conditions that affect transportation.

In terms of the value of all products produced by a nation, the United States has the largest **gross national product (GNP)** in the world, $3,640 billion. GNP is an overall measure of a nation's economic standing, but it does not take into account the concept of GNP in relation to population (GNP per capita). The United States has a GNP per capita of $15,380. The aggregate GNP of a very small country may be low. Austria's, for instance, is $67.2 billion, but the GNP per capita, a measure of the **standard of living**, is $8,892. The Soviet Union has one of the highest GNPs in the world ($1,998 billion) but only a $7,268 GNP per capita.[13] This figure means that the average Soviet citizen has less discretionary income than do citizens

11. Brian Oliver, "U.K. Soccer Advertising in Trouble," *Advertising Age,* July 8, 1985, p. 36.
12. Laurel Wentz, "Local Laws Keep International Marketers Hopping," *Advertising Age,* July 11, 1985, p. 20.
13. *Statistical Abstract of the United States,* 1988, p. 805.

in countries with higher GNPs per capita. Knowledge about per capita income, aggregate GNP, credit, and the distribution of income provides general insights into market potential.

Opportunities for international marketers are not limited to those countries with the highest incomes. Some nations are progressing at a markedly faster rate than they were a few years ago, and these countries—especially in Latin America, Africa, and the Middle East—have tremendous market potential for specific products. However, marketers must understand the political and legal environment before they can convert buying power into actual demand for specific products.

Technological Forces

Much of the marketing technology used in North America and other industrialized regions of the world may be ill suited for developing countries. In addition, the export of technology of strategic importance to the United States may require U.S. Department of Defense approval before foreign sales can occur. For example, the Soviet Union wanted to buy Boeing 747 jet engines, made by General Electric Co., for Russian airlines. When GE applied for the license to export these jet engines to the Soviet Union, its request was denied, yet GE was licensed to sell these same engines to Israel for use on jet fighters.

Political and Legal Forces

A country's political system, national laws, regulatory bodies, national pressure groups, and courts all have great impact on international marketing. A government's policies toward public versus private enterprise, consumers, and foreign firms influence marketing across national boundaries. For example, the Japanese have developed many barriers to imports into their country. Even though they have announced that over the next few years tariffs on 1,853 items will be reduced, many nontariff barriers still make it difficult for American companies to export their products to Japan.[14] Until recently, companies exporting electronic equipment to Japan had to wait for the Japanese government to inspect each item. A government's attitude toward cooperation with importers has a direct impact on the economic feasibility of exporting to that country. The Application on page 797 focuses on the proposed United States and Canada trade pact.

Figure 22.4 summarizes categories of political and legal risk in international markets. Political experts individually rated sixty-one countries according to each nation's (1) likelihood of restricting business and (2) relative political instability. A "high" ranking on either scale means a greater than 30 percent chance of regime change or further business restriction. "Low" is defined as less than 20 percent risk. Thus China, for example, whose regime is considered secure, nonetheless rates high on restrictions.

Differences in political and government ethical standards are illustrated by what the Mexicans call *la mordida*, "the bite." The use of payoffs and bribes is deeply entrenched in many governments. Because U.S. trade and corporate policy, as well as U.S. law, prohibits direct involvement in payoffs and bribes, American firms may have a hard time competing with foreign firms that engage in this practice. Some U.S. firms that refuse to make payoffs are forced to hire local consultants,

14. Lee Smith, "Japan Wants to Make Friends," *Fortune*, Sept. 2, 1985, p. 84.

public relations firms, or advertising agencies—which results in indirect payoffs. The ultimate decision about whether to give small tips or gifts where they are customary must be based on a firm's code of conduct. However, it is illegal for U.S. firms to attempt to make large payments or bribes to influence policy decisions of foreign governments. These actions are covered under the Foreign Corrupt Practices Act of 1977. The act also subjects all publicly held U.S. corporations to demanding internal control and record-keeping requirements related to their overseas operations. Corporations that fail to meet the requirements are subject to civil or criminal prosecution of corporate officers, directors, employees, agents, or stockholders.[15]

15. Jyotic N. Prasad and C. P. Rao, "Foreign Payoffs and International Business Ethics Revisited," in *Marketing Comes of Age,* David M. Klein and Allen E. Smith, eds. (Southern Marketing Association, 1984), pp. 260–264.

FIGURE 22.4

Sixty countries classified by instability and restrictions on business (SOURCE: From Bob Donath, "Handicapping and Hedging the Foreign Investment," *Industrial Marketing,* Feb. 1981, p. 58. Based on the Frost and Sullivan (F&S) World Political Risk Forecast)

	High	Medium	Low
High	El Salvador Iran Zaire	Philippines	Bolivia
Medium	Libya Kenya Nicaragua Nigeria Zambia	Argentina Dominican Republic Canada Ecuador, Egypt Indonesia Morocco, Pakistan Panama, Peru Portugal Tunisia, Turkey Yugoslavia	Brazil Colombia India, Italy Israel South Africa Spain Thailand Uruguay Zimbabwe
Low	China	Algeria Greece Mexico Saudi Arabia Venezuela	Australia Austria Chile, Denmark Finland, France Ireland Japan Kuwait Malaysia Netherlands New Zealand Norway Singapore South Korea Sweden, Taiwan United Kingdom United States West Germany

Political instability (vertical axis)

Restrictions on business (horizontal axis)

United States and Canada Trade Pact

Congressional and Parliamentary leaders in the United States and Canada have yet to give the final go-ahead. But if, as expected, they approve the trade pact recently drawn up after nineteen months of negotiation, markets in the United States and Canada will essentially merge, forming the largest free-trade zone in the world. Although the treaty has its opponents in both countries, supporters say the agreement will open up new markets, boost productivity, and generally provide a shot in the arm for American-Canadian trade, currently worth about $150 billion a year.

First proposed by the Canadian prime minister, the historic pact calls for the elimination of most tariffs and other trade restrictions during a ten-year period so that goods and services can flow more easily each way across the four-thousand-mile United States–Canadian boundary. For example, banks and some telecommunications and service businesses will be able to operate freely in both countries; manufacturing companies in one country that must import parts from the other will not have to pass on the costs of tariffs to customers. Most experts say that the agreement will enable firms in both countries to compete more effectively against Asian and European rivals. It may also offset protectionist tendencies in Congress, which some observers regard as a misguided response to current economic problems.

Not everybody is in favor of the trade agreement, which in some ways is even more sweeping than the 1957 accord that established the European Common Market. Canada already ships 77 percent of its exports to the United States, and some Canadians believe that the treaty jeopardizes their cultural and economic independence, particularly when it comes to energy, entertainment, and financial services. Many Canadians, foreseeing heightened competition with U.S. companies, also fear for their jobs; in one recent survey, 40 percent of those polled predicted that free trade would result in job losses, compared with only 21 percent of those polled three years ago. On the U.S. side, oil and gas producers and those in other troubled industries have expressed doubts that the marketplace can absorb additional competitors. Some U.S. legislators also are unhappy with the treaty's provisions for settling disputes: a panel of U.S. and Canadian experts with the power to review trade legislation.

In the long run, however, arguments for the treaty will probably outweigh those against it. By the year 2000, when all provisions are in effect, the treaty will have enlarged Canada's markets ten times, and the United States will have new access to a market the size of California. Canadians, for example, are expected to ship more minerals, livestock, and forest products southward; U.S. investments in Canada and sales of paper goods, in particular, are likely to jump. Some experts estimate that the gross national products of the two countries could rise 1 to 5 percent, as keener competition spurs companies on both sides to greater efficiency and productivity. The agreement will probably leave some losers in its wake, but other firms will emerge as winners. So far, most companies on both sides seem to regard free trade not as a threat but as an opportunity.

SOURCES: Gordon Bock, "Big Hug from Uncle Sam," *Time*, Oct. 19, 1987, p. 50; Madelaine Drohan, "A Critical Concern," *Maclean's*, Jan. 4, 1988, pp. 42–43; Clyde H. Farnsworth, "Trade Pact Is Seen as Economic Spur by U.S. and Canada," *The New York Times*, Oct. 5, 1987, p. 1; Michael Rose, "Signed But Not Yet Delivered," *Maclean's*, Jan. 11, 1988, p. 15; Edith Terry, Bill Javetski, Steven Dryden, and John Pearson, "A Free-Trade Milestone," *Business Week*, Oct. 19, 1987, pp. 52–53; Edith Terry, Christopher Waddell, Steven J. Dryden, "The U.S.–Canada Trade Pact Is Already Springing Leaks," *Business Week*, Dec. 7, 1987, p. 75; "The Trade Pact Benefits Both Sides," *Business Week*, Oct. 19, 1987, p. 154.

Strategic Adaptation of Marketing Mixes

Strategic marketing planning is discussed in detail in Chapter 18. A planning aid discussed in that chapter is the plotting of competitive strengths and market attractiveness on a two-dimensional matrix. Such a device is most useful for analyzing products within the international context. As Figure 22.5 illustrates, each axis is a linear combination of factors that can be used to define a country's attractiveness from a market view and to assess the level of competition in that country.[16] To develop a matrix, marketers must gather data for a specific product and country. Research style, methodology, and approach to data gathering vary by company.[17]

Once a U.S. firm determines foreign market potentials and understands the foreign environment, it develops and adapts its marketing mix. Creating and maintaining the marketing mix is the final step in developing the international marketing strategy. Only if foreign marketing opportunities justify the risk will a company go to the expense of adapting the marketing mix. Of course, in some situations new products are developed for a specific country. In these cases, there is no existing marketing mix and no extra expense to consider in serving the foreign target market.

Product and Promotion

As Figure 22.6 shows, there are five possible strategies for adapting product and promotion across national boundaries: (1) keep product and promotion the same worldwide, (2) adapt promotion only, (3) adapt product only, (4) adapt both product and promotion, and (5) invent new products.[18]

16. Gilbert D. Harrell and Richard O. Kiefer, "Multinational Strategic Market Portfolios," *MSU Business Topics*, Winter 1981, p. 6.
17. David C. Pring, "Filling Overseas Gaps," *Advertising Age*, Oct. 26, 1981, pp. 5–18.
18. Warren Keegan, *Multinational Marketing Management*, 3rd ed. (Englewood Cliffs, N.J.: Prentice-Hall, 1984), pp. 317–321; Philip Kotler, *Marketing Management: Analysis, Planning and Control*, 6th ed. (Englewood Cliffs, N.J.: Prentice-Hall, 1988), pp. 395–396.

Keep Product and Promotion the Same Worldwide   This strategy attempts to use in the foreign country the product and promotion developed for the U.S. market, an approach that seems desirable wherever possible because it eliminates the expenses of marketing research and product redevelopment. Despite certain inherent risks that stem from cultural differences in interpretation, exporting advertising copy does provide the efficiency of international standardization. As shown in Figure 22.7, the makers of Fibre Trim fibre tablets use the same product and advertisement (with slight alteration) to reach the Singapore market.

Even multinational firms operating in less-developed countries are using standardization, despite wide economic and cultural differences. A recent survey of American and British firms marketing nondurable consumer products in less-developed countries revealed that approximately 70 percent of the firms maintained their original brand names. Only 10 percent used a new local name for their brands, and the remaining 20 percent either used another English brand name or translated the original name to the local language.[19]

Global advertising embraces the same concept as global marketing, discussed earlier in this chapter. An advertiser can save hundreds of thousands of dollars by

19. John S. Hill and Richard S. Still, "Brand Name Decisions in International Marketing: To Adapt or Not to Adapt—(That Is the Question)," in *Marketing Comes of Age,* David M. Klein and Allen E. Smith, eds. (Southern Marketing Association, 1984), pp. 161–163.

FIGURE 22.5

Matrix for plotting products in international marketing (SOURCE: Adapted from Gilbert D. Harrell and Richard O. Kiefer, "Multinational Strategic Market Portfolios," *MSU Business Topics,* Winter 1981, p. 7. Reprinted by permission)

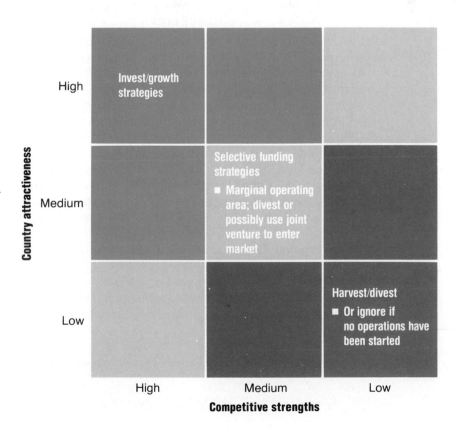

FIGURE 22.6

International product and promotion strategies (SOURCE: Adapted from Warren J. Keegan, "Multinational Product Planning Strategic Alternatives," *Journal of Marketing,* Jan. 1969, pp. 58–62. Published by the American Marketing Association)

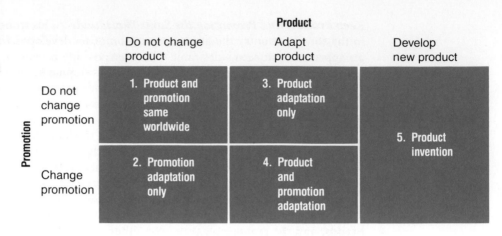

running the same advertisement worldwide. Playtex has combined its thirteen foreign intimate-apparel operations with its U.S. operation. Grey Advertising developed a global advertisement using models who have universal appeal. Clones of the same advertisement in different languages were used globally.[20]

Adapt Promotion Only This strategy leaves the product basically unchanged but modifies its promotion. This approach may be necessary because of language, legal, or cultural differences associated with the advertising copy.

As discussed earlier in this chapter, sales of Affinity Shampoo suffered because the U.S. advertising campaign was translated directly into Spanish. Because of the sensitivity about Spanish women's ages, the advertising slogan had to be changed to appeal to "women who feel young regardless of their age."[21] Promotional adaptation is a low-cost modification compared with the costs of redeveloping engineering and production and physically changing products.

Generally, the strategy of adapting only promotion infuses advertising with the culture of people who will be exposed to it. Often promotion combines thinking globally and acting locally: At company headquarters a basic global marketing strategy is developed, but promotion is modified to fit each market's needs. For example, in the United States, Affinity Shampoo uses a Nancy Reagan lookalike in advertisements, but in England, where Nancy Reagan does not have a great following, a more independent-looking female character is used.[22]

Adapt Product Only The basic assumption in modifying a product without changing its promotion is that the product will serve the same function under different conditions of use. Soap and detergent manufacturers have adapted their products to local water conditions and washing equipment without changing their promotions. Household appliances have been altered to use different types of electricity.

20. "Playtex Kicks Off a One-Ad-Fits-All Campaign," *Business Week,* Dec. 16, 1985, p. 48.
21. Laurel Wentz, "Local Laws Keep International Marketers Hopping," *Advertising Age,* July 11, 1985, p. 20.
22. "Global Brands Need Local Ad Flavor," *Advertising Age,* Sept. 13, 1984, p. 26.

A product may have to be adjusted for legal reasons. Japan has some of the most stringent automobile emission requirements in the world. American automobiles that fail emission standards cannot be marketed in Japan.

Sometimes, products must be adjusted to overcome social and cultural obstacles. Jell-O introduced a powdered gelatin mix that failed in England because the English were used to buying gelatin in jelled form. Resistance to a product is frequently based on attitudes and ignorance about the nature of a new technology. It is often easier to change the product than to overcome technological biases.

Adapt Both Product and Promotion   When a product serves a new function in a foreign market, then both the product and its promotion need to be altered. In Europe, greeting cards provide a space for senders to write messages in their own words, and European greeting cards are cellophane wrapped, which also calls for a product alteration. Both the product and the promotion must be changed because the product's function is different. Adaptation of both product and promotion is the most expensive strategy discussed thus far, but it should be considered if the foreign market appears large enough.

FIGURE 22.7

Fibre Trim uses U.S. product and slightly altered promotion to reach a Singapore market (SOURCE: Courtesy of Fibre Trim)

Invent New Products This strategy is selected when existing products cannot meet the needs of a foreign market. General Motors developed an all-purpose, jeeplike motor vehicle that can be assembled in underdeveloped nations by mechanics with no special training. The vehicle is designed to operate under varied conditions; it has standardized parts and is inexpensive. Colgate-Palmolive Co. developed an inexpensive, all-plastic, hand-powered washing machine that has the tumbling action of a modern automatic machine. The product, marketed in underdeveloped countries, was invented for households that have no electricity. Strategies that involve the invention of products are often the most costly, but the payoff can be great.

Distribution and Pricing

Decisions about the distribution system and pricing policies are important in developing an international marketing mix. Figure 22.8 illustrates different approaches to these decisions.

Distribution A firm can sell its product to an intermediary that is willing to buy from existing market channels in the United States, or it can develop new international marketing channels. It must consider distribution both between countries and within the foreign country.

In determining distribution alternatives, the existence of retail institutions and wholesalers that can perform marketing functions between and within nations is one major factor. If a foreign country has a segmented retail structure consisting primarily of one-person shops or street vendors, it may be difficult to develop new marketing channels for such products as packaged goods and prepared foods. Quite often in Third World countries, certain channels of distribution are characterized by ethnodomination. *Ethnodomination* is when an ethnic group occupies a majority position within a marketing channel. Consider the following examples: Indians own approximately 90 percent of the cotton gins in Uganda; the Hausa tribe in Nigeria dominates the trade in kola nuts, cattle, and housing; Chinese merchants dominate the rice economy in Thailand. Marketers must be sensitive to

FIGURE 22.8

Strategies for international distribution and pricing

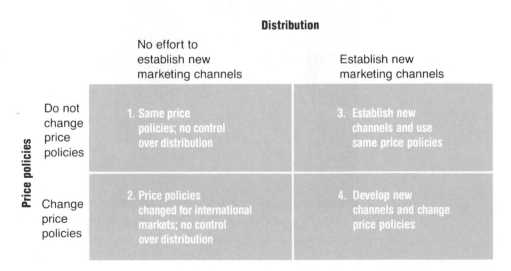

Part VII   Selected Applications

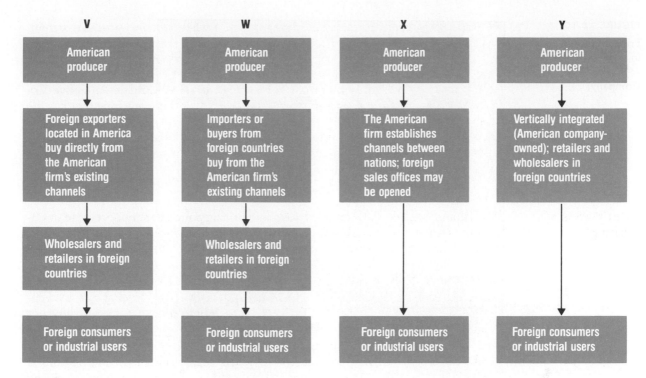

FIGURE 22.9

Examples of international channels of distribution for an American firm

ethnodomination and recognize that the ethnic groups operate in subcultures unique in social and economic organization.[23]

If the product being sold across national boundaries requires service and information, then control of the distribution process is desirable. Caterpillar, for example, sells more than half its construction and earth-moving equipment in foreign countries. Because it must provide services and replacement parts, Caterpillar has established its own dealers in foreign markets. Regional sales offices and technical experts are also available to support local dealers. A manufacturer of paintbrushes, on the other hand, would be more concerned about agents, wholesalers, or other manufacturers that would facilitate the product's exposure in a foreign market. Control over the distribution process would not be so important for that product.

Several international marketing channels are available to American businesses (see Figure 22.9). These marketing channels are not all-inclusive, nor do they exist for all product types. Marketers planning to sell products across national boundaries must work with available intermediaries or bridge the gaps.

Pricing The domestic and foreign prices of products are usually different. For example, the prices charged for Disney videos in Spain may differ from U.S. prices for Disney videos (see Figure 22.10). The increased costs of transportation, supplies, taxes, tariffs, and other expenses necessary to adjust a firm's operations to international marketing can raise prices. A key decision is whether the basic pricing

23. Douglass G. Norvell and Robert Morey, "Ethnodomination in the Channels of Distribution of Third World Nations," *Journal of the Academy of Marketing Science,* Summer 1983, pp. 204–215.

FIGURE 22.10

Prices of Disney videos in Spain (SOURCE: © 1987 The Walt Disney Company)

policy will change (as discussed in Chapter 15). If it is a firm's policy not to allocate fixed costs to foreign sales, then lower foreign prices could result.

American drug manufacturers have been accused of selling drugs in foreign markets at low prices (without allocating research and development costs) while charging American customers high prices that include all research and development expenses. The sale of U.S. products in foreign markets—or vice versa—at lower prices (when all costs have not been allocated or when surplus products are sold) is called **dumping.** Dumping is illegal in many countries if it damages domestic firms and workers.

A cost-plus approach to international pricing is probably the most common method used because of the compounding number of costs necessary to move products from the United States to a foreign country. Of course, our discussion of pricing policies in Chapter 15 points out that understanding consumer demand and the competitive environment is a necessary step in selecting a price.

The price charged in other countries is also a function of foreign currency exchange rates. Fluctuations in the international monetary market can change the prices charged across national boundaries on a daily basis. There has been a trend toward greater fluctuation (or float) in world money markets. A sudden variation in the exchange rate, which occurs when a nation devalues its currency, for example, can have wide-ranging effects on consumer prices. United States' devaluation of the dollar in the 1970s resulted in lower prices for American products in foreign countries and higher prices for imports in the United States.

In the 1980s this trend was reversed. The strong dollar caused the prices of American exports to climb, and the price of many imported products declined. By early 1985, the dollar's exchange value was 90 percent over the average weighted 1970s price of other countries' currencies. The high value of the dollar eliminated many foreign markets for American exporters. After reaching a peak in early 1985, the dollar once again dropped, lowering the prices of American products in other countries. However, it takes time even after prices drop for foreign companies to reorient their purchasing habits away from established trade relationships. For larger American companies, the stakes can be enormous. Packaged goods companies such as Colgate-Palmolive, Procter & Gamble, and Bristol-Myers get as much as 50 percent of their revenues from overseas operations.[24]

Developing International Marketing Involvement

The level of commitment to international marketing is a major variable in deciding what kind of involvement is appropriate. A firm's options range from occasional exporting to expanding overall operations (production and marketing) into other countries. In this section we examine exporting, licensing, joint ventures, trading companies, and direct ownership as approaches to marketing across national boundaries.

Exporting

Exporting is the lowest level of commitment to international marketing and the most flexible approach. A firm may find an exporting intermediary that can perform most marketing functions associated with selling to other countries. This approach entails minimum effort and cost. Modifications in packaging, labeling, style, or color may be the major expenses in adapting a product. There is limited risk in using export agents and merchants because there is no direct investment in the foreign country.

Export agents bring together buyers and sellers from different countries; they collect a commission for arranging sales. Export houses and export merchants purchase products from different companies and then sell them to foreign countries. They are specialists at understanding customers' needs in foreign countries.

Foreign buyers from companies and governments provide a direct method of exporting and eliminate the need for an intermediary. Foreign buyers encourage international exchange by contacting domestic firms about their needs and the opportunities available in exporting. Domestic firms that want to export with a minimum of effort and investment seek out foreign importers and buyers.

---

24. "Who Wins from the Cheaper Dollar," *Fortune*, Aug. 19, 1985, p. 30.

Licensing

When potential markets are found across national boundaries—and when production, technical assistance, or marketing know-how is required—**licensing** is an alternative to direct investment. Exchanges of management techniques or technical assistance are primary reasons for licensing agreements. The licensee (the owner of the foreign operation) pays commissions or royalties on sales or supplies used in manufacturing. Yoplait yogurt is a French yogurt that is licensed for production in the United States; the Yoplait brand tries to maintain a French image. An initial down payment or fee may be charged when the licensing agreement is signed. Licensing is an attractive alternative to direct investment when the political stability of a foreign country is in doubt or when resources are unavailable for direct investment.

Licensing is especially advantageous for small manufacturers wanting to launch a well-known brand internationally. For example, all Spalding sporting products are licensed worldwide. The Questor Corporation owns the Spalding name but produces no products itself. Pierre Cardin has issued five hundred licenses and Yves St. Laurent two hundred to make their products.[25] Löwenbräu has used licensing agreements, including one with Miller in the United States, to increase sales worldwide without committing capital to build breweries.

Joint Ventures

In international marketing, a **joint venture** is a partnership between a domestic firm and a foreign firm or government. Joint ventures are often a political necessity because of nationalism and governmental restrictions on foreign ownership. These ventures are assuming greater global importance because of cost advantages and the number of inexperienced firms entering foreign markets. In environments of scarce resources, rapid technological change, and massive capital requirements, joint ventures may be the best way for underdog firms to attain better positions in global industries. Such partnerships may be used to gain access to marketing channels, suppliers, and technology.[26]

Joint ventures are especially popular in industries that call for large investments, such as natural resources extraction or automobile manufacturing. Control of the joint venture can be split equally, or one party may control decision making. In one example of a joint venture, Toyota Motor Corporation and General Motors joined to produce the Nova automobile. The major components of the car, the engine and transmission, come from Japan; many of the surface elements, such as the grill, radio, seats, and tires, are made in the United States. General Motors and other domestic automobile manufacturers are faced with the dilemma that Japanese companies can produce cars at a cost advantage of $2,000 per unit. The joint venture with Toyota lets GM provide import quality and price competitiveness in an American-branded product.[27]

Increasingly, once a joint venture succeeds, nationalism spurs a trend toward expropriating or purchasing foreign shares of the enterprise. On the other hand, a

25. John A. Quelch, "How to Build a Product Licensing Program," *Harvard Business Review,* May–June 1985, pp. 186–187.
26. Cathryn Rudie Harrigan, "Joint Ventures and Global Strategies," *Columbia Journal of World Business,* Summer 1984, pp. 7–16.
27. Maralyn Edid, "The American Small Car Keeps Getting More Japanese," *Business Week,* June 24, 1985, p. 50.

joint venture may be the only available means for entering a foreign market. American construction firms bidding for business in Saudi Arabia, for example, have found that joint ventures with Arab construction companies gain local support among the handful of people who make the contracting decisions.

Trading Companies

A **trading company** provides a link between buyers and sellers in different countries. A trading company, as its name implies, is not involved in manufacturing or owning assets related to manufacturing. It buys in one country at the lowest price consistent with quality and sells to buyers in another country. An important function of trading companies is taking title to products and undertaking all the activities necessary to move the products from the domestic country to a market in a foreign country. For example, major grain trading companies operating out of home offices in both the United States and overseas control a major portion of the world's trade in basic food commodities, which is valued at more than $50 billion per year. These trading companies sell agricultural commodities that are homogeneous and can be stored and moved rapidly in response to market conditions.

Trading companies reduce risk for companies interested in getting involved in international marketing. A trading company will assist producers with information about products that meet quality and price expectations in domestic or international markets. Additional services a trading company may provide include consulting, marketing research, advertising, insurance, product research and design, legal assistance, warehousing, and foreign exchange.

In 1982, the Export Trading Company Act was passed to facilitate the efficient operation of trading companies in the United States. At least seventy-five major trading companies have been created to help American manufacturers build international markets. Besides allowing banks to invest in trading companies, the Export Trading Act created a new certification procedure that enables companies to apply for limited protection from antitrust laws when conducting export operations. A few major corporations have set up trading companies to market various lines of business abroad. The best known is Sears World Trade, which specializes in consumer goods, light industrial items, and processed foods. A trading company acts like a wholesaler, taking on much of the responsibility of finding markets while facilitating all marketing aspects of a transaction.

Direct Ownership

Once a company makes a long-term commitment to marketing in a foreign nation that has a promising political and economic environment, **direct ownership** of a foreign subsidiary or division is a possibility. Although most discussions of foreign investment concern only manufacturing equipment or personnel, the expenses of developing a separate foreign distribution system can be tremendous. The opening of retail stores in Europe, Canada, or Mexico can require a large investment in facilities, research expenditures, and management costs.

A wholly owned foreign subsidiary may be allowed to operate independently of the parent company so that management can have more freedom to adjust to the local environment. Cooperative arrangements are developed to assist in marketing efforts, production, and management. A wholly owned foreign subsidiary may export products to the home nation. Some American automobile manufacturers import cars built by their foreign subsidiaries. A foreign subsidiary offers important tax, tariff, and other operating advantages. One of the greatest advantages is the cross-cultural approach. A subsidiary usually operates under foreign management, so it can develop a local identity. The greatest danger in such an arrangement comes from political uncertainty: a firm may lose its foreign investment.

Summary

Marketing activities performed across national boundaries are usually significantly different from domestic marketing activities. International marketers must have an in-depth awareness of the foreign environment. The marketing strategy ordinarily is adjusted to meet the needs and desires of foreign markets.

Global marketing strategies are developed to expand a business beyond national boundaries and to achieve a corporate goal of long-term growth. The level of involvement in international marketing can range from casual exporting to globalization of markets. Although most firms adjust their marketing mixes for differences in target markets, some firms are able to standardize their marketing efforts worldwide. That is, they sell the same things the same way everywhere.

Marketers must understand the complexities of the international marketing environment before they can formulate a marketing mix. Environmental aspects of special importance include cultural, social, economic, political, and legal forces. Cultural aspects of the environment that are most important to international marketers include customs, concepts, values, attitudes, morals, and knowledge. Social institutions influence human interaction; international marketers must understand such social institutions as family, religion, education, health, and recreation.

The most prominent economic forces that affect international marketing are those that can be measured by income and resources. Credit, buying power, and income distribution are aggregate measures of market potential. The level of technology helps define economic development within a nation and indicates the existence of methods to facilitate marketing. The level of technology can dictate the structure of the marketing mix.

Political and legal institutions include the political system, national laws, regulatory bodies, national pressure groups, and courts. Foreign policies of all nations involved in trade determine how marketing can be conducted. Ethical standards and internal politics must be dealt with effectively; a firm must decide whether to use a domestic code of ethics or the foreign country's code of ethics.

After a country's environment has been analyzed, marketers must develop a marketing mix and decide whether to adapt product or promotion. Foreign distribution channels are nearly always different from domestic ones. The allocation of costs, transportation considerations, or the costs of doing business in foreign nations will affect pricing. Standardization of international marketing mixes is highly desirable, but most evidence indicates that standardization is regional at best.

There are several ways of getting involved in international marketing. Exporting is the easiest and most flexible method. Licensing is an alternative to direct investment; it may be necessitated by political and economic conditions. Joint ventures or partnerships are often appropriate when outside resources are needed or when there are governmental restrictions on foreign ownership. Trading companies are experts at buying products in the domestic market and selling to foreign markets, thereby taking most of the risk in international involvement. Direct ownership of foreign divisions or subsidiaries is the strongest commitment to international marketing and involves the greatest risk.

Important Terms

International marketing
Multinational enterprise
Globalization of markets
Social institutions
Economic institutions
Political and legal institutions
Culture
Gross national product (GNP)
Standard of living
Dumping

Licensing
Joint venture
Trading company
Direct ownership

Discussion and Review Questions

1. How does international marketing differ from domestic marketing?
2. What must marketers consider before deciding whether to become involved in international marketing?
3. Why are the largest industrial corporations in the United States so committed to international marketing?
4. Why was so much of this chapter devoted to an analysis of the international marketing environment?
5. A manufacturer recently exported peanut butter with a green label to a nation in the Far East. The product failed because it was associated with jungle sickness. How could this mistake have been avoided?
6. Relate the concept of reference groups (Chapter 4) to international marketing.
7. How do religious systems influence marketing activities in foreign countries?
8. Which is more important to international marketers, a country's **aggregate** GNP or its GNP per capita? Why?
9. If you were asked to provide a small tip (or bribe) to have a document approved in a foreign nation where this practice was customary, what would you do?
10. In marketing dog food to Latin America, what aspects of the marketing mix need to be altered?
11. What should marketers consider as they decide whether to license or to enter into a joint venture in a foreign nation?

Cases

22.1 Porsche AG[28]

Founded in 1930 by Dr. Ferdinand Porsche, the company known today as Porsche AG began as a research and development firm only. The original company, called Porsche Konstruktionsburo fuer Motoren-Fahrzeug-Luftfahrzeug und Wasserfahrzeugbau, accepted contracts from individuals and firms to design new automobiles, airplanes, and ships. Prototypes of each design were subsequently built by Porsche and thoroughly tested. If the firm that commissioned the work approved the design, the product was then produced by one of the large manufacturing firms in Germany.

Following the end of World War II, the Porsche family entered a period of hardship, disappointment, and personal tragedy, culminating in Ferdinand Porsche's imprisonment by the French for alleged war crimes, charges that were later determined to be false. In 1948, Porsche's son, Dr. Ferry Porsche, began a company to produce family designed sports cars. Despite depressed economic conditions, the company persevered and prospered. By 1973, Porsche AG had built and sold some 200,000 Porsche automobiles, gaining world recognition for its cars and their promise of "driving in its purest form."

The company today is organized into three distinct divisions located in three suburbs of Stuttgart: the factory, in Zuffenhausen; testing, engineering, and design, in Weissach; and marketing, in Ludwigsburg. All the company's voting shares are in the hands of the Porsche family, to whom the image and reputation of the company are far more important than sales and profits. The family has not set highly aggressive goals for growth. They do want the company to remain independent and to maintain its standards of quality and exclusivity.

Porsche is successful in markets in which the social climate is favorable to people who want to demonstrate their success and the economic climate is conducive to the entrepreneur. Porsche management believes that its customers have high personal goals and a drive to achieve, are not given to compromise, and give their best efforts every time. Although not averse to risk, they prepare thoroughly for new ventures. Porsche customers are goers and doers, but they are not showoffs.

To succeed as a company, Porsche AG must also exhibit some of its customers' traits. Customers must be able to identify with the firm, to see in the company the

---

28. This case was contributed by Lee Ann Heard, Texas A&M University Summer Intern for Porsche AG, Stuttgart, West Germany.

SOURCES: Peter Schutz and Jack Cook, "Porsche on Nichemanship," *Harvard Business Review,* March–April 1986, pp. 98–106; *Plan Your Success,* 2nd ed. (Stuttgart: Dr. Ing. h.c. Ferry Porsche, 1985), pp. 1, 3; Joseph M. Callahan and Lance A. Ealey, "Porsche's Schutz Reveals U.S. Marketing Plans," *Industries,* March 1985, p. 50; Dr. Ing. h.c. Ferry Porsche and John Bentley, *We at Porsche* (Garden City, N.Y.: Doubleday, 1976), p. 263; "Porsche," *Ward's Auto World,* January 1985, pp. 52–53; John A. Russell, "Porsche Puts High Value on Its People, Schutz Says," *Automotive News,* Aug. 4, 1986, p. 64; Richard Morais, "What Price Excellence?", *Forbes,* Nov. 17, 1986, p. 234; Jesse Snyder, "Porsche Looks for New Brand to Sell in U.S.," *Automotive News,* Dec. 15, 1986, p. 1; *Porsche Brochure for Distribution,* Stuttgart: Dr. Ing. h.c. F. Porsche AG, 1984; "It Shortens the Path," *Christophorous,* August 1984.

same characteristics they see in themselves. A Porsche customer must be able to say truthfully, "If I were a car, I would want to be a Porsche." Porsche management believes that its most important asset is the nucleus of loyal customers who love Porsche automobiles.

Porsche's total production for world markets is about 45,000 cars. In 1988 production dropped from record levels in 1986–1987 (more than 50,000 cars) because of price increases related to the dollar/mark exchange rate. In the fiscal year ending 1987, 61 percent of all Porsches were sold in the United States. Owing to price increases and possibly the October 19, 1987, stock market crash, sales in the United States dropped significantly in 1988.

In Germany, 60 percent of all Porsches are picked up at the factory by their owners. Many Americans also elect to take delivery in Stuttgart, although there are about 325 Porsche dealers in the United States. Management has learned much about Porsche customers by spending considerable time visiting with them when they pick up their cars.

The Porsche's popularity stems from its reputation for outstanding performance. Not only are the cars produced in a painstaking fashion, Porsche AG also takes maintenance and repair very seriously. Mechanics servicing Porsches receive five days of classroom instruction each year at the Porsche marketing center in Ludwigsburg, more training than any other car company provides. Until 1984, U.S. Porsche mechanics also flew to Germany for training, but now they receive instruction at Porsche training centers in this country. Through advertising, the company encourages its customers to rely only on Porsche experts for the repair and maintenance of their cars, to prevent the customers, regardless of nationality, from having unsatisfactory experiences with unqualified mechanics. At the same time, the company is further differentiating its product.

For the foreseeable future, Porsche's primary market will remain North America and Western Europe; at the present time the company has few plans to enter new geographic markets. By remaining relatively small, Porsche AG will retain the flexibility that is essential to effective customer service. The company is holding preliminary talks with other foreign car makers, however, to arrange to sell additional automobile brands through its existing North American dealer network. Such an arrangement would fill out Porsche's sports car line with compatible products and make expansion into markets too small to support independent Porsche dealerships feasible. Porsche has also introduced its 959 model to European markets (total production: two hundred cars) and is now developing an airplane engine as well.

Questions for Discussion

1. Porsche is a German company with more than half its market in the United States. What are the implications for marketing strategy development?
2. Porsche is committed not just to excellence in quality but to winning automobile races in which the firm participates. How does this decision relate to Porsche's marketing strategy?
3. Should Porsche produce a lower-priced automobile (below $20,000)? Should it be marketed in the United States, in Europe, or in both regions?

22.2 Parker Pen Uses a Globalization Strategy[29]

When Parker Pen Company decided to launch a global marketing strategy several years ago, some observers were puzzled. Although Parker's name was well-known, the Wisconsin-based company brought limited resources to the task. Annual sales of Parker writing instruments had never exceeded $225 million, and the company had never budgeted more than $20 million a year for advertising. Still, Parker's high-quality products were sold in 154 countries, and marketing executives with experience in such firms as R. J. Reynolds Industries, 3M Company, and Gillette Company were eager to design and implement a global strategy for Parker Pen. In their view, cultural and competitive similarities would be more important than differences, meaning that the same product could be sold the same way in many different markets, and with much lower marketing costs. They believed, in short, that Parker Pen would provide a classic test of global marketing theory.

Parker's new president, James Peterson, also believed that global marketing would be crucial to the survival of the faltering company. The company was founded in 1888 by George S. Parker, a Wisconsin teacher who decided to improve the fountain pens he sold as a sideline. The company's weaknesses had been obscured for years by strong overseas sales and a weak U.S. dollar. At home, not only were competitors introducing mass-marketed, disposable pens, but even as Parker attempted to guard its reputation for quality, the company was losing its share of the domestic expensive-pen market to A. T. Cross Company and Sheaffer Eaton. Furthermore, Parker's manufacturing process was inefficient. New-product development had been neglected, and advertising worldwide, which had been left to local marketers, was handled by more than forty different agencies. Profits were plunging, and most of the profits were generated by Manpower Temporary Services, a Parker subsidiary.

Peterson's first move was to streamline Parker's operations. He cut the payroll from 6,800 employees to about 3,400, reduced the product line from five hundred different writing instruments to one hundred, and spent $20 million to upgrade Parker's manufacturing facilities. Then Peterson and his marketing team embarked on a two-pronged program with far-reaching consequences. They began production of cheap pens that could compete in the under-$3 market (which accounts for 65 percent of all pen sales), and they standardized everything associated with Parker products under a "global umbrella." From then on, all packaging and point-of-sale display materials would use the same striking black motif. The advertising budget would be centralized, and one advertising agency would handle accounts worldwide. A single theme—"Make your mark with a Parker"—would be used for all products and in all markets, and advertisements would feature the same graphics, photography, and typefaces; only the languages of the copy would vary. In addition, advertising would spotlight Parker's new, inexpensive products instead of the quality pens that were the company's trademark.

These two decisions—to produce cheap pens and to use a uniform marketing strategy for all Parker products—were eventually considered major blunders by

---

29. Based on information from Leigh Bruce, "Parker Pen's Script for Recovery," *International Management,* December 1986, p. 43; Kevin Cote, "Parker Pen Finds Black Ink," *Advertising Age,* July 13, 1987, p. 49; David O'Reilly, "The Write Approach," *Marketing,* May 21, 1987, pp. 22–23; Joseph M. Winski and Laurel Wentz, "Parker Pen: What Went Wrong?", *Advertising Age,* June 2, 1986, p. 1.

many inside Parker Pen, including George Parker, nominal chairman of the company. Long-time Parker Pen employees objected that the lower-quality pens ran counter to Parker's carefully nurtured status image. Parker's European managers protested that advertising dollars should remain with the expensive pens because in Europe the cheaper roller-ball pens tended to sell themselves. They also argued that advertising should take into account the differences among markets. For example, in writing instruments the Germans looked for precision, the French wanted a certain snob appeal, and the British were somewhere in between. Furthermore, among the forty advertising agencies Peterson's team dismissed was a London firm largely responsible for turning the United Kingdom into Parker's most profitable market.

However, Parker's new management insisted that the company's future lay in high-tech, high-volume production of cheap pens for a global market, and implementation of the new strategy proceeded. At first, sales of the new roller-ball pen and other writing instruments increased. Then, just as demand was picking up, the automated production line began to shut down—repeatedly. Technical problems at the Wisconsin plant had already created severe product shortages during the previous Christmas selling season, and Parker employees now were forced to return to the assembly lines to take over for the malfunctioning systems. The defect rate soared, and before the problems were resolved, the marketing division set aside strategies and forecasts and sold whatever products were available.

A few months later, the global advertising campaign was launched. In accordance with the "one product, one market" policy, advertisements for different markets had identical layout, illustrations, and text; only the languages in which they were written were different. Because the theme was so general, the advertisements appealed to no one in particular, especially not to those buyers who viewed writing instruments as status symbols. The advertising agency itself disliked the campaign sufficiently to consider resigning the account. Resentment against the global marketing strategy mounted within the company, and when the failure of the advertising campaign could no longer be ignored, Peterson resigned, followed by his handpicked marketing executives. The pen business suffered a $500,000 loss and was purchased early last year by a group of Parker's international managers and a British venture capital company.

Now based in Newhaven, England, Parker Pen Ltd. is a profitable company, with pretax profits last year of $23 million and sales up 22 percent. Although the reorganized firm uses the now-functioning Wisconsin plant and owes some of its success to the greater operating efficiency the former management brought about, the new owners have instituted several policies of their own. Parker's inexpensive pens, which now account for about 40 percent of sales, receive less emphasis in advertising, and all plans to produce disposable pens have been dropped. Instead, the company is working to restore its reputation for quality and reliability. It intends to add perceived value, rather than volume, to its products.

In addition—except for the marketing of the company's new Duofold Centennial model, a $200 pen targeted to a tiny market segment—global advertising has been abandoned. Local managers have considerable leeway in decision making, especially in marketing. Parker Pen Ltd. also grants its managers the option of using the award-winning London advertising agency that the Peterson team had dismissed. The agency now handles Parker accounts in Great Britain, most of Europe, and the United States.

1. Are some products more susceptible to successful marketing through a global marketing approach than others? Explain your answer.
2. Specifically, are writing instruments among the products that can be effectively marketed through global marketing? Why or why not?
3. Evaluate Parker Pen's decision to compete in the under-$3 market.

Part VII   S T R A T E G I C   C A S E

Federal Express Expands Services Internationally

Frederick W. Smith founded Federal Express Corp. in 1973 with part of an $8 million inheritance. At that time, the U.S. Postal Service and United Parcel Service (UPS) were the only means for delivering letters and packages, and they often took several days or more to get packages to their destinations. While a student at Yale in 1965, Smith wrote a paper criticizing the industry and proposed an independent delivery system. He got a C on the paper. Nevertheless, he never lost sight of his vision of an overnight delivery company. Smith recognized that in today's high-tech world, time is money, and he believed that many businesses would be willing to pay more to get letters, documents, and packages delivered overnight. He was right.

Federal Express began shipping packages overnight from Memphis, Tennessee, on April 17, 1973. On that first night of operations, the company handled eight packages, seven of which were mailed from Federal Express employees to each other. Today Federal Express has more than $3 billion in revenues and handles more than half of all overnight package and document transactions within the United States. According to the company, Federal Express does not just transport packages anywhere in the United States and to much of the rest of the world; it moves information for both consumers and industrial customers.

Federal Express offers a valuable service to businesspeople who need letters, documents, and packages delivered overnight. When a customer needs a package shipped, Federal Express sends a courier to pick up the package and take it to a Federal Express office, from where it is trucked to the nearest airport. The package is usually flown to the company's Memphis superhub for sorting and then flown to the airport nearest its destination. The package is then trucked to another Federal Express office, where a courier picks it up and hand delivers it to the correct recipient. All this takes place overnight; 85 percent of all packages are delivered before 10:30 A.M. the next day. Couriers use handheld computers to keep track of packages. Federal Express says that more than 99 percent of its deliveries are made on time.

Federal Express charges $14 for delivery of its Overnight Letter package. Prices vary for larger packages and international shipments. Customers can save $3 by dropping packages off at a Federal Express office instead of having a courier pick it up. Although the U.S. Postal Service currently charges $8.75 for its Express Mail delivery service and the United Parcel Service charges $8.50 for its overnight letter delivery (mid-1988), Federal Express believes it offers customers more service and efficiency for its price.

Federal Express has 12,000 drop boxes in the United States, 165 drive-through centers, and 371 storefront service centers. It owns a fleet of 145 airplanes and 17,200 trucks and vans for handling delivery. The company even has its own weather forecasting service, which permitted 98 percent of its 1987 flights to arrive within fifteen minutes of schedule. Most packages are sorted at the Memphis superhub (in the middle of the night), but nearly 30 percent of all packages and documents are trucked directly to their destination whenever convenient. For international deliveries to the United Kingdom, West Germany, Spain, and eighty-six other countries, Federal Express uses a combination of direct service and independent contractors.

Promotion, Pricing, and Competition

As with other services, promotion of Federal Express' delivery service is difficult because of its intangible nature. Federal Express promotes its service, convenience, efficiency, price, and customer service. Its ongoing campaign, "When it absolutely, positively, has to be there overnight," appealed to businesspeople and was one of the most successful slogans in the service industry. When Federal Express began opening service centers all over the United States, it promoted each one with a huge grand opening celebration, complete with direct mail invitations, radio remotes, and door prizes. It reinforced this promotion with excellent customer relations. In a 1985 campaign to highlight the company's international service, Federal Express used point-of-sale materials and gave a World Atlas to each new customer making an international shipment. The international campaign boosted international volume in the service centers 46 percent.

When the U.S. Postal Service raised its Express Mail to $10.75, Federal Express saw an opportunity for more promotion and launched its "Battle the Bird" campaign. This campaign used direct mailings that included an explanation of the benefits of Federal Express services, an application for a Federal Express account, a listing of nearby drop-off centers, and a coupon good for the 25 cent difference between Express Mail and Federal Express' Overnight Letter. The company also promoted Battle the Bird to its employees with a twenty-four-page information package and a video. The company kept track of everyone who redeemed a coupon and which agent that customer dealt with. It followed up the promotion by sending the customer thank-you letters signed by the agent the customer had dealt with. This effort was designed to build individual store awareness.

Because Federal Express depends on its employees for promoting its service, the company hires the best people it can and offers them the best training and compensation possible. As a result, Federal Express employees are loyal and have very high levels of service and efficiency.

Despite offering a vital service and having motivated employees and successful promotions, Federal Express faces a maturing market for its services. Figures 1 and 2 indicate that competition is squeezing the company's profits. The company that created the overnight delivery service now faces intense competition from the U.S. Postal Service, United Parcel Service, and electronic mail (facsimile—fax—machines and computer links). Many corporations that once sent important docu-

FIGURE 1

Shares of the overnight
air express package de-
livery market, 1986
(SOURCE: Larry Reib-
stein, "Federal Express
Faces Challenges to Its
Grip on Overnight De-
livery," *Wall Street
Journal,* Jan. 8, 1988,
p. 8. Data from Mor-
gan Stanley & Co.

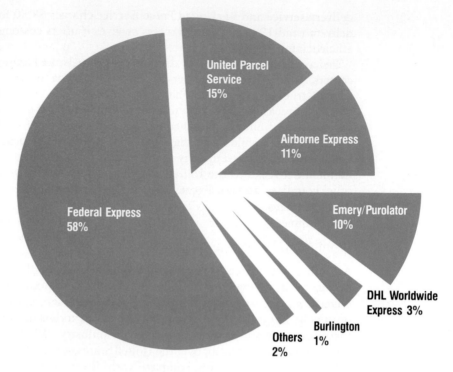

ments overnight via Federal Express now fax those documents or send them via
computer modem. Some experts believe that Federal Express could lose as much as
30 percent of its letter business to electronic mail. Moreover, the intense competition among air express companies has cut Federal's operating profit margin by 5.5
percent, to 11.4 percent in 1987.

The Introduction and Decline of ZapMail

To combat the increase in electronic mail, Federal Express introduced its own
electronic mail service, ZapMail, in 1983. ZapMail involved Federal Express sending a courier to pick up a document and taking it to the nearest Federal Express
office where it was faxed to the Federal Express office nearest the recipient. The
faxed document was then delivered by courier to the recipient's address. ZapMail
was delivered within two hours and cost about $35. If the customer took the
document directly to the Federal Express office, it could be faxed within an hour
for $25.

Federal Express believed that ZapMail was the future of the mail industry and
invested $3 million in the project (it planned to invest a total of $1.2 billion). The
company even planned to launch its own satellites to help carry ZapMail transmissions. During the first years of ZapMail, Federal Express leased thirteen satellite
earth stations from Harris Corporation; the stations were linked to thirteen computer switching centers from Tandem Computer. By November 1984, two
thousand pieces of mail were being transmitted through ZapMail daily, but analysts estimated that nearly ten times that volume was needed for Federal Express to
break even with ZapMail. In 1985, ZapMail service dropped off because of many

technical problems (overloaded switches, disappearing documents, slow transmission; moreover, the space shuttle Challenger, which exploded in January 1986, was to have launched the first Federal Express satellite), and during the period 1984 to 1986, ZapMail lost millions of dollars. In 1986 Federal Express announced that it would discontinue ZapMail despite its huge investment.

Expanding International Operations

Dropping ZapMail allowed Federal Express to focus on expanding its overseas operations, the most rapidly growing area of the overnight express market. Because of the globalization of the economy, businesses need to be able to communicate quickly with employees around the world, with partners in other nations, and with other businesses. Thus Federal Express began international operations in 1975 with shipments to and from the United States' biggest trading partner, Canada. In 1984, Federal Express bought Gelco International, enabling Federal to start operations in Europe and the Far East. The company plans to be the first official air express company flying routes to Japan in 1988. In 1988, the company offered service to eighty-nine countries, and its 1987 sales from international operations were $350 million. Federal Express was also named the official air express carrier for the 1988 Olympic Games in Seoul, a designation that the company used in promotions.

The Future

Federal Express is also counting on the current trend of just-in-time inventory to help boost its revenues. With its sophisticated computer tracking system and overnight delivery, Federal is actually managing the inventories of some customers at its Memphis, Oakland (California), and Newark hubs. IBM is using Federal to ware-

FIGURE 2

Federal Express net income per share, in dollars from continuing operations, year's end May 31 (SOURCE: Larry Reibstein, "Federal Express Faces Challenges to Its Grip on Overnight Delivery," *Wall Street Journal,* Jan. 8, 1988, p. 8. Data from Zachs Investment Research)

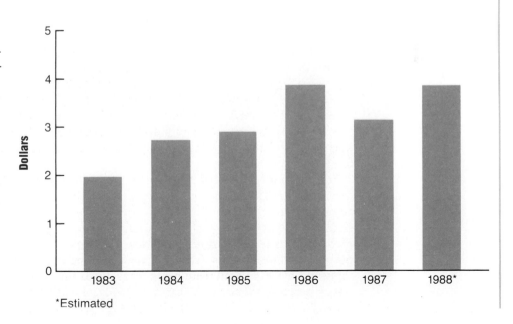

*Estimated

house parts for its workstations, enabling it to cut its delivery costs and close 120 parts depots.

In an effort to retain its leading market share, Federal Express has entered UPS's traditional turf: loading-dock deliveries. The company has expanded its two-day ground delivery service of heavy packages and plans to add still more trucks and vans. If necessary, Smith says the company will cut its prices to compete with UPS, Airborne Express, DHL, and other air express companies. Federal Express also plans to shift its emphasis from letters to packages, which generate higher profits.

Federal Express continues to try to improve its services through more sophisticated computers and customer relations. The company has been highly successful because it recognized a need—overnight delivery of important letters and packages—and it filled that need. Fred Smith's C paper has become an indispensable part of the world of business.

Questions for Discussion

1. Federal Express is an international firm that provides a service for industrial customers. How does the Federal Express marketing strategy permit effective competition with other overnight delivery companies?
2. What challenges does Federal Express face in maintaining a 50 percent share of the overnight delivery market?

SOURCES: Larry Reibstein, "Federal Express Faces Challenges to Its Grip on Overnight Delivery," *Wall Street Journal,* Jan. 8, 1988, pp. 1, 8; "The Rise and Fall of ZapMail: A Postmortem," case prepared by George Lucas, Memphis State University, 1988; "The History," fact sheet provided by Federal Express, 1988; Dean Foust, with Resa W. King, "Why Federal Express Has Overnight Anxiety," *Business Week,* Nov. 9, 1987, pp. 62, 66; 1987 Federal Express Corp. Annual Report; Carl Williams, "The Challenge of Retail Marketing at Federal Express," *Journal of Services Marketing,* Summer 1987, pp. 25–38; John J. Keller, with John W. Wilson, "Why ZapMail Finally Got Zapped," *Business Week,* Oct. 13, 1986, pp. 48–49; John P. Tarpey, "Federal Express Tries to Put More Zip in ZapMail," *Business Week,* Dec. 17, 1984, pp. 110–111; Arthur M. Louis, "The Great Electronic Mail Shootout," *Fortune,* Aug. 20, 1984, pp. 167–172.

Appendix A: Careers in Marketing

Some General Issues

As we note in Chapter 1, between one-fourth and one-third of the civilian work force in the United States is employed in marketing-related jobs. Although there obviously are a multitude of diverse career opportunities in the field, the number of positions in its different areas varies. For example, millions of workers are employed in many facets of sales, but relatively few people work in public relations and marketing research.

Many nonbusiness organizations now recognize that they do, in fact, perform marketing activities. For that reason, marketing positions are increasing in government agencies, hospitals, charitable and religious groups, educational institutions, and similar organizations.

Even though financial reward is not the sole criterion for selecting a career, it is only practical to consider how much you might earn in a marketing job. Table A.1 illustrates top ten salary positions for middle managers in marketing. Note that all these careers relate directly to marketing. A national sales manager may earn $60,000 to $100,000 or an even higher salary. Brand managers make $35,000 to $60,000. A media manager could earn $30,000 to $55,000. Generally, entry-level marketing personnel earn more than their counterparts in economics and liberal arts but not as much as people who enter accounting, chemistry, or engineering positions. Starting salaries for marketing graduates averaged $20,844, according to the 1988 College Placement Council Salary Survey. Marketers who advance to higher-level positions often earn high salaries, and a significant proportion of corporate executives held marketing jobs before attaining top-level positions.

Another important issue is whether you can enjoy the work associated with a particular career. Because you will spend almost 40 percent of your waking hours on the job, you should not allow such factors as economic conditions or status to override your personal goals as you select a lifelong career. Too often, people do not weigh these factors realistically. You should give considerable thought to your choice of a career, and you should adopt a well-planned, systematic approach to finding a position that meets your personal and career objectives.

After determining your objectives, you should identify the organizations that are likely to offer desirable opportunities. Learn as much as possible about these organizations before setting up employment interviews; job recruiters are impressed with applicants who have done their homework.

When making initial contact with potential employers by mail, enclose a brief, clearly written letter of introduction. After an initial interview, you should send a

TABLE A.I

Top salary ranges for
middle managers in
marketing

POSITION	SALARY RANGE
Corporate strategic market planner	$55,000–$ 75,000
National sales manager	60,000– 100,000
International sales	50,000– 75,000
Advertising account supervisors	40,000– 70,000
Sales promotion	40,000– 55,000
Purchasing manager	35,000– 55,000
Product/brand manager	35,000– 60,000
Media manager	30,000– 55,000
Retail sales	25,000– 45,000
Distribution management	40,000– 60,000

brief letter of thanks to the interviewer. The job of getting the right job is important, and you owe it to yourself to take this process seriously.

The Résumé

The résumé is one of the keys to being considered for a good job. Because it states your qualifications, experiences, education and career goals, the résumé is a chance for a potential employer to assess your compatibility with the job requirements. For both the employer's and the individual's benefit, the résumé should be accurate and current.

To be effective, the résumé can be targeted toward a specific position, as Figure A.1 shows. This document is only one example of an acceptable résumé. The job target section is specific and leads directly to the applicant's qualifications for the job. Capabilities show what the applicant can do and that the person has an understanding of the job's requirements. Skills and strengths should be highlighted as to how they relate to the specific job. The achievement section indicates success at accomplishing tasks or goals within the job market and at school. The work experience section includes educational background, which adds credibility to the résumé but is not the major area of focus; the applicant's ability to function successfully in a specific job is the major emphasis.

Common suggestions for improving résumés include deleting useless information, improving organization, using professional printing and typing, listing duties (not accomplishments), maintaining grammatical perfection, and avoiding an overly elaborate or fancy format.[1] One of the biggest problems in résumés, according to a survey of personnel experts, is distortions and lies; 36 percent of the experts thought that this was a major problem.[2] People lie most often about previous salaries and tasks performed in former jobs.

1. Tom Jackson, "Writing the Targeted Resume," *Business Week's Guide to Careers,* Spring 1983, pp. 26–27.
2. Burke Marketing Research for Robert Hall Inc. Reported in *USA Today,* Oct. 2, 1987, p. B-1.

FIGURE A.I

A résumé targeted
toward a specific
position

LORRAINE MILLER
2212 WEST WILLOW
(416) 862-9169

EDUCATION: B.A. Arizona State University 1987 Marketing

POSITION DESIRED: PRODUCT MANAGER WITH AN INTERNATIONAL FIRM PROVIDING FUTURE
CAREER DEVELOPMENT AT THE EXECUTIVE LEVEL.

QUALIFICATIONS:

* communicates well with individuals to achieve a common goal

* handles tasks efficiently and in a timely manner

* knowledge of advertising, sales, management, marketing research, packaging, pricing,
distribution, and warehousing

* coordinates many activities at one time

* receives and carries out assigned tasks or directives

* writes complete status or research reports

EXPERIENCES:

* Assistant Editor of college paper

* Treasurer of the American Marketing Association (student chapter)

* Internship with 3-Cs Advertising, Berkeley, CA

* Student Assistantship with Dr. Steve Green, Professor of Marketing, Arizona State University

* Achieved 3.6 average on a 4.0 scale throughout college

WORK RECORD:

1984 – Present	Blythe and Co., Inc.	
	* Junior Advertising Account Executive	
1982 – Present	Assistantship with Dr. Steve Green	
	* Research Assistant	
1980 – 1982	The Men	
	* Retail sales and consumer relations	
1976 – 1980	Tannenbaum Trees, Inc.	
	* Laborer	

Types of Marketing Careers

In considering marketing as a career, the first step is to evaluate broad categories of
career opportunities in the areas of marketing research, sales, public relations,
industrial buying, distribution management, product management, advertising, retail management, and direct marketing. Keep in mind that the categories described
here are not all-inclusive and that each encompasses hundreds of marketing jobs.

Marketing Research Clearly, marketing research and information systems are vital aspects of marketing
decision making. Marketing researchers spend more than $1 billion each year
surveying Americans to determine their habits, preferences, and aspirations.[3] The

3. Judith George, "Market Researcher," *Business Week Careers,* October 1987, p. 10.

information about buyers and environmental forces that research and information systems provide improves a marketer's ability to understand the dynamics of the marketplace and make effective decisions.

Marketing researchers gather and analyze data relating to specific problems. Marketing research firms are usually employed by a client organization, which could be a provider of goods or services, a nonbusiness organization, the government, a research consulting firm, or an advertising agency. The activities performed include concept testing, product testing, package testing, advertising testing, test-market research, and new-product research.

A researcher may be involved in one or several stages of research, depending on the size of the project, the organization of the research unit, and the researcher's experience. Marketing research trainees in large organizations usually perform a considerable amount of clerical work, such as compiling secondary data from a firm's accounting and sales records and periodicals, government publications, syndicated data services, and unpublished sources. A junior analyst may edit and code questionnaires or tabulate survey results. Trainees also may participate in primary data gathering by learning to conduct mail and telephone surveys, conducting personal interviews, and using observational methods of primary data collection. As a marketing researcher gains experience, the researcher may become involved in defining problems and developing hypotheses; designing research procedures; and analyzing, interpreting, and reporting findings. Exceptional personnel may assume responsibility for entire research projects.

Although most employers consider a bachelor's degree sufficient qualification for a marketing research trainee, many specialized positions require a graduate degree in business administration, statistics, or other related fields. Today, trainees are more likely to have a marketing or statistics degree than a liberal arts degree. Also, trainees who are capable of immediate productivity and more complex tasks are more desirable.[4] Courses in statistics, data processing, psychology, sociology, communications, economics, and English composition are valuable preparations for a career in marketing research.

The U.S. Bureau of Labor Statistics indicates that marketing research provides abundant employment opportunity, especially for applicants with graduate training in marketing research, statistics, economics, and the social sciences. Generally, the value of information gathered by marketing information and research systems will become more important as competition increases, thus expanding the opportunities for prospective marketing research personnel.

The three major career paths in marketing research are with independent marketing research agencies/data suppliers, advertising agency marketing research departments, and marketing research departments in businesses. In a company in which marketing research plays a key role, the researcher is often a member of the marketing strategy team. Surveying or interviewing consumers is the heart of the marketing research firm's activities. A statistician selects the sample to be surveyed, analysts design the questionnaire and synthesize the gathered data into a final report, data processors tabulate the data, and the research director controls and coordinates all these activities so that each project is computed to the client's

---

4. Marcia Fleschner, "Evolution of Research Takes the Profession to New Heights," *Collegiate Edition Marketing News,* March 1986, p. 1.

Appendix A   Careers in Marketing

satisfaction (i.e., consumer and industrial product manufacturers).[5] In marketing research agencies, a researcher deals with many clients, products, and problems. Advertising agencies use research as an ingredient in developing and refining campaigns for existing or potentially new clients.[6]

Salaries in marketing research depend on the type, size, and location of the firm as well as the nature of the positions. Generally, starting salaries are somewhat higher and promotions somewhat slower than in other occupations requiring similar training. Typical starting salaries are $21,000 to $25,000 per year. Salaries range from $14,000 to $18,000 for a junior analyst, $35,000 or more for a senior analyst, and research directors often earn salaries more than $60,000. In addition, the role of marketing in overall corporate planning is becoming more important as companies seek marketing information for strategic planning purposes. Marketing research directors are reporting to higher levels of management than ever before, and the number of corporate vice presidents who receive marketing research as regular input in decision making has doubled in recent years.

Sales

Millions of people earn a living through personal selling. Chapter 13 defines personal selling as a process of informing customers and persuading them to purchase products through personal communication in an exchange situation. Although this definition describes the general nature of many sales positions, individual selling jobs vary enormously with respect to the type of businesses and products involved, the educational background and skills required, and the specific activities sales personnel perform. Because the work is so varied, sales occupations offer numerous career opportunities for people with a wide range of qualifications, interests, and goals. A sales career offers the greatest potential compensation. The following two sections describe what is involved in wholesale and manufacturer sales.

Wholesale Sales Wholesalers perform activities to expedite transactions in which purchases are intended for resale or to be used to make other products. Wholesalers thus provide services to both retailers and producers. They can help match producers' products to retailers' needs and can provide accumulation and allocation services that save producers time, money, and resources. Some activities associated with wholesaling include planning and negotiating transactions; assisting customers with sales, advertising, sales promotion, and publicity; handling transportation and storage activities; providing customers with inventory control and data processing assistance; establishing prices; and giving customers technical, management, and merchandising assistance.

The background wholesale personnel need depends on the nature of the product handled. A drug wholesaler, for example, needs extensive technical training and product knowledge and may have a degree in chemistry, biology, or pharmacology. A wholesaler of standard office supplies, on the other hand, may find it more important to be familiar with various brands, suppliers, and prices than to have technical knowledge about the products. A new wholesale representative may

5. Judith George, "Market Researcher," *Business Week Careers*, October 1987, p. 10.
6. "What It's Like to Work in Marketing Research Depends on Where You Work—Supplier, Ad Agency, Manufacturer," *Collegiate Edition Marketing News*, December 1985, pp. 1 and 3.

begin a career as a sales trainee or hold a nonselling job that provides experience with inventory, prices, discounts, and the firm's customers. A college graduate usually enters the sales force directly out of school. Competent salespersons also transfer from manufacturer and retail sales positions.

The number of wholesale sales positions is expected to grow about as fast as the average for all occupations. Earnings for wholesale personnel vary widely because commissions often make up a large proportion of their incomes.

Manufacturer Sales Manufacturer sales personnel sell a firm's products to wholesalers, retailers, and industrial buyers; they thus perform many of the same activities wholesale salespersons handle. As is the case with wholesaling, the educational requirements for manufacturer sales depend largely on the type and complexity of the products and markets. Manufacturers of nontechnical products usually hire college graduates who have a liberal arts or business degree and give them training and information about the firm's products, prices, and customers. Manufacturers of highly technical products generally prefer applicants who have degrees in fields associated with the particular industry and market involved.

More and more sophisticated marketing skills are being utilized in industrial sales. Industrial marketing originally followed the commodity approach to complete a sale, whereby the right product is in the right place at the right time and for the right price. Today industrial sales use the same marketing concepts and strategies as do marketers selling to consumers.

Employment opportunities in manufacturer sales are expected to experience average growth. Manufacturer sales personnel are well compensated and earn above-average salaries. Most are paid a combination of salaries and commissions, and the highest salaries are paid by manufacturers of electrical equipment, food products, and rubber goods. Commissions vary according to the salesperson's efforts, abilities, and sales territory and the type of products sold.

Public Relations

Public relations encompasses a broad set of communication activities designed to create and maintain favorable relations between the organization and its publics—customers, employees, stockholders, government officials, and society in general. Public relations specialists help clients both create the image, issue, or message they wish to present and communicate it to the appropriate audience. According to the Public Relations Society of America, 120,000 persons work in public relations in the United States. Half the billings found in the 4,000 public relations agencies and firms come from Chicago and New York. The highest starting salaries can also be found there. Expect the average starting salary to be $15,000 or less but salaries can increase rapidly.[7] Communication is basic to all public relations programs. To communicate effectively, public relations practitioners first must gather data about the firm's client publics to assess their needs, identify problems, formulate recommendations, implement new plans, and evaluate current activities.

Public relations personnel disseminate large amounts of information to the organization's client publics. Written communication is the most versatile tool of public relations, and good writing ability is essential. Public relations practitioners must be adept at writing for a variety of media and audiences. It is not unusual for

7. Jan Greenberg, "Inside Public Relations," *Business Week Careers*, February 1988, pp. 46–48.

a person in public relations to prepare reports, news releases, speeches, broadcast scripts, technical manuals, employee publications, shareholder reports, and other communications aimed at both organizational personnel and external groups. In addition, a public relations practitioner needs a thorough knowledge of the production techniques used in preparing various communications.

Public relations personnel also establish distribution channels for the organization's publicity. They must have a thorough understanding of the various media, their areas of specialization, the characteristics of their target audiences, and their policies regarding publicity. Anyone who hopes to succeed in public relations must develop close working relationships with numerous media personnel to enlist their interest in disseminating an organization's communications.

A college education combined with writing or media-related experience is the best preparation for a career in public relations. Most beginners have a college degree in journalism, communications, or public relations, but some employers prefer a business background. Courses in journalism, business administration, marketing, creative writing, psychology, sociology, political science, economics, advertising, English, and public speaking are recommended. Some employers require applicants to present a portfolio of published articles, television or radio programs, slide presentations, and other work samples. Other agencies are requiring written tests that include activities such as writing sample press releases. Manufacturing firms, public utilities, transportation and insurance companies, and trade and professional associations are the largest employers of public relations personnel. In addition, sizable numbers of public relations personnel work for health-related organizations, government agencies, educational institutions, museums, and religious and service groups.

Although some larger companies provide extensive formal training for new personnel, most new public relations employees learn on the job. Beginners usually perform routine tasks such as maintaining files about company activities and searching secondary data sources for information that can be used in publicity materials. More experienced employees write press releases, speeches, and articles and help plan public relations campaigns.

Employment opportunities in public relations are expected to increase faster than the average for all occupations through the 1990s. One caveat is in order, however: Competition for beginning jobs is keen. The prospects are best for applicants who have solid academic preparation and some media experience. Areas that are projected to offer the most opportunity are in public relations agencies in the areas of product publicity, mergers and acquisitions, and financial and investor relations.[8] Abilities that differentiate candidates such as a basic understanding of computers are becoming increasingly important.

Industrial Buying Industrial buyers, or purchasing agents, are responsible for maintaining an adequate supply of the goods and services that an organization needs for operations. In general, industrial buyers purchase all items needed for direct use in producing other products and for use in the day-to-day operations. Industrial buyers in large firms often specialize in purchasing a single, specific class of products, for example, all petroleum-based lubricants. In smaller organizations, buyers may be responsible

8. Jan Greenberg, "Inside Public Relations," *Business Week Careers,* February 1988, p. 47.

for purchasing many different categories of items, including such goods as raw materials, component parts, office supplies, and operating services.

An industrial buyer's main job is selecting suppliers who offer the best quality, service, and price. When the products to be purchased are standardized, buyers may compare suppliers by examining catalogs and trade journals, making purchases by description. Buyers who purchase highly homogeneous products often meet with salespeople to examine samples and observe demonstrations. Sometimes, buyers must inspect the actual product before purchasing; in other cases, they invite suppliers to bid on large orders. Buyers who purchase specialized equipment often deal directly with manufacturers to obtain specially designed items made to specifications. After choosing a supplier and placing an order, an industrial buyer usually must trace the shipment to ensure on-time delivery. Finally, the buyer sometimes is responsible for receiving and inspecting an order and authorizing payment to the shipper.

Training requirements for a career in industrial buying relate to the needs of the firm and the types of products purchased. A manufacturer of heavy machinery may prefer an applicant who has a background in engineering; a service company, on the other hand, may recruit liberal arts majors. Although it is not generally required, a college degree is becoming increasingly important for buyers who wish to advance to management positions. Entry level positions are in the $18,000 to $23,000 range.

Employment prospects for industrial buyers are expected to increase faster than average through the 1990s. Opportunities will be excellent for individuals with a master's degree in business administration or a bachelor's degree in engineering, science, or business administration. In addition, companies that manufacture heavy equipment, computer equipment, and communications equipment will need buyers with technical backgrounds.

Distribution Management

A distribution (or traffic) manager arranges for the transportation of goods within firms and through marketing channels. Transportation is an essential distribution activity that permits a firm to create time and place utility for its products. It is the distribution manager's job to analyze various transportation modes and select the combination that minimizes cost and transit time while providing acceptable levels of reliability, capability, accessibility, and security.

To accomplish this task, a distribution manager performs many activities. First, the individual must choose one or a combination of transportation modes from the five major modes available: railways, motor vehicles, inland waterways, pipelines, and airways. Then the distribution manager must select the specific routes the goods will travel and the particular carriers to be used, weighing such factors as freight classifications and regulations, freight charges, time schedules, shipment sizes, and loss and damage ratios. In addition, this person may be responsible for preparing shipping documents, tracing shipments, handling loss and damage claims, keeping records of freight rates, and monitoring changes in government regulations and transportation technology.

Distribution management employs relatively few people and is expected to grow about as fast as the average for all occupations in the near future. Manufacturing firms are the largest employers of distribution managers, although some traffic managers work for wholesalers, retail stores, and consulting firms. Salaries of experienced distribution managers vary but generally are much higher than the average for all nonsupervisory personnel.

Entry-level positions for distribution management are in the $20,000 to $25,000 per year salary range. Starting jobs are diverse, varying from inventory control, traffic scheduling, operations management, or distribution management. Inventory management is an area of great opportunity because many U.S. firms see inventory costs as high relative to foreign competition, especially that from the Japanese. Just-in-time inventory systems are designed by inventory control specialists to work with the bare minimum of inventory.[9]

Most employers prefer graduates of technical programs or seek people who have completed courses in transportation, logistics, distribution management, economics, statistics, computer science, management, marketing, and commercial law. A successful distribution manager must be adept at handling technical data and be able to interpret and communicate highly technical information.

Product Management

The product manager occupies a staff position and is responsible for the success or failure of a product line. Product managers coordinate most of the marketing activities required to market a product; however, because they hold a staff position, they have relatively little actual authority over marketing personnel. Even so, they take on a large amount of responsibility and typically are paid quite well relative to other marketing employees. Being a product manager can be rewarding both financially and psychologically, but it also can be frustrating because of the disparity between responsibility and authority.

A product manager should have a general knowledge of advertising, transportation modes, inventory control, selling and sales management, sales promotion, marketing research, packaging, pricing, and warehousing. The individual must be knowledgeable enough to communicate effectively with personnel in these functional areas and to make suggestions and help assess alternatives when major decisions are being made.

Product managers usually need college training in an area of business administration. A master's degree is helpful, although a person usually does not become a product manager directly out of school. Frequently, several years of selling and sales management are prerequisites for a product management position, which often is a major step in the career path of top-level marketing executives. The average salary for an experienced product manager is $35,000 to $60,000.

Advertising

Advertising pervades our daily lives. As we detail in Chapter 14, business and nonbusiness organizations use advertising in many ways and for many reasons. Advertising clearly needs individuals with diverse skills to fill a variety of jobs. Creative imagination, artistic talent, and expertise in expression and persuasion are important for copywriters, artists, and account executives. Sales and managerial ability are vital to the success of advertising managers, media buyers, and production managers. Research directors must have a solid understanding of research techniques and human behavior.

9. Nicholas Basta, "Inventory and Distribution," *Business Week's Guide to Careers,* Spring–Summer 1985, p. 23.

Advertising professionals disagree on the most beneficial educational background for a career in advertising. Most employers prefer college graduates. Some employers seek individuals with degrees in advertising, journalism, or business; others prefer graduates with broad liberal arts backgrounds. Still other employers rank relevant work experience above educational background.

"Advertisers look for generalists," says Kate Preston, a staff executive of the American Association of Advertising Agencies, "thus there are just as many economics or general liberal arts majors as M.B.A.s." Common entry level positions in an advertising agency are found in the traffic department, account service (account coordinator), or in the media department (media assistant). Starting salaries in these positions are often quite low but to gain experience in the advertising industry, employees must work their way up in the system. The entry level salaries of media assistants and account coordinators are often $15,000 or less.[10]

A variety of organizations employ advertising personnel. Although advertising agencies are perhaps the most visible and glamorous of employers, many manufacturing firms, retail stores, banks, utility companies, and professional and trade associations maintain advertising departments. Advertising jobs also can be found with television and radio stations, newspapers, and magazines. Other businesses that employ advertising personnel include printers, art studios, letter shops, and package-design firms. Specific advertising jobs include advertising manager, account executive, research director, copywriter, media specialist, and production manager.

Employment opportunities for advertising personnel are expected to decrease in the early nineties as agency acquisitions and mergers continue. General economic conditions, however, strongly influence the size of advertising budgets and, hence, employment opportunities.

Retail Management

More than 20 million people in the United States work in the retail industry.[11] Although a career in retailing may begin in sales, there is more to retailing than simply selling. Many retail personnel occupy management positions. Besides managing the sales force, they focus on selecting and ordering merchandise, promotional activities, inventory control, customer credit operations, accounting, personnel, and store security.

How retail stores are organized varies. In many large department stores, retail management personnel rarely get involved with actually selling to customers; these duties are performed by retail salespeople. However, other types of retail organizations may require management personnel to perform selling activities from time to time.

Large retail stores offer a variety of management positions besides those at the very top, including assistant buyers, buyers, department managers, section managers, store managers, division managers, regional managers, and vice president of merchandising. The following list describes the general duties of four of these positions; the precise nature of these duties varies from one retail organization to another.

10. Vincent Daddiego, "Making It In Advertising," *Business Week Careers,* February 1988, p. 42.
11. Eleanor May, *Future Trends in Retailing* (Cambridge, Mass.: Marketing Science Institute, 1987), p. 1.

A section manager coordinates inventory and promotions and interacts with buyers, salespeople, and ultimate consumers. The manager performs merchandising, labor relations and managerial activities and can rarely expect to get away with as little as a forty-hour work week.

The buyer's task is more focused. In this fast-paced occupation, there is much travel, pressure, and need to be open-minded with respect to new and potentially successful items.

The regional manager coordinates the activities of several stores within a given area. Sales, promotions, and procedures in general are monitored and supported.

The vice president of merchandising has a broad scope of managerial responsibility and reports to the president at the top of the organization.

Traditionally, retail managers began their careers as salesclerks. Today, many large retailers hire college-educated people, put them through management training programs, and then place them directly into management positions. They frequently hire people with backgrounds in liberal arts or business administration. Sales and retailing are the greatest employment opportunities for marketing students.

Retail management positions can be exciting and challenging. Competent, ambitious individuals often assume a great deal of responsibility very quickly and advance rapidly. However, compensation programs for entry-level positions (management trainees) have historically been below average. This situation is changing rapidly with major specialty, department, and discount stores offering entry salaries in the $20,000 to $25,000 range. In addition, a retail manager's job is physically demanding and sometimes entails long working hours. Nonetheless, positions in retail management often provide numerous opportunities to excel and advance.

Direct Marketing

One of the most dynamic areas in marketing is direct marketing, in which the seller uses one or more direct media (telephone, mail, print, or television) to solicit a response. For example, Shell Oil uses its credit card billings (direct mail) to sell a variety of consumer products.

The telephone is a major vehicle for selling many consumer products, such as magazines. Telemarketing is direct selling to customers using a variety of technological improvements in telephone services; it is an estimated $91 billion a year industry creating jobs in sales, marketing strategy, and marketing technology. According to the American Telemarketing Association (Glenview, Illinois), $73 billion of the industry's sales come from business-to-business marketing, not from selling to consumers at home. In addition, the telemarketing industry has been growing an average of 30 percent per year. Starting salaries in telemarketing are $19,000 to $26,000.[12]

The use of direct mail catalogs appeals to market segments such as working women or people who find going to retail stores difficult or inconvenient. Newspapers and magazines offer great opportunity, especially in special market segments. *Golf Digest,* for example, is obviously a good medium for selling golfing equipment. Cable television provides many new opportunities for selling directly to

12. Nicholas Basta, "Telemarketing," *Business Week's Guide to Careers,* Dec. 1985, p. 27.

consumers. Interactive cable will offer a new method to expand direct marketing by developing timely exchange opportunities for consumers.

The volume of goods distributed through direct marketing is a strong indicator of opportunity for careers in this growing area. H. B. Crandall, president of Crandall Associates, New York, stated that job candidates with experience could "write their own ticket." He continued, "People with five years' experience are getting phenomenal salary offers. People with one year's experience are getting offers unheard of in any other marketing field."[13]

The most important asset in direct marketing is experience. Employers often look to other industries to locate experienced professionals. In a choice between an M.B.A. or an individual with a direct marketing background, the experienced individual would be hired.[14] This preference means that if you can get an entry-level position in direct marketing, you will have a real advantage in developing a career.

Jobs in direct marketing include buyers, such as department store buyers, who select goods for catalog, telephone, or direct mail sales. Catalog managers develop marketing strategies for each new catalog that goes into the mail. Research/mail-list management involves developing lists of products that will sell in direct marketing and lists of names that will respond to a direct mail effort. Order fulfillment managers direct the shipment of products once they are sold. Nearly all nonprofit organizations have fund-raising managers who use direct marketing to obtain financial support.[15]

The executive vice president of the advertising agency Young & Rubicam, Inc. in New York stated that direct marketing will have to be used "not as a tactic, but as a strategic tool."[16] Direct marketing's effectiveness is enhanced by periodic analysis of advertising and communications at all phases of contact with the consumer. Direct marketing involves all aspects of the marketing decision. It is becoming a more professional career area that provides great opportunity.

13. Kevin Higgins, "Economic Recovery Puts Marketers in Catbird Seat," *Marketing News,* Oct. 14, 1983, pp. 1, 8.
14. Ibid.
15. Nicholas Basta, "Direct Marketing," *Business Week Careers,* March 1986, p. 52.
16. "Wonderman Urges: Replace Marketing War Muskets with the Authentic Weapon—Direct Marketing," *Marketing News,* July 8, 1983, pp. 1, 12.

Appendix B: Financial Analysis in Marketing

Our discussion in this book focused more on fundamental concepts and decisions in marketing than on financial details. However, marketers must understand the basic components of selected financial analyses if they are to explain and defend their decisions. In fact, they must be familiar with certain financial analyses if they are to reach good decisions in the first place. We therefore examine three areas of financial analyses: cost-profit aspects of the income statement, selected performance ratios, and price calculations.[1] To control and evaluate marketing activities, marketers must understand the income statement and what it says about the operations of their organization. They also need to be acquainted with performance ratios, which compare current operating results with past results and with results in the industry at large. In the last part of the appendix, we discuss price calculations as the basis of price adjustments. Marketers are likely to use all these areas of financial analysis at various times to support their decisions and to make necessary adjustments in their operations.

The Income Statement

The income, or operating, statement presents the financial results of an organization's operations over a period of time. The statement summarizes revenues earned and expenses incurred by a profit center, whether it is a department, brand, product line, division, or entire firm. The income statement presents the firm's net profit or net loss for a month, quarter, or year.

Table B.1 is a simplified income statement for a retail store. The owners of the store, Rose Costa and Nick Schultz, see that net sales of $250,000 are decreased by the cost of goods sold and by other business expenses to yield a net income of $83,000. Of course, these figures are only highlights of the complete income statement, which appears in Table B.2.

The income statement can be used in several ways to improve the management of a business. First, it enables an owner or manager to compare actual results with budgets for various parts of the statement. For example, Rose and Nick see that the total amount of merchandise sold (gross sales) is $260,000. Customers returned merchandise or received allowances (price reductions) totaling $10,000. Suppose

1. We gratefully acknowledge the assistance of Jim L. Grimm, Professor of Marketing, Illinois State University, in writing this appendix.

STONEHAM AUTO SUPPLIES INCOME STATEMENT FOR THE YEAR ENDED
DECEMBER 31, 1988

Net Sales	$250,000
Cost of Goods Sold	45,000
Gross Margin	$205,000
Expenses	122,000
Net Income	$ 83,000

the budgeted amount was only $9,000. By checking the ticket for sales returns and allowances, the owners can determine why these events occurred and whether the $10,000 figure could be lowered by adjusting the marketing mix.

After subtracting returns and allowances from gross sales, Rose and Nick can determine net sales from the statement. They are pleased with this figure because it is higher than their sales target of $240,000. Net sales is the amount the firm has available to pay its expenses.

A major expense for most companies that sell goods (as opposed to services) is the cost of goods sold. For Stoneham Auto Supplies, it amounts to 18 percent of net sales. Other expenses are treated in various ways by different companies. In our example, they are broken down into standard categories of selling expenses, administrative expenses, and general expenses.

The income statement shows that the cost of goods Stoneham Auto Supplies sold during fiscal year 1988 was $45,000. This figure was derived in the following way. First, the statement shows that merchandise in the amount of $51,000 was purchased during the year. In paying the invoices associated with these inventory additions, purchase (cash) discounts of $4,000 were earned, resulting in net purchases of $47,000. Special requests for selected merchandise throughout the year resulted in $2,000 of freight charges, which increased the net cost of delivered purchases to $49,000. Adding this amount to the beginning inventory of $48,000, the cost of goods available for sale during 1988 was $97,000. However, the records indicate that the value of inventory at the end of the year was $52,000. Because this amount was not sold, the cost of goods that were sold during the year was $45,000.

Rose and Nick observe that the total value of their inventory increased by 8.3 percent during the year:

$$\frac{\$52,000 - \$48,000}{\$48,000} = \frac{\$\ 4,000}{\$48,000} = \frac{1}{12} = .0825 \text{ or } 8.3\%$$

Further analysis is needed to determine whether this increase is desirable or undesirable. (Note that the income statement provides no detail concerning the composition of the inventory held on December 31; other records provide this information.) If Nick and Rose determine that inventory on December 31 is excessive, they can implement appropriate marketing action.

Gross margin is the difference between net sales and cost of goods sold. Gross margin reflects the markup on products and is the amount available to pay all other expenses and provide a return to the owners. Stoneham Auto Supplies had a gross margin of $205,000:

TABLE B.2

Operating statement for a retailer

STONEHAM AUTO SUPPLIES INCOME STATEMENT FOR THE YEAR ENDED DECEMBER 31, 1988

Gross Sales			$260,000
Less: Sales returns and allowances			10,000
Net Sales			$250,000
Cost of Goods Sold			
Inventory, January 1, 1988 (at cost)		$48,000	
Purchases	$51,000		
Less: Purchase discounts	4,000		
Net purchases	$47,000		
Plus: Freight-in	2,000		
Net cost of delivered purchases		$49,000	
Cost of goods available for sale		$97,000	
Less: Inventory, December 31, 1988			
(at cost)		52,000	
Cost of goods sold			$ 45,000
Gross Margin			$205,000
Expenses			
Selling expenses			
Sales salaries and commissions	$32,000		
Advertising	16,000		
Sales promotions	3,000		
Delivery	2,000		
Total selling expenses		$53,000	
Administrative expenses			
Administrative salaries	$20,000		
Office salaries	20,000		
Office supplies	2,000		
Miscellaneous	1,000		
Total administrative expenses		$43,000	
General expenses			
Rent	$14,000		
Utilities	7,000		
Bad debts	1,000		
Miscellaneous (local taxes, insurance,			
interest, depreciation)	4,000		
Total general expenses		$26,000	
Total expenses			$122,000
Net Income			$ 83,000

Net Sales	$250,000
Cost of Goods Sold	−45,000
Gross Margin	$205,000

Stoneham's expenses (other than cost of goods sold) during 1988 totaled $122,000. Observe that $53,000, or slightly more than 43 percent of the total, is direct selling expenses:

$$\frac{\$\ 53,000\ \text{selling expenses}}{\$122,000\ \text{total expenses}} = .434 \text{ or } 43\%$$

The business employs three salespersons (one full time) and pays competitive wages for the area. All selling expenses are similar to dollar amounts for fiscal year 1987, but Nick and Rose wonder whether more advertising is necessary because inventory increased by more than 8 percent during the year.

The administrative and general expenses are also essential for operating the business. A comparison of these expenses with trade statistics for similar businesses indicate that the figures are in line with industry amounts.

Net income, or net profit, is the amount of gross margin remaining after deducting expenses. Stoneham Auto Supplies earned a net profit of $83,000 for the fiscal year ending December 31, 1988. Note that net income on this statement is figured before payment of state and federal income taxes.

Income statements for intermediaries and for businesses that provide services follow the same general format as that shown for Stoneham Auto Supplies in Table B.2. The income statement for a manufacturer, however, is somewhat different in that the purchases section is replaced by a section called cost of goods manufactured. Table B.3 shows the entire Cost of Goods Sold section for a manufacturer, including cost of goods manufactured. In other respects, income statements for retailers and manufacturers are similar.

Selected Performance Ratios

Rose and Nick's assessment of how well their business did during fiscal year 1988 can be improved through selective use of analytical ratios. These ratios enable a manager to compare the results for the current year with data from previous years and industry statistics. Unfortunately, comparisons of the current income statement with income statements and industry statistics from other years are not very meaningful because factors such as inflation are not accounted for when comparing dollar amounts. More meaningful comparisons can be made by converting these figures to a percentage of net sales, as this section shows.

The first analytical ratios we discuss, the operating ratios, are based on the net sales figure from the income statement.

Operating Ratios

Operating ratios express items on the income, or operating, statement as percentages of net sales. The first step is to convert the income statement into percentages of net sales, as illustrated in Table B.4.

After making this conversion, the manager looks at several key operating ratios: two profitability ratios (the gross margin ratio and the net income ratio) and the operating expense ratio.

For Stoneham Auto Supplies, these ratios are determined as follows (see Tables B.2 and B.4 for supporting data):

$$\text{Gross margin ratio} = \frac{\text{gross margin}}{\text{net sales}} = \frac{\$205,000}{\$250,000} = 82\%$$

TABLE B.3

Cost of goods sold for a manufacturer

STONEHAM AUTO SUPPLIES INCOME STATEMENT FOR THE YEAR ENDED DECEMBER 31, 1988			
Cost of Goods Sold			
Finished goods inventory, January 1, 1988			$ 50,000
Cost of goods manufactured			
Work-in-process inventory, January 1, 1988		$ 20,000	
Raw materials inventory, January 1, 1988	$ 40,000		
Net cost of delivered purchases	240,000		
Cost of goods available for use	$280,000		
Less: Raw materials inventory, December 31, 1988	42,000		
Cost of goods placed in production		$238,000	
Direct labor		$32,000	
Manufacturing overhead			
Indirect labor	$ 12,000		
Supervisory salaries	10,000		
Operating supplies	6,000		
Depreciation	12,000		
Utilities	10,000		
Total manufacturing overhead		$ 50,000	
Total manufacturing costs		$320,000	
Total work-in-process		$340,000	
Less: Work-in-process inventory, December 31, 1988		22,000	
Cost of goods manufactured			$318,000
			$368,000
Cost of goods available for sale			
Less: Finished goods inventory, December 31, 1988			48,000
Cost of Goods Sold			$320,000

$$\text{Net income ratio} = \frac{\text{net income}}{\text{net sales}} = \frac{\$\ 83{,}000}{\$250{,}000} = 33.2\%$$

$$\text{Operating expense ratio} = \frac{\text{total expense}}{\text{net sales}} = \frac{\$122{,}000}{\$250{,}000} = 48.8\%$$

TABLE B.4

Income statement components as percentages of net sales

STONEHAM AUTO SUPPLIES INCOME STATEMENT AS A PERCENTAGE
OF NET SALES FOR THE YEAR ENDED DECEMBER 31, 1988

		Percentage of net sales
Gross Sales		103.8%
Less: Sales returns and allowances		3.8
Net Sales		100.0%
Cost of Goods Sold		
Inventory, January 1, 1988 (at cost)		19.2%
Purchases	20.4%	
Less: Purchase discounts	1.6	
Net purchases	18.8%	
Plus: Freight-in	.8	
Net cost of delivered purchases		19.6
Cost of goods available for sale		38.8%
Less: Inventory, December 31, 1988 (at cost)		20.8
Cost of goods sold		18.0
Gross Margin		82.0%
Expenses		
Selling expenses		
Sales salaries and commissions	12.8%	
Advertising	6.4	
Sales promotions	1.2	
Delivery	0.8	
Total selling expenses		21.2%
Administrative expenses		
Administrative salaries	8.0%	
Office salaries	8.0	
Office supplies	0.8	
Miscellaneous	0.4	
Total administrative expenses		17.2%
General expenses		
Rent	5.6%	
Utilities	2.8	
Bad debts	0.4	
Miscellaneous	1.6	
Total general expenses		10.4%
Total expenses		48.8
Net Income		33.2%

The gross margin ratio indicates the percentage of each sales dollar available to cover operating expenses and achieve profit objectives. The net income ratio indicates the percentage of each sales dollar that is classified as earnings (profit) before payment of income taxes. The operating expense ratio indicates the percentage of each dollar needed to cover operating expenses.

If Nick and Rose feel that the operating expense ratio is higher than historical data and industry standards, they can analyze each operating expense ratio in Table B.4 to determine which expenses are too high and can then take corrective action.

After reviewing several key operating ratios, in fact, managers will probably want to analyze all the items on the income statement. For instance, by doing so, Nick and Rose can determine whether the 8 percent increase in inventory was necessary.

Inventory Turnover

The inventory turnover rate, or stockturn rate, is an analytical ratio that can be used to answer the question, "Is the inventory level appropriate for this business?" The inventory turnover rate indicates the number of times that an inventory is sold (turns over) during one year. To be useful, this figure is then compared to historical turnover rates and industry rates.

The inventory turnover rate can be computed on cost as follows:

$$\text{Inventory turnover} = \frac{\text{cost of goods sold}}{\text{average inventory at cost}}$$

Rose and Nick would calculate the turnover rate from Table B.2 as follows:

$$\frac{\text{Cost of goods sold}}{\text{Average inventory at cost}} = \frac{\$45,000}{\$50,000} = 0.9 \text{ time}$$

They find that inventory turnover is less than once per year (0.9 time). Industry averages for competitive firms are 2.8 times. This figure convinces Rose and Nick that their investment in inventory is too large and that they need to reduce inventory.

Return on Investment

Return on investment (ROI) is a ratio that indicates management's efficiency in generating sales and profits from the total amount invested in the firm. For example, Stoneham Auto Supplies' ROI is 41.5 percent, which compares well with competing businesses.

We use figures from two different financial statements to arrive at ROI. The income statement, already discussed, gives us net income. The balance sheet, which states the firm's assets and liabilities at a given point in time, provides the figure for total assets (or investment) in the firm.

The basic formula for ROI is

$$\text{ROI} = \frac{\text{net income}}{\text{total investment}}$$

For Stoneham Auto Supplies, net income for fiscal year 1988 is $83,000 (see Table B.2). If total investment (taken from the balance sheet for December 31, 1988) is $200,000, then

$$\text{ROI} = \frac{\$\ 83,000}{\$200,000} = 0.415 \text{ or } 41.5\%$$

The ROI formula can be expanded to isolate the impact of capital turnover and the operating income ratio separately. Capital turnover is a measure of net sales per dollar of investment; the ratio is figured by dividing net sales by total investment. For Stoneham Auto Supplies,

$$\text{Capital turnover} = \frac{\text{net sales}}{\text{total investment}}$$

$$= \frac{\$250,000}{\$200,000} = 1.25$$

ROI is equal to capital turnover times the net income ratio. The expanded formula for Stoneham Auto Supplies is

$$\text{ROI} = (\text{capital turnover}) \times (\text{net income ratio})$$

or

$$\text{ROI} = \frac{\text{net sales}}{\text{total investment}} \times \frac{\text{net income}}{\text{net sales}}$$

$$= \frac{\$250,000}{\$200,000} \times \frac{\$\ 83,000}{\$250,000}$$

$$= (1.25)\ (33.2\%) = 41.5\%$$

Price Calculations

An important step in setting prices is selecting a pricing method, as indicated in Chapter 16. The systematic use of markups, markdowns, and various conversion formulas helps in calculating the selling price and evaluating the effects of various prices. The following sections provide more detailed information about price calculations (Chapter 15).

Markups

As indicated in the text, markup is the difference between the selling price and the cost of the item. That is, selling price equals cost plus markup. The markup must cover cost and contribute to profit; thus markup is similar to gross margin on the income statement.

Markup can be calculated on either cost or selling price, as follows:

$$\text{Markup as percentage of cost} = \frac{\text{amount added to cost}}{\text{cost}} = \frac{\text{dollar markup}}{\text{cost}}$$

$$\text{Markup as percentage of selling price} = \frac{\text{amount added to cost}}{\text{selling price}} = \frac{\text{dollar markup}}{\text{selling price}}$$

Retailers tend to calculate the markup percentage on selling price.

Examples of Markup

To review the use of these markup formulas, assume that an item costs $10 and the markup is $5.

$$\text{Selling price} = \text{cost} + \text{markup}$$

$$\$15 = \$10 + \$5$$

Thus

$$\text{Markup percentage on cost} = \frac{\$\,5}{\$10} = 50\%$$

$$\text{Markup percentage on selling price} = \frac{\$\,5}{\$15} = 33\tfrac{1}{3}\%$$

It is necessary to know the base (cost or selling price) to use markup pricing effectively. Markup percentage on cost will always exceed markup percentage on price, given the same dollar markup, so long as selling price exceeds cost.

On occasion, we may need to convert markup on cost to markup on selling price, or vice versa. The conversion formulas are

$$\text{Markup percentage on selling price} = \frac{\text{markup percentage on cost}}{100\% + \text{markup percentage on cost}}$$

$$\text{Markup percentage on cost} = \frac{\text{markup percentage on selling price}}{100\% - \text{markup percentage on selling price}}$$

For example, if the markup percentage on cost is 33⅓ percent, then the markup percentage on selling price is

$$\frac{33\tfrac{1}{3}\%}{100\% + 33\tfrac{1}{3}\%} = \frac{33\tfrac{1}{3}\%}{133\tfrac{1}{3}\%} = 25\%$$

If the markup percentage on selling price is 40 percent, then the corresponding percentage on cost would be the following:

$$\frac{40\%}{100\% - 40\%} = \frac{40\%}{60\%} = 66\frac{2}{3}\%$$

Finally, we can show how to determine selling price if we know the cost of the item and the markup percentage on selling price. Assume that an item costs \$36 and the usual markup percentage on selling price is 40 percent. Remember that selling price equals markup plus cost. Thus if

$$100\% = 40\% \text{ of selling price} + \text{cost}$$

then

$$60\% \text{ of selling price} = \text{cost}$$

In our example, cost equals \$36. Then

$$0.6X = \$36$$

$$X = \frac{\$36}{0.6}$$

$$\text{Selling price} = \$60$$

Alternatively, the markup percentage could be converted to a cost basis as follows:

$$\frac{40\%}{100\% - 40\%} = 66\frac{2}{3}\%$$

Then the computed selling price would be as follows:

$$\text{Selling price} = 66\frac{2}{3}\% \text{ (cost)} + \text{cost}$$

$$= 66\frac{2}{3}\% \text{ (\$36)} + \$36$$

$$= \$24 + \$36$$

$$= \$60$$

By remembering the basic formula—selling price equals cost plus markup—you will find these calculations straightforward.

Markdowns

Markdowns are price reductions a retailer makes on merchandise. Markdowns may be useful on items that are damaged, priced too high, or selected for a special sales event. The income statement does not express markdowns directly because the change in price is made before the sale takes place. Therefore separate records of markdowns are needed to evaluate the performance of various buyers and departments.

The markdown ratio (percentage) is calculated as follows:

$$\text{Markdown percentage} = \frac{\text{dollar markdowns}}{\text{net sales in dollars}}$$

In analyzing their inventory, Nick and Rose discover three special automobile jacks that have gone unsold for several months. They decide to reduce the price of each item from $25 to $20. Subsequently, these items are sold. The markdown percentage for these three items is

$$\text{Markdown percentage} = \frac{3\ (\$5)}{3\ (\$20)} = \frac{\$15}{\$60} = 25\%$$

Net sales, however, include all units of this product sold during the period, not just those marked down. If ten of these items have already been sold at $25 each, in addition to the three items sold at $20, then the overall markdown percentage would be

$$\text{Markdown percentage} = \frac{3\ (\$5)}{10\ (\$25) + 3\ (\$20)}$$

$$= \frac{\$15}{\$250 + \$60} = \frac{\$15}{\$310} = 4.8\%$$

Sales allowances also are a reduction in price. Thus the markdown percentages should also include any sales allowances. It would be computed as follows:

$$\text{Markdown percentage} = \frac{\text{dollar markdowns} + \text{dollar allowances}}{\text{net sales in dollars}}$$

Discussion and Review Questions

1. How does a manufacturer's income statement differ from a retailer's income statement?
2. Use the following information to answer questions a through c:

Company TEA
Fiscal year ended June 30, 1989

Net Sales	$500,000
Cost of Goods Sold	300,000
Net Income	50,000
Average Inventory at Cost	100,000
Total Assets (total investment)	200,000

   a. What is the inventory turnover rate for TEA Company? From what sources will the marketing manager determine the significance of the inventory turnover rate?

b. What is the capital turnover ratio for fiscal year 1989? What is the net income ratio? What is the return on investment (ROI)?

c. How many dollars of sales did each dollar of investment produce for TEA Company in fiscal year 1989?

3. Product A has a markup percentage on cost of 40 percent. What is the markup percentage on selling price?

4. Product B has a markup percentage on selling price of 30 percent. What is the markup percentage on cost?

5. Product C has a cost of $60 and a usual markup percentage of 25 percent on selling price. What price should be placed on this item?

6. Apex Appliance Company sells twenty units of product Q for $100 each and ten units for $80 each. What is the markdown percentage for product Q?

Glossary

A

Accessory equipment Equipment used in production or office activities; does not become a part of the final physical product.

Accumulation A process through which an inventory of homogeneous products that have similar production or demand requirements is developed.

Administered pricing Process in which the seller sets a price for a product, and the customer pays that specified price.

Advertising A paid form of nonpersonal communication about an organization and/or its products that is transmitted to a target audience through a mass medium.

Advertising appropriation The total amount of money that a marketer allocates for advertising for a specific time period.

Advertising platform The basic issues or selling points that an advertiser wishes to include in the advertising campaign.

Advertising target The group of people toward whom advertisements are aimed.

Agent Marketing intermediary who receives a commission or fee for expediting exchanges; represents either buyers or sellers on a permanent basis.

Aided recall test A posttest method of evaluating the effectiveness of advertising in which subjects are asked to identify advertisements they have seen recently; they are shown a list of products, brands, company names, or trademarks to jog their memory.

Allocation The breaking down of large homogeneous inventories into smaller lots.

Allowance Concession in price to achieve a desired goal; for example, industrial equipment manufacturers give trade-in allowances on used industrial equipment to enable customers to purchase new equipment.

Approach The manner in which a salesperson contacts a potential customer.

Arbitrary approach A method for determining the advertising appropriation in which a high-level executive in the firm states how much can be spent on advertising for a certain time period.

Area sampling A variation of stratified sampling, with the geographic areas serving as the segments, or primary units, used in random sampling.

Artwork The illustration in an advertisement and the layout of the components of an advertisement.

Assessment center An intense training center at which sales candidates are put into realistic, problematic settings in which they must prioritize activities, make decisions, and act on their decisions to determine whether each candidate will make a good salesperson.

Assorting Combining products into collections or assortments that buyers want to have available at one place.

Assortment A combination of similar or complementary products put together to provide benefits to a specific market.

Atmospherics The conscious designing of a store's space to create emotional effects that enhance the probability that consumers will buy.

Attitude Knowledge and positive or negative feelings about an object.

Attitude scale Measurement instrument that usually consists of a series of adjectives, phrases, or sentences about an object; subjects are asked to indicate the intensity of their feelings toward the object by reacting to the statements in a certain way. It can be used to measure consumer attitudes.

Automatic vending Nonstore, nonpersonal retailing; includes coin-operated, self-service machines.

Average cost Total costs divided by the quantity produced.

Average fixed cost The fixed cost per unit produced; it is calculated by dividing the fixed costs by the number of units produced.

Average revenue Total revenue divided by quantity produced.

Average total cost The sum of the average fixed cost and the average variable cost.

Average variable cost The variable cost per unit produced; it is calculated by dividing the variable cost by the number of units produced.

B

Barter The trading of products.

Base-point pricing A geographic pricing policy that includes the price at the factory plus freight charges from the base point nearest the buyer.

Benefit segmentation The division of a market according to the benefits that customers want from the product.

Better Business Bureau A local, nongovernmental regulatory group supported by local businesses that aids in settling problems among specific business firms and consumers.

Bid pricing A determination of prices through sealed bids or open bids.

Bonded storage A storage service many public warehouses provide whereby the goods are not released until U.S. customs duties, federal or state taxes, or other fees are paid.

Brand A name, term, symbol, design, or combination of these that identifies a seller's products and differentiates them from competitors' products.

Brand-extension branding Type of branding in which a firm uses one of its existing brand names as part of a brand for an improved or new product that is usually in the same product category as the existing brand.

Brand manager A type of product manager responsible for a single brand.

Brand mark The element of a brand, such as a symbol or design, that cannot be spoken.

Brand name The part of a brand that can be spoken— including letters, words, and numbers.

Breakdown approach A general approach for measuring company sales potential based on a general economic forecast—or other aggregate data—and the market sales potential derived from it; company sales potential is based on the general economic forecast and the estimated market sales potential.

Breakeven point The point at which the costs of producing a product equal the revenue made from selling the product.

Broker A functional middleman who performs fewer functions than other intermediaries; the primary function is to bring buyers and sellers together for a fee.

Buildup approach A general approach to measuring company sales potential in which the analyst initially estimates how much the average purchaser of a product will buy in a specified time period and then multiplies that amount by the number of potential buyers; estimates are generally calculated by individual geographic areas.

Business analysis Provides a tentative sketch of a product's compatibility in the marketplace, including its probable profitability.

Buy-back allowance A certain sum of money given to a purchaser for each unit bought after an initial deal is over.

Buying allowance A temporary price reduction to resellers for purchasing specified quantities of a product.

Buying behavior The decision processes and acts of people involved in buying and using products.

Buying center The group of people within an organization who are involved in making organizational purchase decisions; these people occupy roles in the purchase decision process, such as users, influencers, buyers, deciders, and gatekeepers.

Buying power Resources such as money, goods, and services that can be traded in an exchange situation.

Buying power index A weighted index consisting of population, effective buying income, and retail sales data. The higher the index number, the greater the buying power.

C

Captioned photograph A photograph with a brief description that explains the picture's content.

Cash-and-carry wholesaler Limited service wholesaler that sells to customers who will pay cash and furnish transportation or pay extra to have products delivered.

Cash discount A price reduction to the buyer for prompt payment or cash payment.

Catalog retailing A type of mail-order retailing in which selling may be handled by telephone or in-store visits and products are delivered by mail or picked up by the customers.

Catalog showrooms A form of warehouse showroom in which consumers shop from a mailed catalog and buy at a warehouse where all products are stored out of buyers' reach. Products are provided in the manufacturer's carton.

Causal study Research planned to prove or disprove that x causes y or that x does not cause y.

Centralized organization An organization in which the

top-level managers delegate very little authority to lower levels of the organization.

Cents-off offer A sales promotion device for established products whereby buyers receive a certain amount off the regular price shown on the label or package.

Channel capacity The limit to the volume of information that a communication channel can handle effectively.

Channel conflict Friction between marketing channel members, often resulting from role deviance or malfunction; absence of an expected mode of conduct that contributes to the channel as a system.

Channel cooperation A helping relationship among channel members that enhances the welfare and survival of all necessary channel members.

Channel of distribution *See* marketing channel.

Channel leadership Guidance a channel member with one or more sources of power gives to other channel members to help achieve channel objectives.

Channel power The ability of one channel member to influence another channel member's goal achievement.

Clayton Act Passed in 1914, this act prohibits specific practices, such as price discrimination, exclusive dealer arrangements, and stock acquisitions, whose effect may substantially lessen competition to tend to create a monopoly.

Client public The direct consumers of the product of a nonbusiness organization; for example, the client public of a university is its student body.

Closing The element in the selling process in which the salesperson asks the prospect to buy the product.

Code of ethics Formalized statement of what a company expects of its employees regarding ethical behavior.

Coding process The process by which a meaning is placed into a series of signs that represent ideas; also called encoding.

Cognitive dissonance Dissatisfaction that may occur shortly after the purchase of a product, when the buyer questions whether he or she should have purchased the product at all or would have been better off purchasing another brand that was evaluated very favorably.

Combination compensation plan A plan by which salespeople are paid a fixed salary and a commission based on sales volume.

Commercialization A phase of new-product development in which plans for full-scale manufacturing and marketing must be refined and settled and budgets for the project must be prepared.

Commission merchant Agent often used in agricultural marketing who usually exercises physical control over products, negotiates sales, and is given broad powers regarding prices and terms of sale.

Communication A sharing of meaning through the transmission of information.

Community shopping center Shopping center that includes one or two department stores and some specialty stores, as well as convenience stores; serves several neighborhoods and draws consumers who are not able to find desired products in neighborhood shopping centers.

Company sales forecast The amount of a product that a firm actually expects to sell during a specific period at a specified level of company marketing activities.

Company sales potential The amount of a product that an organization could sell during a specified period.

Comparative advertising Advertising that compares two or more identified brands in the same general product class; the comparison is made in terms of one or more specific product characteristics.

Competition Generally viewed by a business as those firms that market products similar to, or substitutable for, its products in the same target market.

Competition-matching approach A method of ascertaining the advertising appropriation in which an advertiser tries to match a major competitor's appropriations in terms of absolute dollars or in terms of using the same percentage of sales for advertising.

Competition-oriented pricing A pricing method in which an organization considers costs and revenue secondary to competitors' prices.

Competitive advertising Advertising that points out a brand's uses, features, and advantages that benefit consumers and that may not be available in competing brands.

Competitive structure The model used to describe the number of firms that control the supply of a product and how it affects the strength of competition; factors include number of competitors, ease of entry into the market, the nature of the product, and knowledge of the market.

Component part A finished item ready for assembly or a product that needs little processing before assembly and that becomes a part of the physical product.

Comprehensive spending patterns The percentages of family income allotted to annual expenditures for general classes of goods and services.

Concentration strategy A market segmentation strategy in which an organization directs its marketing efforts toward a single market segment through one marketing mix.

Conflict of interest Results from marketers taking advantage of situations for their own selfish interests rather than for the long-run interest of the business.

Consumable supplies Items that facilitate an organization's production and operations, but they do not become part of the finished product.

Consumer buying behavior The buying behavior of ultimate consumers—those persons who purchase products for personal or household use and not for business purposes.

Consumer buying decision process The five-stage decision process consumers use in making purchases.

Consumer contest A sales promotion device for established products based on the analytical or creative skill of contestants.

Consumer Goods Pricing Act Federal legislation that prohibits the use of price maintenance agreements among producers and resellers involved in interstate commerce.

Consumer jury A panel used to pretest advertisements; it consists of a number of persons who are actual or potential buyers of the product to be advertised.

Consumer market Purchasers and/or individuals in their households who intend to consume or benefit from the purchased products and who do not buy products for the main purpose of making a profit.

Consumer movement A social movement through which people attempt to defend and exercise their rights as buyers.

Consumer movement forces Focus on three different areas: product safety, disclosure of information, and protection of our environment. The major forces in the consumer movement are consumer organizations, consumer laws, consumer education, and independent consumer advocates.

Consumer product Product purchased for ultimate satisfaction of personal and family needs.

Consumer Product Safety Commission A federal agency created to protect consumers by setting product standards, testing products, investigating product complaints, banning products, and monitoring injuries through the National Electronic Surveillance System.

Consumer protection legislation Laws enacted to protect consumers' safety, to enhance the amount of information available, and to warn of deceptive marketing techniques.

Consumer sales promotion method Sales promotion method that encourages or stimulates customers to patronize a specific retail store or to try and/or purchase a particular product.

Consumer spending patterns Information indicating the relative proportions of annual family expenditures or the actual amount of money that is spent on certain types of goods or services.

Consumer sweepstakes A sales promotion device for established products in which entrants submit their names for inclusion in a drawing for prizes.

Containerization The practice of consolidating many items into one container that is sealed at the point of origin and opened at the destination.

Convenience products Relatively inexpensive, frequently purchased items for which buyers want to exert only minimal effort.

Cooperative advertising An arrangement in which a manufacturer agrees to pay a certain amount of a retailer's media costs for advertising the manufacturer's products.

Copy The verbal portion of advertisements; includes headlines, subheadlines, body copy, and signature.

Corporate strategy The strategy that determines the means for utilizing resources in the areas of production, finance, research and development, personnel, and marketing to reach the organization's goals.

Correlation methods Methods used to develop sales forecasts as the forecasters attempt to find a relationship between past sales and one or more variables, such as population, per capita income, or gross national product.

Cost comparison indicator Allows an advertiser to compare the costs of several vehicles within a specific medium relative to the number of persons reached by each vehicle.

Cost-oriented pricing A pricing policy in which a firm determines price by adding a dollar amount or percentage to the cost of a product.

Cost-plus pricing A form of cost-oriented pricing in which first the seller's costs are determined and then a specified dollar amount or percentage of the cost is added to the seller's cost to set the price.

Count and recount A sales promotion method based on the payment of a specific amount of money for each product unit moved from a reseller's warehouse in a given period of time.

Coupon A new-product sales promotion technique used to stimulate trial of a new or improved product, to increase sales volume quickly, to attract repeat purchasers, or to introduce new package sizes or features.

Credence qualities Qualities of services that cannot be assessed even after purchase and consumption; for example, few consumers are knowledgeable enough to assess the quality of an appendix operation, even after it has been performed.

Culture Everything in our surroundings that is made by human beings, consisting of tangible items as well as intangible concepts and values.

Cumulative discount Quantity discount that is aggregated over a stated period of time.

Customary pricing A type of psychological pricing in which certain goods are priced primarily on the basis of tradition.

Customer forecasting survey The technique of asking customers what types and quantities of products they intend to buy during a specific period so as to predict the sales level for that period.

Customer orientation A marketer attempts to provide a

marketing mix that satisfies the needs of buyers in the target market.

Cycle analysis A method of predicting sales whereby a forecaster analyzes sales figures for a period of three to five years to ascertain whether sales fluctuate in a consistent, periodic manner.

D

Dealer listing An advertisement that promotes a product and identifies the names of participating retailers that sell the product.

Dealer loader A gift, often part of a display, that is given to a retailer for the purchase of a specified quantity of merchandise.

Decentralized organization An organization in which decision making authority is delegated as far down the chain of command as possible.

Decline stage The stage in a product's life cycle in which sales fall rapidly and profits decrease.

Decoding process The stage in the communication process in which signs are converted into concepts and ideas.

Defensive advertising Advertising used to offset or lessen the effects of a competitor's promotional program.

Demand curve A line showing the relationship between price and quantity demanded.

Demand-oriented pricing A pricing policy based on the level of demand for the product—resulting in a higher price when demand for the product is strong and a lower price when demand is weak.

Demand schedule The relationship, usually inverse, between price and quantity demanded; classically, a line sloping downward to the right, showing that as price falls, quantity demanded will increase.

Demographic factors Personal characteristics such as age, sex, race, nationality, income, family, life cycle stage, and occupation; also called socioeconomic factors.

Demonstration A sales promotion method manufacturers use temporarily to encourage trial use and purchase of the product or to actually show how the product works.

Department store A type of retail store having a wide product mix; organized into separate departments to facilitate marketing efforts and international management.

Dependent variable A variable contingent on, or restricted to, one or a set of values assumed by the independent variable.

Depression A stage of the business cycle during which there is extremely high unemployment, wages are very

low, total disposable income is at a minimum, and consumers lack confidence in the economy.

Depth (of product mix) The average number of different products offered to buyers in a firm's product line.

Depth interview Personal interview with an open, informal atmosphere; this interview may take several hours. It is used to study motives.

Derived demand A characteristic of industrial demand that arises because industrial demand derives from the consumer demand.

Descriptive studies Type of study undertaken when marketers see that knowledge of the characteristics of certain phenomena is needed to solve a problem; may require statistical analysis and predictive tools.

Direct-cost approach An approach to determining marketing costs in which cost analysis includes direct costs and traceable common costs but does not include nontraceable common costs.

Direct costs Costs directly attributable to the performance of marketing functions.

Direct distribution channels Distribution channels in which products are sold directly from producer to users.

Direct marketing The use of nonpersonal media to introduce products by mail or telephone.

Direct ownership A long-run commitment to marketing in a foreign nation in which a subsidiary or division is owned by a foreign country through purchase.

Discount store Self-service, general merchandise store positioned as having low prices.

Discretionary income Disposable income that is available for spending and saving after an individual has purchased the basic necessities of food, clothing, and shelter.

Disposable income After-tax income.

Distribution center A large, centralized warehouse that receives goods from factories and suppliers, regroups the goods into orders, and ships the orders to customers quickly, with the focus on active movement of goods rather than passive storage.

Distribution variable The marketing mix variable in which marketing management attempts to make products available in the quantities desired with adequate service to a target market and to hold the total inventory, transportation, communication, storage, and materials handling costs as low as possible.

Diversified growth A type of growth that occurs in three forms, depending on the technology of the new products and the nature of the new markets the firm enters; the three forms are horizontal, concentric, and conglomerate.

Drop shipper A limited service wholesaler that takes title to products and negotiates sales but never physically handles products.

Dual distribution A channel practice whereby a producer distributes the same product through two or more different channels.

Dumping The sale of products in foreign markets at lower prices than those charged in the domestic market (when all costs are not allocated or when surplus products are sold).

E

Early adopters Individuals who choose new products carefully and are viewed by persons in the early majority, late majority, and laggard categories as being "the people to check with."

Early majority Individuals who adopt a new product just prior to the average person; they are deliberate and cautious in trying new products.

Economic forces Forces that determine the strength of a firm's competitive atmosphere and affect the impact of marketing activities because they determine the size and strength of demand for products.

Economic institutions An environmental force in international markets made up of producers, wholesalers, retailers, buyers, and other organizations that produce, distribute, and purchase products.

Economic order quantity (EOQ) The order size that minimizes the total cost of ordering and carrying inventory.

Effective buying income Similar to disposable income; it includes salaries, wages, dividends, interest, profits, and rents less federal, state, and local taxes.

Elasticity of demand The relative responsiveness of changes in quantity demanded to changes in price.

Encoding *See* Coding process.

Environmental analysis Process of assessing and interpreting the information gathered through scanning.

Environmental monitoring The process of seeking information about events and relationships in a company's environment to assist marketers in identifying opportunities and in planning.

Environmental scanning The collecting of information regarding the forces in the marketing environment.

Equalized workload method A method of determining sales-force size in which the number of customers multiplied by the number of sales calls annually required to serve these customers effectively is divided by the average number of calls each salesperson makes annually.

Ethical pricing A form of professional pricing in which the demand for the product is inelastic and the seller is a professional who has a responsibility not to overcharge the client.

Exchange Participation by two or more individuals, groups, or organizations, with each party possessing something of value that the other party desires. Each must be willing to give up its "something of value" to get "something of value" held by the other, and all parties must be willing to communicate with each other.

Exclusive dealing A manufacturer forbids an intermediary to carry products of competing manufacturers.

Exclusive distribution A type of market coverage in which only one outlet is used in a geographic area.

Executive judgment A sales forecasting method based on the intuition of one or more executives.

Experience curve pricing A pricing approach in which a company fixes a low price that high-cost competitors cannot match and thus expands its market share; this approach is possible when a firm gains cumulative production experience and is able to reduce its manufacturing costs to a predictable rate through improved methods, materials, skills, and machinery.

Experience qualities Qualities of services that can be assessed only after purchase and consumption (taste, satisfaction, courtesy, and the like).

Experimentation Research in which those factors that are related to or may affect the variables under investigation are maintained as constants so that the effects of the experimental variables may be measured.

Expert forecasting survey Preparation of the sales forecast by experts, such as economists, management consultants, advertising executives, college professors, or other persons outside the firm.

Exploratory studies Type of research conducted when more information is needed about a problem and the tentative hypothesis needs to be made more specific; it permits marketers to conduct ministudies with a very restricted database.

Extensive decision making Considerable time and effort a buyer spends seeking alternative products, searching for information about them, and then evaluating them to determine which one will be most satisfying.

F

Facilitating agency Organization that performs activities that assist in performing channel functions but does not buy, sell, or transfer title to the product; can include transportation companies, insurance companies, advertising agencies, marketing research agencies, and financial institutions.

Family packaging A policy in an organization that all

packages are to be similar or are to include one major element of the design.

Feature article A form of publicity that is up to three thousand words long and usually is prepared for a specific publication.

Federal Trade Commission Made up of five commissioners with the goal of preventing the free enterprise system from being stifled or fettered by monopoly or anticompetitive practices and providing the direct protection of consumers from unfair or deceptive trade practices.

Federal Trade Commission Act (1914) Established the Federal Trade Commission and currently regulates the greatest number of marketing practices.

Feedback The receiver's response to the decoded message.

Field public warehouse A warehouse established by a public warehouse at the owner's inventory location; the warehouser becomes the custodian of the products and issues a receipt that can be used as collateral for a loan.

Fixed cost Cost that does not vary with changes in the number of units produced or sold.

F.O.B. (free-on-board) factory Part of price quotation; used to indicate who must pay shipping charges. For example, F.O.B. factory indicates the price of the merchandise at the factory, before it is loaded onto the carrier vehicle. Thus the buyer must pay for shipping.

Food broker Intermediary that sells food and other grocery products to retailer-owned and merchant wholesalers, grocery chains, industrial buyers, and food processors. Both buyers and sellers use food brokers to cope with fluctuating market conditions.

Franchising An arrangement in which a supplier (franchisor) grants a dealer (franchisee) the right to sell products in exchange for some type of consideration.

Free merchandise A sales promotion method aimed at retailers whereby free merchandise is offered to resellers that purchase a stated quantity of product.

Free samples A new-product sales promotion technique marketers use to stimulate trial of a product, to increase sales volume in early stages of the product's life cycle, or to obtain desirable distribution.

Freight absorption pricing Pricing for a particular customer or geographical area whereby the seller absorbs all or part of the actual freight costs.

Freight forwarders Businesses that consolidate shipments from several organizations into efficient lot sizes, which increases transit time and sometimes lowers shipping costs.

Full-cost approach An approach to determining marketing costs in which cost analysis includes direct costs, traceable common costs, and nontraceable common costs.

Full-service wholesaler A marketing intermediary that provides most services that can be performed by wholesalers.

Functional discount *See* Trade discount.

Functional middleman Marketing intermediary that does not take title to products but usually receives a fee for expediting exchanges.

Functional modifications Changes that affect a product's versatility, effectiveness, convenience, or safety, usually requiring the redesigning of one or more parts of the product.

Functional wholesaler A marketing intermediary that expedites exchanges among producers and resellers and is compensated by fees or commissions.

G

General merchandise wholesaler Full-service merchant wholesaler that carries a very wide product mix.

General public The indirect consumers of the product of a nonbusiness organization; for instance, the general public of a university includes alumni, trustees, parents of students, and other groups.

Generic brand A brand that indicates only the product category (such as *aluminum foil*), not the company name and other identifying terms.

Geographic pricing A form of pricing that involves reductions for transportation costs or other costs associated with the physical distance between the buyer and the seller.

Globalization of markets The development of marketing strategies as if the entire world (or regions of it) were a single entity; products are marketed the same way everywhere.

Good A physical concrete; something you can touch; a tangible item.

Government markets Markets made up of federal, state, county, and local governments, spending billions of dollars annually for goods and services to support their internal operations and to provide such products as defense, energy, and education.

Gross National Product (GNP) An overall measure of a nation's economic standing in terms of the value of all products produced by that nation for a given period of time.

Group interview A method to uncover people's motives relating to some issue, such as product usage, with an interviewer generating discussion on one or several topics among the six to twelve people in the group.

Growth state The product life cycle stage in which sales rise rapidly; profits reach a peak and then start to decline.

H

Heterogeneity Because people typically perform services, there may be variation from one service provider to another or variation in the service provided by a single individual from day to day and from customer to customer.

Heterogeneous market A market made up of individuals with diverse product needs for products in a specific product class.

Horizontal channel integration The combining of institutions at the same level of operation under one management.

Hypothesis A guess or assumption about a certain problem or set of circumstances; reasonable supposition that may be right or wrong.

I

Idea A concept, philosophy, image, or issue.

Idea generation The search by businesses and other organizations for product ideas that help them achieve their objectives.

Illustrations Photographs, drawings, graphs, charts, and tables, used to encourage an audience to read or watch an advertisement.

Implicit bargaining A method of employee motivation that recognizes the various needs of different employees and is based on the theory that there is no one best way to motivate individuals.

Income The amount of money received through wages, rents, investments, pensions, and subsidy payments for a given period.

Incremental productivity method A plan by which a marketer should continue to increase the sales force as long as the additional sales increases are greater than the additional selling costs that arise from employing more salespeople.

Independent variable Variable free from influence of, or not dependent on, other variables.

Individual branding A branding policy in which each product is named differently.

Industrial buying behavior *See* Organizational buying behavior.

Industrial distributor Independent business organization that takes title to industrial products and carries inventories.

Industrial market A market consisting of individuals, groups, or organizations that purchase specific kinds of products for resale, for direct use in producing other products, or for use in day-to-day operations; also called organizational market.

Industrial marketing A set of activities directed toward facilitating and expediting exchanges involving industrial markets and industrial products.

Industrial product A product purchased to be used directly or indirectly to produce other products or to be used in the operations of an organization.

Industrial service Intangible product that an organization uses in its operations, such as financial products and legal services.

Inelastic demand A type of demand in which a price increase or decrease will not significantly affect the quantity demanded.

Inflation A condition in which price levels increase faster than incomes, causing a decline in buying power.

Information inputs The sensations that we receive through our sense organs.

In-home retailing A type of nonstore retailing that involves personal selling in consumers' homes.

Innovators The first consumers to adopt a new product; they enjoy trying new products and tend to be venturesome, rash, and daring.

Input-output data A type of information, sometimes used in conjunction with the SIC system, that is based on the assumption that the output or sales of one industry are the input or purchases of other industries.

Inseparability Because services normally are produced at the same time that they are consumed, the consumer frequently is directly involved in the production process.

Institutional advertising A form of advertising promoting organizational images, ideas, and political issues.

Institutional market A market that consists of organizations that seek to achieve goals other than such normal business goals as profit, market share, or return on investment.

Intangibility Because services are performances, they cannot be seen, touched, tasted, or smelled, nor can they be possessed.

Integrated growth The type of growth that a firm can have within its industry; three possible growth directions include forward, backward, and horizontal.

Intense growth The type of growth that can occur when current products and current markets have the potential for increasing sales.

Intensive distribution A form of market coverage in

which all available outlets are used for distributing a product.

Intermodal transportation Combining and coordinating two or more modes of transportation.

International marketing Marketing activities performed across national boundaries.

Introduction stage The stage in a product's life cycle beginning at a product's first appearance in the marketplace, when sales are zero and profits are negative.

J

Job enrichment A method of employee motivation that gives employees a sense of autonomy and control over their work, with employees being encouraged to set their own goals.

Joint demand A characteristic of industrial demand that occurs when two or more items are used in combination to produce a product.

Joint venture A partnership between a domestic firm and foreign firms and/or governments.

K

Kinesic communication Commonly known as body language, this type of interpersonal communication occurs in face-to-face selling situations when the salesperson and customers move their heads, eyes, arms, hands, legs, and torsos.

L

Labeling An important dimension of packaging for promotional, informational, and legal reasons; regulated by numerous federal and state laws.

Laggards The last consumers to adopt a new product; they are oriented toward the past and suspicious of new products.

Late majority People who are quite skeptical of new products; they eventually adopt new products because of economic necessity or social pressure.

Layout The physical arrangement of the illustration, headline, subheadline, body copy, and signature of an advertisement.

Learning A change in an individual's behavior that arises from prior behavior in similar situations.

Legal forces Forces that arise from the legislation and interpretation of laws; these laws, enacted by government units, restrain and control marketing decisions and activities.

Licensing (international) An arrangement in international marketing in which the licensee pays commissions or royalties on sales or supplies used in manufacturing.

Limited decision making The type of consumer decision making used for products that are purchased occasionally and when a buyer needs to acquire information about an unfamiliar brand in a familiar product category.

Limited-line wholesaler Full-service merchant wholesaler that carries only a few product lines.

Limited service wholesaler A marketing intermediary that provides only some marketing services and specializes in a few functions.

Line family branding A branding policy in which an organization uses family branding only for products within a line, not for all its products.

Long-range plan A plan that covers more than five years.

M

Mail-order retailing A type of nonpersonal, nonstore retailing that uses direct mail advertising and catalogs and is typified by selling by description. The buyer usually does not see the actual product until it is delivered.

Mail-order wholesaler Organization that sells through direct mail by sending catalogs to retail, industrial, and institutional customers.

Mail surveys Questionnaires sent to respondents, who are encouraged to complete and return them.

Major equipment A category of industrial products that includes large tools and machines used for production purposes.

Manufacturer brand Brand initiated by a producer; makes it possible for a producer to be identified with its product at the point of purchase.

Manufacturers' agent An independent business person who sells complementary products of several producers in assigned territories and is compensated through commissions.

Marginal cost The cost associated with producing one more unit of a product.

Marginal revenue (MR) The change in total revenue that occurs after an additional unit of a product is sold.

Market An aggregate of people who, as individuals or as organizations, have needs for products in a product class and who have the ability, willingness, and authority to purchase such products.

Market attractiveness/business position model A two-dimensional matrix designed to serve as a diagnostic tool to highlight SBUs that have an opportunity to grow or that should be divested.

Market density The number of potential customers within a unit of land area, such as a square mile.

Marketing Individual and organizational activities that facilitate and expedite satisfying exchange relationships in a dynamic environment through the creation, distribution, promotion, and pricing of goods, services, and ideas.

Marketing audit A systematic examination of the objectives, strategies, organization, and performance of a firm's marketing unit.

Marketing audit report A written summary produced after the marketing audit has been conducted; it includes recommendations that will increase marketing productivity and develops a recommendation as to the business' general direction.

Marketing channel A group of interrelated intermediaries who direct products to customers; also called channel of distribution.

Marketing concept Managerial philosophy that an organization should try to satisfy customers' needs through a coordinated set of activities that at the same time allows the organization to achieve its goals.

Marketing control process Process that consists of establishing performance standards, evaluating actual performance by comparing it with established standards, and reducing the differences between desired and actual performance.

Marketing cost analysis A method for helping to control marketing strategies whereby various costs are broken down and classified to determine which costs are associated with specific marketing activities.

Marketing databank A file of data collected through both the marketing information system and marketing research projects.

Marketing environment Environment that surrounds both the buyer and marketing mix; consists of political, legal, regulatory, societal, consumer movement, economic, and technological forces. Environmental variables affect a marketer's ability to facilitate and expedite exchanges.

Marketing ethics Relates to a moral evaluation of decisions based on accepted principles of behavior that result in an action being judged right or wrong.

Marketing experimentation A set of rules and procedures under which the task of data gathering is organized to expedite analysis and interpretation.

Marketing function account Classification of costs that indicates which function was performed through the expenditure of funds.

Marketing information system (MIS) System that establishes a framework for the day-to-day managing and structuring of information gathered regularly from sources both inside and outside an organization.

Marketing intelligence Includes all data gathered as a basis for marketing decisions.

Marketing intermediary A member of a marketing channel, primarily merchants and agents, acting to direct products to buyers.

Marketing management A process of planning, organizing, implementing, and controlling marketing activities to facilitate and expedite exchanges effectively and efficiently.

Marketing mix Consists of four major variables: product, price, distribution, and promotion.

Marketing objective A statement of what is to be accomplished through marketing activities.

Marketing-oriented organization An organization that attempts to determine what target market members want and then tries to produce it.

Marketing plan The written document or blueprint for implementing and controlling an organization's marketing activities related to a particular marketing strategy.

Marketing planning A systematic process that involves assessing marketing opportunities and resources, determining market objectives, and developing a plan for implementation and control.

Marketing program A set of marketing strategies that are implemented and used at the same time.

Marketing research The part of marketing intelligence that involves specific inquiries into problems and marketing activities to discover new information so as to guide marketing decisions.

Marketing strategy A plan for selecting and analyzing a target market and creating and maintaining a marketing mix.

Market manager A person responsible for the marketing activities that are necessary to serve a particular group or class of customers.

Market opportunity An opportunity that arises when the right combination of circumstances occurs at the right time to allow an organization to take action toward generating sales from a target market.

Market planning cycle The five-step cycle that involves developing or revising marketing objectives relative to performance, assessing marketing opportunities and resources, formulating marketing strategy, developing the plan for implementation and control, and implementing the marketing plan.

Market requirement Related to customers' needs or desired benefits, the market requirement is satisfied by components of the marketing mix that provide benefits to buyers.

Market sales potential The amount of a product that

specific customer groups would purchase within a specified period at a specific level of industrywide marketing activity.

Market segment A group of individuals, groups, or organizations that share one or more similar characteristics that make them have relatively similar product needs.

Market segmentation The process of dividing a total market into groups of people with relatively similar product needs, for the purpose of designing a marketing mix (or mixes) that more precisely matches the needs of individuals in a selected segment (or segments).

Market share A firm's sales in relation to total industry sales, expressed as a decimal or percentage.

Market test Stage of new-product development that involves making a product available to buyers in one or more test areas and measuring purchases and consumer responses to promotion, price, and distribution efforts.

Markup A percentage of the cost or price of a product added to the cost.

Markup pricing Pricing method whereby the price is derived by adding a predetermined percentage of the cost to the cost of the product.

Mass merchandiser A retail operation that tends to offer fewer customer services than department stores and to focus its attention on lower prices, high turnover, and large sales volume; includes supermarkets and discount houses.

Materials handling Physical handling of products.

Maturity stage A stage in the product life cycle in which the sales curve peaks and starts to decline as profits continue to decline.

Mechanical observation devices Cameras, recorders, counting machines, and equipment to record movement, behavior, or physiological changes in individuals.

Media plan Plan that sets forth the exact media vehicles to be used for advertisements and the dates and times that the advertisements are to appear.

Medium of transmission That which carries the coded message from the source to the receiver or audience; examples include ink on paper or vibrations of air waves produced by vocal cords.

Medium-range plans Plans that usually encompass two to five years.

Megacarrier A freight transportation company that provides many methods of shipment, such as rail, truck, and air service.

Merchandise allowance A sales promotion method aimed at retailers; it consists of a manufacturer's agreement to pay resellers certain amounts of money for providing special promotional efforts, such as setting up and maintaining a display.

Merchant A marketing intermediary who takes title to merchandise and resells it for a profit.

Merchant wholesaler A marketing intermediary who takes title to products, assumes risk, and generally is involved in buying and reselling products.

Missionary salesperson Support salesperson, usually employed by a manufacturer, who assists the producer's customers in selling to their own customers.

Modified-rebuy purchase A type of industrial purchase in which a new-task purchase is changed the second or third time, or the requirements associated with a straight-rebuy purchase are modified.

Money refund A new-product sales promotion technique in which the producer mails a consumer a specific amount of money when proof of purchase is established.

Monopolistic competition A market structure in which a firm has many potential competitors; to compete, the firm tries to develop a differential marketing strategy to establish its own market share.

Monopoly Market structure existing when a firm produces a product that has no close substitutes and/or when a single seller may erect barriers to potential competitors.

Motive An internal energizing force that directs a person's behavior toward his or her goals.

MRO items An alternative term for supplies: supplies can be divided into Maintenance, Repair, and Operating (or overhaul) items.

Multinational enterprise A firm that has operations or subsidiaries in several countries.

Multisegment strategy A market segmentation strategy in which an organization directs its marketing efforts at two or more segments by developing a marketing mix for each selected segment.

Multivariable segmentation Market division achieved by using more than one characteristic to divide the total market; this approach provides more information about the individuals in each segment than does single-variable segmentation.

N

National Advertising Review Board A self-regulatory unit created by the Council of Better Business Bureaus and three advertising trade organizations; screens national advertisements to check for honesty and processes complaints about deceptive advertisements.

Natural account Classification of costs based on what the money is actually spent for; typically a part of a regular accounting system.

Negotiated pricing A determination of price through bargaining even when there are stated list prices and discount structures.

Negotiation Mutual discussion or communication of the terms and methods of an exchange.

Neighborhood shopping center Shopping center that usually consists of several small convenience and specialty stores and serves consumers who live less than ten minutes' driving time from the center.

New product Any product that a given firm has not marketed previously.

New-product development A process consisting of six phases: idea generation, screening, business analysis, product development, test-marketing, and commercialization.

News release A form of publicity that is usually a single page of typewritten copy containing fewer than three hundred words.

New-task purchase A type of industrial purchase in which an organization is making an initial purchase of an item to be used to perform a new job or to solve a new problem.

Noise A condition in the communication process existing when the decoded message is different from what was coded.

Nonbusiness marketing Marketing activities conducted by individuals and organizations to achieve some goal other than ordinary business goals such as profit, market share, or return on investment.

Noncumulative discount One-time price reduction based on the number of units purchased, the size of the order, or the product combination purchased.

Nonprice competititon A policy in which a seller elects not to focus on price and instead emphasizes distinctive product features, service, product quality, promotion, packaging, or other factors to distinguish its product from competing brands.

Nonprofit organization marketing Involves the application of marketing concepts and techniques to such nonprofit groups as hospitals and colleges.

Nonstore retailing Consumers purchase products without visiting a store.

Nontraceable common costs Costs that cannot be assigned to any specific function according to any logical criteria and thus are assignable only on an arbitrary basis.

O

Objective and task approach One approach to determining the advertising appropriation: Marketers first determine the objectives that a campaign is to achieve, then ascertain the tasks required to accomplish those objectives; the costs of all tasks are added to ascertain the total appropriation.

Observation method Researchers record the overt behavior of subjects, noting physical conditions and events. Direct contact with subjects is avoided; instead, their actions are examined and noted systematically.

Odd-even pricing A type of psychological pricing that assumes that more of a product will be sold at $99.99 than at $100.00, indicating that an odd price is more appealing than an even price to customers.

Off-price retailer A store that buys manufacturers' seconds, overruns, returns, and off-season merchandise for resale to consumers at deep discounts.

Oligopoly Competitive structure existing when a few sellers control the supply of a large proportion of a product; each seller must consider the actions of other sellers to changes in marketing activities.

Open bids Prices submitted by several, but not all, sellers; the amounts of these bids are not made public.

Opportunity cost The value of the benefit that is given up by selecting one alternative rather than another.

Order getter A type of salesperson who increases the firm's sales by selling to new customers and by increasing sales to present customers.

Order processing The receipt and transmission of sales order information in the physical distribution process.

Order taker A type of salesperson who primarily seeks repeat sales.

Organizational buying behavior The purchase behavior of producers, government units, institutions, and resellers; also called industrial buying behvior.

Organizational market Individuals or groups who purchase a specific kind of product for one of three purposes: resale, direct use in producing other products, or use in general daily operations; also called industrial market.

Overall family branding A policy whereby all of a firm's products are branded with the same name or at least a part of the name.

P

Patronage motives Motives that influence where a person purchases products on a regular basis.

Penetration price A lower price designed to penetrate the market and thus quickly produce a larger unit sales volume.

Percent of sales approach A method for establishing the advertising appropriation whereby marketers simply multiply a firm's past sales, forecasted sales, or a combination of the two by a standard percentage based on both what the firm traditionally has spent on advertising and what the industry averages.

Perception The process by which an individual selects, organizes, and interprets information inputs to create a meaningful picture of the world.

Perfect competition Ideal competitive structure that would entail a large number of sellers, no one of which could significantly influence price or supply.

Performance standard An expected level of performance against which actual performance can be compared.

Perishability Because of simultaneous production and consumption, unused capacity to produce services in one time period cannot be stockpiled or inventoried for future time periods.

Personal interview survey Face-to-face interview that allows more in-depth interviewing, probing, follow-up questions, or psychological tests.

Personality An internal structure in which experience and behavior are related in an orderly way.

Personal selling A process of informing customers and persuading them to purchase products through personal communication in an exchange situation.

Person-specific factors Factors influencing the consumer buying decision process that are unique to particular individuals.

Persuasion Convincing or prevailing upon an individual or organization to bring about an exchange.

Physical distribution An integrated set of activities that deal with managing the movement of products within firms and through marketing channels.

PIMS (Profit Impact on Marketing Strategy) A Strategic Planning Institute (SPI) research program that provides reports on the products of SPI member firms; these reports assist the member firms in analyzing marketing performance and formulating marketing strategies.

Pioneer advertising A type of advertising that informs persons about what a product is, what it does, how it can be used, and where it can be purchased.

Point-of-purchase materials A sales promotion method that uses such items as outside signs, window displays, and display racks to attract attention, to inform customers, and to encourage retailers to carry particular products.

Political and legal institutions Public agencies, laws, courts, legislatures, and government bureaus.

Political forces Forces that strongly influence the economic and political stability of our country not only through decisions that affect domestic matters but through their authority to negotiate trade agreements and to determine foreign policy.

Population All elements, units, or individuals that are of interest to researchers for a specific study.

Posttest Evaluation of advertising effectiveness after the campaign.

Premiums Items that are offered free or at a minimum cost as a bonus for purchasing.

Press conference A meeting used to announce major news events.

Prestige pricing Setting prices at a high level to facilitate a prestige or quality image.

Pretest Evaluation of an advertisement before it actually is used.

Price The value placed on what is exchanged.

Price competition A policy whereby a marketer emphasizes price as an issue and matches or beats the prices of competitors also emphasizing low prices.

Price differentiation A demand-oriented pricing method whereby a firm uses more than one price in the marketing of a specific product; differentiation of prices can be based on several dimensions, such as type of customers, type of distribution used, or the time of the purchase.

Price discrimination A policy whereby some buyers are charged lower prices than other buyers, which gives those paying less a competitive advantage.

Price elasticity The percentage change in quantity demanded divided by the percentage change in price.

Price leaders Products sold at less than cost to increase sales of regular merchandise.

Price lining A form of psychological pricing in which an organization sets a limited number of prices for selected lines of products.

Price skimming A pricing policy whereby an organization charges the highest possible price that buyers who most desire the product will pay.

Price variable A critical marketing mix variable in which marketing management is concerned with establishing a value for what is exchanged.

Pricing method A mechanical procedure for setting prices on a regular basis.

Pricing objectives Overall goals that describe the role of price in an organization's long-range plans.

Pricing policy A guiding philosophy or course of action designed to influence and determine pricing decisions.

Primary data Information observed and recorded or collected directly from subjects.

Private brand *See* Private distributor brand.

Private distributor brand A brand that is initiated and owned by a reseller; also called private brand.

Private warehouse A storage facility operated by a company for the purpose of distributing its own products.

Problem definition The first step in the research process toward finding a solution or launching a research study; the researcher thinks about how best to discover the nature and boundaries of a problem or opportunity.

Process materials Materials used directly in the production of other products; unlike component parts, they are not readily identifiable.

Procompetitive legislation Laws enacted to preserve competition.

Producer market Market that consists of individuals and business organizations that purchase products for the purpose of making a profit by using them to produce other products or by using them in their operations.

Product Everything (both favorable and unfavorable) that one receives in an exchange; it is a complexity of tangible and intangible attributes, including functional, social, and psychological utilities or benefits. A product may be a good, service, or idea.

Product adoption process The five-stage process of buyer acceptance of a product: awareness, interest, evaluation, trial, and adoption.

Product advertising Advertising that promotes goods and services.

Product assortment A collection of a variety of products.

Product deletion Elimination of some products that no longer satisfy target market customers and contribute to achievement of an organization's overall goals.

Product development A stage in creating new products that moves the product from concept to test phase and also involves the development of the other elements of the marketing mix (promotion, distribution, and price).

Product differentiation Use of promotional efforts to differentiate a company's products from its competitors' products, with the hope of establishing the superiority and preferability of its products relative to competing brands.

Production orientation The viewpoint that increasing the efficiency of production is the primary means of increasing an organization's profits.

Production-oriented organization A firm that concentrates on either improving production efficiency or producing high-quality, technically improved products; it has little regard for customers' desires.

Product item A specific version of a product that can be designated as a unique offering among an organization's products.

Product life cycle Course of product development, consisting of several stages: introduction, growth, maturity, and decline. As a product moves through these stages, the strategies relating to competition, pricing, promotion, distribution, and market information must be evaluated and possibly changed.

Product line A group of closely related products that are considered a unit because of marketing, technical, or end-use considerations.

Product manager Person who holds a staff position in a multiproduct company; responsible for a product, a product line, or several distinct products that are considered an interrelated group.

Product mix The composite of products that an organization makes available to consumers.

Product mix depth *See* Depth of product mix.

Product mix width *See* Width of product mix.

Product modification The changing of one or more of a product's characteristics.

Product-portfolio analysis (BCG approach) A strategic planning approach based on the philosophy that a product's market growth rate and its relative market share are important considerations in determining its market strategy.

Product-portfolio approach An approach to managing the product mix that attempts to create specific marketing strategies to achieve a balanced mix of products that will produce maximum long-run profits.

Product positioning The decisions and activities that are directed toward trying to create and maintain the firm's intended product concept in customers' minds.

Product-specific spending patterns The dollar amounts families spend for specific products within a general product class.

Product variable That aspect of the marketing mix dealing with researching consumers' product wants and planning the product to achieve the desired product characteristics.

Professional pricing Pricing used by persons who have great skill or experience in a particular field or activity, indicating that a price should not relate directly to the time and involvement in a specific case; rather, a standard fee is charged regardless of the problems involved in performing the job.

Professional services Complex and frequently regulated services that usually require the provider to be highly skilled; examples are accounting or legal services.

Projective technique Test in which subjects are asked to perform specific tasks for particular purposes while in fact they are being evaluated for other purposes; assumes that subjects will unconsciously "project" their motives as they perform the tasks.

Promotion The communication with individuals, groups, or organizations to directly or indirectly facilitate exchanges by influencing audience members to accept an organization's products.

Promotion mix The specific combination of promotional methods an organization uses for a particular product.

Promotion variable A major marketing mix component

used to facilitate exchanges by informing an individual or one or more groups of people about an organization and its products.

Prospecting Developing a list of potential customers for personal selling purposes.

Prosperity A stage of the business cycle, during which unemployment is low and aggregate income is relatively high, which causes buying power to be high (assuming a low inflation rate).

Proxemic communication A subtle form of interpersonal communication used in face-to-face interactions when either party varies the physical distance that separates them.

Psychological influences Factors that operate within individuals to partially determine their general behavior and thus influence their behavior as buyers.

Psychological pricing Pricing method designed to encourage purchases that are based on emotional reactions rather than rational responses.

Publicity Nonpersonal communication in news story form, regarding an organization and/or its products, that is transmitted through a mass medium at no charge.

Public relations A broad set of communication activities used to create and maintain favorable relations between the organization and its publics, such as customers, employees, stockholders, government officials, and society in general.

Public warehouses Business organizations that provide rented storage facilities and related physical distribution facilities.

Pull policy Promotion of a product directly to consumers with the intention of developing strong consumer demand.

Purchasing power A buyer's income, credit, and wealth available for purchasing products.

Push money An incentive program designed to push a line of goods by providing salespeople with additional compensation.

Push policy Promotion of a product only to the next institution down the marketing channel.

Q

Quality modification A change that relates to a product's dependability and durability and usually is executed by alterations in the materials or production process employed.

Quality of life The enjoyment of daily living, which is enhanced by leisure time, clean air and water, an unlittered earth, conservation of wildlife and natural re-

sources, and security from radiation and poisonous substances.

Quantity discounts Deductions from list price that reflect the economies of purchasing in large quantities.

Quota sampling Nonprobability sampling in which the final choice of respondents is left to the interviewers.

R

Rack jobbers Middlemen (also called service merchandisers) similar to truck wholesalers but which provide the extra service of cleaning and filling a display rack.

Random factor analysis A method of predicting sales whereby an attempt is made to attribute erratic sales variations to random, nonrecurrent events, such as a regional power failure or a natural disaster.

Random sampling Type of sampling in which all the units in a population have an equal chance of appearing in the sample; probability sampling.

Raw materials Basic materials that become part of a physical product; obtained from mines, farms, forests, oceans, and recycled solid wastes.

Real-estate brokers Brokers who, for a fee or commission, bring buyers and sellers together to exchange real estate.

Receiver The individual, group, or organization that decodes a coded message.

Recession A stage in the business cycle, during which unemployment rises and total buying power declines, stifling both consumers' and businesspersons' propensity to spend.

Reciprocity A practice unique to industrial sales in which two organizations agree to buy from each other.

Recognition test A posttest method of evaluating the effectiveness of advertising; individual respondents are shown the actual advertisement and asked whether they recognize it.

Recovery A stage of the business cycle, during which the economy moves from recession toward prosperity.

Recruiting A process by which the sales manager develops a list of applicants for sales positions.

Reference group A group with which an individual identifies so much that he or she takes on many of the values, attitudes, and/or behaviors of group members.

Regional issues Versions of a magazine that differ across geographic regions and in which a publisher can vary the advertisements and editorial content.

Regional shopping center Type of shopping center that usually has the largest department stores, the widest product mix, and the deepest product lines of all shopping centers in an area; usually at least 150,000 customers in the target area.

Regulatory forces Forces that arise from regulatory units at all levels of government; these units create and enforce numerous regulations that affect marketing decisions.

Reinforcement advertising An advertisement that tries to assure current users that they have made the right choice and tells them how to get the most satisfaction from the product.

Reliability Reliability exists when a sample is representative of the population; it also exists when repeated use of an instrument produces almost identical results.

Reminder advertising Advertising used to remind consumers that an established brand is still around and that it has certain uses, characteristics, and benefits.

Reorder point The inventory level that signals that more inventory should be ordered.

Reseller market Market that consists of intermediaries, such as wholesalers and retailers, that buy finished goods and resell them for the purpose of making a profit.

Retailer An intermediary that purchases products for the purpose of reselling them to ultimate consumers.

Retailer coupon A sales promotion method used by retailers when price is a primary motivation for consumers' purchasing behavior; usually takes the form of a "cents-off" coupon that is distributed through advertisements and is redeemable only at a specific store.

Retailing Focuses on the activities required for exchanges in which ultimate consumers are the buyers.

Robinson-Patman Act Directly influences pricing and promotions policies; the act prohibits price differentials and promotional allowances that are discriminatory.

Role A set of actions and activities that a person in a particular position is supposed to perform, based on the expectations of both the individual and the persons around the individual.

Routine response behavior The type of decision making a consumer uses when buying frequently purchased, low-cost items that require very little search and decision effort.

S

Safety stock Inventory needed to prevent a stockout S(running out of a product).

Sales analysis A process for controlling marketing strategies whereby sales figures are used to evaluate performance.

Sales branches Similar to merchant wholesalers in their operations; they may offer credit, delivery, give promotional assistance, and furnish other services.

Sales contest A sales promotion method used to motivate distributors, retailers, and sales personnel through the recognition of outstanding achievements.

Sales-force forecasting survey Estimation by members of a firm's sales force of the anticipated sales in their territories for a specified period.

Sales office Provides service normally associated with agents; owned and controlled by the producer.

Sales orientation A focus on increasing an organization's sales as the major way to increase profits.

Sales-oriented organization There is a general belief that personal selling and advertising are the primary tools used to generate profits and that most products—regardless of consumers' needs—can be sold if the right quantity and quality of personal selling and advertising are used.

Sales promotion An activity and/or material that acts as a direct inducement, offering added value or incentive for the product, to resellers, salespersons, or consumers.

Sampling Selecting representative units from a total population.

Scientific decision making An approach that involves systematically seeking facts and then applying decision making methods other than trial and error or generalization from experience.

Scrambled merchandising The addition of unrelated products and product lines to an existing product mix, particularly fast-moving items that can be sold in large volume.

Screening ideas A stage in the product development process in which the ideas that do not match organizational objectives are rejected and those with the greatest potential are selected for further development.

Sealed bids Prices submitted to a buyer, to be opened and made public at a specified time.

Search qualities Tangible attributes of services that can be viewed prior to purchase.

Seasonal analysis A method of predicting sales whereby an analyst studies daily, weekly, or monthly sales figures to evaluate the degree to which seasonal factors, such as climate and holiday activities, influence the firm's sales.

Seasonal discounts A price reduction that sellers give to buyers who purchase goods or services out of season; these discounts allow the seller to maintain steadier production during the year.

Secondary data Information compiled inside or outside the organization for some purpose other than the current investigations.

Segmentation variable A dimension or characteristic of individuals, groups, or organizations that is used to divide a total market into segments.

Selective distortion The changing or twisting of currently received information that occurs when a person receives information that is inconsistent with his or her feelings or beliefs.

Selective distribution A form of market coverage in which only some available outlets in an area are chosen to distribute a product.

Selective exposure Selection of some inputs to be exposed to our awareness while many others are ignored because of the inability to be conscious of all inputs at one time.

Selective retention A phenomenon in which a person remembers information inputs that support personal feelings and beliefs and forgets inputs that do not.

Self-concept One's own perception of himself or herself.

Selling agents Intermediaries who market all of a specified product line or the entire output of a manufacturer; they have control over the manufacturer's marketing effort and may be used in place of a marketing department.

Service An intangible that is the result of applying human and mechanical efforts to people or objects.

Service heterogeneity *See* Heterogeneity.

Service inseparability *See* Inseparability.

Service intangibility *See* Intangibility.

Service perishability *See* Perishability.

Sherman Act Legislation passed in 1890 to prevent businesses from restraining trade and monopolizing markets.

Shopping product An item for which buyers are willing to put forth considerable effort in planning and making the purchase.

Short-range plans Plans that cover a period of one year or less.

Single-variable segmentation The simplest form of segmentation is achieved by using only one characteristic to divide—or segment—the market.

Situational factors The set of circumstances or conditions that exist when a consumer is making a purchase decision.

Social class An open aggregate of people with similar social ranking.

Social influences The forces that other people exert on one's buying behavior.

Social institutions An environmental force in international markets, including the family, education, religion, health, and recreational systems.

Social marketing Involves the development of programs designed to influence the acceptability of social ideas or causes.

Social responsibility Relates to how marketing decisions affect society as a whole and various groups and individuals within society.

Societal forces Forces that pressure marketers to provide high living standards and enjoyable lifestyles through socially responsible decisions and activities; the structure and dynamics of individuals and groups and the issues of concern to them.

Socioeconomic factors *See* Demographic factors.

Sorting activities The way channel members divide roles and separate tasks, including the roles of sorting out, accumulating, allocating, and assorting products.

Sorting out The first step in developing an assortment; it involves breaking down conglomerates of heterogeneous supplies into relatively homogeneous groups.

Source A person, group, or organization that has a meaning that it intends and attempts to share with a receiver or an audience.

Special-event pricing Advertised sales or price cutting to increase revenue or lower costs.

Specialty-line wholesaler A merchant wholesaler that carries a very limited variety of products designed to meet customers' specialized requirements.

Specialty product An item that possesses one or more unique characteristics that a significant group of buyers is willing to expend considerable purchasing efforts to obtain.

Specialty retail A type of store that carries a narrow product mix with deep product lines.

Standard Industrial Classification (SIC) System A system developed by the federal government for classifying industrial organizations, based on what the firm primarily produces; also classifies selected economic characteristics of commercial, financial, and service organizations. Code numbers are used to classify firms in different industries.

Statistical interpretation Analysis that focuses on what is typical or what deviates from the average; it indicates how widely respondents vary and how they are distributed in relation to the variable being measured.

Stockout Condition that exists when a firm runs out of a product.

Storyboard A blueprint used by technical personnel to produce a television commercial; combines the copy with the visual material to show the sequence of major scenes in the commercial.

Straight commission compensation plan A plan by which a salesperson's compensation is determined solely by the amount of his or her sales for a given time period.

Straight-rebuy purchase A type of industrial purchase in which a buyer purchases the same products routinely under approximately the same terms of sale.

Straight salary compensation plan A plan by which salespeople are paid a specified amount per time period.

Strategic business unit (SBU) A division, product line, or other profit center within a parent company that sells a distinct set of products and/or services to an identifiable group of customers and competes against a well-defined set of competitors.

Strategic marketing planning A process whereby an organization can develop marketing strategies that, when properly implemented and controlled, will contribute to achieving the organization's overall goals.

Strategic market plan A comprehensive plan that takes into account not only marketing but all other functional areas of a business unit that must be coordinated, such as production, finance, and personnel, as well as concern about the environment.

Strategy The key decision or plan of action required to reach an objective or set of objectives.

Stratified sampling Units in a population are divided into groups according to a common characteristic or attribute; then a probability sample is conducted within each group.

Style modification Modification directed at changing the sensory appeal of a product by altering its taste, texture, sound, smell, or visual characteristics.

Subculture A division of a culture based on geographic regions or human characteristics, such as age or ethnic background.

Superficial discounting A deceptive markdown sometimes called "was-is pricing" (the firm never intended to sell at the higher price); fictitious comparative pricing.

Supermarket A large, self-service store that carries broad and complete lines of food products, and perhaps some nonfood products.

Superstore A giant store that carries all food and nonfood products found in supermarkets as well as most products purchased on a routine basis; sales are much greater than discount stores or supermarkets.

Supplies *See* Consumable supplies.

Support personnel Members of the sales staff who facilitate the selling function but usually are not involved only with making sales.

Survey methods Include interviews by mail or by telephone and personal interviews.

Symbolic pricing A type of psychological pricing in which prices are set at an artificially high level to provide prestige or a quality image.

Syndicated data services External sources of information a marketer uses to study a marketing problem. Examples include American Research Bureau (ARB), Selling Areas Marketing, Inc. (SAMI), the A. C. Nielsen Company Retail Index, the Market Research Corpora-

tion of America (MRCA); they collect general information that is sold to subscribing clients.

T

Tactile communication Interpersonal communication through touching.

Target market A group of persons for whom a firm creates and maintains a marketing mix.

Target public A collective of individuals who have an interest in or concern about an organization, a product, or a social cause.

Technical salesperson Support salesperson who directs efforts toward the organization's current customers by providing technical assistance in system design, product application, product characteristics, or installation.

Technological forces Forces that influence marketing decisions and activities because they affect people's lifestyles and standards of living, influence their desire for products and their reaction to marketing mixes, and have a direct impact on maintaining a marketing mix by influencing all its variables.

Technology The knowledge of how to accomplish tasks and goals.

Technology assessment A procedure whereby managers try to foresee the effects of new products and processes on the firm's operation, on other business organizations, and on society in general.

Telemarketing A form of personal selling whereby highly trained account executives do everything over the telephone that face-to-face salespeople do.

Telephone retailing A type of nonstore retailing based on a cold canvass of the telephone directory or a screening of prospective clients before calling.

Telephone surveys Respondents' answers to a questionnaire are solicited over the telephone, with the answers being written down by the interviewer.

Test-marketing A limited introduction of a product in areas chosen to represent the intended market to determine probable buyers' reactions to various parts of a marketing mix.

Time series analysis A technique in which the forecaster, using the firm's historical sales data, tries to discover patterns in the firm's sales volume over time.

Total costs The sum of fixed costs and variable costs.

Total market approach Approach in which an organization designs a single marketing mix and directs it at an entire market for a specific product category; also called undifferentiated approach.

Total revenue Price times quantity.

Traceable common costs Costs that can be allocated indirectly, using one or several criteria, to the functions that they support.

Trade (functional) discount A reduction off the list price a producer gives to a middleman for performing certain functions.

Trademark A legal designation indicating that the owner has exclusive use of a brand or part of a brand and that others are prohibited by law from using it.

Trade mart A relatively permanent facility that firms can rent to exhibit products year-round.

Trade name The legal name of an organization, rather than the name of a specific product.

Trade salesperson A type of salesperson not strictly classified as support personnel because he or she performs the order-taking function as well.

Trade sales promotion method A category of sales promotion techniques that stimulate wholesalers and retailers to carry a producer's products and to market these products aggressively.

Trade show Allows manufacturers or wholesalers to exhibit products to potential buyers and therefore assists in the selling and buying functions; these shows are commonly held annually at a specified location.

Trading company Companies that provide a link between buyers and sellers in different countries. Trading companies take title to products and provide all the activities necessary to move the product from the domestic country to a market in a foreign country.

Trading stamps A sales promotion method retailers use to attract consumers to specific stores and to increase sales of specific items by giving extra stamps to purchasers of those items.

Traditional specialty retailer A store that carries a narrow product mix with deep product lines.

Transfer pricing The type of pricing used when one unit in a company sells a product to another unit; the price is determined by one of the following methods: actual full cost, standard full cost, cost plus investment, or market-based cost.

Transit time The total time that a carrier has possession of the goods.

Transportation modes Railways, motor vehicles, waterways, pipelines, and airways used to move goods from one location to another.

Trend analysis Analysis that focuses on aggregate sales data, such as company's annual sales figures, over a period of many years to determine whether annual sales are generally rising, falling, or staying about the same.

Truck wholesaler Wholesaler that provides transportation and delivery of products directly to customers for inspection and selection.

Tying contract An agreement by which a supplier agrees to sell certain products to a dealer on the condition that the dealer consent to purchase other products the supplier sells.

U

Unaided recall test A posttest method of evaluating the effectiveness of advertising; subjects are asked to identify advertisements that they have seen or heard recently but are not shown any clues to stimulate their memories.

Undifferentiated approach Occurs when an organization designs a single marketing mix and directs it at an entire market for a specific product; same as total market approach.

Unfair trade practices acts State laws, enacted in more than half the states, that prohibit wholesalers and retailers from selling products below their costs or below their costs plus a certain percentage of markup.

Uniform geographic pricing Sometimes called "postage-stamp price," results in fixed average transportation; used to avoid the problems involved with charging different prices to each customer.

Unit loading Grouping one or more boxes on a pallet or skid.

Unsought products Products purchased because of a sudden need that must be solved (e.g., emergency automobile repairs) or when aggressive selling is used to obtain a sale that otherwise would not take place (e.g., encyclopedias).

V

Validity Said to exist when an instrument does measure what it is supposed to measure.

Variable cost A cost that varies directly with changes in the number of units produced or sold.

Vending *See* Automatic vending.

Venture team An organizational unit established to create entirely new products that may be aimed at new markets.

Vertical channel integration The combining of two or more stages of a marketing channel under one management.

Vertical marketing system A marketing channel in which channel activities are coordinated or managed by a single channel member to achieve efficient, low-cost distribution aimed at satisfying target market customers.

W

Warehouse showroom A type of retail store with high volume and low overhead. Lower costs are effected by shifting some marketing functions to consumers who must transport, finance, and perhaps store merchandise.

Warehouse/wholesale club A large-scale, members-only establishment that combines features of cash-and-carry wholesaling with discount retailing.

Warehousing Designing and operating facilities for storing and moving goods.

Warranty Document that specifies what the producer will do if the product malfunctions.

Wealth The accumulation of past income, natural resources, and financial resources.

Wheeler-Lea Act Makes unfair and deceptive acts or practices unlawful regardless of whether they injure competition.

Wheel of retailing A hypothesis that holds that new types of retailers usually enter the market as low-status, low-margin, low-price operators who eventually evolve into high-cost, high-price merchants.

Wholesaler An intermediary that buys from a producer or another intermediary and sells to another reseller; performs such marketing activities as transportation, storage, and information gathering necessary to expedite exchanges.

Wholesaling All marketing transactions in which purchases are intended for resale or are used in making other products.

Width (of product mix) The number of product lines a company offers.

Willingness to spend A disposition toward expected satisfaction from a product; is influenced by the ability to buy as well as numerous psychological and social forces.

Z

Zone prices Regional prices that vary for major geographic zones as the transportation costs differ.

Name Index

Chex cereals, 352
Chianine Lite Beef, Inc., 147
Chiat Day, 444
Chicken of the Sea tuna, 352
Chief Auto Parts, 428
Chih Kang Wang, 439n
Children's World, 116
Chipello, Christopher J., 49n
Choco-diles snack cakes, 353
Chonko, Lawrence B., 207n
Choudhury, Pravet, 24n
Chow formula feeds, 353
Chrysler Corporation, 461, 477, 565, 619–620, 672, 681, 682(illus.)
Chuck Wagon, 352
Church's Fried Chicken, 429, 550
Cincinnati Microwave, 324–325
Circle K Corp., 428, 430
Citgo Petroleum Corp., 428, 429, 431, 641
Citibank, 640
Citicorp, 371–372, 450
Citrus Hill juices, 702
Clarion cosmetics, 83–85
Clark, Laura, 783n
Clark, Scott, 702n
Clark Equipment Company, 725
Clendinen, Dudley, 254n
Close-Up toothpaste, 276
Coca-Cola Company, 28–31, 149, 201, 236, 238, 240–242, 273, 277, 374, 465, 547–554, 550 (illus.), 553(illus.), 686, 702
Coca-Cola Foods, 344
Code-A-Phone, 266
Cohen, Dorothy, 490(table)
Cohn, Bob, 742n
Cohn, Cathy, 145n
Coke, 554
Coke Classic, 547–554
Coleman, Lynn G., 545n
Coleman, Mel, 147
Coleman, Richard P., 139n, 140(table)
Coleman Natural Beef, 147
Colemar, Lynn, 206n
Colford, Steven W., 77n
Colgate-Palmolive Co., 240, 287, 537, 802
Collischon, David, 223–224
Collischon, Lesley, 223–224
Colt Car Co., 541
Combustion Engineering, 791
Comes, Frank, 715n
Coniston Partners, 777
Connaught Laboratories, 263
Conner, Tim, 524n
Connolly, Joseph, 224n
Connor, Patrick E., 685n
Consumer Distributing, 366

Contadina, 585
Conte, Maria, 530n
Continental Airlines, 453, 620, 621, 622, 624
Continental Baking Company, 352, 353
Continental Glass & Plastic, 411
Conway, John A., 24n
Cook, Jack, 810n
Cook's Magazine, The, 481
Cooper, Philip D., 766n, 769(table), 773(table)
Cooper, Robert G., 260n
Copper 7 intrauterine contraceptive devices, 263
Corsica automobiles, 435
Corwin, Pat, 400n, 422n
Cosby, Bill, 550
Cosby Show, The, 475
Cosmair, 263–264
Cosse, Thomas J., 260n
Costco Wholesale Clubs, 365
Cottinberger, Richard, 44n
Cover Girl cosmetics, 83–84
Covino, Renee M., 365n
Cox, James, 46n
Cox, Jonathan M., 346n
Coyle, John J., 412n
Cracker Jacks snacks, 539
Crane Co., 342
Cravens, David W., 656n
Crazy Eddie home shopping network, 462
Crest for Kids toothpaste, 137
Crest toothpaste, 276, 286, 472, 486
Crete, Michael, 322–323
Crimmins, Ed, 540n
Cross, A.T. Company, 89 and illus., 812
Cross pens, 573
Crowley, Ayn E., 383n
Crowley's department stores, 382
Crown, Judith, 702n
Crown Plaza hotels, 237
Crum & Forster, 643
CSX Corporation, 417, 418(illus.)
Cuneo, Alice Z., 659n
Cunon, John J., 314n
Curley, Jim, 424n
Curran, John J., 28n
Curtis Mathes Corp., 567

Daddiego, Vincent, A10n
Dagnoli, Judann, 282n
Dahl, Jonathan, 25n, 580n, 625n
Dairy Queen, 374, 639
D'Amato, Nancy, 238n
Daniel Starch, 492
Darmon, Rene Y., 526n

Data General, 681(illus.)
Davids, Meryl, 770n
Davidson, Casey, 606n
Davis, Jo Ellen, 625n, 702n
Davis, Tim, 274n
Dawson, Gaye C., 315n
Day, George S., 649n, 650(illus.), 653(illus.)
Day, Ralph L., 177n
DayBridge Learning Centers, 116
Dayco Corporation, 727
Days Inns of America, Inc., 296
Dayton-Hudson Corp., 527
Deakin, Edward B., 678n, 698n
De Bruicker, E. Steward, 234n, 279n
DeGeorge, Gail, 462n
Dehamarter, Richard Thomas, 572n
Delano, Frank, 238n
Del Monte Corp., 246
Delozier, M. Wayne, 439n
Delta Air Lines, Inc., 453, 460–462, 624, 728, 746
Deneuve, Catherine, 545
Deneuve fragrance, 545
Denny's restaurants, 99
DeQuine, Jeanne, 46n
Deschaine, Monique, 584n, 584–585
Desk Pals, 172
Deveny, Kathleen, 737n
Dewey Stevens wine cooler, 352
Diamond Star Motors, 565
Dichter, Ernest, 104n
Didronel, 289
Diet cherry Coke, 551, 553, 554
Diet Coke, 277, 547, 553, 554
Diet Pepsi, 456, 554
Diet Sprite, 554
Dietrich Corp., 284
Di Giorgio Corporation, 703–704
Digital Equipment Corporation (DEC), 635
Dillman, Don A., 202(table)
Diner's Club, 603
Ding Dongs, 353
"Dirty Dancing," 456
Disney, Walt, 254
Disney Channel, 255
Disneyland, 752
Disneyland Tokyo, 254
Disney Store, 255
Disney Sunday Movie, 255
Disney World, 255, 465
Dobrzynski, Judith H., 776n
Dodds, Lynn Strongin, 252n, 282n
Dodge, James, 176n
Dodge automobiles, 620
Dolecheck, Maynard M., 210n
Dolliver, Mark, 477n
Domino's Pizza, 439, 497, 757

Friendly Ice Cream Corp., 282
Frontier Airlines, 620
Fruit of the Loom, 568, 569(illus.), 637 and *illus.*
Fuji, 679
Fuld, Leonard M., 790(table)
Fuller, Alfred, 509
Fuller Brush Company, 369, 509–511, 510(illus.)

Gabel, H. Landis, 609n
Gable, Myron, 380n, 512n
Gabor, Andrea, 254n
Galante, Steven P., 412n
Galek, Thomas, 315n
Gallup, George Jr., 195n
Gallup & Robinson, 492
Gap, The, 366
Garcia, Carlos E., 440n
Gardner, Ella P., 44n
Garino, David P., 246n
Garrison, John, 763n
Gaskamp, Barbara, 6–7
Gaskamp, Virginia, 6–7
Gaski, John F., 316n
Gaston Dupré, 585
Gates, Roger, 200n
Gay, Verne, 213n
G.D. Searle & Co., 263, 289
Gelb, Betsy D., 751(table)
Gelco International, 817
General Electric Co., 15, 17(illus.), 240, 643, 652, 705, 707, 795
General Foods Corporation, 15, 120, 149, 259, 372, 441, 537, 538
General Mills, Inc., 234, 247, 283
General Motors Corp., 17, 200, 435–436, 536, 565, 568, 572, 620, 640, 677, 802, 806
Genuine Draft beer, 638
Geoghegan, Patrick, 145n
Georgaff, David M., 639n
George, Judith, A3n, A5n
George, William R., 754n, 756n
Gerber Products Company, 116, 448, 481
Gersh, Debra, 538n
Gershman, Michael, 248n
Gibson, Richard, 677n
Giese, William, 768n
Giges, Nancy, 555n
G.I. Joe toys, 651
Gillette Company, 272
Gillette European Personal Care Division, 17–18
Gilman, Hank, 173n, 173n
Giorgio fragrances, 618
Glaskowsky, J. Nicholas, 413n

Glocil fluorescent pencils, 172
Gloede, Bill, 467n
Godiva chocolate stores, 358
Goizueta, Roberto C., 547, 549
Gold Bond trading stamps, 545–546
Golden Girls, 255
Goldman, Ellen F., 591n
Good News disposable razors, 20
Good Sam Club, 103
Goodrich, B.F. Co., 236
Goodyear Tire & Rubber Company, 236, 263, 684–685
Gorbachev, Mikhail, 791
Gordon, Ian, 63n
Gottlieb, Carrie, 233n
Gourmet, 481
Gourmet Retailer, The, 584
Graham, Ellen, 138n
Grassmuck, Karen, 584n
Gray, Daniel H., 633n
Grayson, Melvin J., 36n
Great American Chocolate Chip Cookie, 390
Greenberg, Jan, A6n, A7n
Greenhouse, Stephen, 701n
Gresham, Larry G., 57n, 207n, 361n
Grether, E.T., 49n
Grey Poupon mustard, 481
Grimm, Jim L., 246n, A13n
Gross, Amy, 443n, 538n
Gross, Neil, 689n
Grossman, Elliott S., 109n, 112n, 113n
Grover, Ron, 659n
Guardian auto ignition interlock system, 325
Gubernick, Lisa, 431n
Gucci, 305
Guelzo, Carl M., 399n, 401n, 402n, 404n, 410n, 412n
Guess?, 313
Guhring, 683, 684(illus.)
Guiltinan, Joseph P., 225n, 358n, 649n
Gurin, Maurice G., 442n
Guzda, M.K., 104n

Haas, Robert W., 228n, 716n
Haggerty, Betsy, 424n, 427n
Haight, Gordon, 172
Haimann, Theo, 685n
Hair, Joseph F., Jr., 200n
Hall, Carol, 259m, 416n
Hall, Peter, 115n
Hall, Rich, 444
Hall, Trish, 606n
Halston Enterprises, Inc., 90
Hamilton, Joan O.C., 467n

Hammond, John S., 633n, 637n, 654(illus.)
Hammonds, Keith, 467n
Hampton, William J., 566n
Hampton Inns, 237
Handy Dan, 392
Hanes Company, 311, 372, 637 and *illus.*
Hannon, Kerry, 511n
Happy Cat, 352
Happy Dog, 352
Happy Kitten, 352
Hardee's fast foods, 429
Hardee's Food Systems, Inc., 138, 452, 550
Hardie, A.E., 310n
Hargrove, Earnestine, 723n
Harley, Mark, 742n
Harley-Davidson Motor Co., Inc., 23–24, 240, 445
Harper, Doug, 728n
Harrell, Gilbert D., 384n, 798n, 799(illus.)
Harrigan, Cathryn Rudie, 806n
Harrington, Lisa, 416n
Harris, Paul, 769n
Hartley, Robert F., 79n, 359(illus.), 373n, 387(illus.)
Hasbro, Inc., 651–652
Hassenfeld, Stephen, 651
Hawes, Jon M., 239n, 378n
Hawk, Kathleen, 601n
Hawken, Paul, 522n
Hawkins, Del, 384n, 385n
Hawkins, Steve L., 254n
Head, Mitch, 248n
Healey, James R., 580n, 625n
Healthtex clothing, 378
Heard, Lee Ann, 810n
Hearty Chews, 352
Hebert, H. Josef, 625n
Heineken beer, 351
Heinz, H.J., 247, 703
Helene Curtis Industries, 263–264
Heller, Walter H., 329n
Hellstern, Ray, 568n, 613n
Helm, Leslie, 294n, 635n, 674n, 680n
Hemp, Paul, 352n
Hemphill, Gary A., 151n
Hershey, Milton, 282
Hershey Foods Corp., 282–284
Hertz Corporation, 374, 777
Hervey, Jewel, 7n
Heskett, James L., 413n, 744n
Heublein Inc., 36
Hewlett–Packard Co., 671, 732
Hi–C, 551
Hickory Farms, 367

Subject Index

Accessibility, of transportation, 414, 416
Accessory equipment, 229
Accounting, marketing cost analysis and, 688–691
Accumulation, 302–303
Actual full cost transfer pricing, 579
Administered pricing, 732
Administered vertical marketing system, 306
Advertising, 766
  appropriation for, 477–480
  careers in, A9–A10
  comparative, 471
  competitive, 470–471
  cooperative, 540
  defensive, 471
  defining objectives of, 474, 476
  developing campaign for, 473–494, 474(illus.)
  ethics and, 56
  evaluating effectiveness of, 491–493
  executing campaign for, 491
  institutional, 468–469
  message in, 486–491
  nature of, 467–468, 469(table)
  pioneer, 470
  platform for, 477
  product, 469
  in promotion mix, 448, 450
  publicity compared with, 494
  reinforcement, 472
  reminder, 472
  target of, 473–474
  uses of, 468–473
Age, as segmentation variable, 92–93
Agents, 337(illus.), 337–340, 338(table)
  buying direct and, 341–342
  commission merchants as, 339–340

manufacturers', 338–339, 341–342, 724
  selling, 339
Aided recall test, advertising effectiveness and, 492
Airways, 410, 412
Allocation, 303
Allowances
  buy-back, 539
  buying, 539
  merchandise, 540
  pricing and, 578
American Marketing Association Code of Ethics, 57, 58–59(table)
Antitrust legislation, 46–49, 48(table)
Approach, in personal selling, 515
Arbitrary approach, to advertising appropriation, 480
Area sampling, 192
Artwork, for advertising, 489, 490(table), 491
Assorting, 303–304
Assortments, 301
  discrepancy in, 301
  retailing and, 379–380
Atmospherics, retailing and, 382–384
Attitudes, in consumer buying behavior, 132–134
Attitude scale, 133
Audit, marketing, 693, 694–696(table), 697–698
Automatic vending sales, 370, 372
Average fixed cost, 596
Average total cost, 597
Average variable cost, 597

Bargaining, implicit, 678
Barter, 561
Base-point pricing, 579

Behavioralistic segmentation variables, 104–105
Benefit segmentation, 104
Better Business Bureaus, 52–53
Bid pricing, 733
Bonded storage, 404
Brand(s), 235
  generic, 239
  manufacturer, 236
  private distributor, 236
Brand-extension branding, 240
Branding, 235–242
  benefits of, 235–236
  family, 240
  policies for, 238–240
  selecting and protecting brands and, 237–238
  types of brands and, 236–237
Brand licensing, 240–242
Brand manager, 259
Brand mark, 235
Brand name, 235
Breakdown approach, to company sales potential, 108
Breakeven analysis, 600(illus.), 600–601
Breakeven point, 600, 600(illus.)
Bribe, 56
Brokers, 337(illus.), 337, 338(table), 340, 344
Buildup approach, 108
Business, see Organization(s)
Business analysis, new-product development and, 269
Buy-back allowances, for sales promotion, 539
Buyer(s)
  behavior of, selection of distribution channels and, 310–311
  demand of, 593–596

Gender, as segmentation variable, 93
General merchandise wholesalers, 334
General publics, 765
Generic branding, 239
Geographic area
    cost analysis by, 691
    organizing marketing unit by, 675
Geographic pricing, 578–579
Geographic segmentation variables,
    96–100, 98(illus.), 101(illus.)
    for organizational markets, 105
Globalization, of markets, 785–786
Goods, 12
Government markets, 154–155,
    155(table)
Government regulation, see Regulatory forces
Growth stage, marketing strategy in,
    278
Group interview, 131
Growth
    diversified, 659
    integrated, 660
    intense, 658
Growth stage in product life cycle, 233

Heterogeneity, of services, 746
Heterogeneous markets, 88
Honesty, 56
Horizontal channel integration, 307,
    309–310
Hypotheses, in marketing research,
    186

ICC, see Interstate Commerce Commission
Ideas, 12
    generation of, for new products,
        268
    screening, 268–269
Ideas, 12
Illustrations, 489, 491
Image, of store, 384–385
Implementation
    of marketing activities, 676–681
    of marketing plans, 31
Implicit bargaining, 678
Income, 64
    buying, effective, 65
    discretionary, 64
    disposable, 64
    as segmentation variable, 93–94
Income statement, A13–A20
    inventory turnover and, A19
    operating ratios and, A16–A19
    return on investment and, A19–
        A20
    selected performance ratios and,
        A16

Incremental productivity method, for
    determining sales-force size, 522
Independent variable, 193
Individual branding, 239–240
Industrial buying, careers in, A7–A8
Industrial buying behavior, see Organizational buying behavior
Industrial distributors, 334, 724
Industrial market(s), 86
    changing, 161–162
    pricing for, 576–581
    segmentation variables for, 105–106
Industrial marketing, 713–734
    defined, 715
    marketing mixes for, 720–732
    nature of, 715–716
    target markets in, 716–720
Industrial products, 226, 228–231,
    715–716
    marketing channels for, 298(illus.),
        298–299
Industrial services, 230–231
Industrial transactions, characteristics
    of, 155–156
Inelastic demand, 162
Information inputs, in consumer buying behavior, 127
Information search, in consumer buying decision process, 123–124
In-home interviews, 200–201
In-home retailing, 369
Inland waterways, 410
Innovators, product adoption and,
    446–447
Input-output data, 717
Inseparability, of production and consumption of services, 745–746
Inside order takers, 518
Inspection, organizational buying by,
    159
Institutional advertising, 468–469
Institutional markets, 155
Intangibility, of services, 745
Integrated growth, marketing strategy
    and, 660
Intense growth, marketing strategy
    and, 658
Intensive distribution, 307–308
Interest, 562
Intermediaries, 299–304
    functions of, 301–304
    justifications for, 299–301,
        300(illus.), 301(table)
    see also Wholesalers; Wholesaling
Intermodal transportation, 417
International marketing, 781–809
    defined, 783
    developing involvement in, 805–
        808

environment and, 789–796
globalization versus customized
    marketing strategies and, 785–786
marketing intelligence and, 787,
    788(table), 789, 790(table)
marketing mixes and, 798–805,
    799(illus.)
multinational involvement in,
    784(table), 784–785, 785(illus.)
Interpretation, of research findings,
    187–189
Interstate Commerce Commission
    (ICC), 53(table), 409
Interviews
    focus-group, 200
    in-house, 200–201
    shopping mall intercept, 199–200
Introduction stage in product life cycle, 232–233
Intuition, 182
    marketing research differentiated
    from, 185(table)
Inventory control, 406–407, 411–412
Inventory management, physical distribution and, 405–407, 406(illus.),
    407(illus.)

Jobber, rack, 334–335
Job enrichment, 678
Joint demand, 162–163
Joint ventures, international marketing
    and, 806–807
Just-in-time inventory control, 406–
    407, 411–412

Kinesic communication, in personal
    selling, 451

Labeling, 246
Laboratory experimentation, 193–194
Laggards, product adoption and, 447
Late majority, product adoption and,
    447
Laws, see Legal forces; Regulatory
    forces
Layout, of advertisement, 491
Leadership, channel, 315–316,
    317(illus.)
Learning, in consumer buying behavior, 132
Legal forces, 24, 44–50
    in channel management, 317–319
    consumer protection and, 49
    in international marketing, 789,
        795–796, 796(illus.)
    interpreting laws and, 49–50
    pricing and, 576
    procompetitive, 46–49, 48(table)
    see also Regulatory forces